Ephesians

Ephesians

An Exegetical Commentary

Harold W. Hoehner

Published by Baker Academic
a division of Baker Publishing Group
P.O. Box 6287, Grand Rapids, MI 49516-6287
www.bakeracademic.com

Printed in the United States of America

Library of Congress Cataloging-in-Publication Data

Hoehner, Harold W.
Ephesians : an exegetical commentary / Harold W. Hoehner.
p. cm.
Includes bibliographical references and index.
ISBN 10: 0-8010-2614-8 (pbk.)
ISBN 978-0-8010-2614-0 (pbk.)
1. Bible. N.T. Ephesians—Commentaries. I. Title.
BS2695.53 .H64 2002
227′.5077—dc21 2002026053

14 15 16 17 18 19 20 15 14 13 12 11 10 9

Dedicated to our children and their spouses

Stephen and Stacy Hoehner
Susan and Darin McFarland
David and Caren Hoehner
Deborah Hoehner

Who love our Lord and serve him
in various parts of the world

Contents

Preface

This commentary has a long history. It was originally part of a series that was discontinued. Although it later became part of a new commentary series from another publisher, the commentary became too long and no longer fit within that series. Finally, Baker Academic agreed to publish it as a stand-alone commentary, and for this I am grateful.

Several things need to be addressed. First, word studies gained a great impetus with the papyri discoveries beginning in the last half of the nineteenth century. Although there was much discussion on the subject, which sometimes led to excesses, James Barr gave necessary cautions that (1) while the etymology of a word provides a history of the word, it does not signify the word's meaning in various periods of history and (2) the meaning of a word must also be derived from its context rather than given one meaning for all contexts, which he labeled as "illegitimate totality transfer."[1] Thus, the synchronic study of words came to the forefront, but one should not entirely forget the diachronic study of words.[2] Another caution concerns the earlier part of the twentieth century when there was a tendency to see little overlap in the meaning of synonyms, whereas in more recent times there is a tendency to see virtually no difference between them. Does it not make more sense to see that synonyms do overlap but they do not have identical meaning? The shades of meaning may be slight and not of much, if any, significance in some contexts, but still their distinctions should not be totally ignored in every instance. The word studies in this commentary are both diachronic and synchronic. I started with LSJ and discovered the classical sources of a word. Then I investigated the sources and reviewed

1. James Barr, *The Semantics of Biblical Language* (Oxford: Oxford University Press, 1961), 109, 218.

2. Cf. James Barr, "The Synchronic, the Diachronic and the Historical: A Triangular Relationship," in *Synchronic or Diachronic? A Debate on Method in Old Testament Exegesis*, ed. Johannes C. de Moor, Oudtestamentische Studiën, ed. Johannes C. de Moor, vol. 34 (Leiden: E. J. Brill, 1995), 1–14.

the usage in classical times. Normally, I used the Greek text of the Loeb Classical Library. Only on rare occasions—when I was not able to obtain a work—did I use a secondary source. (I translated the primary sources except where I have specifically mentioned a translator.) Then I used the *Accordance* software program to search for and analyze the word(s) in the LXX, MT, NT, and Qumran. I mention the number of times the Greek word is used in the LXX and the number of the times it is found in the canonical books of the OT because these books are a translation of the Hebrew text. Certainly, there was hesitancy in selecting a Hebrew word from among many Hebrew words. My intent was to show how it was generally rendered in the OT and then move on to the NT. In the NT I attempted to see how the word was used generally and then how it was used by Paul, especially in his later life.

Second, regarding textual criticism, I used a "reasoned eclectic" approach. When considering external evidence, I gave more weight to geographical distribution than some. When I first began working on this commentary, I used the textual apparatuses of UBS^3 and NA^{26}, but I have revised my work to comply with the textual apparatuses of UBS^4 and NA^{27}. Surprisingly, the new editions of these textual apparatuses brought many changes. Beyond these apparatuses, I used textual information that is mentioned by Bruce M. Metzger, *A Textual Commentary on the Greek New Testament,* 2d ed. (Stuttgart: Deutsche Bibelgesellschaft, 1994). I tried to be consistent in the use of symbols whether I used UBS^4 or NA^{27}. There are still some inconsistencies. For example, when relying solely on NA^{27}, I used the symbol 𝔐, but when using UBS^4, I used the symbol *Byz* [K L P]. However, when a textual variant in NA^{27} was not in UBS^4, I used the comments in the *Textual Commentary,* hence the symbols may be inconsistent with those used in NA^{27}. Also, I gained help from the commentaries on Ephesians by the church fathers, namely, Ambrosiaster, Chrysostom, Jerome, Oecumenius, Origen, Theodore of Mopsuestia, Theodoret, and Theophylact (based on Migne's text).

Third, I decided not to include a bibliography (aside from the list of commentaries and the bibliography on authorship at the end of the introduction) because it would have added one hundred pages to the commentary. Hence, in the footnotes, I gave full bibliographical data the first time a work was cited. In later references to the same work, I listed only author's last name, title or short title, and page number. The exceptions to this are the works in the list of abbreviations. When referring to commentaries, I gave only author's last name and page number; full bibliographical data is given in the list of commentaries. I should note a few commentaries that may cause confusion. Bruce has produced two commentaries on Ephesians, but I used only his latest one (except in the introduction, where I used both with regard to authorship). Although there are three editions of Dibelius's commentary (1912, 1927, 1953), I used the latest edition, Dibelius-Greeven (except in the excursus of 1:3–14, where he first developed the division of the passage in his 1927 edition, and in his treatment of the household codes, which was first developed in his 1912 edition). Martin has written three commentaries on Ephesians. Outside the introduction, I cite two of them and distinguish them as Martin, "Ephesians," in *The Broadman Bible Commentary* and Martin, *Ephesians, Colossians, and Philemon.* Also, Mitton's works could be confusing since he has a commentary entitled *Ephesians* and a treatise on the authorship of the letter entitled *The Epistle to the Ephesians: Its Authorship, Origin and Purpose.* When I cited his commentary, I listed his last name and the page number, and when I cited the latter work, I gave his last name, the short title *The Epistle to the Ephesians,* and a page number. When I have a question mark after an author's pagination, there is some doubt of the author's support.

Fourth, in regard to the order in listing publications, I typically put the most important work(s) first. After that, I listed the other works in chronological order of publication date to give a sense of history of interpretation. In the listing of commentaries, I do place Schnackenburg (1991) before Bruce (1984) and Lincoln (1990) because I started with the German edition (1982) and later changed the pagination to the English version (1991).

Fifth, with reference to the biblical text, I normally referred to the passages in the English text but noted the differences in the MT or the LXX. This is all based on *Accordance* versification. I used the English titles of the books rather than LXX's titles. For example, I employed 1 Sam rather than 1 Kgdms or Ezra and Neh rather than 2 Esdr. Whenever I use an equal sign (e.g., Matt 12:4 = Mark 2:26 = Luke 6:4), it refers to a parallel passage, usually in the Synoptics. In the listing of scriptural passages, I first cited the most relevant passages, followed by other passages in canonical order. Whenever I place a question mark after a passage of Scripture, I had some doubt regarding its use for that particular instance.

Sixth, when quoting other works, I followed the abbreviations, transliterations, and spellings of the work cited even when they differed from what is used in this commentary

Seventh, it is with deep gratitude that I express my appreciation to the following organizations and people: Dallas Theological Seminary for the generous sabbatical program that enabled me to devote concentrated time to the commentary; the libraries and librarians of Dallas Theological Seminary, Tyndale House, and University Library at Cambridge; Darrell L. Bock, my colleague, for reading the first five chapters at a very early stage and for his suggestions; my son, David, who read parts of the commentary and offered suggestions; and Professor Best for sending me offprints of all his recent articles. I further wish to express my appreciation to the following people who have helped me in various ways, namely, Markus N. A. Bockmuehl, Michael H. Burer, David J. A. Clines, Dorian G. Coover-Cox, Buist M. Fanning III, Donald R. Glenn, Trudy Goff, Wayne A. Grudem, Scott Hafemann, George W. Knight III, William Mounce, Peter T. O'Brien, Stanley E. Porter, Robert Reymond, Judith Siegel, Moisés Silva, Stephen Spencer, Eduard M. Vandermass, Daniel B. Wallace, and Bruce W. Winter. Finally, I wish to express my deeply felt appreciation to my beloved wife, Gini, who read through the entire commentary at least twice, offering suggestions for stylistic changes that enhance clarity.

Abbreviations

AB	Anchor Bible
ABD	*Anchor Bible Dictionary*. Edited by David Noel Freedman et al., 6 vols. New York: Doubleday, 1992
AGJU	Arbeiten zur Geschichte des antiken Judentums und des Urchristentums
Ambrosiaster *Eph*	Ambrosiaster [Pseudonym]. *In Epistolam Beati Pauli ad Ephesios*. *PL*, vol. 17. Paris: Excudebatur et Venit Apud J.-P. Migne Editorem, 1845. Pp. 371–404
AnBib	Analecta Biblica
ANRW	*Aufstieg und Niedergang der römischen Welt: Geschichte und Kultur Roms im Spiegel der neueren Forschung*. Edited by Hildegard Temporini and Wolfgang Haase. Berlin: de Gruyter, 1972–
ASNU	Acta seminarii neotestamentici upsaliensis
ASV	American Standard Version
AusBR	*Australian Biblical Review*
AV	Authorised Version (King James Version)
BAGD	Bauer, Walter. *A Greek-English Lexicon of the New Testament and Other Early Christian Literature*. Revised and augmented by F. Wilbur Gingrich and Frederick W. Danker, 2d ed. Chicago: University of Chicago Press, 1979
BDAG	Bauer, Walter. *A Greek-English Lexicon of the New Testament and Other Early Christian Literature*. Revised and edited by Frederick William Danker, 3d ed. Chicago: University of Chicago Press, 2000
BDB	Brown, Francis, S. R. Driver, and Charles A. Briggs, eds. *A Hebrew and English Lexicon of the Old Testament with an Appendix Containing the Biblical Aramaic*. Oxford: Clarendon, 1907
BDF	Blass, F., and A. Debrunner. *A Greek Grammar of the New Testament and Other Early Christian Literature*. Translated by Robert W. Funk. Chicago: University of Chicago Press, 1961
Best, *Ephesians*	Best, Ernest. *Ephesians*. New Testament Guides, ed. A. T. Lincoln. Sheffield: JSOT Press, 1993
BHT	Beiträge zur historischen Theologie
Bib	*Biblica*
BibLeb	*Bibel und Leben*
BJRL	*Bulletin of the John Rylands University Library of Manchester*
BR	*Biblical Research*
BSac	*Bibliotheca Sacra*

BT	*The Bible Translator*
BWANT	Beiträge zur Wissenschaft vom Alten und Neuen Testament
BZ	*Biblische Zeitschrift*
BZNW	Beiheft zur Zeitschrift für die neuetestamentliche Wissenschaft
CBQ	*Catholic Biblical Quarterly*
Chrysostom *Eph*	Chrysostom. *Ὑπόμνημα εἰς τὴν πρὸς Ἐφεσίους ἐπιστολήν* [*In Epistolam ad Ephesios Commentarius*]. *PL*, vol. 62. Paris: Excudebatur et Venit Apud J.-P. Migne Editorem, 1862. Pp. 9–176
CIG	*Corpus Inscriptionum Graecarum*. Edited by Augustus Boeckhius, Ioannes Franzius, Ernestus Curtius, and Adolphus Kirchhoff, 4 vols. Berlin: Ex Officiana Academica, 1828–77
CQR	*Church Quarterly Review*
GT	Greek Text
DDD	*Dictionary of Deities and Demons in the Bible (DDD)*. Edited by Karel van der Toorn, Bob Becking, and Peter W. van der Horst. Leiden: Brill, 1995
Dibelius-Greeven	Dibelius, Martin. *An die Kolosser, Epheser, an Philemon*. Revised by Heinrich Greeven, 3d ed. HNT, ed. Günther Bornkamm, vol. 12. Tübingen: Mohr, 1953. Pp. 54–100
DLNT	*Dictionary of the Later New Testament & Its Developments*. Edited by Ralph P. Martin and Peter H. Davids. Downers Grove, Ill.: InterVarsity; Leicester: Inter-Varsity, 1997
DNTB	*Dictionary of New Testament Background*. Edited by Craig A. Evans and Stanley E. Porter. Downers Grove, Ill.: InterVarsity; Leicester: Inter-Varsity, 2000
DPL	*Dictionary of Paul and His Letters*. Edited by Gerald F. Hawthorne, Ralph P. Martin, and Daniel G. Reid. Downers Grove, Ill.: InterVarsity; Leicester: Inter-Varsity, 1993
DRev	*Downside Review*
EBib	Études bibliques
EDNT	*Exegetical Dictionary of the New Testament*, ed. Horst Balz and Gerhard Schneider, trans. Virgil P. Howard, James W. Thompson, John W. Medendorp, and Douglas W. Stott, 3 vols. Grand Rapids: Eerdmans, 1990–93
ET	English Translation
ETR	*Études théologiques et religieuses*
EvQ	*Evangelical Quarterly*
EvT	*Evangelische Theologie*
Exp	*Expositor*
ExpTim	*Expository Times*
FRLANT	Forschungen zur Religion und Literatur des Alten und Neuen Testaments
GL	*Geist und Leben*
GNTMT	*The Greek New Testament according to the Majority Text*. Edited by Zane C. Hodges and Arthur L. Farstad. Nashville: Thomas Nelson, 1982
GTJ	*Grace Theological Journal*
HALOT	Koehler, Ludwig, Walter Baumgartner, and Johann Jakob Stamm, eds. *The Hebrew and Aramaic Lexicon of the Old Testament*. Translated and edited under the supervision of M. E. J. Richardson, 5 vols. Leiden: E. J. Brill, 1994–2000

HNT	Handbuch zum Neuen Testament
HS	Hoffmann, Ernst G., and Heinrich von Siebenthal. *Griechische Grammatik zum Neuen Testament*. Riehen, Switzerland: Immanuel, 1985
HTR	*Harvard Theological Journal*
HTS	Harvard Theological Studies
ICC	International Critical Commentary
IBS	*Irish Biblical Studies*
IKZ	*Internationale kirchliche Zeitschrift*
Int	*Interpretation*
JB	Jerusalem Bible
JBL	*Journal of Biblical Literature*
Jerome *Eph*	Jerome. *Commentoriorum in Epistolam ad Ephesios*. *PL*, vol. 26. Paris: Venit Apud Editorem, 1845. Pp. 439–554
JETS	*Journal of the Evangelical Theological Society*
JSNT	*Journal for the Study of the New Testament*
JSNTSup	Journal for the Study of the New Testament Supplement Series
JTS	*Journal of Theological Studies*
KEK	Kritisch-exegetischer Kommentar über das Neue Testament
κτλ.	καὶ τὰ λοῖπα (et cetera)
L&N	Louw, Johannes P., Eugene A. Nida, et al. *Greek-English Lexicon of the New Testament Based on Semantic Domains*, 2 vols. New York: United Bible Societies, 1988
LSJ	Liddell, Henry George, and Robert Scott, comps. *A Greek-English Lexicon*. Revised and augmented by Henry Stuart Jones and Roderick McKenzie, 9th ed. With a Revised Supplement 1996, ed. P. G. W. Glare and A. A. Thompson. Oxford: Clarendon, 1940
LUÅ	Lunds universistets årsskrift
LXX	*Septuaginta*. Edited by Alfred Rahlfs. Stuttgart: Deutsche Bibelgesellschaft, 1979
MHT 1	Moulton, James Hope. *Prolegomena*. Vol. 1, *A Grammar of New Testament Greek*, ed. James Hope Moulton, 3d ed. Edinburgh: T & T Clark, 1908
MHT 2	Moulton, James Hope, and Wilbert Francis Howard. *Accidence and Word-Formation*. Vol. 2, *A Grammar of New Testament Greek*, ed. James Hope Moulton. Edinburgh: T & T Clark, 1929
MHT 3	Turner, Nigel. *Syntax*. Vol. 3, *A Grammar of New Testament Greek*, ed. James Hope Moulton. Edinburgh: T & T Clark, 1963
MHT 4	Turner, Nigel. *Style*. Vol. 4, *A Grammar of New Testament Greek*, ed. James Hope Moulton. Edinburgh: T & T Clark, 1976
MM	Moulton, James Hope, and George Milligan. *The Vocabulary of the Greek Testament*. London: Hodder and Stoughton, 1930
MT	Masoretic Text
NASB	New American Standard Bible
NEB	New English Bible
NA^{25}	*Novum Testamentum Graece*. Edited by Erwin Nestle and Kurt Aland, 25th ed. Stuttgart: Württembergische Bibelanstalt, 1963
NA^{26}	*Novum Testamentum Graece*. Edited by Kurt Aland, Matthew Black, Carlo M. Martini, Bruce M. Metzger, and Allen Wikgren, 26th ed. Stuttgart: Deutsche Bibelstiftung, 1979

NA[27]	*Novum Testamentum Graece*. Edited by Barbara and Kurt Aland, Johannes Karavidopoulos, Carlo M. Martini, and Bruce M. Metzger, 27th rev. ed. Stuttgart: Deutsche Bibelgesellschaft, 1993
NICNT	New International Commentary on the New Testament
NIDOTTE	*The New International Dictionary of Old Testament Theology and Exegesis*, ed. Willem A. VanGemeren, 5 vols. Grand Rapids: Zondervan Publishing House, 1997
NIDNTT	*The New International Dictionary of New Testament Theology*, ed. Colin Brown, 3 vols. Grand Rapids: Zondervan Publishing House, 1975–78
NIV	New International Version
NJB	New Jerusalem Bible
NovT	*Novum Testamentum*
NovTSup	Supplements to Novum Testamentum
NRSV	New Revised Standard Version
NRT	*Nouvelle revue théologique*
NT	New Testament
NTD	Das Neue Testament Deutsch
NTS	*New Testament Studies*
OCD	*The Oxford Classical Dictionary*, 3d ed., ed. Simon Hornblower and Antony Spawforth. Oxford: Oxford University Press, 1996
Oecumenius *Eph*	Oecumenius. *Παύλου ἀποστόλου ἡ πρὸς Ἐφεσίους ἐπιστολή* [*Pauli Apostoli ad Ephesios Epistola*]. *PL*, vol. 118. Paris: Excudebatur et Venit Apud J.-P. Migne Editorem, 1864. Pp. 1169–1258
OJRS	*Ohio Journal of Religious Studies*
OTM	Oxford Theological Monographs
PG	*Patrologiae cursus completus, . . . Series Graeca*. Edited by J.-P. Migne, 161 vols. Paris: Seu Petit-Montrogue, 1857–66
PL	*Patrologiae cursus completus, . . . Series Latina*. Edited by J.-P. Migne, 221 vols. Paris: Excudebat Migne, 1844–64
P.Oxy.	*The Oxyrhynchus Papyri*. Edited by Bernard P. Grenfell, Arthur S. Hunt, et al., 66 vols. London: Egypt Exploration Fund, 1898–1999
RB	*Revue Biblique*
ResQ	*Restoration Quarterly*
RevExp	*Review and Expositor*
RivB	*Rivista biblica*
RSR	*Recherches de science religieuse*
RTR	*Reformed Theological Review*
RSV	Revised Standard Version
RV	Revised Version
SANT	Studien zum Alten und Neuen Testament
SBLDS	Society of Biblical Literature Dissertation Series
SBLSBS	Society of Biblical Literature Sources for Biblical Study
SBT	Studies in Biblical Theology
ScEs	*Science et esprit*
Scr	*Scripture*
SE	*Studia Evangelica*
SIG	*Sylloge Inscriptionium Graecarum*. 3d ed. Edited by Wilhelm Dittenberger, 4 vols. Leipzig: S. Hirzel, 1915–24
SJT	*Scottish Journal of Theology*
SNTSMS	Society for New Testament Studies Monograph Series

ST	*Studia Theologica*
Str-B	Strack, Hermann L., and Paul Billerbeck. *Kommentar zum Neuen Testament aus Talmud und Midrasch*, 6 vols. (Munich: C. H. Beck'sche Verlagsbuchhandlung, 1922–61)
SWJT	*Southwestern Journal of Theology*
TEV	Today's English Version
TBl	*Theologische Blätter*
TBT	*The Bible Today*
TDNT	*Theological Dictionary of the New Testament*, ed. Gerhard Kittel and Gerhard Friedrich, trans. Geoffrey W. Bromiley, 10 vols. Grand Rapids: Eerdmans, 1964–76
TDOT	*Theological Dictionary of the Old Testament*, ed. G. Johannes Botterweck and Helmer Ringgren, trans. John T. Willis, Geoffrey W. Bromiley, David E. Green, and Douglass W. Stott, 11 vols. Grand Rapids: Eerdmans, 1974–2001
Theodore of Mopsuestia *Eph*	Theodore of Mopsuestia. *In Epistolam Pauli ad Ephesios Comentarii Fragmenta*. *PG*, vol. 66. Paris: Excudebatur et Venit Apud J.-P. Migne Editorem, 1859. Pp. 911–22
Theodoret *Eph*	Theodoret. *Ἑρμενεία τῆς πρὸς Ἐφεσίους ἐπιστόλης* [*Interpretatio Epistolae ad Ephesios*]. *PG*, vol. 82. Paris: Excudebatur et Venit Apud J. P. Migne Editorem, 1859, Pp. 508–58
Theophylact *Eph*	Theophylact, *Τῆς τοῦ ἁγίου Παύλου πρὸς Ἐφεσίους ἐπιστολῆς ἐξήγεσις* [*Epistolae divi Pauli ad Ephesios Expositio*]. *PG*, vol. 124. Paris: Excudebatur et Venit Apud J.-P. Migne Editorem, 1864. Pp. 1031–1138
TGl	*Theologie und Glaube*
ThStud	*Theologische Studiën*
TJ	*Trinity Journal*
TLZ	*Theologische Literaturzeitung*
TQ	*Theologische Quartalschrift*
TR	Textus Receptus
TU	Texte und Untersuchungen zur Geschichte der altchristliche Literatur
TWAT	Botterweck, G. Johannes, Heinz-Josef Fabry, and Helmer Ringgren, eds. *Theologisches Wörterbuch zum Alten Testament*, 10 vols. Stuttgart: W. Kohlhammer, 1970–2000
TynBul	*Tyndale Bulletin*
TZ	*Theologische Zeitschrift*
UBS^{1}	*The Greek New Testament*. Edited by Kurt Aland, Matthew Black, Bruce M. Metzger, and Allen Wikgren. London: United Bible Societies, 1966
UBS^{2}	*The Greek New Testament*. Edited by Kurt Aland, Matthew Black, Carlo M. Martini, Bruce M. Metzger, and Allen Wikgren, 2d ed. Stuttgart: Deutsche Bibelgesellschaft, 1968
UBS^{3}	*The Greek New Testament*. Edited by Kurt Aland, Matthew Black, Carlo M. Martini, Bruce M. Metzger, and Allen Wikgren, 3d ed. New York: United Bible Societies, 1975
UBS$^{3\text{corr.}}$	*The Greek New Testament*. Edited by Kurt Aland, Matthew Black, Carlo M. Martini, Bruce M. Metzger, and Allen Wikgren, 3d ed., corrected. Stuttgart: United Bible Societies, 1983

UBS[4] — *The Greek New Testament*, Edited by Barbara Aland, Kurt Aland, Johannes Karvidopoulos, Carlo M. Martini, and Bruce M. Metzger, 4th rev. ed. Stuttgart: United Bible Societies, 1993
VC — *Vigiliae christianae*
VE — *Vox evangelica*
Vg — Vulgate
WBC — Word Biblical Commentary
WD — *Wort und Dienst*
WH — Westcott, Brooke Foss, and Fenton John Anthony Hort. *The New Testament in the Original Greek: Text*. Cambridge/London: Macmillan, 1881
WLQ — *Wisconsin Lutheran Quarterly*
WTJ — *Westminster Theological Journal*
WUNT — Wissenschaftliche Untersuchungen zum Neuen Testament
ZEE — *Zeitschrift für evangelische Ethik*
ZKT — *Zeitschrift für katholische Theologie*
ZNW — *Zeitschrift für die neutestamentliche Wissenschaft*
ZTK — *Zeitschrift für Theologie und Kirche*

Pseudepigraphy

2 Apoc. Bar. — *2 Apocalypse of Baruch*
1 Enoch — *1 Enoch*
Barn. — *Barnabas*
Jub. — *Jubilees*
Pss. Sol. — *Psalm(s) of Solomon*
T. Dan. — *Testament of Dan*
T. Iss. — *Testament of Issachar*
T. Jud. — *Testament of Judah*
T. Lev. — *Testament of Levi*
T. Sim. — *Testament of Simeon*
T. Sol. — *Testament of Solomon*

Qumran/Dead Sea Scrolls

CD — Cairo Genizah copy of the *Damascus Document*
1QH[a] — *Hodayot*[a] or *Thanksgiving Hymns*[a]
1QM — *Milḥamah* or *War Scroll*
1QpHab — *Pesher Habakkuk*
1QS — *Serekh ha-Yaḥad* or *Rule of the Community*
1QSa — *Rule of the Congregation* (Appendix a to 1QS)

Josephus

A.J. — *Antiquitates Judaicae*
B.J. — *Bellum Judaicum*
C. Ap. — *Contra Apionem*

Philo

Decal. — *De Decalogo*
Deus — *Quod Deus sit immutabilis*
Fug. — *De Fuga et Inventione*
Gig. — *De Gigantibus*
Hypoth. — *Hypothetica/Apologia pro Iudaeis*
Jos. — *De Josepho*

Leg. All.	*Legum Allegoriae*
Leg. Gai.	*De Legatione ad Gaium*
Mos.	*De Vita Mosis*
Mut.	*De Mutatione Nominum*
Op. Mund.	*De Opificio Mundi*
Post. C.	*De Posteritate Caini*
Praem.	*De Praemiis et Poenis*
Sobr.	*De Sobrietate*
Somn.	*De Somniis*
Spec.	*De Specialibus Legibus*
Virt.	*De Virtutibus*

Rabbinic Literature

ʾAbot	*ʾAbot*
Qid.	*Qiddušin*
Yeb.	*Yebamot*
Midr. Lev	*Midrash Leviticus*
Midr. Ps.	*Midrash Psalms*
Deut. Rab.	*Deuteronomy Rabbah*
Num. Rab.	*Numbers Rabbah*

Commentaries

In this work I have referred to commentaries on Ephesians only by the author's last name and page number with the exception of Martin who wrote more than one commentary on Ephesians. Although Bruce wrote two commentaries on Ephesians, only the 1984 edition is used in this commentary. In the commentaries below, pagination within brackets signifies the pages which discuss the authorship of Ephesians.

Abbott, T. K. *A Critical and Exegetical Commentary on the Epistle to the Ephesians and to the Colossians*. ICC, ed. S. R. Driver, A. Plummer, and C. A. Briggs. Edinburgh: T & T Clark, 1897, lxiv+191 [ix–xxxi].

Aletti, Jean-Noël. *Saint Paul Épître aux Éphésiens: Introduction, Traduction et Commentaire*. EBib, vol. 42. Paris: Gabalda, 2001 [1–38].

Alford, Henry. *The Greek New Testament: With a Critically Revised Text: A Digest of Various Readings: Marginal References to Verbal and Idiomatic Usage: Prolegomena: and a Critical and Exegetical Commentary*. 5th ed., vol. 3. London: Rivingtons, 1871, 6–26, 68–151 [6–10] [1st ed., 1856].

Allan, John A. *The Epistle to the Ephesians*. Torch Bible Commentaries, ed. John Marsh, David M. Paton, and Alan Richardson. London: SCM, 1959 [14–23].

Ambrosiaster. *In Epistolam Beati Pauli ad Ephesios*. *PL*, vol. 17. Paris: Excudebatur et Venit Apud J.-P. Migne Editorem, 1845, 371–404.

Aquinas, Thomas. *Commentary on Saint Paul's Epistle to the Ephesians*. Translation and introduction by Matthew L. Lamb. Albany, N.Y.: Magi Books, 1966.

Barclay, William. *The Letters to the Galatians and Ephesians*. Rev. ed. The Daily Study Bible. Philadelphia: Westminster, 1976, 61–185 [61–71] [1st ed., 1956].

Barth, Markus. *Ephesians: Introduction, Translation, and Commentary on Chapters 1–3*. AB, ed. William Foxwell Albright and David Noel Freedman, vol. 34. Garden City, N.Y.: Doubleday, 1974 [36–50].

———. *Ephesians: Translation and Commentary on Chapters 4–6*. AB, ed. William Foxwell Albright and David Noel Freedman, vol. 34A. Garden City, N.Y.: Doubleday, 1974.

Beare, Francis W. "The Epistle to the Ephesians." In *The Interpreter's Bible*, ed. George Arthur Buttrick et al., vol. 10. New York: Abingdon, 1953, 595–749 [597–605].

Beet, Joseph Agar. *A Commentary on St. Paul's Epistle to the Ephesians, Philippians, Colossians, and to Philemon*. London: Hodder and Stoughton, 1890, 2–5, 9–13, 271–380 [9–13].

Belser, Johannes Evang. *Der Epheserbrief des Apostels Paulus*. Freiburg im Breisgau: Herdersche Verlagshandlung, 1908 [1–6].

Bengel, John Albert. *Gnomon of the New Testament*. Originally brought out by M. Ernest Bengel, completed with corrections by J. C. F Steudel, 7th ed. Vol. 4, *Containing the Commentary on the Galatians, Ephesians, Philippians, Colossians, I. and II. Thessalonians, I. and II. Timothy, Titus, Philemon, and Hebrews*. Translated by James Bryce. Edinburgh: T & T Clark, 1877, 61–118 [61–62] [1st published in 1742].

Best, Ernest. *A Critical and Exegetical Commentary on Ephesians*. ICC, ed. J. A. Emerton, C. E. B. Cranfield, and G. N. Stanton. Edinburgh: T & T Clark, 1998 [6–36].

Bouttier, Michel. *L'Épître de Saint Paul aux Éphésiens*. Commentaire du Nouveau Testament, ed. J. Zumstein et al., vol. 9B. Genève: Labor et Fides, 1991 [24–35].

Bratcher, Robert G., and Eugene A. Nida. *A Translator's Handbook on Paul's Letter to the Ephesians*. London: United Bible Societies, 1982.

Braune, Karl. *The Epistle of Paul to the Ephesians*. Translated with additions by M. B. Riddle. A Commentary on the Holy Scriptures: Critical, Doctrinal, and Homiletical, with Special Reference to Ministers and Students, ed. John Peter Lange and Philip Schaff, vol. 7. Edinburgh: T & T Clark, 1870 [8–10] [German ed., 1867, 6–7].

Bruce, F. F. *The Epistle to the Ephesians. A Verse by Verse Exposition*. London: Pickering & Inglis, 1961 [11–19].

———. *The Epistles to the Colossians, to Philemon, and to the Ephesians*. NICNT, ed. F. F. Bruce. Grand Rapids: Eerdmans, 1984, 227–416 [229–46].

Caird, G. B. *Paul's Letters from Prison (Ephesians, Philippians, Colossians, Philemon) in the Revised Standard Version*. New Clarendon Bible, ed. H. F. D. Sparks. London: Oxford University Press, 1976, 9–94 [11–29].

Calvin, [Jean]. *The Epistles of Paul the Apostle to the Galatians, Ephesians, Philippians and Colossians*. Translated by T. H. L. Parker. Calvin's Commentaries, ed. David W. Torrance and Thomas F. Torrance. Grand Rapids: Eerdmans; Edinburgh: Oliver & Boyd, 1965, 121–224 [121–23] [1st published in 1548].

Chadwick, Henry. "Ephesians." In *Peake's Commentary on the Bible*. Edited by Matthew Black and H. H. Rowley. London: Thomas Nelson, 1962, 980–84 [980–82].

Chafer, Lewis Sperry. *The Ephesian Letter Doctrinally Considered*. Findlay, Ohio: Dunham; London: Marshall, Morgan & Scott, 1935 [13–17].

Chrysostom, S. John. *Ὑπόμνημα εἰς τὴν πρὸς Ἐφεσίους ἐπιστολήν* [*In Epistolam ad Ephesios Commentarius*]. *PL*, vol. 62. Paris: Excudebatur et Venit Apud J.-P. Migne Editorem, 1862, 9–176.

———. *Homilies on Epistle of S. Paul the Apostle to the Ephesians*. Translated by members of the English Church. A Library of Fathers of the Holy Catholic Church Anterior to the Division of the East and West, vol. 6. Oxford: John Henry Parker, 1840, 99–381.

Conzelmann, Hans. "Der Brief an die Epheser." In *Die Briefe an die Galater, Epheser, Philipper, Kolosser, Thessalonicher und Philemon*, 15th ed. NTD, ed. Gerhard Friedrich and Peter Stuhlmacher, vol. 8. Göttingen: Vandenhoeck & Ruprecht, 1981, 86–124 [86–88] [9th ed., 1962, 56–58].

Dahl, Nils Alstrup with Donald H. Juel. "Ephesians." In *The HarperCollins Bible Commentary*, ed. James L. Mays et al., rev. ed. San Francisco: HarperSanFransico, 2000, 1113–20 [1113–14].

Dale, R. W. *The Epistle to the Ephesians. Its Doctrine and Ethics*. London: Hodder and Stoughton, 1883 [11–16].

Davies, J. Llewelyn. *The Epistles of St. Paul to the Ephesians, the Colossians, and Philemon*. 2d ed. London: Macmillan, 1884 [9–26] [1st ed., 1866, same pages].

Dibelius, Martin. *An die Kolosser, Epheser, an Philemon*. 3d ed. rev. by Heinrich Greeven. HNT, ed. Günther Bornkamm, vol. 12. Tübingen: Mohr, 1953, 54–100 [56–57, 59–60, 63, 78, 83–85, 91–92, 99] [1st ed., 1912, 95–125 (96–97, 99–100, 109, 113–14, 119, 125)].

Dodd, C. H. "Ephesians." In *The Abingdon Bible Commentary*. Edited by Frederick Carl Eiselen, Edwin Lewis, and David G. Downey. New York: Abingdon-Cokesbury, 1929, 1222–37 [1223–25].

Donelson, Lewis R. *Colossians, Ephesians, First and Second Timothy, and Titus*. Westminster Bible Companion, ed. Patrick D. Miller and David L. Bartlett. Louisville, Ky.: Westminster/John Knox, 1996, 57–114 [60–61].

Eadie, John. *A Commentary on the Greek Text of the Epistle of Paul to the Ephesians*. 3d ed. Edited by W. Young. Edinburgh: T & T Clark, 1883. Reprint, idem. *Commentary on the Epistle to the Ephesians*. Grand Rapids: Zondervan, n.d. [xx–xlix] [1st ed., 1854, xiii–xxxvi].

Ellicott, Charles J. *St Paul's Epistle to the Ephesians: with a Critical and Grammatical Commentary, and a Revised Translation*. 5th ed. London: Longmans, Green, 1884 [xi, xvi] [1st ed., 1855, v].

Erasmus' Annotations on the New Testament: Galatians to the Apocalypse. Edited by Anne Reeve and M. A. Screech. Studies in the History of Christian Thought, ed. Heiko A. Oberman et al., vol. 52. Leiden: Brill, 1993, 591–619 [591, 595]. [Originally published: Erasmus of Rotterdam. *In Novum Testamentum Annotationes*. Basel: Froben, 1519].

Ernst, Josef. *Die Briefe an die Philipper, an Philemon, an die Kolosser, an die Epheser*. Regensburger Neues Testament, ed. Otto Kuss. Regensburg: Friedrich Pustet, 1974, 245–405 [245–63].

Ewald, Paul. *Die Briefe des Paulus an die Epheser, Kolosser und Philemon*. Kommentar zum Neuen Testament, ed. Theodor Zahn, vol. 10. Leipzig: A. Deichert'sche Verlagsbuchhandlung, 1905, 13–266 [13–53].

Findlay, G. G. *The Epistle to the Ephesians*. The Expositor's Bible, ed. W. Robertson Nicoll. London: Hodder and Stoughton, 1892 [3–18].

Foulkes, Francis. *The Epistle of Paul to the Ephesians: An Introduction and Commentary.* 2d ed. The Tyndale New Testament Commentaries, ed. Leon Morris, vol. 10. Grand Rapids: Eerdmans, 1989 [22–48] [1st ed., 1963, 17–40].

Gaugler, Ernst. *Der Epheserbrief*. Auslegung neutestamentlicher Schriften, ed. Max Geiger and Kurt Stalder, vol. 6. Zürich: EVZ-Verlag, 1966 [3–14].

Gnilka, Joachim. *Der Epheserbrief*. Herders theologischer Kommentar zum Neuen Testament, ed. Alfred Wikenhauser, Anton Vögtle, and Rudolf Schnackenburg, vol. 10: Fasc. 2. Freiburg: Herder, 1971 [1–52, esp. 1–21, 45–49].

Gore, Charles. *St. Paul's Epistle to the Ephesians: A Practical Exposition*. London: John Murray, 1898 [6–19, 43–45].

Graham, Glenn R. *An Exegetical Summary of Ephesians*. Dallas: Summer Institute of Linguistics, Inc., 1997.

Grosheide, F. W. *De Brief van Paulus aan de Effeziërs*. Commentaar op het Nieuwe Testament, ed. F. W. Grosheide, vol. 9. Kampen: N. V. Uitgeversmaatschappij J. H. Kok, 1960 [5–9].

Harless, G. Chr. Adolph v. *Commentar über den Brief Pauli an die Ephesier.* 2d ed. rev. Stuttgart: Liesching, 1858 [xvii–lxxviii] [1st ed., 1834].

Haupt, Erich. "Die Brief an die Epheser." In *Die Gefangenschaftsbriefe*, 7th ed. KEK, ed. W. Schmidt, vol. 8. Göttingen: Vandenhoeck & Ruprecht, 1897, 38–86 [54–74]; 1–259.

Hendriksen, William. *Ephesians*. New Testament Commentary. Grand Rapids: Baker, 1967 [32–56].

Hitchcock, George S. *The Epistle to the Ephesians: An Encyclical of St. Paul.* London: Burns and Oates, 1913 [12–25].

Hodge, Charles. *A Commentary on the Epistle to the Ephesians*. New York: R. Carter and Brothers, 1856. Reprint, Grand Rapids: Eerdmans, 1954 [ix–xvii].

Hoehner, Harold W. "Ephesians." In *Bible Knowledge Commentary,* ed. John F. Walvoord and Roy B. Zuck, vol. 2. Wheaton, Ill.: Victor Books, 1983, 613–45 [613–14].

Holmes, Mark A. *Ephesians: A Bible Commentary in the Wesleyan Tradition*. Edited by Ray E. Barnwell et al. Indianapolis, Ind.: Wesleyan Publishing House, 1997 [12–15].

Houlden, J. L. *Paul's Letters from Prison: Philippians, Colossians, Philemon, Ephesians*. The Pelican New Testament Commentary, ed. Dennis Nineham. Baltimore: Penguin Books, 1970, 233–341 [235–56].

Hübner, Hans. *An Philemon. An die Kolosser. An die Epheser.* HNT, ed. Andreas Lindemann, vol. 12. Tübingen: Mohr, 1997, 129–277 [11–12, 272].

Hugedé, Norbert. *L'Épître aux Éphésiens*. Genève: Labor et Fides, 1973 [9–10].

Jerome. *Commentoriorum in Epistolam ad Ephesios*. *PL*, vol. 26. Paris: Venit Apud Editorem, 1845, 439–554.

Johnson, Luke Timothy. *Invitation to the NT Epistles III: A Commentary on Colossians, Ephesians, 1 Timothy 2 Timothy, and Titus with a Complete Text from the Jerusalem Bible*. Garden City, N.Y.: Image Books, 1980, 71–136 [17–22].

Johnston, George. *Ephesians, Philippians, Colossians and Philemon*. Century Bible, new ed., ed. H. H. Rowley and Matthew Black. London: Thomas Nelson and Sons, 1967, 4–27 [4–7].

Karavidopoulos, Ioannes D. *Ἀποστόλου Παύλου ἐπιστολὲς πρὸς Ἐφεσίους, Φιλιππησίους, Κολοσσαεῖς, Φιλήμονα*. Ἑρμηνεία Καινῆς Διαθήκης, ed. I. Karavidopoulos, I. Galanis, and P. Vassiliadis, vol. 10. Thessaloniki: Pournaras, 1981 [50–55] [1973 ed., 347–52].

Kitchen, Martin. *Ephesians*. New Testament Readings, ed. John Court. New York: Routledge, 1994 [4–7].

Klöpper, Albert. *Der Brief an die Epheser.* Göttingen: Vandenhoeck & Ruprecht, 1891 [9–35, esp. 9–17].

Koehler, John Ph. *A Commentary on Galatians* and *Paul's Rhapsody in Christ: A Commentary on Ephesians*. Edited by Paul Hensel and Hans Koch. Translated by Gerhard Ruediger and Elmer E. Sauer. Milwaukee, Wis.: Northwestern Publishing House, 2000, 161–529 [163–65, 177–79] [German ed., 1936].

Kreitzer, Larry J. *The Epistle to the Ephesians*. Epworth Commentaries, ed. Ivor H. Jones. Peterborough: Epworth, 1998 [21–30].

Lenski, R. C. H. *The Interpretation of St. Paul's Epistle to the Galatians to the Ephesians and to the Philippians*. Columbus, Ohio: Lutheran Book Concern, 1937. Reprint, Minneapolis: Augsburg, 1961, 325–668 [336–43].

Liefeld, Walter L. *Ephesians*. The IVP New Testament Commentary Series, ed. Grant R. Osborne, D. Stuart Briscoe, and Haddon Robinson. Downers Grove, Ill.: InterVarsity, 1997 [14–20].

Lincoln, Andrew T. *Ephesians*. WBC, ed. David A. Hubbard and Glenn W. Barker; New Testament, ed. Ralph P. Martin, vol. 42. Dallas: Word, 1990 [xlvii–lxxiii].

Lindemann, Andreas. *Der Epheserbrief*. Züricher Bibelkommentare, ed. Hans Heinrich Schmid and Siegfried Schulz, vol. NT 8. Zürich: Theologischer Verlag, 1985 [9–16].

Lock, Walter. *The Epistle to the Ephesians with an Introduction and Notes*. Westminster Commentaries, ed. Walter Lock and D. C. Simpson. London: Methuen, 1929 [11].

Luther, Martin. *Die Briefe an die Epheser, Philipper und Kolosser.* D. Martin Luthers Epistelauslegung, ed. Eduard Ellwein, vol. 3. Göttingen: Vandenhoeck & Ruprecht, 1973, 11–174 [passim] [1st published in 1530–45].

Luz, Ulrich. "Der Brief an die Epheser." In *Die Briefe an die Galater, Epheser und Kolosser,* by Jürgen Becker and Ulrich Luz, 18th ed. NTD, ed. Peter Stuhlmacher and Hans Weder, vol. 8/1. Göttingen: Vandenhoeck & Ruprecht, 1998, 105–80 [108–9].

MacDonald, Margaret Y. *Colossians and Ephesians*. Sacra Pagina Series, ed. Daniel J. Harrington, vol. 17. Collegeville, Minn.: Liturgical Press, 2000 [15–17].

Mackay, John A. *God's Order. The Ephesian Letter and this Present Time*. New York: Macmillan; London: Nisbet, 1953 [10–14].

Macpherson, John. *Commentary on St. Paul's Epistle to the Ephesians*. Edinburgh: T & T Clark, 1892 [32–44].

Martin, Ralph P. "Ephesians." In *The New Bible Commentary*, ed. D. Guthrie et al. London: Inter-Varsity, 1970, 1105–24 [1105–6].

———. "Ephesians." In *The Broadman Bible Commentary*, ed. Clifton J. Allen, vol. 11. Nashville: Broadman; London: Marshall, Morgan & Scott, 1971, 125–77 [125–31].

———. *Ephesians, Colossians, and Philemon*. Interpretation: A Bible Commentary for Teaching and Preaching, ed. James Luther Mays; New Testament ed. Paul J. Achtemeier. Atlanta: John Knox, 1991, 1–79 [2–6].

Masson, Charles. *L'Épître de Saint Paul aux Éphésiens*. Commentaire du Nouveau Testament, vol. 9. Neuchatel: Delachaux & Niestlé, 1953 [226–28].

Meinertz, Max., and Fritz Tillmann. *Die Gefangenschaftsbriefe des Heiligen Paulus*. 4th newly rev. ed. Die Heilige Schrift des Neuen Testaments Übersetzt und Erklärt in Verbindung mit Fachgelehrten, ed. Fritz Tillmann, vol. 7. Bonn: Peter Hanstein, 1931, 50–106 [50–61] [1st ed., 1917, 43–91 (43–52)].

Meyer, Heinrich August Wilhelm. *Critical and Exegetical Handbook to the Epistle to the Ephesians and the Epistle to Philemon*. 4th ed. Translated by Maurice J. Evans, trans. rev. and ed. by William P. Dickson. Critical and Exegetical Commentary on the New Testament, ed. Heinrich August Wilhelm Meyer. Edinburgh: T & T Clark, 1895, 1–353 [1–30] [German ed., 1843].

Mitton, C. Leslie. *Ephesians*. New Century Bible, ed. Ronald E. Clements (OT) and Matthew Black (NT). London: Oliphants, 1976 [2–32].

Morris, Leon. *Expository Reflections on the Letter to the Ephesians*. Grand Rapids: Baker, 1994 [10–12, 28–30, 83–85, passim].

Moule, H. C. G. *The Epistle to the Ephesians*. Cambridge Bible for Schools and Colleges, ed. J. J. S. Perowne. Cambridge: Cambridge University Press, 1886 [22–29].

Muddiman, John. *The Epistle to the Ephesians*. Black's New Testament Commentaries, ed. Morna D. Hooker. London: Continuum, 2001.

Murray, J. O. F. *The Epistle of Paul the Apostle to the Ephesians*. Cambridge Greek Testament for Schools and Colleges, ed. R. St John Parry. Cambridge: Cambridge University Press, 1914 [ix–lxxvi].

Mußner, Franz. *Der Brief an die Epheser*. Ökumensicher Taschenbuchkommentar zum Neuen Testament, ed. Erich Gräßer and Karl Kertelge, vol. 10. Gütersloh: Gütersloher Verlagshaus, 1982 [17–18].

O'Brien, Peter T. *The Letter to the Ephesians*. The Pillar New Testament Commentary, ed. D. A. Carson. Grand Rapids: Eerdmans, 1999 [4–21, 37–47].

Oecumenius. *Παύλου ἀποστόλου ἡ πρὸς Ἐφεσίους ἐπιστολή* [*Pauli Apostoli ad Ephesios Epistola*]. *PL*, vol. 118. Paris: Excudebatur et Venit Apud J.-P. Migne Editorem, 1864, 1169–1258.

Olshausen, Hermann. *Biblical Commentary on St Paul's Epistles to the Galatians, Ephesians, Colossians, and Thessalonians*. Translated by Clergymen of the Church of England. Clarks Foreign Theological Library, vol. 21. Edinburgh: T & T Clark, 1851, 109–284 [117–22] [German ed., 1840, 4:126–31].

Origen. *In Epistolam ad Ephesios*. *PG*, vol. 14. Paris: Excudebatur et Venit Apud J.-P. Migne Editorem, 1862, 1297–98.

Patzia, Arthur G. *Colossians, Philemon, Ephesians*. Good News Commentary New Testament, ed. W. Ward Gasque. San Francisco: Harper & Row, 1984, 102–271 [102–22].

Penna, Romano. *La lettera agli Efesini*. Scritti delle origini cristiane, ed. G. Barbaglio and R. Penna, vol. 10. Bologna: Edizioni Dehoniane, 1988 [13–69, esp. 19–40, 59–69].

Perkins, Pheme. *Ephesians*. Abingdon New Testament Commentaries, ed. Victor Paul Furnish et al. Nashville: Abingdon, 1997 [15–27].

Pokorný, Petr. *Der Brief des Paulus an die Epheser*. Theologisher Handkommentar zum Neuen Testament, ed. Erich Fascher, Udo Schnelle, Joachim Rhode, and Christian Wolff, vol. 10/II. Leipzig: Evangelische Verlagsanstalt, 1992 [34–43].

Rendtorff, Heinrich. "Der Brief an die Epheser." In *Die kleineren Briefe des Apostles Paulus*, 6th ed. NTD, ed. Paul Althaus, vol. 8. Göttingen: Vandenhoeck & Ruprecht, 1953, 56–85 [56–57].

Rienecker, Fritz. *Der Brief des Paulus an die Epheser.* Wuppertaler Studienbibel, ed. Fritz Rienecker. Wuppertal: Brockhaus, 1961 [19–25].

Robinson, J. Armitage. *St Paul's Epistle to the Ephesians. A Revised Text and Translation with Exposition and Notes*. London: Macmillan, 1903. Reprint, London: James Clark, n.d. [11–13, 292–95].

Salmond, S. D. F. "The Epistle of Paul to the Ephesians." In *The Expositor's Greek Testament*, ed. W. Robertson Nicoll, vol. 3. London: Hodder and Stoughton, 1903, 201–95 [217–33].

Sampley, J. Paul. "The Letter to the Ephesians." In *The Deutero-Pauline Letters: Ephesians, Colossians, 2 Thessalonians, 1–2 Timothy, Titus*. Rev. ed. Proclamation Commentaries, ed. Gerhard Krodel. Philadelphia: Fortress, 1993 [1–4] [1st ed., 1978].

Schlatter, Adolf. "Der Brief an die Epheser." In *Erläuterungen zum Neuen Testament*, vol. 7. Stuttgart: Calwer, 1963, 151–249 [152–53] [1st ed., 1908, pt. 11, unable to see, but 1909 printing, 2:545–46].

Schlier, Heinrich. *Der Brief an die Epheser.* 7th ed. Düsseldorf: Patmos, 1971 [22–28] [1st. ed., 1957, same pages].

Schnackenburg, Rudolf. *Ephesians: A Commentary.* Translated by Helen Heron. Edinburgh: T & T Clark, 1991 [24–37] [German ed., 1982, 20–34].

Scott, E. F. *The Epistles of Paul to the Colossians, to Philemon and to the Ephesians*. The Moffatt New Testament Commentary, ed. James Moffatt. London: Hodder and Stoughton, 1930, 119–257 [119–23].

Simpson, E. K. "Commentary on the Epistles to the Ephesians." In *Commentary on the Epistles to the Ephesians and Colossians. The English Text with Introduction, Exposition and Notes*, by E. K. Simpson and F. F. Bruce. NICNT, ed. Ned B. Stonehouse. Grand Rapids: Eerdmans; London: Marshall, Morgan & Scott, 1957, 15–157 [17–19].

Snodgrass, Klyne. *Ephesians*. The NIV Application Commentary, ed. Terry Muck et al. Grand Rapids: Zondervan, 1996 [23–30].

Soden, H. von, ed. *Die Briefe an die Kolosser, Epheser, Philemon; die Pastoral Briefe*. 2d ed. Hand-Commentar zum Neuen Testament, ed. H. J. Holtzmann, R. A. Lipsius, P. W. Schmiedel, and H. von Soden, vol. 3. Freiburg:

Akademische Verlagsbuchhandlung von Mohr, 1893, 79–154 [90–95] [1st ed., 1891, 86–96].

Speyr, Adrienne von. *The Letter to the Ephesians*. Translated by Adrian Walker. San Francisco: Ignatius, 1996 [13–18] [German ed., 1983, 11–15].

Staab, Karl. *Die Thessalonicherbriefe, die Gefangenschaftsbriefe*. 3d ed. Regensburger Neues Testament, ed. Alfred Wikenhauser and Otto Kuss, vol. 7. Regensburg: Friedrich Pustet, 1959, 114–66 [114–18].

Stadelmann, Helge. *Der Epheserbrief*. Bibelkommentars zum Neuen Testament, ed. Gerhard Maier, vol. 14. Neuhausen-Stuttgart: Hänsler, 1993 [20–22].

Stockhausen, Carol L. *Letters in the Pauline Tradition: Ephesians, Colossians, I Timothy, II Timothy and Titus*. Message of Biblical Spirituality, ed. Carolyn Osiek, vol. 13. Wilmington, Del.: Michael Glazier, 1989, 66–125 [66–85].

Stoeckhardt, G. *Commentary on St. Paul's Letter to the Ephesians*. Translated by Martin S. Sommer. Saint Louis: Concordia, 1952 [3–14] [German ed., 1910, 1–11].

Stott, John R. W. *The Message of Ephesians. God's New Society*. The Bible Speaks Today, ed. J. A. Motyer and John R. W. Stott. Downers Grove, Ill.: InterVarsity; Leicester: Inter-Varsity, 1979 [16–22].

Swain, Lionel. *Ephesians*. New Testament Message. A Biblical-Theological Commentary, ed. Wilfrid Harrington and Donald Senior, vol. 13. Dublin: Veritas, 1980 [ix–x].

Synge, F. C. *St Paul's Epistle to the Ephesians: A Theological Commentary*. London: SPCK, 1941 [69–76].

Tanzer, Sarah J. "Ephesians." In *Searching the Scriptures*, ed. Elisabeth Schüssler Fiorenza et al., vol. 2: *A Feminist Commentary*. New York: Crossroad, 1994, 325–48.

Taylor, Walter F., Jr. "Ephesians." In *Ephesians*, by Walter F. Taylor Jr., *Colossians*, by John H. P. Reumann. Augsburg Commentary on the New Testament, ed. Roy A. Harrisville, Jack Dean Kingsbury, and Gerhard A. Krodel. Minneapolis: Augsburg, 1985, 7–103 [9–17].

Theodore of Mopsuestia. *In Epistolam Pauli ad Ephesios Comentarii Fragmenta*. *PG*, vol. 66. Paris: Excudebatur et Venit Apud J.-P. Migne Editorem, 1859, 911–22.

Theodoret. *Ἑρμενεία τῆς πρὸς Ἐφεσίους ἐπιστόλης* [*Interpretatio Epistolae ad Ephesios*]. *PG*, vol. 82. Paris: Excudebatur et Venit Apud J.-P. Migne Editorem, 1859, 508–58.

Theophylact. *Τῆς τοῦ ἁγίου Παύλου πρὸς Ἐφεσίους ἐπιστολῆς ἐξήγεσις* [*Epistolae divi Pauli ad Ephesios Expositio*]. *PG*, vol. 124. Paris: Excudebatur et Venit Apud J.-P. Migne Editorem, 1864, 1031–1138.

Thompson, G. H. P. *The Letters of Paul to the Ephesians, to the Colossians and to Philemon*. Cambridge Bible Commentary, ed. P. R. Ackroyd, A. R. C. Leaney, and J. W. Packer. Cambridge: Cambridge University Press, 1967, 2–102 [5–16].

Turner, Max. "Ephesians." In *New Bible Commentary: 21st Century Edition*, 4th ed., ed. D. A. Carson, R. T. France, J. A. Motyer, and G. J. Wenham.

Downers Grove, Ill.: InterVarsity; Leicester: Inter-Varsity, 1994, 1222–44 [1222].

Turner, Samuel H. *The Epistle to the Ephesians in Greek and English*. New York: Dana, 1856 [xi–xix].

Vosté, Jacobo-Maria. *Commentarius in Epistolam ad Ephesios*. Rome: Collegio Angelico; Paris: Gabalda, 1921 [3–28, 53–74].

Westcott, Brooke Foss. *Saint Paul's Epistle to the Ephesians: The Greek Text with Notes and Addenda*. London: Macmillan, 1906 [xxiii–lxvi, 19–20].

Wette, W. M. L. de. *Kurze Erklärung der Briefe an die Colosser, an Philemon, an die Ephesier und Philipper.* 2d rev. ed. Kurzgefasstes exegetisches Handbuch, vol. 2, pt. 4. Leipzig: Weidmann'sche Buchhandlung, 1847, 86–176 [88–92] [1st ed., 1843, 79–82].

Wettstein, Johann Jakob. *Ἡ Καινὴ Διαθήκη*. Novum Testamentum Graecum, vol. 2. Amsterdam: Ex Officiana Dommeriana, 1752, 238–61.

Wood, A. Skevington. "Ephesians." In *The Expositor's Bible Commentary with the New International Version of the Holy Bible*, ed. Frank E. Gaebelein, vol. 11. Grand Rapids: Zondervan, 1978, 1–92 [3–9].

Zerwick, Max. *The Epistle to the Ephesians*. Translated by Kevin Smyth. New Testament for Spiritual Reading, ed. John L. McKenzie, vol. 16. London: Burns & Oates, 1969 [xiii–xvi, 5–6] [German ed., 1963, 7–11, 21–22].

Introduction

The Letter to the Ephesians is one of the most influential documents in the Christian church. In the last decade of the fourth century the golden-mouthed Chrysostom of Constantinople states in the preamble to his homilies on Ephesians that this letter is full of Paul's sublime thoughts and doctrines which he scarcely utters elsewhere but plainly declares here.[1] John Calvin considered Ephesians as his favorite letter and he preached a series of forty-eight sermons on the book from May 1558 to March 1559.[2] Days before his death on November 24, 1572, John Knox's wife read to him daily Calvin's sermons on Ephesians.[3] Samuel Taylor Coleridge, the great poet and philosopher, wrote (May 25, 1830) regarding Ephesians: "It is one of the divinest compositions of man. It embraces every doctrine of Christianity;—first, those doctrines peculiar to Christianity and then those precepts common to it with natural religion."[4] In 1903 J. Armitage Robinson considered Ephesians as "the crown of St Paul's writings"[5] and in 1929 C. H. Dodd reckoned that Ephesians' *"thought is the crown of Paulinism."*[6] Nearly four decades later F. F. Bruce considered it the "quintessence of Paulinism" because it "in large measure sums up the leading themes of the Pauline epistles, and at the same time the central motive of Paul's ministry as apostle to the Gentiles."[7] In 1974 Markus

1. Chrysostom *Eph* Argumentum (*PG* 62:10).

2. John Calvin, *Sermons on the Epistle to the Ephesians*, trans. Arthur Golding in 1577 and rev. in 1973 [published in French in 1562] (Edinburgh: Banner of Truth Trust, 1973), viii.

3. David Laing, collected and ed., *The Works of John Knox*, vol. 6 (Edinburgh: Thomas George Stevenson, 1864; reprint, New York: AMS Press, 1966), 639, 643.

4. Samuel Taylor Coleridge, *Specimens of the Table Talk* (London: John Murray, 1858), 82.

5. Robinson, vii.

6. Dodd, 1224–25.

7. F. F. Bruce, "St. Paul in Rome. 4. The Epistle to the Ephesians," *BJRL* 49 (spring 1967): 303; reprinted in chap. 36 in idem, *Paul: Apostle of the Heart Set Free* (Grand Rapids: Eerdmans, 1977, 424–40; Bruce, 229. The title "The Quintessence of Paulinism" is

Barth begins his commentary by saying "Ephesians is among the greatest letters under the name of the apostle Paul."[1] Raymond E. Brown stated in 1997: "Among the Pauline writings only Rom can match Eph as a candidate for exercising the most influence on Christian thought and spirituality."[2] In 1999 Peter T. O'Brien claims, "The Letter to the Ephesians is one of the most significant documents ever written."[3] Hence, this letter has been considered to reflect the epitome of Pauline thought and has been very influential in Christian thought.

However, within the last two centuries there has been much debate over various issues regarding Ephesians. In this introduction we will be discussing five issues: authorship, structure and genre, city and historical setting, purpose, and theology of Ephesians. This will be followed by a bibliography for this introduction.

Authorship of Ephesians

Introduction

A study of commentaries on Ephesians or a perusal of NT introductions readily reveal a great debate on the authorship of this book. An investigation of this issue is necessary in order to understand the various aspects of the problem.

Attestation of Pauline Authorship of Ephesians

Ephesians has the earliest attestation of any NT book. Already in the first century or very early second century Clement of Rome (fl. 96), when mentioning "one God and one Christ and one Spirit," may be a reference to Eph 4:4–6.[4] Furthermore, Clement's prayer that God would "open the eyes of our heart that we might know you [God]"[5] is most likely an allusion to Eph 1:17–18. Also, the expression "the

borrowed from Peake, the original occupant of the Rylands Chair in Manchester University, where he used this title for all of Paul's letters including Ephesians, Arthur S. Peake, "The Quintessence of Paulinism," *BJRL* 4 (September, 1917–January, 1918): 285–311.

1. Barth, 3.

2. Raymond E. Brown, *An Introduction to the New Testament*, The Anchor Bible Reference Library, ed. David Noel Freedman (New York: Doubleday, 1997), 620.

3. O'Brien, 1.

4. Clement of Rome *Epistola 1 ad Corinthios* 46.6 (*PG* 1:304); cf. A Committee of the Oxford Society of Historical Theology, *The New Testament in the Apostolic Fathers* (Oxford: Clarendon, 1905), 53. For a discussion of Clement's allusions to the Ephesians, see Donald Alfred Hagner, *The Use of the Old and the New Testaments in Clement of Rome*, NovTSup, ed. W. C. van Unnik et al., vol. 34 (Leiden: Brill, 1973), 222–26.

5. Clement of Rome *Epistola 1 ad Corinthios* 59.3; cf. 36.2 (*PG* 1:281).

senseless and darkened heart"[1] is probably an allusion to Eph 4:18, and "let each be subject to his neighbor"[2] is reminiscent of Eph 5:21. Ignatius (35–107/8), bishop of Antioch, seems to allude to Eph 5:1–2 when he speaks of the Ephesians as imitators of God by their demonstration of love to him.[3] In his letter to Polycarp, Ignatius shows familiarity with the armor of God described in Eph 6:11–17.[4] Furthermore, in the first third of the second century, Polycarp (69–135), bishop of Smyrna, states: "As it is expressed in these Scriptures, 'Be angry and sin not,' and 'Let not the sun go down on your wrath.'"[5] Polycarp quotes from Ps 4:5 and Eph 4:26 and calls both of them Scripture! In other words, he places Ephesians on the same level as the Psalms, making Ephesians the first NT book to be called Scripture by the early church fathers. Earlier in his letter Polycarp's statement "knowing that 'by grace you are saved, not by works, but by the will of God through Jesus Christ,'"[6] is a clear reference to Eph 2:5, 8–9. In addition, Polycarp mentions "the armor of righteousness,"[7] indicating an acquaintance with Eph 6:11–17. Irenaeus (130–200, fl. 175–95), bishop of Lyons, explicitly quotes Eph 5:30 when he remarks, "as blessed Paul declares in his epistle to the Ephesians, that 'we are members of his body, of his flesh, and of his bones.'"[8] He also mentions that the apostle in the epistle to the Ephesians had stated, "In which you also, having heard the word of truth, the gospel of your salvation, in which also believing you were sealed with the Holy Spirit of promise, which is the earnest of our inheritance" (1:13–14a).[9] Again Irenaeus notes that "the apostle says to the Ephesians, 'In whom we have redemption through his blood, the remission of sins' [1:7]; and additionally in the same treatise he says, 'You who formerly were far off have been brought near in the blood of Christ' [2:13]; and 'Abolishing in his flesh, the law of commandments in ordinances'" (2:15).[10] Irenaeus also speaks of "the devil as one of those angels who are placed over the spirit of the air, as the apostle Paul declared in the letter to the Ephesians" (2:2).[11] Clement of Alexandria (150–215) quotes

1. Ibid., 36.2 (*PG* 1:281).

2. Ibid., 38.1 (*PG* 1:284).

3. Ignatius *Ad Ephesios* 1.1–2 (*PG* 5:644). For a critique of Ignatius' references to Ephesians, see Matthias Günther, *Die Frühgeschichte des Christentums in Ephesus*, Arbeiten zur Religion und Geschichte des Urchristentums, ed. Gerd Lüdemann, vol. 1 (Frankfurt am Main: Peter Lang, 1995), 147–59.

4. Ignatius *Ad Polycarpum* 6.2 (*PG* 5:868).

5. Polycarp *Ad Philippenses* 12.1 (*PG* 5:1020).

6. Ibid., 1.3 (*PG* 5:1017).

7. Ibid., 4.1 (*PG* 5:1017–18).

8. Irenaeus *Adversus Haereses* 5.2.3 (*PG* 7:1126).

9. Ibid., 5.8.1 (*PG* 7:1141).

10. Ibid., 5.14.3 (*PG* 7:1163).

11. Ibid., 5.24.4 (*PG* 7:1188).

Eph 5:21–29[1] and Eph 4:13–15[2] as the words of the apostle, and there is no reason to think this was someone other than Paul. Marcion (d. 160) in Rome considered Ephesians a genuine letter of Paul, even though he renamed it the "Epistle to the Laodiceans."[3] Also, Ephesians is listed as one of the Pauline letters in the Muratorian Canon, which many think came from Rome within the last three decades of the second century,[4] though some regard it as a fourth century Eastern list.[5] Furthermore, Tertullian of Carthage (160–220) mentions that the apostle (Paul) had written to the Ephesians regarding Christ's headship of all things in his citation of Eph 1:9–10.[6] In one passage he lists Ephesus, along with Corinth, Philippi, Thessalonica, and Rome, as the places where there were established apostolic churches that received authentic letters from the apostle.[7] Also, in another passage he mentions that these same churches, as well as Galatia, read Paul's letters.[8]

1. Clement of Alexandria *Stromatum* 4.8 (*PG* 8:1275–76).
2. Clement of Alexandria *Paedagogus* 1.5 (*PG* 8:269–70).
3. Tertullian *Adversus Marcionem* 5.17.1 (*PL* 2:512); cf. Adolf von Harnack, *Marcion: Das Evangelium vom fremden Gott. Eine Monographie zur Geschichte der Grundlegung der katholischen Kirche*, 2d ed., TU, ed. Adolf von Harnack and Carl Schmidt, vol. 45 (Leipzig: J. C. Hinrichs'sche Buchhandlung, 1924); John Knox, *Marcion and the New Testament: An Essay in the Early History of the Canon* (Chicago: University of Chicago Press, 1942), 1–76, 158–67, 172–76; Hans von Campenhausen, *The Formation of the Christian Bible*, trans. J. A. Baker (Philadelphia: Fortress; London: A. and C. Black, 1972), 147–67; John J. Clabeaux, *A Lost Edition of the Letters of Paul. A Reassessment of the Text of the Pauline Corpus Attested by Marcion*, Catholic Biblical Quarterly Monograph Series, vol. 21 (Washington, D.C.: Catholic Biblical Association of America, 1989), 26, 94–98, 156.
4. *The Apostolic Fathers*, ed. and trans. J. B. Lightfoot, 2d ed. (London: Macmillan, 1890; reprint, Grand Rapids: Baker, 1981), pt. I, vol. 2, 405–13; Brooke Foss Westcott, *A General Survey of the History of the Canon of the New Testament*, 6th ed. (London: Macmillan, 1889; reprint, Grand Rapids: Baker, 1980), 212; John A. T. Robinson, *Redating the New Testament* (Philadelphia: Westminster; London: SCM, 1976), 319; E. Ferguson, "Canon Muratori. Date and Provenance," in *Studia Patristica*, ed. Elizabeth A. Livingstone, vol. 17, pt. 2 (Oxford: Pergamon, 1982), 677–83; Bruce M. Metzger, *The Canon of the New Testament: Its Origin, Development, and Significance* (Oxford: Clarendon, 1987), 191; F. F. Bruce, *The Canon of Scripture* (Downers Grove, Ill.: InterVarsity, 1988), 158; Wilhelm Schneemelcher, ed., *New Testament Apocrypha*, trans. and ed. R. McL. Wilson, vol. 1 (London: James Clarke; Louisville, Ky.: Westminster/John Knox, 1991), 27–29, 34, 72 n. 37.
5. A. C. Sundberg Jr., "Towards a Revised History of the New Testament Canon," in *SE IV. Papers Presented to the Third International Congress on New Testament Studies held at Christ Church Oxford, 1965. Part I: The New Testament Scriptures*, ed. F. L. Cross, TU, ed. Friedrich Zucher et al., vol. 102 (Berlin: Akademie-Verlag, 1968), 452–61; A. C. Sundberg Jr., "Canon Muratori: A Fourth-Century List," *HTR* 66 (January 1973): 1–41; Geoffrey Mark Hahneman, *The Muratorian Fragment and the Development of the Canon*, OTM, ed. M. F. Wiles et al. (Oxford: Clarendon, 1992), 4, 33, 215–18.
6. Tertullian *De Monogamia* 5 (*PL* 2:935).
7. Tertullian *De Praescriptionibus* 36 (*PL* 2:49).
8. Tertullian *Adversus Marcionem* 4.5.1 (*PL* 2:366).

In arguing his case against Marcion, Tertullian cites Eph 2:12 and states that it is the apostle's (Paul's) letter written to the Ephesians, although, according to Tertullian, the heretics such as Marcion say it was a letter to the Laodiceans.[1] Later in the same work Tertullian again criticizes Marcion for designating the letter to the Ephesians as "the epistle to the Laodiceans," and then Tertullian quotes from Ephesians more than forty times over the course of two chapters.[2]

Arnold correctly asserts that another early source that needs attention is the Gnostic writings.[3] He suggests two works. First, in the *Exegesis on the Soul* (2.6.131), which may be dated around A.D. 200,[4] Eph 6:12 ("for our struggle is not against flesh and blood . . . but against the world rulers of this darkness and the spirits of wickedness") is cited as Paul's words. Second, in the *Hypostasis of the Archons* (2.86.20–25), dated in the third century (some date it in the second century),[5] the same verse is cited as from the "great apostle." The *Epistle of Barnabas* and the *Shepherd of Hermas* contain other possible allusions to Ephesians. The *Epistle of Barnabas*, which is from Alexandria and is dated some time after the temple's destruction in A.D. 70 and before Hadrian rebuilt Jerusalem following the revolt of A.D. 132–35, possibly during Nerva's reign 96–98,[6] refers to a new creation,[7] a possible allusion to Eph 2:10 and 4:22–24. Also, three times it mentions the fact that Christ dwells in us,[8] an allusion to Eph 3:17, and that the community of believers is the temple of the Lord in which God dwells,[9] surely an allusion to Eph 2:21–22. Although some of these concepts could possibly be drawn from 1 and 2 Corinthians, Bartlet suggests that they are a much closer parallel to Ephesians.[10]

1. Ibid., 5.11.12 (*PL* 2:500).
2. Ibid., 5.17–18 (*PL* 2:512–19).
3. Clinton E. Arnold, "Ephesians, Letter to the," in *DPL*, 241.
4. William C. Robinson Jr., "Tractate 6: The Expository Treatise on the Soul," in *Nag Hammadi Codex II,2–7 together with XIII,2*, Brit. Lib. Or.4926(1), and P. Oxy. 1, 654, 655*, ed. Bentley Layton, vol. 2, Nag Hammadi Studies, ed. Martin Krause, James M. Robinson, Frederik Wisse, et al., vol. 21 (Leiden: Brill, 1989), 136.
5. Roger A. Bullard, "Tractate 4: The Hypostasis of the Archons," in *Nag Hammadi Codex II,2–7 together with XIII,2*, Brit. Lib. Or.4926(1), and P. Oxy. 1, 654, 655*, ed. Bentley Layton, vol. 1, Nag Hammadi Studies, ed. Martin Krause, James M. Robinson, Frederik Wisse, et al., vol. 20 (Leiden: Brill, 1989), 220.
6. Jack N. Sparks, ed., *The Apostolic Fathers* (Nashville: Thomas Nelson, 1978), 263; Michael W. Holmes, ed. and rev., *The Apostolic Fathers: Greek Texts and English Translations of Their Writings*, trans. and ed. J. B. Lightfoot and J. R. Harmer, 2d updated ed. (Grand Rapids: Baker, 1999), 272; James Carleton Paget, *The Epistle of Barnabas*, WUNT, ed. Martin Hengel and Otfried Hofius, vol. 64 (Tübingen: Mohr, 1994), 9–30.
7. *Epistle of Barnabas* 6.11.
8. Ibid., 6.14; 16.8–10.
9. Ibid., 6.15; 16.8–10.
10. A Committee of the Oxford Society of Historical Theology [J. V. Bartlet], *The New Testament in the Apostolic Fathers*, 5–6.

The *Shepherd of Hermas* from Rome is difficult to date precisely but some suggest around 140–50.[1] It mentions the grieving of the Holy Spirit[2] which seems to be an allusion to Eph 4:30 and it refers to "one Spirit and one body,"[3] "one faith . . . [one] love,"[4] and "one body, . . . one faith, one love"[5] all likely allusions to Eph 4:2–5. The fact that the concept of "grieving the Holy Spirit" is unusual and that it contains frequent references to one body, spirit, faith, and love in such close proximity, it must be concluded that they "have all the appearance of being imitated from Ephesians."[6]

The Pauline authorship of Ephesians has not only had strong and widespread geographical attestation in the early church, but it has had continued support in recent time. Extensive defense of Pauline authorship has been maintained in recent times by Percy[7] and van Roon.[8]

Dispute over Pauline Authorship of Ephesians

Scholars' Rejection of Pauline Authorship of Ephesians

The first doubt of Pauline authorship was introduced in 1792 by the English clergyman Evanson who felt that it was inconsistent for the writer of Ephesians to claim that he had heard of their faith (1:15–16) when according to Acts Paul had spent more than two years at Ephesus.[9] Some thirty years later Usteri cast doubt on its authenticity because it was so similar to Colossians, which he felt was a genuine letter of Paul.[10] Shortly thereafter de Wette, at first uncertain,[11] later

1. Sparks, *The Apostolic Fathers*, 156; Norbert Brox, *Der Hirt des Hermas*, Kommentar zu den Apostolischen Vätern, ed. N. Brox, G. Kretschmar, and K. Niederwimmer, vol. 7 (Göttingen: Vandenhoeck & Ruprecht, 1991), 23–25; Holmes, *The Apostolic Fathers*, 330–31.

2. Mandate 10.2.1, 2, 4, 5.

3. Similitude 9.13.5.

4. Ibid., 9.17.4.

5. Ibid., 9.18.4.

6. A Committee of the Oxford Society of Historical Theology [J. Drummond], *The New Testament in the Apostolic Fathers*, 106.

7. Ernst Percy, *Die Probleme der Kolosser- und Epheserbriefe*, Skrifter Utgivna av Kingl. Humanistiska Vetenskapssamfundet i. Lund, vol. 39 (Lund: Gleerup, 1946).

8. A. van Roon, *The Authenticity of Ephesians*, trans. S. Prescod-Jokel, NovTSup, ed. W. C. van Unnik et al., vol. 39 (Leiden: Brill, 1974).

9. Edward Evanson, *The Dissonance of the Four Generally Received Evangelists and the Evidence of Their Respective Authenticity Examined* (Ipswich, England: George Jermym, 1792), 261–62.

10. Leonhard Usteri, *Entwickelung des paulinischen Lehrbegriffes mit Hinsicht auf die übrigen Schriften des Neuen Testamentes*, 3d ed. (Zürich: Orill, Füssli, und Compagnie, 1831), 1–8 [1st ed. 1824].

11. Wilhelm Martin Leberecht de Wette, *An Historico-Critical Introduction to the Canonical Books of the New Testament*, trans. from the 5th ed. by Frederick Frothing-

decided it was not a Pauline work because of its many parenthetic and secondary clauses, its verbosity, and its lack of new thoughts. He proposed that it was a clumsy imitation of Paul's letter to the Colossians.[1] This concept was adopted by Baur who thought that Ephesians was to be identified with the postapostolic era and that it was composed early in the second century.[2] The denial of Pauline authorship has had extensive treatment more recently by Goodspeed[3] and Mitton.[4] Brown states, "A fair estimate might be that *at the present moment about 80 percent of critical scholarship holds that Paul did not write Eph.*"[5]

The chart below will enable one to visualize more easily those who have argued for Pauline authorship of Ephesians (left column), those who have changed their views or are uncertain (center column), and those who do not think Paul was the author of Ephesians (right column).[6] The chart is somewhat skewed in favor of the non-Pauline authorship of Ephesians because it focuses on the last two centuries whereas prior to 1792 scholars were almost unanimously in favor of Pauline authorship and because it lists scholars from the Western church (one exception) whereas the Eastern church is almost unanimously in favor of Pauline authorship. In order not to clutter the chart, the bibliographical sources are listed in "Commentaries" or the bibliography regarding authorship, which appears at the end of this introduction. The scholars are listed in chronological order with the dates of their works in parenthesis. These dates are generally the earliest editions of the particular scholar's work(s) although the bibliog-

ham (Boston: Crosby, Nichols, 1858), 274–85 [1st German ed., 1826, 2:254–65, esp. 254–56].

1. De Wette, 88–92 [1st ed., 1843, 79–82].

2. Ferdinand Christian Baur, *Paul the Apostle of Jesus Christ, His Life and Work, His Epistles and His Doctrine. A Contribution to a Critical History of Primitive Christianity*, ed. after the author's death by Eduard Zeller, 2d ed., trans. A. Menzies, vol. 2, Theological Translation Fund Library (London: Williams and Norgate, 1875 [German 1st ed. 1845]), 1–44, esp. 22–44.

3. Edgar J. Goodspeed, *New Solutions of New Testament Problems* (Chicago: University of Chicago Press, 1927), 11–20, 29–64; idem, "The Place of Ephesians in the First Pauline Collection," *ATR* 12 (January 1930): 189–212; idem, *The Meaning of Ephesians* (Chicago: University of Chicago Press, 1933), 3–17.

4. C. Leslie Mitton, *The Epistle to the Ephesians. Its Authorship, Origin and Purpose* (Oxford: Clarendon, 1951).

5. Raymond E. Brown, *The Churches the Apostles Left Behind* (New York: Paulist; London: Geoffrey Chapman, 1984), 47; idem, *An Introduction to the New Testament*, 620.

6. The form of the chart came from my colleague, W. Hall Harris III, *The Descent of Christ: Ephesians 4:7–11 and Traditional Hebrew Imagery*, AGJU, ed. Martin Hengel et al., vol. 32 (Leiden: Brill, 1996), 201–3. For an overview of the discussion on the authorship of Ephesians, see Helmut Merkel, "Der Epheserbrief in der neueren exegetischen Diskussion," in *ANRW*, pt. 2, vol. 25.4 (1987), 3156–3246.

raphy will list a more recent edition (I did not always see the first edition). The list is not exhaustive but hopefully fairly representative of well known scholars in the field. There has been no attempt to favor one side or the other. There are 279 scholars with 390 of their works. Where there is more than one author of a single work (e.g., Kirsopp and Silva Lake or Carson, Moo, and Morris), they will be counted as one author. On the other hand, there are only two authors who are listed twice, namely, McNeile and McNeile/Williams or Wikenhauser and Wikenhauser/Schmid because the author named after the slash revised the former author's work with a different conclusion than the original author. One work difficult to list is the *Introduction to the New Testament* begun by Feine and later revised by Behm and Kümmel. In order to be fair it seems best to list this work three times, namely, under Feine, Feine/Behm, and Kümmel because the *Introduction* became the product of each new reviser. These three listings are in chronological order of their publication so that one can more easily find them on the chart. Muddiman's assessment is difficult to classify precisely because he thinks the final letter is an expansion of a genuine Pauline letter. Hence, with some hesitation, it is classified as a Pauline letter with a question mark (?) after it.

The center column indicates an author's change of view or uncertainty regarding Pauline authorship of Ephesians. Sometimes the uncertainty is noted because the author specifically states his or her uncertainty and at other times authors are listed in this column because it is unclear to this reader which view the author holds. Symbols Y (= Yes), U (= Uncertain), and N (= No) following the slash after the year of publication indicates the author's position. The bibliography is in alphabetical order of scholar but chronological order for works of a particular scholar. Only in the case of Goguel was there a question mark after the affirmative (Y?) because although in his earlier work he considered it not Pauline, later he felt that portions of it were Pauline. Only Schlier and Martin asserted from the beginning that it was not written by Paul; later they considered it Pauline, and finally they reverted to their first position. In the case of Schlier, he doubted Pauline authorship in his earliest work,[1] but in two of his later works he defended Pauline authorship in spite of the Gnostic language[2] and then reverted to his first position as verbally stated to Schnackenburg.[3] Martin first denied Pauline authorship and then two years later accepted it, and only a year later he again denied it.[4]

1. Heinrich Schlier, *Christus und die Kirche im Epheserbrief*, BHT, vol. 6 (Tübingen: Mohr, 1930), passim.

2. Heinrich Schlier, "Die Kirche nach dem Brief an die Epheser," in *Die Kirche im Epheserbrief, Beiträge Kontroverstheologie*, ed. Robert Grosche, Beiheft zur Catholica, no. 1 (Münster: Aschendorffsche Verlagsbuchhandlung, 1949), 82–114; Schlier, 22–28.

3. Rudolf Schnackenburg, *Ephesians: A Commentary*, trans. Helen Heron (Edinburgh: T & T Clark, 1991), 24 n. 16.

4. Ralph P. Martin, "An Epistle in Search of a Life-Setting," *ExpTim* 79 (July 1968): 297–302; Martin, "Ephesians," in *The New Bible Commentary*, 1105–6; Martin, "Ephesians," in *The Broadman Bible Commentary*, 125–31.

For Pauline Authorship	Change or Uncertain	Against Pauline Authorship
Erasmus, Desiderius (1519)		
Luther, Martin (1530–45)		
Calvin, John (1548)		
Bengel, John Albert (1742)		
Paley, William (1790)		
		Evanson, Edward (1792)
Eichhorn, Johann Gottfried (1812)		
		Usteri, Leonhard (1824)
	Wette, Wilhelm Martin Leberecht de (1826/U, 1843/N)	
Harless, G. Chr. Adolph v. (1834)		
Mayerhoff, Ernst Theodor (1838)		
Olshausen, Hermann (1840)		
Meyer, Heinrich August Wilhelm (1843)		
		Baur, Ferdinand Christian (1845)
		Schleiermacher, Friedrich (1845)
Eadie, John (1854, 1883)		
Ellicott, Charles J. (1855)		
Alford, Henry (1856)		
Hodge, Charles (1856)		
Turner, Samuel H. (1856)		
Bleek, Friedrich (1862)		
Davies, J. Llewelyn (1866)		
Braune, Karl (1867)		

For Pauline Authorship	Change or Uncertain	Against Pauline Authorship
		Davidson, Samuel (1868)
		Hoekstra, Sytze (1868)
		Renan, Ernest (1869)
		Ewald, Heinrich (1870)
		Hitzig, Ferdinand (1870)
		Holtzmann, Heinrich Julius (1872)
		Hönig, W. (1872)
		Pfleiderer, Otto (1873, 1887)
		Hilgenfeld, Adolf (1875)
Sabatier, A. (1881)		
Weiss, Bernhard (1882, 1896)		
Dale, R. W. (1883)		
Salmon, George (1885)		
Moule, H. C. G. (1886)		Weizsäcker, Carl von (1886)
Godet, F. (1887, 1893)		
Beet, Joseph Agar (1890)		Brückner, Wilhelm (1890)
		Klöpper, Albert (1891)
		Soden, Hermann von (1891, 1905)
Findlay, G. G. (1892)		
Macpherson, John (1892)		
Lightfoot, J. B. (1893)		
	Jülicher, Adolf (1894/Y, 1899/U)	
Hort, F. J. A. (1895)		
Abbott, T. K. (1897)		

For Pauline Authorship	Change or Uncertain	Against Pauline Authorship
Haupt, Erich (1897)		
McGiffert, Arthur Cushman (1897)		
Gore, Charles (1898)		
Lock, Walter (1898, 1929)		
Zahn, Theodor (1899)		
		Dobschütz, Ernst von (1902)
Robinson, J. Armitage (1903)		
Salmond, S. D. F. (1903)		
Shaw, R. D. (1903)		
		Weinel, H. (1904, 1921)
Bacon, Benjamin Wisner (1905)		
Innitzer, Th. (1905)		
Knowling, R. J. (1905)		
Westcott, Brooke Foss (1906)		Soltau, Wilhelm (1906)
		Wendland, Paul (1907)
		Wrede, William (1907)
Belser, Johannes Evang. (1908)		
Deissmann, Adolf (1908, 1911, 1929)		
Rutherfurd, John (1908)		
Peake, Arthur S. (1909)		
Harnack, Adolf (1910)		
Stoeckhardt, G. (1910)		
Case, Shirley Jackson (1911)		Moffatt, James (1911)
Souter, Alexander B. (1911)		Soden, Hans von (1911)

For Pauline Authorship	Change or Uncertain	Against Pauline Authorship
Coppieters, H. (1912)		Dibelius, Martin (1912, 1937)
Feine, Paul (1913)		Bousset, Wilhelm (1913)
Hitchcock, George S. (1913)		Norden, Eduard (1913)
Murray, J. O. F. (1914)		
Grensted, Lawrence William (1916)		
Meinertz, Max (1917, 1933)		Weiss, Johannes (1917)
Vosté, Jacobo-Maria (1921)		Reitzenstein, R. (1921)
	Goguel, Maurice (1926/N, 1935/Y?, 1946/N, 1947/Y?)	
McNeile, A. H. (1927)		Goodspeed, Edgar J. (1927, 1930, 1933, 1937, 1951)
Zwaan, J. de (1927, 1937)		
Schmid, Josef (1928)		
Dodd, C. H. (1929, 1933)		
Asting, Ragnar (1930)		
Scott, Ernest Findlay (1930, 1932)	Schlier, Heinrich (1930/N, 1949/Y, 1957/Y, 1978/N)	
		Knox, Wilfred L. (1932, 1939)
Roller, Otto (1933)		Bowen, Clayton R. (1933)
		Käsemann, Ernst (1933, 1949, 1958, 1961, 1963, 1966)
		Cadoux, C. J. (1934)
		Ochel, Werner (1934)
Scott, C. A. Anderson (1935)		Knox, John (1935, 1950)
Feine, Paul/Behm, Johannes (1936)		

For Pauline Authorship	Change or Uncertain	Against Pauline Authorship
Koehler, John Ph. (1936)		
Benoit, Pierre (1937, 1963, 1966)		
Lenski, R. C. H (1937)	Lake, Kirsopp and Lake, Silva (1937/U)	
	Manson, T. W. (1939/U, 1956/Y)	Schubert, Paul (1939)
Synge, F. C. (1941)		
Thiessen, Henry Clarence (1943)		Johnston, George (1943, 1962, 1967)
Mowry, Lucetta (1944)		
Michaelis, Wilhelm (1946)		
Percy, Ernst (1946)		
		Mitton, C. Leslie (1948, 1949, 1951, 1956, 1976)
Buck, Charles H., Jr. (1949)		
Dupont, Jacques (1949)		
		Harrison, P. N. (1950, 1964)
		Heard, Richard (1950)
		Brandon, S. G. F. (1951)
Hunter, Archibald M. (1951, 1957)	Dahl, Nils A. (1951/Y, 1962/N, 1962/N, 1978/N, 2000/N)	Maurer, Christian (1951)
Henshaw, T. (1952)	Schnackenburg, Rudolf (1952/Y, 1961/Y, 1982/N)	
Mackay, John A. (1953)	McNeile, A. H./Williams, C. S. C. (1953/U)	Beare, Francis W. (1953)
Rendtorff, Heinrich (1953)		Bultmann, Rudolf (1953)
Wikenhauser, Alfred (1953)		Masson, Charles (1953)
		Sparks, H. F. D. (1953)
Albertz, Martin (1954)		

For Pauline Authorship	Change or Uncertain	Against Pauline Authorship
	Best, Ernest (1955/Y, 1979/N, 1987/N, 1993/N, 1997/N, 1998/N)	
	Mussner, Franz (1955/ Y, 1982/N)	
Barclay, William (1956)		Nineham, D. E. (1956)
Sanders, J. N. (1956)		Schweizer, Eduard (1956, 1989)
Schille, Gottfried (1957)		
Simpson, E. K. (1957)		
		Allan, John A. (1958, 1959)
Cadbury, H. J. (1959)	Brown, Raymond E. (1959/Y, 1984/N, 1997/N)	
Cerfaux, Lucien (1959, 1960, 1962)		
Grosheide, F. W. (1960)	Chadwick, Henry (1960/U, 1962/Y)	
Bruce, F. F. (1961, 1984)		
Guthrie, Donald (1961)		
Rienecker, Fritz (1961)		
Barker, Glenn W. (1962, 1975)		Conzelmann, Hans (1962)
		Kasser, Rodolphe (1962)
Beasley-Murray, G. R. (1963)		Kümmel, Werner Georg (1963)
Brown, Raymond Bryan (1963)		
Foulkes, Francis (1963)		
Grant, Robert M. (1963)		
Zerwick, Max (1963)		
Filson, Floyd V. (1964)		Marxsen, W. (1964)

For Pauline Authorship	Change or Uncertain	Against Pauline Authorship
Harrison, Everett (1964)		Morton, A. Q.; McLeman, James (1964)
Cook, James I. (1965)		Pokorný, Petr (1965, 1992)
Klijn, A. F. J. (1965)		Schmithals, Walter (1965)
Murphy-O'Connor, Jerome (1965, 1995, 1996)		
Gaugler, Ernst (1966)	Cullmann, Oscar (1966/U)	Fuller, Reginald H. (1966)
Gundry, Robert H. (1967)		
Hendriksen, William (1967)		Thompson, G. H. P. (1967)
	Martin, Ralph P. (1968/N, 1970/Y, 1971/N, 1978/N, 1981/N, 1991/N)	Kirby, John C. (1968)
Roon, A. van (1969)		Bornkamm, Günther (1969)
	Dunn, James D. G. (1970/U, 1977/U, 1991/Y, 1997/N, 1997/N, 1998/N)	Houlden, J. L. (1970)
		Gnilka, Joachim (1971, 1996)
		Sampley, J. Paul (1971, 1978)
	Meeks, Wayne A. (1972/U)	Lohse, Eduard (1972)
		Munro, Winsome (1972, 1983)
Hagner, Donald Alfred (1973)	Lincoln, Andrew T. (1973/Y, 1981/Y, 1982/U, 1983/N, 1990/N, 1993/N)	Fischer, Karl Martin (1973)
Hugedé, Norbert (1973)		Klauck, Hans-Josef (1973)
Karavidopoulos, Ioannes D. (1973)		Merklein, Helmut (1973)

For Pauline Authorship	Change or Uncertain	Against Pauline Authorship
Polhill, John B. (1973, 1979, 1996)		Wikenhauser, Alfred/ Schmid, Josef (1973)
Barth, Markus (1974, 1984, 1994)		Barrett, C. K. (1974, 1994)
		Ernst, Josef (1974)
		Perrin, Norman (1974)
		Stuhlmacher, Peter (1974)
		Schenke, Hans-Martin; Fischer, Karl Martin (1975, 1978)
		Vielhauer, Philipp (1975)
Caird, G. B. (1976)		Lindemann, Andreas (1976, 1985)
Hemphill, Kenneth S. (1976, 1988)		
Robinson, John A. T. (1976)		
Vanhoye, A. (1978)		
Wood, A. Skevington (1978)		
Howard, Fred D. (1979)		
Stott, John. R. W. (1979)		
Johnson, Luke Timothy (1980, 1986)		Koester, Helmut (1980, 1995)
Swain, Lionel (1980)		
Black, David Alan (1981)		
Danker, Frederick W. (1982)		
Hoehner, Harold W. (1983)		Collins, Raymond F. (1983, 1988)
Speyr, Adrienne von (1983)		
	Patzia, Arthur G. (1984/U)	Lona, Horacio E. (1984)
		Wake, William C. (1984)

For Pauline Authorship	Change or Uncertain	Against Pauline Authorship
Roberts, J. H. (1985)		Adai, Jacob (1985)
		Taylor, Walter F., Jr. (1985)
Trudinger, Paul (1986, 1988)		Meade, David G. (1986)
		Merkel, Helmut (1987)
	Bauckham, Richard (1988/U)	Penna, Romano (1988)
Arnold, Clinton E. (1989, 1993, 1996)		Puskas, Charles B. (1989)
Mauerhofer, Erich (1989)		Stockhausen, Carol L. (1989)
		Trobisch, David (1989, 1994)
Goulder, M. D. (1991)		Bouttier, Michel (1991)
Moritz, Thorsten (1991, 1996)		Roetzel, Calvin J. (1991)
Yorke, Gosnell L. O. R. (1991)		
Carson, D. A.; Moo, Douglas J.; Morris, Leon (1992)		Furnish, Victor Paul (1992)
Ellis, E. Earle (1992, 1999)		
Hui, Archie Wang Do (1992)		
Stadelmann, Helge (1993)		Faust, Eberhard (1993)
Fay, Greg (1994)		
Fee, Gordon D. (1994)		Fleckenstein, Karl-Heinz (1994)
Morris, Leon (1994)		Kitchen, Martin (1994)
Turner, Max (1994)		
		Günther, Matthias (1995)
		Maclean, Jennifer Kay Berenson (1995)
		Thurston, Bonnie (1995)

For Pauline Authorship	Change or Uncertain	Against Pauline Authorship
Donelson, Lewis R. (1996)		
Harris, W. Hall, III (1996)		
Snodgrass, Klyne (1996)		
Holmes, Mark A. (1997)		Gese, Michael (1997)
Liefeld, Walter L. (1997)		Hübner, Hans (1997)
		Perkins, Pheme (1997, 1998)
		Yoder Neufeld, Thomas R. (1997)
		Dawes, Gregory W. (1998)
		Kreitzer, Larry J. (1998)
		Luz, Ulrich (1998)
Boismard, M.-É. (1999)		
O'Brien, Peter T. (1999)		
McDonald, Lee Martin; Porter, Stanley E. (2000)		MacDonald, Margaret Y. (2000)
Muddiman, John (2001)?		Aletti, Jean-Nöel (2001)

Do 80 percent of the scholars deny Pauline authorship as Brown asserts? In reviewing the numbers it must first be remembered that out of 279 scholars, only seven are categorized as U (Jülicher [his later work], Lake, McNeile/Williams,[1] Cullmann, Meeks, Patzia, Bauckham) while the other five are either Y or N (possibly U in the midst of change). The two charts below will help clarify the actual percentage for and against Pauline authorship of Ephesians. The first chart reckons from a certain period of time to and including 2001. The second chart looks at quarter centuries incrementally from 1801 to 1850 and decades incrementally from 1851 to 2001.

1. There are two editions. The first edition is by A. H. McNeile (*An Introduction to the Study of the New Testament* [Oxford: Clarendon, 1927], 154–63), who accepted Pauline authorship but the second edition was done by C. S. C. Williams in 1953 (165–77), who left it as uncertain. Similar to the work above is the introduction by Alfred Wikenhauser, *New Testament Introduction*, trans. Joseph Cunningham, 2d ed. (New York: Herder and Herder, 1958), 421–30 who accepted Pauline authorship whereas the next major revision was done in 1973 by Josef Schmid who did not accept Pauline authorship.

Pauline Authorship Viewed Totally over the Centuries

Years and Numbers	For Pauline Authorship	Change or Uncertain	Against Pauline Authorship
1519–2001 (279)	151 (54%)	20 (7%)	108 (39%)
1801–2001 (273)	146 (54%)	20 (7%)	107 (39%)
1826–2001 (271)	145 (54%)	20 (7%)	106 (39%)
1851–2001 (264)	141 (54%)	19 (7%)	104 (39%)
1861–2001 (259)	136 (53%)	19 (7%)	104 (40%)
1871–2001 (251)	133 (53%)	19 (8%)	99 (39%)
1881–2001 (247)	133 (54%)	19 (8%)	95 (38%)
1891–2001 (238)	126 (53%)	19 (8%)	93 (39%)
1901–2001 (225)	116 (52%)	18 (8%)	91 (40%)
1911–2001 (206)	102 (49%)	18 (9%)	86 (42%)
1921–2001 (192)	94 (49%)	18 (9%)	80 (42%)
1931–2001 (181)	87 (48%)	16 (9%)	78 (43%)
1941–2001 (165)	80 (48%)	14 (9%)	71 (43%)
1951–2001 (154)	73 (47%)	14 (9%)	67 (44%)
1961–2001 (124)	59 (47%)	7 (6%)	58 (47%)
1971–2001 (91)	41 (45%)	4 (4%)	46 (51%)
1981–2001 (59)	27 (46%)	2 (3%)	30 (51%)
1991–2001 (38)	19 (50%)	0 (0%)	19 (50%)

The second chart reckons the column "Change or Uncertain" differently than the first chart. It reckons according to the author's position on the issue in the particular quarter century or decade. In other words, if in the particular time period the author's work indicates Y, then it will be counted as accepting Pauline authorship and if in the particular time period the author's work indicates N, then it will be counted as rejecting Pauline authorship. The author will be entered only as many times he or she changes. For example, if an author has five works and the first two works indicate acceptance of Pauline authorship and the last three works indicate rejection of Pauline authorship, he or she will be listed once in the column "For Pauline Authorship" and once in the column "Against Pauline Authorship." It must be kept in mind that the acceptance or rejection of Pauline authorship is due to various reasons. This will be discussed below.

It is evident that Brown's estimate that 80 percent of critical scholarship does not think that Paul wrote Ephesians is simply untrue. The closest to that figure is in the decades (second chart) beginning with 1861 (63%), 1871 (100% [note: this contrasts with 1851's 100% for

Pauline Authorship View Incrementally over the Centuries

Years and Numbers	For Pauline Authorship	Change or Uncertain	Against Pauline Authorship
1519–1800 (5)	4 (80%)	0 (0%)	1 (20%)
1801–1825 (2)	1 (50%)	0 (0%)	1 (50%)
1826–1850 (8)	4 (50%)	1 (12%)	3 (38%)
1851–1860 (5)	5 (100%)	0 (0%)	0 (0%)
1861–1870 (8)	3 (37%)	0 (0%)	5 (63%)
1871–1880 (4)	0 (0%)	0 (0%)	4 (100%)
1881–1890 (9)	7 (78%)	0 (0%)	2 (22%)
1891–1900 (14)	11 (79%)	1 (7%)	2 (14%)
1901–1910 (19)	14 (74%)	0 (0%)	5 (26%)
1911–1920 (14)	8 (57%)	0 (0%)	6 (43%)
1921–1930 (11)	7 (64%)	0 (0%)	4 (36%)
1931–1940 (17)	8 (47%)	2 (12%)	7 (41%)
1941–1950 (14)	9 (64%)	0 (0%)	5 (36%)
1951–1960 (32)	20 (63%)	3 (9%)	9 (28%)
1961–1970 (35)	19 (54%)	3 (9%)	13 (37%)
1971–1980 (35)	15 (43%)	1 (3%)	19 (54%)
1981–1990 (26)	8 (31%)	3 (11%)	15 (58%)
1991–2001 (40)	20 (50%)	0 (0%)	20 (50%)

Pauline authorship]), 1971 (54%), 1981 (58%), and 1991 (50%) with only 8, 4, 35, 26, and 40 scholars respectively. The second closest time is the same general periods (first chart), 1971–2001 (51%), 1981–2001 (51%), and 1991–2001 (50%) with 91, 59, and 38 scholars respectively. In fact, the first chart illustrates that, historically, right up to 1960 more scholars favored the Pauline authorship of Ephesians than denied it and there were actually only two periods, 1971–2001 (51%) and 1981–2001 (51%), where more scholars denied Pauline authorship than accepted it. Furthermore, the second chart reveals that the only times that more scholars denied than accepted the Pauline authorship of Ephesians were the decades beginning with 1971 and 1981 with never more than 58 percent (except 1871; see note above). Hence, acceptance of the Pauline authorship of Ephesians has had a long tradition.

Reasons for Rejecting Pauline Authorship of Ephesians

Although rejecting Pauline authorship of Ephesians, Mitton acknowledges the long history of Pauline authorship of this epistle and states that "the burden of proof lies with those who seek to maintain a contrary opinion."[1] The reasons for rejecting Pauline authorship are numerous. Although much has been written on this debate, lack of space prevents a complete recitation of all the arguments. However, a discussion follows regarding six of the major issues surrounding the rejection of the Pauline authorship of Ephesians.

(1) Impersonal nature. According to 1:1 this letter is addressed to the Ephesians (see 1:1 and Excursus 1: Textual Problem in Ephesians 1:1). Paul had first arrived in Ephesus at the end of his second missionary journey in the autumn of A.D. 52 and ministered in the synagogue for a short period of time after which he left for Jerusalem, leaving Priscilla and Aquila there (Acts 18:18–21). He returned in the autumn of 53 on his third missionary journey and remained in Ephesus for a period of two and a half years, leaving in the spring of 56 (Acts 19:1–20:1). In the spring of 57 he visited the elders of Ephesus at Miletus on his way to Jerusalem from Corinth (Acts 20:16–38). Some contend that since Paul had spent considerable time with the Ephesians, it seems remarkable that he speaks of "having heard" of their faith and love (Eph 1:15) and further that he closes the epistle with such a brief and impersonal farewell.[2] In addition, Paul questions whether or not they had heard of the administration of the grace of God given to him to minister to Gentiles, including those at Ephesus (3:2) and also questions their reception of the instruction they received (4:21). Curiously, there are no greetings to individuals in the church at Ephesus. Yet, in letters such as the one addressed to Rome, a place he had never visited, there are extended greetings from him in the last two chapters of the book.

It is possible to explain the impersonal character of Ephesians in a couple of ways. First, Marcion attempts to solve the problem by suggesting a textual problem in 1:1 with reference to the letter's destination. As noted previously, he claims that the saints "in Ephesus" should read "in Laodicea,"[3] making it the letter to the "Laodiceans"

1. Mitton, *The Epistle to the Ephesians*, 25.

2. This is the charge made by the earliest critic of Pauline authorship of Ephesians, Evanson, *The Dissonance of the Four Generally Received Evangelists and the Evidence of Their Respective Authenticity Examined*, 261–62.

3. Cited in Tertullian *Adversus Marcionem* 5.11.12; 5.17.1 (*PL* 2:500; 2:512); cf. also John Rutherfurd, *St. Paul's Epistle to Colossae and Laodicea: The Epistle to the Colossians Viewed in Relation to the Epistle to the Ephesians* (Edinburgh: T & T Clark, 1908), 31–44; Adolf Deissmann, *Light from the Ancient East*, trans. Lionel R. M. Strachan, rev. ed. [4th ed.] (London: Hodder and Stoughton; New York: Harper & Brothers, 1927; reprint, Grand Rapids: Baker, 1965), 237–38; idem, *The New Testament in the Light of Modern Research. The Haskell Lectures, 1929* (Garden City, N.Y.: Doubleday, Doran, 1929), 33; Adolf Harnack, "Die Adresse des Epheserbriefs des Paulus," in *Sitzungsberichte der königlich preussischen Akademie der Wissenschaft*, Sitzung der philosophisch-historischen Classe vom 21. Juli, 1910, no. 37, vol. 2 (Berlin: Verlag der könglichen Akademie der Wissenschaften, 1910), 696–709; reprint in idem, *Kleine Schriften zur alten Kirche*, vol. 2, Opuscula: Sammelausgaben seltener und bisher nicht selbständig

mentioned in Col 4:16. Since we have no record of Paul visiting Laodicea, we would expect him to address the Laodiceans in an impersonal manner. However, as discussed in Excursus 1: Textual Problem in Ephesians 1:1, the best external and internal textual evidence is for the inclusion of "in Ephesus," and there is no manuscript evidence for "in Laodicea." Second, others explain its impersonal character by postulating that this was an encyclical letter. Accordingly the author provided an intentional space for the city's name, which would be inserted by the one who brought the letter to a particular city or perhaps would be filled in by the members of the church as the letter passed from one community to another. Again, there is no manuscript evidence that would support this hypothesis of a blank space. Furthermore, if there were a blank space, the text would have included the preposition ἐν ("in") to show where to insert the city's name; however, none of the manuscripts that omit the city's name have ἐν.[1]

Both these positions do not question Paul's authorship. Those who do question his authorship propose that this work was written by a Pauline imitator. However, in such a case an imitator would likely have included greetings to make it look like a letter from Paul. This, however, was not done. Several approaches attempt to explain Paul's impersonal tone. First, it must be noted that Paul does not give personal greetings in 2 Corinthians, Galatians, 1 and 2 Thessalonians, and Philippians. In fact, Paul had stayed in Corinth for eighteen months (Acts 18:11) and was in Galatia a few months before he wrote the epistle. Even though greetings are absent in these books very few would deny their Pauline authorship.

Second, although the letter specifically addressed those in Ephesus, it may well have been intended for other churches in the area. This was certainly true for the Colossian epistle, which was to be read by the Laodiceans (Col 4:16) even though it was addressed to the Colossians (1:2). By the same token, the Colossians were to read the letter addressed to the Laodiceans (4:16). It is not improbable to think that

erschienener wissenschaftlicher Abhandlungen, ed. Werner Peek, vol. 9.2 (Leipzig: Zentralantiquariat der deutschen demokratischen Republik, 1980), 120–33; Shirley Jackson Case, "To Whom Was 'Ephesians' Written?" *Biblical World* 38 (November 1911): 315–20; M. D. Goulder, "The Visionaries of Laodicea," *JSNT* 43 (September 1991): 15–16; Stanley E. Porter and Kent D. Clarke, "Canonical-Critical Perspective and the Relationship of Colossians and Ephesians," *Bib* 78, no. 1 (1997): 76–77.

1. N. A. Dahl, "Adresse und Proömium des Epheserbriefes," *TZ* 7 (Juli/August 1951): 243–44; updated in idem, *Studies in Ephesians: Introductory Questions, Text- & Edition-Critical Issues, Interpretation of Texts and Themes*, ed. David Hellholm, Vemund Blomkvist, and Tord Fornberg, WUNT, ed. Martin Hengel and Otfried Hofius, vol. 131 (Tübingen: Mohr, 2000), 60–64; Ernest Best, "Ephesians i.1," in *Text and Interpretation: Studies in the New Testament Presented to Matthew Black*, ed. Ernest Best and R. McL. Wilson (Cambridge: Cambridge University Press, 1979), 36–37; idem, *Ephesians*, New Testament Guides, ed. A. T. Lincoln (Sheffield: JSOT Press, 1993), 12.

a letter addressed to a city like Ephesus may have been intended to go elsewhere. Granted that Colossians is personal, but this may be explained by the fact that Colossae and Laodicea were neighboring villages and the people of one community would know those of the other community. On the other hand, Ephesus was not only a commercial and political center in western Asia Minor, but it was also the center of Paul's ministry for that area. It is probable that many other churches within the city and in the immediate vicinity were established by him during his long stay at Ephesus or by his disciples after he departed from there. Hence, it is reasonable to think that this letter would go to the many satellite churches in a wide geographical area and thus lack the personal touch. As mentioned above, Galatians has no personal greetings and was an encyclical letter since it was addressed to the "churches of Galatia" (Gal 1:2).

Third, since Paul had not visited Ephesus for five or six years, there may have been many new believers with whom he had no acquaintance. Thus he may not have wished to single out those he knew, since his emphasis was on the unity of all believers.

Fourth, the fact that Paul prays for them (1:16) and asks for their prayers (6:19–20) indicates some familiarity with the believers in Ephesus. Thus this letter cannot be considered completely impersonal.

In conclusion, the impersonal nature of this letter does not prove that it was not from Paul. In fact, Black thinks that the impersonal character of Ephesians is not out of character with the rest of Paul's epistles and it should not be even considered as an encyclical letter.[1] Furthermore, it seems that the better Paul knew the church, the fewer personal greetings were given. For example, Romans has the most extensive greetings, yet he had never been there. On the other hand, the Thessalonian epistles include no greetings and Paul had been there a few weeks earlier. Perhaps one of the reasons for greetings was to strengthen his credibility. If this is the case, greetings would be most necessary in cities where he had never been. Conversely, it would be least needed in letters to cities where the recipients knew him well. Thus, the impersonal tone of the letter in no way necessitates the denial of Pauline authorship.

Within the letter Paul assumes that the recipients had a personal interest in him. This is seen especially in 6:21–22 where the readers will receive a visit from Tychicus who, in order to encourage them, will tell them about the apostle's personal circumstances and will request prayer on Paul's behalf. Also, they had known of his suffering and imprisonment (3:1, 13; 4:1; 6:20) and he asked them to pray for him that he might be bold in his proclamation of the mystery of the gospel in his trial before Caesar (6:19). It must be concluded then that

1. Black, "The Peculiarities of Ephesians and the Ephesian Address," 59–73; cf. also J. Rendel Harris, "Epaphroditus, Scribe and Courier," *Exp* 8:8 (December 1898): 406–9.

although Paul may not have known some of the believers in Ephesus and the surrounding area, he assumed that they knew about him and thus a bond between the author and these recipients had been established.

(2) Language and style. Much ink has flowed over the language and style of Ephesians in comparison with other Pauline literature. First, with regards to language, many scholars think that Ephesians has too many unique words to be Pauline.[1] Statistics show that Ephesians has 2429 words with a total vocabulary of 530 words.[2] When the data from Morgenthaler was put into a database, it was discovered that forty-one words are used only in Ephesians and eighty-four words in Ephesians are not found elsewhere in Paul's writings but occur elsewhere in the NT.[3] How do these figures compare with other books by Paul? Galatians is suitable for such a comparison because: (1) it is a book with similar characteristics, namely, 2220 words with a total vocabulary of 526 words; and (2) very few people doubt its Pauline authorship. Using the same method, there are thirty-five words (thirty-one not counting proper nouns—Ephesians has no unique proper nouns) only in Galatians and there are ninety (eighty not counting proper nouns) words in Galatians not found elsewhere in Paul but occur elsewhere in the NT. Hence, the unique vocabulary in both Ephesians and Galatians are almost identical even though Galatians is about 10 percent shorter. Yet would this demonstrate that Paul did not write Galatians? Most agree that it does not.

However, some scholars say a number of variations of language and style make Paul's authorship suspect. Harrison, who is renowned for his doubt of the Pauline authenticity of the Pastoral Epistles, states that the number of hapax legomena per page in Ephesians is about the same as in other Pauline epistles.[4] In his earlier work, most of Harrison's charts even indicate that Ephesians is characteristically Pauline to the same or greater degree than the other nine undisputed books.[5]

In conclusion, when one looks at Morgenthaler, one will realize that Paul uses unusual vocabulary in each of his works. This does not prove or disprove Pauline authorship of any work.[6] For example, in

1. Mitton, *The Epistle to the Ephesians*, 8–9; Werner Georg Kümmel, *Introduction to the New Testament*, trans. Howard Clark Kee, 17th ed. (Nashville: Abingdon, 1975), 358.

2. Robert Morgenthaler, *Statistik des neutestamentliche Wortschatzes*, 4th ed. (Zürich: Gotthelf-Verlag, 1992), 164.

3. For similar results, see Raymond F. Collins, *Letters That Paul Did Not Write: The Epistle to the Hebrews and the Pauline Pseudepigrapha*, Good News Studies, vol. 28 (Wilmington, Del.: Michael Glazier, 1988), 142.

4. P. N. Harrison, *Paulines and Pastorals* (London: Villiers, 1964), 48.

5. P. N. Harrison, *The Problem of the Pastoral Epistles* (Oxford: Oxford University Press, 1921), 21, 23, 25, 34, 35, 44, 63, 69, 71, 72.

6. For an interesting analysis of this phenomenon, see John J. O'Rourke, "Some Considerations about Attempts at Statistical Analysis of the Pauline Corpus," *CBQ* 35 (October 1973): 483–90.

Ephesians Paul uses διάβολος, "devil" (4:27; 6:11), rather than σατανᾶς, "Satan," which he uses ten times in his other letters, but διάβολος is a common word used thirty-seven times in the NT. Moreover, both of these terms are used in six NT books written by four different authors, namely, Matthew, Luke, John, Acts, 1 Timothy, and Revelation.[1] For further comments, see the commentary on 4:27. Furthermore, Paul uses unique words in every epistle as the following examples demonstrate. He uses ἱερόν, "temple," only in 1 Cor 9:13 but employs ναός six times in his Corinthian correspondence and eight times in total. He utilizes πορθέω, "to destroy," only in Gal 1:13, 23, while he uses ἀπόλλυμι twelve times in his other writings, and it occurs ninety times in the NT. Paul employs συμπαραλαμβάνω, "to take along," only in Gal 2:1, whereas he uses παραλαμβάνω eleven times in his other letters (including twice in Gal 1:9, 12) and it occurs forty-nine times in the NT. Paul uses the hapax legomenon φθονέω, "to be envious" (Gal 5:26), rather than ζηλόω, which he uses eight times (including the three occurrences in Gal 4:17–18) and eleven times in the NT. There is no reason why Paul could not use unique vocabulary in his letters and also demonstrate flexibility in vocabulary usage. Even Mitton admits, "Several of the undoubtedly genuine epistles have an even higher percentage of words which are not found in the other Pauline writings."[2] Barker has challenged the contention of Goodspeed and Mitton that the use of non-Pauline vocabulary in Ephesians indicates that the author wrote in the last decade of the first century A.D., the period that produced Acts, Revelation, Hebrews, and 1 Peter. Their claim is flawed because when one applies the same criteria to the other Pauline epistles, the evidence demonstrates they have about the same number of non-Pauline words as does Ephesians.[3] It can be concluded, then, that the vocabulary in Ephesians does not necessarily demonstrate a non-Pauline authorship of Ephesians.

The same reasoning can be applied to unique phrases used in Ephesians. Lincoln lists fifteen word combinations or phrases in Ephesians unique to the Pauline literature.[4] For example, five times he used ἐν τοῖς ἐπουρανίοις, "in the heavenlies," rather than his normal usage of οἱ οὐρανοί, "the heaven(s)." In another instance, Christ is uniquely called ὁ ἠγαπημένος, "the beloved one" (1:6). Lincoln also cites ὁ λόγος τῆς ἀληθείας, "the word of truth" (Eph 1:13), but this is found elsewhere in Paul (Col 1:5; cf. also 2 Cor 6:7; 2 Tim 2:15) as well

1. F. J. A. Hort, *Prolegomena to St Paul's Epistles to the Romans and to the Ephesians* (London: Macmillan, 1895), 158.

2. Mitton, *The Epistle to the Ephesians*, 29.

3. Glenn Wesley Barker, "A Critical Evaluation of the Lexical and Linguistic Data Advanced by E. J. Goodspeed and Supported by C. L. Mitton in a Proposed Solution to the Problem of the Authorship and Date of Ephesians" (Th.D. diss., Harvard University, 1962), 13–53.

4. Lincoln, lxv.

as in Jas 1:18. Although not found in other of Paul's writings, some expressions in Ephesians have similar language elsewhere in the NT. For example, the expression τὰ θελήματα τῆς σαρκός, "the wishes of the flesh" (Eph 2:3), is analogous to John 1:13. Also, the expression ὁ πατὴρ τῆς δόξης, "the Father of glory" (Eph 1:17), is expressed similarly in Acts 7:2 as "the God of glory" (see also Matt 16:27; Mark 8:38; Rom 6:4; Phil 2:11; 4:20). Although most of these are unique within Pauline literature, some find resemblances in the NT.[1]

However, many expressions in Galatians are also unique within the Pauline corpus. These include τοῦ δόντος ἑαυτὸν ὑπὲρ τῶν ἁμαρτιῶν ἡμῶν, "the one who gave himself on behalf of our sins" (1:4); ἐκ τοῦ αἰῶνος τοῦ ἐνεστῶτος πονηροῦ, "from the present evil age" (1:4); ἀνάθεμα ἔστω, "let him be accursed" (1:8, 9); ἠναγκάσθη περιτμηθῆναι, "he was [not] compelled to be circumcised" (2:3; 6:12); ἡ ἀλήθεια τοῦ εὐαγγελίου, "the truth of the gospel" (2:5, 14; Col 1:5); τὸ εὐαγγέλιον τῆς ἀκροβυστίας . . . τῆς περιτομῆς "the gospel of uncircumcision . . . of circumcision" (2:7); ἐξ ἀκοῆς πίστεως, "by the hearing of faith" (3:2, 5); ἐξηγόρασεν ἐκ τῆς κατάρας τοῦ νόμου, "[Christ] redeemed [us] from the curse of the law" (3:13); τὸ πλήρωμα τοῦ χρόνου, "the fullness of time" (4:4); πτωχὰ στοιχεῖα, "beggarly elements" (4:9); τῆς χάριτος ἐξεπέσατε, "you have fallen from grace" (5:4); τὰ ἔργα τῆς σαρκός, "the works of the flesh" (5:19); ὁ καρπὸς τοῦ πνεύματος, "the fruit of the Spirit" (5:22); ἀλλήλους προκαλούμενοι, "provoking one another" (5:26); ἀλλήλων τὰ βάρη βαστάζετε, "bear one another's burdens" (6:2); τὸ ἴδιον φορτίον βαστάσει, "he shall bear his own burdens" (6:5); θεὸς οὐ μυκτηρίζεται, "God is not mocked" (6:7); τὸν Ἰσραὴλ τοῦ θεοῦ, "the Israel of God" (6:16); and τὰ στίγματα τοῦ Ἰησοῦ, "the marks of Jesus" (6:17). Again, do these eighteen unique expressions in Galatians prove that Paul did not write this letter? Few, if any, scholars would suggest this. Unique expressions are due to the mood and content of the letter, the recipients of the letter, and the flexibility and ingenuity of the author.

Another cause of perplexity is that the prepositions ἐν and κατά which are used more frequently in Ephesians than in Paul's undisputed letters.[2] However, the same sort of criteria could be used to

1. Vanhoye has made a detailed comparison between Ephesians and Hebrews. Although there does not seem be a direct relationship between the two epistles, he notes many similarities in vocabulary and expressions (e.g., "enlightened," Eph 1:18; Heb 6:4; "foundation of the world," Eph 1:4; Heb 4:3; 9:26; "made with hands" applied to Jewish institutions, Eph 2:11; Heb 9:11, 24). He suggests that both epistles were composed in same apostolic environment and concludes that if Hebrews were written before A.D. 70, then Ephesians can be dated in the sixties. See A. Vanhoye, "L'épître aux Éphésiens et l'épître aux Hébreux," *Bib* 59, no. 2 (1978): 198–230. For a comparison between Ephesians and 1 Peter, see C. L. Mitton, "The Relationship between 1 Peter and Ephesians," *JTS*, n.s., 1 (April 1950): 67–73; Mitton, *The Epistle to the Ephesians*, 176–97.

2. See James Moffatt, *An Introduction to the Literature of the New Testament*, 3d rev. ed., The International Theological Library, ed. Charles A. Briggs and Stewart D. F. Salmond (Edinburgh: T & T Clark, 1918), 387; Lincoln, lxv.

question the authenticity of the undisputed works of Paul. An examination of the use of prepositions per thousand words in Romans, 1 Corinthians, 2 Corinthians, Galatians, Ephesians, Philippians, and Colossians reveals that there is much greater frequency of διά and παρά in Romans, ἐπί, πρός, and ὑπέρ in 2 Corinthians, ἐκ and ὑπό in Galatians, μετά and περί in Philippians, and ἀπό and σύν in Colossians. Must it, therefore, be concluded that these works were not written by Paul? Furthermore, though it is true that ἐν is more frequently used in Ephesians than in the undisputed letters of Paul, it is not as frequent in Ephesians as it is in Colossians, a book many accept as genuinely Pauline. It is true that κατά is used more frequently in Ephesians, but it is also used quite frequently in Galatians; in fact, κατά with the genitive is used much more frequently in Galatians than in other Pauline letters, but it does not follow that Galatians was not Pauline. Hence, though the writer of Ephesians may have used the prepositions ἐν and κατά more frequently than in the undisputed letters of Paul, one cannot reasonably argue that Ephesians is not by the hand of Paul. Furthermore, if an imitator were the writer, he would have likely avoided the use of different vocabulary or phrases which would betray his hand.[1] Cerfaux states that such imitative skills are lacking by imitators of antiquity as seen in the so-called *Letter of the Laodiceans*.[2] In addition, some of Paul's writings were lost (see 1 Cor 5:9; Col 4:16) and it may well be that some of the unique vocabulary in the few existing letters were used with frequency in the lost letters.

Yule, a statistician, applied statistical methods to the study of vocabulary to see if the work *De Imitatione Christi* was written by Thomas à Kempis, as some have doubted. He stated that to make a proper comparison, one needs to have samples of around 10,000 words similar in length and content.[3] The longest in Pauline literature is Romans with 7094 words followed by 1 Corinthians with 6807 words, 2 Corinthians with 4448 words, and Ephesians with 2429 words.[4] Thus, according the guidelines supplied by Yule, the Pauline literature available is too limited to conclusively determine distinguishing characteristics in Paul's writings. Given this, much of the debate surrounding Pauline language must be viewed with caution.[5]

1. Markus Barth, *Israel and the Church: Contribution to a Dialogue Vital for Peace*, Research in Theology, ed. Dietrich Ritschl (Richmond, Va.: John Knox, 1969), 79–80.

2. L. Cerfaux, "The Epistles of the Captivity," in *Introduction to the New Testament*, ed. A. Robert and A. Feuillet, trans. Patrick W. Skehan et al. (New York: Desclee, 1965), 503.

3. G. Udny Yule, *The Statistical Study of Literary Vocabulary* (Cambridge: Cambridge University Press, 1944), 2, 281.

4. Morgenthaler, *Statistik des neutestamentliche Wortschatzes*, 164.

5. A. Q. Morton and James McLeman, *Paul, the Man and the Myth: A Study in the Authorship of Greek Prose* (London: Hodder and Stoughton, 1966), passim, esp. 89–97; summarized in S. Michaelson and A. Q. Morton, "Last Words: A Test of Authorship for Greek Writers," *NTS* 18 (January 1972): 192–208, but severely criticized by P. F.

In addition to the language, the style in which Ephesians is written causes some to question Pauline authorship. Its eight lengthy sentences (1:3–14, 15–23; 2:1–7; 3:2–13, 14–19; 4:1–6, 11–16; 6:14–20) are a case in point.[1] However, van Roon argues that when compared with other Pauline literature, this is not unusual. For instance, the short letter of 2 Thessalonians has proportionally just as many or possibly more long sentences than Ephesians. He also points out that Paul chose to use long sentences in doxologies and prayers (Eph 1:3–14, 15–23; 3:14–19; Rom 8:38–39; 11:33–39; 1 Cor 1:4–8; Phil 1:3–8; 1 Thess 1:2–5; 2 Thess 1:3–10), doctrinal content (Eph 2:1–7; 3:2–13; Rom 3:21–26; 1 Cor 1:26–29; 2:6–9), and parenthetical materials (Eph 4:1–6, 11–16; 6:14–20; 1 Cor 12:8–11; Phil 1:27–2:11).[2] As mentioned in the commentary (1:3), it is not unusual even in the present day to have long sentences in doxologies and prayers. Along with other scholars, Lincoln points out the unusual heavy pleonastic style with compound genitival constructions and repetition of certain phrases.[3] It might be counterargued, however, that the short incisive language and abrupt statements of Galatians are missing from other Pauline letters. Should one then conclude that Galatians is not from Paul? Few, if any, would agree. Rather it is the urgency of the situation that affects Paul's style in Galatians, whereas in other letters containing similar doctrinal concerns, there is a much more deliberate tone. Likewise, in Ephesians there were no pressing problems, thus Paul may have been in a more reflective mood, which allows for the use of long sentences. Kenny suggests that as Paul grew older, his sentences became longer.[4] Furthermore, Turner points out that several stylistic features of Ephesians are similar to that of other Pauline literature, such as the rich use of the genitive, the μὲν . . . δέ construction (e.g., Rom 2:25; 6:11; Eph 4:11), and the ἀρὰ . . . οὖν construction (found only in Romans, Galatians, 1 and 2 Thessalonians, and Ephesians).[5] Consequently, Ephesians is not out of character with the other Paulines in style.[6]

In conclusion, it is extremely difficult to determine authorship on

---

Johnson, "The Use of Statistics in the Analysis of the Characteristics of Pauline Writing," *NTS* 20 (October 1973): 92–100.

1. Lincoln, lxvi; Kreitzer, 21–22.

2. Van Roon, *The Authenticity of Ephesians*, 105–11.

3. Lincoln, lxv–lxvi.

4. Anthony Kenny, *A Stylometric Study of the New Testament* (Oxford: Clarendon, 1986), 110.

5. Nigel Turner, *Style*, vol. 4, *A Grammar of New Testament Greek*, by James Hope Moulton (Edinburgh: T & T Clark, 1976), 84–85.

6. See Kenneth J. Neumann, *The Authenticity of the Pauline Epistles in the Light of Stylostatistical Analysis*, SBLDS, ed. David L. Petersen and Charles Talbert, no. 120 (Atlanta: Scholars Press, 1990), 194–99, 206–11, 213–26; Michael Gese, *Das Vermächtnis des Apostels: Die Rezeption der paulinischen Theologie im Epheserbrief*, WUNT, ed. Martin Hengel and Otfried Hofius, vol. 99 (Tübingen: Mohr, 1997), 85–101.

the basis of language and style.[1] For example, an engineer uses different language and style when he writes to his wife than when he writes to one of his colleagues. When an engineer corresponds with his colleague, he uses the vocabulary and style normally used by engineers when discussing a complex engineering problem, different vocabulary and style when complaining that he had not been promoted, and yet different vocabulary and style when writing a postcard from a vacation spot. A similar scenario can be applied to Paul's situations. In the Galatian epistle he was upset about their quick departure from the gospel he had preached. In Colossians he was concerned with their theological drift. In Ephesians, however, there was no pressing problem. Thus, it would not be unusual for the vocabulary and style to differ in each of these letters. Furthermore, there are reasons for development in vocabulary and style, such as personal growth or new development in ideas or philosophies. Likewise, the advent of computers in more recent times has precipitated changes in language usage and style.

Certainly Ephesians manifests some differences in vocabulary and style, but not enough to discount authenticity. Deissmann proposes that "we cannot speak of 'the' style of Paul because we must distinguish between his different styles."[2] Again, as stated above, only a few writings of Paul are available. Additionally, Cadbury, in response to the suggestion that Ephesians was written by an imitator, states it well by saying, "Which is more likely—that an imitator of Paul in the first century composed a writing ninety or ninety-five per cent in accordance with Paul's style or that Paul himself wrote a letter diverging five or ten per cent from his usual style?"[3] Normally, the imitator of a great writer betrays himself by his inferiority. Therefore, if not written by Paul, it must have been done by someone equal or superior to him. It is unlikely that a superlative writer of this caliber would have been unknown to the first century church. It is much easier to accept that a work like Ephesians would be written by no other than Paul.[4] Ironically, Knox, who does not believe it was written by Paul, admits that Ephesians is "so thoroughly Pauline."[5] The study of sentence symmetry and rhythm substantiates that Ephesians was written by Paul and not an imitator.[6]

1. Cf. Kenny, *A Stylometric Study of the New Testament*, 80–115; see also David L. Mealand, "Positional Stylometry Reassessed: Testing a Seven Epistle Theory of Pauline Authorship," *NTS* 35 (April 1989): 266–86; D. L. Mealand, "The Extent of the Pauline Corpus: A Multivariate Approach," *JSNT* 59 (September 1995): 61–92.

2. Deissmann, *The New Testament in the Light of Modern Research*, 98.

3. H. J. Cadbury, "The Dilemma of Ephesians," *NTS* 5 (January 1959): 101.

4. Ernest Findlay Scott, *The Literature of the New Testament* (New York: Columbia University Press, 1932), 180; O'Brien, 7–8.

5. John Knox, *Chapters in a Life of Paul*, rev. ed. (Macon, Ga.: Mercer University Press, 1987), 19.

6. George K. Barr, "Scale and the Pauline Epistles," *IBS* 17 (January 1995): 22–41; see also idem, "Contrasts in Scale and Genre in the Letters of Paul and Seneca," *IBS* 18 (January 1996): 16–25.

(3) Literary relationships. Both Goodspeed and Mitton propose that when one examines the parallel phrases in Ephesians to the other Pauline letters, one must conclude that Ephesians has far greater parallels to other Pauline epistles than do the undisputed letters have with other Pauline writings.[1] Yet Mitton asserts that Goodspeed is overzealous in his estimate of these parallels. Goodspeed suggests that there are more than 400 passages from eight letters of Paul (Romans, 1 and 2 Corinthians, Galatians, Philippians, 1 and 2 Thessalonians, Philemon) which are reflected in Ephesians but Mitton would omit more than 150 of those examples. Furthermore, Mitton observes that only 416 words in Ephesians (17.3% of Ephesians) have verbatim or remarkably similar correspondence with the eight letters of Paul.[2] However, in critiquing Mitton's analysis, Barker shows that there are far greater parallels between Ephesians and Colossians than between Ephesians and Paul's eight letters. Furthermore, the majority of the verbatim parallels between Ephesians and Paul's eight letters "consist of no more than two or three words, many of which are relatively insignificant."[3] When analyzing the near verbatim parallels, Barker thinks that many are unwarranted such as articles, conjunctions, and particles as well as unwarranted paraphrases or substitutions. For example, Mitton thinks the phrase χάριτί ἐστε σεσῳσμένοι in Eph 2:5 is parallel to δικαιούμενοι δωρεὰν τῇ αὐτοῦ χάριτι in Rom 3:24.[4] Barker notes that only χάριτι has verbal correspondence and it is unlikely that σεσῳσμένοι indicates a literary dependence on δικαιούμενοι.[5] Hence, the proposal of Goodspeed and Mitton will not stand.

More particularly to be noted are the literary relationships between Ephesians and Colossians. Lincoln states, "Most decisive against Paul as author of Ephesians is its dependence on Colossians and its use of other Pauline letters, particularly Romans."[6] The central issue is the

1. Goodspeed, *The Meaning of Ephesians*, 8–12, 79–165; idem, *An Introduction to the New Testament* (Chicago: University of Chicago Press, 1937), 236–37; Mitton, *The Epistle to the Ephesians*, 98–105; 246–47, 255–59.

2. Mitton, *The Epistle to the Ephesians*, 100–106.

3. Barker, "A Critical Evaluation," 68–75, esp. 70.

4. Mitton, *The Epistle to the Ephesians*, 286–87.

5. Barker, "A Critical Evaluation," 75–78, esp. 76.

6. Andrew T. Lincoln and A. J. M. Wedderburn, *The Theology of the Later Pauline Letters*, New Testament Theology, ed. James D. G. Dunn (Cambridge: Cambridge University Press, 1993), 84; cf. also Werner Ochel, *Die Annahme einer Bearbeitung des Kolosser-Briefes im Epheser-Brief in einer Analyse des Epheser-Briefes untersucht*, Inaugural-Dissertation zur Erlangung der Doktorwürde der Philosophischen Fakultät der Philipps-Universität zu Marburg (Würzburg: Konrad Triltsch, 1934), 7–73; C. Leslie Mitton, "Unsolved New Testament Problems. Goodspeed's Theory regarding the Origin of Ephesians," *ExpTim* 59 (September 1948): 324–27; idem, *The Epistle to the Ephesians*, 55–158; Helmut Merklein, "Eph 4,1–5, 20 als Rezeption von Kol 3,1–17 (zugleich eine Beitrag zur Pragmatik des Epheserbriefes)," in *Kontinuität und Einheit: Für Franz Mußner*, ed. Paul-Gerhard Müller and Werner Stenger (Freiburg: Herder, 1981), 194–

literary relationship between Ephesians and Colossians. Scholars state that the closeness of these two epistles is similar to the relationship of the Synoptic Gospels or that of 2 Peter and Jude.[1] Mitton concludes that 26.5 percent of Ephesians is paralleled verbally with Colossians and 34 percent of the shorter Colossians is paralleled in Ephesians.[2] This is not as formidable as it might first appear. By using a database to observe the parallels, it becomes apparent that there are only 246 words shared between the two epistles out of a total of 2429 words for Ephesians and 1574 words for Colossians. Furthermore, when accounting for the multiple use of these 246 words, they make up 2057 words (out of 2429 words) in Ephesians and 1362 words (out of 1574 words) in Colossians. This, of course, includes the multiple use of conjunctions, pronouns, prepositions, and proper nouns (e.g., God, Christ). In fact, shared words that occur twenty-five times or more in Ephesians total thirteen (totaling 1109 words out of 2429) and twenty-five times or more in Colossians total nine (totaling 676 words out of 1574)—46 percent of Ephesians and 43 percent of Colossians. Hence, although there are vocabulary similarities between Ephesians and Colossians, many of the shared words used are the multiple use of conjunctions, pronouns, prepositions, and proper nouns. Beyond this, the similarity in vocabulary is understandable since the two works have similar content.

Conversely, there are thirty-eight words unique to Colossians and sixty-three words in Colossians not found elsewhere in Paul but found elsewhere in the NT (as mentioned above this compares to forty-one words unique to Ephesians and eighty-four words in Ephesians not found elsewhere in Paul but found elsewhere in the NT). Taking this a bit further, there are twenty-one words in Ephesians and Colossians not found elsewhere in Paul but found elsewhere in the NT and only eleven words in Ephesians and Colossians that are not found elsewhere in the NT. One would have thought that if an imitator of Paul had copied from Colossians, far more verbal correspondence would exist between the two epistles, especially when much of the content is similar. Furthermore, in regard to word usage it has been noted that the author of Ephesians uses vocabulary in a way different from that

---

210; Hans Hübner, "Glossen in Epheser 2," in *Vom Urchristentum zu Jesus. Für Joachim Gnilka*, ed. Hubert Frankemölle and Karl Kertelge (Freiburg: Herder, 1989), 392–406; Jennifer Kay Berenson Maclean, "Ephesians and the Problem of Colossians: Interpretation of Texts and Traditions in Eph 1:1–2:10" (Ph.D. diss., Harvard University, 1995), 14–18, 23–105.

1. Lincoln, xlvii.

2. Mitton, *The Epistle to the Ephesians*, 57; cf. also John B. Polhill, "The Relationship between Ephesians and Colossians," *RevExp* 70 (fall 1973): 439–50; A. J. M. Wedderburn, *Baptism and Resurrection: Studies in Pauline Theology against Its Graeco-Roman Background*, WUNT, ed. Martin Hengel and Otfried Hofius, vol. 44 (Tübingen: Mohr, 1987), 76–80.

of Colossians (e.g., "mystery" in Col 1:27 speaks of Christ in the believer whereas in Eph 3:6 it is used of believing Jews and Gentiles united in Christ).[1] Such differences would not be expected from an imitator presumed to have known Paul well.[2]

Up to this point, individual words have been considered, but another interesting element is the linkage of words. Mitton has noted that the greatest number of consecutive words that correspond exactly in the two epistles is seven and this occurs only three times (Eph 1:1–2 = Col 1:1–2; Eph 3:2 = Col 1:25; Eph 3:9 = Col 1:26). There are only two instances of exact correspondence of five consecutive words (Eph 1:7 = Col 1:14; Eph 4:16 = Col 2:9). According to Mitton, in only one place, information regarding the sending of Tychicus (Eph 6:21–22; Col 4:7–8), twenty-nine consecutive words of Colossians are repeated in Ephesians, except for the omission of the words καὶ σύνδουλος (actually there are thirty-two consecutive words; see chart in commentary at 6:21).[3] Because of the close literary correspondence between these two passages, Mitton suggests that the author of Ephesians may have copied it directly from Colossians or that he knew Colossians so well that he reproduced it almost verbatim. After looking at other parallel passages of Ephesians and Colossians, he prefers the latter alternative and concludes that the author of Ephesians must have known Colossians almost by heart.[4] However, why would anyone memorize such insignificant details regarding Tychicus? It seems more reasonable to imagine that Paul wrote both epistles around the same time and that toward the end of the second letter he referred to the conclusion of his first letter, since it was applicable to both. One would think that if the author of Ephesians had known Colossians almost by heart, he would have memorized verbatim the more significant contents of the book for the sake of accuracy in order to convince the recipients that it was Paul's work. Needless to say, there is actually very little consecutive verbal agreement between the two epistles.

Certainly there are thematic parallels between Ephesians and Colossians and much of the materials follow in the same sequence. The chart below is based on the work of Schmid and has been followed by Ernst and Lincoln.[5]

1. Goodspeed, *An Introduction to the New Testament*, 233.

2. Luke Timothy Johnson, *The Writings of the New Testament. An Interpretation* (Philadelphia: Fortress, 1986), 369.

3. Mitton, *The Epistle to the Ephesians*, 58–59; see also Ochel, *Die Annahme einer Bearbeitung des Kolosser-Briefes*, 4–5, 69–71.

4. Mitton, *The Epistle to the Ephesians*, 59, 67.

5. Josef Schmid, *Der Epheserbrief des Apostels Paulus. Seine Adresse, Sprache und literarischen Beziehungen Untersucht*, Biblische Studien, ed. Joh. Göttsberger and Jos. Sickenberger, vol. 22 (Freiburg: Herder, 1928), 412; Ernst, 254–55; Lincoln, xlix; Nils Alstrup Dahl, "Einleitungsfragen zum Epheserbrief," in *Studies in Ephesians: Introductory Questions, Text- & Edition-Critical Issues, Interpretation of Texts and Themes*, ed.

No one questions that there is a relationship between Ephesians and Colossians nor the possibility that the author of the second letter used the first letter. Although some would hold to the priority of Ephesians,[1] most think Colossians was written first.[2] In comparing Ephesians and Colossians there are parallels but there are surely also distinct materials in each epistle. Even Mitton admits that although the author of Ephesians may have been thoroughly familiar with Colossians, he did not know Colossians by heart and, despite borrowing exceedingly freely from Colossians, there is no indication of a rigid or mechanical copying.[3]

Lincoln makes several comparisons between the two epistles.[4] Three will be considered. First, he discusses verbal correspondences within parallel sections. In the first half of the books the greetings are similar, both having "saints" and "faithful in Christ (Jesus)," a combination not found in any other of Paul's epistles. Further, there are verbal correspondences of key words (e.g., redemption, reconciliation, body, flesh, tribulation, ministry, mystery, power) in parallel sections of each epistle. Lincoln contends that this shows that the author of Ephesians "clearly" borrowed from Colossians (Col 1:15–22; Eph 2:11–16). In the last half of the books he cites Ephesians' utilization of Colossians in reference to the putting off of the old humanity and putting on the new (Col 3:5–17; Eph 4:25–5:20), the *Haustafeln* or household codes (Col 3:18–4:1; Eph 5:21–6:9), and the information about the sending of Tychicus (Col 4:7–8; Eph 6:21–22). In response to this

---

David Hellholm, Vemund Blomkvist, and Tord Fornberg, WUNT, ed. Martin Hengel and Otfried Hofius, vol. 131 (Tübingen: Mohr, 2000), 39–48.

1. See Ernst Theodor Mayerhoff, *Der Brief an die Colosser, mit vornehmlicher Berücksichtigung der drei Pastoralbriefe kritisch geprüft*, ed. J. L. Mayerhoff (Berlin: Hermann Schultze, 1838), 72–106. He thinks that Colossians is not genuine but Ephesians is. See also Th. Innitzer, "Zur Frage der Priorität des Epheser-oder des Kolosserbriefes," *ZKT* 29, no. 3 (1905): 579–88; F. C. Synge, *St Paul's Epistle to the Ephesians: A Theological Commentary* (London: SPCK, 1941), 69–76; John Coutts, "The Relationship of Ephesians and Colossians," *NTS* 4 (April 1958): 201–7. Van Roon possibly thinks that Colossians borrowed from Ephesians although he thinks that both epistles depend on an Urtext (van Roon, *The Authenticity of Ephesians*, 413–37).

2. See Heinrich Julius Holtzmann, *Kritik der Epheser- und Kolosserbriefe: Auf Grund einer Analyse ihres Verwandtschaftsverhältnisses* (Leipzig: Wilhelm Engelmann, 1872), 35–129. Holtzmann suggests that neither Ephesians nor Colossians can claim priority throughout and both are partly indebted to the other. The author of Ephesians borrows from an alleged original of Colossians and after finishing Ephesians, he inserts materials from it into the final form of Colossians. This complicated theory has never gained wide acceptance. See also W. Hönig, "Ueber das Verhältniss des Epheserbriefes zum Briefe an die Kolosser," *Zeitschrift für wissenschaftliche Theologie* 15, no. 1 (1872): 63–87; Mitton, *The Epistle to the Ephesians*, 55–56; Gottfried Schille, "Der Autor des Epheserbriefes," *TLZ* 82 (Mai 1957): 325–34; Lincoln, l–lviii.

3. Mitton, *The Epistle to the Ephesians*, 57–58.

4. Lincoln, li–lviii.

Comparison of Ephesians and Colossians

Col	Unique to Col	Parallel Material	Unique to Eph	Eph
1:1–2		Prologue		1:1–2
			Eulogy	1:3–14
1:3–14		Thanksgiving and intercession		1:15–23
1:15–20	Supremacy of Christ in creation and reconciliation			
			Believers' redemption	2:1–10
1:21–23		From alienation to reconciliation to God	(also reconciliation of Jews and Gentiles into one body)	2:11–22
1:24–2:3		Paul's suffering and his ministry of the mystery		3:1–13
2:4–3:4	Warning against false teaching and reminder of true teaching			
			Prayer for strengthened love and doxology	3:14–21
		(head-body of Christ Col 2:19 = Eph 4:15–16)	Exhortation to unity	4:1–16
3:5–11		Rejection of old life and reception of new life		4:17–32
3:12–15		Exhortation to love		5:1–6
			Exhortation to holiness	5:7–14
3:16–17		Exhortation to a wise walk		5:15–21
3:18–4:1		Household code	(Christ and the church 5:23–32)	5:22–6:9
			Spiritual warfare	6:10–17
4:2–4		Exhortation to prayer and proclamation of the mystery		6:18–20
4:5–6	Conduct toward outsiders			
4:7–9		Commendation of Tychicus		6:21–22
4:10–17	Salutations			
4:18	(autograph)	Benediction	(peace and love)	6:23–24

argument, verbal links between the two epistles are also readily explainable if these letters were written by the same person. Since some of the same issues are discussed in both, it would be normal to use the same vocabulary and expressions. Is it not a little overstated to assert that the writer of Ephesians "clearly" borrowed from Colossians?

Second, Lincoln continues his line of argument by attempting to show that there are terminological links outside of major parallel sections. For example, he states: "The turn of the phrase in 1:4, ἁγίους καὶ ἀμώμους κατενώπιον αὐτοῦ, is taken from Col 1:22 but omits its additional καὶ ἀνεγκλήτους. 1:6, 7 incorporates Col 1:13, 14, ἐν ᾧ ἔχομεν τὴν ἀπολύτρωσιν . . . τὴν ἄφεσιν, but substitutes 'in the beloved' for 'in the Son of his love' and 'transgressions' for 'sins,' and adds 'through his blood' in an apparent conflation with Col 1:20."[1] But how does Lincoln know this with such certainty? It appears to be conjectural. It is natural for a single individual to use both similar vocabulary and/or expressions and yet incorporate different emphases for a different audience. This practice is common today. Often an article read to a scholarly society is later rewritten and presented to an audience of laypeople. Although there are changes, much of the vocabulary and expressions will remain the same.

Third, Lincoln discusses the claim by some scholars that Ephesians uses some terms from Colossians with different connotations.[2] For example, the term σῶμα refers to the cosmos in Col 2:19 but to the church in Eph 4:15–16.[3] However, careful examination reveals that in both Col 1:18 and 2:9 σῶμα refers to the church and thus is compatible with the meaning in Ephesians.[4] For another example, some postulate that the word πλήρωμα in Col 1:19 and 2:9 revolves around Christology whereas in Eph 1:23, 3:19, and 4:13 it centers in ecclesiology.[5] However, when one looks at the terms used in the two epistles there is not a great distinction, for in Col 2:10 the cognate verb states that believers (i.e., members of the church) are said to be filled in Christ.[6] Lincoln correctly observes that the argument that other terms are used differently (e.g., οἰκονομία in Col 1:25 and Eph 1:10; 3:2, 9; μυστήριον in Col 1:26–27 and Eph 3:3–6) will not stand when investigated.[7]

1. Ibid., lii.

2. Ibid., liii–liv; cf. also Ochel, *Die Annahme einer Bearbeitung des Kolosser-Briefes*, 3; Mitton, *The Epistle to the Ephesians*, 84–86; David G. Meade, *Pseudonymity and Canon: An Investigation into the Relationship of Authorship and Authority in Jewish and Earliest Christian Tradition*, WUNT, ed. Martin Hengel and Otfried Hofius, vol. 39 (Tübingen: Mohr, 1986; reprint, Grand Rapids: Eerdmans, 1987), 141.

3. Dibelius-Greeven, 84; Mitton, *The Epistle to the Ephesians*, 84.

4. C. F. D. Moule, "E. J. Goodspeed's Theory regarding the Origin of Ephesians," *ExpTim* 60 (May 1949): 224; Lincoln, liii; Donald Guthrie, *New Testament Introduction*, 4th ed. (Downers Grove, Ill.: InterVarsity, 1990), 514.

5. Mitton, *The Epistle to the Ephesians*, 94–97.

6. Lincoln, liv; van Roon, *The Authenticity of Ephesians*, 227–47.

7. Lincoln, liii–lv.

Lincoln concludes that the writer of Ephesians depended on Colossians "in terms of its overall structure and sequence, its themes, and its wording. Yet what is also absolutely clear is that this is a free and creative dependence, not a slavish imitation or copying."[1] He argues that the writer of Ephesians had seen a copy of Colossians, but whether he had memorized it or had a copy when composing Ephesians is uncertain. Further, he conjectures that the writer also made use of other letters in the Pauline corpus (excluding the Pastorals).[2] Later in his introduction, Lincoln argues in more detail that the writer of Ephesians could not have been Paul.[3] His main contention regarding the language and style is that the author of Ephesians used some of the same words and phrases to express different ideas (cf. Eph 5:20 and Col 3:17).

Several things need to be considered in this regard. First, after examining the literary parallels between Ephesians and Colossians, van Roon found few, if any, signs of literary interdependence between the two letters and what evidence was found pointed in the direction of Colossians depending on Ephesians.[4] This runs counter to Lincoln's argument that the writer of Ephesians rightly or wrongly presupposed that Paul (or a disciple of Paul while Paul was yet alive) wrote Colossians and he then used that as his basis when writing Ephesians.[5] Best looks at many parallel passages between Ephesians and Colossians and concludes that it is impossible to determine priority of either letter and shows the difficulties of Ephesians depending on Colossians or Colossians depending on Ephesians.[6] However, internal evidence indicates that both epistles were written by Paul (Eph 1:1; Col 1:1) but nothing in either epistle indicates priority.

Second, on the one hand, Lincoln is careful to point out that the writer of Ephesians did not change the meaning of the same terms used in Colossians.[7] On the other hand, he later argues that the writer used the same terms to express different ideas.[8] It seems that Lincoln wants it both ways. However, a closer look at the ideas expressed in the two epistles reveals that they are not substantially different.

1. Ibid., lv.

2. Ibid., lvi–lviii. Gese suggests that the author of Ephesians depended on other Pauline letters besides Colossians; see Gese, *Das Vermächtnis des Apostels*, 56–78.

3. Lincoln, lxvii–lxx.

4. Van Roon, *The Authenticity of Ephesians*, 413–37, esp. 426, 436; cf. Eta Linnemann, *Biblical Criticism on Trial: How Scientific is "Scientific Theology"?* trans. Robert W. Yarbrough (Grand Rapids: Kregel Publications, 2001), 113–17.

5. Lincoln, lxviii.

6. E. Best, "Who Used Whom? The Relationship of Ephesians and Colossians," *NTS* 43 (January 1997): 72–96, esp. 79, 81, 83, 84, 87, 88, 92–93. Best suggests that Ephesians and Colossians may have been written by two authors of the Pauline school who had discussed Pauline theology (93–96). See also Best, 23; Aletti, 19–21, 315.

7. Lincoln, liii–lv.

8. Ibid., lxvii.

Third, there is no proof that Paul had Colossians in front of him when he wrote Ephesians. Ephesians may have been written from the memory of what he had said and taught over the years. The expression of his thoughts may have varied, due to his own development and the varying needs of his audiences.

Fourth, we are not sure what lapse of time there was between the two epistles. Lincoln states that one should not compare the relationship of Colossians and Ephesians with the relationship of Galatians and Romans because there was a large time lapse between the latter two that cannot be the case for the former two. However, some scholars, especially those who accept the North Galatian theory, would see very little time gap between the composition of Galatians and Romans.[1]

Fifth, it is more likely that the same author would vary to a greater degree than an imitator. An imitator would feel more compelled to use the same vocabulary and expressions than would an author. Applying canonical criticism, Porter and Clarke make an interesting observation. The newly coined term for reconciliation (ἀποκαταλλάσσω) is used in Col 1:20, 22 and Eph 2:16. It would seem that no pseudonymous author of Colossians and/or Ephesians would have coined a new word. Furthermore, if a pseudonymous author of Ephesians used Colossians as his basis he would not have used this newly coined word in Eph 2:16 since it is used differently. It is far more likely that Paul would have coined a new term for use in Colossians and a slightly different use in Ephesians. The use of this word in these books points to Pauline authorship for both books.[2]

Sixth, if the author of Ephesians were an imitator or a disciple of Paul, he most probably would have copied vocabulary, expressions, and content more exactly throughout the letter. As mentioned above there is very little exact wording, and most of it is insignificant.

In conclusion, the literary relationship between Ephesians and Colossians is quite evident. Similar vocabulary and ideas certainly substantiate this. Despite these similarities, Best concludes that the author of Ephesians did not copy or use Colossians and that though both epistles could have been written by Paul, he thinks that it is more likely that they were written by two members of the Pauline school.[3]

1. Cf. Moffatt, *An Introduction to the Literature of the New Testament*, 105, 144; Kümmel, *Introduction to the New Testament*, 304, 311; Günther Bornkamm, *Paul*, trans. M. G. Stalker (New York: Harper & Row, 1971), 241–42; Hans Dieter Betz, *Galatians*, Hermeneia—A Critical and Historical Commentary on the Bible, New Testament ed. Helmut Koester et al. (Philadelphia: Fortress, 1979), 9–12; Robert Jewett, *A Chronology of Paul's Life* (Philadelphia: Fortress, 1979), end chart; Gerd Luedemann, *Paul, Apostle to the Gentiles: Studies in Chronology*, trans. F. Stanley Jones (Philadelphia: Fortress, 1984), 44–100, 263.

2. Porter and Clarke, "Canonical-Critical Perspective," 77–83.

3. Best, "Who Used Whom?" 95–96; Best, 40.

However, it seems appropriate to accept the internal evidence of Ephesians that states that Paul wrote it (1:1–2; 3:1) and to accept that what he wrote is consistent with Colossians and with his other letters. In the end, this solution is more consistent with the evidence. Also, it is much easier to understand the creative differences of an author than to expect them of an imitator or disciple. The differences arise due to differences of purpose, content, time, mood, and audience. This scenario explains the similarities and dissimilarities in wording on specific topics and concerns. It is easier to believe that Paul wrote these two epistles and that when he penned Ephesians he would have similar vocabulary and content on similar topics and would vary in vocabulary when addressing different issues. Is it not possible for an author to use the same words in different epistles or choose to use different vocabulary over some of the same issues? One must also allow for a development in Paul's thought. Certainly the thrust of Colossians is different because he had to deal with heresy, whereas Ephesians offers no indication that he is combating doctrinal error.

(4) Pseudonymity. The question of pseudonymity is an outgrowth of the preceding discussion. If Paul did not write Ephesians, then who did?[1] Throughout the years many suggestions have been made. Barrett suggests that Ephesians may be the oldest of the Pauline pseudepigrapha.[2] Most think the writer was of the Pauline school[3] or a disciple or secretary who was familiar with Paul's thinking.[4] Others

1. For a succinct discussion of this issue, see Arthur G. Patzia, "The Deutero-Pauline Hypothesis: An Attempt at Clarification," *EvQ* 52 (January–March 1980): 27–42.

2. C. K. Barrett, "Pauline Controversies in the Post-Pauline Period," *NTS* 20 (April 1974): 239.

3. Klöpper, 9–17; Hans-Martin Schenke, "Das Weiterwirken des Paulus und die Pflege seines Erbes durch die Paulus-Schule" *NTS* 21 (July 1975): 505–18; this was later incorporated into Hans-Martin Schenke and Karl Martin Fischer, *Einleitung in die Schriften des Neuen Testaments*, Die Briefe des Paulus und Schriften des Paulinismus, vol. 1 (Gütersloh: Gütersloher Verlagshaus, 1978), 174–90; Hans Conzelmann, "Die Schule des Paulus," in *Theologia crucis–signum crucis: Festschrift für Erich Dinkler zum 70. Geburtstag*, ed. Carl Andresen and Günter Klein (Tübingen: Mohr, 1979), 85–96.

4. Moffatt, *An Introduction to the Literature of the New Testament*, 388; Mitton, *The Epistle to the Ephesians*, 261–69; Wilfred Knox, *St. Paul* (New York: D. Appleton, 1932), 146; Pierre Benoit, "L'horizon paulinien de l'Épître aux Ephésiens," *RB* 46 (Juillet 1937): 342–61; (Octobre 1937): 506–25; H. F. D. Sparks, *The Formation of the New Testament* (New York: Philosophical Library, 1953), 72; Schenke, "Das Weiterwirken des Paulus und die Pflege seines Erbes durch die Paulus-Schule," 505–18; J. Paul Sampley, "The Letter to the Ephesians," in *The Deutero-Pauline Letters: Ephesians, Colossians, 2 Thessalonians, 1–2 Timothy, Titus*, rev. ed., Proclamation Commentaries, ed. Gerhard Krodel (Philadelphia: Fortress, 1993), 3–4; Lincoln, lx, lxviii–lxix; Aletti, 31–32; Dahl, "Einleitungsfragen zum Epheserbrief," 48–60, esp. 51–52, 58–60. Boismard proposes that Ephesians was originally written by Paul but was edited with inclusions from Colossians dating around A.D. 80, see M.-E. Boismard, *L'Énigme de la lettre aux Éphesiens*, EBib, no. 39 (Paris: Gabalda, 1999), 11–12, 15, 163–80; Marie-Émile Boismard, "Rm 16,17–20: Vocabulaire et style," *RB* 107 (Octobre 2000): 548–49, 556. In this article

suggest the possibility that the writer may have been a Gentile convert[1] or a Jewish Christian of some official standing.[2] When scholars propose particular individuals, most suggest either Tychicus[3] or Onesimus.[4] Goodspeed's proposal that an unknown writer, later identified as Onesimus, collected Paul's writings and composed Ephesians as an introduction to the collection[5] has not had wide acceptance.[6] Along similar lines Trobisch suggests that the collection of Paul's letters developed in three stages: (1) authorized recensions while Paul was alive (Rom 16 as cover letter, Rom 1–15, 1 and 2 Cor, Gal); (2) expanded editions of published and unpublished letters after Paul's death (Eph, Phil, Col, 1 and 2 Thess); and finally (3) comprehensive editions dealing with letters to individuals (1 and 2 Tim, Titus, Phlm). These stages are determined by the length of the letters in descending order. Therefore, since Ephesians is longer than Galatians, it is not in the first

---

Boismard suggests that Rom 16:17–18a, 20 belonged originally to the Ephesian letter but this has been challenged by Mora (Vincent Mora, "Romains 16,17–20 et la lettre aux Éphésiens," *RB* 107 [Octobre 2000]: 541–47).

1. Goodspeed, *The Meaning of Ephesians*, 16, 32; idem, *The Key to Ephesians* (Chicago: University of Chicago Press, 1956), v–vi.

2. Helmut Merklein, *Das kirchliche Amt nach dem Epheserbrief*, SANT, ed. Vinzenz Hamp and Josef Schmid, vol. 33 (Munich: Kösel, 1973), 44–45, 215–16, 350; Lincoln (lxx) thinks the author was probably "a Jewish Christian admirer of Paul."

3. Friedrich Schleiermacher, *Einleitung ins Neue Testament*, ed. G. Wolde, Literarischer Nachlaß zur Theologie, vol. 3; Sämmtliche Werke, pt. 1, vol. 8 (Berlin: G. Reimer, 1845), 165–66; Wilfred L. Knox, *St Paul and the Church of the Gentiles* (Cambridge: Cambridge University Press, 1939), 203; Mitton, *The Epistle to the Ephesians*, 268; Rodolphe Kasser, "L'autore dell' Epistola agli Efesini," *Protestantesimo* 17 (1962): 74–84.

4. Goodspeed, *An Introduction to the New Testament*, 239; idem, *New Chapters in New Testament Study* (New York: Macmillan, 1937), 32; P. N. Harrison, "The Author of Ephesians," in *SE II. Papers Presented to the Second International Congress on New Testament Studies held at Christ Church Oxford, 1961*, ed. F. L. Cross, TU, ed. Friedrich Zucher et al., vol. 87 (Berlin: Akademie-Verlag, 1964), 595–604.

5. Cf. Edgar J. Goodspeed, *The Formation of the New Testament* (Chicago: University of Chicago Press, 1926), 20–32; idem, *New Solutions of New Testament Problems*, 1–64; idem, *The Meaning of Ephesians*; idem, *An Introduction to the New Testament*, 210–22; idem, "The Place of Ephesians in the First Pauline Collection," *ATR* 12 (January 1930): 189–212; idem, "Ephesians and the First Edition of Paul," *JBL* 70 (December 1951): 285–91; Knox, *Marcion and the New Testament*, 53–60, 172–76; Goodspeed, *The Key to Ephesians*, xiv–xv; John Knox, *Philemon Among the Letters of Paul: A New View of Its Place and Importance* (New York: Abingdon, 1959), 71–90.

6. Cf. Charles H. Buck Jr., "The Early Order of the Pauline Corpus," *JBL* 68 (December 1949): 351–57; Jack Finegan, "The Original Form of the Pauline Collection," *HTR* 49 (April 1956): 85–103; see reply by John Knox, "A Note on the Format of the Pauline Letters," *HTR* 50 (October 1957): 311–14; Collins, *Letters That Paul Did Not Write*, 135; C. K. Barrett, *Paul: An Introduction to His Thoughts*, Outstanding Christian Thinkers Series, ed. Brian Davies (Louisville, Ky.: Westminster/John Knox; London: Geoffrey Chapman, 1994), 154–55.

stage but in the second stage, which means that it was collected and revised after Paul's death.[1] This is speculative and unconvincing because Trobisch's governing rule for determining a collection of letters is by the length of the letters in descending order. Furthermore, this is based on the canonical order of nine corpus editions and not other corpus editions that markedly deviate from the canonical order.[2] Hence, it is a hypothesis built on a tenuous supposition. Fischer suggests that from about A.D. 60 to 100 with the loss of the authority of Paul and the Jerusalem community, there was a need to address issues of the day (e.g., delay of the parousia, church offices) by appealing to names like Paul or Peter in order to gain a hearing and this caused the writers in this period to write pseudonymously.[3] However, Peter and Paul were most likely alive until A.D. 64 and 68 respectively and thus could have written the necessary letters ascribed to them which the early church readily assumed to be the case. It seems the period A.D. 60–100 is based on the bias that Paul could not have written these letters rather than on solid historical grounds. Regardless, it is the argument of many contemporary scholars that Paul was not the author and that the writer of Ephesians used the literary convention of pseudonymity.

This concept is based on the claim that it was a widely used literary practice in the Greco-Roman, Jewish, and Christian cultures.[4] Harrison suggests that the implementation of this literary model carried no

1. David Trobisch, *Die Entstehung der Paulusbriefsammlung: Studien zu den Anfängen christlicher Publizistik*, Novum Testamentum et Orbis Antiquus, ed. Max Küchler und Gerd Theißen, vol. 10 (Freiburg: Universitätsverlag; Göttingen: Vandenhoeck & Ruprecht, 1989), 57–60, 84–104, 117–42, passim; see the more popular version of this in English, idem, *Paul's Letter Collection: Tracing the Origins* (Minneapolis: Fortress, 1994), 48–96, passim.

2. As rightly critiqued by Eugene H. Lovering Jr., review of *Die Entstehung der Paulusbriefsammlung: Studien zu den Anfängen christlicher Publizistik*, by David Trobisch, *JBL* 110 (winter 1991): 736.

3. Karl Martin Fischer, "Anmerkungen zur Pseudepigraphie im Neuen Testament," *NTS* 23 (October 1976): 76–81.

4. Moffatt, *An Introduction to the Literature of the New Testament*, 40–44; Arnold Meyer, "Religiöse Pseudepigraphie als ethisch-psychologisches Problem," *ZNW* 35, nos. 3/4 (1936): 262–79; Goodspeed, *The Meaning of Ephesians*, 12–13; idem, *An Introduction to the New Testament*, 229; Mitton, *The Epistle to the Ephesians*, 222, 259–60; Josef A. Sint, *Pseudonymität im Altertum: ihre Formen und ihre Gründe*, Commentationes Aenipontanae, ed. Karl Jax and Robert Muth, vol. 15 (Innsbruck: Universitätsverlag Wagner, 1960); K. Aland, "The Problem of Anonymity and Pseudonymity in Christian Literature of the First Two Centuries," *JTS*, n.s., 12 (April 1961): 39–49 (this has been reprinted, idem, "The Problem of Anonymity and Pseudonymity in Christian Literature of the First Two Centuries," in *The Authorship and Integrity of the New Testament*, Theological Collections, no. 4 (London: SPCK, 1965), 1–13); Wolfgang Speyer, *Die literarische Fälschung im heidnischen und christlichen Altertum: Ein Versuch Ihrer Deutung*, Handbuch der Altertumswissenschaft, ed. Walter Otto and Hermann Bengston, vol. 1, pt. 2 (Munich: C. H. Beck'sche Verlagsbuchhandlung, 1971); Martin Rist, "Pseudepigraphy

moral stigma. In fact, he claims that the author "was not conscious of misrepresenting the Apostle in any way; he was not consciously deceiving anybody; it is not, indeed, necessary to suppose that he did deceive anybody. . . . They [epistles] went for what they really were, and the warm appreciation with which the best minds in the Church received them, would not be tinged with any misunderstanding as to the way in which they had been written."[1] However, Green cogently argues, "If this assessment were wholly true, and if nobody was taken in by the device, it is hard to see why it was adopted at all."[2] Furthermore, although there was widespread use of pseudepigraphy by the Greeks and Romans, none were accepted as genuine if it were known not to have been written by the author it claimed. Donelson states: "No one ever seems to have accepted a document as religiously and philosophically prescriptive which was known to be forged. I do not know a single example."[3]

More recently Meade seeks to show that pseudonymity, which was allegedly practiced in NT times, had its basis in OT and Jewish writings. He proposes that Second Isaiah (chaps. 40–55), written in light of the Babylonian exile in the sixth century B.C. and Third Isaiah (chaps. 56–66) written in the era of postexilic Jerusalem some time between the second and fourth century B.C., contemporize (*vergegenwärtigen*) First Isaiah (chaps. 1–39) which deals with the Assyrian threats of the eighth century B.C.[4] Meade continues by applying this

---

and the Early Christians," in *Studies in New Testament and Early Christian Literature: Essays in Honor of Allen P. Wikgren*, ed. David Edward Aune, NovTSup, ed. W. C. van Unnik et al., vol. 33 (Leiden: Brill, 1972), 75–91; Norbert Brox, *Falsche Verfasserangaben zur Erklärung der frühchristlichen Pseudepigraphie*, Stuttgarter Bibelstudien, ed. Herbert Haag, Rudolf Kilian, and Wilhelm Pesch, vol. 79 (Stuttgart: KBW, 1975), 41–48; Lewis R. Donelson, *Pseudepigraphy and Ethical Argument in the Pastoral Epistles*, Hermeneutische Untersuchungen zur Theologie, ed. Hans Dieter Betz, Gerhard Ebeling, and Manfred Mezger, vol. 22 (Tübingen: Mohr, 1986), 7–54; Meade, *Pseudonymity and Canon*; James D. G. Dunn, *The Living Word* (Philadelphia: Fortress; Philadelphia: Trinity Press International, 1987), 65–85; Lincoln, lxx–lxxii. For recent doctoral dissertations on pseudonymity, see Curtis Kent Horn, "Pseudonymity in Early Christianity: An Inquiry into the Theory of Innocent Deutro-Pauline Pseudonymity" (Ph.D. diss., Southwestern Baptist Theological Seminary, 1996); Jeremy N. Duff, "A Reconsideration of Pseudepigraphy in Early Christianity" (D.Phil. thesis, University of Oxford, 1998); Terry L. Wilder, "New Testament Pseudonymity and Deception" (Ph.D. thesis, University of Aberdeen, 1998).

1. Harrison, *The Problem of the Pastoral Epistles*, 12; cf. idem, *Paulines and Pastorals*, 14–15.

2. E. M. B. Green, *2 Peter Reconsidered* (London: Tyndale, 1961), 32; so also, Bruce M. Metzger, "Literary Forgeries and Canonical Pseudepigrapha," *JBL* 91 (March 1972): 16.

3. Donelson, *Pseudepigraphy*, 11; cf. also Speyer, *Die literarische Fälschung im heidnischen und christlichen Altertum*, 133–34; Stanley E. Porter, "Pauline Authorship and the Pastoral Epistles: Implications for Canon," *BBR* 5 (1995): 115.

4. Meade, *Pseudonymity and Canon*, 17–43.

procedure of continuity between revelation and tradition in Wisdom literature, Daniel, and *1 Enoch*.[1] Hence, it is his contention that pseudonymity practiced in the OT served as the basis for its practice in the NT, attempting to apply it to the Pastorals, Ephesians, and 2 Peter.[2] But Guthrie rightly observes that this is special pleading because his OT examples are of a different literary genre from those in the NT.[3] Smith concurs by stating that "the major pseudepigraphic forms of the period between Alexander and Titus—apocalyptic visions and Mosaic legal revelations—were direct outgrowths of the earlier Israelite tradition," whereas the forgery of letters (epistolary genre) may reflect Greek influence.[4] Hence, even if one were to accept Meade's procedure of continuity or contemporization within the OT, it is invalid to apply it to NT epistolary genre because the genres are entirely different. Also, Duff points out that "Old Testament pseudepigraphy cannot have functioned as a model for early-Christian pseudepigraphy, since the early-Christians appear not to have thought that there was any Old Testament pseudepigraphy."[5] Furthermore, Meade's hypothesis rests on critical OT presuppositions devised in the last two centuries for which there is no historical evidence either in the Jewish or in the Christian communities. There is no historical evidence in rabbinic, Qumran, or Christian circles for the division of Isaiah into three different authors and eras. Neither can the practice of pseudonymity be confirmed as an acceptable practice at anytime in the history of the church. Nonetheless, Meade suggests that the literary device of pseudonymity for Pauline literature came with the persecution of Domitian and with the rise of heresy, beginning in the first decade of the second century. He claims that these events provoked the need for authoritative Pauline interpretation from a "school" (e.g., the Pastorals) that was later discovered to be pseudonymous but no less authoritative. He further contends that in the second century A.D. the practice of pseudonymity became more difficult and became nonexistent at the closure of the canon.[6]

This scenario, however, has no historical basis. Even Meade admits it lacks the work needed to substantiate it. In fact, it really runs contrary to his OT models where Second Isaiah and Third Isaiah allegedly contemporize First Isaiah centuries later whereas the so-called

1. Ibid., 44–102.

2. Ibid., 103–93.

3. Guthrie, *New Testament Introduction*, 1027.

4. Morton Smith, "Pseudepigraphy on the Israelite Literary Tradition," in *Pseudepigrapha I: Pseudopythagorica—Lettres de Platon Littérature pseudépigraphique juive*, ed. Kurt von Fritz, Entretiens sur l'Antiquité classique, vol. 18, pt. 1 (Vandaeuvres-Genève: Foundation Hardt, 1972), 215.

5. Duff, "A Reconsideration of Pseudepigraphy," 66.

6. Meade, *Pseudonymity and Canon*, 194–203.

imitators of Paul are rarely found one century later contemporizing Pauline literature.

Certainly there were many pseudepigraphical works in Judaism, such as *The Book of Enoch* and *The Testament of the Twelve Patriarchs*, but they were composed centuries after the lives of those named in their works and were never accepted as canonical by the Jews whereas it is proposed that Ephesians was written within a few years after Paul's death and yet had no difficulty being accepted as canonical. To the contrary, it is difficult to imagine that those who knew Paul would have accepted this as Paul's work so shortly after his death if it were truly not his work. Furthermore, most pseudepigraphical works are apocalyptic and not epistolary in form. Of all the known pseudepigraphical writings, only the *Epistle of Jeremy* and the *Letter of Aristeas* are epistolary in form and neither of these are strictly epistles.[1] The *Epistle of Jeremy,* using Jeremiah's name to denounce idolatry and probably composed sometime between the early fourth and late second century B.C., "reads more like a sermon or hortatory address than a letter."[2] Apparently the recipients of this letter never really considered it as coming from the revered prophet Jeremiah or it would have been mentioned by the rabbis or accepted as canonical. The *Letter of Aristeas*, purported to be written by Aristeas to his brother Philocrates about the translation of the Hebrew Scriptures into Greek at the time of Ptolemy II (285–247 B.C.), was composed sometime between the third century B.C. and first century A.D., most likely sometime between 170 and 70 B.C.[3] Because of the historical mistakes, it was easily detected as pseudepigraphical. Neither of these two works were considered genuine and hence canonical either by the Jewish rabbis or by the Christian church in the first century A.D.

In post-NT times many works bore the names of the apostles, for example, the *Gospel of Thomas*, *Gospel of Peter,* and *Apocalypse of Peter.* However, these works were never seriously considered by the early church as genuine (or canonical). The church from its earliest days critically examined many writings with apostolic claims but rejected them either because they were heretical or because they were pseudonymous.[4] Any person who falsely claimed that his work was apos-

1. Guthrie, *New Testament Introduction*, 1012.

2. C. J. Ball, "Epistle of Jeremy," in *The Apocrypha and Pseudepigrapha of the Old Testament in English*, ed. R. H. Charles, vol. 1 (Oxford: Clarendon, 1913), 596; cf. also Sidney S. Tedesche, "Jeremiah, Letter of," in *The Interpreter's Dictionary of the Bible*, ed. George Arthur Buttrick et al., vol. 2 (Nashville: Abingdon, 1962), 822–23.

3. Herbert T. Andrews, "The Letter of Aristeas," in *The Apocrypha and Pseudepigrapha of the Old Testament in English*, ed. R. H. Charles, vol. 2 (Oxford: Clarendon, 1913), 85–87; Günther Zuntz, "Aristeas," in *The Interpreter's Dictionary of the Bible*, ed. George Arthur Buttrick et al., vol. 1 (Nashville: Abingdon, 1962), 220; R. J. H. Shutt, "Letter of Aristeas," in *The Old Testament Pseudepigrapha*, ed. James H. Charlesworth, vol. 2 (Garden City, N.Y.: Doubleday; London: Darton, Longman & Todd, 1985), 7–34.

4. As discussed below, the case of Serapion, Eusebius *Historia Ecclesiastica* 6.12.2–3.

tolic or was from within the apostolic circle was rejected. Lea asserts, "Pseudonymous authorship seems not to have been an acceptable option for the early church."[1] In fact, in one of his earliest letters Paul cautions his readers not to be troubled or anxious by a letter purported to have come from him (2 Thess 2:2).[2] He affirms this at the end of this same epistle by stating that the greeting is by his own hand (3:17). Clearly, Paul was opposed to pseudonymous writings. This view toward pseudonymous works continued after the first century.

Of all the works in epistolary form that claim apostolic authorship, two come to the forefront. The first is the *Epistle to the Laodiceans*. The temptation to fabricate such a work no doubt arose from Col 4:16 where the Colossians were to share their letter from Paul with the Laodiceans and also to read the letter Paul had sent to the Laodiceans (a letter that has been lost). The *Epistle to the Laodiceans* is a feeble compilation of Pauline passages and phrases mainly from Philippians.[3] As early as the Muratorian Canon (ca. A.D. 170–200) the letter to the Laodiceans was considered a letter forged in Paul's name in support of Marcion's heresy.[4] Jerome (A.D. 345–419) certainly regarded the Laodicean letter as a forgery and stated that it was rejected by all.[5] It was finally rejected as "a forged Epistle to the Laodiceans" by the Second Council of Nicea (A.D. 787).[6]

The second writing in epistolary form is *The Acts of Paul and Thecla*. Thecla of Iconium was a female convert, companion, and colleague of Paul who faithfully endured persecutions and whom Paul had commissioned to teach the Word of God. Although this work was

1. Thomas D. Lea, "The Early Christian View of Pseudepigraphic Writings," *JETS* 27 (March 1984): 70.

2. Wilder ("New Testament Pseudonymity and Deception," 113–14, see also 104–13) concludes his discussion on 2 Thess 2:2 by writing "In light of the evidence presented in this section, the correct interpretation of 2 Thessalonians 2:2 appears to be that *Paul did not want to be misrepresented by any teaching falsely attributed to him*. It does not appear that the Paul in this text was particularly motivated by a sense of scruples regarding *his* literary property at all; for, he does not refer to an actual work of his own in this verse. Moreover, he does not appear to have had any specific literary work in mind; for, the description in 2:2 about the false teaching's source is in general terms. But it does seem clear from this text that he would have been upset if someone had written a work which purported to be his. As we have seen, forgery in this regard is a pseudo-author's attempt to claim that his literary property is somebody else's." Cf. also Duff, "A Reconsideration of Pseudepigraphy," 215–22.

3. Wilhelm Schneemelcher, "The Epistle to the Laodiceans," in *New Testament Apocrypha*, ed. Edgar Hennecke, Wilhelm Schneemelcher, and R. McL. Wilson, trans. George Ogg, vol. 2 (London: Lutterworth; Philadelphia: Westminster, 1965), 129.

4. *The Muratorian Canon* 64–65.

5. Jerome *De Viris Illustribus* 5 (*PL* 23:619).

6. J. B. Lightfoot, *Saint Paul's Epistles to the Colossians and to Philemon* (London: Macmillan, 1875), 290; for a study of the problem regarding this letter, see pp. 272–98; Charles P. Anderson, "Who Wrote 'The Epistle from Laodicea'," *JBL* 85 (December 1966): 436–40; idem, "Laodiceans, Epistle to the," in *ABD*, 4:231–33.

popular from the fourth to the sixth centuries, comparatively few church fathers refer to it. Tertullian rejected it as a spurious work in his treatise on baptism[1] written around A.D. 185–195.[2] It is sometimes argued that Tertullian rejected it because it authorized women to teach and baptize, a posture quite different from Paul's view of the role of women in ministry.[3] However, when one examines the text of Tertullian there is no indication that he rejected this work due to heretical teaching but rather because the author was convicted of passing off this work under Paul's name and thus using Paul's reputation for his own purpose. The author of the work protested that he had done it in good faith and that he had done it out of love for Paul. Nevertheless, because of his deception he was removed from his office as presbyter. Packer summarizes it well by stating that "frauds are still fraudulent, even when perpetrated from noble motives."[4] Hence, not only Paul but also the church as early as the second century rejected pseudonymous writings.

There is a tendency to minimize the fraudulence of pseudonymity. For instance, Baur asserts that present-day ethics should not be applied to early church practices and that pseudonymous writings should not be labeled as "deception or wilful forgery."[5] Along the same lines Jülicher asserts that it was common for Christians to use materials from others without indicating their sources and to ascribe them to an apostle's name with clear conscience and without any hint of deception.[6] In more recent times, Mitton states, "If the writer deliberately derived what he wrote from the epistles which Paul had written, and did so that he might the more faithfully represent Paul to a subse-

1. Tertullian *De Baptismo* 17 (*PL* 1:1219–20). For a discussion of this passage by Tertullian, see Wilder, "New Testament Pseudonymity and Deception," 231–41; Duff, "A Reconsideration of Pseudepigraphy," 230–33.

2. Wilhelm Schneemelcher, "Acts of Paul," in *New Testament Apocrypha*, ed. Edgar Hennecke, Wilhelm Schneemelcher, and R. McL. Wilson, trans. R. McL. Wilson, vol. 2 (London: Lutterworth; Philadelphia: Westminster, 1965), 351.

3. Meade, *Pseudonymity and Canon*, 205; Donelson, *Pseudepigraphy*, 18; E. Margaret Howe, "Interpretations of Paul in the Acts of Paul and Thecla," in *Pauline Studies. Essays Presented to F. F. Bruce on His 70th Birthday*, ed. Donald A. Hagner and Murray J. Harris (Grand Rapids: Eerdmans; London: Paternoster, 1980), 34–35; Dennis R. MacDonald, "Thekla, Acts of," in *ABD*, 6:444; Léonie Hayne, "Thecla and the Church Fathers," *VC* 48 (September 1994): 209–10, 215; cf. also Dennis Ronald MacDonald, *The Legend and the Apostle: The Battle for Paul in Story and Canon* (Philadelphia: Westminster, 1983), 17–21, 34–35. MacDonald thinks that this work was dismissed because of unwelcomed eschatological views (84–85).

4. J. I. Packer, *'Fundamentalism' and the Word of God: Some Evangelical Principles* (Grand Rapids: Eerdmans; London: Inter-Varsity, 1958), 184.

5. Baur, *Paul the Apostle of Jesus Christ*, 2:110–11.

6. Adolf Jülicher, *An Introduction to the New Testament*, trans. Janet Penrose Ward, Prefatory Note by Mrs. Humphrey Ward (New York: G. P. Putnam's Sons; London: Smith, Elder, 1904), 52–53; this view was continued in his later editions, cf. idem, *Einleitung in das Neue Testament*, 7th ed. with Erich Fascher, Grundriss der theologischen

quent generation, it might well have been less honest in his case to pass the result off under his own name than to acknowledge it as Paul's."[1] Meade concurs by stating that the "pseudepigrapher really felt that he was a spokesman for the apostle."[2] Aland goes so far as to state, "When the pseudonymous writings of the New Testament claimed the authorship of the most prominent apostles only, this was not a skilful trick of the so-called fakers, in order to guarantee the highest possible reputation and the widest possible circulation for their work, but the logical conclusion of the presupposition that the Spirit himself was the author."[3] Yet, Guthrie correctly points out that the works which are accepted as "genuine are undoubtedly manifestations of the work of the Spirit and yet Paul appends his name."[4] In fact, as Balz observes, following Aland's logic would mean that Paul's ascription of his own name was less directed by the Spirit than the pseudepigraphers of later generations.[5] Guthrie also states, "The idea that the Spirit would lead some to write in their own names and forbid others to do so is inconceivable."[6] Furthermore, if the pseudonymous writers really felt that the Spirit was the author, why would they use an apostle's name rather than designating the Holy Spirit as the author? It is clear that there were writers who used the apostle's name to deceive the recipients of their writings.[7] Nonetheless, whatever the

Wissenschaften, ed. Achelis et al., pt. 3, vol. 1 (Tübingen: Mohr, 1931), 54–55; cf. also J. C. Fenton, "Pseudonymity in the New Testament," *Theology* 58 (February 1955): 55–56; James D. G. Dunn, "Pseudepigraphy," in *DLNT*, 981. Dunn thinks that if the word "pseudonymity" reflects the idea of deliberate deceit and forgery we should not use the term "because they would have fooled nobody!" See Dunn, *The Living Word*, 68. It is unlikely that the pseudonymous writer did not want to deceive, otherwise, he would have used his own name!

1. Mitton, *The Epistle to the Ephesians*, 259–60; cf. also idem, "Important Hypotheses Reconsidered VII. The Authorship of the Epistle to the Ephesians," *ExpTim* 67 (April 1956): 197. Guthrie takes exception to Mitton's argument, see Donald Guthrie, "Tertullian and Pseudonymity," *ExpTim* 67 (August 1956): 341–42.

2. Meade, *Pseudonymity and Canon*, 198–99.

3. Aland, "The Problem of Anonymity and Pseudonymity," 44–45.

4. Guthrie, *New Testament Introduction*, 1025.

5. Horst R. Balz, "Anonymität und Pseudepigraphie im Urchristentum: Überlegungen zum literarischen and theologischen Problem der urchristlichen and gemeinantiken Pseudepigraphie," *ZTK* 66 (Januar 1969): 419.

6. Donald Guthrie, "The Development of the Idea of Canonical Pseudepigrapha in New Testament Criticism," *VE* 1 (1962): 56; reprinted as idem, "The Development of the Idea of Canonical Pseudepigrapha in New Testament Criticism," in *The Authorship and Integrity of the New Testament*, Theological Collections, no. 4 (London: SPCK, 1965), 37.

7. Ellis suggests that the exceptions to this would be writings composed in a style of ancient masters like school exercises were done with no intent of deceiving anyone. See E. Earle Ellis, "Pseudonymity and Canonicity of New Testament Documents," in *Worship, Theology and Ministry in the Early Church: Essays in Honor of Ralph P. Martin*, ed. Michael J. Wilkins and Terence Paige, JSNTSup, ed. Stanley E. Porter et al., vol. 87

possible reasons were for pseudepigraphy, none should be considered valid. Indeed, all attempts to minimize this practice are fallacious rationalizations. Paul, in the middle of the first century, was aware of such a practice, spoke against it (2 Thess 2:2–3), and warned of the danger of its use to propound false doctrine. Furthermore, there is no evidence that there was a shift in thinking between Paul in the middle of the first century (2 Thess 2:2; 3:17) and Tertullian at the end of the second century as Meade suggests. In short, whether or not it was practiced by those outside or within Christianity, pseudepigraphy must be seen as that which was designed to deceive.[1]

Many propose that the idea of "intellectual property" in the current "discussion of legitimate claims to authorship, plagiarism, and copyright laws, played little or no role in ancient literary production"[2] and such is a modern invention.[3] However, such a proposal cannot be maintained in light of the evidence from classical times and the early church.[4] As mentioned above, in the Greco-Roman world no pseudepigraphical writing identified as such was ever considered to have prescriptive or proscriptive authority and was thus rejected.[5] The concept of literary property was already acknowledged in the fifth century B.C. when Herodotus (484–425 B.C.) questioned Homer's authorship of

(Sheffield: JSOT Press, 1992), 223. Ellis suggests that fiction would be another exception using the modern analogy; Robert Graves, *I, Claudius. From the Autobiography of Tiberius Claudius Born B.C. 10, Murdered and Deified A.D. 54* (London: A. Barker, 1934; reprint, New York: Time, 1965). Neither of these exceptions were intended to deceive anyone. Certainly plays in ancient or modern times depicting a person from another period would not deceive an audience.

1. Rist, "Pseudepigraphy and the Early Christians," 75; Martin Rese, "Church and Israel in the Deuteropauline Letters," *SJT* 43, no. 1 (1990): 20; Eduard Verhoef, "Pseudepigraphy and Canon," *Biblische Notizen* 106 (2001): 93, 98. For an examination of motives for the writers of pseudepigraphy, see Metzger, "Literary Forgeries and Canonical Pseudepigrapha," 5–12; P. J. Parsons, "Forgeries, Literary, Greek," *OCD*, 604; Herbert Jennings Rose and P. J. Parsons, "Pseudepigraphical Literature," *OCD*, 1270; Horn, "Pseudonymity in Early Christianity," 55–57; Verhoef, "Pseudepigraphy and Canon," 94–97.

2. Lincoln, lxxi; see also Kreitzer, 27–28; Harrison, *The Problem of the Pastoral Epistles*, 12; Meade, *Pseudonymity and Canon*, 198–99, 206.

3. Frederik Torm, *Die Psychologie der Pseudonymität im Hinblick auf die Literatur des Urchristentums*, Studien der Luther-Akademie, ed. Carl Stange, vol. 2 (Gütersloh: Bertelsmann, 1932), 19.

4. Ellis, "Pseudonymity and Canonicity," 212–24; Duff, "A Reconsideration of Pseudepigraphy," 276, 278; D. A. Carson, "Pseudonymity and Pseudepigraphy," in *DNTB*, 860–61.

5. Donelson, *Pseudepigraphy*, 11. For examples of this, Donelson refers to Speyer, *Die literarische Fälschung im heidnischen und christlichen Altertum*, 112–27 [should be 111–28] and Brox, *Falsche Verfasserangaben zur Erklärung der frühchristlichen Pseudepigraphie*, 71–80. See also Porter, "Pauline Authorship and the Pastoral Epistles," 113–14.

Epigoni and *Cypria*.[1] Also, the writer of 2 Maccabees informs his readers that his work was a condensation of the five-volume work of Jason of Cyren (2 Macc 2:23).[2] Likewise, in Paul's day some used Paul's name to further their purposes (2 Thess 2:2; 3:17) but their writings were not to be heeded because they were false. Similarly, in the early church a pseudepigraphical work was to be rejected as a forgery and worthless.[3] As mentioned above, the *Epistle to the Laodiceans* was rejected from the Muratorian Canon as a letter forged in Paul's name to support Marcion's heresy. Eusebius clearly states that it was a practice of the church to reject pseudepigraphical writings as forgeries put forward by heretics.[4] Hence, there is uniform testimony in the first four centuries of the church that any pseudepigraphical work was to be rejected as a forgery. This perspective is not different from the contemporary view of literary proprietorship.

Furthermore, Meade's idea that *"the discovery of pseudonymous origins or anonymous redaction in no way prejudices either the inspiration or the canonicity of the work"*[5] will not bear the weight of the evidence. For example, Serapion, bishop of Antioch (ca. A.D. 190–211) at first allowed the *Gospel of Peter* to be read. Later when he heard that some were appealing to it for the support of Docetism, he examined it, found it unorthodox, and consequently rejected it as a forgery (ψευδεπίγραφα).[6] A forgery was considered not inspired[7] and thus not canonical.[8] If the opposite were true, one would think that there would be many clear-cut cases in the early church. Hence, the early church fathers were interested in authorship and as Gempf notes, "we have no

1. Herodotus 2.117; 4.32; cf. Parsons, "Forgeries, Literary, Greek," *OCD*, 604.

2. Dunn, "Pseudepigraphy," 978.

3. Jas. S. Candlish, "On the Moral Character of Pseudonymous Books," *Exp* 4th ser., vol. 4 (August 1891): 103; Donelson, *Pseudepigraphy*, 11–12; Ellis, "Pseudonymity and Canonicity," 217–19.

4. Eusebius *Historia Ecclesiastica* 3.25.6–7; cf. also 1.9.2–3; 6.12.3; 9.5.1; 9.7.1.

5. Meade, *Pseudonymity and Canon*, 215–16; cf. also Penna, 65–69; Lincoln, lxxiii; Aletti, 32.

6. Eusebius *Historia Ecclesiastica* 6.12.2–3. For a discussion on Serapion and the *Gospel of Peter*, see Wilder, "New Testament Pseudonymity and Deception," 248–57; Duff, "A Reconsideration of Pseudepigraphy," 225–29.

7. Candlish, "On the Moral Character of Pseudonymous Books," 276.

8. Ellis, "Pseudonymity and Canonicity," 223–24; Porter and Clarke, "Canonical-Critical Perspective," 66–67, 69–72; E. Earle Ellis, *The Making of the New Testament Documents*, Biblical Interpretation Series, ed. R. Alan Culpepper, Rolf Rendtorff, and David E. Orton, vol. 39 (Leiden: Brill, 1999), 322–25; Porter, "Pauline Authorship and the Pastoral Epistles," 118–21; Verhoef, "Pseudepigraphy and Canon," 93, 98. O'Brien, 45, correctly asserts: "The claim is made that because Ephesians is in the canon it is therefore, authoritative. But for the early church the argument went the other way: Ephesians was recognized as apostolic and authoritative, and as a result it was accepted into the canon. Its placement in the canon did not give the letter authority; rather, its authority as an apostolic writing preceded its acknowledgment and inclusion within the canon."

record of their congratulating a pseudonymous author or consciously accepting a single pseudonymous work. We must conclude that if pseudonymous works got into the canon, the church fathers were *fooled* by a transparent literary device that was originally intended *not* to fool anyone."[1]

Finally, if the letter to the Ephesians were written by a pseudonymous author, then the passage regarding information about the author's circumstances (Eph 6:21–22) is pointless.[2] What would Tychicus say about the author? Why would the congregation want to know of Paul's situation when he was already dead? Were they to pray for the dead? It is incongruous for a pseudonymous author to ask the Ephesian believers to pray for Paul when he knew he was no longer living. It is even more preposterous to think that Tychicus would report about Paul's situation if the letter were not by Paul himself. It would mean that Tychicus would be part of the fraud. If the author were pseudonymous, then the Ephesians would not have known who he was, and if they had known who he was, the letter would not be pseudonymous! Also, as O'Brien correctly observes, the strong emphasis on the need for truthfulness (4:15, 24, 25; 5:19; 6:14) would render the author hypocritical when he condemns deceit in 4:25: "having laid aside falsehood, each one of you speak the truth with his neighbor."[3]

In conclusion, therefore, it is more reasonable to accept the fact that Ephesians was authored by Paul as stated in Eph 1:1 and 3:1. This, after all, has been the accepted view throughout church history until the nineteenth and twentieth centuries (see chart above). The arguments for pseudonymity are less than convincing.

(5) Theological distinctions. No one will deny that there are theological distinctions in every book of the NT. However, there are those who suggest that the theological distinctions in Ephesians are of such a magnitude as to indicate that they were not Pauline. Kümmel says that "the theology of Eph makes the Pauline composition of the letter completely impossible."[4] Also, Käsemann states, "In the New Testament it is Ephesians that most clearly marks the transition from the Pauline tradition to the perspectives of the early Catholic era."[5] Though much

1. Conrad Gempf, "Pseudonymity and the New Testament," *Themelios* 17 (January/February 1992): 10.

2. Archibald M. Hunter, *Introducing the New Testament*, 2d ed., rev. and enl. (Philadelphia: Westminster, 1957), 121.

3. O'Brien, 43–44.

4. Kümmel, *Introduction to the New Testament*, 360.

5. Ernst Käsemann, "Ephesians and Acts [trans. Marianne Grobel and Thomas Wieser]," in *Studies in Luke-Acts. Essays Presented in Honor of Paul Schubert Buckingham Professor of New Testament Criticism and Interpretation at Yale University*, ed. Leander E. Keck and J. Louis Martyn (Nashville: Abingdon, 1966), 288, see 288–97; cf. also idem, "Epheserbrief," in *Die Religion in Geschichte und Gegenwart: Handwörter-*

has been written on the theological distinctions,[1] this discussion will be limited to three areas: soteriology, ecclesiology, and eschatology.

First, with regard to soteriology,[2] it is proposed, on the one hand, that in Ephesians the death of Christ and the theology of the cross are less prominent than in other Pauline literature. The cross is only mentioned in 2:16 (which depends on Col 1:20) in connection with the reconciliation of the Jews and Gentiles into one body and Christ's death is mentioned only in the traditional formulations (1:7; 5:2, 25). On the other hand, Christ's resurrection, exaltation, and cosmic lordship are more prominent. In response to this argument, these references do speak to Christ's death as a substitutionary sacrifice for humankind and to say that the reference to the cross depends on Col 1:20 is begging the question as to which of these letters came first. The fact that there are four references to Christ's death in a six-chapter book is noteworthy. Also, the reconciliation of Jews and Gentiles into one body is within the context of the reconciliation of God and humankind on the basis of the cross which, indeed, leads to the exaltation of Christ. However, even understanding this, there is no hint that the exaltation could come without the death of Christ. Furthermore, Christ's exaltation is an emphasis in the NT as a whole. Of note in the Book of Acts are the sermons by Peter (Acts 2:24–36; 3:15–16, 21, 26) and by Paul (Acts 13:30–37), which stress resurrection and exaltation. Also, in his defense speeches, Paul stresses the hope of the resurrection (Acts 23:6; 24:14–15; 26:23). In other letters Paul accentuates resurrection and exaltation (1 Cor 15:3–28; Phil 2:5–11).

It is also suggested that the writer of Ephesians contradicts the teachings of Paul in Romans with respect to the law. They say that Paul's message does not abolish or nullify (καταργέω) the law in Rom 3:31 but, using the same verb, Eph 2:15 states that Christ has nullified it. However, one must look at the context, for certainly the law is in effect for the unbelievers to show them that they are sinners and need to come to God by faith (Rom 3:31) but the law is nullified (καταργέω) for believers (Rom 7:2, 6; Eph 2:15). Further, Paul states that the law came to an end for those who believe (Rom 10:4) and that believers are no longer under it (Gal 3:25).

---

buch für Theologie und Religionswissenschaft, ed. Hans Frhr. v. Campenhausen et al., 3d ed., vol. 2 (Tübingen: Mohr, 1958), 517–20; idem, "Paul and Early Catholicism," in *New Testament Questions of Today*, trans. Wilfred F. Bunge, The New Testament Library, ed. Alan Richardson, C. F. D. Moule, C. F. Evans, and Floyd V. Filson (London: SCM, 1969), 236–51; idem, "The Theological Problem Presented by the Motif of the Body of Christ," in *Perspectives on Paul*, trans. Margaret Kohl, The New Testament Library, ed. Alan Richardson, C. F. D. Moule, C. F. Evans, Floyd V. Filson (London: SCM, 1971), 102–21, esp. 120–21.

1. See Mitton, *The Epistle to the Ephesians*, 16–24; Lincoln, lxiii–lxv; Lincoln and Wedderburn, *The Theology of the Later Pauline Letters*, 91–166.

2. Lincoln, lxiii–lxiv; cf. also Mitton, *The Epistle to the Ephesians*, 20.

In addition, some question the absence of the concept of justification by grace in Ephesians.[1] Granted this terminology is not used but certainly that is the essence of Eph 2:8–10. It is true that the noun (δικαιοσύνη) and verb (δικαιόω) used for justification occur eighty-five times in Paul's writings but sixty-one of these are in Romans and Galatians, the books which specifically address justification. In fact, the noun occurs only once and the verb only twice in the long epistle of 1 Corinthians. Neither the noun nor the verb are found in Colossians, 1 and 2 Thessalonians. The verb is used twenty-seven times by Paul, only four times outside of Romans and Galatians (1 Cor 4:4; 6:11; 1 Tim 3:16; Titus 3:7—hence only twice in the undisputed books). Clearly, specific terms for justification need not be in every Pauline book. Hence, though the terminology regarding salvation in Ephesians differs from the undisputed books, the concepts are the same.[2]

To suggest, as some do, that the words "good works," used in Eph 2:10 in reference to believers, are avoided in the undisputed Paulines is inaccurate. In fact, Paul stresses the "fruit" of the believer (Rom 6:22; Gal 5:22; Phil 1:11, 22; 4:17). This signifies the same thing using different terminology.

Finally, it is alleged that salvation is viewed as something completed in the past by the use of the perfect tense of σῴζω (Eph 2:8–9) and has no future implication. On the contrary, although specific terminology is not employed, the idea is clearly conveyed. Among such references are the enjoyment of salvation in a future consummation (1:10), the sealing of believers until the "redemption of the purchased possession" (1:13–14), the "coming age(s)" (1:21; 2:7), the "day of redemption" (4:30), and the presentation to Christ of the church (the body of believers), which is characterized as glorious "not having a blemish or wrinkle or any such thing" (5:27). There are instances in the undisputed Paulines which mention a past justification (δικαιόω) with no reference to a future salvation (e.g., Gal 2:16–17; 3:24). Thus, though different terms are used in Ephesians, hope of a future salvation is portrayed. It must be understood that the concept that the believer is presently seated with Christ (Eph 2:6) emphasizes the deliverance from the cosmic powers of the preconversion person but in no way implies that salvation is fully realized. A future age is considered in this book (as discussed below).[3] In conclusion then, different ex-

1. Cf. Ulrich Luz, "Rechtfertigung bei den Paulusschülern," in *Rechtfertigung. Festschrift für Ernst Käsemann zum 70. Geburtstag*, ed. Johannes Friedrich, Wolfgang Pöhlmann, and Peter Stuhlmacher (Tübingen: Mohr; Göttingen: Vandenhoeck & Ruprecht, 1976), 369–75.

2. I. Howard Marshall, "Salvation, Grace and Works in the Later Writings in the Pauline Corpus," *NTS* 42 (July 1996): 339–58, esp. 342–45, 355, 357–58; Walter Radl, "σῴζω," *EDNT* 3 (1993): 321.

3. Clinton E. Arnold, *Ephesians: Power and Magic. The Concept of Power in Ephesians in Light of Its Historical Setting*, SNTSMS, ed. G. N. Stanton, vol. 63 (Cambridge:

pressions are used to define soteriology but this is not unique to Ephesians. Allowances must be made for differences in expression, for Paul was not a static but a creative thinker. Though there may be differences, they do not present contradictions with the undisputed Pauline works.

The second theological concern which is troubling to some is ecclesiology.[1] It is suggested that the author of Ephesians employs ἐκκλησία exclusively of the universal church (cf. 1:22; 3:10, 21; 5:23–25, 27, 29, 32) whereas the term in the undisputed Paulines most frequently refers to the local churches. In addition, it is suggested that the emphasis on the church as one body (4:4), universal (1:22–23), built on the apostles and prophets (2:20), and holy and blameless (5:26–27) probably reflects a stage after the ministry of Paul, an emergent catholicism.[2] The point is made that the concept of apostles and prophets as the foundation of the church is somewhat different from Col 2:7 and radically different from 1 Cor 3:11 where Christ is depicted as the only foundation. However, there is ample evidence that these above-mentioned concepts were not only conveyed throughout the undisputed Pauline texts but make sense in the context of Pauline authorship.

Although it is true that Ephesians refers exclusively to the universal church,[3] the idea of the universal church is also conveyed in 1 Corinthians where Paul refers not only to "the church of God which is in Corinth" but also to "all those who in every place call on the name of

---

Cambridge University Press, 1989; reprint, Grand Rapids: Baker, 1992), 147–50; cf. Barrett, *Paul: An Introduction to His Thoughts*, 157.

1. Lincoln, lxiv; cf. also Mitton, *The Epistle to the Ephesians*, 18–20; Dahl, "Einleitungsfragen zum Epheserbiref," 80–81. For a discussion of the ecclesiology of Ephesians according to Chrysostom, see Peter Kohlgraf, *Die Ekklesiologie des Epheserbriefes in der Auslegung durch Johannes Chrysostomus: Eine Untersuchung zur Wirkungsgeschichte paulinischer Theologie*, Hereditas: Studien zur Alten Kirchengeschichte, ed. Ernst Dassmann and Hermann-Josef Vogt, vol. 19 (Bonn: Borengässer, 2001).

2. Käsemann, "Ephesians and Acts," 288; cf. also idem, "The Theological Problem Presented," 102–21, esp. 120–21; J. L. Houlden, "Christ and Church in Ephesians," in *SE VI. Papers Presented to the Fourth International Congress on New Testament Studies held at Oxford, 1969*, ed. Elizabeth A. Livingstone, TU, ed. Veselin Beševliev et al., vol. 112 (Berlin: Akademie-Verlag, 1973), 267–73.

3. Cf. Bruce M. Metzger, "Paul's Vision of the Church. A Study of the Ephesian Letter," *Theology Today* 6 (April 1949): 49–63. Rather than designating it "universal church" O'Brien suggests "heavenly gathering" because the word "church" means "gathering" and since a world-wide gathering could not be accomplished on an earthly plane, such a gathering would be on a heavenly plane as referred to in the contexts of Colossians and Ephesians, see P. T. O'Brien, "The Church as a Heavenly and Eschatological Entity," in *The Church in the Bible and the World. An International Study*, ed. D. A. Carson (Exeter: Paternoster Press; Grand Rapids: Baker, 1987), 93–95; idem, "Church," in *DPL*, 125–26.

our Lord Jesus Christ" (1 Cor 1:2). Also, when Paul argues that the body of Christ is composed of individual members out of which God has appointed apostles, prophets, teachers, and other ministries (1 Cor 12:27–28; Rom 12:4–8), there is no evidence that he limits this to one local body. These remarks are analogous to Eph 4:11. Another example is 1 Cor 12:13 which states that all Christians are baptized into one body (cf. Gal 3:27); thus, here the concept of a universal church takes precedent over a local assembly.[1] Furthermore, Paul's statement that he persecuted the church of God (1 Cor 15:9; Gal 1:13; Phil 3:6) and his exhortation not to offend the church of God (1 Cor 10:32) easily have reference to the universal church. Thus, the idea of a universal church is seen early in Paul's correspondence. As to the lack of specific mention of a local church in Ephesians, this is explainable if one considers this letter to be a circular letter addressed to a number of churches in western Asia Minor. Also, the simplest explanation of the use of the singular "church" rather than the plural "churches" may be due to his theme of unity throughout this book.[2] Lastly, the idea of a universal church in Ephesians indicating an emergent catholicism after Paul's day is untenable. There is no hint of the institutionalization of a worldwide church with offices and duties connected with an interchurch organization. Rather, in Ephesians the universal church is depicted as an organism, not an organization.[3]

With the emphasis on ecclesiology, Käsemann suggests that it overshadows Christology so that Christology has become a function of ecclesiology.[4] Certainly ecclesiology is emphasized in Ephesians but not at the expense of Christology. The church did not come into existence by itself but on the basis on what God has done in Christ.[5] Though the emphasis on the church may be more pronounced in Ephesians than in some of the other letters of Paul, nevertheless, the church's existence and function is always based on Christ's work (Eph 1:22; 5:2, 23–27, 29; see also 1 Cor 1:2; 15:3). According to Merklein the church must become what it already is in Christ through knowing, filling, growing, and building. The integration of Christology and ecclesiology results in ecclesiology being grounded in Christology, namely, that Christ is the ground or basis of the church's existence.[6]

1. Bruce, 237–38.

2. Arnold, *Ephesians: Power and Magic*, 164–65.

3. Bruce, 239.

4. Käsemann, "The Theological Problem Presented," 120–21.

5. Arnold, *Ephesians: Power and Magic*, 163–64; Lincoln and Wedderburn, *The Theology of the Later Pauline Letters*, 138; Barrett, *Paul: An Introduction to His Thoughts*, 155–56; Maclean, "Ephesians and the Problem of Colossians," 63.

6. Helmut Merklein, "Paulinische Theologie in der Rezeption des Kolosser- und Epheserbriefes," in *Paulus in den neutestamentlichen Spätschriften. Zur Paulusrezeption im Neuen Testament*, ed. Karl Kertelge, Quaestiones Disputatae, ed. Karl Rahner and Heinrich Schlier, vol. 89 (Freiburg: Herder, 1981), 48, 51, 62; Schnackenburg, 298; Brevard S. Childs, *The New Testament as Canon: An Introduction* (London: SCM, 1984;

The words "holy and blameless" (5:26–27), with reference to the church, are appropriate in light of the context. Christ loved the church and gave himself for it in order that he might sanctify it with the further purpose that he might present the church to himself as glorious with the final purpose that it might be holy and blameless. Hence, this is not an indicative statement but a purpose statement. Furthermore, as mentioned in the commentary, this final purpose, "holy and without blame," refers to a future day when Christ will come for his church. Although this has reference to the future state of the church, Paul also described the local church at Corinth as God's holy temple (1 Cor 3:17) and as a pure bride (2 Cor 10:2). Thus, to refer to the future church as holy and blameless does not necessarily indicate a stage after Paul's ministry but rather a state which is future to us all.

It is untenable to hold that Ephesians has a different author than Paul because it views the apostles and prophets as the foundation of the church (Eph 2:20) in a way different than that of Col 2:7 and especially that of 1 Cor 3:11 where Christ is the foundation. Authors must be allowed to use different imagery as suits their purposes. In fact, some suggest that there are great diversities in ecclesiologies within the NT that may not always be possible to harmonize.[1] In any case, as mentioned in the commentary, the description given in Eph 2:20 fits well with the imagery given in 1 Cor 3:11. If in Ephesians one views the words "apostles" and "prophets" as genitives of apposition, namely, "the foundation consisting of the apostles and prophets," then Christ becomes the chief cornerstone of that foundation. Though the imagery is changed, it is not a contradiction but an extension of the imagery in 1 Cor 3:11. This may reflect a further development in Paul's thought. The imagery in Col 2:7 does not contradict what is given in Eph 2:20 because it is not discussing the same issue.

Lincoln adds yet another ecclesiological objection. He suggests that the church, as a new creation (Eph 2:11–22), is a replacement of Israel rather than a continuity with Israel that still has a part in God's plan.[2] However, the emphasis in Eph 2:11–22 is that Gentiles, who were formerly excluded, can now be fellow sharers with believing Jews. In other words, Gentile believers join with Jewish believers as fellow citizens. The distinction between the church and Israel is not emphasized because Paul was dealing with a predominantly Gentile audience (2:1–2, 11–13; 4:17–19). This issue simply was not critical in the Ephesian locale. Furthermore, in Pauline literature Israel is men-

Philadelphia: Fortress, 1985; reprint, Valley Forge, Pa.: Trinity Press International, 1994), 327.

1. Max-Alain Chevallier, "L'unite plurielle de l'Eglise d'après le Nouveau Testament," *Revue d'histoire et de philosophie religieuse* 66 (Janvier–Mars 1986): 3–20.

2. Lincoln, lxiv; cf. also idem, "The Church and Israel in Ephesians 2," *CBQ* 49 (October 1987): 605–24; Lincoln and Wedderburn, *The Theology of the Later Pauline Letters*, 158–61.

tioned seventeen times, eleven times in Romans, three times in the Corinthian letters, and once in Galatians, in Ephesians, and in Philippians, and no mention in eight of his letters (or five of the undisputed letters). God's plan for Israel in relationship to the church loomed large in Romans but not in the other correspondence of Paul. Ephesians emphasizes the incorporation of both believing Jews and Gentiles into God's plan but does not elaborate on God's present and future plans for Israel. This omission cannot be used to prove that God's plan for ethnic Israel has ceased but rather indicates that the subject was not relevant to the purpose of the epistle. On the other hand, Moritz cautions that it should not be concluded that there was no Jewish interest in Ephesians. As he points out, there are more OT references in Ephesians than in Galatians and though the church in Ephesus was primarily Gentile, there was a significant Jewish Christian contingent.[1] If there were a good number of Jewish Christians in Ephesus, it seems that Paul would have made the church's replacement of Israel more explicit. As a result of the Holocaust and due to the prevailing pluralistic sentiment, very few scholars presently speak of the church's replacement of Israel. On the other hand, to be fair, Lincoln rightly contends that 2:11–22 speaks of the church as a unity between believing Jews and Gentiles, distinct from Israel, rather than a unity between Christians and Jews or the church and the synagogue as Barth asserts.[2]

In conclusion, though there is more explicit emphasis on the universal church in Ephesians, it is latent in Paul's earlier letters. This emphasis can be explained in two ways. First, it was probably intended as a circular letter to the churches in the Ephesus area. Second, an important thrust of the book is the unity of believers. Certainly, Paul would have included all believers in his exhortation. The teaching in Ephesians regarding the foundation of the apostles and prophets and Israel's place in God's plan are not in opposition to the letters in the Pauline corpus. Again one should not limit Paul's thought and development in ecclesiology. He was a creative thinker and the differences in ecclesiology among his writings may reflect a different emphasis or development in ecclesiological thinking.[3]

Finally, the third theological argument against Pauline authorship

1. Thorsten Moritz, *A Profound Mystery: The Use of the Old Testament in Ephesians*, NovTSup, ed. C. K. Barrett et al., vol. 85 (Leiden: Brill, 1996), 1–8, 213–18; idem, "Reasons for Ephesians," *Evangel* 14 (spring 1996): 8–14.

2. Lincoln, "The Church and Israel in Ephesians 2," 605–24; Lincoln and Wedderburn, *The Theology of the Later Pauline Letters*, 159. Cf. Markus Barth, *The People of God*, JSNTSup, vol. 5 (Sheffield: JSOT Press, 1983); idem, "Conversion and Conversation. Israel and the Church in Paul's Epistle to the Ephesians," *Int* 17 (January 1963): 3–24.

3. Cf. Christopher F. Mooney, "Paul's Vision of the Church in 'Ephesians'," *Scr* 15 (April 1963): 33–43.

concerns eschatology.[1] Some suggest that the constant expectation of the Christ's second coming evidenced in the early years of Paul's ministry has now faded into the background. It is asserted that since Christ has not returned, the emphasis in Ephesians has shifted to the believer's present relationship to Christ in the heavenlies (1:3, 20–21; 2:6)[2] and the believer's maturity in the present age (4:15). In 1 Cor 7 Paul urged the believers to abstain from marriage because of difficult times, but in Eph 5 marriage is elevated to the extent that it is compared with the relationship of Christ and the church. Furthermore, the household code (5:22–6:9) also seems to indicate either a realized eschatology or a remote parousia.

However, to say that the lack of emphasis on the parousia indicates a later writing is invalid because, in fact, there is very little about this subject in Paul's earliest letter, the one to the Galatians. The expression "made us alive together with Christ" (2:5) is not referring to a realized eschatology but is essentially describing what is known as justification in the undisputed letters. It is immediately followed by the words "by grace you have been saved," which certainly substantiates a soteriological rather than a realized eschatological emphasis.[3] Moreover, in Ephesians Paul does express the parousia as the time of redemption of the purchased possession (1:14; 4:30) and although we are presently seated with Christ in the heavenlies (2:6), we will be demonstrated as his riches of grace in the future (2:7). It is not a realized eschatology with no future realization but a present realization of what we are in Christ with a future consummation. Thus, it is not an either/or but a both/and situation. Even Lincoln wants to maintain in Ephesians a Jewish two-age structure where there is a present age and an age to come (1:21).[4] Eschatology is certainly evident in Eph 1:10 which speaks of uniting all creation under Christ's headship. This is not referring to a present realization but a future "fullness of the times."[5] Furthermore, Eph 1:10 speaks of uniting all creation under

1. Lincoln, lxiv; cf. also Mitton, *The Epistle to the Ephesians*, 21–22.

2. Cf. Andreas Lindemann, *Die Aufhebung der Zeit. Geschichtsverständnis und Eschatologie im Epheserbrief*, Studien zum Neuen Testament, ed. Günter Klein, Willi Marxsen, and Wolfgang Schrage, vol. 12 (Gütersloh: Gütersloher Verlagshaus, 1975), 120–25; Lindemann, 38–41.

3. G. F. Wessels, "The Eschatology of Colossians and Ephesians," *Neot* 21, no. 2 (1987): 185–90.

4. Lincoln, lxxxix; cf. also idem, "A Re-Examination of 'the Heavenlies' in Ephesians," *NTS* 19 (July 1973): 481; idem, *Paradise Now and Not Yet. Studies in the Role of the Heavenly Dimension in Paul's Thought with Special Reference to His Eschatology*, SNTSMS, ed. R. McL. Wilson and M. E. Thrall, vol. 43 (Cambridge: Cambridge University Press, 1981; reprint, Grand Rapids: Baker, 1991), 166–68; H. R. Lemmer, "A Multifarious Understanding of Eschatology in Ephesians: A Possible Solution to a Vexing Issue," *Hervormde Teologiese Studies* 46, nos. 1/2 (1990): 102–19.

5. Cf. Stephen S. Smalley, "The Eschatology of Ephesians," *EvQ* 28 (July–September 1956): 154–56.

Christ's headship. Creation obviously has not yet attained this status. Although not stated in the same terms, the undisputed Paulines also convey the concept of the present age (Rom 12:2; Gal 1:4; 2 Cor 4:4) and the future age (1 Cor 6:9–10; 15:50; Gal 5:21). It is true that while the author deals with the present age, a future eschatology in Ephesians is in line with the other Pauline letters.[1]

With regard to marriage it is true that in 1 Cor 7 Paul urged believers not to marry, but he did not forbid marriage (1 Cor 7:9, 27–28, 36, 38). Paul states that this was not a command but his opinion in light of the present distress (7:25–26). What that distress was we do not know, but it could have been a particular situation in Corinth that may not have been applicable elsewhere. Regardless, the reason for the injunction was because of the present distress and not because of the imminent return of Christ. Furthermore, his elevated view of marriage in Ephesians does not contradict what he said in 1 Corinthians. He stated to the Corinthians that if they are not married, they should not seek to change their status; but if they are married, they should remain married even if their spouse is an unbeliever (1 Cor 7:10–16). The author of Ephesians is not discussing a change in status but rather addressing those who are already married. Hence, there is no conflict with what is stated in 1 Corinthians.

Also, it is invalid to say that the appearance of the household code (Eph 5:22–6:9) seems to indicate a realized eschatology or that the parousia is not imminent. There are also household codes in Col 3:18–4:1; 1 Pet 2:18–3:7; 1 Tim 2:8–15; 6:1–10; Titus 2:1–10. Furthermore, in other Pauline literature there are many injunctions for how the Christian should live in the present age, such as the Christian's responsibility to government (Rom 13), relationship of the weak and strong in the church (Rom 14:1–15:13), restoration of a weaker brother/sister (Gal 6:1–5), exhortations to the married and unmarried (1 Cor 7), admonitions to those who preach the gospel with wrong motives (Phil 1), as well as to those who do not work (2 Thess 3:10). Nevertheless, none of these indicate a realized eschatology or that the parousia was not in the forefront of Paul's thinking. Rather, Paul expected that Jesus could come back at any time but was led by the Holy Spirit to give injunctions on how one should live in the meantime. Also, as Arnold correctly observes, the injunction for believers to take up the full armor of God in the light of their ongoing spiritual struggle against the rulers and authorities (Eph 6:10–20) presents a major difficulty for those who advocate a fully realized eschatology in Ephesians. If the authorities and powers are already subject to Christ (1:20–21) and believers in a real sense have been resurrected and are in heaven with

1. Although he does not think Paul wrote Ephesians, Lona thinks that the eschatology of Ephesians is in line with Pauline thinking. See Horacio E. Lona, *Die Eschatologie im Kolosser- und Epheserbrief*, Forschung zur Bibel, ed. Rudolf Schnackenburg and Josef Schreiner, vol. 48 (Würzburg: Echter, 1984), 427–28, 449–50.

Christ, then why does the author warn them of the spiritual warfare? As in other Pauline literature, there is the concept of "already—not yet" in Paul's eschatology.[1]

Although some particular eschatological terminology used in other Pauline literature may not appear in Ephesians, there are certainly many indications within the book that speak of a future eschatology. The author of Ephesians does not portray that the final age had arrived but there will be a day in the future when Christ will head up all things (Eph 1:10) and there will be the redemption of the purchased possession (1:14; 4:30). Instructions for the believers' living in the present age are similar to Paul elsewhere and one cannot infer that the hope of the parousia is remote. Thus, the eschatology of Ephesians is in line with the other Pauline letters.[2]

In conclusion, the letter to the Ephesians may exhibit differences from other letters by Paul. However, they are differences in emphasis possibly due to differences in circumstances. Such a phenomenon can also be observed in the undisputed Paulines. Paul had taught at Ephesus for over two years and may not have felt the need to stress in his letter everything which he had taught while there. Certainly, one needs to be careful not to equate differences in doctrinal emphasis with dissimilarity of authorship unless one can demonstrate contradiction.[3] Paul was not a static but creative thinker and as new situations and/or problems arose, it is not unreasonable to suggest that there would have been development in his thinking.[4] A different emphasis is not indicative of a different author.

(6) Historical considerations. These will be considered from two perspectives: external and internal evidence. First, regarding external evidence, as discussed above, the authorship of Ephesians was not questioned in the history of the church until the last two centuries. In fact, Mitton states:

> The external evidence is wholly on the side of those who maintain Pauline authorship. Among all the early writers of the Christian Church there is never the slightest hint that questions it. Moreover, the epistle seems to be known and quoted as Paul's as early as any of the other Pauline epistles. One of the most difficult tasks for those who reject the tradition of Pauline authorship is to find a satisfactory explanation of this acknowledged fact.[5]

Thus, most of the discussion about Pauline authorship centers around the internal evidence.

1. Arnold, *Ephesians: Power and Magic*, 156–57; O'Brien, 33.
2. For more discussion on this, see Arnold, *Ephesians: Power and Magic*, 145–58.
3. Guthrie, *New Testament Introduction*, 525.
4. Hort, *Prolegomena to St Paul's Epistles*, 123–24.
5. Mitton, *The Epistle to the Ephesians*, 15–16.

Second, with regard to internal evidence, it is thought that the resolution of the Jewish-Gentile controversy seems to reflect a period after Paul's lifetime.[1] Goodspeed asserts that the breakdown of the barrier between Jews and Gentiles, although figurative, makes more sense after the destruction of the temple in A.D. 70. At that time the physical barrier which barred the Gentiles from the temple's court for men of Israel was eliminated.[2] In considering the development of the Jewish-Gentile controversy, one wonders how much of the old Tübingen influence remains. Certainly there was controversy in the early church but not to the extent proposed by the Tübingen school. Furthermore, it is difficult to assess exactly the circumstances of the Jewish-Gentile debate from the contents of Ephesians, let alone from any of the Pauline letters. More importantly, in the context of Eph 2:11–22 Paul is not reporting the historical development of the controversy in the church but is showing what had happened at the cross and its implications to the believers in Ephesus. The work of reconciliation between the Jews and Gentiles was accomplished in the past at the cross and its application to the believers in Ephesus continued to the time of the writing of this letter. Even if one accepts a later stage of the controversy in this letter, could not this be possible if one dates this toward the end of Paul's life? In the end, though, it is difficult, if not impossible, to determine the development of the Jewish-Gentile controversy from Ephesians or any of Paul's letters. Moreover, Goodspeed's suggestion that Ephesians fits better after the destruction of the temple in Jerusalem in A.D. 70 is irrelevant because the physical barrier that separated the court of the Gentiles from the court of the Jews was probably unknown to the Ephesian believers (more on this is discussed in the commentary on 2:14). Hence, this epistle does little to identify the development of the Jewish-Gentile controversy.

There are some who think that the implied author of Ephesians is later than the apostle Paul.[3] The most critical passage is 3:1–13 where it seems to be a description about Paul in the past rather than a reference to his ministry and mission. The author states that the revelation of the mystery was not only given to him but also to other holy apostles and prophets (3:3–6), suggesting a later date than Paul. Also, calling apostles "holy" supports a postapostolic date when apostles were revered (3:5). Furthermore, to be considered "less than the least of all the saints" seems to belittle the apostle more than Paul himself does in 1 Cor 15:9 where he states that he is "the least of all the apostles"

1. Ibid., 16; Lincoln and Wedderburn, *The Theology of the Later Pauline Letters*, 84; Ralph P. Martin, *Reconciliation: A Study of Paul's Theology*, New Foundations Theological Library, ed. Peter Toon and Ralph P. Martin (Atlanta: John Knox, 1981), 159–60; reprint, idem, "Reconciliation and Unity in Ephesians," *RevExp* 93 (spring 1996): 205.

2. Goodspeed, *The Key to Ephesians*, vii.

3. For discussion and literature on the portrayal of Paul, see Best, 40–44 and O'Brien, 33–37.

again suggesting someone later than Paul wrote the letter. However, all this is in keeping with Paul. Even Best, who thinks that Ephesians was not written by the apostle, states that the picture of Paul in Ephesians is basically in harmony with Paul's account of himself in his other letters and hence need not be thought of as postapostolic.[1]

Beginning with Baur and more recently by Käsemann, Schlier, and Conzelmann, among others, it has been proposed that Ephesians parallels Gnostic literature (e.g., the head/body imagery is compared to the Gnostic Redeemer myth) which makes it too late for Paul to have composed this letter.[2] However, as mentioned in the commentary, the Gnostic literature is much too late (second or third century A.D.) to have influenced Ephesians[3] and many of the features that are attributed to Gnosticism can be ascribed to other influences.[4] Hence, the notion that the author of Ephesians borrowed from Gnostic writings is untenable and, therefore, this letter need not have been written by someone after Paul.

Conclusion

The Pauline authorship of Ephesians not only has the earliest attestation of any book of the NT but this attestation continued until the last two centuries. The early attestation is highly significant. The early church was not only closer to the situation but also they were very astute in their judgment of genuine and fraudulent compositions. This overwhelming support for the Pauline authorship of Ephesians should not be easily dismissed.

In the course of this discussion, the various scholars and their views have been identified along with the many reasons given for rejecting Paul's authorship of Ephesians. Although Ephesians differs from other Pauline literature, the differences do not sufficiently argue for the rejection of Pauline authorship of this letter. Variations can be accounted for due to differences in content and differences in the character and needs of the recipients of the letter.[5] Furthermore, it

1. Best, 44.

2. Baur, *Paul the Apostle of Jesus Christ*, 2:7–22; Ernst Käsemann, *Leib und Leib Christi. Eine Untersuchung zur paulinischen Begrifflichkeit*, BHT, vol. 9 (Tübingen: Mohr, 1933), 56–96, 138–39, 156–59; idem, "Epheserbrief," 519–20; Schlier, 19–21, 272–78, passim; Conzelmann, 87–88, 109–11, passim.

3. Guthrie, *New Testament Introduction*, 506. For a discussion on this issue, see Barth, 12–18; Arnold, *Ephesians: Power and Magic*, 7–13. Even if Paul were not the author of Ephesians, Best (87–89) observes there is no indication in the book that the author was motivated by or reacted against Gnosticism.

4. Lincoln and Wedderburn, *The Theology of the Later Pauline Letters*, 89.

5. Murphy-O'Connor suggests that the variances in this epistle may be due to his use of a different amanuensis working under the direction of Paul. He suggests that the amanuensis was a converted Essene. Cf. Jerome Murphy-O'Connor, "Who Wrote Ephesians?" *TBT* 18 (April 1965): 1201–2.

must be accepted that a genius such as Paul is not sterile in his expressions; allowances must be made for development in his own thinking. These elements are evident even in his undisputed letters. Yet further, it is rather limiting to determine Paul's style and vocabulary based only on the writings that are canonical. If more of his writings were available, it would be easier to evaluate variances and consistency of vocabulary and style. Content, mood, and recipients affect the vocabulary and style of an author whether it be in the first or the present century. In fact, repeating the same content in identical or nearly identical circumstances would still produce variations in vocabulary, style, and sentence length. Authors are not machines that duplicate vocabulary and style.

It is fitting to close with a story found at the conclusion of the Cadbury article:

> Many years ago there was in an English school a much beloved bachelor master whom the boys called Puddles. He had, however, decided mannerisms of speech, which showed among other occasions whenever he recited a favourite poem on the prehistoric animal called Eohippus. Once in holiday-time when a large group of his old boys was gathered together at Woodbrooke College to share again his leadership, they arranged to have a little competition to see which of them could most perfectly imitate him in the recitation of his well-known selection. In order to ensure the impartiality of the judges chosen for the contest they were seated in the audience, while the contestants spoke in turn from the stage, but behind the curtain. Unknown to judges and audience Puddles himself slipped in backstage as one of the contestants and when the merits of each were scored by the judges and the winners announced, it was found that Puddles was himself awarded third place in the competition.[1]

Structure and Genre of Ephesians

Structure and Outline of Ephesians

Ephesians, similar to other Pauline letters, is divided into two main parts: doctrine or theology (chaps. 1–3) and duties or ethics (chaps. 4–6). After the prologue (1:1–2) the first portion offers extended praise directed to God for all the spiritual benefits given to those who are in Christ (1:3–14), which is followed immediately by a commendation to the readers for their faith and love and a petition for wisdom and revelation (1:15–23). The readers are reminded of their relationship to God before and after their conversion (2:1–10) and the new union of Jewish and Gentile believers who are now considered one new person, the church (2:11–22). Consequently, there is not only reconciliation of

1. Cadbury, "The Dilemma of Ephesians," 101–2.

human beings to God but also between Jewish and Gentile believers. Having explained this, Paul, in a parenthetical section, describes the mystery which is the union of Jew and Gentile believers in Christ and his ministry in dispensing this mystery to the Gentiles (3:1–13). He concludes the first portion of the letter by praying that the Ephesian believers might be strengthened in love so that the union of Jewish and Gentile believers might be carried out in God's power (3:14–21).

The second portion is the application, or paraenesis, showing how the doctrine translates into the conduct of the believers. This portion is subdivided into six sections, five governed by the imperative "walk" (περιπατέω) which is used five times in conjunction with the inferential conjunction "therefore" (οὖν). They are: (1) to walk in unity (4:1–16); (2) to walk in holiness and not as the Gentiles (4:17–32); (3) to walk in love by imitating God and abstaining from evil practices (5:1–6; (4) to walk in light by not becoming involved with the evildoers and their works (5:7–14); and (5) to walk in wisdom by being controlled by the Holy Spirit in their domestic and public life (5:15–6:9). The sixth section begins with the articular adjective τὸ λοιπόν/τοῦ λοιποῦ, "finally," to indicate that this is the final thing he wants to say before he ends the epistle. Here Paul enjoins them to be strengthened (ἐνδυναμόω) in the Lord in order to be able to stand against evil powers (6:10–20). A short conclusion closes the epistle (6:21–24).[1]

Several links exist between the first and last parts of the book. First, the term "walk" is used in both parts. Negatively, the Ephesians were walking in trespasses and sins (2:1–2) and they are exhorted not to walk as the Gentiles in the futility of their minds (4:17). Positively, a believer is to walk in the good works which God has prepared beforehand (2:10). The elaboration of this is seen in the exhortation to walk worthy of one's calling (4:1). Finally, there is the repeated use of "walk" in the last portion of the letter (4:17; 5:2, 8, 15).

Second, love is a very prominent theme in both sections. Love, both in the verb and noun forms, is found twenty times. In the first part it appears seven times: God chose the believers that they might be holy and blameless in love (1:4); Paul praises God for the grace bestowed on believers in the beloved one, Christ (1:6); Paul commends the Ephesian believers' love for one another (1:15); God exhibits his rich mercy through the great love by which he loved the believers (2:4*bis*); and because the believers have been rooted and grounded in (God's)

1. Regarding the division of Ephesians, Cameron looks not at the content but analyzes its linguistic structure. He observes that there are eight parallel panels (he excludes 6:18–22) that are chiastic in structure though he labels them as palistrophe in structure. These eight parallel panels form the whole letter as a palistrophe. See P. S. Cameron, "The Structure of Ephesians," *Filologia Neotestamentaria* 3 (Mayo 1990): 3–17. Such intricate and subtle patterns seem unlikely for any writer of a letter. Interestingly, the divisions of the epistle are similar to others who derive their structure from the content.

love (3:17), Paul prays that they might be able to comprehend Christ's love (3:19). The theme of love continues in the second half of the book where it appears thirteen times: Paul exhorts believers: to walk worthy of their calling with which God called them in forbearing one another in love (4:2); to walk in unity by being truthful with love (4:15) so that every believer contributes to the growth of the body and thus the body will be built up in love (4:16); to walk in love just as Christ loved us (5:2*bis*). Also, husbands are to love their wives as Christ loved the church (5:25*bis*) and as they love their own bodies (5:28*ter*, 33). Finally, there is a salutation of love with peace from God the father and the Lord Jesus Christ (6:23), and a benediction of grace to all of those who unceasingly love our Lord Jesus Christ (6:24). Frequent occurrences of this concept indicate its importance. Certainly Paul is emphasizing the unity of believing Jews and Gentiles in one body and this can only be based on God's love and the practice of love of the believers for one another (more will be developed below).

Third, the Spirit is prominent in both parts. In the first part of the book the Holy Spirit is the seal (1:13); gives access to the Father (2:18); dwells in the new temple, the body of believers (2:22); reveals the mystery of believing Jews and Gentiles in one body (3:5); and strengthens the inner person (3:16). The Holy Spirit in the last part of the book is characterized as the one who brings about unity of the believers (4:3–4), grieves at sin and seals believers (4:30), is the means by which believers are filled (5:18), is the sword which is the preached Word of God (6:17), and the one in whose power believers are exhorted to pray (6:18).

Fourth, the concept of the body begins in the first part where the church is defined as Christ's body (1:22–23) in which believing Jews and Gentiles are reconciled into one body (2:16). In the second part, reference is made to the unity exhibited in one body (4:4), God's gifted people given for the purpose of building up the body (4:12, 16), the church again described as Christ's body (5:23), and believers as a part of that body (5:30).

Fifth, the concept of the mystery in the first part is introduced (1:9). Although hidden in the past ages (3:9), this mystery has now been revealed by the Holy Spirit to the apostles and prophets (3:4–5) that Jewish and Gentile believers are in one body. In the second part the mystery is seen as the union of Christ and the church rather than Jews and Gentiles (5:32), but the last mention of it refers to Paul making known God's work of uniting believing Jews and Gentiles into one body (6:19).

Sixth, in the first part of the book, the Ephesians before conversion were governed by the evil one (2:2) and in the second part of the book they, who had now been converted to the Lord, were exhorted to be strong in the Lord in order to stand against the schemes of the evil one (6:10–20).

Seventh, the book begins with spiritual blessings (1:3–14) and ends with spiritual warfare (6:10–20). Other links could be developed such as "in Christ" and "in the Lord" but these will suffice to indicate definite structural links between the two parts of the book.

The following outline of Ephesians will be used in this commentary.

- I. The Calling of the Church (1:1–3:21)
    - A. Prologue (1:1–2)
    - B. Praise for God's Planned Spiritual Blessings (1:3–14)
        - 1. The Provision of Spiritual Blessings (1:3)
        - 2. The Basis of Spiritual Blessings (1:4–14)
            - a. God's election for himself (1:4–6)
                - (1) Activity: Election before creation (1:4)
                - (2) Cause: Predestination to sonship (1:5)
                - (3) Goal: Praise of the glory of his grace (1:6)
            - b. God's redemption in Christ (1:7–12)
                - (1) Redemption: Forgiveness of sins (1:7)
                - (2) Wisdom: Mystery of his will (1:8–10)
                    - (a) Provision (1:8)
                    - (b) Manner (1:9)
                    - (c) Goal (1:10)
                - (3) Inheritance: Possession of God (1:11)
                - (4) Goal: Praise of his glory (1:12)
            - c. God's seal with the Spirit (1:13–14)
                - (1) Activity: Sealed with the Spirit (1:13)
                - (2) Duration: Sealed until redemption (1:14a)
                - (3) Goal: Praise of his glory (1:14b)
    - C. Prayer for Wisdom and Revelation (1:15–23)
        - 1. Commendation (1:15–16a)
        - 2. Supplication (1:16b–23)
            - a. The request for wisdom and revelation (1:16b–18a)
            - b. The reason for wisdom and revelation (1:18b–23)
                - (1) What is the hope of his calling (1:18b)
                - (2) What is the wealth of his glorious inheritance (1:18c)
                - (3) What is the greatness of his power (1:19–23)
                    - (a) Its magnitude (1:19)
                    - (b) Its manifestation (1:20–23)
                        - (i) He displayed power in Christ (1:20–21)
                            - (aa) In raising Christ from the dead (1:20a)
                            - (bb) In seating Christ in the heavenlies (1:20b–21)
                        - (ii) He subjected everything under Christ's feet (1:22a)
                        - (iii) He gave Christ to the church as head (1:22b–23)
    - D. New Position Individually (2:1–10)
        - 1. The Old Condition: Dead to God (2:1–3)
            - a. Condition described (2:1)
            - b. Condition delineated (2:2–3)

- (1) Walked according to the temporal values of the world (2:2a)
- (2) Walked according to the ruler of the power of the air (2:2b)
- (3) Lived in the desires of the flesh and mind (2:3)

2. The New Position: Alive in God (2:4–10)
   - a. Action of God's Grace (2:4–6)
     - (1) God made alive (2:4–5)
     - (2) God raised (2:6a)
     - (3) God seated (2:6b)
   - b. Purpose of God's grace (2:7)
   - c. Explanation of God's grace (2:8–10)
     - (1) Salvation by grace (2:8a)
     - (2) Salvation not of humans (2:8b–10)
       - (a) Statement: God's gift (2:8b–9)
       - (b) Reason: God's workmanship (2:10)
         - (i) Statement: God's workmanship (2:10a)
         - (ii) Goal: Created for good works (2:10b)
         - (iii) Purpose: Walk in good works (2:10c)

E. New Position Corporately (2:11–22)
1. Statement of the Union (2:11–13)
   - a. Past disunion (2:11–12)
     - (1) Uncircumcised (2:11)
     - (2) Unprivileged (2:12)
   - b. Present union (2:13)
2. Explanation of the Union (2:14–18)
   - a. Assertion of peace (2:14–16)
     - (1) Destruction of the wall (2:14a)
     - (2) Disengagement of the law (2:14b–16)
       - (a) The fact of the operation (2:14b–15a)
       - (b) The purpose of the operation (2:15b–16)
         - (i) To create one new person (2:15b)
         - (ii) To reconcile both to God (2:16)
   - b. Announcement of peace (2:17–18)
     - (1) Content of the message: Peace (2:17)
     - (2) Result of the message: Access (2:18)
3. Consequence of the Union (2:19–22)
   - a. Fact: New Relationship (2:19)
   - b. Cause: New establishment (2:20–22)
     - (1) The foundation of the building (2:20)
     - (2) The formation of the building (2:21)
     - (3) The function of the building (2:22)

F. Parenthetical Expansion of the Mystery (3:1–13)
1. The Introduction (3:1)
2. The Mystery (3:2–6)
   - a. The administration of God's grace (3:2)
   - b. The revelation of the mystery (3:3–5)
     - (1) The manner of the mystery's disclosure (3:3)
     - (2) The ability to understand the mystery (3:4)

(3) The time of the mystery's disclosure (3:5)
c. The content of the mystery (3:6)
3. The Ministry (3:7–12)
a. The placement into the ministry (3:7–8a)
b. The performance of the ministry (3:8b–9)
(1) To preach the unfathomable wealth of Christ (3:8b)
(2) To enlighten the administration of the mystery (3:9)
c. The purpose of the ministry (3:10–12)
(1) God's wisdom made known to the angelic rulers (3:10)
(2) God's purpose accomplished in Christ (3:11)
(3) God's presence accessible in Christ (3:12)
4. The Injunction (3:13)
G. Prayer for Strengthened Love (3:14–21)
1. The Approach to Prayer (3:14–15)
2. The Appeal in Prayer (3:16–19)
a. Petition stated: to be strengthened in the inner person (3:16–17a)
b. Purpose stated: to comprehend Christ's love and to be filled with God's fullness (3:17b–19)
3. The Ascription of Praise (3:20–21)
II. The Conduct of the Church (4:1–6:24)
A. Walk in Unity (4:1–16)
1. The Basis of Unity (4:1–6)
a. Exhortation to unity (4:1–3)
b. Elements of unity (4:4–6)
2. The Preservation of Unity (4:7–16)
a. The donation of the gifts (4:7–10)
(1) Description of the giving of gifts (4:7)
(2) Validation for the giving of gifts (4:8)
(3) Interpretation of the giving of gifts (4:9–10)
b. The distribution of the gifts (4:11–16)
(1) The provision: gifted persons (4:11)
(2) The immediate purpose: prepare for ministry (4:12)
(3) The final goal: attain maturity (4:13)
(4) The ultimate purpose: grow in unity (4:14–16)
(a) For the individuals (4:14–15)
(i) Negatively: Avoiding Instability (4:14)
(ii) Positively: Development (4:15)
(b) For the body (4:16)
B. Walk in Holiness (4:17–32)
1. Presentation of the Old Person (4:17–19)
a. His nature (4:17–18)
b. His practice (4:19)
2. Presentation of the New Person (4:20–32)
a. His position (4:20–24)
(1) The statement of the instruction (4:20–21a)
(2) The nature of the instruction (4:21b)
(3) The content of the instruction (4:22–24)
(a) Put off the old person (4:22)

- (b) Be renewed by the spirit (4:23)
- (c) Put on the new person (4:24)

b. His practice (4:25–32)
- (1) Do not use falsehood but speak truth (4:25)
- (2) Do use anger but do not sin (4:26–27)
- (3) Do not steal but work to give to needy (4:28)
- (4) Do not use corrupt words but edify with words (4:29–30)
- (5) Do not be malicious but edify in action (4:31–32)

C. Walk in Love (5:1–6)
1. Positive: Walk in Love (5:1–2)
   a. Imitate God (5:1)
   b. Walk in love (5:2)
      (1) Command: love (5:2a)
      (2) Comparison: Christ's love (5:2b)
2. Negative: Abstain from Evil (5:3–6)
   a. Responsibility: Abstain from evil practices (5:3–4)
      (1) In conduct (5:3)
      (2) In conversation (5:4)
   b. Reason: No inheritance for evildoers (5:5–6)
      (1) Evildoers have no inheritance in the kingdom of God (5:5)
      (2) Evildoers receive the wrath of God (5:6)

D. Walk in Light (5:7–14)
1. Do Not Become Involved with Evildoers (5:7–10)
   a. Command: Do not get involved (5:7)
   b. Reason: Christians are changed persons (5:8a)
   c. Command: Walk as children of light (5:8b–10)
      (1) Command to walk as children of light (5:8b)
      (2) Characteristics of the fruit of light (5:9)
      (3) Confirmation of God's pleasure (5:10)
2. Do Not Become Involved with Evildoers' Works (5:11–13)
   a. Command: Do not get involved but expose (5:11)
   b. Reason: Their works are shameful (5:12)
   c. Explanation: Light shows true character of works (5:13)
3. Conclusion: Enlightenment of Christ (5:14)

E. Walk in Wisdom (5:15–6:9)
1. Admonition (5:15–21)
   a. Proper action: Walk wisely (5:15–16)
   b. Proper state: Become wise (5:17–21)
      (1) In thought (5:17)
         (a) Negative: Do not become foolish (5:17a)
         (b) Positive: Understand the Lord's will (5:17b)
      (2) In life (5:18–21)
         (a) Negative: Be not drunk with wine (5:18a)
         (b) Positive: Be filled by the Spirit (5:18b–21)
            (i) The command (5:18b)
            (ii) The consequences (5:19–21)
               (aa) Speaking (5:19a)
               (bb) Singing (5:19b)

(cc) Thanking (5:20)
(dd) Submitting (5:21)
2. Application (5:22–6:9)
a. Wives and husbands (5:22–33)
(1) Responsibility of wives' submission (5:22–24)
(a) Imperative: Submit to husbands (5:22)
(b) Reason: Husband is head (5:23)
(c) Illustration: Church's submission (5:24a)
(d) Application: Wives' submission (5:24b)
(2) Responsibility of husbands' love (5:25–32)
(a) Imperative: Love wives (5:25a)
(b) Illustration: Christ's love (5:25b–27)
(c) Application: Husbands' love (5:28–32)
(i) Responsibility: Love wives as they love their own bodies (5:28)
(ii) Illustration: One cares for his own flesh (5:29a)
(iii) Illustration: Christ cares for his body (5:29b–30)
(iv) Substantiation: Two are one flesh (5:31)
(v) Conclusion: The mystery is great (5:32)
(3) Responsibilities reviewed (5:33)
b. Children and parents (6:1–4)
(1) Responsibility of children's obedience (6:1–3)
(a) Imperative: obey parents (6:1a)
(b) Reason: it is right (6:1b)
(c) Motivation: Old Testament command and promise (6:2–3)
(2) Responsibility of fathers' care (6:4)
(a) Negative: Do not provoke to wrath (6:4a)
(b) Positive: Care for them (6:4b)
c. Servants and masters (6:5–9)
(1) Responsibility of servants' obedience (6:5–8)
(a) Imperative: obey masters (6:5–7)
(b) Reason: God rewards (6:8)
(2) Responsibility of masters' treatment (6:9)
(a) Imperative: Forebear threats (6:9a)
(b) Reason: God judges (6:9b)
F. Stand in Warfare (6:10–20)
1. Put on the Armor (6:10–13)
a. What: Be strong in the Lord (6:10)
b. How: Put on God's armor (6:11a)
c. Why: Stand against the devil's strategy (6:11b–12)
d. Conclusion: Put on God's armor in order to stand (6:13)
2. Stand with the Armor (6:14–16)
a. The mandate: Stand (6:14a)
b. The method: Arm (6:14b–16)
(1) The preparation: Girdle of truth (6:14b)
(2) The chest: Breastplate of righteousness (6:14c)

(3) The feet: Gospel of peace (6:15)
(4) The body: Shield of faith (6:16)
3. Receive the Final Pieces of Armor (6:17–20)
a. The mandate: Take (6:17)
(1) The head: Helmet of salvation (6:17a)
(2) The mouth: Sword of the Spirit (6:17b)
b. The method: Care (6:18–20)
(1) Manner: Praying and watching (6:18)
(2) Petitions: For utterance and bold speech (6:19–20)
G. Conclusion (6:21–24)
1. Information (6:21–22)
2. Salutation (6:23)
3. Benediction (6:24)

Genre of Ephesians

Having looked at the structure and outline of Ephesians, it is necessary to consider the genre of this work. New impetus in the study of the literary form of Paul's writings came with the discovery of large quantities of papyri texts in Egypt in the late nineteenth and early twentieth centuries. These texts contained many letters that reflected a cross-section of ancient Hellenistic life, including a few that revealed rhetorical and literary training, but the majority were business contracts, legal agreements, family affairs, and correspondence between friends. Deissmann, an early scholar in the discussion, made a distinction between "epistles" (i.e., artistic literary works written for public interaction by such writers as Epicurus, Seneca, and Pliny) and "letters" (i.e., un-literary, private, occasional communication, much like our telephone calls today).[1] Paul's letters fall into the latter category although there has been much discussion on whether or not they are to be viewed as private or personal letters. Since Deissmann there has been a great deal of discussion regarding the characteristics and forms of Paul's letters, especially in the last three decades.[2]

1. G. Adolf Deissmann, *Bible Studies. Contribution from Papyri and Inscriptions to the History of the Language, the Literature, and the Religion of Hellenistic Judaism and Primitive Christianity*, trans. Alexander Grieve, 2d ed. (Edinburgh: T & T Clark, 1903), 3–59; idem, *Light from the Ancient East*, 148–49, 233–51. The distinction between "epistle" and "letter" cannot be made in Greek terminology, see M. Luther Stirewalt Jr., *Studies in Ancient Greek Epistolography*, Society of Biblical Literature Resources for Biblical Study, ed. Marvin A. Sweeney, no. 27 (Atlanta: Scholars Press, 1993), 87.

2. Modern discussion of this issue is vast and some key works are selected which are relevant to studies in Ephesians. In chronological order see Francis Xavier Exler, *The Form of the Ancient Greek Letter. A Study in Greek Epistolography*, Ph.D. Dissertation of Catholic University of America (Washington, D.C.: Catholic University of America, 1923); Paul Schubert, *Form and Function of the Pauline Thanksgivings*, BZNW, ed. Hans Lietzmann, vol. 20 (Berlin: Töpelmann, 1939); Paul Schubert, "Form and Function of the Pauline Letters," *Journal of Religion* 19 (October 1939): 365–77; Lucetta

Regarding the form the letter to the Ephesians, as well as the other Pauline epistles, follows the normal pattern of Hellenistic letters, namely, opening, body, and closing. The opening and closing will be addressed first, followed by the main body of the letter.

Mowry, "The Early Circulation of Paul's Letters," *JBL* 63 (June 1944): 73–86; R. L. Archer, "The Epistolary Form in the New Testament," *ExpTim* 63 (July 1952): 296–98; Jack T. Sanders, "The Transition from Opening Epistolary Thanksgiving to Body in the Letters of the Pauline Corpus," *JBL* 81 (December 1962): 348–62; Nils Alstrup Dahl, "The Particularity of the Pauline Epistles as a Problem in the Ancient Church," in *Neotestamentica et Patristica: Eine Freundesgabe, Herrn Professor Dr. Oscar Cullmann zu Seinem 60. Geburtstag Überreicht*, NovTSup, ed. W. C. van Unnik et al., vol. 6 (Leiden: Brill, 1962), 261–71; updated in idem, *Studies in Ephesians*, 165–78; Terence Y. Mullins, "Disclosure. A Literary Form in the New Testament," *NovT* 7 (March 1964): 44–50; Gordon J. Bahr, "Paul and Letter Writing in the Fifth Century," *CBQ* 28 (October 1966): 465–77; Carl J. Bjerkelund, *Parakalô. Form, Funktion und Sinn der parakalô-Sätze in dem paulinischen Briefen*, Bibliotheca Theologica Norvegica, ed. Åge Holter et al., no. 1 (Oslo: Universitetsforlaget, 1967); Béda Rigaux, *The Letters of St. Paul: Modern Studies*, ed. and trans. Stephen Yonick (Chicago: Franciscan Herald, 1968), 117–20; Gordon J. Bahr, "The Superscriptions in the Pauline Letters," *JBL* 87 (March 1968): 27–41; Terence Y. Mullins, "Greetings as a New Testament Form," *JBL* 87 (December 1968): 418–26; William G. Doty, "The Classification of Epistolary Literature," *CBQ* 31 (April 1969): 183–99; M. Luther Stirewalt Jr., "Paul's Evaluation of Letter-Writing," in *Search the Scriptures: New Testament Studies in Honor of Raymond T. Stamm*, ed. J. M. Myers, O. Reimherr, and H. N. Bream, Gettysburg Theological Studies, vol. 3 (Leiden: Brill, 1969), 179–96; John L. White, "Introductory Formulae in the Body of the Pauline Letter," *JBL* 90 (March 1971): 91–97; idem, *The Form and Function of the Body of the Greek Letters: A Study of the Letter-Body in the Non-Literary Papyri and in Paul the Apostle*, 2d ed., cor., SBLDS, ed. Howard C. Kee and Douglas A. Knight, no. 2 (Missoula, Mont.: Society of Biblical Literature, 1972); idem, *The Form and Structure of the Official Petition: A Study in Greek Epistolography*, Dissertation Series, no. 5 (Missoula, Mont.: Society of Biblical Literature, 1972); William G. Doty, *Letters in Primitive Christianity* (Philadelphia: Fortress, 1973); Terence Y. Mullins, "Visit Talk in New Testament Letters," *CBQ* 35 (July 1973): 350–58; Klaus Berger, "Apostelbrief und apostolische Rede/Zum Formular früchristilicher Briefe," *ZNW* 65, nos. 3/4 (1974): 190–231; Peter Thomas O'Brien, *Introductory Thanksgivings in the Letters of Paul*, NovTSup, ed. W. C. van Unnik et al., vol. 49 (Leiden: Brill, 1977); Abraham J. Malherbe, "Ancient Epistolary Theorists," *OJRS* 5 (October 1977): 3–77; Terence Y. Mullins, "Benedictions as a NT Form," *Andrews University Seminary Studies* 15 (spring 1977): 59–64; John L. White, "The Greek Documentary Letter Tradition Third Century B.C.E. to Third Century C.E.," *Semeia* 22 (1982): 89–106; John S. Lown, "Epistle," in *The International Standard Bible Encyclopedia*, ed. Geoffrey W. Bromiley, vol. 2 (Grand Rapids: Eerdmans, 1982), 122–25; John L. White, "Saint Paul and the Apostolic Letter Tradition," *CBQ* 45 (July 1983): 433–44; Klaus Berger, "Hellenistische Gattungen im Neuen Testament," in *ANRW*, pt. 2, vol. 25.2 (1984), 1031–1432; Stanley K. Stowers, *Letter Writing in Greco-Roman Antiquity*, Library of Early Christianity, ed. Wayne A. Meeks, vol. 5 (Philadelphia: Westminster, 1986); J. H. Roberts, "Pauline Transitions to the Letter Body," in *L'apôtre Paul. Personnalité, style et conception du ministère*, ed. A. Vanhoye, Bibliotheca Ephemeridum Theologicarum Lovaniensium, vol. 73 (Leuven: University Press/Uitgeverij Peeters, 1986), 93–99; idem, "Transitional Techniques to the Letter Body in the *Corpus Paulinum*," in *A South African Perspective on the New Testament Essays by South African New*

The Pauline letters open with the author's identity along with the recipient's identity in the form "A to B, greetings." This is expanded by a description of the relationship to God in Christ with epithets de-

---

Testament Scholars Presented to Bruce Manning Metzger during His Visit to South Africa in 1985, ed. J. H. Petzer and P. J. Hartin (Leiden: Brill, 1986), 187–201; Vincent Parkin, "Some Comments on the Pauline Prescripts," *IBS* 8 (April 1986): 92–99; John L. White, *Light from Ancient Letters*, Foundations and Facets: New Testament, ed. Robert W. Funk (Philadelphia: Fortress, 1986), 186–220; Helen Elsom, "The New Testament and Greco-Roman Writing," in *The Literary Guide to the Bible*, ed. Robert Alter and Frank Kermode (Cambridge, Mass.: Harvard University Press, 1987), 561–78; David E. Aune, *The New Testament in Its Literary Environment, Library of Early Christianity*, ed. Wayne A. Meeks, vol. 8 (Philadelphia: Westminster, 1987), 158–225; John L. White, "Ancient Greek Letters," in *Greco-Roman Literature and the New Testament: Selected Forms and Genres*, ed. David E. Aune, SBLSBS, ed. Bernard Brandon Scott, no. 21 (Atlanta: Scholars Press, 1988), 85–105; E. Randolph Richards, *The Secretary in the Letters of Paul*, WUNT, ed. Martin Hengel and Otfried Hofius, vol. 42 (Tübingen: Mohr, 1991); D. Brent Sandy, "Form and Function in the Letters of the New Testament," in *New Testament Essays in Honor of Homer A. Kent, Jr.*, ed. Gary T. Meadors (Winona Lake, Ind.: BMH Books, 1991), 49–68; Leland Ryken, *Words of Delight: A Literary Introduction to the Bible*, 2d ed. (Grand Rapids: Baker, 1992), 431–39; Stanley K. Stowers, "Letters: Greek and Latin Letters," in *ABD*, 4:290–93; Stirewalt, *Studies in Ancient Greek Epistolography*; William G. Doty, "The Epistles," in *A Complete Literary Guide to the Bible*, ed. Leland Ryken and Tremper Longman III (Grand Rapids: Zondervan, 1993), 445–57; Kenneth J. Neumann, "Major Variations in Pauline and Other Epistles in Light of Genre and the Pauline Letter Form," in *Origins and Method: Towards a New Understanding of Judaism and Christianity. Essays in Honour of John C. Hurd*, ed. Bradley H. McLean, JSNTSup, ed. Stanley E. Porter et al., vol. 86 (Sheffield: JSOT Press, 1993), 199–209; Peter T. O'Brien, "Letters, Letter Forms," in *DPL*, 550–53; Stanley E. Porter, "The Theoretical Justification for Application of Rhetorical Categories to Pauline Epistolary Literature," in *Rhetoric and the New Testament: Essays from the 1992 Heidelberg Conference*, ed. Stanley E. Porter and Thomas H. Olbricht, JSNTSup, ed. Stanley E. Porter et al., vol. 90 (Sheffield: JSOT Press, 1993), 100–122; Jeffrey T. Reed, "Using Ancient Rhetorical Categories to Interpret Paul's Letters: A Question of Genre," in *Rhetoric and the New Testament: Essays from the 1992 Heidelberg Conference*, ed. Stanley E. Porter and Thomas H. Olbricht, JSNTSup, ed. Stanley E. Porter et al., vol. 90 (Sheffield: JSOT Press, 1993), 292–324; John L. White, "Apostolic Mission and Apostolic Message: Congruence in Paul's Epistolary Rhetoric, Structure and Image," in *Origins and Method: Towards a New Understanding of Judaism and Christianity. Essays in Honour of John C. Hurd*, ed. Bradley H. McLean, JSNTSup, ed. Stanley E. Porter et al., vol. 86 (Sheffield: JSOT Press, 1993), 145–61; Greg Fay, "Paul the Empowered Prisoner: Eph 3:1–13 in the Epistolary and Rhetorical Structure of Ephesians" (Ph.D. diss., University of Marquette, 1994), 25–105, 314–437; Jerome Murphy-O'Connor, *Paul the Letter-Writer: His World, His Options, His Skills, Good News Studies*, vol. 41 (Collegeville, Minn.: Liturgical Press, 1995); Jeffrey T. Reed, "The Epistle," in *Handbook of Classical Rhetoric in the Hellenistic Period 330 B.C.–A.D. 400*, ed. Stanley E. Porter (Leiden: Brill, 1997), 171–93; Dahl, "Einleitungsfragen zum Epheserbrief," 3–18. For Jewish writings, see P. S. Alexander, "Epistolary Literature," in *Jewish Writings of the Second Temple Period: Apocrypha, Pseudepigrapha, Qumran Sectarian Writings, Philo, Josephus*, ed. Michael E. Stone, Compendia Rerum Iudaicarum ad Novum Testamentum, ed. Y. Aschkenasy et al., sec. 2, vol. 2 (Philadelphia: Fortress; Assen: Van Gorcum, 1984), 579–96.

scribing the sender such as "apostle" and/or "servant" and the epithets describing the recipients as "saints," "beloved," or "church which is at. . . ." The usual Hellenistic greeting (χαίρειν) is replaced by χάρις καὶ εἰρήνη, "grace and peace from God." In Ephesians, it is, "Paul, an apostle of Jesus Christ through the will of God, to the saints in Ephesus, that is, believers in Christ Jesus, grace to you and peace from God our Father and Lord Jesus Christ" (1:1–2). This is a typical Pauline greeting (2 Thess 1:2; Gal 1:3; 1 Cor 1:2; 2 Cor 1:2; Rom 1:7; Phil 1:2; Col 1:2; Phlm 3; Titus 1:2; 1 Tim 1:2; 2 Tim 1:2).[1] Normally after the greetings, Paul gives an introductory thanksgiving for the recipients of the letter (1 Cor 1:4; Phil 1:3; Col 1:3; 1 Thess 1:2; 2 Thess 1:3; Phlm 4). In this epistle he changes the order by giving an extended eulogy (Eph 1:3–14), which resembles some OT blessings (Pss 41:13 [MT 41:14; LXX 40:14]; 72:18–19 [LXX 71:18–19]; 106:48 [LXX 105:48]).[2] This is followed by his thanksgiving in Eph 1:15–23. Paul follows his normal pattern of beginning with the verb of thanksgiving (εὐχαριστέω) followed by ἵνα to express the content of his prayers for the believers (Phil 1:3–11; Col 1:3–14; 1 Thess 1:2–3:13; 2 Thess 1:2–12; 2:13–14; Phlm 4–7). Another intercessory prayer is given in Eph 3:1, 14–19 ending with a doxology in 3:20–21.

The closing in Ephesians, which is similar to other letters by Paul, parallels Hellenistic literature except Paul leaves out the customary health wish[3] and the word for farewell (ἔρρωσο). Typically, Paul concludes with "the grace of our Lord Jesus Christ be with you/your spirit" (Rom 16:20; 1 Cor 16:23; 2 Cor 13:14 [GT 13:13]; Gal 6:18; Phil 4:23; 1 Thess 5:28; 2 Thess 3:18; Phlm 25; cf. Col 4:18). Ephesians 6:23–24 ends similarly with "grace be with all who love our Lord Jesus Christ."[4] Along with Paul's other letters, Eph 6:23–24 includes the terminology of "peace" and/or "love" (1 Cor 16:24; 2 Cor 13:11, 14 [GT 13:13]; 1 Thess 5:23; 2 Thess 3:16), and "faith" (1 Cor 16:13; Titus 3:15).[5]

Although the opening and closing of the letter reveal Hellenistic influences, the body of any letter is by far the most difficult to classify. This is true of present-day practice as well. Even in contemporary correspon-

1. Otto Roller, *Das Formular der paulinischen Briefe: ein Beitrag zur Lehre von antiken Briefe*, BWANT, ed. Albrecht Alt and Gerhard Kittel, ser. 4, vol. 6 (Stuttgart: W. Kohlhammer, 1933), 110–14, 388–93, 529–31, table 3; Gese, *Das Vermächtnis des Apostels*, 30–31.

2. Cf. Peter T. O'Brien, "Ephesians I: An Unusual Introduction to a New Testament Letter," *NTS* 25 (July 1979): 504–16.

3. Cf. Peter Arzt, "The 'Epistolarly Introductory Thanksgiving' in the Papyri and in Paul," *NovT* 36 (January 1994): 38, 45; Jeffrey A. D. Weima, *Neglected Endings: The Significance of the Pauline Letter Closings*, JSNTSup, ed. Stanley E. Porter et al., vol. 101 (Sheffield: JSOT Press, 1994), 34–39.

4. Cf. Roller, *Das Formular der paulinischen Briefe*, 114–16, 394–96, 532, table 4; Weima, *Neglected Endings*, 78–87, 80, table 1.

5. Cf. Roller, *Das Formular der paulinischen Briefe*, 165, 472–74, 577–78, table 6; Weima, *Neglected Endings*, 88–100, 89, table 2.

dence, opening and closing statements tend to be more conventional while the main body of the letter may take all sorts of forms. For example, a business letter may contain a contract, a price agreement for a product, a settlement of a dispute regarding one's rights, a commendation for a job well done, the defense of one's case before a merchant or judge, an announcement of a promotion, or a recommendation as well as many other kinds of information and discussion. On the other hand, a personal letter may express commendation, love, displeasure, encouragement, exhortation, embarrassment, threat, confidential materials, a personal story, family news, instruction, or a combination of these. Both business and personal letters may have a variation of several forms. For instance, parts of a letter may be prose and other parts could include poetic, contractual, or legal forms. Thus, the difficulty in classifying the body of contemporary letters would be true also of the body of Hellenistic[1] and NT letters. For example, Paul's letters contain advice (1 Cor 5:1–6:20; 7:1–40; 8:1–11:34; 12:1–14:40), instruction (Rom 1:18–11:36; 1 Cor 15; Gal 3:7–20; Phil 2:5–11) consolation (1 Thess 4:13–18), reprimand (Gal 1:6–9; 3:1–6), and exhortation (Rom 12:1–15:13; 1 Cor 3:5–4:21; Gal 5–6). Certainly the letter body of Ephesians includes some of these elements.

Ephesians has three parts in the letter body: instruction (1:3–3:21), paraenesis (4:1–6:20), and commendation (6:21–22). In regard to the instructions (1:3–3:21), some dispute that the body of the letter does not begin in 1:3 but in 2:1 after Paul has completed his prayer of thanksgiving. It is true that the beginning of the letter body is difficult to demarcate because so much of it appears to be assimilated in the thanksgiving portion, a feature not uncommon in Paul's writings (1 Cor, Phil, 2 Thess).[2] However, it is even more complicated in Ephesians because there is a eulogy between the opening and the prayer of thanksgiving. Since the eulogy contains instruction concerning God's eternal purpose and plan, it seems best to accept that the body of the letter begins with the eulogy in 1:3–14 followed by the thanksgiving and prayer in 1:15–23. After the thanksgiving Paul continues the instruction regarding sinners who deserve nothing but God's wrath but have become trophies of God's grace due to his gracious work of salvation (2:1–10). He continues his instruction by informing the believers at Ephesus that redeemed sinners have been united with other believers into a corporate unity, in particular Jewish and Gentile believers (2:11–22). Paul elaborates on this union of Jewish and Gentile believers into one new humanity, the church (3:1–13). He then prays for the Ephesians that they might know Christ's strengthened love and exhibit that love toward one another. Positionally they have become one new humanity and now he prays that this might be true experientially in the Ephesian believers' lives (3:14–19). Paul ends this instructional section with a doxology (3:20–21).

1. Cf. White, "The Greek Documentary Letter Tradition," 92–100; Reed, "The Epistle," 186–92.

2. Doty, *Letters in Primitive Christianity*, 34.

The second part of the letter body is the paraenesis (4:1–6:20) beginning with the words Παρακαλῶ οὖν ὑμᾶς, "I exhort you," in 4:1.[1] Having just completed the prayer for the believers to be strengthened with Christ's love (3:14–19), Paul's paraenesis further emphasizes the need for them to demonstrate love for one another. Other Pauline literature such as 1 Thessalonians substantiates the idea that prayer and paraenesis are companions.[2] Paul exhorts the Ephesian believers to proper conduct within their own church community as well as to those outside their fellowship. He concretizes this exhortation by the repetition of περιπατέω, "walk, conduct," in 4:1, 17; 5:2, 8, 15. Lastly, 6:10–11 comments on the necessity of the Lord's strength in order to be able to stand against the schemes of the devil that hinder this righteous walk. Hence, Ephesians is a letter very similar to other Pauline letters, namely, instruction and prayer followed by a paraenetic section.

The third part of the body of Paul's letters normally includes a concluding section, which may incorporate an autobiographical element, an announcement of Paul's visit, or an identification and recommendation of Paul's messenger.[3] In Eph 6:21–22 Paul identifies and recommends his messenger Tychicus who is to relate to them how Paul was doing. These elements are analogous to his other letters (cf. Rom 16:1–2; 1 Cor 16:10–12, 15–18; Col 4:7–9; Phlm 8–20; cf. also 2 Cor 8:16–24; Phil 2:19–30).

Ephesians, on the whole, has many characteristics of a Hellenistic letter. However, some contend that it is not accurate to call it a letter and propose various ideas. Some suggest that it is a theological tractate clothed as a letter.[4] Schlier views it as a "wisdom discourse" with Christ personified as wisdom.[5] Nevertheless, the long paraenesis section (4:1–6:20) argues against a theological tract or a wisdom discourse.[6] Sanders asserts that chapters 1–3 contain early Christian hymns or fragments of them[7] but this view has not gained wide acceptance. Others suggest it was a liturgical document. For instance, Dahl thinks the benediction in 1:3–14 is a blessing said before baptism and that the letter instructs the newly converted Gentiles about the mean-

1. Bjerkelund, *Parakalô*. 15–19, 179–87.

2. Lincoln, xxxix; cf. also Doty, *Letters in Primitive Christianity*, 32; Schubert, *Form and Function of the Pauline Thanksgivings*, 89. Lincoln, Doty, and Schubert think that Eph 3:14–20 is thanksgiving. However, it fits better as a prayer of petition.

3. White, "Ancient Greek Letters," 97.

4. Käsemann, "Epheserbrief," 517, 520; Conzelmann, 86; Andreas Lindemann, "Bemerkungen zu den Adressaten und zum Anlaß des Epheserbriefes," *ZNW* 67, nos. 3/4 (1976): 240; Hans Conzelmann and Andreas Lindemann, *Interpreting the New Testament: An Introduction to the Principles and Methods of N.T. Exegesis*, 8th rev. German ed., trans. Siegfried S. Schatzmann (Peabody, Mass.: Hendrickson, 1988), 208.

5. Schlier, 21–22.

6. Schnackenburg, 23.

7. Jack T. Sanders, "Hymnic Elements in Ephesians 1–3," *ZNW* 56, nos. 3/4 (1965): 214–32.

ing of their baptism.[1] Schille suggests that it was a baptismal liturgy in the form of a letter.[2] Kirby proposes that it was both a prayer (based on the Jewish *berakhah*) and a discourse in the form of a letter that was shaped by Pentecost and that reflected the liturgy of Ephesus (the locale and not destination of the letter) in public worship, possibly at the Eucharist.[3] These suggestions are unlikely for they cannot be demonstrated. There is little, if anything, in the epistle that points to liturgy. Best correctly notes that "the references to baptism are too few for it to have been a baptismal liturgy" (since this was an important event for those converted from paganism) and it is unlikely that it refers to eucharistic liturgy since there is no mention of the Eucharist.[4] The epistle is concerned with broader considerations, the Christian life as a whole. Still others think Ephesians is a sermon or homily. For example, Gnilka thinks this epistle is a liturgical homily in the form of a letter.[5] Lincoln suggests that since Ephesians does not address specific issues and lacks personal greetings typical of other Pauline epistles, it is a written equivalent to an oral presentation and thus should be considered a written equivalent of a sermon or homily.[6] This explanation is plausible but this should not be based on its

1. Dahl, "Adresse und Proömium des Epheserbriefes," 261–64; updated in idem, *Studies in Ephesians*, 325–27; idem, "Gentiles, Christians, and Israelites in the Epistle to the Ephesians," *HTR* 79 (January/April/July 1986): 38; updated in idem, *Studies in Ephesians*, 447. Elsewhere Dahl suggests that "it belongs to a type of Greek letters—genuine and spurious—which substitutes for a public speech rather than for private conversation. The epistolary purpose is to overcome separation and establish contact between sender and recipients, or even to mediate the apostles presence to Gentile Christians who are separated from him in time rather than in space," see idem, "Ephesians, Letter to the," in *The Interpreter's Dictionary of the Bible*, ed. George Arthur Buttrick et al., Supplementary vol. (Nashville: Abingdon, 1962), 268.

2. Gottfried Schille, "Liturgisches Gut im Epheserbrief" (D.Theol. diss., Georg-August-Universität, Göttingen, 1953), 135–51; idem, *Frühchristliche Hymnen* (Berlin: Evangelische Verlagsanstalt, 1962), 20–23, 102–7; idem, "Der Autor des Epheserbriefes," 330–31; cf. also Petr Pokorný, "Epheserbrief und gnostische Mysterien," *ZNW* 53, nos. 3/4 (1962): 160–94; Coutts, "The Relationship of Ephesians and Colossians," 115–27.

3. John C. Kirby, *Ephesians, Baptism and Pentecost: An Inquiry into the Structure and Purpose of the Epistle to the Ephesians* (Montreal: McGill University; London: SPCK, 1968), 125–49, 165–72. Storer suggests that Ephesians was read by the church at Pentecost much like Ruth was in OT times. See R. Storer, "A Possible Link between the Epistle to the Ephesians and the Book of Ruth," in *SE IV. Papers Presented to the Third International Congress on New Testament Studies held at Christ Church, Oxford, 1965*, ed. F. L. Cross, TU, ed. Friedrich Zucher et al., vol. 102 (Berlin: Akademie-Verlag, 1968), 343–46.

4. Best, 61.

5. Gnilka, 33. MacDonald (18) does not think Ephesians is a liturgical tract but letter "greatly influenced by liturgy."

6. Lincoln, xxxix. So also Roy R. Jeal, *Integrating Theology and Ethics in Ephesians: The Ethos of Communication, Studies in Bible and Early Christianity*, vol. 43 (Lewiston,

omission of specific issues or personal greetings. In fact, personal greetings also are omitted in other Pauline epistles, as discussed above. Furthermore, as to specific issues (as well as to identify the audience with certainty), this is also a problem in Romans, yet no one really considers this book uncharacteristic of Pauline literature. Moreover, those who consider Ephesians to be a written equivalent of a sermon or homily must consider a similar assessment for other Pauline letters such as Galatians, Philippians, 1 Corinthians, and/or Romans. Most of these letters were read aloud to an audience very much like a homily.[1] Hendrix proposes that Ephesians is "an epistolary decree in which the author recites the universal benefactions of God and Christ and proceeds to stipulate the appropriate honors, understood as the moral obligations of the beneficiaries."[2] He suggests that this explains some peculiar features such as the long sentences and the exhortations in chapters 4–6, which set forth the obligations of the community as beneficiaries of God and Christ. Although there are resemblances to Greco-Roman inscriptions that indicate the benefits from a head of state (such as an emperor) and the ensuing obligation and loyalty of the recipients of the benefits, they are not in the form of a letter but are inscriptions of official civic resolutions (using a standard literary form) that were publicly displayed in connection with a public ceremony.[3] Since Ephesians has the characteristics of Hellenistic letters and is similar to other Pauline epistles, it seems best to characterize it as an actual letter.

In conclusion, there are various genres within contemporary letters and this was also true in Paul's day.[4] For example, Ephesians contains didactic materials (2:1–22), a eulogy (1:3–14), prayers of thanksgiving (1:15–23) or petition (3:13–19), a doxology (3:20–21), a reprimand

---

N.Y.: Edwin Mellen, 2000), 27–29, 43–51, 70–72, 203–5. Brown (*An Introduction to the New Testament*, 631–33) seems to favor this view although he is vague on this point.

1. So Best, 61–63. Mouton examines Ephesians from linguistic-literary, socio-historical, and rhetorical perspectives in an attempt to determine the implications of the ethical effect it had for the past (first century) and now for the present day. See E. Mouton, "Reading Ephesians ethically: Criteria towards a Renewed Identity Awareness?" *Neot* 28, no. 2 (1994): 359–77.

2. Holland Hendrix, "On the Form and Ethos of Ephesians," *Union Seminary Quarterly Review* 42, no. 4 (1988): 3–15, esp. 9; Frederick W. Danker, *Benefactor: Epigraphic Study of a Graeco-Roman and New Testament Semantic Field* (St. Louis: Clayton, 1982), 451–52.

3. Cf. Bruce W. Winter, *Seek the Welfare of the City: Christians as Benefactors and Citizens, First-Century Christians in the Graeco-Roman World*, ed. Andrew D. Clarke (Grand Rapids: Eerdmans, 1994), 26–33.

4. Cf. Malherbe, "Ancient Epistolary Theorists," 15–17; Detlev Dormeyer, *The New Testament among the Writings of Antiquity*, trans. Rosemarie Kossov (Sheffield: Sheffield Academic Press, 1998), 205–13.

(4:17–19), an encouragement (1:15; 5:1–2), hymnic materials (5:14), and commands (5:25–30). Applying rhetorical criticism to Ephesians, Lincoln suggests that the two major parts of the book utilize two elements of rhetoric. The first half of the book, he contends, is epideictic rhetoric where the speaker or writer tries to establish a sense of community by focusing on certain values and avoiding differences between the writer and the readers. In Eph 1–3 Paul prays for them and focuses on the relationships of believers with God and with fellow believers, particularly Jewish and Gentile believers who are a new entity. The second half of Ephesians is primarily deliberative rhetoric and attempts by persuasive (protreptic) and dissuasive (apotreptic) means to encourage the readers to move in a new direction in the future. Thus, in Eph 4–6 he exhorts the believers to change their behavior in light of their new relationship to Christ and fellow believers.[1] The rhetorical analysis of Ephesians may well have validity; however, it appears somewhat forced.[2] Such an analysis may fit better with Romans or Galatians but even with these one must proceed with caution.

Not only are there different genres but there also is a mixture of styles. For example, there are eight long sentences (1:3–14, 15–23; 2:1–7; 3:2–13, 14–19; 4:1–6, 11–16; 6:14–20) and yet there are short declarations (4:4–6) or commands (5:1, 18, 22, 25; 6:1). Lincoln acknowledges that "in terms of ancient epistolary theory there is nothing to disqualify it [Ephesians] as a letter."[3] It seems best to conclude that Ephesians is an actual letter with a mixture of genre and styles, such as other Hellenistic and Pauline letters. It was a letter to be read to those in Ephesus and probably to the churches in the surrounding communities.

1. Lincoln, xli–xlvii; cf. Berger, "Hellenistische Gattungen im Neuen Testament," 1139–40. Kittredge disagrees with Lincoln's rhetorical analysis by suggesting that the whole of Ephesians is "best characterized as deliberative rhetoric" (Cynthia Briggs Kittredge, *Community and Authority: The Rhetoric of Obedience in the Pauline Tradition*, HTS, ed. Allan D. Callahan et al., vol. 45 [Harrisburg, Pa.: Trinity Press International, 1998], 145–46). For a more extensive application of rhetorical criticism to Ephesians (and a critique of Lincoln), see Fay, "Paul the Empowered Prisoner," 438–666; see also Jeal, *Integrating Theology and Ethics in Ephesians*, 30–43, 62–70.

2. Cf. Aune, *The New Testament in Its Literary Environment*, 203–4; Porter, "Theoretical Justification for Application of Rhetorical Categories," 115–16; Reed, "Using Ancient Rhetorical Categories," 322–24; Elna Mouton, "The Communicative Power of the Epistle to the Ephesians," in *Rhetoric, Scripture and Theology: Essays from the 1994 Pretoria Conference*, ed. Stanley E. Porter and Thomas H. Olbricht, JSNTSup, ed. Stanley E. Porter et al., vol. 131 (Sheffield: Sheffield Academic Press, 1996), 280–307; Reed, "The Epistle," 182–92; Jeffrey A. D. Weima, "What Does Aristotle Have to Do With Paul? An Evaluation of Rhetorical Criticism," *Calvin Theological Journal* 32 (November 1997): 458–68.

3. Lincoln, xl; cf. also Best, *Ephesians*, 14.

City and Historical Setting

The City of Ephesus

Its Mention in Ephesians

Traditionally it is understood that this letter was written to believers in Ephesus of Asia Minor. Because certain manuscripts omit the words "in Ephesus" and because of the impersonal tone of the letter, some doubt that this letter was written by Paul to the Ephesians and this has engendered a great deal of discussion on the destination of this epistle.[1] The textual problem is discussed in more detail elsewhere (see Excursus 1: Textual Problem in Ephesians 1:1) where it is concluded that the words "in Ephesus" were most likely in the original manuscripts. Some suggest that this letter was encyclical and possibly the city name was omitted so that Tychicus or anyone who read the letter could fill in the city's name. However, there is no lacuna in any manuscript, even those which omit "in Ephesus," and no such lacunae exist in examples of letters in the ancient world.[2] Moreover, the manuscripts which omit "in Ephesus" insert no other city in its place.[3] Furthermore, to omit the city name after the participle (τοῖς οὖσιν), would read τοῖς ἁγίοις τοῖς οὖσιν καὶ πιστοῖς ἐν Χριστῷ Ἰησοῦ "to the saints and those who are faithful in Christ Jesus" (cf. RSV, JB, NJB) which is grammatically awkward if not impossible.[4] No other Pauline letter has this construction without the name of the city (see Rom 1:7; 1 Cor 1:1; 2 Cor 1:1; Phil 1:1).

Some conjecture it originally read τοῖς ἁγίοις καὶ πιστοῖς ἐν Χριστῷ Ἰησοῦ, which is similar to Colossians. It is proposed that later when it became known as the Ephesian letter, someone inserted τοῖς οὖσιν ἐν Ἐφέσῳ, "to those who are in Ephesus," from the superscription outside the scroll. With this insertion the text would read (with most manuscripts) τοῖς ἁγίοις τοῖς οὖσιν ἐν Ἐφέσῳ καὶ πιστοῖς ἐν Χριστῷ Ἰησοῦ, "to the saints who are in Ephesus and faithful in Christ Jesus." It is suggested that later a scribe remembered that originally there was no geographical designation and thus omitted ἐν Ἐφέσῳ and hence its omission in 𝔓[46], א, and B.[5] The complexity of this view becomes self-

1. Cf. Ernest Best, "Recipients and Title of the Letter to the Ephesians: Why and When the Designation 'Ephesians'?" in *ANRW*, pt. 2, vol. 25.4 (1987), 3247–79.

2. Roller, *Das Formular der paulinischen Briefe*, 199–212, 520–25.

3. Bruce, 250.

4. Cf. Cadbury, "The Dilemma of Ephesians," 94; Richard Batey, "The Destination of Ephesians," *JBL* 82 (March 1963): 101.

5. Schmid, *Der Epheserbrief des Apostels Paulus. Seine Adresse, Sprache und literarischen Beziehungen Untersucht*, 125–29; Maurice Goguel, "Esquisse d'une solution nouvelle du problème de l'épître aux Éphésiens," *Revue de l'histoire des religions* 111 (Mai–Juni 1935): 254–84; 112 (Juillet–Août 1935): 73–99; Ernest Best, "Ephesians 1.1 Again," in *Paul and Paulinism. Essays in Honour of C. K. Barrett*, ed. M. D. Hooker and S. G. Wilson (London: SPCK, 1982), 276–78.

defeating for it would need "a long and complicated textual development" as Best admits.[1] Moreover, there is simply no textual evidence for this evolution.

Another suggestion is that originally there were two place names, Hierapolis and Laodicea, and when the names were removed the awkward καί (often translated "also") was accidentally retained as seen in 𝔓[46], ℵ, and B.[2] Again this view fails because there is no evidence for the two place names and it is difficult to explain why a scribe, who normally attempts to make the text flow smoothly, would have retained the awkward καί.[3] On the other hand, Dahl proposes that several copies of the letter were made, each with the specific city inserted.[4] However, all the extant manuscripts with a city inserted have only ἐν Ἐφέσῳ. Also, the cost of making several copies of the same letter would have been prohibitive and the transporting of them by Tychicus would have been difficult.

It seems that the best solution is to retain ἐν Ἐφέσῳ for it has good support from external and internal evidence (see Excursus 1: Textual Problem in Ephesians 1:1). The acceptance of this reading has gained supporters[5] (cf. AV, ASV, NASB, NEB, NIV, NRSV). The scenario may well have been not one large church but many house churches in the city of Ephesus and in western Asia Minor. The impersonal nature of the letter has been discussed above; however, if this letter were to be read to several churches in the vicinity, the lack of personal greetings, as in some of the other Pauline letters, is understandable. It is not inconceivable that there were several churches in the area because on his third missionary journey Paul had ministered in Ephesus for around two and a half years. While resident in Ephesus he could well have established many churches, not only in the city but also in outlying villages. However, Ephesus would still have been the center of church activity and hence the letter was addressed to Ephesus.

Its Location

Today ancient Ephesus[6] is located about four miles inland from the Aegean Sea on the west coast of modern-day Turkey. However, the

1. Best, "Recipients and Title of the Letter to the Ephesians," 3250; cf. also idem, "Ephesians 1.1 Again," 277–78.

2. Van Roon, *The Authenticity of Ephesians*, 80–85; Lincoln, 3–4.

3. Best, "Recipients and Title of the Letter to the Ephesians," 3250; Arnold, "Ephesians, Letter to the," 244.

4. Dahl, "Adresse und Proömium des Epheserbriefes," 247–49; updated in idem, *Studies in Ephesians*, 62–63; idem, "The Particularity of the Pauline Epistles as a Problem in the Ancient Church," in *Neotestamentica et Patristica*, 267; updated in idem, *Studies in Ephesians*, 170.

5. Cf. Gnilka, 1–7; Conzelmann, 89; Lindemann, "Bemerkungen zu den Adressaten," 235–51; cf. also idem, *Aufhebung*, 10 n. 5; Lindemann, 10, 19; Conzelmann and Lindemann, *Interpreting the New Testament*, 205.

6. The first excavation of the city was in 1863 by the British archaeologist J. T. Wood followed by David G. Hogarth. Excavations were continued by Austrian archaeologists

first-century geographer Strabo (64/63 B.C.–A.D. 21) described the city as a seaport located at about the middle of the western coast of the Roman province of Asia at the mouth of the Cayster River.[1] Over the years the silting of the Cayster River made Ephesus a gulf city.[2] Around 1000 B.C. the coast line was farther inland, passing Ephesus which was situated on the south side of the harbor. Later, around 300 B.C., with the silting of the river, the coast line had moved westward with Ephesus being on the southeast corner of the gulf. By Roman times the Cayster had silted the area so much that only a narrow harbor remained. This rapid silting was due to an ill-advised engineering scheme under the Pergamenian King Attalus Philadelphius (159–138 B.C.) when he tried to narrow the entrance of the river, attempting to make it deeper for larger ships. Unfortunately, it had the opposite effect.[3] In A.D. 61 the governor of Asia tried to clear the harbor in order to improve the connection between the harbor and the sea.[4] Thus during Paul's time it was difficult for large merchant ships to dock at Ephesus.[5] Perhaps this is why Paul met the Ephesian elders at Miletus when he visited them in A.D. 57.

Its History

The Egyptian Athenaeus (ca. A.D. 200, not to be confused with church father Athanasius A.D. 293–373) relates the legendary version of the founding of the city. According to this legend the founders were having difficulty in selecting a site for the city. They consulted an oracle which told them that they should build a city wherever a fish and a wild boar should point out. Subsequently, some fishermen were cooking a meal when a fish with a live coal jumped out of the fire, fell into

---

such as Josef Keil, Franz Miltner, Fritz Eichler, Hermann Vetters, and Anton Bammer. The Austrian archaeologists have published over the years many of their finds in *Anzeiger der österreichischen Akademie der Wissenschaften—Philosophisch-historische Klasse*. Also, one should consult Oster who has engaged in extensive research into the ancient city of Ephesus and has published a very helpful bibliography (Richard E. Oster, comp., *A Bibliography of Ancient Ephesus*, ATLA Bibliography Series, ed. Kenneth E. Rowe, no. 19 [Metuchen, N.J.: American Theological Library and Scarecrow Press, 1987]). For a brief history of the city as well as a brief history of archaeological excavations, see Peter Scherrer, "Ephesus Uncovered from Latrines to Libraries," *Archaeology Odyssey* 4 (March/April 2000): 26–37.

1. Strabo 14.1.20, 24.

2. Cf. Ibid., 13.3.2.

3. Ibid., 14.1.24.

4. Tacitus *Annales* 16.23.

5. G. H. R. Horsley, "The Inscriptions of Ephesos and the New Testament," *NovT* 34 (April 1992): 134–35. For recent excavations of the harbor, see Heinrich Zabehlicky, "Preliminary Views of the Ephesian Harbor," in *Ephesos Metropolis of Asia: An Interdisciplinary Approach to its Archaeology, Religion, and Culture*, ed. Helmut Koester, HTS, ed. Allen D. Callahan et al., vol. 41 (Valley Forge, Pa.: Trinity Press International, 1995), 201–15, esp. 206–12.

some straw, and ignited a thicket occupied by a wild boar. Frightened, the boar fled and was pursued by the fisherman who felled it where the temple of Athena was later built.[1] In memory of this remarkable fulfillment of the oracle's prediction, an effigy of a wild boar stood beside the main street of the city as late as A.D. 400.[2]

Strabo recounts that around 1100 B.C. the land was occupied by Amazons[3] who named the cities of Ephesus and Smyrna but were driven back by the Ionians who were led by Androculus, one of the numerous sons of the legendary king of Athens. When the Ionians came to the area of Ephesus they made an amicable arrangement with the inhabitants of the area (Carians and Lydians) who were living around the environs of the temple of the great Anatolian mother-goddess.[4] The royal seat of the Ionians was established here. Thus, a new city was founded and the Greeks adopted the native goddess under the name of their own goddess Artemis (Greek name; Diana is the Roman or Latin name).[5] This city of Ephesus occupied the north slope of the theater hill, namely, Mt. Pion. Its prominence among Greek settlements in Ionia was twofold: "first, its harbour, conveniently situated in the middle of the west coast of Asia Minor, at the mouth of the River Cayster, and second, the sanctuary of Artemis, a place of pilgrimage from prehistoric times."[6] Ephesus became a prominent and prosperous city near Mt. Pion for the next 400–500 years.

Over the centuries there was a struggle between the East and the West for control over Asia Minor. In 560 B.C. Croesus (560–546 B.C.), last king of Lydia in western Asia Minor, attacked prosperous Ephesus. The Ephesians tried to defend themselves by tying a rope from the temple of Artemis to the city, a distance of about three-quarters of a mile. It was thought that this action would place them under the goddess' protection but this pious measure did not help. Croesus destroyed the city but not the temple. He transplanted the inhabitants farther inland to the level ground of the temple Artemis. With the Anatolian victory Ephesus became an Anatolian city rather than a Greek city and Artemis became the national deity of Lydia's domain. Cyrus of Persia took over in 546 B.C. and in 499 B.C. Ephesus attempted an unsuccessful revolt against Persia. In 479 B.C. the Ephe-

1. Athenaeus *Deipnosophistae* 8.361.

2. George E. Bean, *Aegean Turkey: An Archaeological Guide* (New York: Frederick A. Praeger, 1966), 160–61.

3. So called in Greek mythology but they cannot be identified. The Amazons were female warriors situated at the borders of the known world.

4. Strabo 14.1.3, 21; cf. Pausanias 7.2.7–9.

5. Artemis can be traced back to at least the eleventh century B.C., see Gerard Mussies, "Pagans, Jews, and Christians at Ephesus," in *Studies on the Hellenistic Background of the New Testament*, ed. Pieter Willem van der Horst and Gerard Mussies, Utrechtse theologische Reeks, vol. 10 (Utrecht: Gegevens Koninklijke Bibliotheek, 1990), 181.

6. Bean, *Aegean Turkey: An Archaeological Guide*, 161.

sians were forced to join the union of the Greek states but seceded at the earliest opportunity (386 B.C.).[1] It appears that the goddess always sided with the Persians against the Greeks.

In the next century power changed from Persian to Greek. The temple of Artemis was set on fire and destroyed by an arsonist named Herostratus.[2] Tradition states that the temple of Artemis burned on the sixth of Hekatombaion (July 22, 356 B.C.), the day of Alexander the Great's birth. A Macedonian remarked that it was no wonder that the temple of Artemis burned down since the goddess was too busy bringing Alexander into the world.[3] The Ephesians immediately began to rebuild a more splendid temple under the architect Cheiracrates.[4] The work was still in progress when Alexander reached Ephesus in 334 B.C. At that time he offered to defray all expenses, past and future, on the condition that a dedicatory inscription be made in his name. This was tactfully declined on the basis that it was inappropriate for a god to dedicate offerings to another god.[5] When the temple was finished it was considered one of the greatest buildings in antiquity.

Lysimachus, one of Alexander's successors, overthrew Antigonus, another of Alexander's successors, in 302 B.C. and founded the modern city of Ephesus.[6] Strabo fills in the details.[7] By 560 B.C. the silt carried down by the Cayster River was encroaching on the city which Croesus had located in a low-lying area near the temple. Foreseeing the inevitable doom of the city, Lysimachus tried to convince the inhabitants to move to the new place he was building. The people refused. Thus, during a heavy rain, he blocked up the sewers of the old city, which made the houses uninhabitable. Around 287 B.C. he built a wall nearly six miles in length on the south side of the city and changed the harbor's location from north of Mt. Pion to the west of it.

After the defeat and death of Lysimachus in 281 B.C. Ephesus and western Asia Minor came under the dominion of the Seleucids and the Ptolemies. With the assistance of King Eumenes II (197–159 B.C.) of Pergamum, the Romans defeated the Seleucid Antiochus III in the battle of Magnesia in 190 B.C.[8] and gave much of the territory, including Ephesus, to Eumenes.[9] Attalus III Philometer, last ruler of Pergamum, died in 133 B.C. and his kingdom was bequeathed to the Romans,[10] thus placing Ephesus under Roman control. Except for the

1. It is a complicated and involved history, cf. Plutarch *Lysander* 5.1–2.
2. Strabo 14.1.22; Plutarch *Alexander* 3.
3. Plutarch *Alexander* 3.
4. Strabo 14.1.23.
5. Ibid., 14.1.22.
6. Pausanias 1.9.7.
7. Strabo 14.1.21.
8. Livy 37.37–45.
9. Polybius 21.45.10.
10. Appian *Μιθριδάτειος* 62; *Bella Civilia* 5.4.

temporary insurrection of the Ephesians in conjunction with King Mithridates of Pontus in 88 B.C. (which was put down by the Romans under Sulla in 84 B.C.), Asia Minor was a Roman province until at least the fifth or sixth century A.D.[1]

Its Structures

Although Ephesus had many wonderful structures such as baths, gymnasiums, a stadium for gladiators and wild animals, and civic and commercial agoras, only the theater and the temple of Artemis will be discussed. They were the two most prominent structures. The theater was probably begun in the second century B.C. and enlarged during Claudius' rule (A.D. 41–54). A two-story stage was erected in Nero's reign (A.D. 54–68) and completed in Trajan's time (A.D. 98–117). The alterations were in progress during Paul's time in Ephesus. It was located on the western slope of Mt. Pion. The theater measured 145 meters (475 feet) wide and 30 meters (98 feet) high. There were three bands of rows, each having twenty-two rows of seats and twelve stairways from the orchestra to the top of the theater. The orchestra measured 11 by 25 meters (37 by 80 feet) and the stage behind the orchestra was 25 by 40 meters (82 by 131 feet) supported by thirty-six pillars. It had a seating capacity of 24,000 people. In this theater the silversmith Demetrius protested against Paul and his message (Acts 19:23–41).

The temple of Artemis or Artemision was rebuilt after the fire in 356 B.C. Over the years there were renovations and additions. According to Pliny (A.D. 23–79), the temple in the first century measured 69 by 130 meters (225 by 425 feet) with 127 columns 18 meters (60 feet) high and 2 meters (6 feet) in diameter.[2] Some think that the breadth and width refer to the temple platform and that the temple itself was 55 by 110 meters (180 by 361 feet) which is an area slightly larger than an American football field (160 by 360 feet including end zones). It was built of marble, Cyprus wood paneling, and cedar roof beams.[3] It was the largest building known in antiquity[4] and was considered one of the seven wonders of the world.[5] For centuries much of life in Ephesus revolved around the temple of Artemis.

1. For a discussion of Ephesus in Roman times, see Dieter Knibbe and Wilhelm Alzinger, "Ephesos vom Beginn der römischen Herrschaft in Kleinasien bis zum Ende der Principatszeit," in *ANRW*, pt. 2, vol. 7.2 (1980), 748–830

2. Pliny *Historia Naturalis* 36.21 §96.

3. Ibid., 16.79 §213.

4. Pausanias 4.31.8; 7.5.4.

5. It was Antipater of Sidon (fl. 120 B.C.) in *Anthologia Graeca* 9.58 who mentioned that the temple of Artemis was one of seven wonders of the world (cf. 8.177).

Its Religions

It is inaccurate to assume that only one religion was practiced in Ephesus for there were many cults and religions in this ancient city,[1] including emperor worship.[2] In fact, it was considered a great honor to be the temple warden (νεώκορος) of the emperor.[3] In A.D. 26 eleven cities in Asia Minor competed to be the temple warden of Tiberius but the Roman Senate, with Tiberius in attendance, passed over Ephesus because the renowned cult of Artemis already dominated the city.[4] It was this city's honor to be the temple warden of Artemis[5] and of her image[6] that fell from the sky (Acts 19:35). Clearly, the cult of Artemis was most prominent and significant in Paul's day and the early church.[7]

1. Richard E. Oster, "Ephesus as a Religious Center under the Principate, I. Paganism before Constantine," in *ANRW*, pt. 2, vol. 18.3 (1990), 1661–1728; cf. also Guy MacLean Rogers, *The Sacred Identity of Ephesos: Foundation Myths of a Roman City* (London: Routledge, 1991); Thorsten Moritz, "'Summing-up all Things': Religious Pluralism and Universalism in Ephesians," in *One God, One Lord in a World of Religious Pluralism*, ed. Andrew D. Clarke and Bruce W. Winter (Cambridge: Tyndale House, 1991), 101–8; Horsley, "The Inscriptions of Ephesos and the New Testament," 149–58; Günther, *Die Frühgeschichte des Christentums in Ephesus*, 21–24.

2. Steven J. Friesen, *Twice Neokoros: Ephesus, Asia and the Cult of the Flavian Imperial Family*, Religions in the Graeco Roman World, ed. R. van den Broek, H. J. W. Drijvers, and H. S. Versnel, vol. 116 (Leiden: Brill, 1993). Cf. W. M. Ramsay, *The Cities and Bishoprics of Phrygia Being an Essay of the Local History of Phrygia from the Earliest Times to the Turkish Conquest*, vol. 1 (Oxford: Clarendon, 1895), 58–60; David Magie, *Roman Rule in Asia Minor to the End of the Third Century after Christ*, 2 vols. (Princeton: Princeton University Press, 1950), 1:637; 2:1497–98 n. 21; A. N. Sherwin-White, *Roman Society and Roman Law in the New Testament* (Oxford: Clarendon, 1963), 88–89; R. A. Kearsley, "Ephesus: *Neokoros* of Artemis," in *New Documents Illustrating Early Christianity: A Review of the Greek Inscriptions and Papyri Published in 1980–81*, ed. S. R. Llewelyn and R. A. Kearsley, vol. 6 (Sydney: Macquarie University, 1992), 203–6; Christine M. Thomas, "At Home in the City of Artemis: Religion in Ephesos in the Literary Imagination of the Roman Period," in *Ephesos Metropolis of Asia: An Interdisciplinary Approach to its Archaeology, Religion, and Culture*, ed. Helmut Koester, HTS, ed. Allen D. Callahan et al., vol. 41 (Valley Forge, Pa.: Trinity Press International, 1995), 107–15; Giancarlo Biguzzi, "Ephesus, Its Artemission, Its Temple to Flavian Emperors, and Idolatry in Revelation," *NovT* 40 (July 1998): 276–90, esp. 280–84.

3. Steven Friesen, "The Cult of the Roman Emperors in Ephesos: Temple Wardens, City Titles, and the Interpretation of the Revelation of John," in *Ephesos Metropolis of Asia: An Interdisciplinary Approach to its Archaeology, Religion, and Culture*, ed. Helmut Koester, HTS, ed. Allen D. Callahan et al., vol. 41 (Valley Forge, Pa.: Trinity Press International, 1995), 229–50.

4. Tacitus *Annales* 4.55. In fact, later buildings for imperial worship were separate from and not on par with the temple of Artemis so that the supremacy of Artemis continued, see S. R. F. Price, *Rituals and Power: The Roman Imperial Cult in Asia Minor* (Cambridge: Cambridge University Press, 1984), 147.

5. Cf. *CIG* 2:2966.7–8?; 2972.6–7; cf. also 2968.c?; 2993.2.

6. The image (διοπετής) is a stone or meteorite that had fallen from heaven or the sky which was regarded as a sacred supernatural object, cf. Dionysius Halicarnassensis 2.66, 71; Appian *Μιθριδάτειος* 53; Herodian 5.3.5; BAGD 199; BDAG 250–51; L&N §2.48.

7. An inscription dated around A.D. 160 states that "the goddess Artemis rules ([π]ροεστῶσα) our city," *SIG* 867.29.

The goddess Artemis has had a long history and went through many transformations due to Anatolian and Greek influences.[1] Numerous statues of her have been found in the excavations in Ephesus. The lower half of the statues have bulls, lions, and sphinxes, probably representing the animal world that the Greek Artemis was supposed to have loved and protected. The upper half has two or three rows of bulbous objects on her chest portraying such things as multiple female breasts, ostrich eggs, grapes, nuts, or acorns among other things,[2] probably depicting Anatolian influence, that is, the life of god embodying and representing the life of nature. Some suggest these characterize fertility but this concept has been questioned.[3] It seems that she was considered the legitimate wife of Ephesus, the protectress and nourisher of the city.[4] Although not much is known, it appears that there were two religious festivals of Artemis (Artemision in March–April and Thargelion in May–June), which included religious processions as well as athletic and theatrical competitions.[5] Little is known about the mystery rites of Arte-

1. For a study of Artemis, see Robert Fleischer, *Artemis von Ephesos und verwandte Kultstatuen aus Anatolien und Syrien*, Études préliminaries aux religions orientales dans l'empire romain, ed. M. J. Vermaseren, vol. 35 (Leiden: Brill, 1973); Lewis Richard Farnell, *The Cults of the Greek States*, vol. 2 (Oxford: Clarendon, 1896), 425–548; Raphaël Tonneau, "Éphèse au Temps de Saint Paul," *RB* 38 (Juillet 1929): 321–63; Thomas, "At Home in the City of Artemis," 85–98; Gerard Mussies, "Artemis Ἄρτεμις," in *DDD*, 167–80; Fritz Graf, "Artemis," in *Der Neu Pauly Enzyklopädie der Antike*, ed. Hubert Cancik and Helmuth Schneider, vol. 2 (Stuttgart: J. B. Metzler, 1997), 53–58.

2. Fleischer, *Artemis von Ephesos*, 74–88; Dieter Knibbe, "Via Sacra Ephesiaca: New Aspects of the Cult of Artemis Ephesia," in *Ephesos Metropolis of Asia: An Interdisciplinary Approach to its Archaeology, Religion, and Culture*, ed. Helmut Koester, HTS, ed. Allen D. Callahan et al., vol. 41 (Valley Forge, Pa.: Trinity Press International, 1995), 142–43.

3. Oster, "Ephesus as a Religious Center under the Principate," 1725–26.

4. Lynn R. LiDonnici, "The Images of Artemis Ephesia and Greco-Roman Worship: A Reconsideration," *HTR* 85 (October 1992): 389–415, esp. 394, 405–7, 409–11; cf. Oster, "Ephesus as a Religious Center under the Principate," 1700–1706.

5. Irene Ringwood Arnold, "Festivals of Ephesus," *American Journal of Archaeology* 76 (January 1972): 17–22; Richard Oster, "The Ephesian Artemis as an Opponent of Early Christianity," *Jahrbuch für Antike und Christentum* 19 (1976): 37–44; idem, "Holy Days in Honour of Artemis," in *New Documents Illustrating Early Christianity*, vol. 4, *A Review of the Greek Inscriptions and Papyri Published in 1979*, ed. G. H. R. Horsley (Sydney: Macquarie University, 1987), 74–82; idem, "Ephesus as a Religious Center under the Principate," 1708–11; Rogers, *The Sacred Identity of Ephesos*, 80–126; Lillian Portefaix, "Ancient Ephesus: Processions as Media of Religious and Secular Propaganda," in *The Problem of Ritual. Based on Papers Read at the Symposium on Religious Rites Held at Åbo, Finland on the 13th–16th of August 1991*, ed. Tore Ahlbäck, Scripta Instituti Donneriani Aboensis, vol. 15 (Åbo, Finland: Donner Institute for Research in Religious and Cultural History; Stockholm: Almqvist & Wiksell International, 1993), 195–210; Knibbe, "Via Sacra Ephesiaca," 141–55; Hilke Thür, "The Processional Way in Ephesos as a Place of Cult and Burial," in *Ephesos Metropolis of Asia: An Interdisciplinary Approach to its Archaeology, Religion, and Culture*, ed. Helmut Koester, HTS, ed. Allen D. Callahan et al., vol. 41 (Valley Forge, Pa.: Trinity Press International, 1995), 157–99.

mis[1] except for the information Strabo provides concerning the cultic practices at the annual celebration of her birth.[2] There is no indication cult prostitution was practiced in this city.[3] However, Ephesus was known as a center for the practice of magic. Metzger states, "Of all ancient Graeco-Roman cities, Ephesus, the third largest city in the Empire, was by far the most hospitable to magicians, sorcerers, and charlatans of all sorts."[4] In Acts 19:18–19, Luke records that the believers divulged the practices of magic and burned their magic books worth 50,000 pieces of silver—that is, 50,000 days' wages![5] This seems to indicate the pervasiveness of the practice of magic and may support the idea that Ephesus could well have been a center for the study of magic.[6] Was the worship of Artemis connected with magic? Arnold states, "Although it has been claimed that the Ephesian Artemis was not by nature a goddess of magic, she does seem to have had a direct link with the magical practices of the time. She was considered a supremely powerful deity and could therefore exercise her power for the benefit of the devotee in the face of other opposing 'powers' and spirits."[7] Horsley rightly cautions that magic may have flourished in Ephesus but not more distinctively than other places.[8] Nevertheless, magic did play a prominent part there. Also, Artemis supposedly was syncretistic in her practices by adapting to cultural and political changes. She was considered sympathetic to the needs of her devotees and was venerated for her supreme power over fate and supernatural powers.[9]

1. Oster, "Ephesus as a Religious Center under the Principate," 1711–13; Rick Strelan, *Paul, Artemis, and the Jews in Ephesus*, BZNW, ed. Erich Gräßer, vol. 80 (Berlin: de Gruyter, 1996), 57–68.

2. Strabo 14.1.20.

3. Although it is difficult to prove the nonexistence of something, Baugh forcefully argues that cult prostitution did not exist in Ephesus, see S. M. Baugh, "Cult prostitution in New Testament Ephesus: A Reappraisal," *JETS* 42 (September 1999): 443–60.

4. Bruce M. Metzger, "St. Paul and the Magicians," *Princeton Seminary Bulletin* 38 (June 1944): 27; Arnold, *Ephesians: Power and Magic*, 14; cf. Paul Trebilco, "Asia," in *The Book of Acts in Its Graeco-Roman Setting*, ed. David W. J. Gill and Conrad Gempf, The Book of Acts in Its First Century Setting, ed. Bruce W. Winter, I. Howard Marshall, and David W. J. Gill, vol. 2 (Grand Rapids: Eerdmans, 1994), 314–15; Clinton E. Arnold, "Ephesus," in *DPL*, 250.

5. Ernst Haenchen, *The Acts of the Apostles: A Commentary*, trans. from the 14th German ed. (1965) by Bernard Noble and Gerald Smith, under the supervision of Hugh Anderson, and with the trans. rev. and brought up to date by R. McL. Wilson (Oxford: Basil Blackwell; Philadelphia: Westminster, 1971), 567.

6. Otto F. A. Meinardus, *St. Paul in Ephesus and the Cities of Galatia and Cyprus* (New Rochelle, N.Y.: Caratzas Brothers, 1979), 91; cf. also R. A. Kearsley, "The Mysteries of Artemis at Ephesus," in *New Documents Illustrating Early Christianity: A Review of the Greek Inscriptions and Papyri Published in 1980–81*, ed. S. R. Llewelyn and R. A. Kearsley, vol. 6 (Sydney: Macquarie University, 1992), 196–202.

7. Arnold, *Ephesians: Power and Magic*, 22; cf. also 23–24.

8. Horsley, "The Inscriptions of Ephesos and the New Testament," 131 n. 109.

9. Oster, "Ephesus as a Religious Center under the Principate," 1701, 1722–25; Arnold, *Ephesians: Power and Magic*, 20–22; Trebilco, "Asia," 316–20.

Its Influence

Politically, Ephesus was the provincial capital of the senatorial province of Asia (Asia Minor). As a senatorial province it was governed by a proconsul (ἀνθύπατοι)[1] who was very powerful and resided in Ephesus (Acts 19:38).[2] In addition, Acts 19:35 mentions the town clerk (ὁ γραμματεύς), an important official who copied, registered, preserved, and published official documents.[3] It was the town clerk in Ephesus who had quieted the riotous crowd and reprimanded them for their conduct before he dismissed them (19:35–41). Under Greek control the members of the senate (ἡ βουλή) were selected annually from the citizens of the city, but in Roman times distinguished citizens remained in the senate for life.[4] Under Greek domain the assembly (ἡ ἐκκλησία) had ultimate control, but in Roman times it was often a rubber stamp for the senate.[5] Acts 19:32 provides a glimpse into the governmental function of the city. When the silversmiths caused a riot the town clerk told the crowd that if they had any further charges, they should utilize the proconsuls or the courts and that any other grievances should be settled in the regular assembly. He then dismissed the assembly (Acts 19:39–41). This incident reveals that the assembly of silversmiths was not a regular meeting and thus could not conduct business. Furthermore, it demonstrates that the town clerk was in control and his authority was recognized.[6]

Commercially, it was the largest trading center in Asia Minor west of the Taurus,[7] which is on the eastern end of Asia Minor. The mouth of the Cayster River provided a harbor for Ephesus (except for the largest

1. For a discussion of the plural, see F. F. Bruce, *The Acts of the Apostles: The Greek Text with Introduction and Commentary*, 3d rev. and enl. ed. (Grand Rapids: Eerdmans, 1990), 421; Colin J. Hemer, *The Book of Acts in the Setting of Hellenistic History*, ed. Conrad H. Gempf, WUNT, ed. Martin Hengel and Otfried Hofius, vol. 49 (Tübingen: Mohr, 1989), 123.

2. For a study on Roman cities in the East, see A. H. M. Jones, *The Cities of the Eastern Roman Provinces*, 2d ed., rev. Michael Avi-Yonah et al. (Oxford: Clarendon, 1971), 28–94; Dieter Nör, "Zur Herrschaftsstruktur des römischen Reiches: Die Städte des Ostens und das Imperium," in *ANRW*, pt. 2, vol. 7.1 (1979), 1–20; cf. also Peter Lampe, "Acta 19 im Spiegel der ephesischen Inschriften," *BZ* 36, no. 1 (1992): 59–70.

3. Arnold Wycombe Gomme and P. J. Rhodes, "Grammateis," *OCD*, 646.

4. Cf. M. Rostovtzeff, *The Social & Economic History of the Hellenistic World*, vol. 1 (Oxford: Clarendon, 1941), 486; Knibbe and Alzinger, "Ephesos vom Beginn der römischen Herrschaft in Kleinasien," 777–83.

5. Rostovtzeff, *The Social & Economic History of the Hellenistic World*, vol. 2, 622.

6. Sherwin-White, *Roman Society and Roman Law in the New Testament*, 88; Trebilco, "Asia," 356–57; Bruce Winter, "The Problem with 'Church' for the Early Church," in *In the Fullness of Times: Biblical Studies in Honour of Archbishop Donald Robinson*, ed. David Peterson and John Pryor (Homebush West, Australia: Lancer, 1992), 206.

7. Strabo 14.1.24. Taurus could refer to a city near Tarsus (ibid., 14.5.10) or an eastern Asia Minor mountain range (ibid., 2.1.1; 2.5.31–32; 11.8.1; 11.12.1–4; 11.14.1; 12.1.1; 12.2.2).

ships in Paul's day) and connected shipping routes of the northern Aegean with Syria and Egypt on the East and with Italy via the Corinthian straits on the West. In addition, Ephesus was privileged, along with Sardis, to be at the western end of what Herodotus called the "Royal Road" (ἡ ὁδὸς ἡ βασιληίη) built by the Persians under Darius I (522–486 B.C.) beginning at Susa (ca. 1700 miles in length).[1] In Roman times it was still a major road in Asia Minor, linking the East to the West. To journey to Rome from Ephesus one would travel north of Troas, cross Macedonia by the Via Egnatia, sail across the Adrian Sea from either Dyrrachium or Aulona to Brundisium, and then traverse to Rome.[2] The fact that Roman milestones showed distances from Ephesus to other cities in Asia Minor indicates the importance of this city.[3] In the same vein, Aristides recounted the importance of Ephesus in all of Asia Minor and compared it in many respects with Athens, the ornament of the whole Greek race.[4] Ephesus was regarded as "the first and greatest metropolis of Asia."[5] With an estimated population between 200,000 and 250,000, its importance ranked only behind Rome and Athens.[6]

Religiously, the worship of Artemis was extensive. Demetrius, a silversmith in Ephesus, claimed that all in Asia Minor and the whole world worshiped Artemis (Acts 19:27). This claim is substantiated by Strabo who mentions that there were temples of Artemis in Magnesia[7] and Perge (Pamphylia)[8] of Asia Minor, in Sparta of Greece,[9] in Massilia (Marseilles, France),[10] and in Hemeroscopeium, Emporium, and Rho-

1. Herodotus 5.52–54.

2. For a study of roads in Asia Minor, see Magie, *Roman Rule in Asia Minor*, 2:786–93, nn. 17–18; W. M. Ramsay, *The Historical Geography of Asia Minor*, Royal Geographical Society Supplementary Papers, vol. 4 (London: John Murray, 1890; reprint, New York: Cooper Square, 1972), 27–62, 164–71; idem, "Roads and Travel (in NT)," in *A Dictionary of the Bible*, ed. James Hastings et al., Extra Volume (Edinburgh: T & T Clark, 1904), 381–85; M. P. Charlesworth, *Trade-Routes and Commerce of the Roman Empire*, 2d ed., rev. (Cambridge: Cambridge University Press, 1926; reprint, Chicago: Ares, 1974), 76–96.

3. D. H. French, "The Roman Road-system of Asia Minor," in *ANRW*, pt., 2, vol. 7.2 (1980), 707.

4. Aristides *Orationes* 23.24–26.

5. Magie, *Roman Rule in Asia Minor*, 2:1496 n. 17; Peter Scherrer, "Ephesos," in *Der Neu Pauly Enzyklopädie der Antike*, ed. Hubert Cancik and Helmuth Schneider, vol. 3 (Stuttgart: J. B. Metzler, 1997), 1082.

6. Meinardus, *St. Paul in Ephesus and the Cities of Galatia and Cyprus*, 54; Richard Oster, "Ephesus, Ephesians," in *Encylopedia of Early Christianity*, ed. Everett Ferguson et al. (New York: Garland, 1990), 301; cf. L. Michael White, "Urban Development and Social Change in Imperial Ephesos," in *Ephesos Metropolis of Asia: An Interdisciplinary Approach to its Archaeology, Religion, and Culture*, ed. Helmut Koester, HTS, ed. Allen D. Callahan et al., vol. 41 (Valley Forge, Pa.: Trinity Press International, 1995), 40–50.

7. Strabo 14.1.40.

8. Ibid., 14.4.2.

9. Ibid., 8.4.9.

10. Ibid., 4.1.4, 5, 8.

dus of Iberia (Spain).[1] Hence, the influence of Artemis was throughout the then-known world with Ephesus as its headquarters. It is here that Paul came to minister on his second and third missionary journeys.

Ephesus was a very influential city in Paul's day. Its influence both as a secular and religious center emanated to the other parts of the Roman Empire.[2] It seems that Paul selected strategic cities from which the influence of the gospel would spread to the surrounding areas. Many cities such as Ephesus were places where the cross-pollination of ideas was present. For Paul the gospel was not secondary to any other religion or philosophy and, consequently, needed to be heard and considered. He states in Rom 1:16 that he is not ashamed of the gospel for it is the power of God to everyone who believes, whether they be Jews or Greeks. In Ephesus he proclaimed the gospel forcefully. Moreover, he remained there for two and a half years and, as he mentioned to the Ephesian elders at Miletus, was able to present "the whole counsel of God" (Acts 20:27).

Historical Setting of Paul's Ministry in Ephesus

The main source of information on Paul's ministry in Ephesus is from Luke's record of Paul's missionary activities and this is abbreviated. The dates of Paul's visits to Ephesus are approximate but are given to provide a historical context.[3]

Paul's First Visit (Autumn 52)

Although early in the second missionary journey Paul wanted to go to Asia, conceivably to Ephesus, the Holy Spirit directed him elsewhere (Acts 16:6). After a ministry of approximately one-and-a-half years in Corinth, Paul, accompanied by Priscilla and Aquila, arrived at

1. Ibid., 3.4.6, 8; 4.1.5.

2. Lemcio suggests that Ephesus was one of the most influential cities in first century Christianity, see Eugene E. Lemcio, "Ephesus and the New Testament Canon," *BJRL* 69 (autumn 1986): 210–34. This is reprinted in Robert W. Wall and Eugene E. Lemcio, *The New Testament as Canon: A Reader in Canonical Criticism*, JSNTSup, ed. Stanley E. Porter et al., vol. 76 (Sheffield: JSOT Press, 1992), 335–60.

3. For a study on the dates of Paul's visits, see Daniel Plooij, *De Chronologie van het Leven van Paulus* (Leiden: Brill, 1918); Harold Hoehner, "Chronology of the Apostolic Age" (Th.D. diss., Dallas Theological Seminary, 1965); George Ogg, *The Odyssey of Paul* (Old Tappen, N.J.: Fleming H. Revell, 1968); John J. Gunther, *Paul: Messenger and Exile. A Study in the Chronology of His Life and Letters* (Valley Forge, Pa.: Judson, 1972); Jewett, *A Chronology of Paul's Life*; S. Dockx, *Chronologies néotestamentaires et Vie de l'Église primitive: Recherches exégétiques* [rev. ed.] (Leuven: Peeters, 1984); Gerd Luedemann, *Paul, Apostle to the Gentiles: Studies in Chronology*, trans. F. Stanley Jones (Philadelphia: Fortress, 1984); Niels Hyldahl, *Die Paulinische Chronologie*, Acta Theologica Danica, ed. Leif Grane, Eduard Nielsen, Hejne Simonsen, and Peter Widmann, vol. 19 (Leiden: Brill, 1986); Rainer Riesner, *Paul's Early Period: Chronology, Mission Strategy, Theology*, trans. Doug Stott (Grand Rapids: Eerdmans, 1998), 212–18, 296–99, 318–23; Knox, *Chapters in a Life of Paul*.

Ephesus. He was well-received there and, in fact, was asked to stay longer but he declined. Promising he would return, Paul departed for Antioch leaving Priscilla and Aquila behind (Acts 18:18–21). Very little is said about Paul's ministry in Ephesus except that he went into the synagogue and reasoned with the Jews. It is likely that the pattern and content of his ministry was similar to other instances in the first and second missionary journeys. Luke does not specify the length of Paul's stay in Ephesus but it seems that it was short, possibly a week or maybe as long as a month. After his departure Apollos arrived in Ephesus. Apollos was well-versed in the Scripture up to the point of the baptism of John the Baptist. Priscilla and Aquila took him aside and gave him additional instruction regarding the Christian faith. Shortly thereafter he left for Corinth (Acts 18:24–19:1).

Paul's Second Visit (Autumn 53–Spring 56)

After spending time in Antioch, Paul departed for his third missionary journey, probably some time in the spring of 53. First, he went to the churches in the areas of Galatia and Phrygia and then arrived again in Ephesus (Acts 18:23; 19:1), possibly in the summer or autumn of 53. There he encountered twelve men who, like Apollos, knew only of the teaching and baptism of John the Baptist. With further instruction by Paul they were baptized in the name of the Lord Jesus, the Holy Spirit fell on them, and they spoke in tongues and prophesied (Acts 19:2–7). Paul taught in the synagogue for three months, but he and a few disciples withdrew when some unbelievers spoke evil of the Christian faith. He then began teaching daily in the lecture hall of Tyrannus, continuing in this way for two years. Many Jews and Greeks in Asia Minor heard the message about Jesus during this time (Acts 19:8–10). Paul performed many miracles and exorcisms of evil spirits, which caused great fear to fall on Jews and Greeks and the Lord Jesus's name to be extolled. People gave up their magic practices and burned their magic books worth 50,000 pieces of silver, equivalent to 50,000 days of income (Acts 19:11–20). Paul's ministry of the Word clearly had a great impact on this city.

However, along with the success of his ministry there also came opposition. Demetrius, a leader of the local silversmiths' trade union, incited a mob at the theater against Christian teaching (Acts 19:23–41).[1] His motive was less religious than economic. Due to Paul's ministry, widespread conversion had occurred. This meant that people were not purchasing the cultic paraphernalia of Artemis, which created a

1. For a historical analysis of the riot, see Robert F. Stoops Jr., "Riot and Assembly: The Social Context of Acts 19:23–41," *JBL* 108 (spring 1989): 73–91; cf. also Werner Thiessen, *Christen in Ephesus. Die historische und theologische Situation in vorpaulinischer und paulinischer Zeit und zur Zeit der Apostelgeschichte und der Pastoralbriefe*, Texte und Arbeiten zum neutestamentlichen Zeitalter, ed. Klaus Berger, François Vouga, Michael Wolter, and Dieter Zeller, vol. 12 (Tübingen: Francke Verlag, 1995), 100–108.

significant income loss for the silversmiths. So Demetrius, in order to sway opinion, persuaded the crowds that Christianity was not only detrimental to their business but it brought disrepute to the goddess Artemis whom all Asia and the world worshiped. Although the worship of Artemis was still the most prominent,[1] the message of Christianity was making inroads in Asia Minor.[2]

According to 1 Cor 16:8 Paul had intended to stay in Ephesus until Pentecost (June 11, 56), but he may have needed to leave sooner because of the uproar in the theater. He may have left Ephesus some time in May, at which time he traveled to Macedonia and Achaia (Acts 19:21; 20:1–2).

In Ephesus Paul's message reached both Jews and Gentiles (Acts 19:10, 17; 20:21). Although Paul began his ministry in the synagogue, Gentiles were converted both times when he ministered there.[3] The letter to the Ephesians emphasizes the unity of believing Jews and Gentiles in one body, namely, the church. Accordingly, the Book of Ephesians matches well with the historical background of the ministry of Paul in Ephesus.

Paul's Meeting with Ephesian Elders at Miletus (Spring 57)

Paul spent the three winter months of A.D. 56–57 in Greece (Acts 20:3), most of the time probably with his friend Gaius in Corinth, the place from which he wrote Romans (Rom 16:23). Subsequently, he began his journey towards Jerusalem, desiring to celebrate Pentecost (May 29, A.D. 57) in the holy city (Acts 19:21; 20:16, 22). He then departed from Corinth to Macedonia where he visited Philippi during the Feast of Unleavened Bread (April 9–16, A.D. 57) and then he traveled to Asia Minor via Troas, Assos, Mitylene, Chios, Trogyllium and finally arrived at Miletus (Acts 20:3–16).[4] There he sent for the Ephe-

1. Some have conjectured that the cult of Artemis was in eclipse as a result of Paul's ministry, e.g., Lily Ross Taylor, "Artemis of Ephesus," in *The Beginnings of Christianity. Part I: The Acts of the Apostles*, ed. F. J. Foakes Jackson and Kirsopp Lake, vol. 5 (London: Macmillan, 1933; reprint, Grand Rapids: Baker, 1979), 255. Oster thinks this is a wrong assessment of the situation based on a misunderstanding of an Ephesian inscription, see Richard Oster, "Acts 19:23–41 and an Ephesian Inscription," *HTR* 77 (April 1984): 233–37.

2. In the light of Artemis's dominance, Strelan's suggestion that Paul's proclamation of the gospel as being largely unsuccessful (*Paul, Artemis, and the Jews in Ephesus*, 126–29, 138–39, 163) is unconvincing. For an appropriate refutation to Strelan's suggestion, see Eckhard Schnabel, "Die ersten Christen in Ephesus. Neuerscheinungen zur frühchristlichen Missionsgeschichte," *NovT* 41 (October 1999): 365, 373–78.

3. For Luke's interest in the Ephesian ministry, see Francis Pereira, *Ephesus: Climax of Universalism in Luke-Acts: A Redaction-Critical Study of Paul's Ephesian Ministry (Acts 18:23–20:1)*, Series X: Jesuit Theological Forum. Studies, no. 1 (Anand, India: Gujarat Sahitya Prakash, 1983).

4. For dates of various feasts, see Plooij, *De Chronologie van het Leven van Paulus*, 85; Jewett, *A Chronology of Paul's Life*, 48.

sian elders and they came to meet him (20:17–18a). It may be that his ship did not go into Ephesus because the harbor was not deep enough for the particular cargo ship he was on or perhaps it simply had no cargo to unload or load at Ephesus.

Paul's ministry to the Ephesian elders at Miletus included a review of his ministry among them (Acts 20:18–21), the declaration of his intention to go to Jerusalem (20:22–24), the statement that he would no longer see them (20:25–27), a warning to them about false teachers (20:28–30), a commendation of them to God (20:31–32), a reminder of his ministry among them (20:33–35), and prayer with them (20:36–38).[1]

Paul's Correspondence from Prison (60–62)

After Paul left Miletus he journeyed to Jerusalem. He caused a stir in Jerusalem and was imprisoned there for a very brief period (Acts 21:27–23:22). Shortly after, he was taken to and imprisoned in Caesarea for two years, A.D. 57–59, where he was tried and where he appealed to Caesar (Acts 23:23–26:32). Subsequently, he traveled to Rome (27:1–28:16) and was imprisoned there for two years, A.D. 60–62 (28:30).

In all four Prison Epistles Paul makes reference to his imprisonment (Eph 3:1; 4:1; 6:20; Phil 1:7, 13, 14, 16, 17; Col 4:3, 10; Phlm 1, 9, 10, 13, 23). Traditionally, it has been thought that these epistles were written while he was imprisoned in Rome. The reason for this view is the natural inference from Acts 27–28 where Luke describes the tortuous journey from Caesarea to Rome. On his arrival in Rome Paul was allowed to live by himself (end of the "we" narrative) in rented private quarters with a soldier guard (Acts 28:16). This continued for the two years of imprisonment (Acts 28:30). Although he was chained to a soldier (Acts 28:20), he was free to receive visitors (Acts 28:17, 23, 30), *custodia militaris*.[2] This corresponds to the Prison Epistles which speak of his imprisonment or chains (Eph 6:20; Phil 1:7, 13; Col 4:18; Phlm 10, 13) and his reception of visitors or friends, namely, Tychicus (Eph 6:21), Timothy (Phil 1:1; 2:19; Col 1:1; Phlm 1; Col 4:7), Epaphras (Col 1:7; 4:12), Epaphroditus (Phil 2:19, 25; 4:18; Phlm 23),

1. Cf. Cheryl Exum and Charles Talbert, "The Structure of Paul's Speech to the Ephesian Elders (Acts 20,18–35)," *CBQ* 29 (April 1967): 233–36; Charles K. Barrett, "Paul's Address to the Ephesian Elders," in *God's Christ and His People. Studies in Honour of Nils Alstrup Dahl*, ed. Jacob Jervell and Wayne A. Meeks (Oslo: Universitetsforlaget, 1977), 107–21; Colin J. Hemer, "The Speeches of Acts: I. The Ephesians Elders at Miletus," *TynBul* 40 (May 1989): 76–85; John J. Kilgallen, "Paul's Speech to the Ephesian Elders: Its Structure," *Ephemerides theologicae Lovanienses* 70 (April 1994): 112–21.

2. For a discussion of Paul's imprisonment in Rome, see Harry W. Tajra, *The Trial of St. Paul: A Juridical Exegesis of the Second half of the Acts of the Apostles*, WUNT, ed. Martin Hengel and Otfried Hofius, vol. 35 (Tübingen: Mohr, 1989), 172–96; idem, *The Martyrdom of St. Paul: Historical and Judicial Context, Traditions, and Legends*, WUNT, ed. Martin Hengel and Otfried Hofius, vol. 67 (Tübingen: Mohr, 1994), 33–72.

Onesimus (Col 4:9; Phlm 10), Jesus or Justus (Col 4:11), Mark and Aristarchus (Col 4:10; Phlm 24), and Luke and Demas (Col 4:14; Phlm 24). Hence, the Roman imprisonment of Paul fits well with the Book of Acts and the Prison Epistles.

However, some question the fact that the Prison Epistles were written from Rome and propose two other alternatives. The first alternative is that Paul wrote the Prison Epistles while he was imprisoned in Caesarea (A.D. 57–59).[1] One reason for this theory is that it is more reasonable to assume that Onesimus traveled to Caesarea than to Rome, for in Caesarea he would have been less likely recognized as a runaway slave. On the contrary, it would seem that Onesimus could be more easily found in a smaller city such as Caesarea and it would be more difficult to contact Paul there than in Rome. Second, those who support a Caesarean imprisonment propose that imprisonment in Rome would pose a distance too great and the time too short for the interchange between him in Rome and the Philippian church. While Paul was in prison such an interchange would have included the following: (1) Philippians heard the news of his imprisonment; (2) Epaphroditus was sent from Philippi to Paul (Phil 4:18); (3) news of Epaphroditus's illness reached Philippi (Phil 2:26); (4) Epaphroditus received the news of the Philippians's grief over his illness (Phil 2:26); (5) Epaphroditus was sent back to Philippi with the Philippian letter (Phil 2:25, 28); and (6) Timothy was to go to Philippi and to return back to Paul with a report of their situation (Phil 2:19–23). However, the problem of time and distance for the news of Epaphroditus' illness in Rome to travel to Philippi is not insurmountable. Many people traveled to various parts of the empire and thus the news going between Rome and Philippi, an important Roman city, could have been carried by any number of people, possibly including Christian couriers in the imperial service.[2] Hence, the theory of a solely Caesarean imprisonment is not convincing or necessary.

1. For a discussion of the Caesarean imprisonment, see Meyer, 18–21; Ernst Lohmeyer, *Die Briefe an die Philipper, an die Kolosser und an Philemon*, 8th ed., KEK, vol. 9 (Göttingen: Vandenhoeck & Ruprecht, 1930), pt. 1, 3–4, 41 n. 5, 43 n. 3, 47; pt. 2, 14–15 [identical to 9th ed., ed. Werner Schmauch, 1953]; Lewis Johnson, "The Pauline Letters from Caesarea," *ExpTim* 68 (October 1956): 24–26; Bo Reicke, "Caesarea, Rome, and the Captivity Epistles," in *Apostolic History and the Gospel. Biblical and Historical Essays Presented to F. F. Bruce on His 60th Birthday*, ed. W. Ward Gasque and Ralph P. Martin (Exeter: Paternoster; Grand Rapids: Eerdmans, 1970), 277–86; Gunther, *Paul: Messenger and Exile*, 91–121; John A. T. Robinson, *Redating the New Testament* (Philadelphia: Westminster; London: SCM, 1976), 60–67, 77–85; Ellis, *The Making of the New Testament Documents*, 266–75; Boismard, *L'Énigme de la lettre aux Éphesiens*, 177–80.

2. Hemer, *The Book of Acts in the Setting of Hellenistic History*, 273–75. For another scenario, see Stephen Robert Llewelyn, "Sending Letters in the Ancient World: Paul and the Philippians," *TynBul* 46.2 (November 1995): 337–56.

The second alternative to the Roman imprisonment is an imprisonment in Ephesus.[1] Scholars propose that the Prison Epistles were written during his imprisonment at Ephesus shortly after the riot there in May of 56. Briefly, the arguments for this view are as follows. First, Paul mentions in 1 Cor 15:32 that he had "fought with beasts at Ephesus" and this is interpreted literally to mean that Paul had been faced with the possibility of being thrown into the arena at Ephesus.[2] However, there is no evidence that such a threat existed. Furthermore, Guthrie argues that it was rare for a Roman citizen to be condemned to the lions and it would not have been contemplated as punishment for temple robbery (as suggested by Duncan).[3] This phrase must be taken figuratively, referring to some physical hardship endured at Ephesus in which there was a real threat on his life.[4] This is certainly not the only time Paul faced danger in his ministry. Second, it is suggested that in 2 Cor 11:23 Paul refers to many imprisonments and yet up to this point in Paul's chronology only the brief imprisonment at Philippi is recorded in Acts 16:23–40. Hence, there must be other imprisonments of which Luke made no mention. Duncan suggests that Paul had a series of three crises or three imprisonments while in Ephesus: one in the summer of 54 in which he wrote Philippians; one in the spring of 55 in which he wrote Colossians, Philemon, and Ephesians; and one in Laodicea in the autumn of 55 in which he wrote a part of 2 Timothy.[5] It is true that 1 and 2 Corinthians speak of trials endured by Paul. Nevertheless, it is

1. For a discussion of the Ephesian imprisonment, see Deissmann, *Light from the Ancient East*, 237–39 [first proposed in his 4th German ed., 1897, 201]; Benjamin W. Robinson, "An Ephesian Imprisonment of Paul," *JBL* 29, no. 2 (1910): 181–89; Edward William Winstanley, "Pauline Letters from an Ephesian Prison," *Exp* 8th ser., vol. 9 (June 1915): 481–98; Clayton R. Bowen, "Are Paul's Prison Letters from Ephesus?" *American Journal of Theology* 24 (January 1920): 112–35; (April 1920): 277–87; Adolf Deissmann, *Paul: A Study in Social and Religious History*, trans. William E. Wilson, 2d ed. (London: Hodder and Stoughton, 1926), 17–18, 20, 248; George S. Duncan, *St. Paul's Ephesian Ministry. A Reconstruction with Special Reference to the Ephesian Origin of the Imprisonment Epistles* (London: Hodder and Stoughton, 1929); idem, "St Paul's Ministry at Ephesus. A Reconstruction," *Theology* 22 (January 1931): 16–23; idem, "A New Setting for St. Paul's Epistle to the Philippians," *ExpTim* 43 (October 1931): 7–11; George L. Hurst, "A Footnote to Paul's Ephesian Ministry," *ExpTim* 43 (February 1932): 235–36; G. S. Duncan, "Some Outstanding New Testament Problems. VI. The Epistles of the Imprisonment in Recent Discussion," *ExpTim* 46 (April 1935): 293–98; idem, "Important Hypotheses Reconsidered VI. Were Paul's Imprisonment Epistles Written from Ephesus?" *ExpTim* 67 (March 1956): 163–66; Donald T. Rowlingson, "Paul's Ephesian Imprisonment: An Evaluation of the Evidence," *ATR* 32 (January 1950): 1–7; Michael Fieger, *Im Schatten der Artemis: Glaube and Ungehorsam in Ephesus* (Bern: Peter Lang, 1998), 157–63. For a recent and lengthy discussion regarding an Ephesian imprisonment, see Thiessen, *Christen in Ephesus*, 111–42.

2. Duncan, *St. Paul's Ephesian Ministry*, 126–31.

3. Guthrie, *New Testament Introduction*, 490–91.

4. Abraham J. Malherbe, "The Beasts at Ephesus," *JBL* 87 (March 1968): 71–80.

5. Duncan, *St. Paul's Ephesian Ministry*, 144–61, 184–216, 298–99. His view of these imprisonments has altered somewhat in later publications. See idem, "Important

reasonable to assume that if they occurred during his time in Ephesus, Luke would have mentioned them because he devotes much space to Paul's ministry in that city. Luke does mention the riot headed by Demetrius but yet nothing of an imprisonment. Furthermore, if imprisonment did occur in Ephesus, it seems strange that there is no reference to it in the Book of Ephesians. Third, the argument for the Ephesian imprisonment is also used for the Caesarean imprisonment in connection with interchange between the Philippian church and the imprisoned Paul. As outlined above in the discussion of a Caesarean imprisonment, it was argued that the six interchanges between the Philippian church and the imprisoned Paul could more easily have been achieved between Philippi and Ephesus than between Philippi and Rome because the distance would not have been as great. Hence, it would more easily fit within the two-year imprisonment. It is true that Ephesus is closer to Philippi than is Rome but the difference in travel time is not as great as one might suspect. The distance by land from Ephesus to Philippi is around 530 miles. Averaging between fifteen to twenty miles per day on foot,[1] it could be traversed in twenty-five to thirty-five days. On the other hand, the distance from Rome to Brundisium is 360 miles, Brundisium to Dyrrachium or Aulona is about a two day journey by sea (75 miles), and Dyrrachium or Aulona to Philippi along the Via Egnatia is around 370 miles. This adds up to 800 miles which could be traversed in thirty-eight to fifty days. Thus, the several journeys can easily fit into the two-year imprisonment in Rome. Hemer notes: "Routes and opportunity, rather than mere distance, are crucial factors, and they point to Rome. Travel elsewhere was more likely to depend on long delays in chartering a passage."[2] Fourth, the extrabiblical materials, such as the Marcionite Prologue to Colossians, which reads, "The apostle already in chains writes to them from Ephesus," are used to support an Ephesian imprisonment but a careful examination of them does not make a convincing argument for this view.[3] Hence, the Ephesian im-

Hypotheses Reconsidered VI. Were Paul's Imprisonment Epistles Written from Ephesus?" 164–65; idem, "Paul's Ministry in Asia—the Last Phase," *NTS* 3 (May 1957): 211–18; idem, "Chronological Table to Illustrate Paul's Ministry in Asia," *NTS* 5 (October 1958): 43–45.

1. The number of miles one can travel by foot depended on weather and road conditions but 15–20 miles a day is reasonable. See Ramsay, "Roads and Travel (in NT)," 386; F. F. Bruce, "Travel and Communication (NT World)," in *ABD*, 6:650; Brian M. Rapske, "Acts, Travel and Shipwreck," in *The Book of Acts in Its Graeco-Roman Setting*, ed. David W. J. Gill and Conrad Gempf, The Book of Acts in Its First Century Setting, ed. Bruce W. Winter, I. Howard Marshall, and David W. J. Gill, vol. 2 (Grand Rapids: Eerdmans, 1994), 6.

2. Hemer, *The Book of Acts in the Setting of Hellenistic History*, 273–74.

3. For interaction in this area as well as other minor points of evidence, see C. H. Dodd, "The Mind of Paul: Change and Development," *BJRL* 18 (January 1934): 69–92; Maurice Jones, "The Epistles to the Captivity: Where Were They Written," *Exp* 8th ser., vol. 10 (October 1915): 289–316; Guthrie, *New Testament Introduction*, 489–95.

prisonment lacks sufficient evidence to be convincing. In Ephesus Paul ministered in the synagogue and in the lecture hall of Tyrannus, and although there was a riot caused by Demetrius there is no evidence of his imprisonment while in that city. Furthermore, Conti makes an incisive observation by noting the friendly attitude of some of the Asiarchs (τῶν Ἀσιαρχῶν) or provincial authorities towards Paul (Acts 19:31) as well as the town clerk's (ὁ γραμματεύς) defense of Paul against the crowd (19:35–40), making it further unlikely that he was imprisoned in Ephesus.[1] Due to this lack of convincing arguments, this theory has not been widely accepted among NT scholars.

In conclusion, the traditional Roman imprisonment has the best biblical support (Acts 25:6–28:31) and continues to be the view of most students of the NT.

The date of the composition of Ephesians is greatly affected by the different theories as to the place of Paul's imprisonment. A Caesarean imprisonment would date the writing sometime between 57 and 59, shortly after Paul's meeting with the elders in Miletus. On the other hand, an Ephesian imprisonment would place the writing of Ephesians in the spring of 55 while he was in Ephesus. In accepting a Roman imprisonment, Ephesians would have been written after his imprisonment in Caesarea (57–59), hence, in the years 60–62.

To date the writing of Ephesians more specifically than his two-year imprisonment in Rome is conjectural but helpful. In an attempt to narrow the date of the Ephesian composition the other Prison Epistles need to be considered. Colossians was sent with Tychicus and Onesimus (Col 4:7–9) and it is reasonable to think that the letter to Philemon was also sent at this time (Phlm 12). Paul instructed Philemon to prepare a guest room for him (Phlm 22) which may indicate an imminent release from prison and hence these epistles may have been written toward the end of his two-year imprisonment. In Phil 2:19, 24 Paul anticipated his release and, therefore, this letter was also written toward the end of his incarceration around the spring of A.D. 62. Nothing is mentioned in Ephesians regarding his release or his hope of visiting them soon. It is possible that this letter was written in the earlier part of his Roman imprisonment, hence, sometime in the latter part of A.D. 60. On the other hand, it is possible that Paul could have sent Ephesians when he sent Colossians because both mention that Tychicus (Eph 6:21; Col 4:7) would report of Paul's situation. This means that Ephesians may have been written toward the end of his Roman imprisonment, some time in late 61 or early 62.[2] Since it is unlikely that Tychicus was sent two different times, the lat-

1. Valentina Conti, "Paolo ad Efeso," *RivB* 37 (Luglio–Settembre 1989): 291–97, 301–3.

2. Hemer (*The Book of Acts in the Setting of Hellenistic History*, 274–75, 403) dates the composition of Ephesians and Colossians in early A.D. 60 and Philippians in the winter of 61–62.

ter view is more probable because of the mention of Tychicus in both letters and because the contents of Ephesians and Colossians are very similar.

Paul's Later Visits (62–67)

Paul's life and journeys after the close of the Book of Acts are uncertain and thus require conjecture. Apparently, Paul expected release from his two-year imprisonment in Rome for he indicates in his letter to Philemon that he expected to be released soon and to revisit his friends in the province of Asia. He urged Philemon to prepare a guest room for him (Phlm 22). If he were released from his Roman incarceration, the incidental references in the Pastorals indicate that he visited Macedonia (1 Tim 1:3), Crete (Titus 1:5), Nicopolis (probably the capital of Epirus) (Titus 3:12), and Asia (2 Tim 4:13, 20). The data in the Pastorals cannot be placed into any period of Paul's life before his imprisonment. For example, the directions of Paul's travel in the Pastorals will not fit with those recorded in the Book of Acts. Thus, the time of Paul's visits to these various places is impossible to determine with any certainty though it seems probable that Paul was released in the spring of 62 and traveled to Macedonia (1 Tim 1:3) remaining there for a good part of a year. It was from Macedonia that Paul addressed Timothy (1 Tim 1:2–3) who was residing in Ephesus. After this it is likely that he spent some time in Spain (Rom 15:24, 28), possibly two years (64–66) and then returned to the East, to Crete (Titus 1:5), Nicopolis (Titus 3:12), and Asia (2 Tim 4:13, 20) before he was arrested and brought to Rome (2 Tim 1:8; 2:9) and executed.

Purpose of Ephesians

Since no particular problem is raised in the book, there has been much discussion over the years on the purpose of Ephesians. When one doubts its authorship, destination, audience, and date of composition, the problem of purpose becomes even more complex. As mentioned above, many suggestions have been proposed such as a theological tract, a wisdom discourse, an early Christian hymn, a baptismal or eucharistic liturgy, or a sermon written by a disciple of Paul or someone who was familiar with Pauline literature (see pp. 74–76). After some discussion, it was concluded that the destination of the letter was Ephesus and the surrounding communities and that Paul the apostle wrote the epistle while imprisoned in Rome. Hence, Paul was addressing people in Asia Minor among whom he had ministered for a period of two-and-a-half to three years (A.D. 53–56) as well as a few days spent with the Ephesian elders at Miletus in the spring of 57.

Having resolved the destination and the authorship questions, the problem of the purpose of the letter is still open for discussion. This problem is not unique to Ephesians. Certainly the Pauline letters such as Galatians, Philippians, and Colossians either explicitly state or their contents reveal the purpose of each. However, this is not always the case. Very few scholars have ever doubted the destination or Pauline authorship of Romans and yet there is a great deal of discussion regarding the purpose of that letter.[1] In fact, Dunn suggests that Paul had several reasons for writing the Roman epistle and there is no reason for him to have had only one purpose in view.[2] This is understandable, for more than one purpose could be listed for other letters of Paul. For example, in 1 Corinthians Paul instructs the recipients on a number of issues and also answers several questions they had raised. This is not entirely foreign to present-day letter writing. However, normally in writing a letter, there is a primary reason or purpose though there may also be subsidiary purposes included.

In the literature concerning the Book of Ephesians various suggestions regarding its purpose have been proposed. As previously stated, some think the letter was written to teach some aspect of church liturgy. Dahl suggests that the letter instructs the newly converted Gentiles on the meaning of their baptism.[3] Kirby suggests that Ephesians presents a renewal of baptismal vows, probably at the Feast of Pentecost.[4] The proponents of this view, however, do not explain why, if this epistle's concern is about baptismal liturgy, there is only one reference to baptism (4:5) and this very reference is not concerned about the ritual of baptism but rather is about one of the elements of unity in the Christian faith.[5] These proposals present very limited purposes for the composition of the book. Considering a broader purpose, Robinson suggests the Book of Ephesians emphasizes that God's purpose for the human race is its unity in Christ exhibited in the corporate life of the church.[6] Chadwick enlarges on this by stating that the epistle stresses

1. For a discussion on the purpose of Romans, see John W. Drane, "Why Did Paul Write Romans?" in *Pauline Studies. Essays Presented to F. F. Bruce on His 70th Birthday*, ed. Donald A. Hagner and Murray J. Harris (Grand Rapids: Eerdmans; London: Paternoster, 1980), 208–27; A. J. M. Wedderburn, *The Reasons for Romans* (Minneapolis: Fortress, 1991). For several articles devoted to this issue, see Karl P. Donfried, ed., *The Romans Debate* (Minneapolis: Augsburg, 1977; reprint, Peabody, Mass.: Hendrickson, 1991).

2. James D. G. Dunn, *Romans 1–8*, WBC, ed. David A. Hubbard and Glenn W. Barker; New Testament ed. Ralph P. Martin, vol. 38A (Dallas: Word, 1988), lv.

3. Dahl, "Adresse und Proömium des Epheserbriefes," 261–64; updated in idem, *Studies in Ephesians*, 325–27; idem, "Gentiles, Christians, and Israelites in the Epistle to the Ephesians," 38; updated in idem, *Studies in Ephesians*, 447; cf. also Schille, "Liturgisches Gut im Epheserbrief," 113–51; Wolfgang Nauck, "Eph. 2,19–22—ein Tauflied?" *Ev*T 13 (Juli/August 1953): 362–71.

4. Kirby, *Ephesians, Baptism and Pentecost*, 145–61.

5. Chrys C. Caragounis, *The Ephesian* Mysterion: *Meaning and Content*, Coniectanea Biblica New Testament Series, vol. 8 (Lund: Gleerup, 1977), 46 n. 83; Arnold, *Ephesians: Power and Magic*, 135.

6. Robinson, 14.

unity of the church and thus demonstrates to the non-Pauline churches their need for unity with the Pauline churches and the Jewish Christians.[1] Similarly, Schmithals suggests that the Pauline communities were to accept the Jewish Christians who had been ousted from the synagogue after Jerusalem's destruction and were also to instruct them regarding the Pauline tradition.[2] Granted there is emphasis on the unity of the church in the epistle, but one is hard-pressed to find any reference to the distinction between Pauline and non-Pauline churches. Also, nothing in Ephesians suggests that the Jewish Christians were under the synagogue's influence. Furthermore, Ephesians seems to argue that the Gentiles needed to feel accepted within the community of faith rather than the Jewish believers needed to be accepted by Gentile Christians. Pokorný thinks the author attempted to refute several Gnostic tendencies.[3] Smith suggests that the author attempted to refute Gentiles who embraced a speculative type of Judaism before their conversion to Christianity and had become arrogant toward the Jews who had become Christians.[4] However, there does not seem to be an apologetic or polemical tone in this letter and these problems are not at all obvious and neither are they really addressed.[5]

Barth sees the Ephesian situation much like the parable of the prodigal son where the son (like the Gentiles) returns not only to the father and the servants but also to the older son (analogous to Israel) who never left home. He claims that the Book of Ephesians shows that Gentiles who were alienated have come into the household of God and must learn to know and obey God "in Christ" by observing what God had done for Israel.[6] However, it is difficult to see this scenario from the text of Ephesians. Furthermore, both Jews and Gentiles needed reconciliation to God (Eph 2:17–18).

Fischer suggests that there was a new episcopacy among the Gentile churches in Asia Minor and that a growing number of Gentile believers despised Jewish Christianity. He suggests that the Book of Ephesians combats this by showing that the church is built on the foundation of the apostles and prophets (4:11–14).[7]

1. Henry Chadwick, "Die Absicht des Epheserbriefes," ZNW 51, nos. 3/4 (1960): 145–53.

2. Walter Schmithals, "The *Corpus Paulinum* and Gnosis," in *The New Testament and Gnosis: Essays in Honour of Robert McL. Wilson*, ed. A. H. B. Logan and A. J. M. Wedderburn (Edinburgh: T & T Clark, 1983), 122.

3. Petr Pokorný, *Der Epheserbrief und die Gnosis. Die Bedeutung des Haupt-Glieder-Gedankens in der entstehenden Kirche* (Berlin: Evangelische Verlagsanstalt, 1965), 21; Pokorný, 43–46.

4. Derwood C. Smith, "The Ephesian Heresy and the Origin of the Epistle to the Ephesians," *OJRS* 5 (October 1977): 78–103.

5. Cf. Lincoln, lxxx.

6. Barth, "Conversion and Conversation," 3–24, esp. 3–5, 24; Barth, 47–48, 58–59.

7. Karl Martin Fischer, *Tendenz und Absicht des Epheserbriefes*, FRLANT, ed. Ernst Käsemann and Ernst Würthwein, vol. 111 (Göttingen: Vandenhoeck & Ruprecht, 1973), 21–39, 79–94.

Yet, there is really nothing in the letter about bishops or deacons and there is nothing of a polemic to indicate that the Gentile Christians despised Jewish Christianity.[1] Along similar lines Martin proposes that the Gentile Christians thought they were independent of Israel and were thus intolerant of the Jewish believers. Martin also suggests that the Gentile Christians misunderstood Paul's teaching and adopted an easygoing moral code (Rom 6:1–12).[2] Again, the text does not necessitate there being a Gentile intolerance toward the Jewish Christians. Furthermore, there is nothing in the text to imply that the Ephesians had a perverted understanding of Paul's teaching on morals. If such were true, it is more likely that the author of Ephesians would have attacked the problem more directly as in 1 Corinthians. Curiously, to support his thesis Martin does not even cite from Ephesians but from Romans. Biguzzi thinks this is an ecumenical letter whereby Jewish Christians plead with Gentile Christian churches not to go their separate way but maintain the peace that was accomplished by Christ.[3] Although individual believing Jews and Gentiles are to maintain unity, there is nothing directly addressed in the book regarding reconciliation of Jewish and Gentile churches.

Lindemann proposes that the believers in Asia Minor were under the Domitian persecution (A.D. 96), suggested by both the military imagery in 6:10–20 and the letter's offer of consolation and encouragement.[4] This, however, is unlikely, for taking up the armor of God does not require a specific persecution. Rather, it is describing the preparations necessary for the spiritual warfare of every believer against the hostile powers of the devil.[5]

Arnold views Ephesians as a pastoral letter that addresses a group of churches in western Asia Minor who had been steeped in the evil spiritual "powers" of the cult of the Ephesian Artemis.[6] He argues that during Paul's two-and-a-half year ministry in Ephesus new converts to Christianity were added and that these new converts were in great fear of the oppressive spiritual "powers" that had plagued them during the time in which they had practiced the religion of the great Artemis. Although they had given up the magical practices and burned their magical papyri (Acts 19:18–19), some of the believers may have

1. Cf. Schnackenburg, 33; Lincoln, lxxx.

2. Martin, "Ephesians," in *The Broadman Bible Commentary*, 126; Martin, *Ephesians, Colossians, and Philemon*, 5.

3. Giancarlo Biguzzi, "Efesini: la misteriosa lettera del muro abbattuto," *Estudios bíblicos* 58, no. 3 (2000): 347–64, esp. 353–58.

4. Lindemann, "Bemerkungen zu den Adressaten," 242–43; Lindemann, 14–15.

5. Schnackenburg, 33–34; Lincoln, lxxx–lxxxi.

6. Arnold, *Ephesians: Power and Magic*, 123–24, 167–72; idem, "Ephesians, Letter to the," 246.

been tempted to syncretize their past magical beliefs and practices with their new-found Christian faith.

Along with this there may have been aberrant teaching about the role of Christianity in connection with these evil "powers." Though there is mention of "powers" in the other letters of Paul (Rom 8:38; 1 Cor 2:6–8; 10:19–21; 15:24–26; Gal 4:3, 9; Phil 2:10) it is more prominent in Ephesians. He proposes that Paul writes this letter to instruct believers in how to deal with those "powers" that were so pervasive in that community. Arnold presents six points to substantiate his idea. Here, they are condensed into three points. First, Paul emphasizes the superiority of the power of God who brings all things, including the evil cosmic powers, under the authority of Christ. Second, the great power of God is available to all believers and thus they do not need to seek additional protection against those powers that once enslaved them and now desire to reassert control over them. They do not need to resort to pagan ritual and practices but rather appropriate this power of God by appropriating his armor through faith and prayer. Third, believers are to realize that supernatural power through magical ritual and practice is for selfish ends, but the supernatural power of God enables believers not only to resist the devil but also to strengthen them to love others as patterned by Christ.

Arnold's scenario provides some valuable insights to the text of Ephesians, but there is insufficient evidence from the letter itself to support this as the main purpose of the letter.[1] Although Arnold feels that his arguments explain the prominence of the power-motif, even he admits that it "is not sufficient to give a full account of the reasons Ephesians was written, or sufficient to explain all of the theological peculiarities of the epistle."[2] Also, his view is based on sources primarily from Egypt that date mostly in the third and fourth century A.D.,[3] and one must be careful not to assume the practices of the third and fourth centuries were exactly the same as those in the first century and that the practices in Egypt were identical with those in Ephesus. This is the same criticism that was leveled against those who impose a second- or third-century Gnosticism on the first century. Furthermore, as Strelan has pointed out, there is no evidence that the Ephesians considered Artemis as evil and demonic.[4]

Schnackenburg suggests two interests: "the idea of the internal unity of the congregation which is intensified by the motif of the one Church founded by Jesus Christ and inseparably bound to him; and the concept of a commitment, growing out of God's calling, to a distinctly Christian way of life which should be distinguished from and

1. Lincoln, lxxxi; Schnackenburg, 33.
2. Arnold, *Ephesians: Power and Magic*, 168.
3. Ibid., 16–17.
4. Strelan, *Paul, Artemis, and the Jews in Ephesus*, 83–85.

contrasted to the unchristian life-style of the environment."[1] Along similar lines Bruce thinks that the letter was written to encourage the Gentile believers to appreciate their heavenly calling and destiny and to walk worthy of that calling.[2] Much of the content of this letter reveals these themes but so do many other of Paul's epistles. O'Brien suggests that the central message of the Ephesians is the cosmic reconciliation and unity in Christ, emerging initially from Eph 1:9–10 where the mystery of God is made known that at the fullness of time God will unite all things in Christ.[3]

Lincoln agrees that the letter addresses broad Christian principles but cautions against attempting to suggest a specific setting for the letter or concluding that there is a specific purpose for the epistle.[4] There is good reason for this conclusion in light of Lincoln's uncertainty regarding the author, the destination, the audience, and the date of its composition. Nonetheless, after he states his caution, Lincoln attempts to reconstruct the situation. He thinks the author was a disciple of Paul writing to second-generation Gentile Christians in Asia Minor whose hopes of the parousia were fading and who needed to grasp who they were in Christ. Thus, they were exhorted to conduct a distinctive lifestyle among those in the world through the power of Christ and the Holy Spirit.[5] This would make it a multipurpose letter that would be applicable to a wide spectrum of believers.

Lincoln's caution against attributing a specific setting and a specific purpose to this letter may be justified. Even those who are convinced of its author, destination, audience, and date of composition should be careful not to be dogmatic about a particular setting or purpose since the letter does not explicitly address a specific problem. One needs only to observe the differences among commentators and students of Ephesians to see that none of them agree on the purpose of this book. Nevertheless, scholars are in agreement regarding certain themes present in the book.

Certainly one theme on which most commentators agree is unity. Patzia has made a good contribution in this area[6] and elements of his research are reflected below, although at times with different statistics.

1. The word "unity" (ἑνότης) is used nowhere else in the NT except Ephesians (4:3, 13).

1. Schnackenburg, 34; Fay, "Paul the Empowered Prisoner," 494. For a discussion of Arnold's and Schnackenburg's views regarding the purpose of Ephesians, see J. H. Roberts, "The Enigma of Ephesians—Rethinking Some Positions on the Basis of Schnackenburg and Arnold," *Neot* 27, no. 1 (1993): 93–106.

2. Bruce, 245.

3. O'Brien, 56–65.

4. Lincoln, lxxxi–lxxxiii; cf. also Muddiman, 40–41.

5. Ibid., lxxxiii–lxxxvii.

6. Patzia, 133–39.

2. The term "one" (ἐν) expresses unity and is used fourteen times: "the both one" (2:14); "one new person" (2:15); "one body" (2:16; 4:4); "one Spirit" (2:18; 4:4); "one hope" (4:4); "one Lord" (4:5); "one faith" (4:5); "one baptism" (4:5); "one God and Father" (4:6); "each one of us" (4:7); "each individual part" (4:16); and "each one of you" (5:33).
3. The phrases "in Christ" (ἐν Χριστῷ), "in whom" (ἐν ᾧ), "in the Lord" (ἐν κυρίῳ), or similar expressions (see Excursus 3: In Christ) occur thirty-eight times in Ephesians and indicate the means by whom or the sphere in whom the unity is achieved.[1]
4. The preposition σύν, "with, together with," is combined with fourteen words. Three times these compound words denote the union between Christ and the believers such as God "made us alive together with (συζωοποιέω) Christ" in 2:5, he "raised us up with (συνεγείρω) Christ," and he "seated us with him (συγκαθίζω) in the heavenly places" in 2:6. The remaining eleven of these combinations refer to the union of Jewish and Gentile believers. These believers are "joined/fitted together" (συναρμολογέω) in 2:21 and 4:16 and "are being built together" (συνοικοδομέω) in 2:22. Believers are portrayed in 4:16 as being "held together" (συμβιβάζω) and in 4:3 they are enjoined to maintain between them the "bond of peace" (σύνδεσμος). They are described in 2:19 as "fellow citizens" (συμπολῖτης) and in 3:6 as "fellow heirs" (συγκληρονόμος), and "fellow members of the body" (σύσσωμος), and "fellow participants of the promise" (συμμέτοχος). Negatively, the believers are not to become fellow participants (συμμέτοχος) with unbelievers (5:7) and are not to participate (συγκοινωνέω) in the unfruitful works of darkness (5:11).
5. This unity is found in the church (ἐκκλησία), a term that is used nine times in the book (1:22; 3:10, 21; 5:23, 24, 25, 27, 29, 32).
6. The church is described "by various metaphors: biological (the body of Christ: 1:22, 23; 2:16; 4:4, 12, 16; 5:23, 30), architectural (the holy temple: 2:20–22; 4:12, 16), and social (the bride: 5:21–33)."[2]
7. The church is depicted as the body which is united under Christ, its head (1:22; 4:15; 5:23), similar to Col 1:18 and 2:19. This is a development in Pauline thought. In 1 Cor 12:12–26 and Rom 12:4–5 the head is considered as simply being one of the members of the body, whereas in Ephesians and Colossians the individual believers are members of the body, the church, who are united under the head, Christ.[3]

1. Cf. John A. Allan, "The 'In Christ' Formula in Ephesians," *NTS* 5 (October 1958): 54–62.

2. Patzia, 133.

3. Koehler suggests that the theme is the church united in Christ, see Joh. Ph. Koehler, "The Real Theme of the Epistle of Ephesians [trans. Irwin J. Habeck]," *WLQ* 65 (April 1968): 116–32 (originally published in German in*TQ* 13 [April 1916]: 103–19).

Unity, then, is a very prominent theme in Ephesians, expressed in the various ways discussed above. But how is this unity to be achieved? Forced unity is unacceptable because it is not genuine; thus, unity must originate from within.

True unity is accomplished when people love one another. The theme of "love" is dominant in Ephesians. Love, both in the verb and noun forms, is found twenty times. The verb form (ἀγαπάω) occurs ten times in Ephesians out of a total of thirty-four times in all of the Pauline letters (including the Pastorals). Hence, nearly one third of all of its occurrences in Pauline literature is in Ephesians. In other words, it occurs 4.12 times out of a thousand words of text but it only appears 0.80 times out of a thousand words in all the other Pauline letters. Outside of Ephesians, the verb appears most frequently in Romans (a much larger book) where it occurs only eight times. The noun form (ἀγάπη) also occurs ten times in Ephesians out of a total of seventy-five times in all of Paul's letters. Hence, one out of every seven-and-a-half times Paul uses the noun, he utilizes it in Ephesians. Regarding the frequency, it again occurs 4.12 times out of a thousand words of text of Ephesians whereas it appears 2.18 times out of a thousand words in all the other letters of Paul. With the exception of 1 Corinthians (occurs fourteen times, nine times in chap. 13), the noun is used more frequently in Ephesians than in the other books attributed to Paul. Combining the noun and verb usage, these words occur twenty times in Ephesians out of one hundred and nine appearances in all of Paul's literature, that is, about one fifth of all their appearances occur in this small letter. In other words, out of every thousand words, the noun or verb occurs 8.23 times in Ephesians whereas they appear in all the other Pauline letters 3.31 times out of a thousand words of text. Hence, the noun or verb form occurs more than twice as many times per thousand words of text in Ephesians than in all the other Pauline letters.

The frequent occurrence of the term love in such a short book is phenomenal. The usage of this term can be divided into four parts. First, out of the twenty times the word appears, five times it refers to God's love, namely, to God's great love for humans (2:4*bis*), to believers being rooted and grounded in God's love (3:17), and to the love and faith that come from God (6:23). The only other link with God is the unique usage in 1:6 where Christ is called "the beloved one," which expresses God's love for Christ. Second, there are three references made to Christ's love. Paul prays that the believer might experience or know Christ's love (3:19), the believer is enjoined to walk in love just as also Christ loved us and gave himself for us (5:2), and Paul enjoins the husband to love his wife as Christ loved the church and gave himself for her (5:25). Third, eleven times it refers to the believers' love for one another. The first half of the book discloses that God chose us in him before the foundation of the world in order that we might be holy and blameless before him in love (1:4). Thus, the believer's conduct should exhibit holiness and blamelessness, with love for one another. Paul states that he had heard of their faith in the Lord Jesus and their love toward all the saints (1:15). Moving into the practical section of the book, "love" is used nine times as Paul exhorts them to love one another. After exhorting them to walk worthy of their calling, he enjoins them to forebear one another in love (4:2); to be truthful with love (4:15); to contribute in the growth of the body so that the body will be built up in love (4:16); and to walk in love just as Christ loved us (5:2). He exhorts the husbands to love their wives as Christ loved the church (5:25, 28*ter,* 33). Fourth, there is a singular reference to the believer's love for Christ in the benediction of grace where it addresses those who unceasingly love our Lord Jesus Christ (6:24).

To summarize it in another way, out of the twenty occurrences of love in Ephesians, there are eight instances of God's or Christ's love for humans, eleven occurrences of the believers' love for one another, and one mention of a person's love of Christ.[1] This frequent use of love seems to furnish the key to the purpose of the book. Apparent are both God's love for people and the believer's love for one another within the new community. Love in action within the community of believers fosters unity, the other prominent theme. Unity without love is possible, but love without unity is not. Love is the central ingredient for true unity, laying the foundation for internal and external unity.

The theme of love is further substantiated when one considers Paul's contacts with the Ephesians. For instance, on the return from his third missionary journey Paul told the Ephesian elders at Miletus (A.D. 57) how he had labored in love by teaching, preaching, and giving. He also warned them to beware of the evil teachers from without and of the professing believers within who would teach perverse things (Acts 20:18–35).[2] After his imprisonment Paul reiterated the theme of love when he wrote from Macedonia to Timothy at Ephesus (ca. A.D. 62), stating that the goal of his instruction was "love that issues from a pure heart and a good conscience and a sincere faith" (1 Tim 1:5). He again warns them of false teachers and their teachings (1:3–20). Hence, Paul's ministry to the Ephesians continually emphasized love.

Except for Paul, the only other time the Ephesian church is addressed is in Rev 2:1–7 (ca. A.D. 95–96).[3] The messenger compliments

1. Barth thinks that the word "love" may sum up the ecclesiology of Ephesians by furnishing the two pillars of the Christian life: love toward God and love toward fellowman, cf. Barth, "Conversion and Conversation," 4. However, this is untenable since there is only one reference to man's love toward God or Christ (6:24).

2. Cf. G. W. H. Lampe, "'Grievous Wolves' (Acts 20:29)," in *Christ and Spirit in the New Testament. In Honour of Charles Francis Digby Moule*, ed. Barnabas Lindars and Stephen S. Smalley (Cambridge: Cambridge University Press, 1973), 253–68.

3. An interesting discussion on the church at Ephesus in relation to Acts 20:18–35, 1 Tim 1, Ignatius' letter to the Ephesians, and Rev 2:1–7 is given by Rudolf Schnackenburg, "Ephesus: Entwicklung einer Gemeinde von Paulus zu Johannes," *BZ* 35, no. 1 (1991): 41–64.

them for their refusal to tolerate false teachers and teaching but reprimands them for their failure to maintain the vibrancy of their first love for Christ (Rev 2:2–6). Their doctrine of separation was the separation *from* the false teachers, but they forgot their separation *to* Christ. One can separate from the false teachers without love for Christ. However, if there is a love for Christ, there more likely will be a separation from false teaching. They had put the proverbial "cart before the horse." By concentrating first on their love for Christ, he would have imbued them with wisdom and power to separate themselves from false teachers and at the same time would have given them the ability and desire to love one another.

In conclusion, the theme of love has a dominant place within the Book of Ephesians and in the other instances where the Ephesian church is addressed. It seems reasonable to conclude that the purpose of Ephesians is to promote a love for one another that has the love of God and Christ as its basis. Paul approaches this very carefully because forced love is not genuine love. He uses the example of God's and Christ's love to the human race in general, and to believers in particular, which serve as the basis of the believers' love for one another. This provides the basis for unity. Possibly realizing that the Ephesians were starting to forsake their first love, Paul wrote this letter to encourage them to love both God and their fellow saints more deeply.

Theology of Ephesians

The teaching in Ephesians is considered the crown or quintessence of Paulinism because in large measure it summarizes the leading themes of the Pauline letters.[1] It is rich with theological themes, many of which are a rehearsal of Pauline theology developed elsewhere in his letters. Some areas of theology are refined or developed to new heights. This is due to further reflection on the subject as well as the necessity to meet the specific needs of the community to which the letter is addressed. Next, some of its theological themes are noted.[2]

Trinity

Ephesians is known as the Trinitarian letter. The activity of the three persons of the Trinity is found in eight passages (Eph 1:4–14, 17; 2:18, 22; 3:4–5, 14–17; 4:4–6; 5:18–20), which are now summarized. In

1. Dodd, 1224–25; Bruce, "St. Paul in Rome," 303.

2. For a discussion of the theology of Ephesians, see Lincoln and Wedderburn, *The Theology of the Later Pauline Letters*, 91–166; cf. also Pheme Perkins, "God, Cosmos & Church Universal: The Theology of Ephesians," in *Society of Biblical Literature 2000 Seminar Papers*, Society of Biblical Literature Seminar Paper Series, no. 39 (Atlanta: Society of Biblical Literature, 2000), 752–73.

the theological portion of the book (chaps. 1–3) Paul teaches that the Trinity is the basis on which spiritual benefits are bestowed on believers by means of the selection of the Father (1:4–6), the sacrifice of the Son (1:7–12), and the seal of the Holy Spirit (1:13–14). Later in the chapter God, who is the Father of our Lord Jesus Christ, gives insight about himself through the Holy Spirit (1:17). Furthermore, the three persons of the Trinity are involved in the access of believing Jews and Gentiles to God, that is, through the work of Christ, united in one Spirit, they have access to the Father (2:18). Hence, the initiation and continuation of a human being's relationship to God involves all three Persons of the Trinity. Paul speaks of God the Father as the one who creates the new person into a holy temple, Christ the Son whose reconciliation is the cornerstone of this new temple, and the Holy Spirit who is the manner by which God dwells in this new structure (2:22). In discussing the mystery Paul states that it is God the Father who reveals the mystery of Christ (believing Gentiles become one with believing Jews in Christ) by means of the Holy Spirit (3:4–5). Later Paul prays to the Father that the Ephesian believers might be strengthened by the Spirit with the result that Christ be permanently at home in them through faith (3:14–17). In the practical portion of the book there is also mention of the work of the Trinity. Paul exhorts believers to walk in unity and shows this by including the Trinity as an integral part in the treatise on unity (4:4–6). The one body of believers is vitalized by one Spirit, so all believers have one hope. That body is united to its one Lord by each member's one act of faith, and his or her identity with him is in the one baptism. One God, the Father, is supreme overall, operative through all, and resides in all. Finally, Paul states that the result of being filled by the Spirit is that believers give thanks to God the Father in the name of Jesus Christ our Lord (5:18–20).

Therefore, the work of Trinity is important in Ephesians. It is the Father to whom believers direct their prayers and the one who is over all and plans or initiates all things. It is the Son through whom believers pray and the one who carries out the Father's plan in redemption, reconciliation, and unification of believers. The Holy Spirit is the one who seals, indwells, and empowers believers. There is need to examine each of these divine persons in more detail.

Fatherhood of God

There are forty references to God as Father in Paul's letters and more references to God as Father in Ephesians than in the other letters: eight times in Ephesians (1:2, 3, 17; 2:18; 3:14–15; 4:6; 5:20; 6:23) whereas only four times each in Romans, Galatians, Colossians, and 1 Thessalonians; three times each in 1 Corinthians, 2 Corinthians, Philippians, and 2 Thessalonians; twice in 1 Timothy; and once each in Philemon and Titus. He is named the Father of glory, the God of our Lord Jesus Christ and proclaimed the Father of all revelation (1:17). He is not only the Father from whom every family in heaven and on earth originates and is named (3:15) but more particularly, as the Father of all believers, he is above all, through all, and in all (4:6) and is in a peculiar sense the Father of our Lord Jesus Christ (1:3). Furthermore, as the Father he bestows grace and peace (1:2; 6:23). It is to him that believers bless or give praise because he has blessed them with all spiritual blessings by choosing them and predetermining their destiny as adopted ones in his family through Jesus Christ (1:3–6). It is to him as Father that believers pray in the name of Christ and in the power of the Spirit (2:18; 3:14; 5:20). Hence, God the Father plays an important role for all in the universe but particularly for believers who are the recipients of his grace and who are to pray to him and praise him for his work on their behalf.

Christology

With the exception of Philippians, 2 Thessalonians, 1 and 2 Timothy, and Philemon, the designations of "Jesus Christ" or "Christ Jesus" occur more frequently per thousand words of text in Ephesians (eighteen times) than in other Pauline epistles.[1] Furthermore, the designation "Christ," when used alone, occurs more frequently per thousand words of text in Ephesians (twenty-six times) than in any other of Paul's letters except Colossians. On the other hand, except for Romans and the Pastorals, the name "Jesus," when used alone, is less frequent per thousand words of text in Ephesians (two times) than in other Pauline epistles. However, the article prefixing the noun "Christ" indicates a title and not only as a name occurs more frequently per thousand words of text in Ephesians (twenty-three times) than in other Pauline epistles (Colossians is a close second).[2] Hence, the use of the term "Christ" is very prominent in the book.

Ephesians 1:13 and 17 state that God is the Father of our Lord Jesus Christ, demonstrating that Christ is distinct from the Father and also affirming him as the Son of God (4:13). He is called the "beloved" (1:6), which is a messianic title demonstrated by the voice from heaven at Christ's baptism (Matt 3:17 = Mark 1:11 = Luke 3:22) and transfiguration (Matt 17:5 = Mark 9:7). The eternity of the Lord is distinctly asserted by the statement that he is the one who existed before the foundation of the world (1:4–5, 11). Jesus is the Christ (1:15; 4:20–21) and Lord (1:2–3, 15, 17; 3:11; 4:5; 5:20; 6:23–24) who became flesh (2:14), died on the cross (2:13, 16; 5:2, 25), was raised from the dead by God (1:20), is now seated at the right hand of God in the heavens (1:20; 4:8), gives gifted people to the church (4:8–11), and gives hope to believers (1:12; 2:12). Christ's divinity is affirmed by the declaration that he has provided redemption for believers (1:7; 2:13; 5:2, 23), that

1. Interestingly, these designations are among the least frequent in Colossians, a fact which would seem unlikely if Ephesians had been written by a Paulinist who was copying from Colossians.

2. Best, 49–50.

is, the forgiveness of sins (1:7; 5:23) which, as the religious leaders had protested to Jesus, is the prerogative of God only (Mark 2:7, 10 = Luke 5:21, 24). Believers are to place their faith in him as their Lord (1:15; 4:5; cf. 3:12). In addition, he reconciles believers to himself and believing Jews and Gentiles to each other (2:16). The Father's predestination of believers to adoption as sons is through Christ (1:5) and believers pray to the Father through Christ (2:18; 5:20). His sovereignty is averred not only as the church's head and the cornerstone of the holy temple wherein the Spirit dwells (2:20–22), but also as the one who has subjected all of God's creation, animate and inanimate, human and angelic, under his feet (1:22) and, in the future, all of creation will be united under him (1:10). Christ is filled with God's fullness (1:23) and fills the church with that fullness (4:10). He possesses unfathomable wealth (3:8) and is with the Father the source of grace (1:2, 7–8). Therefore, Christ, eternal and divine, is not only the cosmic head of all things[1] but also head of the church. Redemption from sin, reconciliation to God, and access to the Father are accomplished through him. The Christology in Ephesians is similar to that of Colossians and is in agreement with the rest of Pauline literature.

Pneumatology

Except for Galatians "Spirit" is used more frequently per thousand words of text in Ephesians (fourteen times) than in any other of Paul's letters. Of these fourteen times only twice does it refer to human spirit (2:2; 4:23). Outside of 2 Thessalonians and Titus the designation of Holy Spirit is used more frequently per thousand words of text in Ephesians than in any other of Paul's letters. Hence, the Spirit plays an important role in Ephesians.

The divinity of the Spirit is asserted when believers are instructed not to grieve the Holy Spirit of God (4:30). As the glory of the Lord filled the tabernacle (Exod 40:34–35) and later the temple (1 Kgs 8:11; 2 Chr 5:14; 7:1–3) in OT times, now in NT times the Spirit of God indwells the new temple, the church, which is the new dwelling place of God (Eph 2:22). He is identified as the promised Holy Spirit (1:13). Joel 2:28–29 specifically makes a promise of God's Spirit for all believers in the new age and in Ezek 36:26–27; 37:14 the promise of the Spirit is given in conjunction with the inauguration of the new covenant. Furthermore, Jesus promised the Spirit to his disciples (Luke 24:49; John 14:16–17; 15:26; cf. also 16:13); believers after Pentecost recognized the fulfillment of this promise (Acts 2:33; Gal 3:14). The basis of the unity of the church is the Trinity (Eph 4:3–6) which affirms the Holy Spirit's divinity and identification with as well as his distinction from the other two persons of the Trinity. The Holy Spirit reveals the person and character of God (1:17) and is also the means

1. Cf. Molly T. Marshall, "The Fullness of Incarnation: God's New Humanity in the Body of Christ," *RevExp* 93 (spring 1996): 189–91.

of revelation of the mystery to his holy apostles and prophets (3:5). He is also identified as God's spoken word to be used against the wicked hosts of the devil (6:17). Furthermore, believers are sealed with the Holy Spirit until the day of redemption (1:13; 4:30) and is the means by which they are filled with God's moral excellence and power (5:18). They are to be empowered by him who is able to do far more than what they ask or think (3:16–20). They are instructed to pray to the Father through Christ in the power of the Spirit (2:18; 6:18).

Hence, the Holy Spirit plays a prominent role in that he reveals the person and message of God and empowers believers to be like Christ and to pray to the Father. The Spirit not only seals believers to indicate God's ownership of them but also he is the means by which believers are filled with God's fullness. Thus, the pneumatology of Ephesians aligns with the rest of the Pauline letters.

Soteriology

Having already discussed soteriology (pp. 50–52), only a brief treatment is needed on the subject. Although the usual terminology for justification is not used in Ephesians, it does not mean that the teaching of salvation in Ephesians is incongruent with other Pauline literature. Paul uses the noun δικαιοσύνη, "justification," and verb δικαιόω, "to justify," eighty-five times, forty-nine times in Romans, twelve times in Galatians, ten times in the Corinthian correspondence, seven times in the Pastorals, four times in Philippians, and three times in Ephesians. They do not appear in the Colossian or Thessalonian correspondence. Their most frequent usage is in the letters dealing specifically with justification. Clearly, the specific terms for justification are not needed in every Pauline book. Some consider the teaching in Eph 2:8–10 an able summary of Paul's doctrine of salvation by grace.[1] This salvation is based on God's grace by means of faith without works (cf. Rom 3:20, 28; 4:2, 6; 9:11, 32; 11:6). The Ephesians were instructed that they formerly had no relationship with God (Eph 2:1–3, 11–12), but that changed when they placed their faith in the work accomplished by Christ's death on the cross (1:7; 2:13, 16; 5:2, 25) with the result that they have access to God the Father (2:18; 3:12). Salvation is not only for the present time but will be consummated in the future since believers are sealed until the day of redemption (1:13–14; 4:30). In that future day the body of believers will be presented to Christ "without blemish or wrinkle or any such thing" (5:27).

Therefore, salvation is a rescue or deliverance from one's former state which means "the same thing as justification and reconciliation."[2] As elsewhere in Paul's writings good works or fruit are not a

1. Mitton, *The Epistle to the Ephesians*, 268–69; Mitton, 99–100; Marshall, "Salvation, Grace and Works in the Later Writings in the Pauline Corpus," 342–45.

2. Radl, "σῴζω," *EDNT* 3 (1993): 321; Best, 51–52.

basis but a result of salvation (Eph 2:10; Rom 6:22; Gal 5:22; Phil 1:11, 22; 4:17). Thus the teaching regarding salvation in Ephesians is, therefore, consistent with other Pauline literature.

Ecclesiology

The term ἐκκλησία, "church," appears nine times in Ephesians (1:22; 3:10, 21; 5:23, 24, 25, 27, 29, 32) where it refers to the universal church with the possible exception in 3:10 where it refers to both the universal and local church.[1] It is depicted biologically as a body: it portrays various members connected to one another as an organic unity in which there is growth (4:16), it is rescued and/or protected (5:23, 25), it is loved and nurtured (5:29), and its head is Christ (1:22; 5:23–24). The church is also described architecturally as the holy temple that has a foundation with Christ as the cornerstone and in which God dwells in the Spirit (2:20–22). As well, the church is viewed psychologically as a "new humanity" or "new person(ality)" (2:15; 4:13). It is also described sociologically as a family unit, the bride of Christ (5:23–32), as two hostile groups which have been reconciled (2:11–22), and as that which is at war with the evil spiritual powers (6:10–20).[2] Its physical location is in the heavenlies (1:3; 2:6), the abode of God (1:20), of Christ (1:3; 2:6), of angels (3:10), and of evil spiritual powers (6:10). The church is also described cultically whereby Christ sanctifies the church in order to present it to himself as glorious, without blemish or wrinkle in order that it might be holy and blameless (5:26–27).

Due to such descriptions of the church, some have contended that the ecclesiology of Ephesians reflects emergent catholicism.[3] However, as argued earlier, Ephesians gives no indication of the institutionalization of the church but rather it portrays the church as a growing and dynamic organism. Moreover, Paul uses universal motifs in his other letters when he refers not only to "the church of God which is in Corinth" but also to "all those who in every place call on the name of our Lord Jesus Christ" (1 Cor 1:2). In speaking of individual members whom God has appointed as apostles, prophets, teachers, and other functions (1 Cor 12:27–28; Rom 12:4–8) he does not seem to limit them to one local body (cf. Eph 4:11). Furthermore, though Ephesians refers to a future church which will be holy and

1. For a discussion of Ephesians' view of the church, see the excursus by Schnackenburg, 293–310; cf. also Rudolf Hoppe, "Theo-logie und Ekklesio-logie im Epheserbrief," *Münchener theologische Zeitschrift* 46, no. 2 (1995): 231–45; O'Brien, 25–29.

2. Cf. Metzger, "Paul's Vision of the Church, 53–54; S. F. B. Bedale, "The Theology of the Church," in *Studies in Ephesians*, ed. F. L. Cross (London: A. R. Mowbray, 1956), 64–75; Hoppe, "Theo-logie und Ekklesio-logie im Epheserbrief," 234–41.

3. Cf. Käsemann, "Ephesians and Acts," 288; cf. also idem, "The Theological Problem Presented," 102–21, esp. 120–21.

blameless (5:26–27), Paul also describes the Corinthian church in his day as God's holy temple (1 Cor 3:17) and as a pure bride (2 Cor 10:2). Hence, the terminology and descriptions used of the church in Ephesians are in keeping with other Pauline literature.

The church's existence and function are based on Christ's work (Eph 1:22; 5:2, 23–27, 29; cf. 1 Cor 1:2; 15:3). Its foundation is composed of apostles and prophets with Christ as the cornerstone (Eph 2:20–22). Christ loves and nourishes the church as a caring bridegroom (5:25–32) and has given gifted people to her for ministry—apostles, prophets, evangelists, and pastor/teacher (4:11)—so that she might not be led into error but continue to grow (4:11–16; cf. also 2:21; 3:18–19). Christ has not only rescued the church from evil powers (2:1–10; 5:23) but also gives enabling strength in order that she might comprehend Christ's love which, in turn, would result in love among fellow saints (3:16–21) and which will enable them to stand against the evil powers in the heavens who desire to rob the church of her blessings (6:10–20). The church is to be characterized by love (Eph 1:4, 15; 2:16; 4:15–16; 5:2, 25, 28–29; 6:23–24).

In conclusion, the church to which the author of Ephesians refers is primarily the universal church and not the local church. This may be due to the fact that it was a circular letter sent to Ephesus and the other churches in the area for the purpose of encouraging the unity of believers in all churches. Certainly Ephesians differs from the other Pauline letters. For example, the church in the other letters is referred to as the body of Christ (Rom 12:4–5; 1 Cor 12:12–13, 27), whereas in Ephesians and Colossians Christ is portrayed as the head of the body (Eph 1:22–23; 4:15–16; 5:23; Col 1:18, 24; 2:19). However, the use of the head and the body in the later letters is not contradictory but complementary. It is more complex and richer. The difference may be due to a further refinement in Paul's thinking occasioned by new situations and/or problems that needed to be addressed in a different way.

Reconciliation

Although reconciliation is taught in Paul's other letters, great emphasis and space is given to it in Ephesians. Beginning in chapter one Paul outlines the eternal plan of God designed to unite all things in Christ (Eph 1:10). Sin caused a great gulf between God and the human race, but by displaying his rich mercy and great love, God provided reconciliation, making it possible for believers to be seated with Christ in the heavenlies (2:1–10). Next, Paul discusses the need for reconciliation not only between God and humans, but also between Jews and Gentiles (2:11–22). Before both were brought near by the blood of Christ there was great hostility between these two groups. By God's grace "one new humanity," the church, was created. In this passage the theme of reconciliation is stressed by the expressions "made the both one" (2:14), "one new person" (2:15), "one body" (2:16), "both have access in one Spirit" (2:18), "fellow citizens" (2:19), "God's household" (2:19), "whole building" (2:21), and "a holy temple" (2:21).[1] It cannot be said that Paul is speaking about a reconciliation between Jews and Gentiles in general but a reconciliation between Jews and Gentiles who believe in Christ. Continuing, Paul explains that this new entity, the church, was not known in previous generations but now has been revealed by the Spirit to the apostles and prophets. Paul himself was commissioned to proclaim this new union to the Gentiles as the unfathomable wealth of Christ. This new entity was according to God's eternal purpose (3:1–12). Again the theme of reconciliation is seen in the expressions "fellow heirs, fellow members of the body, fellow participants of the promise" (3:6), and "we [believing Jews and Gentiles] have the boldness and access" (3:12). Paul then prays that believers might know the love of Christ that surpasses knowledge (3:17–19) desiring that the reconciliation is more than external but a reality of the heart.

The doctrine of reconciliation is developed further in the practical portion of the letter. Paul exhorts them to walk in unity (4:1–3), which is the evidence of reconciliation. This unity, based on the model of the Trinity (4:4–6), is accomplished by Christ who gives gifted individuals to the church (4:7–11) so that the corporate body of believing Jews and Gentiles might continue to be built up until "the unity of the faith" wherein each individual part causes the body to grow up in love (4:12–16). Believers are not to walk like the Gentiles but are to develop an honest and loving relationship with one another (4:17–5:14). They are to walk wisely by understanding the will of their Lord Christ and to be filled by the Spirit, which results in praising, singing, and giving thanks to God the Father through the Lord Jesus Christ—evidence of unity due to reconciliation (5:15–20). Reconciliation is seen in the exhortations within the household code regarding the relationships of wives with husbands, children with parents, and slaves with masters (5:21–6:9). Finally, reconciliation is also seen between the Lord and believers as well as among believers who need to be strengthened in the Lord to be able to stand against the evil spiritual powers in the heavens (6:10–20). Moreover, Paul asks the Ephesians to pray for him so that he might proclaim boldly the mystery of the gospel, that is, the reconciliation of believing Jews and Gentiles (6:18–20).

In conclusion, the theology of reconciliation is prominent in this letter. The heart of reconciliation is love. It is the love of God (2:4) and Christ (3:17–19; 5:2) that is the basis of reconciliation between God and mankind. Also, the reconciliation of believing Jews and Gentiles is to be characterized by love for one another (1:15; 3:17–19; 4:2, 15–

1. Martin, *Reconciliation: A Study of Paul's Theology*, 166–98, esp. 197–98; reprint, Martin, "Reconciliation and Unity in Ephesians," 210–35, esp. 233–34; William W. Klein, "Reading Ephesians: The Glory of Christ in the Church," *SWJT* 39 (fall 1996): 16.

16; 5:2, 25, 28, 33; 6:23). A reconciliation without love is hollow, but a reconciliation with love is a genuine reconciliation demonstrated by a change of heart and a mutual trust of one another.

Bibliography Regarding Authorship

If there is more than one entry for an author, they are listed in chronological order. The pagination following the bibliographic entry refer specifically to the issues of authorship.

Adai, Jacob. *Der Heilige Geist als Gegenwart Gottes in den einzelnen Christen, in der Kirche und in der Welt: Studien zur Pneumatologie des Epheserbriefes*. Frankfurt: Peter Lang, 1985, 17–24.

Albertz, Martin. *Die Botschaft des Neuen Testamentes*. Die Entstehung der Botschaft, vol. 1, pt. 2. Zollikon-Zürich: Evangelischer Verlag, 1952, 167–68.

Allan, John A. "The 'In Christ' Formula in Ephesians." *NTS* 5 (October 1958): 54–62.

Arnold, Clinton E. *Ephesians: Power and Magic. The Concept of Power in Ephesians in Light of Its Historical Setting*. SNTSMS, ed. G. N. Stanton, vol. 63. Cambridge: Cambridge University Press, 1989. Reprint, Grand Rapids: Baker, 1992, 171.

———. "Ephesians, Letter to the." In *DPL*, 238–46.

———. "Introducing Ephesians: Establishing Believers In Christ." *SWJT* 39 (fall 1996): 4–13.

Asting, Ragnar. *Die Heiligkeit im Urchristentum*. FRLANT, ed. Rud. Bultmann and Hermann Gunkel, vol. 46. Göttingen: Vandenhoeck & Ruprecht, 1930, 4–5, 106–8, 145–46, 168–78.

Bacon, Benjamin Wisner. *The Story of St. Paul: A Comparison of Acts and Epistles*. London: Hodder and Stoughton, 1905, 299–302.

Barker, Glenn Wesley. "A Critical Evaluation of the Lexical and Linguistic Data Advanced by E. J. Goodspeed and Supported by C. L. Mitton in a Proposed Solution to the Problem of the Authorship and Date of Ephesians." Th.D. diss., Harvard University, 1962.

———. "Ephesians, Letter of Paul to the." In *The Zondervan Pictorial Encyclopedia of the Bible*, ed. Merrill C. Tenney and Steven Barabas, vol. 2. Grand Rapids: Zondervan, 1975, 316–21.

Barrett, C. K. "Pauline Controversies in the Post-Pauline Period." *NTS* 20 (April 1974): 229–45.

———. *Paul: An Introduction to His Thoughts*. Outstanding Christian Thinkers Series, ed. Brian Davies. Louisville, Ky.: Westminster/John Knox; London: Geoffrey Chapman, 1994, 4, 154–57.

Barth, Markus. "Traditions in Ephesians." *NTS* 30 (January 1984): 3–25.

Barth, Markus, and Helmut Blanke. *Colossians*. Translated by Astrid B. Beck. AB, ed. William Foxwell Albright and David Noel Freedman, vol. 34B. New York: Doubleday, 1994, 114–26.

Bauckham, Richard. "Pseudo-Apostolic Letters." *JBL* 107 (September 1988): 469–94.

Baur, Ferdinand Christian. *Paul the Apostle of Jesus Christ, His Life and Work, His Epistles and His Doctrine. A Contribution to a Critical History of Primitive Christianity.* 2d ed. Edited after the author's death by Eduard Zeller. Translated by A. Menzies, vol. 2. Theological Translation Fund Library. London: Williams and Norgate, 1875, 1–44 [1st German ed., 1845, 417–57].

Beasley-Murray, G. R. "Introduction to the New Testament." In *A Companion to the Bible*, ed. H. H. Rowley. Edinburgh: T & T Clark, 1963, 104–6.

Benoit, Pierre. "L'horizon paulinien de l'Épître aux Ephésiens." *RB* 46 (Juillet 1937): 342–61; (Octobre 1937): 506–25.

———. "Rapports littéraires entre les épîtres aux Colessiens et aux Éphésiens." In *Neutestamentliche Aufsätze. Festschrift für Prof. Josef Schmid zum 70. Geburtstag*, ed. J. Blinzler, O. Kuss, and F. Mußner. Regensburg: Friedrich Pustet, 1963, 11–22.

———. "L'unité de l'Église selon l'épître aux Éphésiens." In *Studiorum Paulinorum Congressus Internationalis Catholicus 1961*, vol. 1, AnBib, vol. 17. Rome: E Pontificio Instituto Biblico, 1963, 55–77.

———. "Paul. Éphésiens (Épître aux)." In *Dictionnaire de la Bible*, Supplément, ed. Henri Cazelles and André Feuillet, vol. 7. Paris: Letouzey & Ané, 1966, 195–211.

Best, Ernest. *One Body in Christ. A Study in the Relationship of the Church to Christ in the Epistles of the Apostle Paul*. London: SPCK, 1955, x–xi, 141, 143, 156, 158.

———. "Ephesians i.1." In *Text and Interpretation: Studies in the New Testament Presented to Matthew Black*, ed. Ernest Best and R. McL. Wilson. Cambridge: Cambridge University Press, 1979, 29–41, esp. 38–39.

———. "Recipients and Title of the Letter to the Ephesians: Why and When the Designation 'Ephesians'?" In *ANRW*, pt. 2, vol. 25.4 (1987), 3247–79.

———. *Ephesians*. New Testament Guides, ed. A. T. Lincoln. Sheffield: JSOT Press, 1993.

———. "Who Used Whom? The Relationship of Ephesians and Colossians." *NTS* 43 (January 1997): 72–96.

Black, David Alan. "The Peculiarities of Ephesians and the Ephesian Address." *GTJ* 2 (spring 1981): 59–73.

Bleek, Friedrich. *An Introduction to the New Testament*. Edited by Johannes Friedrich Bleek. Translated from the 2d German ed. by William Urwick, vol. 2. Clarks Foreign Theological Library, vol. 26. Edinburgh: T & T Clark, 1869, 36–51 [1st German ed., 1862, 2:447–60].

Boismard, M.-E. *L'Énigme de la lettre aux Éphesiens*. EBib, no. 39. Paris: Gabalda, 1999, 9–180.

Bornkamm, Günther. *Paul*. Translated by M. G. Stalker. New York: Harper & Row, 1971, 242 [German ed., 1969, 246].

Bousset, "Paulusbriefe," In *Die Religion in Geschichte und Gegenwart: Handwörterbuch in gemeinverständlicher Darstellung*, ed. Hermann Gunkel et al., vol. 4. Tübingen: Mohr, 1913, 1335–36.

Bowen, Clayton R. "The Place of Ephesians among the Letters of Paul." *ATR* 15 (October 1933): 279–99.

Brandon, S. G. F. *The Fall of Jerusalem and the Christian Church: A Study of the Effects of the Jewish Overthrow of* A.D. *70 on Christianity*. 2d ed. London: SPCK, 1957, 215–16 [1st ed., 1951, same pages].

Brown, Raymond Bryan. "Ephesians among the Letters of Paul." *RevExp* 60 (fall 1963): 373–79.

Brown, Raymond E. "The Semitic Background of the New Testament *Mystery*." *Bib* 39, no. 4 (1958): 426–48; 40, no. 1 (1959): 70–87, esp. 74–84. Reprint, idem. *The Semitic Background of the Term "Mystery" in the New Testament*. Facet Books: Biblical Series, ed. John Reumann, vol. 21. Philadelphia: Fortress, 1968, 56–66.

———. *The Churches the Apostles Left Behind*. New York: Paulist; London: Geoffrey Chapman, 1984, 47–60.

———. *An Introduction to the New Testament*. The Anchor Bible Reference Library, ed. David Noel Freedman. New York: Doubleday, 1997, 627–30.

Brückner, Wilhelm. *Die chronologische Reihenfolge, in welcher die Briefe des Neuen Testaments verfasst sind insofern diese absuleiten ist: sowohl aus ihrer gegenseitigen Uebereinstimmung und gegenseitigen Verschiedenheit, als aus dem in den späteren Briefen gemachten Gebrauch von Worten and Citaten, die in den frühen vorkommen*. Haarlem: De Erven F. Bohn, 1890, 41–56, 257–76, esp. 271–76.

Buck, Charles H., Jr. "The Early Order of the Pauline Corpus." *JBL* 68 (December 1949): 351–57.

Bultmann, Rudolf. *Theology of the New Testament*. Translated by Kendrick Grobe, vol. 2. New York: Charles Scribner's Sons, 1955; London: SCM, 1955, 133–35, 175–80 [German ed., 1953, 479–80, 518–23].

Cadbury, H. J. "The Dilemma of Ephesians." *NTS* 5 (January 1959): 91–102.

Cadoux, C. J. "The Dates and Provenance of the Imprisonment Epistles of St. Paul." *ExpTim* 45 (July 1934): 471–73.

Carson, D. A., Douglas J. Moo, and Leon Morris. *An Introduction to the New Testament*. Grand Rapids: Zondervan, 1992, 305–16.

Case, Shirley Jackson. "To Whom Was 'Ephesians' Written?" *Biblical World* 38 (November 1911): 315–20.

Cerfaux, Lucien. "En faveur de l'authenticité des épîtres de la captivité. Homogénéité doctrinale entre Éphésiens et les Grandes Épîtres." In *Littérature et Théologie Pauliniennes. Recherches Bibliques*, vol. 5. Louvain: Descleé de Brouwe, 1960, 60–71.

———. "The Epistles of the Captivity." In *Introduction to the New Testament*, ed. A. Robert and A. Feuillet. Translated by Patrick W. Skehan et al. New York: Desclee, 1965, 471–509, esp. 493–509 [French ed., 1959].

———. *The Christian in the Theology of St. Paul*. Translated by Lilian Soiron. London: Geoffrey Chapman; New York: Herder and Herder, 1967, 514–24 [French ed., 1962].

Chadwick, Henry. "Die Absicht des Epheserbriefes." *ZNW* 51, nos. 3–4 (1960): 145–53.

Collins, Raymond F. *Introduction to the New Testament*. Garden City, N.Y.: Doubleday, 1983, 142–43, 186–88.

———. *Letters That Paul Did Not Write: The Epistle to the Hebrews and the Pauline Pseudepigrapha*. Good News Studies, ed. Robert J. Karris, vol. 28. Wilmington, Del.: Michael Glazier, 1988, 132–49.

Cook, James I. "The Origin and Purpose of Ephesians." *Reformed Review* 18 (March 1965): 3–18.

Coppieters, H. "Les récentes attaques contre l'authenticité de l'épître aux Éphésiens." *RB* 9 (Juillet 1912): 361–91.

Cullmann, Oscar. *The New Testament: An Introduction for the General Reader*. Translated by Dennis Pardee. Philadelphia: Westminster, 1968, 83–87 [French ed., 1966].

Dahl, Nils Alstrup. "Adresse und Proömium des Epheserbriefes." *TZ* 7 (Juli/August 1951): 241–65.

———. "Ephesians, Letter to the." In *The Interpreter's Dictionary of the Bible*, ed. George Arthur Buttrick et al., Supplementary vol. Nashville: Abingdon, 1962, 268–69.

———. "The Particularity of the Pauline Epistles as a Problem in the Ancient Church." In *Neotestamentica et Patristica: Eine Freundesgabe, Herrn Professor Dr. Oscar Cullmann zu Seinem 60. Geburtstag Überreicht*. NovTSup, ed. W. C. van Unnik et al., vol. 6. Leiden: Brill, 1962, 266–67.

———. "Interpreting Ephesians, Then and Now." *Currents in Theology and Mission* 5 (April 1978): 133–43.

———. "Einleitungsfragen zum Epheserbrief." In *Studies in Ephesians: Introductory Questions, Text- & Edition-Critical Issues, Interpretation of Texts and Themes*, ed. David Hellholm, Vemund Blomkvist, and Tord Fornberg. WUNT, ed. Martin Hengel and Otfried Hofius, vol. 131. Tübingen: Mohr, 2000, 48–60, esp. 58–60.

———. *Studies in Ephesians: Introductory Questions, Text- & Edition-Critical Issues, Interpretation of Texts and Themes*. Edited by David Hellholm, Vemund Blomkvist, and Tord Fornberg. WUNT, ed. Martin Hengel and Otfried Hofius, vol. 131. Tübingen: Mohr, 2000.

Danker, Frederick W. "Ephesians." In *The International Standard Bible Encyclopedia*, ed. Geoffrey W. Bromiley, vol. 2. Grand Rapids: Eerdmans, 1982, 108–14.

Davidson, Samuel. *An Introduction to the Study of the New Testament*. 2d ed., vol. 2. London: Longmans, Green, 1882, 195–230 [1st ed., 1868, 1:372–407].

Dawes, Gregory W. *The Body in Question: Metaphor and Meaning in the Interpretation of Ephesians 5:21–33*. Biblical Interpretation Series, ed. R. Alan Culpepper, Rolf Rendtorff, and David E. Orton, vol. 30. Leiden: Brill, 1998, 198 n. 5.

Deissmann, Adolf. *Paul: A Study in Social and Religious History*. Translated by William E. Wilson. London: Hodder and Stoughton, 1926, 15–18, 24 [1st German ed., 1911, 10–12, 15–16].

———. *Light from the Ancient East*. Rev. ed. [4th ed.]. Translated by Lionel R. M. Strachan. London: Hodder and Stoughton; New York: Harper & Brothers, 1927. Reprint, Grand Rapids: Baker, 1965, 237–38 [1st German ed., 1908, 165–66].

———. *The New Testament in the Light of Modern Research. The Haskell Lectures, 1929*. Garden City, N.Y.: Doubleday, Doran, 1929, 33, 98.

Dibelius, Martin. *A Fresh Approach to the New Testament and Early Christian Literature*. Translated by [D. S. Noel and Gordon Abbott]. The International Library of Christian Knowledge, ed. William Adams Brown and Bertram Lee Woolf. London: Ivor Nicholson and Watson, 1936, 170.

Dobschütz, Ernst von. *Christian Life in the Primitive Church*. Translated by George Bremner. Edited by W. D. Morrison. Theological Translation Library, vol. 18. New York: G. P. Putnam's Sons; London: Williams and Norgate, 1904, 174–89, 93–94 [German ed., 1902, 125–36, 138–39].

Dodd, C. H. "The Message of the Epistles: Ephesians," *ExpTim* 45 (November 1933): 60–66.

Duff, Jeremy N. "A Reconsideration of Pseudepigraphy in Early Christianity." D.Phil. thesis, University of Oxford, 1998.

Dunn, James D. G. *Baptism in the Holy Spirit. A Re-examination of the New Testament Teaching on the Gift of the Spirit in relation to Pentecostalism Today.* SBT, ed. C F. D. Moule, Peter Ackroyd, J. Barr, C. F. Evans, Floyd V. Filson, and G. Ernest Wright, vol. 15. London: SCM, 1970, 152, 158–65.

———. *Unity and Diversity in the New Testament: An Inquiry into the Character of Earliest Christianity.* 2d ed. London: SCM; Philadelphia: Trinity Press International, 1990 [1st ed., same pages].

———. *The Partings of the Ways: Between Christianity and Judaism and Their Significance for the Character of Christianity.* London: SCM; Philadelphia: Trinity Press International, 1991, 75, 76, 82, 149, 249?, 275–76, 309 n. 39.

———. "Pauline Legacy and School." In *DLNT*, 889–90.

———. "Pseudepigraphy." In *DLNT*, 977, 981–82.

———. *The Theology of Paul the Apostle*. Grand Rapids: Eerdmans; Edinburgh: T & T Clark, 1998, 13 n. 39.

Dupont, Jacques. *«Gnosis», la connaissance religieuse dans les épîtres de saint Paul*. Universitas Catholica Lovaniensis: Dissertationes ad gradum magistri in Facultate Theologica consequendum conscriptae, ser. 2, vol. 40. Louvain: E. Nauwelaerts; Paris: Gabalda, 1949, passim.

Eichhorn, Johann Gottfried. *Einleitung in das Neue Testament*. Vol. 3. Leipzig: Weidmannische Buchhandlung, 1812, 249–83, esp. 249–72, 276–83.

Ellis, E. Earle. "Pseudonymity and Canonicity of New Testament Documents." In *Worship, Theology and Ministry in the Early Church: Essays in Honor of Ralph P. Martin*, ed. Michael J. Wilkins and Terence Paige. JSNTSup, ed. Stanley E. Porter et al., vol. 87. Sheffield: JSOT Press, 1992, 220–21.

———. *The Making of the New Testament Documents*. Biblical Interpretation Series, ed. R. Alan Culpepper, Rolf Rendtorff, and David E. Orton, vol. 39. Leiden: Brill, 1999, 105–11, 266–67.

Evanson, Edward. *The Dissonance of the Four Generally Received Evangelists and the Evidence of Their Respective Authenticity Examined*. Ipswich, England: George Jermym, 1792, 261–62.

Ewald, Heinrich. *Sieben Sendschreiben des Neuen Bundes*. Göttingen: Dieterichschen Buchhandlung, 1870, xii, 153–61.

Fay, Greg. "Paul the Empowered Prisoner: Eph 3:1–13 in the Epistolary and Rhetorical Structure of Ephesians." Ph.D. diss., University of Marquette, 1994, 20–24.

Faust, Eberhard. *Pax Christi et Pax Caesaris: Religionsgeschichtliche, traditionsgeschichtliche und sozialgeschichtliche Studien zum Ephesebrief*. Novum Testamentum et Orbis Antiquus, ed. Max Küchler und Gerd Theissen, vol. 24. Freiburg: Universitätsverlag; Göttingen: Vandenhoeck & Ruprecht, 1993, 12–18.

Fee, Gordon D. *God's Empowering Presence: The Holy Spirit in the Letters of Paul*. Peabody, Mass.: Hendrickson, 1994, 658–60.

Feine, Paul. *Einleitung in das Neue Testament*. 5th rev. ed. Leipzig: Quelle & Meyer, 1930, 161–68 [1st ed., 1913].

———. *Einleitung in das Neue Testament*. 8th ed. Newly rev. ed. Johannes Behm. Leipzig: Quelle & Meyer, 1936, 190–94 [This ed. is when Behm became involved. Later ed. is by Kümmel see below.].

Filson, Floyd V. *A New Testament History*. New Testament Library, ed. Alan Richardson, C. F. D. Moule, and Floyd V. Filson. London: Westminster, 1964; London: SCM, 1965, 280–83.

Fischer, Karl Martin. *Tendenz und Absicht des Epheserbriefes*. FRLANT, ed. Ernst Käsemann and Ernst Würthwein, vol. 111. Göttingen: Vandenhoeck & Ruprecht, 1973, 13–26.

Fleckenstein, Karl-Heinz. *Ordnet euch einander unter in der Furcht Christi: Die Eheperkiope in Eph 5,21–33. Geschichte der Interpretation, Analyse und Aktualisierung des Textes*. Forschung zur Bibel, ed. Rudolf Schnackenburg and Josef Schreiner, vol. 73. Würzburg: Echter, 1994, 156–60.

Fuller, Reginald H. *A Critical Introduction to the New Testament*. London: Gerald Duckworth, 1966, 65–68.

Furnish, Victor Paul. "Ephesians, Epistle to the." In *ABD*, 2:535–42.

Gese, Michael. *Das Vermächtnis des Apostels: Die Rezeption der paulinischen Theologie im Epheserbrief*. WUNT, ed. Martin Hengel and Otfried Hofius, vol. 99. Tübingen: Mohr, 1997, 1–27, 250–76.

Gnilka, Joachim. *Paulus von Tarsus: Apostel und Zeuge*. Freiburg: Herder, 1996, 320–21.

Godet, F. "The Epistle to the Gentile Churches." *Exp* 3d ser., vol. 5 (November 1887): 376–91.

———. *Introduction to the New Testament*. Translated by William Affleck, vol. 1. Edinburgh: T & T Clark, 1894, 478–94 [French ed., 1893; apparently there was to be a vol. 2 but it never appeared].

Goguel, Maurice. *Introduction au Nouveau Testament*. Vol. 4, pt. 2. Paris: Leroux, 1926, 431–75.

———. "Esquisse d'une solution nouvelle du problème de l'épître aux Éphésiens." *Revue de l'histoire des religions* 111 (Mai–Juni 1935): 254–84; 112 (Juillet–Août 1935): 73–99 [there are portions of the epistle that are genuine which have no evidence of Gnosticism].

———. *The Birth of Christianity*. Translated by H. C. Snape. London: George Allen & Unwin, 1953; New York: Macmillan, 1954, 328–30 [French ed., 1946, 356–59].

———. *The Primitive Church*. Translated by H. C. Snape. London: George Allen & Unwin; New York: Macmillan, 1964, 65–69, 480–81 [French ed., 1947, 55–59, 511–13] [the ethical elements of the epistle that are genuine].

Goodspeed, Edgar J. *New Solutions of New Testament Problems*. Chicago: University of Chicago Press, 1927, 11–20, 29–64.

———. "The Place of Ephesians in the First Pauline Collection." *ATR* 12 (January 1930): 189–212.

———. *The Meaning of Ephesians*. Chicago: University of Chicago Press, 1933, 3–17.

———. *An Introduction to the New Testament*. Chicago: University of Chicago Press, 1937, 222–39.

———. *New Chapters in New Testament Study*. New York: Macmillan, 1937, 173–79.

———. "Ephesians and the First Edition of Paul." *JBL* 70 (December 1951): 285–91.

Goulder, M. D. "The Visionaries of Laodicea." *JSNT* 43 (September 1991): 15–39.

Grant, Robert M. *A Historical Introduction the New Testament*. 2d ed. New York: Simon and Schuster, 1972, 199–202 [1st ed., 1963].

Grensted, Lawrence William. "Ephesians, Epistle to the." In *Dictionary of the Apostolic Church*, ed. James Hastings, vol. 1. Edinburgh: T & T Clark, 1916, 343–49.

Gundry, Robert H. "'Verba Christi' in 1 Peter: Their Implications Concerning the Authorship of 1 Peter and the Authenticity of the Gospel Tradition." *NTS* 13 (July 1967): 349 n. 1.

Günther, Matthias. *Die Frühgeschichte des Christentums in Ephesus*. Arbeiten zur Religion und Geschichte des Urchristentums, ed. Gerd Lüdemann, vol. 1. Frankfurt am Main: Peter Lang, 1995, 68–75.

Guthrie, Donald. *New Testament Introduction*. 4th ed. Downers Grove, Ill.: InterVarsity, 1990, 496–528 [1st ed., 1961, 99–128].

Hagner, Donald Alfred. *The Use of the Old and the New Testaments in Clement of Rome*. NovTSup, ed. W. C. van Unnik et al., vol. 34. Leiden: Brill, 1973, 222–26, 314–31.

Harnack, Adolf. "Die Adresse des Epheserbriefs des Paulus." In *Sitzungsberichte der königlich preussischen Akademie der Wissenschaft*. Sitzung der philosophisch-historischen Classe vom 21. Juli, 1910, no. 37, vol. 2. Berlin: Verlag der könglichen Akademie der Wissenschaften, 1910, 696–709. Reprint, idem. *Kleine Schriften zur alten Kirche*, vol. 2, Opuscula: Sammelausgaben seltener und bisher nicht selbständig erschienener wissenschaftlicher Abhandlungen, ed. Werner Peek, vol. 9.2. Leipzig: Zentralantiquariat der deutschen demokratischen Republik, 1980, 120–33.

Harris, W. Hall, III. *The Descent of Christ: Ephesians 4:7–11 and Traditional Hebrew Imagery*, AGJU, ed. Martin Hengel et al., vol. 32. Leiden: Brill, 1996, 184, 198–204.

Harrison, Everett F. *Introduction to the New Testament*. Rev. ed. Grand Rapids: Eerdmans, 1971, 331–40 [1st ed., 1964, 310–19].

Harrison, P. N. "Onesimus and Philemon," *ATR* 32 (October 1950): 268–94.

———. "The Author of Ephesians." In *SE II. Papers Presented to the Second International Congress on New Testament Studies held at Christ Church Oxford, 1961*, ed. F. L. Cross. TU, ed. Friedrich Zucher et al., vol. 87. Berlin: Akademie-Verlag, 1964, 595–604. 595–604.

Heard, Richard. *An Introduction to the New Testament*. London: Adam and Charles Black, 1950, 203–6.

Hemphill, Kenneth S. "The Pauline Concept of Charisma: A Situational and Developmental Approach." Ph.D. thesis, University of Cambridge, 1976, 197–210.

———. *Spiritual Gifts: Empowering the New Testament Church*. Nashville: Broadman, 1988, 153–62.

Henshaw, T. *New Testament Literature in the Light of Modern Scholarship*. London: George Allen & Unwin, 1952, 298–307.

Hilgenfeld, Adolf. *Historisch-kritische Einleitung in das Neue Testament*. Leipzig: Fues's Verlag (R. Reisland), 1875, 669–80, esp. 676–80.

Hitzig, Ferdinand. *Zur Kritik paulinischer Briefe*. Leipzig: S. Hirzel, 1870, 1–36.

Hoekstra, S. "Vergelijking van de brieven aan de Efeziërs en de Colossers, vooral uit het oogpunt van beider leerstelligen inhoud." *Theologisch Tijdschrift* 2 (November 1868): 599–652.

Holtzmann, Heinrich Julius. *Kritik der Epheser- und Kolosserbriefe: Auf Grund einer Analyse ihres Verwandtschaftsverhältnisses*. Leipzig: Wilhelm Engelmann, 1872, viii+338.

Hönig, W. "Ueber das Verhältniss des Epheserbriefes zum Briefe an die Kolosser." *Zeitschrift für wissenschaftliche Theologie* 15, no. 1 (1872): 63–87.

Horn, Curtis Kent. "Pseudonymity in Early Christianity: An Inquiry into the Theory of Innocent Deutero-Pauline Pseudonymity." Ph.D. diss., Southwestern Baptist Theological Seminary, 1996.

Hort, F. J. A. *Prolegomena to St Paul's Epistles to the Romans and to the Ephesians*. London: Macmillan, 1895, 65–98, 111–69.

Howard, Fred D. "An Introduction to Ephesians." *SWJT* 22 (fall 1979): 7–23.

Hui, Archie Wang Do. "The Concept of the Holy Spirit in Ephesians and Its Relation to the Pneumatologies of Luke and Paul." Ph.D. thesis, University of Aberdeen, 1992, 1–2, 5–8, 120–24, 195–97, 211, 311–18, 390–95, 402–12.

Hunter, Archibald M. *Interpreting the New Testament, 1900–1950*. Philadelphia: Westminster, 1951, 62–63.

———. *Introducing the New Testament*. 2d ed., rev. and enl. Philadelphia: Westminster, 1957, 120–27 [1st ed., 1946 does not deal with Ephesian authorship].

Innitzer, Th. "Zur Frage der Priorität des Epheser-oder des Kolosserbriefes." *ZKT* 29, no. 3 (1905): 579–88.

Johnson, Luke Timothy. *The Writings of the New Testament. An Interpretation*. Philadelphia: Fortress, 1986, 367–72.

Johnston, George. *The Doctrine of the Church in the New Testament*. Cambridge: Cambridge University Press, 1943, 136–40.

———. "Ephesians, Letter to the." In *The Interpreter's Dictionary of the Bible*, ed. George Arthur Buttrick et al., vol. 2. Nashville: Abingdon, 1962, 108–14.

Jülicher, Adolf. *Einleitung in das Neue Testament*. 7th ed. with Erich Fascher, Grundriss der theologischen Wissenschaften, ed. Achelis et al., pt. 3, vol. 1. Tübingen: Mohr, 1931, 142–43 [1st & 2d ed., 1894, 94–97].

———. "Colossians and Ephesians, Epistles to the." In *Encyclopaedia Biblica*, ed. T. K. Cheyne and T. Sutherland Black, vol. 1. London: Adam and Charles Black; New York: Macmillan, 1899, 860–69.

Käsemann, Ernst. *Leib und Leib Christi. Eine Untersuchung zur paulinischen Begrifflichkeit*. BHT, vol. 9. Tübingen: Mohr, 1933, 138 n. 2.

———. Review of *Probleme der Kolosser- und Epheserbriefe*, by Ernest Percy. *Gomon* 21, nos. 7/8 (1949): 342–47.

———. "Epheserbrief." In *Die Religion in Geschichte und Gegenwart: Handwörterbuch für Theologie und Religionswissenschaft*, 3d ed., ed. Hans Frhr. v. Campenhausen et al., vol. 2. Tübingen: Mohr, 1958, 517–20.

———. "Das Interpretationsproblem des Epheserbriefes." *TLZ* 86 (Januar 1961): 1–8.

———. "Paulus und der Frühkatholizismus." *ZTK* 60 (August 1963): 75–89.

———. "Ephesians and Acts." Translated by Marianne Grobel and Thomas Wieser. In *Studies in Luke-Acts. Essays Presented in Honor of Paul Schubert Buckingham Professor of New Testament Criticism and Interpretation at Yale University*, ed. Leander E. Keck and J. Louis Martyn. Nashville: Abingdon, 1966, 288–97.

Kasser, Rodolphe. "L'autore dell' Epistola agli Efesini." *Protestantesimo* [Rome] 17 (1962): 74–84.

Kirby, John C. *Ephesians, Baptism and Pentecost: An Inquiry into the Structure and Purpose of the Epistle to the Ephesians*. Montreal: McGill University; London: S.P.C.K., 1968, 3–56, 165–72.

Klauck, Hans-Josef. "Das Amt in der Kirche nach Eph 4,1–16." *Wissenschaft und Weisheit* 36 (Juni 1973): 81–86.

Klijn, A. F. J. *An Introduction to the New Testament*. Translated by M. van der Vathorst-Smit. Leiden: Brill, 1967, 99–106 [Dutch ed., 1965; possibly as early as 1961].

Knowling, R. J. *The Testimony of St. Paul to Christ Viewed in Some of Its Aspects*. 3d ed. London: Hodder and Stoughton, 1911, 94–111 [1st ed., 1905, same pages].

Knox, John. *Philemon among the Letters of Paul: A New View of Its Place and Importance*. Rev. ed. New York: Abingdon, 1959, 66, 75–76 [1st ed., 1935, 37].

———. *Chapters in a Life of Paul*. Rev. ed. Macon, Ga.: Mercer University Press, 1987, 8–9 [1st ed., 1950, 19–20].

Knox, Wilfred L. *St. Paul*. New York: D. Appleton, 1932, 146.

———. *St Paul and the Church of the Gentiles*. Cambridge: Cambridge University Press, 1939, 183–203.

Koester, Helmut. *Introduction to the New Testament*. 2 vols. Hermeneia—Foundations and Facets, ed. Robert W. Funk. Philadelphia: Fortress, 1982, 2:267–72 [German ed., 1980, 705–9].

———. "Ephesos in Early Christian Literature." In *Ephesos Metropolis of Asia: An Interdisciplinary Approach to its Archaeology, Religion, and Culture*, ed. Helmut Koester. HTS, ed. Allen D. Callahan et al., vol. 41. Valley Forge, Pa.: Trinity Press International, 1995, 124.

Kümmel, Werner Georg. *Introduction to the New Testament*. 17th ed. Translated by Howard Clark Kee. Nashville: Abingdon, 1975, 357–66 [12th German ed. of Feine-Behm, 1963 is when Kümmel became involved, 257–64].

Lake, Kirsopp, and Silva Lake. *An Introduction to the New Testament*. New York: Harper & Brothers, 1937. Reprint, London: Christophers, 1938, 146–49.

Lightfoot, J. B. "The Destination of the Epistle to the Ephesians." In *Biblical Essays*. London: Macmillan, 1893, 375–96.

Lincoln, Andrew T. "A Re-Examination of 'the Heavenlies' in Ephesians." *NTS* 19 (July 1973): 468–83.

———. *Paradise Now and Not Yet. Studies in the Role of the Heavenly Dimension in Paul's Thought with Special Reference to His Eschatology.* SNTSMS, ed. R. McL. Wilson and M. E. Thrall, vol. 43. Cambridge: Cambridge University Press, 1981. Reprint, Grand Rapids: Baker, 1991, 135.

———. "The Use of the OT in Ephesians." *JSNT* 14 (February 1982): 16–57, esp. 36–37, 44–50.

———. "Ephesians 2:8–10: A Summary of Paul's Gospel?" *CBQ* 45 (October 1983): 617–18.

Lincoln, Andrew T., and A. J. M. Wedderburn. *The Theology of the Later Pauline Letters*, New Testament Theology, ed. James D. G. Dunn. Cambridge: Cambridge University Press, 1993, 78–86.

Lindemann, Andreas. "Bemerkungen zu den Adressaten und zum Anlaß des Epheserbriefes." *ZNW* 67, nos. 3/4 (1976): 235–51.

Lock, Walter. "Ephesians, Epistle to." In *A Dictionary of the Bible*, ed. James Hastings, vol. 1. Edinburgh: T & T Clark, 1898, 714–20.

Lohse, Eduard. *The Formation of the New Testament*. 3d German ed. Translated by M. Eugene Boring. Nashville: Abingdon, 1981, 93–97 [1st German ed., 1972, 57–60].

Lona, Horacio E. *Die Eschatologie im Kolosser- und Epheserbrief*. Forschung zur Bibel, ed. Rudolf Schnackenburg and Josef Schreiner, vol. 48. Würzburg: Echter, 1984, 30–34.

Maclean, Jennifer Kay Berenson. "Ephesians and the Problem of Colossians: Interpretation of Texts and Traditions in Eph 1:1–2:10." Ph.D. diss., Harvard University, 1995, 7–13.

Manson, T. W. "The New Testament and Other Christian Writings of the New Testament Period." In *A Companion to the Bible*, ed. T. W. Manson. New York: Charles Scribner's Sons, 1939, 97–129, esp. 111–13.

———. Review of *The Formation of the Pauline Corpus of Letters*, by C. L. Mitton. *JTS*, n.s., 7 (October 1956): 286–89.

Martin, Ralph P. "An Epistle in Search of a Life-Setting." *ExpTim* 79 (July 1968): 297–302.

———. *New Testament Foundations: A Guide for Christian Students*. Vol. 2, *The Acts, the Letters, the Apocalypse*. Grand Rapids: Eerdmans, 1978, 223–33.

———. *Reconciliation: A Study of Paul's Theology*. New Foundations Theological Library, ed. Peter Toon and Ralph P. Martin. Atlanta: John Knox, 1981, 157–98. Reprint, idem. "Reconciliation and Unity in Ephesians." *RevExp* 93 (spring 1996): 203–35.

Marxsen, W. *Introduction to the New Testament: An Approach to Its Problems*. Translated by G. Buswell. Philadelphia: Fortress, 1968, 187–98 [German ed., 1964].

Mauerhofer, E. "Der Brief an die Epheser. 1. Teil: Einleitende Gedanken." *Fundamentum* 4 (1989): 17–32.

Maurer, Christian. "Der Hymnus von Epheser I als Schlüssel zum ganzen Briefe." *EvT* 11 (Oktober 1951): 151–72.

Mayerhoff, Ernst Theodor. *Der Brief an die Colosser, mit vornehmlicher Berücksichtigung der drei Pastoralbriefe kritisch geprüft*. Edited by J. L. Mayerhoff. Berlin: Hermann Schultze, 1838, 1–6, 72–106.

McDonald, Lee Martin, and Stanley E. Porter. *Early Christianity and Its Sacred Literature*. Peabody, Mass.: Hendrickson, 2000, 482–88.

McGiffert, Arthur Cushman. *A History of Christianity in the Apostolic Age*. Rev. ed. International Theological Library. New York: Charles Scribner's Sons, 1906, 377–85 [1st ed., 1897, same pages].

McNeile, A. H. *An Introduction to the Study of the New Testament*. 2d ed. rev. by C. S. C. Williams. Oxford: Clarendon, 1953, 165–77.

———. *An Introduction to the Study of the New Testament*. Oxford: Clarendon, 1927, 154–63.

Meade, David G. *Pseudonymity and Canon: An Investigation into the Relationship of Authorship and Authority in Jewish and Earliest Christian Tradition*. WUNT, ed. Martin Hengel and Otfried Hofius, vol. 39. Tübingen: Mohr, 1986, 139–57.

Meeks, Wayne A., ed. *The Writings of St. Paul*. A Norton Critical Edition, ed. Herbert J. Muller. New York: W. W. Norton, 1972, 121–23.

Meinertz, Max. *Einleitung in das Neue Testament*. 5th ed. Wissenschaftliche Handbibliothek. Paderborn: Ferdinand Schöningh, 1950, 126–31 [originally a work of Aloys Schaefer, 1898 and rev. by Meinertz in 1913 and 1921 but finally came under Meinertz' name in the 4th ed., 1933].

Merkel, Helmut. "Der Epheserbrief in der neueren exegetischen Diskussion." In *ANRW*, pt. 2, vol. 25.4 (1987), 3156–76.

Merklein, Helmut. *Christus und die Kirche. Die theologische Grundstruktur des Epheserbriefes nach Eph 2,11–18*. Stuttgarter Bibelstudien, ed. Herbert Haag, Rudolf Kilian, and Wilhelm Pesch, vol. 66. Stuttgart: KBW, 1973, 12, 67, 77–81, 85–86, 88–89, 94–95–98, 100–101.

———. *Das kirchliche Amt nach dem Epheserbrief*. SANT, ed. Vinzenz Hamp and Josef Schmid, vol. 33. Munich: Kösel, 1973, 19–54.

Michaelis, Wilhelm. *Einleitung in das Neue Testament: Die Entstehung, Sammlung und Überlieferung der Schriften des Neuen Testaments*. 3d ed. Bern: Berchtold Haller, 1961, 191–200 [1st ed., 1946, 192–200].

Mitton, C. Leslie. "Unsolved New Testament Problems. Goodspeed's Theory regarding the Origin of Ephesians." *ExpTim* 59 (September 1948): 323–27.

———. "Goodspeed's Theory regarding the Origin of Ephesians." *ExpTim* 60 (August 1949): 320–21.

———. *The Epistle to the Ephesians. Its Authorship, Origin and Purpose*. Oxford: Clarendon, 1951, x+346.

———. "Important Hypotheses Reconsidered VII. The Authorship of the Epistle to the Ephesians." *ExpTim* 67 (April 1956): 195–98.

Moffatt, James. "The Problem of Ephesians." *Exp* 8th ser., vol. 2 (September 1911): 193–200.

———. *An Introduction to the Literature of the New Testament*. 3d rev. ed. The International Theological Library, ed. Charles A. Briggs and Stewart D. F. Salmond. Edinburgh: T & T Clark, 1918, 41, 375, 387–89 [1st ed., 1911, same pages].

Moritz, Thorsten. "'Summing-up all Things': Religious Pluralism and Universalism in Ephesians." In *One God, One Lord in a World of Religious Pluralism*, ed. Andrew D. Clarke and Bruce W. Winter. Cambridge: Tyndale House, 1991, 88–111.

———. *A Profound Mystery: The Use of the Old Testament in Ephesians*. NovTSup, ed. C. K. Barrett et al., vol. 85. Leiden: Brill, 1996, 1–8, 213–20 [unclear but allows for Pauline authorship which his other works assert].

———. "Reasons for Ephesians." *Evangel* 14 (spring 1996): 8–14.

Morton, A. Q., and James McLeman. *Christianity in the Computer Age*. New York: Harper & Row, 1964, 24–35, 92–95.

Mowry, Lucetta. "The Early Circulation of Paul's Letters." *JBL* 63 (June 1944): 73–86.

Munro, Winsome. "Col. iii.18–iv.1 and Eph. v.21–vi.9: Evidences of a Late Literary Stratum?" *NTS* 18 (July 1972): 434–47.

———. *Authority in Paul and Peter. The Identification of a Pastoral Stratum in the Pauline Corpus and 1 Peter*. SNTSMS, ed. R. McL. Wilson and M. E. Thrall, vol. 45. Cambridge: Cambridge University Press, 1983, 12–14.

Murphy-O'Connor, Jerome. "Who Wrote Ephesians?" *TBT* 18 (April 1965): 1201–9.

———. *Paul the Letter-Writer: His World, His Options, His Skills*, Good News Studies, vol. 41. Collegeville, Minn.: Liturgical Press, 1995, 34–35, passim.

———. *Paul: A Critical Life*. Oxford: Clarendon, 1996, 356–57.

Mussner, Franz. *Christus, das All und die Kirche. Studien zur Theologie des Epheserbriefes*. Trierer theologische Studien, vol. 5. Trier: Paulinus-Verlag, 1955, 1–8, passim.

Nineham, D. E. "The Case against the Pauline Authorship" In *Studies in Ephesians*, ed. F. L. Cross. London: A. R. Mowbray, 1956, 21–35.

Norden, Eduard. *Agnostos Theos: Untersuchungen zur Formengeschichte religiöser Rede*. Leipzig: B. G. Teubner, 1913, 251 n. 1.

Ochel, Werner. *Die Annahme einer Bearbeitung des Kolosser-Briefes im Epheser-Brief in einer Analyse des Epheser-Briefes untersucht*. Inaugural-Dissertation zur Erlangung der Doktorwürde der Philosophischen Fakultät der Philipps-Universität zu Marburg. Würzburg: Konrad Triltsch, 1934, v+73.

Paley, William. *Horae Paulinæ; or, the Truth of the Scripture History of St. Paul Evinced, by a Comparison of the Epistles Which Bear His Name, with the Acts of the Apostles, and with One Another.* London: R. Faulder, 1790; New York: American Tract Society, n.d., 113–37.

Peake, Arthur S. *A Critical Introduction to the New Testament*. London: Duckworth, 1909, 49–57.

Percy, Ernst. *Die Probleme der Kolosser- und Epheserbriefe*. Skrifter Utgivna av Kingl. Humanistiska Vetenskapssamfundet i. Lund, vol. 39. Lund: Gleerup, 1946, xviii+517.

Perkins, Pheme. "Ephesians: An Introduction." *TBT* 36 (November 1998): 341–44.

Perrin, Norman. *The New Testament: An Introduction. Proclamation and Parenesis, Myth and History.* New York: Harcourt Brace Jovanovich, 1974, 129–32.

Pfleiderer, Otto. *Paulinism: A Contribution to the History of Primitive Theology.* Translated by Edward Peters, vol. 2. London: Williams and Norgate, 1877, 162–93 [1st German ed., 1873, 431–61].

———. *Primitive Christianity: Its Writings and Teachings in Their Historical Connections*. Translated by W. Montgomery. Edited by W. D. Morrison, vol. 3. London: Williams & Norgate; New York: G. P. Putnam's Sons, 1910, 300–322 (see also vol. 1 [1906], 269) [1st German ed., 1887, 684–95].

Pokorný, Petr. *Der Epheserbrief und die Gnosis. Die Bedeutung des Haupt-Glieder-Gedankens in der entstehenden Kirche*. Berlin: Evangelische Verlagsanstalt, 1965, 11–16, 24–25.

Polhill, John B. "The Relationship between Ephesians and Colossians." *RevExp* 70 (fall 1973): 439–50.

———. "An Introduction to Ephesians." *RevExp* 76 (fall 1979): 465–79.

———. "An Overview of Ephesians." *RevExp* 93 (spring 1996): 182–83.

Puskas, Charles B. *An Introduction to the New Testament*. Peabody, Mass.: Hendrickson, 1989, 217–20.

Reitzenstein, R. *Das iranische Erlösungsmysterium: Religionsgeschichtliche Untersuchungen*. Bonn: A. Marcus & E. Weber's Verlag, 1921, 235–36.

Renan, Ernest. *Saint Paul*. Translated by Ingersoll Lockwood. New York: G. W. Carleton, 1869, 10, 13–19, 331–33 [1st French ed., n.d.; earliest dated French ed., 1869].

Roberts, J. H. "The Imprisonment Letters." In *The Pauline Letters: Introduction and Theology*, ed. A. B. du Toit and trans. D. Roy Briggs. Guide to the New Testament, vol. 5. Pretoria: N. G. Kerkboekhandel Transvaal, 1985, 108–17, 130–31.

Robinson, John A. T. *Redating the New Testament*. Philadelphia: Westminster; London: SCM, 1976, 61–65.

Roetzel, Calvin J. *The Letters of Paul: Conversations in Context*. 3d ed. Louisville, Ky.: Westminster/John Knox, 1991, 138–44 [1st ed., 1975—but does not deal with Ephesian authorship].

Roller, Otto. *Das Formular der paulinischen Briefe: ein Beitrag zur Lehre von antiken Briefe*. BWANT, ed. Albrecht Alt and Gerhard Kittel, ser. 4, vol. 6. Stuttgart: W. Kohlhammer, 1933, 199–212, 520–28.

Roon, A. van. *The Authenticity of Ephesians*. Translated by S. Prescod-Jokel. NovTSup, ed. W. C. van Unnik et al., vol. 39. Leiden: Brill, 1974, x+449 [Dutch ed., 1969].

Rutherfurd, John. *St. Paul's Epistle to Colossae and Laodicea: The Epistle to the Colossians Viewed in Relation to the Epistle to the Ephesians*. Edinburgh: T & T Clark, 1908, 19–25, 31–44.

Sabatier, A. *The Apostle Paul: A Sketch of the Development of His Doctrine*. Translated by A. M. Hellier. ed., with an Additional Essay on the Pastorals, by George G. Findlay. London: Hodder and Stoughton, 1891, 229–34 [2d French ed., 1881].

Salmon, George. *A Historical Introduction to the Study of the Books of the New Testament*. 9th ed. London: John Murray, 1899, 423–33 [1st ed., 1885, 475–88].

Sampley, J. Paul. *'And the Two Shall Become One Flesh.' A Study of Traditions in Ephesians*. SNTSMS, ed. Matthew Black, vol. 16. Cambridge: Cambridge University Press, 1971, 1, 3.

Sanders, J. N. "The Case for the Pauline Authorship." In *Studies in Ephesians*, ed. F. L. Cross. London: A. R. Mowbray, 1956, 9–20.

Schenke, Hans-Martin. "Das Weiterwirken des Paulus und die Pflege seines Erbes durch die Paulus-Schule." *NTS* 21 (July 1975): 505–18 [this is later incorporated into his *Einleitung*].

Schenke, Hans-Martin, and Karl Martin Fischer. *Einleitung in die Schriften des Neuen Testaments*, Die Briefe des Paulus und Schriften des Paulinismus, vol. 1. Gütersloh: Gütersloher Verlagshaus, 1978, 174–90.

Schille, Gottfried. "Der Autor des Epheserbriefes." *TLZ* 82 (Mai 1957): 325–34.

Schleiermacher, Friedrich. *Einleitung ins Neue Testament*. Edited by G. Wolde. Literarischer Nachlaß zur Theologie, vol. 3; Sämmtliche Werke, pt. 1, vol. 8. Berlin: G. Reimer, 1845, 163–66.

Schlier, Heinrich. *Christus und die Kirche im Epheserbrief*. BHT, vol. 6. Tübingen: Mohr, 1930, passim.

———. "Die Kirche nach dem Brief an die Epheser." In *Die Kirche im Epheserbrief*. Beiträge Kontroverstheologie, ed. Robert Grosche, Beiheft zur Catholica, no. 1. Münster: Aschendorffsche Verlagsbuchhandlung, 1949, 82–114.

Schmid, Josef. *Der Epheserbrief des Apostels Paulus. Seine Adresse, Sprache und literarischen Beziehungen Untersucht*. Biblische Studien, ed. Joh. Göttsberger and Jos. Sickenberger, vol. 22. Freiburg: Herder, 1928, xxiii+466.

Schmithals, Walter. *Paul & the Gnostics*. Translated by John E. Steely. Nashville: Abingdon, 1972, 239–74 [German ed., 1965].

Schnackenburg, Rudolf. "»Er hat uns mitauferweckt«. Zur Tauflehre des Epheserbriefes." *Liturgisches Jahrbuch* 2 (1952): 159–83.

———. "Gestalt und Wesen der Kirche nach dem Epheserbrief." *Catholica* 15, no. 2 (1961): 104–20, esp. 108, 119. Reprint, idem. "Gestalt und Wesen der Kirche nach dem Epheserbrief." In *Schriften zum Neuen Testament. Exegese in Fortschritt und Wandel*, ed. Rudolf Schnackenburg. Munich: Kösel, 1971, 268–87.

Schubert, Paul. *Form and Function of the Pauline Thanksgivings*. BZNW, ed. Hans Lietzmann, vol. 20. Berlin: Töpelmann, 1939, 1, 8, 33, 37, 44.

Schweizer, Eduard. "Zur Frage der Echtheit des Kolosser- und des Epheserbriefes." ZNW 47, nos. 3–4 (1956): 287.

———. *A Theological Introduction to the New Testament*. Translated by O. C. Dean Jr. Nashville: Abingdon, 1991, 95–98 [German ed., 1989, 90–93].

Scott, C. A. Anderson. *Foot-Notes to St Paul*. Cambridge: Cambridge University Press, 1935, 174.

Scott, Ernest Findlay. *The Literature of the New Testament*. New York: Columbia University Press, 1932, 179–81.

Shaw, R. D. *The Pauline Epistles: Introductory and Expository Studies*. 3d ed. Edinburgh: T & T Clark, 1909, 344–69 [1st. ed., 1903, same pages].

Soden, Hans von. "ΜΥΣΤΗΡΙΟΝ und *Sacramentum* in den ersten zwei Jahrhunderten der Kirche." *ZNW* 12, nos. 2/3 (1911): 188–227, esp. 193–94.

Soden, Hermann von. *The History of Early Christian Literature: The Writings of the New Testament*. Translated by J. R. Wilkinson. Edited by W. D. Morrison. Crown Theological Library, vol. 13. London: Williams & Norgate; New York: G. P. Putnam's Sons, 1906, 284–305 [German ed., 1905, 145–55].

Soltau, Wilhelm. *Das Fortleben des Heidentums in der altchristlichen Kirche*. Berlin: Georg Reimer, 1906, 302–3.

Souter, Alex. "The Epistle to the 'Ephesians' not a Secondary Production." *Exp* 8th ser., vol. 2 (August 1911): 136–41.

———. "The Non-Secondary Character of 'Ephesians'." *Exp* 8th ser., vol. 2 (October 1911): 321–28.

Sparks, H. F. D. *The Formation of the New Testament*. New York: Philosophical Library, 1953, 67–72.

Stuhlmacher, Peter. "'He is our Peace' (Eph. 2:14). On the Exegesis and Significance of Ephesians 2:14–18." In *Reconciliation, Law, & Righteousness: Essays in Biblical Theology*, trans. Everett Kalin. Philadelphia: Fortress, 1986, 192–93 [German ed., 1974, 354–56].

Thiessen, Henry Clarence. *Introduction to the New Testament*. Grand Rapids: Eerdmans, 1943, 239–47.

Thurston, Bonnie. *Reading Colossians, Ephesians, and 2 Thessalonians: A Literary and Theological Commentary*. Reading the New Testament Series, ed. Charles H. Talbert. New York: Crossroad, 1995, 84–87.

Trobisch, David. *Die Entstehung der Paulusbriefsammlung: Studien zu den Anfängen christlicher Publizistik*. Novum Testamentum et Orbis Antiquus, ed. Max Küchler und Gerd Theißen, vol. 10. Freiburg: Universitätsverlag; Göttingen: Vandenhoeck & Ruprecht, 1989, passim.

———. *Paul's Letter Collection: Tracing the Origins*. Minneapolis: Fortress, 1994, 48–54, passim.

Trudinger, Paul. "Computers and the Authorship of the Pauline Epistles: A Brief Rejoinder." *Faith and Freedom* 39 (spring 1986): 24–27.

———. "The Ephesian Milieu." *DRev* 106 (October 1988): 286–96.

Usteri, Leonhard. *Entwickelung des paulinischen Lehrbegriffes mit Hinsicht auf die übrigen Schriften des Neuen Testament*. 3d ed. Zürich: Orill, Füssli, und Compagnie, 1831, 1–8, passim [1st ed., 1824; 2d ed., 1829; 3d ed., 1831; 4th ed., 1834; 6th ed., 1851].

Vanhoye, A. "L'épître aux Éphésiens et l'épître aux Hébreux." *Bib* 59, no. 2 (1978): 198–230.

Verhoef, Eduard. "Pseudepigraphy and Canon." *Biblische Notizen* 106 (2001): 90–98.

Vielhauer, Philipp. *Geschichte der urchristlichen Literatur: Einleitung in das Neue Testament, die Apokryphen und die Apostolischen Väter*. New York: de Gruyter, 1975, 203–15.

Wake, William C. "Numbers, Paul and Rational Dissent." *Faith and Freedom* 37 (spring 1984): 59–72.

Wette, Wilhelm Martin Leberecht de. *An Historico-Critical Introduction to the Canonical Books of the New Testament*. Translated from the 5th ed. by Frederick Frothingham. Boston: Crosby, Nichols, 1858, 274–85 [1st German ed., 1826, 2:254–65, esp. 254–56].

Weinel, H. *St Paul: The Man and His Work*. Translated by G. A. Bienemann. Edited by W. D. Morrison. Theological Translation Library, vol. 21. London: Williams & Norgate; New York: G. P. Putnam's Sons, 1906, 195 [German ed., 1904, 153].

———. *Biblische Theologie des Neuen Testament: Die Religion Jesu und des Urchristentums*. Tübingen: Mohr, 1921, 574–81.

Weiss, Bernhard. *A Manual of Introduction to the New Testament*. Translated by A. J. K. Davidson, vol. 1. London: Hodder and Stoughton, 1888, 339–57 [German ed., 1882].

———. "The Present Status of the Inquiry concerning the Genuineness of the Pauline Epistles." *American Journal of Theology* 1 (April 1897): 377–84. Reprint, idem. *The Present Status of the Inquiry concerning the Genuineness of the Pauline Epistles*. Chicago: University of Chicago Press, 1897, 52–59 [German ed., 1896].

Weiss, Johannes. *The History of Primitive Christianity*. Completed after his death by Rudolf Knopf. 2 vols. Translated and edited by Frederick C. Grant et al. New York: Wilson-Erickson, 1937. Reprint, idem. *Earliest Christianity: A History of the Period* A.D. *30–150*. New York: Harper & Brothers, 1959, 1:150; 2:682, 775 [The first part of the German ed. was published in 1914 before his death. His friend Rudolf Knopf completed the last 3 chapters published in 1917] [German ed., 1914, 109; 1917, 533, 602].

Weizsäcker, Carl von. *The Apostolic Age of the Christian Church*. 3d ed. Translated from the 2d and rev. ed. by James Millar, vol. 2, Theological Translation Library, ed. T. K. Cheyne and A. B. Bruce. London: Williams and Norgate; New York: G. P. Putnam's Sons, 1912, 240–45 [1st German ed., 1886, 560–65].

Wendland, Paul. *Die hellenistisch-römische Kultur in Ihren Beziehungen zu Judentum und Christentum. Die urchristlichen Literaturformen*. 2d and 3d eds. HNT, vol. 1, pts. 2–3. Tübingen: Mohr, 1912, 361–64.

Wikenhauser, Alfred. *New Testament Introduction*. 2d ed. Translated by Joseph Cunningham. New York: Herder and Herder, 1958, 423–30 [1st German ed., 1953, 302–7].

Wikenhauser, Alfred, and Josef Schmid. *Einleitung in das Neue Testament*. 6th ed. Freiburg: Herder, 1973, 481–96 [the change from Pauline authorship to non-Pauline authorship was due to Schmid who had changed his own mind].

Wilder, Terry L. "New Testament Pseudonymity and Deception." Ph.D. thesis, University of Aberdeen, 1998.

Wrede, William. *The Origin of the New Testament*. Translated by James S. Hill. London: Harper & Brothers, 1909, 40–41 [German ed., 1907, 33].

Yoder Neufeld, Thomas R. *'Put on the Armour of God': The Divine Warrior from Isaiah to Ephesians*. JSNTSup, ed. Stanley E. Porter et al., vol. 144. Sheffield: Sheffield Academic Press, 1997, 94–97.

Yorke, Gosnell L. O. R. *The Church as the Body of Christ in the Pauline Corpus: A Re-examination*. Lanham, Md.: University Press of America, 1991, 99–102.

Zahn, Theodor. *Introduction to the New Testament*. 3d German ed. Edited by Melancthon Williams Jacobus and Charles Snow Thayer. Translated by John Moore Trout et al., vol. 1. Edinburgh: T & T Clark, 1909. Reprint, Grand Rapids: Kregel, 1953, 479–522 [1st German ed., 1899, 1:339–68].

Zwaan, J. de. "Le 'Rythme logique' dans l'épître aux Éphésiens." *Revue d'histoire et de philosophie religieuse* 7 (Novembre–Décembre 1927): 554–65.

———. "Ephesen neit 'Deuteropaulinisch' (Eph 5:16)." *Nieuwe theologische Studiën* 20 (Juni 1937): 172–74.

I.

The Calling of the Church (1:1–3:21)

A. Prologue (1:1–2)

The prologue of Ephesians, as in other Pauline letters, follows the normal pattern of Hellenistic openings, namely, the name of the sender, the recipients, and a greeting. As the sender Paul gives his credentials and gives a description of the recipients indicating that both sender and recipients are related to Jesus Christ. His greeting is adorned with theological content.

Text: 1:1. Παῦλος ἀπόστολος Ἰησοῦ Χριστοῦ διὰ θελήματος θεοῦ τοῖς ἁγίοις τοῖς οὖσιν [ἐν Ἐφέσῳ] καὶ πιστοῖς ἐν Χριστῷ Ἰησοῦ· **1:2.** χάρις ὑμῖν καὶ εἰρήνη ἀπὸ θεοῦ πατρὸς ἡμῶν καὶ κυρίου Ἰησοῦ Χριστοῦ.

Translation: 1:1. "Paul, an apostle of Jesus Christ by the will of God, to the saints who are in Ephesus, that is, believers in Christ Jesus, **1:2.** grace to you and peace from God our Father and the Lord Jesus Christ."

Commentary: In the salutation of this letter three items are mentioned: the name of the sender, the recipients, and the greeting itself.

1:1. Παῦλος, "Paul." Immediately the writer of the epistle identifies himself as Paul. There has been much discussion on the authorship of Ephesians, as discussed in the introduction. Paul commonly mentions associates in his epistles.[1] However, this is not the case in Ephesians, Romans, and the Pastorals. If Ephesians is a forgery of Colossians, it seems strange that the writer did not use the more characteristic inclusion of those who accompanied him. Furthermore, there is no textual evidence for any other name besides the apostle's or for the absence of Paul's name.

ἀπόστολος Ἰησοῦ Χριστοῦ,[2] "apostle of Jesus Christ." The term ἀπόστολος, "apostle," is used in classical Greek primarily of ships be-

1. The following people are mentioned as associating with him: Sosthenes in 1 Cor 1:1; Timothy in 2 Cor 1:1; Phil 1:1; Col 1:1; Silas and Timothy in 1 Thess 1:1; 2 Thess 1:1 and "all the brothers who are with me" in Gal 1:1.

2. It is a moot point whether it should read Χριστοῦ Ἰησοῦ as in 𝔓^{46} B D P 0278 33 1505 *pc* it^{b} vg$^{st.\ ww}$ syr^{h}; Ambrosiaster (NA^{27}, UBS^{4}) or Ἰησοῦ Χριστοῦ as in ℵ A F G Ψ

ing sent out for cargo or military expeditions.[1] Infrequently is it used to refer to a single person as an envoy or emissary.[2] It appears only once in the Alexandrinus text of the LXX (1 Kgs 14:6) where שָׁלוּחַ, the passive participle of שָׁלַח, is rendered "to send" or "to send forth."[3] In the context of 1 Kgs 14:6 it is used of Ahijah who was commissioned and empowered to deliver a hard message to Jeroboam's wife who had come to consult him. Although the noun is used only once, the verbs ἀποστέλλω and ἐξαποστέλλω are used 976 times and are translated almost exclusively from שָׁלַח. Therefore, the idea not only included the sending of the messenger but more importantly the authorization of the messenger.[4]

This word was little used among the Hellenistic Jews but Paul commonly used it as a part of the greetings in his epistles to identify himself as an apostle of Christ (Rom 1:1; 1 Cor 1:1; 2 Cor 1:1; Gal 1:1; Col 1:1; 1 Tim 1:1; 2 Tim 1:1; Titus 1:1). It is used four times in Ephesians (1:1; 2:20; 3:5; 4:11). In the NT the term "apostle"[5] is used in three different ways. First, there are the Twelve that Jesus named "apostles" (Matt 10:2–4 = Mark 3:16–19 = Luke 6:13–16; Acts 1:13). This seems to refer to the office of the apostle. Acts 1:21–22 indicates that to qualify as an apostle one must have been with the Lord in his earthly ministry

---

1739 1881 𝔐 it vg^{cl} syr^{p}. However, the latter reading is preferred because it has both ancient manuscripts and wide geographical distribution representing the Alexandrian, Western, and Byzantine traditions. The first reading does not have as good a geographical distribution. Either reading makes the same sense although the normal genitival form is used in the first reading (1 Cor 1:1; 2 Cor 1:1; Col 1:1; 1 Tim 1:1; 2 Tim 1:1; Titus 1:1; cf. also Rom 1:1; Phil 1:1; Phlm 1). Only twice does the genitival form agree with the second reading: Titus 1:1 and Gal 1:1 where the διά precedes it. Therefore, the second reading is the harder reading. If this is the true reading, it would be another indication that the forger did a poor job or did not know Paul very well if he intended to slavishly copy him. For a study on the order of the names, see Werner Kramer, *Christ, Lord, Son of God*, trans. Brian Hardy, SBT, ed. C F. D. Moule, J. Barr, Peter Ackroyd, Floyd V. Filson, and G. Ernest Wright, vol. 50 (London: SCM, 1966), 59–63, 201–6.

1. Lysias 19.21; Demosthenes *Orationes* 18.80, 107; Karl Heinrich Rengstorf, "ἀπόστολος," *TDNT* 1 (1964): 407; Erich von Eicken and Helgo Linder, "Apostle [ἀποστέλλω]," *NIDNTT* 1 (1975): 127.

2. Herodotus 1.21; 5.38.

3. BDB 1018–19; cf. F.-L. Hossfeld and F. van der Velden, "שָׁלַח *šālaḥ*," *TWAT* 8 (1995): 47–68.

4. Eicken and Linder, *NIDNTT* 1 (1975): 127.

5. For a study of apostles, see J. B. Lightfoot, *Saint Paul's Epistle to the Galatians* (London: Macmillan, 1865; reprint, Grand Rapids: Zondervan, n.d.), 92–101; C. K. Barrett, *The Signs of an Apostle* (London: Epworth, 1970). Barrett lists eight persons, or groups of persons, called apostles (C. K. Barrett, "*Sheliaḥ* and Apostle," in *Donum Gentilicium. New Testament Studies in Honour of David Daube*, ed. E. Bammel, C. K. Barrett, and W. D. Davies [Oxford: Clarendon, 1978], 98). For a study of Paul as an apostle, see F. S. Malan, "The Relationship between Apostolate and Office in the Theology of Paul," *Neot* 10 (1976): 53–68; Ernest Best, "Paul's Apostolic Authority—?" *JSNT* 27 (June 1986): 3–25.

and must have witnessed his resurrection body (Acts 1:21–22; 4:33; 2 Pet 1:16; 1 John 1:1). The witness of the Twelve to Christ's resurrection is affirmed by Paul (1 Cor 15:5). Second, there were apostles in addition to the Twelve. There were Barnabas (Acts 14:4, 14; 1 Cor 9:5–7), James, the Lord's brother (1 Cor 15:7; Gal 1:19), and Apollos (1 Cor 4:6, 9), probably Silvanus (1 Thess 1:1; 2:6 [GT 2:7]), Titus (2 Cor 8:23), Epaphroditus (Phil 2:25), and possibly Andronicus and Junia(s)[1] (Rom 16:7). Paul mentions James and all the apostles (1 Cor 15:7) as distinct from Peter and the Twelve (15:5). In Gal 1:18–19 Paul states that when he went up to Jerusalem he visited Peter and he did not visit other apostles except James, the Lord's brother. Hence, Paul recognized apostles beyond the Twelve. These are most likely those who were endowed with the gift of apostleship because they did not meet the above mentioned qualifications for the office. Third, there was Paul who was an apostle (1 Cor 9:1; 15:9) and yet had not been with Jesus in his earthly ministry but did, however, see the Lord in his resurrection body. Hence, he claimed that he was born out of due season (1 Cor 15:8). Rather than trying to include him in either of the two categories above, it is best to see Paul as an exception to the rule and make a third category. It seems that he had the office of an apostle for the following reasons: (1) he used authority as an apostle (1 Cor 4:9; 9:1, 5; 11:5; 12:11–12); (2) he performed miracles (Acts 13:8–11; 14:3; 19:11; 2 Cor 12:12) that seemed to be done by those who had the office (Acts 2:43; 5:15–16; Heb 2:4); (3) his laying on of hands brought the Holy Spirit to the believers (Acts 19:6) such as happened to Peter (Acts 8:17); and (4) his greetings in most all of his letters (see passages above) are similar to those of Peter (1 Pet 1:1; 2 Pet 1:1). It would not be likely that he would have referred to himself as an apostle in his formal greetings if he had only the gift. Thus, this third category is an exception exclusive to Paul.

In the present context Paul has the office of apostle in mind, declaring that he is an official delegate possessed by Jesus Christ for the purpose of propagating his message.[2] The qualifying genitives (Ἰησοῦ Χριστοῦ) express more than mere possession as would be the case of δοῦλος[3] ("slave") found in Rom 1:1; Phil 1:1; Titus 1:1 or δέσμιος ("prisoner") in Phlm 1, 9. Barrett thinks they express both the possessive idea of ownership and the subjective idea of one who has been sent by Jesus Christ.[4] In relating them to the term ἀπόστολος, Paul envisions that he is not only owned by

1. See Ray R. Schulz, "Romans 16:7: Junia or Junias?" *ExpTim* 98 (January 1987): 108–10.

2. Rienecker (28) states one should not translate "apostle" as "envoy" but as "missionary." However, a missionary without proper legal authority is useless. Certainly an envoy has a mission, namely, to represent the one who sent him. Hence, the two concepts cannot be divorced from one another.

3. Abbott, 1.

4. Barrett, *The Signs of an Apostle*, 45.

Christ but is a fully authorized ambassador sent by him. This is seen more fully in Gal 1:1 where Paul is an apostle not appointed by humans or commissioned by any one person but (ἀλλά) by Jesus Christ and God the Father who raised him from the dead. So an apostle is one who is sent out on a mission with fully delegated authority by his master, just as the original disciples whom Jesus selected were sent out.[1]

The apostle had full authority in oral and written proclamation. This can be seen in the oral form with the preaching by Peter (Acts 2:14–40; 3:12–26) and Paul (13:16–41; 17:22–31) and when Peter disciplined Ananias and Sapphira (5:1–10). The written form is seen in the books of the NT, each produced by the power of the Holy Spirit. Another role of an apostle was to establish and build up churches. Jesus was the founder of the church (Matt 16:18) and the apostles were to build on him. Certainly, throughout Acts many churches were established. In fact, Paul makes it clear that the purpose of his preaching was to establish churches and he would not go where this was being done by another (Rom 15:20). In conclusion, it can be said that an apostle was an official delegate of Jesus Christ commissioned for the specific tasks of proclaiming authoritatively the message in oral and written form and of establishing and the building up of churches. More will be discussed in 2:20 and 4:11.

διὰ θελήματος θεοῦ, "by the will of God." These same words are also found in 1 Cor 1:1; 2 Cor 1:1; Col 1:1; 2 Tim 1:1. The διά denotes efficient cause or agency[2] by which Paul received his apostleship. It was not by personal drive or presumptuous human ambition but by God's will and initiative that Paul was made an apostle. Paul was fully cognizant that not only his conversion (Gal 1:15) and his new life

1. Holger Mosbech, "Apostolos in the New Testament," *ST* 2, no. 2 (1948): 170–72. For other studies, see J. B. Lightfoot, "The name and office of an Apostle," in *Saint Paul's Epistle to the Galatians* (London: Macmillan, 1865; reprint, Grand Rapids: Zondervan, n.d.), 92–101; Rengstorf, "ἀποστέλλω, κτλ.," *TDNT* 1 (1964): 398–447; Hans Frhr. von Campenhausen, "Der urchristliche Apostelbegriff," *ST* 1, nos. 1–2 (1947): 96–130; Johannes Munck, "Paul, the Apostle, and the Twelve," *ST* 3, no. 1 (1949): 96–110; Rudolf Schnackenburg, "Apostles before and during Paul's Time [trans. Manfred Kiviran and W. Ward Gasque]," in *Apostolic History and the Gospel. Biblical and Historical Essays Presented to F. F. Bruce on His 60th Birthday*, ed. W. Ward Gasque and Ralph P. Martin (Exeter: Paternoster; Grand Rapids: Eerdmans, 1970), 287–303; Barrett, "*Sheliaḥ* and Apostle," 88–102; John Howard Schütz, *Paul and the Anatomy of Apostolic Authority*, SNTSMS, ed. Matthew Black and R. McL. Wilson, vol. 26 (Cambridge: Cambridge University Press, 1975); Robert W. Herron Jr., "The Origin of the New Testament Apostolate," *WTJ* 45 (spring 1983): 101–31.

2. BAGD 180; BDAG 224–25; A. T. Robertson, *A Grammar of the Greek New Testament in the Light of Historical Research*, 4th ed. (Nashville: Broadman, [1923]), 582; C. F. D. Moule, *An Idiom Book of New Testament Greek*, 2d ed. (Cambridge: Cambridge University Press, 1959), 57; Daniel B. Wallace, *Greek Grammar Beyond the Basics: An Exegetical Syntax of the New Testament* (Grand Rapids: Zondervan, 1996), 434 n. 79; Eadie, 1.

(Phil 2:13; Gal 1:23–24; 2:20) were of God, but, also, his apostleship as a missionary to the Gentiles was of God (Eph 3:1–2, 8, 13; Gal 1:1, 16; 2:2, 8; Rom 1:1, 5; 11:13; 1 Cor 15:9–10; 1 Tim 2:7; 2 Tim 1:11; Acts 9:15; 13:2, 47; 18:6; 22:21; 26:17).

The term θέλημα rarely used in the classical literature, means "wish, will,"[1] something that a human being has that plant life does not have.[2] In the LXX it appears forty-seven times (thirty-four times in the canonical books) and is used with reference to human desire or wish (e.g., 2 Sam 23:6; 1 Kgs 5:8–10 [MT & LXX 5:22–24]; Esth 1:8; Pss 1:2; 28:7 [LXX 27:7]; 107:30 [106:30]), his pleasure (e.g., Eccl 12:1, 10; Isa 58:3, 13), and will (Jer 23:17, 26; Dan 11:16, 36). Also, some passages refer to God's will (Pss 103:7, 21 [LXX 102:7, 21]; 143:10 [LXX 142:10]; Isa 48:14) and his pleasure or delight (Ps 16:3 [LXX 15:3]; Isa 62:4; Jer 9:24 [MT & LXX 9:23]; Mal 1:10). Hence, it has the idea of desire, wish, will, or resolve. This term is used sixty-two times in the NT, twenty-four times by Paul, and of those, seven times in Ephesians (1:1, 5, 9, 11; 2:3; 5:17; 6:6). Only eleven times does it refer to human desire or will (Matt 21:31; Luke 12:47*bis*; 23:25; John 1:13*bis*; 7:17; 1 Cor 16:12) and desire or impulse (1 Cor 7:37; Eph 2:3; 2 Pet 1:21), and once to the devil's will or desire (2 Tim 2:26). In these texts one finds both the idea of pleasure and resolve, depending on the context. The other fifty-one occurrences refer to God's will, and, with the exception of Acts 13:22, it is always in the singular to present the concept that God's will is a powerful unity.[3] God's will is his desire or divine resolve "which cannot remain in the sphere of thought but demands action."[4] It is the doing of God's will that gives God pleasure and glory.

In Ephesians, with the exception of 2:3, this word always refers to God's will. For the present context, Barth prefers the translation "decision," contending that the term "will" might be understood as the fixed plan of an impersonal fate.[5] However, "will" is a commonly used word with reference to living and personal beings both divine and human. With regard to its usage here, it denotes a living and personal being who acts freely according to his character and brings to bear his will on those serving him. It does not seem as impersonal and fatalistic as the word "decision." Regardless, the picture is not that God was capitulating to the whims and desires of human beings but that his will was being worked out in Paul.

[6]**τοῖς ἁγίοις τοῖς οὖσιν ἐν Ἐφέσῳ,** "to the saints who are in Ephesus." The recipients of the letter are addressed as "saints" as in Phil

1. Aeneas Tacticus 2.8; 18.19.
2. Aristotle *De Plantis* 1.1 §815b.21.
3. Gottlob Schrenk, "θέλημα," *TDNT* 3 (1965): 54.
4. Ibid., 57.
5. Barth, 65.
6. The insertion πᾶσιν before τοῖς ἁγίοις is found in ℵ[2] A P 81 326 629 2464 *pc* it[b, f] vg[(cl), st, ww] cop[bo] and 𝔓[46] omits τοῖς. The omission of πᾶσιν is found in ℵ* B D F G Ψ 0278

1:1; Col 1:2; rather than "church(es)" as in 1 Cor 1:1; 2 Cor 1:1; Gal 1:2; 1 Thess 1:1; 2 Thess 1:1; Phlm 2. The term ἅγιος, "saint," originally had "a cultic concept, referring to the quality possessed by things and persons that could approach a divinity."[1] The Hebrew substantive (קֹדֶשׁ) is predominantly impersonal, referring to a place (Exod 3:5; Josh 5:15), to the temple (1 Chr 29:3; Ps 5:7) and its parts (Exod 26:33–34; Ps 28:2), to the sacrifices (Lev 22:12; 23:20) and vessels (1 Sam 21:5–7; 1 Kgs 8:4), and to the Sabbath (Exod 31:14–15; Neh 9:14), among other things. However, a few references allude to people (Exod 22:31; Isa 62:12; Ezra 8:28)[2] and many refer to God's name, which may be conceivably counted as personal since God and his name are inseparable (cf. Lev 22:2, 32; 1 Chr 16:10, 35; Ps 103:1; 105:1; 145:21; Ezek 20:39; 36:20–22; 39:7*bis*, 25, 43:7–8; Amos 2:7). Thus, although the adjective קָדוֹשׁ can refer to impersonal things like a nation (Exod 19:6) or a place (Exod 29:31; Lev 6:16 [MT & LXX 6:9]; 10:13; Ps 46:4; Isa 57:15; Ezek 42:13), its predominant use is personal and can denote God's unique character (Isa 1:14; 5:16; 6:3; Jer 50:29; 51:5; Ezek 39:7; Hos 11:9). It is also used to refer to angels (Job 5:1; 15:15; Ps 89:5, 7; Dan 8:13) and human beings who are called "holy [one(s), people]" (Lev 21:7; Num 6:5, 8; 16:3, 5, 7; Deut 7:6; 14:2; 26:19; 28:9; 2 Kgs 4:9; 2 Chr 35:3; Isa 4:3; Dan 8:24) or "saints" (Pss 16:3; 34:9; 106:16; Hos 11:12 [MT & LXX 12:1]; Zech 14:5 [קַדִּישׁ in Dan 7:18, 21, 22*bis*, 25, 27]).[3] Therefore, both the substantive and the adjective can be used to denote God's unique character, but they can also be used of things, places, and persons. When the term is used to refer to things, places, and persons, it does not in itself connote any inherent holiness, for the basic root can also refer to temple prostitutes, whether they are male (קָדֵשׁ in Deut 23:17 [MT & LXX 23:18]; 1 Kgs 14:24; 15:12; 22:46 [MT & LXX 22:47]; 2 Kgs 23:7; Job 36:14) or female (קְדֵשָׁה in Deut 23:17 [MT & LXX 23:18]; Hos 4:14).[4] Thus the basic idea is that which is consecrated to God or to God's service or, in the case of the temple prostitutes, who are dedicated to the service of temple gods or cultic worship. Similarly, members of the Qumran community were frequently designated as

---

33 1739 1881 𝔐 it[a, r] Victorinus-Rome Jerome. The inclusion of πᾶσιν was probably influenced by the reading in Rom 1:7 (πᾶσιν τοῖς οὖσιν ἐν Ῥώμῃ), but it has limited manuscript support. Its omission is the preferred reading because it is supported by the best and earliest manuscripts with a wide geographical distribution and good genealogical solidarity in the Alexandrian, Western, and Byzantine text-types.

1. BAGD 9; BDAG 10.

2. *Contra* Otto Procksch, "ἅγιος," *TDNT* 1 (1964): 90.

3. BDB 871–72; cf. W. Kornfeld and H. Ringgren, "קדשׁ *qdš*, etc.," *TWAT* 6 (1989): 1181–1200.

4. BDB 873; Kornfeld and Ringgren, *TWAT* 6 (1989): 1200–1201.

"holy ones" (e.g., CD 20:8; 1QS 1:1; 11:18; 1QM 6:6; 12:1–2, 4; cf. 1QS 11:7–9).[1]

So also in the NT ἅγιος can refer to God,[2] Jesus,[3] and the Holy Spirit,[4] which would reveal the unique character of their persons. Furthermore, it can also refer to things,[5] places,[6] angels,[7] and human beings.[8] In these latter categories nothing is inherently or intrinsically unique or holy. There are things (e.g., Rom 11:16) and places (e.g., Matt 4:5) that are not intrinsically holy, and angels who are evil (Matt 25:41; Jude 6; Rev 12:7, 9). With regard to humans, when it is used adjectively, it describes the person as holy, such as John the Baptist (Mark 6:20), the prophets (Luke 1:70; Acts 3:21; 2 Pet 3:2), apostles (Eph 3:5), and children (1 Cor 7:14). When it is used substantively, it is used of those who are called saints (1 Cor 1:2) who may have practiced unholy things (5:1). In fact, the saints of Ephesus were admonished to stop practicing the lifestyle of those who were not saints (Eph 4:25–32). The reason that saints are to abstain from the sins of the ungodly is because their bodies are the temples of the Holy Spirit (1 Cor 6:15–20) and because of their position as saints (Eph 5:3), not because they are not inherently holy in themselves. The idea, then, is that they had the position of saints and thus were to act saintly. They obtained this position because they had appropriated Christ's work to their lives (1 Cor 6:11) rather than gained it by acting saintly. Therefore, in the context of the Bible and of the NT in

1. For a helpful comparison between the Qumran literature and the Book of Ephesians, see Nils Alstrup Dahl, "Ephesians and Qumran," in *Studies in Ephesians: Introductory Questions, Text- & Edition-Critical Issues, Interpretation of Texts and Themes*, ed. David Hellholm, Vemund Blomkvist, and Tord Fornberg, WUNT, ed. Martin Hengel and Otfried Hofius, vol. 131 (Tübingen: Mohr, 2000), 107–44.

2. Luke 1:49; John 17:11; 1 Pet 1:15, 16; Rev 4:8; 6:10.

3. Mark 1:24; Luke 1:35; 4:34; John 6:69; Acts 3:14; 4:27, 30; 1 John 2:20; Rev 3:7.

4. Matt 3:11 = Mark 1:8 = Luke 3:16; Matt 12:32 = Mark 3:29 = Luke 12:10; Matt 1:18, 20; 28:19; Mark 12:36; 13:11; Luke 1:15, 35, 41, 67; 2:25, 26; 3:22; 4:1; 10:21; 11:13; 12:12; John 1:33; 14:26; 20:22; Acts 1:2, 5, 8, 16; 2:4, 33, 38; 4:8, 25, 31; 5:3, 32; 6:5; 7:51, 55; 8:15, 17, 18, 19; 9:17, 31; 10:38, 44, 45, 47; 11:15, 16, 24; 13:2, 4, 9, 52; 15:8, 28; 16:6; 19:2*bis*, 6; 20:23, 28; 21:11; 28:25; Rom 5:5; 9:1; 14:17; 15:13, 16, 19; 1 Cor 6:19; 2 Cor 6:6; Eph 1:13; 4:30; 1 Thess 1:5, 6; 4:8; 2 Tim 1:14; Titus 3:5; Heb 2:4; 3:7; 6:4; 9:8; 10:15; 1 Pet 1:12; 2 Pet 1:21; Jude 20.

5. Matt 7:6?; Luke 1:72; Rom 1:2; 7:12*bis*; 11:16*bis*; 12:1; 16:16; 1 Cor 3:17; 16:20; 2 Cor 13:12; Eph 5:27; 1 Thess 5:26; 2 Tim 1:9; 1 Pet 2:9; 2 Pet 2:21.

6. Matt 4:5; 24:15; 27:53; Acts 6:13; 7:33; 21:28; Eph 2:21; Heb 8:2; 9:1, 2, 3, 8, 12, 24, 25; 10:19; 13:11; 2 Pet 1:18; Rev 11:2; 21:2, 10; 22:19.

7. Mark 8:38 = Luke 9:26; Acts 10:22; Jude 14; Rev 14:10.

8. Mark 6:20; Luke 1:70; 2:23; Acts 3:21; 9:13, 32, 41; 26:10; Rom 1:7; 8:27; 12:13; 15:25, 26, 31; 16:2, 15; 1 Cor 1:2; 6:1, 2; 7:14, 34; 14:33; 16:1, 15; 2 Cor 1:1; 8:4; 9:1, 12; 13:13; Eph 1:1, 4, 15, 18; 2:19; 3:5, 8, 18; 4:12; 5:3; 6:18; Phil 1:1; 4:21, 22; Col 1:2, 4, 12, 22, 26; 3:12; 1 Thess 3:13; 5:27?; 2 Thess 1:10; 1 Tim 5:10; Phlm 5, 7; Heb 3:1; 6:10; 13:24; 1 Pet 1:15; 2:5; 3:5; 2 Pet 3:2, 11; Jude 3; Rev 5:8; 8:3, 4; 11:18; 13:7, 10; 14:12; 16:6; 17:6; 18:20, 24; 19:8; 20:6, 9; 22:11*bis*, 21?.

particular, the term "saint" does not have the cultic concept nor does the saint possess a quality that allows him or her to claim divinity. The term is applied to all believers. The believer can approach God only because he or she has obtained a righteous standing or position on the basis of Christ's work by means of faith. Paul addresses his letter to these people.

With reference to believers the term ἅγιος is used in three senses in the NT.[1] First, very few passages refer to the believer's personal sanctity (Rom 12:1; Eph 1:4; Col 1:22; 1 Pet 1:15–16). Second, a few instances refer to the believers as members of a spiritual community (1 Cor 6:2; Eph 1:18; 2:19; 3:18; Col 1:12; 3:12; 1 Pet 2:5, 9). Third, the overwhelmingly predominate use refers to members of a visible and local body (e.g., Acts 9:13, 32, 41; 26:10; Rom 1:7; 15:26; 1 Cor 1:2). The context determines its usage. Normally the term is in the plural and is one of the most frequent designations of the believers. When used of believers, it is always in the plural.

Paul addresses the saints who reside in Ephesus. The background and description of the city is discussed in the introduction. The inclusion of "in Ephesus" is supported as the best reading. Externally, it has excellent support in the date and character, geographical distribution, and genealogical relationships of the manuscripts. Internally, the inclusion of "in Ephesus" has good support in both the transcriptional and intrinsic probabilities. For further discussion of the textual problem, see Excursus 1: Textual Problem in Ephesians 1:1.

However, one further item needs to be discussed. Kümmel, among others, finds it remarkable that the epistle lacks any sort of relationship with the readers indicated by the fact that he had only heard of their faith and love (1:15), he had to present himself commissioned by God as the missionary to the Gentiles (3:2), he did not address himself to concrete problems, and he alluded to some teaching the Ephesians had heard which was strange to him (4:21–22).[2] Furthermore, a lack of personal attention is evidenced by his failure to mention any individuals in the church where he had labored for three years (Acts 20:31). These problems are not as great as they might appear to be. First, it is possible that he is referring to what he had heard of their faith and love (Eph 1:15) since leaving them.[3] Second, 3:2 must be closely connected to verse 13 where it states that the Ephesians were not to sorrow over his imprisonment but, rather, understand his commission as an apostle to the Gentiles. He was not introducing himself to them but only reminding them that his imprisionment was their glory. Third, he does address a specific problem, namely, that of love both in doctrine and its practice among believers, especially regarding the mutual love between Jewish and Gentile Christians (see Introduc-

1. Ellicott, 1–2.

2. Kümmel, *Introduction to the New Testament*, 352.

3. Guthrie, *New Testament Introduction*, 529–30.

tion). Interestingly, although Romans does not state problems any more concretely, its authencity is not questioned by most. Fourth, in 4:21–22 Paul is not implying that the preaching they had heard was strange to him but that they were to live out what they heard. They were to have the hearing of faith, not just the hearing of the ears. Finally, the fact that he did not mention any individuals could indicate that he did not want to single out certain persons in his short letter, since he knew so many as a result of his extended ministry there.

Furthermore, Paul may have intended this as a circular letter even though he did not specifically state it. Accepting the ἐν Ἐφέσῳ as genuine and yet considering it circular is not a contradiction. There is no real doubt about the destination of the Colossian letter and yet Paul in Col 4:16 tells them to have it read to the church in Laodecia and that, in turn, they were to read the letter he had sent to the Laodecians. Also, since Ephesus was the center of his western Asia Minor ministry and it is probable that the other churches of that area were established by him or his disciples during his long stay at Ephesus, it is reasonable to think that a letter to the Ephesian church would go to the satellite churches in that area. The Book of Galatians, which is not disputed, also lacks personal greetings and this Kümmel readily admits.[1] It, too, was an encyclical letter since it is addressed to the "churches of Galatia" (Gal 1:2). In addition to the Galatian churches, Lenski points out that Paul founded the churches at Corinth and Thessalonica, yet 2 Corinthians and both Thessalonian letters lack personal greetings.[2] On the other hand, Black thinks that the impersonal character of Ephesians is not out of character with the rest of Paul's epistles and thinks it should not be even considered as an encyclical letter.[3]

In conclusion, although it may lack the personal warmth of some of Paul's epistles, it is reasonable to accept that the apostle wrote this letter to the believers at Ephesus where he had an effective ministry in previous years, and possibly even to the surrounding regions to which he had not ministered directly.

καὶ πιστοῖς ἐν Χριστῷ Ἰησοῦ, "that is, believers in Christ Jesus." Without the repeat of the article before πιστοῖς, the phrase is somewhat difficult to interpret. The exact form is unparalleled in Pauline greetings. In Col 1:2 the same basic words are used, but the structure is different (τοῖς ἐν Κολοσσαῖς ἁγίοις καὶ πιστοῖς ἀδελφοῖς ἐν Χριστῷ) where the one article unites the two terms. Although in Col 1:2 no verb "to be" (οὖσιν) is used, it is utilized in Rom 1:1 and Phil 1:1, but neither of these passages have it followed by the conjunction (καί)

1. Kümmel, *Introduction to the New Testament,* 352.

2. Lenski, 334.

3. Black, "The Peculiarities of Ephesians and the Ephesian Address," 59–73; see also J. Rendel Harris, "Epaphroditus, Scribe and Courier," *Exp* 8th ser., vol. 8 (December 1898): 406–9.

with an anarthrous descriptive phrase as in Eph 1:1. Thus, what did Paul mean by this phrase?

The conjunction καί could be translated "and," which could mean that two groups were being addressed, that is, to the saints who were in Ephesus and to those who were faithful.[1] However, the other greetings of Paul do not support this idea. Rather, the picture is that the two appellations refer to one and the same group. In Col 1:1 the one article unites the two. In Rom 1:7 it is "to all in Rome beloved of God, called saints." The beloved and saints are one. In 1 Cor 1:2 it is "to the church of God in Corinth, who have been sanctified in Christ Jesus, called saints." The church and the saints refer to the same group. Thus, in the present context it is better to see καί used as epexegetical or explicative, indicating that both adjectives refer to the same group and is to be translated "that is" or "namely" or omitted in the translation.[2]

The word πιστός can be taken in either the passive sense, that is, one who is faithful or trustworthy (Matt 25:21*bis*, 23*bis*; 1 Cor 4:2; 7:25); or the active sense, namely, one who trusts another, that is, a believer (Acts 10:45; Gal 3:9; 1 Pet 1:21). Lightfoot thinks πιστός is used in the passive sense because the active sense "believing" would add nothing to the aforementioned ἁγίοις.[3] However, in this context the active sense fits better being in agreement with its near parallel use in Col 1:2 where it modifies the noun "brothers." It further defines that the saints are those who are believers in Christ Jesus as opposed to saints of the OT era. Furthermore, the "faithful" saints would not need the exhortations of the epistle nearly as much as the "unfaithful" saints. In this epistle Paul is not contrasting the faithful and unfaithful saints, but he is describing the saints as those who are believers in Christ Jesus. The opposite of a believer is an ἄπιστος, "unbeliever," who is not a saint, one who does not trust Christ. Twice in the NT the two terms are used within the same verse marking the stark contrast (John 20:27; 2 Cor 6:15). Although the word "believers" is anarthrous, it is united to "saints" by the article that precedes "saints."

Because of the single article before "saints," the prepositional phrase ἐν Χριστῷ Ἰησοῦ further defines both the ἁγίοις and πιστοῖς. To have it refer only to πιστοῖς would be strange for it would mean the

1. As does Kirby, *Ephesians, Baptism and Pentecost*, 170. He thinks that the "saints" refer to Jewish Christians and the "faithful" refer to the Gentile Christians. This does not seem plausible for the epistle emphasizes unity of Jewish and Gentile Christians and here the author would encourage the continuance of the division. His proof texts of 2:12 and 19 are not valid, for Paul is showing that Gentiles who were outside God's salvation are now inside and are on equal footing with the saints of the OT.

2. Daniel B. Wallace, "The Semantic Range of the Article-Noun-καί-Noun Plural Construction in the New Testament," *GTJ* 4 (spring 1983): 75–77; idem, *Greek Grammar*, 282; Barth, 68.

3. J. B. Lightfoot, *Notes on Epistles of St Paul from Unpublished Commentaries* (London: Macmillan, 1895; reprint, Grand Rapids: Zondervan, 1957), 310.

"believers" are in Christ Jesus and the "saints" are not. Even if one were to render the πιστοῖς as "faithful" it still would be odd to have only the "faithful" in Christ Jesus but the other saints not in Christ Jesus. Therefore, ἐν Χριστῷ Ἰησοῦ refers back to both ἁγίοις and πιστοῖς. Moreover, the one article that governs both the "saints" and "believers" prevents one from making ἐν Χριστῷ Ἰησοῦ a simple object of only "believers" so as to render it "believing Christ."[1] Rather, Paul is addressing the believers who are in Christ Jesus.

This particular prepositional phrase is used seven times in Ephesians (1:1; 2:6, 7, 10, 13; 3:6, 21). Similiar prepositional phrases are used throughout Ephesians with various connotations that are determined by the individual contexts (see Excursus 3: In Christ). More will be discussed at verse 3. In this context it has the idea of incorporation,[2] the union of believers to Christ.[3] This marks the new era, for the saints are those who are connected with Christ Jesus, something to which the OT saints looked forward. Again the phrase refers to the believer who is in Christ, not to the one who believes Christ. To be in Christ is the result of believing Christ.

The term Χριστός, "Christ,"[4] comes from the OT מָשִׁיחַ, "anointed one," or "Messiah."[5] Today "Christ" is thought of by many as a surname. Early in the church's development the Gentile pagans called the believers in Antioch "Chrsitians" presumably because they followed someone whose name was "Christ" (Acts 11:26; cf. 26:28). However, "Christ" does have more significance than just a last name. In the first sermon preached at Pentecost, Peter emphasized that this crucified Jesus was both Lord and Christ (Acts 2:36). To Paul, the Pharisaic

1. Moule, *Idiom Book*, 108.

2. NEB translates it "believers incorporate in Christ Jesus" and TEV renders it "in union with Christ Jesus."

3. Caird, 31; Barth, 69–71; Ernest Best, *One Body in Christ. A Study in the Relationship of the Church to Christ in the Epistles of the Apostle Paul* (London: SPCK, 1955), 1; cf. also Albrecht Oepke, "ἐν," *TDNT* 2 (1964): 541.

4. For some recent literature on this subject, see L. Cerfaux, *Christ in the Theology of St. Paul*, trans. Geoffrey Webb and Adrian Walker (New York: Herder and Herder; Edinburgh: Thomas Nelson and Sons, 1959), 480–508; Kramer, *Christ, Lord, Son of God*, 19–44, 133–50, 203–14; Ferdinand Hahn, *The Titles of Jesus in Christology: Their History in Early Christianity*, trans. Harold Knight and George Ogg, Lutterworth Library, ed. James Barr, C. F. D. Moule, Dennis E. Nineham, and A. Marcus Ward (London: Lutterworth; New York: World, 1969), 136–239; Nils Alstrup Dahl, "The Messiahship of Jesus in Paul," in *The Crucified Messiah and Other Essays*, ed. Nils Alstrup Dahl (Minneapolis: Augsburg, 1974), 37–47; Walter Grundmann, "χρίω," *TDNT* 9 (1974): 527–62; C. F. D. Moule, *The Origin of Christology* (Cambridge: Cambridge University, 1977), 31–35; Martin Hengel, "'Christos' in Paul," *Between Jesus and Paul: Studies in the Earliest History of Christianity*, trans. John Bowden (London: SCM, 1983), 65–77.

5. Moule, *The Origin of Christology*, 31–35; see also, M. de Jonge, "The Use of the Word 'Anointed' in the Time of Jesus," *NovT* 8 (April–October 1966): 132–48; cf. BDB 603; K. Seybold, "מָשַׁח *māšaḥ*; מָשִׁיחַ *māšîaḥ*," *TDOT* 9 (1998):43–45, 49–54.

Jew, it was blasphemous to identify the crucified Jesus as the Messiah (Gal 3:13; 5:11; 1 Cor 1:23).[1] After his conversion, he preached to the Jews that Jesus was the Son of God and the Christ (Acts 9:20–22; 17:2–3; 18:5).[2] In his letters to predominantly Gentile audiences, he does not emphasize that Jesus was the Christ. However, Dahl argues that the interchangeability of the terms Jesus Christ (e.g., Rom 1:6; 1 Cor 3:11; Gal 1:12) and Christ Jesus (e.g., Rom 3:24; 1 Cor 4:15; Gal 2:4) indicates that Christ is not a fixed proper name. He proposes, rather, that Jesus is his proper name, for there are instances when a title is associated with it as in "Jesus is Lord" (Rom 10:9; 1 Cor 12:3) or "Jesus Christ is Lord" (Phil 2:11) or where he is called "Lord Jesus" (e.g., Rom 14:14; 1 Cor 5:4–5; 11:23; 2 Cor 4:14; 11:31; Phil 2:19) and "Lord Jesus Christ" (e.g., Rom 1:7; 5:1, 11; 13:14; 1 Cor 8:6; Gal 6:14; Eph 6:23; Phil 3:20) but never "Lord Christ" for that would be redundant.[3] Therefore, although Christ is a proper name, it is more than that.[4] When Paul preached to the Jews he tried to convince them that the Jesus who died and rose from the dead was the Christ or the promised Messiah who would bring salvation and the eschatological kingdom. But when the Jews rejected Paul's message, he went to the Gentiles (Acts 18:6; 28:28) and to them he presented Jesus Christ as the only one who could bring them salvation. Christ, who is inseparably united to Jesus,[5] is both a name and title referring to God's anointed on whom all must trust for salvation. It is with him that believers are united and this is what it means to be "in Christ Jesus." The believers are united with the one who provided salvation.

Excursus 1
Textual Problem in Ephesians 1:1

NA[27]

1 Παῦλος ἀπόστολος ⸉Χριστοῦ Ἰησοῦ⸊ διὰ θελήματος θεοῦ τοῖς ἁγίοις ⸀τοῖς οὖσιν ⸋[ἐν Ἐφέσῳ]⸌ καὶ πιστοῖς ἐν Χριστοῦ Ἰησοῦ, **2** χάρις ὑμῖν καὶ εἰρήνη ἀπὸ θεοῦ πατρὸς ἡμῶν καὶ κυρίου Ἰησοῦ Χριστοῦ.

⸋𝔓[46] ℵ* B* 6. 1739; (Mcion[T, E] *cf Inscr.*) ¦ *txt* ℵ[2] A B[2] D F G Ψ 0278. 33. 1881 𝔐 latt sy co

1. Hengel, "'Christos' in Paul," 71.

2. Cerfaux, *Christ in the Theology of St. Paul*, 487.

3. Dahl, "The Messiahship of Jesus in Paul," 38. The only places where he is called Lord Christ are in Rom 16:18 and Col 3:24 and in both cases it contrasts serving the Lord Christ to serving other lords.

4. *Contra* Hahn, *The Titles of Jesus in Christology*, 193.

5. The inseparability of Jesus and Christ is seen in Paul for he talks about the sacrificial death of Jesus (1 Thess 1:10; 4:14; cf. also 5:10; Rom 8:11) and of Christ (e.g., Rom 5:8; 1 Cor 15:3; 2 Cor 5:14–21; Gal 3:13). Thus Jesus and Christ are one and the same person.

UBS^4

1 Παῦλος ἀπόστολος Χριστοῦ Ἰησοῦ διὰ θελήματος θεοῦ τοῖς ἁγίοις τοῖς οὖσιν [ἐν Ἐφέσῳ][1]
καὶ πιστοῖς ἐν Χριστοῦ Ἰησοῦ· **2** χάρις ὑμῖν καὶ εἰρήνη ἀπὸ θεοῦ πατρὸς ἡμῶν καὶ κυρίου Ἰησοῦ Χριστοῦ.

[1]1 {C} ἐν Ἐφέσῳ א^2 A B^2 D F G Ψ^c (Ψ* *illegible*) 075 0150 33 81 104 256 263 365 424* 436 459 1175 1241 1319 1573 1852 1881 1912 1962 2127 2200 2464 *Byz* [K L P] *Lect* it$^{ar, b, d, f, g, o, r}$ vg syr$^{p, h}$ cop$^{sa, bo}$ arm eth geo slav Ps-Ignatius Chrysostom Theodore^{lat}; Victorinus-Rome Ambrosiaster Jerome Pelagius // *omit* 𝔓^{46} א* B* 6 424^c 1739 Marcion$^{acc. to Tertullian}$ Origen^{vid}

Readings	Alexandrian	Western	Byzantine	Others
ἐν Ἐφέσῳ	A Ψ^c	D F G	*Byz* [K L P]	א^2 B^2
	33 81 104 1175 1881			075 0150 256 263 365 424* 436 459 1241 1319 1573 1852 1912 1962 2127 2200 2464
			Lect	
	cop$^{sa, bo}$ vg	it$^{ar, b, d, f, g, o, r}$ (syr^h)	syr^p goth, slav	arm, geo
	Jerome	Ambrosiaster? Pelagius Theodore Victorinus	Chrysostom	Ps-Ignatius
omit	𝔓^{46} א* B* 6 1739			424^c
	(Origen^{vid})	Marcion? Tertullian?		

A great deal of ink has flowed concerning the textual problem ἐν Ἐφέσῳ in Eph 1:1.[1] It is bracketed in both NA^{27} and UBS^4. Looking at the external evidence[2] the oldest Alexandrian uncials 𝔓^{46} (III—Roman numerals indicate centuries) א* (IV) B* (IV) as well as minuscules 6 (XIII), 1739 (X), and a corrector of 424 (XI) omit the words. The inclusion of the words is found in the Alexandrian uncials א^2 (VI/VII), A (V), B^2 (X/XI), Ψ^c (VIII/IX); minuscules 33 (IX), 81 (XI), 104 (XI), 1175 (XI), and 1881 (XIV); and versions cop^{sa} (III), cop^{bo} (IV), vg (IV/V). Although outside of A, the uncials are quite late but the cop$^{sa, bo}$ versions are really early, which may have a tradition behind them earlier than the extant uncials that omit the words. Also, minuscule 33 is an excellent representative of the Alexandrian text-type. In the Western text the inclusion has good representation with D (VI), F (IX), G (IX) in the Greek manuscripts and an abundance of the it$^{ar, b, d, f, g, o, r}$ (V–XV) versions and possibly syr^h (VII) (whose text-type is difficult to identify). In Byzantine tradition the inclusion is seen in *Byz* [K (IX), L (IX), P (VI)] and *Lect* in the Greek manuscripts and syr^p (IV/V), goth (IV), arm (IV/V) in the versions. The inclusion of the words is also found in manuscripts,

1. For a review of the various solutions offered throughout church history, see Schmid, *Der Epheserbrief des Apostels Paulus. Seine Adresse, Sprache und literarischen Beziehungen Untersucht*, 51–129; Percy, *Probleme*, 449–66; Best, "Ephesians i.1," 29–41; Muddiman, 59–62.

2. For classification and dating much help was derived from Kurt Aland and Barbara Aland, *The Text of the New Testament: An Introduction to the Critical Editions and to the Theory and Practice of Modern Textual Criticism*, trans. Erroll F. Rhodes, 2d ed. rev. and enl. (Grand Rapids: Eerdmans; Leiden: Brill, 1989); Bruce M. Metzger, *The Text of the New Testament: Its Transmission, Corruption, and Restoration*, 3d enl. ed. (New York: Oxford University Press, 1992).

which are significantly independent of the Byzantine manuscript tradition including uncials 075 (X) and 0150 (IX) and minuscules 256 263 365 424* 436 459 1241 1319 1573 1852 1912 1962 2127 2200 2464 (IX–XIV). Among the church fathers Origen (III) excludes it but admits there are grammatical difficulties with its exclusion.[1] According to Tertullian (III),[2] Marcion (II) supplies "to the Laodiceans" and it is debated whether or not his original text was wanting or he changed it. Since Tertullian is probably arguing about the superscription, it is difficult to know if even Tertullian's text had ἐν Ἐφέσῳ in it. However, Ambrosiaster (IV), Chrysostom (IV), Pelagius (IV), Victorinus-Rome (IV), Theodore of Mopsuestia (IV/V), Jerome (IV/V), and Pseudo-Ignatius (V) had texts that included the words.

The external evidence must be examined in three areas. First, the date and character of the three early Alexandrian manuscripts for the omission of ἐν Ἐφέσῳ are excellent. However, the date and character of the witnesses for the inclusion of ἐν Ἐφέσῳ are also very good. Support in the Alexandrian text-type includes A and Ψ^{vid} as well as $\aleph^2$ and B^2 and the important minuscules 33 and 81 among others and the early versions $cop^{sa, bo}$ and Vg, all of which give a very good Alexandrian tradition. Furthermore, the date and character of the Western (e.g., D, F, G, it) and Byzantine (e.g., K, L, P syr^p, goth) manuscript tradition for the inclusion of the words are excellent.[3] Second, the geographical distribution of the witnesses that agree in support of the omission of ἐν Ἐφέσῳ is poor, being limited to the Alexandrian text-type, whereas the geographical distribution supporting its inclusion is excellent, being represented by all the text-types. Third, the genealogical relationship of the texts is divided between the two readings in the Alexandrian text. Although within the Alexandrian text-type most would think that the genealogical relationship of the texts favors the omission of ἐν Ἐφέσῳ, nevertheless, the genealogical relationship of the texts for its inclusion is also very good. It seems that within the Alexandrian text-type the genealogical relationship of the texts are approximately equal in evidential weight. Certainly the genealogical relationship of the texts in the Western and Byzantine text-types is decidedly in favor of the inclusion of the words. In conclusion, as to external evidence, it seems improbable to exclude ἐν Ἐφέσῳ from the verse on the basis of only three early manuscripts.[4] Furthermore, when one examines the three early Alexandrian texts, along with all other manuscripts, they all have the superscript ΠΡΟΣ ΕΦΕΣΙΟΥΣ ("To the Ephesians"). Thus, very early this letter was known as the Ephesian letter.

Since the external evidence is overwhelmingly in favor of the inclusion of ἐν Ἐφέσῳ, internal evidence should not be highly determinative. Two additional areas need to be considered: transcriptional and intrinsic probabilities. First, with regards to transcriptional probabilities, normally the more difficult and shorter readings are preferred. Certainly the omission would fit both of these canons. It is a more difficult reading and it is easy to understand why a scribe would insert the words if the original words were missing. It may

1. J. A. F. Gregg, "The Commentary of Origen upon the Epistle to the Ephesians," *JTS* 3 (January 1902): 235; cf. also Aberle, "Ueber eine Aeußerung des Origenes zu Eph. 1,1," *TQ* 34, no. 1 (1852): 108–22.

2. Tertullian *Adversus Marcionem* 5.11.12; 5.17.1 (*PL* 2:500; 2:512).

3. It is generally true that the date of the Western and Byzantine manuscripts are not as early as the Alexandrian. This is not difficult to explain when one considers the conducive climate for many of the Alexandrian manuscripts. If one is concerned with the earliest manuscripts, then the Alexandrian text-type will always win. Is it not fairer to consider which are the earliest manuscripts in each text-type? One cannot expect as early uncials in the Byzantine tradition although there may be early readings in that text-type.

4. As Kümmel, *Introduction to the New Testament*, 353; John Reumann, *Variety and Unity in New Testament Thought*, Oxford Bible Series, ed. P. R. Ackroyd and G. N. Stanton (Oxford: Oxford University Press, 1991), 99, 116.

well have been an accidental omission and that is why it appears in so few manuscripts within only one text-type. It is also the shorter reading. However, Griesbach (who proposed both of these canons) was careful to point out that if the shorter reading utterly lacks sense and is out of keeping with the style of the author, the longer reading is to be preferred.[1] This is certainly true if the omission is accepted.[2] Those who opt for the exclusion find it difficult to offer a viable explanation for its omission.[3] Second, the intrinsic probabilities need to be assessed. The normal construction in the Pauline letters is to have the place name in the dative after the participial construction τοῖς οὖσιν ("to those who are"), as seen in Rom 1:7; 2 Cor 1:1; Phil 1:1 (cf. also a similar construction when he addresses a church: τῇ οὔσῃ in 1 Cor 1:2; 2 Cor 1:1). Some contend that the name of the city was intentionally left out by Paul because it was intended to be an encyclical letter. It is suggested that Paul's envoy Tychichus would have inserted the name of each city he visited or it could have been filled in by members of each church as the letter passed to the various communities.[4] However, this argument is not compelling. First, he had never done this with any other letter. Second, none of the manuscripts, even the three early Alexandrian manuscripts, have a lacuna where Tychichus or the recipients were to insert the city's name, or have only the word ἐν ("in") without the city's name, or even have another city listed in the place of Ephesus.[5] Third, for the name of the city to be omitted after the participle is grammatically awkward, if not impossible,[6] for it would read "to the saints who are, that is, believers in Christ Jesus." On the other hand, Dahl proposes that several copies of the letter were made, each with the specific city inserted.[7] However, all the ex-

1. Cited in Metzger, *The Text of the New Testament*, 120.

2. It creates an impossible grammatical construction, see BDF §413 (3); G. Zuntz, *The Text of the Epistles: A Disquisition upon the Corpus Paulinum* (London: British Academy, 1953), 228 n. 1.

3. Cf. W. C. Shearer, "To whom was the so-called Epistle to the Ephesians actually addressed?" *ExpTim* 4 (December 1892): 129; Lightfoot, "The Destination of the Epistle to the Ephesians," 375–96; Paul Ewald, "Exegetische Miszellen. Zu Eph. 1, 1," *Neue kirchliche Zeitschrift* 15 (1. July 1904): 560–68; P. van Imschoot, "De Destinatariis Epistolae ad Ephesios," *Collationes Grandavenses* 28 (1945): 3–12; Harnack "Die Adresse des Epheserbriefs des Paulus," 696–709; reprint in idem, *Kleine Schriften zur alten Kirche*, 2:120–33; James P. Wilson, "Note on the Textual Problem of Ephesians i. 1," *ExpTim* 60 (May 1949): 225–26; Dahl, "Adresse und Proömium des Epheserbriefes," 241–50; updated in idem, *Studies in Ephesians*, 360–64; Batey, "The Destination of Ephesians," 101; Mark Santer, "The Text of Ephesians I.1," *NTS* 15 (January 1969): 247–48; van Roon, *The Authenticity of Ephesians*, 72–85; Wolfgang Schenk, "Zur Entstehung und zum Verständnis der Adresse des Epheserbriefes," *Theologische Versuche* 6 (1975): 73–78; Best, "Ephesians 1.1 Again," 273–79.

4. Percy, *Probleme*, 461–63. Zuntz (*The Text of the Epistles*, 228 n. 1, 276–77) thinks, due to the insurmountable grammatical problems one has if there is not blank, that the primitive *Corpus Paulinum* had a blank in the text and ἐν Ἐφέσῳ in the margin. Cf. also Dahl, "Adresse und Proömium des Epheserbriefes," 241–50; updated in idem, *Studies in Ephesians*, 60–64; W. Bartlett, "The Saints at Ephesus," *Exp* 8th ser., vol. 18 (November 1919): 327; Moir, "A Mini-Guide to New Testament Textual Criticism," 126.

5. Cf. Lindemann, "Bemerkungen zum den Adressaten und zum Anlaß des Epheserbriefes," 235–39, esp. 236. Even Marcion's insertion of Laodicea is not in the text but in the superscription (see Tertullian *Adversus Marcionem* 5.11.12; 5.17.1 [*PL* 2:500; 2:512]).

6. BDF §413 (3); cf. also Best, "Ephesians i.1," 36–41.

7. Dahl, "Adresse und Proömium des Epheserbriefes," 247–49; updated in idem, *Studies in Ephesians*, 62–63.

tant manuscripts with a city inserted have only ἐν Ἐφέσῳ. Therefore, the internal evidence dealing with both the transcriptional and intrinsic probabilities do not argue against the inclusion of ἐν Ἐφέσῳ.[1]

In conclusion, both the external and internal evidence favor the inclusion of ἐν Ἐφέσῳ.

1:2. χάρις ὑμῖν καὶ εἰρήνη ἀπὸ θεοῦ πατρὸς ἡμῶν καὶ κυρίου Ἰησοῦ Χριστοῦ, "grace to you and peace from God our Father and the Lord Jesus Christ." The exact same wording is used in Rom 1:7; 1 Cor 1:3; 2 Cor 1:2; Gal 1:3; Phil 1:2; 2 Thess 1:2 (some manuscripts omit ἡμῶν); Phlm 3. The greeting is shortened in Col 1:2 and 1 Thess 1:1 whereas in the Pastorals there are differences, although with much of the same wording.[2] Because of the similarity of the greetings, Lohmeyer thought their form was that used in Near Eastern letters, but the content was adopted from an introductory liturgy of the worship service by the early church.[3] Friedrich agrees with Lohmeyer that their form was from the Near East but rejects the idea of the liturgical derivation because of the variety in the wording of the greetings in letters of Paul (cf. Col 1:2; 1 Thess 1:1; 1 Tim 1:2; 2 Tim 1:2; Titus 1:2)[4] as well as other NT letters (cf. 1 Pet 1:2; 2 Pet 1:2; 2 John 3; Jude 2; Rev 1:4).

After indicating the name of the writer and the one addressed, the normal Greek letter opens with the greeting "rejoice" (χαίρειν, χαῖρε, χαίρετε).[5] This greeting was used during Jesus' life (Matt 26:49; 27:29 [= Mark 15:18]; 28:9; Luke 1:28), in the church decree (Acts 15:23), in an official letter (Acts 23:26), and in an epistle (Jas 1:1). No doubt, Paul knew this formula (Acts 15:23; 23:26) but he did not adopt it.[6]

1. Cf. J. Keith Elliott, review of *Text and Interpretation: Studies in the New Testament Presented to Matthew Black*, ed. by Ernest Best and R. McL. Wilson, *TZ* 35 (November/Dezember 1979): 369–70.

2. For a study of Pauline greeting, see Roller, *Das Formular der paulinischen Briefe*, 54–91; Gordon P. Wiles, *Paul's Intercessory Prayers. The Significance of the Intercessory Prayer Passages in the Letters of St. Paul*, SNTSMS, ed. Matthew Black, vol. 24 (Cambridge: Cambridge University Press, 1974), 108–14; Berger, "Apostelbrief und apostolische Rede/Zum Formular früchristilicher Briefe," 190–231; Mullins, "Benedictions as a NT Form," 59–64; White, "Ancient Greek Letters," 85–105.

3. Ernst Lohmeyer, "Probleme paulinischer Theologie. I. Briefliche Grußüberschriften," *ZNW* 26, nos. 2–4 (1927): 161–64, 172–73.

4. Gerhard Friedrich, "Lohmeyers These über 'Das paulinischen Briefpräscript' kritisch beleuchtet," *ZNW* 46, nos. 3–4 (1955): 272–74.

5. Francis Xavier J. Exler, *The Form of the Ancient Greek Letter. A Study in Greek Epistolography*, Ph.D. Dissertation of Catholic University of America (Washington, D.C.: Catholic University of America, 1923; reprint, *The Form of the Ancient Greek Letter of the Epistolary Papyri (3rd c. B.C. – 3rd c. A.D.). A Study in Greek Epistolography*, Chicago: Ares, 1957), 23–68; Judith M. Lieu, "'Grace to You and Peace': The Apostolic Greeting," *BJRL* 68 (autumn 1985): 161–78; cf. also John Lee White, *The Form and Structure of the Official Petition: A Study in Greek Epistolography*, Dissertation Series, no. 5 (Missoula, Mont.: Society of Biblical Literature, 1972), 21–40.

6. Wiles (*Pauls' Intercessory Prayers*, 109–10) observes that though the spelling and the sound are similar, Paul purposefully chose the "radically richer χάρις greeting."

Also, Paul does not use the Jewish greeting "mercy and peace" (Jude 2; *Jub.* 12:29; 22:9; *2 Apoc. Bar.* 78:2),[1] though he adds "mercy" in two of his greetings (1 Tim 1:2; 2 Tim 1:2; cf. also 2 John 3). Rather, he uses in every letter both "grace" and "peace," which apparently had become a distinctively Christian greeting (cf. 1 Pet 1:2; 2 Pet 1:2; 2 John 3; Rev 1:4).[2]

In using χάρις, "grace," Paul begins Ephesians with profound theological import, for χάρις characteristically denotes in the NT (in the LXX it occurs 164 times, seventy-nine times in the canonical books, and is translated sixty-one times from חֵן) God's unmerited or undeserved favor[3] in providing salvation for sinners through Christ's sacrificial death (e.g., Rom 3:23–24; Eph 1:7; 2:8) and enablement[4] for the believer (1 Cor 15:10; Eph 4:7, 29). This word appears 155 times in the NT, 100 times in Paul's literature, twelve times in this small letter to the Ephesians (1:2, 6, 7; 2:5, 7, 8; 3:2, 7, 8; 4:7, 29; 6:24). It is no mere introductory cliche. It is the gospel in one word. The object of this grace is ὑμῖν, "you," the recipients of the letter. Since no verb is supplied in any of the Pauline greetings, it is probably best to assume that the present optative verb "to be" (εἴη) was intended,[5] which expresses a wish "may grace be to you." Paul desires the Ephesians to appreciate, accept, and appropriate God's undeserved favor.

The second term εἰρήνη, "peace," appears in the LXX 290 times (211 times in the canonical books) and almost always translates שָׁלוֹם, which was the common greeting of the Semitic world (Gen 43:23; Judg 19:20; 1 Sam 25:6). The Hebrew term had the idea of "well-being" (Gen 29:6; 43:27; 2 Sam 18:29) in the very broadest sense (e.g., prosperity [Ps 73:3]; between nations [Judg 4:17]; health [Ps 38:3]; sleep [Ps 4:8]; death [Gen 15:15]; salvation [Jer 29:11]).[6] The Greek

1. Cf. Lohmeyer, "Probleme paulinischer Theologie," 159; Berger, "Apostelbrief und apostolische Rede," 197–200.

2. Lieu, "'Grace to You and Peace': The Apostolic Greeting," 167–78.

3. For a study of this word, see Hans Conzelmann and Walther Zimmerli, "χαρίς," *TDNT* 9 (1974): 372–402; Hans-Helmut Esser, "Grace, Spiritual Gifts [χάρις]," *NIDNTT* 2 (1976): 115–24; cf. also *HALOT* 1 (1994); 334–35; D. N. Freedman, J. R. Lundbom, and H.-J Fabry, "חָנַן *ḥānān*; חֵן *ḥēn*, etc.," *TDOT* 5 (1986): 22–36; Terence E. Fretheim, "חנן (*ḥnn* I)," *NIDOTTE* 2:203–6; Klaus Berger, "'Gnade' im frühen Christentum," *Nederlands theologisch Tijdschrift* 27 (Januari 1973): 8–10.

4. For the concept of grace as enablement, see John Nolland, "Grace as Power," *NovT* 28 (January 1986): 26–31.

5. The aorist optative is used in the greetings in 1 Pet 1:2; 2 Pet 1:2; Jude 2. Since there is no aorist for the verb "to be," the present tense is presumed. Another way it could be taken is a present indicative "grace is with you," see C. F. D. Moule, *Worship in the New Testament*, Ecumenical Studies in Worship, ed. J. G. Davies and A. Raymond George, no. 9 (London: Lutterworth, 1961), 78–79.

6. BDB 1022–23; cf. F.-J. Stendebach, "שָׁלוֹם *šālôm*," *TWAT* 8 (1995): 14–46; Walter Eisenbeis, *Die Wurzel* שלם *im Alten Testament*, Beihefte zur Zeitschrift für die alttestamentliche Wissenschaft, ed. Georg Fohrer, vol. 113 (Berlin: de Gruyter, 1969).

term is also broad and must be determined by its context.[1] Out of the forty-three times Paul utilizes it in all his epistles, he uses it eight times in this short letter (1:2; 2:14, 15, 17*bis*; 4:3; 6:15, 23). In Ephesians it is used with differences of meaning in the various contexts, but predominantly it has the idea of the sinners' peace with God (e.g., 2:14, 17) and the believers' peace with one another (e.g., 2:15; 4:3).

Therefore, grace (χάρις) expresses the cause, God's gracious work, and peace (εἰρήνη), the effect of God's work. The grace of God that brings salvation to sinners effects peace between them and God, and that same grace enables believers to live peaceably with one another. It is very possible that the combination of "grace and peace" may have their roots in the benediction of Num 6:24–26 (even though the LXX translates חֵן, "grace," as ἐλεέω, "mercy").

Characteristically, with Paul these words of greetings are followed by ἀπὸ θεοῦ πατρὸς ἡμῶν καὶ κυρίου Ἰησοῦ Χριστοῦ, "from God our Father and Lord Jesus Christ" (Rom 1:7; 1 Cor 1:3; 2 Cor 1:3; Gal 1:3; Phil 1:2; 2 Thess 1:2; Philm 3; cf. also 1 Tim 1:2; 2 Tim 1:2). The preposition ἀπό, "from," indicates the source of the grace and peace as being from God our Father[2] and the Lord Jesus Christ. A look in the concordance reveals that the concept of God as Father is used only fifteen times in the OT and over 260 times in the NT, forty-five times of which are in Paul's correspondence (cf. Eph 1:3; 3:14). This shows the prominence of God the Father in the NT times. Such is in keeping with Jesus' teaching, for he said that one should not call anyone "father" on earth but rather God in heaven is "your father" (Matt 23:9). In the model prayer Jesus taught the disciples to address God as "our Father" (Matt 6:9). In fact, Jesus used the most endearing term Abba, "my father"[3] (Mark 14:36), which was later utilized by Paul to indicate that Christians were truly the sons of God their Father (Rom 8:15; Gal 4:6). Hence, Paul in his greetings can state that grace and peace come from God who is not only called Father but "our" Father. This denotes personal relationship. Furthermore, Paul is stating that grace and peace come not only from God, our Father, but also the Lord Jesus Christ. Paul denotes by the single preposition ἀπό that the source of the grace and peace is from both the Father and the Son.

Because of the frequency of its occurrence in Scripture, one can only summarize the use of the word κύριος, "Lord."[4] ὁ κύριος is the

1. For a study of this word, see Gerhard von Rad and Werner Foerster, "εἰρήνη," *TDNT* 2 (1964): 400–17; Hartmut Beck and Colin Brown, "Peace [εἰρήνη]," *NIDNTT* 2 (1976): 776–83.

2. "Father" is a genitive of simple apposition (Wallace, *Greek Grammar*, 99).

3. Cf. Joachim Jeremias, *The Prayers of Jesus*, trans. John Bowden, Christoph Burchard, and John Reumann, SBT, ed. C. F. D. Moule, J. Barr, Peter Ackroyd, Floyd V. Filson, and G. Ernest Wright, 2d ser., no. 6 (London: SCM; Naperville, Ill.: Allenson, 1967), 11–65.

4. For a more extensive study of this term, see Gottfried Quell and Werner Foerster, "κύριος, κτλ.," *TDNT* 3 (1965): 1039–98; Hans Bietenhard, "Lord, Master [δεσπότης,

noun form of the adjective κύριος, "having power, authority," which in turn is derived from the noun κῦρος, "power," "might." In early classical Greek it was not used as a divine title because the gods were subject to fate just as human beings were, and only in instances where the gods ruled over particular spheres would they be called "lords."[1] However, in the Orient and Egypt the gods were considered the lords of reality. They created humans and thus humans were answerable to them.[2] In Roman times it was used of political leaders. In 12 B.C. the Emperor Augustus was called God and Lord (θεὸς καὶ κύριος). The title "Lord" also was used for Herod the Great, Herod Agrippa I and II.[3] "From the time of Nero (A.D. 54–68), who was described in an inscription as *ho tou pantos kosmou kyrios,* Lord of all the world (*SIG* 814, 31), the title *kyrios* occurs more and more frequently."[4] This was the era when the letter to the Ephesians was written.

κύριος occurs around 8400 times in the LXX (7412 times in the canonical books) translated from אָדוֹן or אֲדֹנָי, which, according to Quell, in the majority of instances (some 6165) is the equivalent to יהוה, "Yahweh," though it is used 192 times to refer to a human master and fifteen times of Ba'al, both of which have the secular idea of "owner."[5] Its usage in post OT Jewish literature appears mixed for there is debate whether it stood for the tetragrammaton (Yaweh).[6] It appears in the NT 717 times, 274 times in Paul's writings and twenty-six times in Ephesians. In the NT it is used in three ways. First, it reflects the secular usage as the "lord" or "owner" of a vineyard (Matt 21:40 = Mark 12:9 = Luke 20:13), masters over slaves (Matt 10:24–25; John 13:16; 15:20; Eph 6:5, 9; Col 3:22; 4:1), or a political leader (Acts 25:26). Second, it is certainly used for God. This usage is seen particularly in the numerous NT quotations from the OT where κύριος stands for Yahweh (e.g., Rom 4:8 = Ps 32:2; Rom 9:28–29 = Isa 10:22–23; Rom 10:16 = Isa 53:1). Third, it is used of Jesus as κύριος. Certainly, this is true in Paul's case because he refers to those who by the Spirit cannot say Jesus is cursed but Jesus is Lord (1 Cor 12:3; cf. Rom 10:9). Jesus is κύριος whom God (θεός) raised from the dead (Rom 10:9) and is seated at God's right hand in the heavenlies (Eph 1:20) and called Lord in verse 17. Even before Jesus' ascension, when Thomas saw the risen Christ he exclaimed, "My Lord and my God" (Ὁ κύριός μου καὶ ὁ θεός μου, John 20:28). Peter expressed it well in his sermon at Pente-

κύριος]," *NIDNTT* 2 (1976): 508–20. Most of the data above is derived from these two sources.

1. Bietenhard, *NIDNTT* 2 (1976): 510.
2. Foerster, *TDNT* 3 (1965): 1048.
3. Ibid., 1049–50.
4. Bietenhard, *NIDNTT* 2 (1976): 511.
5. Quell, *TDNT* 3 (1965): 1058–59.
6. Foerster, *TDNT* 3 (1965): 1081–83; Bietenhard, *NIDNTT* 2 (1976): 512–13.

cost when he stated, “Let all the house of Israel therefore know without any doubt that God has made him both Lord and Christ, this Jesus whom you crucified” (Acts 2:36). This Jesus is the one in whom believers put their faith (Rom 3:22; Gal 2:16; 3:22; Phil 3:9; Col 1:4; 2:5; 1 Tim 3:13; 2 Tim 1:13; 3:15). Out of the twenty-six times κύριος is used in Ephesians, only twice does it refer to masters of slaves (6:5, 9); all the other times it refers to Jesus Christ. Therefore, in the present context of Paul’s greeting to the Ephesians, he states that the believers are to appropriate the grace and peace that comes not only from God the Father, but also from Jesus Christ who is their Lord.

In summary, the prologue of this epistle covers three things: (1) the authorship of Paul who is an apostle of Jesus Christ through the will of God; (2) the identification of the recipients who are the saints in Ephesus, also called believers, who have been united to Christ Jesus; and (3) the expression of greetings summarizing the author’s desire that the recipients appreciate and appropriate the grace that brought salvation and its resulting peace, both of which come from God their Father and the Lord Jesus Christ.

B. Praise for God's Planned Spiritual Blessings (1:3–14)

Normally, after the greeting Paul gives an introductory thanksgiving for the recipients of the letter. In this epistle he changes the order, for before he gives his thanksgiving in verses 15–23, he has in verses 3–14 a pæan of praise for what God has done for the believer.

In the Greek text, 1:3–14 is a single long sentence of 202 words which one frequently quoted scholar considers to be the most monstrous sentence conglomeration (cannot even correctly call it a sentence) that he has ever found in the Greek language![1] Actually in this book there are eight lengthy sentences (1:3–14, 15–23; 2:1–7; 3:2–13, 14–19; 4:1–6, 11–16; 6:14–20). Three of these (1:3–14, 15–23; 3:14–19) are items of praise and prayer. It is not unusual to have lengthy sentences for praise and prayer. Even in our present day it is not uncommon to have long sentences in prayers and doxologies.

There has been much discussion on the form and structure of this passage.[2] At the beginning of the twentieth century it was fashionable

1. Eduard Norden, *Agnostos Theos: Untersuchungen zur Formengeschichte religiöser Rede* (Leipzig: B. G. Teubner, 1913), 253 n. 1. Robbins compares this long sentence with long sentences used by rhetoricians in classical literature and concludes that Eph 1:3–14 can be divided into an eight-period sentence (vv. 3, 4, 5–6, 7–8, 9–10, 11–12, 13, 14) allowing for breathing spaces (Charles J. Robbins, "The Composition of Eph. 1:3–14," *JBL* 105 [December 1986]: 677–87). However, this ruins the unity of the eulogy. Danker has pointed out that this long sentence is short in comparison to some of the recipients' response to Roman benefactors, see Danker, *Benefactor*, 451.

2. For further studies outside of commentaries, cf. Th. Innitzer, "Der 'Hymnus' im Epheserbriefe (1,3–14)," *ZKT* 28, no. 4 (1904): 612–21; H. Coppieters, "La doxologie de la letter aux Éphésiens," *RB* 6 (Janvier 1909): 74–88; Joseph M. Bover, "Doxologiae

to see these verses as a hymn.[1] Various interpreters up to the present time have proposed ways to divide it (Excursus 2: Views and Structures of Eph 1:3–14). Innitzer suggests that, after the doxology in

---

Epistolae ad Ephesios logical partitio," *Bib* 2, no. 4 (1921): 458–60; Ernst Lohmeyer, "Das Proömium des Epheserbriefes," *TBl* 5 (Mai 1926): 120–25; Albert Debrunner, "Grundsätzliches über Kolometrie im Neuen Testament," *TBl* 5 (September 1926): 231–34; Giorgio Castellino, "La dossologia della Lettera agli Efesini (1,3–14): analisi della forma e del contenuto," *Salesianum* 8 (Gennaio–Giugno 1946): 147–67; John T. Trinidad, "The Mystery Hidden in God. A Study of Eph. 1,3–14," *Bib* 31, no. 1 (1950): 1–26; Dahl, "Adresse und Proömium des Epheserbriefes," 250–65; updated in idem, *Studies in Ephesians*, 315–28; Maurer, "Der Hymnus von Epheser I als Schlüssel zum ganzen Briefe," 151–72; J. Coutts, "Ephesians i.3–14 and I Peter i.3–12," *NTS* 3 (January 1957): 115–27; Stanislas Lyonnet, "La bénédiction de Eph. i,3–14 et son arrière-plan judaïque," in *A la Rencontre de Dieu. Mémorial Albert Gelin*, ed. A. Barucq, J. Duplacy, A. George, and H. de Lubac, Bibliothèque de la Faculté Catholique de Théologie de Lyon, vol. 8 (Le Puy: Editions Xavier Mappus, 1961), 341–52; J. Cambier, "La bénédiction d'Eph 1:3–14," *ZNW* 54, nos. 1/2 (1963): 58–104; Gottfried Schille, *Frühchristliche Hymnen* (Berlin: Evangelische Verlagsanstalt, 1965), 65–73; Johannes Schattenmann, *Studien zum Neutestamentlichen Prosahymnus* (Munich: C. H. Beck'sche Verlagsbuchhandlung, 1965), 1–10; Sanders, "Hymnic Elements in Ephesians 1–3," 214–32; Reinhard Deichgräber, *Gotteshymnus und Christushymnus in der frühen Christenheit. Unterschungen zu Form, Sprache und Stil der frühchristlichen Hymnen*, Studien zur Umwelt des Neuen Testaments, ed. Karl Georg Kuhn, vol. 5 (Göttingen: Vandenhoeck & Ruprecht, 1967), 64–76; Helmut Krämer, "Zur sprachlichen Form der Eulogie Eph. 1,3–14," *WD* 9 (1967): 34–46; Kirby, *Ephesians, Baptism and Pentecost*, 84–89, 126–38; Friedrich Lang, "Die Eulogie in Epheser 1,3–14," in *Studien zur Geschichte und Theologie der Reformation. Festschrift für Ernst Bizer*, ed. Luise Abramowski and J. F. Gerhard Goeters (Neukirchen-Vluyn: Neukirchener Verlag, 1969), 7–20; Fischer, *Tendenz und Absicht des Epheserbriefes*, 111–18; Caragounis, *Ephesian* Mysterion, 41–52; Rudolf Schnackenburg, "Die grosse Eulogie Eph. 1,3–14. Analyse unter textlinguistischen Aspekten," *BZ* 21, no. 1 (1977): 67–87; Andrzej Suski, "Eulogia w Liście do Efezjan," *Studia Theologica Varsaviensia* 16 (1978): 19–48; Felice Montagnini, "Christological Features in Ep 1:3–14," in *Paul de Tarse, apôtre de notre temps*, ed. Lorenzo De Lorenzi, Série monographique de «Benedictina» Section paulinienne, vol. 1 (Rome: Abbaye de S. Paul h.l.m., 1979), 529–39; O'Brien, "Ephesians I: An Unusual Introduction to a New Testament Letter," 504–16; Léonard Ramaroson, "'La grande bénédiction' (Ep 1,3–14)," *ScEs* 33 (Janvier–Avril 1981): 93–103; H. R. Lemmer, "Reciprocity between Eschatology and Pneuma in Ephesians 1:13–14," *Neot* 21, no. 1 (1987): 159–82; Pierre Grelot, "La structure d'Éphésiens 1,3–14," *RB* 96 (Avril 1989): 193–209; J. H. Barkhuizen, "The Strophic Structure of the Eulogy of Ephesians 1:3–14," *Hervormde Teologiese Studies* 46, no. 3 (1990): 390–403; Ernest Best, "The Use of Credal and Liturgical Materials in Ephesians," in *Worship, Theology and Ministry in the Early Church: Essays in Honor of Ralph P. Martin*, ed. Michael J. Wilkins and Terence Paige, JSNTSup, ed. Stanley E. Porter et al., vol. 87 (Sheffield: JSOT Press, 1992), 56–58; Ian H. Thomson, *Chiasmus in the Pauline Letters*, JSNTSup, ed. Stanley E. Porter et al., vol. 111 (Sheffield: Sheffield Academic Press, 1995), 46–83; Chantal Reynier, "La bénédiction en Éphésiens 1,3–14," *NRT* 118 (Mars–Avril 1996): 182–99. For a rhetorical analysis of vv. 3–14, see Jeal, *Integrating Theology and Ethics in Ephesians*, 80–93.

1. Innitzer, "Der 'Hymnus' im Epheserbriefe (1,3–14)," 612–21.

verse 3, it should be divided around the three persons of the Trinity with the words of praise ending each section, namely, God the Father in verses 4–6, the Son in verses 7–12, and the Holy Spirit in verses 13–14.[1] Coppieters thinks it is a doxology and he devised a complex structure where after the initial benediction in verse 3a, the three aorist participles mark the major divisions, that is, εὐλογήσας, "having chosen," for verses 3b–4; προορίσας, "having predestined," for verses 5–8; and γνωρίσας, "having made known," for verses 9–14, which is further subdivided by two ἐν ᾧ, "in whom," in verses 11 and 13.[2] Bover also labeled it a doxology, and after the initial blessing (v. 3a), he divided it into three major sections (each with two subsections): first, verses 3b–6 (3b–4 and 5–6); second, verses 7–10 (7–8 and 9–10); and third, verses 11–14 (11–12 and 13–14). The last two divisions are around the Latin "in quo" = ἐν ᾧ, "in whom" (vv. 7, 11, 13).[3] Lohmeyer thought it was a poetic or hymnic structure of four parts (vv. 3–4, 5–8, 9–12, 13–14), the first three with four strophes of three lines and the last with three strophes of three lines. The first three major sections begin with aorist participles (εὐλογήσας [v. 3], προορίσας [v. 5], and γνωρίσας [v. 9]), and the last section also begins with an aorist participle (ἀκούσαντες, "having heard") in verse 13a followed by a corresponding rhyming aorist participle (πιστεύσαντες, "having believed") in verse 13b.[4]

Shortly after his publication Lohmeyer was severely criticized by Debrunner[5] for the arbitrary way he chose his divisions because they not only differ in length but also because his use of participles to mark their beginning is false since the participles depend on other finite verbs.[6] Since Lohmeyer's proposal, many attempts have been made to decipher the structure. Dahl divides it into three parts: first, verse 3, praise to God for having blessed us in Christ; second, verses 4–12, giving more specific details and are subdivided into two points, verses 4–6a and 6b–12 (which are further divided into verses 6b–7, 8–9a, 9b–10, 11–12); and third, verses 13–14, serving as an application to the Gentile recipients.[7] Maurer sees this as a hymn that is the key to the whole epistle, and on the basis of content divides it into four parts: verses 3–4 (theme), 5–8, 9–10, and 11–14.[8] Schille thinks it may be a baptismal or initiation hymn and sees verses 3–4 as the introit which is followed by two strophes

1. Ibid., 614; see also Cambier, "La bénédiction d'Eph 1:3–14," 59–60, 80, 98, 103–4; Fischer, *Tendenz und Absicht des Epheserbriefes*, 113–14.

2. Coppieters, "La doxologie de la letter aux Éphésiens," 85–88.

3. Bover, "Doxologiae Epistolae ad Ephesios logical partitio," 458–60.

4. Lohmeyer, "Das Proömium des Epheserbriefes," 120–22.

5. Debrunner, "Grundsätzliches über Kolometrie im Neuen Testament," 231–34.

6. Cf. Deichgräber, *Gotteshymnus*, 68; Sanders, "Hymnic Elements in Ephesians 1–3," 224.

7. Dahl, "Adresse und Proömium des Epheserbriefes," 260–61; updated in idem, *Studies in Ephesians*, 325.

8. Maurer, "Der Hymnus von Epheser I als Schlüssel zum ganzen Briefe," 154.

(vv. 5–8 and 9–12a), with verses 12b–14 added by a corrector.[1] Masson has six strophes (vv. 3–4, 5–6, 7–9a, 9b–10b, 11–12, 13–14), each of which is subdivided into two parts consisting of four lines each.[2] Schlier sees verse 3 as the benediction, verses 4–10 as the development with reference to the believers and Christ, this having three subpoints (vv. 4–6a, 6b–7, 8–10), and the ending with a double strophe appendix which refers to being "in Christ" (vv. 11–12, 13–14).[3] Cambier in his lengthy study concludes that verse 3, which announces the subject, is the introductory strophe followed by three strophes, each of which are further divided into two or three couplets of an ABA pattern and ends with a formal refrain of "glory" ([1] vv. 4–6—4, 5, refrain 6a; [2] vv. 7–12—7–8a, 8b–10, 11, refrain 12; [3] vv. 13–14—13, 14a, refrain 14b).[4] Basing it on the ancient Greek meter and music, Schattenmann counts the words and syllables and following the heading (v. 3a), he divides it into two main parts with each having two strophes: (1) Above: God's work (vv. 3b–10) with the two strophes of 60 words and 136 syllables each (vv. 3b–6a, 6b–10a) followed by a midway heading (v. 10b–c); and (2) Below: believer's experience (vv. 11–14) with two strophes of 40 words each and 77 and 92 syllables respectively (vv. 11–12, 13–14). At the end of each strophe he has a refrain (vv. 5b–6a, 9b–10a, 12, 14b–c).[5] Krämer felt that the organizing principle of the eulogy is the phrase ἐν Χριστῷ, "in Christ," and one needs to observe the sentences that end with prepositional phrases that begin with ἐν, which will relate back to ἐν Χριστῷ. He divides it into three parts: (1) benediction, verse 3; (2) verses 4–12 (subdivided vv. 4–6, 7–10, 11–12); and (3) verses 13–14.[6] Lang thinks it could be a baptismal eulogy and divides it into three parts: (1) benediction formula, verse 3; (2) first strophe based on active participles of God's actions, verses 4–10 (two half strophes: vv. 4–6, 8–10); and (3) second strophe based on passive main verbs describing the church's reception of God's blessing, verses 11–14 (two half strophes: vv. 11–12, 13b–14).[7] Fischer thinks that the present passage is not a hymn but was based on a hymn. The original hymn had three strophes: first, verses 4–6a; second, verses 7–8 and verse 12a ("to the praise of his glory"); and third, verses 13b–14. He feels that there are many other changes because the hymn has been extensively reconstructed.[8] Schnackenburg does not divide it up according to hymnic, poetic, or thematic structure but according to the formal aspects of linguistic analysis. He divides it into six major sections with two

1. Schille, "Liturgisches Gut im Epheserbrief," 16–24; cf. also idem, *Frühchristliche Hymnen*, 67–69.
2. Masson, 149–51.
3. Schlier, 39–41.
4. Cambier, "La bénédiction d'Eph 1:3–14," 102–4.
5. Schattenmann, *Studien zum Neutestamentlichen Prosahymnus*, 1–10.
6. Krämer, "Zur sprachlichen Form der Eulogie Eph. 1,3–14," 38–41.
7. Lang, "Die Eulogie in Epheser 1, 3–14," 8–14.
8. Fischer, *Tendenz und Absicht des Epheserbriefes*, 111–18.

verses each (vv. 3–4, 5–6, 7–8, 9–10, 11–12, 13–14). The key to his analysis is the relationship of the preposition κατά, "according to," to the verbs in each section (καθώς in v. 4 functions like κατά). Only verses 13–14 do not have the preposition but are to be considered as application for the reader.[1] Ramaroson thinks the eulogy falls into two parts: first, the plan (vv. 3–6a), and second, the purpose (vv. 9b–14), with the final redactor inserting verses 6b–9a, the ideas of which come from Col 1:13b–14, 20.[2] Grelot thinks it is a hymn where the refrain "blessed be God, the Father of our Lord Jesus Christ" (1:3a) is recited between the six strophes (vv. 3b–4, 5–6, 7–8, 9–10, 11–12, 13–14).[3] Clearly, there have been many attempts to divide and interpret these verses. However, no unanimity has resulted from these efforts.

Although there are attempts up to the present time to see this as a hymn with decipherable divisions, a change of attitude about the form and structure of this passage took place in the middle of the twentieth century. Rather than a strictly structured hymn, Dahl,[4] Maurer,[5] Schlier,[6] Barth,[7] Caragounis,[8] and O'Brien[9] think it may be some sort of prologue that summarizes the whole epistle. At this time, more scholars became less certain about the precise division of it.[10] Rather than some Greek meter or rhyme as a key to its understanding, they began to think that this eulogy was born out of a Semitic background. The English word "eulogy" comes from the Greek εὐλογέω/εὐλογία/εὐλογητός, which is a translation of the Hebrew respectively בָּרוּךְ/בְּרָכָה/בָּרַךְ (often in English it is labeled *berakah*) meaning "praise" or "blessing."[11] Kuhn points out that the language and style of Ephesians have evidence of Semitic influence from Qumran literature and that the eulogy of 1:3–14 is the typical Hebrew sentence structure of the Qumran texts.[12] After showing de-

1. Schnackenburg, "Die grosse Eulogie Eph. 1,3–14," 69–78; cf. also Schnackenburg, 47–49.

2. Ramaroson, "'La grande bénédiction' (Ep 1,3–14)," 93–103.

3. Grelot, "La structure d'Éphésiens 1,3–14," 193–209.

4. Dahl, "Adresse und Proömium des Epheserbriefes," 252–57, 262; updated in idem, *Studies in Ephesians*, 317–22, 325.

5. Maurer, "Der Hymnus von Epheser I als Schlüssel zum ganzen Briefe," 167–72.

6. Schlier, 72.

7. Barth, 55, 97.

8. Caragounis, *Ephesian* Mysterion, 45–52.

9. O'Brien, "Ephesians I: An Unusual Introduction," 509–12, 514–16; O'Brien, 93.

10. Sanders, "Hymnic Elements in Ephesians 1–3," 227; Deichgräber, *Gotteshymnus*, 66–67, 72.

11. For a study of "praise" and the distinction between doxology and eulogy, see Deichgräber, *Gotteshymnus*, 24–43.

12. Karl Georg Kuhn, "The Epistle to the Ephesians in the Light of the Qumran Texts," in *Paul and Qumran: Studies in New Testament Exegesis*, ed. and trans. Jerome Murphy-O'Connor (Chicago: Priory Press; London: Geoffrey Chapman, 1968), 116–20, esp. 116–17.

tailed parallels with the Qumran texts, Deichgräber concludes that this introductory eulogy was influenced by Hebraic liturgical form that fits with what is seen in the Qumran texts and definitely not influenced by late rabbinic Judaism.[1] It is thought that although the Qumran texts and Ephesians are independent of one another, they both go back to a common tradition that has their basis in the OT.[2] Thomson depicts 1:3–10 as form of a Jewish *berakah* with a chiastic pattern: intro (v. 3), A (v. 4), B (v. 5), C (v. 6), D (v. 7a–b), C′ (vv. 7c–8), B′ (v. 9a–b), A′ (vv. 9c–10). Verses 11–14 are closely joined to the previous verses but are not chiastic in structure.[3] Van Roon shows that the characteristics of this eulogy have affinities with thought-rhyming of OT Hebrew poetry and yet are in keeping with the environment of the Jewish-Hellenistic style of the first century.[4] Robinson argues that it is not uncommon in both canonical and noncanonical Jewish literature to have a eulogy before the intercessory prayer.[5] Here the euology is followed first by thanksgiving (vv. 15–16)[6] and then intercession (vv. 17–19). Hence, it seems that Paul is expressing praise that is consistent with the Jewish-Hellenistic style of his day, which has its roots in the OT.[7]

In a study of eulogies of the OT, Apocrypha, and Judaism, Caragounis states some of the similarities in wording and form with the eulogy of Eph 1:3–14, but he also notes the differences in content. Furthermore, although the eulogies of Mary and Zecharias (Luke

1. Deichgräber, *Gotteshymnus*, 72–75.

2. Kuhn, "Ephesians in the Light of the Qumran Texts," 120.

3. Thomson, *Chiasmus in the Pauline Letters*, 46–83.

4. Van Roon, *The Authenticity of Ephesians*, 135–45, 182–92.

5. James M. Robinson, "Die Hodajot-formel in Gebet und Hymnus des Früchristentums," in *Apophoreta. Festschrift für Ernst Haenchen zu seinem siebzigsten Geburtstag am 10. Dezember 1964*, ed. W. Eltester and F. H. Kettler, BZNW, ed. Walther Eltester, vol. 30 (Berlin: Alfred Töplemann, 1964), 204.

6. Kirby (*Ephesians, Baptism and Pentecost*, 131) argues that the *berakah* and thanksgiving are one and the same thing and this is the only time it happens in the Pauline corpus which is an indication that the author was not Paul but an imitator of Paul. However, O'Brien ("Ephesians I: An Unusual Introduction," 513) argues that Paul consistently distinguishes between the introductory *berakah* (εὐλογητός), which includes the writer within the sphere of blessing and the thanksgiving (εὐχαριστέω) report, which refers to the recipients. Here Paul uses both the *berakah* and thanksgiving in order to maintain the distinction. Cf. also Kathryn Sullivan, "'Blessed be the God and Father of Our Lord Jesus Christ' Εὐλογητὸς ὁ θεός (Eph 1:3–14)," in *Liturgy for the People: Essays in Honor of Gerald Ellard, S.J., 1894–1963*, ed. William J. Leonard (Milwaukee: Bruce, 1963), 29–37.

7. Cf. Best, 104–14, esp. 105–8, 112. Maclean thinks that much of Eph 1:3–14 is taken from Rom 8:15–34, esp. from Rom 8:28–30, see Jennifer Kay Berenson Maclean, "Ephesians and the Problem of Colossians: Interpretation of Texts and Traditions in Eph 1:1–2:10" (Ph.D. diss., Harvard University, 1995), 106–41. This is not convincing for though there is some overlapping terminology and thought, it is much better to see the OT as its background.

1:46–55, 68–79) are closer to the eulogy of Ephesian 1:3–14, they are still nationalistic. The eulogy in Ephesians is universal in scope, including both Jews and Gentiles, and is revelatory in that God's purpose for the ages is unveiled.[1]

In conclusion, it appears that the eulogy of Eph 1:3–14 is somewhat unique in that its roots are in the OT and in keeping with the Jewish-Hellenistic style, and yet its content goes beyond them. On the one hand, it has been criticized as a grammatically cumbersome sentence of 202 words, but, on the other hand, it has been praised for its fullness of words, liturgical majesty, and perceptible rhythm,[2] and these verses which seem to defy structure are described as "a kaleidoscope of dazzling lights and shifting colours."[3] The attempt to precisely decipher the divisions as a liturgical hymn has proven impossible. Though the grammatical structure is at times difficult to determine, all this is understandable when considered in the context of praise and prayer. However, this assumes that this passage had to fit into some liturgical mold. This seems to be reading too much into this text. Rather, it is more likely to be a spontaneous utterance of praise to God. It is noticeable in the present day that when one offers extemporaneous praise and/or prayer, often long complicated sentences with many subordinate clauses and phrases are used. This is not to say that there is an absence of structure, but rather there is the absence of a neatly divisible structure that can be found in a liturgical hymn or recitation that was carefully thought out and written down. This does not mean there is no plan. Certainly, this eulogy shows development, for one sees that the refrain "to the praise of his glory" (vv. 6, 12, 14) is given after discussing each person of the Trinity in the order of the Father, Son, and Holy Spirit. Also, there is progression from a pronouncement of praise to God (v. 3), to a description of God's great plan and action (vv. 4–12), and finally to its application to the believers at Ephesus (vv. 13–14). Therefore, the abundance of descriptive words of God's purpose, plan, and action in a long complicated sentence is entirely fitting within the scope of a eulogy. The abundance of words does not denote verbosity, but instead it is an attempt to use a multiplicity of words to praise God for his supernatural plan and acts that are almost beyond description. Finally, though it is Paul's praise of God's goodness to him, it also serves as a model to encourage the Ephesian believers to offer praise to God,[4] for believers then and now need to acknowledge the many blessings bestowed by him.

1. Caragounis, *Ephesian* Mysterion, 39–41, 44–45.
2. Masson, 149.
3. Robinson, 19.
4. Lincoln, 44.

Excursus 2
Views and Structures of Eph 1:3–14

Name	View	Division
Innitzer 1904	Hymn	3–6, 7–12, 13–14
Coppieters 1909	Doxology	3a (benediction), 3b–4, 5–8, 9–14 (a–11b–12; b–13–14—ἐν ᾧ)
Bover 1921	Doxology	3a (benediction), 3b–6, 7–10, 11–14 (11–12, 13–14—ἐν ᾧ)
Lohmeyer 1926	Poetic or hymnic	3 participles: 3, 5, 9 so division = 3–4, 5–8, 9–12, 13–14
Debrunner 1926	Doubts Lohmeyer's colometry	
Dibelius 1927, 1953	Liturgy with Semitic influence	3 (introduction), 4–6 (election), 7–10 (redemption), 11–14 (Jews and Gentiles received blessing of election and redemption)
Trinidad 1950	Mystery	3–4, 5–6, 7–10, 11–14
Maurer 1951	Hymn	3–4 (theme), 5–8, 9–10, 11–14
Dahl 1951	Hymn praise to God	3, 4–12 (4–6a, 6b–12 [6b–7, 8–9a, 9b–10]), 13–14
Schille 1952	Baptismal parenesis	3–4 (introit), 5–8, 9–12a
Masson 1953		6 strophes, each 2 parts with 6 lines
Schlier 1957	Hymn of revelation of mystery	3 (benediction), 4–10 (development [4–6a, 6b–7, 8–10]), 11–14 (appendix [11–12, 13–14])
Coutts 1957	Baptism	3–6, 7–12, 13–14
Kuhn 1961	Hymn/genre of blessing	
Lyonnet 1961	Second blessing of Jewish daily prayers before shema	
Cambier 1963	Hymn of revelation of mystery of both Semitic & Greek = Asianic poetry	Refrains 6a, 12, 14b 3 (introduction), 4–6 (4, 5, 6a), 7–12 (7–8a, 8b–10, 11, 12), 13–14 (13, 14a, 14b)
Schattenmann 1965		Rhymes & tonic syllables in classical rhythm; above = God's work 3b–10a; below = believer's experience 11–14
Mußner 1965	Eulogy	
Sanders 1965	Proem (not hymn)	
Deichgräber 1967	Baptismal praise	
Krämer 1967	Eulogy	3 (benediction), 4–12 (4–6, 7–10, 11–12), 13–14 (key = ἐν Χριστῷ)
Kirby 1968	Berakah	3, 4–9, 10–14
Lang 1969	Eulogy	3 (benediction), 4–10 participles active, 11–14 main verbs passive

Name	View	Division
Gnilka 1971	Hymnishce Sprache	Hebrew parallel poetry
Fischer 1973	Not a hymn but hymnic elements	4–6a, 7–8 and12a, 13b and 14
Barth 1974	Hymn for oral Christian tradition	Unity around God's name
Caragounis 1977	Eulogy	
Schnackenburg 1977	Praise	3–4, 5–6, 7–8, 9–10, 11–12, 13–14
Suski 1978	Baptismal hymn	
Montagnini 1979	Christological hymn	
O'Brien 1979	Praise for salvation	
Ramaroson 1981	Eulogy: 2 parts	Plan (3–6a) and purpose (9b–14) (redactor insertion 6b–9a)
Lincoln 1981	*Berakah*	
Robbins 1986	Similar to Greek rhetoricians	8 breathing periods: 3, 4, 5–6, 7–8, 9–10, 11–12, 13, 14
Grelot 1989	Hymn or benediction	3a a refrain to be sung between the 6 strophes 3b–4, 5–6, 7–8, 9–10, 11–12, 13–14
Barkhuizen 1990	Eulogy	3–6, 7–12, 13–14
Fay 1994	*Berakah*	3–4, 5–8, 9–12, 13–14
Thomson 1995	*Berakah* (chiastic vv. 3–10)	intro–3, A–4, B–5, C–6, D–7a–b, C′–7c–8, B′–9a–b, A′–9c–10
Reynier 1996	Blessing of redemption	3–10 (Christ in the eternal plan), 11–14 (11–12—in Christ—"we" = Jews; 13–14—"you" = Gentiles)
Best 1998	Eulogy	3–10 (3 significant participles), 11–14 (first plural verbs)
O'Brien 1999	Eulogy	3, 4–6, 7–8, 9–10, 11–14
Jeal 2000	*Berakah*	Complex structure on praise around salvation and redemption which includes the audience as participants
Muddiman 2001	*Berakah*	3–10 (*berakah* proper), 11–14 (*berakah* expanded)

1. The Provision of Spiritual Blessings (1:3)

Text: 1:3. Εὐλογητὸς ὁ θεὸς καὶ πατὴρ τοῦ κυρίου ἡμῶν Ἰησοῦ Χριστοῦ, ὁ εὐλογήσας ἡμᾶς ἐν πάσῃ εὐλογίᾳ πνευματικῇ ἐν τοῖς ἐπουρανίοις ἐν Χριστῷ,

Translation: 1:3. "Blessed is the God and Father of our Lord Jesus Christ, who has blessed us with every spiritual blessing in the heavenly realms in Christ,"

Commentary: 1:3. This verse marks not only the introduction but also the main sentence of the eulogy.[1] It is in essence a summary of the whole eulogy.[2] It is normal for Paul to have an introductory thanksgiving right after the greetings, but in this letter it is in verse 15 following the eulogy. In 2 Cor 1:3–4 the eulogy takes the place of the introductory thanksgiving. The only other NT epistle that has a eulogy following the greetings is 1 Pet 1:3–12. Peter does not have an introductory thanksgiving in either of these letters.

Εὐλογητὸς ὁ θεὸς καὶ πατὴρ[3] **τοῦ κυρίου ἡμῶν Ἰησοῦ Χριστοῦ,** "Blessed is the God and Father of our Lord Jesus Christ." Paul begins by stating that God is blessed or praised. The word εὐλογητός is a verbal adjective which is not found in classical literature but it appears eighty-seven times in the LXX and is translated forty-three times in the canonical books from the Hebrew passive participle בָּרוּךְ. The Hebrew term is translated "blessed," which has the idea of someone deserving appreciation, honor, and praise.[4] It is used once to bless a thing, namely, wisdom (1 Sam 25:33), a few times to bless people (e.g., Deut 28:6; 33:24; Judg 17:2; Ruth 2:20), but the predominant use is to bless God (e.g., Gen 9:26; 14:20; Exod 18:10; 1 Sam 25:32, 39; 2 Sam 18:28; 1 Kgs 1:48; 1 Chr 29:10; 2 Chr 2:12; Pss 28:6; 41:13; 66:20; 72:18; 119:12; Zech 11:5). Throughout the OT God is blessed or praised for his benefits to humanity as seen in his care (Pss 68:19, 35; 72:18; 119:12; 144:1; Zech 11:5), his provision (Ruth 4:14; 1 Kgs 1:48; 5:7; 8:56; 1 Chr 29:10; 2 Chr 2:12), his response to prayer (Gen 24:27; 1 Kgs 8:15 = 2 Chr 6:4; Pss 28:6; 66:20), and his deliverance from enemies (Gen 14:20; Exod 18:10; 2 Sam 18:28; Pss 41:13; 124:6) and from evil (1 Sam 25:32, 39). Sometimes God is blessed for who he is (Pss 72:19; 89:52; 106:48; 135:21) although usually it is tied with something he has done for the saints. The concept of blessing with reference to God is not expressing a wish, "blessed be God," but rather a declaration, "blessed is God."[5]

1. For a history of interpretation of this verse, see Ernest Best, "Fashions in Exegesis: Ephesians 1:3," in *Scripture: Meaning and Method. Essays Presented to Anthony Tyrrell Hanson*, ed. Barry P. Thompson (Hull, England: Hull University Press, 1987), 79–91; reprint, idem, *Interpreting Christ* (Edinburgh: T & T Clark, 1993), 161–77.

2. Dahl, "Adresse und Proömium des Epheserbriefes," 254; updated in idem, *Studies in Ephesians*, 319–20; Cambier, "La bénédiction d'Eph 1:3–14," 62, 102.

3. The words καὶ πατήρ are omitted only in B. The textual evidence for their inclusion is overwhelming.

4. Josef Scharbert, "ברך *brk*; בְּרָכָה *bᵉrākhāh*," *TDOT* 2 (1977): 288.

5. Robert J. Ledogar, "Verbs of Praise in the LXX Translation of the Hebrew Canon," *Bib* 48, no. 1 (1967): 54. Ledogar points out that the LXX is fairly consistent when translating the passive participle בָּרוּךְ by distinctly using the verbal adjective εὐλογητός, which denotes quality when referring to God, and by using the perfect participle εὐλογημένος, which denotes results when referring to human beings. He cites Gen 14:19–20 as an illustration, for God is blessed (εὐλογητός) and Abraham has been blessed (εὐλογημένος) by God. Cf. A. Campbell King, "Ephesians in the Light of Form Criticism," *ExpTim* 63 (June 1952): 273.

Praise to God was a characteristic component of Jewish prayer which became fixed toward the end of the first century A.D. in the *Shemoneh 'Esreh* or Eighteen Benedictions. They were recited three times daily in the synagogue and each ended with the refrain, "Blessed are you, O Lord."[1] Therefore, blessing God or calling God blessed is not something new to the people of the NT era.

In the NT εὐλογητός is used eight times and it is never used of people but only of God (Mark 14:61; Luke 1:68; Rom 1:25; 9:5; 2 Cor 1:3; 11:31; Eph 1:3; 1 Pet 1:3). At Jesus' trial it was used in the place of "God" by the high priest when he asked Jesus, "Are you the Christ, the Son of the Blessed?" (Mark 14:61). It was the Jewish custom to avoid the use of the name God and hence the use of "blessed," which indicates their thought that God is one who is blessed or the one who deserves praise. Normally, in Jewish literature it is appended to "the Holy One," and thus God would be addressed as "the Holy One, Blessed is He."[2] At the circumcision of his son John, Zechariah blessed the Lord God of Israel (Luke 1:68) for the promised salvation from sin. Three times (Rom 1:25; 9:5; 2 Cor 11:31) God is one who is (to be) blessed "forever" (εἰς τοὺς αἰῶνας). The only other times the term is used is when it is used as an introduction to a eulogy (Eph 1:3; 2 Cor 1:3; 1 Pet 1:3). In all of these instances the exact same words are used (εὐλογητὸς ὁ θεὸς καὶ πατὴρ τοῦ κυρίου ἡμῶν Ἰησοῦ Χριστοῦ). εὐλογητός is a verbal adjective, which means that as an adjective it agrees with the noun it qualifies in number, gender, and case; and as a verb, it denotes action but is absent of tense and voice.[3] It is from the verb εὐλογέω, "to speak well of," and hence reflects the idea of praise or praiseworthy. Since it is timeless, God is (to be) blessed or praised forever (εἰς τοὺς αἰῶνας) as stated in Rom 1:25; 9:5; 2 Cor 11:31. The omitted verb "to be" could be the present imperative (ἔστω), "let God be blessed/praised," as it is in Ps 72:17 [LXX 71:17], which is in the context of εὐλογητός (v. 18) and 2 Chr 9:8; or the present optative (εἴη) "may God be blessed/praised" as it is in Ps 113:2 [LXX 112:2] and Job 1:21; or more likely the present indicative (ἐστί), "blessed is God," as Paul states in Rom 1:25 (cf. 2 Cor 11:31).[4] The omission of the verb "to be" is common in eulogies.

1. For a discussion and a copy of them in English, see Emil Schürer, *The History of the Jewish People in the Age of Jesus Christ (175 B.C.–A.D. 135)*, new English version rev. and ed. by Geza Vermes, Fergus Millar, and Matthew Black, vol. 2 (Edinburgh: T & T Clark, 1979), 454–63.

2. Gustaf Dalman, *The Words of Jesus Considered in the Light of Post-Biblical Jewish Writings and the Aramaic Language*, trans. D. M. Kay (Edinburgh: T & T Clark, 1909), 200.

3. MHT 1:221; Robertson, *Grammar*, 372–73; 1095–97.

4. Scharbert suggests that it could be the present participle of the verb "to be" (ὤν) but how would one translate it—"God who is blessed"? See Josef Scharbert, "Die Geschichte der bārûk-Formel," *BZ* 17, no. 1 (1973): 20. It seems better to use the indicative because there is need of a finite verb here and Scharbert's example for his suggestion is Rom 1:25, which uses the finite verb "to be" (ἐστίν).

The expression "the God and Father of our Lord Jesus Christ" is frequently used (cf. Rom 15:6; 2 Cor 1:3; 11:31; Col 1:3; 1 Pet 1:3). The Christian eulogy is rich because it describes God also as "Father" (cf. 1:2; 3:14; 5:20). Whereas "father" is rarely used of God in the OT (fifteen times out of 1448 occurrences) and in Palestinian Judaism, in the NT it is the predominent use (245 times out of 413 occurrences).[1] Hence, he is both the God and Father of our Lord Jesus Christ. This denotes that Jesus Christ is the Son of God.

The genitives that follow, τοῦ κυρίου ἡμῶν Ἰησοῦ Χριστοῦ, "of our Lord Jesus Christ," have been interpreted in two ways. First, some think the genitives refer only to "Father" and would render it "Blessed be God, who is the Father of our Lord Jesus Christ."[2] Second, others think that "God" and "Father" are in apposition and the genitives depend on both and so translate it "Blessed be the God and Father of our Lord Jesus Christ."[3] The second view is best for the following reasons. First, the Granville Sharp rule applies here whereby the copulative καί connects two personal, singular, non-proper nouns, the first noun preceded by an article and the second noun, which is anarthrous, further describing the first noun (the first named person).[4] Hence, "Father" further describes "God." Second, in verse 17 Paul explicitly writes "God of our Lord Jesus Christ," where God is further described as "the Father of glory," and so the genitives in verse 3 surely refer to both "God" and "Father." Third, it is certainly clear that God and Father are to be joined as one and the same in Rev 1:6 (καὶ ἐποίησεν ἡμᾶς βασιλείαν, ἱερεῖς τῷ θεῷ καὶ πατρὶ αὐτοῦ, "and he made us a kingdom, priests to his God and Father") and in 1 Cor 15:24 (ὅταν παραδιδῷ τὴν βασιλείαν τῷ θεῷ καὶ πατρί, "when he delivers the kingdom to the God and Father").[5] Therefore, the genitives go back to both "God" and "Father."

The genitival prepositional phrase "of our Lord Jesus Christ" denotes four things: (1) his personal relationship to the believer ("our Lord"); (2) his name ("Jesus"); (3) his Lordship ("Jesus is Lord" was an early confession of the church, as in Acts 2:36; 8:16; 10:36; 11:17; 19:5; Rom 10:9; 14:9; 1 Cor 12:3; 2 Cor 4:5; Phil 2:11); and (4) his title ("Christ"), which is more than just a name, denotes that he is the promised Messiah who would bring salvation (see discussion of Χριστός above in v. 1).

1. Otfried Hofius, "Father [ἀββά]," *NIDNTT* 1 (1975): 617–18.

2. Syriac Peshitta; Theodore of Mopsuestia *Eph* 1:3 (*PG* 66:912); Ellicott, 4; Meyer, 34.

3. Chrysostom *Eph* 1:3 (*PG* 62:10–11); Jerome *Eph* 1:3 (*PL* 26:446); Theophylact *Eph* 1:3 (*PG* 124:1034–35); Alford, 3:69; Eadie, 11–12; Abbott, 4; Robinson, 142; Westcott, 6; Schlier, 42.

4. Wallace, *Greek Grammar*, 270–74, 671, 735.

5. Westcott, 6.

God is blessed or worthy of praise. He is the God who also is the Father of our Lord Jesus Christ. Since there is no verb "to be" expressed, it could be a statement of a wish or a declaration. The latter is preferred. But why? Certainly God is worthy of praise because of who he is. But it is difficult to praise someone if nothing is known about him. The next part of the verse as well as verses 4–14 give reasons why the believer is to praise God.

ὁ εὐλογήσας ἡμᾶς, "who has blessed us." The reason God is to be praised is because he blessed us. The aorist participle comes from εὐλογέω which literally means "I speak well" (εὖ + λεγέω). In classical Greek it sometimes refers to the ability to speak well (used with the noun λογία), but usually it refers to "speaking well of," "praising," or "extoling someone."[1] This concept is not difficult to find in Greek literature. However, although there are a few references to a human praising or blessing the gods,[2] there is only one instance of a god blessing a human.[3] Rather, the term ὄλβος is used to denote that the gods lavished happiness on humans, especially worldly happiness.[4] In brief then, the concept of blessing is infrequent in classical literature.[5]

There is a marked difference in the OT because εὐλογέω occurs 461 times in the LXX, 297 times in the canonical books. In the canonical books, it is a translation of the Hebrew בָּרַךְ except for twenty-three instances (nine times it is used without referring to any Hebrew word; fourteen times it is a translation of ten different Hebrew words). Most frequently it is translated from the Piel stem.[6] Much study has been done on the Hebrew word[7] and its basic idea is "to bless." To be more specific, when God is the object of a person's blessing, it has the idea of "praise" and when a person is the object of God's blessings, it has the idea of "happiness, success, an increase of earthly possessions" (e.g., Gen 27:4, 33, 34; 49:28; Pss 5:12; 65:11 [MT 65:12; LXX 64:12]; 67:6–7 [MT 67:7–8; LXX 66:7–8]; Hag 2:19). When one petitions God to bless someone (e.g., Num 6:23, 24, 27; Pss 28:9 [LXX 27:9]; 67:1 [MT 67:2; LXX 66:2]) it means that he petitions God to grant success to that person.[8] It is the opposite of curse, which means to be exposed

1. Hermann W. Beyer, "εὐλογέω," *TDNT* 2 (1964): 754.

2. E.g., Pan in *CIG* 3:4705b.2; Isis in *CIG* 3:4705c.3.

3. Euripides *Supplices* 925–27.

4. LSJ 1213.

5. Beyer, "εὐλογέω," *TDNT* 2 (1964): 755.

6. For a specific breakdown of stem usage, see Joseph Thuruthumaly, *Blessing in St Paul (Eulogein in St Paul)*, Pontifical Institute Publications, vol. 35 (Alwaye, Kerala, India: Pontifical Institute of Theology and Philosophy, 1981), 17.

7. For bibliography, see Scharbert, *TDOT* 2 (1977): 279–80 n. 1; cf. also Christopher Toll, "Ausdrücke für »Kraft« im Alten Testament mit besonderer Rücksicht auf die Wurzel BRK," *Zeitschrift für die alttestamentliche Wissenschaft* 94, no. 1 (1982): 111–23.

8. Scharbert, *TDOT* 2 (1977): 293; cf. A. Murtonen, "The Use and Meaning of the Words *lᵉbårek* and *bᵉråkåh* in the Old Testament," *VT* 9 (April 1959): 158–77.

to destruction (cf. Lev 26, Deut 27–28; Ps 37:22 [LXX 36:22]). Therefore, to be blessed by God means to receive benefits from God in the sense of possessions, prosperity, or power. For example, when Isaac blessed Jacob, Esau pleaded to have the blessings also (Gen 27).

In the NT εὐλογέω is used forty-two times in various ways. First, like the OT it is used thirteen times as "praise" where God is the object (Matt 14:19 = Mark 6:41 = Luke 9:16; Matt 26:26 = Mark 14:22; Mark 8:7; Luke 1:64; 2:28; 24:30, 53; 1 Cor 10:16; 14:16; Jas 3:9). Second, it is used seven times of people blessing or praising Jesus (Matt 21:9 = Mark 11:9, 10 = Luke 19:38 = John 12:13; Matt 23:39 = Luke 13:35). Third, it is used eight times of persons blessing other persons (Luke 1:42*bis*; 2:34; Heb 7:1, 6, 7; 11:20, 21), which invokes God's enablement for success. Fourth, there are five cases where it is used in a new way in that persons are to bless or desire good to those who curse them (Luke 6:28; Rom 12:14*bis*; 1 Cor 4:12; 1 Pet 3:9). Fifth, twice it is used of Jesus blessing people (Luke 24:50, 51), which has the idea of calling on God's power for enablement. Finally, it is used seven times where God is the subject who "provides with benefits"[1] (Matt 25:34; Luke 1:28; Acts 3:25, 26; Gal 3:9; Eph 1:3; Heb 6:14). This last category fits this context well. God is the subject and he provides benefits to "us" (ἡμᾶς), the believers. As Mary was the object of God's gracious provision of being chosen to bear Jesus (Luke 1:28, 42), so believers today are the object of God's blessing, enrichment, or provision of benefits. The "us" refers to both Paul and the recipients of the letter ("the saints," v. 1). Here the substantival participle[2] seems to summarize the activity of God (being aorist may give the idea of the past activity of God) and gives a causal idea. The believers bless God who has blessed them, or the believers praise God because he has benefited them. But with what did God benefit the believer? The following phrase answers this question.

ἐν πάσῃ εὐλογίᾳ πνευματικῇ, "with every spiritual blessing." Here the preposition ἐν with the dative is the instrumental use that follows the Hebrew בְּ[3] and is translated "with." The πάσῃ shows the quantity. It can be translated "all" but here, because of the absence of the article, it is preferable to translate it "every,"[4] which emphasizes God's benefit to believers of every kind of blessing.[5] The specifics of these blessings are given in verses 4–14, beginning with God's election in the past and God's redemption both in the present and in the future.

1. BAGD 322; BDAG 408.

2. For a study of participial formulas of praise, cf. Gerhard Delling, "Partizipiale Gottesprädikationen in den Briefen des Neuen Testaments," *ST* 17, no. 1 (1963): 1–59, esp. 14–15.

3. BDF §§4 (3), 195, 219; MHT 3:252–53. Deichgräber (*Gotteshymnus*, 23) gives examples of this usage in OT and Qumran texts.

4. BDF §275 (3).

5. BAGD 631; BDAG 784.

The noun εὐλογία, "blessing," is a cognate to the verb εὐλογέω discussed above. It has the idea of "a good speech or word," "blessing," or "praise."[1] In the LXX it occurs a hundred times and in the canonical books it appears seventy times and sixty-three times it translates בְּרָכָה, which means "blessing." Interestingly, the noun is seldom used for praise (2 Chr 20:26; Neh 9:5). The basic idea seems to be prosperity or benefit, as in the case of the father blessing his posterity, that is, he had the power to provide benefits or prosperity (e.g., Gen 27:35, 36, 38, 41; 28:4; 49:25*ter*, 26*bis*; Isa 44:3). Outside of the family context the prosperity of material things is also mentioned (e.g., Lev 25:21; Prov 10:22; Isa 65:8; Mal 3:10). Such blessings are contrasted with curses which bring one to desolation (e.g., Gen 27:12; Deut 11:26, 27, 29; 23:5 [MT & LXX 23:6]; 28:2, 8; 30:1, 19; Neh 13:2; Ps 109:17 [LXX 108:17]; Prov 11:26; Mal 2:2*bis*). However, the dispensing of prosperity or benefits was not through magical power, as was the case in many tribal religions of that day, but always through the sovereign God with a personal will who brought Abraham out of Ur and Israel out of Egypt. He could bestow prosperity and benefits. In the NT εὐλογία is used sixteen times, nine times by Paul. It is used once of fine speech, that is, flattering words (Rom 16:18). Five times it denotes praise (1 Cor 10:16; Jas 3:10; Rev 5:12, 13; 7:12). It is used four times as a gift or bounty (2 Cor 9:5*bis*, 6*bis*). Finally, six times it is used of obtaining benefits (Rom 15:29; Gal 3:14; Eph 1:3; Heb 6:7; 12:17; 1 Pet 3:9). It is this last category that is in agreement with so many of the OT references and it makes the best sense in the present context.

The benefit or enrichment is further defined as "spiritual" (πνευματικῇ). In the OT the benefits were primarily material, such as prosperity and physical protection (e.g., Gen 49:25; Deut 28:2–8, 12; 30:9, 19; Mal 3:10). The adjective πνευματικός in classical Greek refers to wind, air, and breath[2] and is not used in the LXX. In the NT it is used twenty-six times and all by Paul except twice (1 Pet 2:5*bis*). In trying to define the word it is interesting to notice to what it is contrasted in various contexts. First, in 1 Cor 2:14–3:4 Paul twice contrasts different persons. (1) The spiritual person who can discern all things is in contrast to the natural (ψυχικός, "soulish") person who is not able to receive the things pertaining to the spirit of God (2:14–16), namely, the wisdom of God described in 1:18–2:13, which is the power of God to transform one's life through the crucified Christ. (2) The spiritual person is contrasted to immature Christians (σάρκινος/σαρκικός) who did not and later desired not to accept the things pertaining to the Spirit (3:1–4). Thus, the spiritual person is the one who knows and wants that which is of the Spirit of God. Second, there is the contrast between the spiritual body, which is the resurrected body animated by

1. LSJ 720.
2. Ibid., 1424.

the Spirit of God and fit for heaven, and the natural (ψυχικόν) body which is animated by the soul and is fit for this age only (1 Cor 15:44–46). Third, Paul contrasts the spiritual things that engender the proclamation of the gospel and the material (σαρκικά) things that engender resources for the maintenance of physical body (Rom 15:27; 1 Cor 9:11). In conclusion, that which is spiritual pertains to things of the Spirit of God and is supernatural having its source in God and is in contrast to that which is natural and has as its source earthly human beings or things. Therefore, "spiritual benefits" have their source in the Spirit of God, are supernatural, and are applicable at the present time to believers who are on earth. The spiritual gifts (1 Cor 12:1; 14:1; Rom 1:11), wisdom (Col 1:9), and spiritual persons (Gal 6:1) are to aid the believer to function on this earth in the present time. For a believer to live effectively in society, he or she needs benefits that have their source in God. So God has blessed the believer with every spiritual benefit necessary for his or her spiritual well-being.

ἐν τοῖς ἐπουρανίοις, "in the heavenly realms." This phrase further elaborates on the sources of the spiritual blessings, which are not only from the Spirit of God but also from the heavenlies. The word ἐπουράνιος in classical Greek can refer to the place where the gods dwell and from which they come[1] or, when used substantively, it can be used synonymously with God.[2] It appears five times in the LXX and only once in the canonical books, once in Ps 68:14 [MT 68:15; LXX 67:15] where it refers to the Almighty (שַׁדַּי) and a possible textual variant in Theodotion Dan 4:26 [Codex A] where it refers to the heavens (שְׁמַיָּא) denoting God's rule. Hence, in both instances it refers to God and his rule. In the NT it occurs nineteen times,[3] five of which are in Ephesians (1:3, 20; 2:6; 3:10; 6:12). Paul contrasts the glories of heavenly and earthly (ἐπίγεια) bodies (1 Cor 15:40*bis*), suggesting that though the natural person bears the image of that which is from the earth, he will bear the image of the heavenly person after the resurrection (15:48, 49). It is in this same context that Paul contrasts the natural and spiritual bodies, the latter being animated by the Spirit of God (15:44–46). Thus, the spiritual body has been transformed by the Spirit from heaven who fits it for heaven. The spiritual body and the heavenly person are one and the same, that which is imperishable and is able to inherit the kingdom of God. There are other explicit references contrasting earthly and heavenly things or realms (cf. John 3:12; Eph 1:20; 2:6; 3:10; 6:12; Phil 2:10; 2 Tim 4:18; Heb 8:5; 9:23; 11:16; 12:22). In using ἐπουράνιος the author to the Hebrews indicates that the call (3:1) and gift (6:4) have their source in heaven as opposed to earth. This agrees well with the present context, for the spiritual benefits that come from heaven are for the believers united with Christ, who as-

1. Homer *Ilias* 6.129; *Odyssea* 17.484.
2. Theocritus 25.5; cf. Homer *Ilias* 6.131.
3. This does not include the reading in Matt 18:35 which is in some manuscripts.

cended into heaven (1:20; 2:6).[1] Thus, spiritual benefits come from the Spirit as well as from the heavens. Although the adjective could be masculine ("among heavenly beings"), it better suits its five occurrences in Ephesians to take it as neuter ("in the heavenly places/realms").[2] Unique to Ephesians, it is always used with the same prepositional phrase (ἐν τοῖς ἐπουρανίοις). In the other four instances it always denotes a location[3] and this makes the most sense in the present context. Caragounis suggests that though the spheres of ἐπουράνιος and οὐρανός, "heaven," overlap, they are not identical. οὐρανός begins with the air space where birds fly and continues all the way up to God's throne, while ἐπουράνιος refers to the higher layers of space, from God's throne down to the sphere where cosmic powers reside and operate.[4] Hence, the spiritual blessings are from the heavenly places or realms and for the benefit of the believer here and now.[5] To put it another way, the believer's life is "conditioned by transcen-

1. Lincoln, "A Re-Examination of 'the Heavenlies' in Ephesians," 470; W. Hall Harris III, "'The Heavenlies' Reconsidered: Οὐρανός and Ἐπουράνιος in Ephesians," *BSac* 148 (January–March 1991): 73–74.

2. Hugo Odeberg, *The View of the Universe in the Epistle to the Ephesians*, LUÅ, n.s. 1, vol. 29, no. 6 (Lund: Gleerup, 1934), 7; Wesley Carr, *Angels and Principalities. The Background, Meaning and Development of the Pauline Phrase Hai Archai Kai Hai Exousiai*, SNTSMS, ed. R. McL. Wilson and M. E. Thrall, vol. 42 (Cambridge: Cambridge University Press, 1981), 94–95; Bruce, 253–54.

3. In 1:20 the place where Christ is at the right hand of God; 2:6 where believers are raised and seated with Christ; 3:10 where the mystery of the church is made known to the spiritual powers; and 6:12 where the believer's struggle is with the evil powers; cf. Schlier, 44–48; Percy, *Probleme*, 181; Gnilka, 63–66; Barth, 78–79; Odeberg, *View of the Universe*, 7; cf. also R. H. Charles, "The Seven Heavens: An Early Jewish and Christian Belief," *ExpTim* 7 (December 1895): 115. Lightfoot denies this by saying "the heaven, of which the Apostle here speaks, is not some *remote locality*, some *future abode*. It is heaven which lies within and about the true Christian" (see Lightfoot, *Notes on Epistles of St Paul*, 312). However, Gibbs comments on Lightfoot's statement by saying, "Such an interpretation of Eph. 1:3 is in defiance, however, of the same phrase in Eph. 6:12" (see John G. Gibbs, *Creation and Redemption. A Study in Pauline Theology*, NovTSup, ed. W. C. van Unnik et al., vol. 26 [Leiden: Brill, 1971], 130).

4. Caragounis, *Ephesian* Mysterion, 150–52.

5. Odeberg, *View of the Universe*, 9. However, Odeberg (12–13) thinks that the "heavenlies" are the spiritual realities of the church in Christ thereby eliminating the local sense as a part of the celestial regions distinct from the terrestrial or earthly realms. Nevertheless, it seems more in line with the text to view that believers operate simultaneously in two realms: they live in their bodies on earth (Eph 3:1; 6:10–20) but their spiritual enrichment is from the heavenlies (1:3) and their struggle is not with flesh and blood but with spiritual foes in the heavenlies (6:12; cf. 3:10). For discussion on this, see Lincoln, "A Re-Examination of 'the Heavenlies' in Ephesians," 468–83, esp. 478–81; Caragounis, *Ephesian* Mysterion, 150–51; Lincoln, 20; Best, 116–17. Clemens does not like "heavenly places" because he feels that it is vague and has the sense of aloofness (John S. Clemens, "Note on the Phrase ἐν τοῖς ἐπουρανίοις," *ExpTim* 2 [March 1891]: 140). He likes to think of it as "having special reference to *conditions* of life and being" and would translate it "heavenly sphere." However, to translate it "heavenly places" or

dence."[1] Later this epistle mentions evil hosts in the heavenlies (3:10) and the believer's struggle with them in the present day (6:12). This is in keeping with the OT portrayal of God and Satan conversing with one another in heaven (Job 1:6–12) and the struggle between the good and evil angels in heaven and on earth (Dan 10:13, 20). Hence, the concept of the heavenlies as a source of spiritual blessings and power is rooted in the OT rather than some Gnostic notion of transcendence interacting with human existence wherein the believer is called to make decisions.[2] Thus, in receiving the spiritual benefit from the heavenly places it is in the midst of satanic attack and interference. The spiritual benefits for the believers are from the heavenlies and the unbelievers' opposition to the believers find their source in wicked spiritual leaders who also reside in the heavenlies (6:12). In other words, the struggles in the heavenlies are also played out on earth. Hence, the believers reside on earth having been enriched with every spiritual blessing in the heavenlies necessary for their spiritual well-being.

ἐν Χριστῷ, "in Christ." This prepositional phrase is used one other time (4:32) and is like the more complete phrase (ἐν Χριστῷ Ἰησοῦ) used seven times in the letter (1:1; 2:6, 7, 10, 13; 3:6, 21).[3] Ever since the monumental work of Deissmann[4] at the end of the nineteenth century, there has been much discussion regarding the interpretation of this prepositional phrase. He found 164 occurrences of the formula "in Christ" (or "in the Lord") in Paul's letters (excluding Colossians, Ephesians, and the Pastorals) and gave it a local and mystical sense indicating the intimate fellowship of the Christian with the living spiritual Christ. In a later work he explains "Christ is Spirit; therefore He can live in Paul and Paul in Him. Just as the air of life, which we breathe, is 'in' us and fills us, and yet we at the same time live in this air and breathe it, so it is also with the Christ-intimacy of the apostle Paul: Christ in him, he in Christ."[5] However, this suggests a mystical and impersonal Christ.[6] Büchsel and Neugebauer think that one cannot give a uniform exegesis of the phrase but must derive its meaning

---

"realms" denotes the source of the blessings for the believer and they are relevant to him or her here and now on earth.

1. R. G. Hamerton-Kelly, *Pre-Existence, Wisdom, and the Son of Man. A Study of the Idea of Pre-existence in the New Testament*, SNTSMS, ed. Matthew Black and R. McL. Wilson, vol. 21 (Cambridge: Cambridge University Press, 1973), 179.

2. As supposed by some like Schlier, 44–48. Lincoln (20) also sees it from a Jewish background.

3. The phrase which takes on various forms in Ephesians is seen in Excursus 3: In Christ.

4. G. Adolf Deissmann, *Die neutestamentliche Formel "in Christo Jesu"* (Marburg: N. G. Elwert'sche Verlagsbuchhandlung, 1892); see also Clarence B. Hale, *The Meaning of "in Christ" in the Greek New Testament* (Dallas: Summer Institute of Linguistics, 1991).

5. Deissmann, *Paul*, 140.

6. Best, *One Body in Christ*, 9.

from each individual context.[1] In many cases it may have the idea of instrumentality "through Christ"[2] but surely it can have the local sense of "the 'place' in whom the believers are and in whom salvation is."[3] With this is the incorporation of the believer with the head, Christ, which is analogous to the scriptural declarations that all the nations shall be blessed in Abraham (Gen 12:3; 18:18) and all humankind dies in Adam (1 Cor 15:22).[4] The present context seems to indicate that there is a definite union between the believer and Christ.[5] Allan challenges this by proposing that the phrase "in Christ" in Ephesians occurs nearly twice as many times as in other Pauline literature, and that in Ephesians it does not have the local or corporate idea (rather, it has the instrumental sense) that is present in the other letters of Paul.[6] Lincoln has rightly critiqued Allan by saying:

> However his thesis both overestimates the extent to which "in Christ" is a formula of incorporation in Paul and underestimates the extent to which its use in Ephesians involves incorporation. . . . But it is particularly hard to avoid the more intensive incorporative connotation in 2:6 where believers are said to have been raised and seated in the heavenly realms together with Christ "in Christ Jesus."[7]

1. Friedrich Büchsel, "»In Christus« bei Paulus," *ZNW* 42 (1949): 141–58; Fritz Neugebauer, "Das Paulinische 'In Christo'," *NTS* 4 (January 1958): 124–38; cf. also A. J. M. Wedderburn, "Some Observations on Paul's Use of the Phrases 'in Christ' and 'with Christ'," *JSNT* 25 (October 1985): 84–86; William B. Barcley, *"Christ in You": A Study in Paul's Theology and Ethics* (Lanham, Md.: University Press of America, 1999).

2. Büchsel, "»In Christus« bei Paulus," 141–58, esp. 144–45, 156–57; Allan, "The 'In Christ' Formula in Ephesians," 59.

3. Best, *One Body in Christ*, 8, 29; cf. also Moule, *The Origin of Christology*, 61–63; Nicholas Thomas Wright, "The Messiah and the People of God: A Study in Pauline Theology with Particular Reference to the Argument of the Epistle to the Romans" (D.Phil. thesis, University of Oxford, 1980), 10–27; Lincoln, 21.

4. Wedderburn, "Some Observations on Paul's Use of the Phrases 'in Christ' and 'with Christ'," 88–89.

5. Neugebauer thinks that one can make a distinction between Χριστός as the personified indicative indicating the one who was crucified and resurrected who is related to the church and κύριος as the personified imperative retaining a functional concept, see Neugebauer, "Das Paulinische 'In Christo'," 127–28; cf. also Wright, "The Messiah and the People of God," 49. This holds true for the most part in Ephesians, for the phrases ἐν Χριστῷ Ἰησοῦ, ἐν Χριστῷ, ἐν τῷ Χριστῷ Ἰησοῦ are found in the doctrinal part of the book (chaps. 1–3) (1:1, 3, 10, 12, 20; 2:6, 7, 10, 13; 3:6, 11, 21) and only once in the application portion (4:32). On the other hand the phrases ἐν κυρίῳ, ἐν τῷ κυρίῳ Ἰησοῦ are found mainly in the application portion of the book (chaps. 4–10) (4:1, 17; 5:8; 6:1, 10, 21) and only twice in the doctrinal section (1:15; 2:21). Hence, our position is in Christ and we are to obey in the Lord or we are to become in the Lord what we are in Christ. Kramer (*Christ, Lord, Son of God*, 141–50, 177–82) gives caution in taking this too far.

6. Allan, "The 'In Christ' Formula in Ephesians," 54–62. The idea of incorporation in Christ is also rejected by Büchsel, "»In Christus« bei Paulus," 141–58, esp. 144–45, 156–58.

7. Lincoln, 22.

Therefore, the local sense, the believer incorporated in Christ, gives the best sense in this context as also in verse 1. With birth a person is identified with the human race whose head is Adam. When Adam sinned all people came under the tyranny of sin which brought death to all humans (Rom 5:12–14). Christ who knew no sin became a human being and took on him the sin of human beings and died to pay its penalty in behalf of humankind, thus propitiating God's wrath (Rom 3:23–26; 2 Cor 5:18–21; Gal 3:13; Phil 2:6–8). Anyone who believes God's provision in Christ becomes united to a new head (Rom 5:15–6:11). Hence, the believer is "in Christ." The believer, who is united with Christ who is in heaven, partakes of the spiritual benefits from the heavenlies. This was a new concept for the Ephesians for they had been worshipers of Artemis who was the local deity on earth.

In conclusion, God is praised because he has enriched believers with every spiritual benefit in the heavenlies in Christ. To declare God is blessed implies that praise is due. To declare the believer blessed implies that the spiritual benefits have been given. However, though spiritual benefits have been given, believers need to appropriate them. An analogy of this is God's promise to Joshua (1:3) that every place in the Promised Land on which he places his foot has already been given to him in accordance with God's promise to Moses. Although it had been given, it was not a reality until Joshua placed his foot on it. As it would have been presumptuous for Joshua to pray for the land that had been given to him, so is it likewise presumptuous for the believer to ask for the spiritual benefits already given to him or her. The only reason Israel did not obtain the land in Ai (Josh 7) was because there was sin in the camp, not because they did not pray. In fact, the first time Joshua prayed was after the defeat at Ai and God told him to stop praying and deal with the sin that caused the defeat (Josh 7). The reason the believer does not receive spiritual benefits is not because God is in some way stingy and he or she must plead for them, but because believers are not appropriating by faith what God has already bestowed in their behalf. The problem is not with God but with the believer. This enrichment is further described in verses 4–14. Although God had promised the people of Israel material prosperity and physical protection, he has not promised this for the believer in this age. Rather, he has promised every spiritual benefit for the entire spiritual well-being of the believer.

In summary, the following list answers several questions in regard to spiritual blessings.

1. Who has given these benefits? God who is the object of praise and the subject of the blessings.
2. To whom has he given these blessings? Believers.
3. With what has he blessed them? With every spiritual benefit.
4. Where has he blessed them? In the heavenlies.
5. How has he blessed them? In Christ.

Excursus 3
In Christ

The expression "in Christ" and its parallels occur thirty-six times in the Book of Ephesians, and if the other similar expressions listed below are included, the total is thirty-nine times.

ἐν Χριστῷ

1:3—ἐν τοῖς ἐπουρανίοις ἐν Χριστῷ (location)
4:32—ὁ θεὸς ἐν Χριστῷ ἐχαρίσατο ἡμῖν (sphere or location)

ἐν Χριστῷ Ἰησοῦ

1:1—τοῖς . . . πιστοῖς ἐν Χριστῷ Ἰησοῦ (incorporation)
2:6—ἐν τοῖς ἐπουρανίοις ἐν Χριστῷ Ἰησοῦ (location)
2:7—ἐν χρηστότητι ἐφ᾽ ἡμᾶς ἐν Χριστῷ Ἰησοῦ (location)
2:10—κτισθέντες ἐν Χριστῷ Ἰησοῦ (sphere or location)
2:13—νυνὶ δὲ ἐν Χριστῷ Ἰησοῦ (location)
3:6—συμμέτοξα τῆς ἐπαγγελίας ἐν Χριστῷ Ἰησοῦ (location)
3:21—αὐτῷ ἡ δόξα ἐν τῇ ἐκκλησίᾳ καὶ ἐν Χριστῷ Ἰησοῦ (sphere or location)

ἐν τῷ Χριστῷ

1:10—ἀνακεφαλαιώσασθαι τὰ πάντα ἐν τῷ Χριστῷ (location)
1:12—τοὺς προηλπικότας ἐν τῷ Χριστῷ (location)
1:20—ἣν ἐνήργησεν ἐν τῷ Χριστῷ (sphere or location)

ἐν τῷ Χριστῷ Ἰησοῦ

3:11—ἣν ἐποίησεν ἐν τῷ Χριστῷ Ἰησοῦ τῷ κυριῷ ἡμῶν (sphere or location)

ἐν τῷ Ἰησοῦ

4:21—καθώς ἐστιν ἀλήθεια ἐν τῷ Ἰησοῦ (location)

ἐν κυρίῳ

2:21—αὔξει εἰς ναὸν ἅγιον ἐν κυρίῳ (sphere)
4:1—ἐγὼ ὁ δέσμιος ἐν κυρίῳ (sphere or location)
4:17—λέγω καὶ μαρτύρομαι ἐν κυρίῳ (sphere)
5:8—ἦτε γάρ ποτε σκότος, νῦν δὲ φῶς ἐν κυρίῳ (sphere)
6:1—ὑπακούετε τοῖς γονεῦσιν ὑμῶν [ἐν κυρίῳ] (sphere?)
6:10—ἐνδυναμοῦσθε ἐν κυρίῳ (sphere)
6:21—Τύχικος . . . πιστὸς διάκονος ἐν κυρίῳ (sphere)

ἐν τῷ κυρίῳ Ἰησοῦ

1:15—ἀκούσας τὴν καθ᾽ ὑμᾶς πίστιν ἐν τῷ κυρίῳ Ἰησοῦ (sphere or location)

ἐν αὐτῷ

1:4—καθὼς ἐξελέξατο ἡμᾶς ἐν αὐτῷ (sphere, relational, or instrumental)
1:9—κατὰ τὴν εὐδοκίαν αὐτοῦ ἣν προέθετο ἐν αὐτῷ (location)
1:10—τὰ ἐπὶ τοῖς οὐρανοῖς καὶ τὰ ἐπὶ τῆς γῆς ἐν αὐτῷ (location)
2:15—ἵνα τοὺς δύο κτίσῃ ἐν ἑαυτῷ/αὐτῷ (textual variant; sphere or location)
2:16—ἀποκτείνας τὴν ἔχθραν ἐν αὐτῷ (means, most likely refers to the cross)

4:21—εἴ γε αὐτὸν ἠκούσατε καὶ ἐν αὐτῷ ἐδιδάχθητε (sphere or location)

ἐν ᾧ

1:7—ἐν ᾧ ἔχομεν τὴν ἀπολύτρωσιν (sphere or location)
1:11—ἐν ᾧ καὶ ἐκληρώθημεν προορισθέντες κατὰ πρόθεσιν (sphere or location)
1:13—ἐν ᾧ καὶ ὑμεῖς ἀκούσαντες τὸν λόγον τῆς ἀληθείας (sphere or location)
1:13—ἐν ᾧ καὶ πιστεύσαντες ἐσφραγίσθητε τῷ πνεύματι τῆς επαγγελίας τῷ ἁγίῳ (location)
2:21—ἐν ᾧ πᾶσα οἰκοδομὴ συναρμολογουμένη αὔξει εἰς ναὸν ἅγιον ἐν κυρίῳ (sphere or location)
2:22—ἐν ᾧ καὶ ὑμεῖς συνοικοδομεῖσθε εἰς κατοικητήριον τοῦ θεοῦ (sphere or location)
3:12—ἐν ᾧ ἔχομεν τὴν παρρησίαν καὶ προσαγωγὴν (sphere)
4:30—τὸ πνεῦμα τὸ ἅγιον τοῦ θεοῦ, ἐν ᾧ ἐσφραγίσθητε (instrumental)

Other Expressions

1:6—ἐν τῷ ἠγαπημένῳ (location)
2:5—συνεζωοποίησεν τῷ Χριστῷ (association)
2:13—ἐγενήθητε ἐγγὺς ἐν τῷ αἵματι τοῦ Χριστοῦ (instrumental)

2. The Basis of Spiritual Blessings (1:4–14)

Having stated that God is praised because he has enriched the believer with every spiritual benefit for his spiritual well-being, Paul now explains that these spiritual benefits are based on the work of the three persons of the Trinity: the selection of the Father (vv. 4–6), the sacrifice of the Son (vv. 7–12), and the seal of the Holy Spirit (vv. 13–14). This division is obvious in the text because of the inclusion of the three persons of the Godhead and also because there is a similar refrain at the end of each person's work (vv. 6, 12, 14).

a. God's Election for Himself (1:4–6)

The action described in these verses is assigned to the Father. Although there is no specific mention of the Father in this passage, it is certainly implied. First, certainly God is the subject of the whole passage. Since the verses following this section explicitly mention Christ (vv. 10, 12) and the Holy Spirit (v. 13), it seems safe to assume that in this section Paul is referring to the only remaining person of the Trinity, the Father. Second, God is already called Father in verse 2. Third, immediately after this pæan of praise, Paul prays on behalf of the Ephesians to God (continuing to be the subject of the present passage) who is called the Father of glory (v. 17). Fourth, this epistle is known for the abundant references to the Trinity (1:17; 2:18, 22; 3:4–5, 14–17; 4:4–6; 5:18–20) and hence it seems unlikely that the Father would be left out in this context. Three subjects are discussed in this passage: election (v. 4), predestination (v. 5), and praise (v. 6).

(1) Activity: Election before Creation (1:4)

Text: 1:4. καθὼς ἐξελέξατο ἡμᾶς ἐν αὐτῷ πρὸ καταβολῆς κόσμου, εἶναι ἡμᾶς ἁγίους καὶ ἀμώμους κατενώπιον αὐτοῦ ἐν ἀγάπῃ,

Translation: 1:4. "just as he chose us in him before the foundation of the world, that we might be holy and blameless before him in love,"

Commentary: 1:4. καθὼς ἐξελέξατο ἡμᾶς, "just as he chose us." The adverbial conjunction καθώς is normally thought of as comparative conjunction and is translated "just as" (NASB, NRSV), "even as" (ASV, RSV), or "according as" (AV) and it is so used in 4:17, 21, 32; 5:2, 25, 29.[1] It suggests that the manner in which God blesses believers is through the three persons of the Trinity. The spiritual benefits are the election of the Father, the redemption of the Son, and the seal of the Holy Spirit. These are sufficient for the well-being of the believer. However, the conjunction can also have a causal sense, especially when, as here, it introduces a sentence. Thus it may be translated "because," "since," or "inasmuch as."[2] This use of the conjunction is seen in other of Paul's writings (Rom 1:28; 1 Cor 1:6; 5:7; Phil 1:7)[3] as is in this epistle (5:3). This rendering means that the work of the three persons of the Trinity is the basis for every spiritual enrichment of the believer stated in verse 3. However, as Ellicott thinks, it is probably best to include both the manner (4:32; 5:3, 25, 29) and cause,[4] as may be the case in 4:4. This means that the election of the Father, the redemption of the Son, and the seal of the Holy Spirit are themselves spiritual benefits as well as being the basis for every spiritual benefit.

The words ἐξελέξατο ἡμᾶς, "he chose us," are very comforting for the believer. Syntactically the verb is the only finite verb in verses 4–14 that is not within a relative clause. In the study of the word "to choose" several observations can be made (see Excursus 4: Election). First, in most instances in the OT and NT, as it is here, God is the subject. Second, the subject did not choose in a vacuum but in the light of all known options. God chose "us" from the whole human race. Third, there is no indication of any dislike towards those not chosen. It is not a rejection with disdain. The choice of Levi for the priesthood does not imply anything negative about the other tribes. Furthermore, nowhere is election contrasted with reprobation. It speaks only of those who are chosen and nothing of those not chosen. Fourth, it is in the middle voice, as is in almost every instance, indicating a personal interest[5] in the one chosen. Hence, God chose with great personal interest rather than a ran-

1. Gaugler, 29–30; Salmond, 247; Bengel, 4:65; Alford, 3:70.

2. Eadie, 18; Abbott, 6; Schlier, 48–49; cf. Thaddäus Soiron, *Die Kirche als der Leib Christi. Nach der Lehre des hl. Paulus exegetisch, systematisch und in der theologischen wie praktischen Bedeutung dargestellt* (Düsseldorf: Patmos, 1951), 133.

3. BDF §453 (2); HS §277c; BAGD 391; BDAG 494; Percy, *Probleme*, 243–45; Barth, 79.

4. Ellicott, 6.

5. Wallace, *Greek Grammar*, 38, 419–21, 428.

dom impersonal choice. Fifth, the one who is chosen has no legal claim on the one who chooses. In fact, it is clear in Scripture that human beings come short of his glory and do not even seek him (Rom 3:10–11). God did not choose anyone because they were holy and thus had a legal claim to be chosen. On the contrary, all people are sinners and deserve rejection. There was no obligation on God's part to choose anyone but he freely chose some and this is evidence of his great grace. The point is that if God had not taken the initiative, no one would have his everlasting presence and life. The real problem is not why he had not chosen some, but why he chose any. No wonder God is to be praised.

The object of the choice is "us." This has reference to Paul and the recipients of the letter (v. 1). One cannot argue that this has reference to a collective election because of the plural pronoun "us."[1] Paul would not have used the singular pronoun, for he was not writing to an individual but to the church as a whole. On the other hand, he is not implying that only those in the Ephesian church were chosen. If this were the case he would have used the plural "you" (ὑμᾶς). Rather Paul uses ἡμᾶς to include himself with the Ephesian church. The recipients of the choice, "us," comprise a body or group of believers. Still, chosen individuals make up this group. As individuals receive the blessings in verse 3 and individually are sealed in verse 13, so individuals are the objects of God's election.[2] This should comfort the believer, for he chose "us" from among the whole human race. Yet the chosen individuals are united with one another as a new family unit, the church, the body of Christ (2:11–3:13; 4:1–16; cf. Rom 8:29).

ἐν αὐτῷ,[3] "in him." This prepositional phrase refers back to "in Christ" in verse 2 and means that God chose "us" in connection with Christ. It does not mean that God chose us through faith in Christ (διὰ τῆς εἰς αὐτον πίστεως) as suggested by Chrysostom[4] because this would destroy God's freedom of choice. If this were the case, believers by their faith would have a legal claim whereby God must choose them. Nor is it as the Barths,[5] Bengel,[6] and possibly even Calvin[7] propose

1. As William G. MacDonald, "The Biblical Doctrine of Election," in *The Grace of God, the Will of Man*, ed. Clark H. Pinnock (Grand Rapids: Zondervan, 1989), 219–26; William W. Klein, *The New Chosen People: A Corporate View of Election* (Grand Rapids: Zondervan, 1990), 179–80; Carey C. Newman, "Election and Predestination in Ephesians 1:4–6a: An Exegetical-Theological Study of the Historical, Christological Realization of God's Purpose," *RevExp* 93 (spring 1996): 239; Best, 120, 124.

2. Edwin D. Roels, *God's Mission: The Epistle to the Ephesians in Mission Perspective* (Franeker: T. Wever, 1962), 47–48; O'Brien, 99; *contra* Best, 119–20.

3. The prepositional phrase ἐν αὐτῷ is replaced by ἑαυτῷ in only F and G.

4. Chrysostom *Eph* 1:3 (*PG* 62:12).

5. Barth, 107–9; Karl Barth, *Church Dogmatics*, trans. G. T. Thompson, G. W. Bromiley, et al., ed. G. W. Bromiley and T. F. Torrance, vol. 2, pt. 2 (Edinburgh: T & T Clark, 1957), 94–194.

6. Bengel, 4:65.

7. Calvin, 125.

that Christ is the elect and we are in him because the object of the verb "chose" is "us" and not "Christ." Nor is it because God, by means of his foresight or omniscience, knew who would have faith in him, which then became the basis of his election of them.[1] This suggests more than the passage claims and, furthermore, verse 5 states that God's selection was done on the basis of the good pleasure of his will. Rather it could be one of two views. One view is that it could be regarded as a dative of sphere, which connotes the idea that we are chosen in Christ as the head and representative of the spiritual community just as Adam is the head and representative of the natural community.[2] The other view is that it could be relational or instrumental in the sense that God chose believers in connection with or through Christ's work of redemption.[3] This latter interpretation is preferable because it expresses that God chose the believer for his glory and that it had to be done in connection with the redemption accomplished in Christ. God cannot bring sinful humans into his presence forever without Christ having paid for sin.

πρὸ καταβολῆς κόσμου, "before the foundation of the world." This denotes the time of the election. The noun καταβολή is a compound of κατα-, "down," and βολή, "throw," and hence the idea of "throwing down." The noun is rarer and later than the verb καταβάλλω with the same basic meaning "to throw down." The verb is used of "throwing down" seed in the ground[4] (sowing), of "throwing down" seed in a female[5] (conception), or of the notion of giving birth to a new idea (person's thought).[6] It is used of stones being thrown down for the foundation or the starting point of a building.[7] The noun form can have the same sense of a starting point. Although the verb is used in OT canonical books, the noun is not. In the NT the noun is used eleven times (Matt 13:35; 25:34; Luke 11:50; John 17:24; Eph 1:4; Heb 4:3; 9:26; 11:11; 1 Pet 1:20; Rev 13:8; 17:8). In all cases but Heb 11:11[8] the word "world" follows it denoting the beginning or foundation of the world. In every case the word is preceded by a preposition: once by εἰς, "into" (Heb 11:11), three times by πρό, "before" (John 17:24; Eph 1:4; 1 Pet 1:20), and the other seven times by ἀπό, "from." When used with the preposition ἀπό, it has the meaning "from the beginning or

1. Abbott, 6.

2. Ellicott, 6; Eadie, 20.

3. Allan, "The 'In Christ' Formula in Ephesians," 57; Hendriksen, 75–76; Newman, "Election and Predestination in Ephesians 1:4–6a," 238–39.

4. Menander *Georgos* 37; Galen *De Naturalibus Facultatibus* 1.6.3.

5. Galen *De Naturalibus Facultatibus* 1.6.3. The noun καταβολή is so used in Philo *Op. Mund*. 45 §132; Lucian *Amores* 19.

6. Demosthenes *Orationes* 24.154.

7. Plato *Leges* 7 §803a; cf. 2 Macc 2:13.

8. It has to do with Sarah's conception and is fraught with difficulties, cf. Philip Edgcumbe Hughes, *A Commentary on the Epistle to the Hebrews* (Grand Rapids: Eerdmans, 1977), 471–74.

foundation of the world." For example, Jesus revealed by parables what was hidden since the beginning of the world (Matt 13:35). Hence, it has the idea that something has been in process from the beginning of the world. With the preposition πρό, it has the meaning that an action occurred before the foundation or creation of the world. Thus, in John 17:24 Jesus states that God loved him before the foundation of the world. In 1 Pet 1:20 it declares that Christ was foreknown before the foundation of the world. In Eph 1:4 God chose us before the foundation of the world. Therefore, God chose the believer before the world was even created, that is, in eternity past.[1] As God chose Jacob over Esau before they were born or had done anything to merit God's favor (Rom 9:11), so God chose us before the world began.[2] Lincoln rightly notes that this implies the preexistence of Christ but not the preexistence of the church as thought by some early Christian writings (2 Clem 14:1). It is not the church but the election of believers in the church that precedes the foundation of the world.[3]

εἶναι ἡμᾶς ἁγίους καὶ ἀμώμους κατενώπιον αὐτοῦ, "that we might be holy and blameless before him." The present infinitive of the verb "to be" (εἶναι) expresses the purpose of election and ἡμᾶς, "we," is the accusative subject of the infinitive. The purpose for those chosen by God is to be holy and without blame. The word "holy" (here as a predicate adjective) has already been discussed at verse 1 in connection with the word "saints." It was seen there that although its adjectival use in the OT can refer to impersonal things like a nation (Exod 19:6) or a place (Exod 29:31; Lev 6:16 [MT & LXX 6:9]; 10:13; Ps 11:4 [LXX 10:4]; Isa 57:15; Ezek 42:13), its predominant use is personal and can denote God's character (Isa 1:4; 5:16; 6:3; Jer 50:29 [LXX 27:29]; 51:5 [LXX 28:5]; Ezek 39:7; Hos 11:9) as unique. A nation that is holy is to be different from other nations, a place that is holy such as the tabernacle or temple is different from other places, God who is holy is different from other gods, and so people who are holy are to be different from other people. Since God has selected the believer to be his possession, the believer should reflect God's character. Both in the OT and NT (Lev 11:44; 1 Pet 1:16) the believer is enjoined to be holy be-

1. *Contra* Brunner who confuses the distinction between creation and election (Emil Brunner, *Dogmatics*, vol. 1, *The Christian Doctrine of God*, trans. Olive Wyon [London: Lutterworth, 1949], 306–13). Coenen attempts to get rid of the purely temporal idea by saying that "it refers to a decision rooted in the depths of God's nature, like his *prognōsis* (foreknowledge) or *prothesis* (purpose)" (Lothar Coenen, "Elect, Choose [ἐκλέγομαι]," *NIDNTT* 1 [1975]: 542). But this is allegorizing the plain meaning of the text. Surely, God's chosing was in God's purpose but here it is specifically denoting the temporal aspect of it.

2. For a discussion of the rabbinic interpretation of Ps 74:2 that God chose his people before the creation of the world, see Otfried Hofius, "»Erwählt vor Grundlegung der Welt« (Eph 1_4)," *ZNW* 62, nos. 1/2 (1971): 123–28.

3. Lincoln, 24.

cause God is holy. God did not chose anyone because they were holy but he chose them in order that they might be holy.[1]

God not only chose the believer to be holy but also "blameless." The word ἄμωμος, "without blame," which is used eight times in the NT, is an alpha privative of μῶμος used only in 2 Pet 2:13 meaning "blame, defect, blemish."[2] Hence, ἄμωμος means "one who is without reproach" or "blameless" either physically or morally.[3] In the OT the people were to offer animals for sacrifice that had no blemish (Exod 29:1; Lev 1:3; 4:3) and so in the NT Christ is offered as an unblemished sacrifice before God (Heb 9:14; 1 Pet 1:19). The Scriptures speak of Christ presenting the believers before God without blemish (Eph 5:27; Col 1:22; Jude 24) and it follows that the redeemed are to live unblemished or blameless lives before unbelievers (Phil 2:15; Rev 14:5). As those in the Aaronic line could not have any physical defects if they were to serve as priests (Lev 21:16–24), so the believer in Christ will not have any moral defects before God. In the present context it speaks of God having chosen the believers in order that they might be holy and without blame.

The term κατενώπιον, used two other times in the NT (Col 1:22; Jude 24), is an improper preposition[4] whose object is a genitive as αὐτοῦ is here, meaning "before him, in the presence of him." God chose his elect with the purpose that they might be holy and blameless before him. The "him" refers to God and not Christ because Christ is not the object but the instrument through whose redemption God can bring the chosen into the presence of himself. This enhances the middle voice of ἐξελέξατο, which substantiates that God chose the believers for his benefit, namely, to be holy and blameless before him. Does this refer to the earthly life of the believer or to the future when the believer stands in his presence? The latter is preferred. First, because the words κατενώπιον αὐτοῦ, "before him," seem to indicate it. Second, the other instance in Ephesians (5:27) speaks of Christ's sanctification of the church in order that in the future he might present it before Christ without blemish. However, there is a necessary correlation between what God is going to do in the future for the believers and what he is presently doing for them. Since he is preparing believers to go into his presence holy and without blame, certainly that is what he desires for them now, as seen in Phil 2:15 where Christians were to be

1. Jerome makes this point, see Elizabeth A. Clark, "The Place of Jerome's Commentary on Ephesians in the Origenist Controversy: The Apokatastasis and Ascetic Ideals," *VC* 41 (June 1987): 159–60.

2. BAGD 531; BDAG 663.

3. F. Hauck, "ἄμωμος," *TDNT* 4 (1967): 830; G. H. R. Horsley, *New Documents Illustrating Early Christianity*, vol. 3, *A Review of the Greek Inscriptions and Papyri Published in 1978* (Sydney: Macquarie University, 1983), 41.

4. Moule, *Idiom Book*, 85; BDF §214 (5). It is an adverb functioning as a preposition, cf. MHT 3:277; BAGD 421; BDAG 531.

blameless in a crooked and perverted generation (cf. Rev 14:5). Hence, the purpose of election is that believers are to be holy and without blame before God, which presupposes that humans are unholy. Paul develops this latter concept in 2:1–5.

ἐν ἀγάπῃ, "in love." Two things need to be discussed: the meaning of the word "love" and what the phrase qualifies. The word for love[1] is an important word in Ephesians. The noun form (ἀγάπη) is used nineteen times in the LXX (fifteen times in the canonical books), 116 times in the NT, and seventy-five times by Paul out of which he uses it ten times in this small Book of Ephesians. The verb form (ἀγαπάω) is used 278 times in the LXX (210 times in the canonical books), 143 times in the NT, thirty-four times by Paul, and ten times in Ephesians. While it is interesting that Paul uses the noun in Ephesians ten out of the seventy-five occurrences in all his literature, it is extraordinary that he uses the verb in this epistle one out of three times in all his works.

In the classical period the verb was used frequently from Homer onwards with the idea of showing or treating with affection.[2] In contrast to ἐράω, the subject of ἀγαπάω makes a free choice toward whom it shows affection, whereas ἐράω is an impulsive act towards the object. The subject of ἀγαπάω selects and keeps the object of one's love, whereas ἐράω seeks satisfaction wherever it can.[3] Hence, the subject of ἀγαπάω is free to select and is faithful in its affection toward its object, whereas the subject of ἐράω is in bondage to impulse and seeks fulfillment of self in whomever the object might be. One is unselfish and the other is selfish. Outside of the Bible, the noun is not found in classical literature before the NT era.

Out of the 211 times the verb ἀγαπάω is used in the canonical LXX, 171 times it is translated from אָהֵב and the remaining times it is translated from eighteen different Hebrew words or there is either no Hebrew word from which it is translated or its identification is doubtful. The Hebrew verb (which the LXX translates ἀγαπάω) denotes both divine (Deut 4:37; 7:13; Jer 31:3 [LXX 38:3]; Hos 14:4 [MT & LXX 14:5]; Mal 1:2*ter*) and human (Gen 29:18, 20, 30; Lev 19:18, 34; Deut 6:5; Cant 3:1–4; Hos 3:1) love as well as love toward inanimate objects such as wisdom (Prov 8:17, 21), sleep (Prov 20:13), death (Prov 8:36), discipline, knowledge (Prov 12:1), and the good (Amos 5:15). With re-

1. For a thorough study of the word, see C. Spicq, *Agapè dans le Nouveau Testament*, EBib, 3 vols. (Paris: Gabalda, 1958–59); cf. also the ET which leaves out the technical footnotes and appendicies (idem, *Agape in the New Testament*, trans. Marie Aquinas McNamara and Mary Honoria Richter, 3 vols. [St. Louis: B. Herder Book, 1963–66]); cf. also Victor Estalayo-Alonso, "Agape en la Carta a los Efesios," *Estudios teológicos* 1 (Enero–Junio 1974): 79–127.

2. Homer *Odyssea* 23.214.

3. Ethelbert Stauffer, "ἀγαπάω," *TDNT* 1 (1964): 37; Walther Günther, "Love [ἀγαπάω]," *NIDNTT* 2 (1976): 539.

gards to the noun ἀγάπη, all fifteen times it is used in canonical literature of the LXX, it is translated from אַהֲבָה. In all these instances it refers to human love (2 Sam 13:15; Eccl 9:1, 6; Cant 2:4, 5, 7), but the Hebrew noun is also used in the OT of divine love (Isa 63:9; Jer 31:3; Hos 11:4; Zeph 3:17). In conclusion, the most frequent Hebrew verb and noun for love denote a selective conscious act of concern toward the person or object loved.[1] The subject is free to make a selective choice in the direction of this love in contrast to the undirected love that is unselective or universal as seen in ἐράω or ἔρως.[2] The Hebrew verb (אָהַב) and noun (אַהֲבָה) discussed are most frequently translated by the Greek verb (ἀγαπάω) and noun (ἀγάπη). There is a close correspondence between them. It is on this base that the NT builds.

Two common Greek words for love are never used in the NT: στοργή (appears four times in LXX but never in canonical books), having the idea of family love or affection, as borne out by the negative adjective ἄστοργος, "unloving," used only in Rom 1:31 and 2 Tim 3:3 (not in LXX) and ἔρως (used only three times in the LXX: Ps 35:11 [LXX 34:11]; Prov 7:18; 30:16), expressing a possessive love and used mainly of physical love. The most common prebiblical word for love is φιλέω, meaning a love with affection in connection with friendship. This is used only thirty-three times in the LXX (twenty-seven times in the canonical books) and although it is the second most frequent word for love in the NT, it is used only twenty-five times, twice by Paul (1 Cor 16:22; Titus 3:15). Again, in the NT the verb ἀγαπάω is used of God's love within the Godhead (John 3:35; 14:31; Eph 1:6), God's love for human beings (John 14:21; Rom 8:37; Gal 2:20; 2 Thess 2:16; 1 John 4:10) and a human being's love for God (Rom 8:28; 1 Cor 2:9; 8:3; Eph 6:24; 1 Pet 1:8; 1 John 5:2) and other humans (John 13:34; 15:12; Rom 13:8–9*ter*; 2 Cor 11:11; 12:15*bis*; Gal 5:14; Eph 5:25, 28*ter*, 33; Col 3:19; 1 Thess 4:9) as well as love for things (2 Tim 4:8, 10). In the NT[3] the noun ἀγάπη is used as an attribute of God (1 John 4:8, 16); love within the Godhead (Col 1:13), God's love toward humans (e.g., Rom 5:5, 8; 2 Cor 5:14; Eph 2:4; 3:17, 19; 1 John 3:1; 4:10); and human beings' love for one another (e.g., Rom 13:10; 1 Cor 13:1–3; Gal 5:13; Eph 1:15; 4:2, 15, 16; 5:2; 6:23; Phil 1:9; 1 Thess 3:6; 1 Tim 1:5; Titus 2:2; Philm 5, 7, 9) and for things (Rom 12:9; 2 Thess 2:10). God's own love is the example of love for one another (1 John 4:7–12, 16–18; Eph 5:2). Paul describes love as not being jealous, boastful, arrogant, disgraceful, selfish, irritable, and unrighteous, but rather as patient, kind, righteous, and enduring (1 Cor 13:4–8). This is in contrast to ἔρως as summarized

1. Gerhard Wallis, "אָהַב *ʾāhabh*," *TDOT* 1 (1977): 105.

2. Stauffer, "ἀγαπάω," *TDNT* 1 (1964): 39; Günther, "Love [ἀγαπάω]," *NIDNTT* 2 (1976): 539.

3. Of necessity many references to love in the NT in both the verb and noun forms are not listed with the exception of Ephesians where they are all listed except for the noun in the present passage (1:4).

by Morris when he writes, "*erōs* has two principal characteristics: it is a love of the worthy and it is a love that desires to possess. *Agapē* is in contrast at both points: it is not a love of the worthy, and it is not a love that desires to possess. On the contrary, it is a love given quite irrespective of merit, and it is a love that seeks to give."[1] In conclusion, a proper concept of love (for both ἀγαπάω and ἀγάπη) is based on God's love in that he extends it to the undeserving and unloving as seen in his continuing love for the sinner and the wayward believer. Love, then, is seeking the highest good in the one loved. Ultimately, for the believer the highest good is the will of God for him or her.

Although both the verb and noun speak of God's love for a human being and a human being's love for God, the predominant use is love between humans. Such use for the verb in Paul's letters is fourteen out of thirty-four times and in Ephesians it is six out of ten times, and such use for the noun in Paul's letters is fifty-seven out of seventy-five and in Ephesians it is six out ten times if one includes the present context. It seems best to view it in this context as love exhibited between humans.

The next problem is to determine what the prepositional phrase ἐν ἀγάπῃ, "in love," qualifies. There are three views. The first view held by some commentators is that it goes back to ἐξελέξατο, "he chose," in verse 4.[2] It would reflect that God's choice is born in God's love and counters the idea of random choice with God having no interest in the objects of his choice. However, this view is not accepted by present day commentators. First, it would seem that if Paul wanted to show God's love in election, he would not have removed it so far from the verb it modifies. Second, the very act of election is an evidence of God's love and needs no additional phrase to express this concept. Third, the predominant use of ἀγάπη in Ephesians refers to the believer's love and not God's love. This seems to be the case in this context.

The second view held by some commentators[3] and translations

1. Leon Morris, *Testaments of Love: A Study of Love in the Bible* (Grand Rapids: Eerdmans, 1981), 128.

2. Oecumenius *Eph* 1:4 (*PG* 118:1173); Dibelius-Greeven, 60; cf. Ernst Gaugler, "Heilsplan und Heilsverwirklichung nach Epheser 1, 3–2, 10," *Internationale kirchliche Zeitschrift* 20 (Oktober–Dezember 1930): 206; Spicq (*Agapé*, 2:210–11; ET 2:256–57) sees God's love in election and wants to make this parallel to predesination in v. 5; Caragounis, *Ephesian* Mysterion, 85–86.

3. Chrysostom *Eph* 1:4–5 (*PG* 62:13; Jerome *Eph* 1:5 (*PG* 26:448; Theodoret *Eph* 1:5 (*PG* 82:509); Theophylact *Eph* 1:5 (*PG* 124:1036); Bengel, 4:65–66; Samuel H. Turner, 12; Eadie, 28–30; Beet, 275–76; Ellicott, 7; Meyer, 38–39; Abbott, 8; Ewald, 69–70; Schlier, 52–53; Grosheide, 18; Rienecker, 55; Hendriksen, 78–79; Johnston, 9–10; Martin, "Ephesians," in *The Broadman Bible Commentary*, 135; Mitton, 50–51; Bratcher and Nida, 13; Schnackenburg, 54; Best, 122–23; Speyr, 29; cf. Percy, *Probleme*, 268; C. H. van Rhijn, "Ouden Neiuw over den Epheser-brief," *ThStud* 29, no. 4 (1911): 259–60; James Moffatt, "Four Notes on Ephesians," *Exp* 8th ser., vol. 10 (July 1915): 89–91; Kazimierz Romaniuk, *L'Amour du Père et du Fils dans la Sotériologie de Saint Paul*, 2d ed. rev. and cor., AnBib, vol. 15a (Rome: Biblical Institute Press, 1974), 203–7; Franz

(Peshitta,[1] RSV, NASB, TEV, NIV) joins ἐν ἀγάπῃ with προορίσας, "predestine," in verse 5. The proponents of this view say that to have it qualify "holy and without blame" seems awkward, for it does not follow immediately after the two adjectives but after the words κατενώπιον αὐτοῦ, "before him." Furthermore, they say that there is no Pauline example of ἐν ἀγάπῃ modifying ἁγίους καὶ ἀμώμους and that the tenor of the passage focuses on the gracious acts of God toward believers rather than the believers' actions before God or humans. Thus, they conclude that it is very fitting to see God's predestination born in love. Nevertheless, in the first place, to have the prepositional phrase modify the two adjectives, though it follows "before him," is not awkward. In fact, to reverse the order would be even more awkward for the tenor of the passage is meant to show that the purpose of those chosen is to be holy and blameless, not before other humans, but before God himself and this is perfectly blended with love. To have ἐν ἀγάπῃ intervene between "holy and blameless" and "before him" would spoil the dramatic effect of God's sovereign grace in fully preparing sinners for his presence. Second, although it is true that there is not another Pauline example of ἐν ἀγάπῃ modifying ἁγίους καὶ ἀμώμους, there are only two other places (Eph 5:27; Col 1:22) where Paul uses the adjectives together. This hardly makes a case. In fact, in the Eph 5:27 passage the ἐν ἀγάπῃ would be redundant because the whole context is love. Third, in Jude 24 ἄμωμος is followed by a further defining prepositional phrase (ἐν ἀγαλλιάσει, "with great joy"), as it is in the present context. Fourth, one does not need ἐν ἀγάπῃ to modify προορίσας in order to show that God's predestination is based in love; the very act of predestination is a demonstration of God's love. Finally, to have ἐν ἀγάπῃ modify the participle "predestine" seems to make verses 5b–6 (κατὰ . . . ἠγαπημένῳ) redundant.

The third view that is held by many commentators[2] and translations (Vg, AV, RV, ASV, NEB, JB, NJB, NRSV) is that ἐν ἀγάπῃ is united with ἁγίους καὶ ἀμώμους, "holy and without blame," in verse 4. This makes

---

Mussner, "People of God according to Ephesians 1.3–14 [trans. Eileen O'Gorman]," *Concilium* 10 (December 1965): 54–60; Kōshi Usami, *Somatic Comprehension of Unity: The Church in Ephesus*, AnBib, vol. 101 (Rome: Biblical Institute Press, 1983), 89 n. 71; Newman, "Election and Predestination in Ephesians 1:4–6a," 242, 246 n. 42.

1. Cf. Alain-G. Martin, "Quelques remarques sur le texte syriaque de l'Épître aux Éphésiens," *ETR* 66, no. 1 (1991): 100.

2. Ambrosiaster *Eph* 1:4 (*PL* 17:373–74); Calvin, 126; Wettstein, 2:239; Hodge, 34–35; Alford, 3:71–72; Moule, 47; Lightfoot, *Notes on Epistles of St Paul*, 313; Salmond, 250–51; Robinson, 27; Westcott, 9; Scott, 140; Lenski, 359–60; Gaugler, 33; Hugedé, 27; Ernst, 271; Caird, 35; Barth, 79–80; Bruce, 256; Lincoln, 17, 24–25; cf. Trinidad, "The Mystery Hidden in God. A Study of Eph. 1,3–14," 6–7; E. Mauerhofer, "Der Brief an die Epheser. 3. Teil: 1,3–4," *Fundamentum* 2 (1990): 30–32; O'Brien, 101; G. Schrenk, "ἐκλέγομαι," *TDNT* 4 (1967): 175 n. 113; cf. Caragounis, *Ephesian* Mysterion, 84–85 n. 24.

the most sense. First, within the present context the verbs and participles describing God's actions *always* precede the qualifying phrases:[1]

v. 3—"the one who blessed us . . . with every spiritual blessing"
v. 4—"he chose us . . . in him before the foundation of the world"
v. 5—"having predestined us . . . to adoption"
v. 6—"he bestowed grace on us . . . in the beloved"
v. 7—"we have the redemption . . . through his blood"
v. 8—"he lavished on us . . . with all wisdom and insight"
v. 9—"Having made known the mystery . . . according to his good pleasure"
v. 9—"he purposed . . . in him"
v. 10—"to head up all things . . . in Christ"
v. 11—"having been predestined . . . according to his purpose"

The only exception to this in the entire passage is where there is the introductory relative pronoun (ἧς, vv. 6, 8). Hence, for ἐν ἀγάπῃ to modify προορίσας is inconsistent with the structure of the context. Second, four out of the five times Paul uses ἐν ἀγάπῃ in Ephesians, it follows the clauses it modifies (Eph 4:2, 15, 16; 5:2) and is so used by Paul in other places (Col 2:2; 1 Thess 5:13; cf. also other words, 1 Tim 4:12; 2 Tim 1:13).[2] Third, the use of ἐν ἀγάπῃ in those four instances in Ephesians always refer to human love and not divine love. Fourth, the other nine times the noun "love" (ἀγάπη) appears in Ephesians, it refers six times to human love (1:15; 4:2, 15, 16; 5:2; 6:23). Fifth, it is fitting to have love joined with holiness and blamelessness. They balance each other out. In the Qumran literature it is common to have two or more expressions that are similar and are effected by the terms "with" or "in."[3] Hence, in this passage holiness and blamelessness are effected by love. To have love without righteousness is to have love without a standard of right and wrong, and to have righteousness without love lacks warmth and personal interest. In reality, both work in harmony because love is the essence of all virtue for it fulfills the whole law.[4] God has restored what humans lost in the fall. He is both love and holy and a person is to manifest love with holiness as a result of being elected. This will be fully realized in the future when believers will stand in God's presence. However, if it is true that they will be holy and blamless before him in love, the purpose of God's work in believers today is to produce holiness within them and love toward one another. That which will be perfected in the future has its necessary corollary today. Believers are to be holy and blameless before him in love, as well as before their fellow human beings in order to show

1. Alford, 3:71.
2. Lightfoot, *Notes on Epistles of St Paul*, 313.
3. Kuhn, "Ephesians in the Light of the Qumran Texts," 119–20.
4. Zerwick, 16.

God's work and character in them. In conclusion, it seems best to see ἐν ἀγάπῃ united with ἁγίους καὶ ἀμώμους. Thus, God chose us that we might stand in his presence holy and blameless before him in love.

Excursus 4
Election

This excursus will consist of two parts: a study of the word and a discussion of Markus Barth's excursus on the doctrine of election.

A Study of ἐκλέγομαι

Classical Usage

Two basic uses of the word exist in the classical era.[1] First, in the active it means "to pick" or "single out,"[2] especially of rulers, oarsmen, and soldiers.[3] The passive means "to be selected" or "chosen."[4] The middle voice means "to pick out for oneself," "choose," or "select,"[5] for example, selectively "to pick or pull out" one's gray hairs.[6] Second, it can mean "to levy taxes" or "tribute."[7] The last use is infrequent and makes little or no sense in the context of Eph 1:4.

LXX Usage

In the LXX it occurs 139 times and in the canonical books it appears 125 times out of which 109 times it translates בָּחַר (which is used a total of 172 times in the MT), nine times it translates six other Hebrew words, and the remaining seven times either it translates no specific Hebrew word or its identification is doubtful. Out of the 139 occurrences, it appears 126 times in the aorist tense and 130 times in the middle voice. The field of meaning of the Hebrew and Greek is substantially the same. The Hebrew word conveys the idea of a carefully, conceived choice, whether it was David's selection of stones for his sling (1 Sam 17:40), God's choice of a people (Deut 7:6–7; 1 Kgs 3:8), a place for his name (Deut 12:5; 1 Kgs 8:16–17), the selection of the priesthood (Num 16:5, 7; 17:5 [MT & LXX 17:20]; Deut 18:5), or the choice of a king (1 Sam 10:24; 2 Sam 6:21; 1 Chr 28:5).[8] Of the 172 times the Hebrew word is used, God is the subject ninety-five times (85 out of 109 times in the LXX).

Three things may be noted about its use in the OT. First, all the options are known before the choice is made. The following are a few examples. After Lot surveyed all the land, he decided to take the Jordan valley (Gen 13:11). His decision was based on knowledge. After Moses presented the options of life versus death and blessings versus curses, he asks the people to choose the way that leads to life for their descendants (Deut 30:19). In the selection of Israel's new king, David was chosen after Samuel had seen all of Jesse's sons (1 Sam 16:1–13 esp. vv. 11–13; 1 Chr 28:4, 5). From among all the nations of the world, God chose Israel (Deut 14:2). In the above instances the choice was not made in a vacuum but only after all the options are known. Second, in no case was the object or per-

1. LSJ 511.
2. Thucydides 4.59.2.
3. Plato *Respublica* 7.15 §535a; Xenophon *Historia Graeca* 1.6.19; Xenophon *Anabasis* 2.3.11 respectively.
4. Plato *Alcibiades* 1 §121e; Xenophon *Memorabilia* 3.5.2.
5. Herodotus 1.199; 3.38.
6. Aristophanes *Equites* 908; *Frag*. 410.
7. Thucydides 8.44.4.
8. Horst Seebass, "בָּחַר *bāchar*," *TDOT* 2 (1977): 74–87.

son not chosen spurned or regarded with dislike.[1] Once again, the choice of David can be used as an illustration. When God chose David his brothers were rejected but not despised. So also with the selection of Israel. His choice did not signify that he hated the other nations. The same holds true in the selection of Levi for the priesthood (Deut 18:5) and Judah for political leadership (1 Chr 28:4; cf. Gen 49:8). God did not despise the other tribes. Third, the choice is made because of the subject's preference and not because the selected recipient had some legal claim on the subject. The sons of God chose wives who were beautiful (Gen 6:2). Lot chose the land that was most favorable to him (13:11). God chose Israel because he loved them and not because he was obligated to them in some way (Deut 7:6–8; 10:15). This shows that the subject has personal interest in his choice and it is neither a random or an impulsive whim nor is it because he is indebted in some way to the object.

In conclusion, the OT use of the word denotes that the subject chose in the light of all known options and that this choice was made freely and not due to a dislike toward any other option or because the object of choice had any legal claim on the one making the choice. The majority of the time God is the subject.

Koine Usage

This period (300 B.C.–A.D. 550) is in substantial agreement with the classical and OT periods. In the first century B.C. there is the example of people exhorted to make a proper choice.[2] In a court record that can be dated in Trajan's rule (A.D. 98–117), possibly in A.D. 109, a settlement of a will was discovered that indicated that the husband had the right to choose one son as appointed heir.[3] Here again we notice the same basic idea of a careful selection out of known options where the subject can freely make a choice according to his or her own preference with no idea of dislike toward the options not selected.

NT Usage

The verb is used twenty-two times in the NT: eleven times in Luke (Luke 6:13; 9:35; 10:42; 14:7; Acts 1:2, 24; 6:5; 13:17; 15:7, 22, 25); five times in John (6:70; 13:18; 15:16*bis*, 19); four times in Paul (1 Cor 1:27–28*ter*; Eph 1:4); and the other two times in Mark 13:20 and Jas 2:5. It is always an aorist middle with the exception of the textually difficult Luke 9:35[4] where it is either a middle or a passive perfect. As noted, there is consistent use of the aorist in both the OT and the NT. Although the aorist does not help in defining objectively the sort of action,[5] it is interesting that the authors did not use the present or perfect,

1. Some may point out that an exception to this statement is Ps 78:67–68 [LXX 77:67–68] where God rejected the tent of Joseph and chose the tribe of Judah. However, rejection does not necessarily import dislike. The point is that God selected Judah's Jerusalem for the temple rather than continuing in Ephraim's (Joseph's son) Shiloh where the tabernacle had been located. Furthermore, a few verses earlier (v. 59) he rejected Israel because of her disobedience and yet the context of the Psalm is God's rescue of Israel whom he loved. He did not like her disobedience, but this does not mean he dislikes her. Third, since this is the only possible, though doubtful, exception to the ninety-five times where God is the subject, the burden of proof is against God's personal dislike of Joseph. It was a matter of choice—he chose Judah over Joseph.

2. *SIG* 736.45.

3. *P.Oxy.* 42:3015.22–23.

4. The reading "chosen" is limited primarily to the Alexandrian family and is the more difficult reading. The other reading "beloved" has very good textual tradition with good geographical distribution but could be a harmonization of the other Gospels.

5. Frank Stagg, "The Abused Aorist," *JBL* 91 (June 1972): 222–31; Charles R. Smith, "Errant Aorist Interpreter," *GTJ* 2 (fall 1981): 205–26; D. A. Carson, *Exegetical Fallacies* (Grand Rapids: Baker, 1984), 72–74.

which would have defined more specifically the author's conception of the action. Thus, the context determines the kind of action.

Again, some of the same characteristics seen in classical and OT literature prevail in the NT. First, in all cases (except possibly Luke 9:35 if taken passively) a choice was made out of multiple known options. For example, Jesus selected the twelve disciples out of all those who were following him (Luke 6:13; John 13:18; 15:19), the church selected seven deacons out of all the number (Acts 6:5), the Jerusalem Council chose Paul and Barnabas to go to Antioch to deliver the council's decrees (Acts 15:22, 25), God chose the foolish of this world to shame the wise (1 Cor 1:27–28*ter*), and God chose the poor of this world to be rich in faith and heirs of the kingdom (Jas 2:5). Second, as in the OT there is no dislike toward the objects not chosen. When Jesus chose the twelve disciples (Luke 6:13), it does not mean he spurned the other disciples. Even when God chose the foolish, weak, and nobodies of this world, to shame respectively the wise, strong, and somebodies of the world (1 Cor 1:27–28), the intent was not to despise the world but to show the world that one does not come to know God because of worldy status. As Schrenk notes, the idea of reprobation is nowhere explicitedly contrasted with God's choosing.[1] Therefore, when God chooses persons as his own, it does not mean that there is a dislike for the persons not chosen. On the other hand, there is no indication that the persons who are chosen have some legal claim on God and thereby God is obligated to chose them. The act of choosing is one of grace and not one of debt. Third, the middle voice is always used (possible exception is Luke 9:35), which indicates personal interest. Moule observes that although the middle may have primarily denoted the reflexive idea for certain periods, it is not true for NT usage. Rather the middle "calls attention to the whole subject being concerned in the action."[2] It shows personal interest. Two illustrations of this are Mary's choice to hear Jesus rather than help Martha (Luke 10:42) and the people who chose places of honor at a marriage feast (14:7). On the other hand, the significance of the middle usage of ἐκλέγομαι should not be pushed too far, because by NT times the word had become a deponent[3] and the very act of choosing would have indicated personal interest. Nevertheless, it does have some significance, for this word was used instead of some other word that could have eliminated the personal interest aspect. It is noteworthy that in every context the personal interest is evident. Fourth, as in the OT the most frequent subject is God. Out of the twenty-two times it is used in the NT, either God or Jesus choses in sixteen instances. The four times Paul uses the word (1 Cor 1:27–28*ter*; Eph 1:4), God is the subject.

In conclusion, the use of ἐκλέγομαι in the NT mirrors its use in the classical, OT, and koine usage. The choice was not made in a vacuum but with all the options known. The subject chose not because of a dislike toward those not chosen nor because the recipients had some legal claim that obliged the subject to choose them. The middle voice expresses the fact that the subject chooses with intense personal interest toward the object rather than an impersonal random selection. Finally, most frequently God is the subject and in all cases it shows God's grace in that he takes the initiative.

Applying this study to the context of Eph 1:4 shows that God is the one who chooses the believer. His choice of the believer is in light of all the known options, namely, the entire human race. There is no reference in this context, as in any other context, to those not chosen, and hence there is no indication of dislike toward other human beings. The middle

1. Schrenk, *TDNT* 4 (1967): 175.

2. Moule, *Idiom Book*, 24; Robertson states: "The only difference between the active and middle voices is that the middle calls especial attention to the subject. In the active voice the subject is merely acting; in the middle the subject is acting in relation to himself somehow" (*Grammar*, 804). Cf. also MHT 1:156; 3:54.

3. It was active in early Attic Greek (MHT 3:55).

voice expresses personal interest in God's choice. The believer is chosen for God's own benefit. The whole action shows God's grace in taking the initiative. It shows that he freely chose the believer due to his grace and not because he was obligated to do so because the believer had some legal claim on God. As in most other cases in the OT and NT, the aorist is used. Although the aorist itself does not describe the action, here the past action is denoted by the descriptive prepositional phrase that follows: "before the foundation of the world." Schrenk states that this is the only time the word is used in the NT "with an express accent on eternity."[1] Hence, knowing all the options, God chose with personal interest the believer (who had no legal claim on God) in eternity past.

A Discussion of the Doctrine of Election

Much has been written about the doctrine of election over the centuries. This attempt is not intended to be a comprehensive discussion of the development of the doctrine. Rather it is merely an interaction with Markus Barth's excursus "Election in Christ vs. Determinism."[2]

Barth's view is that God's election by grace (Eph 1:4–5; cf. Rom 11:5) is quite different from a "principle or axiom of absolute determinism. There are six distinctive reasons why Ephesians cannot be considered the charter for the eternal predestination of one part of mankind for bliss, the other for hell, and a seventh reason which by itself is decisive."[3]

First, he states, "The tone of the statements made on God's decision is adoring rather than calculating or speculative. God himself is being praised, not a fate or system above God, or a scheme created by him."[4] It is true that election is not speculative but a loving and carefully thought-out action of God as discussed above. Certainly there is no hint that there is a scheme above God, rather, one created by him. However, one basic supposition which must not be overlooked is the fact that if there were no plan (scheme?) of election, no one would ever come into the presence of God. The Scripture is clear that all are lost and that none seek God (Rom 3:10–11). The greatest example of this is the attitude of Adam and Eve after they had sinned. Even though they had known what it was like to live in perfect fellowship with God without sin, they did not seek God after the fall. Instead, it was God who took the initiative to seek and restore them. The point is that humans are destined for an eternal separation from God and the only saving factor is the gracious act of God's selection. No humans have any legal claim on God's grace, for all are sinners and deserve nothing but God's wrath. This is why it is correct to say that the passage is one of praise to God because the believer can praise him for the grace obtained that was not deserved. Barth adds that Eph 1 manifests a single attitude and act of God's love and no hint of a double destiny for humankind that would reflect a double edge to God's will, for example, love and hatred, as portrayed in Rom 9:13, 18. This is confusing the issue. It is not that God has two destinies. Rather, sin has one destiny and God another. Since human beings do not seek God, the only destiny is separation from God forever. It is the sheer grace of God that allows any person to have another destiny. Barth's citation of Rom 9:13 goes back to Mal 1:2–3, which says, "Jacob I loved, but Esau I hated." However, the real problem here is not why God hated Esau but why he loved Jacob. Also, it should be noted that this statement is not as harsh as it might first appear, for it is "an idiomatic way of expressing in Hebrew 'I have chosen Jacob rather than Esau', and corresponds to use of the verb

1. Schrenk, *TDNT* 4 (1967): 175.

2. Barth, 105–9. For a discussion of the similarities and differences between Eph 1 and the Islamic religion with regards to election and predestination, see Colin Sedgwick, "Predestination, Pauline and Islamic: A Study in Contrasts," *VE* 26 (1996): 69–91.

3. Barth, 105.

4. Ibid.

'love' in an 'election' sense, as in Hos. 11:1."[1] There is no implication of personal animosity towards Esau, although his descendants did nurse resentment and hostility towards Jacob and thus brought judgment on themselves.[2] This same Semitic form of expression is used in the Gospels as in Luke 14:26. When Jesus states that if anyone comes to him and does not hate his father, mother, wife, children, brother, sisters, and even himself, he cannot be his disciple, Jesus does not mean that a person must hate all his family. Rather it corresponds to Matt 10:37–39 where Jesus declares that he who loves father, mother, son, daughter, or self more than they love him is not worthy of him. The emphasis is not on the one hated but on the one chosen as the object of love. In respect to Jacob and Esau, the emphasis is on the fact that God elected to love Jacob rather than a decision to hate Esau. The other passage that Barth cites is Rom 9:18, which states that God has mercy on whomever he wills and hardens the heart of whomever he wills. Admittedly, this is a difficult verse, but when examining the context, it becomes obvious that Paul is demonstrating God's freedom to act. He is not bound by a person's will. In addition, nothing in the passage indicates that Paul is talking about two eternal destinies. He is, instead, discussing God's actions towards people in a temporal sense, such as when he demonstrated mercy to Moses and hardened the heart of Pharaoh.[3] Nothing indicates that Moses received salvation and Pharaoh did not. In conclusion, then, it is inappropriate for Barth to use this passage as an example of double destiny.

Second, Barth states:

> The election of men is not one among several features of an impersonal omnipotent rule or disposition of a deity over all created things. . . . Mechanical predetermination calls forth the reaction of marionettes to the wire-pulling artist: there may be blind submission and compliance; there may also be fruitless rebellion or mechanical failure.[4]

This statement is only a caricature of the doctrine of election. Barth states that rather than being "subject to the whims of fate or to an anonymous predetermining force," the picture in Eph 1 is of the relationship of a loving Father to his children which results in praise of the Father's love.[5] But that is exactly what the word study of ἐκλέγομαι has shown. God's election is one of grace and love that is very personal, a fact enhanced by the use of the middle voice. God's act of love is further accentuated by the fact of his initiative in the election of those who do not seek him. Furthermore, the word study shows that God's election was not a whim of fate but the careful loving selection of individuals. Finally, to have a plan does not rule out personal interest. For example, when parents plan for their children's future education, there is intense personal involvement. Therefore, Barth's assessment of election is inaccurate.

Third, Barth complains that the author of Ephesians lacks originality because he does not engage in philosophical discussions about the ramifications of election but rather is dependent on OT statements about it. Barth acknowledges that the OT passages view

1. Rex Mason, *The Books of Haggai, Zechariah, and Malachi*, Cambridge Bible Commentary, New English Bible, ed. P. R. Ackroyd, A. R. C. Leaney, and J. W. Packer (Cambridge: Cambridge University Press, 1977), 141.

2. Joyce G. Baldwin, *Haggai, Zechariah, Malachi*, The Tyndale Old Testament Commentaries, ed. D. J. Wiseman (Grand Rapids: Eerdmans; London: Tyndale, 1972), 223.

3. For a good discussion on this problem, see John Piper, *The Justification of God. An Exegetical and Theological Study of Romans 9:1–23*, 2d ed. (Grand Rapids: Baker, 1993), 151–81.

4. Barth, 105.

5. Ibid.

election with a particularist perspective in electing a partriarch, tribe, king, or the whole of Judah or Israel, but that the author of Ephesians has a universalistic outlook that includes not only Israel but all nations in God's love, peace, and worship (Eph 1:11–14; 2:1–3:6).[1] However, Barth contradicts himself. How can it be said, on the one hand, that the author of Ephesians depends of the OT statements about election, which are particularistic, and yet, on the other hand, say that the letter to the Ephesians has a universalistic slant on election? It is true that Paul does depend on the OT concept of election, but God's election is not universalistic as Barth proposes, for God chooses individuals from Israel as well as from all nations. Barth follows his father here.[2] However, nothing in the NT indicates that all are elect. Some from every ethnic background are elect but that is quite different from saying that all from every ethnic group are elect. If all were elect, then the term is bankrupt of meaning. The whole tone of the NT is particularistic, for the broad way leads to destruction and the narrow way leads to eternal life (Matt 7:13–14; 22:14; cf. also John 6:37, 44; 10:3; 14:6; Rom 9:16).

Fourth, Markus Barth states that "the eternal election of Jews and Gentiles is not a mystery that must remain hidden. . . . The gospel is the publication of the secret of election."[3] This statement confuses the doctrine of election with the gospel message. God has revealed the mystery of Jew and Gentile united into one body but this is not the gospel. Rather it is the result of believing the gospel. Although God has revealed many things, there is no indication that he has revealed everything. In light of this, the gospel is not secret but the identification of God's elect is his alone to know.

Fifth, Barth says:

> Election cannot be identified with an event of the remote past or with a timeless divine will. . . . God elects not only before the creation of the world but He is and remains the electing God when his grace is poured out, when sins are forgiven, when revelation opens the eyes of man's mind, and when the seal of the Spirit quickens the dead and assembles those dispersed. . . . In sum, election is an event which is still being fulfilled.[4]

Barth cites Eph 1:4–14 to show that election precedes the world's time and space, but then, with no scriptural support, presumes that election continues into the present. He confuses God's election before time and space with the implementation of the plan within time and space. To prove his point he uses the illustration of the completion of a medieval cathedral according to a planner's specifications long after the planner dies. However, this contradicts his own view because the architect had completed the plans before he died and the builders simply carried out his plans after he died. In the same way, God's election was determined before the world began and he implements it in time and space. Another flaw in the illustration of the architect is that Barth presses this illustration too far. God is both the architect and the builder and has interest in seeing his plan fulfilled. Barth states that since God does not die, he carries out the plan. This does not pose a problem because it makes a distinction between the planning and the carrying out of the plan. Hence, God is not still in the process of planning (i.e., presently electing) but only the carrying out the plan.

1. Ibid., 105–6.
2. Karl Barth, *Church Dogmatics*, trans. G. T. Thompson, G. W. Bromiley, et al., ed. G. W. Bromiley and T. F. Torrance, vol. 2, pt. 2 (Edinburgh: T & T Clark, 1957), 195–305.
3. Barth, 106.
4. Ibid.

Sixth, Barth states:

> Awareness of God's election is given together with the awareness of the forgiveness of sins. Election means resurrection from the dead. It is not derived from the experience that one part of mankind has a holy, happy, or successful life while another appears condemned to frustration and misery. The elect know they have been engulfed by the same death which, because of sin, has come over all mankind. . . . Awareness of election is neither a church steeple from which to view the human landscape nor a pillow to sleep on. But it is a stronghold in times of temptations and trials.[1]

On the surface there is no problem with these statements. However, what does Barth mean by the term "awareness"? Does he mean, as it seems, that all are elect but only some are aware of it? To suggest this is to begin with a wrong premise. Although all are engulfed by death because of sin, it does not follow that all are elect. The dichotomy is not between the elect who are aware of it and those who are not, but between the elect and nonelect.

While, according to Barth, the six preceding arguments distinguish election from a determinism (i.e., a part of humankind is destined for bliss and the other for hell), a seventh reason is decisive because it deals with the main feature of Eph 1:3–14, namely, "that the election of the saints was made 'in Christ.'"[2] His argument has several facets. First, he claims that "Christ has a passive role in election. He is the epitome of the beloved (1:6), the first on whom God set his favor (1:9), or briefly, the first elect."[3] This is a rather curious interpretation. First, Paul states that Christ is the beloved and not the epitome of the beloved (1:6). Second, Christ is not totally passive because God makes known the mystery of his will in Christ (1:9). Third, it is a great leap to conclude that Christ is the first elect. Again he follows his father.[4] To support his point, Markus Barth cites 1 Pet 1:20 but this does not reveal that Christ was the first elect but that in the foreknowledge of God Christ was destined to be manifested for the purpose of redemption. Again, Barth confuses election with salvation. Election is the beginning point and salvation is the means by which to carry out the election.

Second, Barth argues that Christ is the revelation, making known "the secret of God's decision," namely, that God entrusted Christ to head up all things in heaven and on earth (Eph 1:8–10) and the saints are resuscitated from their death in sins (2:5–6) on the basis of Christ's resurrection (1:20). "Resurrection from death, together with Christ, is the content of election. Apart from the revelation given in the resurrection of Christ there is no election."[5] In response to this argument, it must be noted that the believer's resurrection with Christ is not the content of election but rather the result of the gospel which is the means by which God's plan of election is carried out. This is again confusing the plan and the means by which it is accomplished.

Third, Barth states, "Christ is also the means or instrument of election. 'Through him' the adoption of many children is to be carried out (1:5); 'through his blood' they are liberated and forgiven. God administers and carries out election through Jesus Christ."[6] This statement has no problem. However, it does seem to contradict his first point.

1. Ibid., 106–7.
2. Ibid., 107.
3. Ibid.
4. Barth, *Church Dogmatics*, 2, pt. 2, 94–194.
5. Barth, 107.
6. Ibid.

Fourth, Barth declares, "The commission given to Christ lifts him far beyond the level of an impersonal tool, an intangible sphere, or an agent who fulfills his role mechanically. Rather Jesus Christ's function in election is that of a free, responsible, active agent."[1] Again, these statements have no problems. In the word study we discovered no indication that election was impersonal. Certainly, God chose but Christ was involved in carrying out the plan. Hence, the personal involvement of both persons of the Trinity negates any idea of that which is impersonal or mechanical. Barth's insistence earlier that Christ's role in election was passive contradicts his present point that Christ was an active agent.

Barth concludes this part of the discussion by stating that "the formula 'in Christ' denotes the concentration, summation, revelation, and execution of God's own decision in one person, that is, the Messiah on whom the Jews had set their hope (1:12)."[2] Although this statement has much to commend it, it goes too far. Christ is the center of the revelation but in this passage he is not portrayed as the object of election. The ἡμᾶς, "us," is the object of the verb "he chose" and the prepositional phrase "in Christ" may refer to the sphere of the election or more likely it could be the relational or instrumental idea that God chose believers in connection with or through Christ's work of redemption. Barth's construct is that Christ is the elect, and since all human beings are in Christ, then all are elect. This is completely foreign to the context of this passage as well as the entire NT. Certainly, Christ was chosen as the means to carry our God's plan of salvation, but that is not classified as election. The elect are those chosen by God to enjoy his favor forever, and the means to this objective is the redemption by Christ. Once redeemed, the elect are in Christ. Therefore, the object of God's election is not Christ but "us" and the prepositional phrase "in Christ" denotes that the election was in connection with or through Christ.

In concluding the whole discussion, Barth argues that election that is defined as an absolute decree dividing humankind into two distinct groups is inadequate and contrary to Eph 1. Rather he contends that it is a matter of God's heart in his personal relationship of love with his Son in his mission, death, and resurrection. Further, he argues that for a god to have a fixed decree would make his continuance unnecessary, but God's election process involves the Father watching and hearing the Son's prayers, seeing his agony, raising him from the dead, and pouring out the Spirit on the many so that the Son's blood will not have been spilled in vain.[3] Again, Barth confuses the decree of election and the means whereby it is carried out. To have a fixed decree does not make God unnecessary, for he is involved in carrying out the decree. Furthermore, a fixed decree does not make God impersonal and remote for he exhibits his love not only to the Son but also to humankind. For example, the decision of parents to have children does not render them impersonal towards their children after birth. In addition, Barth seems to be inconsistent in his rejection of a fixed decree on the one hand and his insistence that Christ must fulfill God's will on the other hand. We must remember that a decree only expresses God's will. Finally, Barth states that the Father does not permit Christ's blood to be spilled in vain. The implication seems to be that all of humankind will be affected. Barth asserts that Christ is elected and all are in Christ and hence are all elected. Is this not forcing all people into something they may not want? Is this Barth's idea of a decree or will of God? This view furthers the idea of universalism, which is contrary to the whole tenor of Scripture.

In the end, no one seeks God and yet in his sovereign grace he chooses some for everlasting life in his presence. His selection was made with full knowledge of all the options and with intense personal interest, not in a random impersonal manner. Believers may take

1. Ibid.
2. Ibid., 107–8.
3. Ibid., 108–9.

comfort in the fact that what God has begun in eternity past will be completed in eternity future.

(2) Cause: Predestination to Sonship (1:5)

Text: 1:5. προορίσας ἡμᾶς εἰς υἱοθεσίαν διὰ Ἰησοῦ Χριστοῦ εἰς αὐτόν, κατὰ τὴν εὐδοκίαν τοῦ θελήματος αὐτοῦ,

Translation: 1:5. "having predestined us to adoption as sons through Jesus Christ to himself, according to the good pleasure of his will,"

Commentary: 1:5. προορίσας ἡμᾶς εἰς υἱοθεσίαν, "having predestined us to adoption as sons." The participle comes from the verb προορίζω, which is a compound from ὁρίζω, "to set a boundary, determine, separate," from which we derive the idea of a horizon, and the prepositional prefix προ-, "before" (not before others, but before time). Hence it means "to determine beforehand, mark out beforehand, predestine." It is a late and rarely used word in classical literature from fourth century B.C. onwards[1] and never used in the LXX. In the NT it is used only six times (Acts 4:28; Rom 8:29, 30; 1 Cor 2:7; Eph 1:5, 11), five times by Paul, and twice in Ephesians. Twice it is used with a thing as its object (Acts 4:28; 1 Cor 1:27). The other four times persons are objects. However, when people are the objects of predestination, there are two accusatives. God has predestined *us* to *something*. Cremer notes that the primary interest is not the *who* but to *what* is one predestined.[2] Although the action of the verb precedes history, the *who* belongs to history and the *what* talks about the eternal future. In conclusion, it means that one's destiny is determined beforehand.[3] The active voice indicates that God did it. It is interesting to notice that both the choosing and predetermining are governed by πρό, "before." God did these things before the creation of the earth.

How this aorist participle προορίσας is related to the finite verb ἐξελέξατο is a matter that needs discussion.[4] There are four views. First,

1. Demosthenes *Orationes* 31.4 codices, BAGD 709; BDAG 873.

2. Hermann Cremer, *Biblico-Theological Lexicon of New Testament Greek*, 4th ed. with Supplement, trans. William Urwick (Edinburgh: T & T Clark, 1895), 462.

3. According to Allen, it may have its background from Ps 2 in that "God 'decreed of old (προορίσας) that we should become his adopted sons through Jesus Christ'." See Leslie C. Allen, "The Old Testament Background of (προ)ὁρίζειν in the New Testament," *NTS* 17 (October 1970): 108.

4. Although election and predestination are involved with one another, they are distinct. Both Barth (*Church Dogmatics*, vol. 2, pt. 2, 13) and Brunner (*Dogmatics*, vol. 1, *The Christian Doctrine of God*, 321–46) confuse the distinction and make them one and the same thing. For a dicussion of predestination and its relationship to election, human responsibility, and calling, see Erich Mauerhofer, "Der Brief an die Epheser. 4. Teil: 1,5–6," *Fundamentum* 3 (1990): 17–25. For a discussion of the similarities and differences between Eph 1 and the Islamic religion with regards to election and predestination, see Sedgwick, "Predestination, Pauline and Islamic: A Study in Contrasts," 69–91.

some think the relationship is temporal, where the participle's action would be antecedent, at least logically, to that of the finite verb.[1] They feel that since this was done by God in eternity, the sequence of events is impossible to determine. Furthermore, because it is an aorist participle, it does not necessarily denote antecedent action but can describe contemporaneous action with an aorist finite verb.[2] Also, recent studies show that when the aorist participle precedes the main verb, there is a tendency toward antecedent action, and when it follows the main verb, as here, there is a definite tendency toward contemporaneous action with the main verb.[3] Second, other commentators think it is a participle of manner with action contemporaneous to the finite verb, which could be translated "in that he predestined us, he chose us."[4] This, however, seems to be a needless duplication. Third, it may be a participle of means indicating that God chose by predestinating. Normally, the participle of means is contemporaneous with the time of the main verb[5] as here. Fourth, it could be viewed as a causal participle, thus giving reason for the election and could be rendered "because of having predestined us, he chose us."[6] It is difficult to choose between the third and fourth views. However, the last option seems to make the most sense. In the counsels of God, the reason he chose the saints out of (ἐκ) the mass of humanity is because he predetermined their destiny.

The prepositional phrase εἰς υἱοθεσίαν, "to sonship," refers to what the saint has been predestined. The preposition εἰς denotes direction or appointment,[7] that is, he predestined us "to" adoption. The word υἱοθεσία is used five times in the NT and only by Paul (Rom 8:15, 23; 9:4; Gal 4:5; Eph 1:5). It is used as early as the second century B.C., meaning "to adopt."[8] The definition of the word has not changed over the years, but the legal ramifications of adoption vary in different settings.[9] There are three views regarding the setting of this word. First, some think that it has a Jewish background.[10] Although there is no le-

1. Alford, 3:72; Ellicott, 7–8.

2. BDF §339 (1).

3. Stanley E. Porter, *Verbal Aspect in the Greek of the New Testament with Reference to Tense and Mood*, Studies in Biblical Greek, ed. D. A. Carson, vol. 1 (New York: Peter Lang, 1989), 383–84.

4. Meyer, 39; Salmond, 251.

5. Wallace, *Greek Grammar*, 629.

6. Abbott, 8.

7. Cf. Albrecht Oepke, "εἰς," *TDNT* 2 (1964): 428.

8. *SIG* 581.102 (200–197 B.C.); Diodorus Siculus 31.26.1; *SIG* 765.11 (41 B.C.).

9. For a more detailed study of υἱοθεσία, see James M. Scott, *Adoption as Sons of God: An Exegetical Investigation into the Background of ΥΙΟΘΕΣΙΑ in the Pauline Corpus*, WUNT, ed. Martin Hengel and Otfried Hofius, vol. 48 (Tübingen: Mohr, 1992), 3–117.

10. Thornton Whaling, "Adoption," *Princeton Theological Review* 21 (April 1923): 223–35; William H. Rossell, "New Testament Adoption—Graeco-Roman or Semitic?" *JBL* 71 (December 1952): 233–34; Daniel J. Theron, "'Adoption' in the Pauline Corpus,"

gal custom for adoption in the Jewish law, the closest thing to it is the levirate marriage whereby if a man died childless, his brother was to marry the widow and raise up children to be heirs of his brother's estate (Deut 25:5–10). However, this is never identified as adoption. The Nuzi documents from the patriarchal age portray the adoption of slaves, which may be akin to Eliezer being adopted as heir by Abraham (Gen 15:2) and Jacob by Laban (Gen 29:14–30). However, there is no indication of a legal code for adoption when Israel received the law. The Greek word υἱοθεσία is not found in the LXX. Nonetheless, there was the concept that every firstborn Israelite belonged to God (Num 3:11–13) and also the idea that the nation Israel was considered the firstborn of God, with God as their father (Exod 4:22; Jer 31:9). In this sense Paul saw Israel as the adopted son (Rom 9:4). However, nowhere does the OT speak of Israelites being adopted into a different family or into God's family as other Pauline references portray. In conclusion, the institution of adoption of individuals into a family is not portrayed in the OT.

The second view is that Paul's concept of adoption comes from the Greek background[1] where during his life a man may adopt a male citizen to receive both the legal and religious privileges and responsibilities of a real son.[2] The real problem with this view is that although the Greek word is used, it is highly improbable that the people of the first century A.D. would be following Greek law when the Romans had overtaken the Greek territory more than a century ago. Hence, it is implausible that Paul relied on the Greek law and customs in his use of υἱοθεσία, for in all five instances he was addressing people who lived under Roman law.

The third alternative is that Paul had in mind the Roman law and practice.[3] This is the most reasonable alternative because the people

EvQ 28 (January–March 1956): 6–14; Martin W. Schoenberg, "Huiothesia: The Adoptive Sonship of the Israelites," *American Ecclesiastical Review* 143 (October 1960): 261–73; idem, "Huiothesia: The Word and the Institution," *Scr* 15 (October 1963): 115–23; idem, "St. Paul's Notion on the Adoptive Sonship of Christians," *Thomist* 28 (January 1964): 51–75; James I. Cook, "The Concept of Adoption in the Theology of Paul," in *Saved by Hope: Essays in Honor of Richard C. Ouderluys*, ed. James I. Cook (Grand Rapids: Eerdmans, 1978), 133–44; Brendan Byrne, *'Sons of God'—'Seed of Abraham'. A Study of the Idea of the Sonship of God of All Christians in Paul against the Jewish Background*, AnBib, vol. 83 (Rome: Biblical Institute Press, 1979).

1. W. M. Ramsay, *A Historical Commentary on St. Paul's Epistle to the Galatians* (London: Hodder and Stoughton, 1899), 339–41; Paul Feine, *Theologie des Neuen Testaments*, 8th ed. (Berlin: Evangelische Verlagsanstalt, 1953), 227 n. 1; Peter Wülfing von Martitz, "υἱοθεσία," *TDNT* 8 (1972): 398; and possibly C. F. D. Moule, "Adoption," in *The Interpreter's Dictionary of the Bible*, ed. George Arthur Buttrick et al., vol. 1 (Nashville: Abingdon, 1962), 48–49.

2. Cf. Mark Golden, "Adoption, Greek," *OCD*, 12–13.

3. Abbott, 9; Salmond, 251; Francis Lyall, "Roman Law in the Writings of Paul—Adoption," *JBL* 88 (December 1969): 458–66; idem, *Slaves, Citizens, Sons: Legal Meta-*

he was addressing were under Roman rule; Paul was born a Roman citizen, which he prized (Acts 22:28); and the practice of adoption was carried out by the Caesars for succession of power and would have been common knowledge for those under Rome's rule.

In order to understand adoption one must understand the structure of the Roman family. The father had absolute power (*patria potestas*) over the members of his family so that he could even take the life of a member of his family and that act would not be considered murder (see comments on 5:23). With regard to property, he had full legal ownership of everything the family had and could dispose of it as he willed.[1] On the other hand, in the Greek family the father did not have absolute power over his family nor was he the legal owner of all the family's property. Under Roman law the procedure of adoption had two steps. In the first step, the son had to be released from the control of his natural father. This was done by a procedure whereby the father sold him as a slave three times to the adopter. The adopter would release him two times and he would automatically again come under his father's control. With the third sale, the adoptee was freed from his natural father. Regarding the second step, since the natural father no longer had any authority over him, the adopter became the new father with absolute control over him, and he retained this control until the adoptee died or the adopter freed him. The son was not responsible to his natural father but only to his newly acquired father. The purpose of this adoption was so that the adoptee could take the position of a natural son in order to continue the family line and maintain property ownership. This son became the *patria potestas* in the next generation.[2]

The saints chosen by God are predestined as adopted sons (and daughters) of God. This means that believers, formerly labeled as "sons of disobedience" and "children of wrath" (Eph 2:2–3), have absolutely no responsibility and/or obligation to their old father the devil (cf. John 8:38, 44), the ruler of the realm of the air (Eph 2:2). Rather, they are now God's sons and daughters and he controls their

phors in the Epistles (Grand Rapids: Zondervan, 1984), 67–99; Trevor Burke, "Pauline Adoption: A Sociological Approach," *EvQ* 43 (April 2001): 119–34.

1. John Crook, "Patria Potestas," *Classical Quarterly* 17 (May 1967): 113–22; Richard Saller, "*Patria potestas* and the Stereotype of the Roman Family," *Continuity and Change* 1 (May 1986): 7–22; W. K. Lacey, "*Patria Potestas*," in *The Family in Ancient Rome: New Perspectives*, ed. Beryl Rawson (Ithaca, N.Y.: Cornell University Press; London: Croom Helm, 1986), 121–44; Barry Nicholas and Susan M. Treggiari, "Patria Potestas," *OCD*, 1122–23; Eva Marie Lassen, "The Roman Family: Ideal and Metaphor," in *Constructing Early Christian Families: Family as Social Reality and Metaphor*, ed. Halvor Moxnes (London: Routledge, 1997), 104–6; Jane F. Gardner, *Family and* Familia *in Roman Law and Life* (Oxford: Clarendon, 1998), 1–4, 117–26, 270–72.

2. Lyall, *Slaves, Citizens, Sons*, 86–87; Adolf Berger, Barry Nicholas, and Susan M. Treggiari, "Adoption, Roman Adoptio," *OCD*, 13; cf. Gardner, *Family and* Familia *in Roman Law and Life*, 126–45.

lives and property. Since God does not die, the saints will always be under his control. The father has a right to discipline his sons (Heb 12:5–11). Although this may sound foreboding, it is not. It must be remembered that under Roman law the reason for adoption was to continue a family name and its property. The point is that the one adopted acquired a new status, privilege, and property that would not have been available under his old father. There would be no reason for adoption if it were disadvantageous. The adoption brought great gains to the adoptee. Likewise, the saints were under the tyrant the devil who was their slavemaster and who brought destruction. In contrast, the saints have a new father who is unselfish, loving, and caring and wants the very best for his sons and daughters, the believers. Although believers are adopted into God's family, its full realization for the believers will be enjoyed at the time of their resurrection (Rom 8:23)[1] when their old father the devil will no longer tempt them to return to him.

Adoption is never used of Christ because he has always been the Son of God by nature, and unlike humans, he does not need to be adopted from his natural state into a new relationship with God as father. Hence, the sense is that since God has predetermined the destiny of the saints to be adopted into God's family, he, knowing all the options, selected them out of all the mass of humanity.

διὰ Ἰησοῦ Χριστοῦ εἰς αὐτόν, "through Jesus Christ to himself." This shows through whom the adoption is. The prepositional phrase διὰ Ἰησοῦ Χριστοῦ indicates the agency of the believer's adoption. The preposition (διά) has the idea of "passing between" two objects[2] and hence can be translated "through." It is through or by means of the work of Christ discussed in the following verses that makes it possible for the sinner to be adopted into the family of God.

The following prepositional phrase εἰς αὐτόν is thought by some to refer to Christ.[3] It is thought that this is parallel in thought to Col 1:16b–20 where all things were created by him and for him. Also, in Eph 4:13–15 it refers to the body of Christ being built up to the goal of the stature of the fullness of Christ. However, it is more likely to refer to God the Father.[4] The reasons are as follows. First, the whole context is praise to God the Father. In verse 4 God is the subject of the choice, "us" is the object of the choice in connection with Christ, and

1. Cf. Augusto Drago, "La nostra adonzione a figli di Dio in *Ef.* 1,5," *RivB* 19 (Aprile–Giugno 1971): 203–19, esp. 215–19. Burke thinks that there has been a lack of eschatological emphasis and Christological focus in the discussion of adoption, cf. Trevor J. Burke, "The Characteristics of Paul's Adoptive Sonship (HUIOTHESIA) Motif," *IBS* 17 (April 1995): 62–74.

2. Robertson, *Grammar*, 581.

3. Aquinas, chap. 1, lec. 1, vv. 1–6a (47–48); Schlier, 54; Gnilka, 73; Ernst, 272.

4. Theodoret *Eph* 1:5 (*PG* 82:509); Oecumenius *Eph* 1:5 (*PG* 118:1173); Calvin, 127; Ellicott, 8; Lightfoot, *Notes on Epistles of St Paul*, 314; Meyer, 40; Abbott, 9; Schnackenburg, 55; Lincoln, 9, 25; Best, 126; O'Brien, 103 n. 64.

the purpose is that we might be holy and blameless before God the Father. Again in verses 5–6 the predestination is according to the will of God and for this he is to be praised. Thus, the Father fits much better than the Son in these verses. Second, in verse 5 the words κατὰ τὴν εὐδοκίαν τοῦ θελήματος αὐτοῦ ("according to the good pleasure of his will") that immediately follow εἰς αὐτόν read much more smoothly if the phrase refers to God the Father and not to Christ. Third, throughout the context when the objects of the preposition are referring to deity, the prepositions ἐν ("in") and διά ("through") are used in connection with Christ (vv. 3, 4, 5, 6, 9, 10, 11, 12, 13), whereas the prepositions εἰς and κατά are used in connection with God the Father (vv. 4, 5, 6, 7, 9, 11, 12, 14). Hence, it better fits the pattern of the use of prepositions if this refers to the Father rather than Christ.

In conclusion then, the weight of the evidence points to this prepositional phrase referring to God the Father rather than Christ. The preposition εἰς denotes direction and relationship, and thus is translated "to" and "into," connoting the coming to and into God's family. Therefore, God predestined us to be adopted as his sons (and daughters), this adoption came through Christ, and this finally brings us to God in order to have fellowship with him as our father.

κατὰ τὴν εὐδοκίαν τοῦ θελήματος αὐτοῦ, "according to the good pleasure of his will." This gives the standard by which God's actions were accomplished. The preposition κατά with the accusative denotes standard. The standard is the good pleasure of God's will. The noun εὐδοκία is a Judeo-Christian word not found in classical literature. In the LXX it is used twenty-eight times (only ten times in the canonical books), seven of which are in the Psalms and are translated from רָצוֹן. The Hebrew word is used fifty-four times and all but sixteen times it is used to describe God's (as opposed to person's) actions. In the NT the word occurs nine times, seven of which speak of God's actions (Matt 11:26; Luke 2:14;[1] 10:21; Eph 1:5, 9; Phil 2:13; 2 Thess 1:11) and twice of a human being's actions (Rom 10:1; Phil 1:15). There are three connotations of the word: (1) it can describe purpose, will, desire (God's, 1 Chr 16:10; Matt 11:26; human's, Ps 145:16 [LXX 144:16]; Rom 10:1); (2) it can denote goodwill or benevolence (God's, Ps 51:18 [MT 51:20; LXX 50:20]; Phil 2:13?; human's, Phil 1:15) and (3) it can mean good pleasure, satisfaction, well-pleasing (cf. God's, Ps 19:14 [MT 19:15; LXX 18:15]; Eph 1:9; human's, Ps 141:5 [LXX 140:5]; 2 Thess 1:11).[2] It is this third sense that fits the concept in the present context. God's predestination of adopted sons into his family

1. The two major variants in this verse could refer to the goodwill/pleasure of human beings or of God. The preferred reading is speaking of God's good pleasure. See Bruce M. Metzger, *A Textual Commentary on the Greek New Testament*, 2d ed. (Stuttgart: Deutsche Bibelgesellschaft, 1994), 111.

2. For a more thorough study of the word, see Gottlob Schrenk, "εὐδοκία," *TDNT* 2 (1964): 747.

was not unpleasant but rather expresses his good pleasure. Barth summarizes it well when he says, "Not a grim Lord watching over the execution of his predetermined plan, but a smiling Father is praised. He enjoys imparting his riches to many children."[1]

What good pleasure is he speaking about? The θελήματος, "will," is probably a genitive of source showing that the good pleasure comes from his will. For more discussion on "will" (θέλημα), see verse 1. In the NT when εὐδοκία is used of God it speaks of God's sovereignty. In the context of Eph 1:5 and 9, God's good pleasure is expressed freely from his own will, which is not influenced by any other person or thing.[2]

In conclusion, predestination puts more emphasis on the "what" than the "who." God took the initiative to predetermine our destiny as adopted sons into the family of God. He accomplished this through (διά) his Son Jesus Christ to bring us to (εἰς) God himself. This was done all according (κατά) to his pleasure freely operating from his own will. Because he has predestined us, he chose us out of all humanity. These actions are not only the basis of every spiritual blessing but also are the spiritual blessings themselves. Is it any wonder that God is to be praised!

(3) Goal: Praise of the Glory of His Grace (1:6)

Text: 1:6. εἰς ἔπαινον δόξης τῆς χάριτος αὐτοῦ ἐν ᾗ ἐχαρίτωσεν ἡμᾶς ἐν τῷ ἠγαπημένῳ,

Translation: 1:6. "to the praise of the glory of his grace with which grace he has bestowed on us in the beloved one,"

Commentary: 1:6. This marks the end of the first strophe of praise revolving around the first person of the Trinity, God the Father. Having discussed the activity and cause of the Father's election, Paul shows the goal, that is, the praise of the glory of his grace.

εἰς ἔπαινον δόξης τῆς χάριτος αὐτοῦ, "to the praise of the glory of his grace." It is to be noted that there are three occurrences of εἰς in verses 5–6: the first one has the idea of direction or appointment, the second indicates direction and relationship, and the third points to goal or end. All of the actions of the Father have as their goal the praise to God.

The word for praise (ἔπαινος) from the earliest times in Greek literature has had the idea of "praise, approval, applause."[3] It is used only ten times in the LXX. Of the five times it appears in the canonical books, it translates three Hebrew words. Three of the five (Ps 22:3, 25 [MT 22:4, 26; LXX 21:4, 26]; 35:28 [LXX 34:28]) are a translation of תְּהִלָּה, a term used frequently in the OT (fifty-nine times) meaning "praise" or "glory." In the NT it is used eleven times, nine times by

1. Barth, 81.
2. Schrenk, *TDNT* 2 (1964): 747.
3. Herbert Preisker, "ἔπαινος," *TDNT* 2 (1964): 586.

Paul and twice by Peter. It is used four times of people's praise of both human beings and God (Rom 13:3; 2 Cor 8:18; Phil 4:8; 1 Pet 2:14), two times of God's praise of human beings (Rom 2:29; 1 Cor 4:5), and five times of human beings' praise of God (Eph 1:6, 12, 14; Phil 1:11; 1 Pet 1:7). In this context it is the praise of God by the believers.

The next word δόξα has changed in its usage. In classical Greek it had the idea of "(my) opinion"[1] or "reputation (opinion of others)."[2] Its use in the Bible gives a different picture. In the LXX it occurs 448 times, in the canonical books 276 times and is translated from twenty-five different Hebrew words, around 180 of which are translated from the one Hebrew word, כָּבוֹד. This word basically comes from the idea of something that is "weighty" in a person and hence the idea of "significance" or "importance."[3] This personal "weightiness" makes an impact on others. Seldom is the word used to show honor to humans (Gen 45:13; 1 Chr 29:28) but frequently it is used with reference to God's great name (Pss 66:2 [LXX 65:2]; 79:9 [LXX 78:9]) or to refer to the greatness of his deity (Pss 29:1–3 [LXX 28:1–3]; 96:7–8 [LXX 95:7–8]; 115:1 [LXX 113:9]; Isa 42:12; Jer 13:16).[4] In the LXX the Greek word δόξα has become identical with the Hebrew word כָּבוֹד.[5] In the NT the word is used 166 times, seventy-seven times by Paul, and eight times in Ephesians. Rather than following the Greek usage, the NT follows the LXX in the sense of "reputation" and "power" and further it also expresses the "divine mode of being" referring to divine honor, splendor, power, and radiance.[6] Although there are references to a human's glory (e.g., Matt 6:29; 1 Cor 11:7), predominantly it refers to God's. Basically, δόξα has the idea of the reflection of the essence of one's being, the summation of all of one's attributes, whether it refers to God or a human being. The essence of one's being makes an impact, whether good or bad, on others; this impact of one's essential being is that of one's reputation or glory. Because of how God has revealed himself, one thinks of his reputation in categories of splendor, power, and radiance. That reputation is a result of his essential being. Therefore, a human being is to glorify (in the sense of magnify or praise) God because of his glory, reflecting his essential being.

The word "grace" has already been discussed in verse 2. It refers to God's unmerited or undeserved favor in providing salvation for sin-

1. Sophocles *Trachiniae* 718; Herodotus 8.132; Thucydides 5.105.2.

2. Herodotus 5.91; Thucydides 2.11; Demosthenes *Orationes* 2.15.

3. *HALOT* 2 (1995): 457–58; M. Weinfeld, "כָּבוֹד *kāḇôḏ*," *TDOT* 7 (1995): 23; cf. BDB 458–59.

4. Gerhard von Rad, "δόξα," *TDNT* 2 (1964): 241.

5. Gerhard Kittel, "δόξα," *TDNT* 2 (1964): 242; cf. Jarl E. Fossum, "Glory כבוד δόξα," in *DDD*, 665–67.

6. Kittel, *TDNT* 2 (1964): 247–48; BAGD 203–4; BDAG 257. For a more thorough discussion, see Carey C. Newman, *Paul's Glory-Christology: Tradition and Rhetoric*, NovTSup, ed. C. K. Barrett et al., vol. 69 (Leiden: Brill, 1992).

ners through Christ's sacrificial death and enablement for believers. Here it focuses on God's undeserved favor.

Having discussed the various words, one needs to see how the words relate to each other. A series of genitives was a style used in both classical and NT Greek, especially by Paul (Eph 1:18, 19; 4:13; 6:10; Rom 8:21; 9:23; 2 Cor 4:4; Col 1:13, 27; 2:12; 1 Thess 1:3). Each genitive is dependent on the one preceding it, and usually the last genitive is possessive, as is the case here,[1] hence, "his grace." Another grammatical phenomenon is what is called the canon of Apollonius, where when two nouns follow one another, either both have the article or neither have it. However, Philo and the NT do not always follow this rule, especially when the first noun follows a preposition as is here. This may have been due to Hebrew influence. Therefore, although the first noun is anarthrous, as here, it is made definite by a defining genitive.[2] Hence, it would not be "a glory of his grace" but "the glory of his grace."[3]

To classify the first and second genitives is very difficult, but the third (αὐτοῦ) is possessive as mentioned above. Three views of dealing with the series of genitives are now given, each of which will be followed by a literal translation and an illustrative translation and then an assessment of the view.

In evaluating the various views, two things must be kept in mind: first, that there is a repetition of εἰς ἔπαινον δόξης αὐτου,[4] "to the praise of his glory," in verses 6, 12, and 14 and it is most probable that these three phrases are parallel in thought since each follow the actions of the three persons of the Trinity; and second, in verse 6 there is the addition of τῆς χάριτος, "of grace," which is used to make a transition to the last part of the verse.

In the first view, the first genitive (δόξης) is attributive of praise (ἔπαινον) and the second genitive (τῆς χάριτος) is objective: "for the glorious praise of his grace"[5] or "to the godly praise of his grace." But this seems to miss the point because it is not describing a human's glorious praise of God's grace but rather one's praise of God's glory. Furthermore, it seems to make even less sense in verses 12 and 14 to translate it "for his glorious praise" when there is no object of praise as in verse 6. For the second view, the first genitive is attributive of the second: "to the praise of his glorious grace" (RSV, NIV, NRSV)[6] or "to the praise of God's essential being's grace." However, this seems to imply more than the text states for Paul is not talking about the praise of his

1. MHT 3:218; HS §172; BDF §168 (2); Robertson, *Grammar*, 503.

2. MHT 3:179–80; Moule, *Idiom Book*, 114–15.

3. For a Qumran parallel to this expression, see 4Q511 frag. 1:7; 1Q28b 4:25, cf. Deichgräber, *Gotteshymnus*, 73.

4. For a similar expression in the Qumran material, see 1QH[a] 9:31–32 [1:31–32]; 11:23 [3:23].

5. Bruce, 258; Lenski, 363.

6. Scott, 142; Houlden, 268; Patzia, 132.

grace but the praise of God's glory for his grace. Also, the commentators and translations are inconsistent in their translation of the phrase in verses 12 and 14. With the third view, the first is an objective genitive of praise and the second is a genitive of quality: "to the praise of the glory of his grace" (AV, ASV, NASB, JB, NJB)[1] or "to the praise of God's essential being for his gracious quality." This view seems to satisfy the demands of the context, for it has a consistent translation of the phrase in verses 6, 12, and 14 and it makes for an easy transition to the next part of the verse where it picks up on "grace." Furthermore, the genitive of quality or definition reflects a Hebraic influence denoting a particular quality of someone or something. This would normally have been accomplished by an adjective in classical Greek.[2] Here it defines or denotes the quality of the grace of God's glory or essential being. Therefore, it is praise to God's essential being, his glory, for his graciousness as seen in his acts of electing and predestinating. God's essential being is the summation of all his attributes. Its manifestation is God's gracious actions of the election and predestination whereby he adopted sons according to the good pleasure of his will. This is why the believer is to praise his glory or his essential being.

ἐν ᾗ[3] **ἐχαρίτωσεν ἡμᾶς,** "with which grace he has bestowed on us." Having mentioned grace, Paul begins the next relative clause with ἐν plus the feminine dative singular relative pronoun ᾗ, which has χάριτος "grace" as its antecedent. The verb for grace, ἐχαρίτωσεν, is the aorist indicative third person singular of χαριτόω. It does not appear in the classical literature before NT times and occurs only once in the LXX (Sir 18:17). It appears only twice in the NT (Luke 1:28; Eph 1:6). There are two ways the verb can be interpreted. First, it is thought of as a subjective endowment which looks at the state of the individual who has been infused with grace so that one is made gracious and is favorably acceptable to God (AV).[4] Chrysostom illustrates this by say-

1. Chrysostom *Eph* 1:6 (*PG* 62:13); Eadie, 36; Ellicott, 9; Hodge, 38; Meyer, 42; Abbott, 10; Salmond, 252–53. One must note that the designation of the "genitive of quality" is not given by these commentators.

2. BDF §165; MHT 1:73–74; 3:212–14; Maximilian Zerwick, *Biblical Greek; Illustrated by Examples*, trans. Joseph Smith, Scripta Pontificii Instituti Biblici, vol. 114 (Rome: Pontificii Instituti Biblici, 1963) §§40–41; Percy, *Probleme*, 189–91, 250–52.

3. This reading ἐν ᾗ is in א[2] D (F) G Ψ 𝔐 it[d, g] vg syr[h] Theodoret Oecumenius Theophylact. The other reading ἧς is accepted by NA[27] and UBS[4] and is supported by 𝔓[46] א* A B P 0278 6 33 81 330 365 424[c] 436 1175 1319 1739 1837 1881 1908 2127 2464 *pc* Origen Chrysostom Euthalius. Admittedly, the second reading has good early Alexandrian evidence and is the more difficult reading where the ἧς is by attraction to the antecedent in the place of ἥν, the cognate accusative (BDF §294 [2]; Robertson, *Grammar*, 716). However, whereas the second reading has only the Alexandrian tradition, the first reading has a much better geographical distribution with good representatives from the Western and Byzantine tradition. With either reading the sense is not altered.

4. Chrysostom *Eph* 1:6 (*PG* 62:13); Theodoret *Eph* 1:6 (*PG* 82:509); Oecumenius *Eph* 1:6 (*PG* 118:1173); Theophylact *Eph* 1:6 (*PG* 124:1037); Calvin, 127.

ing it is like taking a poor, old, ill clad, and famished leper and turning him into a rich, healthy, well attired, and satiated youth. Internally believers have been changed so that they are acceptable to God. This is really foreign to all biblical teaching. The second view is that it is an objective bestowal of grace on the believers (Peshitta, Vg, RSV, NASB, NEB, NIV).[1] The believer is visited with grace. He has been ingratiated with grace. This fits with the context where it speaks of God's gracious provision. In the immediately preceding context he talks about the gracious acts of God in election and predestination, and the verses immediately after this verse speak of redemption and forgiveness and nothing of an infusion of God's grace. Furthermore, this relative clause goes back to "grace" and Paul does not use it as the subjective human grace, even in 4:29. This sense agrees with its only other use in Luke 1:28 where God bestowed favor in choosing Mary as the mother of Jesus. This is further substantiated in verses 29–30 where Mary was troubled and Gabriel enjoins her not to fear God's grace in choosing her, a sense which is strange if she were endowed with grace. The context emphasizes God's choice rather than Mary's acceptability. Therefore, the believers are acceptable to God not because he has infused grace in them, but because God has bestowed grace[2] on them.

ἐν τῷ ἠγαπημένῳ,[3] "in the beloved one." The preposition ἐν denotes a close personal relationship[4] and the article with the participle individualizes it,[5] namely, the grace God has bestowed on us in close relationship to the beloved one. This designation "beloved one" is used of people in the OT (Deut 21:15; 33:12; 2 Sam 1:23; Prov 4:3; Isa 5:1; Jer 11:15; 12:7; Hos 3:1) and in the NT (Rom 9:25; Col 3:12; 1 Thess 1:4; 2 Thess 2:13). It is also used of God in the OT (Isa 5:1*bis*, 7). In the NT it is used as a title of Christ only in Eph 1:6. However, it is very similar

1. Bengel, 4:67; Alford, 3:73; Eadie, 37–39; Ellicott, 9–10; Lightfoot, *Notes on Epistles of St Paul*, 315; Meyer, 42–43; Abbott, 10–11; Salmond, 253; Westcott, 10; Schlier, 56; Barth, 81–82; Bruce, 252. For a review of translations in older English translations, see W. H. Griffth Thomas, "Ephesians i.6," *ExpTim* 29 (September 1918): 561.

2. It is unfortunate that English does not have a verb for grace, and so "to bestow grace" probably best captures the idea. For a brief discussion of this problem, see James Matthew, "Exact Renderings," *ExpTim* 23 (December 1911): 138; F. V. Pratt, "Ephesians i.6," *ExpTim* 23 (April 1912): 331.

3. The additional reading υἱῷ αὐτοῦ which is supported in D* F G 629 it$^{ar, b, d, f, (g), o, r}$ vg^{cl} syr^{h**} cop$^{sa, (bo)}$ Adamantius Theodotus-Ancyra Victorinus-Rome Ambrosiaster Latin mss$^{acc. to Jerome}$ Pelagius^{lem} Augustine is an evident gloss and is not acceptable because it is basically in only one text-type. The omission of these words has the overwhelming support of the manuscripts, viz., 𝔓^{46} א A B D^{2} Ψ 075 0150 6 33 81 104 256 263 365 424 436 459 1175 1241 1319 1573 1739 1852 1881 1912 1962 2127 2200 2464 *Byz* [K L P] *Lect* vg$^{ww, st}$ syr$^{p, pal}$ arm geo slav Origen$^{acc. to Jerome}$ Didymus^{vid} Chrysostom Theodore^{lat} Jerome mss $^{acc. to Jerome}$ Pelagius^{com} Orosius.

4. Cf. BAGD 259; BDAG 327–28.

5. Wallace, *Greek Grammar*, 233–34.

to the verbal adjective ἀγαπητός, "beloved,"[1] in conjunction with the noun "son" where the Father calls Jesus "beloved Son" at the baptism (Matt 3:17 = Mark 1:11 = Luke 3:22), at the transfiguration (Matt 17:5 = Mark 9:7 = Luke 9:35?; 2 Pet 1:17), and is implied in the parable of the wicked husbandmen (Mark 12:6 = Luke 20:13). In Col 1:13 Jesus is called "the Son of his love." Hence, although unique to Eph 1:6, reference to Jesus as the "beloved one" is in keeping with other passages. The church fathers used this title to designate Jesus Christ.[2] Barth strongly regards this as a messianic title of Jesus.[3] Robinson and Schlier suggest "the beloved one" used for Israel (Jeshurun [יְשֻׁרוּן] in OT: Deut 32:15; 33:5, 26; Isa 44:2) was a messianic title used by the Jews before the Christians used it as a messianic title for Jesus.[4] However, Lincoln appropriately points out that neither present "any hard evidence for its pre-Christian usage in such a way."[5] Nevertheless, in the NT God the Father calls his Son the beloved One, which is evidence of his love for him. Since believers are in Christ, they are also the object of God's love.

Believers are to bless God who has benefited them with every spiritual blessing. The first is the work of God the Father who has elected them in Christ in eternity before the creation of the world that they might be holy before him. He elected them from the mass of all humanity because he had already predetermined their destiny as adopted sons into God's family, all in accordance with God's good pleasure. The goal of all this was to cause believers to praise the glorious father for his grace which he has bestowed on them in his beloved Son Christ. This reference to Christ furnishes a transition to the second person of the Trinity discussed in verses 7–12.

b. God's Redemption in Christ (1:7–12)

The father's plan of adoption into his family could only be accomplished through Jesus Christ. Having stated the Father's plan, Paul naturally speaks next about Christ who made provision for that plan. In the discussion of the work of the second person of the Trinity, Paul shows that God provides redemption in Christ (v. 7), provides wisdom to understand the mystery of his will (vv. 8–10), and recognizes his inheritance in the believers (v. 11).

(1) Redemption: Forgiveness of Sins (1:7)

Text: 1:7. ἐν ᾧ ἔχομεν τὴν ἀπολύτρωσιν διὰ τοῦ αἵματος αὐτοῦ, τὴν ἄφεσιν τῶν παραπτωμάτων, κατὰ τὸ πλοῦτος τῆς χάριτος αὐτοῦ,

1. Cf. its use in *Ascension of Isaiah* esp. 3:13.
2. *Barn.* 3:6; 4:3, 8; Acts of Paul and Thecla 1.
3. Barth, 82.
4. Robinson, 229–33; Schlier, 56.
5. Lincoln, 26.

Translation: 1:7. "in whom we have redemption through his blood, the forgiveness of sins, according to the wealth of his grace,"

Commentary: 1:7. ἐν ᾧ ἔχομεν[1] τὴν ἀπολύτρωσιν, "in whom we have redemption." The ἐν ᾧ "in whom" relates back to the immediately preceding words referring to Christ, the beloved one. The preposition ἐν, "in," is not to be taken as outward means or agency as διά, "by, through," would express, but it denotes location or sphere and here specifically indicates an internal close relationship;[2] hence, redemption is integrally connected with Christ. This view of the preposition is well illustrated in Col 1:16 where Paul uses three prepositions to refer to creation. He states that all things were created "in" him (ἐν, internal connection), "through" him (διά, external means), and "for" him (εἰς, goal). The present tense for ἔχομεν, "we have," is the best reading and means that redemption is an ongoing state.[3] Best states: "The present tense implies redemption and forgiveness are present possessions and this is in keeping with AE's [Author of Ephesians] stress on the present nature of salvation."[4]

The word used here for redemption (ἀπολύτρωσις) is used ten times in the NT, seven times by Paul, three times in Ephesians (1:7, 14; 4:30). It is used infrequently in classical literature and Abbott concludes that it means "'holding to ransom' or 'release on receipt of ransom,' not 'payment of ransom.'"[5] Morris challenges this conclusion by stating that Abbott always takes the substantive in the active sense and not the middle. In examining the passages Abbott used plus four additional passages,[6] Morris concludes that the middle sense is not only satisfactory in all of the passages but it is demanded in eight or nine of the instances and consequently means that "there is the payment of a ransom price to secure the desired release."[7] Dodd disagrees and feels that in the NT the main point is the setting free and that the

1. The aorist ἔσχομεν is found in very few manuscripts: ℵ* D* Ψ 104 1505 *pc* cop Irenaeus[latpt]. Although it is represented in two text-types, the representation is very sparse.

2. BAGD 259; BDAG 327–28.

3. Cf. Buist M. Fanning, *Verbal Aspect in New Testament Greek*, OTM, ed. J. Barton, R. C. Morgan, B. R. White, J. MacQuarrie, K. Ware, and R. D. Williams (Oxford: Clarendon, 1990), 206; Wallace, *Greek Grammar*, 521–22.

4. Best, 129.

5. Abbott, 12 cites Plutarch *Pompey* 24.4; Josephus *A.J.* 12.2.3 §27; Philo *Quod Omnis Probus Liber Sit* 17 §114*bis*; Diodorus Siculus *Frag*. 37.5.3; Dan 4:34 [LXX].

6. Namely, *Letter of Aristeas* 12.33*bis*; W. R. Paton and E. L Hicks, *The Inscriptions of Cos* (Oxford: Clarendon, 1891), no. 29.7; *Scholia in Luciani Peregrin* 13 (Scholia in Lucianum, ed. Hugo Rabe [Lipsiae: B. G. Teubner, 1906], 220); see Leon Morris, *The Apostolic Preaching of the Cross*, 3d ed. (London: Tyndale; Grand Rapids: Eerdmans, 1965), 16 n. 2, 17 n. 5; 18 n. 1.

7. Morris, *Apostolic Preaching*, 18, cf. 16–18, 40–44; cf. also Herman Ridderbos, *Paul: An Outline of His Theology*, trans. John Richard de Witt (Grand Rapids: Eerdmans, 1975), 193–97; Erich Mauerhofer, "Der Brief an die Epheser. 5. Teil: 1,7–9," *Fundamentum* 4 (1990): 19–21.

payment of price is lost.[1] However, this is not borne out if one examines its use in inscriptions[2] and the NT. The context in three instances certainly demands price (Rom 3:24; Eph 1:7; Heb 9:15), referring to Christ's death by which the price was paid for freeing us.[3] Four times it is used of the future redemption of believers from the earthly sphere (Luke 21:28; Rom 8:23; Eph 1:14; 4:30) and although there is nothing specific in the context to denote payment, Morris states accurately that the future redemption is based on Christ's payment at the cross.[4] Although Col 1:14 does not mention payment, it is parallel to Eph 1:7 which does have the payment of Christ's death.[5]

The last two passages to be considered are more difficult. Hebrews 11:35 includes nothing specific about a payment of ransom, but it implies that women refused to renounce their faith in order to be released or redeemed from torture. Instead, they chose martyrdom in order to obtain a better resurrection.[6] Clearly, there is a need of payment of price to secure release. The final passage is 1 Cor 1:30 where redemption is listed with righteousness and sanctification. Certainly, since righteousness is obtained through Christ's death, it can be implied that redemption also is obtained by payment of his death. Hence, the NT usage of ἀπολύτρωσις refers to one set free on the basis of a ransom paid to God by Christ's death.[7] It is granted that the main import of this word is release or setting free rather than payment, but it does not exclude the latter as some think.[8] It is not either/or but both/and.

διὰ τοῦ αἵματος αὐτοῦ, "through his blood," explicitly states the cost of the ransom. The preposition διά expresses means[9] that is outward and it often follows ἐν, "in,"[10] an internal close relationship

1. C. H. Dodd, "Some Problems of New Testament Translation," *BT* 13 (July 1962): 151; so also Best, 130.

2. Cf. Deissmann, *Light from the Ancient East*, 323–31.

3. Morris, *Apostolic Preaching*, 42–46.

4. Ibid., 48.

5. Cf. Maclean, "Ephesians and the Problem of Colossians," 33–41.

6. Benjamin B. Warfield, "The New Testament Terminology of 'Redemption,'" *Princeton Theological Review* 15 (April 1917): 240.

7. BAGD 96; BDAG 117; cf. Stanislas Lyonnet and Léopold Sabourin, *Sin, Redemption, and Sacrifice. A Biblical and Patristic Study*, trans. Fidelis Buck, AnBib, vol. 48 (Rome: Biblical Institute Press, 1970), 79–103; Karl Wennemer, "'ΑΠΟΛΥΤΡΩΣΙΣ Römer 3,24–25a," in *Studiorum Paulinorum Congressus Internationalis Catholicus 1961*, vol. 2, AnBib, vol. 18 (Rome: E Pontificio Instituto Biblico, 1963), 283–88; William Barclay, *New Testament Words* (London: SCM, 1964), 189–96.

8. Frederick R. Swallow, "'Redemption' in St Paul," *Scr* 10 (January 1958): 21–27; F. Büchsel, "λύω, κτλ.," *TDNT* 4 (1967): 354–55; David Hill, *Greek Words and Hebrew Meanings: Studies in the Semantics of Soteriological Terms*, SNTSMS, ed. Matthew Black, vol. 5 (Cambridge: Cambridge University Press, 1967), 73–74; Robinson, 148; Caird, 36–37; Lincoln, 28.

9. HS §184f; BAGD 180; BDAG 224.

10. HS §177a.

mentioned above. The διά defines more precisely how redemption was accomplished. It was not only in connection with Christ, which could refer to his life, but, more specifically, it was by Christ's death. However, it is more than mere death because the blood speaks of sacrificial death. The OT writings very carefully indicated that the shedding of blood was involved in sacrifice. Sacrificial animals were not killed by strangulation. The shedding of blood is necessary (Lev 17:11; Eph 2:13; 1 Pet 1:19) for without it there is no forgiveness of sins (Heb 9:22), and Paul makes it clear that God has been propitiated in Christ's redemption, which was in connection with his blood (Rom 3:24–25), and that one is justified by means of Christ's blood (Rom 5:9). Therefore, the ransom price in connection with deliverance was the sacrificial death of Christ. Certainly, there are numerous references in the NT which refer to the blood of Christ as the ransom price for our sins (Acts 20:28; 1 Pet 1:18–19; Rev 1:5; 5:9; cf. 1 Cor 6:20; 7:23).

τὴν ἄφεσιν τῶν παραπτωμάτων, "the forgiveness of sins," is appositional to redemption and further defines it. It is the immediate result of release from sin's bondage by the payment of Christ's sacrificial death. The substantive ἄφεσις is used in classical literature of the release of captives[1] and the cancellation or release from a legal charge,[2] financial obligation,[3] or punishment.[4] In the LXX it occurs fifty times (forty-five times in the canonical books) and is translated from eleven Hebrew words to denote "release" (Lev 25:41; Deut 15:1–3, 9; 31:10; Isa 58:6), "amnesty" (Esth 2:18), "liberty" (Lev 25:10; Isa 61:1; Jer 34:8 [LXX 41:8]; 34:15, 17*bis* [LXX 41:15, 17*bis*]; Ezek 46:17), and "jubilee," which marked the release of slaves, debt, and property every fifty years in Israel (Lev 25:11–13, 28*bis*, 30–31, 33, 40, 50, 52, 54; 27:17–18, 21, 23–24). It is used seventeen times in the NT: twice about the release of captives (Luke 4:18*bis* quoting Isa 61:1; 58:6) and the other occurrences about the forgiveness of sin. The synonym πάρεσις, used only in Rom 3:25, means "passing by" sins, which has the idea of a temporary suspension of punishment for sins committed before the cross, whereas ἄφεσις is the permanent cancellation of or release from the punishment for sin because it has been paid for by Christ's sacrifice.[5]

The noun παράπτωμα is used to indicate a false step, mistake, fault, or error.[6] It is used twenty-two times in the LXX (fourteen times in the canonical books) and is translated primarily from מַעַל, "unfaithful,

1. Polybius 1.79.12.

2. Plato *Leges* 9 §869d.

3. Demosthenes *Orationes* 24.45–46.

4. Diodorus Siculus 20.44.6.

5. Richard Chenevix Trench, *Synonyms of the New Testament*, 10th ed. (London: Kegan Paul, Trench, 1886; reprint, Grand Rapids: Eerdmans, 1958), 118–19; cf. also Rudolf Bultmann, "ἀφίημι, ἄφεσις, παρίημι, πάρεσις," *TDNT* 1 (1964): 509–12.

6. Polybius 9.10.6; 15.23.5; 16.20.5; Diodorus Siculus 19.100.3.

treacherous act" (Ezek 14:13; 15:8; 18:24; 20:27), עָוֶל, "injustice, unrighteousness" (Ezek 3:20; 18:26*bis*),[1] and פֶּשַׁע, "transgression, rebellion" (Job 36:9; Ezek 14:11; 18:22). The tone in the LXX is much sharper than in classical literature because it indicates a conscious and deliberate false step, or error before a holy and righteous God. In the NT it is used nineteen times, sixteen times by Paul, three of which are in Ephesians (1:7; 2:1, 5). It is used synonymously with ἁμαρτία, "mistake, failure to reach a goal," in classical literature.[2] The term ἁμαρτία occurs 535 times in the LXX and 411 times in the canonical books and is translated around 300 times from חָטָא and its derivatives, meaning "miss (a goal or way), go wrong, sin"[3] (Exod 32:31; Deut 19:15; Isa 53:12), about sixty-five times from עָוֹן, meaning "iniquity, guilt, punishment for iniquity"[4] (Gen 15:16; Isa 5:18; Jer 14:7), and fifteen times from פֶּשַׁע, meaning "transgression, rebellion" (Prov 10:19; Isa 53:5, 12*bis*). It appears 173 times in the NT, sixty-four times in Paul, but only once in Ephesians (2:1). However, it is used in the parallel passage to the present verse (Col 1:14). It is also synonymous with ἁμάρτημα, which has the idea of mistake or false step.[5] In the Bible all three of these words denote more than an inadvertent mistake. Rather they denote a conscious and willful act against God's holiness and righteousness. Human beings are held responsible for these acts of treachery against God and sin needs to be punished. The use of the plural indicates the acts of sin or violence against God.

However, this verse shows that as a result of redemption in Christ through his blood, God has cancelled or forgiven sins and the necessary punishment that goes with them. Redemption is the cause and forgiveness is the effect. God is not lenient with sin because sin had to be paid in order for the sinner to be set free. The effect of this payment is the cancellation of or release from all the obligations caused by sin. Christ in his sacrificial death has taken the punishment for us. The supreme sacrifice of Christ clearly shows that God does not take sin lightly.

κατὰ τὸ πλοῦτος τῆς χάριτος[6] αὐτοῦ, "according to the wealth of his grace," demonstrates the supreme cost of Christ's sacrifice for sinners. The preposition shows that God's redemption and forgiveness were

1. Cf. J. Schreiner, "עָוֶל *ʿāwel*, etc.," *TDOT* 10 (1999): 522–30.

2. In Polybius 16.20.5, he uses both of these terms synonymously.

3. BDB 306–10; cf. K. Koch, "חָטָא *chāṭāʾ*, etc.," *TDOT* 4 (1980): 309–19.

4. BDB 730–31; K. Koch, "עָוֹן *ʿāwōn*, etc.," *TDOT* 10 (1999): 546–62.

5. For further study on these three words, see Wilhelm Michaelis, "πίπτω, κτλ.," *TDNT* 6 (1968): 170–72; Wolfgang Bauder, "Sin [ἀδικία, ἁμαρτία, παράβασις, παράπτωμα]," *NIDNTT* 3 (1978): 585–86; Gustav Stählin, "ἁμαρτάνω, ἁμάρτημα, ἁμαρτία," *TDNT* 1 (1964): 293–96.

6. Instead of χάριτος, the reading χρηστότητος is found in A 365 *pc* cop^{bo}. The first reading is definitely preferred, for the second reading has very few manuscripts supporting it. It may well have its origin from Rom 2:4 (τοῦ πλούτου τῆς χρηστότητος αὐτοῦ).

not "out of" but "according to" the wealth of his grace. The noun πλοῦτος is used twenty-two times in the NT, fifteen times by Paul, five of which are in Ephesians (1:7, 18; 2:7; 3:8, 16). It basically comes from the idea of "full, filled" (πλε[F]ω, πλη-),[1] and thus from the classical to the NT period it means to have abundance, riches, or wealth. The translation "wealth" is preferred because it depicts singularity as opposed to many kinds of riches. This word is followed by a genitive of the thing, which is χάρις "grace, unmerited favor," a word that has already been discussed (vv. 2, 6). This is followed by a possessive genitive (αὐτοῦ, "his"), which indicates that it is God's grace. It took the wealth of God's grace to redeem and forgive the sinner.[2] The cost of sin was the supreme sacrifice of God's Son Jesus Christ.

In conclusion, sin is a violation of God's holiness and righteousness and the violater must be punished. God sacrificed his Son, Christ, whereby he provided the payment for sins committed and set the sinner free from sin's punishment. The effect of this was the cancellation of sin's obligation resulting in the permanent release from the guilt and punishment of sin. All this was accomplished according to the standard of God's wealth of grace.

(2) Wisdom: Mystery of His Will (1:8–10)

Paul now is going to discuss God's grace that is given to enable believers to understand his will. This is divided into three parts: its provision (v. 8), its manner (v. 9), and its goal (v. 10).

(a) Provision (1:8)

Text: 1:8. ἧς ἐπερίσσευσεν εἰς ἡμᾶς ἐν πάσῃ σοφίᾳ καὶ φρονήσει

Translation: 1:8. "which he has lavished on us with all insight and discretion"

Commentary: 1:8. ἧς ἐπερίσσευσεν εἰς ἡμᾶς, "which he lavished on us." The singular feminine genitive relative pronoun ἧς is in direct attraction[3] to the antecedent χάριτος, "grace." What case the relative pronoun should be depends on how one views the verb ἐπερίσσευσεν. The verb is an aorist indicative of περισσεύω and has the basic idea of overabundance either of things[4] or persons.[5] It is used only nine times in the LXX (three times in the canonical books, viz., 1 Sam 2:33, 36; Eccl 3:19) and thirty-nine times in the NT, twenty-six times by Paul,

1. Friedrich Hauck and Wilhelm Kasch, "πλοῦτος, πλούσιος, πλουτέω, πλουτίζω," *TDNT* 6 (1968): 319.

2. Similar thoughts are expressed in the Qumran community (1QH[a] 8:21 [16:12]; 19:28–30 [11:28–30]).

3. Robertson, *Grammar*, 716.

4. Sophocles *Electra* 1288; Philo *Jos*. 40 §243; Josephus *A.J.* 16.2.2 §19.

5. Polybius 18.35.5; Philo *Quis Rerum Divinarum Heres* 39 §191; Josephus *A.J.* 19.1.18 §150.

and only this one time in Ephesians. It can be used intransitively of things, "to be present in abundance" (Mark 12:44) or of persons, "to have an abundance" (Rom 15:13); or it can be used transitively of things, "to have an abundance" (Matt 13:12) or of persons, "to cause one to abound" (Luke 15:17).[1] In this context it is used of persons, but is it used transitively or intransitively? There are three ways this could be interpreted. First, it could be taken intransitively and the genitive relative pronoun ἧς used as an attraction for the dative relative pronoun ᾗ meaning "wherein he has abounded" (AV).[2] However, there is no example in the NT of a dative relative representing a genitive. Second, it could be taken transitively and the genitive relative pronoun ἧς used as the object of the verb ἐπερίσσευσεν, much like Luke 15:17 ("have an abundance of bread"), and hence it would translate "of which he abounded toward us." Unfortunately, this makes the sentence rather clumsy. Third, the verb can be taken transitively and although the relative pronoun ordinarily would be accusative (ἣν), it is a genitive relative pronoun ἧς since it is attracted to its antecedent χάριτος, a feature which is not uncommon in the NT.[3] This is the position taken by most commentators.[4] Thus, it would be translated "which he abounded to us" or as some modern translations "which he lavished on us" (RSV, NASB, NEB, NIV, NRSV). This seems the best solution. Therefore, the grace which provided redemption, God lavished on the believers. As Theophylact states, God poured this grace unsparingly on us.[5] With the combination of τὸ πλοῦτος and ἐπερίσσευσεν, the overwhelming abundance of God's grace is clearly demonstrated.

ἐν πάσῃ σοφίᾳ καὶ φρονήσει, "with all insight and discretion." In connection with this prepositional phrase, three problems must be discussed: (1) the meaning, (2) to whom it refers; and (3) to what it is connected. First, in regard to the meaning, two words must be considered. The first word σοφία, "wisdom," referred in its earliest use to an unusual ability in a practical skill (like the skill of a carpenter),[6] but later it was restricted to theoretical and intellectual knowledge and, in its final development, a wise person was one who united the theoretical knowledge with practice.[7] It is prominent in the OT, for it appears in the LXX 248 times and in the canonical books it occurs 142 times and is translated about 130 times from חָכְמָה and the remaining instances translated from five other Hebrew words. The OT concept was not of solely theoretical knowledge but a combination of theoretical and practical knowledge with the idea of skillful living (Exod 35:31,

1. BAGD 650–51; BDAG 805.
2. Calvin, 127.
3. BDF §294.
4. E.g., Eadie, 44; Abbott, 14; Schnackenburg, 56; Lincoln, 29.
5. Theophylact *Eph* 1:7 (*PG* 124:1039).
6. Homer *Ilias* 15.412.
7. Ulrich Wilckens, "σοφία," *TDNT* 7 (1971): 467.

35; Prov 2:10; 4:11; 10:13) and true wisdom apparent in those who fear the Lord (Prov 9:10; Job 28:28). In the NT it is used fifty-one times, twenty-eight times by Paul, three of which are in Ephesians (1:8, 17; 3:10). Of the twenty-eight times Paul uses this word, it occurs fifteen times in 1 Cor 1:17–2:13 where he is contrasting human and divine wisdom. These references indicate that human self-reformation cannot change people. Only the crucified Christ, which is the wisdom of God, generates the power that can transform people. This is the power and wisdom of God (1:18, 21–25). Thus wisdom is the true insight of known facts or "insight into the true nature of things."[1] The best wisdom is that which has been revealed by God. Thus, it is insight into the true nature of God's revelation.

The second word to be discussed is φρόνησις which is very close in meaning to σοφία. Its use is not altogether clear because at times in Plato's writings φρόνησις takes the place of σοφία.[2] Yet, in general, he seems to think that σοφία refers to intellectual knowledge and that φρόνησις refers to practical knowledge.[3] The noun φρόνησις appears in the LXX sixty-one times. In the canonical LXX it occurs thirty-seven times, and it is translated ten times from תְּבוּנָה, "understanding," nine times from חָכְמָה, "wisdom,"[4] and six times from בִּינָה, "understanding."[5] All three of these Hebrew words are also translated σοφία, which indicates that these two words overlap in meaning. The word φρόνησις is used of knowledge of God's understanding (Isa 40:28), of the superiority of a person's understanding as opposed to physical strength (Prov 24:5), of cleverness (Job 5:13), and, in wisdom literature, of discernment or discretion (Prov 1:2; 8:14; 9:6, 16; 14:29; 19:8). In the NT it is used only twice (Luke 1:17; Eph 1:8). In Luke it speaks of John the Baptist's ministry of turning hearts toward the Lord and turning the disobedient to the "wisdom," "discernment," or "discretion" of the righteous. This refers to the practical living of the righteous. In Eph 1:8 it has the idea of understanding the relevance of God's revelation in the present time. In this context it is used with σοφία and it speaks of the practical side of wisdom. A good translation is "discretion." A study of the use of the two words together needs to made.

The use of these two Greek words is seen often in Proverbs (3:13, 19; 7:4; 8:1; 10:23; 16:16). They are called companions of a wise person (7:4). The words are synonymous but σοφία seems to emphasize insight and φρόνησις seems to emphasize understanding in a practical way. Proverbs 10:23 sums up these emphases very well: "as doing evil is a sport (pleasure) to a fool, so is wisdom (חָכְמָה σοφία) to a person of

1. Lightfoot, *Notes on Epistles of St Paul*, 317.

2. Plato *Leges* 10 §906b.

3. Georg Bertram, "φρόνησις," *TDNT* 9 (1974): 221.

4. BDB 315; cf. H.-P. Müller and M. Krause, "חָכַם *chākham*; חָכָם *chākhām*; חָכְמָה *chokhmāh*; חָכְמוֹת *chokhmôth*," *TDOT* 4 (1980): 364–85.

5. Helmer Ringgren, "בִּין *bîn*; בִּינָה *bînāh*; תְּבוּנָה *tᵉbhûnāh*," *TDOT* 2 (1977): 105–7.

understanding (תְּבוּנָה φρόνησις)." People of understanding or discretion have pleasure in wisdom because they know how it will benefit them practically. This fits well with Greek literature. As mentioned above, Plato seems to make this distinction and this is borne out in other Greek literature. Aristotle states that σοφία is both scientific and intuitive knowledge of the most honorable things in nature, whereas φρόνησις is concerned with the affairs and action of people.[1] Philo asserts that σοφία is for the worship of God and φρόνησις is for the regulation of human life.[2] Hence, the first is more theoretical and the latter is the more practical application of knowledge. However, one must realize that they do overlap. On the one hand, it is an error to make them identical but on the other hand, it is an error to make them completely distinct.

The adjective πάσῃ, "all," modifies both the words "insight" and "discretion." When this adjective is used with an anarthrous singular noun, it emphasizes individuality meaning "every kind of, all sorts of."[3] As Harless suggests, it denotes extension and not intensity, making the abstract nouns concrete, for example, not all power but every kind of power that exists, not all endurance but every kind of endurance there is.[4] Hence, it means not all insight and discretion but every kind of insight and discretion that exists.

Second, to whom does this prepositional phrase refer? Some think it refers to God, namely, that in all of God's insight and discretion he lavished his grace on us,[5] while others think it refers to believers, namely, God lavished on us his grace of all insight and discretion.[6] The latter view is most likely for several reasons. First, the use of πάσῃ with an anarthrous abstract would be unfitting of God's wisdom (connotes every kind of wisdom of God), which could imply that God's wisdom is incomplete. Second, the context indicates that believers have been given wisdom so that they can discern the mysteries of God's will (v. 9). Third, later in the context (v. 17) Paul prays that believers might be given wisdom and revelation. Fourth, the analogy in Col 1:9, "in order that you might be filled with the knowledge of his will in all wisdom and understanding," certainly points to Christians as recipients of insight and discretion. Fifth, support of the "manifold wisdom of God" in 3:10 for "all of God's insight and discretion" is not valid because he is talking about the exercise of his manifestation rather than talking about the essence of God's wisdom. Thus, it is best

1. Aristotle *Ethica Nicomachea* 6.7.5–7 §1141b.4–23; *Magna Moralia* 1.34.14–16 §1196b.3.

2. Philo *Praem*. 14 §81.

3. BAGD 631; BDAG 783.

4. Harless, 33.

5. Alford, 3:74; Eadie, 45; Best, 132–33.

6. Eadie, 46; Ellicott, 12; Lightfoot, *Notes on Epistles of St Paul*, 317; Abbott, 15; Salmond, 257; Schnackenburg, 56–57.

to accept that the insight and discretion refers to the believer as a result of God's grace rather than referring to those attributes of God which cause his grace.

Third, to what is this prepositional phrase connected? Some would connect it with the following participle describing the manner in which God made known the mystery of his will ("with all wisdom and discretion he made known to us the mystery of his will," e.g., RSV, NASB, TEV, NRSV).[1] Others think it goes with the preceding verb qualifying that which God lavished, that is, his grace on the believers ("he lavished on us with all insight and discretion," e.g., AV, RV, ASV, NEB, JB, NIV, NJB).[2] The last alternative is best for the following reasons. First, in the present context the qualifying phrases always follow the verbs and participles. This was discussed at verse 4. Second, the context demands it, for it indicates that God is going to make known the mystery of his will to the believers, and this is possible because they have received insight and discretion. Third, the later context (vv. 17–21) is analogous, for Paul prays that they might receive wisdom and revelation in order to know God's program for the believer.

In conclusion, God's grace which provided redemption and the forgiveness of sins also lavishes on us all insight and wisdom. One must have not only the benefits of grace but also the benefits of insight and discretion in order to live wisely. For example, those who receive God's gracious redemption and forgiveness of sin gain insight into the fact that God no longer holds them guilty for their sins because they have been paid for. Furthermore, because of the freedom from the bondage of sin, believers will discern that their new freedom is not for self-consumption but freedom to serve the living God. This is only a beginning point, for the next verses show that this insight and discretion that God gives the believer is for the purpose of understanding God's plan for the ages.

(b) Manner (1:9)

Text: 1:9. γνωρίσας ἡμῖν τὸ μυστήριον τοῦ θελήματος αὐτοῦ, κατὰ τὴν εὐδοκίαν αὐτοῦ ἣν προέθετο ἐν αὐτῷ

Translation: 1:9. "having made known to us the mystery of his will, according to his good pleasure which he purposed in him"

Commentary: 1:9. γνωρίσας[3] ἡμῖν, "having made known to us." The aorist participle γνωρίσας is from γνωρίζω, which from the earliest

1. Chrysostom *Eph* 1:8–9 (*PG* 62:14); Jerome *Eph* 1:9 (*PL* 26:452); Theodoret *Eph* 1:9 (*PG* 82:512); Eadie, 45, 48–49; Gnilka, 77; Best, 132–33.

2. Ambrosiaster *Eph* 1:8 (*PL* 17:374); Oecumenius *Eph* 1:5–8 (*PG* 118:1176); Ellicott, 12; Abbott, 15; Schnackenburg, 56–57; Bruce, 260; Lincoln, 17, 29; O'Brien, 107–8; Mauerhofer, "Der Brief an die Epheser. 5. Teil: 1,7–9," 25.

3. The aorist infinitive γνωρίσαι is found only in F G (lat) and thus does not have good textual support.

times has had the meaning "to make known, reveal."[1] It occurs sixty-eight times in the LXX, sixty-three times in the canonical books (including Theodotion Daniel). It is translated from five Hebrew words but fifty-four times from יָדַע and fifty times from the Hiphil form of this verb or Aphel form of the Aramaic יְדַע, which gives it the same meaning. It is used of God making known his will (Ps 16:11 [LXX 15:11]; 25:4 [LXX 24:3]; 103:7 [LXX 102:7]; 143:8 [LXX 142:8]; Ezek 20:11) and making known that which is secret (Dan 2:5, 23, 28, 45; 5:17; 7:16; 8:19). The same sense carries over into the NT where it is used of God making known his power (Luke 2:15; Rom 9:22–23; cf. 2 Pet 1:16), his will (John 15:15), and most prominently used of making known the mysteries that have been kept secret until the present time (Rom 16:26; Eph 1:9; 3:3, 5, 10; 6:19; Col 1:27).[2] It is this use about which the present context is concerned. The action of the participle is contemporaneous with the finite verb in verse 8,[3] which indicates the manner in which he bestowed grace, namely, he made known to us the mystery of his will. The adverbial participle of manner tells how the action of the main verb is accomplished. The pronoun ἡμῖν, "us," indicates that God has made known his mystery not just to Paul or a few select believers but to all believers. This is consistent with use of the pronoun in the context (cf. vv. 4, 5, 6, 8).

τὸ μυστήριον τοῦ θελήματος αὐτοῦ, "the mystery of his will." The concept of μυστήριον has been discussed more thoroughly in an excursus (see Excursus 6: Mystery). It refers to something in ages past, hidden in God (3:9) and unable to be unravelled or understood by human ingenuity or study. It has now been revealed by the Holy Spirit to his holy apostles and prophets (3:4–5) who in turn have made it manifest to everyone. In 1 Cor 2:7 it is connected with the wisdom of God, which is the crucified Christ who is the power of God for salvation to those who believe. In Eph 2:11–3:13 the concept is further developed on the foundation of the crucified Christ where believing Jews and Gentiles are united into one, the body of Christ. More will be discussed later in that context. The present context deals with making known the mystery of his will. The genitives τοῦ θελήματος are objective and the pronoun αὐτοῦ is possessive and hence, the mystery concerning God's own will. The mystery of his will is concerned with that will or plan of God that was hidden in God and is now made known to believers. For a discussion on "will" (θέλημα), see verse 1. The following prepositional phrase indicates God's attitude in making known his plan.

1. Aeschylus *Prometheus Vinctus* 487; Polybius 2.37.4; Plutarch *Fabius Maximus* 21.3.

2. Cf. Rudolf Bultmann, "γνωρίζω," *TDNT* 1 (1964): 718.

3. Ernest De Witt Burton, *Syntax of the Moods and Tenses in New Testament Greek*, 3d ed. (Chicago: University of Chicago Press, 1898) §139; Porter, *Verbal Aspect*, 384; Wallace, *Greek Grammar*, 625.

κατὰ τὴν εὐδοκίαν αὐτοῦ,[1] "according to his good pleasure." This prepositional phrase does not modify τὸ μυστήριον τοῦ θελήματος αὐτοῦ because it needs no further definition. Nor does this phrase modify that which follows προέθετο ἐν αὐτῷ. Rather, it modifies γνωρίσας in the same way προορίσας was declared to be κατὰ τὴν εὐδοκίαν τοῦ θελήματος αὐτοῦ in verse 5.[2] The preposition κατά with the accusative denotes standard. The standard of making known the secret plan of his will is God's good pleasure or his satisfaction. For a discussion of εὐδοκία, see verse 5. This secret plan of his will was not given begrudgingly but with God's pleasure.

ἣν προέθετο ἐν αὐτῷ, "which he purposed in him." Because of the feminine singular relative pronoun ἥν, this refers back to God's good pleasure. In the NT the verb προτίθημι occurs only three times, always in the middle (Rom 1:13; 3:25; and here). Literally, it means "to set before" in a local sense, for example, food.[3] It can also have the idea "to resolve, purpose."[4] It appears in the LXX twelve times, eight times in the canonical books, translated from three different Hebrew words (two occurrences have no corresponding Hebrew words) and it has the meaning "to set before" (Exod 29:23; 40:4, 23; Ps 54:3 [MT 54:5; LXX 53:5]; 86:14 [LXX 85:14]). In the NT in one context it most likely has the idea "to display" (Rom 3:25), but in the other two contexts it has the idea "to purpose." For example, in Rom 1:13 Paul states that he had often purposed to come to the Romans but was prevented. Thus, God made known to believers the mystery of his will according to his good pleasure which he purposed or resolved in him.

The words ἐν αὐτῷ[5] can refer to God (AV)[6] or to Christ (RSV; NASB; NEB, TEV, JB, NIV, NJB, NRSV).[7] To have the pronoun refer to God would make it reflexive "himself." Thus God purposed or resolved in himself the good pleasure of doing his own will. Those who hold that this refers to God the Father argue: (1) throughout this passage God is the subject and it would be inconsistent to make Christ the subject;

1. αὐτοῦ is omitted by D F G it^{b} vg^{mss} Victorinus-Rome probably because the following ἐν αὐτῷ seemed redundant. Its inclusion should be retained since it is omitted only in Western texts, and its inclusion has the support of the other text-types.

2. Salmond, 258.

3. Hesoid *Theogonia* 537.

4. Plato *Phaedrus* 259e.

5. The reflexive pronoun ἑαυτῷ is found in P, thus it has very weak textual support.

6. Chrysostom *Eph* 1:9 (*PG* 62:15; Calvin, 128; Hodge, 47; Eadie, 50; Ellicott, 13; Meyer, 46–47; Salmond, 259; Hugedé, 34; Speyr, 44–45.

7. Theodoret *Eph* 1:10 (*PG* 82:512); Oecumenius *Eph* 1:9 (*PG* 118:1176); Theophylact *Eph* 1:9 (*PG* 124:1040); Bengel, 4:67; Alford, 3:76; Lightfoot, *Notes on Epistles of St Paul*, 318; Robinson, 32; Westcott, 13; Lenski, 370; Josef Könn, *Die Idee der Kirche. Bibellesungen über den Epheserbrief* (Einsiedeln/Köln: Benzinger, 1946), 42–43; E. F. Ströter, *Die Herrlichkeit des Leibes Christi. Der Epheserbrief* (Bern: Siloah, 1952), 14; Schlier, 63; Gaugler, 49; Hendriksen, 85; Caird, 38; Barth, 85; Schnackenburg, 57; Bruce, 261; Lincoln, 31; Mauerhofer, "Der Brief an die Epheser. 5. Teil: 1,7–9," 31–32.

(2) verse 5 serves as a parallel referring to God as the subject and the εἰς αὐτόν referring to God the father; and (3) it would be strange to have the pronoun here followed by Christ who is named in the next verse, for it would appear tautologous. On the other hand, to have ἐν αὐτῷ refer to Christ would mean that which God purposed in making known the mystery was in connection with Christ. Those who consider that ἐν αὐτῷ refers to Christ argue that: (1) throughout this passage the ἐν with a pronoun or personal pronoun is used in connection with Christ (vv. 3, 4, 6, 10, 11, 12, 13) whereas εἰς is used in connection with God the Father (vv. 5, 6, 12, 14); (2) it makes better sense and is not tautologous with the next verse but, in fact, is required by the next verse which expands the concept of the connection of Christ to the good pleasure of God's will; (3) to have it refer to God seems "pointless because the middle voice of the verb is already reflexive and needs no added phrase to express the idea 'in himself.'"[1] This latter view makes the best sense in the context.

God made known the secret plan of his will which was according to his good pleasure which he purposed or set beforehand in Christ, or as in the NEB, "such was his will and pleasure determined beforehand in Christ." The purpose of the Father was to be effected in Christ. Christ was the basis and goal of that mystery. Christ would provide the sacrifice and thus it would be possible to culminate all things in him, as outlined in the next verse. This was the secret of God's will that could not be unraveled by human ingenuity or study.

(c) Goal (1:10)

Text: 1:10. εἰς οἰκονομίαν τοῦ πληρώματος τῶν καιρῶν, ἀνακεφαλαιώσασθαι τὰ πάντα ἐν τῷ Χριστῷ, τὰ ἐπὶ τοῖς οὐρανοῖς καὶ τὰ ἐπὶ τῆς γῆς ἐν αὐτῷ,

Translation: 1:10. "in the administration of the fullness of the times, to unite under one head all things in Christ, the things in heaven and the things on earth in him"

Commentary: 1:10. εἰς οἰκονομίαν, "in the administration." This prepositional phrase modifies not γνωρίσας but the immediately preceding verb προέθετο. How is the preposition εἰς to be taken? One has to look ahead to the infinitive ἀνακεφαλαιώσασθαι which complements προέθετο.[2] According to his good pleasure God purposed to unite, under one head, all things in Christ. The preposition εἰς could denote: (1) reference—"God purposed with reference to the fullness of the times to unite under one head all things"; (2) purpose—"God purposed for the administration of the fullness of the times to unite under one

1. Lenski, 370.

2. This construction borders on purpose and is used with verbs "to wish," "to strive," "to be able" (BDF §392 [1]). Here the verb is "to purpose" and hence God purposes to head up all things in Christ.

head all things";[1] or (3) time—"God purposed in (at the time of) the administration of the fullness of the times to unite under one head all things." All make good sense. However, views (2) and (3) make better sense than view (1) in the context. View (2) corresponds with purpose expressed by the verb (v. 9) and the complementary infinitive (v. 10). View (3) corresponds with the following phrase which expresses time. It is difficult to choose between the last two views but view (3) is preferred because the purpose is already strongly expressed (v. 9), making view (2) seem to be redundant. What is God purposing in Christ? It is not activity of administration but rather, unification of all things in Christ under one head (v. 10). Thus, it seems that since this phrase is talking about time, it is best to see it as temporal, a use of εἰς that is not uncommon in the NT.[2] Again, what is God purposing in Christ? It is to unite under one head all things in Christ. When will this occur? It is at the time of the administration of the fullness of time. Hence, Paul is talking about when God's purpose will be carried out.

The term οἰκονομία has two nuances: first, the position or office of an administrator as used of an administration or management of a household,[3] or of a state;[4] and, second, of the activity of administrating and thus arrangement, order, plan, strategy.[5] In the LXX it occurs only twice (Isa 22:19, 21) where it refers to the office of administration. In the NT it is used nine times, six times by Paul, three times in Ephesians (1:10; 3:2, 9). Outside of Paul only Luke (Luke 16:2–4) uses the term. He uses it to refer both to the office (vv. 3–4) and to the activity of administration (v. 2). Besides Ephesians, Paul uses it three times: once to refer to his apostolic office of preaching the gospel without pay (1 Cor 9:17; in 4:1 he describes himself and fellow messengers as administrators [οἰκονόμους] of God's mysteries), once as an odd usage meaning "training" (1 Tim 1:4),[6] and once where it could refer to either the office or the activity or both the office and the activity (Col 1:25).[7] More will be discussed in the respective contexts of Eph 3:2 and 9. In Eph 1:10 it has the second meaning, the activity of

1. Bockmuehl thinks that the mystery of God's will is to gather up everything in the fullness of time. See Markus N. A. Bockmuehl, *Revelation and Mystery in Ancient Judaism and Pauline Christianity*, WUNT, ed. Martin Hengel and Otfried Hofius, vol. 36 (Tübingen: Mohr, 1990), 199–200.

2. BAGD 228–29; BDAG 289.

3. Plato *Apologia* 36b; *Respublica* 6.11 §498a; Xenophon *Oeconomicus* 1.1.

4. Josephus *A.J.* 2.5.7 §89.

5. Polybius 4.67.9; 10.16.2; Diodorus Siculus 1.81.3; G. H. R. Horsley, *New Documents Illustrating Early Christianity*, vol. 2, *A Review of the Greek Inscriptions and Papyri Published in 1977* (Sydney: Macquarie University, 1982), 92; cf. Gibbs, *Creation and Redemption*, 120–23.

6. BAGD 560; BDAG 698; Otto Michel, "οἰκονομία," *TDNT* 5 (1967): 153; J. Reumann, "Οἰκονομία-Terms in Paul in Comparison with Lucan *Heilsgeschichte*," *NTS* 13 (January 1967): 156.

7. Reumann, "Οἰκονομία-Terms in Paul," 157, 165.

an administrator and can be translated "administration" (NASB) or "dispensation" (Old Latin, Vg, AV, ASV). The translation of the NEB and NIV, "to be put into effect," makes good sense. Some think οἰκονομία means "a plan of salvation,"[1] but that is not what this passage is addressing.[2] Rather, it is talking about God's activity of administration, as all the verbs describing his activities make clear. Hence, God purposed in Christ, in the administration (or the carrying out) of the fullness of the times, to unite under one head all things in Christ.

τοῦ πληρώματος τῶν καιρῶν, "of the fullness of the times." The term πλήρωμα is more fully discussed in Excursus 5: A Study of πλήρωμα. Basically, it has the idea of fullness, completeness, entirety. In this context πλήρωμα does not have the theological implications it has in verse 23, but rather it is merely descriptive. When it is used with reference to time, it has the idea of the state of being full[3] in the sense of completeness or having reached its goal. The term is further defined by the genitives τῶν καιρῶν, "of the times." Two terms for time in the NT are χρόνος and καιρός. Generally, it has been thought that χρόνος refers to the objective impersonal measurement of time, whereas καιρός refers to time as an opportune moment.[4] Similarly, Eynikel and Hauspie conclude that in the LXX, χρόνος normally refers to an indefinite period of time while καιρός notes a critical time.[5] Lindemann maintains a sharp distinction between these two terms: χρόνος refers to a duration of time and καιρός refers not to a climax of history but a combination of the past, present, and future into one temporal unity and hence the cessation of time, as the title of his book suggests (*Die Aufhebung der Zeit*).[6] Lincoln thinks that Lindemann's view is highly unlikely with no supporting evidence.[7] A strict division between these two words has been criticized as being inaccurate because there are examples of both words used interchangeably.[8] Ac-

1. Cf. Gaugler, 49–50, 233–47; Schnackenburg, 57; Michel, *TDNT* 5 (1967): 152; Oscar Cullmann, *Salvation in History*, trans. Sidney G. Sowers (London: SCM, 1967), 76–77.

2. Masson, 144 n. 6; Reumann, "Οἰκονομία-Terms in Paul," 164; Reumann shows that this was the case among the church fathers, see John Reumann, "*Oikonomia* = 'Covenant'; Terms for *Heilsgeschichte* in Early Christian Usage," *NovT* 3 (December 1959): 282–92.

3. BAGD 672; BDAG 830.

4. John Marsh, *The Fulness of Time* (London: Nisbet, 1952), 19–22; John A. T. Robinson, *In the End God*, Religious Perspectives, ed. Ruth Nanda Anshen, vol. 20 (New York: Harper & Row, 1968), 55–67.

5. Erik Eynikel and Katrin Hauspie, "The Use of καιρός and χρόνος in the Septuagint," *Ephemerides theologicae Lovanienses* 73 (December 1997): 385.

6. Lindemann, *Aufhebung*, 94–95.

7. Lincoln, 32.

8. A. L. Burns, "Two Words for 'Time' in the New Testament," *AusBR* 3 (March/December 1953): 7–22; James Barr, *Biblical Words for Time*, 2d (rev.) ed., SBT, no. 33 (London: SCM, 1969), 21–49.

cordingly, it is better to allow their individual contexts to determine the meaning. Parallel wording to Eph 1:10 is in Gal 4:4 where Paul states that "when the fullness of time came (ὅτε δὲ ἦλθεν τὸ πλήρωμα τοῦ χρόνου), God sent for his Son." Barr thinks in cases like these two passages "which speak of the 'time' or 'times' which God has appointed or promised, the two words are most probably of like meaning."[1] However, Burns poses the question of whether the plural form in Eph 1:10 has any significance.[2] It seems that in Galatians the fullness of time speaks of a particular point of time in history when God brought forth his Son. In Ephesians the plural appears to point to the fullness or totality of the times or epochs of history. The only other time the plural of καιρός is used with a derivative of πληρόω is in Luke 21:24, and there it speaks of Gentile domination over Jerusalem ("until the times of the Gentiles are fulfilled") at which time the Messiah will come to rule on earth. Hence, the "times" are completed when Messiah rules. This is analogous to Eph 1:10, for the mystery of his will is made known according to his good pleasure which he purposed in Christ for the administration of fullness of the "times," which is that future earthly messianic kingdom. This earthly messianic kingdom had been promised in the OT (e.g., Gen 12:1–4; 2 Sam 7:14–17; Isa 2:1–4; 11:1–5; Jer 23:3–8; 31:31–37; Dan 2:35, 44–45; Hos 3:4–5; Amos 9:11–15; Zeph 3:14–20; Zech 14:16–21), discussed in the Gospels (e.g., Matt 24:29–31; 25:31–46; Luke 1:31–33; 2:25), not fulfilled at Christ's ascension (Acts 1:6–7), and hoped for by the church (e.g., Acts 3:19–21; 15:13–18; Rom 11:25–27; Rev 20:1–6). Lindemann opposes this idea for he thinks all temporal categories have ceased in Christ and one cannot make a distinction between history and eschatology.[3] Lincoln rightly criticizes him on this point by saying, "This is to ignore completely the apocalyptic background of the terminology of this verse, its context in early Christian eschatology, and the continuity between Ephesians and Paul's gospel."[4] What is going to happen in that future messianic kingdom? Paul explains this next.

ἀνακεφαλαιώσασθαι τὰ πάντα ἐν τῷ Χριστῷ, "to unite under one head all things in Christ." The verb ἀνακεφαλαιόω is defined in three ways. First, in classical literature it means "to sum up an argument" in a speech.[5] It is used in a couple of manuscripts of the LXX (Theodotian and Quinta) in Ps 72:20 [LXX 71:20] meaning "to gather together" the prayers of David. In the NT the only other place this word

1. Barr, *Biblical Words for Time*, 44.

2. Burns, "Two Words for 'Time' in the New Testament," 20.

3. Lindemann, *Aufhebung*, 95–96.

4. Lincoln, 32.

5. Dionysius Halicarnassensis *De Lysia* 9. Maclean made a study of over 400 occurrences in the *Thesaurus Linguae Graecae* and arrived at the same conclusion, viz., to summarize an argument or discussion, Maclean, "Ephesians and the Problem of Colossians," 51–58.

is used is in Rom 13:9 where the "second table" of the law is "summed up" in the command to love one's neighbor. Hence, it has the idea "to sum up"[1] or to bring all the parts into a coherent whole. Second, due to the ἀνα- prefix, some of the versions (Old Latin, Vg, Peshitta) and church fathers thought it connoted repetition or renewal.[2] Barth states that these church fathers used this as a polemic against the dualism of Marcion and the Gnostics in order to teach them that God's creation was not abolished but restored in Christ.[3] This view of repetition or renewal is not taught in Scripture and yet Irenaeus, who taught this view, uses this word in other contexts to mean "to sum up" with reference to verbal statements.[4] Third, it has the idea "to head up," thus making Christ the head. Chrysostom wanted to make very sure, by a long explanation, that it is more than summing up, for it is the summing up under Christ's headship.[5] The main contention against this sense is that it would be derived from the noun κεφαλή ("head") rather than κεφάλαιον ("main point, summary") and Barth thinks it is "an unwarranted etymological adventure."[6] In fact, Chrysostom states that the meaning of ἀνακεφαλαιώσασθαι is "union" (συνάψαι),[7] otherwise, it seems that Paul would have used "head" (κεφαλή). Furthermore, some feel that the idea of Christ's headship is not introduced until verse 22.[8]

It seems best not to accept one view exclusively but to consider elements of all three views to gain a correct perspective. First, to bring the diverse elements into union there must be someone to head it up. It certainly cannot be said that Christ is the sum of the various parts of the universe. Second, it cannot be asserted dogmatically that the idea of Christ's headship is not introduced until verse 22 since this present verse may contain the concept of headship without using the

1. Cf. *Barn.* 5.11.

2. Irenaeus *Adversus Haereses* 1.10.1 (*PG* 7:549B); Tertullian *De Monogamia* 5; Ambrosiaster *Eph* 1:10 (*PL* 17:374); Jerome *Eph* 1:10 (*PL* 26:454); Aquinas *Lec* 3; 1:10; cf. John McHugh, "A Reconsideration of Ephesians 1.10b in the Light of Irenaeus," in *Paul and Paulinism. Essays in Honour of C. K. Barrett*, ed. M. D. Hooker and S. G. Wilson (London: SPCK, 1982), 302–9; J. G. Bookless, "The Summing up of All Things in Christ," *Indian Journal of Theology* 12 (July–September 1963): 107–10; Martin, "Quelques remarques sur le texte syriaque de l'Épître aux Éphésiens," 100; Gibbs, *Creation and Redemption*, 119–20.

3. Barth, 90; Lightfoot, *Notes on Epistles of St Paul*, 322.

4. Irenaeus *Adversus Haereses* 1.9.2 (*PG* 7:541A).

5. Chrysostom *Eph* 1:10 (*PG* 62:16). Cf. Kohlgraf, *Die Ekklesiologie des Epheserbriefes in der Auslegung durch Johannes Chrysostomus*, 222, 239–53.

6. Barth, 91 n. 93; cf. MHT 2:395. Earlier Best (*One Body in Christ*, 120 n. 3, 147–48) thought it was derived from κεφαλή but more recently he is not so definitive (Best, 140). For a study of the church fathers' use of the verb, see Jean-Marc Dufort, "La récapitulation paulinienne dans l'exégèse des Pères," *ScEccl* 12 (Janvier 1960): 21–38.

7. Chrysostom *Eph* 1:10 (*PG* 62:16).

8. Alford, 3:76; Eadie, 54.

specific word "head." Third, to use Chrysostom to prove that ἀνακεφαλαιόω means only "union" is overstating the case because he goes into great detail to show that Christ is head (κεφαλή) over angels and humans and that the union effected is by the one and same head (κεφαλή).[1] Furthermore, although the noun κεφάλαιον can have the idea of "summary" or "sum" of money (Acts 22:28), it connotes more than this because it has the idea of "the main point"[2] to which others are subordinate (Heb 8:1). Hence, there is union of other points under the main point. Therefore, God's purpose in Christ is to unite all things for himself (middle voice) under one head. Consequently, the translation "to unite under one head" appears to capture the idea. Finally, although Barth[3] and Schlier[4] find the second view unacceptable because it is not taught in Ephesians, it does need serious consideration. The phrase "all things under one head" suggests an element of renewal or recapitulation.[5] Lincoln thinks that the prefix ἀνα- seems to indicate a restoration of harmony with Christ as the central focal point, similar to the reconciliation expressed in Col 1:20. Both passages presuppose that the universe had come into chaos on account of sin and that God will restore it to its original harmony in Christ.[6] Hence, all three elements need to be brought into focus, namely, that God will bring together all things and restore the whole creation under one head.[7] Although this may not be taught elsewhere in Ephesians, it is taught here and in other parts of the NT. More will be said of this restoration in the discussion of the next phrase.

The phrase "all things in Christ" (τὰ πάντα ἐν τῷ Χριστῷ) shows what and in whom the summation occurs. There is further elaboration in the words that follow. Suffice it to say, God is going to head up the union "in the Christ" (ἐν τῷ Χριστῷ). The preposition ἐν refers to the local sense that God is going to unite and head up all things in the Christ. The article preceding "Christ" occurs frequently in this epistle (twenty-three times—1:10, 12, 20; 2:5, 13; 3:1, 4, 8, 11, 17, 19; 4:7, 12, 13, 20; 5:2, 5, 14, 23, 24, 25, 29; 6:5), nearly 27 percent of all Pauline usage. This form not only particularizes the name but also the office and/or the title of "the Messiah" (cf. v. 1). Again, the point is that the

1. Chrysostom *Eph* 1:10 (*PG* 62:16).

2. Thucydides 4.50.2.

3. Barth, 91–92.

4. Heinrich Schlier, "ἀνακεφαλαιόομαι," *TDNT* 3 (1965): 682.

5. Cf. P. J. Hartin, "ἀνακεφαλαιώσασθαι τὰ πάντα ἐν τῷ Χριστῷ (Eph 1:10)," in *A South African Perspective on the New Testament Essays by South African New Testament Scholars Presented to Bruce Manning Metzger during His Visit to South Africa in 1985*, ed. J. H. Petzer and P. J. Hartin (Leiden: Brill, 1986), 230–31.

6. Lincoln, *Paradise Now and Not Yet*, 143.

7. The present writer did not see the study of this term by M. Kitchen, "The ἀνακεφαλαίωσις of All Things in Christ: Theology and Purpose in the Epistle to the Ephesians" (Ph.D. thesis, University of Manchester, 1989). However, a summary of his thinking on this term is found in his commentary (Kitchen, 36–42).

Messiah will unite and head up all things. Best accepts the common view that "in the early church 'Christ' quickly ceased to be a title and became a name" and wonders why the author of Ephesians revives the titular nature of "Christ."[1] It may well be that Paul is attempting to show that the summation of all things will occur in Israel's promised Messiah. Later in 2:11–22 Paul develops the idea that Gentiles who were alienated from the citizenship of Israel and strangers to the covenants of promise are united with believing Jews by the death of the promised Christ into a new entity, the church.

τὰ ἐπὶ[2] τοῖς οὐρανοῖς καὶ τὰ ἐπὶ τῆς γῆς ἐν αὐτῷ, "the things in heaven and the things on earth in him," further describe the immediately preceding words τὰ πάντα, "the all things." The two articles (τά) before both prepositions[3] refer back to the τὰ πάντα. Thus the "all" is defined as "those things in the heavens and those things on the earth." The two prepositions are followed first by the dative, which may denote position, and second by the genitive, which may show extension over,[4] but more likely it is just a stylistic variation (cf. Acts 27:44).[5]

What, then, do the words τὰ πάντα, "the all things," have reference to? There are several views. First, they could refer to redeemed humans who are both in heaven and on earth,[6] but this seems to be a strange way of expressing it and causes one to wonder why the neuter is used. Second, they could refer to the church[7] since this is what is expressed in verses 22–23, but here more than the church is in view. Third, some think that the things in the heavens are angels and the things on earth are (redeemed) people,[8] but this dichotomy is artificial and difficult to decipher from the context. Fourth, Caird proposes that the things on earth refer to reconciled humanity who are carrying out God's work, and the things in the heavens refer to the invisible forces such as the political, economic, social, and religious power that compete for the allegiance of humans and the control of their destiny and

1. Best, 143.

2. The reading ἐν is found in A F G K P Ψ 33 81 104 365 1175 1739 1881 2464 *pm* syr[h] and has good geographical spread but is missing some main manuscripts in the Alexandrian and Western texts. Another reading is τε ἐν in ℵ[2] 323 945 *pc* Ambrosiaster, but it is very weak. The ἐπί is supported in 𝔓[46] ℵ* B D L 6 629 630 1241 1505 *pm*, and is the preferred reading because it has not only good geographical support but it also has good manuscripts represented in each of the text-types.

3. Cf. Robertson, 766.

4. Westcott, 14.

5. Moule, *Idiom Book*, 49; MHT 3:271–72.

6. Hodge, 51.

7. Schlier, 65–66; Ernst, 277–78; Schnackenburg, 60–61; cf. also Heinrich Schlier, *Die Zeit der Kirche. Exegetische Aufsätze und Vorträge* (Freiburg: Herder, 1956), 171; Allan, "The 'In Christ' Formula in Ephesians," 58; Maclean, "Ephesians and the Problem of Colossians," 60–64.

8. Chrysostom *Eph* 1:10 (*PG* 62:16); Calvin, 129–30; Bengel, 4:68; Moule, 23; Hendriksen, 87.

must be brought within the unifying purpose of God. Caird thinks that "Paul's *heaven* is neither the eternal abode of God nor yet a Platonic realm of perfect reality of which earth is but an imperfect copy."[1] Caird's attempt to make Paul's heaven a human environment rather than a transcendent reality flies in the face of biblical evidence. The picture here is not of human victory over the invisible powers but rather of God's initiative to head up all things in heaven and on earth in Christ. And fifth, most commentators see the words "all things" as referring to God's creation, animate and inanimate, which are going to be united under Christ.[2] This view best fits the description and it is in harmony with other NT teaching. As already mentioned, in Col 1:20 Paul speaks of the reconciliation of all things.

The location of the "things" is both in heaven and on earth.[3] The plural form (τοῖς οὐρανοῖς) "heavens" most likely reflects the Hebrew שָׁמַיִם, "heaven" rather than the number of heavens, as speculated by the apocryphal apocalyptic and rabbinic sources. Hence, at least here, a two-tier universe is portrayed which, however, does not rule out the possibility of more than two levels in 4:7–10 (τὰ κατώτερα μέρη τῆς γῆς). The "things" in both realms are creations of God, which is consistent with the OT cosmology that states "in the beginning God created the heavens and the earth" (Gen 1:1; 14:19, 22; Pss 121:2; 124:8; 146:6; cf. Col 1:16). In the future the "things" in heaven (including both good and evil spiritual forces [cf. 6:12]) along with the "things" on earth will face a judgment (Isa 51:6; Hag 2:6; Heb 12:26). Ultimately, however, both the "things" in heaven and the "things" on earth will be united under Christ.

1. Caird, 39–40.

2. E.g., Alford, 3:76; Salmond, 262; Murray, 23; Barth, 91–92; Bruce, 262. Cf. also Eadie, 57; Ellicott, 15; Meyer, 51–52; Abbott, 19; Gnilka, 65; Best, 139; O'Brien, 112; Franz Mussner, *Christus, das All und die Kirche. Studien zur Theologie des Epheserbriefes*, Trierer theologische Studien, vol. 5 (Trier: Paulinus-Verlag, 1955), 64–68; Michael Neary, "The Cosmic Emphasis of Paul," *Irish Theological Quarterly* 48, nos. 1/2 (1981): 19–20; Friedrich Schröger, "Zur komischen Ekklesiologie des Epheserbriefes: Eine Reflexion über einen besseren Umgang mit der Schöpfung," in *"Deiner in Eurer Mitte". Festschrift für Dr. Antonius Hofmann Bischof von Passau zum 75. Geburtstag*, ed. Rainer Beer et al., Schriften der Universität Passau: Reihe Katholische Theologie, vol. 5 (Passau: Passavia Universitätsverlag, 1984), 118–19; Margaret Y. MacDonald, *The Pauline Churches: A Socio-historical Study of Institutionalization in the Pauline and Deutero-Pauline Writings*, SNTSMS, ed. G. N. Stanton, vol. 60 (Cambridge: Cambridge University Press, 1988), 154–55.

3. Cf. Lincoln, "A Re-Examination of 'the Heavenlies' in Ephesians," 479–80; Harris, "'The Heavenlies' Reconsidered," 75–76. For a discussion of the cosmology of the first century, see Timothy B. Cargal, "Seated in the Heavenlies: Cosmic Mediators in the Mysteries of Mithras and the Letter to the Ephesians," in *Society of Biblical Literature 1994 Seminar Papers*, ed. Eugene H. Lovering Jr., Society of Biblical Literature Seminar Papers Series, ed. Eugene H. Lovering Jr., no. 33 (Atlanta: Scholars Press, 1994), 804–21.

The prepositional phrase ἐν αὐτῷ, "in him," should be in verse 10 as most texts have it (TR[ed], NA[27], UBS[4], GNTMT, AV, ASV, NEB, NIV) and not a part of verse 11 (TR[ed], WH, RSV, NASB, JB, NJB, NRSV). Accordingly, there should be no punctuation before it and a minor punctuation after it. This prepositional phrase serves in two ways: first, it reasserts that God is going to unite all things in Christ, and second, it serves as a transition to the next verse.

When will Christ head up all things? It seems best to see this in two stages. The initial stage refers to the present time, which is based on Christ's work on the cross (1:7; 2:16) and his exaltation (1:20–21; 2:6–7) whereby all things are subjected to Christ and God has given him to the church as head over everything, including the church (1:22). The spiritual powers which had control over human beings were broken by Christ's death and resurrection (2:1–6). Believers can be victorious through God's power, the same power which resurrected Christ (1:19–20). Even in the midst of battle believers are given the ability to stand against the spiritual foes (6:10–20). However, the present verse seems to speak not only of the initial stage of the present age, but more particularly to a final stage. This is in keeping with Christ's exaltation over all power not only in this age but in the age to come (1:20–21). This ultimate stage speaks of the time yet future when God is going to unite all of creation under Christ's headship in the fullness of time, the eschatological age of Messiah's rule to which all creation looks foward. It is, therefore, not referring primarily to the present age, for the devil and his hosts are still active in opposing God (Eph 2:2; 6:11–13; cf. 1 Pet 5:8) and are not yet completely united under Christ's headship.[1] To be sure, the defeat of the devil's power was accomplished at the cross, but a greater event is in store for all believers. As mentioned above, the earthly messianic age was promised in the OT, discussed in the Gospels, not totally fulfilled at the ascension, and hoped for by the church. However, it is not only the church that has this hope, but all of creation. Romans 8:19–23 states that the whole of creation is groaning and waiting for the day of release from curse. This will not occur before the second coming of Christ.[2] In 1 Cor

1. *Contra* Lindemann, *Aufhebung*, 95–99; Roels, *God's Mission*, 274–94; Sterling Rayburn, "Cosmic Transfiguration," *CQR* 168 (April–June 1967): 162–68; Hartin, "ἀνακεφαλαιώσασθαι τὰ πάντα ἐν τῷ Χριστῷ (Eph 1:10)," 234; Klaus Wegenast, *Das Verständnis der Tradition bei Paulus und in den Deuteropaulinen*, Wissenschaftliche Monographien zum Alten und Neuen Testament, ed. Günther Bornkamm and Gerhard von Rad, vol. 8 (Neukirchen: Neukirchener Verlag, 1962), 131; Gnilka, 81; Lona, *Die Eschatologie im Kolosser- und Epheserbrief*, 272–77. On the other hand, see Caragounis, *Ephesian* Mysterion, 144; Lincoln, *Paradise Now and Not Yet*, 167–68; Lemmer, "A Multifarious Understanding of Eschatology in Ephesians," 115–16; Moritz, "'Summing-up all Things'," 96–99.

2. Cf. Franz Mussner, "Geschichtstheologie des Epheserbriefes," in *Studiorum Paulinorum Congressus Internationalis Catholicus 1961*, vol. 2, AnBib, vol. 18 (Rome: E Pontificio Instituto Biblico, 1963), 59–63.

15:24–28 Paul outlines that Christ is going to destroy the existing powers and put all things in subjection to himself and then hand them over to the Father. In Rev 19–21, John describes Christ's victory over the earthly rulers, the binding of Satan, and his rule for a 1000 years. All this is a depiction of the subjection by Christ of all things in heaven and on the earth. It is that time that is called "the fullness of the times" for which all of creation, animate and inanimate, has longed for throughout history. The millennium and the eternal state are the times when chaos will be removed and universal peace will be established under the leadership of Christ (Isa 2:2–4; 11:1–10). Therefore, the fullness of time refers to the future unification of all things under the headship of Christ. It does not primarily refer to the present church age but the future messianic age. That will be the time of restoration and harmony under one head.

In summary, believers have experienced the abundance of God's grace in the redemption of Christ and in the provision of all insight and wisdom. This wisdom and insight have made known to them the secret plan of God, namely, that at the fullness of time God will unite in his dear Son Christ all the things in heaven and on earth. So Christ is the provision of redemption and the one in whom God unites all things in heaven and on earth.

(3) Inheritance: Possession of God (1:11)

Text: 1:11. ἐν ᾧ καὶ ἐκληρώθημεν προορισθέντες κατὰ πρόθεσιν τοῦ τὰ πάντα ἐνεργοῦντος κατὰ τὴν βουλὴν τοῦ θελήματος αὐτοῦ

Translation: 1:11. "in whom also we were made a heritage having been predestined according to the purpose of the one who is working all things according to the counsel of his will"

Commentary: 1:11. ἐν ᾧ καὶ ἐκληρώθημεν, "in whom also we were made a heritage." The preposition with the relative pronoun (ἐν ᾧ) relates this verse back to Christ mentioned in verse 10. The conjunction καί is most likely adjunctive ("also"), which enhances this next section. It has been suggested that Paul is making a contrast between "we," Jewish Christians, and "you," Gentile Christians in verse 13.[1] If this were the case, one would think that Paul would have used the pronoun ἡμεῖς, "we," to emphasize that.[2] This inheritance is true for both Jewish and Gentile Christians. The καί is not qualifying an unexpressed pronoun but, rather, the action of the verb (ἐκληρώθημεν), thus expressing the believers' acquisition of that which God had purposed in Christ in verse 9.[3] The subject of the entire doxology is God, but the emphasis has changed from what God has done, expressed in the active voice, to

1. Barth, 92; D. W. B. Robinson, "Who Were 'the Saints'?" *RTR* 22 (June 1963): 51–52; O'Brien, 115; *contra* Best, 144–45.

2. Meyer, 56; cf. Cambier, "La bénédiction d'Eph 1:3–14," 91–92.

3. Ellicott, 15; Meyer, 56.

what the believers receive from God, expressed in the passive voice. One must remember that the focal point is Christ, for it is in him that God accomplishes his purposes and the believers receive those benefits. This context demonstrates that God not only purposed to unite all things in the one head, Christ, in the future "fullness of the time," but that the believers of this present age would "also" be God's inheritance.

The verb ἐκληρώθημεν[1] is an aorist passive from κληρόω, which occurs only here in the NT. In classical literature it had two basic senses: (1) "to appoint by lot,"[2] "to cast lots,"[3] or the middle usage, "to obtain by lot";[4] and (2) "to allot, assign, appoint, apportion."[5] It appears only three times in the LXX (1 Sam 14:41; Isa 17:11*bis*) and the only clear use is in 1 Sam 14:41 where it is used in conjunction with the same verb compounded (in 14:42*bis*, 47). Both of these are translated from לָכַד meaning "to take by lot" or "to acquire."[6] Because of the various ways this word can be rendered in the classical literature and because this is the only occurrence in the NT, the exact nuance for this context is difficult. There are four views.[7] (1) The passive acts as a middle and hence has the idea "to obtain a lot"[8] and is translated "we have obtained an inheritance" (AV, NASB, NRSV).[9] However, this is inconsistent with the use of the passives in this passage.[10] (2) It is a simple passive with the idea that God chose as though it were by lot and is translated "we were obtained by lot" (Vg, Peshitta, RSV). Chrysostom, a defender of this view, attempts to show that Paul did not think God chose by chance, for in the very next clause Paul explains that it was God's predestination, which was according to the purpose of his will that was involved in that choice and that is parallel to his election in verse 4. Chrysostom uses Rom 8:28, 30 to support his point.[11] The problem with this view is that it bankrupts the meaning of the verb used here since it would have the same meaning as "to choose" in verse 4 and "to call" in Rom 8:28, 30. The verb should retain some idea of a "lot" or "portion" (κλῆρος) because the point does not deal with the acquisition of the portion but the portion itself.[12] Although this view defends

1. This is replaced by ἐκλήθημεν ("we were called") in A D F (*) G but it is apparently a gloss of the preferred reading of ἐκληρώθημεν, which is found in א B P 𝔐 vg.

2. Isocrates 7.22; Aristotle *Politica* 4.7.3 §1294b.8.

3. Euripides *Ion* 416.

4. Euripides *Troades* 29; also in the middle it can mean "to cast lots" (see Lysias 6.4).

5. Thucydides 6.42.1; in the passive Euripides *Hecuba* 100.

6. Cf. BDB 539–40; H. Gross, "לָכַד *lāḵaḏ*," *TDOT* 8 (1997): 1–4; Werner Foerster, "κληρόω," *TDNT* 3 (1965): 764. The term is used unclearly twice in Isa 17:11.

7. For a discussion of the views, see the various commentators, esp. Alford, 3:77–78; Eadie, 58–59; Ellicott, 15–16; Abbott, 19–20; Salmond, 263–64; Barth, 92–94, 118.

8. Cf. Euripides *Troades* 29.

9. Hodge, 55–56; Cremer, *Biblico-Theological Lexicon*, 358–59; Gaugler, 50–51.

10. Ellicott, 15.

11. Chrysostom *Eph* 1:11 (*PG* 62:17); cf. also Aquinas *Lec*. 5; 1:11.

12. Eadie, 58.

the freedom of God's choice, it puts the emphasis in the wrong place inasmuch as it attributes God's choice to chance rather than to his gracious will.[1] (3) It is a passive with the sense that the believer receives a portion or a share of what God has and could be translated "we were made partakers of the inheritance" or "we were assigned/appointed a portion/inheritance" (NEB, JB, NJB).[2] The strength of this view is that it fits well in the present context with both where the believers receive redemption, the forgiveness of sins (v. 7), and where believers receive the seal of the Spirit as the earnest of their inheritance (vv. 13–14). This also coincides with the parallel passage in Col 1:12 where the believers share in the inheritance of the saints (or possibly angels). (4) It is a passive with the idea that the believer is viewed as God's inheritance and could be translated "we were made a heritage (of God)" (RV, ASV).[3] The strength of this view is that it has OT precedent where Israel is called God's possession (Deut 4:20; 7:6; 14:2) or heritage (Deut 9:26, 29; 32:9; cf. 1QS 2:2).

Views (3) and (4) are preferred over the first two views. View (3) refers to the believers' possession and view (4) to God's possession. It is difficult to choose between these last two views but view (4) is preferred for the following reasons. First, it is more consistent with its usage because "to be assigned a thing," as in view (3), seems legitimate only when "the accusative of the object assigned is expressed."[4] Second, view (4) fits well with the participle (προορισθέντες) immediately following, for it makes more sense that the believer was predestined as God's possession rather than that the believer was predestined as his own possession. Third, view (4) makes much better sense with the grammatical structure of εἰς followed by the infinitival construction in verse 12 (εἰς τὸ εἶναι ἡμᾶς κτλ.). View (3) would read "we were made partakers of an inheritance . . . in order that we might praise him," whereas view (4) would read "we are God's possession . . . in order that we might praise him." This coincides with Israel as God's possession for she too was to praise him. Fourth, for this term to refer to the believers' possession of redemption, the forgiveness of sins, and the sealing of the Spirit is redundant. Rather, it is because of these benefits that the believers are God's possession. This takes it a step further. Not only do believers possess these benefits, but moreover, God possesses the believers because of all he has done for them.

In conclusion, then, it seems best to take it as passive and see it as referring to the believers assigned as God's inheritance or heritage.

1. Meyer, 56–57.

2. Calvin, 127, 130; Eadie, 59; Meyer, 56; Abbott, 20; Hendriksen, 87–88; Schnackenburg, 62.

3. Bengel, 4:68; Alford, 3:77; Ellicott, 15–16; Salmond, 263–64; Robinson, 146; Barth, 93–94, 118; Bruce, 263.

4. Robinson, 146.

προορισθέντες κατὰ πρόθεσιν[1] τοῦ τὰ πάντα ἐνεργοῦντος, "having been predestined according to the purpose of the one who is working all things." As in verse 5 the participle προορισθέντες has the same meaning "to determine beforehand, mark out beforehand, predestine," and it also functions in the same way in connection with the finite verb, namely, causally. Since it follows the verb, the action of the participle is most likely contemporaneous with the finite verb.[2] The only difference here is that the participle is in the passive rather than the active, as in verse 5. This is understandable since in verse 5 God is the subject and the main verb is active (deponent) with an active participle modifying it. In the present verse the passive finite verb shows that believers are the recipients of the action and the participle coincides with it. Therefore, the reason we become God's heritage is because our destiny as his inheritance was predetermined beforehand by him. Again, as noted in verse 5, the verb "to predestine" is more interested in the "what" than the "who." In this context the destiny is God's heritage and because of this, we were assigned to be God's heritage.

The preposition κατά with the accusative shows the standard by which the predestination was done: it was done according to the standard of the purpose of the one who is working all things. The noun πρόθεσις is used in two ways in classical literature: (1) something that is public or open before the public, such as a body lying in state[3] or a public notice;[4] and (2) plan or purpose.[5] In the LXX it occurs eighteen times (eleven times in the canonical books) and is used in the same two ways, for it is used of the showbread that was laid out before God (e.g., Exod 40:4, 23; 1 Chr 9:32; 23:29; 28:16; 1 Macc 1:22; 2 Macc 10:3) and used of purpose (2 Macc 3:8; 3 Macc 1:22; 2:26; 5:12, 29). Again in the NT this noun is used in the same two ways. It occurs twelve times: four times it refers to the table of showbread (Matt 12:4 = Mark 2:26 = Luke 6:4; Heb 9:2) and the other eight times it refers to purpose; three times to human purpose or resolve (Acts 11:23; 27:13; 2 Tim 3:10) and five times to God's purpose (Rom 8:28; 9:11; Eph 1:11; 3:11; 2 Tim 1:9). It conveys the idea that God who purposes is faithful to carry it out.[6] Hence, in this context the idea of "purpose" fits well since it has been expressed already in the verb form in verse 9 where God made known the mystery of his will according to the good pleasure of his will which he "purposed" or "resolved" in Christ. In the im-

1. The manuscripts which insert τοῦ θεοῦ either before or after πρόθεσιν are D F G 81 104 365 1175 *pc* it[a] vg[mss] cop[sa, boms] Ambrosiaster. This is not an acceptable reading because it is primarily out of one text-type.

2. Porter, *Verbal Aspect*, 384.

3. Plato *Leges* 12 §§947b; 959a, e; Demosthenes *Orationes* 43.64.

4. Aristotle *Politica* 6.5.6 §1322a.10.

5. Demosthenes *Orationes* 18.167; Aristotle *Analytica Priora* 1.32 §47a.5; Polybius 5.35.2.

6. Christian Maurer, "προτίθημι, πρόθεσις," *TDNT* 8 (1972): 166.

mediate context it has the idea that the predestined inheritance as God's possession was according to the purpose, resolve, or decision of the one who is working all things.

The genitives τοῦ τὰ πάντα ἐνεργοῦντος that follow πρόθεσιν are possessive inasmuch as this purpose belongs to the one who works all things. The participle ἐνεργοῦντος is from ἐνεργέω, which is derived from the adjective ἐνεργός from which we get our English word "energy."[1] The verb occurs only seven times in the LXX (four times in the canonical books: Num 8:24; Prov 21:6; 31:12; Isa 41:4) and has the idea of performing or working. In the NT it is used twenty-one times, all of them by Paul except three (Matt 14:2 = Mark 6:14; Jas 5:16). Predominantly, it refers to the working of God's will in the life of believers. This may include the concept of infusion with supernatural power.[2] It occurs four times in Ephesians (1:11, 20; 2:2; 3:20) and refers to God's power with the exception of 2:2 where it speaks of the devil's power which is now working in unbelievers. In the present context τοῦ τὰ πάντα ἐνεργοῦντος is active and transitive with the accusative of the thing referring to God as he takes an active part in all things. The present tense refers to God's continual activity toward the purpose that he resolved in eternity past. The "all things" (τὰ πάντα) refers to all of God's providence and must not be restricted to God's redemptive plan. This coincides with verse 10 where "all things" are described as "those things in heaven and those things on earth." How God accomplishes this will now be discussed.

κατὰ τὴν βουλὴν τοῦ θελήματος αὐτοῦ, "according to the counsel of his will." Again κατά with the accusative refers to standard. Therefore, God who works all things always does it according to the standard of the counsel of his will. The definition and relationship of βουλή and θέλημα have long been debated. This is the fourth time θέλημα is used in this chapter (vv. 1, 5, 9, 11). Verse 1 includes a more detailed study of the word. In that study it is concluded that it has the idea of "desire, will, resolve."

The noun βουλή in classical literature conveyed the meaning of "will" or "determination,"[3] "counsel" or "advice,"[4] and "deliberation."[5] It is used also for a council or senate.[6] This latter idea makes sense because it is in a council or senate where deliberation takes place. Of the 172 occurrences in the LXX, it appears 125 times in the canonical books and

1. For further study, see Robinson, 241–47; Georg Bertram, "ἐνεργέω, κτλ.," *TDNT* 2 (1964): 652–54.

2. Cf. Kenneth W. Clark, "The Meaning of ἐνεργέω and καταργέω in the New Testament," *JBL* 54 (June 1935): 97–98.

3. Homer *Ilias* 1.5.

4. Ibid., 1.258; 24.652.

5. Aristotle *Ethica Nicomachea* 3.3.1 §1112a.19; Demosthenes *Orationes* 9.46.

6. Senate at Athens—Herodotus 9.5; at Argos—7.149; Roman Senate—Dionysius Halicarnassensis 6.69.1.

it is translated seventy-seven times from the Hebrew עֵצָה meaning "counsel, advice."[1] Schrenk has summarized the OT into four categories: (1) the first stage of inward deliberation (Deut 32:28; Prov 2:11; 8:12; 11:14); (2) the final result of inward deliberation for the purpose of advice or counsel (Gen 49:6; 2 Sam 15:31; 1 Kgs 12:8); (3) the gathering of people to serve on a council in order to deliberate and make a resolution (1 Chr 12:19); and (4) divine counsel (Pss 33:11 [LXX 32:11]; 73:24 [LXX 72:24]; Prov 19:21; Isa 5:19; 14:26; Jer 49:20 [LXX 30:14]).[2] Hence, the idea of deliberation is always evident, whether it involves an individual decision or the input of a group of people who discuss an idea for the purpose of counsel or advice. In the NT it is used twelve times: six times it refers to the counsels of human beings (Luke 23:51; Acts 4:28; 5:38; 27:12, 42; 1 Cor 4:5) and the other six times to the counsels of God (Luke 7:30; Acts 2:23; 13:36; 20:27; Eph 1:11; Heb 6:17). In these instances various meanings are conveyed: inward deliberation (1 Cor 4:5), the result of deliberation (Luke 23:51; Acts 4:28), gathering of people to reach agreement (Acts 27:12, 42), and divine counsel or plan (Luke 7:30; Acts 2:23; 20:27; Heb 6:17). Hebrews 6:17 defines the character of God's counsel as being unchangeable. In conclusion, the term gives a sense of deliberation: therefore, decisions and plans are not based on a whim but on careful thought and interaction.

In conclusion, βουλή describes the intelligent deliberation of God and θέλημα expresses the will of God which proceeds from the deliberation. Therefore, the genitive θελήματος is objective, followed by the possessive genitive αὐτοῦ. Thus, God's will comes from the deliberation. The sovereign work of God is very evident. We were allotted an inheritance as God's possession because he predestined it according to the purpose (πρόθεσις) of the one who works all things according to the deliberation or counsel (βουλή) that issues forth his will (θέλημα). The idea that God acts capriciously is completely foreign to the context. His will is carefully thought out.

Therefore, we are God's heritage because it was predestined for us and this is according to the purpose of God who continually works out his purpose in his entire providence according to his will after deliberation.

(4) Goal: Praise of His Glory (1:12)

Text: 1:12. εἰς τὸ εἶναι ἡμᾶς εἰς ἔπαινον δόξης αὐτοῦ τοὺς προηλπικότας ἐν τῷ Χριστῷ·

Translation: 1:12. "in order that we, the ones who already hoped in Christ, might be to the praise of his glory;"

Commentary: 1:12. As verse 6 marked the end of the first strophe of this eulogy, this verse marks the end of the second strophe which re-

1. BDB 420; L. Ruppert, "עֵצָה *ʿēṣâ*," *TDOT* 6 (1990): 163–85.

2. Gottlob Schrenk, "βούλομαι, βουλή, βούλημα," *TDNT* 1 (1964): 633–34; cf. also Hermann Müller, "Will, Purpose [βούλουμαι, θέλω]," *NIDNTT* 3 (1978): 1016.

volved around the second person of the Trinity, Christ. The second strophe considered God's gracious act of redemption in his Son, made known the mystery of his will to head up all things in Christ, and revealed the heritage he has in the saints which he had predestined according to his will. Paul is now going to show that the goal of this is for the praise of God's glory.

εἰς τὸ εἶναι ἡμᾶς εἰς ἔπαινον δόξης αὐτοῦ, "in order that we might be to the praise of his glory." εἰς τό with the infinitive can express purpose or result[1] and in this context it expresses purpose.[2] It expresses the purpose, not of the participle προορισθέντες, but of the finite verb ἐκληρώθημεν, "we were made a heritage," in verse 11. Therefore, we were made a heritage in order that we might be to the praise of his glory. The "praise of his glory" is praise given for the reflection of God's essential being as already discussed in more detail at verse 6.[3]

τοὺς προηλπικότας ἐν τῷ Χριστῷ, "the ones who already hoped in Christ." These words present the major problem of this verse. The perfect participle comes from προελπίζω, a rare word in classical literature meaning "to hope for before,"[4] never in the LXX, and only here in the NT. The articular participle is in apposition to the pronoun "we" (ἡμᾶς).[5]

The main problem is not the meaning of the word but to whom it refers. There are two main views and within each view there are two options. (1) Some scholars think the "we" in the previous phrase refers to Jews and the "you" in verse 13 refers to Gentile Christians. The two options within this view are as follows. Some hold that this refers to Jews before Christ who had their hope in the Messiah.[6] Others think it refers to Jewish Christians who heard before Gentile Christians.[7] It is felt by those who hold this view (regardless of which option) that the shift between "we" and "you" is more than a reference to

1. BDF §402 (2); MHT 3:143.

2. Burton, *Moods and Tenses* §409; Robertson, *Grammar*, 991, 1071.

3. Cf. also François Dreyfus, "Pour la louange de sa glorie (*Ep 1,12.14*). L'origine vétéro-testamentaire de la formule," in *Paul de Tarse, apôtre de notre temps, ed. Lorenzo De Lorenzi*, Série monographique de «Benedictina» Section paulinienne, vol. 1 (Rome: Abbaye de S. Paul h.l.m., 1979), 233–48.

4. Posidippus 27.8 in *Comicorum Atticorum Fragmenta*, ed. Theodor Kock, vol. 3 (Leipzig: B. G. Teubner, 1888), 344.

5. Cf. Robertson, 778.

6. Ambrosiaster *Eph* 1:11–12 (*PL* 17:374–75); Hodge, 59; Alford, 3:78; Meyer, 57–59; Salmond, 265; Vosté, 110–11; Schlier, 68; Rienecker, 66–67; Barth, 130–33; Mußner, 49–50.

7. Bengel, 4:68–69; Eadie, 62; Ellicott, 16–17; Abbott, 21; Robinson, 34–35; Westcott, 15; Thompson, 37; Ernst, 279; Caird, 40–41; Mitton, 57; Bruce, 264; O'Brien, 116–17; cf. Augustyn Jankowski, "L'espérance messianique d'Israël selon la pensée paulinienne, en partant de *Proelpizein* (Ep 1,12)," in *De la Tôrah au Messie. Études d'exégèse et d'herméneutique bibliques offertes à Henri Cazelles pour ses 25 anées d'enseignement à l'Institut Catholique de Paris (Octobre 1979)*, ed. Maurice Carrez, Joseph Doré, and Pierre Grelot

the addressee and sender. In the next chapter Paul talks about the difference between the Jews and Gentiles and so this is in keeping with the distinction between the Jews and Gentiles. (2) Other scholars regard the "we" as Paul and those with him and the "you" as the Ephesian believers. The two options within this view are the following. Some think that the "we" could refer to Paul and his fellow workers who speak in a pontifical manner to the church much as in 2 Cor 1:4–24 or, at least, some kind of distinction between the apostles and readers.[1] Others think that the interchange of "we" and "you" has no significance but is normal epistolary style.[2]

Interpretation (2) is the most plausible. Furthermore, the two options within this interpretation are not really that distinct and can be considered together. It is an apostle with his fellow workers who write to the church at Ephesus and they express common interests and experiences, not a reprimand. Interpretation (1) is untenable for the following reasons. First, up to verse 12 the "we" in the eulogy stands for all Christians who are in Christ and there is no indication in verse 12 that the "we" refers particularly to the Jews.[3] Although distinctions are drawn later in the epistle, there is no indication of that here. Second, the personal pronoun "we" (ἡμᾶς) of verse 12 refers to the same people as the ἡμᾶς in verses 5 and 8. Consequently, it cannot be limited to Jewish Christians or, for that matter, Jews before Christ.[4] Third, "our inheritance" in verse 14 is not just for Jewish Christians but for all.[5] It would be strange for verse 12 to refer to Jewish Christians, verse 13 to Gentile Christians, and verse 14 back to Jewish Christians. A similar use of terms exists in Col 1:9–14 in somewhat the

(Paris: Descleé, 1981), 475–78; MacDonald, *The Pauline Churches*, 94; Thomson, *Chiasmus in the Pauline Letters*, 77–79; Maclean, "Ephesians and the Problem of Colossians," 19–21.

1. Trinidad, "The Mystery Hidden in God. A Study of Eph. 1,3–14," 21–23; cf. R. A. Wilson, "'We' and 'You' in the Epistle to the Ephesians," in *SE II. Papers Presented to the Second International Congress on New Testament Studies held at Christ Church Oxford, 1961*, ed. F. L. Cross, TU, ed. Friedrich Zucher et al., vol. 87 (Berlin: Akademie-Verlag, 1964), 676–80; Donald Jayne, "'We' and 'You' in Ephesians 1,3–14," *ExpTim* 85 (February 1974): 151–52.

2. Theophylact *Eph* 1:12 (*PG* 124:1041); Ewald, 85–86; Moule, 52; Lenski, 380; Dibelius-Greeven, 61–62; Masson, 146 n. 3; Conzelmann, 92; Gaugler, 52; Hendriksen, 87–88; Gnilka, 83–84; Schnackenburg, 63–64; Best, 147; Erich Mauerhofer, "Der Brief an die Epheser. 8. Teil: 1,12–13," *Fundamentum* 3 (1991): 22–24; Lincoln, 37–38, 88; cf. also Percy, *Probleme*, 266–67 n. 16; Dahl, "Adresse und Proömium des Epheserbriefes," 259–60; updated in idem, *Studies in Ephesians*, 323–24; Werner Bieder, "Das Geheimnis des Christus nach dem Epheserbrief," *TZ* 11 (September/Oktober 1955): 334; Roels, *God's Mission*, 52–56; Cambier, "La bénédiction d'Eph 1:3–14," 92–95; Lindemann, *Aufhebung*, 100–101.

3. Dahl, "Adresse und Proömium des Epheserbriefes," 259–60; updated in idem, *Studies in Ephesians*, 323–24.

4. Cf. Percy, *Probleme*, 267 n. 16.

5. Lindemann, *Aufhebung*, 101 n. 82.

same context and similarily cannot be thought of as a distinction between Jewish and Gentile Christians. Fourth, the "hope" mentioned in verse 12 is no different than the hope which Gentile Christians have in the parallel passage of Col 1:5. Also, 1 Cor 15:19 mentions that the Gentiles have hope "in Christ," indicating that it is not limited to the Jewish hope in Messiah. Fifth, Paul really does not take up the discussion of the Jews and Gentiles "until 2:11 and even then in 2:11–3:21 'we' is used of all believers, Jews and Gentiles, not just Jewish Christians."[1] Hence, it is best to accept that Paul is not making a distinction between Jews and Christians. Rather, he is talking about the common hope of all believers.

In light of this, the prepositional prefix προ- in προηλπικότας refers not to the Jews who had hoped in the Messiah before his coming or to Jewish Christians who had their hope in Christ before the Gentile Christians but it refers to the hope of all Christians. There are three possible interpretations. First, it conveys that all believers have hope before Christ appears to head up all things. The problem with this is that it would give the prefix προ- no meaning, for all hope looks forward to the desired event. Second, it refers to the hope that "already" exists before the apostle even writes. The perfect tense would emphasize the completed action with continuing results and thus it is the hope in Christ that the believers previously had but continue to have in the present. In the parallel passage of Col 1:5 Paul refers to the hope that was brought about by the gospel that they had already heard (προηκούσατε).[2] Third, a simpler explanation could be that it refers to all believers reading this epistle because of their knowledge and experience of God's redemption, revelation of his mystery, and the hope for the consummation of the times in Christ discussed in verses 7–11. In other words "we believers who already have hope because of the work of God in Christ (vv. 7–11) bring praise to his glory." This is similar to 3:3 where Paul elaborates on the mystery of which he had already written (προέγραψα) in the immediately preceding context of 2:11–22. More particularly since this infinitival clause goes back to ἐκληρώθημεν in verse 11, it indicates that the believers' position as God's inheritance gave them hope and further, reference is made in verse 12 to that hope as having already existed. Although either the second or the third interpretation is acceptable in this context, the third is preferred.

The prepositional phrase ἐν τῷ Χριστῷ, "in Christ," following a verb does present a problem. It is rare to have the construction of an ἐν following a verb.[3] However, there is the example of this in Mark 1:15

1. Lincoln, 38.

2. Cambier ("La bénédiction d'Eph 1:3–14," 94–95) suggests that the πρό- is tautological to emphasize that when they heard the message, they had "hope-confidence" or confident hope. However, "hope" without the prefix really has this nuance.

3. Cf. Moule, *Idiom Book*, 81, 205.

translated "believe in the gospel" (πιστεύετε ἐν τῷ εὐαγγελίῳ).[1] More pointedly, there are examples of "hope" followed by ἐν in 2 Kgs 18:5; Hos 10:13; Phil 2:19; 1 Cor 15:19. In this passage ἐν τῷ Χριστῷ is used in the local sense, that is, the believers' hope is in the Christ, the promised Messiah in whom the righteous from the beginning of time have had their hope. In 1 Cor 15:19 the verb "hope" is followed by ἐν Χριστῷ, which again shows where believers place their hope.

In conclusion, then, the believers are God's heritage (v. 11) in order that they, who already have their hope in Christ, might be to the praise of his glory.

c. God's Seal with the Spirit (1:13–14)

The Father's plan to adopt people into his family was accomplished through Jesus Christ and made a reality in them by the ministry of the Holy Spirit. Having stated the Father's plan and the Son's provision for that plan, Paul now discusses the Holy Spirit's ministry to make it a reality in those who believe. As good as the plan and provision may be, it is useless unless it can be appropriated by individuals by means of the Holy Spirit. In this discussion of the work of the Holy Spirit, Paul shows the Spirit's activity of sealing, the duration of the sealing, and finally, offers praise to God for his work.

(1) Activity: Sealed with the Spirit (1:13)

Text: 1:13. ἐν ᾧ καὶ ὑμεῖς ἀκούσαντες τὸν λόγον τῆς ἀληθείας, τὸ εὐαγγέλιον τῆς σωτηρίας ὑμῶν, ἐν ᾧ καὶ πιστεύσαντες ἐσφραγίσθητε τῷ πνεύματι τῆς ἐπαγγελίας τῷ ἁγίῳ,

Translation: 1:13. "in whom you also having heard the word of truth, the gospel of your salvation, in whom having also believed, you were sealed with the Holy Spirit of promise,"

Commentary: 1:13. ἐν ᾧ καὶ ὑμεῖς,[2] "in whom you also," can be understood in four different ways. (1) One needs to supply an elliptical verb "to be" (ἐστέ) rendering it "you are also in him" as we are (NIV).[3] However, it seems odd that Paul did not include it here since he does have the infinitival form in the previous verse. (2) It refers back to the participle, προηλπικότας, "the ones who already hoped in Christ" in verse 12. In this case, one needs to supply ἠλπίκατε (or προηλπίκατε if in verse 12 it refers to Christ's second advent) to give a modified sense

1. Possibly also in John 3:15, depending on a textually debatable reading.

2. The variant ἡμεῖς is supported by א[2] AK L Ψ 326 629 630 1241 2464 *al* whereas the reading in the text is supported by 𝔓[46] א*,c B D F G 33 1739 1881 𝔐 lat syr cop Irenaeus[lat] which is preferred for it has good manuscript representation and good geographical distribution.

3. Alford, 3:78–79; Meyer, 60; Westcott, 16; Hendriksen, 89–90; Barth, 94–95; Bruce, 294.

of the word so that it has the meaning "you also trusted in Christ" as we did (AV, JB, NJB).[1] The problem with this interpretation is that a different word is needed and a different meaning given to the newly adopted word. (3) It refers back to ἐκληρώθημεν in verse 11 and would mean "in whom you were also made God's heirs (κλῆρος) or possession."[2] The problem with this view is that the antecedent is so far removed. Normally, these three views are taken by those who think the distinction is between Jewish and Gentile Christians, but that idea is not necessary to the views. (4) It connects with the central theme of being "in Christ" and relates it to the main verb of the present verse (ἐσφραγίσθητε) so that "you also were sealed in him" (RV, ASV, RSV, NASB, NRSV),[3] indicating location. This view does the best justice to the second relative prepositional phrase (ἐν ᾧ καί) since it would be considered resumptive. Conversely, the other views have to view it in reference to something different as the word (λόγον) or the gospel (εὐαγγέλιον), and this is inconsistent with its use throughout the eulogy that uniformly refers to Christ. Nevertheless, one problem with this view is that Paul consistently places the modifiers after the main verb.[4] However, here a relative propositional phrase relates it back to the prepositional phrase "in Christ" in verse 12 which, in turn, follows the verbal form. This is consistent with its use in verse 11 where the ἐν ᾧ καί refers back to ἐν αὐτῷ of verse 10. Also, in this verse Paul wants to show two things that occur at the time one is sealed (ἐν ᾧ καὶ . . . ἐν ᾧ καί) and this is the best way to do it. Thus, Paul is showing that "in him/whom" refers back to Christ, who is central in the eulogy, and the pronoun (ὑμεῖς) is the nominative of the main verb (ἐσφραγίσθητε) in the verse.

There is a change in the personal pronoun from ἡμᾶς in verse 12 to ὑμεῖς in verse 13. As mentioned in verse 12 it is improbable that this is a change from "we" Jews (ἡμᾶς) to "you" Gentiles (ὑμεῖς) for it seems highly unlikely that Paul is talking about "we" Jews in verse 12, "you" Gentiles in verse 13, then back to "we" Jews in verse 14. It is simply a distinction between those who are with Paul as opposed to the believers at Ephesus.

ἀκούσαντες τὸν λόγον τῆς ἀληθείας, τὸ εὐαγγέλιον τῆς σωτηρίας ὑμῶν,[5] "having heard the word of truth, the gospel of your salvation." The relation of the aorist participle (ἀκούσαντες) to the main verb (ἐσφραγίσθητε) will be discussed below in connection with "believing"

1. Calvin, 130; Hodge, 61.
2. Olshausen, 145–46; Harless, 66.
3. Eadie, 63; Ellicott, 17–18; Abbott, 22; Salmond, 266–67; Robinson, 146; Schlier, 53; Best, 148; Adai, *Der Heilige Geist als Gegenwart Gottes*, 62–63.
4. See discussion of this in v. 4 in connection with ἐν ἀγάπῃ.
5. The variant ἡμῶν found in K Ψ 323 630 945 1505 2464 *al* has a rather limited support of manuscripts whereas the reading in the text has the overwhelming support of manuscripts with wide geographical distribution.

(πιστεύσαντες). The word for truth (ἀλήθεια) already has been discussed thoroughly.[1] It occurs frequently in classical literature and its basic idea is that which is in contrast to a lie[2] or that which is reality or actual as opposed to that which is false.[3] In the LXX it occurs 197 times and in the canonical books it appears 129 times and is translated from seven different Hebrew words; and of these, about ninety times it is from אֱמֶת, which according to Jepsen essentially conveys the idea of "reliability." When speaking of God, it referes to one who is faithful and thus "in whose word and work one can place complete confidence."[4] In the NT it is used 109 times, forty-seven times by Paul, six of which are in Ephesians (1:13; 4:21, 24, 25; 5:9; 6:14). It is used in contrast to a lie (Rom 1:25; 2 Cor 7:14) or falsehood (Eph 4:25). It can also indicate reality (Eph 4:21) or demonstrate the idea of uprightness or righteousness (Eph 4:24; 5:9). However, it is also used "of the content of Christianity as the absolute truth" and this is how it is used in the present context and in 6:14.[5] Hence, it has the idea of reality in contrast to the falsehood of other religions.

In this context the genitive could be: (1) attributive "true word, the gospel"; (2) objective and thus "the word about or concerning the truth"; (3) a genitive of apposition, that is, "the word which is truth"; or (4) a genitive of content "the word of which the truth is the very substance and essence."[6] This means that the word or message is one of truth. The last option is preferred. The following words (τὸ εὐαγγέλιον τῆς σωτηρίας ὑμῶν) only explain further: it is the gospel of their salvation. The term "gospel" is used seventy-six times in the NT, sixty times by Paul, and four times in Ephesians (1:13; 3:6; 6:15, 19). Originally it connoted a "reward for good news" but later it referred to the message itself, namely, "good news,"[7] and the genitive following it

1. Cf. Gottfried Quell, Gerhard Kittel, and Rudolf Bultmann, "ἀλήθεια, κτλ.," *TDNT* 1 (1964): 232–51; Anthony C. Thiselton, "Truth [ἀλήθεια]," *NIDNTT* 3 (1978): 874–902; Daniel J. Theron, "Aletheia in the Pauline Corpus," *EvQ* 26 (January 15th 1954): 3–18; Jerome Murphy-O'Connor, "Truth: Paul and Qumran," in *Paul and Qumran: Studies in New Testament Exegesis*, ed. and trans. Jerome Murphy-O'Connor (Chicago: Priory Press; London: Geoffrey Chapman, 1968), 179–230.

2. Homer *Ilias* 24.407; *Odyssea* 11.507; Herodotus 1.116.

3. Thucydides 2.41.2; 4.120.3; Polybius 10.40.5.

4. Alfred Jepsen, "אֱמֶת *ʾemeth*," *TDOT* 1 (1977): 313.

5. BAGD 35–36; BDAG 42; Bultmann, *TDNT* 1 (1964): 244; Thiselton, *NIDNTT* 3 (1978): 884–85.

6. Ellicott, 18.

7. BAGD 317; BDAG 402. For a thorough study of "gospel," see Peter Stuhlmacher, "The Theme: The Gospel and the Gospels," in *The Gospel and the Gospels*, ed. Peter Stuhlmacher, trans. John Vriend (Grand Rapids: Eerdmans, 1991), 1–25, esp. 19–23; idem, "The Pauline Gospel," in *The Gospel and the Gospels*, ed. Peter Stuhlmacher, trans. John Vriend (Grand Rapids: Eerdmans, 1991), 149–72; cf. also P. T. O'Brien, *Gospel and Mission in the Writings of Paul: An Exegetical and Theological Analysis* (Grand Rapids: Baker; Carlisle: Paternoster, 1995), 77–81.

most likely is one of content, namely, "the gospel which has for its contents salvation."[1] The term "salvation" indicates rescue or deliverance, as seen later in the epistle (in the verb form) referring to the sinner who is dead in trespasses and is saved or delivered by grace (2:5). The truth of the message is the good news of deliverance of people from their bondage to sin. Many different messages proclaimed by the world as deliverance are false and bring people into greater bondage. Those messages contain faleshood and deception, whereas here Paul is showing the message of truth—the good news of deliverance.

ἐν ᾧ καὶ πιστεύσαντες, "in whom having also believed." This second ἐν ᾧ[2] is a resumption of the first one in the verse (indicating sphere or location) and hence its antecedent is also ἐν τῷ Χριστῷ, "in Christ," in verse 12 and is in close connection to the main verb ἐσφραγίσθητε.[3] The conjunction καί is not connected to the implied ὑμεῖς but is adjunctive ("also") to the πιστεύσαντες[4] because it is not only the hearing but also the believing that is necessary for the sealing. There is some debate about the preposition ἐν following πιστεύω since this is rare in the NT (Mark 1:15; John 3:15?), but most think in this context it has reference to sphere.[5] However, it is best to consider the preposition as resumptive and thus join it with the main verb.[6]

The aorist participles in relation to the main verb could be causal, "because you heard and believed, you were sealed," or better still they could be regarded as temporal. Although the action could be logically antecedent to the main verb, "after having heard and believed, you were sealed," it is better to consider it contemporaneous,[7] "when you heard and believed, you were sealed." The moment one hears and believes the gospel of salvation, he or she is sealed. The AV gives the idea that sometime after they heard and believed, they were sealed. Rather, the picture is that when they heard, they believed and hence were sealed. This negates the idea that they heard the gospel over a period

1. Eadie, 64; Ellicott, 18; Meyer, 60; Salmond, 267.

2. Delebecque thinks that this "double relative" or "complex relative" (ἐν ᾧ) was borrowed from classical Greek having the idea "within whom." See Édouard Delebecque, "L'hellénisme de la «relative complexe» dans le Nouveau Testament et Principalement chez saint Luc," *Bib* 62, no. 2 (1981): 229–38, esp. 233.

3. Robertson, *Grammar*, 396.

4. Salmond, 270.

5. Cf. Robertson, *Grammar*, 453; Moule, *Idiom Book*, 80–81. This is based on Deissmann, *Die neutestamentliche Formel "in Christo Jesu,"* 46–47, 103 n. 4.

6. Robertson, *Grammar*, 540; MHT 1:67 n. 2; Wallace, *Greek Grammar*, 625 n. 33. As noted above (comment on 1:5), Porter (*Verbal Aspect*, 383–85) observes that when the aorist participle precedes the main verb, as here, there is a tendency toward antecedent action, and when it follows the main verb, there is a definite tendency toward contemporaneous action with the main verb. However, Porter is quick to say that there are exceptions to this rule and the present context seems to be one of them.

7. BDF §339 (1); Burton, *Moods and Tenses* §132; Harless, 70; *contra* Eadie, 64; Meyer, 61.

of time and then finally believed. On the contrary it should be regarded that the hearing was the hearing of faith (Rom 10:14–17) and, thus, it was at that point in time that they "also" believed. It may be true that they heard the gospel superfically many times, but at one point in time they really heard and at that time they believed. This becomes the obedience of faith (Rom 1:5).

ἐσφραγίσθητε, "you were sealed." This verb is the aorist passive of σφραγίζω[1] and is used in classical literature meaning: (1) to close with a seal to denote security,[2] (2) to mark with a seal to authenticate,[3] (3) to certify genuineness,[4] and (4) to denote identification,[5] especially the identification of ownership.[6] In the LXX it occurs thirty-one times (twenty-one times in the canonical books) and nineteen times it translates חָתַם, meaning "to seal, attest by seal, seal up."[7] Again it is used to denote: (1) security (Deut 32:34; Job 14:17; Cant 4:12; Isa 8:16; Dan 6:17 [MT & LXX 6:18); (2) authentication (1 Kgs 21:8 [LXX 20:8]; Esth 8:10; Jer 32:10–11 [LXX 39:10–11]); (3) genuineness (Esth 8:8, 10); and (4) identification (Neh 10:1 [MT & LXX 10:2]; Esth 3:10) and ownership (Jer 32:44 [LXX 39:44]). In the NT it occurs fifteen times out of which eight are in Revelation and only four times are in Paul (Rom 15:18; 2 Cor 1:22; Eph 1:13; 4:30). Once more, some of the same ideas for its use prevail: (1) to seal in order to avoid tampering, denoting security (Matt 27:66; Rom 15:28; Eph 4:30; Rev 20:3); (2) to authenticate (John 6:27); (3) to certify genuineness (John 3:33); and (4) to denote identification of ownership (2 Cor 1:22; Eph 4:30; Rev 7:3–5, 8). In this context the sealing refers to ownership. This fits well with the previous verses because the believers are God's heritage (v. 11) and thus belong to him. Many think this refers to baptism (or possibly confirmation),

1. For a study of this word, see Eldon Woodcock, "The Seal of the Holy Spirit," *BSac* 155 (April–June 1998): 139–50; Rodney Thomas, "The Seal of the Spirit and the Religious Climate of Ephesus," *ResQ* 43 (third quarter 2001): 155–59.

2. Aeschylus *Eumenides* 828.

3. Third century B.C., *The Hibeh Papyri: Part I*, ed. with trans. and notes by Bernard P. Grenfell and Arthur S. Hunt (London: Egypt Exploration Fund, 1906), 39.15; 72.19; second century B.C., *Inscriptiones Graeciae Septentrinalis, pars I, Inscriptiones Phocidis, Locridis, Aetoliae, Acarnaniae, insularum maris Ionii*, ed. Wilhelm Dittenberger, Inscriptiones Graecae, vol. 9.1 (Berlin: Apud Georgium Reimerum, 1897), 61.78, 95; *Inscriptiones insularum maris Aegaei praeter Delum, fasc. v, Inscriptiones Cycladum*, ed. Friedrich Hiller von Gaertringen, Inscriptiones Graecae, vol. 12.5 (Berlin: Apud Georgium Reimerum, 1909), 833.14; 835.31; *Inscriptiones Deli, fasc. IV, Inscriptiones Deli liberae: Decreta foedera, Catalogi dedicationes varia*, ed. Pierre Roussel, Inscriptiones Graecae, vol. 11.4 (Berlin: Apud Georgium Reimerum, 1914), 1065.28; cf. LSJ 1742.

4. Herodotus 2.38.

5. Euripides *Iphigenia Taurica* 1372.

6. Herodotus 2.113.

7. BDB 367–68; B. Otzen, "חָתַם *ḥāṯam*," *TDOT* 5 (1986): 263–69.

denoting identification.[1] This idea is derived from Rom 4:11 where it refers to Abraham's circumcision as a seal of his righteousness. It is thought that this is transferred to baptism for the Christian. Although there may have been some church fathers who made this deduction, it is a great leap and really foreign not only to this context but to the whole NT.[2] Barth gives a lengthy discussion on why this is not referring to baptism.[3] Caragounis rightly discerns that it is curious and inexplicable that a letter devoted to baptism mentions the term only once (4:5), not for the rite itself but merely as one of the points that constitute the Christian faith.[4] On the other hand, Lincoln suggests that this is not talking about water baptism but the baptism of the Spirit.[5] This, however, confuses the ministries of the Spirit. Baptism of the Spirit places the believer in the body of Christ (1 Cor 12:13) whereas the sealing of the Spirit indicates God's ownership of the believer. Thomas thinks that the sealing of the Spirit is the Christians' talisman to protect them from the magical influence and power prevalent in western Asia Minor.[6] There is no hint in the context to give any credence to this suggestion.

τῷ πνεύματι τῆς ἐπαγγελίας τῷ ἁγίῳ, "with the Holy Spirit of promise." Up to this point it has been concluded that God is the one who seals, the believers are the ones who are sealed, and Christ is the location or sphere in which the sealing is accomplished. Now the dative τῷ πνεύματι . . . τῷ ἁγίῳ shows that the Spirit is the means or instrument of the seal[7] and hence can be translated "by/with the Holy

1. Cf. Schlier, 69–70; Gaugler, 54; Schnackenburg, 65–66. Cf. also Nils Alstrup Dahl, "Dopet i Efesierbrevet," *Svensk Teologisk Kvartalskrift* 21 (1945): 85–103, esp. 85–87, 99–100; G. W. H. Lampe, *The Seal of the Spirit. A Study in the Doctrine of Baptism and Confirmation in the New Testament and the Fathers* (London: Longmans, Green, 1951), 5, 57; Coutts, "Ephesians i.3–14 and I Peter i.3–12," 125; Rudolf Schnackenburg, *Baptism in the Thought of St. Paul. A Study in Pauline Theology*, trans. G. R. Beasley-Murray (Oxford: Basil Blackwell, 1964), 86–89; Mussner, "People of God according to Ephesians 1.3–14 [trans. Eileen O'Gorman]," *Concilium* 10 (December 1965): 57–58; Kirby, *Ephesians, Baptism and Pentecost*, 153; Ronald Fung, "The Doctrine of Baptism in Ephesians," *Studia Biblica et Theologica* 1 (March 1971): 6–7; Hans Halter, *Taufe und Ethos. Paulinische Kriterien für das Proprium christlicher Moral*, Freiburger theologische Studien, ed. Remigius Bäumer, Alfons Deissler, and Nehmut Reidlinger, vol. 106 (Freiburg: Herder, 1977), 229–33; Allen Mawhinney, "Baptism, Servanthood, and Sonship," *WTJ* 49 (spring 1987): 52–58.

2. Cf. Eadie, 66; Ellicott, 18; Meyer, 62–63; Abbott, 22; Salmond, 268.

3. Barth, 135–44; Best, 150–51; O'Brien, 120; cf. also G. R. Beasley-Murray, *Baptism in the New Testament* (London: Macmillan, 1962), 171–74; Gerhard Delling, *Die Taufe im Neuen Testament* (Berlin: Evangelische Verlagsanstalt, 1963), 105–6; Hui, "The Concept of the Holy Spirit in Ephesians," 287–90; Woodcock, "The Seal of the Holy Spirit," 148–49; Thomas, "The Seal of the Spirit and the Religious Climate of Ephesus," 163–66.

4. Caragounis, *Ephesian* Mysterion, 46 n. 83.

5. Lincoln, 40; cf. Mauerhofer, "Der Brief an die Epheser. 8. Teil: 1, 12–13," 31–32.

6. Thomas, "The Seal of the Spirit and the Religious Climate of Ephesus," 166.

7. Robertson, *Grammar*, 533; Wallace, *Greek Grammar*, 162, 165–66.

Spirit of promise." The τῷ ἁγίῳ is placed at the end to emphasize the personal righteous character of the Spirit. A study of ἅγιος has been made in 1:1 (cf. also 1:4) and there it was concluded that when it refers to God, Jesus Christ, or the Holy Spirit, the word depicts the unique character of the person. All three persons of the Trinity are involved with the believers' relationship to God.

Although the genitive ἐπαγγελίας, "of promise," could be considered as having an active sense, "the Spirit confirms the promise of salvation,"[1] it is best to see it as having a passive sense, "the Spirit which was promised."[2] The genitive is attributive,[3] "the promised Holy Spirit." Chrysostom claims that the Spirit was promised by the prophets (see esp. Joel 2:28–29) and by Christ.[4] The former seems to speak of the Spirit promised when the new covenant was to be initiated (Ezek 36:26–27; 37:14; cf. also 39:29) and the latter specifically refers to Christ's promise to his disciples that he would send the Spirit (Luke 24:49; John 14:16–17; 15:26; Acts 2:33; Gal 3:14; cf. also John 16:13; Acts 1:5; 10:47).

In conclusion, God seals the believers in Christ with the promised Holy Spirit when they have not only heard but also believed the gospel of salvation. The sealing with the Spirit must not be confused with the other ministries of the Spirit. The indwelling of the Spirit refers to his residence in every believer (Rom 8:9; 1 John 2:27). The baptizing ministry of the Spirit places believers into the body of Christ (1 Cor 12:13). The filling by the Spirit is the control of the Spirit over believers' lives (Eph 5:18). The sealing ministry of the Spirit is to identify believers as God's own and thus give them the security that they belong to him (Eph 1:13; 4:30; 2 Cor 1:22). The very fact that the Spirit indwells believers is a seal of God's ownership of them. Fee says it well: "The Spirit, and the Spirit alone, marks off the people of God as his own possession in the present eschatological age."[5]

One further note is that the indwelling, baptizing, and sealing ministries of the Spirit are bestowed on every believer at the moment of conversion. There are no injunctions regarding them because they are an integral part of the gift of salvation. This is not to be confused with the exhortation to believers to be repeatedly filled by the Spirit from

1. Calvin, 132.

2. Chrysostom *Eph* 1:14 (*PG* 62:18); Theophylact *Eph* 1:13 (*PG* 124:1041); Eadie, 65; Ellicott, 19; Meyer, 62–63; Salmond, 268; Abbott, 22–23; Schlier, 71; Schnackenburg, 65.

3. Moule (*Idiom Book*, 175, 176) calls it an adjectival genitive probably under Semitic influence. Howard (MHT 2:485) says: "An unidiomatic use of the genitive of definition may perhaps be termed the Hebraic genitive." Sellin thinks it is a genitive of quality, see Gerhard Sellin, "Über einige ungewöhnliche Genitive im Epheserbrief," *ZNW* 83, nos. 1/2 (1992): 89–90.

4. Chrysostom *Eph* 1:14 (*PG* 62:18).

5. Gordon D. Fee, *God's Empowering Presence: The Holy Spirit in the Letters of Paul* (Peabody, Mass.: Hendrickson, 1994), 670.

the moment of their conversion to the end of their lives here on earth. To summarize, at the moment of conversion, the believers are sealed with the Spirit, indicating God's ownership of them.

(2) Duration: Sealed until Redemption (1:14a)

Text: 1:14a. ὅς ἐστιν ἀρραβὼν τῆς κληρονομίας ἡμῶν, εἰς ἀπολύτρωσιν τῆς περιποιήσεως,

Translation: 1:14a. "who is the initial installment of our inheritance, until the redemption of the purchased possession"

Commentary: 1:14a. ὅς[1] ἐστιν ἀρραβὼν τῆς κληρονομίας ἡμῶν, "who is the initial installment of our inheritance." The masculine relative pronoun ὅς relates back to πνεῦμα in verse 13. It is masculine, rather than neuter, not to demonstrate the personality of the Holy Spirit but because it agrees with the predicate nominative ἀρραβών.[2] The word ἀρραβών is used of earnest money or caution money, which refers to a down payment that was forfeited if the purchase was not completed.[3] It was the first installment with a guarantee that the rest would follow. As a Semitic loan word, it appears only three times in the LXX and is transliterated from עֵרָבוֹן, having the idea of a pledge (Gen 38:17,

1. The ὅ reading is found in 𝔓[46] A B F G L P 075 6 81 104 256 263 365 459 1175 1319 1505 1573 1739 1881 1912 1962 2127 *l* 422 *l* 596 it[b, d, g] syr[p] slav Irenaeus[lat] Origen[lem] Marcellus Didymus[dub1/2] Chrysostom[lem] Cyril (NA[27], UBS[4]). The ὅς reading is found in א D Ψ 0150 33 424 436 1241 1852 2200 2464 *Byz Lect* it[ar, f, o] vg Didymus[dub1/2] Chrysostom[comm] Didymus[lat] Theodore[lat] Victorinus-Rome Ambrosiaster Ambrose Jerome Pelagius Augustine Ps-Vigilius Varimadum and NA[25]. The editors of UBS[4] give ὅ a "B" rating (though UBS[3] rates it "C") and in their discussions they indicate it was difficult to decide which was the better reading. Certainly, the external evidence is quite evenly divided. The date and character of manuscripts probably slightly favor the ὅς reading for although the Alexandrian text does not have the earliest manuscripts, it does have good representation of early manuscripts in the Western and Byzantine texts. Regarding geographical distribution, the ὅς reading is better but the other reading is not poor. Genealogically, the Alexandrian and Western texts are split but the Byzantine text-type is united with ὅς. In conclusion, the weight of the evidence for the external evidence is quite even. If pushed to the corner, it seems that ὅς has only a slight edge. Internal evidence does not seem to give much help either. In transcription it is easy to see why a scribe may have dropped the final sigma if the manuscript were written in uncials (ΤΩΑΓΙΩΟΣΕΣΤΙΝ). Normally, one would think that ὅ is preferred because that would relate back to the neuter πνεύματι, "Spirit," as a neuter article does in 1 Cor 2:11. On the other hand, in Gal 3:16 and Eph 6:17 the relative pronoun agrees with the predicate nominative rather than the antecedent. In conclusion, the internal evidence could go either way. In the end it seems that it is quite evenly divided and the reading ὅς is preferred only because the external evidence gives it a slight edge. Either way the sense remains the same.

2. Eadie, 66; Lincoln, 10; Best, 151 n. 71; O'Brien, 120 n. 131; Wallace, *Greek Grammar*, 332 n. 44, 338; idem, "Greek Grammar and the Personality of the Holy Spirit" (paper delivered at the Annual Meeting of the Institute for Biblical Research, Denver, CO, November 17, 2001), 14–17.

3. Isaeus 8.23; Aristotle *Politica* 1.4.5 §1259a.14.

18, 20).[1] In koine Greek it continues to convey the idea of earnest money with further payments guaranteed. For example, a woman selling a cow received 1000 drachmas as ἀρραβών.[2] It occurs only three times in the NT (2 Cor 1:22; 5:5; Eph 1:14). In 2 Cor 1:22 it states that God sealed the believers and gave them the Holy Spirit in their hearts as a down payment of more to come. In 2 Cor 5:5 Paul explains that believers, while in their present "earthly dwelling," are given the Spirit as a deposit or guarantee of their future "heavenly dwelling." It is sometimes translated "pledge" (Vg, NASB, NEB, JB, NJB, NRSV) but this is really inaccurate because the pledge is returned when the full payment is made (cf. Gen 38:17–20), whereas ἀρραβών is a portion of the whole payment. Chrysostom states that it is "a part of the whole" (μέρος ἐστὶ τοῦ παντός).[3] Bauer states that it "is a payment which obligates the contracting party to make further payments."[4] It is better to translate it "earnest" (AV, RV, ASV), "deposit guaranteeing" (NIV), or "initial installment." All of these indicate that much more is sure to come. In Eph 1:14 the promised Holy Spirit is the present deposit or initial installment of the believers' future inheritance.[5]

The word κληρονομία is the compound[6] of κλῆρος, "land received by lot, allotment," and νέμω, "to dispense, distribute," and thus, "a portion that is given," hence "inheritance"[7] or "possession."[8] In the LXX it occurs 211 times and in the canonical books it appears 165 times, translated from six Hebrew words. Of these, approximately 140 times it is from נַחֲלָה, meaning "possession, property, inheritance."[9] It is used of inheritance of personal property (Gen 31:14; Num 18:20, 23; 27:7–11; 32:18; Deut 12:9), of tribal land (Num 26:54*bis*, 56; 11:23), of national land (1 Kgs 8:36; Jer 2:7; 3:19; 10:16), and of the nation Israel as God's inheritance (Deut 32:9; 1 Sam 10:1; 26:19; 1 Kgs 8:51, 53; Isa 19:25; 47:6). In the koine period it continues to have the idea of inheritance or property.[10] In the NT it occurs fourteen times, five times in

1. E. Lipiński, "עֵרָבוֹן *ʿērāḇôn*," *TDOT* 11 (2001): 328–30.
2. MM 79.
3. Chrysostom *Eph* 1:14 (*PG* 62:18).
4. BAGD 109; BDAG 134.
5. For a study of this word in this context, see Barnabas Ahern, "The Indwelling Spirit, Pledge of Our Inheritance (Eph. 1:14)," *CBQ* 9 (April 1947): 179–89; A. J. Kerr, "Ἀρραβών," *JTS*, n.s., 39 (April 1988): 92–97; Woodcock, "The Seal of the Holy Spirit," 150–54, 159–60. Origen sees the down payment not as "flat sum, but is a deposit made in proportion to the ultimate inheritance to be received by each of the saints," see Richard A. Layton, "Recovering Origen's Pauline Exegesis: Exegesis and Eschatology in the *Commentary on Ephesians*," *Journal of Early Christian Studies* 8 (fall 2000): 381–82, 406.
6. Johannes Eichler, "Inheritance, Lot, Portion [κλῆρος, μέρος]," *NIDNTT* 2 (1976): 296.
7. Isocrates 19.43; Demosthenes *Orationes* 43.3; Aristotle *Politica* 5.7.12 §1309a.24.
8. Aristotle *Ethica Nicomachea* 7.13.6 §1153b.33.
9. BDB 635; E. Lipiński, "נָחַל *nāḥal*; נַחֲלָה *naḥᵃlâ*," *TDOT* 9 (1998): 321–33.
10. MM 346–47.

Paul's writings, three times in Ephesians (1:14, 18; 5:5). The word is used of inheritance of property or possessions (Matt 21:38 = Mark 12:7 = Luke 20:14; Luke 12:13; Acts 7:5; Gal 3:18; Heb 11:8), of an eternal inheritance (Acts 20:32; Eph 1:14; 5:5; Col 3:24; Heb 9:15; 1 Pet 1:4), and of the saints as God's inheritance (Eph 1:18). In the present context it refers to the believers' eternal inheritance, their gain of heaven because of the Father's election, the Son's redemption, and the Spirit's sealing.[1] The genitive (κληρονομίας) is possibly a genitive of purpose showing that the purpose of the earnest is for our inheritance, but more likely it is a partitive genitive showing that the earnest of the Holy Spirit is only part of our entire inheritance. The pronoun ἡμῶν is a possessive genitive showing that it is "our" inheritance. Because we have been adopted into God's family with all the privileges, we have an inheritance from God.[2] This inheritance qualifies believers to live eternally in heaven in the presence of God.[3] We have a little bit of heaven in us, namely, the Holy Spirit's presence, and a guarantee of a lot more to come in the future.

εἰς ἀπολύτρωσιν τῆς περιποιήσεως, "until the redemption of the purchased possession." The word "redemption" (ἀπολύτρωσις) has already been discussed at verse 7. It means to release or set free on the basis of a ransom paid to God by Christ's death. The most difficult part of this prepositional phrase is the word περιποίησις. Although rarely used in classical literature, it has the idea of "preservation"[4] and the verb περιποιέω similarly means "to preserve, to keep safe."[5] Moreover, it can also mean "to acquire, to gain possession

1. For a discussion of inheritance, although for the most part excluding reference to Ephesians, see James D. Hester, *Paul's Concept of Inheritance. A Contribution to the Understanding of Heilsgeschichte*, Scottish Journal of Theology Occasional Papers, no. 14 (Edinburgh: Oliver and Boyd, 1968). Although Kerrigan thinks that ultimately inheritance is eternal life, he thinks the tokens of inheritance now are in some way connected to the mystery revealed in Ephesians (Alexander Kerrigan, "Echoes of Themes from the Servant Songs in Pauline Theology," in *Studiorum Paulinorum Congressus Internationalis Catholicus 1961*, vol. 2, AnBib, vol. 18 [Rome: E Pontificio Instituto Biblico, 1963], 222–25). This seems rather unlikely for there is nothing in the context to indicate that inheritance is linked with mystery.

2. Hammer thinks that "inheritance" in Romans and Galatians refers to the past and in Ephesians it refers to the future and that this is another indication that Ephesians is deutero-Pauline (Paul L. Hammer, "A Comparison of *klēronomia* in Paul and Ephesians," *JBL* 79 [September 1960]: 267–72). This is overstating the case, as ably argued by D. R. Denton, "Inheritance in Paul and Ephesians," *EvQ* 54 (July–September 1982): 157–62.

3. Kennedy has confused κληρονόμος, "heir," and κληρονομία, "inheritance," so that he interprets the present passage as gaining sonship (H. A. A. Kennedy, "St. Paul's Conception of the Spirit as a Pledge," *Exp* 6th ser., vol. 4 [October 1901]: 276–78). However, because the believers are heirs, they will receive an inheritance, viz., heaven, and the two terms are to be distinguished.

4. Plato *Definitiones* 415c.7.

5. Herodotus 3.36; Thucydides 2.25.2.

of."[1] περιποίησις is used only three times in the LXX with the concept of "preservation" (2 Chr 14:13 [MT & LXX 14:12]) but, also, of "possession" (Hag 2:9; Mal 3:17). Both concepts continue in the koine literature.[2] In the NT it is used five times. Excluding the present passage, it refers once to preservation or safe-keeping (Heb 10:39) and otherwise is used with the idea of "acquisition, possession." In 1 Thess 5:9 God did not appoint the believers to wrath but to the acquisition of salvation through Christ. In 2 Thess 2:14 God calls the believer through the gospel to obtain or acquire the glory of our Lord Jesus Christ. In 1 Pet 2:9 the believers are called "the people for his possession."

It can be seen that the noun may have an active sense of "acquiring, obtaining," as in the two Thessalonian passages cited above. In the present context it would mean the redemption of the believers' acquisition, namely, their inheritance, translated in the RSV as "until we acquire possession of it."[3] On the other hand, the noun can have the passive sense of "having been acquired, possessed." This would refer to the redemption of believers who have been acquired by God as the NEB renders it, "when God has redeemed what is his own" (so also AV, RV, ASV, NASB, JB, NIV, NJB, NRSV).[4] The passive makes much more sense in the present context. It is used much in the same way as 1 Pet 2:9 which may go back to Mal 3:17 or possibly Isa 43:21 where it refers to an OT concept that the redeemed people of God are God's possession. In the present context the believers are considered God's possession by the very fact that he has chosen, redeemed, and adopted them. Hence, in this context περιποιήσεως would be classed as an objective genitive[5] meaning the setting free of God's own possession. A parallel idea is given in Rom 8:23 where believers who have been adopted into God's family (Rom 8:15; Eph 1:5) have the firstfruits of the Spirit and are now eagerly waiting for Christ's return to fully realize their adoption, the redemption of their bodies. Another parallel al-

1. Thucydides 1.9.2; 15.1; Xenophon *Anabasis* 5.6.17.

2. MM 508.

3. Abbott, 24; Dibelius-Greeven, 62–63; Schlier, 71–72; Schnackenburg, 45, 67; Best, 152–53; cf. Carlo Kruse, "Il significato di περιποίησις in *Eph*. 1,14," *RivB* 16 (Dicembre 1968): 465–93.

4. Chrysostom *Eph* 1:14 (*PG* 62:19); Oecumenius *Eph* 1:13–14 (*PG* 118:1180); Hodge, 66; Alford, 3:80–81; Eadie, 69–70; Ellicott, 20; Meyer, 63–65; Salmond, 269–70; Robinson, 148; Westcott, 17–18; Gnilka, 87; Caird, 42; Barth, 97; Bruce, 266–67; O'Brien, 122; cf. Percy, *Probleme*, 188–89 n. 15; Lyonnet and Sabourin, *Sin, Redemption, and Sacrifice*, 115–17.

5. Cf. MHT 3:215; Zerwick, *Biblical Greek* §46; cf. Ernst Käsemann, "Ephesians and Acts," [trans. Marianne Grobel and Thomas Wieser] in *Studies in Luke-Acts. Essays Presented in Honor of Paul Schubert Buckingham Professor of New Testament Criticism and Interpretation at Yale University*, ed. Leander E. Keck and J. Louis Martyn (Nashville: Abingdon, 1966), 295. Sellin thinks it is genitive of apposition or an epexegetical genitive (see Sellin, "Über einige ungewöhnliche Genitive im Epheserbrief," 91–92).

ready mentioned is 2 Cor 5:5 where Paul speaks of the Holy Spirit as the earnest until the future resurrection.

Now that the different words have been discussed, it necessary to see how the words relate to each other. First, the preposition εἰς could be joined to the immediately preceding verb "to be" (ἐστίν) but more likely it is joined to "we were sealed" (ἐσφραγίσθητε). The preposition may indicate purpose,[1] denoting that the believers were sealed with the Holy Spirit "for the purpose of the redemption of the possession" (NASB, JB, NJB), but it really makes good sense to indicate time[2] so that they were sealed "until the redemption of the possession" (AV, RSV, NEB, NIV, NRSV). This coincides with the only other mention in Ephesians (4:30) of the sealing with the Spirit where it states "by whom you were sealed until the day of redemption" (εἰς ἡμέραν ἀπολυτρώσεως). Second, the redemption here is different from that of verse 7. In verse 7 "we" have redemption by which the effect was the forgiveness of sins. Here the redemption concerns God's possession. So there are two redemptions or more accurately two phases of redemption. The first phase was in the past, which set us free from sin and its obligation. The second phase is future when Christ comes for the saints.[3] This will set us free from the presence of sin. We are "already" set free from sin's penalty and power "but not yet" from its presence and temptations. In the meantime we have the initial installment, the ministry of the Holy Spirit as our portion.

(3) Goal: Praise of His Glory (1:14b)

Text: 1:14b. εἰς ἔπαινον τῆς δόξης αὐτοῦ.

Translation: 1:14b. "to the praise of his glory."

Commentary: 1:14b. εἰς ἔπαινον τῆς δόξης αὐτοῦ, "to the praise of his glory." This is the third time a refrain similar to this has been expressed (cf. vv. 6 and 12). It occurs after each time the work of each person of the Trinity is extolled. The genitive is objective and the glory refers to the reflection of God's essential being as discussed in more detail at verse 6. God sealed the believers with the Holy Spirit of promise until the day he redeems them, his possession, and for this he is to be praised.

1. Ellicott, 19–20; Salmond, 269; Lincoln (42) thinks it speaks of goal.

2. Eadie, 70; Schlier, 71–72; Schnackenburg, 67; cf. BAGD 228; BDAG 289; Adai, *Der Heilige Geist als Gegenwart Gottes*, 74.

3. Schnackenburg, 66–67; Lincoln, 42; Lincoln, *Paradise Now and Not Yet*, 167; Lona, *Die Eschatologie im Kolosser- und Epheserbrief*, 419–22, 427.

C. Prayer for Wisdom and Revelation (1:15–23)

Having completed the magnificent eulogy, Paul prays for the Ephesians. It could be called the prayer for those who have everything because the believers have every spiritual benefit for their spiritual welfare, including election, predestination, adoption, grace, redemption, forgiveness, insight, understanding, knowledge of the mystery of his will, and sealing with the Holy Spirit. Paul's desire is for the Ephesian believers to deepen their relationship with the God who has enriched them with every spiritual benefit and to experience those benefits in a deeper way. Normally Paul gives his introductory thanksgiving immediately after the greeting. In this epistle he includes the greeting (vv. 1–2), a pæan of praise for what God has done for the believer (vv. 3–14), and now the thanksgiving and prayer (vv. 15–23). As usual, Paul begins the prayer with commendation (vv. 15–16a) and then he presents his supplication before God on behalf of them (vv. 16b–23).[1] This prayer is the second of the eight long sentences in this epistle (1:3–14, 15–23; 2:1–7; 3:2–13, 14–19; 4:1–6, 11–16; 6:14–20) with 169 words. Three of these (1:3–14, 15–23; 3:14–19) are items of praise and prayer. It is not unusual to have lengthy sentences for praise and prayer.

1. Commendation (1:15–16a)

Text: 1:15. Διὰ τοῦτο κἀγώ ἀκούσας τὴν καθ' ὑμᾶς πίστιν ἐν τῷ κυρίῳ Ἰησοῦ καὶ τὴν ἀγάπην τὴν εἰς πάντας τοὺς ἁγίους, **1:16a.** οὐ παύομαι εὐχαριστῶν ὑπὲρ ὑμῶν

1. For a rhetorical analysis of this thanksgiving and praise, see Jeal, *Integrating Theology and Ethics in Ephesians*, 94–110.

Translation: 1:15. "For this reason I also having heard of your faith in the Lord Jesus and the love toward all the saints, **1:16a.** I never cease giving thanks for you"

Commentary: 1:15. Διὰ τοῦτο κἀγώ, "For this reason I also." διὰ τοῦτο, "for this reason," refers back to verses 3–14,[1] especially to verses 13–14.[2] In light of all of the spiritual benefits that God has given to believers (especially since the Ephesians heard and believed the gospel and were sealed with the promised Holy Spirit), Paul has reason to give thanks and prays on their behalf. The κἀγώ, "I also," emphatically makes a contrast between God's actions in verses 3–14 and his. Furthermore, it specifically points to Paul in contrast to the "we/us" in verses 3–12, 14 and also sets him as the author apart from the recipients designated by "you" in verse 13. Paul is saying that because of all that has happened to the believers at Ephesus, he now has something to say.[3]

ἀκούσας τὴν καθ' ὑμᾶς πίστιν ἐν τῷ κυρίῳ Ἰησοῦ, "having heard of your faith in the Lord Jesus." Paul begins by stating what he had heard concerning the Ephesians' faith and love. The aorist participle ἀκούσας "having heard," could be causal, or perhaps better, temporal.[4] It refers to that time between the report about them and the writing of the epistle. After (or because) he had heard about them, he continually gives thanks. Since there is only hearsay acquaintance with the readers' faith and love, some suggest that this letter could not have been written by Paul who spent nearly three years in Ephesus and would have personally known the believers.[5] However, as mentioned in the introduction, Paul had not been in Ephesus for five or six years, and there were probably many new believers with whom he had no personal acquaintance. Also, this was probably a circular letter[6] and he may have been personally unacquainted with many in the satellite churches in western Asia Minor.

As stated, Paul had heard about their faith in the Lord Jesus. The expression τὴν καθ' ὑμᾶς πίστιν is a Hellenistic circumlocution (cf. Acts 17:28; 18:15; Rom 1:15) for a possessive pronoun denoting a close re-

1. Chrysostom *Eph* 1:15 (*PG* 62:23); Oecumenius *Eph* 1:15–20 (*PG* 118:1180); Abbott, 24–25; Hendriksen, 95; Schnackenburg, 72.

2. Some think it has reference to only vv. 13–14: Theophylact 1:15 (*PG* 124:1044); Eadie, 72; Ellicott, 20; Meyer, 66; Salmond, 270; Schlier, 75; Gaugler, 56.

3. Maclean ("Ephesians and the Problem of Colossians," 70–87, esp. 70–73) suggests that twenty words in Eph 1:15–17 are taken from Col 1:3–4, 9. However, though the two texts have similar or identical words, this is not an indication that Ephesians borrowed from Colossians because many of the words are common vocabulary of eulogy and thanksgiving. Furthermore, a close examination of the two texts reveals that few words are consecutive and that in Colossians the subject is first person plural while in Ephesians it is first person singular.

4. Wallace, *Greek Grammar*, 627.

5. Cf. Mitton, 66; Patzia, 163–64; Lincoln, lx, 54.

6. Cf. Martin, *Ephesians, Colossians, and Philemon*, 21.

lationship.[1] Literally, it is "the faith with regards to you" or more simply "your faith." Ellicott thinks that since the possessive genitive (ὑμῶν) follows "faith" some sixteen times in Paul's letters, this unique form would seem to indicate that the κατά is distributive, referring to the faith of the community, "the faith which is among you."[2] However, it seems better to think of this unique form as not only indicating simple possession but indicating an active faith in Christ (cf. πιστοῖς, v. 1) that is a peculiar possession of theirs.[3] This is substantiated by the article (τήν) that introduces the expression and would be literally translated "the faith with regards to you." Following is the prepositional phrase ἐν τῷ κυρίῳ Ἰησοῦ, which shows that their faith was "in the Lord Jesus." Although it is infrequent in the NT to have the preposition ἐν follow the noun "faith" (Rom 3:25; Eph 1:15; Col 1:4; 1 Tim 3:12; 2 Tim 3:15) and even rarer to have it follow the verb (Mark 1:15; John 3:15?), in all these passages it has the idea of sphere or location.[4] They had placed their faith in the Lord Jesus. This is not only the initial act of faith mentioned in verse 13, but a continuing faith in the Lord Jesus. The fact that this was an ongoing faith is evidenced by the reports Paul had received and by their continued love for one another mentioned next. This is new for the Ephesians, for they had originally placed their trust in Artemis and now their faith is in the Lord Jesus.

καὶ τὴν ἀγάπην τὴν εἰς πάντας τοὺς ἁγίους,[5] "and the love toward all the saints." Paul not only had heard about their vertical relationship

1. Robertson, *Grammar*, 608; BDF §224 (1); Moule, *Idiom Book*, 58; Zerwick, *Biblical Greek* §130; SH §184k.

2. Ellicott, 21.

3. Cf. Eadie, 74.

4. Moule, *Idiom Book*, 81, 108; MHT 3:263.

5. There is a mixture of textual readings: (1) καὶ τὴν ἀγάπην τὴν εἰς πάντας τοὺς ἁγίους is found in א² D² (D* G omit 2d τήν) Ψ 075 0150 6 424 1241 1852 1912 1962 2200 *Byz* [K L] *Lect* (*l* 884) it$^{ar, b, d, f, o}$ vg syr^{h} cop$^{(sa), bopt}$ arm eth geo slav (Gregory-Nyssa) Chrysostom Theodore^{lat} Victorinus-Rome Ambrosiaster Pelagius; (2) καὶ τὴν εἰς πάντας τοὺς ἁγίους is in 𝔓^{46} א* A B P 33 1739 1881 *l* 921 cop^{bopt} Origen Jerome Augustine; and (3) καὶ τὴν εἰς πάντας τοὺς ἁγίους ἀγάπην is supported by 81 104 256 263 365 436 459 1175 1319 1573 2127 (2464 *omit* τήν) *l* 60 *l* 596 Cyril. The third reading is not a serious option. The second reading has good Alexandrian tradition but it is limited to that text-type in both the uncials and minuscules and may well have been a result of a transcriptional accident (Metzger, *Textual Commentary*, 2d ed., 533; cf. also Ian A. Moir, "A Mini-Guide to New Testament Textual Criticism," *BT* 36 [January 1985]: 122–29). Also, internally this reading is without precedent for it would mean that Paul had heard about their "faith [exercised] toward the saints." Souter tries to get around this by translating it "faith among the saints" (Alex. Souter, "An Interpretation of Eph. i.15," *ExpTim* 19 [October 1907]: 44). But this is really strained to say the least. Maclean ("Ephesians and the Problem of Colossians," 71–72, 82–87) accepts the shorter reading with the result that the Ephesian believers are reprimanded for their lack of love. The first reading, though weak in the Alexandrian text-type, is the preferred reading. It has good support from the manuscripts outside the Alexandrian text-type, giving each of them genealogical solidarity. It also has good geographical representation.

but also their horizontal relationship. Both the conjunction καί and the first article τήν connect the love with the participle "having heard" so that Paul had not only heard of their faith but also "the love." The term "love," which has already been discussed (cf. v. 4), has the idea of that which seeks to give rather than possess, always seeking highest good or the will of God in the one loved. The second article τήν acts as a mild relative pronoun so that the love has focus rather than being a mere abstract concept. Following this is the preposition εἰς, indicating direction. Thus this love that seeks the highest good in the one loved is directed toward all the saints, not toward some who may be more lovable. Used in the plural, "the saints" (cf. vv. 1, 4, 13), refer to believers who belong to a local church. This love is not to the whole world but to the saints. The believers are to love one another in order to show the world that they are disciples of the Lord (John 13:35).

1:16a. οὐ παύομαι εὐχαριστῶν ὑπὲρ ὑμῶν, "I never cease giving thanks for you." This really goes back to "for this reason" at the beginning of verse 15, and the intervening clause further substantiates Paul's reason for thanksgiving. He not only gives thanks for the Ephesians because they had received all spiritual benefits and more particularly had been sealed with the Spirit when they heard and believed, but he also gives thanks because of their continuing faith in Christ and love toward the saints. The verb (with the negative particle) οὐ παύομαι, "I never cease," is a present middle and is always followed by a complementary nominative participle,[1] as here, "giving thanks." This statement complements the Ephesians' actions. As they continue to believe and love, Paul is continually giving thanks and praying for them. "Never ceasing to give thanks" may be hyperbolic, for this was the common style of ancient letters and it simply means that Paul did not forget the believers at his regular time of prayer.[2]

Over the years there has been much discussion on Paul's thanksgiving.[3] The present participle εὐχαριστῶν is from the verb εὐχαριστέω,

1. Robertson, *Grammar*, 1102; MHT 3:159; Wallace, *Greek Grammar*, 646.

2. O'Brien, *Introductory Thanksgivings in the Letters of Paul*, 21–22.

3. Schubert, *Form and Function of the Pauline Thanksgivings*; Sanders, "The Transition from Opening Epistolary Thanksgiving to Body in the Letters of the Pauline Corpus," 348–62; Robert J. Ledogar, *Acknowledgment: Praise-Verbs in the Early Greek Anaphora* (Rome: Casa Editrice Herder, 1968); Wiles, *Paul's Intercessory Prayers*; P. T. O'Brien, "Thanksgiving and the Gospel in Paul," *NTS* 21 (October 1974): 144–55; idem, *Introductory Thanksgivings in the Letters of Paul*; idem, "Ephesians I: An Unusual Introduction to a New Testament Letter," 504–16; idem, "Thanksgiving within the Structure of Pauline Theology," in *Pauline Studies. Essays Presented to F. F. Bruce on His 70th Birthday*, ed. Donald A. Hagner and Murray J. Harris (Grand Rapids: Eerdmans; London: Paternoster, 1980), 50–66. Arzt thinks that the formal "introductory thanksgivings" have no support from the letters contemporary with NT times. See Arzt, "The 'Epistolarly Introductory Thanksgiving' in the Papyri and in Paul," 29–46. For a response to Arzt, see Jeffrey T. Reed, "Are Paul's Thanksgivings 'Epistolary'?" *JSNT* 61 (March 1996): 87–99.

which originally had the meaning "to bestow a favor"[1] but later meant "to be thankful" or "to give thanks."[2] In the LXX it appears only in the noncanonical books (Jdt 8:25; 2 Macc 1:11; 12:31; 3 Macc 7:16; Ode 14:8; Wis 18:2) and always means "to give thanks." This same meaning continues in NT times.[3] In the NT it occurs thirty-eight times: thirteen times in the Gospels and Acts; one time in Revelation; twenty-four times in the Pauline epistles; and twice in Ephesians (1:16; 5:20). The word continues to have the same meaning in the NT although primarily pertaining to thanksgiving to God (only twice for thanks to people, Luke 17:16; Rom 16:4).[4] After a careful study of the word, Ledogar concludes that in the first century B.C. it denoted "to thank, to give thanks, to return thanks," more often than "to be thankful" and "it signifies always *the outward expression in word or deed of the interior sentiment of gratitude for a favor received*."[5] His investigation of Philo (20 B.C.–A.D. 50) shows that the word continued to mean "to thank," thus expressing an outward sentiment of gratitude.[6] Hence, in NT times it, no doubt, has this meaning.

Schubert concluded that there are two types of introductory thanksgiving statements and that the one in the present context fits the first type, namely, where it begins with εὐχαριστέω (or its equivalent; here οὐ παύομαι εὐχαριστῶν) and is followed by one or more nominative masculine participles modifying the main verb. Also, these participles are always followed by a final subordinate clause (or clauses) introduced by ἵνα or ὅπως or εἰς τό with the infinitive (here ἵνα).[7] However, Schubert thinks that the thanksgiving here is superfluous after the eulogy, giving evidence that Ephesians is pseudo-Pauline.[8] This has been refuted by Barth who proposes that Paul had the freedom to use different styles. For example, in 2 Cor 1 there is only a benediction and in Galatians there is no benediction or thanksgiving.[9] Although the reasons for Paul's thanksgiving are varied in his

1. LSJ 738.

2. Polybius 4.72.7; 16.25.1; Diodorus Siculus 16.11.1; 20.34.5; Epictetus *Dissertationes* 1.4.32; 1.10.3.

3. Josephus *A.J.* 16.4.5 §127; 20.1.2 §12; *B.J.* 1.10.9 §214; 2.1.1 §2; Philo *Spec.* 1.38 §211; 2.29 §175.

4. Hans Conzelmann, "εὐχαριστέω, εὐχαριστία, εὐχάριστος," *TDNT* 9 (1974): 411; Hans-Helmut Esser, "Thank, Praise, Eucharist [αἰνέω, εὐχαριστία]," *NIDNTT* 3 (1978): 818.

5. Ledogar, *Acknowledgment*, 92.

6. Ibid., 98.

7. Schubert, *Form and Function of the Pauline Thanksgivings*, 35, 54–55. Schubert states regarding the second type: "The second type is structurally characterized, first, by a causal ὅτι-clause immediately following and subordinate to the principal εὐχαριστῶ-clause and, second, by a consecutive clause, following and subordinate to the ὅτι-clause, introduced by ὥστε" (35).

8. Ibid., 8, 44.

9. Barth, 161 n. 50.

different epistles (frequently faith, love, and hope or a variation of these serve as the immediate bases), the ultimate basis for thanksgiving is always linked with the gospel, including concern that it be properly received.[1] Both of these factors are in the present context.

Paul continually gives thanks ὑπὲρ ὑμῶν, "on behalf of them," or more simply "for them." Such an attitude of thankfulness for others is all too often neglected. The genuine concern of the apostle is obvious. Thus, he never ceased to give thanks for progress in their faith and love and to entreat God on their behalf. However, he not only continued to give thanks but, as seen in the following text, he prayed for them.

2. Supplication (1:16b–23)

The second part of Paul's prayer is his entreaty for them before God. There has been debate about the length of this prayer. Some would say that it probably ends in verse 19[2] and that verses 20–23 present a new hymn of praise,[3] while others think that the prayer continues to 2:10.[4] There is no indication in the text of a break between verses 19 and 20 and to try to reconstruct a hymn in verses 20–23 is problematic.[5] The prayer ends in verse 23 and does not continue into chapter 2. This will be discussed more fully in 2:1.

Having commended them (1:15–16a), he now makes his supplication (1:16b–23) in the form of only one request (1:16b–18a) and then gives his reason (1:18b–23). The prayer can be set out in the following way:

Request: ἵνα ὁ θεὸς . . . δώῃ ὑμῖν πνεῦμα σοφίας καὶ ἀποκαλύψεως ἐν ἐπιγνώσει αὐτοῦ (1:17)
  Purpose: εἰς τὸ εἰδέναι ὑμᾶς (1:18b)
    Content:
      (1) τίς ἐστιν ἡ ἐλπὶς τῆς κλήσεως αὐτοῦ (1:18b)
      (2) τίς ὁ πλοῦτος τῆς δόξης τῆς κληρονομίας αὐτοῦ ἐν τοῖς ἁγίοις (1:18c)

1. O'Brien, "Thanksgiving within the Structure of Pauline Theology," 56–57; cf. also O'Brien, "Thanksgiving and the Gospel in Paul," 148–52.

2. Cf. Schubert, *Form and Function of the Pauline Thanksgivings*, 8; Schlier, 75; O'Brien, "Ephesians I: An Unusual Introduction," 505, 514; Schnackenburg, 71, 72; Bruce, 271.

3. Dibelius-Greeven, 64; Schlier, 75; Barth, 153–54; Schnackenburg, 72; Bruce, 271–72; cf. Schille, "Liturgisches Gut," 114–16; Fischer, *Tendenz und Absicht des Epheserbriefes*, 118–20. Schnackenburg (72) thinks that vv. 19c–23 present a Christological-ecclesialogical excursus and Ernst (284) thinks that vv. 20b–23 give a confession.

4. Sanders, "The Transition from Opening Epistolary Thanksgiving to Body," 356–57; idem, "Hymnic Elements in Ephesians 1–3," 218–23.

5. Deichgräber, *Gotteshymnus*, 161–65.

(3) τί τὸ ὑπερβάλλον μέγεθος τῆς δυνάμεως αὐτοῦ εἰς ἡμᾶς τοὺς πιστεύοντας (1:19)
  Evidence:
    (a) ἐνήργησεν ἐν τῷ Χριστῷ (1:20)
      (1) ἐγείρας αὐτὸν ἐκ νεκρῶν (1:20a)
      (2) καθίσας ἐν δεξιᾷ αὐτοῦ . . . (1:20b)
    (b) πάντα ὑπέταξεν ὑπὸ τοὺς πόδας αὐτοῦ (1:22a)
    (c) αὐτὸν ἔδωκεν κεφαλὴν ὑπὲρ πάντα τῇ ἐκκλησίᾳ (1:22b)

Request: that God . . . may give to you the Spirit of insight and revelation in the knowledge of him (1:17)
  Purpose: in order that you might know (1:18b)
    Content:
      (1) what is the hope of his calling (1:18b)
      (2) what is the wealth of his glorious inheritance in the saints (1:18c)
      (3) what is the surpassing greatness of his power toward us who believe (1:19)
        Evidence:
          (a) which power he exercised in Christ (1:20)
            (1) by raising him from the dead (1:20a)
            (2) by seating him at his right hand . . . (1:20b)
          (b) he subjected everything under his feet (1:22a)
          (c) he gave him as head over everything to the church (1:22b)

a. The Request for Wisdom and Revelation (1:16b–18a)

Text: 1:16b. μνείαν ὑμῶν ποιούμενος ἐπὶ τῶν προσευχῶν μου, **1:17.** ἵνα ὁ θεὸς τοῦ κυρίου ἡμῶν Ἰησοῦ Χριστοῦ, ὁ πατὴρ τῆς δόξης, δώῃ ὑμῖν πνεῦμα σοφίας καὶ ἀποκαλύψεως ἐν ἐπιγνώσει αὐτοῦ, **1:18a.** πεφωτισμένους τοὺς ὀφθαλμοὺς τῆς καρδίας [ὑμῶν]

Translation: 1:16b. "making mention of you in my prayers, **1:17.** that the God of our Lord Jesus Christ, the Father of Glory, may give to you the Spirit of insight and revelation in the knowledge of him, **1:18a.** since the eyes of your heart have been enlightened,"

Commentary: 1:16b. μνείαν ὑμῶν[1] ποιούμενος ἐπὶ τῶν προσευχῶν μου, "making mention of you in my prayers." The word μνεία is used seven times in the NT and it is used exclusively by Paul. It has the idea of "remembrance, memory" of someone (Phil 1:3; 1 Thess 3:6; 2 Tim 1:3) and when it is used with the middle voice of ποιέω, "I do, make,"

1. The inclusion of ὑμῶν is in D[2] (ˢ F G) Ψ 𝔐 lat vg syr. The omission of ὑμῶν is supported by 𝔓[46] ℵ A B D* 33 81 326 1175 1739 1881 *pc* Hilary (NA[27], UBS[4]). The inclusion is to be preferred mainly because of geographical distribution. It is weak in the Alexandrian text but it does have representation of the pronoun in the various versions. On the other hand, the omission of it is almost exclusively by the Alexandrian text-type. Inter-

as it is here, it has the idea of "mentioning"[1] those individuals in one's prayers (Rom 1:9; Eph 1:16; 1 Thess 1:2; Phlm 4).[2] The preposition ἐπί with the genitive has a temporal sense of "in/at the time of,"[3] indicating that Paul mentioned them when he was praying. The word προσευχή in classical literature had the idea of a prayer or a vow.[4] In the LXX the noun appears 112 times and in the canonical books it appears sixty-eight times and is translated from three Hebrew words but nearly sixty-five times from תְּפִלָּה, meaning "prayer" (2 Sam 7:27; 1 Kgs 8:29, 38, 45, 54; Ps 69:13 [MT 69:14; LXX 68:14]; Isa 56:7*bis*).[5] It occurs in the NT thirty-six times, seven times in the Synoptics, nine times in Acts, fourteen times in Paul, and twice in Ephesians (1:16; 6:18). It always has the idea of prayer or supplication to the eternal God or the place of prayer.[6] Again one sees that Paul not only gives thanks but also in his time of prayer he intercedes on behalf of the believers in Ephesus. The plural form "prayers" along with "I never cease" seems to indicate the plurality of his prayers in which he constantly mentions them.

1:17. ἵνα ὁ θεὸς τοῦ κυρίου ἡμῶν Ἰησοῦ Χριστοῦ, "that the God of our Lord Jesus Christ." The conjunction ἵνα normally indicates purpose (cf. Rom 1:11; Eph 2:7), but it can also denote result (cf. John 9:2; Gal 5:17; Rev 9:20), and, in the case of prayer, it can denote content (Matt 24:20; 26:41; 1 Cor 14:13).[7] This is the case here. At times it is difficult to distinguish between purpose and content, for when praying for God to perform his purpose in one's life, that request is also the content of the prayer.

The one who is addressed in prayer is "the God of our Lord Jesus Christ." This is similar to verse 3 ("the God and Father of our Lord Jesus Christ"; cf. also Rom 15:6; 2 Cor 1:3; 11:31; Col 1:3?; 1 Pet 1:3) although there are some differences. The form in the present context

---

nally, the inclusion is preferred. In the NT μνεία is used seven times exclusively by Paul, normally with the personal pronoun. However, the only other time the personal pronoun (in connection with μνεία) is omitted in NA[27] is in 1 Thess 1:2. Nevertheless, even there the inclusion of the personal pronoun has better support than its omission. Hence the style of Paul argues for its inclusion. If one omits it, one needs to supply the personal pronoun "you" as most of the translations do.

1. Cf. Plato *Phaedrus* 254a.

2. BAGD 524; BDAG 654; cf. Robinson, 279–80.

3. BDF §234 (8); BAGD 286; BDAG 367.

4. Earlier εὐχή, Homer *Odyssea* 10.526; Herodotus 1.31; Sophocles *Electra* 636; later προσευχή, Philo *Leg. Gai.* 371 §600; Josephus *B.J.* 5.9.4 §388.

5. BDB 813; E. Gerstenberger and H.-J Fabry, "פלל *pll*, etc.," *TDOT* 11 (2001): 568–72.

6. BAGD 713; BDAG 878–79; Heinrich Greeven, "προσεύχομαι, προσευχή," *TDNT* 2 (1964): 807–8; Hans Schönweiss, "Prayer [προσεύχομαι, κτλ.]," *NIDNTT* 2 (1976): 867–69.

7. Moule, *Idiom Book*, 145; Burton, *Moods and Tenses* §§200, 203; Wallace, *Greek Grammar*, 475.

is unique.[1] The Arians misconstrued it to mean that Christ was not the eternal Word but was the created Son of God who prayed and worshiped his Creator. The Arians failed to distinguish between the subordination of the Son to the Father, and the unity of essence of both the Son and the Father.

As already discussed at verse 3 the genitival prepositional phrase "of our Lord Jesus Christ" shows four things: (1) his personal relationship with the believer ("our Lord"); (2) his name ("Jesus"); (3) his Lordship ("Jesus is Lord" was an early confession of the church, Acts 2:36; 8:16; 10:36; 11:17; 19:5; Rom 10:9; 14:9; 1 Cor 12:3; 2 Cor 4:5; Phil 2:11); and (4) his title ("Christ") more than just a name, it denotes that he is the promised Messiah who would bring salvation (cf. v. 1).

ὁ πατὴρ τῆς δόξης, "the Father of glory," a further description of God, is unique in Jewish and NT traditions.[2] He is called "the God of glory" (Ps 29:3 [LXX 28:3]; Acts 7:2), "the Lord of glory" (Num 24:11; 1 Cor 2:8), and "the king of Glory" (Ps 24:7, 8, 9, 10 [LXX 23:7, 8, 9, 10]; 1QM 12:8; 19:1). As discussed at verse 6, the meaning of "glory" is the reflection of the essence of one's being, the summation of all of one's attributes. The essence of one's being makes an impact from which one's reputation emerges. Because of the way in which God has revealed himself, his reputation displays splendor, power, and radiance. In the immediate context God has revealed himself in election, predestination, redemption, revelation of his will, and the sealing with the Holy Spirit. All of these characterize gracious acts which bring praise of his glory (vv. 6, 12, 14). In the present verse he epitomizes this by saying that he is the Father of glory. The genitive (δόξης) could be attributive "the glorious father" (NIV) which would denote God as the source of his splendor.[3] It seems better to label the genitive as characteristic quality, that is, the Father is characterized by his glory.[4] He is not only a glorious Father but the Father to whom all glory belongs (NEB "the all-glorious Father") or of whom glory is the characteristic feature. It is to this kind of God that Paul prays.

δώῃ[5] ὑμῖν, "[God] may give to you." The real syntactical debate is whether the verb is an aorist optative (δῴη) or subjunctive (δώῃ). On the whole grammarians think that this must be subjunctive because the final optative, although not quite obsolete in NT times, would be

1. For a discussion of similar phrases, see Sellin, "Über einige ungewöhnliche Genitive im Epheserbrief," 94–96.

2. Although this is unique, the phrase ὁ θεὸς τῆς δόξης is frequently used in the Jewish literature and the NT (cf. Sellin, "Über einige ungewöhnliche Genitive im Epheserbrief," 93–94, esp. n. 36).

3. Barth, 148.

4. Eadie, 81; Ellicott, 23; cf. Robertson, *Grammar*, 398.

5. Another form of the subjunctive (δῷ) is found only in B 1739 1881 *pc*.

an artificial construction.[1] Except for the Atticists and much later writers (first to third century A.D.), the final optative does not follow a present tense as would be the case here.[2] Therefore, Paul is praying that God may give to them, the Ephesian believers, the content of the request expressed in the next words.

πνεῦμα σοφίας καὶ ἀποκαλύψεως, "the spirit of insight and revelation." The words σοφία and ἀποκάλυψις need to be discussed first. The word σοφία has already been discussed at verse 8 as meaning the true insight of known facts or insight into the true nature of things and thus best translated as "insight." The second word ἀποκάλυψις in the verb form comes from καλύπτω, meaning "to cover, to hide, to conceal,"[3] and ἀπο-, "from." Hence, it has the meaning "to unveil, to disclose" something that had previously been hidden. The noun is used from first century B.C. onwards, meaning "disclosure, revelation."[4] The noun is used only four times in the LXX (1 Sam 20:30; Ode 13:32; Sir 11:27; 22:22). In the 1 Samuel reference it speaks of Jonathan's mother's "nakedness" revealing what should be hidden (for a study of the verb form, see 3:5). Although in the LXX the "spirit of wisdom" seldom appears (Exod 31:3; 35:31; Isa 11:2; Wis 1:6; 7:7), the "spirit of revelation" never occurs. It is used eighteen times in the NT, thirteen times by Paul, and twice in Ephesians (1:17; 3:3). In the NT it always has theological significance, referring to the unveiling of those things which were hidden in God and unknown to humans. It is "not the impartation of knowledge, but the actual unveiling of intrinsically hidden facts."[5] Therefore, revelation is some hidden thing or mystery of God that is unveiled by God and cannot be discovered by human investigation.

Much discussion has been raised over the "spirit," whether it refers to the Holy Spirit or to the human spirit. Able students of the Scriptures have been on both sides of the issue. Some of those who think it refers to the human spirit base it on the anarthrous usage. However, being anarthrous does not necessitate it to be a human spirit, for clearly there are numerous references in the NT to the Holy Spirit with no preceding article (cf. Rom 8:4, 5, 9*ter*, 13, 14; Gal 5:5, 16). Others who argue that it refers to the human spirit[6] point to genitives that follow πνεῦμα, as in the cases of the spirit of "bondage" (Rom 8:15), "stupor" (11:8), "meekness" (Gal 6:1), and "timidity" (2 Tim

1. MHT 1:196–97; BDF §§369 (1); 386 (3); Robertson, *Grammar*, 983; Moulton (MHT 1:55) thinks the subjunctive seems to be "a syntactical necessity."

2. MHT 3:129.

3. LSJ 871.

4. Plutarch *Aemilius Paulus* 14.3.

5. Albrecht Oepke, "ἀποκαλύπτω, ἀποκάλυψις," *TDNT* 3 (1965): 591; cf. also Wilhelm Mundle, "Revelation [ἀποκαλύπτω, δηλόω, ἐπιφάνεια, χρηματίζω]," *NIDNTT* 3 (1978): 312–15.

6. Chrysostom *Eph* 1:15–20 (*PG* 62:23); Abbott, 28; Westcott, 22–23; Lenski, 393; Barth, 148; Bruce, 269; Wallace, *Greek Grammar*, 90–91.

1:7). Thus, this view contends that in the present context it refers to the attitude or spiritual disposition toward insight and the openness to revelation. Those who think that it refers to the Holy Spirit[1] do so because the qualities of wisdom and revelation cannot be generated by humans. This second view is preferred for seven reasons. First, although the first view can define the "spirit of wisdom" as "a wise disposition," it cannot explain the "spirit of revelation," for revelation (ἀποκάλυψις) is not the understanding of the hidden things but the disclosing of them.[2] The human spirit cannot disclose the hidden mysteries of God. Second, Lincoln argues that the context of the book supports that revelation is by God's Spirit and not the human spirit.[3] In 3:3 the mystery was made known to Paul by revelation and in 3:5 the mystery was revealed (verb form) to the holy apostles and prophets by the Spirit. Paul continues by stating the contents of the mystery (3:6) and shows that this intricate wisdom of God will be made known to the angelic forces by the church (3:10). Third, Meyer has pointed out that whenever πνεῦμα, "spirit," is the predicate of "to give," as is the case in this verse, it always refers to the objective spirit, whether it be divine or demonical (e.g., Luke 11:13; John 3:34; Acts 8:18; 15:8; Rom 5:5; 1 Thess 4:8; 1 John 3:24).[4] As mentioned above, Rom 8:15 ("spirit of bondage") is used to support the human spirit view. However, this verse most likely is a reference to the Holy Spirit. The spirit of "bondage" is contrasted to the spirit of "adoption" and seems certain to refer to the Holy Spirit who did not lead them back into bondage but rather brought about their adoption.[5] It is not a disposition of adoption. Fourth, those who do hold to the first view generally state that the disposition is not self-generated but generated by the Holy Spirit. So ultimately the source is the Holy Spirit. It seems more logical, therefore, to begin with the Holy Spirit. Fifth, other genitival expressions such as "Spirit of truth" (John 15:26), "Spirit of his Son" (Gal 4:6), and "Spirit of God" (Matt 12:28) refer to the Holy Spirit. Sixth, this corresponds to verse 8 where God has graciously "lavished on us all insight and discretion."[6] Now Paul prays that God may give them the Spirit that makes possible insight and discloses hidden mysteries.

1. Oecumenius *Eph* 1:15–20 (*PG* 118:1181); Theophylact *Eph* 1:17 (*PG* 124:1045); Calvin, 134; Bengel, 4:70; Hodge, 71–72; Eadie, 82–84; Ellicott, 23; Meyer, 69–70; Salmond, 273–74; Robinson, 38–39; Masson, 153; Schlier, 77–79; Gaugler, 62; Hendriksen, 96–97; Schnackenburg, 74; Lincoln, 57; Best, 162–63; O'Brien, 132; Erich Mauerhofer, "Der Brief an die Epheser. 11. Teil: 1,17.18," *Fundamentum* 2 (1992): 17–18; Hui, "The Concept of the Holy Spirit in Ephesians," 292–95; Fee, *God's Empowering Presence*, 674–76.

2. Salmond, 273–74.

3. Lincoln, 57.

4. Meyer, 70 n. 1.

5. C. E. B. Cranfield, *The Epistle to the Romans*, vol. 1, ICC, ed. J. A. Emerton and C. E. B. Cranfield (Edinburgh: T & T Clark, 1975), 396–97.

6. Schlier, 79.

Seventh, as Schnackenburg shows, this verse corresponds to the field of meaning in 1 Cor 2:6–16 where it states that the Holy Spirit imparts wisdom and knowledge and reveals the secret counsels of God.[1] The whole point of that passage is that humans cannot know the things of God by their own ingenuity. Thus, in conclusion, it seems this refers to the Holy Spirit.

Yet two major problems attend this view. First, how can Paul pray for God to give them the Holy Spirit when he has already been imparted, and second, how can these genitives be categorized? To answer the initial question, the second one must first be addressed. It is best to consider that these genitives denote characteristic quality. The Spirit is characterized as one who gives insight and unveils God's hidden mysteries. The genitives denote special manifestations of the Spirit.[2] Regarding the first problem, Paul is not praying that they be given the Holy Spirit for he has already been imparted to them. Rather, he is praying for a specific manifestation of the Spirit so that the believers will have insight and know something of God's mysteries as a result of the Holy Spirit's revelation. However, the request does not end here. Paul has a specific objective for the Spirit who gives insight and unveils.

ἐν ἐπιγνώσει αὐτοῦ, "in the knowledge of him." Much study has been devoted to ἐπίγνωσις, "knowledge,"[3] partly to see if it had a different meaning than γνῶσις. Bultmann thinks that it is difficult "to find any strict distinction" between the two words in the LXX, Philo, and the NT.[4] The function of the prepositional prefix ἐπι-, according to Lightfoot, is to intensify and hence it indicates "a larger and more thorough knowledge"[5] than γνῶσις. Robinson, in disagreeing with Lightfoot, thinks the ἐπί is not intensive but directive and hence, whereas γνῶσις signifies breadth and looks at knowledge in the full and abstract sense, "ἐπίγνωσις is knowledge directed towards a particular object, perceiving, discerning, recognizing."[6] This latter idea seems to be the correct assessment of the word and it fits well with this context. The genitive pronoun (αὐτοῦ) following it is objective and thus "denotes the object of the knowledge."[7] Hence, the knowledge is

1. Schnackenburg, 74 n. 12.

2. Ellicott, 23.

3. Robinson, 248–54; Rudolf Bultmann, "γινώσκω, κτλ.," *TDNT* 1 (1964): 689–719; Kathryn Sullivan, "Epignosis in the Epistle of St. Paul," in *Studiorum Paulinorum Congressus Internationalis Catholicus 1961*, vol. 2, AnBib, vol. 18 (Rome: E Pontificio Instituto Biblico, 1963), 405–16; Robert E. Picirelli [*sic*], "The Meaning of 'Epignosis'," *EvQ* 47 (April–June 1975): 85–93.

4. Bultmann, *TDNT* 1 (1964): 707.

5. J. B. Lightfoot, *Saint Paul's Epistles to the Colossians and to Philemon* (London: Macmillan, 1875; reprint, Grand Rapids: Zondervan, n.d.), 138; cf. Eadie, 85.

6. Robinson, 254. For a slight variation of Robinson, see Picirelli [*sic*], "The Meaning of 'Epignosis'," 91–92.

7. Robinson, 254.

directed toward God and not Christ as Calvin thinks.[1] It is "the perception of God's will or the recognition of him in his self-revelation in Jesus Christ."[2] It is to know God intimately. This corresponds very closely with Col 1:9–10 where Paul prays that they will be filled with the knowledge of his will in all spiritual wisdom and understanding and further that they will increase in the knowledge of God.

This prepositional phrase must now be considered as a whole. The preposition ἐν denotes the sphere in which the action takes place.[3] Some connect this prepositional phrase with what follows—"in the knowledge of him the eyes of your heart have been enlightened."[4] But this does not flow well, especially with the perfect participle in the following clause (v. 18a). Eadie thinks the prepositional phrase is joined especially to "revelation" (ἀποκάλυψις),[5] but it is much more natural for it to go back to both of the characteristic genitives of insight and revelation.[6]

Therefore, Paul prays that God would give the Holy Spirit's insight and disclosure in the sphere or area of the knowledge of God himself. This corresponds to 1 Cor 2:10–16 where the Holy Spirit searches the deep things of God and reveals them to the believer. The deep things of God are God's wisdom and power to change individuals through the crucified Christ. In the present context the believer is to come to know him intimately and as a result the believer will become acquainted with God's actions described in the following verses. Hence, it is not facts about God that are most important but knowing him personally and intimately. One can know many facts about the leader of a nation through the news media, but that is quite different from personally knowing that leader as his or her family does. Thus, one acquires this knowledge of God not only by facts from the Bible but by the Holy Spirit's giving insight and disclosure in the knowledge of God himself. In the end, philosophy says "Know yourself" whereas Christianity says "Know your God, through the Holy Spirit." One final thing that needs to be said is that this knowledge of God is available to all Christians and not just to the apostles, prophets, or a select group within the community.[7]

1. Calvin, 134.

2. C. F. D. Moule, "A Note on the Knowledge of God," Appendix III in *The Epistles of Paul the Apostle to the Colossians and to Philemon*, Cambridge Greek Testament Commentary, ed. C. F. D. Moule (Cambridge: Cambridge University Press, 1957), 160.

3. Ellicott, 23–24.

4. Chrysostom *Eph* 1:15–20 (*PG* 62:24); Theophylact *Eph* 1:17 (*PG* 124:1045); Olshausen, 149; Abbott, 28.

5. Eadie, 84.

6. Ellicott, 24; Salmond, 274–75.

7. Bockmuehl, *Revelation and Mystery*, 200; *contra* Gnosticism, see Elaine Hiesey Pagels, *The Gnostic Paul: Gnostic Exegesis of Pauline Letters* (Philadelphia: Fortress, 1975), 117.

Again all three persons of the Trinity are mentioned in this verse, namely, God, the father of our Lord Jesus Christ, who gives insight about himself through the Holy Spirit. This fits well with Ephesians' abundant references to the Trinity (cf. 1:4–14, 17; 2:18, 22; 3:4–5, 14–17; 4:4–6; 5:18–20).

1:18a. πεφωτισμένους τοὺς ὀφθαλμοὺς τῆς καρδίας [ὑμῶν][1] "since the eyes of your heart have been enlightened." The perfect passive participle πεφωτισμένους comes from the verb φωτίζω which has the idea "to give light, to light (up), to illuminate," "to enlighten."[2] The eye is metaphorically the avenue through which light flows to the heart or mind. In all literature καρδία, "heart," refers to the physical organ but more frequently it is used figuratively to refer to the seat of the moral and intellectual life.[3] In classical literature καρδία, "heart," is used to refer to the physical organ of humans and beast[4] but more frequently it refers to the seat of feelings and emotions,[5] of will or volition,[6] and of thought and understanding.[7] In nature it is used of the middle or core of a plant.[8] Hence, figuratively, the heart is the very center of a person, beast, or plant. In the LXX the term occurs 935 times (744 times in the canonical books) and rarely does it have reference to the physical organ (e.g., 2 Kgs 9:24; see also 1 Sam 25:37; 2 Sam 18:14). In the NT "heart" occurs 156 times (157 times if one accepts Acts 8:37 as genuine), fifty-two in Paul's writings, six of which are in Ephesians (1:18; 3:17; 4:18; 5:19; 6:5, 22), and it never refers to the physical organ. In biblical usage the heart can be the seat of feelings and emotions (Deut 28:47; Ps 34:18 [MT 34:19; LXX 33:19]; John 16:6, 22; Eph 6:22), the place of God's residence (Rom 5:5; Eph 3:17), the seat of religious and moral conduct both positively (1 Sam 12:20; Jas 4:8; Eph 6:5) and negatively (Exod 4:21; Rom 2:5; Eph 4:18), of will or volition (1 Kgs 8:17; 1 Cor 4:5; Eph 5:19), and, as it is in the present verse, of thought and understanding (Deut 28:28; Job 34:10, 34; Dan 2:30; Matt

1. The manuscripts that omit ὑμῶν—𝔓[46] B 6 33 1175 1739 1881 arm (Marcion[acc. to Tertullian]) Origen (Cyril-Jerusalem) Didymus[4/5] Didymus[dub] Cyril—are few and basically all Alexandrian. Its inclusion is found in ℵ A D F G Ψ 075 0150 0278 81 104 256 263 365 424 436 459 1241 1319 1573 1852 1912 1962 2127 2200 2464 *Byz* [K L P] *Lect* it[ar, b, d, f, (g), o] vg syr[p, h, pal] cop[sa, bo, fay] eth geo slav Gregory-Nyssa Didymus[1/5] Ammonas Chrysostom (Severian) Victorinus-Rome Ambrosiaster Jerome Pelagius Augustine, which represent good representative manuscripts from the various text-types, and thus has good geographical distribution. This is certainly the best reading.

2. BAGD 873; BDAG 1074.

3. For a thorough study of heart, see Friedrich Baumgärtel and Johannes Behm, "καρδία," *TDNT* 3 (1965): 605–13.

4. E.g., Homer *Ilias* 10.94; 13.442; Plato *Symposium* §215e; Aeschylus *Eumenides* 861; Aristotle *Historia Animalium* 2.15 §506a.5; 2.17 §508a.30.

5. Homer *Odyssea* 17.489; *Ilias* 9.646.

6. Sophocles *Antigone* 1105.

7. Homer *Ilias* 21.441; Pindar *Olympian Odes* 13.16.

8. Theophrastus *Historia Plantarum* 1.2.6; 3.14.1.

12:34 = Luke 6:45; Rom 1:21; 10:6; cf. also 1QS 2:3; 4:2). Hence, the "eyes of the heart"[1] denotes enlightenment of thought and understanding. The word "heart" is in the singular, denoting that it belongs to each person of the group.[2] An almost identical expression is given by Clement of Rome where the prayer to God is, "open the eyes of our heart to know you" (ἀνοίξας τοὺς ὀφθαλμοὺς τῆς καρδίας ἡμῶν εἰς τὸ γινώσκειν σε).[3] One difference is the use of the aorist imperative rather than a perfect participle. However, it may well be that these words are from Ephesians since the context in Clement is of knowing God, which is the same as Ephesians. Since Clement's letter is dated sometime between A.D. 75–110, it would show that Ephesians was recognized early.

The real problem with this clause is its syntactical connection. There are six ways this can be taken, but these can be divided into two major alternatives. The first alternative is to have πεφωτισμένους τοὺς ὀφθαλμούς refer back to δώῃ and thus be a part of the request. There are three variations of this alternative. (1) Some take πεφωτισμένους τοὺς ὀφθαλμούς as the second predicate of δώῃ which would be translated, "that God may give you the Spirit of insight and revelation in the knowledge of him [and] the enlightenment of the eyes of your heart" (NASB, NEB, JB, NIV, NJB).[4] The criticism of this view is that it does not really reckon with the perfect participle. It seems that if Paul were to employ a participle in this manner, he would probably have used an aorist participle. Normally, one would expect another aorist subjunctive. (2) Some would see the participial construction as being in apposition to πνεῦμα, "Spirit," and would translate it the same way as view (1).[5] Again, as in view (1), this view does not reckon with the perfect participle. (3) Others take it as a circumstantial participle of result of the gift of the Spirit and would translate it, "that God may give you the Spirit of insight and revelation in the knowledge of him resulting in the enlightenment of the eyes of your heart."[6] Nevertheless, to express a result with the participle is rare and to make it subsequent to the giving of the Spirit seems awkward in light of the fact that it is perfect participle.

The second major alternative is to see πεφωτισμένους τοὺς ὀφθαλμούς not as a part of the request, but an ancillary thought to the request. There are three variations of thought about this. (1) It is possible that πεφωτισμένους τοὺς ὀφθαλμούς is in apposition to ὑμῖν (v. 17) and would be translated, "that God may give you, who had the eyes of your heart

1. Cf. its use in *Corpus Hermeticum* 4.11; 7.1, 2.

2. MHT 3:23.

3. Clement of Rome *Epistola 1 ad Corinthios* 59.3.

4. Ewald, 98; Gaugler, 63; Gnilka, 90 n. 6; Hugedé, 55; Schnackenburg 74; Bruce, 270; Mauerhofer, "Der Brief an die Epheser. 11. Teil: 1,17.18," 22.

5. Olshausen, 149; Harless, 98; Abbott, 28–29; Lenksi 395; Hendriksen, 98 n. 38.

6. Alford, 3:83; Ellicott, 24; Meyer, 72–73.

enlightened, the Spirit of insight and revelation in the knowledge of him." This makes more sense except for the question of why it was put in the accusative rather than the dative. (2) Some think that it is an accusative absolute that looks back to ὑμῖν in verse 17 and is closely tied to εἰς τὸ εἰδέναι ὑμᾶς in the latter part of verse 18. It can be translated like view (1) or, "that God may give you the Spirit of insight and revelation in the knowledge of him, already having had the eyes of your heart enlightened" (AV, RV, ASV, RSV, NRSV).[1] In some ways this view is a refinement of view (1). Although the accusative absolute is infrequent, it is used in Acts 26:3 (cf. 1 Cor 16:6; Rom 8:3) and possibly Eph 2:1, 5. (3) It is an accusative absolute that anticipates the ὑμᾶς in the immediately following infinitival clause and could be translated, "in order that you, who had the eyes of your heart enlightened, might know." This is paralleled in 3:17 where you have two nominative absolutes that look forward to the following ἵνα clause in 3:18.[2] Although this is an attractive view, it does not read as easily as view (2). It seem that Paul would have put the accusative absolute after ὑμᾶς to make his intentions clearer. It is more difficult to read because it loads too much into the latter half of verse 18.

In conclusion, the second major alternative is better than the first one. Of this alternative, view (2) is preferred while keeping in mind that the accusative absolute does look forward to the following ὑμᾶς. Hence, πεφωτισμένους τοὺς ὀφθαλμούς looks back to ὑμῖν in verse 17 and forward to ὑμᾶς in the latter part of verse 18. Thus it could be translated, "that God may give *you* the Spirit of insight and revelation in the knowledge of him, [*you*] having had the eyes of your heart enlightened, in order that *you* might know. . . ." Viewing the participle as causal and taking more notice of its passive voice, it would better read, "that God may give you the Spirit of insight and revelation in the knowledge of him, since the eyes of your heart have been enlightened, in order that you might know. . . ."[3] The point being made is that Paul is praying that God may give them the Spirit of insight and revelation, not an impossible request because the believers in Ephesus already have had their understanding enlightened.

But what is this enlightenment and when did it occur? Some want to explain it as baptism.[4] However, this is completely foreign to the context.[5] Noyen thinks it speaks of the enlightenment of the mystery to the Gentiles as confirmed in 3:8–9 where the unsearchable riches of Christ are preached to the Gentiles to enlighten (φωτίσαι) them of the

1. Bengel, 4:70; Eadie, 86–87; Salmond, 275; Westcott, 24; Simpson, 38 n. 31; Barth, 149; Lincoln, 47.

2. This suggestion was personally given to me by Darrell L. Bock.

3. Wallace, *Greek Grammar*, 631 n. 47.

4. Justin Martyr *Apologia* 1.61.12; 65.1; Lock, 26; Schlier, 79–80; Patzia, 144; cf. Dahl, "Dopet i Efesierbrevet," 87.

5. Barth, 149–50; Schnackenburg, 74.

dispensation of the mystery.[1] However, the immediate context is not addressing the issue of the mystery. Rather, it is concerned that they might know God more intimately. It is best to think that since the Ephesian believers were chosen, redeemed, and sealed, they were enlightened the moment they heard and believed (vv. 3–14). This makes good sense of the perfect passive participle, for they had once been enlightened with continuing results of enlightenment.[2]

In conclusion then, Paul prays that God might give them the Spirit to procure the insight and revelation of their knowledge of God. This was possible because their understanding had already been enlightened at the moment of belief. Again, the reason Paul made this request was because of his great desire that they know God more intimately. Why did he want this for the believers? This will be discussed next.

b. The Reason for Wisdom and Revelation (1:18b–23)

Having stated his request that the Ephesians might know God intimately, Paul now states the purpose of such knowledge. This intimate knowledge would make believers aware of: (1) the hope of his calling (v. 18b); (2) the wealth of the glory of his inheritance in the saints (v. 18c); and (3) the greatness of his power in us (vv. 19–23). These are not three separate prayer requests but a declaration of the three areas to be comprehended concerning the purpose of the one request (for a structural layout of the prayer, see 1:16b).

(1) What Is the Hope of His Calling (1:18b)

Text: 1:18b. εἰς τὸ εἰδέναι ὑμᾶς τίς ἐστιν ἡ ἐλπὶς τῆς κλήσεως αὐτοῦ,

Translation: 1:18b. "in order that you might know what is the hope of his calling,"

Commentary: 1:18b. εἰς τὸ εἰδέναι ὑμᾶς, "in order that you might know." εἰς τό with the infinitive is predominantly used by Paul and most frequently it expresses purpose.[3] This certainly fits well in this context. Much discussion has been generated over the distinctions or similarities of οἶδα and γινώσκω.[4] Most conclude that the distinctions are slight and each occurrence must be determined by its use in the context. Although γινώσκω generally means "to find something out," in

1. Carlos Noyen, "Foi, charité, espérance et «connaissance» dans les Epîtres de la Captivité," *NRT* 94 (Novembre 1972): 901–7, esp. 902–4.

2. Cf. Fanning, *Verbal Aspect*, 416–18.

3. MHT 1:218–19; Burton, *Moods and Tenses* §409; cf. also BDF §402 (2); MHT 3:143; Robertson, *Grammar*, 991, 1071–72, 1087.

4. Heinrich Seesemann, "οἶδα," *TDNT* 5 (1967): 116–19; Donald W. Burdick, "Οἶδα and Γινώσκω in the Pauline Epistles," in *New Dimensions in New Testament Studies*, ed. Richard N. Longenecker and Merrill C. Tenney (Grand Rapids: Zondervan, 1974), 344–56; Moises Silva, "The Pauline Style as Lexical Choice: ΓΙΝΩΣΚΕΙΝ and Related Verbs,"

this context εἰδέναι has this same nuance because Paul wanted the Ephesians to know something that was previously unknown to them.[1] Paul wanted them to discover three things, each introduced by the interrogative pronoun τίς, "what" (for a structural layout of the prayer, see 1:16b).

τίς ἐστιν ἡ ἐλπὶς τῆς κλήσεως αὐτοῦ, "what is the hope of his calling" is the first concept Paul wanted them to understand. The word ἐλπίς has the basic idea of "hope, expectation,"[2] which can easily be dashed.[3] Also, it has the sense of "confidence," the kind, for example, the Peloponnesians had in their navy.[4] In the LXX the noun is used 116 times, seventy-eight times in the canonical books translated from seventeen different Hebrew words. About one-fourth of the time it translates תִּקְוָה, which means "hope" (e.g., Job 5:16; 7:6; Prov 26:12). In Greek thought hope consists merely of a consoling dream of the imagination designed to forget the present troubles but yet leaving one with many uncertainties. On the other hand, in the OT the hope of the righteous is directed toward the eternal God who will protect and ultimately deliver if not now, certainly in the future.[5] In the NT ἐλπίς is used fifty-three times, thirty-six times by Paul, and three times in Ephesians (1:18; 2:12; 4:4). The NT's concept of hope is built on the OT and has the elements of expectation, a trust in God, and the patient waiting for God's outworking of his plan.[6] The ultimate hope for Christians is to be with their Lord (Rom 5:4–5; 8:20, 24–25; 12:12; 15:13; Gal 5:5; Col 1:5; Titus 1:2) and they eagerly wait for his coming, unlike the heathen who have no hope (Eph 2:12; 1 Thess 4:13–18; 5:8; Titus 2:13; 1 John 3:3). Hope in the present context is not the objective hope, that hope which is laid up for the believer (Col 1:5; Rom 8:24) but the subjective hope of all believers. One needs to realize that subjective hope is based on objective hope, a hope that looks back to God's work of redemption in 1:3–14, especially in 1:9–10 where Paul relates that all things are going to be headed up in Christ. Neverthe-

---

in *Pauline Studies. Essays Presented to F. F. Bruce on His 70th Birthday,* ed. Donald A. Hagner and Murray J. Harris (Grand Rapids: Eerdmans; London: Paternoster, 1980), 184–207; Richard J. Erickson, "*Oida* and *Ginōskō* and Verbal Aspect in Pauline Usage," *WJT* 44 (spring 1982): 110–22.

1. Silva, "Pauline Style," 202, 207 n. 42.

2. Sophocles *Oedipus Tyrannus* 158; *Ajax* 478; *Antigone* 330; Euripides *Troades* 633.

3. Euripides *Iphigenia Taurica* 414; *Supplices* 479.

4. Thucydides 2.89.10.

5. Rudolf Bultmann, "ἐλπίς, κτλ.," *TDNT* 2 (1964): 522–23.

6. Ibid., 530–31. Robertson thinks that hope is primarily concerned with unity and reconciliation between Jewish and Gentile believers. See A. C. Robertson, "'Hope' in Ephesians 1:18: A Contextual Approach," *Journal of Theology for Southern Africa* 55 (March 1986): 62–63. However, the context is not about the unity of believers but about knowing God and a part of that is knowing the hope that comes from one being called to salvation.

less, in this verse Paul is referring to the subjective hope. Hope for believers is not the world's wishful thinking, but the absolute certainty that God will make true what he has promised.

The genitive that follows (κλήσεως, "calling") could be a genitive of source, "hope has its origin in his call" or more likely a subjective genitive "hope produced by his calling" (cf. 4:4). The noun κλῆσις is used in classical Greek for "a call" for attention, "summons,"[1] a "summons" to court,[2] or an "invitation" to a feast.[3] The noun is used only three times in the LXX (Jer 31:6 [LXX 38:6]; Jdt 12:10; 3 Macc 5:14) and has the meaning of summons or invitation. In the NT it is used eleven times, nine times by Paul, three times in Ephesians (1:18; 4:1, 4). It can have the idea of a "vocation" (1 Cor 7:20), or a summons or invitation (Phil 3:14), but the other passages refer to a "call" in a religious sense, an "invitation, summons" by God (Rom 11:29; Eph 4:1, 4; 2 Thess 1:11; Heb 3:1). It is closely linked with election (1 Cor 1:26; 2 Pet 1:10; 2 Tim 1:9), for inherent in the verb form is the idea of God's foreknowledge and predestination—he called and justified (Rom 8:29–30). In the present context κλῆσις refers to the believers' call of God to salvation, since they were chosen by the Father to be his and have been adopted into God's family. The pronoun αὐτοῦ, "his," is a possessive genitive and hence it is God's call to them to partake in his salvation and become part of his family. Because believers are called by God into his family, they have hope. Their hope is an absolute certainty. This whole clause looks back into the past because the hope was produced by the call of God on their lives.[4]

(2) What Is the Wealth of His Glorious Inheritance (1:18c)

Text: 1:18c. τίς ὁ πλοῦτος τῆς δόξης τῆς κληρονομίας αὐτοῦ ἐν τοῖς ἁγίοις,

Translation: 1:18c. "what is the wealth of his glorious inheritance in the saints,"

Commentary: 1:18c. τίς[5] ὁ πλοῦτος τῆς δόξης τῆς κληρονομίας αὐτοῦ ἐν τοῖς ἁγίοις, "what is the wealth of his glorious inheritance in the saints." This is the second concept Paul wanted the Ephesians to comprehend. Thus, he requests that they might know God intimately in order that they might know first, the hope of his calling and now sec-

1. Plato *Symposium* 172a; Xenophon *Cyropaedia* 3.2.14.

2. Aristophanes *Nubes* 875, 1189.

3. Xenophon *Symposium* 1.7; Demosthenes *Orationes* 19.32; Plutarch *Pericles* 7.4.

4. Cf. Dietrich Wiederkehr, *Die Theologie der Berufung in den Paulusbriefen*, Studia Friburgensia, vol. 36 (Freiburg: Universitätsverlag, 1963), 199–210, esp. 205.

5. The inclusion of a καί before τίς is supported by $\aleph^{2}$ D^{1} Ψ 𝔐 it^{a} vg^{cl} syr Jerome, but its omission is supported by $\mathfrak{P}^{46}$ ℵ* A B D* F G 0278 33 81 104 1175 1739 1881 *pc* lat $vg^{st,\ ww}$ Ambrosiaster Pelagius. The omission has far better manuscript tradition from each text-type outside the Byzantine and it also has good geographical distribution. The omission is to be accepted.

ond, the wealth of his glorious inheritance in the saints. The word πλοῦτος was briefly discussed at verse 7 (it also occurs in 2:7; 3:8, 16) and has the idea of "abundance, riches, or wealth." The reason for using "wealth" rather than "riches" for our translation is because it expresses singular abundance rather than just one of many kinds of riches.

As in verse 6 here is a series of genitives which is characteristic of Paul (cf. Eph 1:19; 4:13; 6:10; Col 1:13, 27; 2:12; 2 Cor 4:4; 1 Thess 1:3; Rom 8:21; 9:23). Each genitive is dependent on the one preceding it and usually the last genitive is possessive, as is the case here.[1] Each of the genitives will be discussed in order. The first genitive is δόξης which is from δόξα a term that has been discussed at verse 6 where it was concluded that it is the reflection of the essence of one's being, the summation of all of one's attributes, whether referring to God or humans. It is a reflection of the essential character of someone or characteristics of something.

The word κληρονομία occurred in verse 14 and basically means property, possession, or inheritance. In that case, it was used of the believers' inheritance which is their share in heaven. Here it is the other way around. The possessive pronoun αὐτοῦ shows that it is God's inheritance. The genitival relationship of these words is difficult to decipher. Some commentators do not discuss the problem.[2] Others state that they do not want to weaken the weightiness of the matters mentioned by a resolution of the genitives into adjectives and hence translate it, "the wealth of the glory of his inheritance" (AV, ASV, NASB).[3] Some suggest that the first genitive is attributive and translate it "the glorious wealth of his inheritance."[4] Others propose that the second genitive is attributive and translate it "the wealth of his glorious inheritance" (RSV, NIV, NRSV).[5] It is difficult to decide, but the last two alternatives are the most viable. Of these it seems that the last alternative (cf. v. 6) is best because it would place greater stress on God's inheritance in the saints.

The prepositional phrase that follows (ἐν τοῖς ἁγίοις) has been interpreted in various ways. Some think it cannot go back to "inheritance" because the possessive pronoun αὐτοῦ comes in between.[6] However, one must remember that the possessive pronoun is at the end of a series of genitives and the prepositional phrase could well be joined to "inheritance." Furthermore, in 1:4 and 2:1 the possessive pronoun is

1. MHT 3:218; HS §172; BDF §168 (2); Robertson, *Grammar*, 503.

2. Robinson, 40, 150; Westcott, 25; Gaugler, 68–69; Gnilka, 91; Schlier, 84; Barth, 151 (Barth's translation is "*what glorious riches are to be inherited among the saints*," but he does not discuss the problem); Schnackenburg, 75.

3. Alford, 83; Eadie, 89; Ellicott, 25; Meyer, 74; Abbott, 30; Bouttier, 84.

4. Scott, 155; Bruce, 270; Hendriksen, 99; Snodgrass, 74.

5. Hodge, 76; Caird, 45; Mitton, 68; Lincoln, 59.

6. Ellicott, 25; Abbott, 30; Meyer, 75.

between the noun and the prepositional phrase beginning with ἐν. Also, it is concluded that it could be joined to "wealth," which would not change the interpretation since "inheritance" is epexegetical to "wealth." In addition, some propose that the preposition ἐν is translated "among" (NEB, JB, NJB, NRSV),[1] indicating that believers have an inheritance of their share in heaven in the future. However, this is confusing for it is not talking about "our" inheritance, but "his" inheritance. It seems best to translate ἐν as "in" (AV, RV, ASV, RSV, NASB, NIV) meaning that God's inheritance is located in the saints. The saints refer not to angels[2] but to the believers[3] as discussed at verse 1 (cf. also vv. 4, 13, 15). This corresponds to verse 11 where the believer is assigned as God's inheritance. Because of his choosing, redeeming, adopting, and sealing us, we are his possession. Thus, his possession is located in the saints. He will fully gain his inheritance when the saints are removed from this earth and come into his presence. Therefore, not only do we have an inheritance (v. 14) but he also has an inheritance (vv. 11, 18).

To summarize, Paul prayed that we would come to know God more intimately in order that we might know the wealth of his glorious inheritance in the saints. It shows that the believers are valuable to God because he purchased them in order to inherit them. This inheritance will be fully realized in the future. Therefore, whereas the hope that was produced by his calling looked back to the past, his inheritance in the saints will be fully realized in Christ's coming to get his saints.

(3) What Is the Greatness of His Power (1:19–23)

Paul prayed that they might know God more intimately in order to comprehend three things. The first dealt with the past, where the hope was produced by the calling of his people to himself. The second dealt with the future when God will gain his inheritance at the coming of Christ. Now Paul deals with the third area, that is, the greatness of his power which God directs toward believers (for a structural layout of the prayer, see 1:16b). Whereas the first and second concepts to be understood dealt with the past and future respectively, the third deals with the power of God in the present time toward believers. This may be the reason Paul spends more time on this area.

1. Eadie, 89–90; Ellicott, 25; Meyer, 74–75; Abbott, 30; Lincoln, 59.

2. "Angels" is suggested as a possibility by P. Benoit, "Ἅγιοι en Colossiens 1.12: Hommes ou Anges?" in *Paul and Paulinism. Essays in Honour of C. K. Barrett*, ed. M. D. Hooker and S. G. Wilson (London: SPCK, 1982), 87–88, 95; cf. also Schlier, 84; Gnilka, 91; Schnackenburg, 75; Best, 167–68; Lincoln, *Paradise Now and Not Yet*, 144. However, Lincoln has changed his view in his commentary (59–60).

3. Chrysostom *Eph* 1:15–20 (*PG* 62:23); Alford, 3:83–84; Eadie, 89–91; Ellicott, 25; Meyer, 74–75; Abbott, 30; Salmond, 276; Westcott, 24; Gaugler, 69; Bruce, 270–71; Lincoln, 59–60.

(a) Its Magnitude (1:19)

Text: 1:19. καὶ τί τὸ ὑπερβάλλον μέγεθος τῆς δυνάμεως αὐτοῦ εἰς ἡμᾶς τοὺς πιστεύοντας κατὰ τὴν ἐνέργειαν τοῦ κράτους τῆς ἰσχύος αὐτοῦ.

Translation: 1:19. "and what is the surpassing greatness of his power toward us who believe according to the mighty working of his power."

Commentary: 1:19. καὶ τί τὸ ὑπερβάλλον μέγεθος τῆς δυνάμεως αὐτοῦ, "and what is the surpassing greatness of his power." Paul heaps one word on another to express the greatness of God's power that is available to the believer. The participle ὑπερβάλλον from ὑπερβάλλω means "to throw over or beyond a mark"[1] and metaphorically it can be translated "surpass, excel, exceed."[2] This verb occurs only six times in the LXX (Sir 5:7; 25:11; 2 Macc 4:13, 24; 7:42; 3 Macc 2:23) where it means "to surpass, exceed." In the NT it is used five times and only by Paul (2 Cor 3:10; 9:14; Eph 1:19; 2:7; 3:19) and can be translated "surpassing, extraordinary, exceeding."[3] The neuter noun μέγεθος occurs only here in the NT and it means "greatness" or "magnitude."[4] Thus it is the surpassing greatness.

The word δύναμις is the first of four words for power in this verse. Although dynamite is derived from this word, there is no suggestion here or anywhere in the Bible that God's power is instantaneous or explosive. Furthermore, dynamite was not invented until at least a millennium after NT times. Rather, it has the idea of "power, ability, capability of acting."[5] It is used 583 times in the LXX, 373 times in the canonical books translated from twenty-six different Hebrew words. Of these, about 160 times from חַיִל or חֵיל, meaning "strength, efficiency, ability,"[6] and about 130 times from צָבָא, a technical term meaning "host, army"[7] and thus "ability, power, competence."[8] In the NT it occurs 119 times, forty-nine times in Paul, five times in Ephesians (1:19, 21; 3:7, 16, 20) and continues to carry the idea of "power, abil-

1. Homer *Ilias* 23.843, 847.

2. Aeschylus *Prometheus Vinctus* 923; Plato *Politicus* 24 §283e.

3. BAGD 840; BDAG 1032; Gerhard Delling, "ὑπερβάλλω, ὑπερβαλλόντως, ὑπερβολή," *TDNT* 8 (1972): 520–21.

4. Walter Grundmann, "μέγεθος," *TDNT* 4 (1967): 544; G. H. R. Horsley, *New Documents Illustrating Early Christianity*, vol. 4, *A Review of the Greek Inscriptions and Papyri Published in 1979* (Sydney: Macquarie University, 1987), 107.

5. Aristotle *Metaphysica* 9.5.1 §1047b.31; 8.5 §1049b.24; 9.1 §1051a.5; Plato *Respublica* 5.21 §477c–d; cf. also Otto Schmitz, "Der Begriff δύναμις bei Paulus. Ein Beitrag zum Wessen urchristlicher Begriffsbildung," in *Festgabe für Adolf Deissmann zum 60. Geburtstag 7. November 1926* (Tübingen: Mohr, 1927): 139–67; Walter Grundmann, *Der Begriff der Kraft in der neutestamentliche Gedankenwelt*, BWANT, ed. Albrecht Alt and Gerhard Kittel, 4th ser., vol. 8 (Stuttgart: W. Kohlhammer, 1932).

6. BDB 298–99; H. Eising, "חַיִל *chayil*," *TDOT* 4 (1980): 348–55.

7. BDB 838–39; H. Ringgren, "צָבָא *ṣāḇāʾ*," *TWAT* 6 (1989): 872–75.

8. Walter Grundmann, "δύναμαι, κτλ.," *TDNT* 2 (1964): 285; Gerhard Friedrich, "δύναμις," *EDNT* 1 (1990): 356.

ity." By way of contrast, the verb form of this word used with a negative particle is seen in Rom 8:7–8 where Paul states that the natural person does not have the power, ability, or capability to please God. Hence, this power or ability is that which is capable for the task and is determined by what it is modified. Here it is modified by the possessive personal pronoun αὐτοῦ, "his," and thus it is talking about God's power, the ability of God himself. It is no wonder that Paul calls it the surpassing greatness of his power.

εἰς ἡμᾶς[1] **τοὺς πιστεύοντας,** "toward us who believe." The preposition εἰς indicates direction and it relates back to "his power," which means that the goal of knowing God intimately is that we might know his great power that is directed toward "us." This "can probably be understood to include the sense of ἐν, 'in' (cf. 3:20 where God's power is said to be at work within believers)."[2] Paul further defines the "us" as those "who believe." It is normal for a participle to have an article when in apposition to the personal pronoun[3] and the article serves as a relative pronoun. Paul is not saying that the power is available at moments of belief, but rather he is stating that the power is available to "believers." Here again the "us" indicates Paul's identification with the believers in Ephesus.

κατὰ τὴν ἐνέργειαν τοῦ κράτους τῆς ἰσχύος αὐτοῦ, "according to the mighty working of his power." This prepositional phrase does not modify "toward us who believe" but modifies "the surpassing greatness of his power."[4] The preposition κατά with the accusative denotes standard. Having mentioned the surpassing greatness of God's power, Paul is now going to show that it is literally "according to the power of the power of his power." Paul lists a series of three words for power used to describe the standard of the surpassing greatness of God's power. There is a need to look briefly at each of the words and then analyze the phrase as a whole.[5]

The first word, ἐνέργεια, like the verb form, which has already been discussed at verse 11, is derived from the noun ἐνεργός from which we get our English word "energy."[6] According to Aristotle ἐνέργεια is "actual" power whereas δύναμις is "potential" power.[7] It is active energy as opposed to potential energy. "In Greek grammar *energeia* has one

1. The reading ὑμᾶς is found in D* F G P 33 104 629 1175 *al* it Ambrosiaster, which is limited almost exclusively to the Western text-type and therefore is not acceptable.

2. Lincoln, 61.

3. Robertson, *Grammar*, 778.

4. *Contra* Eberhard Nestle, "Little Contributions to the Greek Testament," *ExpTim* 14 (October 1902): 35–36.

5. For a study of these words, see Clark, "The Meaning of ἐνεργέω and καταργέω in the New Testament," 3–101; Arnold, *Ephesians: Power and Magic*, 73–75.

6. For further study, see Robinson, 241–47; Bertram, *TDNT* 2 (1964): 652–54; Barclay, *New Testament Words*, 77–84.

7. Aristotle *Metaphysica* 9.5.1 §1047b.31; 8.5 §1049b.24; 9.1 §1051a.5.

technical meaning; it means the *active* mood of the verb in contradistinction to the *passive*."[1] ἐνέργεια is used eight times in the LXX, only in noncanonical books and hence no Hebrew original (Wis 7:17, 26; 13:4; 18:22; 2 Macc 3:29; 3 Macc 4:21; 5:12, 28). In Wis 7:17; 13:4; 18:22 it refers to cosmic powers, otherwise, all the other passages refer to God's power. In the NT it occurs eight times and is used only by Paul, three times in Ephesians (1:19; 3:7; 4:16). It always refers to supernatural power: once of satanic power (2 Thess 2:9), while the others allude to God's power directly (Eph 1:19; 3:7; Phil 3:21; Col 1:29; 2:12; 2 Thess 2:11) or indirectly (Eph 4:16). In conclusion, ἐνέργεια is supernatural power that is in actual operation. It is the active exercise of supernatural power.

The next word, κράτος, means "strength, might,"[2] like physical strength[3] or "mastery, victory" as in a war.[4] Out of the fifty-one times this word occurs in the LXX, it appears only eighteen times in the canonical books and these are translated from nine different Hebrew words denoting "strength, might" of God (Job 12:16; Ps 62:12 [MT 62:13; LXX 61:13]; 90:11 [LXX 89:11]; Isa 40:26), of human beings (Deut 8:17; Job 21:23; Ps 59:9 [MT 59:10; LXX 58:10]), and of nature (Ps 89:9 [MT 89:10; LXX 88:10]). In the NT it is used twelve times, four times by Paul, twice in Ephesians (1:19; 6:10) and it always has reference to supernatural power: once of the devil (Heb 2:14), and the other eleven times of God. It is used in doxologies to extol the power or dominion of God (1 Pet 5:11; Jude 25; Rev 5:13) and of Christ (1 Tim 6:16; 1 Pet 4:11; Rev 1:6; 5:13), which has victory over all contrary powers. The verb form, κρατέω, makes the power obvious, for it means primarily to grasp, seize, or capture (Matt 9:25 = Mark 5:41; Matt 14:3 = Mark 6:17; Matt 26:48, 50, 55 = Mark 14:44, 46, 49; Rev 20:2). It is from κράτος from which we get theocracy, the rule of God; autocracy, absolute rule; democracy, the rule of the people; and plutocracy, the rule of the wealthy. Therefore, κράτος has the meaning of "strength, might, dominion, mastery."

The final word to be discussed is ἰσχύς, prominent in early Greek literature but later waned, denotes "strength, power, might, ability" that is possessed[5] like the strength of human beings.[6] It is the second most frequently used word for power in the canonical LXX, occurring 347 times (255 times in canonical books) and translated from twenty-seven Hebrew words, specifically, about 100 times from כֹּחַ, which

1. Barclay, *New Testament Words*, 79.

2. For further study, see Wilhelm Michaelis, "κράτος (θεοκρατία), κτλ.," *TDNT* 3 (1965): 905–10; Georg Braumann, "Strength [κράτος]," *NIDNTT* 3 (1978): 716–18.

3. Homer *Ilias* 7.142.

4. Ibid., 1.509; 6.387.

5. For further study, see Walter Grundmann, "ἰσχύω, κτλ.," *TDNT* 3 (1965): 397–402; Georg Braumann, "Strength [ἰσχύς]," *NIDNTT* 3 (1978): 712–14.

6. Hesiod *Theogonia* 146, 823; Sophocles *Philoctetes* 104.

means "strength, power," whether it be of God (Ps 65:6 [MT 65:7; LXX 64:7]; Jer 10:12), humans (Judg 16:5–19, 30; Ps 31:10 [MT 31:11; LXX 30:11]), or animals (Job 39:11, 21; Prov 14:4).[1] It generally denotes inherent strength. In the NT it is used ten times, three times in Paul (2 Thess 1:9), and twice in Ephesians (1:19; 6:10). It has reference to the strength of humans (Mark 12:30 = Luke 10:27; Mark 12:33), and of angels (2 Pet 2:11); the power of strength of God (Eph 1:19; 6:10; 2 Thess 1:9; 1 Pet 4:11); and it is used in doxologies to praise the might of Christ (Rev 5:12) and God (7:12). It continues to have the idea of a power or strength that can be possessed.

How do these words for power relate to each other? All four terms are closely related and overlap with one another. First, ἰσχύς speaks of the inherent strength or of power possessed. Second, κράτος is close to ἰσχύς but denotes even more emphatically the presence and significance of the strength or force of power, or the ability to overcome resistance,[2] or more at the visible aspect of strength, perhaps its supremacy.[3] Third, ἐνέργεια stresses the activity of power, namely, it is power in action. Fourth, δύναμις, found earlier in this verse, denotes capacity in view of its ability or potential power. By way of illustration, a bulldozer has the ability, capacity, and potential of routing out trees (δύναμις). By looking at it, one senses its inherent strength (ἰσχύς) but when its engine roars and it begins to move, its power of mastery becomes obvious (κράτος). However, when it comes to a tree and knocks it over one sees the activity of its power (ἐνέργεια). Similarly, Calvin illustrates the use of these words by stating that ἰσχύς is like the root, κράτος the tree, and ἐνέργεια the fruit.[4] It seems that δύναμις is the more general term and that the other terms support it, as is the case in this passage. Again these words overlap and the point of using all of these words is not so much to emphasize their distinctiveness but to enforce the idea of God's abundant power available to all believers.

In looking at other NT passages where any of these terms occur together, there are never more than two in any one passage and not enough of these to establish any order of the words. In the present context it is necessary to see what kind of genitival relationship is in the prepositional phrase, κατὰ τὴν ἐνέργειαν τοῦ κράτους τῆς ἰσχύος αὐτοῦ. As in verses 6 and 18 here is a series of genitives that is characteristic of Paul (cf. Eph 4:13; 6:10; Col 1:13, 27; 2:12; 2 Cor 4:4; 1 Thess 1:3; Rom 8:21; 9:23). Each genitive is dependent on the one preceding it, and usually the last genitive is possessive, as is the case here,[5] hence, "his strength." The other two genitives could be attributive but what

1. BDB 470–71; H. Ringgren, "כֹּחַ *kōaḥ*," *TDOT* 7 (1995): 122–28.
2. Abbott, 31; Westcott, 25–26.
3. Michaelis, *TDNT* 3 (1965): 908.
4. Calvin, 135.
5. MHT 3:218; HS §172; BDF §168 (2); Robertson, *Grammar*, 503.

are they modifying? It could be interpreted as "the mighty working of his strength" (AV) or "the working of his mighty strength" (RSV, JB, NIV, NJB, NRSV). The first of these makes better sense. What kind of potential power? It is the mighty working or the masterful activity of power making κράτους attributive to ἐνέργειαν. The next genitive (ἰσχύος) could be possessive or it could even refer to source, in which case this mighty working comes from God's inherent strength. Outside of the NT, with the exception of ἐνέργεια, a combination of these terms was used in the magical papyri of the third and fourth centuries A.D. However, in them the petitioner implores the angelic powers to use magical incantations in order to gain ascendancy over people. This is in direct contrast to the scriptural principal of knowing God and his power.[1]

In conclusion, Paul states that the end of knowing God intimately is that we might know what is the surpassing greatness of his ability or potential power which is according to the mighty activity of power derived from his inherent strength. This power is directed to all who believe. It is this kind of power that is needed to survive the satanic hostile powers and worldly system that surrounds us.

(b) Its Manifestation (1:20–23)

As already mentioned in verse 16, some think that the prayer ends at verse 19 and that verse 20 begins a new hymn of praise. However, this is not likely because grammatically the following relative pronoun would indicate that the prayer is continuing. Furthermore, Paul picks up on ἐνέργεια and uses the verb form in verse 20, showing continuity between verses 19 and 20. Also, verses 20–23 are a very fitting conclusion to his request for their knowledge of God's power on their behalf.[2] It is one thing to state the concept of power, but it is quite another to show how this power operates. That is what he is going to do in verses 20–23. God has directed toward the believers that same power that he exercised in Christ by raising him from the dead and seating him at his right hand, that subjected all things under his feet, and that gave him to the church as head. There is a continuity between what God worked in Christ and what he is working in believers through the centuries up to and including the present time.[3] As sug-

1. Arnold, *Ephesians: Power and Magic*, 74–75.

2. Maclean argues that Eph 1:20–23 is directly dependent on 1 Cor 15:20–28 although the author of Ephesians disagrees in some points from Paul in 1 Cor 15 ("Ephesians and the Problem of Colossians," 140–76). Although there are similar concepts in the two passages, each is addressing an entirely different subject. Hence, it is unlikely that Eph 1:20–23 is borrowing from 1 Cor 15. Gese (*Das Vermächtnis des Apostels*, 223–28), on the other hand, thinks Eph 1:19–23 is a systematization of various Pauline expressions on power and applies them to the situation of the Ephesian church. This is unconvincing for Paul often referred to the need of God's power and it seems that Paul's desire for God's power in the Ephesian believers' lives is a natural outflow of the present context rather than a compilation of various Pauline expressions on power.

3. Gese, *Das Vermächtnis des Apostels*, 226–28.

gested by a previous illustration, there is a difference between describing what a bulldozer can do and seeing what it can actually do.

The structure of this section is as follows. The relative pronoun ἥν in verse 20 ties verses 20–23 back to ἐνέργειαν in verse 19. The relative pronoun is the object of the verb (ἐνήργησεν, v. 20) of which God is the subject. This finite verb is followed by two additional finite verbs (ὑπέταξεν and ἔδωκεν, v. 22), each introduced with the conjunction καί. Accordingly it reads, God exercised the power in Christ (v. 20), and subjected all things under Christ's feet, and gave Christ as head over everything to the church (v. 22). The participles (ἐγείρας and καθίσας) in verse 20 follow the first of these three finite verbs in verse 20 and modify it by showing how God worked in Christ. So the structure is composed of three finite verbs with two participles modifying the first verb (for a structural layout of the prayer, see 1:16b). Verse 23 is joined to verse 22 by the relative pronoun ἥτις and thus subordinate to verse 22b. Barth states that God is the grammatical subject of verses 20–22 and the church is in verse 23.[1] However, it must be realized that verse 23 is introduced with a relative pronoun to elucidate the church rather than to give the impression that Paul has changed subjects. God remains as the subject throughout the passage, for he gave Christ as head to the church which is his body.

As mentioned in verse 16, to make these four verses a Christological hymn is begging the question. There is no uniformity in scholarly discussions on its form and construction. Certainly, Christ is exalted in this passage but that is to be expected when the intent is to show how God's power worked in Christ. It is best to think that Paul is explaining God's work without trying to formulate some sort of hymn that was used in the early church. There is a tendency to read early church or present day church liturgy back into the NT times.

(i) He Displayed Power in Christ (1:20–21)

(aa) In Raising Christ from the Dead (1:20a)

Text: 1:20a. ἣν ἐνήργησεν ἐν τῷ Χριστῷ ἐγείρας αὐτὸν ἐκ νεκρῶν

Translation: 1:20a. "Which power he exercised in Christ by raising him from the dead"

Commentary: 1:20a. ἣν ἐνήργησεν[2] ἐν τῷ Χριστῷ, "Which power he exercised in Christ." The noun ἐνέργειαν in verse 19 is the antecedent of the present relative pronoun ἥν, which is a cognate accusative,

1. Barth, 153.

2. The perfect form of the verb ἐνήργηκεν is found in A B 81 *pc* and NA[25] while the aorist form ἐνήργησεν is found in ℵ D F G Ψ 0278 33 1739 1881 𝔐. The aorist form is preferred because it has good representative manuscripts from the various geographical areas, whereas the perfect form is found only in the Alexandrian text. Furthermore, internally the aorist is consistent with the other verbs and participles. *Contra* Lincoln, 47.

meaning that it repeats the content of the verb:[1] "the working which he worked." The verb ἐνήργησεν has already been discussed at verse 11, showing that its source is from the adjective ἐνεργός, from which we get our word "energy." It always has in mind power that is active; hence, in this context it seems that to translate it "exerted" or "exercised" best conveys that idea. The prepositional phrase ἐν τῷ Χριστῷ denotes sphere or place;[2] hence, God's power was exercised "in connection with Christ," "in the case of Christ," or "in the person of Christ."[3] The article clearly delineates that God worked his power in *the* Christ, the anointed one of whom the OT prophesied that God would work in him (cf. Isa 11:2).

ἐγείρας αὐτὸν ἐκ νεκρῶν, "by raising him from the dead." The participle could be temporal denoting contemporaneous action with the main verb, "which God exercised in him when he raised him from the dead,"[4] or it could express means,[5] showing how he exercised the power "by raising him from the dead." It is difficult to decide between the two choices, but the expression of means is preferred since the temporal element is included because Christ's resurrection is unique. The plural for the "dead" (νεκρῶν) is normal and the preposition ἐκ indicates separation; thus, Christ was raised out of all those who had died and who remain buried in the earth. "Other places in Paul's writings which liken the resurrection of Christ with the power of God are 1 Cor 6:14, Rom 1:4, and Phil 3:10."[6] This resurrection power is truly an expression of active power, for although Lazarus was raised from the dead, he died again and returned to the grave. On the other hand, God did more than raise Christ from the dead. This is seen in the next participle.

(bb) In Seating Christ in the Heavenlies (1:20b–21)

Text: 1:20b. καὶ καθίσας ἐν δεξιᾷ αὐτοῦ ἐν τοῖς ἐπουρανίοις **1:21.** ὑπεράνω πάσης ἀρχῆς καὶ ἐξουσίας καὶ δυνάμεως καὶ κυριότητος καὶ παντὸς ὀνόματος ὀνομαζομένου, οὐ μόνον ἐν τῷ αἰῶνι τούτῳ ἀλλὰ καὶ ἐν τῷ μέλλοντι·

Translation: 1:20b. "and by seating him at his right hand in the heavenly realms **1:21.** above every ruler and authority and power and dominion and every name that is named, not only in this age but also in the one to come;"

1. Robertson, *Grammar*, 716; MHT 2:419; Moule, *Idiom Book*, 32.
2. BAGD 258; BDAG 326; Oepke *TDNT* 2 (1964): 541.
3. Robertson, *Grammar*, 587.
4. If it is temporal, recent studies show that when the aorist participle precedes the main verb, there is a tendency toward antecendent action, and when it follows the main verb, as it does here, there is a definite tendency toward contemporaneous action with the main verb as already mentioned in 1:5 (see Porter, *Verbal Aspect*, 381–84; cf. also Wallace, *Greek Grammar*, 624, 625).
5. Wallace, *Greek Grammar*, 630; cf. Burton, *Moods and Tenses* §447.
6. Lincoln, 61.

Commentary: 1:20b. καὶ καθίσας[1] ἐν δεξιᾷ αὐτοῦ ἐν τοῖς ἐπουρανίοις,[2] "and by seating him at his right hand in the heavenly realms." This is the second way God has exercised his power in Christ. He has not only raised Christ, as he did Lazarus, but he also seated him at his right hand. The NT writers often used Ps 110:1—"The Lord said to my Lord: 'Sit at my right hand until I make your enemies your footstool'"—to demonstrate that when Jesus was resurrected he also became the exalted Lord.[3] To sit at the right hand of God is a "symbol of divine power."[4] Hence, God not only exercised power in Christ in the resurrection but also gave him the place of honor (Matt 26:64; Heb 1:3–4, 13; 8:1; 10:12–13; 12:2) with which comes authority (Matt 28:18). In the future, humans and angels will stand before God and worship him, but Christ is not thus portrayed. Rather, he is presently seated at God's right hand. The location of this is seen in the prepositional phrase "in the heavenlies" (ἐν τοῖς ἐπουρανίοις). As discussed at verse 3, this prepositional phrase, unique to Ephesians, is used five times (1:3, 20; 2:6; 3:10; 6:12) and denotes the place where God dwells. From there every spiritual benefit is derived (1:3). This prepositional phrase only reinforces that Christ is seated in the presence of God at his right hand. However, as Lincoln points out, one must not equate the functions of "at the right hand" and "in the heavenlies" because the former is a symbol of sovereignty.[5] This is in contrast to the position of believers (2:6) and satanic forces (6:12) who are in the heavenlies, but neither are at the right hand of God. This is reserved only for Christ. It displays sovereignty at the present time and indicates his authority over the world and the church. This will be seen further in verse 22. The main point of the passage, then, is that God exercised his power in raising Christ and then seated him at his right hand. This is an exalted

1. The participle καθίσας is found in 𝔓[92vid] ℵ A B 0278 33 81 104 365 1175 1505 1739 1881 2464 249 *pc* it[a, f, g, t] vg Marcion Eusebius Victorinus-Rome. The finite verb ἐκάθισεν is found in D F G Ψ 𝔐 it[b r] Ambrosiaster Chrysostom Theodoret Oecumenius Theophylact. The finite verb has the support of the Western text and the Byzantine tradition but may have only followed the Western tradition. The participle has the solid support of the Alexandrian text-type and some Western support among the versions and fathers. Thus, it has the support of the earliest traditions. Internally, it makes good sense to show the exhibition of God's power by raising and seating Christ in the heavenlies. Hence, the participle is the preferred reading.

2. The reading οὐρανιοῖς is found only in B 365 629 *pc* syr[p] Victorinus-Rome and should not be considered as genuine.

3. Cf. W. R. G. Loader, "Christ at the Right Hand—Ps. cx.1 in the New Testament," *NTS* 24 (January 1978): 199–217, esp. 209–10; Lincoln, "The Use of the OT in Ephesians," 40–41; Herbert W. Bateman IV, "Psalm 110:1 and the New Testament," *BSac* 149 (October–December 1992): 438–53; Dunn, *The Partings of the Ways*, 190–93; cf. also Walter Wink, *Naming the Powers: The Language of Power in the New Testament*, vol. 1, *The Powers* (Philadelphia: Fortress, 1984), 20–64.

4. Walter Grundmann, "δεξιός," *TDNT* 2 (1964): 37.

5. Lincoln, "A Re-Examination of 'the Heavenlies' in Ephesians," 472.

position with all authority (cf. Matt 28:18) and this same power is available to believers to appropriate in their lives. The above argument is based on the textual reading of the aorist participle καθίσας rather than the finite verb ἐκάθισεν. However, if one accepts the finite verb as the true reading, the sense is altered only slightly. It would mean that God first exercised his power in Christ by raising him from the dead and, second, he seated Christ at his right hand.

1:21. ὑπεράνω πάσης ἀρχῆς καὶ ἐξουσίας καὶ δυνάμεως καὶ κυριότητος, "above every ruler and authority and power and dominion." The adverb ὑπεράνω is used as an improper preposition with the genitive. Some think that because it is not ἄνω but ὑπεράνω it is intensive and should be translated "far above."[1] It occurs twenty-two times in the LXX and although it may possibly denote "far above" (Deut 26:19; 28:1), it normally denotes "above." Some examples of this usage are the dedication of the Jerusalem wall where some of the people stood "above" the Tower of Furnaces (Neh 12:38) and others stood "above" the Gate of Ephraim by the Old Gate (Neh 12:39), or where it speaks of the gourd that made shade "over" Jonah's head (Jonah 4:6). If the gourd were "high above" it would not have shaded him. It is used two other times in the NT (Eph 4:10; Heb 9:5) and certainly in Heb 9:5, which speaks of the cherubim "over" the mercy seat, it cannot be translated "far above" but "above, over." The other two uses speak of "above" in a spatial sense or, as here, rank. It is true that Christ is far above all other authorities, but this is not defined by ὑπεράνω but by the fact that he is at the right hand of God. Therefore, it is best not to translate it "far above" (AV, RV, ASV, RSV, NASB, NEB, JB, NIV, NJB, NRSV) but "above" (TEV).[2]

Paul now mentions the powers over which Christ rules. A brief discussion of each term[3] will be followed by a comparison of the list of rulers in similar passages. Before discussing the various powers, it needs to be observed that the adjective πάσης can be translated "all" but here, due to it being anarthrous singular, it is preferable to translate it "every."[4] This expresses that Christ's position in the heavenlies is above "every kind of"[5] power that exists.

The first word, ἀρχή, "always signifies 'primacy' whether in time: 'beginning,' *principium*, or in rank: 'power,' 'dominion,' 'office.'"[6] Cer-

1. Chrysostom *Eph* 1:15–20 (*PG* 62:25); Theophylact *Eph* 1:20–21 (*PG* 124:1048); Oecumenius *Eph* 1:20–23 (*PG* 118:1184); Eadie, 102; L&N §87.31.

2. Horsley, *New Documents Illustrating Early Christianity*, vol. 3, *A Review of the Greek Inscriptions and Papyri Published in 1978*, 87.

3. For a discussion of the terms, see Wink, *Naming the Powers*, 13–17, 20–21; Arnold, *Ephesians: Power and Magic*, 52–54; Daniel G. Reid, "Principalities and Powers," in *DPL*, 748–49.

4. BDF §275 (3).

5. BAGD 631; BDAG 784.

6. Gerhard Delling, "ἀρχή," *TDNT* 1 (1964): 479.

tainly, in the present context it refers to rank in rule. It is the one who is in first place or power.[1] In the LXX it occurs 227 times and in the canonical books it appears 164 times translated from twenty-four Hebrew words which speak of position of power (Gen 40:13, 21) or denotes a leader (Neh 9:17; Hos 11:1). In the NT it is used fifty-five times, eleven times by Paul, three times in Ephesians (1:21; 3:10; 6:12). Most frequently it has reference to the beginning of time but it can refer to power or dominion. It can speak of spiritual or secular leaders (Luke 12:11; 20:20; Titus 3:1) or angelic leadership (Eph 3:10; 6:12; Col 1:16).[2] In the present context possibly it could denote a human ruler but more likely an angelic ruler.

The second word, ἐξουσία, is derived from ἔξεστιν, meaning "that which is permitted," in other words, the freedom to act. Thus the noun denotes "freedom of choice, the right to act" and hence "authority."[3] In the LXX it occurs seventy-seven times and in the canonical books twenty-eight times, translated from six Hebrew words. The most prominent word actually is the Aramaic שָׁלְטָן, meaning "dominion, power" with reference to the Son of man's everlasting dominion over the whole world (Dan 7:12, 14*ter*, 26, 27*bis*).[4] The second most used Hebrew word is מֶמְשָׁלָה, which can mean "rule" or "authority" (Ps 136:8–9 [LXX 135:8–9]) but it also can denote "realm" or "kingdom," that is, sphere of power (2 Kgs 20:13; Pss 114:2 [LXX 113:2]).[5] It occurs in the NT 102 times, twenty-seven in Paul, and four times in Ephesians (1:21; 2:2; 3:10; 6:12). In the NT the plural form can refer to spiritual or secular leaders or authorities (Luke 12:11; 20:20; Rom 13:1–3; Titus 3:1). In the singular form, as in the present context, it often has reference to "government."[6] It may also refer to evil spiritual powers (Eph 6:12; 1 Cor 15:24). Normally the term means "authority" although it can have reference to "domain, realm, kingdom" (Luke 22:53; 23:7; Eph 2:2; Col 1:13).[7] In this particular context it refers to authority, and although it possibly could refer to human authority, it more likely refers to angelic authority.[8]

1. Aristotle *Politica* 3.8.4 §1284b.2; Herodotus 1.6.

2. Delling, *TDNT* 1 (1964): 482–84; Konrad Weiss, "ἀρχή," *EDNT* 1 (1990): 162–63; David E. Aune, "Archai Ἀρχαί," in *DDD*, 146–49.

3. Plato *Symposium* 182e; Thucydides 7.12.5.

4. BDB 1115; cf. *HALOT* 5 (2000): 1995; Philip J. Nel, "שׁלט (*šlṭ*)," *NIDOTTE* 4 (1997): 124–25.

5. BDB 605–6; H. Gross, "מָשַׁל *māšal*; מֹשֵׁל *mōšel*; מִמְשָׁל *mimšāl*; מֶמְשָׁלָה *memšālâ*," *TDOT* 9 (1998): 68–71.

6. Werner Foerster, "ἐξουσία," *TDNT* 2 (1964): 565.

7. BAGD 278; BDAG 353; Foerster, *TDNT* 2 (1964): 565, 567.

8. Cf. Matthew Black, "Πᾶσαι ἐξουσίαι αὐτῷ ὑποταγήσονται," in *Paul and Paulinism. Essays in Honour of C. K. Barrett*, ed. M. D. Hooker and S. G. Wilson (London: SPCK, 1982), 74–82, esp. 76–80; Ingo Broer, "ἐξουσία," *EDNT* 2 (1991): 11; Hans-Dieter Betz, "Authorities ἐξουσίαι," in *DDD*, 232–33.

The third word, δύναμις, has already been discussed at verse 19 with reference to the concept of power. In its use in Ephesians (1:19, 21; 3:7, 16, 20) it consistently has reference to the abstract sense of power, although the present context seems to be a bit more concrete and thus could refer to human power, although more likely it is a reference to angelic power that is subject to Christ's power.[1] Arnold observes that the LXX uses this term "to refer to 'the hosts of heaven' (2 Kings 17:16; 21:3, 5; 23:4f.), which Israel is prohibited from worshiping (Deut 4:19)."[2]

The final word, κυριότης, is rarely used outside the NT. In the NT it occurs only four times (Eph 1:21; Col 1:16; 2 Pet 2:10; Jude 8). Basically, it means the "'power or position as lord.'"[3] It is used of God's authority, which is despised by the false teachers (2 Pet 2:10; Jude 8). In Col 1:16 Paul states that κυριότητες were created by God along with thrones, principalities, and authorities, whether in reference to human or angelic beings. In the present context a good rendering would be "lordship" or "dominion" with reference to "a special class of angelic powers."[4]

Having looked at the terms briefly, we will now compare them to other passages listing authorities and rulers.[5] Outside of 1 Pet 3:22, only Paul gives a list of rulers (always in the same order with the exception of Col 1:16). Three times Paul lists three authorities, and twice they are listed in the following order: ἀρχή, ἐξουσία, and δύναμις (Eph 1:21; 1 Cor 15:24) and once κυριότης, ἀρχή, and ἐξουσία (Col 1:16). Ten times two powers are listed in the following order: ἀρχή and ἐξουσία (Luke 12:11; 20:20; 1 Cor 15:24; Eph 1:20; 3:10; 6:12; Col 1:16; 2:10, 15; Titus 3:1), once ἀρχή and δύναμις (Rom 8:38), and once ἐξουσία and δύναμις (1 Pet 3:22).

There are some observations to be made regarding the passages cited above. First, certain terms are used much more frequently than others: ἀρχή and ἐξουσία are mentioned eight times each, δύναμις four times, and κυριότης twice. Second, the names themselves (ἀρχή [ruler],

1. Grundmann, *TDNT* 2 (1964): 307–8; Friedrich, *EDNT* 1 (1990): 358; Hans-Dieter Betz, "Dynamis δύναμις," in *DDD*, 509–14.

2. Arnold, *Ephesians: Power and Magic*, 53.

3. Werner Foerster, "κυριότης," *TDNT* 3 (1965): 1096.

4. BAGD 460–61; BDAG 579; cf. Arnold, *Ephesians: Power and Magic*, 54.

5. For further study on this subject, see G. H. C. Macgregor, "Principalities and Powers: The Cosmic Background of Paul's Thought," *NTS* 1 (October 1954): 17–28; Cyril H. Powell, *The Biblical Concept of Power* (London: Epworth, 1963), 161–72; Barth, 170–83; Carr, *Angels and Principalities*, 47–114; cf. also G. B. Caird, *Principalities and Powers. A Study in Pauline Theology* (Oxford: Clarendon, 1956); Heinrich Schlier, *Principalities and Powers in the New Testament* (Freiburg: Herder; London: Burns & Oates, 1961), 11–39; Peter T. O'Brien, "Principalities and Powers: Opponents of the Church," in *Biblical Interpretation and the Church: Text and Context*, ed. D. A. Carson (Exeter: Paternoster, 1984), 110–50, esp. 125–47; Wink, *Naming the Powers*, 13–26; Arnold, *Ephesians: Power and Magic*, 51–56; Reid, "Principalities and Powers," 749–52.

ἐξουσία [authority], δύναμις [power], κυριότης [lordship or dominion]) used of human government indicate their political function in the cosmic order (cf. 2:2; 3:10; 6:12).[1] Third, there is a general order of titles but this order is violated at times and thus it is difficult if not impossible to denote hierarchy. Fourth, there is a definite influence from Jewish sources, although one should not exclude the pagan environment.[2] Fifth, Christ is over all these powers. Sixth, Christ's supremacy, in some cases, is already accomplished (Eph 1:21; 3:10; Col 2:10, 15; 1 Pet 3:22) while in others it is yet to be demonstrated (1 Cor 15:14). Seventh, some of these refer to heavenly powers (Eph 3:10; 6:12) and others to earthly rulers (Titus 3:1). Eighth, the terms do not denote impersonal entities[3] but personal beings.

In conclusion, the four terms in the present passage are abstract and difficult to pin down. There is debate as to whether these terms refer to human or angelic authorities[4] or whether they are good or evil powers. Carr thinks the terms have reference to angels and archangels of God and are not demonic or evil.[5] However, in the context of the book it seems that these rulers are angelic and also evil in character.[6] In the present context, Christ is seated at the right hand of the Father and this may be an allusion to Ps 110 where God will make the ene-

1. Pierre Benoit, "Pauline Angelology and Demonology. Reflexions on the Designations of the Heavenly Powers and on the Origin of Angelic Evil According to Paul," *Religious Studies Bulletin* 3 (January 1983): 11–13.

2. O'Brien, "Principalities and Powers: Opponents of the Church," 127–33; Arnold, *Ephesians: Power and Magic*, 52–54; Wink, *Naming the Powers*, 13–26.

3. As Walter Wink, *Engaging the Powers: Discernment and Resistance in a World of Domination*, vol. 3, *The Powers* (Minneapolis: Fortress, 1992), 8–9. Wink's demythologizing the powers as bereft of spiritual essence relegating them as institutional powers or oppressive political structures (*Naming the Powers*, 60–67, 99–148) has been rightly critiqued by Arnold, *Ephesians: Power and Magic*, 47–51. For further elaboration of Wink's view, see Walter Wink, *Unmasking the Powers: The Invisible Forces That Determine Human Existence*, vol. 2, *The Powers* (Philadelphia: Fortress, 1986), 41–68; idem, *The Powers That Be: Theology for a New Millennium* (New York: Doubleday, 1998), 14–62.

4. Morrison does not think that in Paul's time power can be broken down into "earthly" and "spiritual," see Clinton Morrison, *The Powers That Be. Earthly Rulers and Demonic Powers in Romans 13:1–7*, SBT, ed. C F. D. Moule, J. Barr, Floyd V. Filson, and G. Ernest Wright, vol. 29 (London: SCM, 1960), 68–80. Although a case for this possibly may be made in the Book of Romans, it seems, as argued above, that the powers in Ephesians are angelic rulers as opposed to Lotz who prefers to see them as solely earthly powers in Asia Minor, see John Paul Lotz, "The *homonoia* Coins of Asia Minor and Ephesians 1:21," *TynBul* 50, no. 2 (1999): 185–88.

5. Carr, *Angels and Principalities*, 98–99.

6. Cf. O'Brien, "Principalities and Powers: Opponents of the Church," 127–28; Wink, *Naming the Powers*, 13–26; James R. Hollingshead, *The Household of Caesar and the Body of Christ: A Political Interpretation of the Letters from Paul* (Lanham, Md.: University Press of America, 1998), 37–38. Maclean ("Ephesians and the Problem of Colossians," 156–59) argues that the powers are not malevolent or hostile to God or Christ unlike 1 Cor 15:20–28, hence, the author of Ephesians disagrees with Paul in 1 Cor 15.

mies of Christ his footstool. Furthermore, other references to "powers" in this letter clearly affirm that they are evil (6:11–12, 16; 4:8, 27).[1] In 6:12 Paul specifically states that "our struggle is not against flesh and blood but against the rulers, against authorities, against the mighty world of this darkness, against the spiritual wickedness in the heavenlies." Hence, these powers most likely are angelic and evil and wish to rob us of our spiritual benefits. The point is clear that Christ is over these authorities and they will not have the final victory.[2] The struggle between God and these evil powers is real and in the present day the battle rages between these angelic powers and believers, individually and corporately.[3] The central point of this passage is that believers have the power that raised and seated Christ far above every power. We are to appropriate that power in light of the spiritual warfare that is portrayed in chapter 6.

καὶ παντὸς ὀνόματος ὀνομαζομένου, "and every name that is named." One interpretation proposes that the name refers to spiritual beings with divine powers which one invokes and worships.[4] The problem with this view is that this changes the subject of the verb from God to humans. This would indicate that humans choose the name or spiritual being they worship, whereas the context signifies God as the subject. He is the one who has designated the names and has exalted Christ above every name.[5] A better interpretation is that God is the namer, as seen in the OT where he gave a new name to Abram (Gen 17:5) and to Jacob (Gen 32:28), and even determined the number of stars and gave all of them their names (Ps 147:4). Thus in the present context after naming specific authorities (v. 21a) over which Christ has authority, Paul indicates that every name that God cites is under Christ's authority (v. 21b).[6] It is a comprehensive state-

---

But, as argued above, the context of Ephesians indicates that these powers are evil and need to be defeated. This is substantiated by the fact that Christ is going to rule over them, an indication that these powers must be overcome and are therefore hostile.

1. Arnold, *Ephesians: Power and Magic*, 56; cf. also Benoit, "Pauline Angelology and Demonology," 13–16.

2. Ernst R. Wendland, "Contextualizing the Potentates, Principalities and Powers in the Epistle to the Ephesians," *Neot* 33, no. 1 (1999): 211–12.

3. Spiritual powers tend to be minimized in our Western culture but they were real to those in Paul's day and they should be considered real in the present day. After examining spiritual powers in Ephesians, Wendland and Hachibamba investigate the concept of spiritual powers from the perspective of contemporary Zambian Tonga people and list seven principles for communicating the gospel effectively in that context (Ernst R. Wendland and Salimo Hachibamba, "A Central African Perspective on Contextualizing the Ephesian Potentates, Principalities, and Powers," *Missiology* 28 [July 2000]: 341–63).

4. Mitton, 72–73; Caird, 47.

5. Thomas G. Allen, "God the Namer: A Note on Ephesians 1.21b," *NTS* 32 (July 1986): 472–73.

6. Ibid., 473–74.

ment specifying that regardless of designation or title a ruling power may have whether in heaven or on earth, it is inferior to Christ who is at the right hand of God. This corresponds to Phil 2:9 where God has highly exalted Christ and bestowed on him the name which is above every name. Arnold insightfully observes that the only time the verb occurs in Acts (19:13), it is linked with the noun (as here) in the account of itinerant Jewish exorcists in Ephesus who pronounced the name of the Lord Jesus over those who had evil spirits.[1] Again, as earlier in this verse, the anarthrous singular παντός is better translated "every," expressing "every kind of name" that is mentioned or claimed. Therefore, Jesus as Lord is greater than any other title, whether in heaven or on earth.[2]

οὐ μόνον ἐν τῷ αἰῶνι τούτῳ ἀλλὰ καὶ ἐν τῷ μέλλοντι, "not only in this age but also the one to come." This is another comprehensive clause, for Christ is not only above all those with various titles and positions, but he will also continue his position at the right hand of God, forever. Hence, Christ is not only above all at the right hand of God but he is also there permanently. This is the only place in Paul's letters that "this age" and "the one to come" occur together.[3] The Bible divides time into three periods: the past, which cannot be changed but which the saints are encouraged to review for lessons of faith (1 Cor 10:11); the present, where people are responsible to God and his will; and the future, for which people are urged to prepare. It is in the future that God will usher in the new age where he will judge and bless humans. In the Bible there is more emphasis on the present than either on the past or on the future. In Ephesians there is much emphasis on the present, for we are told that presently we are redeemed (1:7; 2:5), are seated in the heavenlies with Christ (2:6), are his workmanship (2:10), and are given all the practical injunctions for godly living (cf. chaps. 4–6; e.g., 5:16). All this indicates the reality of the present age. The present context bears this out because it states that Christ is at the right hand of God with full authority in "this age." However, it does not end there. This context also states that there is "also the one [age] to come." This is borne out where it states that in the future God will, in the fullness of times, unite all things in Christ (1:10), redeem his purchased possession (1:14), demonstrate the riches of his grace in the saints (2:7), redeem those he has sealed (4:30), inherit the kingdom of God (5:5), present his church spotless (5:27), and reward be-

1. Arnold, *Ephesians: Power and Magic*, 55.

2. In accordance with Lotz's ("The *homonoia* Coins of Asia Minor and Ephesians 1:21," 187) suggestion that the author of Ephesians was asserting that Christ, not the Emperor, was the only one who could bring harmony to the political rivalries in Asia Minor, these would appear as "provocative and seditious words." However, Paul was not addressing the political rivalries of Asia Minor but the conflicts within the spiritual world.

3. Hill, *Greek Words and Hebrew Meanings*, 188.

lievers for their good deeds (6:8). Hence, in Ephesians there is not the cessation of time as suggested by Lindemann[1] but there is a time division between the present and future ages.[2] The word αἰών, "age," consistently refers to "age" or a period of time in Ephesians (1:21; 2:2, 7; 3:9, 11, 21*bis*; cf. also Col 1:26).[3] For a further study of this word, see comment on 2:2.

The future age has always been viewed in the Bible as "the age to come," that is, the messianic age (cf. Matt 12:32; Mark 10:30). It is the time when Messiah will rule with justice and put down all other powers or authorities that oppose him.[4] Messiah is going to demonstrate that though many attempt to usurp his power, he has a permanent position at the right hand of God.

(ii) He Subjected Everything under Christ's Feet (1:22a)

Text: 1:22a. καὶ πάντα ὑπέταξεν ὑπὸ τοὺς πόδας αὐτοῦ,

Translation: 1:22a. "and he subjected everything under his feet,"

Commentary: 1:22a. καὶ πάντα ὑπέταξεν ὑπὸ τοὺς πόδας αὐτοῦ, "and he subjected everything under his feet." The magnitude of God's power described in verse 19 is great and has been manifested first in his work in Christ by raising him from the dead and by seating him at his right hand in the heavenlies, and now second in subjecting everything under Christ's feet. The ὑπέταξεν is coordinate with the previous ἐνήργησεν (v. 20) joined with the conjunction καί. The first demonstration of God's power had to do with Christ's resurrection and the establishment of Christ's position of authority. The last two are going to show God's power in Christ by Christ's dominion over all creation and over the church in particular (for a structural layout of the prayer, see 1:16b).

It is one thing to be given the position of authority, that is, seated at the right hand of the Father; it is quite another to be allowed to exercise that authority. The first evidence of the reality of Christ's power is the subjection of everything under his feet. This is a quotation from Ps 8:6 [MT & LXX 8:7], even though there is nothing mentioned of Messiah in Ps 8 but, rather, it is about humans whom God created as the vice-regents to rule over the creation. However, Heb 2:6–9 states that the first Adam lost control over the creation when sin entered into the world. When applied to Ps 8, the writer of Hebrews shows that the last Adam was given control over what the first Adam had lost (2:6–8). Although Paul in 1 Cor 15:24–28 applies Ps 8:7 to the overthrow of the enemies in conjunction with Ps 110:1 where it states, "Sit at my right hand until I make your enemies your footstool," in the

1. Lindemann, *Aufhebung*, 56–59, 94–97, 104–6, 129–33, 230–32.

2. Lincoln, *Paradise Now and Not Yet*, 170–74.

3. Cf. Wessels, "The Eschatology of Colossians and Ephesians," 195.

4. Cf. Jung Young Lee, "Interpreting the Demonic Powers in Pauline Thought," *NovT* 12 (January 1970): 64–66.

present context the overthrow of the enemies is not explicitly stated. It is nevertheless implied by: (1) the very idea of subjecting; (2) the fact that everything is subjected; (3) that subjection is under his feet; and (4) that Christ is at the right hand of God (v. 20). It could be argued that some of these reasons stand or fall together because they are all part of a citation from Ps 8 but of course Paul wanted to use the whole quotation to enforce his point, otherwise, he could have cited the first half of the verse and omitted the last half.[1]

The verb ὑποτάσσω appeared first in Hellenistic times where it meant to place or arrange under or be subordinated.[2] It is a part of the ταγ- word group signifying order or arrangement (see τάγμα in 1 Cor 15:23) and with the prepositional prefix ὑπο-, the word literally means "'to order oneself under' a leader."[3] It occurs twenty-nine times in the LXX but only sixteen times in the canonical LXX and is translated from ten different Hebrew words with the same basic idea of subordination (1 Chr 22:18; 29:24; Ps 8:6 [MT & LXX 8:7]; 18:47 [MT 18:48; LXX 17:48]; 47:3 [MT 47:4; LXX 46:4]). In the NT it is used thirty-eight times, twenty-three times by Paul (e.g., Rom 8:7, 20; 13:1, 5; 1 Cor 15:27–28 [six times]), and three (possibly four) times in Ephesians (1:22; 5:21, 22?, 24). Again, it has the same basic meaning "to be subject, to be subordinate."[4] A good example of this is in Rom 8:7 where Paul states that the mind-set of the flesh is hostile to God because it is not subject to the law of God, nor can it be. Hence, for Christ to subject everything, enemies must be overthrown. It must be kept in mind that the subject of the verb is God who subjected everything under Christ's feet. This fact empowers Christ to accomplish the subjection of all things.

Again, as in verse 21 the anarthrous πάντα should be translated "everything" to indicate that every single thing is to be subjected to Christ. The πάντα in Ps 8 has reference to Adam's dominion over all animal creation, but the author of Hebrews applies this to Christ as having dominion over all creation and that is the force of the present context. The "everything" subjected under his feet would have reference to inanimate things and animate creatures, human and angelic beings. Hence, Christ has been given the right to exercise his control over everything in God's creation as verses 20–21 make clear.

The metaphorical language "under his feet" has the idea of victory over enemies. It is used of the winner of a duel who places his foot on the neck of his enemy who has been thrown to the ground,[5] like

1. For a discussion of the use of Pss 8 and 110 in the present Ephesian context, see Moritz, *A Profound Mystery*, 9–22; Gese, *Das Vermächtnis des Apostels*, 190–93.

2. Polybius 3.36.7; Plutarch *Pompeius* 64; *Nicias* 23.4.

3. Ceslas Spicq, *Theological Lexicon of the New Testament*, trans. and ed. James D. Ernest, vol. 3 (Peabody, Mass.: Hendrickson, 1994), 424 n. 2.

4. Cf. Gerhard Delling, "ὑποτάσσω," *TDNT* 8 (1972): 41–45.

5. Diodorus Siculus 17.100.8; cf. BAGD 696; BDAG 858.

Joshua who had his generals place their feet on the necks of the five defeated Amorite kings (Josh 10:24; cf. 2 Sam 22:39). Similarly, everything is subjected under Christ's feet, meaning that everything is currently under his control, both friends and enemies. This coincides with 1 Pet 3:22 where it states that Christ has gone to heaven and is at the right hand of God, having the angels, authorities, and powers subject to him.

What are the implications of Christ's exaltation in relation to the cosmic powers? There are some who think Ephesians is talking about a realized eschatology whereby the cosmic powers also have been subjected as a consequence of Christ's exaltation. Hence, the destruction of the cosmic powers is not at the parousia but at the exaltation of Christ.[1] Yet, in 6:12 Paul warns believers of the evil powers that presently war against them and urges them to put on the armor of God,[2] which indicates that the cosmic powers are still active. In reality Christ is at the right hand of the Father and everything has been subjected under his feet, but the full exercise of that power will not be evident until his return.[3] This corresponds to 1 Cor 15:24–28 where it states that God has subjected everything under Christ's feet and that in the end, Christ will subject all enemies and will hand the kingdom over to God the Father. At the present, the manifestation of this control is not always evident to us, for there are many inequities, injustices, disasters, unholy actions, and evidences of outright defiance against Christ and God. However, Christ is exercising control without it being obvious to humankind. Without his control, things would be much worse. Hence, he has the right to exercise his control but chooses not to fully exercise it immediately in every instance of violation against God's holy character. Certainly, a basic and important illustration of his present use of authority is his current ability to rescue sinners from the most despicable powers of all, Satan and sin, which will be discussed in the next chapter. To summarize, God does have a plan and everything must follow according to that plan which will culminate at Christ's return where the exercise of his control will be very evident.

(iii) He Gave Christ to the Church as Head (1:22b–23)

Text: 1:22b. καὶ αὐτὸν ἔδωκεν κεφαλὴν ὑπὲρ πάντα τῇ ἐκκλησίᾳ, **1:23.** ἥτις ἐστὶν τὸ σῶμα αὐτοῦ, τὸ πλήρωμα τοῦ τὰ πάντα ἐν πᾶσιν πληρουμένου.

1. Lindemann, *Aufhebung*, 209–10; Lindemann, 30–31; see also Franz-Josef Steinmetz, *Protologische Heils-Zuversicht: Die Strukturen des soteriologischen und christologischen Denkens im Kolosser- und Epheserbrief*, Frankfurter theologische Studien, ed. Heinrich Bacht, Josef Haspecker, and Otto Semmelroth, vol. 2 (Frankfurt: Josef Knecht, 1969), 81–82.

2. Wessels, "The Eschatology of Colossians and Ephesians," 191.

3. Cf. Wink, *Engaging the Powers*, 139–43, 349 n. 21.

Translation: 1:22b. "and he gave him as head over everything to the church, **1:23.** which (indeed) is his body, the fullness of him who is being filled entirely."

Commentary: 1:22b. καὶ αὐτὸν ἔδωκεν κεφαλὴν ὑπὲρ πάντα τῇ ἐκκλησίᾳ, "and he gave him as head over everything to the church." This marks the final demonstration of God's power (for a structural layout of the prayer, see 1:16b). There needs to be a discussion of the terms before putting them together as a whole.

First, some think that the verb ἔδωκεν is equivalent to ἔθηκεν, yielding "he appointed"[1] him as head to the church (RSV, NEB, JB, NIV, NJB, NRSV). However, the meaning of the word "he gave" makes good sense in this context and in 4:11, as well as 1 Cor 12:18, 28.

Second, there has been much discussion regarding the concept of the word κεφαλή, "head." From the earliest times κεφαλή refers most often to the physical head of a human being or an animal[2] but also it refers to the coping of a wall[3] or head or mouth (singular) of a river.[4] In the LXX the word appears over 400 times and in the canonical books it occurs 336 times and around 300 times it translates רֹאשׁ, which refers to the head of a human being (Gen 28:18; Exod 29:7), an animal (Gen 3:15; Exod 29:19), a tribe (Exod 6:14; Judg 11:8), or a tower (Gen 11:4).[5] The term is used seventy-five times in the NT, eighteen times by Paul, and four times in Ephesians (1:22; 4:15; 5:23*bis*). Bedale thinks that the term denotes not so much the sense of ruler or authority but more the idea of "source," as the head of a river.[6] Grudem has challenged this concept because he does not find

1. Calvin, 138; Gaugler, 74; Barth, 157–58; BAGD 193; BDAG 242.

2. Aeschylus *Septem contra Thebas* 525; Sophocles *Ajax* 238; Herodutus 2.39.

3. Xenophon *Cyropaedia* 3.3.68.

4. Callimachus *Aetia* 2.46.

5. BDB 910–11; cf. W. Beuken and U. Dahmen, "רֹאשׁ *roʾš*, etc.," *TWAT* 7 (1990): 272–77, 282–83.

6. Stephen Bedale, "The Meaning of κεφαλή in the Pauline Epistles," *JTS*, n.s., 5 (October 1954): 211–15; cf. also idem, "The Theology of the Church," 68–72. Others who have argued for source are Berkeley and Alvera Mickelsen, "The 'Head' of the Epistles," *CT* 25 (February 20, 1981): 20–23 [264–67]; idem, "What Does *Kephalē* Mean in the New Testament?" in *Women, Authority & the Bible*, ed. Alvera Mickelsen (Downers Grove, Ill.: InterVarsity, 1986), 97–110; Philip Barton Payne, "Response: What Does *Kephalē* Mean in the New Testament?" in *Women, Authority & the Bible*, ed. Alvera Mickelsen (Downers Grove, Ill.: InterVarsity, 1986), 118–32; Catherine Clark Kroeger, "Appendix III: The Classical Concept of *Head* as 'Source'" in Gretchen Gaebelein Hull, *Equal to Serve: Women and Men in the Church and Home* (Old Tappen, N.J.: Fleming H. Revell, 1987), 267–83; Gordon D. Fee, *The First Epistle to the Corinthians*, NICNT, ed. F. F. Bruce (Grand Rapids: Eerdmans, 1987), 502–3 n. 42; Gilbert Bilezikian, "A Critical Examination of Wayne Grudem's Treatment of *kephalē* in Ancient Greek Texts," an appendix in *Beyond Sex Roles. What the Bible Says About a Woman's Place in Church and Family*, 2d ed. (Grand Rapids: Baker, 1990), 215–52; C. C. Kroeger, "Head," in *DPL*, 375–77.

one instance of it having the meaning "source, origin" in his investigation of 2336 instances of κεφαλή in Greek literature. He proposes that in most instances it refers to the physical head of a human being or animal, but when it is used metaphorically of a person, it means "ruler, person of superior authority or rank."[1] However, Cervin has written a rebuttal to Grudem's article and concludes that the normal sense of the word is neither "source" nor "authority over" or "leader" but "preeminence."[2] Another round of lengthy discussions between Grudem and Cervin has clarified the difference between them. Both Grudem and Fitzmyer maintain that κεφαλή inherently conveys the idea of leadership or authority,[3] whereas Cervin and Perriman think that it denotes only preeminence or prominence and that the idea of authority comes from the context and not from the word itself.[4] The latter view is better, for words must be seen in their context. Certainly, when this word is used in relationship to Christ, it refers to his authority over the church (Eph 5:23; Col 1:18), although in Col 2:10 it speaks of him being head of all rule and au-

1. Wayne Grudem, "Does κεφαλή ('head') Mean 'Source' or 'Authority Over' in Greek Literature? A Survey of 2,336 Examples," *TJ* 6 (spring 1985): 38–59; also printed in idem, "Appendix 1: Does *kephalē* ('head') Mean 'Source' or 'Authority Over' in Greek Literature? A Survey of 2,336 Examples," in George W. Knight III, *The Role Relationship of Men and Women: New Testament Teaching*, rev. ed. (Chicago: Moody, 1985), 49–80; updated in idem, "Appendix 1: The Meaning of *Kephalē* ('Head'): A Response to Recent Studies," in *Recovering Biblical Manhood and Womanhood: A Response to Evangelical Feminism*, ed. John Piper and Wayne Grudem (Wheaton, Ill.: Crossway, 1991), 425–68, 534–41; idem, "The Meaning of κεφαλή ('Head'): An Evaluation of New Evidence, Real and Alleged," *JETS* 44 (March 2001): 25–65; cf. also Beuken and Dahmen, *TWAT* 7 (1990): 277–79; Heinrich Schlier, "κεφαλή," *TDNT* 3 (1965): 673–81; Colin Brown and Karlfried Munzer, "Head [κεφαλή]," *NIDNTT* 2 (1976): 156–63; BAGD 430; BDAG 542.

2. Richard S. Cervin, "Does Κεφαλή Mean 'Source' or 'Authority over' in Greek Literature? A Rebuttal," *TJ* 10 (spring 1989): 85–112.

3. Wayne Grudem, "The Meaning of Κεφαλή ('Head'): A Response to Recent Studies," *TJ* 11 (spring 1990): 3–72; Joseph A. Fitzmyer, "Another Look at ΚΕΦΑΛΗ in 1 Corinthians 11.3," *NTS* 35 (October 1989): 503–11; idem, *Kephalē* in I Corinthians 11:3," *Int* 47 (January 1993): 52–59.

4. Richard S. Cervin, "ΠΕΡΙ ΤΟΥ ΚΕΦΑΛΗ: A Rejoinder," Unpublished manuscript (1991), 1–39 [used by permission of the author]; A. C. Perriman, "The Head of a Woman: The Meaning of κεφαλή in I Cor. 11:3," *JTS*, n.s., 45 (October 1994): 602–22, esp. 616–19; idem, *Speaking of Women: Interpreting Paul* (Leicester: Apollos, 1998), 13–33, 42–43. Cf. also Terrence Alexander Crain, "The Linguistic Background to the Metaphoric Use of Κεφαλη in the New Testament" (B.D. Thesis, Perth: Murdoch University, 1990). For a similar conclusion with more discussion on "head" as a metaphor, see Gregory W. Dawes, *The Body in Question: Metaphor and Meaning in the Interpretation of Ephesians 5:21–33*, Biblical Interpretation Series, ed. R. Alan Culpepper, Rolf Rendtorff, and David E. Orton, vol. 30 (Leiden: Brill, 1998), 122–49; Edmundo de Los Santos, *La novedad de la metáfora κεφαλή-σῶμα en la carta a los Efesios*, Tesi Gregorianna, Serie Teologia, vol. 59 (Rome: Editrice Pontificia Università Gregoriana, 2000), 58–61, 348–49.

thority.[1] In the present context Christ has subjected all things under his feet and God gave him (as head over all things) to the church.

Third, ἐκκλησία has always had the meaning of "assembly," such as a group of citizens who gather to vote on issues.[2] In the LXX it occurs a hundred times and in the canonical books it appears seventy-seven times nearly always translated from קָהָל, meaning "assembly, congregation" (Deut 18:16; 31:30; 1 Sam 17:47; 1 Kgs 8:14, 22, 55, 65; Pss 22:22 [MT 22:23; LXX 21:23]; 149:1; Mic 2:5).[3] It is used 114 times in the NT, sixty-two times by Paul, and nine times in Ephesians (1:22; 3:10, 21; 5:23, 24, 25, 27, 29, 32). Its only mention in the Gospels is in Matt 16:18 and 18:17*bis* where Jesus speaks respectively of its founding and the process of discipline within an assembly or church. Except for Acts 7:38, where Stephen speaks of the OT congregation in the wilderness, and 19:32, 39, 40, which refers to a secular assembly in Ephesus, it always refers to the church that was predicted in Matt 16:18, begun at Pentecost, and consisting of people who put their trust in Jesus Christ (Acts 11:26). It can refer to house churches (Rom 16:5; 1 Cor 16:19), to a church in a village or city (1 Cor 1:2; 1 Thess 1:1), to several churches in a province or country (Acts 15:41; Gal 1:2, 22; 1 Cor 16:1), or to the universal church (1 Cor 12:28; 15:9; Gal 1:13; Phil 3:6; Col 1:18, 24; all references in Ephesians). Thus, in the present context it speaks of Christ's relationship to the universal church.[4]

Having discussed the terms, some grammatical observations need to be noted in order to see how the words relate to one another. The subject is God, the object is αὐτόν (Christ), and the predicate accusative is κεφαλήν "head." The problem is the relationship of ὑπὲρ πάντα to the rest of the sentence. Scholars have given various proposals. Four will be discussed.

1. *Contra* Robinson, who states: "Christ is never spoken of as the head of things in general in a metaphorical way, though His universal lordship is of course everywhere presupposed." See John A. T. Robinson, *The Body. A Study in Pauline Theology*, SBT, ed. T. W. Manson, H. H. Rowley, Floyd V. Filson, and G. Ernest Wright, vol. 5 (London: SCM, 1952), 66.

2. Aristotle *Politica* 3.9.2 §1285a.11; Thucydides 1.87.6; 2.22.1; Herodotus 3.142; Polybius 4.34.6. For the secular use of the term, cf. Winter, "The Problem with 'Church' for the Early Church," 205–7.

3. BDB 874–75; H.-J. Fabry, "קָהָל *qāhāl*, etc.," *TWAT* 6 (1989): 1205–9.

4. For further study, see Karl Ludwig Schmidt, "ἐκκλησία," *TDNT* 3 (1965): 501–36; Lothar Coenen, "Church [ἐκκλησία]," *NIDNTT* 1 (1975): 291–305; Jürgen Roloff, "ἐκκλησία," *EDNT* 1 (1990): 410–15; Winter, "The Problem with 'Church' for the Early Church," 207–8. As mentioned in the introduction, instead of calling it "universal church" O'Brien suggests "heavenly gathering" because the word "church" means "gathering" and since a worldwide gathering could not be accomplished on an earthly plane, such a gathering would be on a heavenly plane as referred to in the contexts of Colossians and Ephesians, see O'Brien, "The Church as a Heavenly and Eschatological Entity," 93–95; idem, "Church," 125–26.

The first view is that κεφαλὴν ὑπὲρ πάντα is in apposition to αὐτόν and is translated, "he gave him, the head over everything, to be head of the church" (JB, NJB).[1] In other words God gave Christ, who is the head over everything in creation, as seen in the first part of this verse, to be the head of the church. But with this view one has to assume, as Meyer does, that a second κεφαλήν just before τῇ ἐκκλησίᾳ must be understood. This has some merit but the repetition of "head" creates a complex grammatical construction.

The second view proposes that κεφαλήν is a predicate accusative and is thus a double accusative with αὐτόν and is translated, "he gave him as head over everything to the church."[2] This is very much like the first view but has a little better construction. This assumes the contents of the first part of the verse. Since Christ is the head of everything in creation, he, as the head of everything, has been given by God to the church. His headship over the church is implied but not explicitedly stated. The problem with this view is that there is no progress regarding his headship over the church. It only restates his headship over the creation and this would be unique in the NT. The only point that is clear in this and the first view is that God gave Christ to the church.

The third option sees ὑπὲρ πάντα further defining κεφαλήν, thus Christ was appointed as the supreme head (NEB).[3] The apostles and prophets were heads of the church(es) but the ὑπὲρ πάντα more closely defines that Christ was above them all. There are three problems with this view. First, it almost demands that ἔδωκεν be translated "he appointed," which is not the normal meaning of the word as discussed above. Second, it makes the ὑπὲρ πάντα dependent on ἔδωκεν, which is highly unlikely because no such construction is found in the LXX or NT. Third, there is no implied contrast with πάντα[4] and furthermore nothing in the context would imply that Christ is being compared with others in the church. Therefore, this is not an acceptable proposal.

The fourth view proposes that the prepositional phrase ὑπὲρ πάντα is attributive to κεφαλήν and means that not only is everything in creation subjected to him but also Christ is given as head over everything to the church.[5] This is analogous to the second view in that it sees κεφαλήν as the predicate accusative. However, the present view shows

1. Chrysostom *Eph* 1:15–20 (*PG* 62:26); Meyer, 82; Schlier, 89; Barth, 156; Schnackenburg, 70, 79–80.

2. Alford, 3:86; Eadie, 105–6; Ellicott, 30; Caird, 48.

3. Olshausen, 157–58.

4. Eadie, 105.

5. Abbott, 34; Bruce, 274–75; cf. also Stig Hanson, *The Unity of the Church in the New Testament. Colossians and Ephesians*, ASNU, vol. 14 (Uppsala: Almquist & Wiksells Boktrycker; København: Einar Munkgraar, 1946), 127; Mussner, *Christus, das All und die Kirche*, 30–31; Best, *One Body in Christ*, 146–47; Clinton E. Arnold, "Jesus Christ: 'Head' of the Church (Colossians and Ephesians)," in *Jesus of Nazareth: Lord and Christ. Essays on the Historical Jesus and New Testament Christology*, ed. Joel B. Green and Max Turner (Grand Rapids: Eerdmans; Carlisle: Paternoster, 1994), 364–65.

progress in the argument for he has finished with Christ's cosmic relationship in the first half of the verse and now is dealing with Christ's ecclesiastical relationship. Furthermore, ἔδωκεν retains its normal sense of "he gave." This view is similar to the third view, except that it does not say that Christ is over other heads of the church. Although it is not explicitly stated that Christ is the head over the church, "a clear implication of the thought that the one who is head over all is given to the Church is that he is also head of the Church."[1] This view fits very nicely with Col 1:15–18 where Christ is both the originator and sustainer of all creation and the head over everything in the church. This also coincides well with Eph 5:23–24 where it states that the church is under the headship of Christ. The first part of verse 22 states that Christ has subjected everything in creation, in the second part of the verse it states that Christ is the head of all things and that he was given to the church (which began at Pentecost[2]) thus implying that he is head of church. One must not confuse the issue by saying that the creation and the church are one and the same[3] but rather they are distinct and his relationship to each is different.

One final question needs to be addressed, namely, how is the dative construction τῇ ἐκκλησίᾳ to be taken? There are three interpretations: first, it could be taken as a dative of reference or respect, that is, God appointed Christ as head over everthing with respect to the church; second, it could be taken as dative of advantage, in which case God appointed or made Christ the head over everything for the church (RSV, NIV, NRSV); or third, it could be taken as a dative of indirect object, in which case God gave Christ to the church (AV, RV, ASV, NASB, NEB). The third option is preferred because it allows ἔδωκεν to be translated normally as "he gave," while the first two interpretations would make it necessary to translate the verb "he appointed" or "he made." In fact, as Howard points out, ἔδωκεν is never used in the Pauline corpus as meaning "to appoint, to make" but always "to give" and always with an explicit or implied indirect object. He concludes: "This is precisely the usage we find in Ephesians and Colossians without exception, the dative case always being used to express the indirect object (Eph. i. 17, 22; iii. 2, 7, 8, 16; iv. 7, 8, 11, 27, 29; vi. 19; Col. i. 25)."[4] The reason that this dative phrase is placed last in the sentence is to make an easy link to the relative pronoun which introduces a further elaboration of the church in verse 23.

In conclusion, this verse speaks of two manifestations of power:

1. Lincoln, 68. Kittredge (*Community and Authority*, 124) disagrees and thinks that Christ is over all things "on behalf of the church."

2. *Contra* Lindemann (*Aufhebung*, 212) who thinks that the church existed before it was given to Christ.

3. Ernst, 296–97.

4. George Howard, "The Head/Body Metaphors of Ephesians," *NTS* 20 (April 1974): 353.

first, God has subjected everything in creation under Christ's feet; and second, God gave Christ to the church as head over everything, which thus implies that he is head over the church. Certainly there is progression of thought with regards to the role of Christ.

1:23. ἥτις ἐστὶν τὸ σῶμα αὐτοῦ, "which (indeed) is his body." Although there is debate regarding the distinction between the relative and the indefinite relative pronouns,[1] it seems that the indefinite relative pronoun does carry a qualitative force so that it could be rendered "which, in fact, is," or "which indeed is." Here we have the identification of the church, over which Christ is the head, as his body.

The word σῶμα, "body,"[2] normally refers to the physical body of a human or animal.[3] It occurs 132 times in the LXX, seventy-four times in the canonical books and always refers to human bodies, except the four times it refers to animal bodies (Gen 15:11; Ezek 1:11, 23; Dan 7:11).[4] In the NT it occurs 142 times, in Paul's writings ninety-one times, in Ephesians nine times (1:23; 2:16; 4:4, 12, 16*bis*; 5:23, 28, 30). It is used in the NT primarily of the human body, though twice it refers to celestial and terrestrial bodies (1 Cor 15:40*bis*), twice to animal bodies (Heb 13:11; Jas 3:3), three times to plant bodies (1 Cor 15:37, 38*bis*), eight times to Christ's body in connection with the Lord's supper (Matt 26:26 = Mark 14:22 = Luke 22:19; 1 Cor 10:16, 17; 11:24, 27, 29), and sixteen times to the church, the body of Christ (Rom 12:5; 1 Cor 10:17; 12:13, 27; Eph 1:23; 2:16; 4:4, 12, 16*bis*; 5:23, 30; Col 1:18; 24; 2:19; 3:15).[5] With the exception of Eph 5:28, in Ephesians it is always used metaphorically as a reference to the body of Christ, the church. In the present context this is certainly true, for the relative clause defines the church as "his body."

Paul clearly states that believers are members of the body of Christ (Rom 12:4–5; 1 Cor 12:12–14, 27; Eph 5:30).[6] However, there are two

1. Robertson, *Grammar*, 726–27; MHT 1:91–92; 3:49–50; BDF §293 (4); Zerwick, *Biblical Greek* §§215–20.

2. For a thorough study of body, see Robert H. Gundry, Sōma *in Biblical Theology, with Emphasis on Pauline Anthropology*, SNTSMS, ed. Matthew Black, vol. 29 (Cambridge: Cambridge University Press, 1976); cf. also Dawes, *The Body in Question*, 150–67.

3. Herodotus 1.139; Sophocles *Philoctetes* 51.

4. Cf. J. A. Ziesler, "Σῶμα in the Septuagint," *NovT* 25 (April 1983): 133–45.

5. Besides the body of Christ it is, though rarely, used of a body of people; cf. T. W. Manson, "A Parallel to a N.T. Use of σῶμα," *JTS* 37 (October 1936): 385. However, as Manson points out, "the uniqueness of the N.T. phrase resides not in the word but in the qualifying genitive. The body is not τὸ σῶμα τῶν Χριστιανῶν but τὸ σῶμα τοῦ Χριστοῦ." It is Christ's body.

6. For a discussion on the body of Christ, see Best, *One Body in Christ*, 85–95; Robert Jewett, *Paul's Anthropological Terms. A Study of Their Use in Conflict Sayings*, AGJU, ed. Otto Michel and Martin Hengel, vol. 10 (Leiden: Brill, 1971), 201–50; Gosnell L. O. R. Yorke, *The Church as the Body of Christ in the Pauline Corpus: A Re-examination* (Lanham, Md.: University Press of America, 1991), 1–126, esp. 1–15; G. M. M. Pelser, "Once More the Body of Christ in Paul," *Neot* 32, no. 2 (1998): 525–45; Best, 189–96.

new things revealed in Ephesians and Colossians about the body of Christ. First, the body of Christ, referring to the whole assembly of believers, is specifically identified as the "church" in the singular (Eph 1:22–23; 5:23; Col 1:18, 24). This is not to say that there was no earlier concept of this, although not specifically labeled, because in 1 Cor 12:27–28 Paul uses the words "body" and "church" synonymously, and, in fact, he persecuted the "church" of God (Gal 1:13; 1 Cor 15:9; Phil 3:6). Second, and more importantly, Christ is designated as head of the body (Eph 1:22–23; 4:15–16; 5:23; Col 1:18, 24; 2:19). Although "head" is used in the illustration of the body in 1 Cor 12:21, it is not identified as being Christ, as it is in Colossians and Ephesians, but rather, as one of the members of the body. Ridderbos, among others, suggests that in Ephesians and Colossians the "head" and "body" are two distinct metaphors and though related to each other should not be combined as one metaphor. This is more clearly seen in the application of the head-body relationship to the marriage relationship in Eph 5:23–33 where one would not postulate that since the church without Christ lacks a head, so wives apart from their husbands are incomplete persons.[1] However, whenever "head" is mentioned in Ephesians (1:22; 4:15; 5:23) and Colossians (1:18; 2:10, 19), the "body" is mentioned in the same context, indicating that the two metaphors are combined.[2] Therefore, there appears to be development in Paul's discussion of the body of believers, indicated by the identification of Christ as head.[3] Imbelli sums it up well when he states, "But whereas in Rom. and 1 Cor. the implicit identification was the following: church = body = Christ; in Eph the relation is richer and more com-

1. Ridderbos, *Paul*, 379–81; Yorke, *The Church as the Body of Christ in the Pauline Corpus*, 104–11; John K. McVay, "Head, Christ as," in *DPL*, 378.

2. Andrew Perriman, "'His body, which is the church. . . .' Coming to Terms with Metaphor," *EvQ* 62 (April 1990): 136; Dawes, *The Body in Question*, 119–20, 248–50; cf. Caird, 49, 78.

3. For further discussion on these two elements, see Pierre Benoit, "Body, Head, and *Pleroma* in the Epistles of the Captivity," in *Jesus and the Gospels*, trans. Benel Weatherhead, vol. 2 (New York: Seabury Press; London: Darton, Longman & Todd, 1974), 59–78; P. Benoît, "L'Église corps du Christ," in *Populus Dei. Studi in onore del Card. Alfredo Ottaviani per il cinquantesimo di sacerdozio: 18 marzo 1966*, vol. 2 (Rome: Communio [published as a part of the periodical *Communio* 11], [1969]), 971–1002 (reprinted in idem, *Exégèsis et Theologie*, vol. 4 [Paris: Cerf, 1982], 205–37); Perriman, "'His body, which is the church. . . .' Coming to Terms with Metaphor," 123–42; Schnackenburg, 298–302; James D. G. Dunn, "'The Body of Christ' in Paul," in *Worship, Theology and Ministry in the Early Church: Essays in Honor of Ralph P. Martin*, ed. Michael J. Wilkins and Terence Paige, JSNTSup, ed. Stanley E. Porter et al., vol. 87 (Sheffield: JSOT Press, 1992), 146–62. Field thinks that the change in the use of the metaphor was done by Paul's disciple(s) who wrote Colossians and Ephesians (Barbara Field, "The Discourses Behind the Metaphor 'the Church is The Body of Christ' as Used by St Paul and the 'Post-Paulines'," *Asia Journal of Theology* 6 [April 1992]: 90–91, 103–4).

plex and may be schematized thus: church = body, Christ = head, body + head = Christ."[1]

How does Paul view the relationship of the head with the body? The Jews, Stoics, and a philosopher like Aristotle saw the heart as the seat of life. On the other hand, physicians in the past such as Hippocrates (469–399 B.C.) and Galen (ca. A.D. 129–199) had thought that the brain directed the members of the body. Philosophers such as Plato, and later Philo, followed this model.[2] Both elements are in Paul's writings for he talks about the heart as an expression of will or volition (1 Cor 4:5; Eph 5:19; 6:22) and of thought and understanding (Rom 1:21; 10:6; Eph 1:18), but he also talks about the head as the source of sustenance of the body (Col 2:19; Eph 4:15–16). Paul's companion Luke, the physician (Col 4:14), may have informed him of the role that the head plays in controlling the body.[3] In the present context it is clear that the ascended Christ is preeminent over all and that God subjects "everything" under his feet and gave Christ to the church as head over everything. It is the church that is directed by Christ or, in other words, it is the body that is directed by the head.

It is interesting to note that in the NT the body of Christ is made analogous only to the human body, and thus there is a clear rather than an abstract idea of its function and the relationship of the various members of the body to each other (cf. Rom 12:4–5; 1 Cor 12:14–27). One good reason to use the human body as an analogy is that it conveys the idea of an organic unity that is animated by the head. It is not like a corporation where the employees may have no relationship with the head and/or other employees. On the contrary, the body depicts that each member is integrally bound to the head and to each other. This is appropriate for this context because of the contrast it presents. God subjected all creation under his feet, including friends and enemies alike. On the other hand, he gave Christ, the head of everything, to the church whose members have an integral relationship with Christ. The members of the body of Christ are bound to each other and are related to Christ as our redeemer, sustainer, and head.

Having discussed the head, body, and church, there needs to be a mention of the origin of these concepts. Several scholars think that their origin was from the Gnostic redeemer myth in which the first man (Urmensch) seems to be both the redeemer and head of the entire universe which is his body. This first man or savior saves himself and as a result of this saves the human race. Some think these ideas

1. Robert P. Imbelli, "'. . . Dwelling Place for God in the Spirit,'" *Dunwoodie Review* 6 (May 1966): 190.

2. Barth, 187–88; Dawes, *The Body in Question*, 129–32. For a good discussion on this, see Arnold, "Jesus Christ: 'Head' of the Church (Colossians and Ephesians)," 352–58.

3. Benoit, "Body, Head, and *Pleroma* in the Epistles of the Captivity," 2:74.

are already found in the earlier epistles of Paul,[1] while others think they are found only in Ephesians and Colossians.[2] This theory was immediately questioned because the Gnostic texts on which they built their hypothesis were written after the NT period and because the Pauline presentation of the church as the body of Christ is quite different from that presented in the Gnostic materials.[3] It is the church, not the whole world, that is the body of Christ. It has been shown that the concepts of the "redeemed-redeemer" and the union of the "redeemed-redeemer" with the cosmos were based on the Iranian Manichaean writings of the third century A.D. and there is no evidence to suppose that these concepts existed before then.[4] It is better to assume that the origin of the concepts of the head, body, and church, although possibly latent in the OT where God redeems, leads, and sustains his people Israel,[5] was revealed to the apostles in the development of the first-century church and was spelled out in Paul's letters.[6] Again one must not confuse the church and the cosmos. Christ is Lord

1. Käsemann, *Leib und Leib Christi*, 137–86; Rudolf Bultmann, *Theology of the New Testament*, trans. Kendrick Grobel, vol. 1 (New York: Charles Scribner's Sons; London: SCM, 1952), 178–80.

2. Schlier, 91–96; idem, "Zum Begriff der Kirche im Epheserbrief," *TBl* 6 (Januar 1927): 12–17; idem, *Christus und die Kirche im Epheserbrief*; Heinrich Schlier and P. Vicktor Warnach, *Die Kirche im Epheserbrief*, Beiträge Kontroverstheologie, Beiheft zur Catholica, ed. Robert Grosche, no. 1 (Münster: Aschendorffsche Verlagsbuchhandlung, 1949); Schlier, *TDNT* 3 (1965): 676–78; Schmidt, *TDNT* 3 (1965): 509–13; Petr Pokorný, "Σῶμα Χριστοῦ im Epheserbrief," *EvT* 20 (Oktober 1960): 456–64; idem, *Der Epheserbrief und die Gnosis*.

3. Cf. Ernst Percy, *Der Leib Christi (Σῶμα Χριστοῦ) in den paulinischen Homologumena und Antilegomena*, LUÅ, vol. 38 (Lund: Gleerup; Leipzig: Otto Harrossowitz, 1942), 39–54; Hanson, *The Unity of the Church in the New Testament* 113–16; Mussner, *Christus, das All und die Kirche*, passim; Jewett, *Paul's Anthropological Terms*, 230–37; Perkins, 52–53.

4. Cf. Carsten Colpe, *Die religionsgeschichte Schule Darstellung und Kritik ihres Bildes vom gnostischen Erlösermythus*, FRLANT, ed. Rud. Bultmann, vol. 60 (Göttingen: Vandenhoeck & Ruprecht, 1961), 140–93; Hans-Martin Schenke, *Der Gott »Mensch« in der Gnosis. Ein religionsgeschichtlicher Beitrag zur Diskussion über die paulinischen Anschauung von der Kirche als Leib Christi* (Göttingen: Vandenhoeck & Ruprecht, 1962), 16–33, 155–56, passim.

5. A. M. Dubarle, "L'origine dans l'Ancient Testament de la notion paulinienne de l'Église corps du Christ," in *Studiorum Paulinorum Congressus Internationalis Catholicus 1961*, vol. 1, AnBib, vol. 17 (Rome: E Pontificio Instituto Biblico, 1963), 231–40. In connection with the mystery in Ephesians, Lemmer suggests that one should understand the "body of Christ" in the light of early Jewish mysticism (Richard Lemmer, "ἡ οἰκονομία τοῦ μυστηρίου τοῦ ἀποκεκρυμμένου ἐν τῷ θεῷ—Understanding 'body of Christ' in the Letter to the Ephesians," *Neot* 32, no. 2 [1998]: 459–95). Although an interesting proposal, one must question whether or not the people in Western Asia Minor would have had the background in understanding Jewish mysticism, which Lemmer attempts to argue for.

6. *Contra* Carsten Colpe, "Zur Leib-Christi-Vorstellung im Epheserbrief," in *Judentum, Urchristentum, Kirche. Festschrift für Joachim Jeremias*, ed. Walther Eltester,

over the cosmos and head over the church. The church, Christ's body, is never called the cosmos.

τὸ πλήρωμα τοῦ τὰ πάντα ἐν πᾶσιν πληρουμένου, "the fullness of him who is being filled entirely." Because these words can be taken in so many different ways, much has been written on them.[1] The words and the possible alternatives will first be examined, then it will be necessary to scrutinize the combination of the alternatives to these words.

There is need for a brief discussion of the words. First, πλήρωμα is more fully discussed in Excursus 5: A Study of πλήρωμα. When it is used with the corresponding verb (πληρόω), as is the case here, it nor-

---

BZNW, ed. Walther Eltester, vol. 26 (Berlin: Alfred Töplemann, 1960), 172–87. He feels that although the concept of the body did not come from the Gnostic soteriological myth developed by Käsemann and Schlier, it also did not come from Christian sources but rather from philosophical speculation in the process of trying to adapt Jewish thinking to the Gentile situation. For a discussion of the Hellenistic or Hellenistic-Jewish influences on the ecclesiology of Ephesians, see Hoppe, "Theo-logie und Ekklesiologie im Epheserbrief," 231–45.

1. A good summary of the problems and views, see Roy Yates, "A Re-examination of Ephesians 1:23," *ExpTim* 83 (February 1972): 146–51, which is a condensation of idem, "A Re-examination of Ephesians 1:23" (M.Litt. thesis, University of Cambridge, 1969). Cf. also J. Armitage Robinson, "The Church as the Fulfilment of the Christ: A Note on Ephesians i.23," *Exp* 5th ser., vol. 7 (April 1898): 24–59; A. E. N. Hitchcock, "Ephesians i.23," *ExpTim* 22 (November 1910): 91; F. R. Montgomery-Hitchcock, "The Pleroma as the Medium of the Self-Realisation of Christ," *Exp* 8th ser., vol. 24 (August 1922): 135–50; idem, "The Pleroma of Christ," *CQR* 125 (October–December 1937): 1–18; C. F. D. Moule, "A Note on Ephesians i.22, 23," *ExpTim* 60 (November 1948): 53; C. F. D. Moule, "'Fulness' and 'Fill' in the New Testament," *SJT* 4 (March 1951): 79–86; Josef Gewieß, "Die Begriffe πληροῦν und πλήρωμα im Kolosser- und Epheserbrief," in *Vom Wort des Lebens. Festschrift für Max Meinertz zur Vollendung des 70. Lebensjahres 19. Dezember 1950*, ed. Nikolaus Adler, Neutestamentliche Abhandlungen I. Ergänzungsband, ed. M. Meinertz (Münster: Münster Aschendorffsch Verlagsbuchhandlung, 1951), 128–41; A. Feuillet, "L'Eglise plérôme du Christ d'après Ephés., I,23," *NRT* 78 (Mai 1956): 449–72; (Juin 1956) 593–610 (cf. idem, *Le Christ sagesse de Dieu: D'après les Épîtres pauliniennes*, EBib [Paris: Gabalda, 1966], 275–319); A. R. McGlashan, "Ephesians i.23," *ExpTim* 76 (January 1965): 132–33; Russell Fowler, "Ephesians i.23," *ExpTim* 76 (June 1965): 294; R. Hermans and L. Geysels, "Efesiërs 1,23: Het pleroma van Gods heilswerk," *Bijdragen Tijdschrift voor Filosofie en Theologie* 28 (Juli, Augustus 1967): 279–93; Josef Ernst, *Pleroma und Pleroma Christi. Geschichte und Deutung eines Begriffs der paulinischen antilegomena*, Biblische Untersuchungen, ed. Otto Kuss, vol. 5 (Regensburg: F. Putset, 1970), 105–20; Barth, 200–210; Ignace de la Potterie, "Le Christi Plérôme de l'Eglise (Ep 1,22–23)," *Bib* 58, no. 4 (1977): 500–524; P. D. Overfield, "Pleroma: A Study in Content and Context," *NTS* 25 (April 1979): 384–96; Pierre Benoit, "The 'plèrôma' in the Epistles to the Colossians and the Ephesians," *Svensk exegetisk årsbok* 49 (1984): 136–58; Sheldon Sawatzky, "*Pleroma* in Ephesians 1:23," *Taiwan Journal of Theology* 11 (March 1989): 107–15; Roy R. Jeal, "A Strange Style of Expression: Ephesians 1:23," *Filologia Neotestamentaria* 10 (Mayo–Noviembre 1997): 129–38; Los Santos, *La novedad de la metáfora κεφαλή-σῶμα*, 67–89.

mally has the idea of "completeness, the absence of any lacunae." The noun can be taken actively, "that which fills," or passively, "that which is filled."

Second, the verb πληρόω is used most frequently with the genitive and in the active sense it means "to fill" containers[1] or "to man" the ships[2] and metaphorically "to satisfy desires."[3] In the passive it means "to be filled" with breath[4] or it can refer to ships that were manned;[5] metaphorically, it means "to be filled with fear."[6] In the middle it is used of one who "mans a ship himself."[7] It can be a middle with an active idea of "manning his own ship,"[8] or it can be a middle with a passive idea, such as "furnishing ships with crews."[9] It appears 109 times in the LXX, seventy-six times in the canonical books and is translated sixty-four times from מָלֵא, which in the active sense means "to fill water in the seas" (Gen 1:22) or "to fulfill what God promised" (1 Kgs 8:15; 2 Chr 6:4), and in the passive sense "the earth be filled with the glory of the Lord" (Ps 72:19 [LXX 71:19]) or "the ear shall not be filled with hearing" (Eccl 1:8).[10] In the NT it is used eighty-six times, twenty-three times by Paul, four times in Ephesians (1:23; 3:19; 4:10; 5:18). It is used in the active sense to refer to the Holy Spirit filling the believers at Pentecost (Acts 2:2) or as a metaphor as "sorrow filling the hearts" (John 16:6). In the passive it used to assert that the "house was filled with the fragrance of the ointment" (John 12:3) or as a metaphor, "to be filled with unrighteousness" (Rom 1:29) or "the word of the Lord might be fulfilled" (Matt 1:22; 2:15, 17). There is no example of a middle use of this verb in the NT with the possibly exception of the present context. In this verse it is either middle or passive in form, and thus it is either "the one who fills himself" or "the one who is being filled." More will be said below.

Third, the words τὰ πάντα ἐν πᾶσιν need to be addressed briefly. The word πᾶς can be used as an adjective, "each, every" (Luke 3:9; Rom 3:4; Eph 1:21); as a substantive, "everyone, everything" (Matt 10:22; Eph 1:22); and adverbially, "in every way, in all respects" (1 Cor 10:33; Eph 4:15),[11] or "wholly, entirely, absolutely."[12] The words τὰ πάντα ἐν πᾶσιν occur in 1 Cor 12:6 and 15:28 and with the addition of καί in Col 3:11. In 1 Cor 12:6 it could be taken adverbially, that is, God works al-

1. Herodotus 3.123.
2. Ibid., 1.171.
3. Plato *Gorgias* 494c.
4. Aeschylus *Septem contra Thebas* 464.
5. Thucydides 1.29.3.
6. Plato *Leges* 9 §865e.
7. Isaeus 11.48.
8. Xenophon *Historica Graeca* 6.2.14, 35; Plutarch *Alcibiades* 35.5.
9. Demosthenes *Orationes* 17.28.
10. Cf. L. A. Snijders, "מָלֵא *mālēʾ*," *TDOT* 8 (1997): 297–300.
11. BAGD 631–33; BDAG 782–84.
12. Moule, *Idiom Book*, 160.

ways or continually, or it could have two separate ideas, namely, God works all things in everyone. The same could be said for the other two passages and thus these examples are not really helpful in interpreting the present phrase. Therefore, these words can be taken either adverbially or adjectivally. This must be determined after the rest of the verse is analyzed.

Having looked at the words, two things need to be considered next. First, πλήρωμα is in apposition either to αὐτόν of verse 22, speaking of the fullness of Christ, or to σῶμα of verse 23, denoting the church as the fullness of Christ. Those who think it refers to Christ claim that they cannot see anywhere in the NT that the church is the completeness of Christ.[1] Furthermore, they consider that this interpretation (that the fullness referring to Christ as the fullness of God) is consistent with Eph 4:10 as well as Col 1:19 and 2:9.[2] However, this view has some real problems. First, it has problems syntactically, for πλήρωμα is far removed from αὐτόν (v. 22); moreover, πλήρωμα is neuter, whereas αὐτόν is masculine. This view makes the intervening words (ἥτις ἐστὶν τὸ σῶμα αὐτοῦ) "a useless insertion, and worse than useless, as serving only to separate πλ. from ἔδωκεν."[3] Furthermore, those who hold that πλήρωμα is in apposition to αὐτόν in verse 22 have to plead a lax construction, as if written under the influence of emotion.[4] Admittedly, there are cases of lax construction in Paul's letters, but in this case there is no indication of his writing under the influence of emotion. It is much more natural for πλήρωμα to be in apposition to σῶμα because these words are not only close in proximity, but they also agree in gender, case, and number. Second, it is true that Christ is spoken of as the fullness of God in other passages, but that does not preclude a different concept here. And third, to say that the alternative view means that the church is the completion of Christ is not necessarily true. This will be discussed below.

Second, a consideration of the different constructs of πλήρωμα and πληρουμένου need to be considered. There are six views. (1) Robinson takes the πλήρωμα as active, πληρουμένου as passive, and the τὰ πάντα ἐν πᾶσιν as adverbial, giving the sense that the church is the completion of Christ in all respects.[5] This means that Christ is incomplete and is moving toward completeness when all the members are incorporated.[6] This has the support of early versions (Peshitta, Itala, Vg) and

1. Moule, "'Fulness' and 'Fill' in the New Testament," 81; Yates, "A Re-examination of Ephesians 1:23," 148; La Potterie, "Le Christi Plérôme de l'Eglise (Ep 1,22–23)," 507–21.

2. Hitchcock, "Ephesians i.23," 91; Moule, "A Note on Ephesians i.22, 23," 53.

3. Abbott, 38.

4. Hitchcock, "Ephesians i.23," 91; McGlashan, "Ephesians i.23," 133.

5. Robinson, 42–45, 255–59; so also Yates, "A Re-examination of Ephesians 1:23," 149–51.

6. Newport J. D. White, "The Catholic Church and the Summing up of all Things in Christ," *Exp* 8th ser., vol. 21 (March 1921): 206, 209–12.

commentators.[1] The real problem with this view is that nowhere in the NT is there any hint that the church completed Christ but rather that Christ completed the church (cf. Eph 3:19; 4:10, 13; Col 2:9–10). Those who accept this view refer to Col 1:24 where Paul states that his sufferings fill up or complete the sufferings of Christ. However, in that context it specifies a full complement to the *action* of Christ's sufferings by the believers' sufferings in this age rather than a complement to the *person* of Christ by the inclusion of believers into the church. Furthermore, Eph 4:13 indicates that it is the church that is growing into the measure of the stature of the fullness (πληρώματος) of Christ. Another problem with this view is that it makes the phrase τοῦ τὰ πάντα ἐν πᾶσιν πληρουμένου redundant because there is no need to say that Christ is being filled with all things (or in every way) if the church completes Christ.[2]

(2) Some see the πλήρωμα as active, πληρουμένου as middle with a reflexive idea and the τὰ πάντα ἐν πᾶσιν as adjectival, giving the sense that the church complements Christ because he himself fulfills all things in all.[3] Montgomery-Hitchcock writes, "As Christ is in us and we are in Christ, Christ becomes all things to us and we become all things through Christ. In this sense we may be said to fulfil Him who fulfils Himself in the *pleroma* of His self-realization."[4] The two problems with this view are: (a) that it is a very difficult view to understand and it seems that one needs to read much more into it than what seems obvious, and (b) as mentioned above there is no example of a middle use of this verb in the NT.

(3) Some see the πλήρωμα as active, πληρουμένου as middle with an active sense, and the τὰ πάντα ἐν πᾶσιν as adjectival. This signifies the church as the completion of Christ who fills all things in all (AV, RV, ASV, RSV, NASB, NIV, NRSV).[5] Three problems with this view are: (a) erroneously viewing the church as the completion of Christ, as dis-

1. Chrysostom *Eph* 1:15–20 (*PG* 62:26; cf. also Kohlgraf, *Die Ekklesiologie des Epheserbriefes in der Auslegung durch Johannes Chrysostomus*, 266–67); Jerome *Eph* 1:23 (*PL* 26:462–63; Aquinas, chap. 1, lec. 8, vv. 22–23 (82–83); Calvin, 138; cf. also Yates, "A Reexamination of Ephesians 1:23," 149–51; Overfield, "Pleroma: A Study in Content and Context," 393.

2. Dawes, *The Body in Question*, 244.

3. Hendriksen, 103–6; Montgomery-Hitchcock, "The Pleroma as the Medium of the Self-Realisation of Christ," 135–50; idem, "The Pleroma of Christ," 1–18.

4. Montgomery-Hitchcock, "The Pleroma as the Medium of the Self-Realisation of Christ," 150; idem, "The Pleroma of Christ," 18.

5. Abbott, 35–38. A similar view is suggested by Korting who views the participle πληρουμένου as both active and passive much like the Hebrew Hophal which is the passive of the causative Hiphil and hence can be translated "the fullness of him who is made (caused) (by God) to fill all things in all." See Georg Korting, "Das Partizip in Eph 1,23," *TGl* 87, no. 2 (1997): 260–65. It is not certain how Korting takes the noun. Furthermore, although Paul was undoubtedly familiar with Semitic structure, one is uncertain that he had the Hophal in mind in this context.

cussed in view (1) above; (b) deriving an active sense from a middle form when Paul could have used an active form as he does in 4:10;[1] and (c) understanding the precise meaning of τὰ πάντα ἐν πᾶσιν.

(4) Some argue that the πλήρωμα is passive and πληρουμένου is middle with a reflexive idea and the τὰ πάντα ἐν πᾶσιν is adverbial and indicates that the church is filled by Christ who completely fills for himself.[2] The problem with this view is understanding the reflexive idea of how he completely fills for himself. What does that mean?

(5) Some view the πλήρωμα as passive and the πληρουμένου as a middle with an active sense and τὰ πάντα ἐν πᾶσιν as adverbial, connoting that the church is filled by Christ who fills all things completely or entirely.[3] This view encounters the last two problems mentioned for view (3). It is not clear if Christ completely fills only the church or the universe as well.

(6) Some take both πλήρωμα and πληρουμένου as passives and τὰ πάντα ἐν πᾶσιν adverbially. This would indicate that the church is filled by Christ who is being filled (by God) entirely or in every way (JB, NEB, NJB).[4] Yates criticizes this view on two grounds: (a) it accepts the lexical rule that -μα endings are always passive, irrespective of the context (so Lightfoot); and (b) it assumes πλήρωμα is never passive but always active throughout the NT.[5] The first criticism is valid and the second is patently untrue. However, it seems best to accept πλήρωμα as passive, not because of its -μα ending but because of its usage in the context. Out of the seventeen times πλήρωμα is used in the NT, it is passive at least ten times (excluding the present context). A few examples follow. With reference to fullness, there is the incident where the baskets were filled with broken pieces of bread (Mark 6:43; 8:20) and the concept of that which God fills (Eph 3:19; 4:13; Col 1:19; 2:9). With reference to quantity, Paul speaks of his coming to Rome in the fullness of blessings or being filled with blessings (Rom 15:29) and refers to the hardening of Israel until the fullness of the Gentiles or when the full number of Gentiles come in (Rom 11:25). With ref-

1. Best, *One Body in Christ*, 143 n. 2.

2. Eadie, 112–15; Ellicott, 31; Salmond, 281–82; McDonald, 221 (but τὰ πάντα refers to the cosmos and ἐν πᾶσιν "is added for emphasis").

3. Alford, 3:87; Masson, 156; Gaugler, 80–81; Caird, 49; Barth, 159, 205–9; Mußner, 57; Schnackenburg, 81; Lincoln, 76–77; Muddiman, 96; cf. also Hanson, *The Unity of the Church in the New Testament*, 127–29; Mussner, *Christus, das All und die Kirkche*, 30, 59–60; Roels, *God's Mission*, 240–47; Lona, *Die Eschatologie im Kolosser- und Epheserbrief*, 317; Arnold, *Ephesians: Power and Magic*, 82–85; Los Santos, *La novedad de la metáfora κεφαλή-σῶμα*, 86–87.

4. Lightfoot, *Colossians*, 257–63; Westcott, 28; Wilfred L. Knox, *St Paul and the Church of the Gentiles* (Cambridge: Cambridge University Press, 1939), 163–65; Robinson, *The Body*, 69; Best, *One Body in Christ*, 143–44; Feuillet, "L'Eglise plérôme du Christ d'après Ephés., I,23," 450–59; Feuillet, *Le Christ Sagesse de Dieu d'après les Épitres pauliniennes*, 287–92; Dawes, *The Body in Question*, 244–45; Jeal, "A Strange Style of Expression: Ephesians 1:23," 137–38; for a view close to this, see Chadwick, "Die Absicht des Epheserbriefes," 152; Best, 185, 188; O'Brien, 150–51.

5. Yates, "A Re-examination of Ephesians 1:23," 148.

erence to time, the goal or plan is filled by time (Gal 4:4; Eph 1:10). Other examples could be given, but these are sufficient to make the point that πλήρωμα can be passive as well as active (Matt 9:16 = Mark 2:21). The context must determine whether it is active or passive. In this context the passive fits much better, as will be discussed below. As for Yates, his dilemma is that he does not want to accept it as a passive, yet neither does he want an active sense where the church complements Christ, so he chooses to make πλήρωμα antecedent to αὐτόν in verse 22. However, this is a far more cumbersome construction, as discussed above. Besides this, he accepts the participle as middle with an active sense and minimizes the significance of voice in making an exegetical decision.[1] The use of the middle with an active sense for πληρόω finds no support in the NT[2] and rarely elsewhere. This is especially true when the active form is used in this epistle (4:10). Therefore, Yates' wrong assertion that πλήρωμα is never passive in the NT has made him posit a view that is cumbersome and fraught with problems.

Of the six views examined, views (4) and (6) seem most viable. Of the two, view (6) seems the most fitting. Having attempted to answer some of the criticisms against this view, I will mention some of its positive features. First, πλήρωμα can be used passively, signifying the result of filling which denotes completion of the church. Second, this use of πλήρωμα fits well in the present context and coincides with the rest of the NT in that Christ completes the church rather than the church completes Christ. Third, it makes good syntactical sense because πλήρωμα is in apposition to σῶμα, which is near to it and corresponds in gender, number, and case. This is preferable to it being in apposition to αὐτόν in verse 22, which is not of the same gender. Furthermore, its great distance syntactically from πλήρωμα almost makes the intervening words unnecessary. Fourth, by accepting the participle (πληρουμένου) as passive,[3] it makes reference to Christ being filled by God's πλήρωμα, as Paul taught in Col 1:19 and 2:9 which state that God was pleased that all the fullness dwelt in Christ. That fullness with which Christ is being filled is that which fills the church or "he who fills the Church is himself being filled."[4] In other words, God's fullness which is filling Christ is filling the church. This agrees with Eph 4:10 where Christ has descended to fill all things. In 1:23 the church is Christ's fullness and in 4:13 Christ's fullness is the measurement which the body of believers must attain.[5] Fifth, the words τὰ

1. Ibid., 146, 149.

2. Westcott, 28.

3. La Potterie, "Le Christi Plérôme de l'Eglise (Ep 1,22–23)," 503–7.

4. Best, *One Body in Christ*, 143; see also Chantal Reynier, "L'apport irremplaçable de l'épître aux Éphésiens en matière de catéchèse," *Lumen Vitae* 52 (Septembre 1997): 275–84.

5. John Macpherson, "The use of the Word '*Pleroma*' in Ephesians and Colossians," *Exp* 2d ser., vol. 4 (December 1882): 464–65.

πάντα ἐν πᾶσιν make sense adverbially, for as the church is receiving the fullness from Christ, he is being filled wholly, entirely, absolutely, or in every way by God.

Before completing the discussion on this passage, four things need to addressed. First, it should be noted that the participle πληρουμένου is present tense, denoting that God's filling of Christ is not static but constant. In the same way Christ's filling of the church is alive and fresh. His power is new for every challenge and opportunity, for every hardship and triumph of believers, individually and collectively. This power is especially needed in struggles against evil powers known to the Ephesian believers.

Second, the word fullness must be defined. In Col 1:19 and 2:9 it indicates God's deity and in Eph 4:10 it refers to God's gifts to the church. In Eph 3:19 Paul prays that all believers might be filled with God's fullness. In these contexts, fullness seems to point to God's moral excellence, perfection, and power. Particularly in 3:19 being filled with God's fullness is to know the love of Christ. On the other hand, in the present context power is the center of the discussion, for God was demonstrating his power in that he gave Christ to the church as head over everything. The church, his body, is being filled with the moral excellence and power of God by Christ who in turn is being filled with the moral excellence and power of God. The fullness is not the Gnostic concept of the complex spiritual world of the Godhead where there are emanations of aeons to enlighten humans about their reconciliation. Rather, it is the character, essence, and power of God that is filling the church. Lightfoot summed it up well when he wrote, "All the Divine graces which reside in Him are imparted to her; His 'fulness' is communicated to her: and thus she may be said to be His pleroma (i.23). This is the ideal Church."[1]

Third, to what do the words τὰ πάντα ἐν πᾶσιν refer? They can be translated literally "all things in/with all things" or adverbially as "wholly, entirely, absolutely." Some think these words have reference to Christ's filling the cosmos in every respect.[2] This seems to fit well with the use of πάντα in verse 22 where "everything" is subjected to Christ. However, as mentioned above, it seems better to consider that this has reference to God's character, essence, and power, with particular emphasis on power since this is the main point of the context. The reasons for this are: (1) τὰ πάντα ἐν πᾶσιν is not the same as πάντα; (2) it seems strange to have moved from creation to the church and then to revert back to creation; and (3) it does not necessitate making πληρουμένου a middle with an active sense since this is never done in the NT and rarely elsewhere, and since he could have used the active form as he does later in this letter (4:10).

1. Lightfoot, *Colossians*, 263.

2. Schnackenburg, 83–84; Lincoln, 77; Arnold, *Ephesians: Power and Magic*, 84–85.

Fourth, there has been some debate on whether God or Christ is the means of the fullness. Both seem to be plausible, for Christ is the one who fills the church and God is the one who fills Christ. However, in this context it is God who gave Christ to the church and Christ who fills the church; thus, he is the means. It is not as some church fathers think that the Father is the "fullness" and Christ is the body.[1] Rather, as God fills Christ with the fullness of moral excellence and power, so Christ fills the church with the fullness of moral excellence and power. Therefore, the main assertion in this verse is that Christ is the agent who fills the church, as opposed to the relationship of God to the saints or to the church.[2]

This marks the end of Paul's prayer begun in verse 15. To summarize this prayer (for a structural layout of the prayer, see 1:16b), Paul requests that believers might know God more personally and intimately. The purpose of this personal and intimate knowledge is that they might know three things: (1) the hope of his calling, which looks in the past; (2) the wealth of his glorious inheritance, which looks into the future when it will be fully realized in Christ's coming to take his saints; and (3) the greatness of his power, which looks at the present day. Paul spends most of his time on this last segment. The greatness of God's power in the present age is not only described but is also demonstrated when: (1) he exercised it in Christ by raising and seating him; (2) subjected all things under Christ's feet; and (3) gave him to the church as head. The fullness of God's power and attributes are given to the church by Christ, who in turn is being filled with them completely. Hence, Paul's prayer is built on the fact that God has enriched believers with every spiritual benefit for their spiritual well-being. He prays that believers will deepen their relationship with God and experience in a deeper way the spiritual benefits with which they have been enriched.

Excursus 5
A Study of πλήρωμα

The term πλήρωμα, which is derived from the adjective πλήρης, has been much discussed.[3] In classical literature it has both the active sense, "that which fills," such as wine

1. Theodoret *Eph* 1:23 (*PG* 82:517); cf. Theodori Episcopi Mopsuesteni, *Epistolas b. Pauli Commentarii, The Latin Version with the Greek Fragments with an Introduction Notices and Indices*, ed. H. B. Swete, vol. 1 (Cambridge: Cambridge University Press, 1880–82), 141 n. 2.

2. Fay ("Paul the Empowered Prisoner," 486–500) proposes that vv. 22–23 express the presuppositional proposition of the discourse on unity in the church whereby God made Christ the cosmic lord "and he gave him as head over everything to the church, which is his body, the fullness of him who is being filled entirely." This proposition is developed in the rest of the book.

3. Lightfoot, *Colossians*, 257–73; Robinson, 255–59; Feuillet, "L'Eglise plérôme du Christ d'après Ephés., I,23," 459–61; M. Bogdasavich, "The Idea of *Pleroma* in the Epistles to the Colossians and Ephesians," *DRev* 83 (April 1965): 118–30; Gerhard Delling,

fills the cup[1] or a crew or cargo fills a ship;[2] and the passive sense, "that which is filled, brought to fullness," such as a full number of ships,[3] full number of citizens of a city.[4] Furthermore, this term can denote the idea of "totality, sum, entirety," as the total number of years of life,[5] total number of members of the senate,[6] or a full or complete supply of materials.[7] In discussing the above and other passages, some have suggested that substantives ending with -μα have a strictly passive sense (and -σις the active sense), but Lightfoot corrected this notion by suggesting that substantives ending with -μα are passive in the sense that "they give the *result* of the agency involved in the corresponding verb."[8] Robinson, on the one hand, criticizes Lightfoot for relying too heavily on the -μα ending to determine it as a passive rather than letting the context determine whether it is passive or active. On the other hand, Robinson goes on to show that Lightfoot's rule is valid if substantives ending with -μα have with them corresponding verbs from the same root, for example, πρᾶγμα "a deed" is the result of "doing" (πράσσω) and δόμα "a gift" is the result of "giving" (δίδωμι).[9] Accordingly, the result of filling is completeness, totality, entirety. Hence, the word πλήρωμα basically means "completeness, the absence of any lacunae."[10]

In the LXX πλήρωμα occurs fifteen times having the idea of fullness of content and thus totality as in the fullness of the sea (1 Chr 16:32; Pss 96:11 [LXX 95:11]; 98:7 [LXX 97:7]) and earth or land (Pss 24:1 [LXX 23:1]; 50:12 [LXX 49:12]; 89:11 [MT 89:12; LXX 88:12]; Jer 8:16; 47:2 [LXX 29:2]; Ezek 12:19; 19:7; 30:12; cf. also Eccl 4:6*bis*). All but two times it translates מְלֹא and twice πλήρωσις translates this Hebrew word (Deut 33:16; Ezek 32:15) meaning "fullness," a fact which shows that the endings do not necessarily determine whether they are active or passive.[11] In koine Greek it continues to have the idea of "full, complete."[12]

In the NT πλήρωμα occurs seventeen times, five times in the Gospels, twelve times in Paul's writings, and four of these in Ephesians (1:10, 23; 3:19; 4:13). It refers to fullness of content, such as the leftover bread that filled the baskets (Mark 6:43; 8:20), a patch on a garment (Matt 9:16 = Mark 2:21) or contents of the earth (1 Cor 10:26 quoting Pss 24:1 [LXX 23:1]; 50:12 [LXX 49:12]). It also refers to a full number of people (Rom 11:12, 25) and to a sense of totality or entirety, such as Jesus' fullness of grace (John 1:16), God's essence (Col 1:19), or deity (Col 2:9); Paul's coming in the fullness of the blessings of Christ (Rom 13:10); believers' maturing to the fullness of Christ (Eph 4:13); filled with God's full-

"πλήρωμα," *TDNT* 6 (1968): 298–305; Ernst, *Pleroma und Pleroma Christ*; Overfield, "Pleroma: A Study in Content and Context," 384–96; Pierre Benoit, "The 'plèrôma' in the Epistles to the Colossians and the Ephesians," 136–58; Hans Hübner, "πλήρωμα," *EDNT* 3 (1993): 110–11.

1. Euripides *Troades* 824.

2. Thucydides 7.12.3; Philo *Mos.* 2.12 §62.

3. Herodotus 8.43, 45.

4. Aristotle *Politica* 2.4.13 §1267b.16; 3.8.1 §1284a.5.

5. Herodotus 3.22.

6. Dio Cassius 52.42.1.

7. Diodorus Siculus 2.12.2.

8. Lightfoot, *Colossians*, 257; BDF §109 (2).

9. Robinson, 256–57.

10. Delling, *TDNT* 6 (1968): 298.

11. Moule, "'Fulness' and 'Fill' in the New Testament," 82–83; cf. also James Barr, *The Semantics of Biblical Language* (Oxford: Oxford University Press, 1961), 141–44; cf. Snijders, *TDOT* 8 (1997): 306–7.

12. MM 520.

ness (Eph 3:19); and the church, the body, as the fullness of Christ (Eph 1:23). Its use to convey completeness can be seen in the phrase "fullness of time" (Gal 4:4; Eph 1:10). It is used once to convey the idea of the completion or fulfillment of the law (Rom 13:10). Clearly, in all NT uses it maintains the idea of the result of filling, that is, fullness, completeness, entirety.

The word πλήρωμα was frequently used by the Gnostics.[1] It is a technical term used by the most influential Gnostic school, the Valentinian Gnostics (second century A.D.) for a complex spiritual world of thirty aeons (intermediaries) arranged in fifteen pairs who emanated from the primordial pair, Depth and Silence. The last created aeon, Sophia ("wisdom"), disturbed the πλήρωμα, which led to her fall whereby she was excluded from the πλήρωμα and this meant that part of the Godhead was lost. She became the creator of the evil material world of which humans are a part. In order to bring Sophia back into harmony with πλήρωμα, two new aeons, Christ and the Holy Spirit, were created. Christ came by adopting Jesus' body probably at baptism and departing from it just before the crucifixion to restore her and to enlighten humans with knowledge (γνῶσις) of their essential identity with the Godhead which also will lead to their ultimate restoration. With the discovery of the Nag Hammadi library more information has been gained regarding Gnosticism. This material has helped to clarify some nuances of the Gnostic use of the word πλήρωμα, although in essence it retains the definition outlined in Valentinian Gnosticism. Notwithstanding, there are some real difficulties in accepting the Gnostic concept of πλήρωμα as relevant to NT studies. First, Gnostic literature is second century A.D., well after the NT era. Some postulate that the fully developed Gnosticism of the second century was already present in pre-Christian Gnosticism (or "Gnosis" which is a more inclusive term than 2d century Gnosticism) and therefore, influenced NT thought.[2] However, since there are no pre-Christian Gnostic documents, these scholars inappropriately use second- and third-century documents to support pre-Christian Gnostic thought and its influence on early Christianity within the NT in the first century.[3] It is inappropriate to foist second century thinking on the first

1. Gnostic teaching and how it relates to the NT is much debated. See Hans Jonas, *The Gnostic Religion: The Message of the Alien God and the Beginnings of Christianity* (Boston: Beacon, 1958); Robert McL. Wilson, *The Gnostic Problem: A Study of the Relations between Hellenistic Judaism and the Gnostic Heresy* (London: A. R. Mowbray; New York: AMS, 1958); idem, *Gnosis and the New Testament* (Oxford: Basil Blackwell, 1968); Edwin M. Yamauchi, *Pre-Christian Gnosticism: A Survey of the Proposed Evidences*, 2d ed. (Grand Rapids: Baker, 1983); A. H. B. Logan and A. J. M. Wedderburn, eds., *The New Testament and Gnosis: Essays in Honour of Robert McL. Wilson* (Edinburgh: T & T Clark, 1983); Charles W. Hedrick and Robert Hodgson Jr., eds., *Nag Hammadi, Gnosticism, and Early Christianity* (Peabody, Mass.: Hendrickson, 1986); Kurt Rudolph, "Gnosticism," in *ABD*, 2:1033–40; Alastair B. Logan, *Gnostic Truth and Christian Heresy: A Study in the History of Gnosticism* (Edinburgh: T & T Clark, 1996).

2. Cf. Bultmann, *Theology of the New Testament*, 1:164–83, esp. 164–72; idem, *Primitive Christianity in Its Contemporary Setting*, trans. R. H. Fuller (London: Thames and Hudson, 1956), 162; G. Quispel, "Gnosticism and the New Testament," *VC* 19 (June 1965): 72–73, 82–85; this is reprinted in *The Bible in Modern Scholarship: Papers Read at the 100th Meeting of the Society of Biblical Literature, December 28–30, 1964*, ed. James Philip Hyatt (Nashville: Abingdon, 1965), 259–60, 268–71.

3. Cf. Robert McLachlan Wilson, "Response to G. Quispel's 'Gnosticism and the New Testament'," in *The Bible in Modern Scholarship; Papers Read at the 100th Meeting of the Society of Biblical Literature, December 28–30, 1964,* ed. James Philip Hyatt (Nashville: Abingdon, 1965), 272–78, esp. 273–75; idem, *Gnosis and the New Testament*, 24; idem, "Twenty Years After," in *Colloque international sur les textes de Nag Hammadi*

century. Furthermore, even a church father such as Ignatius (35–107/8) uses πλήρωμα in the same sense as the NT. Since he does not make a polemic against the Gnostic concept of it, it would indicate that the later second-century perception of πλήρωμα had not yet become known.[1] Second, the concept of πλήρωμα in Gnosticism is altogether different from what is presented in the NT and should not be taken seriously.[2] After careful study of πλήρωμα in the Nag Hammadi materials, Evans concludes, "it would seem apparent that whereas nowhere in the New Testament does *pleroma* function in the Valentinian sense at least one aspect of Pauline usage (i.e., reconciliation/restoration) is represented in the gnostic writings. I would also suggest that not one of the occurrences of *pleroma* in the Pauline corpus indicates gnostic thought either on the part of the author or on the part of his opponents."[3] Hence, one must not try to foist Gnostic ideas of the word into the NT era.

Although in the OT the noun πλήρωμα is never used to describe God's essence, glory, power, or presence of God, the verb "to fill" and the adjective "full" are used to describe filling with God's presence or essence.[4] For example, the OT refers to the concept of the glory of God which filled the temple of God (1 Kgs 8:10, 27) and the earth (Ps 72:19 [LXX 71:19]; Jer 23:24).[5] Hence, Paul's use of πλήρωμα to describe Christ being filled with fullness of God's essence is in line with the OT teaching of God's filling certain things with his essence, presence, power, or glory. This view is far more plausible than to think Paul adopted the Gnostic concept of fullness.

In conclusion, it is best to determine the usage of πλήρωμα within its context. Only there can one ascertain if it has an active or passive sense. For a further discussion of this, see the comments on 1:23.

(Québec, 22–25 août 1978), ed. Bernard Barc, Bibliothèque Copte de Nag Hammadi, ed. Jacques-É. Ménard, Paul-Hubert Poirier, and Michel Roberge, section «Études» 1 (Québec: Les Presses de l'Université Laval; Louvain: Peeters, 1981), 64–67; idem, "Nag Hammadi and the New Testament," *NTS* 28 (July 1982): 292–93; Yamauchi, *Pre-Christian Gnosticism*, 170–86, 190–93; Charles W. Hedrick, "Introduction: Nag Hammadi, Gnosticism, and Early Christianity—A Beginner's Guide," in *Nag Hammadi, Gnosticism, & Early Christianity*, ed. Charles W. Hedrick and Robert Hodgson Jr. (Peabody, Mass.: Hendrickson, 1986), 2–7; Logan, *Gnostic Truth and Christian Heresy*, xvii–xxi.

1. Lightfoot, *Colossians*, 264.

2. Cf. ibid., 265–70; Overfield, "Pleroma: A Study in Content and Context," 384–96; Violet MacDermot, "The Concept of Pleroma in Gnosticism," in *Gnosis and Gnosticism: Papers Read at the Eighth International Conference on Patristic Studies (Oxford, September 3rd–8th 1979)*, ed. Martin Krause, Nag Hammadi Studies, ed. Martin Krause, James M. Robinson, Frederik Wisse, et al., vol. 17 (Leiden: Brill, 1981), 76–81; Perkins, 52–53.

3. Craig A. Evans, "The Meaning of πλήρωμα in Nag Hammadi," *Bib* 65, no. 2 (1984): 264.

4. Barth, 204.

5. Cf. Sverre Aalen, "Begrepet πλήρωμα i Kolosser-og Efeserbrevet," *Tidsskrift for Teologi og Kirke* 23 (1952): 49–67; Gerhard Münderlein, "Die Erwählung durch das Pleroma," *NTS* 8 (April 1962): 264–76; Ernst, *Pleroma und Pleroma Christi*, 22–40; Barth, 203–5; Sawatzky, "*Pleroma* in Ephesians 1:23," 112.

D. New Position Individually (2:1–10)

In chapter 1 Paul revealed God's eternal plan in choosing those who are predestined to sonship into God's family by means of the redemption accomplished by Christ and the sealing of the Holy Spirit to those who hear and believe the word of the gospel. Paul prayed that believers would know God intimately and personally, and realize what is the hope of his calling, his glorious inheritance in the saints, and his mighty power toward them. By raising and seating Christ, God exerted this power in Christ, subjected the cosmic powers under his feet, and gave him as head to the church and thus head over all believers. In chapters 2 and 3 Paul explains the execution of this eternal plan by showing how God makes sinners into saints and builds them into the church, the body of Christ. In 2:1–10 Paul states how sinners, who deserve nothing but God's wrath, become trophies of his grace.

Paul begins a new thought at this point. Some think that the conjunction καί, "and," indicates that 2:1–10 is a continuation of 1:15–23 and could be translated with "also you."[1] However, the conjunction is not connecting the series: God exerted his power in Christ (1:20a) *and* he put all things in subjection to him (22a) *and* he gave him to the church (22b) *and* he quickened you who were dead (2:1, 5). The reason for this is twofold: first, the previous two καίs are always followed by a main verb, whereas here it is followed by a participle, an adjective, and a noun, and then followed by another καί which is followed by a noun and pronoun. Second, in 1:20–23 God was acting in relationship to Christ, whereas here (cf. 2:5) God is acting in behalf of sinners. It seems that 1:23 is a fitting conclusion to the foregoing clause and that the καί in 2:1 furnishes the bridge to begin a new section,[2]

1. Gaugler, 82–83; Schnackenburg, 87–88; cf. Léonard Ramaroson, "Une lecture de Éphésiens 1,15–2,10," *Bib* 58, no. 3 (1977): 388–410.

2. As do Alford, 3:88; Ellicott, 32; Meyer, 90–91; Abbott, 38; Salmond, 282; Robinson, 47–48; Hendriksen, 109–10; Mitton, 80; Barth, 212; Lincoln, 84.

connecting the ὑμᾶς with all that has been previously said in chapter 1.[1] Therefore, these verses are a commentary on 1:19, in that the great power toward us has been demonstrated historically in Christ and is now being demonstrated by making sinners into saints. The ὑμᾶς is selected to give prominence to those Ephesians who are recipients of his grace. In 1:19 the power of God is toward all of us who believe and in 2:1 God's power is toward those who were dead in trespasses and sins and deserve nothing but his wrath. In other words, his power began operating in the Ephesians before they were believers. In conclusion, chapter 1 emphasizes our relationship to the three persons of the Trinity and chapter 2 emphasizes God's activity towards us.

Regarding the structure of this section, verses 1–7 form one sentence that possibly extends to the end of verse 10.[2] Although there are normally periods after verses 7 and 9, it may well be that the γάρ, "for," used in both verses 8 and 10 only give reason to the immediately preceding clauses. This sentence with 124 words is the third of eight long sentences in this epistle (1:3–14, 15–23; 2:1–7; 3:2–13, 14–19; 4:1–6, 11–16; 6:14–20). Regardless of where the sentence ends, the grammatical subject is not given until verse 4 ("God") and the main verbs are in verses 5–6 ("made alive with" . . . "raised together with" . . . "seated together with"). The object of each of these verbs is "us," that is, believers. Therefore, the main assertion of this section is that God has made sinners alive, raised them up, and seated them with Christ. All other clauses in these verses are subordinate to this main assertion. Many translations blur this by introducing additional finite verbs in verses 1–3 (as "hath he quickened/did he quicken/he made alive" and "were dead" [AV, RV, ASV, RSV] or simply "were dead" [NASB, NEB, TEV, JB, NIV, NJB, NRSV]) to those already mentioned in verses 5–6. In addition to this, there is a frequent interchange between the first person plural ("we/us" in vv. 3, 4, 5, 6, 7, 10) and second person plural ("you" in vv. 1, 2, 8), which empahsizes all that we have in common.

1. The Old Condition: Dead to God (2:1–3)

This is a parenthetical section describing the believers' condition before they experienced the power of God that transformed their lives. As mentioned above, the subject and verbs do not occur until

1. Denbow thinks that 1:21b–23 is a parenthesis and that the accusative ὑμᾶς in 2:1 is parallel to the in αὐτόν 1:20 and thus it should read "When he raised him and you from the dead, you being dead in trespasses and sins" (Walter H. Denbow, "A Note on Ephesians ii.1," *Congregational Quarterly* 35 [January 1957]: 62–64). The problem with Denbow's view is that he does not observe the structure of 1:20–22 with four main verbs connected with three καίs. If anything, the parenthesis is not 1:21b–23 but 2:1–3.

2. For a rhetorical analysis of 2:1–10, see Jeal, *Integrating Theology and Ethics in Ephesians*, 130–46.

verses 4–6 and, therefore, this section is introduced in verse 1 by a participle and the three finite verbs in verses 2–3 are in relative clauses that explain verse 1.

a. Condition Described (2:1)

Text: 2:1. Καὶ ὑμᾶς ὄντας νεκροὺς τοῖς παραπτώμασιν καὶ ταῖς ἁμαρτίαις ὑμῶν,

Translation: 2:1. "And you being dead in your transgressions and sins,"

Commentary: 2:1. Καὶ ὑμᾶς ὄντας νεκροὺς τοῖς παραπτώμασιν καὶ ταῖς ἁμαρτίαις ὑμῶν, "And you being dead in your transgressions and sins." The first six words of verses 1 and 5 are identical, except for the pronouns (ἡμᾶς for ὑμᾶς). Paul does not complete verse 1 but digresses to an exposition of our old condition in verses 2–3. The apostle chooses not to explain the grace of God until he makes inescapably clear the desperate need of human beings.

Καὶ ὑμᾶς, "and you." The conjunction with the pronoun marks the transition from the previous verse in chapter 1 to the present chapter. In other words, that power of God historically and presently operating in Christ is also working in "you." The "you" makes it emphatic and very personal even though it is plural. Paul is addressing the readers directly.

ὄντας νεκροὺς, "being dead" shows the state or condition before God took action. The present participle of the verb "to be" denotes the action that occurred before the main verbs in verses 5–6, "representing the imperfect,"[1] and thus shows their ongoing condition as dead before God's gracious act of making them alive. As mentioned in 1:18 this participial construction could be accusative absolute, which would mean that though the pronouns "you/we" are repeated in the main clause, they are not the subject(s) of the main clause and are, therefore, loosely related. It could be labeled a concessive participle, "although you were dead."[2] Regardless, it depicts the state or condition before God's action.

The adjective (predicate accusative) "dead" must certainly describe their spiritual and not physical condition, for the next two verses show that they were very much alive physically. The prodigal son was considered dead or lost from home, but when he returned home he was reckoned as alive or found (Luke 15:24, 32). This concept of spiritual death would be familiar to the readers of this letter for the same language was used in Greek philosophy. It can especially be seen in Stoic writings,[3] in Hellenistic Judaism, where Philo speaks of the es-

1. BDF §339 (3); cf. several examples in Moule, *Idiom Book*, 101, 206.

2. Wallace, *Greek Grammar*, 634.

3. Epictetus *Dissertationes* 1.3.3; 9.19; 2.19.27; 3.23.28; Rudolf Bultmann, "νεκρός, νεκρόω, νέκρωσις," *TDNT* 4 (1967): 892; Lothar Coenen, "Death, Kill, Sleep [νεκρός]," *NIDNTT* 1 (1975): 443–44.

trangement of the wicked from God as true death in contrast to physical death,[1] and also in rabbinic literature.[2] The Qumran community mentions a redemption from the grave and resurrection from Sheol, or purification from sin and resurrection from the dust, speaking of their present salvation (1QH[a] 11:19 [3:19]; 19:10–14 [11:10–14]). As those who are physically dead cannot communicate with the living, so also those who are spiritually dead cannot communicate with the eternal living God and thus are separated from God. They are lost and need to be found. They are dead and need to be made alive.

τοῖς παραπτώμασιν καὶ ταῖς ἁμαρτίαις[3] ὑμῶν, "in your transgressions and sins." The two terms παράπτωμα and ἁμαρτία have already been discussed at 1:7 where it was concluded that they are synonyms to denote a conscious and deliberate false step. They connote more than an inadvertent mistake for they express a conscious and willful action against God's holiness and righteousness and thus a failure to live as one should. Human beings are responsible for these acts of treachery against God. The datives could indicate cause[4] ("because of your transgressions and sins") or be instrumental[5] ("by your transgressions and sins") or preferably indicate sphere[6] ("in your transgressions and sins"). The parallel passage of Col 2:13, "dead in transgressions and the uncircumcision of the flesh," would seem to rule out the causal and instrumental sense in that they were not dead because of or by their uncircumcision of the flesh. Barth prefers to leave it vague so that it would denote "the cause, the instrument, the manifestation, the realm, and the consequence of death."[7] Sphere leaves it vague enough to capture these various ideas. Alford's illustration of "sick in a fever"[8] shows the cause and condition. Sin is the cause of the spiritual death[9] of people and they remain in that dead condition until God acts.

This verse describes the condition or state of a person before the gracious act of God. Dead people cannot communicate and have no power to bring life to themselves. It is the power of God that is directed toward us that gives us life.

1. Normally he uses θάνατος, see Philo *Leg. All.* 1.24, 33 §§76, 108; 3.14 §52; *Quod Deterius Potiori Insidiari Soleat* 20 §70; *Deus* 19 §89; *Fug.* 10, 15, 21 §§55, 78, 113; *Praem.* 12 §§70, 72; νεκρός in *Somn.* 2.9 §66.

2. Wedderburn, *Baptism and Resurrection*, 63.

3. In place of ἁμαρτίαις, B has ἐπιθυμίαις which should not be seriously considered.

4. Ellicott, 32; Meyer, 91; HS §177b.

5. Salmond, 283; Westcott, 29; cf. Erich Mauerhofer, "Der Brief an die Epheser. 15. Teil: 2,1," *Fundamentum* 2 (1993): 17.

6. Alford, 3:88; Eadie, 119; Wallace, *Greek Grammar*, 154, 155.

7. Barth, 213.

8. Alford, 3:88.

9. For a discussion of sin and its relationship to death, see Ernest Best, "Dead in Trespasses and Sins (Eph. 2.1) [Essays in Honour of Antony Tyrrell Hanson]," *JSNT* 13 (October 1981): 15–19.

b. Condition Delineated (2:2–3)

Having stated our spiritual condition, Paul now is going to give fuller details to substantiate his claim. This spiritual condition is delineated in three ways.

(1) Walked according to the Temporal Values of the World (2:2a)

Text: 2:2a. ἐν αἷς ποτε περιεπατήσατε κατὰ τὸν αἰῶνα τοῦ κόσμου τούτου,

Translation: 2:2a. "in which you formerly walked according to the age of this world,"

Commentary: 2:2a. ἐν αἷς ποτε περιεπατήσατε, "in which you formerly walked." The preposition ἐν emphasizes the sphere of the walk and the relative pronoun αἷς takes the gender of the nearer noun, although it refers to both nouns. As mentioned above, although the participle is present tense, the condition refers to the past as the enclitic particle ποτέ, "formerly, once," substantiates. Hence, in former times they were living day to day in this condition. The literal sense of περιπατέω, "to walk around," is frequently used in classical literature,[1] in the OT (Gen 3:8; Exod 21:19; Judg 21:24; Job 38:16), and in the NT (Matt 4:18; Acts 3:8, 9, 12; 14:10; Rev 2:1; 21:24). Infrequently in classical literature[2] the term is used metaphorically, "to live," expressing the ethical walk, as is also the case in the LXX where it is so used in only five (2 Kgs 20:3; Prov 8:20; Eccl 11:9; Isa 59:9; Sir 13:13) out of the thirty-eight times it occurs. The verb occurs ninety-five times in the NT: forty-six times in the Gospels and Acts where it is used literally, except for four times when it is used metaphorically (Mark 7:5; John 8:12; 12:35; Acts 21:21), and forty-nine times in the rest of the NT where it is used metaphorically except twice (Rev 2:1; 21:24). The prominence of the literal sense in the Gospels and Acts is understandable since much of the text is narrative, whereas the metaphorical sense is prominent in the rest of the NT where most of the text is didactic. Therefore, in Paul's use of it thirty-two times, eight times in Ephesians (2:2, 10; 4:1, 17*bis*; 5:2, 8, 15), it is always used metaphorically, speaking of one's conduct or lifestyle, both negatively (e.g., Eph 2:2; 1 Cor 3:3; Col 3:7; 2 Thess 3:11) and positively (Eph 4:1; 5:2; Rom 6:4; Gal 5:16). In Ephesians it is used negatively only in this verse and in 4:17. The other six times it is used positively and marks the outline divisions for the second half of the book. Thus, one's conduct is a very important issue in this book. This immediate passage shows the Ephesians' walk before their conversion.

κατὰ τὸν αἰῶνα τοῦ κόσμου τούτου, "according to the age of this world. . . ." The preposition κατά, "according to," with the accusative in-

1. Aristophanes *Equites* 744; *Vespae* 237; Demonsthenes 54.7.
2. Philodemus *De Liberate* 23.3.

dicates the standard by which the Ephesians had walked before regeneration. The noun αἰών normally denotes "time" or "age." In the LXX it occurs 738 times and in the canonical books it appears 417 times and consistently has reference to "age" or "time" with only five possible exceptions (Sir 38:34; Tob 3:2?; Wis 13:9; 14:6?; 18:4) that could be rendered "world."[1] In the NT the noun αἰών normally has reference to time, either a specifically limited period of time, as in 1:21 and 3:9 (cf. Matt 13:39–40, 49; Gal 1:4; Heb 9:26), or an unlimited time, as in 3:21 (John 6:51, 58; Gal 1:5). It can also have reference to the world (Matt 13:22 = Mark 4:19; 1 Tim 6:17; 2 Tim 4:10; Tit 2:12; Heb 1:2; 11:3). Certainly, it is not a personal aeon of Gnosticism,[2] for Paul (and the NT) never uses αἰών to refer to personal power but instead uses τῶν ἀρχόντων τοῦ αἰῶνος τούτου "the rulers of this age" (1 Cor 2:6, 8) or ὁ θεὸς τοῦ αἰῶνος "the god of this age" (2 Cor 4:4) to denote personal power.[3] Though it may have the nuance of the spirit of the age or worldview in the sense of "way, lifestyle, practice, principle" (NEB, JB, TEV, NIV, NJB), the temporal aspect is very much in view and it would be consistent with Paul's usage elsewhere in Ephesians (1:21; 2:7; 3:9, 11, 21*bis*).[4] The reader or hearer of the letter in the first century would assume it is temporal in this verse since it was so used a few lines before in 1:21.[5] Normally it is translated "course" (AV, RV, ASV, RSV, NASB, NRSV) but it could be translated "age" or "era," depicting a span of time. The next term κόσμος, "world," is used to describe the created material world as in 1:4 but it can also refer to the ethical world, which is the satanically organized system that hates and opposes all that is godly (cf. John 15:18, 23; 18:36; 1 Cor 3:19). The second sense fits best with the present context. The genitive could be attributive, "this worldly age or era," but it is more likely descriptive, "age of this world," meaning the era characterized by this ungodly world in contrast to the age to come, which will be of a different character.[6] Wink labels the present age as "the era of the Fall."[7] In other words the unregenerate are found "'conforming to the standards of the present world order'."[8] They go along with what is fashionable and acceptable and are not out of step with the rest of the world, hence, they embrace temporal values. They are concerned only with activities and values of

1. It is a translation of עוֹלָם but never meaning "world," as suggested by Lincoln, 95.

2. *Contra* Hermann Sasse, "αἰών," *TDNT* 1 (1964): 207–8; cf. also Schlier, 101–2; Steinmetz, *Protologische Heils-Zuversicht*, 61; Lindemann, *Aufhebung*, 108–9. Percy (*Probleme*, 259–61) opposes the Gnostic idea.

3. Lincoln, 94–95.

4. Alford, 3:89; Ellicott, 33; Meyer, 93–94; Abbott, 40; Salmond, 283; Robinson, 48, 153; Westcott, 29; Mitton, 82–83; Caird, 51; Bruce, 281; Lincoln, 94–95; Carr, *Angels and Principalities*, 100; Arnold, *Ephesians: Power and Magic*, 59–60; Wink, *Engaging the Powers*, 59–60.

5. Arnold, *Ephesians: Power and Magic*, 59; Lincoln, 94–95.

6. Bruce, 281 n. 17; cf. Wallace, *Greek Grammar*, 79–81.

7. Wink, *Engaging the Powers*, 60.

8. Caird, 51.

the present age and are not concerned with God and eternal values or with the judgment to come.

(2) Walked according to the Ruler of the Power of the Air (2:2b)

Text: 2:2b. κατὰ τὸν ἄρχοντα τῆς ἐξουσίας τοῦ ἀέρος, τοῦ πνεύματος τοῦ νῦν ἐνεργοῦντος ἐν τοῖς υἱοῖς τῆς ἀπειθείας·

Translation: 2:2b. "according to the ruler over the realm of the air, the spirit that now works in the sons of disobedience;"

Commentary: 2:2b. κατὰ τὸν ἄρχοντα τῆς ἐξουσίας τοῦ ἀέρος, "according to the ruler over the realm of the air." This is the second prepositional phrase beginning with κατά that describes the walk before conversion. Not only is the standard of the unregenerate in accordance with the temporal values of the world, but it is also in accordance with or under the control[1] of the ruler of the realm of the air. The term ἄρχων is used in classical literature to mean "ruler, commander, captain"[2] or "chief, king, lord"[3] and it is used 634 times in the LXX (544 times in the canonical books) to denote leaders of nations (Exod 15:15), tribes (Num 7:18, 24, 30, 36), and armies (2 Sam 24:2). Infrequently, it is used of angelic beings (Dan 10:13) or angelic beings as patrons of specific nations (Theodotian Dan 10:20–21; 11:5; 12:1).[4] In the NT it occurs thirty-seven times and outside of the Gospels and Acts it occurs only five times (Rom 13:3; 1 Cor 2:6, 8; Eph 2:2; Rev 1:5). It is used to denote Roman and Jewish officials (Luke 14:1; 18:18; 23:13; 24:20; John 3:1; Acts 3:17; 4:26) and is used of Jesus as the leader of the kings of earth (Rev 1:5). However, it is also used of Satan who is the prince of demons (Matt 9:34; 12:24–26 = Mark 3:22–25 = Luke 11:15–18) and ruler of this world, whose power has been broken by Christ (John 12:31; 14:30; 16:11). Later in Ephesians he is identified as the devil (4:27; 6:11) and the evil one (6:16). In the present context it is used of the devil as leader and is best translated "ruler." The next term ἐξουσία was discussed at 1:21 with the conclusion that it has the idea of "the right to act" and can thus be translated "authority, government, power" or "domain, realm, kingdom." Although some translate it in the present context as "power" or "authority,"[5] it is bet-

1. As suggested by Best, 202. Best notes that the author of Ephesians "is hardly saying that unbelievers lived 'after the manner of the ruler of the power of the air', i.e., in the same way as the devil lives. The preposition rather implies that in some way they have come under the control of the devil. In Rom 8.4 to walk κατὰ πνεῦμα must mean under the control of the Spirit as κατὰ σάρκα (cf. also 2 Cor 10.2) means to walk controlled by the flesh."

2. Sophocles *Ajax* 668; Herodotus 5.33.

3. Aeschylus *Persae* 73.

4. David E. Aune, "Archon Ἄρχων," in *DDD*, 157.

5. Aquinas, chap. 2, lec. 1, vv. 1–3 (86); Alford, 3:89; Meyer, 95; Abbott, 41; Salmond, 284; Gaugler, 86–88; Adai, *Der Heilige Geist als Gegenwart Gottes*, 253–54.

ter translated as "domain" or "realm"[1] (cf. Luke 22:53; 23:7; Col 1:13). The genitive ἐξουσίας is a genitive of subordination indicating that the devil is the ruler over the realm of the air.[2]

The final term ἀήρ, "air," was thought in ancient times to be that which filled the space between the earth and moon. The Greeks thought this term referred to the lower impure air, the home of the spirits, as opposed to the higher pure air, the ether.[3] It appears ten times in the LXX (only twice in the canonical books: 2 Sam 22:12; Ps 18:11 [MT 18:12; LXX 17:11]) and seven times in the NT. It appears four times in the Pauline letters and only here in Ephesians. It refers to that place above the earth (Acts 22:23; Rev 9:2; 16:17) where Christ will meet his saints (1 Thess 4:17) and is also used idiomatically "to beat the air" (1 Cor 9:26) or "to speak into the air" (1 Cor 14:9). In the present context it is the place or sphere of the activity of the devil. It denotes both universality[4] and locality.[5] Philo makes the distinction between the physical elements of earth, water, and fire, which can be localized, and air, which is unseen and cannot be localized.[6] Although today we might conceptualize it as a spiritual matrix of inauthentic living, ideologies, or *Zeitgeist*,[7] in Paul's day the air was considered as "the dwelling place of evil spirits."[8] Also, this air is not impersonal but, as Philo asserts, it is the abode of living beings, which the other philosophers identified as demons whereas the Scriptures label them as angels or messengers.[9] Job (1:7) speaks of Satan going to and fro on the earth. Paul calls him "the evil one" who controls this evil world (1 John 5:19) and also calls him "the god of this age" (2 Cor 4:4). He and his emissaries presently rule from heaven (Eph 6:12) but, according to John, they will be cast from heaven to earth in the middle of the tribulation (Rev 12:7–17). Although he will continue to retain his power over the world for a time (Rev 12–13), he will eventually lose it, be bound for a thousand years (20:1–3), and ultimately will be cast into the lake of fire (20:10).

Therefore, the unregenerate not only walk according to the values of the present age but also under the control of the leader who rules over this evil world. The next clause further explains his operation in the world of people.

1. Chrysostom *Eph* 2:1–3 (*PG* 62:31–32); Eadie, 123; Ellicott, 34; Dibelius-Greeven, 66; Schlier, 102; Hendriksen, 112–13 n. 51; Gnilka, 115; Barth, 214, 215; Bruce, 282; Lincoln, 95; BAGD 278; BDAG 353; Foerster, *TDNT* 2 (1964): 565, 567; Arnold, *Ephesians: Power and Magic*, 60 (although later [148] he labels it "authority").

2. Wallace, *Greek Grammar*, 104.

3. Hans Bietenhard, "Demon, Air, Cast Out [ἀήρ, δαιμόνιον]," *NIDNTT* 1 (1975): 449.

4. Carr, *Angels and Principalities*, 103; Wink, *Naming the Powers*, 83–84.

5. Arnold, *Ephesians: Power and Magic*, 60–61 (although later he translates it "authority" [148]).

6. Philo *Gig*. 1 §2; *Somn*. 1.22 §134.

7. As does Wink, *Naming the Powers*, 84.

8. Arnold, *Ephesians: Power and Magic*, 60–61.

9. Philo *Somn*. 1.19, 20 §§134–35, 140–41; cf. also *Gig*. 1 §2.

τοῦ πνεύματος τοῦ νῦν ἐνεργοῦντος, "the spirit that now works." This clause more specifically describes the preceding clause. Before attempting to see how it relates to the preceding clause, it is necessary to discuss the word πνεῦμα, "spirit." Paul uses the word "spirit" 142 times and thirty-three times it refers to something or someone other than the Holy Spirit. There are four possible alternatives. (1) It could refer to an evil spirit, namely, the spirit of the evil one who now works in the sons of disobedience. Certainly, the Gospels do mention "evil spirits" (Luke 7:21; 8:2) and/or "unclean spirit(s)" (Mark 1:27 = Luke 4:36; Matt 10:1 = Mark 6:37; Mark 3:11; Luke 6:18). In the story of the Gadarene/Gerasene demoniac(s) (Matt 8:28–34 = Mark 5:1–20 = Luke 8:26–39) Mark speaks of an unclean spirit (5:2, 8), whereas Matthew speaks of demons (8:31) and Luke speaks of the unclean spirit (8:27, 29) as one and the same as a demon (8:30, 33, 35–37). Acts 5:16 and 8:7 mention "unclean spirits" and 19:12–16 mentions "evil spirit(s)" (cf. 1 John 4:1–6). However, Paul never uses the terms "unclean spirit(s)" or "evil spirit(s)" although he does use "deceitful spirits" (1 Tim 4:1), "different spirit," and five times, "demons" (1 Cor 10:20–21). (2) There are instances when "spirit" refers to an attitude. Paul mentions the "spirit of gentleness" (1 Cor 4:21; Gal 6:1), "spirit of faith" (2 Cor 4:13), or "not . . . a spirit of cowardliness but a spirit of power and love and self-control" (2 Tim 1:7). Outside of Paul's writing there is mention of the "spirit of the poor" (Matt 5:3) and "a quiet and gentle spirit" (1 Pet 3:4). (3) In Qumran teaching one discovers the mixture of a personal spirit and a spirit of influence. It was thought that God appointed equally for every person two spirits, the spirit of truth and the spirit of deceit/injustice. It is asserted that the spirit of truth springs from a source of light and the children of righteousness are ruled by the Prince of Light and/or the Angel of Truth. The children of righteousness exhibit many fine characteristics such as a spirit of humilty, patience, abundant compassion, eternal goodness, understanding, zeal for just laws, and love toward all the sons of truth, among other things. On the other hand, the spirit of deceit springs from a source of darkness and the children of deceit are ruled by the Angel of Darkness. They walk in paths of darkness and exhibit greed, irreverence, deceit, pride, haughtiness, dishonesty, trickery, cruelty, abominable deeds of lust and lewdness, and a blasphemous tongue, among other things. This spirit of falsehood attempts to lead the children of righteousness astray. These two spirits will continue in human beings until the day of visitation (1QS 3:13–4:26).[1] (4) It could have reference to an "inward" or immaterial part of a person (in contrast to the flesh), "as the source and seat of insight, feeling, and will"[2] of human beings. Paul uses such phrases as "with my spirit" (Rom 1:9),

1. Cf. Kuhn, "Ephesians in the Light of the Qumran Texts," 152; Lincoln, 97–97.

2. BAGD 675; BDAG 833; cf. also Eduard Schweizer, "Πνεῦμα, πνευματικός, κτλ.," *TDNT* 6 (1968): 434–37; James D. G. Dunn, "Spirit, Holy Spirit [πνεῦμα]," *NIDNTT* 3 (1978): 693–94.

"the Spirit himself bears witness to/with our spirit" (8:16), no one knows a person's thoughts except the "spirit of man" (1 Cor 2:11), the destruction of the person in order that "his spirit" may be saved in the day of the Lord Jesus (5:5), or the unmarried woman is to be holy in body and in "spirit" (7:34; cf. also 2 Cor 7:1; Gal 6:18; 1 Thess 5:23; 2 Thess 2:2; 2 Tim 4:22; Phlm 25). Outside of Paul's writings the NT mentions that "the spirit is willing but the flesh is weak" (Matt 26:41 = Mark 14:38), Jesus "perceived in his spirit" (Mark 2:8; cf. 8:12), Mary's "spirit" delighted in God (Luke 1:46), John the Baptist grew strong "in spirit" (Luke 1:80), when revived, Jairus's daughter's "spirit" returned (Luke 8:55), Jesus was "troubled in his spirit" (John 13:21), in his death Jesus "yielded up his spirit" (Matt 27:50; Luke 23:46; John 19:30), and Stephen yielded his "spirit" to Jesus (Acts 7:59). Of these options, view (2) is unlikely because Paul normally uses a descriptive genitive following "spirit," which is not the case in the present context. The difficulty with view (3) is that it is out of character for Paul to portray a dichotomy within a person, namely, an evil and a good spirit within a person. Paul states in Rom 8:9 that believers are not in the flesh but in the spirit, which indicates that they are in one category or the other but not both simultaneously. Although view (1) is possible, the most likely alternative is view (4). Thus, it is that spirit in human beings that is now working in the sons of disobedience.

It should be noted that whichever one of these two alternatives is preferred depends on the connection of τοῦ πνεύματος to the preceding clause, and this is difficult to determine. Again, there are four basic views. (1) Some suggest that τοῦ πνεύματος is in apposition to the immediately preceding genitive τοῦ ἀέρος, "of the air."[1] This makes good sense, for in Greek the word πνεῦμα is "air" and would naturally relate back to the "air" just mentioned. Also, it is the nearest antecedent in the same case. This view would allow "spirit" to refer to the spiritual disposition and/or the personal spirit. As was discussed above, the air is that abode of angels or messengers of the devil, and thus the spirit of the devil through his emissaries is that which is now working in the sons or daughters of disobedience. However, a genitive of apposition should clarify the previous noun. "The air, namely, spirit" does not clarify what is meant by "air." Is it saying that the abode of the angels of the devil is the spirit that is now working in the sons or daughters of disobedience? (2) Others suggest that τοῦ πνεύματος is in apposition to τῆς ἐξουσίας.[2] The major problem with this is that there is a change

1. Chrysostom *Eph* 2:1–3 (*PG* 62:32); Schlier, 104; Barth, 215; Caird, 51; Hugedé, 69–70; Bruce, 283. Hilaire de Poiters supports this view from Pss 118 and 128 as well as from a faulty variant in Eph 6:12. See Jean Doignon, "Variations inspirées d'origène sur le «prince de l'air» (Ep 2,2) chez Hilaire de Poitiers," *ZNW* 81, nos. 1/2 (1990): 143–48; Erich Mauerhofer, "Der Brief an die Epheser. 16. Teil: 2,2 und 3," *Fundamentum* 3 (1993): 29–30.

2. Bengel, 4:73; Hodge, 101; Alford, 3:90; Eadie, 129.

in genders—a neuter noun referring back to the feminine. Furthermore, it does not make much sense because can one say "the authority which is spirit" or "the authority, namely, spirit"? (3) It is thought by some that τοῦ πνεύματος is in apposition to τὸν ἄρχοντα and thus refers to the personal spirit, meaning that the ruler (the devil) himself is the one who now works in the sons or daughters of disobedience.[1] The problem with this view is that "a gen. of apposition never involves two personal nouns. 'The ruler of the spirit' does not mean 'the ruler who is spirit.'"[2] Moreover, one would expect the accusative case to be in agreement with τὸν ἄρχοντα.[3] (4) Others propose that it is parallel with τῆς ἐξουσίας, "of the realm," governed by τὸν ἄρχοντα, "the ruler."[4] This makes the most sense. Along with τῆς ἐξουσίας, τοῦ πνεύματος is best classified as a genitive of subordination, "the ruler over the realm of the air, [the ruler over] the spirit that now works in the sons of disobedience." Hence, if "spirit" refers to an evil spirit, then Paul is saying that the devil is the ruler over the evil "spirit." Such a statement does little to clarify the context as it is already obvious that this is the case. However, if "spirit" refers to immaterial or inward part of a person, then Paul is saying that the devil rules over the inward person, a function he now performs in the sons or daughters of disobedience. This interpretation makes the most sense.

The adverb of time νῦν, "now," is in contrast to the Ephesian believers' ποτέ, "former," walk.[5] The spiritual disposition is now working in unbelievers. The participle ἐνεργοῦντος is from ἐνεργέω, which is derived from the adjective ἐνεργός, from which we get our English word "energy." In the brief discussion of this word in 1:11, it was concluded that it meant to perform or work, generally denoting supernatural power. Here it is used of the spirit of the devil which is active in unbelievers.

ἐν τοῖς υἱοῖς τῆς ἀπειθείας, "in the sons of disobedience." The preposition ἐν locates where this spirit is now working, namely, in the sons of disobedience. The use of υἱός or τέκνον (mostly in the plural) followed by a genitive of the abstract noun is like a Hebrew idiom with בֵּן, and it is found frequently in the LXX.[6] This form of expression "is

1. Cf. Aquinas, chap. 2, lec. 1, vv. 1–3 (87); Dibelius-Greeven, 65–66; Masson, 158 n. 5; Gnilka, 115 n. 5; Hendriksen, 114; Bratcher and Nida, 41; Patzia, 156; Best, 205; O'Brien, 160 n. 29; cf. Lindemann, *Aufhebung*, 110.

2. Wallace, *Greek Grammar*, 100 n. 74.

3. Lincoln, 96.

4. Meyer, 98–99; Abbott, 42; Robinson, 154–55; Lincoln, 96; Wallace, *Greek Grammar*, 100, 104.

5. For a discussion of the contrast of ποτέ and νῦν in Eph 2, see Peter Tachau, *„Einst" und „Jetzt" im Neuen Testament: Beobachtungen zu einem urchristlichen Predigtschema in der neutestamentliche Briefliteratur und zu seiner Vorgeschichte*, FLANT, ed. Ernst Käsemann and Ernst Würthwein, vol. 105 (Göttingen: Vandenhoeck & Ruprecht, 1972), 134–43.

6. Deissmann, *Bible Studies*, 161–66; cf. Robertson, *Grammar*, 651–52; MHT 2:441; 4:84, 90; Zerwick, *Biblical Greek* §§42–43.

due to the more vivid imagination of the oriental, who viewed any very intimate relationship—whether of connection, origin or dependence—as a relation of sonship, even in the spiritual scene."[1]

The term ἀπειθεία is derived from ἀπειθής and from the time of Xenophon onwards it has meant "disobedience."[2] It is an alpha privative from πειθός/πειθώ and has the idea of that which is persuasive or convincing. The term ἀπειθεία occurs only four times in the LXX but never in the canonical books (4 Macc 8:9, 18; 12:3; *Pss. Sol.* 17:20), and ἀπειθής appears eight times meaning "disobedient, rebellious" (Num 20:10; Deut 21:18; Isa 7:16; 30:9; Jer 5:23; Zech 7:12; Sir 16:6; 47:21). In the NT ἀπειθεία occurs only seven times (Rom 11:30, 32; Eph 2:2; 5:6; Col 3:6; Heb 4:6, 11) and has the idea of "disobedience" or "unbelief." Disobedience comes from unbelief, for the person is not persuaded or convinced to trust what has been stated. The genitive is one of quality that could be labeled as an attributive genitive, "disobedient sons,"[3] or simply a descriptive genitive, "sons of disobedience."[4] So, the unregenerate are characterized as disobedient because they do not believe in what God has provided. It shows that unbelief is more than the absence of trust—it is a defiance against God. Thus, it is no wonder they are called the sons of disobedience for they follow their commander who is the prototype of disobedience.

In conclusion, the unregenerate Ephesians walked according to the values of the present age. Not only were they in step with the world, but they also went according to the wishes of the ruler (the devil) who is in control of the spiritual atmosphere and that spirit is presently working in the sons of disobedience. Since the world system is controlled by the devil, it is not surprising that the unregenerate do what the rest of the world does. Futhermore, the unconverted not only are under the pressure of the world system and its commander's control, but they also enjoy it, as the next verse shows.

(3) Lived in the Desires of the Flesh and Mind (2:3)

Text: 2:3. ἐν οἷς καὶ ἡμεῖς πάντες ἀνεστράφημέν ποτε ἐν ταῖς ἐπιθυμίαις τῆς σαρκὸς ἡμῶν ποιοῦντες τὰ θελήματα τῆς σαρκὸς καὶ τῶν διανοιῶν, καὶ ἤμεθα τέκνα φύσει ὀργῆς ὡς καὶ οἱ λοιποί·

Translation: 2:3. "among whom also we all were formerly living in the desires of our flesh doing the wishes of the flesh and the reasoning processes, and we were by nature the children of wrath as even the rest."

Commentary: 2:3. ἐν οἷς καὶ ἡμεῖς[5] πάντες ἀνεστράφημέν ποτε, "among whom also we all were formerly living." There are a couple of

1. Deissmann, *Bible Studies*, 161.

2. Xenophon *Memorabilia* 3.5.5; Dionysius Halicarnassensis 9.41.1.

3. Robertson, *Grammar*, 496–97.

4. Wallace, *Greek Grammar*, 79 n. 24, 81.

5. καὶ ὑμεῖς is found in A* D* 81 326 365 *pc* and is omitted in F G L but καὶ ἡμεῖς is found in 𝔓[46] ℵ A[c] B D[1] Ψ 0278 33 1739 1881 𝔐 lat syr cop[sa, bo] Tertullian. The first read-

changes from the two previous assertions of the unregenerate's state of spiritual death: (1) the two previous assertions began with κατά followed by an accusative, whereas here it begins with a prepositional relative phrase ἐν οἷς, and (2) the first two assertions are in second person plural whereas here it is first person plural.[1]

The prepositional relative phrase ἐν οἷς is not rendered "in which," referring back to the trespasses of verse 1,[2] but is translated "among whom," joining this clause with the immediately preceding prepositional phrase ἐν τοῖς υἱοῖς τῆς ἀπειθείας, "in the sons of disobedience."[3] The following words καί ἡμεῖς πάντες are in contrtast with καὶ ὑμᾶς in verse 1 and the conjunction is best seen as an adjunctive and thus translated "also we all." The contrast that Paul is making is thought by some to be between Paul as a Jew and the Ephesians as Gentiles,[4] but more likely it is between him as writer and the Ephesians as recipients.[5] The addition of "all" creates an insuperable objection against "we" as referring only to the Jews.[6] All humans in the unregenerate state are in the same condition of rebellion against God. Furthermore, does the use of the first person plural in verses 4–7 and 10 mean that only Jews are the objects of God's love and workmanship? Moreover, the use of the second person plural in verses 5 and 8 "does not imply that only Gentiles need to be saved by grace!"[7] It is best, therefore, not to make this distinction between Jews and Gentiles on the basis of

ing is primarily Western whereas the last reading is preferred because it has good manuscripts from the Alexandrian text and is solid in the Byzantine tradition and thus has a fairly good geographical distribution.

1. For a history of interpretation on v. 3, see Joannes Mehlmann, *Natura Filli Irae Historia interpretationis Eph 2,3 ejusque cum doctrina de Peccato Originali nexus*, AnBib, vol. 6 (Rome: E Pontificio Instituto Biblico, 1957).

2. As Robinson, 49, 155; Ramaroson, "Une lecture de Éphésiens 1,15–2,10," 397.

3. As Alford, 3:90; Eadie, 130; Ellicott, 35; Meyer, 100; Abbott, 43; Salmond, 285; Hendriksen, 114; Bruce, 283; Barth, 216; Lincoln, 97; Wallace, *Greek Grammar*, 336. Wedderburn (*Baptism and Resurrection*, 76 n. 2) thinks that here is an instance of the author of Ephesians awkwardly echoing the neuter of Col 3:7. However, the Colossians passage is not exactly parallel with the present passage. Also, who is to say that the author of Ephesians was looking at Col 3:7 and confusing the masculine with the neuter?

4. Abbott, 43; Schlier, 66, 100; Barth, 212; Bruce, 280; O'Brien, 161; Peter T. O'Brien, "Divine Analysis and Comprehensive Solution: Some Priorities from Ephesians 2," *RTR* 53 (September–December 1994): 131, 135–36; Biguzzi, "Efesini: la misteriosa lettera del muro abbattuto," 351, 355–56.

5. Eadie, 130–31; Ellicott, 35; Gaugler, 88–89; Schnackenburg, 92; Lincoln, 88; Best, 208; Mauerhofer, "Der Brief an die Epheser. 15. Teil: 2,1," 14–15; Jeal, *Integrating Theology and Ethics in Ephesians*, 133 n. 298; cf. Wallace, *Greek Grammar*, 399; Francis Watson, "Writing the Mystery: Christ and Reality in the Letter to the Ephesians" (paper delivered at the 2000 Annual Meeting of the American Academy of Religion and the Society of Biblical Literature, Nashville, TN, November 19, 2000), 3 n. 3, 4–5.

6. Ellicott, 35.

7. Peter Richardson, *Israel in the Apostolic Church*, SNTSMS, ed. Matthew Black, vol. 10 (Cambridge: Cambridge University Press, 1969), 150.

pronouns. It is not until verse 11 that Paul makes a distinction between Jews and Gentiles.

The main verb ἀναστρέφω has had a long history of a wide range of meaning. From the earliest times it has had the literal idea "to turn upside down, turn around, turn back, convert"[1] and the figurative meaning of human conduct "to conduct oneself, walk, behave."[2] Although it occurs 111 times in the LXX, it appears eighty-eight times in the canonical books and seventy times it translates שׁוּב, meaning "to turn around, return" (Gen 14:17; Judg 3:19; Jer 3:7*bis*; Ezek 46:9)[3] and only six times from הָלַךְ, which can mean "to return" (e.g., 1 Sam 3:5, 9; Jer 41:14 [LXX 48:14]) but can also mean "to walk" before God or according to his commandments (Prov 8:20; 20:7).[4] This double range of meanings continues in the NT where it occurs nine times: twice "to return, turn over" (Acts 5:22; 15:16) and seven times "to walk, conduct oneself, behave, live" (2 Cor 1:12; Eph 2:3; 1 Tim 3:15; Heb 10:33; 13:18; 1 Pet 1:17; 2 Pet 2:18). In the present context the latter meaning fits well and most English versions translate it "to live," which makes good sense. Our translation "were living" is attempting to depict a repeated action of life before conversion. It corresponds to the verb "to walk" in verse 2. Although the present tense is used, the activity occurred before their conversion, as in verse 2, indicated by the enclitic particle ποτέ, "formerly, once." The noun form (ἀναστροφή) is used in Eph 4:22 to depict the believer's lifestyle before becoming a Christian.

ἐν ταῖς ἐπιθυμίαις τῆς σαρκὸς ἡμῶν, "in the desires of our flesh." The sphere of their walk is seen in the preposition ἐν, "in." The noun ἐπιθυμία has from early usage[5] meant "desire," both good, as a desire for water,[6] and bad, as a desire to steal.[7] In the LXX it is used eighty-two times (thirty-eight times in the canonical books) and is translated from eight Hebrew words but twenty-one times from אָוָה or תַּאֲוָה, expressing both a good desire, as for food (Deut 12:15, 20), for righteousness (Prov 10:24; 11:23); or a bad desire, as opposing God's will (Num 11:4, 34) or desiring wickedness (Ps 112:10 [LXX 111:10]; cf. also Pss 140:8 [MT 140:9; LXX 139:9]).[8] In the NT it is used thirty-eight times, nineteen times by Paul and twice in Ephesians (2:3; 4:22).

1. Homer *Ilias* 23.436; Sophocles *Philoctetes* 449; Herodotus 1.80.5; Thucydides 4.43.4.

2. Xenophon *Anabasis* 2.5.14; Aristotle *Ethica Nicomachea* 2.1.7 §1103b.20; Polybius 1.9.7; 23.17.10.

3. BDB 996–1000; cf. H.-J. Fabry and A. Graupner, "שׁוּב *šûḇ*, etc.," *TWAT* 7 (1990): 1120–69.

4. Cf. BDB 229–37; F. J. Helfmeyer, "הָלַךְ *hālakh*," *TDOT* 3 (1978): 388–403.

5. For a study of its usage in Greek philosophy, see Friedrich Büchsel, "ἐπιθυμία, ἐπιθυμέω," *TDNT* 3 (1965): 168–69.

6. Thucydides 7.84.2; cf. 4.81.2.

7. Plato *Leges* 9 §854a; cf. Xenophon *Memorabilia* 1.2.64.

8. BDB 15–16; Günter Mayer, "אָוָה *ʾāvāh*; אַוָּה *ʾavvāh*; תַּאֲוָה *taʾăvāh*; מַאֲוַיִּים *maʾăvyyîm*," *TDOT* 1 (1977): 134–37.

In three instances it refers to a neutral or good desire, as when it speaks of Jesus' desire to eat the passover with the disciples (Luke 22:15), Paul's desire to be with Christ (Phil 1:23), and his desire to be with the Thessalonians (1 Thess 2:17). The other thirty-five times it has a bad connotation, as the desire for impurity (Rom 1:24; 2 Pet 2:10), sin (Rom 6:12), covetousness (Rom 7:7, 8), and opposition to God's will (1 Pet 4:2). Therefore, the moral character of the desire is determined by the object named. In the present context, the following genitive attests that our desires are bad and the plural may point to "a feeling of comprehensiveness: all our intentions are evil."[1]

The term σάρξ has been much discussed and will only be summarized here.[2] From the beginning, along with bones, sinews, and blood, it has had reference to the material part of the body[3] and hence, is different from the gods who have no flesh but are ascribed mind, intelligence, and reason.[4] Unlike the soul it is transitory and will pass away.[5] It is used also to depict the seat of lusts and affections.[6] In the LXX it occurs 211 times and 158 times in the canonical books and 144 times it is a translation of בָּשָׂר, meaning "flesh."[7] It can refer to the material of which animals and humans are composed (Gen 2:21; 40:19; Lev 4:11; Job 2:5) or the whole person, not just the physical aspects (Pss 16:9 [LXX 15:9]; 63:1 [MT 63:2; LXX 62:2]). The flesh is transitory (Isa 40:6) and is weak and limited in comparison to God (Ps 78:39 [LXX 77:39]; Isa 31:3; Jer 17:5). The primary reference is to that of the material substance of humans and animals and very little is said about the moral connotations of the flesh. However, Gen 6:12 speaks of the corruption of the flesh, referring to the human race as a whole in its rebellion against God. In Eccl 2:3; 5:6 [MT & LXX 5:5]; 11:10 it refers to the inclination of the flesh to moral excess. In the Qumran community it can have reference to a human body (1QS 3:8–9), but there is much more emphasis on its powerlessness (1QH[a] 7:21 [15:21]) and its sinfulness (1QS 4:20; 11:9; 1QH[a] 5:13–14 [13:13–14]; 7:15–16 [15:16–17]; cf. 18:22–23 [10:22–23]).

1. Best, 209.

2. For a study of this word, see Alexander Sand, *Der Begriff »Fleisch« in den paulinischen Hauptbriefen*, Biblische Untersuchungen, ed. Otto Kuss, vol. 2 (Regensburg: Friedrich Pustet, 1967); Jewett, *Paul's Anthropological Terms*, 49–166, 453–56; Eduard Schweizer, Friedrich Baumgärtel, and Rudolf Meyer, "σάρξ, σαρκικός, σάρκινος," *TDNT* 7 (1971): 98–151; Horst Seebass and Anthony C. Thiselton, "Flesh [σάρξ]," *NIDNTT* 1 (1975): 671–82; Robert G. Bratcher, "The Meaning of *Sarx* ("Flesh") in Paul's Letters," *BT* 29 (1978): 212–18.

3. Plato *Phaedo* 45, 47 §§96d, 98d; *Symposium* 207d; cf. also Aeschylus *Agamemnon* 72.

4. Epictetus *Dissertationes* 2.8.2.

5. Homer *Odyssea* 11.219–22; cf. Plato *Leges* 12 §959c.

6. Plutarch *Moralia: De virtute et vitio* 3 §101b; *Moralia: Consolatio ad Apollonium* 13 §107f.

7. Cf. N. P. Bratsiotis, "בָּשָׂר *bāśār*," *TDOT* 2 (1977): 317–32.

In the NT σάρξ is used 147 times, ninety-one times by Paul, and nine times in Ephesians (2:3*bis*, 11*bis*, 14; 5:29, 31; 6:5, 12). It can refer to the material substance of animals and humans (1 Cor 15:39; 2 Cor 12:7; Eph 6:12) that is transitory (1 Pet 1:24; John 17:2) and is weak and limited in power (Rom 8:3). It is used to speak of the material substance of Christ's earthly existence (Rom 1:3; 8:3; Eph 2:15; Heb 2:14; 5:7). However, in contradistinction to the OT, the flesh often denotes the moral dynamics of fallen humanity.[1] The flesh is that which opposes God (Rom 8:5–8; Gal 3:3; 5:16–17). The unregenerate incline toward the things of the flesh (Rom 8:5), which produce works that are contrary to the character of God (Gal 5:19–21). Hence, one who lives in the flesh is depicted as one whose existence is apart from God and thus opposed to God and his ways. The believer is considered as one who no longer lives in the flesh but in the Spirit (Rom 8:9). This means that he no longer follows the desires of the flesh but the will of God. Certainly, the believer's earthly existence continues in a material body called "flesh" but he desires to live not in its power but in the power of God (Gal 2:20) and to see Jesus' life manifested in it (2 Cor 4:10–11). In conclusion, the term "flesh" can be neutral, referring to the material substance of the body, or it can have an ethical dimension, which speaks of the natural inclinations of the whole person to oppose God's will and ways.

Of the nine times σάρξ occurs in Ephesians, only in this verse (where it occurs twice) is it used with a negative ethical connotation. The other seven times the term "flesh" is neutral, referring to the material substance of a person. It is used of the flesh of Jesus (2:14 [NA[27], UBS[4], NEB, TEV, JB, NJB, NRSV]; 2:15 [AV, RV, ASV, RSV, NASB, NIV]) and also in 2:11 where Paul speaks of those who were Gentiles in the flesh, as opposed to Jews, thus marking the distinction between two peoples who are not in Christ (cf. v. 13). In the present context the genitival relationship to the plural "desires" is subjective and thus it is the flesh that produces the desires. The desires of the flesh are parallel to the works of the flesh listed in Gal 5:19–21. Therefore, the unregenerate's behavior before conversion was within the sphere of the impulses of our (ἡμῶν) flesh. The next clause further explains this behavior.

ποιοῦντες τὰ θελήματα τῆς σαρκὸς καὶ τῶν διανοιῶν, "doing the wishes of the flesh and the reasoning processes." The plural participle ποιοῦντες is most likely a participle of manner modifying ἀνεστράφημεν ("were living") by showing how the desires of the flesh were being carried out, namely, by "doing" the will of the flesh. This is not a needless repetition, for it is one thing for the flesh to have desires but another

1. Schweizer has shown that although Paul was influenced by the OT and Qumran, the Hellenistic influence is noticed because σάρξ was used by Greek authors to denote the source or the essential character of the ungodly or the sinful (Eduard Schweizer, "Die hellenistische Komponente im neutestamentlichen σάρξ-Begriff," *ZNW* 48, nos. 3–4 [1957]: 237–53).

to act on those desires. The present tense shows an action that regularly occurs. This agrees with verse 1 where it states that our death was in the sphere of transgressions and sins. The word θέλημα, "wish," was discussed at 1:1 where it was concluded that it has the idea of desire, wish, will, or resolve. Out of the sixty-two times it is used in the NT only eleven times does it refer to human desire or will as it does in this context and only here is it in the plural (Acts 13:22 is a quotation from the LXX where θέλημα is often plural). Here it is better translated "wishes" than "will" in order to depict the plural and yet retain the idea of will or determination. This makes it parallel in thought to ἐν ταῖς ἐπιθυμίαις, "in the desires," earlier in this verse.

The following two genitives σαρκὸς . . . διανοιῶν are subjective genitives indicating the wishes of the flesh and the mind. Consequently, we were not only living in the sphere of the desires of flesh, but we were doing the wishes or dictates of the flesh. Thus, our life in the flesh was not accidental or forced but desirable and natural. Furthermore, we were doing the wishes of the "thoughts" or "reasoning processes." The term διάνοια has the idea of "thought, reflection, intention"[1] or "process of thinking, reasoning process."[2] It occurs sixty-nine times in the LXX and forty-four times in the canonical books; all but eleven times it is translated from לֵב or לֵבָב, meaning "heart, inner person, mind, will" (Gen 17:17; Exod 28:3; 35:35; Num 15:39; Deut 28:28; Prov 2:10).[3] In the NT it is used twelve times, three times by Paul (Eph 2:3; 4:18; Col 1:21). The NT use of this word has been influenced by the LXX rather than Greek philosophy.[4] It has the idea of the "ability to think, faculty of knowledge, understanding" and is parallel to the OT idea of the heart, inner person, or the thoughts of the heart.[5] It expresses calculations formed by a thinking mind and is best translated "thoughts, reasoning processes." Elsewhere, Paul expresses it as the mind-set of the flesh which opposes God and his moral character (Rom 8:5–7). Hence, the unregenerate does the wishes of the flesh and of the reasoning processes, showing that it is more than an occasional lapse but rather a deliberate or premeditated activity of flesh and the mind. The participle "doing" is the outward manifestation of the inward wishes of the flesh and thoughts. This coincides with Paul's assertion that human beings used the reasoning processes to reject God and consequently they became futile in their thinking and their senseless minds became darkened. Though they thought they were

1. Herodotus 1.46, 90; 2.169; Plato *Phaedo* 63c; Aristotle *Metaphysica* 1.5.10 §986b.10.

2. Plato *Sophista* 263d; Aristotle *Metaphysica* 6.1.5 §1025b.25.

3. BDB 523–25; cf. H.-J. Fabry, "לֵב *lēḇ*; לֵבָב *lēḇāḇ*," *TDOT* 7 (1995): 412–34.

4. J. Behm, "διάνοια," *TDNT* 4 (1967): 965.

5. Günther Harder and Jürgen Goetzmann, "Reason, Mind, Understanding [νοῦς, σύνεσις]," *NIDNTT* 3 (1978): 127.

wise, they became fools (Rom 1:21–22) and used their reasoning process to rationalize their sinful activity (2:15). Hence, unbelievers were not only confronted by the external satanic powers but also the internal powerful desires of the flesh.

καὶ ἤμεθα[1] τέκνα φύσει[2] ὀργῆς, "and we were by nature children of wrath." This sentence is not a further extension of the last clause, but instead the coordinating conjunction (καί) makes it parallel with the beginning of the verse: "we all were formerly living in the desires of our flesh." The term τέκνα, "children," is similar to υἱοῖς, "sons," mentioned in verse 2, but it denotes a closer relationship to the parent. The word "son" has "the thought of individual freedom, and the dignity or responsibility of personal choice,"[3] while "child" depicts a close relationship and dependence on the parent. One does not call an eighteen-year-old male in the family a child but a son. Thus to be a son of disobedience is one who by his own choice disobeyed God. To be a child of wrath is one who by his relationship to his parent or ancestor comes under God's wrath, as will be discussed below. Hence, the unregenerate not only has the distinction of being called a son of disobedience but also a child of wrath!

The term φύσις has been much debated.[4] First, it can denote origin, source, or descent, as lineal descent.[5] Second, it can have the idea of the natural condition, state, or quality,[6] like the natural lay of the land[7] or the nature of the existence of the gods.[8] Third, it can refer to the created world or nature.[9] It appears only in the noncanonical books of the LXX (twelve times) and it has the same range of meanings. It appears fourteen times in the NT, all in Paul's writings except Jas 3:7*bis* and 2 Pet 1:4, and only in this verse in Ephesians. The first

1. There is dispute over the two forms of the imperfect first person plural. The form ἤμεθα is found in 𝔓[46] ℵ B 17 73 wheras ἦμεν is found in A D E F G P 𝔐 Clement Chrysostom Theodoret Oecumenius. Although the second reading has better geographical distribution than the first, it is inconsequential which reading is preferred.

2. The order φύσει τέκνα is found in A D E F G L P 3 37 latt vg arm and the reverse, τέκνα φύσει, is found in ℵ B K Chrysostom Oecumenius. The first reading is primarily Western with some Alexandrian and Byzantine support. The second reading has a good representation of Alexandrian and Byzantine traditions and thus is preferred. It is a toss-up and the meaning does not change, although there may be a difference of emphasis.

3. John Massie, "Two New Testament Synonyms, Υἱὸς and Τέκνον," *Exp* 1st ser., vol. 11 (February 1880): 151.

4. For a discussion of the term, see Aristotle *Metaphysica* 5.4.1–8 §§1014b.16–1015a.19; cf. also Helmut Köster, "φύσις, φυσικός, φυσικῶς," *TDNT* 9 (1975): 251–77; Günther Harder, "Nature [φύσις]," *NIDNTT* 2 (1976): 656–62.

5. Herodotus 7.134; Sophocles *Electra* 325; Polybius 3.6.9; 12.3; 11.2.2.

6. Aristotle *Metaphysica* 5.4.3–5 §1014b.27–35.

7. Herodotus 2.5.

8. Diodorus Siculus 3.9.1.

9. Sophocles *Antigone* 345; Plato *Respublica* 4 §429d.

sense, that of origin or descent, is seen in Gal 2:15 where Paul speaks of being a Jew by nature or descent (cf. Rom 2:27). The second sense, that of a natural condition or quality, is seen in reference to the natural branches of the olive tree (Rom 11:21, 24*ter*). The third sense, that of the nature of the created world, is seen in Paul's illustration from nature with regard to long hair (1 Cor 11:14) or the misuse of the natural relations between men and women (Rom 1:26). In the present context, the third sense definitely does not fit. Neither does the second, although some would interpret it as a natural quality, so that when "left to ourselves," we are destined to suffer wrath, the consequence of sin.[1] However, the first sense, that of origin or descent, seems to fit best in the present context. The dative could be instrumental[2] or causal. We were, because of our ancestors, children of wrath. It is the natural endowment or condition inherited from our ancestors, particularly from Adam (Rom 5:12–21), that brings wrath.[3] This fits well with the term τέκνα, "children," who have a close relationship to parents.

The word ὀργή[4] can have the meaning of "temperament" or "disposition,"[5] but it also can have the idea of "anger" or "wrath."[6] Wrath was an outstanding characteristic of the Greek gods, thus they needed to be placated.[7] It appears 300 times in the LXX, 234 times in the canonical books translated from fourteen Hebrew words, but around 100 times from אַף, the most used Hebrew word for anger or wrath. It is the word for "nose" (Isa 2:22), which comes from the verb אָנֵף, "to snort," hence, "to be angry."[8] Anger in the OT refers both to human (Gen 39:19; 2 Sam 12:5; Prov 21:14) and more often to divine anger (Exod 32:10, 11; Deut 29:28 [MT & LXX 29:27]; Isa 5:25). In the NT it is used thirty-six times, twenty-one times by Paul, three times in Ephesians (2:3; 4:31; 5:6). Only five refer to human anger or wrath (Eph 4:31; Col 3:8; 1 Tim 2:8; Jas 1:19, 20), while the others refer to God's wrath. Clearly, in the present context, it refers to God's wrath. The genitive form of "wrath" could be descriptive,[9] as children who

1. Moule, *Idiom Book*, 174; cf. Köster, *TDNT* 9 (1975): 274–75; Meyer, 103–7.

2. Robertson, *Grammar*, 530. Lincoln (99) appropriately illustrates the instrumental use by citing Gal 2:15 which states "we who are Jews by nature."

3. BAGD 869; BDAG 1069; Calvin, 141–42; Alford, 3:91; Eadie, 134–37; Ellicott, 37; Barth, 231; Bruce, 284–85. For a survey on theological interpretations of original sin in connection with this verse, see David L. Turner, "Ephesians 2:3c and *Peccatum Originale*," *GTJ* 1 (fall 1980): 195–219.

4. For a more detailed study of this word, see Hermann Kleinknecht et al., "ὀργή κτλ.," *TDNT* 5 (1967): 382–447; Hans-Cristoph Hahn, "Anger, Wrath [ὀργή]," *NIDNTT* 1 (1975): 107–13.

5. Herodotus 6.128; Thucydides 1.140.1.

6. Herodotus 3.25; 6.85; Thucydides 4.122.5.

7. Kleinknecht, *TDNT* 5 (1967): 385–88.

8. BDB 60; Elsie Johnson, "אָנֵף *ʾānaph*," *TDOT* 1 (1977): 351.

9. Cf. Robertson, *Grammar*, 497.

are under God's wrath, but it is more likely a genitive of direction or purpose[1] and hence the unregenerate are children destined to God's wrath. What a horrible dilemma. It is saying that unbelievers have a close relationship to God's wrath rather than to God himself. This is reminiscent of the wrath of God that is presently revealed due to the sin and disobedience of human beings (Rom 1:18–3:20; John 3:36). Paul makes it very clear in Romans that it is their willful acts of transgression and disobedience that bring this wrath. Humans deserve God's wrath because when they could know God, they willfully turned away (Rom 1:19–21). Moreover, they not only turn away but they hate God (Rom 1:30).

ὡς καὶ οἱ λοιποί, "as even the rest." Again, the distinction between the "you" and "we" may be between Gentiles and Jews or recipients of the letter and its author. In any case, these words refer to the rest of the human beings who are in the dilemma described in verses 1–3. We were not the only ones who were the children of wrath, but all the rest of humanity has the same title and destiny.

Paul paints a dark picture of a person without redemption. This verse pictures what a human being does—lives in the desires of his or her flesh and thoughts; and what a human being is—a child destined to God's wrath. The problem is both personal and universal.

To summarize verses 1–3, Paul is showing that we are dead in transgressions and sins. This is delineated in three ways. First, we did what everybody else did—walked according the era of this ungodly world. Second, we did what the devil wanted—walked according to the ruler of the realm of the air. Third, we enjoyed it because we did what pleased our flesh and thoughts. Hence, the temporal values we had before conversion not only fit into the pattern of the world and satanic forces but it also into the pattern of our desires.[2] We did what came naturally because it naturally fit into the patterns external and internal to us. This is evidence that we were dead in transgressions and sins and we, with all other people, were children destined for God's wrath. It was a vicious circle that seemed to have no escape. Lincoln correctly links this to original sin discussed in Rom 5:12–21 where our natural ancestor, Adam, sinned and so we by nature are sinners.[3] Accordingly, there is no way that men and women by themselves are able to escape this terrible dilemma. It is only God's intervening grace that can deliver us. It is this initiative that Paul discusses next.

1. Cf. BDF §166; Wallace, *Greek Grammar*, 101.

2. Cf. Clinton E. Arnold, *Powers of Darkness: Principalities & Powers in Paul's Letters* (Downers Grove, Ill.: InterVarsity, 1992), 125–26.

3. Lincoln, 99.

2. The New Position: Alive in God (2:4–10)

a. Action of God's Grace (2:4–6)

Having discussed the terrible situation of the unregenerate, Paul now demonstrates the gracious act of God in redeeming people from their desperate straits. This is in keeping with Paul's style, for in Rom 1:18–3:20 Paul demonstrates the sinfulness of human beings and the need to have a right standing before God and then reveals God's redemption in Christ in 3:21–31. Structurally, verses 1–3 form an anacoluthon to disclose humankind's desperate dilemma before Paul introduces God as the subject in verse 4 and the main verbs describing God's gracious act of deliverance in verses 5–6. Sanders thinks that verses 4–7 have traits of an early Christian hymn,[1] but his construction is not convincing.

(1) God Made Alive (2:4–5)

In verse 4 the subject, God, is introduced and described. In contrast to humankind's desperate condition depicted in verses 1–3, the richness of God's character is described in verse 4 and his gracious act of enlivenment explained in verse 5.

Text: 2:4. ὁ δὲ θεὸς πλούσιος ὢν ἐν ἐλέει, διὰ τὴν πολλὴν ἀγάπην αὐτοῦ ἣν ἠγάπησεν ἡμᾶς, **2:5.** καὶ ὄντας ἡμᾶς νεκροὺς τοῖς παραπτώμασιν συνεζωοποίησεν τῷ Χριστῷ,—χάριτί ἐστε σεσῳσμένοι—

Translation: 2:4. "But God being rich in mercy, because of his great love with which he loved us, **2:5.** even when we were dead in transgressions made us alive together with Christ,—by grace you are saved—"

Commentary: 2:4. ὁ δὲ θεὸς πλούσιος ὢν ἐν ἐλέει, "But God being rich in mercy." The adversative coordinating conjunction δέ, "but," introduces God's actions toward sinners in contrast to their plight in verses 1–3. The sinners described in verses 1–3 could only anticipate God's wrath, but the two letter conjunction introduces the wonderful news of God's grace. The contrast is actually with verse 1, for verses 2–3 are only relative sentences further describing what was stated in verse 1. Therefore, δέ, "but," is the proper conjunction to be used after a digression or parenthesis, as is the case here.[2]

Finally, after the digression which describes the sinners' plight, God is introduced as the grammatical subject and the subject of the gracious act of redemption. The rest of the verse describes this gracious God. He is one who is rich in mercy. Aristotle in his discourse on

1. Sanders, "Hymnic Elements in Ephesians 1–3," 218–20.

2. G. B. Winer, *A Treatise on the Grammar of New Testament Greek, Regarded as a Sure Basis for New Testament Exegesis*, trans. W. F. Moulton, 3d ed., rev. (9th English ed.) (Edinburgh: T & T Clark, 1882), 553.

ἔλεος, "mercy," states that it is an emotional concern for those who undeservedly suffered some calamity. Those who have suffered or think that they might suffer the same disaster are most likely to feel the pity or mercy.[1] It appears 352 times in the LXX and 238 times in the canonical books translated from seven Hebrew words, but over 200 times it is from חֶסֶד, meaning "steadfast, loyal, or covenant love."[2] It is used of God who shows his mercy to his people with whom he has made a covenant (1 Kgs 8:23; Ps 89:49 [MT 89:50; LXX 88:50]; Isa 63:7) and a person is to show mercy to God based on a mutual relationship (Hos 6:4, 6).[3] Because God has made a covenant with his people Israel, he is faithful in extending his mercy to them. This same concept of God's covenant love continues in the Qumran literature (e.g., 1QS 1:8, 22; 2:1, 4; 1QM 12:3; 14:4, 8, 9).[4] However, it is all too easy to see its use in the OT as something legal when, actually, it should be received as God's kindness, sensitivity, and actions of loving-kindness.[5] In the NT it is used twenty-seven times, ten times by Paul, and only in this passage in Ephesians. It sometimes has the idea of compassion or pity on those who are suffering undeserved misfortune. Mercy shown to another human being is illustrated in the good Samaritan's action (Luke 10:37) and is enjoined (Matt 9:13; 12:7 [both from Hos 6:6]; Jas 2:13; 3:17). It is also used in greetings (1 Tim 1:2; 2 Tim 1:2; 2 John 3; Jude 2) and a benediction (Gal 6:16). Except for the two Hebrew songs in Luke (1:50, 54, 72, 78), mercy in the NT does not refer to a covenant relationship but rather to loving-kindness or, as the Greeks such as Aristotle expressed it, pity or compassion toward those who are suffering misfortune.[6]

In the present context it is God's compassion or pity on the sinners who are suffering the calamity of sin. In this instance, the calamity of

1. Aristotle *Rhetorica* 2.8.1–16 §§1385b–86b, esp. 2.8.2 §1385b. For further study on the word, see Rudolf Bultmann, "ἔλεος, ἐλεέω," *TDNT* 2 (1964): 477–85.

2. Nelson Glueck, *Ḥesed in the Bible*, trans. Alfred Gottschalk, intro. by Geral A. Larue, ed. Elisas L. Epstein (Cincinnati: Hebrew Union College, 1967; reprint, New York: KTAV, 1975); cf. also Gordon R. Clark, *The Word* Hesed *in the Hebrew Bible*, Journal for the Study of the Old Testament Supplement Series, ed. David J. A. Clines and Philip R. Davies, no. 157 (Sheffield: Sheffield Academic Press, 1993).

3. Cf. H.-J. Zobel, "חֶסֶד *ḥesed*," *TDOT* 5 (1986): 44–64.

4. For the many references to God's covenant loyalty in the Qumran community, see Hans-Helmut Esser, "Mercy, Compassion [ἔλεος, οἰκτιρμός, σπλάγχνα]," *NIDNTT* 2 (1976): 595.

5. Recently there has been a challenge to Glueck's analysis of חֶסֶד. See Francis I. Andersen, "Yahweh, the Kind and Sensitive God," *God Who Is Rich in Mercy. Essays Presented to Dr. D. B. Knox*, ed. Peter T. O'Brien and David G. Peterson (Homebush West, Australia: Anzea; Grand Rapids: Baker, 1986), 41–88.

6. For a study of the word in Greco-Roman times, see Bruce F. Harris, "The Idea of Mercy and Its Graeco-Roman Context," *God Who Is Rich in Mercy. Essays Presented to Dr. D. B. Knox*, ed. Peter T. O'Brien and David G. Peterson (Homebush West, Australia: Anzea; Grand Rapids: Baker, 1986), 89–105.

sin is not something undeserved, yet God extends his mercy toward sinners because he loves them and knows that they are helplessly entrapped in their own snare. They have nothing to commend them to God. However, as Aristotle argues, the person who is most compassionate is one who has suffered a similar calamity. This is in keeping with God's extension of mercy toward sinners, for he suffered the consequences of sin in his Son's death. This is the evidence of God's grace. The present participle ὢν does not denote cause, for that is given in the following clause beginning with διά. Rather, the participle "characterizes (in the form of a secondary predicate of time, 'being as He is;' . . .) the *general* principle under which the divine compassion was exhibited."[1] The adjective πλούσιος shows that God's mercy is not miserly, but rich. The preposition ἐν expresses the sphere in which God is rich, namely, in mercy. Thus, God being rich in mercy, exhibits his character.

διὰ τὴν πολλὴν ἀγάπην αὐτοῦ[2] **ἣν ἠγάπησεν**[3] **ἡμᾶς,** "because of his great love with which he loved us." The former clause describes God's richness in mercy; this clause, introduced by the preposition διά, states the cause[4] for this demonstration of mercy, that is, God's love. The noun ἀγάπη and the verb ἀγαπάω, "love," were discussed at 1:4 where it was concluded that it is a love that seeks the highest good in the one loved. There, too, it is given irrespective of merit and to those who are undeserving, just as in the present context. Paul uses the cognate accusative (cf. 1:3, 6, 20)[5] to give an intensity of meaning. The intensity of love is further expressed by the adjective πολλήν, "great," and by the possessive pronoun αὐτοῦ "his" thus showing that it is "his great" love. Undoubtedly, there is a relationship between the adjectives "rich" (πλούσιος) in mercy and God's "great" (πολλήν) love.[6] The relative clause (ἣν ἠγάπησεν ἡμᾶς) signifies that the action of love is directed toward us. The verb is a constative aorist which views the entire action without reference to its beginning, its progress, or its end.[7] The specific action of this great love is given in vv. 5–6. This is similar

1. Ellicott, 37.

2. The αὐτοῦ is omitted in 𝔓[46] D* F G it[b] Ambrosiaster Augustine but included in א A[vid] B C D[1] Ψ 0278 33 1739 ([s] 1881) 𝔐 it[ac, f] vg syr Clement Jerome. With the exception of 𝔓[46], it is omitted only in the Western tradition, which is not sufficient to warrant its omission.

3. The relative pronoun with the verb ἣν ἠγάπησεν is replaced with ἠλέησεν in 𝔓[46] it[b, d] Ambrosiaster, but again, with the exception of 𝔓[46], it is only in the Western text. For an interpretation with ἠλέησεν as the correct reading, see Ramaroson, "Une lecture de Éphésiens 1,15–2,10," 388–410. He sees Eph 1:15–2:10 as one unit.

4. Robertson, *Grammar*, 584; cf. Spicq, *Agape in the New Testament*, 2:72.

5. Cf. Robertson, *Grammar*, 478; BDF §153 (2); MHT 2:419; Moule, *Idiom Book*, 32; HS §151a.

6. Lona, *Die Eschatologie im Kolosser- und Epheserbrief*, 253.

7. Robertson, *Grammar*, 833; Burton, *Moods and Tenses* §39; Moule, *Idiom Book*, 13; Fanning, *Verbal Aspect*, 255–56.

to 1:19–23 where in verse 19 the magnitude of his power toward us is described, but in verses 20–23 the actual manifestation of his power is demonstrated. The pronoun ἡμᾶς, "us," refers to the "we all" in verse 3, which includes both Jews and Gentiles and/or both the recipients and the author of the letter. Certainly, this love of God for sinners is demonstrated in Christ's sacrifice for them as so clearly seen in Rom 5:5, 6, 8; 8:35–39 and later in the present epistle (Eph 5:2, 25).

In conclusion, in these verses God's character is portrayed as rich in mercy, the cause or motivation is his great love, and the basis is his grace. The latter will be demonstrated in the next verse.

2:5. καὶ ὄντας ἡμᾶς νεκροὺς τοῖς παραπτώμασιν,[1] "even when we were dead in transgressions" is basically a restatement of verse 1 with only a change of persons in the pronoun from ὑμᾶς, "you," to ἡμᾶς, "we," and the omission of καὶ ταῖς ἁμαρτίαις ὑμῶν, "and in your sins." In this regard, two things are to be noted. First, the change of pronouns does not indicate a distinction between the Jews ("we") and the Gentiles ("you"), but it is far more likely an identification of the author with the readers (cf. v. 3). In fact, Wilson demonstrates that in Ephesians "we" consistently refers to all Christians and "you" always refers to a much smaller group distinct from other Christians (cf. 2:13–14, 17).[2] Second, the omission of καὶ ταῖς ἁμαρτίαις ὑμῶν, "and in your sins," does not suggest that Paul identified himself as a transgressor with the Gentile recipients, but rather he as a Jew would not have considered himself "a sinner of the Gentiles" as depicted in Gal 2:15–17. This is too subtle a distinction for, as discussed at 1:7, παράπτωμα and ἁμαρτία are synonymous, denoting a conscious and deliberate false step. Furthermore, in Gal 2:17 Paul, as a Jew, realized that he too found himself a sinner before God along with the Gentiles. Therefore, since "transgressions" and "sins" are synonymous, probably Paul is only summarizing and, with the change of the pronouns, he is truly identifying with the Gentile readers. Both Jews and Gentiles before conversion are spiritually dead before God.

The conjunction καί is not a simple copula[3] since the two ideas of "because of his great love with which he loved us" and "we being dead

1. There are various readings in place of τοῖς παραπτώμασιν. There is τοῖς σώμασιν, "the bodies," in 𝔓[46], but this is the only manuscript and it is nonsensical. The reading ταῖς ἁμαρτίαις is found in D* (F G have the singular τῇ ἁμαρτίᾳ), but this is only replacing the accepted reading probably coming from v. 1. It is not acceptable because it comes from one geographical area. The reading τοῖς παραπτώμασιν καὶ ταῖς ἁμαρτίαις is a repetition of v. 1 found only in Ψ and Origen[lat], and it is unacceptable because it does not have enough manuscript support. Another reading is τοῖς παραπτώμασιν καὶ ταῖς ἐπιθυμίαις found only in B and a, but it is not acceptable because of the lack of manuscript support. It is best to accept the reading τοῖς παραπτώμασιν, which is found in ℵ A D[2] 0278 33 1739 1881 𝔐 cop Clement, which has good support from the Alexandrian and Byzantine text-types and thus has reasonably good geographical distribution.

2. Wilson, "'We' and 'You' in the Epistle to the Ephesians," 678–79.

3. As thought by Meyer, 109; Best, 214.

in sins" are not coordinate.[1] Nor is it a resumption of καί in verse 1.[2] Preferably this conjunctive has an ascensive idea ("even")[3] qualifying the participle, thus intensifying the greatness of God's mercy. The following participle (ὄντας) could be concessive and with the conjunction would be translated "even though." However, it is more likely temporal (as in most translations) and thus translated "even when" or "even while" we were dead in transgressions, God is rich in mercy. With the present tense of the participle, Paul shows that we being dead in transgressions was concurrent with God being rich in mercy. Hence, one is a state of deadness and the other is the action of mercy.

συνεζωοποίησεν τῷ Χριστῷ,[4] "[God] made us alive together with Christ." Having introduced and described the subject in verse 5, now Paul introduces the first of a series of three main verbs, all of which are rarely used words. This first verb, συζωοποιέω, is not found in classical literature or in the LXX but only in Eph 2:4 and Col 2:13. Paul created the word from συν-, "with," and ζωοποιέω, "to make alive," and hence the meaning "to make alive together [with someone]." The verb ζωοποιέω is used in classical literature as "to make alive" with reference to the birth of animals or the growth of plants.[5] It appears only eight times in the LXX translated from חָיָה, "to live," either in the Piel or Hiphil forms, with the resultant meaning "to make alive." When the Syrian king sent a letter to the king of Israel to ask him to cure the leprosy of Naaman, the king of Israel rhetorically asked, "Am I God who is able to kill and make alive" (2 Kgs 5:7)? In the NT it is used eleven times, seven times by Paul. Except for the illustration of the seed dying and coming to life (1 Cor 15:36), all the references point to one of the persons of the Trinity who has the ability to enliven. It can speak of life brought forth by God, as in the case of Isaac (Rom 4:17),

1. Abbott, 47.

2. As thought by Dibelius-Greeven, 67; Gaugler, 91–92; Best, "Dead in Trespasses and Sins (Eph. 2.1)," 14–15; Schnackenburg, 94.

3. Alford, 3:92; Eadie, 141; Ellicott, 38; Abbott, 47; Salmond, 287; Barth, 211, 219; Bruce, 41; Lincoln, 46; O'Brien, 166 n. 50.

4. The reading τῷ Χριστῷ is found in א A D G Ψ 075 0150 6 81 104 256 263 365 424 436 459 1175 1241 1319 1573 1739 1852 1881 1912 1962 2127 2200 2464 *Byz* [K L P] *Lect* it$^{b, d, f, o}$ vg$^{ww, st}$ slav Clement Origen^{lem} Ps-Athanasius Cyril-Jerusalem Didymus Didymus^{dub} Theodore^{lat} Cyril Theodoret Jerome Pelagius Augustine. The reading σὺν τῷ Χριστῷ appears in it^{gtxt} syr$^{p, (h), pal}$ (Origen^{lat}) Hilary Jerome$^{com1/4}$. The reading ἐν τῷ Χριστῷ is found in 𝔓^{46} B 33 *l* 60 *l* 599 it$^{ar, g, v, r}$ vg^{cl} cop$^{sa, bo}$ arm eth geo Chrysostom Victorinus-Rome Ambrosiaster Ambrose. The second reading is primarly a Western reading and is not acceptable. The third reading has a good representation of the Alexandrian text but not the other text-types and thus lacks geographical distribution. The first reading is to be accepted because it has good representative manuscripts from the various text-types and thus has an early date, good character of the manuscripts from the various text-types, and good geographical distribution.

5. Aristotle *Historia Animalium* 27 §555b.9; *De Generatione Animalium* 1.21 §730a.2; Theophrastus *De Causis Plantarum* 3.22.4.

or the future resurrection of the physical body (1 Cor 15:22, 45), or the spiritual life produced in the believer (John 5:21; 6:63; Rom 8:11; 2 Cor 3:6). This last sense fits the present context.[1] As mentioned above, Paul combines this verb, giving life, with the preposition "with" so it means "to make alive together." Having been dead in transgressions and sins, God in his mercy and because of his love made us alive together with Christ. The aorist is constative, viewing the entire action without reference to its beginning, its progress, or its end. The dative that follows (τῷ Χριστῷ) is governed by the prepositional prefix of the verb (συνεζωοποίησεν). This is substantiated by the parallel passage (Col 2:13) where the same verb is used and is followed by the preposition σύν. Therefore, the dative would be a dative of association,[2] hence, we were made alive together with Christ.

This phrase "making alive together with Christ" has reference to spiritual life and not the physical resurrection of the believer. Christ died physically, we were dead spiritually. Christ was raised physically (1:20), we were raised together with Christ spiritually. We were dead spiritually and now he made us alive spiritually. Paul was fond of relating the believer's identification with (συν-) Christ, as seen in Rom 6 where the believer died spiritually, was buried, and was raised with Christ.[3] There is a difference in Eph 2:5, however, for in this passage Paul emphasizes the fact that we were dead in trespasses instead of the fact that we have died with Christ. Nevertheless, the concepts are not altogether different. In Romans Paul states that we died with Christ as he died to pay the obligation of our sins and in this identification with his death, we were also buried with him, raised up to the newness of life, and will be united with him in the future resurrection (Rom 6:3–11). Ephesians states that we were dead in our trespasses but were made alive with Christ to the newness of life. However, our identification with Christ does not end in the newness of life but continues until the time that we are resurrected with him (1 Thess 4:14, 17; Phil 1:23; cf. 2 Cor 5:8). In John 5:21–24 Jesus asserts that as the Father raises the dead and gives them life, so also the Son gives life to whom he wills; whoever believes in the Son has eternal life presently and will not come into judgment but is passed from death to life. This

1. Cf. Brendan McGrath, "'*Syn*' Words in Saint Paul," *CBQ* 14 (July 1952): 220–21.

2. Robertson, *Grammar*, 529; Wallace, *Greek Grammar*, 160.

3. For more study in the area of our identification with Christ, see Ernst Lohmeyer, "Σὺν Χριστῷ," in *Festgabe für Adolf Deissmann zum 60. Geburtstag 7. November 1926* (Tübingen: Mohr, 1927), 218–57; Jacques Dupont, *ΣΥΝ ΧΡΙΣΤΩΙ: L'Union avec le Christ suivant saint Paul* (Bruges: L'Abbaye De Saint-André; Louvain: E. Nauwelaerts; Paris: Desclée de Brouwer, 1952); Robert C. Tannehill, *Dying and Rising with Christ: A Study in Pauline Theology*, BZNW, ed. Walter Eltester, vol. 32 (Berlin: Töpelmann, 1967); Eduard Schweizer, "Dying and Rising with Christ," *NTS* 14 (October 1967): 1–14; Walter Grundmann, "σύν–μετά with the Genitive, κτλ.," *TDNT* 7 (1971): 766–97, esp. 786–94; Murray J. Harris, "Appendix: Prepositions and Theology in the Greek New Testament," *NIDNTT* 3 (1978): 1206–7.

new life occurred at the time of our conversion for in the immediate context there is mention that salvation is by grace and the means is by faith and not works (vv. 5b, 8–9). Chrysostom said if Christ the first-fruits lives, so do we, for God has quickened both Christ and us.[1]

—χάριτί[2] ἐστε σεσῳσμένοι— "—by grace you are saved—" is a parenthetical outburst that will be repeated in verse 8.[3] It is to assure the reader, who has been made alive together with Christ, that his salvation is based on God's grace. God's response to the sinners' plight is one of mercy, the motive for his compassion is his love for them, and the basis for his action is his grace. The word χάρις, "grace," was discussed at 1:2 (cf. also 1:6, 7) where it was concluded that it is God's unmerited or undeserved favor. First, it provides salvation for sinners through the sacrificial death of Christ, and second, it enables believers to live acceptably before God. It appears 164 times in the LXX, seventy-nine times in the canonical books translated from eight Hebrew words, sixty-one times from חֵן. It is used of a superior who grants favor to an inferior (Gen 34:11; 39:4, 21; Exod 11:3; 12:36; 1 Sam 16:22) and the occasional times it is used in connection with God (Exod 33:12, 13, 16–17; Num 11:11; 32:5; 2 Sam 15:25; Ps 84:11 [MT 84:12; LXX 83:12]; Zech 12:10), it signifies undeserved favor, synonymous with ἔλεος.[4] Hence, it continues to be used as unmerited or unde-

1. Chrysostom *Eph* 2:5 (*PG* 62:32).

2. The first reading χάριτι appears in $\mathfrak{P}^{46}$ ℵ A D^{2} Ψ 075 0150 6 33 81 104 263 424 459 1175 1241 1739 1852 1881 1912 1962 2200 2464 *Byz* [K L P] *Lect* vg$^{ww, st}$ syr^{h} (eth) slav Didymus Theodore^{lat} Theodoret Jerome. The second reading χάριτι γάρ found in 256 365 436 1319 1573 2127 (*l* 597 δέ *for* γάρ) vg^{ms} syr^{pal} cop$^{sa,(bo)}$ arm lacks good manuscript support. The third reading with the relative pronoun οὗ preceding χάριτι is found in (D* τῇ χάριτι) F G it$^{ar, b, d, f, g, o}$ vg^{cl} syr^{p} Victorinus-Rome Ambrosiaster Pelagius Augustine, and it is basically all in the Western text-type and lacks wide geographical support. Moreover, it is a reading that tries to clarify that it is God's grace. Therefore, the first reading is preferred because it has an early date, good character, good geographical distribution, and it is the more difficult reading.

3. This parenthetical expression repeated in v. 8 is unusual and is considered a gloss by Hübner, "Glossen in Epheser 2," 392–406. Granted there is a sudden change from first person plural to second person plural in v. 5 and a return to the first person plural in v. 10. However, one must allow an author to change persons, especially in this context when Paul is overwhelmed by the grace of God exhibited to those who deserve nothing but the wrath of God. Furthermore, there is no textual evidence of a scribal insertion. Also, as Best (229) points out, there are other places in Ephesians where the author suddenly switches between first and second person plural (e.g., 1:12–13; 2:13–14).

4. Freedman, Lundbom, and Fabry, *TDOT* 5 (1986): 22–36; Zimmerli, *TDNT* 9 (1974): 376–87; Esser, *NIDNTT* 2 (1976): 116–18; cf. also Gillis P. Wetter, *Charis: Ein Beitrag zur Geschichte des ältesten Christentums*, Untersuchungen zum Neuen Testament, ed. Hans Windisch, vol. 5 (Leipzig: J. C. Hinrichs'sche Buchhandlung, 1913); Joseph Wobbe, *Der Charis-Gedanke bei Paulus: Ein Beitrag zur Ntl Theologie*, Neutestamentliche Abhandlung, ed. M. Meinertz, vol. 13 (Münster: Aschendorffsche Verlagsbuchhandlung, 1932); Darrel J. Doughty, "The Priority of ΧΑΡΙΣ," *NTS* 19 (January 1973): 163–80; Berger, "'Gnade' im frühen Christentum," 1–25.

served favor. It appears in the NT 155 times, in Paul 100 times, and in Ephesians twelve times (1:2, 6, 7; 2:5, 7, 8; 3:2, 7, 8; 4:7, 29; 6:24) with the same meaning. It is used in this verse as a dative of means, instrument,[1] or cause,[2] expressing that salvation is "by grace" or "on the basis of grace." The omission of the article "tends to emphasize the inherent qualities of abstract nouns"[3] and hence the enhancement of the gracious act of God toward sinners, who deserved nothing but wrath. Certainly, its place at the beginning of this parenthetical expression gives emphasis to grace, especially since the pattern in Ephesians is quite consistent in placing qualifiers after the verbs, as discussed at 1:4. Thus, it is necessary to realize the desperate situation of the unregenerate, then to recognize that grace alone is able to provide salvation.

The term σεσῳσμένοι is a perfect passive participle of σῴζω, "save," which has the idea of deliverance or rescue from danger.[4] From classical times it connoted deliverance from the dangers of war or the sea,[5] from disease,[6] or from the wrath of the gods.[7] It occurs 348 times in the LXX, 291 times in the canonical books translating sixteen Hebrew words. About 175 times it is translated from יָשַׁע, "to make wide, spacious," as opposed to the narrowness of oppression or being hemmed in. About 160 times translates this Hebrew word in the Hiphil stem (יָשַׁע), meaning "to deliver, save" (1 Sam 23:2, 5; Pss 106:8, 10, 21, 47 [LXX 105:8, 10, 21, 47]; 119:94, 146 [118:94, 146]; Isa 33:22; 43:3, 11).[8] In the NT the word is used 106 times, twenty-nine times by Paul, and only here and verse 8 in Ephesians. Again, it has the idea of being delivered or saved from danger, such as drowning in the sea (Matt 14:30; Acts 27:2), from disease (Matt 9:22 = Mark 5:34 = Luke 8:48; 17:19), and from eternal separation from God (Matt 10:22; John 10:9; Acts 2:21; Acts 15:1; Rom 10:9, 13; 1 Cor 5:5; 1 Thess 2:16). This last sense fits the present context.[9] Due to the dilemma of being dead in transgressions and sins, there was no hope of deliverance from God's wrath outside of God's grace. Although in the Pauline letters the term has many references to the future salvation (5:9–10; 13:11; 1 Cor 3:15;

1. Robertson, *Grammar*, 533; MHT 3:240; Moule, *Idiom Book*, 44.

2. Wallace, *Greek Grammar*, 167–68. Wallace states that the dative of cause is better translated "by grace" or "on the basis of grace" rather than "because of grace."

3. MHT 3:176; Zerwick, *Biblical Greek* §176; cf. BDF §258 (2); cf. Wallace, *Greek Grammar*, 249–50.

4. For a study of the word, see Werner Foerster and Georg Fohrer, "σῴζω κτλ.," *TDNT* 7 (1971): 965–1024; Wilhelm Mundle, Colin Brown, and Walter Schneider, "Redemption, Loose, Ransom, Deliverance, Release, Salvation, Saviour [λύω, λύτρον, ῥύομαι, σῴζω, σωτήρ]," *NIDNTT* 3 (1978): 177–223, esp. 205–16.

5. Homer *Ilias* 15.290; Plato *Symposium* 220d.

6. *SIG* 620.14 (188 B.C.).

7. Homer *Odyssea* 5.130; Diodorus Siculus 11.92.3–4.

8. BDB 446–47; cf. J. F. Sawyer and H.-J Fabry, "ישׁע *yšʿ*, etc.," *TDOT* 6 (1990): 441–63.

9. *Contra* Foerster, *TDNT* 7 (1971): 994.

5:5; 1 Tim 4:16; 2 Tim 4:18), there are numerous references to salvation as a present experience (Rom 8:24; 1 Cor 1:18, 21; 15:2; 2 Cor 2:15; 2 Thess 2:10; 2 Tim 1:9; Titus 3:5).[1]

The passive voice is labeled by some grammarians as a divine passive where God clearly is the subject.[2] Sinners are being saved by God's gracious act. The perfect tense expresses a completed action with continuing results in the present time. The completed action occurred at the moment of their conversion. Here the perfect periphrastic intensifies the present results of being saved.[3] Although it could be translated "you have been saved" (ASV, RSV, NASB, TEV, JB, NIV, NJB, NRSV), the translation "you are saved" (AV, NEB) better conveys the continuing results of being saved. In other words, God, by his grace, initially saves, but by that same grace he keeps believers safe or saved from God's wrath and from sin's grip of death from which they are delivered. On the other hand, one must not think that the perfect tense in itself guarantees future deliverance. It is the God behind the perfect tense that guarantees the future deliverance.

In summary, Paul's parenthetical exclamation expressing the sheer grace of God in salvation was prompted by verses 4 and 5. In verse 6 Paul uses the next two main verbs. These further underscore God's grace.

(2) God Raised (2:6a)

Text: 2:6a. καὶ συνήγειρεν

Translation: 2:6a. "and raised us up with him"

Commentary: 2:6a. καὶ συνήγειρεν, "and raised us up with him." This is the second of the three main verbs that go with the subject "God" in verse 5. Note the logical progression—we are made alive from the dead and then we are resurrected with him. This verb συνεγείρω is used three times in the LXX where it speaks of assisting to raise something heavy (Exod 23:5), of sheol arousing the spirits of the dead (Isa 14:9), and of raising up fallen things (4 Macc 2:14). In the NT it is used only here and in Col 2:12 and 3:1 where it speaks of being raised with Christ. Like the compound verb in verse 5, the aorist is constative, viewing the entire action without reference to its beginning, its progress, or its end. Normally, resurrection is considered as something yet future. But in both Col 2:12 and 3:1 and here, it talks about a resurrection in conjunction with Christ's resurrection, and since Christ's resurrection is in the past, it is not talking about a future resurrection. Thus, the believers' spiritual resurrection is in conjunction with Christ's physical resurrection. As he died physically, we

1. Lincoln, 104.

2. Wallace, *Greek Grammar*, 437–38.

3. Cf. MHT 1:127; BDF §352; Fanning, *Verbal Aspect*, 319; Porter, *Verbal Aspect*, 468; Wallace, *Greek Grammar*, 575, 649.

were dead spiritually; so also as he was raised physically (1:20), we were raised spiritually. This talks about the believers' positional resurrection and not their future physical resurrection (e.g., 1 Thess 4:16; 1 Cor 15; Rom 8:23; Phil 3:21; 2 Tim 2:11, 18). When Christ was resurrected, all power was given to him (Matt 28:18; Rom 1:4). So too, Christians identified with Christ, and those in whom Christ dwells presently have this same power in them. The new resurrected life demands new values. It is summed up well in Col 3:1–2 which says, "If therefore you have been raised with Christ, seek the things above, where Christ is seated at the right hand of God; set your mind on things above, not on things on earth."

(3) God Seated (2:6b)

The third main verb is given in verse 6b, indicating another facet of God's marvelous grace.

Text: 2:6b. καὶ συνεκάθισεν ἐν τοῖς ἐπουρανίοις ἐν Χριστῷ Ἰησοῦ,

Translation: 2:6b. "and seated us with him in the heavenly realms in Christ Jesus,"

Commentary: 2:6b. καὶ συνεκάθισεν ἐν τοῖς ἐπουρανίοις ἐν Χριστῷ Ἰησοῦ, "and seated us with him in the heavenly realms in Christ Jesus." The verb συγκαθίζω simply means to be seated together with someone and is used six times in the LXX (Gen 15:11; Exod 18:13; Num 22:27; Jer 16:8; 1 Esdr 9:6, 16). In the NT it occurs only in Eph 2:6 and Luke 22:55 where it has reference to those who, having seized Christ, kindled a fire in the middle of the high priest's courtyard and sat down together. In the present context, not only has God made us alive and raised us with Christ, but he also has seated us with Christ in the heavenlies in Christ Jesus. Like the two previous compound verbs in verses 5 and 6a, the aorist is constative, viewing the entire action without reference to its beginning, its progress, or its end. As God raised and seated Christ in the heavenlies physically (1:20), so has God raised and seated us together with Christ in the heavenlies spiritually.[1] The phrase ἐν τοῖς ἐπουρανίοις, "in the heavenlies," was discussed at 1:3 where it was concluded that the noun should be regarded as neuter, thus meaning the place of heavenly realms. From this position the believer derives every spiritual benefit. Hence, the position of being seated with Christ in the heavenlies gives the believer a heavenly status with heavenly power to overcome the power of sin and death. The believers are not only in the heavenlies but also in Christ Jesus. This last prepositional phrase is not connected to the previous prepositional phrase "in the heavenly realms" but is joined to the verb "to be seated together with him." This is not redundant, for it

1. Cf. Beat Weber, "'Setzen'-'Wandeln'-'Stehen' im Epheserbrief," *NTS* 41 (July 1995): 478; McGrath, "'*Syn*' Words in Saint Paul," 219–20.

underscores the reason we are seated in the heavenlies with Christ, namely, because we are in him. It is our union with Christ that gives us the right to be in the heavenly places. Although we are in the heavenlies positionally, we remain on the earth to live a resurrected life in connection with the resurrected Christ. God, who has benefited us with every spiritual blessing (1:3), enables us. Ephesians 2:10 states that the believer is created for good works here on earth. The idea of being seated in the heavenlies is not from a Gnostic concept of salvation.[1] Mussner has pointed out the parallels in Qumran literature where members of the community thought they had already been purified from sin and had entered into the company of the eternal host (1QH[a] 11:19–20 [3:19–22]; 19:10–12 [11:10–12]).[2] Although there are some similarities, the central thrust in the present context is that we are in the heavenlies because of our sole relationship to Christ.[3]

There is a tendency among many interpreters to think of the three main verbs in verses 5–6 as referring to Christian baptism.[4] They refer to a parallel passage in Col 2:12–13 where there is a specific reference to baptism. But there are differences. First, in the Colossians passage there is a tendency to allow baptism to dominate the exegesis, when that along with circumcision is only one part of it. The main point of that passage is the believer's burial and resurrection to a new life.[5] Second, there is no mention of baptism in the present context, and since this is not the main point of the parallel passage,

1. Conzelmann, 66; Schille, *Frühchristliche Hymnen*, 56–57.

2. Franz Mussner, "Contributions Made by Qumran to the Understanding of the Epistle to the Ephesians," in *Paul and Qumran: Studies in New Testament Exegesis*, ed. and trans. Jerome Murphy-O'Connor (Chicago: Priory Press, 1968), 166–67.

3. Lincoln, "A Re-Examination of 'the Heavenlies' in Ephesians," 473.

4. Schlier, 109–11; Schnackenburg, 94–95; cf. idem, "»Er hat uns mitauferweckt.« Zur Tauflehre des Epheserbriefes," 167–74; Mussner (*Christus, das All und die Kirche*, 91–94) who argues against Schlier's and Käsemann's Gnostic interpretation agrees with them in the baptism motif here; Schnackenburg, *Baptism in the Thought of St. Paul*, 73–74; Ernst Käsemann, *New Testament Questions of Today*, trans. W. J. Montague and Wilfred F. Bunge (London: SCM, 1969), 19, 125; Fung, "The Doctrine of Baptism in Ephesians," 7–8; Halter, *Taufe und Ethos*, 236–39; Lincoln, *Paradise Now and Not Yet*, 147–50; cf. also Edvin Larsson, *Christus als Vorbild. Eine Untersuchung zu den paulinischen Tauf- und Eikontexten*, trans. Beatrice Steiner, ASNU, vol. 23 (Uppsala: Gleerup; København: Einar Munkgraar, 1962), 105–8; Viktor Warnach, "Taufwirklichkeit und Taufbewußtsein nach dem Epheserbrief," in *Leben aus der Taufe*, ed. Theodor Bolger Limburgh (Limburgh: ARS Liturgica Maria Laach, 1963/64), 39–43; Franz Mußner, "Eph 2 als ökumenisches Modell," in *Neues Testament und Kirche für Rudolf Schnackenburg*, ed. Joachim Gnilka (Freiburg: Herder, 1974), 329–31; Wayne A. Meeks, "In One Body: The Unity of Humankind in Colossians and Ephesians," in *God's Christ and His People. Studies in Honour of Nils Alstrup Dahl*, ed. Jacob Jervell and Wayne A. Meeks (Oslo: Universitetsforlaget, 1977), 213; Lona, *Die Eschatologie im Kolosser- und Epheserbrief*, 360–64; MacDonald, *The Pauline Churches*, 142–43.

5. Peter T. O'Brien, *Colossians, Philemon*, WBC, ed. David A. Hubbard and Glenn W. Barker; New Testament ed. Ralph P. Martin, vol. 44 (Waco, Tex.: Word, 1982), 119.

it seems to force the issue to make the present context a baptismal passage.[1] Third, it is difficult to see the connection between being seated together with Christ and water baptism.[2] Fourth, the present context refers to death before conversion and not a burial ritual after conversion.[3]

Instead of baptism, Allen suggests that the use of συν- compounds may well speak of corporate solidarity between Christ and the believers. This is similar to the Semitic understanding of the one and the many usually discussed under the rubric of a corporate personality.[4] Our resurrection and being seated with him in the heavenlies is a present reality, even though it must not be seen as a fully realized eschatology.[5] As mentioned above, there is a future aspect of our salvation. It is similar to Rom 8:15 where we have received the spirit of adoption and 8:23 where we eagerly await for adoption, the redemption of our bodies.

In summary, we are no longer dead in our trespasses. Rather we are alive in the heavenlies with Christ. What we have is both a present and future reality. On the one hand, we have a realized eschatology but, on the other hand, we wait for this eschatology to be fully realized. This corporate solidarity is a reality now but in the future its reality will be enlarged as we fully bond with our Savior, with new bodies and without sin. The next verse points to the future aspect of our salvation.

b. Purpose of God's Grace (2:7)

Text: 2:7. ἵνα ἐνδείξηται ἐν τοῖς αἰῶσιν τοῖς ἐπερχομένοις τὸ ὑπερβάλλον πλοῦτος τῆς χάριτος αὐτοῦ ἐν χρηστότητι ἐφ᾽ ἡμᾶς ἐν Χριστῷ Ἰησοῦ.

Translation: 2:7. "in order that he might demonstrate in the coming ages the surpassing wealth of his grace in kindness toward us in Christ Jesus."

Commentary: 2:7. ἵνα ἐνδείξηται, "in order that he might demonstrate." The conjunction ἵνα indicates the purpose expressed in the three main verbs in verses 5–6 (συνεζωοποίησεν . . . συνήγειρεν καὶ

1. Cf. Erich Mauerhofer, "Der Brief an die Epheser. 18. Teil: 2,5b–7," *Fundamentum* 1 (1994): 20.

2. James D. G. Dunn, *Baptism in the Holy Spirit. A Re-examination of the New Testament Teaching on the Gift of the Spirit in relation to Pentecostalism Today*, SBT, ed. C. F. D. Moule, Peter Ackroyd, J. Barr, C. F. Evans, Floyd V. Filson, and G. Ernest Wright, vol. 15 (London: SCM, 1970), 160.

3. Cf. Barth, 234.

4. Thomas G. Allen, "Exaltation and Solidarity with Christ: Ephesians 1.20 and 2.6," *JSNT* 28 (October 1986): 103–20.

5. *Contra* Lindemann, *Aufhebung*, 125; Gese, *Das Vermächtnis des Apostels*, 159, 169. Layton discusses Origen's tension between a realized and futuristic eschatology, see Layton, "Recovering Origen's Pauline Exegesis," 382–86, 407–8.

συνεκάθισεν). The reason God quickened, raised, and seated believers together with Christ is that he might demonstrate his grace in the coming ages. The word ἐνδείκνυμι occurs fourteen times in the LXX and occurs in the NT eleven times, all of which are in Paul, except twice (Heb 6:10, 11), and is only here in Ephesians. It has the meaning "to show, demonstrate."[1] The active form rarely occurs in classical literature but never in the NT. Thus the middle form here has the active sense. If it had the middle sense ("he demonstrates for himself"), it seems that the pronoun αὐτοῦ would be redundant. Barth sees this as a legal term with the idea "to prove, give evidence," and thus it is God's cosmic lawsuit, using the church as proof of God's goodness, especially to the Gentiles.[2] However, this seems to be an exaggeration because normally this sense uses the active form,[3] and also in this context God does not appear to be in a trial situation. He simply wants to show to the cosmic audience his gracious generosity. None of its uses in the NT bears this lawsuit imagery. In the case of Pharaoh (Rom 9:17 quoting Exod 9:16) God wanted to show his power in Pharaoh rather than have a lawsuit to prove his power. Thus, in this context God wants to demonstrate or show his grace.

ἐν τοῖς αἰῶσιν τοῖς ἐπερχομένοις, "in the coming ages." This prepositional phrase indicates the time when God will demonstrate his kindnesses. The preposition ἐν, "in," with the dative gives both the point and duration of time,[4] and thus, in this context refers to that period of the coming ages. The noun αἰών can have a reference either to an unlimited time (John 6:51, 58; Gal 1:5) or to a specifically limited period of time as in 1:21, 2:2, and 3:9 (cf. Matt 13:39–40, 49; Gal 1:4; Heb 9:26), but certainly it does not refer to a personal aeon of Gnosticism.[5] Again, here it seems to speak of a specifically limited period of time. Whereas in 1:21 the time period is the present age, here the participle ἐπερχομένοις directs it to the future time. To what future time is Paul referring? It may be interpreted in one of three ways. First, it could be speaking of the succeeding future ages beginning with the first century right up until the parousia.[6] This is indicated in 3:10 where the manifold wisdom of God is *now* made known through the church to the rulers and authorities in the heavenlies. Second, it may refer to the future after the parousia as in 1:21, indicated by ἐν τῷ μέλλοντι, "in the coming age," which is in contrast to "this (present) age."[7] Third, it may refer to a combination of the first two options

1. BAGD 262; BDAG 331–32.
2. Barth, 238–42.
3. Abbott, 50.
4. BDF §200.
5. Cf. Schlier, 113–15; Schille, *Früchristiliche Hymnen*, 57–58; Lindemann, *Aufhebung*, 129–31.
6. Alford, 3:93; Eadie, 147; Ellicott, 39.
7. Olshausen, 173; Meyer, 112; Abbott, 50; Salmond, 288.

where it speaks of the future succeeding ages beginning in the first century and continuing into the future after the parousia.[1] This seems to be the best interpretation. The present tense of the participle supports the notion of continuous successive ages, including the present and future messianic ages. God is continually going to demonstrate his kindness in the succeeding ages. Ultimately, it is in the future age that this grace will be fully appreciated. At the present time, we are limited because of our sinful and human limitations and take for granted the abundance of grace. In the future, with a new body and without sin, we will be able to fully appreciate the surpassing greatness of the wealth of his grace.

τὸ ὑπερβάλλον πλοῦτος[2] **τῆς χάριτος αὐτοῦ,** "the surpassing wealth of his grace." The participle ὑπερβάλλον from ὑπερβάλλω was discussed at 1:19. In the NT it is used only by Paul (2 Cor 3:10; 9:14; Eph 1:19; 2:7; 3:19) and can be translated "surpassing, extraordinary, exceeding."[3] In 1:19 it is used of the surpassing greatness of God's power in us, in 3:19 it speaks of the surpassing greatness of Christ's love, and here it speaks of the surpassing greatness of God's grace. The next words πλοῦτος τῆς χάριτος αὐτοῦ are found in 1:7 where it was concluded that πλοῦτος means to have abundance, riches, or wealth and is best translated "wealth" because it depicts singularity rather than one of many kinds of riches (cf. also 1:18). The word "grace" is discussed at 1:2 (cf. also 1:6, 7; 2:5) where it was concluded that it has the idea of "unmerited favor." Therefore, God is going to demonstrate the surpassing wealth of his grace.[4] This is further defined by the following prepositional phrase.

ἐν χρηστότητι ἐφ' ἡμᾶς ἐν Χριστῷ Ἰησοῦ, "in kindness toward us in Christ Jesus." Here is a cluster of three prepositional phrases. This cluster can be connected either to the immediately preceding phrase, showing the sphere of his grace, in his kindness, or it can go back to the main verb, indicating God's demonstration of the wealth of his grace by means of his kindness or preferably in the sphere of his kindness. Either construction gives the same basic idea. The term χρηστότης is found twenty-six times in the LXX and fifteen times in the canonical books, all in the Psalms, and is always translated from טוֹב/

1. Caird, 53; Bruce, 288; O'Brien, 173; idem, "Divine Analysis and Comprehensive Solution," 140–41; cf. Lemmer, "A Multifarious Understanding of Eschatology in Ephesians," 116.

2. The masculine form τὸν ὑπερβάλλοντα πλοῦτον is in D[1] Ψ 0278 𝔐, but the neuter form τὸ ὑπερβάλλον πλοῦτος is found in 𝔓[46] ℵ(* *h. t.*) A B D* F G 6 33 81 1175 1739 1881 2464 *l* 249*pc* (ℵ* should not be included as in NA[27] because the verse is omitted). The neuter reading should be accepted because of good representative manuscripts in the Alexandrian and Western text-types.

3. BAGD 840; BDAG 1032; Delling, *TDNT* 8 (1972): 520–21.

4. Similarly expressed by the Qumran community (1QH[a] 8:21 [16:12]; 19:28–30 [11:28–30]).

טוֹבָה/טוּב, meaning "good, goodness"[1] (Pss 14:1, 3 [LXX 13:1, 3]; 21:3 [MT 21:4; LXX 20:4]; 31:19 [MT 31:20; LXX 30:20]; 68:10 [MT 65:12; LXX 65:11]). In the NT it occurs ten times and is used only by Paul and only here in Ephesians. Again it has the idea of "goodness, kindness, generosity"[2] (Rom 2:4; 3:12 [from Ps 14:3, LXX 13:3]; 11:22*bis*; 2 Cor 6:6; Gal 5:22; Col 3:12; Titus 3:4) and is derived from the adjective χρηστός, that which is appropriate.[3] The adjective is used in Luke 5:39 of wine that has mellowed with age, and it is used of Christ's yoke (Matt 11:30), which is not harsh.[4] Thus, in both of these passages it has the idea of that which is fitting or appropriate. The preposition ἐν, "in," denotes the sphere of the action. Hence, in this context it has the idea that God will demonstrate the wealth of his grace in the sphere of that which is his goodness or kindness appropriate to God. It describes the entire work of salvation.[5] The second prepositional phrase (ἐφ' ἡμᾶς) is introduced by the preposition ἐπί (with the accusative), which shows direction,[6] indicating that this kindness is directed toward us. The third prepositional phrase (ἐν Χριστῷ Ἰησοῦ) is introduced with ἐν, "in," which could give the idea of "in connection with," but preferably it gives the location of the action of kindness. The work of kindness located in Christ Jesus is the wonderful salvation wrought by him and not by us. Because we are located in Christ we were made alive with him, raised with him, seated with him in the heavenlies, hence the kindness of God toward us. Our own efforts would have been rejected by God, but we are accepted because we are in Christ.

Hence, the action of God's love was in conjunction with Christ to make us alive, to raise us, and to seat us in the heavenlies in Christ Jesus for the purpose of demonstrating in the successive ages the surpassing wealth of his grace in the sphere of his appropriate kindness directed toward us who are located in Christ Jesus. This description of our salvation which we did not merit is further delineated in verses 8–10.

c. Explanation of God's Grace (2:8–10)

These verses explain the surpassing wealth of his grace he showed in his kindness towards us (v. 7), expanding on the parenthetical outburst made in verse 5. Paul is going to explain that salvation is totally of grace and nothing of human effort.

1. BDB 375; I. Höver-Johag, "טוֹב *ṭôḇ*; טוּב *ṭûḇ*; יטב *yṭb*," *TDOT* 5 (1986): 296–317.

2. BAGD 886; BDAG 1090.

3. Konrad Weiss, "χρηστότητος," *TDNT* 9 (1974): 491.

4. Trench, *Synonyms of the New Testament*, 234.

5. Lech Remigius Stachowiak, *Chrestotes. Ihre biblisch-theologische Entwicklung und Eigenart*, Studia Friburgensia, vol. 17 (Freiburg: Universitätsverlag, 1957), 63–66.

6. BAGD 289; BDAG 366; Moule, *Idiom Book*, 49.

(1) Salvation by Grace (2:8a)

Text: 2:8a. τῇ γὰρ χάριτί ἐστε σεσῳσμένοι διὰ πίστεως·

Translation: 2:8a. "For by grace you are saved through faith,"

Commentary: 2:8a. τῇ γὰρ χάριτί ἐστε σεσῳσμένοι διὰ[1] πίστεως, "For by grace you are saved through faith." Having stated the action of God's grace and the reason for the demonstration of the riches of his grace, Paul now explains this gracious salvation of God. The words expressed above are the same words in the parenthetical expression in verse 5 with three exceptions. First, there is the explanatory γάρ, "for," by which Paul is going to explain that this salvation is truly of God's grace and does not originate or result from the efforts of humans. Second, there is the article τῇ before "grace." In Greek the abstract noun can occur with or without the article. In verse 5 "grace" is without the article, but here it is with the article. The use of the article in the present context has been thought to refer to a concrete application of the abstract noun, namely, the work of redemption as a concrete historical fact.[2] However, it seems that the anarthrous use in verse 5 is also speaking of the concrete historical incident. It is better to see this article as used anaphorically, namely, the grace to which Paul made reference in verse 5 is again being discussed in the present context.[3] Third, the addition of the words διὰ πίστεως, "through faith," denote the subjective means by which one is saved. Paul expresses the means of faith twenty-one times by ἐκ πίστεως (Rom 1:17*bis*; 3:26, 30; 4:16*bis*; 5:1; 9:30, 32; 10:6; 14:23*bis*; Gal 2:16; 3:7, 8, 9, 11, 12, 22, 24; 5:5) and fourteen times by διὰ [τῆς] πίστεως (Rom 3:22, 25, 30, 31; 2 Cor 5:7; Gal 2:16; 3:14, 26; Eph 2:8; 3:12, 17; Phil 3:9; Col 2:12; 2 Tim 3:15). Three observations can be made. First, ἐκ πίστεως is found in only Romans and Galatians, whereas διὰ [τῆς] πίστεως is found in Romans, 2 Corinthians, Galatians, Ephesians, Philippians, Colossians, and 2 Timothy. Second, the phrases are synonymous when used in the same verse with the same meaning in Rom 3:30 and Gal 2:16. Third, διὰ [τῆς] πίστεως is used in Paul's later writings such as the Prison Epistles and it is used three times in Ephesians (2:8; 3:12, 17). Hence, Paul's expression διὰ πίστεως is commonly used to express the means by which one is saved.

In this explanatory portion, as in verse 5, "grace" is a dative of means, instrument, or cause, expressing that salvation is "by" grace and is mentioned first for the sake of emphasis, especially since in

1. The inclusion of the article (τῆς) is found in A D[2] Ψ 1881 𝔐 but it is omitted by ℵ B D* F G P 0278 6 33 104 1175 1505 1739 1881 2464 *pc* cop[bo]. The second reading is preferred because it has better representation in both the Alexandrian and Western text-types. Its inclusion can be easily accounted for by a scribe who thought that "faith" needed to be particularized as it is in some languages (cf. HS §133a).

2. Zerwick, *Biblical Greek* §176; MHT 3:176.

3. BDF §258 (2); Winer, *Grammar*, 148 n. 6; Wallace, *Greek Grammar*, 250.

Ephesians the qualifiers normally follow rather than precede the verbs (cf. 1:4). Only on the basis of grace are people delivered from their desperate situation of sinfulness which separates them from God. The terms and the periphrastic construction of ἐστε σεσῳσμένοι, "you are saved," were discussed at verse 5, emphasizing the completed action with continuing results of one's salvation. Although the perfect tense denotes the completed action with continuing results, the perfect periphrastic seems to give more emphasis on the continuing results.[1] This salvation delivers people who are dead in transgressions and are eternally separated from God and can only expect God's wrath. On the basis of God's grace one has been saved from God's wrath and continues in God's safe keeping. Again, though it could be translated "you have been saved" (ASV, RSV, NASB, TEV, JB, NIV, NJB, NRSV), the translation "you are saved" (AV, NEB) better conveys the continuing results of being saved. Whereas "grace" is the objective cause or basis of salvation, "through faith" is the subjective means by which one is saved. This is important, for the salvation that was purchased by Christ's death is universal in its provision, but it is not universal in its application. One is not automatically saved because Christ died, but one is saved when one puts trust in God's gracious provision. Calvin states that a person must receive by faith the salvation offered to him or her by the hand of God.[2] A good illustration of this is the life of Abraham whereby his faith (ἡ πίστις αὐτοῦ) was reckoned for righteousness (Rom 4:5). Notice, it was Abraham's own (αὐτοῦ) faith that gave him a right standing. However, faith is never thought of as a work, for the preceding verse (v. 4) explicitly states that if a righteous stand before God were obtained by works, it would not be according to grace but according to obligation. Verse 5 continues by saying that it is to those who do not work but believe in the one who justifies the ungodly that their faith reckons to them a right standing. This is confirmed in the present context in Ephesians, for following the above statement Paul reinforces the idea that this salvation was not by means of any kind of works done by humans but solely by faith.

Although the word "faith" is often used by believers, it is vague in the minds of many. The word πίστις, "faith," basically means "trust, confidence" in people or gods.[3] The word appears fifty-nine times in

1. Cf. BDF §352; MHT 1:127; Moule, *Idiom Book*, 18–19; Fanning, *Verbal Aspect*, 319; Porter, *Verbal Aspect*, 468. Wallace, *Greek Grammar*, 575, 649.

2. Calvin, 144. There is, at times, a tendency to minimize faith as the means of salvation. Some scholars believe that regeneration precedes faith, but that goes against the present context. There is nothing in this context to indicate that regeneration is the means of salvation and in some way faith follows. For a good discussion on this, see Roy L. Aldrich, "The Gift of God," *BSac* 122 (July–September 1965): 248–53.

3. Hesiod *Opera et Dies* 372; Sophocles *Oedipus Tyrannus* 1445; *Oedipus Coloneus* 611, 950; Thucydides 1.120.5.

the LXX and the thirty-two times it occurs in the canonical books it is always translated from the basic root of אָמַן or אֱמוּנָה, meaning "trusting, faithfulness, fidelity"[1] (Deut 32:20; 1 Sam 26:23; 1 Chr 9:22; Prov 12:17, 22; Jer 5:1, 3). In the NT it is used 243 times, 142 times by Paul and eight times in Ephesians. Much study has been done on the word,[2] but again it basically has the idea of "trust, reliance, faith." As one who trusts in a chair for support because it is trustworthy, so one trusts in God's gracious salvation because God is reliable or trustworthy. In short, one does not work to support oneself in the chair, nor does one work to obtain salvation. Rather, one relies on what God has accomplished in his Son at the cross 2000 years ago.

(2) Salvation Not of Humans (2:8b–10)

To make it clear, Paul not only presents the source of salvation, but he also states the opposite, namely, what is not the source of salvation. Salvation is of God and not of humans.

(a) Statement: God's Gift (2:8b–9)

Text: 2:8b. καὶ τοῦτο οὐκ ἐξ ὑμῶν, θεοῦ τὸ δῶρον· **2:9.** οὐκ ἐξ ἔργων, ἵνα μή τις καυχήσηται.

Translation: 2:8b. "and this is not of yourselves, it is the gift of God; **2:9.** not of works, lest anyone should boast."

Commentary: 2:8b. καὶ τοῦτο οὐκ ἐξ ὑμῶν, θεοῦ τὸ δῶρον, "and this is not of yourselves, it is the gift of God." The conjunction καί, "and," seems to be more than a mere connective, especially with a demonstrative pronoun following it. It seems to function epexegetically, namely, "that is to say," and yet it is best translated "and."[3] The real problem is with the demonstrative pronoun τοῦτο, "this." Barth states, "The neuter pronoun 'this' may refer to one of three things: the 'grace,' the verb 'saved,' the noun 'faith.'"[4] Some commentators think that it refers to πίστεως, the nearest preceding noun.[5] A serious objection to this is that the feminine noun does not match the neuter gender of the pronoun. The same problem is raised with "grace," a feminine noun. Some would have it refer back to ἐστε σεσῳσμένοι,[6] but again the antecedent would be a masculine participle. Furthermore, to refer back to

1. BDB 53; cf. Alfred Jepsen, "אָמַן *ʾāman*, etc.," *TDOT* 1 (1977): 292–323.

2. See Rudolf Bultmann and Artur Weiser, "πιστεύω κτλ.," *TDNT* 6 (1968): 174–228; Otto Michel, "Faith [πίστις]," *NIDNTT* 1 (1975): 593–606.

3. Robertson, *Grammar*, 1181–82; BDF §442 (9); Wallace, *Greek Grammar*, 334–35. Taking this conjunction with the demonstrative pronoun, Turner (MHT 3:45) translates them "and indeed." Cf. BAGD 393; BDAG 495.

4. Barth, 225.

5. Chrysostom *Eph* 2:8 (*PG* 62:33); Theodoret *Eph* 2:8 (*PG* 82:521); Jerome *Eph* 2:8–9 (*PL* 26:470); Bengel, 4:75; Moule, 73; Westcott, 32; Robert H. Countess, "Thank God for the Genitive," *JETS* 12 (spring 1969): 118–20.

6. Alford, 3:94; Eadie, 152; Meyer, 114.

any one of these words seems to be redundant. Rather than any particular word it is best to conclude that τοῦτο refers back to the preceding section.[1] This is common and there are numerous illustrations of such in Ephesians. For example, in 1:15 τοῦτο refers back to the contents of 1:3–14, in 3:1 it refers back to 2:11–22, and in 3:14 it refers back to 3:1–13. Therefore, in the present context, τοῦτο refers back to 2:4–8a and more specifically 2:8a, the concept of salvation by grace through faith.[2]

The next words οὐκ ἐξ ὑμῶν, "is not of yourselves," express that salvation does not have its origin or source (ἐκ) with humans. Rather, as expressed in the first part of the verse, its basis is grace and, as shown in verses 4–5, its origin is in God and his love. Paul continues by saying that it is the gift of God (θεοῦ τὸ δῶρον). In classical literature the word δῶρον, "gift," refers to "votive gift" or "offering" to a god,[3] or a gift from the gods,[4] as well as a "present" given as a tribute[5] or for a bribe.[6] It appears 173 times in the LXX and 158 times it occurs in the canonical books (translates sixteen Hebrew words but seventy-six times it translates קָרְבָּן and thirty-one times it translates מִנְחָה) where it most often signifies a cultic offering (Gen 4:4; Lev 1:2*bis*, 3, 10; 2:1*bis*, 4*bis*; Num 5:15; 7:10–13; Deut 12:11; 1 Chr 16:29; Jer 33:11 [LXX 40:11]), but it is also used of people who give gifts to God (Isa 18:7; Ps 68:29 [MT 68:30; LXX 67:30]) and to one another (Gen 24:53; 32:13, 18, 20, 21), as well as presenting tribute (Judg 3:15, 17, 18*bis*; 1 Chr 18:2, 6) and giving bribes (Exod 23:8*bis*; Deut 10:17; 16:19*bis*; 1 Sam 8:3; Ps 15:5 [LXX 14:5]; Prov 15:27).[7] It appears nineteen times in the NT and only in the present passage in the Pauline literature. It is used of people giving to one another (Matt 2:11; Rev 11:10) and to God (Luke 21:1, 4). Most of the time it is used of cultic offerings (Matt 5:23, 24; 8:4; 23:18, 19; Heb 5:1; 8:3, 4; 9:9; 11:4) and only once is there a reference of the gift of God given to humans (Eph 2:8).[8] The genitive could be possessive, "God's gift," or more likely a genitive of origin, "gift from God." In the present passage, the gift of God does not refer to "faith" but rather it refers to the whole concept of salvation. The contrast is stark not only in the words themselves but also in their position in the sentence. The

1. Theophylact *Eph* 2:8 (*PG* 124:1056); Calvin, 144; Alford, 3:94; Abbott, 51; Salmond, 289; Robinson, 156–57; Schlier, 115; Gaugler, 98; Gnilka, 129; Schnackenburg, 98; Bruce, 289–90; Lincoln, 112; Best, 226; O'Brien, 175; Muddiman, 110–11; Robertson, *Grammar*, 704.

2. Cf. Wallace, *Greek Grammar*, 334–35.

3. Homer *Ilias* 1.213; 6.293.

4. Homer *Ilias* 20.265; *Odyssea* 18.142.

5. Homer *Ilias* 17.225.

6. Demosthenes *De Corona* 18.109; Aristotle *Athenaion politeia* 55.5.

7. BDB 898–99; cf. H.-J. Fabry, "קָרְבָּן *qŏrbān*," *TWAT* 7 (1990): 165–71.

8. Friedrich Büchsel, "δῶρον," *TDNT* 2 (1964): 166–67; Herwart Vorländer, "Gift [δῶρον]," *NIDNTT* 2 (1976): 40–43.

words καὶ τοῦτο οὐκ ἐξ ὑμῶν, θεοῦ τὸ δῶρον are literally "and this is not of yourselves, of God is the gift." In conclusion, the "gift" is that which is outside of ourselves and is to be received. Therefore, the gift of salvation has its origin in God, its basis is grace, and it is received by means of faith.

2:9. οὐκ ἐξ ἔργων, "not of works." Paul continues by saying that the origin of salvation not only does not come from within a person but it is also not from his or her works or efforts. He consistently shows that works or works of the law are an antithesis to grace. In Rom 11:16 he states, "if it is by grace it is no longer from works, otherwise, grace is no longer grace" (cf. also 2 Tim 1:9; Titus 3:5). Hence, as in verse 8, grace is the means or instrument of our salvation. Furthermore, on numerous instances Paul makes the stark contrast between works and faith (cf. Rom 3:20, 28; 4:1–5; 9:32; Gal 2:16; 3:2–5, 7, 9). However, Romans and Galatians refer to the "works of the law,"[1] whereas the present context refers only to "works." But it needs to be realized that in Romans and Galatians Paul is dealing with many Jews, whereas in Ephesians he is dealing primarily with Gentiles. In fact, "law" (νόμος) is mentioned only once in Ephesians (2:15) where Paul reminds them that Christ has rendered the law inoperative in order that he might create in himself the two (believing Jews and Gentiles) into one new person. Furthermore, it is incorrect to think that "works of the law" is really different from "works." "Works" is a broad term referring to human effort, which is the same as "works of the law" in a Jewish con-

1. There has been a great debate regarding Paul and the law since Sander's epoch-making book, E. P. Sanders, *Paul and Palestinian Judaism: A Comparison of Patterns of Religion* (London: SCM, 1977). Dunn proposes that the "works of the law" is thought by Paul as *"particular observances of the law like circumcision and the food laws"* including special days and feasts and thus *"these feast observances were widely regarded as characteristically and distinctively Jewish."* See James D. G. Dunn, "The New Perspective on Paul," *BJRL* 65 (spring 1983): 107, cf. also 95–122. This article is reprinted with an additional note responding to those who criticized the view. See idem, *Jesus, Paul and the Law: Studies in Mark and Galatians* (Louisville, Ky.: Westminster/Knox, 1990), 183–241. The view is refined and broadened so that the "works of the law" refers to a mode of existence distinctly determined by the law whereby the individual Israelite is identified as belonging to the people of God as distinct from other nations, see idem, "Works of the Law and the Curse of the Law (Galatians 3.10–14)," *NTS* 31 (October 1985): 523–42, esp. 527–32 and the reprint with an additional note, idem, *Jesus, Paul and the Law*, 219–25, 237–41; idem, "Yet Once More—'The Works of the Law': A Response," *JSNT* 46 (June 1992): 99–117. Cf. also idem, *The Partings of the Ways*, 117–39; idem, "4QMMT and Galatians," *NTS* 43 (January 1997): 147–53. This view has been challenged. See Stephen Westerholm, *Israel's Law and the Church's Faith: Paul and His Recent Interpreters* (Grand Rapids: Eerdmans, 1988), 117–19, 143–44; C. E. B. Cranfield, "'The Works of the Law' in the Epistle to the Romans," *JSNT* 43 (September 1991): 89–101; Thomas R. Schreiner, "'Works of Law' in Paul," *NovT* 33 (July 1991): 217–44; Donald A. Hagner, "Paul and Judaism—The Jewish Matrix of Early Christianity: Issues in the Current Debate," *BBR* 3 (1993): 111–30; Joseph A. Fitzmyer, *According to Paul: Studies in the Theology of the Apostle* (New York: Paulist, 1993), 23.

text.[1] This is clearly seen in Romans where Paul states that one is justified without the "works of the law" (3:20, 28) and then he illustrates it in the life of Abraham who was justified not by "works" since he was before the law (4:1–5); however, that was also true in David's life who was after the law (4:6). Other examples within Romans (9:11 [AV, RV, ASV, RSV, NASB, NEB], 12 [NA[27], UBS[4], JB, NIV, NJB, NRSV], 32; 11:6) indicate that Paul uses "works" with the same meaning as "works of the law," that is, human effort.

Again, as in verse 8, we are saved by means (διά) of faith. As mentioned above, grace is the objective instrumental basis of our salvation, and faith is the subjective means by which we are saved. Therefore, salvation is obtained not by anything inherent in a human nor by his or her external efforts but is obtained by trusting God who saves a person on the basis of his grace. From God's vantage point it is his grace not a human being's works that is the basis of salvation. From a human's vantage point, it is faith and not works that is the means to salvation.

ἵνα μή τις καυχήσηται, "lest anyone should boast." The conjunction ἵνα could be purpose, "in order that no one should boast," or result, "so as that no one may boast." It is difficult to choose between the options because when God is involved, one must realize that what God purposes will result. Accordingly, because salvation cannot be obtained due to some inherent good or by good works but only by faith, boasting is excluded (Rom 3:27). A person is not to boast about his or her efforts (1 Cor 1:29; 3:21) but only in God (Rom 5:11; 1 Cor 1:31; 2 Cor 10:17; Phil 1:26; 3:3) or the cross of Christ (Gal 6:14). Certainly, if one could obtain salvation from within oneself or by one's own works or efforts, there would be a lot of boasting (Rom 4:2). Lincoln says it well: "Boasting perverts human autonomy by making it the object of trust."[2] In contrast, this salvation is the gift of God obtained by faith and thus one can bring praise only to God and not to self or self-effort.

Since the Pauline keywords "justify" (δικαιόω) and "justification" (δικαιοσύνη) are absent, some scholars surmise that Ephesians is not written by Paul.[3] These two terms occur eighty-five times in Paul's writings, but sixty-one of these are in Romans and Galatians, the books which specifically address justification. In fact, the noun occurs

1. Lincoln, 112–13; Lincoln and Wedderburn, *The Theology of the Later Pauline Letters*, 131–32, 135–36; Marshall, "Salvation, Grace and Works in the Later Writings in the Pauline Corpus," 345–48, 355–57.

2. Lincoln, 113.

3. See Ulrich Luz, "Rechtfertigung bei den Paulusschülern," in *Rechtfertigung. Festschrift für Ernst Käsemann zum 70. Geburtstag*, ed. Johannes Friedrich, Wolfgang Pöhlmann, and Peter Stuhlmacher (Tübingen: Mohr; Göttingen: Vandenhoeck & Ruprecht, 1976), 369–75. Lindemann (*Aufhebung*, 137) thinks the terminology used in vv. 5–8 are "totally unPauline."

only once and the verb only twice in the long epistle of 1 Corinthians. Neither the noun or verb are found in Colossians or 1 and 2 Thessalonians. The verb is used twenty-seven times by Paul, only four times outside of Romans and Galatians (1 Cor 4:4; 6:11; 1 Tim 3:16; Titus 3:7 [hence only twice in the undisputed books]). Though the specific terminology of justification is absent from the present context, the concept of salvation is the same.[1] Radl states, "Deliverance can thus mean the same thing as justification and reconciliation."[2] It is on the basis of grace by means of faith without any works. We need to grant Paul the freedom to express the same concepts with different terms. On the other hand, Maclean observes that many of the soteriological terms used in Eph 2:5–9 parallel those used in Rom 3:21–30, especially in 3:24–27 (χαρίς, ἔνδειξις/ἐνδείκνυμι, διὰ πίστεως, δωρεάν/δῶρον, ἔργα, καύχησις/καυχάομαι), and concludes that the author of Ephesians depended literarily on Rom 3:21–30.[3] Dependence is difficult to prove but it does signify that concept of salvation is clear in both passages though not always using the same terminology.

In conclusion, verses 8–9 spell out salvation in summary form. Its source is God, its basis is by grace, and it is obtained as a gift by means of faith. It is external to human beings and becomes a reality to them when they appropriate it by faith. This salvation is not something that is inherent in a person nor can it be gained by his or her efforts. Hence, a person cannot boast of any self-achievement but must boast in the gracious gift of God.

(b) Reason: God's Workmanship (2:10)

It becomes apparent that the reason that this salvation is not from humans or their efforts is because we are God's workmanship.

(i) Statement: God's Workmanship (2:10a)

Text: 2:10a. αὐτοῦ γάρ ἐσμεν ποίημα,

Translation: 2:10a. "For we are his workmanship,"

Commentary: 2:10a. αὐτοῦ γάρ ἐσμεν ποίημα, "For we are his workmanship." The conjunction γάρ, "for," tells us why this salvation is not of human origin or by human works. The reason is that "we" (recipients of salvation) are "his" (God's) workmanship. The possessive pronoun, αὐτοῦ, "his," placed first in the sentence emphasizes that it is God's workmanship.[4] The word ποίημα,[5] "workmanship," is used in

1. Marshall, "Salvation, Grace and Works in the Later Writings in the Pauline Corpus," 342–45, 355, 357–58; cf. Gese, *Das Vermächtnis des Apostels*, 160–68, 170.

2. Walter Radl, "σῴζω," *EDNT* 3 (1993): 321.

3. Maclean, "Ephesians and the Problem of Colossians," 177–205, esp. 189–205.

4. Robertson, *Grammar*, 681; MHT 3:190; Winer, *Grammar*, 193.

5. It may be from where the English word for "poem" comes; cf. "Notes of Recent Exposition," *ExpTim* 11 (April 1900): 292–93. A poem is something that is crafted by the poet.

classical times for the work of a craftsman, such as the making of a crown.[1] It is used twenty-nine times in the LXX, occurring twenty-eight times in the canonical books (twenty times in Ecclesiastes), and all but one time is translated from מַעֲשֶׂה, meaning "deed," "work" or a "work of art."[2] It is used of God's works (Pss 64:9 [MT 64:10; LXX 63:10]; 92:4 [MT 92:5; LXX 91:5]; 143:5 [LXX 142:5]; Eccl 3:11; 8:9, 17*bis*; 11:5) and of a person's deeds, both good (1 Sam 19:4; Eccl 2:4, 11, 17; 3:22; 8:14) and evil (Eccl 4:3; 8:14). It is also used of a person's skillful work or art (Eccl 4:4; Isa 29:16). In the NT it is used only here and in Rom 1:20. In Rom 1:20 it refers to God's creation (as in Pss 92:4 [MT 92:5; LXX 91:5]; 143:5 [LXX 142:5]), but in the present context it is used of God's new creation. The first reference speaks of the physical handiwork of God and the second refers to the spiritual re-creation of God in the individual believer's life. Both of these passages speak of the crafted work of God. God's masterwork or "his workmanship" is a good translation. This workmanship of God differs from human works (ἔργων) in verse 9.

The change from second person plural in verses 8–9 to first person plural in verse 10 is not a Jewish and Gentile difference, for Jews were to be saved by grace through faith and Gentiles are also God's workmanship. Rather, it is the author's identification with his audience.

(ii) Goal: Created for Good Works (2:10b)

Text: 2:10b. κτισθέντες ἐν Χριστῷ Ἰησοῦ ἐπὶ ἔργοις ἀγαθοῖς οἷς προητοίμασεν ὁ θεός,

Translation: 2:10b. "having been created in Christ Jesus for good works which God prepared beforehand,"

Commentary: 2:10b. κτισθέντες ἐν Χριστῷ Ἰησοῦ, "having been created in Christ Jesus." The word κτίζω, meaning "to create," is used in the NT only of God's acts of creation in both the physical (Matt 19:4; Mark 13:19; Rom 1:25; Eph 3:9; Col 1:16; 1 Tim 4:3; Rev 4:11*bis*; 10:6) and spiritual realms (Eph 2:10, 15; 4:24; Col 1:16; 3:10). The participle κτισθέντες is passive, indicating that the believer is the recipient of the action and may indicate attendant circumstance, but more likely denotes cause. Thus, the reason that God's workmanship is different from human works (v. 9) is because believers are a new creation in Christ Jesus. In 2 Cor 5:17 Paul states that if anyone is in Christ Jesus, he or she is a new creation (καινὴ κτίσις). In Gal 6:15 Paul states that the important thing is not that one is a Jew (circumcised) or a Gentile (uncircumcised) but a new creation (καινὴ κτίσις). Paul states in Eph 4:24 that the new person (καινὸν ἄνθρωπον) has been created (κτισθέντα) in righteousness and holiness of truth. Some see a baptism

1. Herodotus 7.84; cf. 4.5.

2. BDB 795–96; *HALOT* 2 (1995): 616–17; Eugene Carpenter, "עשׂה (*ʿśh* I)," *NIDOTTE* 3 (1997): 551.

motif in the new creation,[1] but that is foreign to the context. The sphere or location of this new creation is "in Christ Jesus" (ἐν Χριστῷ Ἰησοῦ). This was described in verses 5–6 where together with Christ we were made alive, raised, and seated in the heavenlies in Christ Jesus. Thus, the reason we are God's workmanship is because we are a new creation in Christ Jesus. But what is the purpose of all this? This is discussed next.

ἐπὶ ἔργοις ἀγαθοῖς οἷς προητοίμασεν ὁ θεός, "for good works which God prepared beforehand." The preposition ἐπί with the dative can denote purpose or goal,[2] as it does in this context. Hence, the goal of being created in Christ Jesus is for good works. God's workmanship is not achieved by good works, but it should result in good works as God has purposed them (Titus 2:14; 3:8). The attributive adjective ἀγαθοῖς, which describes the works as good, normally has a moral as well as a beneficial connotation.[3] In other words, we are created in Christ Jesus for works that are morally and beneficially good for us, for those around us, and for God.

The relative pronoun οἷς presents a real grammatical problem. Eadie mentions several interpretations and their adherents.[4] Briefly, the three main views are: (1) it is a dative of destination translated "to which God prepared us beforehand," but the omission of the pronoun ἡμᾶς, "us," is fatal to this view; (2) it is masculine and is translated "for whom God prepared us beforehand," but the antecendent ἡμεῖς, "we," is too remote (vv. 3, 7?), whereas the nearest antecedent (ἔργοις ἀγαθοῖς), as well as the following pronoun (αὐτοῖς), refer to the works and not people; and (3) acceptable to most, the οἷς is for ἅ by attraction and is translated "which [good works] God prepared beforehand," which is simple and common in the NT.[5] The word προετοιμάζω, meaning "to prepare beforehand," is used in the NT only here and in Rom 9:23 both of which have God as the subject. The prefix προ- would in-

1. Cf. Ferdinand Hahn, "Taufe und Rechtfertigung. Ein Beitrag zur paulinischen Theologie in ihrer Vor- und Nachgeschichte," in *Rechtfertigung. Festschrift für Ernst Käsemann zum 70. Geburtstag*, ed. Johannes Friedrich, Wolfgang Pöhlmann, and Peter Stuhlmacher (Tübingen: Mohr; Göttingen: Vandenhoeck & Ruprecht, 1976), 101–3; Edvin Larsson, *Christus als Vorbild. Eine Untersuchung zu den paulinischen Tauf- und Eikontexten*, trans. Beatrice Steiner, ASNU, vol. 23 (Uppsala: Gleerup; København: Einar Munkgraar, 1962), 105–8; Warnach, "Taufwirklichkeit und Taufbewußtsein nach dem Epheserbrief," 39–43; Mußner, "Eph 2 als ökumenisches Modell," 329–31.

2. Robertson, *Grammar*, 605; Moule, *Idiom Book*, 50; BDF §235 (4); Zerwick, *Biblical Greek* §129; HS §184j β; BAGD 287; BDAG 366; G. H. R. Horsley, *New Documents Illustrating Early Christianity*, vol. 1, *A Review of the Greek Inscriptions and Papyri Published in 1976* (Sydney: Macquarie University, 1981), 46; David P. Kuske, "Exegetical Brief: Does Ephesians 2:10 Teach Sanctification or Not?" *WLQ* 92 (winter 1995): 51–52.

3. BAGD 2–3; BDAG 3–4; Erich Beyreuther, "Good, Beautiful, Kind [ἀγαθός, καλός, χρηστός]," *NIDNTT* 2 (1976): 98; Cremer, *Biblico-Theological Lexicon*, 3–6.

4. Eadie, 158–59.

5. Robertson, *Grammar*, 716; HS §289e; Winer, *Grammar*, 185–86.

dicate that God prepared these good works before the believer was created in Christ Jesus, most likely as a part of his plan in eternity past. This corresponds with 1:4 where it states that God "chose us in him before the foundation of the world in order that we might be holy and blameless before him in love." Hence, God not only chose his own before the foundation of the world to be holy and without blame, but he also prepared beforehand good works for them. But what good works did God prepare beforehand? It is the good works or conduct, given in chapters 4–6, that proceed from salvation. Before coming to faith, human beings exist in the sphere of bad works and were the objects of God's wrath. When they come to faith they are not left in a vacuum of no activity, but they have in this new creation works already prepared by God in eternity past. Not only did God predetermine eternal glory for the believers (1:5, 11; 2:6–7), but he has prepared beforehand good works for their present life.[1] This is grace from beginning to end. But what is the purpose of these good works prepared in advance? That is addressed next.

(iii) Purpose: Walk in Good Works (2:10c)

Text: 2:10c. ἵνα ἐν αὐτοῖς περιπατήσωμεν.

Translation: 2:10c. "in order that we might walk in them."

Commentary: 2:10c. ἵνα ἐν αὐτοῖς περιπατήσωμεν, "in order that we might walk in them." Several things need to be noted. First, the conjunction ἵνα, "in order that," shows the purpose of the good works prepared beforehand. We are God's workmanship because we were created in Christ Jesus for the goal of good works in order that we might walk in them. Second, the verb "walk" is an ingressive aorist subjunctive which "expresses the coming about of conduct which contrasts with prior conduct."[2] The only prior use of this verb in Ephesians is in 2:2 where it describes the walk of the unbeliever who is dead in transgressions and sins. Third, the use of "walk" in 2:10 suggests that these are the same works outlined for the believer in chapters 4–6 because the dominant theme of those chapters is the believer's "walk" (4:1, 17; 5:2, 8, 15). Fourth, it is interesting to notice that we are "to walk in them" and not "to work in them." God has prepared beforehand good works for believers that he will perform in and through them as they walk by faith in his power. It is not doing a work *for* God but God doing a work *in* and *through* the believer (Phil 2:13). Hence, the good works, also, cannot be a cause for boasting, as is the case in our salvation, because both elements are accomplished by God's grace by means of faith. If no good works are evident, it may indicate that that one is not a believer, because what God has purposed in the believer is not being accomplished. Works are not the

1. Klein, *The New Chosen People,* 188.
2. BDF §337 (1).

means of salvation—only faith is. But works are an evidence of salvation—God's working in the believer his prepared works. Verses 8–10 depict the essence of the gospel, probably the best summary in the Pauline corpus.[1] It is grace from start to finish.

In conclusion, 2:1–10 demonstrates that though people were spiritually dead and deserving only God's wrath, God, in his marvelous grace, has provided salvation through faith by making us alive, raising us, and seating us in the heavenlies in Christ Jesus. The origin of salvation is God, the basis is grace, the means is faith. Our salvation is not only a one time act of conversion, but also includes the activity of his workmanship in whom and through whom he performs the good works he has already prepared in advance.

Does this section refer to individual believers or believers as a collective group? Certainly, from 2:11 onwards Paul develops the idea of individual believers united with other believers into one body, but has he already begun developing this idea before verse 11? In reading 2:1–10 it seems that he is continuing to deal with the concept of individual believers that he had developed in chapter 1. He is showing that individual sinners were redeemed. Having delineated this, he is ready to develop the concept of the body beginning with 2:11 and following. To extrapolate the body concept from 2:1–10, the latter portion of the chapter must be read into these verses. It is necessary to establish the groundwork, that is, the individual saint's relationship to God, before Paul develops the relationship to each other in a body.[2] It is true that the church as a body is mentioned in 1:22–23 but it was pointing out that the same power, God's, that made Christ the head over everything is the same power resident in the individual believer. Thus, it does not refer to individual believers' relationship to each other.

1. C. Crowther, "Works, Work and Good Works," *ExpTim* 81 (March 1970): 170. For further discussion of the various themes of salvation in connection with other Pauline literature, see Andrew T. Lincoln, "Ephesians 2:8–10: A Summary of Paul's Gospel?" *CBQ* 45 (October 1983): 617–30; cf. also Mußner, "Eph 2 als ökumenisches Modell," 326–27; Luz, 134.

2. Cf. Rudolf Schnackenburg, "L'idée de «Corpus du Christ» dans la lettre aux Ephésiens; perspective pour notre temps," in *Paul de Tarse, apôtre de notre temps*, ed. Lorenzo De Lorenzi, Série monographique de «Benedictina» Section paulinienne, vol. 1 (Rome: Abbaye de S. Paul h.l.m., 1979), 667–69.

E. New Position Corporately (2:11–22)

Individual sinners have obtained the gracious gift of salvation on the basis of God's grace by faith. That is not the end. They are not left alone but are united with other believers into a corporate unity. In 2:11–22 Paul discusses this union of redeemed Jews and Gentiles in the church, Christ's body (cf. 1:22–23).[1] This forms the basis of the discussion for the rest of the epistle. As stated in the introduction, the dominant theme of this epistle is love, and certainly no union can be truly successful unless love is its basis and mode of operation. Ephesians 2:11–22 divides into three sections: the statement of the union (vv. 11–13), the explanation of the union of believing Jews and Gentiles into one "new humanity" (vv. 14–18), and the consequences of that union (vv. 19–22).

1. Statement of the Union (2:11–13)

The first thing Paul discusses about this union is that it is accomplished in Christ. Although Jews and Gentiles had nothing to do with

1. For a history of interpretation of Eph 2:11–22, see William Rader, *The Church and Racial Hostility: A History of Interpretation of Ephesians 2:11–22*, Beiträge zur Geschichte der biblischen Exegese, ed. Oscar Cullmann et al., vol. 20 (Tübingen: Mohr, 1978). Giavini suggests a highly complex chiastic structure of 2:11–22 with "having made the both one" (v. 14) as the central core. He has two chiasms, one within the other. First, he has C (11–12), B (13), A (14a, he is our peace): X (14b–16): A′ (17a, he came and preached peace), B′ (17b–18), C′ (19–20). Second, he has a chiasm within X: a (v. 14, he made the both one), b (destroyed the middle wall of partition), c (the hostility), d (in his flesh): e (v. 15, having rendered inoperative the law of commandments in decrees): a′ (in order that he might create in himself the two into one new person, so

each other before Calvary, both Jews and Gentiles who are in Christ have been united by the blood of Christ. Thus, it is not Jews and Gentiles per se that have been united but Jews and Gentiles in Christ that have been united by the work of Christ. This is really no baptismal motif as some suggest.[1]

a. Past Disunion (2:11–12)

Before discussing the union, Paul wants to state clearly the issue of the great gulf between Jews and Gentiles. Paul shows that the Jews considered the Gentiles uncircumcised, indicating that they had no favor with God because they lacked the covenant seal. Furthermore, not only were they not circumcised but they had none of the privileges that God graciously gave to the Jews. This is a similar pattern to 2:1–6 where Paul clearly states the dilemma of human beings prior to the gracious act of God's love, namely, redemption. In that context it spoke of the transfer from sinner to saint, and here it is a description of the transference of the hostility between the Jews and Gentiles to that of reconciliation in Christ.

(1) Uncircumcised (2:11)

Text: 2:11. Διὸ μνημονεύετε ὅτι ποτὲ ὑμεῖς τὰ ἔθνη ἐν σαρκί, οἱ λεγόμενοι ἀκροβυστία ὑπὸ τῆς λεγομένης περιτομῆς ἐν σαρκὶ χειροποιήτου,

Translation: 2:11. "Therefore remember that formerly you, the Gentiles in the flesh, the ones who are called 'uncircumcision' by the so-called 'circumcision' which is performed in the flesh by hands,"

---

making peace), b´ (v. 16, and that he might reconcile them both in one body to God through the cross), c´ (the hostility has been killed), d´ (in himself, by it [the cross]). See Giovanni Giavini, "La Structure Littéraire d'Eph ii.11–22," *NTS* 16 (January 1970): 209–11. This is an interesting analysis, but it is highly complicated as well as being inconsistent in that with the upper case he goes backwards (CBA) and then forwards (A´B´C´) whereas with the lower case he goes forward both times (abcd:e:a´b´c´d´). He admits that it is an inconsistent chiastic pattern. It seems highly unlikely that any author would have purposely constructed such a complicated chiastic pattern. Other chiastic structures have been proposed by Kirby: A (11a), B (11b), C (12a), D (12b), E (12c), F (12d), G (13a), H (13b), I (14a), J (14b), K (14c–15a), K´ (15b–c), J´ (15d–16b), I´(16c), H´ (17a), G´ (17b), F´(18), E´ (19a), D´ (19b), C´ (20), B´ (21), A´ (22) (*Ephesians, Baptism and Pentecost*, 156–57); and Thomson: A (11a), B (11b–c), C (12a), D (12b), E (12c), F (12d), G (13 [subdivided]), H (14 [subdivided]), I (15a), I´ (15b), H´ (15c–16 [subdivided]), G´ (17 [subdivided]), F´ (18), E´ (19a), D´ (19b), C´ (20), B´ (21), A´ (22) (*Chiasmus in the Pauline Letters*, 84–115, esp. 93, who refined what had been proposed by Kenneth Ewing Bailey, *Poet and Peasant: A Literary Cultural Approach to the Parables in Luke* [Grand Rapids: Eerdmans, 1976], 63). All of these chiastic structures seem to be highly complex and again it is doubtful that Paul constructed this with a chiastic structure in mind. For a rhetorical analysis of 2:11–22, see Jeal, *Integrating Theology and Ethics in Ephesians*, 146–63.

1. Cf. Dahl, "Dopet i Efesierbrevet," 89–90.

Commentary: 2:11. Διὸ[1] μνημονεύετε, "Therefore remember." Paul begins this section with the strong inferential conjunction διό (from δι᾽ ὅ), which can be translated "therefore, for this reason,"[2] to alert the Gentiles of the unenviable position of their having no relationship with God. The conjunction not only draws from the immediately previous sentence but from 2:1–10, which delineates the universal depravity of humans and God's redemptive grace. Although all people were in a desperate situation, Paul implies that the Gentiles were worse off (and were considered far off, v. 13) than the Jews since God had given Israel the revelation of the OT along with certain privileges which the Gentiles did not have. But this is only one side of the coin, for he is also going to show that though the Gentiles were far from God, the Jews also had to be brought to God. Therefore, both are now in Christ and have the same standing and privileges before him. Nevertheless, it is important for the Gentiles to remember their peculiar dilemma in the past. The present imperative may suggest continuance, and hence the Gentiles were to continue to remember their former plight.

ὅτι ποτὲ ὑμεῖς τὰ ἔθνη ἐν σαρκί, "that formerly you, the Gentiles in the flesh." The ὅτι, "that," introduces the content of what the Ephesian Gentiles were to hear. Immediately following, for emphasis, is the enclitic particle ποτέ, indicating time which can be properly translated "formerly" in contrast to the "now" in verse 13. It refers to the time before either the Jews or the Gentiles had obtained the gracious gift of salvation, and Paul reminds them of how they were viewed by the Jews. The pronoun ὑμεῖς is in the first part of the sentence for emphasis which is further described by τὰ ἔθνη ἐν σαρκί, "the Gentiles in the flesh." The article τά denotes a whole class[3] and the fact that it is not repeated before ἐν σαρκί indicates one idea with the noun.[4] They are not just "Gentiles" but "Gentiles in the flesh." The reference "in the flesh" could denote what they were before they were "in Christ" (v. 13).[5] Although this has validity, the Jews also were "in the flesh" and hence before God neither Jews nor Gentiles were "in Christ." However, in the immediate context the contrast is between Jews and

1. This conjunction, omitted by 104 it[d] Victorinus-Rome Ambrosiaster, is replaced by διὰ τοῦτο in F G. It can be seen that there is no strong support for either of these options. The conjunction διό is found in all the other manuscripts and thus it has good representative manuscripts from a wide geographical spread.

2. BAGD 198; BDAG 250; Einar Molland, "Διο, Einige syntaktische Beobachtungen," in *Serta Rudbergiana*, ed. H. Holst and H. Mørland, Symbolae Osloenses, Fasc. Supplet. IV (Oslo: A. W. Brøgger, 1931), 43–52; reprinted in idem, "Διο: Einige syntaktische Beobachtungen," in *Opuscula Patristica*, ed. Einar Molland, Biblotheca Theologica Norvegica, ed. Åge Holter, Johan B. Hygen, Alv Kragerud, and John Nome, Nr. 2 (Oslo: Universitetsforlaget, 1970), 9–16.

3. Winer, *Grammar*, 132; cf. BDF §262.

4. Winer, *Grammar*, 169; cf. BDF §272; Robertson, *Grammar*, 782–83.

5. Barth, 254.

Gentiles as evidenced in their flesh or body. Paul is stating that the Jews considered the Gentiles inferior just by what can be observed in the flesh. Paul proceeds to describe this.

οἱ λεγόμενοι ἀκροβυστία, "the ones who are called 'uncircumcision.'" The Gentiles were designated as "uncircumcised." The term ἀκροβυστία, "uncircumcision," is anarthrous and thus is given the qualitative force of contempt in this context. It is derived from the adjective ἄκρος, which means "running up to a point" or "that which stands on the outer edge," and from the verb βύω, which means "to stop up" or "close"; hence, it means "foreskin."[1] Therefore, with contempt the Jews considered "the Gentiles in the flesh" as those with foreskins.

ὑπὸ τῆς λεγομένης περιτομῆς ἐν σαρκὶ χειροποιήτου, "by the so-called 'circumcision' which is performed in the flesh by hands." Here Paul identifies "the so-called circumcision" as those who label Gentiles as "foreskins." The verb form of the term περιτομῆς, "circumcision," literally means "to cut around" with a view to remove,[2] and hence it is the cutting off of the foreskin. The Jews were widely known in the ancient world as those who were circumcised.[3] They were proud of the distinctive of circumcision, a God-ordained covenantal sign that goes back to Abraham (Gen 17:9–14). Paul, in his preconversion days, was proud to state that he was "circumcised on the eighth day" (Phil 3:5), and it seems that Jews were zealous to have Gentiles circumcised so that they would come under the covenant (Gal 6:12–13; cf. 5:2–6, 11; Phil 3:2–3). The prepositional phrase "in the flesh" has reference to where this circumcision was done. This is further defined by the genitival adjective of means χειροποιήτου, namely, "being performed with the hands." This word is used in the OT of making idols (Isa 2:18; 10:11) and in all the other occurrences in the NT it is used of constructing a temple (Mark 14:58; Acts 7:48; 17:24; Heb 9:11, 24). This adjective always depicts what a person does with his or her hands in contrast to the work of God.[4] Physical circumcision is in contrast with circumcision of the heart (Rom 2:28–29; Phil 3:2–3; Col 2:11). In the present context the contrast is between the Jew who has this physical mark in his flesh and the Gentile who has his foreskin, and is thus disdained by the Jew. The gracious work of Christ in the lives of both Jew and Gentile profoundly changed this situation.

Some suggest that the description of the Gentiles as "Gentiles in the flesh" who are called "uncircumcision" and that of the Jews as

1. Karl Ludwig Schmidt, "ἀκροβυστία," *TDNT* 1 (1964): 225.

2. Rudolf Meyer, "περιτέμνω, περιτομή, ἀπερίτμητος," *TDNT* 6 (1968): 73.

3. Ernest Best, "Ephesians 2.11–22: A Christian View of Judaism," in *Text as Pretext: Essays in Honour of Robert Davidson*, ed. Robert P. Carroll, Journal for the Study of the Old Testament Supplement Series, ed. David J. A. Clines and Philip R. Davies, vol. 138 (Sheffield: JSOT Press, 1992), 48.

4. Eduard Lohse, "χειροποίητος, ἀχειροποίητος," *TDNT* 9 (1974): 436.

"circumcision which is performed in the flesh by hands" suggest that some period of time had elapsed since Paul disputed with the Jews during the time of his ministry. The fact that the author asked them to remember who they were indicates that he was addressing a second generation of Gentile believers, some time after Paul.[1] These descriptions are not proofs of late date and authorship.[2] Paul is using these descriptions only to make it vivid and to remind the Gentiles not to forget their past alienation from God and the great disparity between them and the Jews. Believing Gentiles now have the privilege to be united with believing Jews in one body. The Gentiles, who were probably in the majority, could easily forget history and look with arrogance toward the Jews. This is not unlike what Paul did in Rom 11:11–24 (esp. vv. 17–20).

(2) Unprivileged (2:12)

Text: 2:12. ὅτι ἦτε τῷ καιρῷ ἐκείνῳ χωρὶς Χριστοῦ, ἀπηλλοτριωμένοι τῆς πολιτείας τοῦ Ἰσραὴλ καὶ ξένοι τῶν διαθηκῶν τῆς ἐπαγγελίας, ἐλπίδα μὴ ἔχοντες καὶ ἄθεοι ἐν τῷ κόσμῳ.

Translation: 2:12. "that you were at that time without Christ, being alienated from the citizenship of Israel and strangers to the covenants of promise, having no hope and without God in the world."

Commentary: 2:12. ὅτι ἦτε τῷ καιρῷ ἐκείνῳ, "that you were at that time." The ὅτι is resumptive of the ὅτι in verse 11. In verse 11 Paul asks the Gentiles to remember how the Jews contemptuously considered their lack of the external sign of circumcision, and now he continues by asking them to remember that they also lacked five privileges that God had given to the nation Israel. The imperfect verb ἦτε, "were," and the temporal datives τῷ καιρῷ ἐκείνω, "at that time" (which designate a point of time[3]) refer back to the period corresponding to that of the enclitic particle ποτέ in verse 11, that is, the extended period of time[4] before conversion in which they did not have these five privileges.

χωρὶς Χριστοῦ, "without Christ." The improper preposition χωρίς is translated "without" (AV, NRSV) or "separate(d) from" (RV, ASV, RSV, NASB, NEB, JB, NIV, NJB). The Gentiles were not only separate from Christ personally, which was true also of many Jews, but morever they had no national hope of the Messiah as did Israel. Israel had this hope because of OT revelation of the promised Messiah (e.g., Gen 49:10; Deut 18:15; Pss 2; 45:3–5, 17 [MT 45:4–6, 18; LXX 44:4–6, 18]; 89:22–

1. Cf. Beare, 10:599, 649; Ralph P. Martin, *Reconciliation: A Study of Paul's Theology*, 159–60; reprint, idem, "Reconciliation and Unity in Ephesians," 205; Lincoln, 136.

2. Cf. Caird, 55.

3. BDF §200 (4); MHT 3:243.

4. Barr, *Biblical Words for Time*, 41; Burns, "Two Words for 'Time' in the New Testament," 17.

25 [MT 89:23–26; LXX 88:23–26]; 110 [LXX 109]; Isa 7:14; 9:1–7 [MT & LXX 8:23–9:6]; 42:1–4; Mic 5:1–4 [MT & LXX 4:14–5:2]; Dan 7:13–14; Zech 9:9–10). This hope continued among the Jews after the close of the OT canon.[1] One of the privileges Paul claims that the Jews had was that Messiah would come from Jewish lineage (Rom 9:4–5). The Jews felt that a deliverer would come and rescue them from their enemies. Hence, another possible translation of "without Christ" could be "without the Messiah."

ἀπηλλοτριωμένοι τῆς πολιτείας τοῦ Ἰσραήλ, "being alienated from the citizenship of Israel," further expands the idea of Gentiles without Christ. The participle derived from ἀπαλλοτριόω is used only two other times in the NT (Eph 4:18; Col 1:21), always in a perfect participial form, meaning "excluded" or "alienated."[2] It is dependent on the imperfect finite verb "to be" (ἦτε), followed by the genitives of separation, and expresses the manner of being separated from Christ, namely, "having been alienated from the citizenship of Israel." This citizenship is the second privilege the Gentiles lacked and never had. The perfect tense gives emphasis on the continuing results of alienation up to the time of the writing of this epistle. This is followed by a genitive of separation (τῆς πολιτείας),[3] which in turn is followed by a possessive genitive (τοῦ Ἰσραήλ), hence alienated from the citizenship that belongs to Israel.

The term πολιτεία is used in classical Greek with reference to citizenship,[4] or with reference to a commonwealth or state.[5] It appears eight times in the LXX but not in the canonical books. In Maccabees it generally has reference to a way of life (e.g., 2 Macc 8:17; 4 Macc 17:9). Hence, the term can be taken in three ways: citizenship, commonwealth or state, or a way of life or conduct. The term appears only twice in the NT. In Acts 22:28 it refers to a Roman commander who has purchased his "citizenship." In the present context, although earlier commentators thought πολιτεία referred to "a manner of life" (Vg),[6] the more recent commentators think it refers either to the state or commonwealth (AV, RV, ASV, RSV, NASB, NRSV) of Israel[7] or to citizenship or membership (JB, NIV, NJB) of Israel.[8] Of these last two interpretations, the first has reference to a commonwealth, state, or body poli-

1. Cf. *Targum Neofiti I* Gen 49:9–12; Exod 12:42; Num 24:7, 17, 19.

2. BAGD 80; BDAG 96.

3. MHT 3:235; Wallace, *Greek Grammar*, 108.

4. Herodotus 9.34; Thucydides 6.104.2.

5. Thucydides 1.127.3; Aristotle *Politica* 1.5.12 §1260b.21.

6. Chrysostom *Eph* 2:11–12 (*PG* 62:37); Jerome *Eph* 2:12 (*PL* 26:472); Theophylact *Eph* 2:12 (*PG* 124:1057); Aquinas, chap. 2, lec. 4, vv. 11–13 (100).

7. Bengel, 4:77; Alford, 3:95–96; Eadie, 164–65; Ellicott, 44–45; Meyer, 122; Abbott, 57–588; Salmond, 292; Westcott, 35; Hendriksen, 129; Lincoln, 137; O'Brien, 189; BAGD 686; BDAG 845.

8. Ewald, 134; Schlier, 120; Gaugler, 103; Barth, 257–58; Schnackenburg, 109–10; Best, 241; cf. Rudolf Schnackenburg, "Die Politeia Israels in Eph 2,12," in *De la Tôrah*

tic, whereas the last has reference to a citizenship, a figurative sense of belonging to a group, here the privileged community of Israel chosen by God as recipients of the promise. In the present context the last view is preferred because the whole context discusses the privileges of belonging to a group of people who had a relationship with God. Furthermore, in verse 19 Paul states that we are fellow citizens with all the saints, not with fellow countrymen. In addition, the meaning of citizenship is more inclusive than the meaning of state or commonwealth because one can be a resident of a state and not be a citizen and hence would not feel a part of that state. On the other hand, a citizen can feel that he belongs to a state, whether or not he is living in it. The Ephesians could relate well to this concept for they knew what it was like to live within the political state of Rome without being a citizen of Rome with all the accompanying privileges. Besides, in reality there was no commonwealth of Israel functioning as an independent state in Paul's day. Rather it was part of the commonwealth or political state of Rome. Moreover, it is doubtful that the Greek believers of Asia would have sought to be members of the political state of Israel.[1] What they sought was the citizenship of Israel because of the special privileges God bestowed on her. Up to this time, some Gentiles were admitted into Judaism as proselytes, but as a whole, Gentiles were excluded and thus alienated from the citizenship of Israel.

καὶ ξένοι τῶν διαθηκῶν τῆς ἐπαγγελίας, "and strangers to the covenants of promise." The third lack of the Ephesians before conversion is that they had no relationship to the covenants God had made with his people Israel. The word ξένος means in general a "stranger, foreigner"[2] who is allowed to be in a country but with no rights, except what has been agreed to by treaty. In the LXX it occurs twenty times and in the canonical books it appears nine times, five times from נָכְרִי, with the same essential meaning of "foreigner"[3] (Ruth 2:10; 2 Sam 15:19; Ps 69:8 [MT 69:9; LXX 68:9]; Eccl 6:2; Lam 5:2). In the NT it is used fourteen times, three times by Paul (Rom 16:23; Eph 2:12, 19) with the idea of "stranger, foreigner."[4] In the present context it is anarthrous, which gives a qualitative force to it,[5] meaning that the Gentiles were truly foreigners to the covenants of promise. This is en-

au Messie. Études d'exégèse et d'herméneutique bibliques offertes à Henri Cazelles pour ses 25 anées d'enseignement à l'Institut Catholique de Paris (Octobre 1979), ed. Maurice Carrez, Joseph Doré, and Pierre Grelot (Paris: Descleé, 1981), 467–74; Hermann Strathmann, "πολιτεία," *TDNT* 6 (1968): 534–35.

1. Strathmann, *TDNT* 6 (1968): 534.

2. Hesiod *Opera et Dies* 225; Sophocles *Oedipus Coloneus* 13

3. BDB 648; B. Lang and H. Ringgren, "נכר *nkr*; נֵכָר *nēkār*; נָכְרִי *nokrî*," *TDOT* 9 (1998): 423–29.

4. For further study, see Gustav Stählin, "ξένος κτλ.," *TDNT* 5 (1967): 1–36.

5. Robertson, *Grammar*, 782.

hanced by the genitives of separation (τῶν διαθηκῶν)[1] following "strangers." The use of the plural "covenants" is significant, for out of the thirty-three times it is used in the NT it is always singular except in three cases (Rom 9:4; Gal 4:24; Eph 2:12). Hence, the plural "covenants" must be taken seriously.[2] Another factor that needs to be considered in the discussion of these covenants is that they are the covenants of "promise." Certainly a promise or promises are contained in the covenants, but the term ἐπαγγελία, "promise," appears only eight times in the LXX, three times in the canonical books (Esth 4:7; Ps 56:8 [MT 56:9; LXX 55:9]; Amos 9:6), appearing more often in later Jewish writings (1 Esdr 1:7; 1 Macc 10:15; 4 Macc 12:9; Ode 12:6; *Pss. Sol.* 12:6; Josephus *A.J.* 2.9.4 §219; 3.1.5 §24; Philo *Mut.* 37 §201).[3] It is used fifty-two times in the NT, twenty-six times by Paul, and four times in Ephesians (1:13; 2:12; 3:6; 6:2).

Hendriksen proposes that "covenants" refer to the *one* covenant of grace with *many* reaffirmations and hence the plural designation "covenants."[4] This is a concocted theological covenant derived from many proof texts from various contexts but has no real basis in Scripture. Scripture does not have a covenant called the "covenant of grace." Also, why would the Gentiles be "strangers" to the covenant of grace since the covenant of grace has nothing to do with national distinctions? Moreover, using the term "reaffirmations" does not do justice to the plural "covenants." This theory should not be taken seriously for it is an example of theology controlling exegesis rather than exegesis controlling theology.

Calvin thought the plural referred to the "tables" of the Mosaic law[5] but it is never so designated in the NT. The Mosaic law is designated three ways: most often as νόμος (e.g., Matt 7:12; Rom 2:12–15; Gal 2:16*ter*; Heb 7:5, 19, 28*bis*; Jas 2:10); as νομοθεσία (Rom 9:4), which is listed with αἱ διαθῆκαι, indicating that the covenants were different from the Mosaic law; or as the singular διαθήκη when it is contrasted with the "new covenant" (e.g., 2 Cor 3:6, 14; Heb 8:6, 8, 9*bis*, 10; 9:4*bis*, 15*bis*, 20). Hence, the plural form of the word rules out the possiblity of reference to the Mosaic covenant. Furthermore, not only are these covenants plural but they are also designated as the covenants of "promise." The Mosaic law cannot be thought of as a covenant of promise for it is a conditional covenant, meaning that God would bless the nation Israel when it collectively obeyed him. In fact, the Mosaic law and the promise to Abraham are starkly contrasted in Rom 4:13–17 and Gal 3:6–4:31. Also, Paul lists the Mosaic covenant

1. MHT 3:215; Moule, *Idiom Book*, 41; Robertson, *Grammar*, 516.
2. Winer, *Grammar*, 221; BDF §141 (8); MHT 3:27.
3. This idea comes from Best although I was unable to use some of the passages he suggests (see Best, "Ephesians 2.11–22: A Christian View of Judaism," 56).
4. Hendriksen, 130.
5. Calvin, 148.

separately from the covenants (of promise) (cf. Rom 9:4).[1] Finally, the Mosaic law has been rendered inoperative for those who are in Christ (Rom 7:1–6; 10:4; Gal 2:19; 3:24–25). How could it be a covenant of promise if it has been replaced by the new covenant?

Best suggests that the "covenants" refer to the Abrahamic covenant (Gen 12, 15) and the new covenant (Jer 31:31–34) and that Christians believe that the first covenant made with Abraham has been replaced by the new covenant which was fulfilled in Christ in connection with the eucharist.[2] However, throughout the NT the new covenant replaces the Mosaic covenant and not the Abrahamic covenant.

It is best to consider that the covenants of promise refer to the unconditional covenants. The primary covenant of promise mentioned in Rom 4 is the Abrahamic covenant which promises land, seed, and blessings (Gen 12:1–4; 13:14–18; 15:1–21; 17:1–21). The other covenants of promise that enhance the Abrahamic covenant are the Davidic covenant (2 Sam 7:12–17; 23:5; Pss 89:3, 27–37, 49 [MT 89:4, 28–38, 50; LXX 88:4, 28–38, 50]; 132:11–12 [LXX 131:11–12]) and the new covenant (Jer 31:31–34; 32:38–40; Ezek 36:23–36). These three specific covenants are unconditional and correspond to the covenants of promise mentioned in the present context. Thus, both the plurality and the promise aspects demanded in this context are taken into account. The reason the Gentiles in Ephesus were "strangers" to these covenants is because they were covenants that God made with the nation Israel that contained promises for that nation. The particular promises were land, seed, and blessing. First, Israel as a nation had been promised a land from the days of Abraham right until the last prophet in the OT (Jer 16:15; 23:3–8; Ezek 11:17; 34:13; 36:24, 28; 39:25–29; Hos 1:10–11; Joel 3:17–21; Amos 9:11–15; Mic 4:4–7; Zeph 3:14–20; Zech 8:4–8). Second, Israel was promised a continued seed whereby the nation of Israel would continue to exist, but more particularly the seed of David that would bring forth the Messiah who would head up that nation (Ps 89:3–4, 34–36 [MT 89:4–5, 35–37; LXX 88:4–5, 35–37]; Isa 9:6–7; Jer 23:5–6; 30:8–9; 33:14–17, 20–21; Ezek 37:24–25; Hos 3:4–5; Amos 9:11; Zech 14:3–9). And third, they were promised the blessing of the new covenant by which they would know God and have the law written in their hearts rather than on tablets of stone (Jer 31:31–34; Ezek 11:19–20; 16:60–62; 36:24–28; 37:26–28; cf. also Isa 59:21; 61:8–9). Gentiles did not have the covenants of promise and thus were alienated or excluded from them. This has changed, as will be discussed at 2:13–22, esp. verses 19–22.

1. *Contra* O'Brien (189 n. 139) who thinks that in the present context the "covenants" refer to the Abrahamic covenant and the Mosaic covenant. However, in the present context Paul refers to the Mosaic covenant not as "covenant" but as "the law of commandments in decrees" (2:15) which seems to indicate a distinction between the covenants of promise and the Siniatic covenant.

2. Best, 242.

ἐλπίδα μὴ ἔχοντες, "having no hope." Hope is the fourth privilege the Gentiles lacked. This logically follows the last deficiency, for if they lacked the covenants of promise then they would also lack hope. A study of the word ἐλπίς, "hope," is made in 1:18 where it was concluded that believers in the OT as well as in the NT have an eager expectation of the future as they trust in the outworking of God's plan. It was an objective hope based on the promises of God. The fact that it is anarthrous would not limit their lack of hope to a specific thing such as the lack of *the* messianic hope. It is, rather, the more general idea of lacking any kind of hope.[1] Its position in the sentence enhances their hopelessness. The present participle gives an action of what regularly occurred before the main verb (μνημονεύετε)[2] and, hence, they were to remember that in the former times they were continually without any sort of hope. The negative particle μή is normal with participles[3] and thus it does not denote some sort of significance indicated by some commentators.[4] Because the Gentiles did not have Israel's privilege of God's revelation, they had nothing to look forward to. They had no expectation that God would work in their lives. They had no knowledge of salvation that would include a future resurrection and life eternal. They had no idea of future messianic deliverance and blessings.

καὶ ἄθεοι ἐν τῷ κόσμῳ, "and without God in the world." This is the fifth and final lack of the Gentiles. The adjective ἄθεος is the word from which we derive the English word "atheist." In classical literature it is used in the sense of one who does not believe in the gods,[5] or one who is ungodly or impious, or one who has a disdain toward the gods and their laws,[6] or one who is abandoned by the gods.[7] It is not found in the LXX and only here in the NT. The Gentiles accuse the Jews[8] and the Christians[9] of being atheists because they do not believe in the gods. In the present context, the reference to God is not to some pagan deity but to the one true God revealed in the Scriptures. The Gentiles may have felt abandoned by the God of Scripture, but God purposed that Israel was to be a priest among the nations (Exod 19:5–6) and thus Gentiles were accepted to participate in the worship of the true God (Exod 12:48; 1 Kgs 8:41–43; Isa 11:10). Furthermore, the Jews may have rebuffed the Gentiles because of God's many warnings

1. Salmond, 292; Abbott, 58–59.
2. Moule, *Idiom Book*, 206.
3. Robertson, *Grammar*, 1137; BDF §430; MHT 3:284–85.
4. E.g., Salmond, 292; Abbott, 59.
5. Plato *Apologia* 26c.
6. Pindar *Pythain Odes* 4.162; Aeschylus *Eumenides* 151; Sophocles *Trachiniae* 1036.
7. Sophocles *Oedipus Tyrannus* 661.
8. Josephus *C. Ap.* 2.14 §148.
9. Justin Martyr *Apologia* 1.6, 13; *Martyrdom of Polycarp* 9.2a. Polycarp also accused the pagans of being atheists (ibid. 9.2b).

for them not to mix with pagan idolatrous worship. Still, it may well be that the Gentiles were impious or ungodly in their conduct because they did not know God's revelation. However, it seems that the primary intent of this passage is that they did not believe in God. Though they believed in many gods, they neither believed in nor desired the one true God (Rom 1:18–23). They were without God in this world. The prepositional phrase "in the world" probably has reference both to their lack of hope and to their unbelief in God. The Ephesians were in this world without any hope or trust in God, the creator and redeemer.

In conclusion, Paul asks the Ephesians to remember their situation before conversion when they were considered uncircumcised by the Jews. They were a people who lacked five distinct privileges that the Jews enjoyed. These were provided to Israel because God revealed himself and made covenants with this nation. It does not mean that the Jews took full advantage of this privileged situation, as seen in both the OT and NT, but they had a distinct advantage over the Gentiles. Paul shows next that though the Jews had advantages over the Gentiles in the past, God has made it possible for both Jews and Gentiles in Christ to be equal before God. This does not mean that the nation Israel becomes the church, for Israel still exists as a separate entity apart from the church (Rom 9:1–5).[1] Paul demonstrates that believing Jews and Gentiles become the church (Eph 2:13–22) but that unbelieving Jews and Gentiles still remain as two separate entities distinct from the church (1 Cor 10:32).

b. Present Union (2:13)

The following verse contrasts the past condition of the Ephesians with their present state, subsequent to their conversion.

Text: 2:13. νυνὶ δὲ ἐν Χριστῷ Ἰησοῦ ὑμεῖς οἵ ποτε ὄντες μακρὰν ἐγενήθητε ἐγγὺς ἐν τῷ αἵματι τοῦ Χριστοῦ.

Translation: 2:13. "But now in Christ Jesus you who formerly were far away have been brought near by the blood of Christ."

Commentary: 2:13. νυνὶ δὲ ἐν Χριστῷ Ἰησοῦ, "But now in Christ Jesus," denotes the contrast between their present condition and that prior to conversion. There are three notes of contrast. First is the adversative δέ, "but." Second is νυνί, "now," which expresses their present condition and this is in contrast to the time indicated by ποτέ, "formerly," (v. 11)[2] and τῷ καιρῷ ἐκείνῳ, "in that time," (v. 12) which denote the time before conversion. Third is the change in locale to indicate relationships; before conversion they were χωρὶς Χριστοῦ "sepa-

1. Cf. Martin Rese, "Die Vorzüge Israels in Röm. 9,4f. und Eph. 2,12. Exegetische Anmerkungen zum Thema Kirche und Israel," *TZ* 31 (Juli/August 1975): 211–22.

2. Tachau, *„Einst" und „Jetzt" im Neuen Testament*, 140–41.

rated from Christ" (v. 12), but now are ἐν Χριστῷ Ἰησοῦ, "in Christ Jesus." Again the preposition ἐν with the dative denotes location and also relationship. Thus, their position is really "in Christ Jesus" rather than "in the world" (v. 12) or "dead in trespasses and sins" (vv. 1, 5). Those who were separated from Christ are now in Christ Jesus. This is a radical change. The name "Jesus" is added to be sure that the Gentiles as well as the Jews would be cognizant that Christ the Messiah is identified as the Jesus who was on earth.

ὑμεῖς οἵ ποτε ὄντες μακρὰν ἐγενήθητε ἐγγὺς, "you who formerly were far away have been brought near." The pronoun ὑμεῖς, "you," which refers back to "you, the Gentiles in the flesh" in verse 11, is emphatic by its mere mention as well as its repetition in the context. Paul gives two more contrasts. First is the contrast of the Gentiles who were μακράν, "far away," and are now ἐγγύς, "near."[1] Lincoln rightly points out that the terms "far" and "near" were used in the OT to describe the Gentile nations as "far off" (Deut 28:49; 29:22; 1 Kgs 8:41; Isa 5:26; Jer 5:15) while describing Israel as "near" (Ps 148:14).[2] The idea of "come or brought near" was also used in Qumran when one became a member of the community and in the rabbinic literature for the "far," the non-Israelite, who was accepted as a proselyte in Israel.[3] However, in the present context the reference is to their being brought near to God, "not by being turned into a Jew, but by being included along with the Jew *in Christ Jesus*."[4] The Jews were near to God because they had the revelation of God, which explained their approach to God. The Gentiles, lacking this revelation, were far away but by the work of Christ had been brought near to God. Second, the repetition of the enclitic particle ποτέ (cf. v. 11) specifies by implication what the Gentiles "formerly" were in contrast to what they are now. The adverb "now" is not used because the emphasis is on the action "having been brought near," which occurred when they trusted in Christ's blood. However, that state of their nearness continued even after they read this letter. Although the participle is present tense in form, it refers to a repeated action that is determined by the enclitic particle ποτέ, which indicates that they were formerly far away.[5] Some, thinking this is a Gnostic document, attempt to see the νυνὶ . . . ποτέ as a contrast not of the temporal but of two existential situations.[6] However, the whole context argues for the temporal contrast between the Gentiles' past and present relationship to God. The verb ἐγενήθητε, "have been brought," is a passive which indicates that the Gentiles were re-

1. Cf. MHT 3:226.

2. Lincoln, 138–39.

3. J. A. Loader, "An Explanation of the Term *Prosēlutos*," *NovT* 15 (October 1973): 270–77.

4. Caird, 56–57.

5. Robertson, *Grammar*, 1115, 1139.

6. Steinmetz, *Protologische Heils-Zuversicht*, 66; Lindemann, *Aufhebung*, 155.

cipients of God's action rather than a result of self-effort as already discussed at 2:8–10. The aorist may indicate an emphasis on past action of Christ's death as the means by which the "drawing near" of the Gentiles was accomplished. To consider this a reference to baptism seems farfetched.[1] The method by which they were drawn near is the subject of the next phrase.

ἐν τῷ αἵματι τοῦ[2] Χριστοῦ, "by the blood of Christ." The preposition ἐν shows the instrumental means or cause of bringing the Gentiles near. This preposition has much the same import as διά in verse 7. Smith contends that the "blood of Christ" refers to the circumcision of Christ because of the mention of circumcision which is performed in the flesh by hands in verse 11.[3] But this is unwarranted for the context speaks of Christ's death on the cross (v. 16) as that which achieved the reconciliation, not his circumcision. Rather, the significance of the "blood of Christ," discussed in 1:7, speaks of the sacrificial death of Christ which was necessary to propitiate God's demand of holiness (cf. Rom 3:25; 5:9; 1 Cor 10:16, 11:25, 27; cf. Heb 9:12, 14; 10:19, 29; 13:12, 20; 1 Pet 1:2, 19; 1 John 1:7). Here again, as frequently in Ephesians, the article precedes the noun "Christ" emphasizing that by the blood of Israel's promised Messiah, reconciliation was accomplished. As the sacrificial death of Christ is the only means of redemption, so also is it the only means of reconciliation.[4] The cost of bringing the Gentile *near* was dear.

In conclusion, the Gentiles, in contrast to the Jews, were far off because they lacked privileges which God had given to the Jews. This status also affected the relationship between Jews and Gentiles. Yet God took the initiative to bring the Gentiles near to God. This union needs further explanation, specifically what it achieved. That is what Paul discusses next in verses 14–18.

2. Explanation of the Union (2:14–18)

Having discussed the new union of Jews and Gentiles in Christ in light of their former disunion, Paul now gives a further explanation of how this union was accomplished. This is an important section to understand, for it gives insight into the deep rift between the Jews and Gentiles before Christ and what God did in Christ to bring the two entities into one entity.

1. As does Fung, "The Doctrine of Baptism in Ephesians," 8–9.

2. The article τοῦ is omitted by only 𝔓[46] and B (0278) which is not sufficient enough to reject it.

3. Derwood Cooper Smith, "Jewish and Greek Traditions in Ephesians 2:11–22" (Ph.D. diss., Yale University, 1970), 44–50; idem, "The Ephesian Heresy and the Origin of the Epistle to the Ephesians," 86–90.

4. Bruce, 295.

This particular section is a distinct unit of thought, most likely a digression. It begins in verse 14 with the conjunction γάρ, "for," and ends in verse 18. Verse 19 begins a new section marked with the conjunctions ἄρα οὖν, "consequently therefore." There has been much speculation regarding the origin of this section. Some have thought that its origin is from a pre-Christian Gnostic redeemer myth which speaks of the union of heavenly and earthly worlds in mythological terminology,[1] but that is generally not accepted today because it just does not fit the context.[2] Rather, the context speaks of the reconciliation of redeemed Jews and Gentiles to each other and to God from whom both were estranged. Others have thought of it as an early Christian hymn,[3] but this has also been called into question.[4] Even among its advocates there is disagreement as to where the hymn ends[5] and how it is to be divided. Others think it speaks of the believ-

1. Schlier, *Christus und die Kirche im Epheserbrief*, 18–37; Schlier and Warnach, *Die Kirche im Epheserbrief*, 83–88; Schlier, 122–40; Ernst Käsemann, "Meditationen: Epheser 2,17–22," in *Exegetische Versuche und Besinnungen*, vol. 1 (Göttingen: Vandenhoeck & Ruprecht, 1964), 280–83; Pokorný, *Der Epheserbrief und die Gnosis*, 114–15; Lindemann, *Aufhebung*, 161–70; Gerhard Wilhelmi, "Der Versöhner-Hymnus in Eph 2:14ff," *ZNW* 78, nos. 1/2 (1987): 145–52.

2. Cf. Mussner, *Christus, das All und die Kirche*, 80–84, 88–97; Derwood Smith, "The Two Made One: Some Observations on Eph. 2:14–18," *OJRS* 1 (April 1973): 34–54; Michael S. Moore, "Ephesians and 2:14–16: A History of Recent Interpretation," *EvQ* 54 (July–September 1982): 163–68; Wessels, "The Eschatology of Colossians and Ephesians," 195–97; Barth, 261–62; Schnackenburg, 113.

3. Schille, "Liturgisches Gut im Epheserbrief" 3–9; Pokorný, "Epheserbrief und gnostische Mysterien," 182–84; Schille, *Früchristliche Hymnen*, 24–31; Sanders, "Hymnic Elements in Ephesians 1–3," 216–18; Joachim Gnilka, "Christus unser Friede—en Friedens-Erlöserlied in Eph 2,14–17. Erwägungen zu einer neutestamentliche Friedenstheologie," in *Die Zeit Jesu. Festschrift für Heirich Schlier*, ed. Günther Bornkamm and Karl Rahner (Freiburg: Herder, 1970), 190–207; Gnilka, 147–52; Jack T. Sanders, *The New Testament Christological Hymns. Their Historical Religious Background*, SNTSMS, ed. Matthew Black, vol. 15 (Cambridge: Cambridge University Press, 1971), 14–15, 88–92; Klaus Wengst, *Christologische Formeln und Lieder des Urchristentums*, Studien zum Neuen Testament, ed. Günter Klein, Willi Marxsen, and Wolfgang Schrage, vol. 7 (Gütersloh: Gütersloher Verlagshaus, 1972), 181–86; Christoph Burger, *Schöpfung und Versöhnung: Studien zum liturgischen Gut im Kolosser- und Epheserbrief*, Wissenschaftliche Monographien zum Alten und Neuen Testament, ed. Ferdinand Hahn and Odil Hannes Steck, vol. 46 (Neukirchen-Vluyen: Neukirchener Verlag, 1975), 117–39, 144–57.

4. Deichgräber, *Gotteshymnus*, 165–67; Helmut Merklein, "Zur Tradition und Komposition von Eph 2,14–18," *BZ* 17, no. 1 (1973): 79–102; idem, *Christus und die Kirche. Die theologische Grundstruktur des Epheserbriefes nach Eph 2,11–18*, Stuttgarter Bibelstudien, ed. Herbert Haag, Rudolf Kilian, and Wilhelm Pesch, vol. 66 (Stuttgart: KBW, 1973); Peter Stuhlmacher, "'He is our Peace' (Eph. 2:14). On the Exegesis and Significance of Ephesians 2:14–18," in Reconciliation, *Law, & Righteousness: Essays in Biblical Theology*, trans. Everett Kalin (Philadelphia: Fortress, 1986), 182–85; Barth, 261. Käsemann argues from style that it could not be a baptismal hymn, see Käsemann, "Meditationen: Epheser 2,17–22," *Exegetische Versuche und Besinnungen*, 282; Best, 247–50.

5. Sanders, *The New Testament Christological Hymns*, 14.

ers' baptism[1] but there is no hint of this in the whole context. Merklein thinks that Eph 2:11–22 has close verbal similarities with the cosmic Christological hymn in Col 1:15–23 and that in particular the reconciliation mentioned in Col 1:21–23 is applied to the reconciliation of the Jews and Gentiles in Eph 2:14–18.[2] The problems with this view are twofold: (1) the verbal similarities are not that close (only nineteen words out of 238 in Eph 2:11–22); and (2) the reconciliation in Colossians is between God and human beings (as also in Eph 2:18) and not between two factions of people. It is easiest to see this as an explanatory digression to emphasize for the reader the means by which Jews and Gentiles have been reconciled to each other and to God, possibly based on Isa 57:19 ("Peace, peace, to the far and to the near, says the Lord; and I will heal him"),[3] though Isaiah is talking about Jews living "near" at home and those living "far away" in dispersion. It is not unusual for Paul to digress in order to give a fuller explanation of what he had just stated. Faust suggests that the *Pax Romana* serves as background to Christ's proclamation of peace in the present context. After the Jewish War (A.D. 66–70) the Romans reestablished peace with the Jews, similar to the reconciliation of Jews and Gentiles in Christ mentioned in this passage.[4] However, this view assumes that Ephesians was a pseudepigraphic tract written to the

1. Léonard Ramaroson, "'Le Christ, notre Paix' (Ep 2,14–18)," *ScEs* 31 (September–December 1979): 373–82; Warnach, "Taufwirklichkeit und Taufbewußtsein nach dem Epheserbrief," 44; Meeks, "In One Body," 215. Sahlin attempts to make a correspondence between circumcision and baptism. In Judaism the division between the heathen and the Jew was circumcision, whereas the division between the Jews/Gentiles and the church is baptism, the circumcision in Christ. Baptism makes peace between between Jews and Gentiles and makes them a new person, namely, the Israel of God (see Harald Sahlin, "'Die Beschneidung Christi.' Eine Interpretation von Eph. 2:11–22," Symbolae biblicae upsalienses, vol. 12 [Lund: Gleerup; København: Ejnar Munksgaard, 1950], 13–15). The problem with this view is that one has to read into the passage much more than what is obvious. Also, the new person is not the Israel of God but a whole new entity.

2. Merklein, "Paulinische Theologie in der Rezeption des Kolosser- und Epheserbriefes," 52–62 [republished in idem, *Studien zu Jesus und Paulus*, WUNT, ed. Martin Hengel and Otfried Hofius, vol. 43 (Tübingen: Mohr, 1987), 436–46]; Merklein, "Zur Tradition und Komposition von Eph 2,14–18," 79–102. For a discussion of a possible Vorlage, see Best, "The Use of Credal and Liturgical Materials in Ephesians," 61–64.

3. Stuhlmacher thinks that vv. 13–18 present a Christological exegesis of Isa 9:5–6; 52:7; 57:19; cf. Stuhlmacher, "'He is our Peace' (Eph. 2:14)," 187–91. But that seems to be reading more into the passages than they will bear, for there is no hint that those far away are brought near (v. 13). For a more extensive study of this, see Smith, "Jewish and Greek Traditions in Ephesians 2:11–22," 8–33; cf. also idem, "The Two Made One," 34 and n. 8; Moritz, *A Profound Mystery*, 31–42; Gese, *Das Vermächtnis des Apostels*, 117–33.

4. Eberhard Faust, *Pax Christi et Pax Caesaris: Religionsgeschichtliche, traditionsgeschichtliche und sozialgeschichtliche Studien zum Ephesebrief*, Novum Testamentum et Orbis Antiquus, ed. Max Küchler und Gerd Theissen, vol. 24 (Freiburg: Universitätsverlag; Göttingen: Vandenhoeck & Ruprecht, 1993), 115–81, 360–426, 471–83.

Gentile Christians in Asia Minor and dated after the Jewish War. Furthermore, there is nothing in Ephesians to indicate that the background of reconciliation of believing Jews and Gentiles was the reestablishment of peace between the Romans and the Jews. The passage clearly indicates that the hostility between Jews and Gentiles could not be reconciled by human ingenuity but was accomplished in Christ.

This section is divided into two major parts: the assertion of peace (vv. 14–16) and the announcement of peace (vv. 17–18).

a. Assertion of Peace (2:14–16)

Because of what Christ did on the cross, there is peace between the Jews and Gentiles in this new union. Much had to be dismantled for this peace to be a reality. The law which was so important to the Jew could longer be the operating principle, otherwise the old rift would reappear. The structure of his argument for this section is the main assertion is given in 2:14a ("he is our peace") followed by several participles in 2:14b–16 which support the main assertion.

(1) Destruction of the Wall (2:14a)

The first thing needed was to break down of the middle wall of partition, the barrier that divided Jews and Gentiles outside of Christ. The root of the problem had to be addressed.

Text: 2:14a. Αὐτὸς γάρ ἐστιν ἡ εἰρήνη ἡμῶν, ὁ ποιήσας τὰ ἀμφότερα ἓν καὶ τὸ μεσότοιχον τοῦ φραγμοῦ λύσας, τὴν ἔχθραν,

Translation: 2:14a. "For he is our peace, who made the both one and who destroyed the middle wall of partition, the hostility,"

Commentary: 2:14a. Αὐτὸς γάρ ἐστιν ἡ εἰρήνη ἡμῶν, "For he is our peace." Having defined the union, Paul introduces this section with an explanatory γάρ, "for," in order to explain how this union was accomplished. The personal pronoun αὐτός, "he," is at the beginning for the sake of emphasis. Now that the Gentiles, who were saved by his grace, are in Christ and have been brought near by his blood, Paul emphatically places this personal pronoun at the beginning in order that the reader will not miss the point. He, the one in whom the Gentiles are, is our peace. Before, there was hostility but now the one who brought us near is "our peace." Peace is an abstract idea that is personified in Christ.[1] This personification is supported by NT grammar. When the subject is anarthrous but "the article is used in the predicate the article is due to a previous mention of the noun (as well known or promi-

1. Grob thinks the subject in this whole passage is God and not Christ, the objects of the reconciliation are Jews and Gentiles, and the means is the cross and Christ (Francis Grob, "L'image du corps et de la tête dans l'Épître aux Ephésiens," *ETR* 58, no. 4 [1983]: 497). However, it seems that Christ is the subject of the reconciliation because: (1) the αὐτός in v. 14a matches with the αὐτοῦ, the last word of the same verse; (2) both the Jew

nent) or [as in the case here] to the fact that the subject and the predicate are identical."[1] Thus, it means "he in his own person"[2] is peace. In this passage it is difficult to determine if that peace refers to the Gentiles' peace with God or their peace with the Jews. That is not important at this juncture for Paul wants to emphasize that Christ is our peace, setting the stage for his later insights. Paul will, within this section, show that the peace is primarily between the Jewish and Gentile believers and secondarily between human beings and God.[3]

In the word study of "peace" in 1:2 it was concluded that it has the broadest idea of "well-being" and that out of the forty-three times Paul uses it, eight times it is in Ephesians, half of which are in this section (vv. 14, 15, 17*bis*). In this context the word indicates a lack of hostility and a mutual acceptance between those who were hostile or appeared to be hostile.[4] Both elements are important. It is not only a lack of hostility but it is also acceptance or friendship. Two nations may not be at war with one another, but that does not necessarily mean that they accept one another or have a friendly relationship. Therefore, Christ is the one who makes possible this lack of hostility and a mutual acceptance. Finally, this peace is ἡμῶν, "ours." As discussed at verse 3, although some want to make a distinction between the pronouns by positing that the first person plural pronouns refer to the Jews and the second person plural pronoun refers to the Gentiles, this distinction is not convincing. Certainly, in this text the pronoun "our" cannot have reference to Jews as opposed to Gentiles but must refer to all believers regardless of whether they are Jews or Gentiles.

ὁ ποιήσας τὰ ἀμφότερα ἓν, "who made the both one." Now Paul defines how that peace accomplishes its goal. The articular aorist participle (ὁ ποιήσας) refers back to the personal pronoun (αὐτός), which refers to Christ. Although the aorist does not help in defining objectively the sort of action,[5] it is interesting that Paul did not use the present or

---

and Gentile are reconciled "to God" (v. 16) and one would think that if God were the subject then it would read "to himself"; and (3) "he preached peace" seems to refer to Christ preaching through his apostles rather than God preaching.

1. Robertson, *Grammar*, 768–69; cf. Winer, *Grammar*, 142 n. 1 (it is Moulton's comment).

2. Salmond, 294.

3. One must keep these priorities in order. It is true that we personally have peace because of what Christ has done, but it is wrong in this context to make that the primary thing, as does Wulf, when the primary point of "our peace" refers to the peace between Jews and Gentiles who are in Christ, that new person that Paul will develop in v. 15. Cf. Friedrich Wulf, "»Er selbst ist unser Friede« (Eph 2,14)," *GL* 30 (1957): 85–89, esp. 88.

4. The idea that this peace refers to the OT sacrificial peace offering is suggested by F. D. Coggan, "A Note on Ephesians ii.14: αὐτὸς γάρ ἐστιν ἡ εἰρήνη ἡμῶν," *ExpTim* 53 (April 1942): 242. This seems foreign to the context and has been ably refuted by Norman Snaith, "Further Note on Ephesians ii.14," *ExpTim* 53 (July 1942): 325–26.

5. Stagg, "The Abused Aorist," 222–31; Smith, "Errant Aorist Interpreters," 205–26; Carson, *Exegetical Fallacies*, 72–74.

perfect which would define more specifically the author's conception of the action. The present tense signifies an action that occurs regularly, which would mean that Christ is making peace in his present heavenly ministry. The perfect signifies the continuing results of his death on the cross. Rather, the aorist may denote action occurring in the past (aorist participle normally suggest antecedent time to that of the main verb) because it is explained in verse 13 that the Gentiles were brought near because of what Christ did historically on the cross. The point is that the present context is trying to emphasize that the peace mentioned was accomplished by Christ's death on the cross. It is not what God is *doing* but what he *did* 2000 years ago. What is this peace? It is the peace he made between the Jews and Gentiles who are now one in Christ. Since they are one, acceptance replaces hostility.

It is common for the verb ποιέω, "to do," to be followed by a double accusative.[1] Here it is followed by τὰ ἀμφότερα ἓν, "the both one." The form of the substantival adjective could have been any of the three genders. It is masculine in verses 16 and 18 but here in verse 14 it is neuter. Thus, in this verse it would seem to eliminate the idea that τὰ ἀμφότερα refers to God and humans as one. Rather, "the both" refer to the two parties, systems, or classes under which the Jews and Gentiles were grouped and which God made one. The neuter makes good grammatical sense here.[2]

Therefore, the expression "the one having made the both one" explains how "he is our peace." Where formerly there was disunity, now there is unity between Jews and Gentiles in the person of Christ. But this still does not state how this was accomplished. Paul explains this in the next comment.

καὶ τὸ μεσότοιχον τοῦ φραγμοῦ λύσας, "and who destroyed the middle wall of partition." The former clause began the explanation (γάρ) of how Christ is our peace and the present clause introduced by the conjunction καί ("and") is a continuation of that explanation. Again, an aorist participle (λύσας) is used, which parallels the aorist participle (ὁ ποιήσας) in the previous clause. The aorist participle is from λύω, basically meaning "to destroy, break down."[3] The words τὸ μεσότοιχον τοῦ φραγμοῦ, "the middle wall of partition," need to be discussed. The noun μεσότοιχον is rarely used in classical literature,[4] not used in the LXX, and occurs only here in the NT. It is from τοῖχος, "wall," and μέσος, "middle," hence, the middle or dividing wall. The following word φραγμός is used to denote "fencing in, blocking up,"[5] "railing" of a bridge,[6] or "fortification."[7] Of the twenty-one times it appears in the LXX, it oc-

1. Robertson, *Grammar*, 480.
2. BDF §138.
3. BAGD 483; BDAG 606–7.
4. Cf. LSJ 1108; Carl Schneider, "μεσότοιχον," *TDNT* 4 (1967): 625.
5. Sophocles *Oedipus Tyrannus* 1387.
6. Herodotus 7.36 (527.30).
7. Ibid., 7.142 (568.7).

curs eighteen times in the canonical books and is translated from four different Hebrew words but half of the times from גָּדֵר or גְּדֵרָה, meaning "hedge" or "fence," as around a vineyard or field (Num 22:24*bis*; Nah 3:17), or "fence" or "wall" to keep intruders out (Pss 62:3 [MT 62:4; LXX 61:4]; 80:12 [MT 80:13; LXX 79:13]; Prov 24:31; Eccl 10:8). The purpose of a wall or fence is for protection. In the NT it is used four times (Matt 21:33 = Mark 12:1; Luke 14:23; Eph 2:14). When it occurs in the Gospels it is used of a fence or hedge to protect the vineyard or fields from intruders. The genitive appears to function appositionally,[1] thus the middle wall which consists of a partition. A wall stands between two parties to separate them. To what does this refer?

First, it is thought by some[2] to refer to the one and half meter (four and a half foot) wall in the Jerusalem temple precincts that separated the court of the Gentiles from the court of the Jews with an inscription in Greek[3] and Latin prohibiting the entrance of a foreigner under the threat of the death penalty as mentioned by Josephus.[4] But this is not valid because: (1) there is no reference to the Jerusalem wall in this context; (2) the Jerusalem wall is never called by the designation given in the present context (inscription on the wall and Josephus designate it δρύφακτος); (3) the wall in Jerusalem was still standing when Paul wrote this letter; and (4) it was probably unfamiliar to the average person in the churches around Ephesus.

Second, it is thought by some to refer to the curtain in the Jerusalem temple between the holy place and the holy of holies.[5] But this is untenable because it was a curtain and not a wall, and because the curtain separated all men, including the Jews, except the high priest

1. Robertson, *Grammar*, 498; BDF §167; MHT 3:215; Sellin, "Über einige ungewöhnliche Genitive im Epheserbrief," 96; Gaugler, 108; Lincoln, 141.

2. Bengel, 4:78; Olshausen, 181; Abbott, 61; Hendriksen, 133; Mitton, 105–6; Bruce, 297–98; James E. Howard, "The Wall Broken: An Interpretation of Ephesians 2:11–22," in *Biblical Interpretation: Principles and Practices. Studies in Honor of Jack Pearl Lewis*, ed. F. Furman Kearley, Edward P. Myers, and Timothy D. Hadley (Grand Rapids: Baker, 1986), 303; Craig McMahan, "The Wall is Gone!" *RevExp* 93 (spring 1996): 262.

3. Two Greek inscriptions have been uncovered. The first one was found in 1871 and it measures 57 centimeters (22 1/2 inches) high, 85 centimeters (33 1/2 inches) long, and 37 centimeters (14 1/2 inches) thick and is now located in the Archaeological Museum in Istanbul (Ch. Clermont-Ganneau, "Une stèle du temple de Jérusalem," *Revue Archéologique* 23 [Avril 1872]: 214–34, 290–96). The inscription reads Μηθένα ἀλλογενῆ εἰσπορεύεσθαι ἐντὸς τοῦ περὶ τὸ ἱερὸν τρυφάκτου καὶ περιβόλου. ὃς δ᾽ ἂν ληφθῇ, ἑαυτῶι αἴτιος ἔσται διὰ τὸ ἐξακολουθεῖν θάνατον: "Let no foreigner enter within the partition and enclosure surrounding the temple. Whoever is arrested will himself be responsible for his death which will follow" (inscription in Deissmann, *Light from the Ancient East*, 80). The second inscription is only a fragment found in 1935 and is now located in the Rockefeller Museum in Jerusalem (J. H. Iliffe, "The θάνατος Inscription from Herod's Temple. Fragment of a Second Copy," *Quarterly of the Department of Antiquities in Palestine* 6, no. 1 [1936]: 1–3).

4. Josephus *A.J.* 15.11.5 §417; *B.J.* 5.5.2 §§193–94.

5. Alford, 3:97; Ellicott, 47–48; Mussner, *Christus, das All und die Kirche*, 84.

who entered once a year into the holy of holies. The wall in the present context separated Jews and Gentiles.

Third, Schlier thinks it comes from Gnostic texts and refers to a cosmic wall that separates the heavenly *pleroma* from the lower world.[1] This is unlikely because the separation is not between the celestial and terrestial but between Jews and Gentiles.[2] Furthermore, Schlier's sources for his theory are too late and postdate Paul (second or third century A.D.)[3] as well as the fact that "the crucial word μεσότοιχον is missing from all the literature."[4]

Fourth, others have thought that it refers to the Mosaic law.[5] Some rabbis thought of the wall as the "fence" around the law.[6] However, that spoke more about the protection around the law than the hostility mentioned in this context.[7] Nevertheless, in later rabbinics, rather than the law surrounded by a fence, the fence was identified as the law itself which protected Israel from pagan practices.[8] The law required the Jews to be holy and separate. Thus they could not eat with Gentiles or intermarry with them.[9] Right within the present context the law of circumcision marked a real separation between Jews and Gentiles. This often led to a hostility of Jews towards Gentiles[10] and was a cause of Gentile hatred of the Jews.[11] Therefore, the law, which may have included many minute scribal additions, was to be strictly

1. Schlier, *Christus and die Kirche im Epheserbrief*, 18–26; idem, 124–33; Dibelius-Greeven, 69; Gaugler, 108–9; Pokorný, "Epheserbrief und gnostische Mysterien," 182–83; Fischer, *Tendenz und Absicht des Epheserbriefes*, 133; Lindemann, *Aufhebung*, 161–66; Lindemann, 47–49.

2. Hanson, *The Unity of the Church in the New Testament*, 143.

3. Barth, 286.

4. Best, 255.

5. Eadie, 173; Robinson, 160–61; Westcott, 37; Schnackenburg, 114; Lincoln, 141–42. Barth states the various interpretations but is not decisive himself. He thinks that Christ broke down every division and frontier between men, whether it be race, politics, morals, nations, etc. Cf. Barth, 282–91, 306–7; Markus Barth, *The Broken Wall. A Study of the Epistle to the Ephesians* (Valley Forge, Pa.: Judson, 1959; London: Collins, 1960), 33–45.

6. *m. ʾAbot* 1:1; *Letter of Aristeas* [probably second century B.C.] 139: "When therefore our lawgiver [Moses], equipped by God for insight into all things, had surveyed each particular, he fenced us about with impregnable palisades and with walls of iron, to the end that we should mingle in no way with any of the other nations, remaining pure in body and in spirit, emancipated from vain opinions, revering the one and mighty God above the whole of creation. . . ." 142: "And therefore, so that we should be polluted by none nor be infected with perversions by associating with the worthless persons, he has hedged us about on all sides with prescribed purifications in matters of food and drink and touch and hearing and sight." For more references, see Barth, 284 nn. 130–31.

7. Barth, 284; cf. Sellin, "Über einige ungewöhnliche Genitive im Epheserbrief," 97.

8. Cf. *Midr. Lev.* 26:2.

9. Barth, 285; Caird, 58–59; Dunn, *The Partings of the Ways*, 82.

10. For discussion and sources, see Str-B, 3:588–91; cf. also 1:359–63.

11. Tacitus *Historiae* 5.1–13.

observed by the Jews and was at the same time offensive to the Gentiles, thus causing hostility between Jews and Gentiles. Consequently, it makes good sense to consider that the "wall of partition" was not a literal wall but a metaphorical wall that divided Jews and Gentiles.[1] Often an attitude of superiority crept in that in turn engendered hostility.[2] This metaphorical wall of partition was destroyed.

τὴν ἔχθραν, "the hostility." The noun ἔχθρα has the meaning of "'hostility' as such, irrespective of the underlying disposition or of its manifestation or otherwise visible form."[3] It occurs twenty times in the LXX (thirteen times in the canonical books); it expresses hatred or hostility towards groups (Gen 3:15),[4] nations (Ezek 35:5),[5] and individuals (Num 35:20, 22; Prov 10:18). In the NT it occurs six times, expressing hostility toward persons (Luke 23:12; Gal 5:20), groups of people (Eph 2:14), and God (Rom 8:7; Eph 2:16; Jas 4:4). Here the hostility is not between God and people[6] but between the two groups of people, namely, Jews and Gentiles. This is seen in the immediately preceding words "the middle wall of partition" and in the preceding context (vv. 11–13) where it speaks of the great divide between these two groups. Furthermore, the contrast to the emnity is the εἰρήνη, "peace," which is mentioned four times in the immediate context (vv. 14, 15, 17*bis*), all of the instances speaking of the peace between Jews and Gentiles.

The problem with the above word is how it relates to the words before and after it, including the first part of verse 15. The UBS[3] punctuation apparatus (this helpful feature is excluded from UBS[4]) shows four different ways that it is punctuated in the various Greek texts and translations. In order to see the problem more clearly, a text will be written out, a translation given, a summary of its meaning stated, and some of the texts and versions listed for each of the punctuations. This will be followed by a discussion of the views. (1) τὸ μεσότοιχον τοῦ φραγμοῦ λύσας, τὴν ἔχθραν, ἐν τῇ σαρκὶ αὐτοῦ, τὸν νόμον τῶν ἐντολῶν ἐν δόγμασιν καταργήσας, which the NEB translates, "in his own body of flesh and blood has broken down the enmity which stood like a dividing wall between them; for he annulled the law with its rules and regulations." This conveys the idea that the destruction of that wall

1. Best, 256–57.

2. One can see this pride as early as second century B.C. in the *Letter of Aristeas* 152: "For most of the rest of mankind defile themselves by their promiscuous unions, working great unrighteousness, and whole countries and cities pride themselves on these vices. Not only do they have intercourse with males, but they even defile mothers and daughters. But we have been kept apart from such things."

3. Werner Foerster, "ἐχθρός, ἔχθρα," *TDNT* 2 (1964): 811.

4. Thucydides 2.68.2.

5. Ibid., 3.10.4.

6. As Chrysostom *Eph* 2:13–15 (*PG* 62:39; cf. also Kohlgraf, *Die Ekklesiologie des Epheserbriefes in der Auslegung durch Johannes Chrysostomus*, 137–38); Theophylact *Eph* 2:14 (*PG* 124:1060–61); Oecumenius *Eph* 2:14–18 (*PG* 118:1197).

(which was the hostility) took place in his flesh because he annulled the law. This is punctuation is in UBS[1–3], GNTMT, NEB, TEV, and NRSV.[1] (2) τὸ μεσότοιχον τοῦ φραγμοῦ λύσας, τὴν ἔχθραν ἐν τῇ σαρκὶ αὐτοῦ,[2] τὸν νόμον τῶν ἐντολῶν ἐν δόγμασιν καταργήσας, which could be translated, "having destroyed the middle wall of partition, the hostility in his flesh, by rendering inoperative the law of the commandments in decrees." This conveys the meaning that Christ destroyed the wall, the hostility which was in his flesh, by rendering the law inoperative. This view is found in the TR, WH, NA[26, 27], and UBS[3corr., 4] but not found in any of the more popular English translations.[3] (3) τὸ μεσότοιχον τοῦ φραγμοῦ λύσας, τὴν ἔχθραν ἐν τῇ σαρκὶ αὐτοῦ, τὸν νόμον τῶν ἐντολῶν ἐν δόγμασιν καταργήσας, which the NASB translates, "broke down the barrier of the dividing wall, by abolishing in his flesh the enmity, *which is* the law of commandments *contained* in decrees." This conveys the idea that the law is that hostility and that Christ put it to death in his flesh. Many English translations follow this punctuation as it is seen in AV, RV, ASV, NASB, JB, NJB.[4] (4) τὸ μεσότοιχον τοῦ φραγμοῦ λύσας, τὴν ἔχθραν, ἐν τῇ σαρκὶ αὐτοῦ τὸν νόμον τῶν ἐντολῶν ἐν δόγμασιν καταργήσας, which is translated by the NIV, "has destroyed the barrier, the dividing wall of hostility, by abolishing in his flesh the law with its commandments and regulations." This gives the idea that Christ destroyed the wall, which was the hostility, by means of making the law inoperative in his flesh. This punctuation is found in NA[25], RSV, and NIV.[5]

View (1) places the "the hostility" in apposition to the "the middle wall of partition," having "in his flesh" governed by λύσας. Thus, the middle wall of partition is destroyed in his flesh. This suggests that the middle wall of partition between the Jews and Gentiles was destroyed in Christ's death. The real problem with this view is that it particularizes the meaning too much. It is true that he bore our sins in his flesh but

1. Alford, 3:97; Ellicott, 48; Abbott, 61–62; Salmond, 295.

2. Baljon thinks that the words τὴν ἔχθραν ἐν τῇ σαρκὶ αὐτοῦ, "the emnity in his flesh," are very difficult to understand and, therefore, are a marginal gloss inserted to explain τὴν ἔχθραν ἐν αὐτῷ "the emnity in himself" in v. 16 (J. M. S. Baljon, "Opmerkingen op het gebied van de Conjecturaalkritiek: de Brief aan Epheziërs," *ThStud* 3, no. 2 [1885]: 151–52). But this is mere speculation with no textual evidence to support his claim.

3. Calvin, 150–51; Westcott, 37; Rienecker, 97–98.

4. Bengel, 4:79; Robinson, 161; Schlier, 125; Barth, 264; Bruce, 298; Lincoln, 142; cf. J. H. A. Hart, "The Enmity in His Flesh: Ephesians ii.14, 15," *Exp* 6th ser., vol. 3 (February 1901): 135–41; Lindemann, *Aufhebung*, 173. Feine's view is somewhat similar, except he thinks the ἔχθραν in v. 14 begins a parenthesis which ends with the ἔχθραν in v. 16. Therefore, he destroyed the middle wall of partition, having killed the hostility in himself (P. Feine, "Eph. 2,14–16," *Theologische Studien und Kritiken* 72, no. 4 [1899]: 540–74, esp. 541–46).

5. Eadie, 174–75; Meyer, 129–30; Gaugler, 109; Gnilka, 141; Hugedé, 84–85; Schnackenburg, 115; cf. also Percy, *Probleme*, 281; Mussner, *Christus, das All und die Kirche*, 83; Rudolf Schnackenburg, "Zur Exegese von Eph 2,11–22: Im Hinblick aus das Verhältnis von Kirche und Israel," in *The New Testament Age: Essays in Honor of Bo Reicke*, ed. William C. Weinrich, vol. 2 (Macon, Ga.: Mercer University Press, 1984), 482–83.

this is not talking about the general hostility of human beings toward God but the hostility between Jews and Gentiles. View (2) is similiar to view (1), except that the "hostility which was in his flesh" is in apposition to the middle wall of partition. The same criticisms of view (1) would also be leveled against this view. In addition, since "in his flesh" is in apposition to "the hostility," it would seem to require τήν before ἐν τῇ σαρκὶ αὐτοῦ. View (3) is accepted by most of the English translations but it raises some real problems. First, it makes "the hostility" in apposition to the law. Nowhere in Scripture is the law presented as hostile. It is that which is good (Ps 19:7 [MT 19:8; LXX 18:8]; Rom 7:12, 16), holy (Rom 7:12), spiritual (Rom 7:14), and a delight (Ps 1:2; Rom 7:22). It may cause hostility (Rom 7:8–11), but in itself it is not hostile (Rom 7:12). Second, this would necessitate that the hostility is between humans and God, whereas in this context it is talking about the hostility between Jews and Gentiles. Third, it forces the participle καταργήσας to be rendered "put to death" when really it means "to make inoperative." Thus, if this is the correct rendering, it would mean that the hostility is inoperative but not destroyed. This seems to be inconsistent, for it indicates that the middle wall of partition is destroyed but that the law, which is in apposition to it, is not destroyed but only inoperative. Fourth, the law is not put to death at the cross, but "the emnity, considered as a condition, *is* definitely put to death in Christ and through his cross (ἀποκτείνας τὴν ἔχθραν, vs. 16)."[1] Fifth, it makes the prepositional phrase ἐν τῇ σαρκὶ αὐτοῦ inexplicable in that it is between the two nouns of apposition and yet it has no relation to either.[2] Hence, this view has too many problems to make it acceptable. View (4) is the most acceptable. This view puts "the hostility" in apposition to "the middle wall of partition" like view (1), but the prepositional phrase ἐν τῇ σαρκὶ αὐτοῦ is governed by καταργήσας rather than λύσας and this is different than the other three views. Thus, the hostility between Jews and Gentiles has been destroyed, and this was accomplished by making the law inoperative for those who are in Christ. This is consistent with other places in Paul's writings where he states that the believer has been rendered inoperative from the law or that the believer is not under the Mosaic law (Rom 7:1–6; 10:4; Gal 2:19; 3:24–25). In brief, as stated earlier, there was hostility between Jews and Gentiles. This came about because many Jews misused the law. The stipulations of the law were to protect the Jew from the practices of the world. Israel was to be a kingdom of priests (Exod 19:6) as a testimony to God. They were to keep the law which provided opportunity to witness to their Gentile neighbors of God's wonderful deliverance and care. Rather than using the law as a witness, it became the tool that enabled them to look down on the Gentiles whom they considered sinners. Hence, this caused hostility between Jews and Gentiles. Due to this and the tenacity with which they practiced their law, they were considered

1. Roels, *God's Mission*, 126.
2. Abbott, 62.

by the Gentiles as prideful and stubborn. Their observance of regulations was well known, and even Julius Caesar exempted the Jews from Roman military service because they would not work on the Sabbath nor eat the normal rations of the soldiers.[1] Hence, it was not the law that was hostile but the wrong conception and use of the law, which resulted in hostility on both sides. To solve the problem, the law was rendered inoperative in Christ's flesh and therefore, Jews and Gentiles in Christ would not have the law as the modus operandi, thus destroying the hostility which existed between them.

(2) Disengagement of the Law (2:14b–16)

Having discussed the destruction of the wall, Paul now shows how and for what purpose that destruction was accomplished. He proposes that it was done by making the law inoperative for believers for the purpose of creating one new person.

(a) The Fact of the Operation (2:14b–15a)

Text: 2:14b. ἐν τῇ σαρκὶ αὐτοῦ, **2:15a.** τὸν νόμον τῶν ἐντολῶν ἐν δόγμασιν καταργήσας,

Translation: 2:14b. "in his flesh, **2:15a.** by having rendered inoperative the law of commandments in decrees,"

Commentary: 2:14b. ἐν τῇ σαρκὶ αὐτοῦ, "in his flesh." This prepositional phrase refers to the crucified Christ[2] and is parallel with the phrase "by the blood of Christ" in verse 13 and "through the cross" in verse 16.[3] It is governed by the participle καταργήσας, "having rendered inoperative," and is placed first in the clause for emphasis, for it was only in his flesh that the law was rendered inoperative. It shows the locale of this accomplishment.

2:15a. τὸν νόμον τῶν ἐντολῶν ἐν δόγμασιν[4] καταργήσας, "by having rendered inoperative the law of commandments in decrees." The first thing to be discussed is the aorist participle καταργήσας, "having rendered inoperative." Verses 14–15 contain three aorist masculine participles (ποιήσας, λύσας, and καταργήσας). The first two are parallel to each other because they are joined by the coordinating conjunction

1. Juvenal *Satires* 14.96–106.

2. Certainly not to the circumcision of Christ as proposed by Smith, "The Ephesian Heresy and the Origin of the Epistle to the Ephesians," 88. This is highly questionable and foreign to the context.

3. Hans-Jürgen Findeis, *Versöhnung-Apostolat-Kirche: Eine exegetische-theologische und rezeptionsgeschichtliche Studie zu den Versöhnungsaussagen des Neuen Testaments (2 Kor, Röm, Kol, Eph)*, Forschung zur Bibel, ed. Rudolf Schnackenburg and Josef Schreiner, vol. 40 (Würzburg: Echter, 1983), 476; Romano Penna, *Paul the Apostle: A Theological and Exegetical Study*, trans. Thomas P. Wahl, vol. 2 (Collegeville, Minn.: Liturgical Press, 1996), 37–40.

4. The reading ἐν δόγμασιν is omitted from only $\mathfrak{P}^{46}$ and vg^{ms}, which is not sufficient to reject it.

καί, and since there is no conjunction between the second and the third participle, the third participle is dependent on the second one. This last participle further describes the destruction of the middle of partition. It could be a participle of manner showing how it was destroyed or, more likely, a participle of means indicating the means by which it was destroyed.[1] The word καταργέω is rarely used in classical literature where it has the idea of "being idle, inactive."[2] In the LXX it occurs only four times (Ezra 4:21, 23; 5:5; 6:8) and is always translated from the Aramaic בְּטֵל, meaning "to cease."[3] It was used in connection with the rebuilding of the temple and meant "to hinder" or "to cease" from rebuilding. In the NT it occurs twenty-seven times, all of which are in Paul's writing, except in Luke 13:7 where it is used of the unproductive use of the land and in Heb 2:14 where it speaks of Christ's ability to nullify or render inactive the devil's power of death. It occurs only here in Ephesians. In Paul's writings it consistently means "to render inoperative, nullify, invalidate" (cf. Rom 3:3, 31; 4:14; 6:6; 7:2, 6);[4] hence, in this context to translate it "to put death" or "to destroy" is incorrect. The law was not put to death or destroyed but has been rendered inoperative or nullified for the believer.

The law is now introduced, and the term ὁ νόμος must refer to the whole Mosaic law and not just the ceremonial law as some suggest.[5] The genitive following it (τῶν ἐντολῶν) is a genitive of content or apposition "the law consisting of commandments" meaning that the law had many specific commands.[6] The prepositional phrase that follows (ἐν δόγμασιν) is descriptive, defining the nature of the commandments to be rendered "consisting in"[7] ordinances or decrees.[8] The term δόγμα

1. Wallace, *Greek Grammar*, 630.

2. Euripides *Phoenissae* 753.

3. BDB 1084; *HALOT* 5 (2000): 1832; John Arthur Thompson and Elmer Martens, "בטל (*bṭl*)," *NIDOTTE* 1:650.

4. Gerhard Delling, "καταργέω," *TDNT* 1 (1964): 452–54; James I. Packer, "Abolish, Nullify, Reject [καταργέω, ἀθετέω, ἐξουδενέω]," *NIDNTT* 1 (1975): 73–74.

5. E.g., Calvin, 151; Eadie, 175; Hendriksen, 135. Faust (*Pax Christi et Pax Caesaris*, 120–21) thinks that the ceremonial law was the dividing wall and thus creating the enmity between Jews and Gentiles.

6. L&N §33.330; Gottlob Schrenk, "ἐντολή," *TDNT* 2 (1964): 551–52; cf. also Sellin ("Über einige ungewöhnliche Genitive im Epheserbrief," 91), who labels it a partitive genitive and thinks that the genitive qualifies or specifies τὸν νόμον.

7. Robertson, *Grammar*, 589; Moule, *Idiom Book*, 45, 79; MHT 1:103; 3:265; MM 210.

8. Roetzel's idea that this signifies misdirected human commandments that were added by a redactor to avoid the impression that the law of commandments has been destroyed is highly speculative; cf. Calvin J. Roetzel, "Jewish Christian – Gentile Christian Relations. A Discussion of Ephesians 2:15a," *ZNW* 74, nos. 1/2 (1983): 81–89, esp. 86. For an evaluation of Roetzel's view, see Martin Kitchen, "The Status of Law in the Letter to the Ephesians," in *Law and Religion: Essays on the Place of the Law in Israel and Early Christianity*, ed. Barnabas Lindars (Cambridge: James Clark & Co, 1988), 145–47.

in classical Greek first had the idea of an "opinion, belief"[1] and in philosophy it had the idea of "doctrine"[2] from which we derive the word "dogma"; it also means "public ordinance or decree."[3] In the LXX it is used seventeen times, once in a canonical book (Dan 6:12 [MT & LXX 6:13]) and the rest in the later books as a public decree (Theodotion Dan 2:13; 3:10). In the NT it is used five times. In Luke 2:1 (only time it is singular) and Acts 17:7 it refers to the decrees of Caesar. In Acts 16:4 it refers to the "decisions" reached by the apostles in the Jerusalem Council. In Col 2:14 it is used of "regulations" and in the present context it refers to the individual statutes of the commandments of the Mosaic law.[4] It is best translated as "ordinances" or "decrees" which were God's will for the nation of Israel. The law of Moses, the content of which are the commandments consisting of decrees, has been rendered inoperative for believers in Christ and hence the hostility between Jewish and Gentile Christians has been destroyed.

Since the whole Mosaic law has been rendered inoperative for Jewish and Gentile believers in Christ, it is a false dichotomy to distinguish between the moral and ceremonial laws, making only the ceremonial laws inoperative.[5] Christ is the end of the whole law for believers (Rom 10:4) and we as believers are no longer under that pedagogue (Gal 3:25).[6] In fact, we have died to the law (Rom 7:1–6). Does this mean that there are no laws in the Mosaic law that the believer of today is obligated to obey? Only those that have been reiterated in the NT. We are under the new covenant, and the old covenant has been done away. It is no longer our

1. Plato *Respublica* 7 §538c; *Sophista* 265c; *Leges* 1 §644d.

2. Strabo 15.1.59; Philo *Gig.* 11 §52; Josephus *A.J.* 15.5.3 §136.

3. Andocides 4.6; Demosthenes *Orationes* 5.19; Dionysius Halicarnassensis 8.87.3.

4. The Peshitta translates δόγμα as "particular commandment" or "a prescription" (cf. Paul Joüon, "Notes philologiques sur quelques versets de l'Épître aux Éphésiens," *RSR* 26 [Octobre 1936]: 458).

5. As does Hendriksen (135) following Grosheide (45); cf. also Erich Mauerhofer, "Der Brief an die Epheser. 22. Teil: 2,13–16," *Fundamentum* 1 (1995): 24–25. The Mosaic Law, therefore, includes both the moral and ceremonial laws (Best, 260). Also, it is incorrect to deduce, as McEleney does, that only those decrees (δόγμα) that are listed by the apostles in the Jerusalem Council in Acts 16:4 are done away with by Christ's death. They are laws of touch and taste followed by the strict school which put a barrier between Jews and Gentiles (Neil J. McEleney, "Conversion, Circumcision and the Law," *NTS* 20 [April 1974]: 339–40). This is being selective and highly subjective when the word is used so infrequently in the NT. Balla's suggestion is that not the whole Mosaic law was abolished but only those laws that marked Israel off from other nations (Peter Balla, "Is the Law Abolished According to Eph. 2:15?" *European Journal of Theology* 3, no. 1 [1994]: 14–16). This is unconvincing because there is nothing in the context that makes such a distinction and that only these laws were abolished.

6. In recent times much discussion has been devoted to this issue. See the various articles from different points of view in Wayne G. Strickland, gen. ed., *The Law, the Gospel, and the Modern Christian: Five Views* (Grand Rapids: Zondervan, 1993), see esp. the articles by Wayne G. Strickland, "The Inauguration of the Law of Christ with the Gospel of Christ: A Dispensational View," 229–79 and Douglas Moo, "The Law of Christ

modus operandi.[1] Christ has fulfilled it and it is no longer operative, and this applies to both Gentile and Jewish believers who are in Christ. To be sure, Paul was opposed to antinomianism for he states that he was under the law of Christ (lit. "in-law of Christ," ἔννομος Χριστοῦ) (1 Cor 9:21) and was to fulfill the law of Christ (τὸν νόμον τοῦ Χριστοῦ) (Gal 6:2). Much debate has been generated over these statements, but suffice it to say that the least one could say is that the law of Christ is expressed in the new covenant, that is, the NT.

Therefore, Paul's progression in the argument is that Christ has destroyed the symptom, that is, the enmity between Jews and Gentiles, by making inoperative the root or cause, namely, the law of commandments in decrees. Hence, the nullification of the Mosaic law has great significance for Jews and Gentiles in Christ. Why did God do this? Paul will deal with this next.

(b) The Purpose of the Operation (2:15b–16)

Paul now states the purpose of rendering inoperative the Mosaic law. The purpose is twofold: first, to create a new person; and second, to reconcile both Jews and Gentiles to God.

(i) To Create One New Person (2:15b)

Text: 2:15b. ἵνα τοὺς δύο κτίσῃ ἐν ἑαυτῷ εἰς ἕνα καινὸν ἄνθρωπον ποιῶν εἰρήνην

Translation: 2:15b. "in order that he might create in himself the two into one new person, so making peace"

Commentary: 2:15b. ἵνα τοὺς δύο κτίσῃ ἐν ἑαυτῷ[2] εἰς ἕνα καινὸν[3] ἄνθρωπον, "in order that he might create in himself the two into one

---

as the Fulfillment of the Law of Moses: A Modified Lutheran View," 319–76; cf. also Thomas R. Schreiner, *The Law and Its Fulfillment: A Pauline Theology of Law* (Grand Rapids: Baker, 1993).

1. Wessels' suggestion that legalism can be permitted and is even useful in the Christian life is unacceptable; cf. Martin Wessels, "'Peace'. Ephesians 2:11–22," *Unitas Fratrum* 10 (1981): 119.

2. The reading αὐτῷ is found in 𝔓[46] ℵ* A B F P 33 104 326 1175 1739 1881 *l* 249 *pc* (NA[27], UBS[4]), whereas ἑαυτῷ is found in ℵ[2] D G Ψ 𝔐 latt Marcion[T] Epiphanius Chrysostom Theodoret Oecumenius Theophylact. The first reading has very good manuscript evidence from the Alexandrian text but only F from the Western text and this is not the best representative of that text-type. The second reading has good representative manuscripts from the Western and Byzantine text-types and not the best representative from the Alexandrian text (Ψ). A minority on the committee for UBS[3] strongly preferred the rough breathing of αὑτῷ (Bruce M. Metzger, *A Textual Commentary on the Greek New Testament* [London: United Bible Societies, 1971], 602). WH's text reads αὑτῷ. The second reading is preferred because of good representatives from the text-types mentioned above and because of good geographical distribution. This is the easier reading because if one accepts the first reading, one still translates it reflexively (cf. Wallace, *Greek Grammar*, 325).

3. The reading κοινόν is found only in 𝔓[46] F G and καὶ μόνον is only in K, neither of which are sufficient to overthrow the reading of the text in UBS[4] and NA[27].

new person," states the first purpose of rendering inoperative the law of commandments, consisting in decrees, namely, to create one new person. The conjunction ἵνα indicates purpose. τοὺς δύο immediately follows ἵνα because Paul had discussed the division of the two groups, Jews and Gentiles. Whereas the neuter form of the substantival adjective τὰ ἀμφότερα was used in verse 14 because it referred to two parties, systems, or classes under which Jews and Gentiles were grouped, here they are conceived concretely as persons, and thus the masculine τοὺς δύο is used. Also, the masculine is used in view of the following ἄνθρωπον. The two persons become one new person. As discussed at 2:10 the verb κτίζω in the NT always has God as the subject of creation, whether it be in spiritual or physical realms. Here the subject is Christ, the second person of the Trinity, who creates "in himself the two into one new person." The preposition with the reflexive pronoun (ἐν ἑαυτῷ) indicates the sphere or location of this creation.

The purpose was to create in himself one new person out of the two persons.[1] The preposition εἰς gives direction. The word "one" (ἕνα) makes a definite contrast to the "two" (δύο) hostile groups, which they once were when outside of Christ. Some of the older lexicographers tried to make a sharp distinction between the adjective καινός, "new," emphasizing new in character or quality, and the synonym νέος, "new," emphasizing new in time.[2] That may have been true in earlier times but by NT times this difference had pretty much evaporated.[3] Both of these adjectives have the idea of newness in the qualitative and temporal senses. This is evident when καινός is used in Eph 4:24 and νέος is used in the parallel passage in Col 3:10. In the present context καινός is used to show that Christ has created a whole new person entirely different from the two former persons, namely, Jews and Gentiles. It is not that Gentiles become Jews[4] as Gentile proselytes did in

1. Mussner ("Contributions Made by Qumran to the Understanding of the Epistle to the Ephesians," 174–76) tries to show that the creation into a new person is paralleled in the Qumran materials. However, it really does not coincide, for in the Qumran literature, unity comes when one enters into the eternal heavenly community rather than an earthly community.

2. Cf. William Barclay, "The One, New Man," in *Unity and Diversity in New Testament Theology: Essays in Honor of George E. Ladd*, ed. Robert A. Guelich (Grand Rapids: Eerdmans, 1978), 73–81; Trench, *Synonyms of the New Testament*, 219–25; Cremer, *Biblico-Theological Lexicon*, 321–22.

3. MM 314–15; R. A. Harrisville, "The Concept of Newness in the New Testament," *JBL* 74 (June 1955): 69–79; Hermann Haarbeck, Hans-Georg Link, Colin Brown, "New [καινός, νέος]," *NIDNTT* 2 (1976): 670; cf. also L&N §§58.71; 67.115.

4. *Contra* Dunn (*The Partings of the Ways*, 149) who sees the Jews and Greeks to "have been recreated in the Israelite of God's purpose (cf. Eph. 2.15), wherein Gentiles are united with Christ, become members of the commonwealth of Israel, participate in the covenants of promise, and rejoice in hope and in the knowledge of God, brought near by the blood of Christ (2.12–13), 'no longer strangers and sojourners' (2.19)." But the context shows that he preached peace to both far and near (v. 17) and he makes a whole new entity.

pre-NT times[1] nor that Jews become Gentiles, but both become "one new person" or "one new humanity," a third entity. This is different from those who were called "God-fearers" (e.g., Acts 10:2, 22). These were Gentiles who accepted God and the Jewish Scriptures but were not circumcised and therefore not fully accepted by the Jews. What is presented in the context is a whole new humanity where Jewish and Gentile believers in Christ fully accept one another because they are one new entity. Best, among others, suggests that the "new person" refers not to two groups united into one corporate person but individual believers who are a new humanity, as Paul describes elsewhere "for neither is circumcision anything, nor uncircumcision, but a new creature" (Gal 6:15), and "if any person be in Christ, he is a new creature" (2 Cor 5:17), and "put on the new person" (Eph 4:24).[2] He asserts that otherwise there is no need to change from neuter (τὰ ἀμφότερα ἕν) in verse 14, to masculine (τοὺς δύο κτίσῃ ἐν αὐτῷ εἰς ἕνα καινὸν ἄνθρωπον) in verse 15, and back to neuter (ἐν ἑνὶ σώματι) in verse 16. However, the context argues for two entities which become one new corporate entity. The new corporate person, who is called "one body" (ἑνὶ σώματι) in verse 16, refers to the church.[3] The change of genders is understandable, as explained in the preceding paragraph. Furthermore, later in 4:13 Paul does picture the two groups, Jews and Gentiles, as a single individual of a mature person. Therefore, in the present context, Paul refers to a whole new race that is formed. A new race that is raceless! This coincides with Paul's admonition not to offend three groups of people: the Jews, the Greeks/Gentiles, and the church of God (1 Cor 10:32). The Jews and the Greeks/Gentiles are presented as unconverted and the church is that which is composed of Jewish and Gentile believers. They are not Jews or Gentiles but a body of Chris-

1. For a brief discussion of a Gentile becoming a proselyte to Judaism, see Smith, "Jewish and Greek Traditions in Ephesians 2:11–22," 142–43.

2. Best, *One Body in Christ*, 152–54; Masson, 166 n. 5; Best, 261–63; cf. also Mussner, *Christus, das All und die Kirche*, 87; Smith, "The Two Made One," 41–43; Allan, "The 'In Christ' Formula in Ephesians," 60–61. Jerome thinks that this new person will receive angelic natures. This is really foreign to the context. See Clark, "The Place of Jerome's Commentary on Ephesians in the Origenist Controversy," 157.

3. Barth, 309; Schnackenburg, 115; Bruce, 299–300; O'Brien, 200; Roels, *God's Mission*, 128–33; cf. Hanson, *The Unity of the Church in the New Testament*, 144–46; Rudolf Schnackenburg, *God's Rule and Kingdom*, trans. John Murray (Freiburg: Herder; Edinburgh: Nelson 1963), 304–5; Merklein, *Christus und die Kirche*, 45–50; Darrell L. Bock, "'The New Man' as Community in Colossians and Ephesians," in *Integrity of Heart, Skillfulness of Hands: Biblical and Leadership Studies in Honor of Donald K. Campbell*, ed. Charles H. Dyer and Roy B. Zuck (Grand Rapids: Baker, 1994), 161; Moritz, "'Summing-up all Things'," 102–4; Gese, *Das Vermächtnis des Apostels*, 134–37. Lindemann (*Aufhebung*, 167–70) suggests that the "new person" refers to the redeemed in connection with the redeemer of the Gnostic redeemer myth. This complicated view is based on materials that postdate the NT and is so foreign to the context that it is not worth serious consideration.

tians who make up the church.[1] This creates unity among the believers in the church, for they are in Christ.[2] It is this community to which Jesus made reference when he said to Peter, "I will build my church" (Matt 16:18).

ποιῶν εἰρήνην, "so making peace." The present participle expresses the result of the creation of the two into one new person.[3] In this case, the "so making peace" explains "he is our peace" in verse 14. It has been a long process from verse 14 to the present verse. Paul had to show that Christ made Jews and Gentiles one, destroyed the middle wall of partition, and rendered inoperative the law of commandments. That, in turn, was the purpose for the creation of one new person which resulted in peace. This is opposite of the hostility expressed in verse 14. Again, the unity of believers is stressed.

At this point, one needs to observe the text carefully. The text does not suggest that Christ's death brought about a universal redemption so that all Jews and Gentiles are reconciled.[4] Most Jews and Gentiles would not concede that they are reconciled to each other. Nor does the text propound that Gentiles have been accepted into the people of God, namely, Israel, as suggested by Barth[5] who maintains that since faith is not mentioned in the context, all Jews and Gentiles are united by Christ and it is not limited to "Jewish- and Gentile-born *Christians* only."[6] In fact, he states that every Jew is included, "be he a faithful observer of the law or a rebellious trespasser, a Pharisee or a Sadducee, orthodox or secularized."[7] Hence, there is no need to preach a message of salvation to the Jews.[8] On the contrary, the present context assumes that only believing Jews and believing Gentiles make up this

1. Cf. excursus to Eph 3:5 by Erich Mauerhofer, "Der Brief an die Epheser. 27. Teil: 3,4–6," *Fundamentum* 3 (1996): 16–19. In the second century the Letter to Diognetus (1.1) depicts Christians as a third race distinct from Israel and the Gentiles.

2. Rey espouses that with baptism one puts on the new person. There is nothing about baptism in this context. Furthermore, he seems to confuse Christ (the new Adam) with the "new person" (the body of believers) (Bernard Rey, "L'homme nouveau d'après S. Paul," *Revue des sciences philosophiques et théologiques* 48 [Octobre 1964]: 168–70). Christ is not the "new person" but the "new Adam." The church is the "new person." Christ is the "new Adam" and because of him we who are in him are the "new person." On this point, Barth puts it well when he states that if the new person is Christ, then Christ created him in himself (*Israel and the Church*, 87).

3. Wallace, *Greek Grammar*, 639.

4. Howard, "The Wall Broken," 302–5.

5. Markus Barth, *Israel und die Kirche im Brief des Paulus an die Epheser*, Theologische Existenz Heute, ed. K. G. Steck and G. Eichholz, vol. 75 (Munich: Chr. Kaiser, 1959); idem, "Conversion and Conversation," 3–24; idem, *Jesus, Paulus und die Juden*, Theologische Studien, ed. Karl Barth and Max Geiger, vol. 91 (Zürich: EVZ-Verlag, 1967), 76–78; Barth, 310–11; idem, *The People of God*, 45–72.

6. Barth, *Israel and the Church*, 95, see also 74–75.

7. Barth, 255; see also idem, *The Broken Wall*, 122, 128.

8. Barth, *Israel and the Church*, 108–15.

new entity. First, in 1:15 Paul commended them for their "faith" in the Lord Jesus Christ. Second, in the immediately preceding context Paul states that Gentiles are saved by grace through "faith" and are his workmanship in Christ (vv. 8–10). He continues by arguing that Gentiles who were far off but now in Christ were brought near by the blood of Christ (redemption and forgiveness, 1:7), that both Jews and Gentiles were reconciled through the cross, and that the message of peace was preached to those far off (Gentiles) and to those near (Jews) (vv. 13–17). The whole context is speaking about a community of faith, believing Jews and believing Gentiles, not all human beings.[1] Both believing Jews and believing Gentiles have been united into one body, a fact on which Paul will elaborate in the next chapter (cf. also 4:5, one "faith"). There is then a need for the church to preach the good news of Christ's redemption and reconciliation to both Jews and Gentiles with the result that those who believe will then belong to this new entity. Also, Best correctly points out that Barth's view "robs the newness (v. 15) of its newness and gravely diminishes the discontinuity before and after Christ if all that has happened is in effect a widening of the boundaries of Israel by the addition of Gentile believers."[2] The text is clear. Only those in Christ Jesus, whether they had been near or far, are brought near by the blood of Christ. The union is not between Jews and Gentiles but between redeemed Jews and Gentiles who are in Christ.[3]

(ii) To Reconcile Both to God (2:16)

This verse considers the second purpose for the law to be rendered inoperative. It is not only for the purpose of creating one new person from two distinct groups but also to reconcile both of them to God himself.

Text: 2:16. καὶ ἀποκαταλλάξῃ τοὺς ἀμφοτέρους ἐν ἑνὶ σώματι τῷ θεῷ διὰ τοῦ σταυροῦ, ἀποκτείνας τὴν ἔχθραν ἐν αὐτῷ.

Translation: 2:16. "and that he might reconcile them both in one body to God through the cross, by which the hostility has been killed."

Commentary: 2:16. καὶ ἀποκαταλλάξῃ, "and that he might reconcile." The coordinating conjunction (καί) makes the two subjunctive verbs (κτίσῃ and ἀποκαταλλάξῃ) parallel. Thus, beginning with the conjunction ἵνα in verse 15b, Paul is stating, "in order that he [Christ]

1. Ernst Percy, review of *Israel und die Kirche im Brief des Paulus an die Epheser*, by Markus Barth, *TLZ* 86 (März 1961): 199–200; Rese, "Church and Israel in the Deuteropauline Letters," 28–29; cf. Günter Klein, "Der Friede Gottes und der Friede der Welt: Eine exegetische Verfgewisserung am Neuen Testament," *ZTK* 83 (August 1986): 338–39.

2. Best, 268.

3. Lincoln, "The Church and Israel in Ephesians 2," 605–24; O'Brien, 203–4; see also Bruce W. Fong, "Addressing the Issue of Racial Reconciliation according to the Principles of Eph 2:11–22," *JETS* 38 (December 1995): 565–80.

might create in himself . . . and that he might reconcile. . . ." The verb ἀποκαταλλάσσω, meaning "to reconcile," is never found prior to Paul. It is found only here and in Col 1:20, 22, and it is thought that he coined the word.[1] The two prepositional prefixes (ἀπο- and κατα-) may be an intensified form of ἀλλάσσω. In the NT God is never the object of ἀποκαταλλάσσω or καταλλάσσω, but only people (or things in Col 1:20).[2] Although Morris insists that both God and people need to be reconciled, he admits that there is no indication of this in the immediate context.[3] He makes a point that διαλλάσσω in Matt 5:24 has the same basic meaning as καταλλάσσω and thus concludes that both sides need reconciliation.[4] This is a weak supposition, however, for διαλλάσσω is used only in Matt 5:24 and should not determine the meaning of καταλλάσσω. Furthermore, the context in Matthew speaks of two human beings who need reconciliation. On the other hand, in contexts of the reconciliation of God and humans, καταλλάσσω and ἀποκαταλλάσσω are always used where God is the one who reconciles and the human being is the one being reconciled (Rom 5:10*bis*; 2 Cor 5:18, 19, 20; Col 1:20, 22), which is also true for the noun καταλλαγή (Rom 5:11; 11:15; 2 Cor 5:18, 19). This is certainly the case here, for Christ made the law inoperative in order that he might create in himself one new person and also might reconcile the two entities, who are now one, to God. Next, the objects of the reconciliation are discussed.

τοὺς ἀμφοτέρους ἐν ἑνὶ σώματι, "them both in one body," are the objects of the reconciliation. It is thought by some that the "one body" refers to Christ's human body on the cross[5] but this is improbable. The usage "his body" would be more appropriate if this were the case.[6] Rather, these words state in another way what was already mentioned in verse 15b, "the two . . . into one new person." This body is the incorporated body of Jewish and Gentiles believers in Christ known as the church (cf. Col 3:15; 1 Cor 10:17; Eph 4:4).[7] Again, the masculine is used here because Jews and Gentiles are seen concretely as persons who are reconciled to God. It must be understood that the

1. Friedrich Büchsel, "ἀποκαταλλάσσω," *TDNT* 1 (1964): 258. For a more recent study of the word, see Stanley E. Porter, *Καταλλάσσω in Ancient Greek Literature, with Reference to the Pauline Writings*, Estudios de Filología Neotestamentaria, ed. Juan Mateos, vol. 5 (Córdoba: Ediciones el Almendro, 1994), 169–71, 185–89.

2. Büchsel, *TDNT* 1 (1964): 258–59.

3. Morris, *Apostolic Preaching*, 233; cf. also Gese, *Das Vermächtnis des Apostels*, 137–41.

4. Morris, *Apostolic Preaching*, 236.

5. Chrysostom *Eph* 2:16 (*PG* 62:40–41; cf. also Kohlgraf, *Die Ekklesiologie des Epheserbriefes in der Auslegung durch Johannes Chrysostomus*, 269–71); Theodoret *Eph* 2:16 (*PG* 82:524); Bengel, 4:79.

6. Eadie, 180; Abbott, 66.

7. Dawes (*The Body in Question*, 160) thinks that the body refers to the church but adds a caution that it is not distinct from Christ, hence "an implicit identification of the Church and Christ." Cf. also Los Santos, *La novedad de la metáfora κεφαλή-σῶμα*, 156–57, 352.

reconciliation spoken of here is not between Jews and Gentiles "into" one body, for that would necessitate an εἰς rather than ἐν and the verb would have been διαλλάσσω (cf. Matt 5:24) rather than ἀποκαταλλάσσω. That particular reconciliation of Jews and Gentiles has already been discussed at verse 15. Rather, it is speaking of those believing Jews and Gentiles, who are in one body, as reconciled "to God." This is different from Col 1:20 where "all things" rather than "those both in one body" are the objects of reconciliation.

τῷ θεῷ διὰ τοῦ σταυροῦ, "to God through the cross." The indirect object (τῷ θεῷ) denotes to whom the corporate body of believing Jews and Gentiles are reconciled, namely, God. This was done "by means of the cross" (διὰ τοῦ σταυροῦ). It is Christ who reconciles Jews and Gentiles to God through his death on the cross. The work of Christ on the cross is described in verse 13, "by the blood of Christ" (ἐν τῷ αἵματι τοῦ Χριστοῦ), and in verse 14, "in his flesh" (ἐν τῇ σαρκὶ αὐτοῦ). This work of Christ is described in 1:7 as redemption "through his blood" (διὰ τοῦ αἵματος αὐτοῦ). This seems reversed from what is normally presented, namely, first the reconciliation of individuals to God and then to each other. However, in the present context of verses 14–18 the main point is the reconciliation of believing Jews and Gentiles rather than reconciliation to God. Furthermore, Paul had already dealt with individual reconciliation to God in 2:1–10, 13. Regardless, one thing should not go unnoticed, namely, both the reconciliation to God and to each other was by means of Christ's death. Reconciliation exacted a heavy price, the death of God's Son.[1] Reconciliation between human beings and God is mentioned elsewhere by Paul and it is always mentioned in connection with the sacrifice of Christ (Rom 5:10; 2 Cor 5:18–21; Col 1:20). In applying canonical criticism, Porter and Clarke make an interesting observation. The newly coined term for reconciliation (ἀποκαταλλάσσω) is used only here and in Col 1:20, 22, as mentioned above. It is a word that fits within Pauline thought. However, it would seem that no pseudonymous author (of Colossians and Ephesians) would have coined a new word nor would he have used it in Ephesians since it is used differently than in Colossians (if he used Colossians as a basis of Ephesians). The use of this word in these books points to Pauline authorship for both books.[2]

ἀποκτείνας τὴν ἔχθραν ἐν αὐτῷ,[3] "by which the hostility has been killed." Three things need to be discussed. First, the hostility (τὴν ἔχθραν) is not the same as that which is mentioned in verse 14. There it speaks of the hostility between Jews and Gentiles, but here it speaks of hostility between God and human beings. The reason for the

1. For a study of sacrifice in connection with reconciliation of Jews and Gentiles, see Barth, *The Broken Wall*, 33–45.

2. Porter and Clarke, "Canonical-Critical Perspective," 77–81.

3. The reading ἐν ἑαυτῷ is found in F G *pc* latt and should not be accepted because it is limited to the Western text-type.

change is due to the change of contexts. In verses 14–15 Paul deals with the union of believing Jews and Gentiles into one new humanity, but here in verse 16 he discusses the reconciliation of this body of Jews and Gentiles to God. Second, the aorist participle ἀποκτείνας, "has been killed," modifies the aorist subjunctive ἀποκαταλλάξῃ. Possibly, it may denote a temporal significance whereby the action of killing the emnity was antecedent to, or more likely, contemporaneous with[1] the reconciliation of the one body of Jews and Gentiles to God. However, more likely, the participle shows the means of the reconciliation of the one body of Jews and Gentiles to God, namely, by the destruction of the hostility between God and human beings. Third, the prepositional phrase ἐν αὐτῷ could be translated reflexively as "in himself," but a preferable translation is "by it," referring back to the cross[2] because (a) the cross is its nearest antecedent, (b) the participle speaks of Christ's death which was on the cross, and (c) it was there that the problem of hostility was actually resolved. Thus, the preposition ἐν indicates the means by which the hostility was put to death, that is, the cross.

b. Announcement of Peace (2:17–18)

Paul has explained how peace was accomplished, first between believing Jews and Gentiles and second between them and God. He now discusses the proclamation of that peace, both its content and its result.

(1) Content of the Message: Peace (2:17)

Text: 2:17. καὶ ἐλθὼν εὐηγγελίσατο εἰρήνην ὑμῖν τοῖς μακρὰν καὶ εἰρήνην τοῖς ἐγγύς·

Translation: 2:17. "And coming he preached peace to you who were far off and peace to those who were near;"

Commentary: 2:17. καὶ ἐλθὼν εὐηγγελίσατο, "And coming he preached." The coordinating conjunction καί, "and," could connect with the previous two aorist subjunctives in verse 16 in an *ad sensum* agreement, but this is highly unlikely. It is much better to consider the present statement parallel to "he is our peace" in verse 14. He is not only our peace but he also preached peace. The aorist participle ἐλθών, meaning "to come," is not superfluous,[3] but rather denotes the actual activity in connection with the proclamation of peace. It could be a participle of attendant circumstance, that is, "he came and

1. BDF §339. Recent studies show that when the aorist participle precedes the main verb, there is a tendency toward antecedent action and when it follows the main verb, as it is here, there is a definite tendency toward contemporaneous action with the main verb (see Porter, *Verbal Aspect*, 383–84).

2. MHT 3:43; HS §139j; Zerwick, *Biblical Greek* §211.

3. MHT 3:453, 485; 4:89–90.

preached peace" (AV, RV, ASV, RSV, NASB, NEB, TEV, NIV, NRSV), but more likely it is a temporal participle, "after/when he came, he preached peace." But to what does his coming refer? Some have thought that it refers to his ministry here on earth[1] or the forty days between his resurrection and ascension.[2] However, it cannot refer to those periods of time. It must be after Christ's crucifixion, for that served as the basis of the peace proclaimed. Also, it cannot be at the time of his earthly ministry, before and after his death and resurrection, because in the present verse it states that he preached this message of peace to both Jews and Gentiles, and there is no record that he preached to Gentiles while on earth. In his earthly ministry Christ preached almost entirely to the Jews (Matt 10:5–6; 15:24–27), and the present verse is primarily addressed to Gentile Christians. It is better to assume that on the basis of the peace he accomplished, it was proclaimed by him to Jews and Gentiles by means of the ministry of the Holy Spirit through his apostles (cf. Eph 3:5–6).[3] Hence, the process would be as follows: he came, accomplished peace in his reconciling death, then preached peace. Lincoln thinks of it "as a retrospective reference to vv. 14–16, i.e., to that coming of Christ which climaxed in his reconciling death." Thus, the preaching of peace resulted from what was accomplished on the cross.[4] This has some merit although it seems that the text actually states "he preached" rather than stating "these things speak" or "his death proclaims."

The main verb εὐαγγελίζομαι is used fifty-four times in the NT, twenty-one times by Paul, and twice in Ephesians (2:17; 3:8). After an extensive discussion Friedrich contends that in Greek literature it is the announcement of news which often does not correspond to the facts (e.g., false stories of victory to boost morale), whereas in the NT the content of the message is Jesus himself. In the NT it is not active or creative but rather reveals and instructs.[5] The point is that the message which is preached is the not the invention of the preacher, but the proclamation of that which has been faithfully handed down. Furthermore, it "is not just speaking and preaching: it is proclamation with full authority and power."[6] As was discussed at 1:13, the noun has the idea of "good news" and the verb conveys the same idea. In

1. Chrysostom *Eph* 2:17–22 (*PG* 62:43); Harless, 244–46; Mitton, 109; Mussner, *Christus, das All und die Kirche*, 101; Fischer, *Tendenz und Absicht des Epheserbriefes*, 131–32; Stuhlmacher, "'He is our Peace' (Eph. 2:14)," 191.

2. Bengel, 4:79–80.

3. Eadie, 185; Ellicott, 50; Abbott, 66–67; Gnilka, 145–46; Schnackenburg, 118; Bruce, 300; Karl Olav Sandnes, *Paul—One of the Prophets?: A Contribution to the Apostle's Self-understanding*, WUNT, ed. Martin Hengel and Otfried Hofius, vol. 43 (Tübingen: Mohr, 1991), 229.

4. Lincoln, 148–49. Cf. Gese, *Das Vermächtnis des Apostels*, 120–23.

5. Gerhard Friedrich, "εὐαγγελίζομαι," *TDNT* 2 (1964): 711–12.

6. Ibid., 720.

the present context it specifies the good news of peace that is being preached.

εἰρήνην ὑμῖν τοῖς μακρὰν καὶ εἰρήνην[1] τοῖς ἐγγύς, "peace to you who were far off and peace to those who were near." The verb εὐαγγελίζομαι is normally followed by the "accusative of the thing and the dative of person."[2] Here the accusative of the thing, "peace," is mentioned twice and the datives of persons are "to you who were far off" and "to those who were near."[3] The preceding context helps us determine the content of the peace and the recipients of the message. First, the recipients of the message, namely, those who were far away, were the unredeemed Gentiles who were without Christ and alienated from Israel and her covenants (vv. 12–13). Those who were near were the unredeemed Jews who had the covenants of promise, had hope, and had God in this world (v. 12). Second, the message of peace was preached to both groups as indicated by the word "peace" being repeated for each group. The content of that peace is that which has just been discussed in the previous verses: the peace between Jews and Gentiles and the peace between them and God. Each group had to learn two things. They had to learn that because of Christ's work on the cross, there is peace horizontally between the two groups and they had become "one new humanity." Further, there is peace vertically between them and God. The Gentiles are addressed first because they were "far off," being completely outside of God's covenantal program and possibly because Paul was an apostle to the Gentiles.

Paul may well have been thinking of Isa 57:19 where peace is repeated twice and the recipients were the far and the near.[4] However, in that context it referred to Jews who were "near" at home and to Jews who were "far" away in the worldwide dispersion. As already stated, in the present context Paul speaks of Gentiles who were far off and Jews who were near in terms of covenantal relationships, although these Jews geographically could be either nearby or far away from the land

1. The repeat of εἰρήνην here is omitted by Ψ 𝔐 syr[h] Marcion[T] Tyconius but retained in 𝔓[46] ℵ A B D F G P 33 365 1175 1739 1881 2464 *pc* it[d, g] cop[sa, bo] arm eth *al* Cyprian Eusebius Didymus (cf. Metzger, *Textual Commentary*, 2d ed., 534; Ian A. Moir, "The Text of Ephesians Exhibited by Minuscule Manuscripts Housed in Great Britain—Some Preliminary Comments," in *Studies in New Testament Language and Text. Essays in Honour of George D. Kilpatrick on the Occasion of His Sixty-fifth Birthday*, ed. J. K. Elliott, NovTSup, ed. W. C. van Unnik et al., vol. 44 [Leiden: Brill, 1976], 315). The reading should be retained for it has solid Alexandrian and Western support, whereas the omission has only solid Byzantine support and only Ψ from the Alexandrian text and the syr[h], which could be either Western or Caesarean.

2. Robertson, *Grammar*, 483; HS §174d.

3. These adverbs (μακράν and ἐγγύς) have an adjectival idea (cf. Robertson, *Grammar*, 547).

4. For a discussion of the use of Isa 57:19 in Eph 2:17, see Lincoln, "The Use of the OT in Ephesians," 25–30; Lincoln, 146–48; Moritz, *A Profound Mystery*, 42–55; cf. Findeis, *Versöhnung-Apostolat-Kirche*, 473–83.

of Israel. In fact, Smith, in citing many Jewish sources, shows that the near-far language consistently refers to Jews with only one exception (*Num. Rab.* 8:4), where it refers to Gentile proselytes.[1] Thus, it can only be surmised that Paul may have used the imagery of the Isaiah passage, but we cannot dogmatically presume he implements its meaning.

This verse reinforces the idea of the formation of an entirely new entity. Both the "far" and "near" hear the message of peace. If the Gentiles actually became Jews, then the near would not need the message of peace; rather those who were far away would enter into the fold of the near. On the contrary, the picture is that the "near" also need a message of peace, and on acceptance they, with the Gentiles, enter the new fold, the church. It is the new humanity that is created. What makes it new is not the message but the new community the message produces. One needs to note, as Barth does, that the message was not to the Gentiles at the Jews' expense nor to the Jews at the Gentiles' expense, but that Christ's sacrifice was for both sides and they are both joined together in Christ.[2]

Most of the discussion of this chapter revolves around Gentiles who are brought near, but little about Jews with whom the Gentile believers have been united. Dahl wonders why the author of Ephesians mentions nothing about the Jewish Christians' attempt to foist some of their Jewish customs on Gentile believers as indicated in other NT literature (Gal 2:11–14; Acts 21:20–21).[3] However, Ephesians is dealing with a predominantly Gentile audience (2:1–2, 11–13; 4:17–19); hence, Jewish Christian concerns may not have been an issue. Furthermore, there is really very little discussion of the controversy in other Pauline letters with the exception of Galatians.

(2) Result of the Message: Access (2:18)

Having explained the preaching of peace to those who were far away and to those who were near, Paul now discusses the result of that message.

Text: 2:18. ὅτι δι' αὐτοῦ ἔχομεν τὴν προσαγωγὴν οἱ ἀμφότεροι ἐν ἑνὶ πνεύματι πρὸς τὸν πατέρα.

Translation: 2:18. "so that through him we both have the access in one Spirit to the Father."

1. Smith, "Jewish and Greek Traditions in Ephesians 2:11–22," 11–14; idem, "The Ephesian Heresy and the Origin of the Epistle to the Ephesians," 79–86.

2. Barth, "Conversion and Conversation," 11–12.

3. Nils Alstrup Dahl, "Gentiles, Christians, and Israelites in the Epistle to the Ephesians," *HTR* 79 (January/April/July 1986): 35–38. This same article is printed as a separate publication, see idem, "Gentiles, Christians, and Israelites in the Epistle to the Ephesians," in *Christians among Jews and Gentiles: Essays in Honor of Krister Stendahl on His Sixty-fifth Birthday*, ed. George W. E. Nickelsburg with George W. MacRae (Philadelphia: Fortress, 1986), 35–38; updated in idem, *Studies in Ephesians*, 444–47.

Commentary: 2:18. ὅτι δι᾽ αὐτοῦ ἔχομεν τὴν προσαγωγὴν οἱ ἀμφότεροι, "so that through him we both have the access." The ὅτι is not to be translated "that" in order to indicate the content of the preaching,[1] for that has already been signified as "peace." Nor is it to be translated "because, for" to indicate the reason for the peace.[2] To say that Christ preached peace to Jews and Gentiles because we have access does not make good sense. Rather, it is better to translate it "so that" to indicate result.[3] Hence, Christ preached peace to Jews and Gentiles with the result that we both have access to the Father. The prepositional phrase δι᾽ αὐτοῦ, "through him," is placed immediately after the ὅτι for the sake of emphasis. It is only through Christ that we have the privilege which Paul is about to discuss. The pronoun "we" here cannot refer to Jews as opposed to Gentiles ("you") but must refer to both Jews and Gentiles who believe (cf. vv. 3, 14).[4] Again, as in verse 16, Paul uses the masculine form of the substantival adjective οἱ ἀμφότεροι to view them concretely as persons from both Jews and Gentiles who together enjoy the privilege of access. In light of verses 14 and 16 this does not mean "we both *alike* have access" but rather "we both *together* have access."[5]

The noun προσαγωγή is used only three times in the NT (Rom 5:2; Eph 2:18; 3:12). It is can be used transitively with the sense of "introduction" to a person such as a king[6] or intransitively with the idea of access or approach to a harbor or to land.[7] It is not used in the LXX. Some think that in the present verse it is used transitively with the idea of being brought to God.[8] However, because peace has been established in verse 17 and because in the present verse the verb is present tense, it seems that the intransitive sense is better. Because of the peace accomplished, we have continual access. It is something we

1. Haupt, 91; Gnilka, 146; Adai, *Der Heilige Geist als Gegenwart Gottes*, 163; Heinrich Rendtorff, "Der Brief an die Epheser," in *Die kleineren Briefe des Apostles Paulus*, 6th ed., NTD, ed. Paul Althaus, vol. 8 (Göttingen: Vandenhoeck & Ruprecht, 1953), 68; Gnilka, 146.

2. Bengel, 4:80; Hodge, 143; Alford, 3:99; Meyer, 139; Salmond, 297; Westcott, 39; Schlier, 139; Gaugler, 119; Findeis, *Versöhnung-Apostolat-Kirche*, 483; Lincoln, 149; Fee, *God's Empowering Presence*, 682 n. 79.

3. Eadie, 186; Ellicott, 51; Robinson, 66; Masson, 168; Mussner, *Christus, das All und die Kirche*, 104; Mitton, 110; Schnackenburg, 106–7; Luz, 140. The conjunction ὅτι can be used to denote result, cf. BAGD 589; BDAG 732; Robertson, *Grammar*, 1001; MHT 1:249; 3:318; BDF §456 (2); F.-M. Abel, *Grammaire du Grec biblique suivie d'un Choix de Papyrus*, 2d ed., EBib (Paris: Gabalda, 1927), 353; HS §279a; Wallace, *Greek Grammar*, 677.

4. Wallace, *Greek Grammar*, 398.

5. Fee, *God's Empowering Presence*, 683.

6. Xenophon *Cyropaedia* 7.5.45.

7. Polybius 9.41.1; 10.1.6; Plutarch *Aemilius Paulus* 13.5.

8. Chrysostom *Eph* 2:17–22 (*PG* 62:43); Eadie, 186–87; Ellicott, 51; Meyer, 139–40; Barth, 268.

possess.[1] This is true of the other two uses of the word in the NT. In the OT the Jews had access to God by means of the temple, but now in a new transcending way both Jews and Gentiles have equal access to God.[2] This access represents the freedom of approach. It breathes the idea of being familiar yet with no idea of contempt. To whom do we have this access? The remainder of the verse answers this question.

ἐν ἑνὶ πνεύματι πρὸς τὸν πατέρα, "in one Spirit to the Father." Although some think that the preposition ἐν should indicate the means by which we have access to the Father (AV, NIV),[3] that was shown to have been already accomplished through Christ as mentioned earlier in the verse (δι᾽ αὐτοῦ). It is preferable to see it as sphere (RV, ASV, RSV, NASB, NEB, TEV, JB, NJB, NRSV) in which both parties have common access.[4] The numeral ἑνί, "one," fortifies the idea of unity.[5] The use of the preposition with the numeral emphasizes both being reconciled ἐν ἑνὶ σώματι τῷ θεῷ, "in one body to God" (v. 16), and both having access ἐν ἑνὶ πνεύματι πρὸς τὸν πατέρα, "in one Spirit to the Father." This coincides with the fact that the body of Christ is united in one Spirit (4:4; 1 Cor 12:13), which is the Holy Spirit who empowers the union of Jews and Gentiles in their access to God. This access is πρὸς τὸν πατέρα, "to the Father." The preposition πρός can denote a friendly relationship and can be translated "to, toward, with, before."[6] Because of Christ's work, God is approachable. Without Christ's work sinful humans could not approach God.

Here, as in other parts of Ephesians, there is the involvement of the three persons of the Trinity (cf. 1:4–14, 17; 2:18, 22; 3:4–5, 14–17; 4:4–6; 5:18–20). In 1:4–14 it took the work of the three persons of the Trinity to redeem humans. Here the three persons of the Trinity are involved in the believers' access to God. Through the work of Christ united in one Spirit, believing Jews and Gentiles have access to the Father. The initiation and continuation of a person's relationship to God involves all three persons of the Trinity.

1. Alford, 3:99; Abbott, 67; Salmond, 298; Robinson, 162; Gaugler, 119; Schnackenburg, 118; Best, 273; O'Brien, 209 n. 218; cf. Karl Ludwig Schmidt, "προσαγωγή," *TDNT* 1 (1964): 133–34.

2. Lincoln, 149; cf. Franz Mussner, "Kirche als Kultgemeinde nach dem Neuen Testament," in *Praesentia Salutis. Gesammelte Studien zu Fragen und Themen des Neuen Testamentes, Kommentare und Beiträge zum Alten und Neuen Testament* (Düsseldorf: Patmos, 1967), 262–66 (this article was originally published in *Liturgisches Jahrbuch* 6 [1956]: 50–67).

3. Chrysostom *Eph* 2:17–22 (*PG* 62:43); Oecumenius *Eph* 2:14–18 (*PG* 118:1197, 1200); Theophylact *Eph* 2:18 (*PG* 124:1064); Calvin, 154.

4. Alford, 3:99; Ellicott, 51; Salmond, 298; Gaugler, 119; Barth, 267–68; Schnackenburg, 118; Mussner, *Christus, das All und die Kirche*, 104.

5. Mussner, *Christus, das All und die Kirche*, 104; Adai, *Der Heilige Geist als Gegenwart Gottes*, 173.

6. BAGD 710; BDAG 874.

In conclusion, in 2:14–18 Paul explains the union of Jews and Gentiles in four different ways: (1) "having made the *both one*" (v. 14); (2) "might create in himself the *two* into *one* new humanity" (v. 15); (3) "might reconcile them *both* in *one* body" (v. 16); and (4) "we *both* have the access in *one* Spirit" (v. 18). Clearly, this new union replaces the old enmity. Before conversion they were Jews and Gentiles, and after conversion they are one new person in Christ, called the Christians.[1] It is through Christ's death that both are brought together in one body (v. 16) and one Spirit (v. 18).[2]

3. Consequence of the Union (2:19–22)

Paul announced the union (vv. 11–13) and explained how it makes believing Jews and Gentiles into one "new humanity" (vv. 14–18). He now defines the consequences of that union (vv. 19–22). The suggestion by Nauck that this section is a baptismal hymn[3] is untenable. Nothing in the passage suggests the death, burial, and resurrection of the one being baptized. Rather, it is a fitting didactic conclusion to verses 11–18.

a. Fact: New Relationship (2:19)

Paul now discusses the consequential facts of the union of Jewish and Gentile believers. He states these both in terms of what they are not and in terms of what they are.

Text: 2:19. ἄρα οὖν οὐκέτι ἐστὲ ξένοι καὶ πάροικοι, ἀλλὰ ἐστὲ συμπολῖται τῶν ἁγίων καὶ οἰκεῖοι τοῦ θεοῦ,

Translation: 2:19 "So then you are no longer foreigners and aliens, but you are fellow citizens with the saints and members of God's household,"

Commentary: 2:19. ἄρα οὖν[4] οὐκέτι ἐστὲ ξένοι καὶ πάροικοι, "So then you are no longer foreigners and aliens." The combination of ἄρα

1. This is the opposite of Sigal's suggestion that the bond comes between Jews and Gentiles when the Jews recognize the Gentiles' salvation through Christ and the Gentiles recognize the Jews' salvation is attained without Christ—in other words, recognize each other's salvation, see Phillip Sigal, "Aspects of Dual Covenant Theology: Salvation," *Horizons in Biblical Theology* 5 (December 1983): 24–28.

2. R. Schnackenburg, "Christus, Geist und Gemeinde (Eph. 4:1–16)," in *Christ and Spirit in the New Testament. In Honour of Charles Francis Digby Moule*, ed. Barnabas Lindars and Stephen S. Smalley (Cambridge: Cambridge University Press, 1973), 283–85.

3. Nauck, "Eph. 2,19–22—ein Tauflied?" 362–71.

4. The conjunction οὖν is omitted by $\mathfrak{P}^{46vid}$ F G Ψ 1881 *pc* syr^{p}. Although this has Western attestation, it is weak in the Alexandrian and Byzantine text-types. Its inclusion has better attestation.

οὖν is not used in classical literature, except in the interrogative form (ἆρα οὖν), or in the LXX. It appears twelve times in the NT, and only in Paul's writings (Rom 5:18; 7:3, 25; 8:12; 9:16, 18; 14:12, 19; Gal 6:10; Eph 2:19; 1 Thess 5:6; 2 Thess 2:15). Both conjunctions are inferential and the combination of both only reinforces each other to denote a conclusion of the previous section and to introduce the logical consequence.[1] On the one hand, ἄρα could be translated "so, as a result, consequently,"[2] and, on the other hand, οὖν can be rendered "so, therefore, consequently, accordingly, then."[3] The two together may be translated "consequently therefore, so then." Although both are logical, ἄρα primarily expresses "a lively feeling of interest,"[4] and in this context the real interest would be the conclusion Paul makes from what he stated in verse 13 and on which he elaborates in verses 14–18.

In his inferential conclusion, Paul first declares what the Gentiles are not. They are no longer foreigners and aliens. The first word ξένος was discussed at verse 12 and it means, in general, a "stranger, foreigner" who is allowed to be in a country but with no rights, except that which has been agreed to by treaty. The second word πάροικος can have the idea of "dwelling near,[5] neighbor,"[6] but in later Greek it refers to an "alien, foreigner" who is a resident alien without national rights.[7] In the LXX it is used thirty-one times (twenty-six times in the canonical books), mostly translated either from גֵּר, meaning "sojourner"[8] (Gen 15:13; 23:4; Exod 18:3; Deut 14:21; Ps 39:12 [MT 39:13; LXX 38:13]), or from תּוֹשָׁב, again meaning "sojourner"[9] (Exod 12:45; Lev 22:10; 25:6; Num 35:15). It occurs only four times in the NT (Acts 7:6 [citing Gen 15:13], 29; Eph 2:19; 1 Pet 2:11) meaning "foreigner, alien" temporarily living in a land that is not theirs. Both ξένοι and πάροικοι basically mean "foreigners," but they do have a

1. Margaret E. Thrall, *Greek Particles in the New Testament: Linguistic and Exegetical Studies*, New Testament Tools and Studies, ed. Bruce M. Metzger, vol. 3 (Leiden: Brill, 1962), 10–11.

2. BAGD 104; BDAG 127. There is no literal translation but one must translate according to the context, as is shown by Kenneth Willis Clark, "The Meaning of αρα," in *Festschrift to Honor F. Wilbur Gingrich: Lexicographer, Scholar, Teacher, and Committed Christian Layman*, ed. Eugene Howard and Ronald Edwin Cocroft (Leiden: Brill, 1972), 70–84, esp. 80–84.

3. BAGD 593; BDAG 736.

4. J. D. Denniston, *The Greek Particles*, 2d ed. (Oxford: Clarendon, 1954), 33.

5. Sophocles *Antigone* 1155.

6. Thucydides 3.113.6; Herodotus 7.235.

7. Diodorus Siculus 13.47.4; for further studies, see Karl Ludwig and Martin Anton Schmidt, "πάροικος," *TDNT* 5 (1967): 841–53.

8. BDB 158; Diether Kellermann, "גּוּר *gûr*; גֵּר *gēr*; גֵּרוּת *gērûth*; מְגוּרִים *m^eghûrîm*," *TDOT* 2 (1977): 439–49.

9. BDB 444; *HALOT* 4 (1999): 1712–13; A. H. Konkel, "תּוֹשָׁב (*tôšāb*)," *NIDOTTE* 4:284; cf. also W. D. Davies, *Paul and Rabbinic Judaism. Some Rabbinic Elements in Pauline Theology*, 4th ed. (Philadelphia: Fortress, 1980), 113–14.

small distinction.[1] The first is a more temporary stay than the second. The ξένος is a stranger who happens to be in a foreign land whereas the πάροικος is a resident alien.[2] By way of illustration, the first is like a tourist traveling in a foreign land which has an agreement with the traveler's land of origin that gives him travel rights. The second is like person who is legally residing in a foreign country with a residence visa. Neither are citizens nor do they have all the privileges of the citizens in that land. Paul expresses negatively that they are no longer temporary foreigners or permanent aliens of a state that was once foreign to them. Paul next gives the positive aspect of their identity.

ἀλλὰ ἐστὲ[3] συμπολῖται τῶν ἁγίων καὶ οἰκεῖοι τοῦ θεοῦ, "but you are fellow citizens with the saints and members of God's household." The adversative conjunction ἀλλά marks a strong contrast from the negative just stated. The word συμπολῖτης is used in classical literature to denote "fellow citizen."[4] It is not found in the LXX and occurs only here in the NT. Without the prepositional prefix (i.e., πολῖτης) it means "citizen" and is the opposite of ξένος, "foreigner."[5] The prefix συν-, "with," enhances the meaning to indicate that they are not only "citizens" but "fellow citizens" with the saints.[6] This stresses unity and peace yet again. The word "saints" was discussed at 1:1 (cf. also 1:4, 13, 15, 18) and it was concluded that the saints are those who had obtained a righteous standing or position before God on the basis of Christ's work by means of faith. There are basically two views regarding the identity of these saints, namely, that they are angels or that they are redeemed human beings. The thought that the "saints" or "holy ones" in this passage refer to angels is due to Qumran influence (e.g., 1QS 11:7–8; 4Q174 3:2–6 [1:2–6]).[7] However, this concept is out

1. Lincoln (150) eliminates the distinction between these two words. One argument he uses is that both ξένος and πάροικος are translated from גֵּר, but when one observes the LXX, ξένος is translated only once (Job 31:32), whereas πάροικος is translated twelve times (about half of the times it is translated from Hebrew) from גֵּר. Although they are synonyms, it does not mean that they do not carry some distinction.

2. Barclay, *New Testament Words*, 285.

3. There is a καί preceding the ἐστέ in manuscripts 1739 and 1881. However, this evidence is too minute to be accepted as a genuine reading. There is the omission of ἐστέ in D[1] Ψ 𝔐 Jerome but again, the evidence is too slim for this proposal, for it is only solid in the Byzantine text. The reading retaining ἐστέ is found in א A B C D* F G 33 104 1175 2464 *pc* latt, which is strong in both the Alexandrian and Western text-types and should be accepted.

4. Euripides *Heraclidae* 826; Josephus *A.J.* 19.2.2 §175.

5. Stählin, *TDNT* 5 (1967): 2; McGrath, "'*Syn*' Words in Saint Paul," 222.

6. For a study of the use of the συν- prefix in this context, see Carl B. Hoch Jr., "The Significance of the *syn*-Compounds for Jew-Gentile Relationships in the Body of Christ," *JETS* 25 (June 1982): 177–81.

7. Cf. Bertil Gärtner, *The Temple and the Community in Qumran and the New Testament. A Comparative Study in the Temple Symbolism of the Qumran Texts and the New Testament*, SNTSMS, ed. Matthew Black, vol. 1 (Cambridge: Cambridge University

of keeping with the present context. The reference to alienation from the citizenship of Israel (v. 12) certainly precludes the idea of the saints as angels, therefore, it must refer to the redeemed people of the old covenant. Correspondingly, after conversion they are fellow citizens not with angels but with the redeemed. In addition, nothing in the context pertains to angels.[1] Furthermore, throughout Ephesians when the term is used substantively, it refers to humans who are redeemed (1:15, 18; 3:8, 18; 4:12; 5:3; 6:18) and never to angels. In conclusion, believing Gentiles are no longer foreigners but fellow citizens with the saints (redeemed humans) who have trusted God.

Some suggest that in the early history of the church "the saints" referred to Jewish Christians (Acts 9:13, 32, 41; 26:10; Rom 15:25, 26, 31; 1 Cor 16:1; 2 Cor 8:4; 9:1, 12) and later it included Gentile Christians.[2] It is true that "the saints" mentioned in the passages in Acts are Jewish Christians because they refer to Jews believing in Christ who resided in Judea before there was a missionary effort to the Gentiles. Furthermore, as Lincoln rightly points out, the Pauline references that address the collection for saints are not speaking about Jewish Christians in general but the Jerusalem church in particular.[3] "Saints" used in the other passages do refer to Jewish Christians, yet not as a technical term to designate them as Jewish Christians. Rather they are Christians who happen to be Jewish.

The genitive denotes relationship or association: "fellow citizens *with* the saints."[4] This is quite different from the Qumran concept[5] where the house built in the last days will allow no Ammonites, Moabites, half-breeds, foreigners, or strangers to enter, but only ritually and morally clean Israelites (4Q174 3:3–4 [1:3–4]; cf. 1QH[a] 14:27 [6:27]). Rather, the saints have become a part of the company of the redeemed of all ages beginning with Adam and not, as some suggest, just with those since the day of Abraham who were identified as

Press, 1965), 63–64; Georg Klinzing, *Die Umdeutung des Kultus in der Qumrangemeinde und im Neuen Testament*, Studien zur Umwelt des Neuen Testaments, ed. Karl Georg Kuhn, vol. 7 (Göttingen: Vandenhoeck & Ruprecht, 1971), 186; Lincoln, *Paradise Now and Not Yet*, 151; Derwood C. Smith, "Cultic Language in Ephesians 2:19–20: A Test Case," *ResQ* 31 (fourth quarter 1989): 214.

1. Cf. Benoit, "Ἅγιοι en Colossiens 1.12: Hommes ou Anges?" 87.

2. Procksch, *TDNT* 1 (1964): 106; Mussner, *Christus, das All und die Kirche*, 105–6; Roels, *God's Mission*, 145; Caird, 60; Faust, *Pax Christi et Pax Caesaris*, 184–87.

3. Lincoln, 151.

4. Wallace, *Greek Grammar*, 129.

5. Franz Mussner, "Was ist die Kirche? Die Antwort des Epheserbriefs," in *"Deiner in Eurer Mitte". Festschrift für Dr. Antonius Hofmann Bischof von Passau zum 75. Geburtstag*, ed. Rainer Beer et al., Schriften der Universität Passau: Reihe Katholische Theologie, vol. 5 (Passau: Passavia Universitätsverlag, 1984), 86; Elisabeth Schüssler Fiorenza, "Cultic Language in Qumran and in the New Testament," *CBQ* 38 (April 1976): 173.

Jews.[1] However, Smith rightly contends that Gentiles were not allowed to be a part of the spiritual temple until they were brought near by the blood of Christ at which time they are no longer foreigners and aliens but fellow citizens of the household of God.[2] This is quite different from the Qumran community where there is no indication that any foreigner will ever be accepted other than Israelites. The point in Ephesians is to welcome the Gentiles as part of the holy temple (v. 21) and as fellow citizens equal with the Jews who also come by the blood of Christ.

They are not only fellow citizens with the saints but they are also of God's household. The word οἰκεῖος is used "of/for household affairs/property"[3] or of persons "of the same household" in the sense of family or kin.[4] In the LXX it occurs nineteen times (seventeen times in the canonical books) mostly translated from either שְׁאֵר, "blood relation"[5] (Lev 18:6, 12, 13; 21:2; 25:49; Num 27:11), or דּוֹד, "uncle, beloved," speaking of one who is in the family[6] (1 Sam 10:14–16; 14:50; Amos 6:10). In addition to the present context it is used only two other times in the NT: in Gal 6:10 Paul speaks of the "household of faith" and in 1 Tim 5:8 he speaks of the believer's provision for "his own family." It implies a close intimate family. In the present context it speaks of membership in God's household. The genitive most likely denotes possession. Believers are considered members of the family of God[7] and hence the translation "members of God's household." Whereas, ξένος is the opposite of συμπολῖτης, so is πάροικος, "a resident alien," opposite of οἰκεῖος, "family members of a household." As illustrated above, although a resident alien may live in a foreign country, he is not a part of the "family" of the nation in which he is residing. Paul uses different imagery in the passage: here it is a household and in verses 20–22 it is a temple in which the Spirit of God dwells.

One should also notice how the two-level progression of reconciliation developed in verses 11–18 coincides with the parallels of opposites in verse 19. The first level shows that the Gentiles were outside the citizenship of Israel (v. 12) and considered foreigners (v. 19). This matches with the idea that now because of Christ's work, both they and the Jews have been made one (vv. 14–15) and they are considered

1. Salmond, 298–99; Mussner, *Christus, das All und die Kirche*, 105–6; Robinson, "Who Were 'the Saints'?" 52; Edward A. McDowell, "The Doctrine of the Church in the Epistle to the Ephesians," *SWJT* 6 (October 1963): 55.

2. Smith, "Cultic Language in Ephesians 2:19–20," 215–16.

3. Herodotus 2.37; Sophocles *Antigone* 661.

4. Herodotus 3.65; 4.65; Thucydides 1.9.2.

5. BDB 985; H. Ringgren, "שְׁאֵר *šᵉʾer*," *TWAT* 7 (1990): 931–33.

6. BDB 187; J. Sanmartin-Ascaso, "דּוֹד *dôdh*," *TDOT* 3 (1978): 143–56.

7. Otto Michel, "οἰκεῖος," *TDNT* 5 (1967): 134; David G. Horrell, "From ἀδελφοί to οἶκος θεοῦ: Social Transformation in Pauline Christianity," *JBL* 120 (summer 2001): 305.

fellow citizens with the saints (v. 19). The second level shows that the Gentiles had no relationship to God by covenant, had no hope, and were without God (v. 12) and considered resident aliens (v. 19). This corresponds with the idea that now both they and the Jews, together in one body, have been reconciled to God (v. 16) and are considered members of God's family (v. 19).

Finally, the question must be asked, "With whom are the saints fellow citizens and members of the household of God?" Although various views have been proposed, three need to be discussed briefly. (1) The saints are fellow citizens with Jewish Christians.[1] But this goes against the present context that talks about unbelieving Jews and unbelieving Gentiles who became the new creation. This text does not distinguish between Jewish Christians and Gentiles Christians. If one is a Christian, then he or she is neither a Jew nor a Gentile. (2) The saints mentioned in this passage are fellow citizens with Israel and members of God's household, with the idea that the church is the continuing Israel.[2] Three reasons are given for this view. (a) Paul discusses in the context the "one new humanity" (v. 15), the "one body" (v. 16). However, this does not mean that Gentiles are incorporated into Israel (nor vice versa), but rather that both believing Jews and believing Gentiles are incorporated into one new "race, class," namely, the church. In the past scholars readily accepted the idea of the church's replacement of Israel, but as a result of the Holocaust and due to the prevailing pluralistic sentiment, very few scholars presently speak of the church's replacement of Israel. (b) Paul specifically states that the Gentiles who have become "fellow citizens with the saints" are members of "God's household" (v. 19). However, he did not say that they have become a part of Israel. Paul clearly states that the Gentiles before conversion were alienated from the citizenship of Israel (v. 12), but he declares that after conversion they became fellow citizens with the saints and not with Israel. Believing Gentiles together with the believing Jews have become "fellow citizens with the saints" of all ages, even those before the formation of Israel. Thus, the

1. Dibelius-Greeven, 71; Caird, 60; Philipp Vielhauer, *Oikodome: Das Bild vom Bau in der christlichen Literatur vom Neuen Testament bis Clemens Alexandrinus*, Inaugural-Dissertation for Ruprecht-Karls-Universität in Heidelberg (Karlsruhe-Durlach: Verlagsdruckerei Gebr. Tron, 1939), 123–24; J. J. Meuzelaar, *Der Leib des Messias: Eine exegetische Studie über den Gedanken vom Leib Christi in den Paulusbriefen* (Assen: Koninklijke Van Gorcum & Comp., 1961), 63–64; Roels, *God's Mission*, 145; Judith Gundry-Volf, "'The One' and 'The Two': Jews, Gentiles and the Church in Ephesians" (Paper delivered at the 2000 Annual Meeting of the American Academy of Religion and the Society of Biblical Literature, Nashville, TN, November 19, 2000), 1–28, esp. 5–8, 22–26.

2. Alford, 3:99; Westcott, 40; Barth, 269–70; Barth, *Israel and the Church*, 79–117; MacDonald, *The Pauline Churches*, 95–96; cf. Wolfgang Schweitzer, "Überlegungen zum Verhältniss von Christen und Juden nach Epheser 2,11–22," *WD* 20 (1989): 262–63; Penna, *Paul the Apostle*, 2:38.

concept of "God's household" includes the redeemed who had lived before God singled out Israel as a nation. (c) Paul explains that this new entity, called the church, is "built on the foundation of the apostles and the prophets with Christ Jesus being the cornerstone" (v. 20). Thus, it is proposed, the new entity is built on and is a continuation of the old entity, namely, Israel. However, this is a "new" entity and not a continuation of something old, and thus its beginning is not in the OT but on the day of Pentecost. It is true that believing Gentiles are incorporated with the redeemed of all ages (v. 19), but the incorporation in the present context is the incorporation of both believing Jews and Gentiles into the "one new humanity," which distinctly began when the church came into existence at Pentecost. As mentioned above, this new entity is built on the foundation of the apostles and prophets (v. 20), not on OT covenants, promises, and/or prophets.[1] (3) The saints are fellow citizens with the redeemed of all ages.[2] This view makes the most sense. Before Abraham, there were saints who were members of the household of God. After Abraham, the saints were those Jews who truly believed God, as did their father Abraham (Rom 4:12). These were fellow saints of former generations who were members of the household of God. In the present time, those Jews and Gentiles redeemed by Christ's death have formed a new entity called the church. Those in the new entity are saints who are fellow citizens with all the saints of past generations, who are also members of God's household. None of the succeeding generation of saints replaces the former generation, but all join as members of God's household or family. Though there may be distinctions, they are all fellow citizens. Though there may be differences, there are no inferiors or superiors. All the saints of every generation believed that God was involved with their redemption and reconciliation. They all had access to God and they all had fellowship with God and other saints. The believers today are neither Jews nor Gentiles but are Christians who pray and give praise to God as all the saints in former generations.

b. Cause: New Establishment (2:20–22)

Having discussed the consequential fact of the new relationship which Gentile believers have, Paul now discusses the cause of it, namely, the new establishment portrayed as a holy temple in which God dwells. This figure of God dwelling in a temple is derived from

1. Best (267–69), in a detached note entitled "Israel and the Church," comes to the same conclusion that the church is not a continuation of Israel. The church is the "third race," unbelieving Jews and Gentiles making up the other two.

2. Chrysostom *Eph* 5:17–22 (*PG* 62:43); Eadie, 191; Meyer, 141; Abbott, 69; Robinson, 67; Masson, 169; Gaugler, 120; Hendriksen, 141; Mitton, 110; Schnackenburg, 121; Bruce, 302; Lincoln, 150–51; Merklein, *Das kirchliche Amt nach dem Epheserbrief*, 132; Best, "Ephesians 2.11–22: A Christian View of Judaism," 59–60.

the OT. Paul will show the temple's foundation (v. 20), formation (v. 21), and function (v. 22).

(1) The Foundation of the Building (2:20)

In this verse Paul explains the foundation and cornerstone of the new holy temple.

Text: 2:20. ἐποικοδομηθέντες ἐπὶ τῷ θεμελίῳ τῶν ἀποστόλων καὶ προφητῶν, ὄντος ἀκρογωνιαίου αὐτοῦ Χριστοῦ Ἰησοῦ,

Translation: 2:20. "having been built on the foundation of the apostles and prophets, Christ Jesus himself being the cornerstone,"

Commentary: 2:20. ἐποικοδομηθέντες ἐπὶ τῷ θεμελίῳ, "having been built on the foundation." Paul makes a transition in his metaphor from those who belong to a household (οἰκεῖος) in verse 19 to that of a building in which the Spirit of God dwells (ἐποικοδομηθέντες . . . οἰκοδομή . . . συνοικοδομεῖσθε . . . κατοικητήριον) in verses 20–22. The aorist passive participle ἐποικοδομηθέντες may signify a temporal idea, indicating that the readers of this letter have already built on the foundation at the time of their conversion,[1] or, more likely, it may denote cause, namely, the reason we are fellow citizens with the saints and members of God's household is because we have been built on the foundation of the apostles and prophets. The passive emphasizes that we who are in one body are recipients of the action. God is the subject of the building. The following preposition ἐπί with the accusative would imply motion (1 Cor 3:12; Rom 15:20) but with the genitive or dative, as here, it denotes place—"on" or "upon" which the structure is built.[2] The word θεμέλιος means "foundation," which speaks of the beginnings of something that is coming into being,[3] a term that is synonymous to καταβολή in 1:4. The nature of the foundation is explained next.

τῶν ἀποστόλων καὶ προφητῶν, "of the apostles and prophets." Five items need to be considered. First, there is only one article for both nouns. This "does not necessarily identify the Apostles and Prophets as one and the same persons,"[4] but the one article may indicate that "groups more or less distinct are treated as one for the purpose in hand."[5]

1. Lincoln, 152.

2. BAGD 286, 288; BDAG 363, 364; SH §184j. Some try to make a distinction between the genitive and dative: the genitive denotes locality of a loose proximity; and the dative suggests a more exact superposition of something upon something (Ellicott, 52; Abbott, 69–70). This seems to make too fine a distinction, for one can cite contrary examples (cf. BAGD 286–88; BDAG 363–66).

3. BAGD 355–566; BDAG 449.

4. Salmond, 299.

5. Robertson, *Grammar*, 787; MHT 3:181; Wallace, "Semantic Range of the Article-Noun-καί-Noun Plural Construction," 82.

Second, the genitives have been interpreted in various ways. (1) Some think they are possessive genitives: "the apostles' and prophets' foundation."[1] But Ellicott has pointed out that this would mix up the θεμέλιος, "foundation" and ἀκρογωνιαῖος, "cornerstone."[2] It states that the foundation belongs to the apostles and yet, on the other hand, Christ is the cornerstone, the main stone of the foundation. Therefore, Christ belongs to the apostles! (2) Others see these as subjective genitives or genitives of agency or originating cause: "the foundation laid by the apostles and prophets."[3] This refers to doctrine preached by the apostles and prophets with Christ as the cornerstone of that doctrine. Those who propound this use of the genitive suggest that two passages support this view: 1 Cor 3:10–11, where Paul, as a wise architect, laid the foundation which is Christ; and Rom 15:20, where Paul specifically states that he will not build on another person's foundation. However, there are some problems with this view. First, it makes Christ both the foundation and the cornerstone. If the foundation is the apostolic doctrine about Christ, what is the content of the cornerstone's teaching? It would appear to be the same teaching, making Christ redundant as the cornerstone.[4] Also, to make Christ personal, as Ellicott does,[5] seems to be inconsistent and confusing with the nonpersonal (teaching).[6] Second, the parallel passages mentioned above do not support this view of the genitive. The first parallel passage is 1 Cor 3:10–11, which states that each believer builds his or her works on the foundation of Christ. However, in the present context there is nothing about building works on the foundation. The second parallel text is Rom 15:20 where Paul states that he will not build on another person's foundation. But this text refers to the establishment of new local churches, whereas in the present context Paul is not speaking about the foundation of a local church. Aside from this, if one uses Rom 15:20 as a text to support the view that the foundation is the doctrine taught by the apostles and prophets, then why would not Paul want to build on it? Did he have a different doctrine? Third, in 1 Cor 3:10–11 Paul specifically states that he laid (ἔθηκα) the foundation, whereas in Ephesians he does not. Ultimately, the interpretation of one passage cannot be imposed on another, especially when they are not addressing the same issue. (3) Still other interpreters regard these as genitives of apposition: "the foundation consisting of the

1. Alford, 3:100.

2. Ellicott, 53.

3. Ambrosiaster *Eph* 2:20 (*PL* 17:380); Calvin, 154–55; Bengel, 4:80; Harless, 257–58; Meyer, 142; Ellicott, 53; Salmond, 299; Hendriksen, 142 n. 75; Sandnes, *Paul—One of the Prophets?* 229.

4. Wayne A. Grudem, *The Gift of Prophecy in 1 Corinthians* (Washington, D.C.: University Press of America, 1982), 87.

5. Ellicott, 53.

6. Abbott, 70; Grudem, *The Gift of Prophecy in 1 Corinthians*, 87.

apostles and prophets."[1] This view is the most consistent. First, the imagery depicted in the present context is that Christ, as a person (αὐτοῦ Χριστοῦ Ἰησοῦ = Christ Jesus himself and not Christ's own teaching), is the cornerstone, the apostles and prophets, as persons, are the foundation, and the saints, as persons, are the building. Second, this coincides with 4:11 and more specifically 1 Cor 12:28 which states, "God placed or appointed (ἔθετο) in the church first apostles, second prophets, . . ." as foundations for ministry. Third, the aorist rather than a present passive participle is used to indicate a summarizing aspect normally referring to past time (aorist participles usually indicate antecedent time to that of the main verb) rather than a repeated action.[2] If it were talking about the doctrine on which the church is built, then there ought to be a present or perhaps a perfect tense to indicate a repeated action representing a continuing effect of the teaching throughout the readers' lives and throughout the centuries of the church. However, if it is referring to persons, it is fitting for the aorist to be used to indicate past time of the apostles and prophets as that first foundation. Fourth, this view corresponds well with Rev 21:14 where the twelve apostles, along with the twelve tribes of Israel, are the foundations of the new city of Jerusalem. In the end, it seems best to view these genitives as appositional, indicating that the apostles and prophets are the historic persons who first formed the universal church. The relationship of this concept to Christ as the cornerstone will be discussed below.

The third thing to be considered is the identity of the apostles and prophets. Since the term "apostle" was discussed in greater detail at 1:1, only a brief discussion is in order here. An apostle is one who is sent out on a mission with fully delegated authority by his master Jesus Christ, as the original disciples whom Jesus selected were sent out to minister (cf. also 4:11). Three kinds of apostles in the NT have been mentioned: those who had been with Jesus in his ministry and had witnessed his resurrection (Acts 1:21–22), Paul who was born out of season (1 Cor 15:8–9), and those who received the gift of apostleship as mentioned in 4:11. The first two categories are to be regarded as offices, whereas the last as a spiritual gift to the church. In the present context Paul is most likely referring to all three categories. Regarding who and what function they had, it was concluded in the study in 1:1 that an apostle was an official delegate of Jesus Christ, commissioned

1. Chrysostom *Eph* 2:17–22 (*PG* 62:43); Oecumenius *Eph* 2:19–22 (*PG* 118:1200); Theophylact *Eph* 2:20 (*PG* 124:1065); Olshausen, 190; Hodge, 149–50; Abbott, 70–71; Robinson, 163; Schlier, 142; Gaugler, 121; Barth, 271; Mitton, 112; Schnackenburg, 122–23; Bruce, 304; Lincoln, 153; cf. also Grudem, *The Gift of Prophecy in 1 Corinthians*, 84–88; R. Schnackenburg, "Die Kirche als Bau: Epheser 2.19–22 unter ökumenischem Aspekt," in *Paul and Paulinism. Essays in Honour of C. K. Barrett*, ed. M. D. Hooker and S. G. Wilson (London: SPCK, 1982), 261, 264–65; Wallace, *Greek Grammar*, 100.

2. Grudem, *The Gift of Prophecy in 1 Corinthians*, 89. Grudem probably presses the once-for-all action more than is justified.

for the specific tasks of proclaiming authoritatively the message in oral and written form and establishing and building up churches.

The prophets are listed along with other gifts to the church (1 Cor 12:28; Eph 4:11; cf. Rom 12:6). There is much debate on this subject and it is beyond the scope of this work to go into great detail.[1] After a study of prophets, Forbes concludes that the prophets of the Hellenistic world were quite different from the prophets of early Christianity, and the more likely background for the term is to be found in the Septuagint and the Judaism of the synagogues.[2] Briefly, it seems that the prophet is one who is endowed by the Holy Spirit with the gift of prophecy for the purpose of edification, comfort, and encouragement (1 Cor 14:3, 31), as well as for the purpose of understanding and communicating the mysteries and revelation of God to the church (12:10; 13:2; 14:6, 22, 30–31). As was true with the OT prophets, the NT prophetic gift also included a predictive element (1 Thess 3:4; 4:6, 14–18; Gal 5:21) that was not a part of the other gifts such as teaching.[3] In the NT the prophet was not to be overcome by some uncontrolled estatic force, but he was to control himself when he received revelation (1 Cor 14:29–32; Rev 1:9–11). In light of an incomplete canon, the prophets may well have received revelation to complete what was needed so that every person could be presented perfect before God (Eph 4:12; Col 1:28). In conclusion, it seems that both the apostle and the prophet were involved in revelation.

In many ways the NT apostle, including the apostle Paul (1 Cor 13:9; 14:6),[4] functioned much like an OT prophet.[5] However, Grudem takes this a bit further when he proposes that the apostles rather than the NT prophets correspond more closely with the OT prophets. He claims that OT prophets and NT apostles spoke with divine authority, whereas NT prophets, who were not apostles, did not prophesy with absolute divine

1. For more study on this, see Gerhard Friedrich, "προφήτης," *TDNT* 6 (1968): 828–61; Theodore M. Crone, *Early Christian Prophecy: A Study of Its Origin and Function* (Baltimore, Md.: St. Mary's University Press, 1973), esp. 205–30; Carl Heinz Peisker and Colin Brown, "Prophet [προφήτης]," *NIDNTT* 1 (1975): 74–92; E. Earle Ellis, *Prophecy and Hermeneutic in Early Christianity: New Testament Essays*, WUNT, ed. Martin Hengel, Joachim Jeremias and Otto Michel, vol. 18 (Tübingen: Mohr, 1978); David Hill, *New Testament Prophecy* (London: Marshall, Morgan & Scott, 1979; Atlanta: John Knox, 1980); Grudem, *The Gift of Prophecy in 1 Corinthians*; Wayne A. Grudem, *The Gift of Prophecy in New Testament and Today* (Westchester, Ill.: Crossway, 1988); David E. Aune, *Prophecy in Early Christianity and the Ancient Mediterranean World* (Grand Rapids: Eerdmans, 1983), esp. 189–217; Christopher Forbes, *Prophecy and Inspired Speech in Early Christianity and Its Hellenistic Environment*, WUNT, ed. Martin Hengel and Otfried Hofius, vol. 75 (Tübingen: Mohr, 1995), esp. 188–250.

2. Forbes, *Prophecy and Inspired Speech*, 216–17. Hui observes the similarities and differences between prophecy in Judaism and Pauline pneumatology, see Archie Hui, "The Spirit of Prophecy and Pauline Pneumatology," *TynBul* 50, no. 1 (1999): 93–115.

3. Forbes, *Prophecy and Inspired Speech*, 222–29, 236; cf. also Aune, *Prophecy in Early Christianity and the Ancient Mediterranean World*, 91, 247–48, 317–18.

4. Grudem, *The Gift of Prophecy in 1 Corinthians*, 53.

5. Aune, *Prophecy in Early Christianity and the Ancient Mediterranean World*, 202.

authority, and their prophecy could even be in partial error (e.g., errors in Agabus' prophecy [Acts 21:10–11]).[1] The problem with Grudem's view is threefold. First, it would be more natural that OT prophets correspond with NT prophets than with apostles.[2] The recipients of this epistle would likely make this correspondence. This would be a consistent use of "prophet" throughout the Bible, whereas "apostles" are distinct though they may have overlapping functions. Further elaboration regarding the identity of NT prophets and apostles is given below. Second, Grudem's bifurcation of the NT prophets into two groups: (1) those who were also apostles and spoke with absolute authority, as did OT prophets or Scripture; and (2) those who were not also apostles whose words, although not absolutely authoritative, were for encouragement has no tenable basis in the NT. Third, it seems strange that Christ would give the prophetic gift which lacked authority and, in fact, could be in error. In the OT anyone who gave nonauthoritative prophecy was considered a false prophet (Deut 13). In the NT prophets were to be tested: if true, then their words would be deemed authoritative; if not true they were considered false prophets (1 Cor 14:29–31; 2 Pet 2; 1 John 4:1; Jude 11–16).[3] Thus, it is best to consider that there were overlapping functions with reference to NT prophets and apostles, much like many ministries today. However, each had a different emphasis. The emphasis for the apostle was more of the divine commission to a specific task; for the prophet, however, it was the communication of divine revelation.

The fourth thing to be considered is the relationship between the apostles and prophets. Grudem[4] lists four ways in which they are related to each other: (1) the teachings of apostles and prophets; (2) apostles who are also prophets;[5] (3) apostles and OT prophets;[6]

1. Grudem, *The Gift of Prophecy in 1 Corinthians*, 7–113, esp. 53–82, 110–13; idem, *The Gift of Prophecy in New Testament and Today*, 60–64, 87–88, 96–102.

2. Aune, *Prophecy in Early Christianity and the Ancient Mediterranean World*, 195–97; Max Turner, "Spiritual Gifts Then and Now," *VE* 15 (1985): 16. For a discussion of the similarities of and differences between the OT and NT prophetic gift, see F. David Farnell, "The New Testament Prophetic Gift: Its Nature and Duration" (Th.D. diss., Dallas Theological Seminary, 1990), 193–274.

3. F. David Farnell, "Fallible New Testament Prophecy/Prophets? A Critique of Wayne Grudem's Hypothesis," *The Master's Seminary Journal* 2 (fall 1991): 173–74.

4. Grudem, *The Gift of Prophecy in 1 Corinthians*, 82–84. For a discussion of these views, see 82–105; cf. also idem, *The Gift of Prophecy in New Testament and Today*, 46–63.

5. Harless, 259–60; Adolphe Monod, *Explication de L'Épître de Saint Paul aux Éphésiens* (Paris: Libraire de ch. Meyrvois, 1867), 139–40; Hort, *Prolegomena to St Paul's Epistles*, 145–48; idem, *The Christian Ecclesia. A Course of Lectures on the Early History and Early Conceptions of the Ecclesia and Four Sermons* (London: Macmillan, 1897), 165–68; Paul Joüon, "Notes de Philologie paulinienne," *RSR* 15 (Décembre 1925): 532–34; Hill, *New Testament Prophecy*, 139; Grudem, *The Gift of Prophecy in 1 Corinthians*, 97–105; idem, *The Gift of Prophecy in New Testament and Today*, 57–63; Erich Mauerhofer, "Der Brief an die Epheser. 24. Teil: 2,20," *Fundamentum* 4 (1995): 21–23.

6. Chrysostom *Eph* 2:17–22 (*PG* 62:43–44); Theodoret *Eph* 2:20 (*PG* 82:525); Calvin, 155; Lenski, 451–53; Mußner, 93; Mussner, *Christus, das All und die Kirche*, 108.

and (4) apostles and NT prophets.[1] View (1) refers not to the apostles and prophets themselves but to their teaching, and this is incongruent with the present context since it speaks of persons and not teaching. Grudem rightly assesses that this view may be tenable for 1 Cor 3:10–15 but inappropriate for the present context. View (2), favored by Grudem, proposes that rather than two groups (NT apostles and NT prophets), it is one group (NT apostle-prophets). He argues that this is possible grammatically since there is only one article for both nouns, but as pointed out above, that does not necessarily make them one and the same. In fact, Wallace remarks that to make them one and the same would be suspect because there is no other example in the NT where two nouns (in a noun + noun construction) refer to two identical groups.[2] Furthermore, in the NT there is no indication that an apostle is necessarily a prophet or vice versa. Certainly, when Paul instructs the Corinthians regarding the conduct of the prophets, there is no indication that they were apostles (1 Cor 14:29–32). If these prophets were apostles, then Paul is instructing apostles how to conduct themselves! In addition when Paul lists the gifts in Eph 4:11, he mentions that there are "some apostles and some prophets," indicating that these are two different groups as opposed to "some apostles and prophets," indicating that they are one and the same. Thus option (2) is not convincing. View (3) suggests that this refers to apostles and OT prophets but it is problematic for the following reasons. First, the order is wrong, for if he meant OT prophets, it would have been logical to list them first. Second, the same order, first apostles and then prophets, is given when Paul lists the various gifted individuals who are to benefit the church (4:11; cf. 1 Cor 12:28, 29). Third, in the context Paul states that before Christ there was a great gulf between Jews and Gentiles, but by Jesus' death God created a new person called the church and made the law inoperative. Hence, if this refers to the OT prophets it confuses the issue, for it implicates an OT institution with an entirely new entity, thus blurring the distinction Paul is making. Fourth, in Eph 3:5 Paul speaks of the mystery (i.e., the church = believing Jews and believing Gentiles in one body) which was hidden in former generations but is now revealed to "his holy apostles and

1. Bengel, 4:80; Hodge, 148–49; Alford, 3:100; Eadie, 193–95; Ellicott, 53; Meyer, 143; Abbott, 72; Salmond, 299–300; Robinson, 163; Schlier, 142; Conzelmann, 70; Gaugler, 121; Hendriksen, 142; Zerwick, 71; Gnilka, 157; Caird, 61; Mitton, 112; Barth, 314–17; Schnackenburg, 122; Bruce, 304; Lincoln, 153; Best, 283; O'Brien, 214–15; Aune, *Prophecy in Early Christianity and the Ancient Mediterranean World*, 404 n. 72; Sandnes, *Paul—One of the Prophets?* 232–36; Wallace, *Greek Grammar*, 284–86; cf. also Richard B. Gaffin Jr., *Perspectives on Pentecost: Studies in New Testament Teaching on the Gifts of the Holy Spirit* (Phillipsburg, N.J.: Presbyterian and Reformed, 1979), 93–96.

2. Wallace, "Semantic Range of the Article-Noun-καί-Noun Plural Construction," 82. Cf. also Farnell, "Fallible New Testament Prophecy/Prophets? A Critique of Wayne Grudem's Hypothesis," 157–79; R. Fowler White, "Gaffin and Grudem on Eph 2:20: In Defense of Gaffin's Cessationists Exegesis," *WTJ* 54 (fall 1992): 303–20.

prophets by the Spirit." Certainly, this statement makes it clear that the prophets were contemporaries with the apostles, both receiving from the same Spirit the revelation of the former hidden mystery.[1] Fifth, it negates the metaphor of Christ as the cornerstone in relationship to the rest of the foundation.[2] The cornerstone is the first stone laid in a building to be followed by the foundation. If this refers to OT prophets, it would imply that they were a part of the foundation before the cornerstone was laid. View (4) proposes that these are apostles and NT prophets. This is the most plausible view for the following reasons. First, the order of apostles before prophets suggests it. Second, the present context discusses God's creation of the "new person" (v. 15), that is, the church, and this is completely distinct from the old order where the law caused hostility between Jews and Gentiles. Now with the law inoperative, the new person is built, not on prophets from the old order, but on the apostles and prophets of the new order. Third, the mystery of believing Jews and Gentiles incorporated into one body was hidden to former generations, which would include the OT prophets, but *now* is revealed to *Christ's* holy apostles and prophets (3:5). The words in 3:5 are listed in the same order as the present verse, that is, apostles before the prophets. Fourth, Eph 4:11 states that the apostles and prophets were given to the church as foundational gifted people who were to prepare saints for ministry and to build up this new body, the church. Again, the apostles are mentioned before prophets in 4:11 as in the present verse. Also, since the apostles and prophets are given for the effective function of the new order, it is inconceivable that these refer to OT prophets. Fifth, since in this metaphor Christ is the cornerstone in the context of his suffering, the first stone of the foundation, it must refer to NT prophets who are a part of the foundation of this new work called the church. In conclusion then, the prophets mentioned here must be NT prophets who form the foundation along with the apostles.

The fifth item to be considered is the makeup of the foundation. In 1 Cor 3:11 Jesus Christ is the foundation, whereas in the present verse the apostles and prophets are the foundation. This is not an insurmountable problem and can be answered in several different ways. First, it is not unreasonable for Paul to use a building metaphor "in two different ways for two different purposes."[3] Second, it is possible that the apostles who laid the foundations (1 Cor 3:10; Rom 15:2) thought of themselves as the foundation stones.[4] Third, this may be a development of Pauline thought, that is, though earlier Christ is portrayed as the foundation, later he is portrayed as the cornerstone, the most important stone of the foundation and the building as a whole

1. Eadie, 194.
2. Grudem, *The Gift of Prophecy in 1 Corinthians*, 91.
3. Caird, 61; Barth, 271; Bruce, 304–5.
4. Best, *One Body in Christ*, 164.

(see the following comments). This is analogous to the development of Christ's relationship with the church. In the earlier letters the church is the body of Christ (Rom 12:4–5; 1 Cor 12:12–13, 27), whereas in the later letters Christ is the head of the body (Eph 1:22–23; 4:15–16; 5:23; Col 1:18, 24; 2:19). In the present context the church's foundation consists of apostles and prophets and the main stone of the foundation is the cornerstone, Christ himself. Thus, this passage is not in contradiction to 1 Cor 3:11 but is a complement, a fuller development of thought.

ὄντος ἀκρογωνιαίου αὐτοῦ[1] **Χριστοῦ Ἰησοῦ,** "Christ Jesus himself being the cornerstone." This is a genitive absolute, which means that it has "no syntactical connection with any part of the sentence."[2] It does connect to the idea of a foundation of apostles and prophets by giving further information about the foundation's construction, namely, that Christ Jesus is the cornerstone. The meaning of word ἀκρογωνιαῖος has been greatly debated. The word does not occur in classical literature but is found in the LXX only in Isa 28:16 where it translates פִּנָּה. It has the basic meaning of "corner," as the corner of a street (Prov 7:8, 12), corner of a roof (Prov 21:9; 25:24), corner of a house (Job 1:19), corner of an altar (Exod 27:2; 38:2), and corner of a city wall (Neh 3:24, 31), but in the Isaiah context it most likely means "cornerstone"[3] (cf. 1QS 8:7; 4Q259 2:16). Besides the present context, this word occurs in the NT only in 1 Pet 2:6, which is a quotation of Isa 28:16.

The older commentators have rendered it "cornerstone,"[4] but because of a proposal by Jeremias that it should be rendered "capstone, topstone,"[5] some recent commentators have followed suit.[6] Jeremias' main support for his theory is the apocryphal work *Testament of Solomon* (22:7–23:4) which speaks about the stone at the top of a gateway to the temple. Further attestation that the word ἀκρογωνιαῖος means "topstone" can be found in two places in the OT translation by Symmachus. One of these is 2 Kgs 25:17 where it is translated three times from כֹּתֶרֶת, meaning "capital" of a column, which the LXX does

1. The word λίθου "stone" is inserted here in D* F G 629 latt Origin[pt] Chrysostom. This is not acceptable because it is only in the Western tradition.

2. Robertson, *Grammar*, 1131; Wallace, *Greek Grammar*, 102.

3. BDB 819; M. Oeming, "פִּנָּה *pinnâ*," *TDOT* 11 (2001): 586–89.

4. Chrysostom *Eph* 2:17–22 (*PG* 62:44); Theodoret *Eph* 2:20 (*PG* 82:525); Theophylact *Eph* 2:20 (*PG* 124:1065); Calvin, 155; Bengel, 4:80; Harless, 258; Alford, 3:101; Eadie, 198–99; Ellicott, 53–54; Meyer, 144–45; Abbott, 70; Salmond, 300; Robinson, 163–64.

5. Joachim Jeremias, "Κεφαλὴ γωνίας—Ἀκρογωνιαῖος," *ZNW* 29, nos. 3/4 (1930): 264–80; Joachim Jeremias, "Eckstein—Schlußstein," *ZNW* 36, nos. 1–2 (1937): 154–57; Joachim Jeremias, "ἀκρογωνιαῖος," *TDNT* 1 (1964): 792.

6. Dibelius-Greeven, 72–73; Schlier, 142; Conzelmann, 70; Gnilka, 158; Caird, 61; Barth, 271, 317–19; Bruce, 304–6; Lincoln, 154–56; cf. Best, *One Body in Christ*, 165–66; F. F. Bruce, "New Wine in Old Wine Skins: III. The Corner Stone," *ExpTim* 84 (May 1973): 231–35.

not translate but transliterates (χωθαρ). The other occurrence is in Ps 118:22 [LXX 117:22] from לְרֹאשׁ פִּנָּה and is translated literally in the LXX as κεφαλὴν γωνίας meaning "head of a corner." Its application in the present context would be that the apostles and prophets are the foundation and Christ is the capstone of the church, similar to another metaphor where he is the head of the body.

However, this meaning of ἀκρογωνιαῖος has been challenged by McKelvey,[1] and many recent commentators continue to accept the traditional view.[2] As mentioned previously, Jeremias' most important text for his theory is from the apocryphal work *Testament of Solomon* (22:7–23:4) of the second/third century A.D. which is not only late but irrelevant since it is not talking about the top of a gateway to the temple but rather the corner of the temple (22:7), or later, the end of the temple (22:8).[3] Furthermore, the translation of Symmachus is of little value for not only is it late (second century A.D.) but also, while known to have been a readable translation, it lacks verbal accuracy. Symmachus' rendering of a "capital" of a column as ἀκρογωνιαῖος meaning "capstone" demonstrates his inaccuracy, since a capstone is the crown of a building and not a stone on the top of a pillar. Furthermore, with regards to Ps 118:22 [LXX 117:22], the "head" of the corner may well refer to the extremity or end rather than the height of the corner, as McKelvey shows from common usage of the word.[4]

When Paul used this metaphor he may well have had Isa 28:16 in mind since this is the only place ἀκρογωνιαῖος is used in the LXX. It states:

1. R. J. McKelvey, "Christ the Cornerstone," *NTS* 8 (July 1962): 352–59; cf. also R. J. McKelvey, *The New Temple: The Church in the New Testament*, OTM, ed. H. Chadwick et al. (Oxford: Oxford University Press, 1969), 114, 195–204; G. H. Whitaker, "'The Chief Corner-Stone,'" *Exp* 8th ser., vol. 22 (December 1921): 470–72; Josef Pfammatter, *Die Kirche als Bau. Eine exegetisch-theologische Studie zur Ekklesiologie der Paulusbriefe*, AnBib, vol. 110 (Rome: Libreria Editrice dell' università Gregoriana, 1960), 97–99, 140–51; Karl Th. Schäfer, "Zur Deutung von ἀκρογωνιαῖος Eph 2,20," *Neutestamentliche Aufsätze. Festschrift für Prof. Josef Schmid zum 70. Geburtstag*, ed. J. Blinzler, O. Kuss, and F. Mußner (Regensburg: Friedrich Pustet, 1963), 218–24; Mussner, *Christus, das All und die Kirche*, 108–11.

2. Könn, 113–14; Masson, 170 n. 1; Foulkes, 94–95; Gaugler, 120–21; Hendriksen, 142–43; Thompson, 51–52; Zerwick, 71–72; Martin, "Ephesians," in *The Broadman Bible Commentary*, 148; Hugedé, 92–95 and n. 94; Mitton, 112–13; Mußner, 93–95; Schnackenburg, 123–24; Speyr, 112; O'Brien, 216–18; cf. also Percy, *Probleme*, 328–35, 485–88; Merklein, *Das kirchliche Amt nach dem Epheserbrief*, 144–52; Schnackenburg, "Die Kirche als Bau," 263–64; Ursula Maiburg, "Christus der Eckstein. Ps. 118,22 und Jes. 28,16 im Neuen Testament und bei den lateinischen Vätern," in *Vivarium: Festschrift Theodor Klauser zum 90. Geburtstag*, ed. Ernst Dassmann and Klaus Thraede (Münster: Aschendorffsche Verlagsbuchhandlung, 1984), 247–56; Mauerhofer, "Der Brief an die Epheser. 24. Teil: 2,20," 23–24.

3. McKelvey, *The New Temple*, 198.

4. McKelvey, "Christ the Cornerstone," 354.

> Therefore thus says the Lord God, "Behold, I am laying in Zion for a foundation a stone, a tested stone, a precious cornerstone [ἀκρογωνιαῖος], of a sure foundation: 'He who believes will not be in haste.'" (RSV)

Here it speaks of the cornerstone that is part of the foundation. McKelvey has shown that in the history of Jewish interpretation of Isa 28:16, it has always been interpreted as "cornerstone" and not "topstone."[1] Whether or not Paul was thinking of this verse in Isaiah, the concept is the same, namely, a foundation with a cornerstone.[2] Moreover, even Jeremias is forced to admit that in this one pre-Christian text (Isa 28:16) the word means "cornerstone."[3]

In the present context, the concept of "cornerstone" is far better than "capstone." First, it is true that Paul pictures Christ as the head of the church, but that is not under discussion here. Paul speaks about the foundation of the apostles and prophets and "Christ Jesus himself the cornerstone" follows immediately. It is not likely that Paul would jump from the concept of a foundation directly to the concept of a final capstone. It is much more likely that he continues the picture of the foundation. Second, the previous context (2:14–18) portrays Christ as the beginning point of this new person, the church, rather than the finishing point. The cornerstone is the focal and beginning point of the foundation and the subsequent structure. Hence, the cornerstone is far more fitting to this portrayal than a capstone. Third, the immediate context (vv. 19–22) depicts the building as growing and not yet completed.[4] It is improbable that Paul would introduce the idea of a final "capstone" when the building is not yet completed. Fourth, although Paul uses the imagery of a building with a different purpose in 1 Cor 3:10–11, nevertheless he states there that he laid the foundation which is Christ, and this corresponds well with cornerstone in the present context.[5] It would not correspond well with the concept of the capstone. Fifth, if Christ is the capstone, then Christ's relationship with the apostles and prophets is unclear.[6] However, if he is the cornerstone, then he is the main stone of the foundation and the apostles and prophets align with him.

What is the significance of a cornerstone? In today's world the cornerstone is sometimes positioned into place at the time of the dedication of the building, after its construction is completed. That was not the case in ancient times. The cornerstone was the first stone laid. The builder was

1. Ibid., 355–57.

2. Smith thinks that it is a reference to Isa 28 ("Jewish and Greek Traditions in Ephesians 2:11–22," 169–73).

3. Jeremias, *TDNT* 1 (1964): 792.

4. Mitton, 113.

5. Schnackenburg, "Die Kirche als Bau," 263.

6. Merklein, *Das kirchliche Amt nach dem Epheserbrief*, 151.

very careful to properly set this stone. Lloyd states, "The *acrogoniaios* here is the primary foundation-stone at the angle of structure by which the architect fixes a standard for the bearings of the walls and cross-walls throughout."[1] In fact, in Isa 28:16 it is called a testing stone or literally "a stone of testing." It is that stone by which every other stone in the foundation and the superstructure must be measured. Thus, the building of the new person, the church, must be in conformity with the cornerstone, Christ Jesus. The pronoun αὐτοῦ refers to Christ, not to the cornerstone or to the foundation (θεμελίῳ),[2] to give emphasis to the fact that he is the one by which all things are measured.

The cornerstone was the most important stone in the whole building. All other stones were to be in line with it. Christ himself is the living cornerstone and the apostles and the prophets who make up the rest of the foundation needed to be correctly aligned with Christ. All succeeding believers are built on that foundation, causing their lives to be measured with Christ.

(2) The Formation of the Building (2:21)

Paul continues by discussing the formation of the building, now that its foundation has been identified.

Text: 2:21. ἐν ᾧ πᾶσα οἰκοδομὴ συναρμολογουμένη αὔξει εἰς ναὸν ἅγιον ἐν κυρίῳ,

Translation: 2:21. "in whom the whole building being fitted together grows into a holy temple in the Lord,"

Commentary: 2:21. ἐν ᾧ πᾶσα οἰκοδομή,[3] "in whom the whole building." The prepositional phrase ἐν ᾧ refers back to Christ who is the cornerstone. The preposition ἐν denotes the locale or sphere of the action; thus it is in Christ that the whole structure rests or has its ground.[4] The adjective πᾶσα without the article has caused discus-

1. W. Watkiss Lloyd, "Notes: Eph. ii.20–22," *Classical Review* 3 (November 1889): 419.

2. As does Bengel, 4:80.

3. The inclusion of the article before this word (hence, πᾶσα ἡ οἰκοδομή) is found in ℵ[1] A C P 075 6 81 326 1739[c] 1881 1912 *l* 751 cop[sa, bo] arm eth Origen[acc. to 1739] Chrysostom[lem] Theophylact. Its omission is attested by ℵ* B D F G Ψ 0150 33 104 256 263 365 424 436 459 614 1175 (1241) 1319 1573 1739* 1852 1962 2127 2200 2464 *Byz* [K L] *Lect* Clement Origen Basil Chrysostom[com] Theodoret. One sees that the inclusion of the article is found basically in the Alexandrian text-type. However, its exclusion is found in the Western and Byzantine texts as well as a good Alexandrian tradition (ℵ* B Ψ 33 104 1739* Clement). Hence, this has not only good date and character but also good geographical distribution and genealogical relationships. It is more likely that copyists would have inserted the article for clarification rather than to have omitted it. Therefore, the omission of the article is the best reading.

4. Delebecque ("L'hellénisme de la «relative complexe»," 229–38, esp. 233) thinks that this "double relative" or "complex relative" (ἐν ᾧ) was borrowed from classical Greek, having the idea "within whom."

sion. Generally, when it is anarthrous it is rendered "every, each," and thus it is translated "each several building" in the RV and ASV and "every structure" in the JB and NJB.[1] However, it is translated "all the building" in the AV and "the whole building/structure" in the RSV, NASB, NEB, TEV, NIV, NRSV. Is this rendering justifiable? It is for the following reasons. First, the context is talking about one structure on one foundation and as opposed to many structures. Second, in the NT there are instances when the anarthrous constructions are rendered "all" or "whole." For example, such cases are abstract nouns, as "with all insight/wisdom" (1:8), "all authority" (Matt 28:18), and in the case of geographical proper names as "all Jerusalem" (Matt 2:3) or "all Israel" (Rom 11:26). Other instances such as "all the face of the earth" (Acts 17:26), "all creation" (Col 1:15), "all flesh" (Acts 2:17; Rom 3:20), and "all the house of Israel" (Acts 2:36) are sufficient examples to indicate that the anarthrous πᾶς can be translated "all, whole, entire."[2] Hence, this rendering is entirely fitting in this context.[3]

The word οἰκοδομή, "building," is used by the classical writers of a building or the act of building.[4] It occurs sixteen times in the LXX (five times in the canonical books) and although it can have the idea of a structure (Ezek 40:2; Sir 22:16), the primary sense is the act of building, both in the canonical (translates from the verb בָּנָה meaning "to build"[5] in Ezek 17:17) and in the noncanonical (1 Esdr 2:26; 4:51; 5:60, 70, 71; 6:6, 21; Tob 14:5; 1 Macc 16:23; Sir 40:19) literature. It is used eighteen times in the NT, fifteen times by Paul, four times in Ephesians (2:21; 4:12, 16, 29). Outside of the present context the word is used five times of a finished building (Matt 24:1 = Mark 13:1–2; 1 Cor 3:9; 2 Cor 5:1) and twelve times of the act of building (Rom 14:19; 15:2; 1 Cor 14:3, 5, 12; 14:26; 2 Cor 10:8; 12:19; 13:10; Eph 4:12, 16, 29). In the present context οἰκοδομή has to refer to the act of building because the following participle and main verb denote that the

1. As Meyer, 146–47; Abbott, 74; Salmond, 300–301; Westcott, 41; Masson, 170–71; Schlier, 143; Mitton, 115.

2. Cf. Zerwick, *Biblical Greek* §190; Moule, *Idiom Book*, 95; BDF §275 (3); Wallace, *Greek Grammar*, 253 n. 99; Calvin, 155; Alford, 3:101; Eadie, 200; Ellicott, 54; Robinson, 164; Dibelius-Greeven, 73; Gaugler, 123; Hendriksen, 143 n. 77; Gnilka, 159; Barth, 271–72; Schnackenburg, 124 n. 60; Bruce, 307; Lincoln, 156; Erich Mauerhofer, "Der Brief an die Epheser. 25. Teil: 2,21–22," *Fundamentum* 1 (1996): 17–18. For the use of πᾶς in the NT and more particularly in the present context, see J. William Johnston, "The Use of Πᾶς in the New Testament" (Ph.D. diss., Dallas Theological Seminary, 2002), 243–56.

3. *Contra* Robertson, *Grammar*, 772; Winer, *Grammar*, 138 n. [1]; Meyer, 146–47; Abbott, 73–75; Salmond, 300–301; Westcott, 41; Masson, 170; Fred L. Fisher, "The Doctrine of the Church in Ephesians," *SWJT* 6 (October 1963): 37.

4. Aristotle *Ethica Nicomachea* 5.10.7 §1137b.30; Diodorus Siculus 1.46.4; Plutarch *Lucullus* 39.2.

5. BDB 124; Siegfried Wagner, "בָּנָה *bānāh*," *TDOT* 2 (1977): 166–78.

building is still in the process of construction.[1] It must be kept in mind that the building portrayed here is not inanimate but a living and growing organism.

συναρμολογουμένη αὔξει, "being fitted together grows." The participle συναρμολογέω is used only here and 4:16. Paul coined this word by adding the prepositional prefix συν- to the rare verb ἁρμολογέω, meaning "to join" or "pile together" stones for a tomb.[2] Hence, it would have the resultant meaning "to join, fit together,"[3] especially in regard to a construction made of stones.[4] Today the process of fitting stones together is rather simple because mortar is used. In that day with no use of mortar, there was an elaborate process of cutting and smoothing the stones so that they fit exactly next to each other.[5] The prepositional prefix συν-, which is common in Ephesians only, intensifies the fitting together. It speaks of the inner unity or harmony among believers[6] who, before their conversion, were at enmity with one another. The present passive participle describes the manner of their growth. Specifically, as recipients of God's grace, they grow by being carefully fitted together rather than growing apart individually from one another. Notice that it is not self-initiative that causes the growth but the gracious action of God who fits individual believers with each other and with the foundation and cornerstone. If ancient masons used an elaborate process to fit the stones together, one can be assured that God, even more, by his grace is carefully fitting together the individuals who are a part of his building. His desire is to bring inner unity in order that corporate growth can occur.

The main verb αὔξει, a present active indicative from αὔξω, is used intransitively (so used only in Isa 61:11; Col 2:19; and here) meaning "to grow,"[7] indicating a living organism that continues to increase. The present tense verb along with the preceding participle shows the continuance of the growth process. Lindemann thinks that there is a paradox between the imagery of a building growing into a holy temple in the Lord and a finished body of Christ.[8] However, the imagery of the body of Christ does not necessarily imply that there is no growth. Certainly, the "body" suggests the idea of a living organism and a living organism is never static but is continually developing. Thus, there

1. If one wanted to retain the idea of an anarthrous πᾶς meaning "every," one could render it "in whom every act of building being fitted together grows into a holy temple in the Lord." The problem remains that the imagery in this context seems to be one building that is growing into a holy temple. That seems to be the sense of not only the noun but also the main verb "to grow."

2. *Anthologia Graeca* 7.554.2 (1st centurty A.D.).

3. Cf. BDF §119 (1).

4. Christian Maurer, "συναρμολογέω," *TDNT* 6 (1968): 855.

5. For a detailed study of this word, see Robinson, 260–63.

6. McGrath, "'*Syn*' Words in Saint Paul," 222.

7. BAGD 121; BDAG 151; BDF §101.

8. Lindemann, *Aufhebung*, 189.

is no real contradiction or paradox. It is not the future tense looking forward to some eschatological temple like that anticipated by the Qumran community, but it is the present tense dealing with a present temple that is not finished and continues to grow.[1]

εἰς ναὸν ἅγιον ἐν κυρίῳ, "into a holy temple in the Lord." The preposition εἰς shows the direction of the growth and can be translated "to" or better in this context "into." The direction of growth is into a ναὸν ἅγιον, "a holy temple." Two common words are used for temple: ἱερόν, which occurs seventy-two times in the NT, and is used exclusively in the Gospels and Acts, with the exception of 1 Cor 9:13; and ναός, which occurs forty-five times in the NT, eight times in Paul's writings (1 Cor 3:16, 17*bis*; 6:19; 2 Cor 6:16*bis*; Eph 2:21; 2 Thess 2:4). Some claim that there is no distinction between the words,[2] but when one looks carefully at the use of the words, a distinction becomes apparent. The word ἱερόν refers to the whole sacred area of the Jewish temple, including the three courts: the court of the Gentiles, the court of women (Jewish), and the court of Israel (men). Within this last court was the court of priests and inside the court of priests was the sacred building called ναός,[3] the second term for temple. This distinction between ἱερόν and ναός seems to be consistent in classical literature and in the LXX[4] and is consistently maintained throughout the NT. The term ἱερόν is used when Jesus found the money changers in the temple (Matt 21:12 = Mark 11:15 = Luke 19:45 = John 2:14–15). The Ephesian equivalent was the temple (ἱερόν) in Ephesus belonging to the goddess, Artemis, who was worshiped throughout the world (Acts 19:27). On the other hand, the term ναός (derived from ναίω, which means "to dwell") is consistently used in the NT of the sacred place where God dwells which, in the Jewish temple, would be the holy place and the holy of holies (Matt 27:51 = Mark 15:38 = Luke 23:45). Likewise, in heathen temples it was the place where the gods were thought to dwell (Acts 17:24). The Ephesian silversmiths made shrines (ναός) to commemorate Artemis' residence in Ephesus (Acts 19:24). In application to the present context, it means that this building is growing into a holy ναός, a place where God dwells, as seen in the next verse.

1. R. H. L. Williams, "Some Theological Pressures Towards Christian Unity," *Canadian Journal of Theology* 7 (July 1961): 187.

2. Gottlob Schrenk, "ἱερόν," *TDNT* 3 (1965): 235; Otto Michel, "ναός," *TDNT* 4 (1967): 882.

3. Josephus *A.J.* 15.11.5 §§417–20. This distinction is also seen in depicting Solomon's temple (see Josephus *A.J.* 8.3.9 §§95–96).

4. For more study on this, see Trench, *Synonyms of the New Testament*, 10–12; G. Lacey May, "Temple Or Shrine?" *ExpTim* 62 (August 1951): 346–47; B. F. Westcott, "Some Lessons of the Revised Version of the New Testament," *Exp* 3d ser., vol. 6 (August 1887): 94–95; Fred H. Chase, "Note on the Word ναός in Ephesians ii. 21," *Exp* 3d ser., vol. 6 (October 1887): 318–19.

The next word ἅγιος has already been discussed at 1:1 (cf. also 1:4, 13, 15, 18; 2:19) where it was concluded that a thing which is holy is that which is consecrated and set aside for God's use. Here then, the building is to grow into a holy temple, a place set aside for God. The final prepositional phrase ἐν κυρίῳ does not modify the main verb αὔξει[1] for that would be redundant. It could modify ναόν, which would then be rendered "a temple holy in the Lord,"[2] but more likely it modifies ναὸν ἅγιον, "holy temple in the Lord."[3] The prepositional phrase ἐν κυρίῳ, "in the Lord," has reference not to God but to Christ as it consistently does throughout the epistle (4:1, 17; 5:8; 6:1, 10, 21). It denotes the sphere in which this holy temple is: it is in Christ. Hence, this temple which is set aside for God's use is not in Artemis but in Christ. This building, which is the "new person," is growing into the holy temple in Christ. The temple of the OT was where God had dwelt. The temple of Ephesus was where Artemis purportedly dwelt. The temple of the Qumran literature was considered the future habitation of God and where only the ritually and morally clean Israelite would be able to enter (1QS 5:5–6; 8:4–26; 4Q174 3:2–6 [1:2–6]).[4] However, the temple mentioned in Ephesians is the presently growing body of believing Jews and Gentiles and the residence of God. Furthermore, as to the Qumran literature, the tone of judgment for those allowed to enter the future temple is entirely missing in Ephesians.

The emphasis here has been on the unified growth of this building, the body of believers, into the temple. This temple in Ephesians lets all those who trust in Christ become a living and growing holy temple in which God dwells. The emphasis is not individual growth but corporate growth. Paul elaborates on this in the following verse.

(3) The Function of the Building (2:22)

The foundation and the formation of the building have been established. Paul now discusses the function of the building. It is the habitation of God.

Text: 2:22. ἐν ᾧ καὶ ὑμεῖς συνοικοδομεῖσθε εἰς κατοικητήριον τοῦ θεοῦ ἐν πνεύματι.

Translation: 2:22. "in whom you also are being built together into a dwelling place of God in the Spirit."

1. As do Oecumenius *Eph* 2:19–22 (*PG* 118:1200); Meyer, 148; Barth, 273.

2. As Harless, 263; Abbott, 75.

3. So Alford, 3:101–2; Eadie, 203; Ellicott, 55; Winer, *Grammar*, 186.

4. For a discussion of the temple of the Qumran community and its relationship to the NT, see Gärtner, *The Temple and the Community in Qumran and the New Testament*, esp. 16–46, 60–66; Georg Klinzing, *Die Umdeutung des Kultus in der Qumrangemeinde und im Neuen Testament*, esp. 184–91; Smith, "Cultic Language in Ephesians 2:19–20," 207–17.

Commentary: 2:22. ἐν ᾧ καὶ ὑμεῖς συνοικοδομεῖσθε, "in whom you also are being built together." Some think that the prepositional phrase ἐν ᾧ refers back to ναὸν ἅγιον ἐν κυρίῳ (v. 21).[1] But most commentators think it refers back to ἐν κυρίῳ (v. 21b),[2] which in turn refers back to ἐν ᾧ (v. 21a), which in turn refers back to Χριστοῦ Ἰησοῦ (v. 20).[3] Since it refers to Christ it is best rendered "in whom," referring to the sphere or location. The reason for this is because it is the nearest antecedent and also because within the context this same prepositional phrase refers to Christ. The conjunction καί is adjunctive and is translated "also." The personal pronoun ὑμεῖς, "you," is emphatic because Paul is returning back to the second person plural used in verses 19–20 (he uses third person singular in v. 21) referring to the Gentiles who were foreigners and aliens and are now fellow citizens with the saints and God's household (v. 19). Verse 21 speaks of the building process, whereas verse 22 speaks of the people who make up the building. These believing Gentiles, with believing Jews, were being built on the foundation of the apostles and prophets. Now he specifically refers to the Gentiles again and states that they are συνοικοδομεῖσθε, "being built together." This verb, which is a combination of the prepositional prefix συν- and the verb οἰκοδομέω, occurs only here in the NT. It is used of a wall being built together with huge stones[4] or of the columns being built in or together with the walls.[5] In the LXX it is used only in 1 Esdr 5:68 [LXX 5:65] where the enemies of Israel offered to build the temple together with them. Hence, it basically means "to build in" or "to build together." The συν- prefix can have one of two meanings. First, it could have the idea of being built *along* with other believers, namely, the Jews, which would fit with the idea of "fellow citizens" (v. 19) or the idea of enemies building the temple *along* with Israel (1 Esdr 5:68 [LXX 5:65]).[6] Second, it could connote the idea of being built *together* with other believers. In this way Jews and Gentiles are brought *together* in Christ as individual pieces of this structure and are being formed as one new building on the foundation of the apostles and prophets. Believing Jews and Gentiles become an inherent part of the building.[7] This would coincide with the idea of "being fitted together" (v. 21) as stones are being pieced together in a wall.[8] This second view is preferred because it is consistent

1. Aquinas, chap. 2, lec. 6, vv. 19–22 (117); Eadie, 204.

2. Bengel, 4:81; Harless, 264; Alford, 3:102; Ellicott, 55; Meyer, 148; Abbott, 75; Salmond, 301; Gaugler, 124; Schnackenburg, 124; Lincoln, 157; Best, 288.

3. Lincoln (158) bypasses ἐν κυρίῳ and goes directly to ἐν ᾧ in v. 21, making vv. 21 and 22 parallel.

4. Thucydides 1.93.5.

5. Diodorus Siculus 13.82.3.

6. Abbott, 76; Robinson, 166.

7. McGrath, "'*Syn*' Words in Saint Paul," 223.

8. Alford, 3:102; Eadie, 205; Ellicott, 55; Meyer, 148–49; Salmond, 301; Otto Michel, "συνοικοδομέω," *TDNT* 5 (1967): 148.

with the imagery of the immediately preceding words of *being fitted* into a building that grows into a holy temple in the Lord, and with the following words where the process *being fit* together results in a building where God dwells. Again, the image stresses unity. The verb is not an imperative,[1] for "the whole passage is descriptive, not hortatory."[2] Rather, it is a present indicative with the tense again indicating the continuance of the building. The voice in form could be middle, but that would indicate that we are the ones who are building this dwelling place. It seems more fitting to the context that it is passive, denoting God's gracious activity in the building.

εἰς κατοικητήριον τοῦ θεοῦ,[3] "into a dwelling place of God." As in verse 20 the preposition εἰς shows the direction of the building and can be translated "to" or better in this context "into." The direction of growth is into a κατοικητήριον τοῦ θεοῦ, "a dwelling place of God." The adjective is derived from οἰκέω, "to dwell," with the prepositional prefix κατα-, "down," and with the -τήριον suffix, which denotes place.[4] Hence it has the idea of the "place of deep or settled dwelling." This word is not found in classical literature but is found twenty times in the LXX (eighteen times in the canonical books), primarily from: (1) the verb יָשַׁב, meaning "to sit, remain, dwell"[5] (Exod 15:17; 1 Kgs 8:39, 43, 49; 2 Chr 6:30, 33, 39; 2 Kgs 19:15 = Isa 37:15–16; Ps 33:14 [LXX 32:14]) and the corresponding masculine noun מוֹשָׁב, meaning "seat, assembly, dwelling-place, dwelling"[6] (Exod 12:20; Ps 107:4, 7 [LXX 106:4, 7]); and (2) from the masculine noun מָעוֹן, meaning "refuge, habitation"[7] (2 Chr 30:27; Jer 9:11 [MT & LXX 9:10]; Nah 2:11 [MT & LXX 2:12]) and the corresponding feminine noun מְעֹנָה, meaning "den, habitation"[8] (Ps 76:2 [MT 76:3; LXX 75:3]; Jer 21:13; Nah 2:12 [MT & LXX 2:13]). Most of the references speak of God's dwelling place either in heaven (1 Kgs 8:39, 43, 49 = 2 Chr 6:30, 33, 39; 2 Chr 30:27; Ps 33:14 [LXX 32:14]) or in the temple with his people Israel (1 Kgs 8:13; Ps 76:2 [MT 76:3; LXX 75:3]). Besides the present context, the only other place in the NT that κατοικητήριον occurs is in Rev 18:2, which refers to fallen Babylon as the dwelling place of demons. Babylon is depicted as that which opposes God, so imagery of the dwelling place of demons is fitting in contradistinction with heaven as the dwelling place of God. The genitive that follows (τοῦ θεοῦ) is possessive, denoting that this place of settled dwelling is God's

1. As suggested by Calvin, 156.

2. Alford, 3:102.

3. Instead of θεοῦ, Χριστοῦ is found in B, which is not sufficient evidence to warrant it as a genuine reading.

4. BDF §109 (9); MHT 2:342–43.

5. BDB 442; M. Görg, "יָשַׁב *yāšaḇ*; מוֹשָׁב *môšāḇ*," *TDOT* 6 (1990): 421–38.

6. BDB 444; Görg, *TDOT* 6 (1990): 426, 430.

7. BDB 732–33; H. D. Preuss, "מָעוֹן *māʿôn*; מְעֹנָה *mᵉʿōnâ*," *TDOT* 8 (1997): 449–52.

8. BDB 733; Preuss, *TDOT* 8 (1997): 450.

in reference to the body of believers. It is not only a dwelling place but a deep or settled dwelling place. It has the idea of a dwelling place that is firmly rooted. It signifies the endurance and permanence of God's inhabitance in the body of believers. This is the ἅγιος ναός, "holy temple," in which God dwells, as mentioned in the previous verse. Not made with hands, it is a living temple in which God is pleased to dwell.

ἐν πνεύματι, "in the Spirit." There are three interpretations of this phrase. First, some commentators render it adjectively as "spiritual," meaning God's spiritual dwelling place (NEB, NRSV).[1] They were thinking of a spiritual temple as opposed to a stone one built by the Jews, similar to 1 Pet 2:5 where the believers are built into a "spiritual house" (οἶκος πνευματικός). "But there is no suggestion of this in the context; and as the whole is so distinctly figurative, it would be worse than superfluous to add this definition."[2] In the context there is a contrast made between the enmity between Jews and Gentiles before Christ's redemptive work and the peace they enjoy since his death, but no contrast between the two kinds of temples. Second, some think ἐν πνεύματι indicates the mere means of συνοικοδομεῖσθε and is rendered "you are being built together by means of the Spirit" (AV).[3] Calvin combines this interpretation with the first one.[4] The problem with the second interpretation is that it is far removed from the verb it modifies. Third, most interpreters think it does not modify the verb "being built together" but rather the immediately preceding words regarding "God's dwelling place," indicating that the holy temple is God's dwelling place "by the Spirit" (TEV, NIV) or "in the Spirit" (RV, ASV, RSV, NASB, JB, NJB).[5] This parallels verse 21 which states that the building grows into a holy temple "in the Lord." Whereas in verse 21 the temple was in the sphere of Christ, this verse may be describing "the manner of God's dwelling in this holy temple, *viz., in the Spirit*."[6] Or it may refer to the means or instrument of God's dwelling, namely, "by/with the Spirit."

God, who is in heaven, was pleased in OT times to dwell first in the tabernacle and later in the temple. Now in the NT times he dwells in the "temple" in two ways. In 1 Cor 6:19 Paul refers to the body of indi-

1. Chrysostom *Eph* 2:17–22 (*PG* 62:44); Theophylact *Eph* 2:22 (*PG* 124:1065); Oecumenius *Eph* 2:19–22 (*PG* 118:1200); Robinson, 72; Scott, 179; Schlier, 145; Mußner, 96; Hanson, *The Unity of the Church in the New Testament*, 134; Mußner, "Eph 2 als ökumenisches Modell," 333; Ronald Y. K. Fung, "Some Pauline Pictures of the Church," *EvQ* 53 (April–June 1981): 101, 105.

2. Abbott, 76.

3. Theophylact *Eph* 2:22 (*PG* 124:1065); Oecumenius *Eph* 2:19–22 (*PG* 118:1200); Hodge, 154; Meyer, 149–50; Salmond, 301.

4. Calvin, 156.

5. Bengel, 4:81; Alford, 3:102; Eadie, 207; Abbott, 76; Lincoln, 158.

6. Roels, *God's Mission*, 150.

vidual Christians as being the temple (ναός) of the Holy Spirit whereas in 1 Cor 3:16 he speaks of the church as the temple (ναός) in which the Holy Spirit dwells (οἰκέω). The present passage is not a reference to his dwelling in individual believers (e.g., Rom 8:9; 1 John 2:27) but to his dwelling in the corporate body of believers, the church (cf. 1 Cor 3:16; 2 Cor 6:16).[1] God's dwelling place in the church, the temple, is that which is settled and abiding in the person of the Holy Spirit.

Again as in other passages in Ephesians one sees the Triune God in operation (cf. 1:4–14, 17; 2:18, 22; 3:4–5, 14–17; 4:4–6; 5:18–20). It is God the Father, the subject of the passage, who is creating this new person into a holy temple. Christ through his work of reconciliation is the cornerstone of this new temple of which the apostles and prophets are the foundation stones. It is a living and dynamic structure that continues to grow by God's gracious power. The Holy Spirit is the manner by which God dwells in this new structure he is creating. Although the Holy Spirit resides in each individual believer, he resides also in the corporate body of believers called the holy temple, the church. This concept of the corporate body of believers as a temple indwelt with the Holy Spirit is seen elsewhere in Paul (1 Cor 3:16).

The relevance to the people of Ephesus is obvious. Before their conversion the Jews thought of God as dwelling in the temple made with hands. On the other hand, the Ephesians thought of the goddess Artemis as the one who dwelt in the renowned temple at Ephesus. This temple was considered one of the seven wonders of the world (see Introduction). These were two diametrically different views of who God was and where he resided. After conversion, both believing Jews and Gentiles must view God and his dwelling place in a drastically different way. They have been made one new person, growing into a holy temple. God's abode is in this new creation. Before, both Jews and Gentiles could see the stone buildings in which their God or gods dwelt, but now the one true God is dwelling in them, the collective entity called the church. In 1:23 it is God who fills Christ with the fullness of moral excellence and power and Christ who fills the church. In the present context it is God in the person of the Holy Spirit who dwells in this corporate body made up of redeemed Jews and Gentiles called the church.

1. Adai, *Der Heilige Geist als Gegenwart Gottes*, 185.

F. Parenthetical Expansion of the Mystery (3:1–13)

In 2:11–22 Paul has explained the union of Jewish and Gentiles believers into one new person in Christ. He now proceeds to offer a prayer on behalf of these believers. However, just as he begins, he stops abruptly in the middle of his sentence (at the end of 3:1) and digresses to the subject of the mystery of Christ. He describes the mystery and his responsibility to make it known. After this digression he resumes his prayer beginning in verse 14.

Regarding the style, it is not unusual for Paul to digress before he continues his train of thought (Rom 5:13–17; 15:23–28).[1] It is understandable in the present context because Paul had just revealed in some detail the union of believing Jews and Gentiles and with the digression he intended to enhance his previous comments. In this digression he emphasizes three things: his responsibility to make known the mystery, when and to whom this new revelation came, and the content of the mystery. In addition to the digression, another matter of style needs to be mentioned, that is, the length of the sentences. This section consists of a long sentence, verses 2–13. With 189 words this is the fourth long sentence out of the eight in the epistle (cf. 1:3–14, 15–23; 2:1–7; 3:2–13, 14–19; 4:1–6, 11–16; 6:14–20). In this particular context, if one considers that this is a digression, a long sentence is understandable. Even today it is not unusual for digressions to involve one long and cumbersome sentence. Van Roon discusses the length of Paul sentences with some detail.[2]

1. For a discussion of the parenthesis in the NT, see Robertson, *Grammar*, 435. Fay ("Paul the Empowered Prisoner," 532–61, 667–83) is not convinced that this is a digression or a parenthesis. He suggests that Ephesians is a deliberative document for the maintenance of peace between Jews and Gentiles and that 3:1–13 is a strategically synthesized composition on reconciliation to support the main argument for unity in the church.

2. Van Roon, *The Authenticity of Ephesians*, 105–11.

1. The Introduction (3:1)

This verse is the introduction to his prayer. As stated above, he abruptly digresses from this prayer at the end of the verse and resumes his prayer in verse 14.

Text: 3:1. Τούτου χάριν ἐγὼ Παῦλος ὁ δέσμιος τοῦ Χριστοῦ [Ἰησοῦ] ὑπὲρ ὑμῶν τῶν ἐθνῶν—

Translation: 3:1. "For this reason I, Paul, the prisoner of Christ Jesus in behalf of you Gentiles—"

Commentary: 3:1. Τούτου χάριν, "For this reason." The adverbial accusative χάριν from χάρις used as a preposition, which generally follows the word it governs, as here, indicates reason, and is thus translated "for this reason."[1] With this connector, Paul refers back to 2:11–22 where he had pointed out that Jews and Gentiles in Christ are now a "new person." Mitton, who does not accept the Pauline authorship of Ephesians, states that these two words are not found in Paul's genuine letters.[2] However, χάριν alone is used by Paul to express reason in Gal 3:19 as well as in disputed Pauline books (1 Tim 5:14; Titus 1:11). Another weakness in Mitton's argument is that this word is used only nine times in the entire NT. Consequently, it is not only misstating but overstating the case to say that because Paul does not use it in his genuine letters, it shows that this letter is not genuine. This is only one way of expressing "for this reason," for he could have used διό (cf. Eph 2:11; 3:13; 4:8, 25; 5:14) and διά τοῦτο (cf. Eph 1:15; 5:17; 6:13) as he does frequently in all his letters.

His next words, ἐγὼ Παῦλος ὁ δέσμιος τοῦ Χριστοῦ Ἰησοῦ, "I, Paul, the prisoner of Christ Jesus," are interpreted in two different ways. (1) The Syriac Peshitta and some commentators[3] supply the verb "I am" (εἰμί) which would render it, "for this reason I Paul am the prisoner of Christ Jesus." This makes it a complete sentence, rather than an incomplete sentence, but with no proper introductory conjunction. It denotes that Paul's imprisonment was precipitated by his presentation of the indwelling of the Holy Spirit in the new temple, the body of believers. In other words, his message to believing Gentiles regarding fellow citizenship with Jewish believers had caused his imprisonment by the hand of some Jews in Jerusalem. Abbott has shown the shortcomings of this view.[4] First, it gives too much emphasis to his imprisonment by making it the main point rather than an incidental remark. Second, if he meant to emphasize his incarceration, one would expect δέσμιος without an article to give a qualitative force. It would also be inappropriate to have

1. BAGD 877; BDAG 1078–79; cf. also Robertson, *Grammar*, 488, 505; Moule, *Idiom Book*, 198.

2. Mitton, 118.

3. Chrysostom *Eph* 3:1 (*PG* 62:43); Theophylact *Eph* 3:1 (*PG* 124:1068); Meyer, 153.

4. Abbott, 77; cf. also Eadie, 209–10; Ellicott, 56.

the article if ὁ δέσμιος were the predicate.[1] Furthermore, if the article is included, then Paul states "I am *the* prisoner of Christ Jesus" and this is out of character for him. Third, if the imprisonment is the main point, then the two phrases "for this reason" and "in behalf of you Gentiles" are redundant. It would seem that if Paul was imprisoned because of his declaration of Gentile fellow citizenship, then to repeat "in behalf of you Gentiles" is unnecessary. Fourth, ὁ δέσμιος is best considered in apposition to ἐγὼ Παῦλος as in 4:1. (2) Most commentators interpret this construction as an abrupt halt in the middle of his sentence in order to digress. This digression is intended to enhance what he had just stated, after which he returns to his new thought in verse 14 where again the words τούτου χάριν are repeated followed by the verb κάμπτω, "I bend my knees."[2] Briefly, Paul had just revealed that the "new person" had been created, composed of believing Jews and Gentiles in which God's Spirit dwells. It is at this point that Paul is going to pray for strengthened love toward one another as the outworking of this new union. However, before he offers this prayer he breaks into the middle of the sentence and gives additional information regarding the content and recipients of the mystery and Paul's responsibility to dispense this mystery to the Gentiles. When he completes this digression, he resumes with the words τούτου χάριν (v. 14) and prays that their mutual love would be strengthened (vv. 14–21). With this view, the use of the article with "prisoner" is not significant because it is only an incidental remark. Most agree that it is best to see this as a sentence that is incomplete until after his digression in verses 2–13.

ἐγὼ Παῦλος, "I, Paul." Besides here, the exact combination of these two words are found only five times in Paul (2 Cor 10:1; Gal 5:2; Col 1:23; 1 Thess 2:18; Phlm 19). In all these instances Paul appears to be speaking directly with a friendly tone. Here Paul explains that he, as the author of this letter (1:1),[3] is personally suffering in their behalf. There is no sense of egotism but rather the sense of personal involvement. He had received and revealed to them the revelation that believing Jews and Gentiles are one body and now is suffering the consequences of declaring that revelation. As he personally (κἀγώ, 1:15) had heard of their faith, now he was personally suffering for their acceptance of his message.

1. Winer, *Grammar*, 708.

2. Alford, 3:102–3; Eadie, 210; Ellicott, 56; Abbott, 77; Salmond, 302; Gaugler, 125; Barth, 327; Schnackenburg, 130; Bruce, 309; Lincoln, 167, 172–73; Erich Mauerhofer, "Der Brief an die Epheser. 26. Teil: 3,1–3," *Fundamentum* 2 (1996): 22–23. It was thought by Oecumenius (*Eph* 3:7–11 [*PG* 118:1204]) that Paul resumed his thought in v. 8 rather than in v. 14, but as Eadie states (209), v. 8 is inseparable from vv. 6–7. Furthermore, the repetition of τούτου χάριν in v. 14 seems to indicate a resumption of thought.

3. It is not an indication of a pseudonymous author, see Mauerhofer, "Der Brief an die Epheser," 23–24.

ὁ δέσμιος τοῦ Χριστοῦ [Ἰησοῦ,][1] "the prisoner of Christ Jesus." In addition to this context, Paul designates himself as a prisoner of Christ four other times: "a prisoner of Christ Jesus" (Phlm 1 and 9), "the prisoner in the Lord" (Eph 4:1), and "his prisoner" (2 Tim 1:8). Later in the present letter, he describes himself as an ambassador in chains (6:20). The genitives (τοῦ Χριστοῦ Ἰησοῦ, "of Christ Jesus") denote not only possession, depicting Paul as Christ's prisoner, but also denote cause, for it was the cause of Christ that made him a prisoner.[2]

ὑπὲρ ὑμῶν τῶν ἐθνῶν[3]**—,** "in behalf of you Gentiles—." This is the only time in his writings that Paul mentions that his imprisonment was in behalf of the Gentiles. Certainly, Paul's special mission was to the Gentiles (Acts 9:15; 22:21; 26:17–18; Gal 1:16; 2:7–9; Rom 1:5; 11:13; 1 Tim 2:7). Because of this, the Jews claimed that he was distorting God's revelation and thus were instrumental in obtaining his imprisonment in Jerusalem (Acts 21:20–36) from where he was taken to Caesarea, tried, and appealed to Caesar (Acts 24:23–25:12). He was then taken to Rome and imprisoned while waiting for his accusers to arrive (Acts 27–28). Altogether he spent four years in prison: two years in Caesarea and another two years in Rome. While in Rome he wrote to the Ephesians about his imprisonment. Therefore, because of his mission to the Gentiles he suffered incarceration. This is why he states that he was a prisoner in their behalf. He did not want pity, for it was their glory, as expressed in verse 13. After speaking these words, he stops abruptly and begins his digression in verses 2–13.[4]

1. There are six readings. The first τοῦ Χριστοῦ Ἰησοῦ is found in 𝔓^{46} ℵ^{2} A B D^{2} 075 0150 33 81 104 263 424 436 459 1175 1241 1739 1912 2464 *Byz* [K L P] *Lect* it$^{ar, f}$ vg syr^{h} cop$^{samss, bo}$ geo^{2} Origen Cyril$^{1/2}$ Jerome$^{2/6}$ Pelagius. The second reading τοῦ Ἰησοῦ Χριστοῦ appears in (6 *omit* τοῦ) 630 1881 2200 *l* 884 it^{b} vg^{mss} syr^{p} cop^{sams} arm geo^{1} slav (Chrysostom) (Cyril$^{1/2}$) Ambrose$^{1/2}$ Jerome$^{4/6}$. The third reading τοῦ Χριστοῦ is in ℵ* D* F G 256 1319 1573 1852 2127 (365) *pc* it$^{d, g, o}$ cop^{samss} eth Victorinus-Rome Ambrosiaster Hilary$^{1/2}$. The fourth reading τοῦ κυρίου Ἰησοῦ is found in C Ψ (Hilary$^{1/2}$ Ambrose$^{1/2}$ *omit* κυρίου). The fifth reading ἐν Χριστῷ is found in 365, and the sixth reading ἐν Χριστῷ Ἰησοῦ appears in *l* 156 *l* 170 *l* 617. Only the first and third readings are serious contenders whereas the second reading is a transposition of words from the first reading. The omission of Ἰησοῦ in the third reading is seen primarily in the Western text-type with the exception of ℵ*. Its inclusion, as in the first and second readings, is solidly in the Alexandrian and Byzantine text-types and thus has better attestation than its exclusion. It represents good geographical distribution as well as good genealogical relationships. The first reading has the best attestation.

2. Winer, *Grammar*, 236; HS §159; Wallace, *Greek Grammar*, 82 n. 30; Mauerhofer, "Der Brief an die Epheser. 26. Teil: 3,1–3," 25.

3. The addition of πρεσβεύω, "I am an ambassador," found in D 104* *pc* and κεκαύχημαι, "I have gloried," found in 2464 *pc* have not enough support to merit their acceptance. A scribe may have inserted the first reading from 2 Cor 5:20, the only other time it is used in the NT, and the second reading from Rom 11:13, where Paul stated that he glories (δοξάζω) in his ministry as an apostle to the Gentiles.

4. For a rhetorical analysis of 3:2–13, see Jeal, *Integrating Theology and Ethics in Ephesians*, 164–75.

2. The Mystery (3:2–6)

Paul breaks into the middle of his sentence to begin a long sentence of digression (vv. 2–13) to explain the mystery (vv. 2–6) and his ministry to make it known to the Gentiles (vv. 7–13). In verses 2–6 he states his responsibility to dispense the mystery (v. 2), when and to whom it was revealed (vv. 3–5), and what is its content (v. 6).

a. The Administration of God's Grace (3:2)

Text: 3:2. —εἴ γε ἠκούσατε τὴν οἰκονομίαν τῆς χάριτος τοῦ θεοῦ τῆς δοθείσης μοι εἰς ὑμᾶς,

Translation: 3:2. —"surely you have heard of the administration of the grace of God that was given to me for you,"

Commentary: 3:2. —εἴ γε ἠκούσατε, "—surely you have heard." The dash at the end of verse 1 and at the beginning of verse 2 is inserted to indicate to the reader the break in Paul's sentence. The conditional conjunction εἴ introduces the reader to the first part of the protasis of a first class conditional sentence that will continue until the end of verse 12 and the conjunction διό in verse 13 introduces the apodosis of this conditional sentence. The following enclitic particle γέ is often added, as is the case here, to the conjunction (εἴ) either to give emphasis to it ("if indeed," 1 Cor 4:8) or to add a concessive nuance ("inasmuch as," John 4:2).[1] Here, although both connotations seem possible, the emphasis is on the latter. On the one hand, it heightens the protasis on the conditional sentence but, on the other hand, it concedes that Paul's distinct ministry was already familiar to the Ephesians. In translations, the intensity is shown by translating it "if so be" (RV, ASV) or "if indeed" (NASB) and the concessive idea is expressed when translating it "assuming" (RSV, NRSV) or "surely" (NEB, TEV, JB, NIV, NJB). Thrall thinks the sense is: "At any rate if you have heard . . . as I know you have."[2] This particle is important, for if it were excluded, it would connote that the Ephesians had not heard of the particular ministry of Paul even though he had been with them two or three years. It would imply that the writer was a stranger to the Ephesians and would legitimately bring into question the Pauline authorship of this letter.[3] However, the enclitic particle gives assurance that they had heard of the mystery and his ministry and consequently they should not be disheartened at his present suffering spelled out in the

1. BAGD 152; BDAG 190; Robertson, *Grammar*, 1148*bis*; cf. BDF §439 (2); MHT 3:331.

2. Thrall, *Greek Particles in the New Testament*, 88; cf. also Norbert Baumert, *Täglich Sterben und Auferstehen. Der Literalsinn von 2 Kor 4,12–5,10*, SANT, ed. Vinzenz Hamp and Josef Schmid, vol. 34 (Munich: Kösel, 1973), 381–82.

3. As do Abbott, 78; Mitton, 120; Lincoln, 173.

apodosis (v. 13). Having not been at Ephesus for five or six years, Paul, by this particle, gently reminds them of what they had heard when he was there. He then proceeds to spell out fully the mystery and his ministry so as to crystalize in their minds what they had been taught by him. Besides here, the combination of εἴ γε is used only in 4:21; 2 Cor 5:3; Gal 3:4; Col 1:23. In Eph 4:21 it presupposes that they had heard of Christ; 2 Cor 5:3 presupposes being clothed with immortality;[1] in Gal 3:4 it assumes that their sufferings were not in vain;[2] and in Col 1:23 it denotes confidence that they will continue in the faith.[3] Hence, the translation "surely" seems best to convey the intended meaning.[4] Paul assumes that they had heard (ἠκούσατε) of the mystery and his ministry when he was there with them and that they, no doubt, continued to hear of his ministry since he had left them.

τὴν οἰκονομίαν τῆς χάριτος τοῦ θεοῦ, "of the administration of the grace of God." In addition to the present verse, the term οἰκονομία is used in 1:10 and 3:9. It was discussed at 1:10 where it was concluded that it has two nuances: first, the position or office of an administrator; and second, the activity of administration. Moreover, it was pointed out that the exact nuance of this term is further dependent on the relationship of the gentives that follow. In this context Reumann suggests that the possible meanings for οἰκονομία "can denote Paul's activity as a steward; his office given him by God's grace; the administration of the grace given to him; or God's plan, and God's administration thereof; or some combination of these senses." He then concludes that it is a combination of both the administration of the mystery and the activity of administration, namely, making known the mystery.[5] Certainly, this has some validity because it is too easy to make a distinct dichotomy excluding any relationship of the options to each other. Surely, the adminstrator has to administrate something—that which has been delegated to him. It seems, however, that in this verse there is more emphasis on the position or office of an administrator than on the activity that naturally follows. In other words, the Ephesians had heard of Paul's position of an administra-

1. Alfred Plummer, *A Critical and Exegetical Commentary on the Second Epistle of St Paul to the Corinthians*, ICC, ed. S. R. Driver, A. Plummer, and C. A. Briggs (Edinburgh: T & T Clark, 1915), 147; Victor Paul Furnish, *II Corinthians*, AB, ed. William Foxwell Albright and David Noel Freedman, vol. 32A (Garden City, N.Y.: Doubleday, 1984), 267; Ralph P. Martin, *2 Corinthians*, WBC, ed. David A. Hubbard and Glenn W. Barker; New Testament ed. Ralph P. Martin, vol. 40 (Waco, Tex.: Word, 1986), 105.

2. Lightfoot, *Galatians*, 135–36; Betz, *Galatians*, 135 n. 69; F. F. Bruce, *The Epistle of Paul to the Galatians. A Commentary on the Greek Text*, The New International Greek Testament Commentary, ed. I. Howard Marshall and W. Ward Gasque (Grand Rapids: Eerdmans; Exeter: Paternoster, 1982), 150.

3. O'Brien, *Colossians, Philemon* 69.

4. Eadie, 211; Ellicott, 57; Meyer, 154; Salmond, 302–3; Gaugler, 128; Barth, 328; Schnackenburg, 130.

5. Reumann, "Οἰκονομία-Terms in Paul," 165.

tor. Mitton has argued that what is conveyed here is something quite different from what is stated in Col 1:25 and other Pauline epistles, thus demonstrating that Ephesians cannot be Pauline.[1] Col 1:25 states, "the administration of God that was given to me for you," whereas the present context states, "the administration of the grace of God that was given to me for you." Mitton contends that the clause "that was given to me for you" modifies "administration" in Col 1:25, whereas in Eph 3:2 it modifies "grace." However, Reumann argues that though the emphasis in Eph 3:2 may be different, it is not at all out of line with Pauline thinking. In the present verse Paul is merely continuing his emphasis on grace (1:6–7; 2:5–8). This is consistent with the idea that the administration given to Paul as an apostle to the Gentiles is an outcome of God's grace (3:7–8), and this is also consistent with other Pauline literature (Rom 1:5; 15:15; 1 Cor 3:10; Gal 2:9).[2] More will be discussed below in connection with τῆς δοθείσης μοι εἰς ὑμᾶς.

The next concern is regarding the following genitives: τῆς χάριτος τοῦ θεοῦ. The final genitive (τοῦ θεοῦ) is either a genitive of possession, "God's grace," or origin, "grace that comes from God." The first genitive (τῆς χάριτος) is a little more difficult to pinpoint. Some think it is a subjective genitive "grace that revealed the administration of God";[3] others see it as an adjectival genitive "the gracious administration of God";[4] but most see it as either an objective genitive, "administration concerning the grace of God,"[5] or a genitive of reference, "administration with reference to the grace of God."[6] Either of these last two constructions seem to be the most plausible. Grace normally means "unmerited favor" (cf. 1:2, 6, 7; 2:5, 7, 8), but here it has a more restrictive sense of administration, that is, of the grace which refers to the mystery of believing Jews and Gentiles as one body that Paul is treating in this passage.[7] This is not unusual, for Paul uses some sort of a restricted sense in other places, usually with a particular combination of words (ἡ χάρις ἡ δοθεῖσά μοι), in connection with his mission to the Gentiles (Rom 12:6; 15:15; 1 Cor 3:10; Gal 2:9; Eph 3:7–8; 4:29).[8] In the present context, Paul talks about the unmerited favor involved in the revelation of the mystery. Therefore, he describes what the Ephesians had heard about his administration regarding God's unmerited favor. In addition, Paul's responsibility was to explain it to his readers. In

1. Mitton, *The Epistle to the Ephesians*, 93, 245; Mitton, 125–26.

2. Reumann, "Οἰκονομία-Terms in Paul," 156–57, 163–65; cf. also van Roon, *The Authenticity of Ephesians*, 175; Lincoln, 174.

3. Chrysostom *Eph* 3:2 (*PG* 62:44–45); Oecumenius *Eph* 3:1–6 (*PG* 118:1201).

4. Percy, *Probleme*, 342–43.

5. Alford, 3:103; Meyer, 155; Abbott, 79; Schlier, 148.

6. Ellicott, 57; Salmond, 303.

7. Caragounis, *Ephesian* Mysterion, 97–98.

8. Robinson, 176.

verse 7 it will be seen that grace is necessary not only for the revelation of the mystery, but also for enablement to make known the mystery.

Dispensationalists could construe that Paul is speaking of the administration of grace in contrast to the dispensation of the law, thus negating that there was grace in the OT. However, most dispensationalists deem that God's grace was abundantly exhibited in the OT. This particular context could be labeled more specifically as the dispensation of a "special" grace which was given to Paul. This "special" grace is the revelation of the mystery regarding the church, which is composed of believing Jews and Gentiles united into one body. Hence, rather than call it a dispensation of grace, a better designation would be the dispensation or administration of the church. This clearly shows that God is operating in a different way in the present day. Before the cross Gentiles would have had to become Jews, whereas now Gentiles do not become Jews nor do Jews become Gentiles but both become one "new person," the church. The idea of the church is not exclusively Paul's, as will be seen in verse 5. It was already revealed to Peter and the early apostles in Acts 10–11 and later at the Jerusalem Council in Acts 15. However, Paul was the one to whom God graciously gave the ministry of dispensing this mystery and this was in connection with his specific role as an apostle to Gentiles.

τῆς δοθείσης μοι εἰς ὑμᾶς, "that was given to me for you." The genitive τῆς δοθείσης could relate back to τὴν οἰκονομίαν,[1] similar to the parallel in Col 1:25 (κατὰ τὴν οἰκονομίαν τοῦ θεοῦ τὴν δοθεῖσάν μοι εἰς ὑμᾶς) as discussed above. This would mean that the administration was given to Paul. Although this does have some validity, most commentators see the genitive τῆς δοθείσης as depending directly on the previous genitive τῆς χάριτος. The reason for this is fourfold: (1) it is the nearest antecedent; (2) it is in the genitive rather than the accusative case, which Paul could have used if he clearly meant to qualify τὴν οἰκονομίαν as he did in Col 1:25; (3) the giving in relationship to grace is used two other times in the present context (vv. 7, 8); and (4) the words ἡ χάρις ἡ δοθεῖσά μοι are a common combination in Paul (Rom 12:3; 15:15; 1 Cor 3:10; Gal 2:9; Eph 3:7; cf. also Rom 12:6; 1 Cor 1:4; Eph 3:8; 4:29; 2 Tim 1:9; Jas 4:6*bis*; 1 Pet 5:5). Therefore, it appears that a special grace relevant to this context was given to Paul. This is merely a minor difference with Colossians.

Although the pronoun μοί, "me," indicates that this grace was given to Paul, the following prepositional phrase εἰς ὑμᾶς, "to/for you" shows that it was to be imparted to the recipients of this letter. The preposition εἰς may indicate direction "toward you,"[2] but more probably it functions much like a dative of advantage "for you."[3] Although Paul's mission was to all Gentiles, it must be observed that the inclu-

1. Possibly Abbott (79), although he is not clear.
2. Ellicott, 57.
3. BAGD 229; BDAG 290–91.

sion of Gentiles into one body is true only for those who believe and not for every Gentile, even unbelievers, as some suggest.[1] This is made clear in verse 6 where "the Gentiles are fellow heirs, and fellow members of the body, and fellow participants of the promise in Christ through the gospel." The "Gentiles" in this context are believers who have been delivered from God's wrath.

In this first stage of the protasis, Paul tells his readers that he assumed that they had heard of the administration of grace given to him in their behalf. He elaborates more on the content in verse 6. In the meantime, Paul discusses the revelation of this grace, which is called the mystery.

b. The Revelation of the Mystery (3:3–5)

Now that Paul's ministry of the adminstration of God's grace has been made clear, he now discusses the revelation of the content of the administration, namely, the mystery. This is divided into three parts: (1) how the mystery was revealed (v. 3); (2) the ability to understand the mystery (v. 4); and (3) the initial revelation of the mystery in the NT era to the apostles and prophets (v. 5).

(1) The Manner of the Mystery's Disclosure (3:3)

Paul is first careful to explain that he received the mystery by revelation. He wanted to prevent the misconception that it was developed by his own or someone else's ingenuity.

Text: 3:3. [ὅτι] κατὰ ἀποκάλυψιν ἐγνωρίσθη μοι τὸ μυστήριον, καθὼς προέγραψα ἐν ὀλίγῳ,

Translation: 3:3. "that by revelation the mystery was made known to me, as I wrote before briefly,"

Commentary: 3:3. [ὅτι][2] κατὰ ἀποκάλυψιν ἐγνωρίσθη[3] μοι τὸ μυστήριον, "that by revelation the mystery was made known to me." The

1. E. Best, "The Revelation to Evangelize the Gentiles," *JTS*, n.s., 35 (April 1984): 24; cf. Barth, "Conversion and Conversation," 3–24; idem, *The People of God*, 45–72.

2. The ὅτι does not appear in 𝔓⁴⁶ B F G it$^{b, d}$ cop$^{sa^{ms}}$ Ambrosiaster but is included in ℵ A C D Ψ 33 1739 1881 𝔐 it^{a} vg syr cop$^{sa/mss, bo}$. Both readings have a fair representation in the Alexandrian and Western text-types. However, the inclusion is better in the Alexandrian tradition because it does have the predominant representation from the Coptic versions, which are early, and does have the vg. It is split in the Western text. The Byzantine text includes it. Therefore, the inclusion does have good date and character of manuscripts, it has excellent geographical distribution, and it has good genealogical relationships, except in the Western text-type. There is no real good reason for omitting it.

3. A γάρ precedes this word only in F and G and the aorist indicative active third person singular ἐγνώρισε is found in D^{2} and 𝔐. The present reading is found in 𝔓⁴⁶ ℵ A B C D* P Ψ 6 33 81 104 365 1175 1505 1739 1881 2464 *pc* lat syr Clement. Certainly, the present reading has overwhelming support in date and character, geographical distri-

conjunction ὅτι often follows verbs that denote sense perception,[1] as hearing (ἠκούσατε) in this context (v. 2), and is in apposition to οἰκονομίαν, "administration," introducing an objective sentence rendered as "how that" or "that," as it is in the translation above.

This is immediately followed by the prepositional phrase κατὰ ἀποκάλυψιν, "by revelation," and its place in the sentence shows its importance. The preposition κατά with the accusative normally denotes the standard,[2] but here it also denotes the manner by which the mystery was made known to Paul, namely, "by revelation." This is virtually the same as διά ἀποκαλύψεως in Gal 1:12. The word ἀποκάλυψις was discussed at 1:17 and has the meaning of unveiling or disclosing something that had been previously hidden. In the NT it has the theological significance of the unveiling of that which was previously hidden in God and unknown to humans. It is not the acquisition of knowledge by diligent searching but the unveiling of facts instrinsically hidden. This idea is further enhanced by the aorist passive verb ἐγνωρίσθη, which is from γνωρίζω, meaning "to make known, reveal," as seen in the study of the word in 1:9. Its most prominent use in the NT is "making known" the mysteries that have been kept secret (Rom 16:26; Eph 1:9; 3:3, 5, 10; 6:19; Col 1:27).[3] The aorist views the action as completed.[4] The passive voice reinforces the fact that the mystery was made known by revelation rather than discovered by human ingenuity. This is further heightened by the dative pronoun μοί, which shows that Paul was the recipient rather than the originator of the knowledge of the mystery.

Finally, that which was made known to Paul by revelation is τὸ μυστήριον, "the mystery." A discussion of this word can be found in an excursus (see Excursus 6: Mystery) where it is concluded that the mystery was hidden in God (v. 9) and cannot be unravelled or understood by human ingenuity or study.[5] It is not something that is mysterious but rather a revealed secret to be understood by all believing people and not just a few elite.[6] Verse 5 substantiates this. Hence, in verse 3 Paul states only that this mystery was made known to him by revelation, and in verse 6 the content of the mystery is given. Reumann[7] interestingly observes that four out of the six times Paul mentions

---

bution, and in genealogical relationships in the Alexandrian and Western texts. Therefore, the present reading should be accepted as the genuine reading.

1. BAGD 588; BDAG 731.

2. Cf. BAGD 407; BDAG 512.

3. Cf. Bultmann, *TDNT* 1 (1964): 718.

4. Fanning, *Verbal Aspect*, 153.

5. Cf. Heinrich Schlier, "Die Kirche als das Geheimnis Christi (Nach dem Epheserbrief)," *TQ* 134, no. 4 (1954): 385–96; this is reprinted: in idem, *Die Zeit der Kirche*, 299–307.

6. "New Testament Lexicography," *CQR* 29 (January 1890): 276.

7. Reumann, "Οἰκονομία-Terms in Paul," 157.

οἰκονομία, "administration," the word "mystery" is in close proximity to it (Eph 1:10; 3:2, 9; Col 1:25; although not so in 1 Cor 9:17 and 1 Tim 4:11). Certainly here the imagery is of Paul as administrator of the mystery which has been revealed to him. This mystery is in contrast to and superior to the popular Lydian-Phrygian mysteries.[1] The mysteries of the mystery religions were secrets known only to initiates, whereas the mystery in the present context is made known not only to Paul but also to the apostles and prophets (v. 5), to all people (v. 9), and to all rulers and the authorities in the heavenly places (v. 10).

It is not clear when this mystery was made known to Paul by revelation. It may well have been at the time of his Damascus experience where he is told to go to the Gentiles (Acts 9:15–16; 26:17–18; Gal 1:16), or perhaps when he first returned to Jerusalem (Acts 22:21). However, it is possible that he received the revelation of the mystery at different stages. Certainly this occurred earlier, for when Peter baptized the Gentile, Cornelius, he was criticized by some in Jerusalem (Acts 11:1–3). Even in A.D. 49, sixteen years after the crucifixion and the inception of the church, the Jerusalem Council debated about the inclusion of the Gentiles (Acts 15). It took years to understand this new concept completely. In the present passage, Paul explains fully what this mystery is that he received by revelation. There is no doubt that this book presents a further development than his earlier epistles of the concept of Jews and Gentiles in one body.

καθὼς προέγραψα ἐν ὀλίγῳ, "as I wrote before briefly." The verb προγράφω is used only four times in the NT (Rom 15:4; Gal 3:1; Eph 3:3; Jude 4) and means "to write before(hand)."[2] The prepositional phrase ἐν ὀλίγῳ could be translated "in a few words" if the plural were used, but since it is singular, it means "in brief,"[3] or in the adverbial sense, "briefly," as in the above translation. The exact expression is used with reference to time in Acts 26:28 where Agrippa II asks Paul if he can persuade him to be a Christian "in a short time." Hence, it has the idea of brevity.

However, the problem is to determine when, beforehand, Paul wrote about the mystery. Some have speculated that he wrote another letter to the Ephesians regarding the mystery,[4] but this is improbable since we have no manuscript evidence to support this nor is there any specific mention in this epistle of a previous letter.[5] Because it speaks of brevity, Davies conjectures that Paul is referring to the few words about the mystery in Rom 16:25–27,[6] but it is highly unlikely that the

1. Arnold, *Ephesians: Power and Magic*, 126–27; Kearsley, "The Mysteries of Artemis at Ephesus," 202.

2. BAGD 704; BDAG 867; Porter, *Verbal Aspect*, 228.

3. BAGD 563; BDAG 703; BDF §195.

4. Chrysostom *Eph* 3:3 (*PG* 62:45); Calvin, 158.

5. Theodoret *Eph* 3:1–4 (*PG* 82:525).

6. Llynfi Davies, "'I wrote afore in few words' (Eph. iii.3)," *ExpTim* 46 (September 1935): 568.

Ephesian church would have had a copy of Romans and it seems from the present context that Paul was writing to the Ephesians and not to the Romans. Bruce suggests that possibly Paul is referring to Col 1:25–27 because the Colossian church was close and the Ephesians could have had access to this letter.[1] Albeit, it is more probable that he is referring to the mystery previously mentioned in the present epistle. Possibly it has reference to the "mystery" in 1:9,[2] but there it refers to the mystery of God's will in very general terms rather than discussing specifically the mystery of the embodiment of Jews and Gentiles in the church. Ellicott suggests that it refers to the immediately preceding clause (ἐγνωρίσθη μοι τὸ μυστήριον), but this is unlikely since no brief description of it is given. Most likely he is alluding to 2:11–22[3] where he states that Jews and Gentiles are "created into one new person" (2:15) and are "in one body" (2:16). This fits well with the content of the mystery as given in 3:6. Apparently, in the present context he is only elaborating on what had already been discussed. Although some suggest that since brevity is mentioned it refers to 2:13–22[4] or 2:14–16,[5] which is the core of the mystery, in the end it is most likely that Paul was referring to 2:11–22 or a portion of this passage. The aorist verb would be considered an epistolary aorist where the writer looks at his letter as the readers did.[6]

Excursus 6
Mystery

This excursus is primarily interested in a word study of mystery although there will be some discussion on related theological issues. The term μυστήριον has been thoroughly discussed among NT scholars[7] from the inception of early church history. The history of the

1. Bruce, 312.

2. Alford, 3:103; Barth, 329.

3. Meyer, 156; Abbott, 79–80; Salmond, 303; Dibelius-Greeven, 74; Schlier, 149; Gaugler, 130; Gnilka, 164; Schnackenburg, 132; Lincoln, 175; Percy, *Probleme*, 350; Merklein, *Das kirchliche Amt nach dem Epheserbrief*, 215–16; Mussner, "Was ist die Kirche?" 84–85.

4. Eadie, 214.

5. Bruce, 312.

6. Robertson, *Grammar*, 845; Wallace, *Greek Grammar*, 563, 565 (Wallace labels it as "immediate past aorist/dramatic aorist").

7. For further study, see Robinson, 234–40; Edwin Hatch, *Essays in Biblical Greek* (Oxford: Clarendon, 1889), 57–62; Bieder, "Das Geheimnis des Christus nach dem Epheserbrief," 329–43; Hugo Rahner, *Greek Myths and Christian Mystery*, trans. Brian Barrershaw (London: Burns & Oates, 1963); K. Prümm, "Mystères," in *Dictionnaire de la Bible, Supplément*, ed. Henri Cazelles, vol. 6 (Paris: Letouzey & Ané, 1960), 4–225; G. Bornkamm, "μυστήριον," *TDNT* 4 (1967): 802–28; Raymond E. Brown, *The Semitic Background of the Term "Mystery" in the New Testament*, Facet Books: Biblical Series, ed. John Reumann, vol. 21 (Philadelphia: Fortress, 1968) (this is a reprint of articles by idem, "The Pre-Christian Semitic Concept of 'Mystery'," *CBQ* 20 [October 1958]: 417–43; idem, "The Semitic Background of the New Testament *Mystery*," *Bib* 39, no. 4 [1958]: 426–48;

word is almost impossible to determine because it could come from μύω meaning "to close, to shut" the mouth or lips,[1] or from μυέω, meaning "to be initiated into the mysteries,"[2] or possibly a combination of both. The technical noun form (usually in the plural) referring to a mystery cult or secret rite first appeared in the seventh century B.C.[3] In its cultic use among the Greeks the mystery was shared only among the initiates of the cult, and they vowed not to disclose the mystery to the noninitiates.[4] This is not the nature of the mystery discussed in Ephesians, for it was for all,[5] and in fact, the church was the vehicle for the revelation of the mystery to the world and angelic powers, both good and bad (Eph 3:9–10).

In the LXX μυστήριον occurs eighteen times and in the canonical books it appears eight times, all of them in Daniel (2:18, 19, 27, 28, 29, 30, 47*bis*) always translating the Aramaic רָז,[6] referring both to the contents and to the interpretation of Nebuchadnezzar's dream. The important thing to notice in this incident is that nobody except God could reveal the contents and the interpretation of the dream. In examining the LXX literature outside the canon, Bornkamm shows that there are references to pagan mystery cults (Wis 14:15, 23) and idolatrous practices (μύστης) (Wis 12:5) and he concludes that these and other passages cited "display no more than influence; the mysteries here are linked neither with sacramental rites nor with the Gnostic redemption myth."[7]

Since μυστήριον occurs in the LXX only in exilic and postexilic books other terms should be considered. One frequently used word, סוֹד (Ps 25:14 [LXX 24:14]; Amos 3:7; Jer 23:18,

40, no. 1 [1959]: 70–87); Pierre Benoit, "Qumran and the New Testament," in *Paul and Qumran: Studies in New Testament Exegesis*, ed. and trans. Jerome Murphy-O'Connor (Chicago: Priory Press; London: Geoffrey Chapman, 1968), 1–30; Kuhn, "Ephesians in the Light of the Qumran Texts," 115–31; Coppens, "'Mystery' in the Theology of Saint Paul and Its Parallels at Qumran," 132–58; Mussner, "Contributions Made by Qumran to the Understanding of the Epistle to the Ephesians," 159–78; Karl Prümm, "Mystery," in *Encyclopedia of Biblical Theology*, ed. Johannes B. Bauer, trans. Joseph Blenkinsopp et al., vol. 2 (London: Sheed and Ward, 1970), 598–611; Barth, 123–27; Gerd A. Wewers, *Geheimnis und Geheimhaltung im rabbinischen Judentum*, Religionsgeschichte Versuche und Vorarbeiten, ed. Walter Burkert and Carsten Colpe, vol. 35 (Berlin: de Gruyter, 1975); Caragounis, *Ephesian* Mysterion, 117–35; Romano Penna, *Il «Mysterion» Paolino*, Supplementi alla *Rivista Biblica*, vol. 10 (Brescia: Paideia, 1978); Devon H. Wiens, "Mystery Concepts in Primitive Christianity and in its Environment," in *ANRW*, pt. 2, vol. 23.2 (1980), 1248–84; A. E. Harvey, "The Use of Mystery Language in the Bible," *JTS*, n.s., 31 (April 1980): 320–36; Bockmuehl, *Revelation and Mystery*, passim, esp. 2, 223–25, 228–30; Louis Bouyer, *The Christian Mystery: From Pagan Myth to Christian Mysticism*, trans. Illtyd Trethowan (Edinburgh: T & T Clark, 1989), 5–18, 106–8; Andreas J. Kostenberger, "The Mystery of Christ and the Church: Head and Body, 'One Flesh'," *TJ* 12 (spring 1991): 79–94; Chantal Reynier, *Évangile et mystère: Les enjeux théologiques de l'épître aux Éphésiens*, Lectio Divina, vol. 149 (Paris: Cerf, 1992).

1. Plato *Phraedrus* 251d; *Anthologia Graeca* 7.630; 15.40.6.

2. Plato *Epistulae* 7 §333e; Herodotus 8.65.

3. Heraclitus *Frag*. 14 in *Die Fragmente der Vorsokratiker*, ed. Hermann Diels; 5th ed. by Walther Kranz, vol. 1 (Berlin: Weidmannische Buchhandlung, 1934), 154; Herodotus 2.51.

4. Bornkamm, *TDNT* 4 (1967): 803–8.

5. Rahner, *Greek Myths and Christian Mystery*, 29; cf. A. H. Armstrong, "Mystery and Mysteries," *DRev* 80 (July 1962): 219–22.

6. Cf. BDB 1112; *HALOT* 5 (2000): 1980.

7. Bornkamm, *TDNT* 4 (1967): 814.

22; Job 15:8; cf. נִסְתָּרֹת in Deut 29:28), means "secret council." It is used also of the secret decisions rendered by an assembly, either in heaven or on earth. In the OT there is the concept of a heavenly council (cf. Job 1–2; 15:8; Pss 82, 89 [LXX 81, 88]) where God gives his decree to be carried out by the angels. The communication to humankind of God's secret or hidden plan was through the prophets who were caught up in visions and would see and hear the heavenly council. Although סוֹד is never translated μυστήριον in the LXX, in later Jewish literature such as the Apocrypha and Qumran it was used to denote secrets or mysteries.[1] Hence, God's heavenly council is where his secret or hidden plans existed and these plans were considered by the later Jewish writers to be God's mysteries. The following is a brief discussion of these later sources.

Jewish apocalyptic literature constantly emphasizes the fact that God's being and actions are great mysteries to humans (*1 Enoch* 63:3). It was considered that these mysteries which were kept in heaven were revealed to an enraptured seer (71:3–5; cf. also 9:6; 40:2; 46:2). The seer comprehended these things as heavenly realities that would be experienced by the righteous in the end time (52:1, 4; 90:20–39). The mysteries were initially given only to seers who would selectively pass them on only to the wise (4 Ezra 12:36–38; 14:5–6, 45–47). These mysteries included the judgment of people's deeds, good and bad, by the Elect One or the Son of Man who knows their deeds (*1 Enoch* 38:3; 49:2–4; 61:9) and will judge sinners and reward the righteous (62:2–16; 103:2–9). There is going to be a new order in the day of the Elect One when the righteous will be resurrected and live forever (5:7; 61:5).

As in Jewish apocalyptic literature, the Qumran literature also includes the idea of mysteries (primarily from סוֹד, רָז, נִסְתָּרֹת) known only to God and hidden from humankind (1QS 11:5–6; 1QH[a] 9:6–20 [1:6–20]) but revealed to the Teacher of Righteousness who is to reveal them to the community (cf. 1QH[a] 9:21 [1:21]; 10:13–14 [2:13–14]; 12:27–28 [4:27–28]; cf. 1QS 11:3; 1QM 14:14). Those who are fully initiated in the community are to appropriate the truths of the mysteries (1QS 9:18–19) but keep them hidden from the uninitiated (1QS 4:6, 17, 22). Besides, it was considered that outsiders were unable to obtain and understand the hidden knowledge (1QS 5:11; 1QH[a] 5:13–14 [13:13–14]). The initiates looked forward to a future victory of the sons of light over the sons of darkness at which time evil will vanish and righteousness will rule (1Q27 frag. 1 i:7). When this final age is achieved, it will endure forever (1QpHab 7:2, 7, 13).

In the NT the word μυστήριον is used twenty-seven[2] times, twenty times by Paul, six times in Ephesians (1:9; 3:3, 4, 9; 5:32; 6:19). First, the references outside of Paul will be examined. In the Gospels (Matt 13:11 = Mark 4:1 = Luke 8:10) it is used by Jesus to explain that he spoke in parables so that the disciples could learn the mysteries (singular only in Mark) of the kingdom of God which would remain hidden from the unbelieving. Certainly, some things concerning the kingdom were generally known because Jesus introduced many of his parables with the phrase "the kingdom of God is like." However, because of their faith, the disciples were provided more insight into the program of God for the ages in which Jesus was involved. The Jews had expected God to bring in his physical kingdom, but the disciples learned that this kingdom would first appear in a spiritual form beginning with Jesus' ministry and last until his return to set up that expected apocalyptic physical kingdom, which will include the judgment of the wicked and the vindication of the righteous.

1. Brown, *The Semitic Background of the Term "Mystery" in the New Testament*, 4–5. Brown has proved to be helpful in his discussion of "mystery" in Jewish literature.

2. Some think that it also occurs in 1 Cor 2:1, but it does not have the good manuscript or geographical support that μαρτύριον, "testimony," does.

The other four references outside of Paul are in the Book of Revelation (1:20; 10:7; 17:5, 7). In 1:20 "mystery" is used the same way as in Dan 2 and is defined by the use of symbols and followed by an interpretation: the seven stars represent the seven angels of the seven churches, and seven golden lampstands represent the seven churches. In 10:7 the trumpet call of the seventh angel signifies that the mystery of God is fulfilled. This refers to the final arrival of the kingdom long awaited by the saints of both the OT and NT, for after the blowing of the trumpet, voices in heaven are heard saying, "The kingdom of this world has become the kingdom of our Lord and of his Christ, and he shall reign for ever and ever" (11:15). This is very thing for which the apocalypists looked (*2 Apoc. Bar.* 85:10; 4 Ezra 14:5). Whereas in the Synoptics discussion of the mystery embraced the process as well as the end, only the end is described here. Revelation 17:5, 7 portray the mystery of a sumptuously attired harlot sitting on a scarlet beast. In the remainder of the chapter John interprets this mystery of the woman and the beast as personifying the epitome of wickedness who has taken control of the world kingdoms and who has attacked the Lamb and his followers and is finally overthrown (cf. also 2 Thess 2:7, 1Q27 frag. 1 i:7).

Next to be considered are those references in Paul's writings outside of Ephesians. Immediately after relating the simile of the olive tree, Paul explains to the Romans the mystery of Israel's present hardness and future deliverance (Rom 11:25). Clearly, the understanding of the mystery is available to all believers and is not restricted to the few belonging to some particular community. In Rom 16:25 he speaks of the mystery as having been hidden in past ages and is now revealed, namely, that Christ is the one who provides salvation for all.

In 1 Cor 2:7 the mystery, equated with the wisdom of God, is revealed as the crucified Christ who is the power of God for salvation. Because God has revealed it through the Spirit (2:10), all believers (not only the few) are able to understand it (1:21) though it is more fully understood by the mature (2:6). In 4:1 the word is plural (only two other times is it plural in Paul[1] [1 Cor 13:2; 14:2]) where Paul states that God has required him to be a faithful administrator of the mysteries. In 13:2 Paul uses hyperbolic language when he declares that if he has the gift of prophecy, understands all mysteries, has all knowledge and all faith, and does not have love, he is nothing. The "all mysteries" refers to the comprehension of all the puzzles of life, including all the plans of God. In 14:2 those who use another language to speak of mysteries may be speaking in the Spirit, but the lack of interpretation renders him incomprehensible. In 15:51 the mystery concerns the future when all saints, dead or alive, will be changed at the time of the resurrection. Although some passages in Jewish literature mention the judgment of sinners and the reward of the righteous, none of them describe the transformation of living saints at the time of the resurrection.

In Col 1:26–27 the mystery which had been hidden and is now manifest to the saints is that Christ is among or in them, the hope of glory. Here there is no reference to the future, just the present reality for the believer. In 2:2–3 Paul reveals his desire that believers have full understanding and thus comprehend God's mystery, namely, Christ in whom all the treasures of wisdom and knowledge are hid. Again in Col 4:3 the mystery of Christ refers to the proclamation of Christ's salvation. All of these Colossian passages where Paul specifically mentions mystery always refer to the present reality of Christ's salvation, with no reference to future implications.

In 2 Thess 2:7 Paul portrays the mystery of lawlessness operative in the world that will greatly increase when the restraining ministry of the Holy Spirit is removed but will finally be destroyed by Christ himself. Part of the mystery involving God's program is to allow the devil's program of evil to continue until Christ's return. Consequently, this passage deals with both the present evil and the future judgment of evil (cf. 1Q27 frag. 1 i:7).

1. *Contra* Prümm, "Mystery," 607.

The last Pauline references to mystery, outside of Ephesians, are in 1 Tim 3:9, 16. Here believers are told that one qualification for a deacon is that he must hold the mystery of faith. Later in the same context Paul speaks of the mystery of godliness, which declares this to be Christ who became incarnate, was resurrected, and is now proclaimed and believed among all nations. In short, the mystery of faith seems to refer to what is believed, the content of faith, and the mystery of godliness refers to Christ, the object of faith (cf. *1 Enoch* 58:5).[1]

The term "mystery" occurs six times in Ephesians, more than in any other NT book. In 1:9 Paul speaks of making known the mystery of God's will according to his purpose which he set forth in Christ in that all things in heaven and earth will be headed up in Christ. So in eternity past God planned for all things to be headed up in Christ in the future. This mystery is made known to all believers. In chapter 3 (vv. 3, 4, 9) the concept of the mystery is most fully developed. In 3:3 Paul states that the mystery was made known to him by revelation and that he had written about it briefly before. Most likely he is referring to the previous context that speaks of both Jews and Gentiles as being brought near as members of the same household, which is built on the foundation of the apostles and prophets with Christ as the cornerstone (2:11–22). Furthermore, 3:4–5 points out that the mystery was not known in former generations but is now revealed to his holy apostles and prophets by the Spirit. Clearly, the mystery was not revealed to one seer or apostle but to many. The content of the mystery given in verse 6 is that Gentiles are fellow heirs, in the same body, and fellow partakers of the promise in Christ Jesus through the gospel. It states in verse 9 that Paul was responsible to preach this gospel and to make known to all human beings the administration of the mystery which had been hidden for ages in God. How was this going to be manifested? In verse 10 it speaks of the church as the vehicle of the wisdom of God to all rulers and powers in heaven. The mystery, once hidden and now revealed to the holy apostles and prophets, is the union of believing Jews and Gentiles (on the basis of Christ's redemption) in one body, the church. Paul's mission was to proclaim this to all people and then the church was to make it known to the angelic powers in the heavens. Paul's mission has no place for secrecy; it is to be openly shared. In Eph 6:19 Paul asks believers to pray for him that when he has opportunity he would boldly proclaim the mystery of the gospel. This request probably has reference not to the message of the gospel but to the union of believing Jews and Gentiles in one body. The final passage to be studied is 5:32 and is considered last because of the difficulties it presents. After quoting Gen 2:24, Paul speaks of the mystery as profound, and though he could be referring to the one flesh concept of husband and wife as one would normally interpret it, he more likely applies it metaphorically to the union of Christ and the church. Brown acknowledges that this use of the word "mystery" is an allowable usage in the Semitic background, but he is unable to adduce a perfect parallel.[2] It is certainly a different use than in the rest of Ephesians.[3]

It would be helpful to keep in mind the following observations when considering mystery in the NT. First, some scholars hold that the NT's use of μυστήριον reflects the influence of the mystery religions that existed at the time of early Christianity.[4] This view is not as

1. Brown, *The Semitic Background of the Term "Mystery" in the New Testament*, 67–68.
2. Ibid., 66.
3. Robinson, 239; Bockmuehl, *Revelation and Mystery*, 204–5; Dawes, *The Body in Question*, 179–81, 190–91, 225–27; *contra* Harvey, "The Use of Mystery Language in the Bible," 326; Kostenberger, "The Mystery of Christ and the Church: Head and Body, 'One Flesh'," 91–92; Reynier, *Évangile et mystère*, 189–92.
4. Wilhelm Bousset, *Kyrios Christos*, trans. John E. Steely (Nashville: Abingdon, 1970); Richard Reitzenstein, *Hellenistic Mystery-Religions: Their Basic Ideas and Significance*, trans. John E. Steely, Pittsburgh Theological Monograph Series, ed. Dikran Y.

readily accepted today because on closer examination the assumed parallels seem forced and scholars seem to think that the ideas in Jewish literature are more in line with NT ideas than that of the mystery religions. Thus, there is no connection between NT mystery and the Greek mysteries, which were shared only by the initiates of the cult who vowed not to disclose the mysteries to those outside the cult.

Second, the concept of mystery in Jewish sources in the OT, Apocrypha, Pseudepigrapha, and Qumran materials furnishes a good background for the concept of mystery in the NT and exhibits parallel ideas. (1) Jewish literature frequently mentions mysteries known only to God, and in the NT Paul speaks of the mystery being hidden in God in ages past (Eph 3:9). (2) The Jewish materials place much emphasis on the last days when the judgment of the wicked and vindication of the saints will occur. Mystery in the NT does not put much emphasis on this point, but it does have an element of this in the Gospels and Revelation. However, the differences are greater. (1) Jewish literature has much to say about the future Elect One who will reveal mysteries. In contrast, Christ, the NT equivalent to the Elect One, reveals very little concerning the mystery. (2) Jewish sources teach that the Elect One divulges his mysteries to an enraptured seer who had the mysteries revealed to him in heavenly splendor, whereas in the NT the mystery was revealed to the holy apostles and prophets with little or no description of how the mystery was revealed.[1] (3) Further, in Jewish literature the seer was to tell the content of the mysteries only to the closed community and they were not to tell anyone outside of that community, whereas in the NT the holy apostles and prophets were entrusted with the knowledge of the mystery and were to make it known publicly. (4) While Jewish writings are concerned largely with the future, the NT entwines mystery teaching with present realities to a greater extent. Thus, whereas the former puts more emphasis in God's reign in heaven to be realized later on earth, the latter places more significance on God's reign on earth with another phase to be realized in the future. (5) Finally, Jewish literature dwells on God's holiness and wrath, while the NT is mainly concerned with God's redemptive act and love.

Third, it is helpful to keep in mind that the NT concept of the mystery is most fully developed in Ephesians. While in Paul's other epistles the mystery focuses on Christ's redemption that includes Gentiles, in Ephesians the mystery is that believing Jews and Gentiles are now one in the body of Christ. This does not contradict Paul's other writings because the one body of believers is based on Christ's redemption as readily seen in Eph 2:11–22. This does not imply that the body of Christ is not present in Paul's other epistles but it is not labeled as the mystery. In other words, the mystery in Ephesians is a further extension of what is stated in the other of Paul's letters and the rest of the NT.

In conclusion, the mystery mentioned in Ephesians was hidden in God in ages past (3:9). It was something that could not be understood by human ingenuity or study. God revealed it to the apostles and prophets by the Spirit (3:4). Now that it is revealed, it is open to everyone and it is simple to understand and thus not relegated to an intellectual minority. Ephesians views God's sacred secret as believing Jews and Gentiles united into one

---

Hadidian, vol. 15 (Pittsburgh: Pickwick Press, 1978); Bultmann, *Theology of the New Testament*, 1:63–183; Bultmann, *Primitive Christianity in Its Contemporary Setting*, 156–61; Pokorný, "Epheserbrief und gnostische Mysterien," 160–94; Pokorný, *Der Epheserbrief und die Gnosis*.

1. This does not imply that there are no experiences of unusual circumstances recorded in the NT when the apostles received revelation, for certainly Paul (Acts 9; 2 Cor 132:1–4) and John (Rev 1:9–20) had experiences of unusual circumstances. What we mean is that virtually nothing is known about how the mystery of the church was revealed. It states that the holy apostles and prophets received it (Eph 3:3–5), not how they received it.

body. In the OT Gentiles could be a part of the company of God, but they had to become Jews in order to belong to it. In the NT Gentiles do not become Jews nor do Jews become Gentiles. Rather, both believing Jews and Gentiles become one new entity, Christians (Eph 2:15–16). That is the mystery.

(2) The Ability to Understand the Mystery (3:4)

Now that the Ephesians understand that it was Paul who was entrusted with the mystery, they need further insight into this mystery of Christ.

Text: 3:4. πρὸς ὃ δύνασθε ἀναγινώσκοντες νοῆσαι τὴν σύνεσίν μου ἐν τῷ μυστηρίῳ τοῦ Χριστοῦ,

Translation: 3:4. "whereby when reading it you are able to perceive my insight into the mystery of Christ,"

Commentary: 3:4. πρὸς ὃ δύνασθε ἀναγινώσκοντες νοῆσαι, "whereby when reading it you are able to perceive." The preposition with the relative pronoun πρὸς ὅ is the same construction as in 2 Cor 5:10 and is difficult to translate. Essentially, it can be translated "in accordance with,"[1] "in reference to which,"[2] or "whereunto,"[3] and is rendered by Reicke, "where you may (turn,) read and understand."[4] The English versions reflect the difficulty, for it is translated "whereby" (AV, RV, ASV), "when" (RSV), "and by referring to" (NASB), "and by" (NEB), "in" (NIV), "of it" (JB, NJB), and "of which" (NRSV). Basically, it directs one's attention back to what was just stated. The translation "whereby" seems to catch the essence of this. The present participle ἀναγινώσκοντες stresses the temporal aspect; in other words, while one is reading (or hearing read) the passage in the previous context, he or she will understand it.

It is not uncommon to have the present indicative δύνασθε complemented by an aorist infinitive, as is the case here with νοῆσαι. The verb δύναμαι means "to be able" or "to be capable of."[5] The infinitive νοῆσαι from νοέω essentially means "to perceive," both by one's senses[6] or by one's mind.[7] In the LXX νοέω occurs thirty-one times and in the canonical books it appears twenty-four times and translates seven Hebrew words, but eleven times (eight of which are in Proverbs) it translates בִּין, meaning "to discern, perceive,"[8] both with the senses (Prov 23:1; 29:19; Jer 2:10) and more frequently with the

1. BAGD 710; BDAG 875.
2. Eadie, 215.
3. J. S. Purton, "Notes on Ephesians iii,3, 4," *Exp* 2d ser., vol. 7 (March 1884): 237–38.
4. Bo Reicke, "πρός," *TDNT* 6 (1968): 722.
5. Grundmann, *TDNT* 2 (1964): 284.
6. Homer *Ilias* 15.422; 24.294.
7. Ibid., 11.599; *Odyssea* 13.318.
8. BDB 106–7; *HALOT* 1 (1994): 122. Terence E. Fretheim, "בין (*byn*)," *NIDOTTE* 1 (1994): 652–53.

mind (Prov 1:2, 6; 8:5; 19:25; 20:24; Jer 23:20). It is used fourteen times in the NT, five times by Paul (Rom 1:20; Eph 3:4, 20; 1 Tim 1:7; 2 Tim 2:7), again having the same idea of perceiving with the senses (Matt 15:17 = Mark 7:18; Matt 24:15 = Mark 13:14; Rom 1:20) and more often with the mind (Matt 16:9 = Mark 8:17; Matt 16:11; John 12:40; Eph 3:4, 20; 1 Tim 1:7; 2 Tim 2:7; Heb 11:3). In the present context it conveys a sense of being able to perceive or understand. Paul wants the Ephesians to read the previous section so that they can perceive or understand his insight. The aorist infinitive may be constative, "to perceive as a whole," or it may be ingressive with the idea "to realize."[1] The former is preferable because he did not want them to realize only what they were reading but to understand fully the mystery he is about to explain.

τὴν σύνεσίν μου ἐν τῷ μυστηρίῳ τοῦ Χριστοῦ, "my insight into the mystery of Christ." The noun σύνεσις literally means "union, joining," as of two rivers,[2] and in a transferred sense, "comprehension, understanding, insight."[3] It appears 126 times in the LXX (seventy-six times in the canonical books) and translates six Hebrew words. Eight occurrences translate בִּין (Ps 32:9 [LXX 31:9]; Isa 10:13; 29:14; Dan 1:17), which was discussed in the immediately preceding paragraph, and eight instances translate the verb שָׂכַל (1 Chr 28:19; Job 22:2; Dan 1:17) or the noun שֶׂכֶל/שֵׂכֶל (1 Sam 25:3; Ps 111:10 [LXX 110:10]; Prov 13:15; 1 Chr 22:12) meaning "prudence, insight, understanding" (cf. also 2 Chr 1:10).[4] These last forms are found in the Qumran literature (1QH[a] 20:20 [12:20]; 1QS 9:18) in reference to God giving "insight" into the mysteries.[5] Best observes that the phrase σύνεσις (συνίημι) ἐν is not in classical or Hellenistic Greek but is found in the Greek OT, particularly in Daniel (1:17; esp. in Theodotion Dan 1:4, 17; 9:13, 23; 10:1, 11) it is "used of the understanding of dreams and visions and implicitly associated with revelations."[6] In the NT it is used only seven times (Mark 12:33; Luke 2:47; 1 Cor 1:19 [quotation from Isa 29:14]; Eph 3:4; Col 1:9; 2:2; 2 Tim 2:7). It has the basic idea of insight or understanding. This is illustrated in Luke 2:47 where the insight of the twelve-year-old Jesus amazed the temple teachers, and in 1 Cor 1:19 where it states that the insight of the world's wise will be destroyed by God. In this context Paul is eager for them to perceive his insight. It should be noted that the personal pronoun does not signify egotism

1. MHT 1:117.
2. Homer *Odyssea* 10.515.
3. Thucydides 2.62.5; 3.82.7.
4. BDB 968; cf. K. Koenen, "שָׂכַל *śāḵal*; שֶׂכֶל *śēḵael*; מַשְׂכִּיל *maśkîl*," *TWAT* 7 (1990): 781–95.
5. For a discussion of the mysteries in Qumran, see Joseph Coppens, "'Mystery' in the Theology of Saint Paul and Its Parallels at Qumran," in *Paul and Qumran: Studies in New Testament Exegesis*, ed. and trans. Jerome Murphy-O'Connor (Chicago: Priory Press; London: Geoffrey Chapman, 1968), 132–58, esp. 134–37, 149–52.
6. Best, 303.

on Paul's part. He makes it clear in verse 3 that it was made known to him by revelation and in verse 5 that it was revealed to him by the Holy Spirit. Furthermore, in verse 8 he claims to be the least of the saints. Paul's main purpose is to assist the Ephesians in their insight into that which has already been revealed to him. He now proceeds to enlarge on the subject of this insight.

Normally one would expect an article before the prepositional phrase ἐν τῷ μυστηρίῳ (cf. Rom 7:5; 8:39; 2 Cor 9:3; 1 Thess 1:8; 2 Thess 3:14), especially to avoid confusion or ambiguity. But it is not needed here for three reasons: (1) τὴν σύνεσίν μου ἐν τῷ μυστηρίῳ forms one composite idea; (2) it was common to have no article following σύνεσις but rather to have the preposition ἐν immediately follow it (Josh 1:7; 2 Chr 34:12; Dan 1:17; cf. 1 Esdr 1:33: τῆς συνέσεως αὐτοῦ ἐν τῷ νόμῳ κυρίου);[1] and (3) the mystery has already been mentioned, so it is clear that it is a specific mystery. This construction (σύνεσίν . . . ἐν) makes good sense, for it connotes "insight in/into" a matter. This makes sense in Hebrew, and similar constructions are seen in the Qumran literature.[2] The preposition ἐν has a local import, indicating in or into what Paul has insight.

The term mystery is discussed briefly in the previous verse and its content will be given in verse 6. The following genitive (τοῦ Χριστοῦ) most likely is an objective genitive meaning that the mystery is about or is concerning Christ.[3] Others have classified it as a genitive of apposition, which corresponds well with the parallel passage in Col 1:27 where it speaks of the glory of this mystery among the Gentiles, which is Christ in you (ὅ ἐστιν Χριστὸς ἐν ὑμῖν).[4] However, as Abbott points out, there is a difference because in Col 1:27 it is not "Christ" but "Christ in you" that constitutes the mystery.[5] Although there is a difference between these two passages, this difference should not be exaggerated. Some use this difference to demonstrate that the two epistles were not written by the same author.[6] However, the difference is not so much content as emphasis. In Col 1:27 Paul states that Christ is resident in individual Gentile believers, whereas in Ephesians he emphasizes that both Jews and Gentiles are fellow partakers.[7] Colossians emphasizes the Christological aspect and Ephesians focuses more on

1. BDF §269 (2); MHT 3:187; Robertson, *Grammar*, 783; Winer, *Grammar*, 170.

2. Kuhn, "Ephesians in the Light of the Qumran Texts," 118–19.

3. Eadie, 215; Abbott, 80–81; Salmond, 304; Gaugler, 131.

4. Alford, 3:104; Ellicott, 59; Meyer, 157; cf. Barth, 331; Bruce, 313; cf. Penna, *Il «Mysterion» Paolino*, 67–68.

5. Abbott, 80; cf. Gese, *Das Vermächtnis des Apostels*, 237.

6. Mitton, *The Epistle to the Ephesians*, 86–89; Lincoln, 176.

7. Percy, *Probleme*, 379–82; Barth, 331; Bruce, 86 n. 216; O'Brien, *Colossians, Philemon*, 87; Michael Wolter, "Verborgene Weisheit und Heil für die Heiden. Zur Traditionsgeschichte und Intention des »Revelationsschemas«," *ZTK* 84 (Juni 1987): 308–10; cf. Wedderburn, *Baptism and Resurrection*, 77 n. 4.

the ecclesiological element.[1] Thus, it is not a different author but a different situation with a distinct emphasis. There will be more discussion of this in verse 6. Returning to the subject at hand, it seems best to take the genitive as an epexegetical genitive or a genitive of apposition, that is, the mystery is that which consists of Christ. Hence, the mystery is Christ or the Messiah.

(3) The Time of the Mystery's Disclosure (3:5)

Paul has just disclosed to the Ephesians the mystery which had been revealed to him, that is, the union of believing Jews and Gentiles in one body. In verse 5 he clarifies exactly when and to whom this mystery first became known.

Text: 3:5. ὃ ἑτέραις γενεαῖς οὐκ ἐγνωρίσθη τοῖς υἱοῖς τῶν ἀνθρώπων ὡς νῦν ἀπεκαλύφθη τοῖς ἁγίοις ἀποστόλοις αὐτοῦ καὶ προφήταις ἐν πνεύματι,

Translation: 3:5. "which in other generations was not made known to people as it has now been revealed to his holy apostles and prophets by the Spirit,"

Commentary: 3:5. ὃ ἑτέραις γενεαῖς οὐκ ἐγνωρίσθη τοῖς υἱοῖς τῶν ἀνθρώπων, "which in other generations was not made known to people." The antecedent to the relative pronoun ὅ is μυστηρίῳ in verse 4 and ultimately it goes back to μυστήριον in verse 3. In fact, the portion beginning with καθώς in verse 3 and including all of verse 4, could be a parenthesis in which he expresses his intent in explaining the mystery, namely, so that they could have the same insight as he. If this construct is accepted, then the present verse follows nicely after verse 3a. There Paul states that the mystery was made known to him by revelation, and he continues in the present verse by saying that it was not made known in other generations. Whether or not one accepts this construction, the meaning is not altered.

The dative of ἑτέραις γενεαῖς is temporal,[2] thus speaking of the times before Paul's generation. The reason for the plural is to signify that since it was not revealed before Paul's day (indicated by νῦν, "now"), it refers to all previous generations. Furthermore, the adjective ἑτέραις connotes that the generations were of a different kind[3] to that of Paul's day. The word γενεά occurs 236 times in the LXX and it appears 184 times in the canonical books. Over 150 times it is translated from דֹּר/דּוֹר, meaning "period, age, generation" (Gen 7:1; 9:12; Exod 3:15).[4] It is frequently used of the period covered by a genera-

1. Seyoon Kim, *The Origin of Paul's Gospel*, 2d ed. rev. and enl., WUNT, ed. Martin Hengel and Otfried Hofius, vol. 4 (Tübingen: Mohr, 1984), 23–24; Bockmuehl, *Revelation and Mystery*, 202; cf. Gese, *Das Vermächtnis des Apostels*, 237.

2. Robertson, *Grammar*, 523; BDF §200 (4); MHT 3:243; Moule, *Idiom Book*, 43.

3. BAGD 315; BDAG 399; cf. also Hermann W. Beyer, "ἕτερος," *TDNT* 2 (1964): 702–3.

4. BDB 189–90; D. N. Freedman, J. Lundbom, and G. J. Botterweck, "דּוֹר *dôr*," *TDOT* 3 (1978): 169–81.

tion of humans (Gen 15:16; Exod 1:6). In the NT it occurs forty-three times, thirty-three times in the Synoptics, and only four times in Paul's writings (Eph 3:5, 21; Phil 2:15; Col 1:26) with the same basic meaning of "age" or "generation."[1] This matches well with the parallel passage in Col 1:26 where it states that the mystery was hid from the ages (αἰώνων) and the generations (γενεῶν).

The aorist passive verb ἐγνωρίσθη, "was made known," is a repeat of verse 3 but in the reverse. Here Paul declares that the mystery was not made known to other generations. The passive indicates that the previous generations were ignorant of the mystery—it was something that could not be acquired by self-assertion, only by revelation. But who in the past was ignorant of the mystery? According to Paul it was τοῖς υἱοῖς τῶν ἀνθρώπων, literally "to the sons of men." Bengel thinks that the phrase "sons of men" refers primarily to the OT prophets because Ezekiel was often called "son of man" (e.g. Ezek 2:1, 3, 6, 8; 3:1, 3, 4).[2] Along the same lines Barth thinks that the phrase "sons of men" does not refer to men in general but to elect servants of God. He gives two reasons: (1) in the Gospels it states that "many prophets and righteous ones (or, kings) desired to see what you see and did not see it" (Matt 13:17 = Luke 10:24); and (2) in Eph 3:5 Paul makes a parallel affirmation: the mystery of Christ was "revealed to his holy apostles and prophets."[3] There are four objections to this view. First, when the phrase "sons of men" is used in the OT (Gen 11:5 and Ps 12:1, 8 [MT 12:2, 9; LXX 11:2, 9]; 45:2 [MT 45:3; LXX 44:3]; 53:2 [MT 53:3]), it has reference to human beings. The term is never used in the plural (sons of men) to refer to prophets or an elect group of men. The designation in Ezekiel is always (ninety-four times) in the singular (son of man). Second, in the NT outside the present context, the only other time the phrase "sons of men" occurs is in Mark 3:28; its parallel, Matt 12:31, has only "men."[4] Third, the reference to Matt 13:17 [= Luke 10:24] is not really relevant because Jesus is referring to his advent and its effects by means of parables; there is nothing about the new creation called the church. Fourth, Barth's analogy in 3:5 is not adequate because he does not distinguish between what is revealed and what is made known. In other words, revelation is limited to apostles and prophets, but the content of the revelation is made known to all people, even the heavenly powers (vv. 2–4, 9–10). Since the mystery was not revealed to the prophets of the OT, it was not known by any person in past generations. Therefore, it is preferable to conclude that the phrase "sons of men" refers to human beings in general and not to a select group of men.

1. Friedrich Büchsel, "γενεά," *TDNT* 1 (1964): 663.
2. Bengel, 4:82–83.
3. Barth, 333.
4. Abbott, 81.

ὡς νῦν ἀπεκαλύφθη, "as it has now been revealed." Paul discloses that this mystery, which was not known in past generations, has now been revealed. A problem centers around the adverbial conjunction ὡς, "as," and results in two different views. First, some take this comparative conjunction as restrictive (a comparison of degree), which means that the mystery was partially revealed in the OT but now has been fully revealed in the church age.[1] Second, some scholars consider this comparative conjunction ὡς to be descriptive (a comparison of kind), which means that no revelation of this mystery was given in the OT but that it was revealed for the first time in the NT era.[2]

The second view is a better interpretation for the following five reasons. (1) Although the restrictive sense for ὡς is more common,[3] the descriptive sense is also used. In the English language we use both the restrictive sense ("I am not as good a teacher as you are") and the descriptive sense ("I am not a teacher as you are"). An example of the restrictive use in the NT occurred at Pentecost. The Jews accused the disciples of being drunk. Peter responded that they were not drunk *as* those Jews thought, since it was only the third hour (Acts 2:15). It does not refer to a degree of drunkenness but rather a lack of it. Furthermore, there is a causal use of ὡς in the NT,[4] which would fit the present context. Matthew 6:12 states, "And forgive our debts *because* we also have forgiven our debtors" (parallel passage in Luke 11:4 has γάρ). John 19:33 says, "But when they came to Jesus, they did not break his legs *because* they saw that he was already dead." In the present context it would mean that the mystery was not made known in other generations because only now has it been revealed to his holy

1. Chrysostom *Eph* 3:5 (*PG* 62:45); Theophylact *Eph* 3:5 (*PG* 124:1068–69); Aquinas, chap. 3, lec. 1, vv. 1–6 (122–23); Calvin, 160; Hodge, 163; Eadie, 217; Moule, 89; Meyer, 159; Abbott, 82; Salmond, 304; Robinson, 77; Westcott, 45; Hendriksen, 145; Caird, 64; Caragounis, *Ephesian* Mysterion, 102 n. 24. This apparently is the view of Origen and Jerome, see Ronald E. Heine, "Recovering Origen's Commentary on Ephesians from Jerome," *JTS*, n.s., 51 (October 2000): 489–98, 506–10.

2. Masson, 173; Schlier, 150; Gaugler, 132; Gnilka, 167; Mitton, 121–22; Barth, 333–34; Schnackenburg, 133; Bruce, 313–15; Lincoln, 177; Best, 305–6; O'Brien, 232 n. 30; Adai, *Der Heilige Geist als Gegenwart Gottes*, 151; Bockmuehl (*Revelation and Mystery*, 201 n. 39) states: "The point is not one of degrees of revelation"; Peter T. O'Brien, "Paul's Missionary Calling within the Purposes of God," in *In the Fullness of Times: Biblical Studies in Honour of Archbishop Donald Robinson*, ed. David Peterson and John Pryor (Homebush West, Australia: Lancer, 1992), 138–39; Mauerhofer, "Der Brief an de Epheser," 19; cf. also Günter Klein, *Die Zwölf Apostel: Ursprung und Gehalt einer Idee*, FRLANT, ed. Rud. Bultmann, vol. 77 (Göttingen: Vandenhoeck & Ruprecht, 1961), 69–71.

3. Mare assumes that because the restrictive sense is more common, it must have that meaning here. See W. Harold Mare, "Paul's Mystery in Ephesians 3," *Bulletin of the Evangelical Theological Society* 8 (spring 1965): 83–84. One must consider the context rather than frequency of use to determine the interpretation for any given passage.

4. Cf. BDF §453 (2); Robertson, *Grammar*, 963–64; MHT 3:320; Wallace, *Greek Grammar*, 674.

apostles and prophets by the Spirit. Although the causal use is possible, the descriptive use best fits the context. (2) The context would support the descriptive sense, for Paul wrote in verse 9 that this mystery was hidden (ἀποκεκρυμμένου) for ages in God. (3) The verb ἀπεκαλύφθη in verse 5 means "to uncover, unveil" something that has previously been completely covered or hidden. There is no indication of a partial uncovering of the mystery in the OT. If, then, it was hidden from view, it could only be made known (γνωρίζω) after it was unveiled. (4) The parallel passage in Col 1:26 does not use the adverbial conjunction ὡς but rather the adversative conjunction δέ and reads, "the mystery which has been hidden for ages and for generations but now was made manifest to his saints." This corresponds with Rom 16:25–26 where Paul states that the mystery was kept secret for ages but (δέ) now has been manifested. (5) The emphatic position of the temporal adverb νῦν, "now," agrees with Col 1:26 and Rom 16:26 in the use and position of the same temporal adverb which marks the contrast between the past and present ages.[1] The same temporal adverb in Eph 3:10 further substantiates this: "In order that the manifold wisdom of God (which is the mystery of Jews and Gentiles united in one body) might *now* be made known to the rulers and authorities in the heavenly places through the church." If the heavenly hosts in OT times did not know of this mystery, it is most unlikely that the people of that era would have known about it. In fact, the heavenly hosts learned of the mystery through the church (which was formed after the death of Christ, 2:11–22). In conclusion, it seems best to interpret the adverbial conjunction ὡς as descriptive. Accordingly, the mystery that was known to no one before the NT era is now revealed to his holy apostles and prophets.

Accepting this view does not exclude the fact that there were no references to Gentile blessings (Gen 12:3; 22:18; 26:4; 28:14) or Gentile inclusion within Israel (Lev 19:34; Deut 10:18–19; 1 Kgs 8:41–43). However, in all these passages there was never the suggestion that Jews and Gentiles were one body. On the contrary, a Gentile had to become a Jew to be fully accepted within Israel. There are many passages which allude to Gentiles being blessed along with Israel (Isa 2:1–4; 11:10; 49:6; 60:1–3; 61:5–6; Jer 3:17; Zech 8:20–23; 14:16–19), but they do not refer to the past but rather to the future kingdom (cf. Acts 3:18–20). Again, there is no portrayal of one body; rather Israel and the Gentiles remain distinct, though both will enjoy God's blessing. The body of believers is an entirely new concept in the NT. A discussion of the concept of the body is also found in 1 Cor 12:12–25.

1. Steinmetz thinks the "now" in contrast to the "then" is strictly theological and not chronological (*Protologische Heils-Zuversicht*, 66). However, the whole context denotes a chronological change from former times to the present time (2:11–13). With the chronological change there is also a theological change, namely, the Gentiles were formerly in the flesh and now in Christ Jesus.

The two distinct features of the body of Christ given in 1 Cor 12:13 are: (1) that Jews and Gentiles are not distinguished from one another and (2) that entrance into the body is by the baptism of the Spirit, a ministry of the Spirit which began after the death of Christ.[1] These two features were absent in OT times. Hence, the mystery of Jews and Gentiles as one body was entirely hidden in God (v. 9) and only revealed in the NT era.

The verb ἀποκαλύπτω comes from καλύπτω, meaning "to cover, hide, conceal,"[2] and ἀπο-, "from," and hence it has the meaning "to uncover, disclose, reveal" something that has been previously hidden.[3] In the LXX it occurs 111 times and in the canonical books it appears eighty-nine times and translates nine Hebrew words, but seventy-six times it translates גָּלָה, meaning "to uncover, disclose, reveal" (Lev 18:6–9; Num 22:31; 24:4, 16; 1 Sam 2:27*bis*; 3:7; Isa 53:1).[4] In the NT it is used twenty-six times, thirteen times by Paul, and only here in Ephesians (not used at all in Revelation), although the noun form appears in Eph 1:17 (cf. word study) and 3:3. It maintains the idea of unveiling something that has been hidden (Rom 1:17–18; 1 Cor 2:10; Gal 1:16). In the NT it always has the theological significance that what was hidden in God and unknown to humans has now been unveiled. It is "not the impartation of knowledge, but the actual unveiling of intrinisically hidden facts. . . ."[5] Therefore, revelation is some hidden thing or a mystery of God that is unveiled by God and cannot be discovered by human investigation. In the present context, it is the uncovering of a mystery that has been hidden in God throughout the ages (vv. 5, 9). Both this verb and ἐγνωρίσθη are passives to indicate that it was only God who could reveal the mystery. Lincoln rightly calls them divine passives.[6] The following phrase discloses the recipients of this revelation.

τοῖς ἁγίοις ἀποστόλοις[7] **αὐτοῦ καὶ προφήταις ἐν πνεύματι,** "to his holy apostles and prophets by the Spirit." First, it is necessary to identify the nouns "apostles" and "prophets" and then the modifiers. A study of these words has already concluded that an apostle is an official delegate of Jesus Christ (see 1:1; 2:20; cf. also 4:11), commissioned for the specific tasks of proclaiming authoritatively the message in oral and written form and of establishing and building up the churches. A prophet is one who is endowed by the Holy Spirit with the gift of prophecy for the purpose of edification, comfort, encouragement

1. Charles C. Ryrie, "The Mystery of Ephesians 3," *BSac* 123 (January–March 1966): 27.
2. LSJ 871.
3. Plato *Protagorus* 352a; Herodotus 1.119; Plutarch *Alexander* 55.7.
4. BDB 162–63; Hans-Jürgen Zobel, "גָּלָה *gālāh*; גּוֹלָה *gôlāh*; גָּלוּת *gālûth*," *TDOT* 2 (1977): 481–86.
5. Oepke, *TDNT* 3 (1965): 591; cf. also Mundle, *NIDNTT* 3 (1978): 312–15.
6. Lincoln, 177.
7. The word ἀποστόλοις is omitted from B it[b] Ambrosiaster, which is not sufficient evidence to sustain its omission.

(1 Cor 14:3, 31), and the enablement to understand and communicate the mysteries and revelation of God to the church (12:10; 13:2; 14:22–25, 30–31) and his prophecy may include a predictive element (1 Thess 3:4; 4:6, 14–18; Gal 5:21). Best thinks that the use of the plural for the apostles and prophets may indicate that they received revelation as a group rather than individually.[1] However, in verse 3 Paul, one of the apostles, personally received the revelation of the mystery (κατὰ ἀποκάλυψιν ἐγνωρίσθη μοι τὸ μυστήριον). Consistently in the NT revelation was given to individuals, such as Cornelius (Acts 10:3–7), Peter (10:13–16), Agabus (11:28; 21:11), and Paul (18:9–10). The plural nouns indicate, rather, that the revelation, believing Jews and Gentiles united into one body, was given to many and not just to Paul. Again here, as in Eph 2:20, the one article for both nouns does not mean that they are identical. The groups may well be distinct but are treated as one for the purpose of discussion.[2] Furthermore, it is proposed that the prophets here are NT prophets, as in 2:20 (where it is discussed more fully), for the following reasons. First, the same order is used in listing apostles before prophets, as in 2:20, where it speaks about the foundation of the new temple, the church. Second, in 4:11 the apostles and prophets, again listed in the same order, were given as foundational gifted people for the purpose of preparing saints for ministry and building up this new body, the church. Third, the present verse talks about the revelation of the mystery which has been revealed in the NT era and not OT times (note νῦν earlier in this verse). Furthermore, there is no indication that the OT prophets received revelation to evangelize the Gentiles.[3] The imagery here is of prophets who were contemporaries of the apostles, thus, NT prophets.

Scholars debate whether the adjective ἁγίοις, "holy," and the possessive pronoun αὐτοῦ, "his," qualify only ἀποστόλοις[4] or both ἀποστόλοις and προφήταις.[5] As mentioned in the previous paragraph there is only one article for both nouns, which most likely indicates that though apostles and prophets are distinct they are treated as one group and similarly the adjective and pronoun most likely qualify both. Both received revelation and both belong to God. Regarding the pronoun αὐτοῦ, it could refer either to Christ[6] or to God.[7] God is a bet-

1. Best, "The Revelation to Evangelize the Gentiles," 24–25.

2. Robertson, *Grammar*, 787; cf. Wallace, "Semantic Range of the Article-Noun-καί-Noun Plural Construction," 82.

3. Ernest Best, "Ministry in Ephesians," *IBS* 15 (October 1993): 148.

4. As Eadie, 218–19; Gaugler, 133; Hendriksen, 154 n. 83; Schnackenburg, 133–34; Lincoln, 178–79; Luz, 145; cf. discussion, Merklein, *Das kirchliche Amt nach dem Epheserbrief*, 188–89.

5. As do Alford, 3:104; Meyer, 159–60; Salmond, 305; Robinson, 77–78; Masson, 173; Schlier, 150; Gnilka, 167 n. 5; Mitton, 122; Barth, 335; Bruce, 315; Bouttier, 143–44; Best, 307.

6. Abbott, 82; Westcott, 46; Gaugler, 133; Schnackenburg, 133–34.

7. Eadie, 218; Meyer, 160; Salmond, 304; Bruce, 314; Lincoln, 178–79.

ter choice because: (1) God is the implied subject of ἐγνωρίσθη and ἀπεκαλύφθη,[1] and (2) it is clearly God in the parallel passage of Col 1:26.

The adjective ἁγίοις, "holy," is considered by some a sign of nonapostolic authorship of the letter since it is a title of veneration used by a later generation of Christians and because the parallel passage in Col 1:26 uses the same word as a substantive meaning "saints."[2] It is thought that Paul would not likely apply the term "holy" to those with the same commission as his. Although this is the only instance that apostles are designated "holy," it was common in the NT to call prophets "holy" (Luke 1:70; Acts 3:21; 2 Pet 3:2). If ordinary Christians are called "saints" (i.e., "holy"; e.g., Rom 1:7; 1 Cor 1:2; 2 Cor 1:1; Eph 1:1) and "holy brothers" (Heb 3:1), certainly there is no reason that this expression could not be used to describe both the apostles and prophets as "holy."[3] In the word study in 1:1 it was concluded that the term "holy" applied to those who were ordinary Israelites (Deut 7:6; 14:2; 26:19), to priests (Lev 21:7), to those who took the Nazarite vow (Num 6:5, 8), and to prophets (2 Kgs 4:9). Both the substantive and the adjective can be used of things, places, and persons, and it does not in itself connote any inherent holiness. Thus, the basic idea is that which is consecrated to God or to God's service. The Qumran literature states that one who was twenty could join the holy congregation (1QSa 1:9) and at twenty-five could serve in the lower ranks of the holy congregation (1QSa 1:12). It also mentions the Council of Holiness (QSa 2:9; 1QM 3:5). These people were not egotists. The designation of the congregation and council as "holy" was simply a recognition of the fact that they were separated or set aside for the congregation and/or council. In application to the present context, it may well be that Paul was just showing that God had revealed the mystery to certain ones who were set aside to receive the revelation and, consequently, pass it on to all. An alternative interpretation suggests that Paul was not including himself as one of the holy apostles because he had already established that the mystery had been made known to him (v. 3). It may be that he attrib-

1. Meyer, 160; Salmond, 304; Lincoln, 178–79.

2. De Wette, 128; Mitton, *The Epistle to the Ephesians*. 19, 85, 236, 245; idem, "Unsolved New Testament Problems. Goodspeed's Theory regarding the Origin of Ephesians," 325; cf. Best, 20, 308. However, most commentators do not really see the designation "holy" apostles and prophets as a real serious objection to Pauline authorship. See Ellicott, 60; Abbott, 82; Salmond, 304; Robinson, 78; Masson, 173 n. 5; Schlier, 150; Gaugler, 133; Caird, 65; Barth, 335; Schnackenburg, 134–35; Bruce, 315; cf. Percy, *Probleme*, 335–36; Schille, "Der Autor des Epheserbriefes," 327–29.

3. Faust (*Pax Christi et Pax Caesaris*, 195–97) states that the adjective ἁγίος means "Jewish" and hence "Jewish apostles and prophets." This term occurs fifteen times in Ephesians and when it is used as an adjective, as here, its always has the sense of "holy" (1:4, 13; 2:21; 3:5; 4:30; 5:27) and never the sense of "Jewish." In light of this, Best (307 n. 16) rightly declares that "it would not have been easy for readers to see that a special meaning was intended here."

uted the term "holy" to these apostles and prophets (to whom the mystery was revealed) out of respect. It was a term he had used previously in reference to the Jerusalem apostles (Gal 2:6, 9). Also, it is consistent with his exhortation to Christians on other occasions to think more highly of others than themselves (Rom 12:10; Phil 2:3). In fact, in the present context he considers himself the least of all saints (v. 8). Although the first interpretation is preferred, either view eliminates the necessity of considering this letter written in a later generation.

Finally, the mystery is revealed ἐν πνεύματι, "by the Spirit." To what this prepositional phrase refers back grammatically is disputed among the commentators. There are three views. First, some think it modifies only the prophets, so "prophets in the Spirit" parallels "holy apostles."[1] But this is superfluous because they would not have been prophets if they had not revealed the mystery by means of the Spirit. Second, others see this as a prepositional phrase modifying both the holy apostles and prophets, since they are joined by one article.[2] Third, it is thought by most commentators to refer back to the verb to indicate that it was revealed by the Spirit.[3] This is the best view. This corresponds to the Spirit of revelation in 1:17. The preposition ἐν is instrumental, expressing the means by which God reveals the mystery to the holy apostles and prophets. This emphasizes the divine aspect in the revelation of the mystery as opposed to human ingenuity. As elsewhere in Ephesians (1:4–14, 17; 2:18, 22; 3:4–5, 14–17; 4:4–6; 5:18–20), the three persons of the Trinity are mentioned: The Father reveals the mystery of Christ by the Holy Spirit.

In conclusion, this is an important verse, for it explains when and to whom the mystery was revealed. This mystery was not known before the NT era. Only after the death of Christ was it revealed to the holy apostles and prophets by means of the Holy Spirit. Verses 3–5 clearly show that the mystery was not revealed to Paul alone but also to the apostles and prophets. Furthermore, the mystery was revealed to the apostles and prophets, not by Paul, but by the Holy Spirit. This contradicts the ultradispensationalists' claim that the mystery was given only or first to Paul. It was the apostle Paul's responsibility to disseminate this mystery to Gentiles. This will be discussed later. First, the content of the mystery will be examined.

1. Eadie, 218–19; Schlier, 150–51; Gaugler, 134; Merklein, *Das kirchliche Amt nach dem Epheserbrief*, 189.

2. Alford, 3:104; Ellicott, 60.

3. Meyer, 160; Abbott, 82; Salmond, 305; Robinson, 78; Masson, 173–74; Gnilka, 167; Barth, 334; Bruce, 314–15; Lincoln, 180; Best, 308; Kendell H. Easley, "The Pauline Usage of *Pneumati* as a Reference to the Spirit of God," *JETS* 27 (September 1984): 305; Hui, "The Concept of the Holy Spirit in Ephesians," 296–97.

c. The Content of the Mystery (3:6)

The administration and the revelation of the mystery have been discussed. Paul is now going to define it.

Text: 3:6. εἶναι τὰ ἔθνη συγκληρονόμα καὶ σύσσωμα καὶ συμμέτοχα τῆς ἐπαγγελίας ἐν Χριστῷ Ἰησοῦ διὰ τοῦ εὐαγγελίου,

Translation: 3:6. "that the Gentiles are fellow heirs, and fellow members of the body, and fellow participants of the promise in Christ Jesus through the gospel,"

Commentary: 3:6. εἶναι τὰ ἔθνη συγκληρονόμα καὶ σύσσωμα, "that the Gentiles are fellow heirs, and fellow members of the body." The present infinitive εἶναι is wrongly translated "should be" in the AV. It is not expressing purpose but is epexegetical or appositional, denoting the content of the mystery, and could be translated "that is" or "namely."[1] Paul uses three adjectives as predicate accusatives[2] to express that Gentiles now are fellow members with the Jews. All three adjectives have a συν- prefix to emphasize the union between Jews and Gentiles in the body of Christ. This is a common stylistic feature of Paul.[3] Therefore, the word "fellow" before each English translated word is used not only to bring continuity in the Greek, but also to reinforce the idea of union. The same idea of union is conveyed in 2:5–6, 19, 21–22.

The first term συγκληρονόμος is not found in either classical literature or the LXX but is found in a couple of inscriptions,[4] in Philo,[5] and four times in the NT (Rom 8:17; Eph 3:6; Heb 11:9; 1 Pet 3:7). It means "he who receives, or will receive, something along with another,"[6] or more simply a "joint heir" (NEB) or "fellow heir" (AV, RV, ASV, RSV, NASB, NRSV). It is not the same as Rom 8:17 where believers are joint heirs with Christ, speaking in Christological and soteriological terms. Rather, here it is expressing in an ecclesiological manner the fact that Gentiles are joint heirs with Jews.[7] The difference is also seen in the genitive that follows this noun, for only in Rom 8:17 is it followed by a genitive of persons, whereas in the other three passages it is followed by a gentive of thing.[8] Although the word is not used in

1. Robertson, *Grammar*, 1078, 1089; Winer, *Grammar*, 400.

2. Wallace, *Greek Grammar*, 192.

3. MHT 4:84.

4. Deissmann, *Light from the Ancient East*, 92.

5. Philo *Leg. Gai.* 10 §67.

6. Werner Foerster, "συγκληρονόμος," *TDNT* 3 (1965): 781.

7. Hammer, "A Comparison of *klēronomia* in Paul and Ephesians," 271–72; cf. Penna, *Il «Mysterion» Paolino*, 72–75; Kerrigan, "Echoes of Themes from the Servant Songs in Pauline Theology," 2:225.

8. Horsley, *New Documents Illustrating Early Christianity*, vol. 1, *A Review of the Greek Inscriptions and Papyri Published in 1976*, 135.

Gal 3:26–29, the same concept is presented.[1] At this point in the discussion the concept of believing Jews and Gentiles as "fellow heirs" was understandable to the Ephesians because of Paul's previous disclosures in Eph 2:14 (made both one), 2:19 (fellow citizens), 2:20 (same foundation), and 2:21 (fitted together). Logically then, believing Gentiles also would be fellow heirs.[2]

The second word σύσσωμος, joined with the first word by the copulative καί, is not found before NT times, is only here in the NT, and may well have been coined by Paul. It means that they are of the same body and it is designed to express a close relationship to the body of Christ.[3] Thus the translation literally would be "concorporate,"[4] but a smoother rendering is "members of the same body" or "fellow members of the body." Both believing Jews and Gentiles are in the body of Christ, so Gentiles are fellow members of the body with Jews. The growth of this body depends on the head who is Christ, and each of the members functions dependently on the other members of the body in order to contribute to the growth of the body (4:15–16). Again, this concept has been mentioned already in 2:14–22 for they are both created into one new humanity (2:15), both in one body (2:16), both growing into a holy temple (2:21), and both being built together as the place where God dwells in the Spirit (2:22).

καὶ συμμέτοχα τῆς ἐπαγγελίας,[5] "and fellow participants of the promise." The third adjective συμμέτοχος, also connected with the former two adjectives by καί, is a rare word that is used of plant life that needs heat and cold as well as dry and wet, and none of these are ever separated from its "partner."[6] It is used also of an "accomplice" in a plot.[7] In the NT it occurs only in Ephesians (3:6; 5:7) and means "sharing with them, casting one's lot with them" or, as translated above, "fellow participant."[8] Again, this concept has already been seen in the earlier section (2:14–22) because believing Jews and Gentiles

1. Denton, "Inheritance in Paul and Ephesians," 161.

2. Wolter, "Verborgene Weisheit und Heil für die Heiden," 308; cf. McGrath, "'*Syn*' Words in Saint Paul," 220.

3. Eduard Schweizer, "σύσσωμος," *TDNT* 7 (1971): 1080. This cannot mean "fellow slave" as suggested by Erwin Preuschen, "σύνσωμος Eph 3, 6," *ZNW* 1, no. 1 (1900): 85–86.

4. Robinson, 78; Barth, 337.

5. The inclusion of αὐτοῦ is found in D[1] F G Ψ 𝔐 it[a] vg[cl] syr[h] Ambrosiaster but is omitted from 𝔓[46] ℵ A B C D* P 33 81 365 1175 1739 1881 2464 *pc* it[b] vg[st, ww] cop Chrysostom Jerome. The inclusion has good Western and Byzantine representation and the omission has fairly good Western representation and solid Alexandrian representation. It is quite evenly distributed, and whichever reading is accepted does not alter the meaning. Internally, it seems to be redundant, for whose promise would Paul be talking about except God's? Furthermore, the pronoun αὐτοῦ does not follow "promise" anywhere else in the NT. It seems that it is best omitted.

6. Aristotle *De Plantis* 1.1 §816b.20.

7. Josephus *B.J.* 1.24.6 §486.

8. Cf. McGrath, "'*Syn*' Words in Saint Paul," 221.

are both created into one new humanity (2:15), both fellow citizens and members of God's household (2:19), both being fitted together (2:21), and both being built together into a dwelling place of God (2:22).

The genitive of ἐπαγγελίας, "promise," is objective and depends only on συμμέτοχα and not all three adjectives. Although the "promise" is not specified, it probably alludes to the covenants of promise from which the Gentiles were excluded before the NT era (2:12). Although before the cross Gentiles could come under the pale of the covenants of promise, they had to become Jews to do so. Now in the NT era Gentiles are fully accepted and are fellow participants of the promise. This promise includes the Messiah, salvation, and enablement of the Holy Spirit. In Gal 3 Paul discloses that the Gentile believer has obtained the promise of the Spirit equally (v. 14), for there is no difference between Jew or Gentile, slave or free, male or female (v. 28). Furthermore, Gentile believers are Abraham's offspring, heirs according to promise (v. 29). Both believing Gentiles and Jews are under the blessings of the new covenant (2 Cor 3; Heb 8).

Care must be taken not to make Gentile believers a part of Israel.[1] There is a delicate balance between what applies specifically to the nation Israel and what applies to the church. Three different views are offered regarding this. First, some believe that all the promises of the OT covenants are applied to the church in the present day. However, there is no indication in the NT that the church should claim the Promised Land for its possession. This was promised specifically to the nation Israel. Second, others take the spiritual promises in the covenants literally but allegorize the land promises. Again, nowhere in the NT is there any indication of this. On what basis can one allegorize parts of the covenant and interpret other parts literally? There is no basis on which one can allegorize the promise of the land which God made to Israel. If this unconditional covenant were not fulfilled, then God's integrity is at stake. Acts 3:19–21 clearly indicates that there will be a time future to our day when the covenants will be fulfilled literally. Furthermore, this view would make the church the "new Israel," and this is contrary to the whole point of Eph 2:11–22 where the "new person" is distinct from the nation Israel. Gentiles do not become Jews but rather Jews and Gentiles become "one new person." The church is not the new Israel but a distinct body of believers made up of believing Jews and Gentiles.[2] Third, some take the covenants of promise literally. In this case, however, only those promises restated in the NT apply to the church and those that are not men-

1. As does Stephen L. Lortz, "The Literal Interpretation of Ephesians 3:6 and Related Scriptures," *Journal from the Radical Reformation* 8 (winter 1999): 8–10, 12.

2. Cf. Robert L. Saucy, "The Church as the Mystery of God," in *Dispensationalism, Israel and the Church: The Search for Definition*, ed. Craig A. Blaising and Darrell L. Bock (Grand Rapids: Zondervan, 1992), 132–37, 155.

tioned apply to the nation Israel and are yet to be fulfilled. There is no indication in the NT that the land promises made to Israel are for the church's possession. In conclusion, the third interpretation seems to fit best with the facts presented in the NT.

ἐν Χριστῷ Ἰησοῦ διὰ τοῦ εὐαγγελίου, "in Christ Jesus through the Gospel." The second of these two prepositional phrases modifies the first and the two depend on the three adjectives just discussed. Therefore, the first prepositional phrase (ἐν Χριστῷ Ἰησοῦ) shows the locale of the three adjectives, namely, "the Gentiles are fellow heirs in Christ, and fellow members of the body in Christ, and fellow participants of the promise in Christ." The second prepositional phrase (διὰ τοῦ εὐαγγελίου) shows the means by which believing Gentiles become one with believing Jews in Christ.[1] As discussed at 1:13, the term "gospel" is used four times in Ephesians (1:13; 3:6; 6:15, 19) and basically connotes "good news,"[2] not only the good news of Christ's death that provides salvation for Gentiles but also the good news that they are one in Christ Jesus with believing Jews. Gentiles did not gain equal status by circumcision or any other religious ceremony, but by the gospel.[3]

In conclusion, the mystery is not that Gentiles would be saved because the OT gives evidence for their salvation, but rather that believing Jews and Gentiles are together in Christ. This concept was revolutionary for Jews and Gentiles alike. The only way this information can be obtained is through the gospel, the good news concerning the effect of Christ's death on all human beings.

3. The Ministry (3:7–12)

Paul has finished his discussion of the mystery. He has explained his administration of it, how and when it was revealed, and the content of it (vv. 2–6). Now he will discuss his placement into the ministry with the attending responsibility to impart the knowledge of the mystery to the Gentiles. Some commentators see a break between verses 7 and 8.[4] This is a possibility because verse 7 begins with a relative pronoun whereas verse 8 begins a new sentence. However, it is more likely that the break is between verses 6 and 7 and that verse 7 is a transition verse. The relative pronoun at the beginning of verse 7 unites the previous discussion of the mystery in verses 2–6 with the discussion of his channel of the mystery in verses 7–13. In addition to

1. Winer, *Grammar*, 486 n. 2.

2. BAGD 317–18; BDAG 402–3; Stuhlmacher, "The Theme: The Gospel and the Gospels," 1–25, esp. 19–23; idem, "The Pauline Gospel," 149–72; cf. also O'Brien, *Gospel and Mission in the Writings of Paul*, 77–81.

3. Caragounis, *Ephesian* Mysterion, 104.

4. Cf. Robinson, 169; Schnackenburg, 128–29, 136; Bruce, 317; Best, 316; O'Brien, 240 n. 70.

being transitional, verse 7 also informs the readers of Paul's placement into the ministry, a fact which is developed in verses 8–13.

a. The Placement into the Ministry (3:7–8a)

As Paul discusses his placement into the ministry, he makes mention of his feeling of unworthiness. He then explains the means by which he will acommplish the task, namely, through God's power.

Text: 3:7. οὗ ἐγενήθην διάκονος κατὰ τὴν δωρεὰν τῆς χάριτος τοῦ θεοῦ τῆς δοθείσης μοι κατὰ τὴν ἐνέργειαν τῆς δυνάμεως αὐτοῦ, **3:8a**. ἐμοὶ τῷ ἐλαχιστοτέρῳ πάντων ἁγίων ἐδόθη ἡ χάρις αὕτη,

Translation: 3:7. "of which I was made a minister according to the gift of God's grace which was given to me according to the working of his power, **3:8a.** to me, who am less than the least of all the saints, was this grace given,"

Commentary: 3:7. οὗ ἐγενήθην διάκονος, "of which I was made a minister." The relative pronoun οὗ relates back to the εὐαγγελίου "gospel" in verse 6. Paul was made a minister of this gospel. The word διάκονος is used of a king's servant.[1] It occurs only six times in the LXX, translated from either נַעַר or the Piel of שָׁרַת. Both refer to a "servant" of a king (Esth 1:10; 2:2; 6:3, 5; Prov 10:4; 4 Mac 9:17).[2] It is used twenty-nine times in the NT, twenty-one times by Paul, and twice in Ephesians (3:7; 6:21). It is used of a "waiter" at a wedding feast (John 2:5, 9), a servant of a king (Matt 22:13), a disciple who is a servant of Christ (Matt 20:26 = Mark 10:43–44 = Luke 22:26), a minister (2 Cor 3:6; Col 1:23), and a "deacon" of a church (1 Tim 3:8, 12). It is a synonym of δοῦλος, which emphasizes the servile relationship of a servant to a master, whereas διάκονος emphasizes the activity of a servant.[3] In the present context the stress is on activity, namely, Paul's declaration of the mystery to the Gentiles or, as verse 9 states it, he is "enlightening" all of the mystery (v. 9).[4] The passive verb ἐγενήθην underscores the idea that God put him into that service. This is substantiated in the rest of the verse.

κατὰ τὴν δωρεὰν τῆς χάριτος τοῦ θεοῦ τῆς δοθείσης[5] μοι, "according to the gift of God's grace which was given to me." The preposition

1. Herodotus 4.71, 72; Aeschylus *Prometheus Vinctus* 942; Sophocles *Philoctetes* 497.

2. BDB 655, 1058; cf. H. F. Fuhs, "נַעַר *naʿar*, etc.," *TDOT* 9 (1998): 480–84; K. Engelkin, "שׁרת *šrt*," *TWAT* 8 (1995): 496–507.

3. Trench, *Synonyms of the New Testament*, 32; Klaus Hess, "Serve, Deacon, Worship [διακονέω, λατρεύω, λειτουργέω]," *NIDNTT* 3 (1978): 584; Rudolf Tuente, "Slave [δοῦλος]," *NIDNTT* 3 (1978): 596.

4. E. Earle Ellis, "Paul and His Co-Workers," *NTS* 17 (July 1971): 441–45 (reprinted in idem, *Prophecy and Hermeneutic in Early Christianity,* 7–13).

5. The reading τὴν δοθεῖσαν appears in D[2] Ψ 1739 1881 𝔐. The reading τῆς δοθείσης is found in 𝔓[46] ℵ A B C D* F G I P 33 81 104 326 365 1175 2464 *pc*. The second reading is

κατά with the accusative denotes standard or norm and can be translated "in accordance with, in conformity with, corresponding to."[1] The standard of his service corresponded to the gift of the grace of God that was given to him. The word δωρεά is used in the classical literature as meaning a "gift, bounty."[2] In the LXX it occurs thirty-five times, in the canonical books twenty-three times, all but once in the adverbial accusative δωρεάν. Nineteen times it is translated from חִנָּם, meaning: (1) without payment, "gratis, for nothing" (Gen 29:15; Exod 21:2, 11; 2 Sam 24:24; Job 1:9; Isa 52:3; Jer 22:13); (2) "without cause, undeserved" (1 Sam 19:5; 25:31; Ps 35:7 [LXX 34:7]); or (3) "in vain" (Mal 1:10).[3] In the NT it is used eleven times, five times by Paul, twice in Ephesians (3:7; 4:7), and it always refers to a gift that God graciously gives. It is a gift; thus it is unearned or undeserved, for which there can be no payment. In the present context it is the gift of the grace of God that was given to Paul.

The word χάρις, "grace," was discussed at 1:2 (cf. also 1:6, 7; 2:5, 7, 8; 3:2) where it was concluded that it is God's unmerited or undeserved favor, both in the provision of salvation for sinners through Christ's sacrificial death (e.g., Rom 3:23–24; Eph 1:7; 2:8) and in the enabling power for the believer in performing the tasks that God gives him (1 Cor 15:10; Eph 4:7, 29).[4] Certainly in this context grace is referring to God's enabling power to minister. The genitive τῆς χάριτος is most likely a genitive of apposition meaning "according to the gift which is grace." The following genitive τοῦ θεοῦ is a possessive genitive or genitive of source showing that it is God's gift of grace or more specifically, God's gift which is his enabling power. The genitival participle τῆς δοθείσης modifies grace, showing that God's grace of enabling power was given to Paul. This passive participle further demonstrates that Paul is the recipient of the enabling power rather than the source of it. That Paul was made a minister of the gospel is an evidence of grace, but that he was given a gift of grace that enables him to perform the duties of ministry is further evidence of God's unmerited favor toward his servant Paul. Briefly then, in verse 2 the administration of grace was given, and in the present verse the ability to administer that grace was given. One further note, on the basis of the aorist tense (cf. also vv. 2, 8) Kim suggests that this grace was given at the time of the Damascus road experience.[5] However, to base the time of this rev-

---

the one to be accepted because it has good representation for the various text-types, good geographical distribution, and good genealogical relationships within each text-type except the Byzantine.

1. BAGD 407; BDAG 512.

2. Herodotus 2.140; 6.130; Aeschylus *Prometheus Vinctus* 340; Sophocles *Ajax* 1032.

3. BDB 336; *HALOT* 1 (1994): 334; Terence E. Fretheim, "חִנָּם (*ḥinnām*)," *NIDOTTE* 2:203–4.

4. Nolland, "Grace as Power," 26–31.

5. Kim, *The Origin of Paul's Gospel*, 25–26.

elation of the mystery on the aorist tense is dubious and unacceptable.[1] When he received the revelation is simply unknown.

κατὰ τὴν ἐνέργειαν τῆς δυνάμεως αὐτοῦ, "according to the working of his power." Again, the preposition κατά with the accusative denotes standard. Here, the standard is the working of his power. The two synonyms for power have been used before in this letter. First, ἐνέργεια was discussed at 1:19 where it was concluded that it is supernatural power that is in actual operation, an active exercise of supernatural power. Second, δύναμις, from which we derived our English word "dynamic," was also discussed at 1:19 (cf. also 1:21) where it was concluded that it means "power, ability, capability of acting." It is that power or ability that is capable for the task and is determined by what it is modified. Here, it is modified by the possessive personal pronoun αὐτοῦ, "his." Thus, it speaks of God's power; its ability is the ability of God himself. The word ἐνέργεια denotes the activity of power whereas δύναμις denotes the capacity in view of its ability, specifically God's ability. Here τῆς δυνάμεως is most likely a subjective genitive. Thus, it is according to the activity of power produced by God's ability.

Some suggest that this prepositional phrase (κατὰ τὴν ἐνέργειαν τῆς δυνάμεως αὐτοῦ) should be parallel with the preceding prepositional phrase (κατὰ τὴν δωρεὰν τῆς χάριτος τοῦ θεοῦ τῆς δοθείσης μοι)[2] and that both be connected to the main verb and its object (ἐγενήθην διάκονος), suggesting that Paul was not only given the initial gift of God's grace but that he also has the continuation of God's power during the course of his ministry. The problem with this view is that there is no coordinating conjunction to make parallel these two prepositional phrases beginning with κατά. Also, as mentioned above, the grace that is given in this verse does not refer to the initial gift of God's grace but rather to his enabling power for ministry. A better proposal is that this prepositional phrase is connected to the immediately preceding τῆς δοθείσης μοι,[3] which would indicate that the gift of grace or enabling power which was given to Paul corresponded to the activity (or working) of power produced by God's own dynamic ability.

In conclusion, Paul was made a minister of the gospel and was able to carry out this awesome responsibility by the gracious gift of unmerited favor of enablement that was given to him. That enablement corresponded to the activity of God's dynamic ability to convey the mystery. God does not give responsibility without the provision of his power to carry it out. In the end God is to be praised, for humans can neither initiate nor accomplish the work in their own power.

1. Porter, *Verbal Aspect*, 183–84.

2. As Westcott, 47; Caragounis, *Ephesian* Mysterion, 105.

3. Alford, 3:105; Eadie, 223; Ellicott, 62; Meyer, 162; Abbott, 84; Schlier, 151; Lincoln, 182.

3:8a. ἐμοὶ τῷ ἐλαχιστοτέρῳ πάντων ἁγίων[1] ἐδόθη ἡ χάρις αὕτη, "to me, who am less than the least of all the saints, was this grace given." This is a parenthetical statement.[2] It is a sudden outburst of amazement that God would use him, giving him not only the responsibility but also the power to communicate this gospel to all people. Paul felt he did not deserve this honor. To indicate that this is a parenthetical statement, we have set it off in commas rather than using a period at the end of verse 7 which creates a new sentence with verse 8 as the editors of NA[27] and UBS[4] do. WH set this clause off by a dash before and after, to indicate that it is a parenthesis.

The personal pronoun ἐμοί, "to me," is emphatic, not only because it is expressed but also because it is placed first in this parenthetical statement. The next word τῷ ἐλαχιστοτέρῳ has been discussed extensively because it is a comparative formed on the superlative ἐλάχιστος,[3] which would be literally translated "leaster" and is rendered "less than the least" (AV, RV, ASV, NEB, TEV, JB, NIV, NJB) or "the very least" (RSV, NASB, NRSV). The comparison that Paul wants to make is not with apostles (as in 1 Cor 15:9) but with πάντων ἁγίων, "all saints." Hence, we have the genitive of comparison.[4] The anarthrous[5] adjective πάντων means "all," not some of the saints. A study of the term ἅγιος was made in 1:1 (cf. also 1:4, 13, 15, 18; 2:19, 21) where we concluded that it is a common designation for believers, especially if it is in the plural as here. Paul wishes to convey that he considers himself to be less than the least of all believers who have been given this grace. "The expression 'least of all the saints', rather than 'least of the apostles', perhaps expresses a sense of solidarity between Paul and the early Christians."[6] This is not false modesty but a true humility. There are two reasons for this sentiment. First, he considered himself to be the foremost of sinners and not worthy of the salvation God graciously gave (1 Tim 1:15). Second, he had blasphemed and persecuted Christ (1 Tim 1:13; Acts 9:4–5; 26:11, 14–15) and persecuted the church, trying to destroy it (1 Cor 15:9; Gal 1:13; Phil 3:6; cf. Acts 7:58; 8:1–3; 9:1–2, 4–5, 7–8; 26:9–11, 14–15). Thus, he felt unworthy not only of God's grace for salvation but also God's grace in appointing him to preach the gospel and to be an apostle to the Gentiles (1 Tim 2:7). This is an important indication of Paul's authorship of Ephesians. Such deprecation likely would not have been expressed about Paul by a pseudonymous author.[7]

1. Only 𝔓[46] omits ἁγίων; thus, it should remain in the text.

2. Harless, 290; Westcott, 47.

3. Robertson, *Grammar*, 278, 663, 670*bis*; BDF §60 (2); MHT 1:236; 2:166; 3:31; Moule, *Idiom Book*, 98; Wallace, *Greek Grammar*, 302.

4. Robertson, *Grammar*, 516; Wallace, *Greek Grammar*, 302.

5. This adjective does not need an article before it or before the noun it modifies. See Robertson, *Grammar*, 773*bis*; MHT 3:200; BDF §275 (1); Zerwick, *Biblical Greek* §188.

6. MacDonald, *The Pauline Churches*, 125–26.

7. Cf. Beare, 10:669; Barth, 363; Bruce, 318–19; *contra* Lincoln, 183. On this point, Wallace interacts with Lincoln (*Greek Grammar*, 302).

In conclusion, it was to Paul that "this grace was given" (ἐδόθη ἡ χάρις αὕτη), the same grace as mentioned in the previous verse, namely, the grace that enabled him to be a minister of the gospel and the enabling grace which gave him the power of God to proclaim it.

b. The Performance of the Ministry (3:8b–9)

God not only made Paul a minister of the gospel but also provided power to carry it out. Now Paul explains the activity and content of his ministry.

(1) To Preach the Unfathomable Wealth of Christ (3:8b)

Text: 3:8b. τοῖς ἔθνεσιν εὐαγγελίσασθαι τὸ ἀνεξιχνίαστον πλοῦτος τοῦ Χριστοῦ

Translation: 3:8b. "to preach to the Gentiles the unfathomable wealth of Christ"

Commentary: 3:8b. [1]**τοῖς ἔθνεσιν εὐαγγελίσασθαι,** "to preach to the Gentiles." The dative phrase τοῖς ἔθνεσιν is placed first to give emphasis to whom Paul is to minister. He was appointed to be the apostle to the Gentiles (Acts 9:15; 22:21; Rom 11:13; Gal 2:8–9; 1 Tim 2:7). The infinitive εὐαγγελίσασθαι could denote purpose but better defines the function of one who was made a minister described in verse 7: "I was made a minister . . . to preach among the Gentiles."[2] This infinitive is the verbal form of the noun εὐαγγέλιον, "gospel," mentioned in verse 6. The verb, like the noun, conveys the idea of proclaiming the good news. It is used only one other time in Ephesians (2:17) where Jesus, by means of his messengers, proclaims peace to Jews and Gentiles. The word study in 2:17 revealed that in Greek literature the announcement of the news did not always correspond to the facts (e.g., false stories of victory to boost morale), whereas in the NT the content of the message is Jesus himself. In the NT the messenger of the good news does not create or invent the content but rather reveals and instructs what has been faithfully handed down. This was Paul's commission.

τὸ ἀνεξιχνίαστον πλοῦτος τοῦ Χριστοῦ, "the unfathomable wealth of Christ." It is normal for the verb εὐαγγελίζομαι to have "the accusative of the thing and dative of the person"[3] and in this case the dative

1. The preposition ἐν is found in D F G Ψ 33 1739 1881 𝔐 latt Chrysostom Theodoret. It is omitted from 𝔓[46] ℵ A B C P 81 104 2464 *pc* cop. The inclusion of this preposition is supported by the Western and Byzantine texts and some Alexandrian manuscripts, whereas the omission is supported only by the Alexandrian text. However, there is a great tendency in the Western and Byzantine texts to add words for clarification. Hence, the shorter reading is preferred.

2. If one does not accept v. 8a as a parenthesis, then this infinitive in v. 8b can be in apposition to "this grace" (ἡ χάρις αὕτη) in v. 8a (Robertson, *Grammar*, 1078; MHT 3:139). However, it could indicate the purpose of the finite verb ἐδόθη: "this grace was given to preach the unsearchable riches of Christ."

3. Robertson, *Grammar*, 474, 483.

of person is "the Gentiles" and the accusative of the thing is "the unfathomable wealth of Christ." Having discussed above the dative of person, it is now necessary to discuss the accusative of the thing (τὸ ἀνεξιχνίαστον πλοῦτος τοῦ Χριστοῦ). The noun πλοῦτος was discussed at 1:7 (cf. also 1:18; 2:7) and means "abundance, riches, wealth." The translation "wealth" is preferred because it depicts singularity rather than one of many kinds of riches. This noun is followed by the genitive τοῦ Χριστοῦ, which is most likely a possessive genitive denoting that it is Christ's wealth. "AE [author of Ephesians] uses the article here with Christ and may be deliberately emphasising Jesus as the Jewish Messiah in whose riches the Gentiles participate."[1] The adjective ἀνεξιχνίαστον which describes this wealth is not found in classical literature and is found only four times in the LXX (Job 5:9; 9:10; 34:24; Ode 12:6) where twice (Job 5:9; 9:10) it is translated from the Hebrew construct אֵין חֵקֶר, meaning "unsearchable."[2] In the NT this word is used only here and in Rom 11:33 and has the idea of that which is "not to be traced out,"[3] "indetectable,"[4] "uninvestigable, unsearchable,"[5] "inscrutable, incomprehensible, fathomless."[6] Salmond rightly observes that it is unsearchable "not in the sense of *inexhaustible*, but rather in that of *unfathomable*."[7] In other words, it is beyond man's ability to investigate; thus it is translated "unfathomable." Origen and Jerome suggest that the reason that Paul is able to preach that which is unfathomable is because it was revealed by God and can now be perceived by the people.[8]

Paul, though considering himself unworthy, had the responsibility and privilege to preach in God's power to the Gentiles the unfathomable wealth of Christ.

(2) To Enlighten the Administration of the Mystery (3:9)

Paul is not only to preach the unfathomable wealth of Christ to the Gentiles but he is also to enlighten all people of the administration of this hidden mystery.

Text: 3:9. καὶ φωτίσαι [πάντας] τίς ἡ οἰκονομία τοῦ μυστηρίου τοῦ ἀποκεκρυμμένου ἀπὸ τῶν αἰώνων ἐν τῷ θεῷ τῷ τὰ πάντα κτίσαντι,

1. Best, 318.

2. BDB 350; *HALOT* 1 (1994): 348; Gordon H. Matties and R. D. Patterson, "חֵקֶר (*ḥēqer*)," *NIDOTTE* 2: 254.

3. R. E. Thomas, "Ephesians iii.8," *ExpTim* 39 (March 1928): 283.

4. Erik Peterson, "ἀνεξιχνίαστος," *TDNT* 1 (1964): 358.

5. Ioannes Mehlmann, "Ἀνεξιχνίαστος = Investigabilis (Rom 11,33; Eph 3,8)," *Bib* 40, no. 3 (1959): 902–14.

6. BAGD 65; BDAG 77.

7. Salmond, 306.

8. See Heine, "Recovering Origen's Commentary on Ephesians from Jerome," 498–99, 511.

Translation: 3:9. "and to enlighten all what is the administration of the mystery which had been hidden for ages in God who created all things,"

Commentary: 3:9. καὶ φωτίσαι [πάντας],[1] "and to enlighten all." The coordinating conjunction and the infinitive (καὶ φωτίσαι πάντας) make this parallel to the previous infinitival statement (εὐαγγελίσασθαι τὸ ἀνεξιχνίαστον πλοῦτος) in verse 8b. The word φωτίζω occurs only one other time in Ephesians (1:18) where it means "to enlighten, illumine." It has the same idea in this context where it involves the disclosure of the mystery, literally "to bring to light."[2] More than preaching or teaching, it is an explanation to enable the recipients to understand the mystery that is being disclosed. However, the coordinating conjunction linking the two infinitives suggest that to preach the unfathomable wealth of Christ is also to enlighten all of that wealth, namely, the mystery that has been hidden in the past. The adjective following the infinitive (πάντας) cannot be an accusative of reference "to enlighten with respect to all things" of the "mystery" because it would need to be a neuter gender, as it is later in this verse. Rather, it is an accusative of direct object, referring to "all human beings." Although it would have been humanly impossible for Paul literally to enlighten every living person at that time, it does mean that he felt a responsibility to all humanity to both Jews and Gentiles, especially to the Gentiles as mentioned in verse 8b, because his main mission was to the Gentiles. This feeling of indebtedness is very similar to that conveyed in Rom 1:14.

τίς ἡ οἰκονομία[3] **τοῦ μυστηρίου,** "what is the administration of the mystery." Not only is there the accusative of person (πάντας) but the accusative of the thing. This is expressed in the nominative case, something that is not uncommon in Greek syntax.[4] The word οἰκονομία was discussed at 1:10 and 3:2 and has two nuances: first, the position or office of an administrator; second, the activity of administrating. Although the nuances are intertwined and both may be in view,[5] the emphasis in 1:10 is on the activity of the administrator, whereas the emphasis in 3:2 and 9 is on the arrangement or plan of

1. The πάντας is omitted from ℵ* A 0150 6 424[c] 1739 1881 Cyril[1/2] Ambrosiaster[1/2] Hilary Jerome Augustine and NA[25]. It is included in 𝔓[46] ℵ[2] B C D F G Ψ 075 33 81 104 256 263 365 424* 436 459 1175 1241 1319 1573 1852 1912 1962 2127 2200 2464 *Byz* [K L P] *Lect* it[ar, b, d, f, g, o] vg syr[p, ph] cop[sa, bo] arm eth slav Marcion[acc. to Adamantius and Tertullian] Didymus[dub] Chrysostom (Severian) Theodore[lat] Cyril[1/2] Victorinus-Rome Ambrosiaster[1/2] Pelagius Varimadum. The inclusion of πάντας should be accepted for it has overwhelming support of all the text-types.

2. Hans Conzelmann, "φῶς κτλ.," *TDNT* 9 (1974): 347–48; cf. BAGD 873; BDAG 1074.

3. The TR and only 31[mg] have κοινωνία (AV "fellowship") which is not at all acceptable. Metzger (*Textual Commentary*, 2d ed., 535) correctly calls it an interpretative gloss.

4. BDF §405; MHT 3:146; Robertson, *Grammar*, 489–90.

5. Reumann, "Οἰκονομία-Terms in Paul," 164.

the mystery. Here it could have the idea of strategy.[1] Paul's responsibility is to enlighten all as to what is the strategy or administration of the mystery. Hence, this mystery was made known to him (v. 3), its content was described (v. 6), and now its adminstration (plan) is to be disclosed.

τοῦ ἀποκεκρυμμένου, "which had been hidden." The adjectival genitive participle (τοῦ ἀποκεκρυμμένου) modifies τοῦ μυστηρίου indicating its concealment. The participle is from ἀποκρύπτω, used in classical literature to mean "to hide from, conceal, cover."[2] In the LXX it occurs eighteen times and in the canonical books it appears eight times and translates three different Hebrew words, but four times it translates סָתַר, meaning "to conceal, hide" (Pss 19:6 [MT 19:7; LXX 18:7]; 119:19 [LXX 118:19]; Prov 27:12; Isa 40:27).[3] In the NT it is used only four times (Luke 10:21; 1 Cor 2:7; Eph 3:9; Col 1:26) and again it means "to conceal, hide." The concept of the mystery's concealment corresponds well with the fact that it was uncovered or unveiled (see word study of ἀποκαλύπτω, v. 5) to the apostles and prophets (v. 5). The perfect tense expresses a completed action with continuing results.[4] The mystery was hidden and continued to be so for the time expressed in the following prepositional phrase.

ἀπὸ τῶν αἰώνων, "for the ages." This tells the duration of time in which the mystery was hidden. There are two ways this prepositional phrase could be understood.[5] First, there is the view that αἰών refers to demonic or angelic beings or both.[6] Thus, some interpreters suggest that it was hidden from (ἀπό) the Gnostic aeons. It is thought that verse 10 supports this view, for although the mystery may have been hidden from angelic beings, it was made known to those who are called rulers and authorities.[7] There are some problems with this view: (1) Paul uses temporal contrast (νῦν, "now") in verse 10; (2) the parallel passage in Col 1:26 has the same construction with the addition of "generations," which has the temporal significance of a period or age (cf. Eph 3:5); and (3) it is based on late postapostolic texts which should not read into the apostolic times.

A second interpretation is that αἰών refers to time (as in 1:21; 2:2, 7; 3:11, 21*bis*).[8] This is a better interpretation for the following reasons:

1. Horsley suggests "arrangement, plan" (*New Documents Illustrating Early Christianity*, vol. 2, *A Review of the Greek Inscriptions and Papyri Published in 1977*, 92).

2. Homer *Ilias* 11.718; Herodotus 7.28, 45, 226; Thucydides 2.53.1.

3. Cf. S. Wagner, "סָתַר *sāṯar*; סֵתֶר *sēṯer*, etc.," *TDOT* 10 (1999): 363–68.

4. Fanning, *Verbal Aspect*, 416–18.

5. Barth, 343–44.

6. Dibelius-Greeven, 75; Schlier, 154–56; BAGD 28; BDAG 33.

7. Steinmetz, *Protologische Helis-Zuversicht*, 64; Lindemann, *Aufhebung*, 223.

8. Masson, 175; Gaugler, 142; Gnilka, 172; Mitton, 127; Schnackenburg, 138; Bruce, 319–20; Lincoln, 184–85. Best (321) suggests that the plan was hidden prior to creation for "it was no afterthought but part of God's intention from the beginning."

(1) it is the consistent use of the term in Ephesians (cf. 1:21; 2:2, 7; 3:11, 21*bis*); (2) it makes good sense of the temporal adverb (νῦν) in verse 10; (3) it is in keeping with the previous context (v. 5) where Paul states that the mystery was not known to other generations but is now (νῦν) known; (4) its use of the term in verse 11 refers to time and not to persons; (5) it makes good sense with the parallel passages in Col 1:26 where he uses both "ages" and "generations" (ἀπὸ τῶν αἰώνων καὶ ἀπὸ τῶν γενεῶν) to connote a temporal framework and in Rom 16:25 where it states that the revelation of the mystery was kept secret for long ages past (κατὰ ἀποκάλυψιν μυστηρίου χρόνοις αἰωνίοις σεσιγημένου); and (6) the prepositional phrase (ἀπ' αἰῶνος) consistently refers to the past ages (Luke 1:70; Acts 3:21; 15:18). In conclusion, then, this most likely refers to time rather than to demonic and angelic beings.

The noun αἰών with the preposition ἀπό could be translated "from the ages," in other words, God did not reveal the mystery during the past ages but it is "now" made known (v. 10). However, the preposition can also be translated "since";[1] thus, the mystery was hidden since the ages began or from the beginning of time.[2] Accordingly, the translation "for the ages" conveys the basic meaning of this prepositional phrase. Therefore, the mystery of the church has been hidden in God for all the ages until the present time. Once again, then, Paul makes it clear that the concept of the church was not evident in the OT.

ἐν[3] τῷ θεῷ τῷ τὰ πάντα κτίσαντι,[4] "in God who created all things." Having discussed the existence and time frame of the mystery, Paul now discusses where this mystery was concealed. The preposition ἐν denotes sphere or location. Thus, the mystery was hidden in God, inaccessible to human beings who lacked the ability to discover it. The relative clause τῷ τὰ πάντα κτίσαντι, "who created all things," speaks of God's omnipotent power. Barth states, "This is the only place in which Ephesians refers to the first [creation] rather than the new creation."[5] However, since God has created all things, the new creation would also be included. Possibly this was to remind the recipients of the letter that God was in control of everything and that the revelation of the mystery (the creation of the new humanity) was in keeping with his plan and timing. In other words, his plan was to create this new entity called the church and his timing was to reveal it in the NT era. Moreover, this cre-

1. BAGD 87; BDAG 105.

2. Mussner, *Christus, das All und Die Kirche*, 26.

3. The preposition ἐν is omitted in only ℵ* 614 Marcion and has the overwhelming support of all other manuscripts.

4. The addition of διὰ Ἰησοῦ Χριστοῦ is found in D² (*ˢ* 0278) 1881 *Byz* [K L P] syr** whereas its omission is attested in 𝔓⁴⁶ ℵ A B C D* F G P Ψ 33 81 365 1175 13191505 1611 1739 2127 2464 *pc* latt syrᵖ cop. The omission is the acceptable text because it is supported solidly by the Alexandrian and Western text-types, whereas the inclusion basically has the support of only the Byzantine text.

5. Barth, 344.

ation is sustained by the one who is the creator of all things. It is important to note that God's omnipotence is important to Paul because he depended on that enabling power to proclaim the wonders of the mystery. He will next discuss the purpose of this ministry.

c. The Purpose of the Ministry (3:10–12)

Paul has explained that he had been placed in the ministry of the gospel with God's enabling grace (vv. 7–8a) to preach the unsearchable wealth of Christ and to enlighten all of humanity concerning the mystery which had been hidden in God (vv. 8b–9). Next, the purpose of Paul's ministry is discussed, namely, that God's wisdom accomplished in Christ might be made known to the angelic rulers (vv. 10–12).

(1) God's Wisdom Made Known to the Angelic Rulers (3:10)

It is remarkable that God purposed to make known his manifold wisdom, the mystery, to heavenly rulers through the church rather than telling them directly.

Text: 3:10. ἵνα γνωρισθῇ νῦν ταῖς ἀρχαῖς καὶ ταῖς ἐξουσίαις ἐν τοῖς ἐπουρανίοις διὰ τῆς ἐκκλησίας ἡ πολυποίκιλος σοφία τοῦ θεοῦ,

Translation: 3:10. "in order that the manifold wisdom of God might now be made known to the rulers and the authorities in the heavenly realms through the church,"

Commentary: 3:10. ἵνα γνωρισθῇ νῦν,[1] "in order that [the manifold wisdom of God] might now be made known." The subject of this purpose clause is at the end of the Greek sentence and will be discussed later. The verb γνωρισθῇ is an aorist subjunctive passive from γνωρίζω meaning "to make known, reveal" (see a brief study of this word in 1:9). The real problem is to determine to what this purpose clause is connected. There are four prevailing views. (1) Some would relate it back to the immediately preceding τοῦ ἀποκεκρυμμένου ἀπὸ τῶν αἰώνων, "which had been hidden for ages," in verse 9 (NEB, TEV),[2] that is, the mystery was hidden in past ages, in order that the wisdom of God might *now* be made it known to angelic leaders. This view has the advantage of close proximity with the opposites close at hand: the γνωρισθῇ corresponds with ἀποκεκρυμμένου and the νῦν with ἀπὸ τῶν αἰώνων. The problem with this view is that it seems unlikely that the reason the mystery was hidden from humans in past ages was solely to enlighten the angelic leaders by means of the church. (2) Others relate the purpose clause back to ἐδόθη ἡ χάρις αὕτη, "this grace was given," in verse 8a (RSV, NRSV).[3] This emphasizes that the purpose of

1. The adverb νῦν is omitted only in F G 629 lat syr^{p} Tertullian Victorinus-Rome, which is insufficient evidence to sustain its omission.

2. Meyer, 167; Abbott, 88; Winer, *Grammar*, 575.

3. Alford, 3:106; Ellicott, 64; Salmond, 308; Best, 322.

Paul's ministry was specifically to enlighten the angelic leaders. The merit of this view is that it refers back to a finite verb. The disadvantage of this view is that this finite verb is part of a parenthetical statement. (3) Others would relate the purpose clause back to the two infinitives εὐαγγελίσασθαι τὸ ἀνεξιχνίαστον πλοῦτος τοῦ Χριστοῦ . . . καὶ φωτίσαι πάντας, "to preach the unsearchable wealth of Christ . . . and to enlighten all," in verses 8–9.[1] This view is not very different from view (2) for the infinitives ultimately depend on ἐδόθη ἡ χάρις αὕτη in verse 8a. This view makes better sense than view (2) because Paul was given grace to preach and enlighten with the purpose or result[2] that angelic leaders are informed of God's wisdom through the church. (4) Finally, it could go back to the same two infinitives in verses 8–9, mentioned in view (3), that define the function of ἐγενήθην διάκονος, "I was made a minister," in verse 7. This view does not refer back to ἐδόθη ἡ χάρις αὕτη in verse 8a, which is considered parenthetical. The only real drawback with this view is that it is necessary to go all the way back to verse 7 for the main verb. However, view (4) seems the most consistent with the text as a whole. In verse 7 Paul was made a minister of the gospel, the function of which was to preach the unsearchable wealth of Christ (v. 8b) and to enlighten all of the mystery (v. 9). The purpose or result of his ministry, then, is that the mystery (manifold wisdom of God) be made known to angelic leaders by means of the church (v. 10). Wink suggests that it is the task of the church to preach to the "powers."[3] However, Arnold points out that the text never states that task but rather declares that "the wisdom of God will be made known (passive voice) through the church," specifically, the harmonious coexistence of Jewish and Gentile believers is a testimony to the "powers."[4]

The adverb νῦν, "now," contrasts the mystery which in the past had been hidden (τοῦ ἀποκεκρυμμένου ἀπὸ τῶν αἰώνων) to the present revelation (vv. 5, 9). The "now" period began with the inception of the church, the time when Jews and Gentiles in Christ formed one body. Paul's next comments refer to the additional recipients of the revelation.

ταῖς ἀρχαῖς καὶ ταῖς ἐξουσίαις ἐν τοῖς ἐπουρανίοις διὰ τῆς ἐκκλησίας, "to the rulers and the authorities in the heavenly realms through the church." A study of "ruler" and "authority" was made in 1:21 where it was concluded that ἀρχή signifies primacy in power and hence "leader, ruler," and that ἐξουσία comes from ἔξεστιν, which indicates the freedom to act, giving the noun the sense of the right to act, implying "authority." Ten times these two terms for power are listed in

1. Eadie, 230; Meyer, 167; Abbott, 88; Schlier, 153; Gaugler, 143 Gnilka, 173–74; Lincoln, 185.

2. It is extremely difficult to distinguish between purpose and result when God is involved, for what God purposes will result.

3. Wink, *Naming the Powers*, 89, 95–96.

4. Arnold, *Ephesians: Power and Magic*, 63; cf. Wink, *Engaging the Powers*, 368 n. 19.

the order of the present passage (Luke 12:11; 20:20; 1 Cor 15:24; Eph 1:21; 3:10; 6:12; Col 1:16; 2:10, 15; Titus 3:1) and can refer to either human or angelic leaders. In the present context they are in the plural (probably indicating more than one leader) and refer to heavenly beings as opposed to earthly ones. It should be noted that the term ἐπουράνιος, "heavenlies," does not refer to heavenly beings for it would make no sense to say that angelic leaders are in the heavenly beings.[1] Rather, it refers to the heavenly places where angelic beings reside and operate over the human world.[2] The problem is to determine the nature of these beings. In 6:12 these residents of the heavenlies have been identified as evil rulers who are in conflict with believers, thus indicating that this is not a physical but a spiritual warfare. On the other hand, the reference in 1:21 could refer to either good or evil authorities and this does not help to determine their character in the present passage. It is not acceptable to conclude, however, that since they are evil in 6:12 they must be exclusively so in the present verse. In Ephesians the term "heavenlies" refers to the source of the believers' spiritual benefits (1:3), where Christ presently resides at the right hand of the Father (1:20), and where believers are positionally raised and seated with Christ (2:6). Hence, the heavenlies is the place where both good and evil leaders reside and attempt to influence humans. Such a concept may be difficult to understand, but in fact it is parallel to the idea that there are good and evil humans living together on earth.[3] As a matter of fact, God and Satan are seen conversing with one another in heaven (Job 1:6–12) and a struggle between good and evil angels is portrayed in heaven and on earth (Dan 10:13, 20). Therefore, it seems acceptable to suppose that both good and evil beings are being informed of the manifold wisdom of God. More will be said regarding this at the end of this verse.

The prepositional phrase διὰ τῆς ἐκκλησίας, "through the church," is very interesting because it shows the intermediate agent through which the angelic leaders are informed; it was through the church and not directly from God. We must remember that the church refers to the one body of believing Jews and Gentiles, a concept developed earlier in this letter. Wallace rightly suggests that the text implies that "God's wisdom should be displayed by what the church collectively does, rather than via its mere existence (which would be expressed by ἐν ἐκκλησίᾳ)."[4] This is the second time in this letter that the term "church" is used. It was first mentioned in 1:22 where God gave Christ to the church, which is his body. Accordingly, the church is the means

1. Cf. Martin Dibelius, *Die Geisterwelt im Glauben des Paulus* (Göttingen: Vandenhoeck & Ruprecht, 1909), 231–32.

2. Benoit, "Pauline Angelology and Demonology," 13.

3. Clemens, "Note on the Phrase ἐν τοῖς ἐπουρανίοις," 140; Harris, "'The Heavenlies' Reconsidered," 79.

4. Wallace, *Greek Grammar*, 434.

by which the angelic leaders are informed of the mystery. The church in this verse refers to not only the universal church but also local visible church.[1] Believing Jews and Gentiles in a local assembly united in one body is made known to the rulers and authorities in the heavenly realms. The following phrase identifies the content which relates to these heavenly beings.

ἡ πολυποίκιλος σοφία τοῦ θεοῦ, "the manifold wisdom of God." Finally, the subject of the sentence is stated. It may well have been put last for emphasis. The word σοφίᾳ, "wisdom," was discussed at 1:8 and 17 where it was concluded that it refers to the true insight into known facts. The best wisdom is that which has been revealed by God, for this is the means by which one gains insight into the true nature of God's plan. The following genitive τοῦ θεοῦ, "of God," denotes possession or source. It is wisdom that belongs to God and comes from him. The adjective πολυποίκιλος is a compound word from πολύς, "much, many," and ποίκιλος. The latter adjective (ποίκιλος) is a common word in classical literature meaning "many/various/rich colors" along side each other, woven, or embroidered.[2] In the LXX it appears twenty-six times (in the canonical books twenty times) and is used in reference to Joseph's coat of many colors (Gen 37:3). The two adjectives combined serve to heighten the idea of multiplicity. On those rare occasional uses outside the NT, it refers to intricate embroidery[3] or flowers of many colors.[4] This is the only occurrence in the NT and it has the idea of "most varied,"[5] or "(very) many sided."[6] It alludes to the variegated facets of God's wisdom,[7] not with reference to redemption[8] but to the unification of Jews and Gentiles into one new person in Christ. In past history God, in his wisdom, has dealt with humankind in a variety of ways. For example, his dealings with people before Abraham differed from his dealings after he made a covenant with Abraham. Likewise, there was another change when Israel became a nation under Moses. Accordingly, in this NT era the unification of believing

1. Best, 325–26; O'Brien, 26–27, 246.

2. Homer *Ilias* 5.735; 10.30; Aeschylus *Agamemnon* 923, 926, 936.

3. Euripides *Iphigenia Taurica* 1149.

4. Eubulus *Athenaeus Deipnosophistae* 105.2 §15.679d.

5. Heinrich Seesemann, "πολυποίκιλος," *TDNT* 6 (1968): 485.

6. BAGD 687; BDAG 847.

7. In an excursus Schlier (159–66) suggests that this multisided wisdom has its origins in a Jewish Gnostic interpretation of Hellenistic Isis theology. This is based on much later literature. Schlier's view is critiqued by Nils Alstrup Dahl, "Das Geheimnis der Kirche nach Eph. 3,8–10," *Zur Auferbauung des Leibes Christi. Festgabe für Professor D. Peter Brunner zum 65. Geburtstag am 25. April 1965*, ed. Edmund Schlink and Albrecht Peters (Kassel: Johannes Stauda, 1965), 63–75, esp. 67–71; updated in idem, *Studies in Ephesians*, 349–63, esp. 353–58.

8. *Pace* Steinmetz who thinks that the cross of Christ is implied in the wisdom of God, see Franz-Josef Steinmetz, "Die Weisheit und das Kreuz. Marginalien zum Kolosser- und Epheserbrief," *GL* 72 (1998): 112–26, esp. 118–20.

Jews and Gentiles into one body is another change. Therefore, the manifold wisdom of God must refer to this mystery which Paul has been explaining from 2:11 to the present verse.

In conclusion, Paul declares that the multisided or intricate wisdom of God is made known to angelic leaders through the instrumentality of the church. Throughout the ages good angels have tried to decipher God's plan (1 Pet 1:12) but were unable to do so. No doubt, evil angels also had wanted to know God's plans in advance in order to frustrate them. In fact, the animosity between Jews and Gentiles may well have been encouraged by the evil angels. However, this animosity was also a natural one, for in the past God had allowed Gentiles to come to him by becoming Jews, as already mentioned in 3:6. The Jews had considered themselves superior to the Gentiles because of the covenants God had made with them and because much of God's revelation was directed to them.

Equality between Jews and Gentiles was beyond the comprehension of any human being and any angelic being. Nevertheless, contrary to all prior thought, Paul has been showing that the mystery is the church, composed of believing Jews and Gentiles united into one body. They are "fellow heirs, and fellow members of the body, and fellow participants of the promise in Christ" (3:6). This was a revolutionary new concept. Through the church, the angelic leaders, both good and evil, gain knowledge of the manifold wisdom of God. It is a defeat for evil angels who would like to continue to engender animosity between Jews and Gentiles in order to frustrate the plan of God. The formation of the church is tangible evidence that the evil angelic leaders' power has been broken, demonstrating that even the most diverse elements of creation are subject to Christ.[1] As mentioned above, it must be emphasized that the church does not preach to the "powers" as suggested by Wink[2] but that the union of Jews and Gentiles in one body must be acknowledged by the "powers" to be a display of the multifaceted wisdom of God. This union is an evidence of the grace of God.

(2) God's Purpose Accomplished in Christ (3:11)

Text: 3:11. κατὰ πρόθεσιν τῶν αἰώνων ἣν ἐποίησεν ἐν τῷ Χριστῷ Ἰησοῦ τῷ κυρίῳ ἡμῶν,

Translation: 3:11. "according to the eternal purpose which he accomplished in Christ Jesus our Lord,"

Commentary: 3:11. κατὰ πρόθεσιν[3] τῶν αἰώνων, "according to the eternal purpose." This prepositional phrase indicates that this mani-

1. Lincoln, "A Re-Examination of 'the Heavenlies' in Ephesians," 474–75; Roy Yates, "Principalities and Powers in Ephesians," *New Blackfriars* 58 (November 1977): 517.

2. Wink, *Naming the Powers*, 89, 95–96.

3. Instead of πρόθεσιν, πρόγνωσιν is read in Clement. This reading has insufficient manuscript evidence to warrant its acceptance.

fold wisdom of God was not the result of a last minute idea which God had. Israel's rejection of their Messiah did not make it necessary for God to create hastily a new plan, namely, the church. The preposition κατά with the accusative denotes standard and it is connected to γνωρισθῇ, "might [now] be made known," in verse 10. In other words, the demonstration to angelic leaders of God's multifaceted wisdom was according to the standard of God's eternal purpose. In a study of the noun πρόθεσις in 1:11, we concluded that it portrayed plan or purpose with the idea that God will always carry out his purpose. The following genitive τῶν αἰώνων (found in 1:21; 2:2, 7; 3:9, 11, 21*bis*) could be objective,[1] "purpose which is carried out in the ages," or possessive,[2] "purpose which runs through history," but more likely it is attributive, "eternal purpose."[3] This fits well with the plural form which is a Hebraism for "eternity."[4] Here again, it has a temporal force rather than a reference to personal aeons in God's purpose.[5] Thus, it was in God's eternal plan for the church to be the means by which angelic leaders learn of this manifold wisdom of God.

ἣν ἐποίησεν ἐν τῷ Χριστῷ Ἰησοῦ τῷ κυρίῳ ἡμῶν, "which he accomplished in Christ Jesus our Lord." The relative pronoun ἥν, "which," connects with πρόθεσιν, "purpose." There are two interpretations of this relative clause, depending on how one renders the verb ἐποίησεν. First, the verb can have the idea "to conceive, form" and could be rendered "according to the eternal purpose which he planned or resolved in Christ Jesus our Lord" (NASB, JB, NJB).[6] The verb is so used in Mark 3:6 and 15:1. It suggests that in eternity past God conceived his purpose in the person of Christ. Hence, God's purpose is not cold and impersonal but focused in Christ. Second, the verb can mean "to accomplish, achieve" and may be rendered "according to the eternal purpose which he accomplished in Christ Jesus our Lord" (RSV, NEB, TEV, NIV, NRSV).[7] The verb is so used in Eph 2:3 as well as in Matt 21:31 and John 6:38. This interpretation indicates that God's purpose was brought to fulfill-

1. As Schlier, 157; Lona, *Die Eschatologie im Kolosser- und Epheserbrief*, 303.

2. As Alford, 3:107; Ellicott, 65; Meyer, 170; Abbott, 89–90; Salmond, 309–10; Robinson, 80, 171.

3. As Hendriksen, 160; Barth, 346; Schnackenburg, 141; Bruce, 322; Lincoln, 189. Similar would be the genitive of quality as suggested by Sellin, "Über einige ungewöhnliche Genitive im Epheserbrief," 99–100; Eadie, 235; Masson, 176 n. 5; Gnilka, 177.

4. MHT 3:25; 4:91; cf. also Sasse, *TDNT* 1 (1964): 199.

5. *Contra* Schlier, 157–58; Steinmetz, *Protologische Helis-Zuversicht*, 64; Lindemann, *Aufhebung*, 228.

6. Calvin, 164; Bengel, 4:84; Harless, 301–2; Alford, 3:107; Ellicott, 65; Abbott, 90; Robinson, 172; Schlier, 157–58; Gaugler, 146; Hendriksen, 160–61; Gnilka, 177; Bruce, 318 n. 47; Best, 328; cf. Caragounis, *Ephesian* Mysterion, 109–10.

7. Theodoret *Eph* 3:10–11 (*PG* 82:529); Olshausen, 199–200; Eadie, 236; Moule, 92; Meyer, 170–71; Salmond, 310; Westcott, 49; Masson, 176 n. 5; Caird, 67; Mitton, 128; Barth, 346–47; Schnackenburg, 141; Lincoln, 189; O'Brien, 248.

ment in Christ Jesus' death. Thus, it is not the conception of the plan in Christ but the achievement of the plan in Christ's death. This view is preferred because: (1) it makes better sense of the tense of the verb, otherwise, a present or perfect tense would be expected; (2) the use of the active verb (ποιέω) rather than a middle (as in 1:16 and 4:16) indicates that the plan is not being formed but has been accomplished;[1] (3) the use of ποιέω, in the active form elsewhere in Ephesians (2:3, 14, 15; 3:20; 6:6, 8, 9), has the idea of achieving or accomplishing; (4) the inclusion of believing Jews and Gentiles into one body was, in fact, accomplished by Christ's death; and (5) the use of Christ's historical name points to his plan already having been accomplished in Christ historically.[2] Therefore, God's purpose has been accomplished in Christ and that is the basis of the formation of the church, the mystery made known to all mankind and to the angelic leaders.

The final prepositional phrase (ἐν τῷ Χριστῷ Ἰησοῦ τῷ κυρίῳ ἡμῶν) uses the full title of Christ to enhance the idea that God's purpose was accomplished in the historical Jesus when he died on the cross about thirty years before the Ephesians received this letter or about two thousand years ago for the present day believer. The preposition indicates sphere or locale in which God's purpose was fulfilled. The full title of Christ is given, though not in the same word order, in 1:3 and 17. As discussed in those contexts, this title shows four things: (1) his Lordship ("Jesus is Lord" was an early confession of the church, Acts 2:36; 8:16; 10:36; 11:17; 19:5; Rom 10:9; 14:9; 1 Cor 12:3; 2 Cor 4:5; Phil 2:11); (2) his name ("Jesus"); (3) his title ("Christ") which is more than just a name, because it denotes that he is the promised Messiah who would bring salvation to both Jews and Gentiles and make it possible for both to be created into one new person; and (4) his personal relationship to believers ("our Lord").

(3) God's Presence Accessible in Christ (3:12)

Having established that God's eternal plan was accomplished in the death of Christ Jesus our Lord, Paul proceeds to explain the wonderful privilege enjoyed by believers, namely, free access to their heavenly Father.

Text: 3:12. ἐν ᾧ ἔχομεν τὴν παρρησίαν καὶ προσαγωγὴν ἐν πεποιθήσει διὰ τῆς πίστεως αὐτοῦ.

Translation: 3:12. "in whom we have the boldness and access with confidence through faith in him."

Commentary: 3:12. ἐν ᾧ ἔχομεν τὴν παρρησίαν καὶ προσαγωγὴν ἐν πεποιθήσει,[3] "in whom we have the boldness and access with confi-

1. Barth, 346–47.

2. Olshausen, 200.

3. The term πεποιθήσει is replaced by τῷ ἐλευθερωθῆναι in only D*, but the manuscript evidence is too scanty to be considered very seriously.

dence." The preposition with the relative pronoun ἐν ᾧ, "in whom," relates back to Christ as the sphere in whom we have access to the Father. The word παρρησία was first used in reference to the Athenians' freedom of speech[1] that was characterized by frankness and could be misused due to a lack of restraint in what was said.[2] It occurs twelve times in the LXX (only five times in the canonical books) and is translated only once with certainty from a Hebrew word. Even with these infrequent references, the theme of freedom seems to dominate. However, in the NT it is used thirty-one times, eight times by Paul, and twice in Ephesians (3:12; 6:19). It conveys openness, speaking freely, concealing nothing (Mark 8:32; John 7:4, 13, 26; 10:24; 11:14, 54; Phil 1:20; Col 2:15), boldness or candor (Acts 2:29; 4:13, 29, 31; 28:31; 2 Cor 3:12), and confidence (2 Cor 7:4). The basic idea is freedom to speak without restraints. Lack of restraints encourages confident speech. In the present context, because the believer is in Christ, he can speak freely, boldly, or openly to the Father,[3] and with the absence of restraints "he can approach God with confidence. He can stand before the Ruler and Judge free and erect, not lowering his head, able to bear his presence."[4] Moses' and David's frankness with God (e.g., Exod 32:11–13; 33:12–23; Pss 6, 13, 69) and Jesus' honesty at Gethsemane (Matt 26:36–44 = Mark 14:32–39 = Luke 22:40–44) are illustrations of boldness and confidence before God. However, this boldness before God is not presumptuous or arrogant but humble and with a sense of awe. "Without Christ they may shout rashly at him and go unheard but with Christ believers may speak boldly knowing that they will be heard."[5] Van Unnik proposes that this does not have reference to our freedom of speech as we approach God mentioned in 2:18 but

1. Euripides *Hippolytus* 422; *Ion* 672; *Bacchae* 668; *Phoenissae* 391; Aristophanes *Thesmophoriazusae* 541; for a discussion of the Athenians' freedom of speech, see Max Radin, "Freedom of Speech in Ancient Athens," *AJP* 48 (July, August, September 1927): 215–30.

2. Plato *Phaedrus* 240e; *Respublica* 8.11 §557b.

3. For a study of the word, see W. C. van Unnik, "The Christian's Freedom of Speech in the New Testament," *BJRL* 44 (March 1962): 466–88 (reprinted in *Sparsa Collecta: The Collected Essays of W. C. van Unnik*, Part Two, NovTSup, ed. C. K. Barrett, A. F. J. Klijn, and J. Smit Sibinga, vol. 30 [Leiden: Brill, 1980], 269–89); idem, "The Semitic Background of παρρησία in the New Testament," in *Sparsa Collecta: The Collected Essays of W. C. van Unnik*, Part Two, NovTSup, ed. C. K. Barrett, A. F. J. Klijn, and J. Smit Sibinga, vol. 30 (Leiden: Brill, 1980), 290–306; Manuel Isidro Alves, *Il Cristiano in Cristo. La presenza del cristiano davanti a Dio secondo S. Paolo*, Dissertatio ad Lauream (Rome: Pontificio Istituto Biblico, 1980), 129–38; Stanley B. Marrow, "*Parrhēsia* and the New Testament," *CBQ* 44 (July 1982): 431–46; David E. Fredrickson, "Παρρησία in the Pauline Letters," in *Friendship, Flattery, and Frankness of Speech: Studies on Friendship in the New Testament World*, ed. John T. Fitzgerald, NovTSup, ed. A. J. Malherbe, D. P. Moessner, et al., vol. 82 (Leiden: Brill, 1996), 163–83.

4. Heinrich Schlier, "παρρησία," *TDNT* 5 (1967): 883.

5. Best, 329.

rather it must refer to the freedom to proclaim the mystery.[1] However, in the context Paul is clearly attempting to show that both believing Jews and Gentiles as one entity have access to God.

The noun προσαγωγή is already used in 2:18 and occurs one other time in the NT (Rom 5:2). In the study of the word in 2:18 it was concluded that it implied access, freedom of approach. It suggests familiarity without contempt. Whereas παρρησία gives the idea of the freedom of address, προσαγωγή has the idea of freedom of approach. Only one article governs both παρρησία and προσαγωγή, which may indicate it is a hendiadys, emphasizing the idea of free access to God.

The noun πεποίθησις belongs to late Greek found in the LXX only in 2 Kgs 18:19 where Rabshakeh asks Hezekiah for the basis of his confidence. Philo speaks about confidence in moral excellence.[2] It is used only six times in the NT, all in Paul's writings (2 Cor 1:15; 3:4; 8:22; 10:2; Eph 3:12; Phil 3:4), and is best rendered "confidence." The preposition ἐν most likely denotes manner and thus could be translated "with confidence." The prepositional phrase could modify only προσαγωγή but it more likely modifies both nouns. It reinforces the concept of free speech and free access. Paul continues by explaining the method by which this is accomplished.

διὰ τῆς πίστεως αὐτοῦ, "through faith in him." The preposition διά shows the means by which believers can have freedom of speech and freedom of approach before God (see 2:8). It is through faith. The classification of the pronoun αὐτοῦ has caused some discussion in recent years. Some expositors propose that this is a subjective genitive rather than an objective genitive, meaning that it speaks of Christ's faithfulness.[3] This fits well with the present context, namely, the body of believers have free access with confidence through the faithfulness of Christ on behalf of the church. However, others suggest that this should still be considered an objective genitive,[4] and thus the object of faith is Christ Jesus our Lord. This view emphasizes the believers'

1. Van Unnik, "The Christian's Freedom of Speech in the New Testament," 475.

2. Philo *De Virtutibus* 41 §226.

3. Barth, 347; Best, 330; O'Brien, 249 n. 114; George Howard, "Notes and Observations on the 'Faith of Christ'," *HTR* 60 (October 1967): 460; D. W. B. Robinson, "'Faith of Jesus Christ'—a New Testament Debate," *RTR* 29 (September–December 1970): 75; Richard B. Hays, *The Faith of Jesus Christ: An Investigation of the Narrative Substructure of Galatians 3:1–4:11*, SBLDS, ed. William Baird, no. 56 (Chico, Calif.: Scholars Press, 1983), 160, 166; cf. also George Howard, "The 'Faith of Christ'," *ExpTim* 85 (April 1974): 212–15; Sam K. Williams, "Again *Pistis Christou*," *CBQ* 49 (July 1987): 431–47; Morna D. Hooker, "ΠΙΣΤΙΣ ΧΡΙΣΤΟΥ," *NTS* 35 (July 1989): 321–42; Thomas F. Torrance, "One Aspect of the Biblical Conception of Faith," *ExpTim* 68 (January 1957): 111–14; Wallace, *Greek Grammar*, 115–16.

4. MHT 3:263 n. 2; Winer, *Grammar*, 232; Lincoln, 190; C. F. D. Moule, "The Biblical Conception of 'Faith'," *ExpTim* 68 (February 1957): 157; Arland J. Hultgren, "The *Pistis Christou* Formulation in Paul," *NovT* 22 (July 1980): 248–63; Erich Mauerhofer, "Der Brief an die Epheser. 29. Teil: 3,10–13," *Fundamentum* 1 (1997): 20.

faith rather than the faithfulness of Christ. The choice between these options is difficult; however, the latter is preferred. On the other hand, some suggest that rather than accepting the genitive as either subjective or objective, it should include both meanings.[1] Hence, believers have faith in Christ's faithfulness to God on behalf of the church.

In this verse the main verb (ἔχομεν) is in the present tense indicating repeated action. Accordingly, we can with confidence continually speak freely to God and boldly enter God's presence. For the Gentiles, in particular, this was astounding news. The Gentiles were uncircumcised, alienated from the blessings of God, and were far off from God (2:11–13). Now they can come into God's presence with no fear and speak openly and frankly to him.

4. The Injunction (3:13)

Finally, Paul concludes his long explanation by furnishing the apodosis to the sentence.

Text: 3:13. διὸ αἰτοῦμαι μὴ ἐγκακεῖν ἐν ταῖς θλίψεσίν μου ὑπὲρ ὑμῶν, ἥτις ἐστὶν δόξα ὑμῶν.

Translation: 3:13. "Therefore, I ask you not to lose heart in my tribulations on behalf of you, which is your glory."

Commentary: 3:13. διό, "Therefore." This is a strong inferential conjunction (from δι' ὅ), which can be translated "therefore, for this reason."[2] It is used here to alert the readers that he is introducting the apodosis of a long conditional sentence. As stated in verse 2 Paul uses εἴ γε to introduce the first class conditional sentence, which could be translated "if indeed" (NASB), "if so be" (RV, ASV), or as Thrall translates it, "At any rate if you have heard . . . as I know you have."[3] This captures both the conditional aspects and the concession that the Ephesians had indeed heard of Paul and his ministry in connection with the mystery. In this context, the point is that if the Ephesians truly understand all that he has explained in verses 2–12, then (διό) it will be possible for them to acquiesce to his following request.

αἰτοῦμαι μὴ ἐγκακεῖν[4] ἐν ταῖς θλίψεσίν μου ὑπὲρ ὑμῶν, "I ask you not to lose heart in my tribulations on behalf of you." The verb αἰ-

1. Williams, "Again *Pistis Christou*," 431–37; Hooker, "ΠΙΣΤΙΣ ΧΡΙΣΤΟΥ," 340–42.

2. BAGD 198; BDAG 250; cf. Molland, "Διο, Einige syntaktische Beobachtungen," in *Serta Rudbergiana*, 43–52; reprinted in idem, "Διο: Einige syntaktische Beobachtungen," in *Opuscula Patristica*, 9–16.

3. Thrall, *Greek Particles in the New Testament*, 88; cf. also Baumert, *Täglich Sterben und Auferstehen*, 381–82.

4. The reading ἐγκακεῖν is found in 𝔓[46] א A B D* 33 81 326 *pc* cop whereas ἐκκακεῖν is found in C D[2] F G Ψ 0278 1739 1881 𝔐. The textual evidence is quite evenly divided although the second reading is somewhat better in its geographcial distribution, but the

τοῦμαι is a present middle indicative from αἰτέω meaning "to request." Although earlier commentators wanted to make a great distinction between the active and middle voices, the only apparent distinction is that the active was used to make requests of God (although this is not true in v. 20) and the middle was used in commercial or official relationships, such as is the case here.[1] Trench tries to make a case that this word was used by an inferior to make a request of a superior[2] but this has been thoroughly refuted.[3] Actually, it is better interpreted as a request by Paul to his readers, acting in his capacity of an apostle. The infinitive ἐγκακεῖν is from ἐγκακέω or ἐκκακέω,[4] meaning "to act/treat badly."[5] This word never occurs in the LXX, but it is in Symmachus' translation of Gen 27:46; Num 21:5; Prov 3:11; Isa 7:16 (cf. also Jer 18:12) and is used with the idea of "becoming weary, tired." In the NT it is used only six times (Luke 18:1; 2 Cor 4:1, 16; Gal 6:9; Eph 3:13; 2 Thess 3:13). In Luke 18:1 it introduces a parable by stating that one ought not grow weary or lose heart while praying. The remaining passages also convey "do not lose heart" or "be discouraged."[6]

The real difficulty in this part of the verse is determining whether Paul is asking God or the Ephesians to pray that he not disgrace his high calling by losing heart[7] or whether he is requesting the Ephesians not to lose heart due to his afflictions.[8] The second interpretation is preferred because, as the apodosis, it concludes that if they truly understood his presentation of the mystery and his ministry, it would be logical for him to ask them not to lose heart. Second, he states at the end of the present verse that he is suffering for their (ὑμῶν) glory; thus, the Ephesians are the subject of the request. Third,

---

first reading has older manuscripts. The meaning is not altered because it is the same word with different spellings.

1. BDF §316 (2); MHT 1:160–61; Gustav Stählin, "αἰτέω (αἰτέομαι)," *TDNT* 1 (1964): 191–92.

2. Trench, *Synonyms of the New Testament*, 144.

3. E. A., review of *Synonyms of the New Testament*, by Richard Cheneuix Trench, *North American Review* 114 (January 1872): 171–89, esp. 182–89.

4. The two words are really one and the same. See Baumert, *Täglich Sterben und Auferstehen*, 326–30.

5. Polybius 4.19.10.

6. BAGD 215; BDAG 272; L&N §25.288; Walter Grundmann, "ἐγκακέω," *TDNT* 3 (1965): 486.

7. Peshitta; Jerome *Eph* 3:13 (*PL* 26:485); Theodoret *Eph* 3:13 (*PG* 82:529); Bengel, 4:84; Harless, 305; G. H. P. Thompson, "Ephesians iii.13 and 2 Timothy ii.10 in the Light of Colossians i.24," *ExpTim* 71 (March 1960): 188; cf. Baumert, *Täglich Sterben und Auferstehen*, 324–26.

8. Chrysostom *Eph* 3:13 (*PG* 62:51); Jerome *Eph* 3:13 (*PL* 26:485); Theophylact *Eph* 3:13 (*PG* 124:1073–74); Aquinas, chap. 3, lec. 4, vv. 13–17 (136); Alford, 3:108; Eadie, 238; Ellicott, 67; Meyer, 172; Abbott, 91–92; Salmond, 311; Robinson, 173; Westcott, 50; Schlier, 166; Gaugler, 148; Barth, 348; Schnackenburg, 142; Bruce, 323; Lincoln, 191; Best, 330–31; O'Brien, 251.

the possessive pronoun μου, "my," following θλίψεσιν, "tribulations," "would be superfluous if the apostle were praying for himself."[1] Hence, it seems best to see Paul asking the Ephesians not to lose heart because of his afflictions.

The afflictions (ἐν ταῖς θλίψεσιν) mentioned here do not refer to his whole ministry but rather to his imprisonment[2] in Rome on behalf of them (ὑπὲρ ὑμῶν). No doubt, at this time he was waiting for the Jews to bring accusations against him before Caesar. In fact, after his arrest and trial in Jerusalem some Jews attempted to take his life after which he was delivered to Caesarea (Acts 23:12–35). There, after a trial and a request by some of the Jewish leaders to have him returned to Jerusalem to be retried, Paul appealed to Caesar (24:1–25:11) and that was when he was sent to Rome (chaps. 27–28). The main contention of the Jews against Paul was that he taught people to overthrow the law of Moses and brought Gentiles into the Jerusalem temple (21:28 [cf. 24:18]; 24:5–6; 25:7–8). In this way Paul was suffering tribulations because of his ministry among Gentiles, including the Ephesians. Paul's willingness to suffer on their behalf is confirmed in a letter written in this same time period of Roman imprisonment where he states that he was willing to be poured out as a drink offering for the faith of the recipients (Phil 2:17). In this spirit Paul cautions Ephesian believers not to lose heart.

ἥτις ἐστὶν δόξα ὑμῶν,[3] "which is your glory." There are two things to observe about the indefinite relative pronoun: (1) rather than being indefinite in function (not untypical in NT times), it specifically refers back to "tribulations,"[4] and (2) it agrees in number with its predicate rather than its antecedent.[5] Although it is definite in this context, it still connotes a qualitative sense[6] and, in addition, gives a causal sense.[7] Consequently, the reason that they should not lose heart due to his sufferings was because it was their glory. The word "glory" was discussed at 1:6 (cf. also 1:12, 14, 17, 18; 3:16, 21) where we concluded that it is the summation of all of one's attributes and thus one's reputation and/or honor. Although the other references to this word in

1. Abbott, 92.

2. Thompson, "Ephesians iii.13 and 2 Timothy ii.10 in the Light of Colossians i.24," 188.

3. The personal pronoun ὑμῶν appears in ℵ A B D F G Ψ 075 0150 6 256 263 365 424 1175 1241 1852 1881 1962 2200 2464 *Byz* [K L P] *Lect* it$^{ar, b, d, f, g, o}$ vg syr$^{p, h}$ cop$^{sa, bo}$ arm eth geo slav Origen Chrysostom Theodore^{lat} Victorinus-Rome Ambrosiaster Jerome Pelagius Augustine. The other reading ἡμῶν is found in 𝔓^{46} C 33 81 104 436 459 1537 1739 1912 2127 cop^{boms}. The first reading is preferred because of good representation in all the text-types. Therefore, it has date and character, good genealogical relationships, and good geographical distribution.

4. Robertson, *Grammar*, 728; cf. Winer, *Grammar*, 209–10 n. 3.

5. Robertson, *Grammar*, 729; HS §263e; Winer, *Grammar*, 206–7.

6. Winer, *Grammar*, 210 n. 3.

7. HS §290b.

Ephesians refer to God's glory, it can also have reference to human glory (Matt 6:29; 1 Cor 11:7; cf. Gen 45:13; Isa 8:7; 10:12; 17:3, 4) as it does in the present context. Stated in another way, because of the reputation or honor enjoyed by them as new creatures in Christ, Paul suffered in Roman imprisonment. It might seem unusual to take glory in another's suffering. This, however, has a similarity in Christ's death. One does not specifically glory because of Christ's suffering but rather glories because his death made possible the honor of being a new creature in Christ. In the present context, the point is that if Paul had never carried out his ministry of the mystery to the Ephesians, he would not have been in prison and the Ephesians would never have been introduced to Christ. In other words, his imprisonment is tangible evidence that he preached the unsearchable riches of Christ to the Gentiles and in particularly to the Ephesians. Hence, his imprisonment is their glory and should not cause them grief.

Lincoln proposes that this glory refers to eschatological glory, the glorification of believers. He bases this conclusion on the fact that Paul has stated elsewhere that sufferings are a condition for glorification (Rom 8:17–18; 2 Cor 4:17) and that in this passage Paul's sufferings are for the Ephesian believers' glorification.[1] This is an interesting concept but it seems unlikely. References relating to suffering and glory are never on behalf of others, even as Lincoln admits. The same person who suffers will be glorified. The exception to this is Christ who suffered on behalf of humans and those who trust him for their salvation.

Briefly then, the Ephesians are admonished not to lose heart over Paul's imprisonment on their behalf. His imprisonment was the glory which they enjoyed because they were now creatures in Christ, for it was Paul who proclaimed the mystery to them. Because of his ministry among Gentiles the Jews brought accusations against him which resulted in his imprisonment in Rome.

1. Lincoln, 192; Best, 331–32.

G. Prayer for Strengthened Love (3:14–21)

This is Paul's second prayer in Ephesians. His first prayer (1:15–23) for the believers in Ephesus was for them to know God intimately so that they might know the following three things: first, referring to the past, that they might be acquainted with the hope of his calling; second, referring to the future, that they will understand the wealth of God's gracious inheritance; and finally, referring to the present, that they would know the surpassing greatness of his power toward them. Paul's desire is for the Ephesian believers to deepen their relationship with God who has enriched them with every spiritual benefit (1:3–14) and to experience in a deeper way those benefits.

In the present context (3:14–21), the focus of his prayer is that the Ephesians might know Christ's strengthened love which surpasses all knowledge. Just prior to this, Paul had developed the doctrine of the mystery of the church where Jewish and Gentile believers are positionally "one new person" (2:15), the body of Christ. He now prays that they may be united experientially in Christ's love. This passage can be divided into three parts. First, homage to God is declared (vv. 14–15). Second, his prayer for the Ephesians is expressed, namely, that they might genuinely know and experience Christ's love and consequently demonstrate it toward each other (vv. 16–19). Third, praise to God is given, ascribing to him glory thoughout all generations (vv. 20–21). Hence, Paul's first prayer (1:15–23) for believers was to know God intimately and experience his power, and his second prayer (3:14–21) is for believers to know the power of Christ's love and to experience Christ's love for one another.[1]

1. For a rhetorical analysis of this prayer, see Jeal, *Integrating Theology and Ethics in Ephesians*, 110–29.

Before discussing the content of the second prayer, we need to review Paul's structure in this section. After developing the concept of the mystery of Jewish and Gentile believers who are united into one body in Christ (2:11–22), Paul prepares to pray (3:1), then digresses to explain further his role as administrator and dispenser of the mystery to the Gentiles (vv. 2–13). Finally, he returns to pray for their unity (v. 14). With 86 words this prayer is the fifth of eight long sentences (vv. 14–19) in this epistle (cf. 1:3–14, 15–23; 2:1–7; 3:2–13, 14–19; 4:1–6, 11–16; 6:14–20). Three of these long sentences are in the form of prayer and/or praise (1:3–14; 1:15–23; 3:14–21). As previously concluded, prayers, past and present, are often composed of lengthy sentences. He ends this prayer with a doxology (vv. 20–21) which serves as a transition from the doctrinal portion of the letter (chaps. 1–3) to the paraenetic portion (chaps. 4–6).[1]

1. The Approach to Prayer (3:14–15)

In these two verses Paul resumes what he started to say in verse 1 of this chapter. Paul, the servant of God, addresses God as Father in accordance with his new relationship to him.

Text: 3:14. Τούτου χάριν κάμπτω τὰ γόνατά μου πρὸς τὸν πατέρα τοῦ κυρίου ἡμῶν Ἰησοῦ Χριστοῦ, **3:15.** ἐξ οὗ πᾶσα πατριὰ ἐν οὐρανοῖς καὶ ἐπὶ γῆς ὀνομάζεται,

Translation: 3:14. "For this reason I bow my knees before the Father of our Lord Jesus Christ, **3:15.** from whom every family in heaven and on the earth is named,"

Commentary: 3:14. Τούτου χάριν, "For this reason." This marks the resumption of the sentence begun in verse 1 which was interrupted by the long digression of verses 2–13.[2] As mentioned in verse 1 the adverbial accusative χάριν from χάρις is used as a preposition that generally follows the word it governs. It indicates the reason and hence is translated "for this reason."[3] This phrase encompasses Paul's discourse in 2:11–22, namely, the unity of Jews and Gentiles in Christ as one "new person." Immediately following this discourse he prepares to pray for their unity. At this point, however, he digresses in order to elaborate further on the mystery and his responsibility to dispense it. The prayer expressed in 3:14–21 would fit well after 2:11–22, but with more information gained from the digression in 3:2–13, the content of the prayer is all the more forceful.

1. Best, 335; O'Brien, 254.
2. Robertson, *Grammar*, 435; Moule, *Idiom Book*, 198.
3. BAGD 877; BDAG 1078–79; cf. also Robertson, *Grammar*, 488, 505; Moule, *Idiom Book*, 198.

κάμπτω τὰ γόνατά μου πρὸς τὸν πατέρα τοῦ κυρίου ἡμῶν Ἰησοῦ Χριστοῦ,[1] "I bow my knees before the Father of our Lord Jesus Christ." The verb κάμπτω is used only four times in the NT (Rom 11:4; 14:11; Eph 3:14; Phil 2:10). In Rom 11:4, Paul quotes 1 Kgs 19:18 where God tells Elijah that 7000 men have not bowed the knee to Baal; in Rom 14:11 Paul quotes Isa 45:23 where God declares that he alone is God and every knee will bow and every tongue will give praise to him; and in Phil 2:10 (again quoting Isa 45:23) Paul states that God has highly exalted Christ and that at the name of Jesus every knee shall bow whether they are in heaven, on earth, or under the earth. Hence, in these passages the bending of the knee conveys worship or submission to a supernatural power.

In the present context Paul prostrates himself before God, who is called "Father," in order to petition him in prayer. In 3:12 Paul mentioned that all believers have access to God and here he exemplifies this. The words κάμπτω τὰ γόνατά μου are a metonomy of adjunct simply meaning "I pray." There are ample examples in the Scriptures of varied postures for prayer, including on one's knees (Ezra 9:5; Ps 95:6 [LXX 94:6]; Dan 6:10; Luke 22:41; Acts 7:60), as well as lying prostrate (Num 16:45; Josh 7:6; Ezra 10:1; Matt 26:39 = Mark 14:35), head between the knees (1 Kgs 18:42), and standing (1 Sam 1:26; 1 Kgs 8:22; Mark 11:25; Luke 18:11, 13). The preposition πρός may indicate direction "to" or preferably relationship "before."[2] The person before whom Paul prays and the object of his prayer is "the Father of our Lord Jesus Christ." The term "Father," with reference to God, is used frequently in Ephesians (1:2, 3, 17; 2:18; 3:14; 4:6; 5:20; 6:23) and is discussed more fully in 1:2, 3. God is rarely addressed as "Father" in

1. The reading πατέρα τοῦ κυρίου ἡμῶν Ἰησοῦ Χριστοῦ is found in א^{2} D F G Ψ 075 104 424* 436 459 1241 1852 1881 1912 2200 2464 *Byz* [K L] *Lect* it$^{ar, b, d, f, g, o}$ vg syr$^{p, h}$ arm slav (Valentinians$^{acc. to Hippolytus}$) Origen^{lat} Gregory-Nyssa Chrysostom Marcus-Eremita Theodore^{lat} Theodoret Victorinus-Rome Ambrosiaster Latin mss$^{acc to Jerome}$ Pelagius Augustine$^{6/8}$ Varimadum. The reading πατέρα is found in 𝔓^{46} א* A B C P 0150 33 81 256 263 365 424^{c} 1175 1573 1739 1962 2127 *l* 596 vg^{ms} syr^{pal} cop$^{sa, bo}$ eth geo Origen (Methodius) Basil-Ancyra Athanasius Cyril-Jerusalem (Didymus^{dub}) Cyril John-Damascus Jerome Augustine$^{2/8}$ Ps-Vigilius (NA^{27}, UBS^{4}). Metzger (*Textual Commentary*, 2d ed., 533) states that the first reading is a gloss suggested by 1:3. However, although this is a possibility, it seems that there is enough manuscript attestation to verify it. The second reading is very strong only in the Alexandrian text. The first reading does have some Alexandrian attestation (Ψ 104 vg) and it is very strong in both the Western and Byzantine text-types. It is primarily on the basis of geographical distribution that the first reading is accepted. Furthermore, internally this is the only time in the NT where this form is used, for every other place it is "God the Father of our Lord Jesus Christ" or "God and Father of our Lord Jesus Christ." Hence, it is not really a gloss of 1:3. Regardless of which reading one accepts, the meaning is not altered for it is established in 1:3 that God is the Father of our Lord Jesus Christ.

2. Erich Mauerhofer, "Der Brief an die Epheser. 30. Teil: Kap. 3,14–15," *Fundamentum* 2 (1997): 32.

the OT (fifteen times out of 1448 occurrences) but in the NT this title is frequently used (245 times out of 413 occurrences).[1] Believers are the sons of God and address God as "Father, Abba" (Rom 8:15; Gal 4:6) as Jesus had addressed him (Mark 14:36). For example, in Eph 1:17 the prayer is addressed not only to "the God of our Lord Jesus Christ," but also to "the Father of glory." If one accepts the reading of the genitives (τοῦ κυρίου ἡμῶν Ἰησοῦ Χριστοῦ) that follow "God," they are genitives of relationship denoting that Christ is the Son of God. In the next verse, Paul further describes the identity of the "Father."

3:15. ἐξ οὗ πᾶσα πατριὰ ἐν οὐρανοῖς[2] καὶ ἐπὶ γῆς ὀνομάζεται, "from whom every family in heaven and on the earth is named." The prepositional relative pronoun ἐξ οὗ denotes origin "out of whom" or "from whom," which could refer back to "our Lord Jesus Christ," but it is much more likely to refer to the "Father," for he is not only the Father of our Lord Jesus Christ but also the origin of what Paul discusses next. Furthermore, it appears that Paul uses a play on words, for the immediately following noun is πατριά, which most naturally refers back to πατέρα, "Father."

The real problem of this verse is to understand what Paul means in his use of πατριά. Some think it refers to the concept of fatherhood, as coming from God the Father.[3] But this is unlikely because πατριά never conveys the abstract concept of "fatherhood" (πατρότης, in Latin *paternitas*).[4] In classical times it could have the idea of lineage or descent from the father's side[5] and the idea of a clan or tribe[6] which had the original father or patriarch as the head. In the LXX it appears 175 times (156 times in the canonical books), about a third of which occur in Numbers and another third in 1 Chronicles. Basically, the word has the sense of a "family" headed by a father (Exod 12:3; 1 Chr 23:11) or a larger unit of several families that make up a tribe or clan with a common father (Exod 6:17, 19; Num 2:34; 4:22; 17:2*bis* [MT & LXX 17:17*bis*]).[7] In the NT it occurs only three times (Luke 2:4; Acts 3:25; Eph 3:15). In Luke 2:4 it refers to Joseph being of the "family" of David. In Acts 3:25 Peter quotes the OT conflation of Gen 12:3 ("in you shall all the families of the earth be blessed") and 22:18 ("in your seed shall all the nations of the earth be blessed"), both of which give a national sense. The thought

1. Hofius, *NIDNTT* 1 (1975): 617–18.

2. Rather than οὐρανοῖς the reading οὐρανῷ is found in P 0278 81 104 365 945 1175 *al* it[a] vg[mss] syr[hmg] Hilary Epiphanius[pt] which, however, has not sufficient evidence to justify its acceptance.

3. Theodoret *Eph* 3:14–15 (*PG* 82:530); Theophylact *Eph* 3:14–15 (*PG* 124:1074); Robinson, 83–84, 174; Percy, *Probleme*, 277–78 n. 30; F. M'Kenzie, "Exposition of Ephesians iii.15," *ExpTim* 2 (January 1891): 93–94.

4. Eadie, 241; Gaugler, 151; Barth, 368; Schnackenburg, 147.

5. Herodotus 3.75; cf. also 2.143.

6. Ibid., 1.200.

7. Gottlob Schrenk, "πατριά," *TDNT* 5 (1967): 1016; Frederick Fyvie Bruce, "Name [ὄνομα]," *NIDNTT* 2 (1976): 655.

is that the nation is composed of many families, all of which have originated from one father. In the present context, it seems to have reference to "family." The anarthrous adjective πᾶσα could be translated "all" or "whole" family (AV, NIV), as in 2:21, but in this phrase it seems more appropriate to accept the normal grammatical usage meaning "every" family (RV, ASV, RSV, NASB, NEB, TEV, JB, NJB, NRSV).[1]

Paul further qualifies this by saying that every family in heaven and on earth is named (ἐν οὐρανοῖς καὶ ἐπὶ γῆς ὀνομάζεται). It is difficult to know exactly what he means by this statement. As mentioned above, there is a play on words, for Paul prays before or to πατέρα out of whom every πατριά is named. Basically, Paul seems to be saying that God the Father names every family in heaven and on earth. This began when God named Adam the son of God (Luke 3:38). However, God usually does it through the human father who names his own children, as Abram named Ishmael (Gen 16:15) and Isaac (21:3), Jacob named Benjamin (35:18),[2] and David named Solomon (2 Sam 12:24). At times, God tells the father what he should name his children, as he told Isaiah to name his child Maher-shalal-hash-baz (Isa 8:3); Hosea to name his children Jezreel, Lo-ruhamah, and Lo-ammi (Hos 1:4, 6, 9); Zacharias to name his son John [the Baptist] (Luke 1:13, 59–63); and Joseph to name God's Son Jesus (Matt 1:21, 25). In the rabbinic tradition the son is always identified with the father, for example, "Joseph ben/bar [son of] Simeon" indicating the importance of the father's place in the lineage and probably his role in naming the children. The present tense of the verb would seem to indicate that God is still naming every family because he is still creating them. Thus, every family, whether in heaven or on the earth, has its origin in God as creator. Because of the context, some restrict the "family" only to the redeemed,[3] and those of the family in heaven may refer to departed Christians.[4] However, in keeping with the preceding context (v. 10), it more likely has reference to the angelic beings.[5] Furthermore, God is called the Father of spirits (Heb 12:9) and Father of lights (Jas 1:17), which probably have reference to the angelic realm. This concept of heaven and earth is similar to Eph 1:10 where it states that Christ will head up all things in heaven and on earth. In the present context the heavenly families are linked to the earthly families in their common dependence on the Father.[6] Schnackenburg thinks it

1. Robertson, *Grammar*, 772; Moule, *Idiom Book*, 94, 95; Winer, *Grammar*, 137–38; Johnston, "The Use of Πᾶς in the New Testament," 158–59.

2. All the rest of Jacob's children are named by his wives (Gen 29:32, 33, 34, 35; 30:6, 8, 11, 13, 18, 20, 21, 24; 35:18).

3. Hodge, 180; Mitton, 131–32; Mauerhofer, "Der Brief an die Epheser. 30. Teil: Kap. 3,14–15," 35–36.

4. Mitton, 132.

5. Alford, 3:109; Ellicott, 68; Salmond, 312; Gaugler, 151; Barth, 381; Lincoln, 202.

6. Harris, "'The Heavenlies' Reconsidered," 80.

has reference only to good angels.[1] This view, however, is unacceptable for three reasons: (1) no such limitation is in the text, (2) the text specifically identifies "every" family and not some or certain families, and (3) it would appear inconsistent to exclude evil angels and yet include all humans.

To summarize, God the Father is the one who creates (3:9) and thus names every family in heaven and on earth. He is a God who is alive and acting in the present time, rather than a god who has died and is no longer active in history. God's ability to create and name every family in heaven and on earth stresses his sovereignty and his fatherhood. He is the one who is able to perform more than we ask or think, as expressed in the doxology in verses 20–21. It should be noted that the early disciples of Jesus extolled God as the sovereign Lord who created heaven, earth, and sea (Acts 4:24). It is to this sovereign God that Paul prays the following prayer.

2. The Appeal in Prayer (3:16–19)

Having described to whom he prays, Paul next expresses his one request. This portion can be divided into two parts: petition (3:16–17a) and purpose (3:17b–19). It can be laid out as follows:

Request: ἵνα δῷ . . . κραταιωθῆναι . . . ἔσω ἄνθρωπον (3:16)
  Result: κατοικῆσαι τὸν Χριστὸν . . . ἐν ταῖς καρδίαις ὑμῶν (3:17)
    Purpose: ἵνα ἐξισχύσητε καταλαβέσθαι (3:18)
      Result: γνῶναί τε . . . ἀγάπην τοῦ Χριστοῦ (3:19a)
        Purpose: ἵνα πληρωθῆτε εἰς πᾶν τὸ πλήρωμα τοῦ θεοῦ (3:19b)

Request: that he may grant you . . . to be strengthened . . . in the inner person (3:16)
  Result: so that Christ may dwell in your hearts (3:17)
    Purpose: you might be able to comprehend (3:18)
      Result: and so to know Christ's love (3:19a)
        Purpose: that you might be filled up to all the fullness of God (3:19b)

a. Petition Stated: To Be Strengthened in the Inner Person (3:16–17a)

Paul had declared that believing Jews and Gentiles are one new person in Christ (2:11—3:13). Although positionally that is true, Paul now petitions God for unity among believers who come from such different backgrounds.

1. Schnackenburg, 147.

Text: 3:16. ἵνα δῷ ὑμῖν κατὰ τὸ πλοῦτος τῆς δόξης αὐτοῦ δυνάμει κραταιωθῆναι διὰ τοῦ πνεύματος αὐτοῦ εἰς τὸν ἔσω ἄνθρωπον, **3:17a.** κατοικῆσαι τὸν Χριστὸν διὰ τῆς πίστεως ἐν ταῖς καρδίαις ὑμῶν,

Translation: 3:16. "in order that he may grant you according to the wealth of his glory to be strengthened with power through his Spirit in the inner person, **3:17a.** so that Christ may dwell in your hearts through faith,"

Commentary: 3:16. ἵνα δῷ ὑμῖν κατὰ τὸ πλοῦτος τῆς δόξης αὐτοῦ, "in order that he may grant you according to the wealth of his glory." As mentioned in 1:17 the conjunction ἵνα normally indicates purpose (cf. Rom 1:11; Eph 2:7), but sometimes it denotes result (cf. John 9:2; Gal 5:17; Rev 9:20). In the context of prayer, however, it can denote content (Matt 24:20; 26:41; 1 Cor 14:13; Eph 1:17). This is the case here.[1] In the case of prayer, it is difficult to distinguish between purpose and content. Paul prays δῷ ὑμῖν, "[God] may grant/give to you." There is a debate as to whether the verb is optative (δῴη) or subjunctive (δῷ).[2] On the whole grammarians think that this must be subjunctive because the final optative, although not quite obsolete in NT times, would be an artificial construction.[3] Except for the Atticists and much later writers (first to the third century A.D.) the final optative does not follow a present tense as it does here.[4] Therefore, Paul prays that God may give to them, the Ephesian believers, the content of the request expressed later in the sentence. Before he makes the request Paul indicates the standard of God's giving by the preposition κατά with the accusative, namely, he does not give "out of" but "according to" the wealth of his glory (κατὰ τὸ πλοῦτος τῆς δόξης αὐτοῦ). As discussed at 1:7 πλοῦτος is best translated "wealth" in order to depict singularity rather than one of many kinds of riches. Throughout this letter Paul stresses God's wealth that is poured out on the believer. As mentioned at 1:6, δόξα, "glory," conveys the idea of the reflection of the essence of one's being, the summation of all of one's attributes. The following genitive αὐτοῦ, "his," is possessive, denoting God's glory. Therefore, in this phrase Paul is looking ahead to his request of God, which he is about to articulate on behalf of the Ephesians. In essence, he asks God to grant that forthcoming request according to the wealth of his essen-

1. Moule, *Idiom Book*, 145; Burton, *Moods and Tenses* §§200, 203; Wallace, *Greek Grammar*, 475.

2. The optative (δῴη) is found in P D E 𝔐 Chrysostom Theodoret whereas the subjunctive (δῷ) is found in 𝔓[46] ℵ A B C F G; cf. *Novum Testamentum Graece*, 8th ed., ed. Constantinus Tischendorf, vol. 2 (Leipzig: Giesecke & Devrient, 1872; reprint, Graz, Austria: Akademische Druck- u. Verlagsanstalt, 1965), 680. Although there is good evidence for each, the second reading is preferred because of good characteristic manuscripts that have an early date.

3. Robertson, *Grammar*, 309, 327; cf. also MHT 1:196–97; BDF §§369 (1); 386 (3); Moulton (MHT 1:55) thinks the subjunctive seems to be "a syntactical necessity."

4. MHT 3:129.

tial being. After he has made this appeal, he then proceeds to make the request.

δυνάμει κραταιωθῆναι διὰ τοῦ πνεύματος, "to be strengthened with power through his Spirit." Two words for power are used here. The first is δύναμις, which has the meaning of "power, ability, capability of acting," denoting capacity in view of its ability as already defined in 1:19 (cf. also 1:21; 3:7). The dative is instrumental and thus translated "with power." The second word is the complementary infinitive[1] κραταιωθῆναι from κραταιόω. It is a late construction from κραταιός replacing the infrequent word κρατύνω. Outside the Bible it is found only in Philo where it means "to strengthen" by exercise.[2] In the LXX it occurs sixty-one times and in the canonical books it appears fifty-six times and translates twelve Hebrew words. Thirty times it translates חָזַק, which means "to be *or* grow firm, strong, strengthen" (1 Sam 4:9; 1 Kgs 20:22, 23*bis*, 25 [LXX 21:22, 23*bis*, 25]; Neh 6:9).[3] In the NT it is used only four times and always in the passive voice: Luke 1:80 and 2:40 state that Jesus grew and "became strong" in spirit and wisdom; in 1 Cor 16:13 Paul exhorts believers to stand firm in the faith, be courageous, "be strong"; and in the present context Paul prays that God may grant the Ephesians "to be strengthened with power or ability." The passive voice reinforces the idea that it is God who gives the strength; it is not self-endowed. Similar expressions ("to be strengthened with power") are found in the Qumran literature (1QH[a] 15:17, 19 [7:17, 19]; 20:35 [12:35]; 1QM 10:5).[4] The fact that it is God's power is further underscored by the following prepositional phrase διὰ τοῦ πνεύματος αὐτοῦ "through his Spirit." While in 1:17 the Holy Spirit bestows insight and disclosure into the knowledge of God, here the Spirit acts as agent. In this capacity God enables believers to be strengthened with his power.[5] This is not new or unusual, for already in the first prayer (1:15–23) Paul prayed that believers might know God's power that he directs toward them. Hence, it is through God's Spirit that the believer is to be strengthened with God's ability to act.

εἰς τὸν ἔσω ἄνθρωπον, "in the inner person." Paul now specifies that this was to be an inner strength as opposed to a physical strength. Some would make the preposition εἰς directional and render it "into, toward" (as in 1:19), but this does not make much sense and does not translate well.[6] Others translate it "with reference to, with re-

1. It is also categorized as an epexegetical infinitive; cf. Robertson, *Grammar*, 1086.

2. Philo *De Agricultura* 37 §160; *De Confusione Linguarum* 22 §§101, 103; cf. Wilhelm Michaelis, "κραταιόω," *TDNT* 3 (1965): 912.

3. BDB 304–5; F. Hesse, "חָזַק *chāzaq*, etc.," *TDOT* 4 (1980): 301–8.

4. Kuhn, "Ephesians in the Light of the Qumran Texts," 117–18.

5. Arnold, *Ephesians: Power and Magic*, 88.

6. Alford, 3:109; Eadie, 244; Ellicott, 69; Abbott, 95; Salmond, 313; Barth, 369–70, 391.

spect to," which makes it distinctive from ἐν (JB, NJB).[1] Possibly it could have the sense "to do something for someone."[2] However, in this context it seems best to understand it as static, having a sense of locale like ἐν. Thus it would be translated "in" (AV, RV, ASV, RSV, NASB, NEB, TEV, NIV, NRSV).[3]

The adverb ἔσω, "inner," occurs nine times in the NT. Six times it is used as "inside" a building, such as when Peter was "inside" the courtyard of the high priest (Matt 26:58; Mark 14:54), when Jesus was brought "into" the palace (Mark 15:16), when the disciples were inside the room at the time that Jesus appeared to Thomas (John 20:26), when the guards of the jail reported that the apostles were not "inside" the jail (Acts 5:23), and when Paul exhorted the Corinthians to judge those "inside" the church (1 Cor 5:12). The other three times Paul uses "inner" with reference to a person (ὁ ἔσω ἄνθρωπος), an adjectival use of the adverb.[4] In Rom 7:22 Paul refers to the law of God as being in the "inner" person which is also called "my mind" and is the opposite of the law of sin in the flesh (vv. 23, 25).[5] In fact, later in Rom 12:2 Paul uses the term to exhort believers to be transformed by the renewing of the "mind." In 2 Cor 4:16 Paul speaks of our "inner" person being renewed day by day while our "outer" person (only time for ἔξω ἡμῶν ἄνθρωπος) is perishing.[6] Hence, the inner person is the heart or mind of the believer whereas the outer person is the physical body that is wasting away.[7] In the present context it is the innermost being of the believer which is to be strengthened with God's power. That innermost being corresponds with the heart of the believer in the following verse.[8] It does not, as Barth suggests, refer to Jesus Christ himself[9] or to the "new" person mentioned in 2:15 but rather to the innermost part of individual believers. This inner person is the object of God's working.[10] Both in Rom 7 and 2 Cor 4 Paul depicts the believer as helpless without God's power. This corresponds with the present context where it speaks of the inner person's need to be

1. Meyer, 178; Winer, *Grammar*, 496, 520; Zerwick, *Biblical Greek* §110.

2. BDF §206 (3).

3. Robertson, *Grammar*, 591–93; MHT 3:256; cf. BDF §205.

4. Robertson, *Grammar*, 766.

5. Gaugler, 152.

6. Erich Mauerhofer, "Der Brief an die Epheser. 31. Teil: Kap. 3,16," *Fundamentum* 3 (1997): 18.

7. Jewett, *Paul's Anthropological Terms*, 460; Hans Dieter Betz, "The Concept of the 'Inner Human Being' (ὁ ἔσω ἄνθρωπος) in the Anthropology of Paul," *NTS* 46 (July 2000): 315–41. Betz does not deal with Eph 3:16, probably because he does not accept Pauline authorship of this letter. Both Jewett (391–401) and Betz (317–24) have good discussions of the history of research regarding the "inner person."

8. Gundry, Sōma *in Biblical Theology*, 137.

9. Barth, 392.

10. Johannes Behm, "ἔσω," *TDNT* 2 (1964): 699; cf. Hui, "The Concept of the Holy Spirit in Ephesians," 107–10.

strengthened with power through God's Spirit. In summary then, Paul prays that the Father from whom every family originates and by whom each is named would grant strength to the believers in Ephesus (according to the wealth of his essential being) with active power through the Holy Spirit in the inner person. The following words explain the important reason for making such a request.

3:17a. κατοικῆσαι τὸν Χριστὸν διὰ τῆς πίστεως ἐν ταῖς καρδίαις ὑμῶν, "so that Christ may dwell in your hearts through faith." The infinitive κατοικῆσαι is from κατοικέω, which is composed of οικέω, meaning "to live, dwell"[1] or "to take up one's abode," and κατά, which when used in regard to place means "down"; hence, the word means "to dwell, reside, live, inhabit, colonize, settle down."[2] In the LXX it occurs 643 times and in the canonical books it appears 583 times. It translates fourteen Hebrew words, but nearly 500 times it translates יָשַׁב, meaning "to sit, remain, dwell" (Gen 11:2, 31; 13:12; 2 Sam 7:5, 6; 1 Kgs 8:27).[3] In the NT it is used forty-four times, mainly in Acts and Revelation and only three times by Paul (Eph 3:17; Col 1:19; 2:9). It is used intransitively, meaning "to dwell, reside, settle (down)" (Matt 2:23; 4:13; Acts 1:20 [quoting Ps 69:25 (MT 69:26, LXX 68:26)]; 2:5; 7:2, 4, 48); and transitively, meaning "to inhabit" (Acts 1:19; 2:14; 4:16).[4] In the present context it is used intransitively, meaning "to dwell, settle down." It seems that κατοικέω is a little more intensive than οικέω, although the latter also frequently translates יָשַׁב in the LXX. However, Paul normally uses οικέω (Rom 7:17, 18, 20; 8:9, 11; 1 Cor 3:16; 7:12, 13; 1 Tim 6:16) or ἐνοικέω (Rom 8:11; 2 Cor 6:16; Col 3:16; 2 Tim 1:5, 14) to express the idea of dwelling (neither term is used elsewhere in the NT). Thus κατοικέω connotes a settled dwelling, as opposed to παροικέω, a temporary sojourn (Luke 24:18; Heb 11:9).[5] This permanence of dwelling is seen in the two other occasions that Paul uses the term where he states that all of the fullness of God's deity dwells in Christ (Col 1:19; 2:9). Here in Ephesians Christ[6] is the one who dwells in the believer.

Before further consideration of the implications of Christ's indwelling, we need to look at the syntactical relationship of κατοικῆσαι to the rest of the sentence. There are three views.[7] First, some consider κατοικῆσαι to be parallel with κραταιωθῆναι with both dependent on ἵνα δῷ in verse 16—"that he may grant you to be strengthened in the inner person and that Christ may dwell in your hearts."[8] This view has three

1. Homer *Ilias* 14.116; Herodotus 1.56.
2. Sophocles *Philoctetes* 40; Herodotus 7.164.
3. BDB 442–43; Görg, *TDOT* 6 (1990): 424–29.
4. Otto Michel, "κατοικέω," *TDNT* 5 (1967): 153; BAGD 424; BDAG 534.
5. Spicq, *Agape in the New Testament*, 2:258–59.
6. Christ is the nominative *ad sensum* (MHT 3:230).
7. Robertson, *Grammar*, 1086, 1087, 1090.
8. Abbott, 96; Westcott, 51; Dibelius-Greeven, 77; Masson, 180; Gaugler, 154; Gnilka, 184; Bruce, 326–27; Lincoln, 197, 206; Best, 341; O'Brien, 258 n. 151.

problems: (1) there is no coordinating conjunction to indicate the parallelism of κατοικῆσαι with κραταιωθῆναι, (2) it must reach a long way back to ἵνα δῷ, and (3) there is no progress of thought. Furthermore, would Paul pray for Christ to dwell in the heart of believers? The second view is that κατοικῆσαι serves as an epexegetical infinitive to κραταιωθῆναι—"that he may grant you to be strengthened in the inner person, namely, that Christ may dwell in your hearts."[1] This is possible, although as with the first alternative it has to reach way back to ἵνα δῷ. Again, would Paul pray for Christ to dwell in believers' hearts? The third alternative is that it is a contemplative result of the previous infinitive κραταιωθῆναι—"that he may grant you to be strengthened in the inner person so that, being strengthened, Christ may dwell in your hearts."[2] This is the better view because it does not have to reach all the way back to ἵνα δῷ, for it is not a contemplative result of ἵνα but of the complementary infinitive κραταιωθῆναι. Also, this allows for progress in the prayer for the believer to be strengthened with the result that Christ may dwell in his heart. This differs from the second view in that it does not explain the previous infinitive but shows the result of receiving strength. Thus, it can be translated, "that he may grant you to be strengthened in the inner person so Christ may dwell in your hearts."

The strengthening in the inner person results in the deep indwelling of Christ by means of faith (διὰ τῆς πίστεως, see the use of this phrase in 2:8) and this takes place in the hearts of believers (ἐν ταῖς καρδίαις ὑμῶν). This demonstrates both the work of God's Spirit in strengthening the believer and the subjective means by which the believer obtains this.[3] However, it is not a reference to Christ's indwelling at the moment of salvation (Rom 8:10; 2 Cor 13:3, 5; Gal 2:20; cf. Col 1:27). Instead, it denotes the contemplated result, namely, that Christ may "be at home in," that is, at the very center of or deeply rooted in believers' lives.[4] Christ must become the controlling factor in attitudes and conduct. The "heart" (cf. 1:18 for a study of "heart") is the core of a person and is synonymous with the "inner person" in verse 16. On the positive side, the heart is the center of a person where there is enlightenment (1:18), integrity of worship (5:19), and motivation for obedience (6:5). On the negative side, hardness of

1. Meyer, 180; Schlier, 169; Schnackenburg, 149; Fee, *God's Empowering Presence*, 696.

2. Alford, 3:110; Eadie, 246–47; Ellicott, 70; Salmond, 314; Barth, 369–70.

3. Ellicott, 70.

4. Erich Mauerhofer, "Der Brief an die Epheser. 32. Teil: Kap. 3,17a," *Fundamentum* 19, no. 1 (1998): 23–24; Scaria Mattam, "Eph 3:17: A Study of the Indwelling of Christ in St. Paul," *Bible Bhashyam* 6 (March 1980): 136–37. Barcley thinks that the expression "Christ in you" in Col 1:27 is only a variation of "that Christ may dwell in your hearts" in Eph 3:17 (Barcley, *"Christ in You": A Study in Paul's Theology and Ethics*, 22). As mentioned above there is a difference of meaning between these two passages.

heart characterizes one who is alienated from the life of God (4:18). This very center of a person is to be strenghtened by the Holy Spirit, resulting in the deep indwelling of Christ in one's heart by faith. Hence, here in Ephesians the indwelling involves the individual believer as opposed to the corporate indwelling mentioned in 2:21–22.

Interestingly, once again, as elsewhere in Ephesians (cf. 1:4–14, 17; 2:18, 22; 3:4–5, 14–17; 4:4–6; 5:18–20), Paul includes the Trinity: the Father (v. 14), the Spirit (v. 16), and the Son (v. 17). All three persons of the Trinity are very involved in the redemption and growth of believers. Here Paul prays to the Father that they be strengthened by the Spirit with the result that Christ be deeply rooted in the lives of the believers through faith.

b. Purpose Stated: To Comprehend Christ's Love and to Be Filled with God's Fullness (3:17b–19)

Having stated the petition, Paul now gives the reason for the prayer: he wants the Ephesians to understand Christ's love and consequently have a deep love for one another.

Text: 3:17b. ἐν ἀγάπῃ ἐρριζωμένοι καὶ τεθεμελιωμένοι, **3:18.** ἵνα ἐξισχύσητε καταλαβέσθαι σύν πᾶσιν τοῖς ἁγίοις τί.τὸ πλάτος καὶ μῆκος καὶ ὕψος καὶ βάθος, **3:19.** γνῶναί τε τὴν ὑπερβάλλουσαν τῆς γνώσεως ἀγάπην τοῦ Χριστοῦ, ἵνα πληρωθῆτε εἰς πᾶν τὸ πλήρωμα τοῦ θεοῦ.

Translation: 3:17b. "in order that you, being rooted and grounded in love, **3:18.** might be able to comprehend with all the saints what is the breadth and length and height and depth, **3:19.** and so to know the love of Christ which surpasses knowledge, in order that you might be filled up to all the fullness of God."

Commentary: 3:17b. ἐν ἀγάπῃ ἐρριζωμένοι καὶ τεθεμελιωμένοι, "[in order that you,] being rooted and grounded in love." Two items warrant discussion: (1) to whose love does it refer; and (2) what is the syntactical relationship of the participles to the context? The word "love" (ἀγάπη) was discussed at 1:4 (cf. also 1:15; 2:4) where we concluded that this word for love seeks the highest good in the one loved. The noun, being anarthrous, is common among abstract nouns,[1] especially when it occurs after a preposition. The absence of a defining genitive makes it difficult to delineate to whose love it refers. There are three views regarding this. First, some of the early fathers thought it referred to Christ's love.[2] Second, some think it refers to God's love[3] or God's love in Christ.[4] The problem with both of these views is that they do not have a defining genitive—Χριστοῦ, θεοῦ, or αὐτοῦ. Third, most think it

1. BDF §258; MHT 3:176–77.
2. Chrysostom *Eph* 3:18–19 (*PG* 62:51); Theophylact *Eph* 3:16–17 (*PG* 124:1076).
3. Schnackenburg, 150; Best, 343; O'Brien, 260.
4. Calvin, 168; Gaugler, 155; Bruce, 327.

has reference to the believer's love, or as some label it, "the grace of love."[1] This makes reasonably good sense because of the lack of a defining genitive and because the next verse mentions love with the defining genitive (ἀγάπην τοῦ Χριστοῦ). This appears to clarify that these two verses are speaking about two different aspects of love. Having said this, it must be realized that, even after salvation, this grace of love does not have its source in human beings, but in God.[2] Christian love always has its source in God's love. The believers' experience of God's love is discussed in chapter 1 and now they are to exhibit this love. Believers' love is mentioned often in this epistle (cf. 1:4, 15; 4:2, 15, 16; 5:2; 6:24).[3]

Regarding the syntactical relationship of the two participles, there are four views. First, some view them as the third request in the prayer, seeing them as substitutes for optatives[4] (TEV)—"that you might be strengthened . . . that Christ might dwell in your hearts . . . that you might be rooted and grounded in love." But this structure is an abnormal way to express it. Second, some think they are imperatives[5]—"be rooted and grounded in love." However, imperatives occurring in the middle of Paul's prayer request are unlikely. Third, others who label them as irregular nominatives consider them a result of the preceding clause—"the result of Christ's dwelling in your hearts is that you are rooted and grounded in love" (NRSV).[6] The perfect tense would argue against this, for it does not describe the condition into which believers are coming. Rather their condition is already assumed. Fourth, some consider them joined to the following ἵνα clause[7]—"having been rooted and grounded (causal participles [?])[8] in love in order that you might be able to comprehend with all the saints" (AV, RV, ASV, RSV, NASB, NEB, JB, NIV, NJB). This view fits best here. There are other examples of this kind of construction in the NT (Rom 11:31; 1 Cor 9:15; 2 Cor 2:4; Gal 2:10; John 13:29; Acts 19:4).[9] Also, the perfect

1. Alford, 3:110; Eadie, 249; Ellicott, 71; Meyer, 182; Abbott, 98; Salmond, 314; Robinson, 85; Westcott, 52; Masson, 181; Gnilka, 185; Mitton, 133; Lincoln, 207; Caragounis, *Ephesian* Mysterion, 75 n. 89.

2. Barth, 371.

3. Lincoln, 207.

4. Dibelius-Greeven, 77; Gaugler, 155; Gnilka, 185; Schnackenburg, 149; Lincoln, 197; MHT 1:182; Arnold, *Ephesians: Power and Magic*, 98.

5. Schlier, 170; Barth, 371; cf. also Porter, *Verbal Aspect*, 377. Barth argues that participles can be imperatives (371 n. 23). There is no problem with this but it does not fit in this context. Wallace questions that these participles are imperatives (*Greek Grammar*, 652).

6. Alford, 3:110; Eadie, 248–49; Ellicott, 70; Abbott, 96–97; Salmond, 315; Mitton, 133; Bruce, 327; Caragounis, *Ephesian* Mysterion, 75.

7. Meyer, 180; Westcott, 51–52; Masson, 181; Hendriksen, 172 n. 95; Best, 342; O'Brien, 259–60; BDF §468 (2); Winer, *Grammar*, 715.

8. Wallace, *Greek Grammar*, 631 n. 47.

9. Some commentators (cf. Alford, 3:110; Ellicott, 70–71; Abbott, 97; Salmond, 315) do not think these passages are applicable, but they do not state the rationale for their

tense, which emphasizes the resulting state,[1] makes good sense, for it assumes that they are rooted and grounded for the purpose of having the ability to comprehend the love of Christ which is mentioned next. Furthermore, the nominative case of these participles fits well with the subject of the following verb, namely, "that you, being rooted and grounded in love, might be able to comprehend with all the saints. . . ." Otherwise, there would be syntactical difficulty because the participles are not in agreement with any of the preceding words. Finally, this syntactical relationship is similar to 1:18, albeit the perfect participle is an accusative absolute. Hence, before Paul begins his new clause, he states that they have been rooted and grounded in love; on that basis he makes a further claim for them.

The two metaphors here express the same idea by different figures; one is from agriculture and the other from architecture. The first participle is from ῥιζόω, which has the idea "to cause to root" with the passive sense "to become firmly rooted."[2] It appears only five times in the LXX (Isa 40:24; Jer 12:2; Sir 3:28; 24:12; *Pss. Sol.* 14:4) with the same meaning "to take root." It occurs only twice in the NT (Col 2:7; Eph 3:17), both of which refer to the personal roots of believers.[3] The second participle is from θεμελιόω, meaning "to found, lay the foundation of"[4] a building. It appears forty-one times in the LXX (thirty-seven times in the canonical books) meaning "to lay the foundation" (Josh 6:26; 1 Kgs 7:47; 16:34; 2 Chr 8:16) or "to found, establish" (Pss 24:2 [LXX 23:2]; 78:69 [LXX 77:69]; 119:152 [LXX 118:152]; Prov 3:19; Isa 14:32). Twenty-seven times it translates יָסַד, meaning "to establish, found, lay the foundation."[5] Paul uses the same two basic figures in Col 2:7, being rooted and built up in Christ. In 1 Cor 3:9 he summarizes his argument with figures of a farmer and builder where both illustrate that one receives rewards on the basis of good works. In the present context Paul states that believers are firmly rooted and grounded in love. This root and foundation of love refers to God having chosen them, predestined them, bestowed them in the beloved, redeemed them, made them a heritage, sealed them with the Holy Spirit, made them alive, raised and seated them in the heavenlies, and placed them equally in one new person in the body of Christ. Therefore, for the believer, the origin of this love is God's love. Having established this root and foundation, Paul makes his next appeal.

3:18. ἵνα ἐξισχύσητε καταλαβέσθαι σὺν πᾶσιν τοῖς ἁγίοις, "in order that you [being rooted and grounded in love] might be able to

---

evaluation. In looking at these passages it must be admitted that none of them have two participles but in principle they parallel what we have here. Therefore, it seems likely that Paul meant these two participles to be connected with the following clause.

1. Fanning, *Verbal Aspect*, 416–18.

2. Homer *Odyssea* 13.163; 7.122; Xenophon *Oeconomicus* 19.9; Herodotus 1.64.

3. Cf. Christian Maurer, "ῥιζόω," *TDNT* 6 (1968): 990.

4. BAGD 356; BDAG 449.

5. BDB 413–14; R. Mosis, "יָסַד *yāsad*, etc.," *TDOT* 6 (1990): 109–11, 114–20.

comprehend with all the saints." The finite verb ἐξισχύω is a rare word meaning "to have strength enough, be able," as the ability to restrain the forces of nature[1] or the ability to influence someone.[2] The word appears once in the LXX (Sir 7:6 [Codex B]) with the same meaning, "to be able," and occurs only here in the NT. The aorist middle infinitive καταλαβέσθαι comes from καταλαμβάνω, which means in the active and passive sense "to seize, lay hold of,"[3] and in the middle means "to grasp, understand, comprehend" mentally.[4] In the LXX this term occurs 123 times and in the canonical books it appears seventy-five times where it translates eighteen Hebrew words, forty-four times for either לָכַד, meaning "to capture, seize, take" (Num 21:32; Josh 8:19; 19:47 [LXX 19:48]; 2 Sam 12:26, 27, 29),[5] or the Hiphil of נָשַׂג, meaning "to reach, overtake" (Gen 31:25; 44:4; Deut 19:6; 1 Sam 30:8*ter*; 2 Kgs 25:5; Isa 59:9).[6] In the NT it occurs fifteen times and seven times in Paul (Rom 9:30; 1 Cor 9:24; Eph 3:18; Phil 3:12*bis*, 13; 1 Thess 5:4) and is defined primarily as "to seize, overtake" (Mark 9:18; John 12:35; 1 Cor 9:24; Phil 3:12*bis*, 13) but also "to grasp, comprehend, understand" mentally (John 1:5; Acts 4:13; 10:34; 25:25; Eph 3:18).[7] This sense of the term fits best in this context.

At this point a summarization may be helpful. First, the infinitive καταλαβέσθαι is complementary to the aorist subjunctive ἐξισχύσητε just as in verse 16 the infinitive κραταιωθῆναι complements the aorist subjunctive δῷ. In this context the subjunctive with the complementary infinitive gives a perfective force "to 'be strong enough' to apprehend, a strength exerted till its object is attained."[8] Second, it is best to consider that ἵνα in the present verse relates back to the infinitive of result in verse 17, thus introducing the purpose for it. It is not parallel with the one in verse 16 because there is no coordinating conjunction between them to indicate any sort of parallelism.[9] Furthermore, the conjunction ἵνα in verse 16 denotes content and the one here denotes purpose. In other words, "that God may grant you to be strengthened in the inner person with the result that Christ may dwell in your hearts *in order that* you, having been rooted and grounded in love, might be able to comprehend" with all the saints (σύν πᾶσιν τοῖς ἁγίοις) the truth presented in

1. Strabo 17.1.3.

2. Josephus *B.J.* 1.23.2 §451.

3. Herodotus 6.39; Thucydides 1.126.5.

4. Dionysius Halicarnassensis 2.66.6; Josephus *A.J.* 8.6.5 §167; Philo *Mos.* 1.50 §278.

5. BDB 539–40; *HALOT* 2 (1995): 530; Gross, *TDOT* 8 (1997): 1–4.

6. BDB 673; cf. J. Hausmann, "נָשַׂג *nāśag*," *TDOT* 10 (1999): 40–44.

7. For a thorough discussion of comprehension and the content of what is comprehended (in vv. 18–19) in light of Gnostic interpretations, see Jacques Dupont, *«Gnosis», la connaissance religieuse dans les épîtres de saint Paul*, Universitas Lovaniensis: Dissertationes ad gradum magistri in Facultate Theologica consequendum conscriptae, ser. 2, vol. 40 (Louvain: E. Nauwelaerts; Paris: Gabalda, 1949), 493–528.

8. MHT 2:310.

9. *Contra* Arnold, *Ephesians: Power and Magic*, 86, 89, 94, 98.

verse 19. Here, as earlier (1:1, 4, 13, 15, 18; 2:19, 21; 3:8), the ἅγιοι, "saints," refers to believers and not angels. Growth in the individual believer cannot occur in isolation but must be accomplished in context with other believers. Furthermore, true growth cannot occur by association with only certain believers, ones preferred because they are of the same socioeconomic, intellectual, or professional status. Paul prays that it might be accomplished in association with *all* the saints.

τί τὸ πλάτος καὶ μῆκος καὶ ὕψος καὶ βάθος,[1] "what is the breadth and length and height and depth." The indirect question introduced with τί expresses the object of what is to be comprehended. The one article (τό) with the four words indicates that, although they are distinct, they are to be treated as one.[2] The four words, expressing measurement, have generated many unusual interpretations.[3] For example, Bengel thinks they refer to the dimensions of the spiritual temple, the church, in connection with the fullness of God in verse 19. Hence, he interprets it the following way: "For the *breadth* of the fulness and of the love of Christ is signified, and that too in respect of all men and all peoples; and its *length*, extending through all ages, ver. 21: as also its *depth*, which no creature can fathom; and its height [*sic*], iv. 8, such as no enemy can reach."[4] Calvin rightly assesses that many of the fanciful interpretations may be subtlety pleasing but have nothing to do with the meaning.[5] Other more coherent views include the following. Some prefer to view these words as a merism where the parts (especially when opposites are expressed) signify the whole. Other principal interpretations are that these words are a mystery of grace in redemption,[6] a spiritual temple or heavenly city (Rev 21:16),[7] the shape of the cross of Christ,[8] a Gnostic idea of Christ's crucified body

1. This order of the words ὕψος καὶ βάθος appears in 𝔓[46] B C D F G I P 0278 0285 33 81 (ˢ 326) 365 1175 *pc* lat cop Origen[txt 1739mg] but is transposed in א A Ψ (1505) 1739 1881 𝔐 syr[h] (Origen) Jerome[part]. The order of the words makes no difference to the interpretation. The evidence is quite evenly divided. The first reading is preferred because it has better representation in the Alexandrian text-type than the second reading, and it is also well supported by the Western text.

2. Robertson, *Grammar*, 787; Winer, *Grammar*, 159.

3. For a discussion of the various interpretations, cf. Eadie, 251–55; Meyer, 183–84; Dupont, *«Gnosis», la connaissance religieuse dans les épîtres de saint Paul*, 476–89; Feuillet, *Le Christ sagesse de Dieu*, 292–319; Barth, 395–97; Lincoln, 208–13.

4. Bengel, 4:86; cf. F. Godet, "The Epistle to the Gentile Churches," *Exp* 3d ser., vol. 5 (November 1887): 391.

5. Calvin, 168.

6. Chrysostom *Eph* 3:18–19 (*PG* 62:51); Theodoret *Eph* 3:18 (*PG* 82:532); Theophylact *Eph* 3:18 (*PG* 124:1076); Oecumenius *Eph* 3:18–21 (*PG* 118:1209–12); Harless, 322–23; Alford, 1:111; Robinson, 86, 176; Gaugler, 156–57; Zerwick, 93; Schnackenburg, 150–52; Percy, *Probleme*, 310–11.

7. Bengel, 4:86; Eadie, 254–55; Dibelius-Greeven, 77; Schlier, 172–73; Rienecker, 123–24; Edward Spurrier, "Note on Ephesians iii.18," *ExpTim* 2 (April 1891): 164.

8. Jerome *Eph* 3:16–19 (*PL* 26:491); Augustine *Epistulae* 55.14 (25) (*PL* 33:216); 140.25 (62) (*PL* 33:564); *Sermon* 103.14 (15) (*PL* 38:371); 165.2 (2) (*PL* 38:903); *De doct-*

which fills the earth,[1] the love of God,[2] the wisdom of God,[3] the power of God,[4] and the love of Christ.[5]

Although some of the last mentioned interpretations are commendable, the last three are the most worth considering. The first interpretation, namely, the idea of the wisdom of God is seen in 3:10 where Paul speaks about the multifaceted wisdom of God in uniting Jews and Gentiles into one body. In 1 Cor 2 Paul contrasts the wisdom of humans with the wisdom of God in connection with God's power to change lives through the crucified Christ. In the OT there are numerous references to the wisdom of God (e.g., Job 11:5–9; 12:13–16; 28:12–28; 30:1–39). However, it is unikely that the immediate context is concerned with God's wisdom since his wisdom is unsearchable and inscrutable (Rom 11:33–35 cites Isa 40:13–14 and Job 41:11 [MT & LXX 41:3]). As such, how then can "all the saints" comprehend it (Eph 3:18)?

The second interpretation suggests that these words refer to God's power. Based on magical papyri,[6] Arnold suggests that it is speaking about the vastness of the power of God. He believes that, in observing the magical texts, the dimensional terminology is not spatial but

---

rina christiana 2.41 (62) (*PL* 34:64); Gerhart B. Ladner, "St. Gregory of Nyssa and St. Augustine on the Symbolism of the Cross," in *Late Classical and Mediaeval Studies in Honor of Albert Mathias Friend, Jr.*, ed. Kurt Weitzmann (Princeton: Princeton University Press, 1955), 88–95.

1. Schlier, 173–75; Conzelmann, 74; Johnston, 16; Houlden, 304–5.

2. Chrysostom *Eph* 3:18–19 (*PG* 62:51); Theodore of Mopsuestia *Eph* 3:18–19 (*PG* 66:917); Monod, 202–4; Moule, 99; David B. Capes, "Interpreting Ephesians 1–3: 'God's People in the Mystery of His Will'," *SWJT* 39 (fall 1996): 30.

3. Westcott, 52; Barth, 396–97; Bruce, 328; A. Feuillet, "L'Eglise plérôme du Christ d'après Ephés., I,23," *NRT* 78 (Juin 1956): 599–602; idem, *Le Christ sagesse de Dieu*, 298–312; Nils Alstrup Dahl, "Cosmic Dimensions and Religious Knowledge (Eph 3:18)," in *Jesus und Paulus: Festschrift für Werner Georg Kümmel zum 70. Geburtstag*, ed. E. Earle Ellis and Erich Gräßer (Göttingen: Vandenhoeck & Ruprecht, 1975), 57–75; updated in idem, *Studies in Ephesians*, 365–88.

4. Arnold, *Ephesians: Power and Magic*, 89–96.

5. Aquinas, chap. 3, lec. 5, vv. 18–21 (145–46); Calvin, 168–69; Hodge, 188–89; Meyer, 184; Abbott, 99–100; Ellicott, 72; Salmond, 315; Ewald, 175–76; Scott, 197; Masson, 182; Hendriksen, 173; Thompson, 59; Gnilka, 186–89; Caird, 70; Mitton, 134; Mußner, 111–12; Patzia, 202; Lincoln, 212–13; Stadelmann, 142; Best, 346; O'Brien, 263; Erich Mauerhofer, "Der Brief an die Epheser. 33. Teil: Kap. 3,17b–18," *Fundamentum* 19, no. 2 (1998): 23–24; Mussner, *Christus, das All and die Kirche*, 71–74; Spicq, *Agape in the New Testament*, 2:263; van Roon, *The Authenticity of Ephesians*. 262–66; Watson, "Writing the Mystery: Christ and Reality in the Letter to the Ephesians," 7–9.

6. *Papyri graecae magicae* 4.464–85; see *Papyri graecae magicae. Die griechischen Zauberpapyri*, 2d ed., trans. and ed. Karl Preisendanz; 2d rev. ed. Karl Preisendanz, Ernst Heitsch, and Albert Henrichs, Sammlung Wissenschaftlicher Commentare, ed. A. Abt et al., vol. 1 (Stuttgart: Teubner, 1973), 88–89; *The Greek Magical Papyri in Translation, including the Demotic Spells*, ed. Hans Dieter Betz (Chicago: University of Chicago Press, 1986), 47–48; Clinton E. Arnold, "Magical Papyri," in *DNTB*, 666–70.

rather refers to the dynamics of supernatural power.[1] This interpretation has much to commend it, but it does depend on magical texts from Egypt that date in the third and fourth centuries A.D. and it thus assumes that the Ephesian audience had knowledge of similar formulations in the first century. Even if they did have similar formulations, it seems unlikely that Paul would have based his prayer on these magical formulations from which the Ephesians had recently been delivered. Furthermore, nothing in this entire epistle indicates a dependence on magical formulas. Regardless, the recipients of this letter would have been familiar with dimensional terminology because, as Arnold suggests, Paul employs such words in reference to the power of God in Rom 8:39. The terms ὕψωμα (not ὕψος), "height," and βάθος, "depth," convey that nothing (whether these words refer to members of the angelic realm or to spatial distance) can separate believers from the love of Christ. Furthermore, "'height' and 'depth' are juxtaposed to 'angels,' 'principalities,' and 'powers.'"[2]

Without being dogmatic, it seems that the third interpretation is best, namely, that the four dimensions refer to the love of Christ. The context itself is about Christ who dwells deeply in believers' hearts (v. 17) and believers who are to know the love of Christ (v. 19). Verse 19 explains the parts of verse 18. The spacial dimensions fit well with the agricultural (ἐρριζωμένοι) and architectural (τεθεμελιωμένοι) figures in verse 17 where they refer to the love in which believers are rooted and grounded. Ultimately, this love is the love of Christ as Paul develops this passage. Abbott has expressed it well when he writes: "The four words seem intended to indicate, not so much the thoroughness of the comprehension as the vastness of the thing to be comprehended."[3] Furthermore, as with the previous interpretation, Rom 8:39 could be used for support because the "height" and "depth" is used in connection with the love of Christ. This love of Christ is enormous to comprehend as the next verse indicates.

3:19. γνῶναί τε τὴν ὑπερβάλλουσαν τῆς γνώσεως ἀγάπην τοῦ Χριστοῦ, "and so to know the love of Christ which surpasses knowledge." The postpositive conjunction τέ introduces this clause. Although it is nearly impossible to state explicitly the difference of meaning between it and other coordinating conjunctions, it can generally be claimed to express an internal logical relationship (whereas καί is an external relationship) and probably can be translated in this context as "and so."[4] As mentioned in 1:18, the distinction and similarities between οἶδα and γινώσκω have been much discussed and most conclude that little distinction exists. Each occurrence must be determined by its use in the context. Generally, it may be said that γινώσκω gives the

1. Arnold, *Ephesians: Power and Magic*, 90–95.

2. Ibid., 94.

3. Abbott, 99.

4. BDF §443 (3); Moule, *Idiom Book*, 197; BAGD 807; BDAG 993.

sense of acquiring knowledge[1] and indeed, in this context it has the idea of acquiring theological[2] but, more particularly, experiential knowledge. The aorist infinitive most likely expresses result.

There is a parallelism in Paul's request (for a structural layout of the prayer, see 3:16). The first part has the ἵνα of content followed by the aorist subjunctive δῷ. This is followed by the complementary infinitive κραταιωθῆναι, which is followed by the infinitive of result κατοικῆσαι. The second part has the ἵνα of purpose followed by the aorist subjunctive ἐξισχύσητε. This is followed by the complementary infinitive καταλαβέσθαι, which is followed by the infinitive of result γνῶναι.

The object of the knowledge is τὴν ἀγάπην . . . τοῦ Χριστοῦ, "the love . . . of Christ." As mentioned in verse 18 the word "love" (ἀγάπη) was discussed at 1:4 (cf. also 1:15; 2:4; 3:18) where we concluded that this kind of love means seeking the highest good in the one loved. In that verse the abstract noun was anarthrous, but here the article is given in order to introduce the participial clause (τὴν ὑπερβάλλουσαν τῆς γνώσεως). The genitive τοῦ Χριστοῦ cannot be objective, meaning "our love to Christ," because of the participial clause which states that love surpasses knowledge.[3] Rather, it is a subjective genitive, meaning "Christ's love to us," or possessive genitive, "Christ's love."

Paul further describes the love of Christ by the participial clause τὴν ὑπερβάλλουσαν τῆς γνώσεως, "which surpasses knowledge." The participle ὑπερβάλλουσαν from ὑπερβάλλω means "to throw beyond" and is used only by Paul in the NT (2 Cor 3:10; 9:14; Eph 1:19; 2:7; 3:19). It can be translated "surpassing, extraordinary, exceeding."[4] Following the participle is a genitive of comparison (τῆς γνώσεως).[5] The repetition of the same idea but with the contrasting senses of γνῶναι and γνώσεως has caused some discussion.[6] It could be that the distinction is between religious experience and theoretical knowledge[7] or that it is between the knowledge that is rooted and grounded in love and mere knowledge.[8] However, it seems simplest to consider that to comprehend the love of Christ is beyond the capability of any human being. The very fact that Christ's love expressed itself in his willingness to die on behalf of sinners is in itself beyond one's comprehension. The reality of Christ's love is overwhelming to all believers, from the point of conversion and continuing as growth in the knowledge of Christ progresses. No matter how much knowledge we have of Christ and his work, his love surpasses that knowledge. The more we know of his

1. Erickson, "*Oida* and *Ginōskō* and Verbal Aspect in Pauline Usage," 121.
2. Bultmann, *TDNT* 1 (1964): 718.
3. Salmond, 316.
4. BAGD 840; BDAG 1032; Delling, *TDNT* 8 (1972): 520–21.
5. Robertson, *Grammar*, 519.
6. Howard (MHT 2:419) lists these words as tautology.
7. Ellicott, 73.
8. Alford, 3:111.

love, the more we are amazed by it. Paul is not denegrating knowledge, for it is greatly emphasized in this epistle (1:9, 17, 18; 3:3–5, 9; 4:13; 5:17). He even requests it in this very prayer (vv. 18, 19a), but here he wishes to stress Christ's love as that which is beyond human comprehension.[1]

ἵνα πληρωθῆτε εἰς πᾶν τὸ πλήρωμα τοῦ θεοῦ,[2] "in order that you might be filled up to all the fullness of God." The ἵνα is not parallel with either the ἵνα in verse 16 or the ἵνα in verse 18 because no coordinating conjunction(s) indicate(s) this. Rather the ἵνα here introduces the final purpose of the prayer that believers might be able to comprehend the love of Christ "in order that they might be filled up to all the fullness of God." This ἵνα clause is the summation of the two previous ἵνα clauses (vv. 16, 18).

The aorist passive subjunctive verb πληρωθῆτε is from πληρόω. The word was discussed at Eph 1:23 (cf. also 4:10; 3:19; 5:18) where it was concluded that the passive should be translated as "to be filled." The noun πλήρωμα occurs four times in Ephesians (1:10, 23; 3:19; 4:13) and was discussed in Excursus 5: A Study of πλήρωμα. In this study it was concluded that in all NT usage, it maintains the idea of the result of filling as fullness, completeness, entirety. It was observed that when it was used with the corresponding verb (πληρόω), as here, it normally has the idea of "completeness, the absence of any lacunae." The noun can be taken actively as "that which fills" or passively as "that which is filled," and in the present context the passive makes the most sense, hence, "you might be filled with fullness."

The genitive that follows (τοῦ θεοῦ) is possessive. The preposition εἰς indicates movement toward a goal[3] and thus could be translated "up to the level of" or "to the measure of" (NIV) or "filled unto" (RV, ASV) or, as we have translated it, "filled up to" (NASB). This implies that believers will never be filled as God is filled but should move toward that goal. The πᾶν with the article is rendered "all" and thus can be translated "filled up to all the fullness of God." In 1:23 we concluded that the church was being filled with God's moral excellence and power. In the present context to be filled up to God's fullness is to

1. Lincoln, 213.

2. There are three readings. First, the reading πληρωθῆτε εἰς πᾶν τὸ πλήρωμα τοῦ θεοῦ is found in ℵ A C D F G Ψ 075 0150 6 (81 πληροφορηθῆτε) 104 256 263 365 424 436 459 1241 1573 1739 1852 1912 1962 2127 2200 2464 *Byz* [K L P] *Lect* (*l* 593) it^b, d, f, g^ vg syr^p, h, pal^ cop^bo^ arm (eth) geo slav^mss^ Athanasius Marcellus Gregory-Nyssa Macarius/Symeon^2/3^ (Chrysostom) Severian Theodore^lat^ Cyril Victorinus-Rome Ambrosiaster Hilary Ambrose Jerome Pelagius. The second reading πληρωθῆτε εἰς πᾶν τὸ πλήρωμα τοῦ Χριστοῦ appears in 1881 *l* 921 it^ar, o^ (vg^ms^) Macarius/Symeon^1/3^. The third reading πληρωθῇ πᾶν τὸ πλήρωμα τοῦ θεοῦ is found in 𝔓^46^ B 0278 (33 *add* εἰς ὑμᾶς *after* θεοῦ) 462 1175 *l* 596 cop^sa^ slav^ms^. The first reading has overwhelming support from all the text-types. The second reading's support is marginal and the third reading has only a few Alexandrian manuscripts. The last two readings are not strong enough to invalidate the first reading.

3. Winer, *Grammar*, 272; BAGD 229; BDAG 289–90.

know the love of Christ. The fullness of the Godhead is only in Christ, and only through him is a believer made complete (Col 2:9–10). Though in Christ this divine fullness ideally belongs to a believer, Paul prayed that it might be experientially realized in each one (cf. Eph 4:13). Experiencing God's moral excellence, perfection, and power would result in love between Jewish and Gentile believers. Positionally they are one in Christ (2:11–3:13), experientially they are to love one another as one in him. Then Jesus' statement that "all people will know that we are his disciples if we love one another" (John 13:35) will ring true among the unconverted in the community. Before redemption real animosity existed between Jews and Gentiles and between these two groups and God. God's redemptive work through his Son transformed them into his workmanship (Eph 2:1–10). God then took these redeemed Jews and Gentiles and made them into one body, creating a new person encompassing reconciliation between the two groups as well as a collective reconciliation to God (2:11–3:13). In other words, theologically the two former enemies are now one in Christ. However, more is involved than a theological reconciliation. There must be experiential reconciliation. Hence, Paul's prayer in this context is that they may know the love of Christ and in knowing this they might be filled with God's moral excellence, perfection, and power. It is, then, a combination of God's righteousness and God's love that must be experienced by believers. This prayer paves the way for the practical outworking of their position in Christ, which is outlined in chapters 4–6 of this letter.

Briefly, Paul's prayer for the Ephesians is that God would strengthen them in the inner person, resulting in Christ effectively dwelling in them for the purpose that they, having been rooted and grounded in love, might be able to comprehend with all the saints the wonders of Christ's love, resulting in their experiential knowledge of Christ's love that surpasses all knowledge for the final purpose of being filled up with God's moral character which reflects God's character.

Paul's first prayer for the Ephesians (1:15–23) was offered in order that they might know God and his power. His second prayer, in the present context, is a plea for them to comprehend Christ's love which, in turn, would cause them to love their fellow saints. This prayer is the climax of his discussion on the unification of Jews and Gentiles in Christ, thus, becoming one new person. Paul desired that what was true positionally would be true experientally in the lives of the Ephesian believers. This experiential knowledge of Christ's love is not only for individual believers but it is to be applied to the corporate unity. Unity of Jewish and Gentile believers is evidence of God's power. "A divided church, instead of being a sign of God's conquering power in Christ, reflects the negative message of a victory by the forces of evil."[1] The body of believers is to experience Christ's love.

1. Roberts, "The Enigma of Ephesians," 104.

3. The Ascription of Praise (3:20–21)

Paul ends his prayer with a doxology.[1] This doxology is a very fitting conclusion not only to the prayer but also to the previous section in which the mystery was unveiled (2:11–3:13) and indeed, to the entire first three chapters. It also serves as a transition in preparation for the last three chapters.

Text: 3:20. Τῷ δὲ δυναμένῳ ὑπὲρ πάντα ποιῆσαι ὑπερεκπερισσοῦ ὧν αἰτούμεθα ἢ νοοῦμεν κατὰ τὴν δύναμιν τὴν ἐνεργουμένην ἐν ἡμῖν, **3:21.** αὐτῷ ἡ δόξα ἐν τῇ ἐκκλησίᾳ καὶ ἐν Χριστῷ Ἰησοῦ εἰς πάσας τὰς γενεὰς τοῦ αἰῶνος τῶν αἰώνων, ἀμήν.

Translation: 3:20. "Now to him who is able to do infinitely beyond all that we ask or think according to the power that works in us, **3:21.** to him be glory in the church and in Christ Jesus to all generations, for ever and ever. Amen."

Commentary: 3:20. Τῷ δὲ δυναμένῳ ὑπὲρ[2] πάντα ποιῆσαι ὑπερεκπερισσοῦ ὧν αἰτούμεθα ἢ νοοῦμεν, "Now to him who is able to do infinitely beyond all we ask or think." In this verse one is immediately struck by the use of the words for power (δύναμαι, δύναμις, ἐνεργέω). They refer to divine power. The conjunction δέ, "now," gives an adversative force changing from the recipients of the letter to God, the one who is to be praised.[3] The one who is addressed must be God because he is the nearest referent (v. 19) and because Christ is mentioned in verse 21.[4] The present participle τῷ δυναμένῳ from δύναμαι means "to be able" or "to be capable of,"[5] and the dative form indicates the direction of the address or praise, "to the one who is able." The preposition ὑπέρ with the accusative gives "the sense of excelling, surpassing *over and above, beyond, more than*"[6] and with the anarthrous πάντα, it would literally be translated "beyond everything." Translating πάντα as "everything" encompasses every minute thing we might ask or think. Bengel suggests that ὑπέρ be used adverbially ("more than").[7] How-

1. King ("Ephesians in the Light of Form Criticism," 273–74) states that there are two main types of doxologies: (1) a type that begins with the word "blessed" as in 1:3; and (2) a type ascribing "glory" to God as in the present text.

2. The preposition ὑπέρ appears in ℵ A B C I^{vid} Ψ 075 0150 0278 0285 6 33 81 104 256 263 365 424 436 459 1175 1241 1573 1739 1852 1881 1912 1962 2127 2200 2464 *Byz* [K L P] *Lect* it$^{ar, o}$ syr$^{p, h, pal}$ cop$^{sa, bo}$ arm geo slav Chrysostom Theodore^{lat} Theodoret Victorinus-Rome Ambrosiaster Jerome Augustine$^{1/9}$ Ps-Vivilius. It is omitted from 𝔓^{46} D F G *l* 593 it$^{b, d, f, g}$ vg Pelagius Augustine$^{8/9}$. Although its omission has some Alexandrian support, its inclusion has solid Alexandrian and Byzantine support and is the preferred reading.

3. Ellicott, 74; Salmond, 317; Herbert G. Miller, "The Rendering of Δέ in the New Testament," *ExpTim* 15 (September 1904): 553.

4. Best, 349.

5. Grundmann, *TDNT* 2 (1964): 284.

6. BAGD 839; BDAG 1031; cf. Harald Riesenfeld, "ὑπέρ," *TDNT* 8 (1972): 515.

7. Bengel, 4:87.

ever, πάντα is not the object of the infinitive ποιῆσαι as he suggests, but it is the object of the preposition ὑπέρ. Thus, ὑπέρ functions as a preposition. Furthermore, if one takes ὑπέρ adverbially, it becomes redundant with the adverb ὑπερεκπερισσοῦ.[1] When used as a preposition, the resulting sense is that God "is able do beyond all that we ask or think." The adverb ὑπερεκπερισσοῦ appears three times in the NT (Eph 3:20; 1 Thess 3:10; 5:13), it is the "highest form of comparison imaginable"[2] and can be translated "exceedingly, infinitely" or "very far in excess of."[3] It would be natural to think that the relative pronoun ἅ would be used preceding αἰτούμεθα ἢ νοοῦμεν rather than the genitive plural ὧν, with πάντα as its antecedent, but its use may be due to an attraction to the genitive of comparison ὑπερεκπερισσοῦ.[4] A similar construction with αἰτέω is found in Matt 18:19. It could be literally translated "to the one who is able to do beyond everything, very far in excess of that which we ask or think" (cf. word study in 3:4). In other words, his ability far surpasses not only what we verbalize in prayer but also beyond our wildest imaginations. Earlier, Paul had prayed that they would be strengthened with power through the Spirit (v. 16) and now Paul gives praise to God for that power. Paul continues by discussing the means by which believers can appropriate this power.

κατὰ τὴν δύναμιν τὴν ἐνεργουμένην ἐν ἡμῖν, "according to the power that works in us." The preposition κατά with the accusative denotes standard. The noun δύναμις was discussed at 1:19 (cf. also 1:21; 3:7, 16) where we concluded that it means "power, ability, capability of acting"; thus, the word δύναμις refers to that power or ability that is capable for the task and is determined by what it is modified. Here it is modified by the participle τὴν ἐνεργουμένην. This participle is from ἐνεργέω, which was discussed at 1:11 (cf. also 1:20; 2:2). We concluded that it is derived from the noun ἐνεργός from which we get our English word "energy." Since it always connotes active power, in this context it seems best to translate it "working" so as to underscore the repeated action of the present tense. It is best to take it as the middle voice to indicate that the power that is working is not impersonal but rather the power of his Spirit mentioned in verse 16. The locale of this power is expressed in the prepositional phrase ἐν ἡμῖν, "in us." Thus, it is appropriate and right that God should be praised not only for past activity but also for his powerful work in the hearts of believers (vv. 16–17)[5] at this present time.

In conclusion, no human or angel (cf. 3:10) could ever imagine that Jews and Gentiles could function together in one body. However, with

1. Cf. Alford, 3:111; Ellicott, 74; Meyer, 187; Moule, *Idiom Book*, 42.

2. BAGD 840; BDAG 1033; cf. BDF §185 (1).

3. Moule, *Idiom Book*, 86.

4. Robertson, *Grammar*, 647; BDF §185 (1); Moule, *Idiom Book*, 42.

5. Erich Mauerhofer, "Der Brief an die Epheser. 35. Teil: Kap. 3,20.20," *Fundamentum* 19, no. 4 (1998): 19.

God's infinite and matchless power of love in the life of each believer, Paul expresses confidence that this is entirely possible.

3:21. αὐτῷ ἡ δόξα ἐν τῇ ἐκκλησίᾳ καὶ[1] ἐν Χριστῷ Ἰησοῦ, "to him be glory in the church and in Christ Jesus." The personal pronoun αὐτῷ, "to him," is a rhetorical repetition of the pronoun to emphasize the great subject of the ascription of praise. The verb understood is probably an optative of the verb "to be" (εἴη), expressing a wish or desire. The term δόξα, "glory," was discussed at 1:6 (cf. 1:12, 14, 17, 18; 3:13, 16) and now appears for the last time in this letter. It conveys the reflection of the essence of one's being, the summation of all of one's attributes. In this context it specifically refers to God' splendor, power, and radiance. Paul gives glory to God because of his essential character, a practice which should be observed by all believers. We have a tendency to petition God while we ignore his right to praise, not only for what he has done but also for who he is.

In the following, Paul indicates where God is to be praised: ἐν τῇ ἐκκλησίᾳ καὶ ἐν Χριστῷ Ἰησοῦ, "in the church and in Christ Jesus" (see discussion on "in Christ" in 1:3). Lincoln has observed that this is the only doxology where the phrases "in the church" and "in Christ Jesus" are both used.[2] There are two things which need to be discussed: (1) whether the coordinating conjunction is to be accepted; and (2) the significance of the order, namely, the church is mentioned before Christ Jesus. If the coordinating conjunction καί, "and," is omitted, it would connote that the praise is to God in the church which is in Christ Jesus. If this view is accepted then the problem of order no longer exists. It would indicate that God is praised for his display of power and love that exists in the church due to the unification of believing Jews and Gentiles into one body which is in Christ Jesus. However, the conjunction should be accepted as genuine because of the good textual critical evidence as discussed in footnote 1.

We will now discuss the second problem, namely, the order. Barth finds the order "startling" because human beings are mentioned before their Messiah.[3] In fact, the words are transposed in some manuscripts (D* F G), but there is not very good evidence to support such a reading. However, the present order is not as much of a problem as it may appear. Paul simply wants to praise God for his creation, the church into which believing Jews and Gentiles are united. Furthermore, he wants to give glory in Christ Jesus who is the head of this church and in whom the union was accomplished (cf. 2:16, 19). Barth

1. The conjunction καί is absent from D^2 Ψ 𝔐 vg^{mss} syr $cop^{sa^{mss}, bo^{ms}}$ Cassiodorus, but it appears in $𝔓^{46}$ ℵ A B C (ʃ D* F G) 0278 6 33 81 104* 365 614 1175 1241^S 1739 1881 *al* vg $cop^{sa^{ms}, bo}$. Its inclusion is the better reading because of the geographical distribution of the Alexandrian and Western text-types whereas it is omitted primarily from the Byzantine tradition.

2. Lincoln, 217.

3. Barth, 375.

even admits that in 4:4–6 the church is mentioned before God because the church is the locus of God's praise.[1] Indeed, the church is central to the entire context. Christ Jesus is mentioned because the church could not have come into existence without him. He fulfilled all the righteous demands of the law, thus destroying the enmity between Jews and Gentiles (2:14). Praise is rendered for genuine reconciliation, not just cessation of hostility but genuine love for one another. Therefore, God is to be glorified in the church because his power and splendor are displayed there and he is glorified in Christ Jesus because Christ's work, which pleased the Father, made the church possible.

εἰς πάσας τὰς γενεὰς τοῦ αἰῶνος τῶν αἰώνων, "to all generations, for ever and ever." This is a unique ending to a prayer or doxology. Both the terms "generation" and "age" are used. It is an apparent mixture of both time and eternity. Bengel correctly proposes that the generations (τὰς γενεάς) refer to periods of human life which ultimately are terminated and engulfed into the ages (αἰῶνος), periods of the divine economy where generations no longer exist.[2] The term αἰών is used of time elsewhere in this epistle (1:21; 2:2, 7; 3:9, 11). Normally, NT doxologies have a repetition of the plural form of αἰών (Gal 1:5; Phil 4:20; 1 Tim 1:17; 2 Tim 4:18; Heb 13:21; 1 Pet 4:11; Rev 1:6; 4:9; 5:13; 7:12), but here we find both the singular and plural form (cf. Jude 25). The repetition of αἰών in both singular and plural forms may be intended to emphasize longevity or, as in this case, eternity.[3] The preposition εἰς gives the direction of the praise: "to" or "throughout" all generations. Therefore, God is to be glorified "forever and ever" beginning in this age and continuing into eternity. Mitton suggests that this expression is an "imprecise accumulation of Greek words."[4] However, Abbott states it well when he says: "But when we consider the difficulty of giving a logical analysis which shall be also grammatical of our own 'world without end,' we may be content to accept the meaning without seeking to analyse the expression."[5]

ἀμήν, "Amen." This marks the end of his prayer and doxology. The term is not used in classical literature and appears only twelve times in the LXX, three times in the canonical books: twice it is used by the people in response to prayer (1 Chr 16:36; Neh 8:6) and once by the people expressing agreement with Nehemiah's statement (Neh 5:13). It translates the verb אָמַן, which means "to confirm, support."[6] It is used 129 times in the NT, fifteen times by Paul and only here in Ephe-

1. Ibid., 376.
2. Bengel, 4:87.
3. BAGD 27; BDAG 32; cf. Robertson, *Grammar*, 408, 660; Moule, *Idiom Book*, 175.
4. Mitton, 137.
5. Abbott, 104.
6. BDB 52–53; cf. *HALOT* 1 (1994): 64; R. W. L. Moberly, "אמן (*ʾāmēn*)," *NIDOTTE* 1:428.

sians. Paul almost exclusively uses it to end doxologies. Basically, it is used to confirm what has been said and thus could also be translated "let it be" or "truly."[1] Here, it is a "yes" to the praise just expressed.[2] This does not reflect pride on Paul's part, as though he were confirming or praising his own composition. Rather, he is overwhelmed by God's glory and in a sense is saying, "Let me repeat that again." Perhaps he included it to invoke his readers to respond the same way since they had also experienced God's grace and power.

This "amen" not only concludes his doxology and prayer but also concludes the doctrinal section of the epistle. It is a truly fitting response to the powerful message that Paul has imparted in these three chapters.

1. BAGD 45; BDAG 53.
2. Heinrich Schlier, "ἀμήν," *TDNT* 1 (1964): 337.

II.

The Conduct of the Church (4:1–6:24)

Paul now applies the doctrine that he expounded in the first three chapters. All knowledge has two components: pure and applied. It is important to embrace both components, for the exclusion of one becomes an exercise in futility. The field of medicine is a good example of this. If only purely theoretical research takes place, the public never benefits from that knowledge. On the other hand, the practice of medicine without pure research excludes the possibility of new discoveries for cures of diseases. Thus, in theology, head knowledge alone will make little difference in individual or corporate lives, and practice without theological knowledge has the potential to lead to heretical practice. It is essential, therefore, that a proper balance be maintained. Such a balance is modeled by Paul in his literature, for he consistently presents doctrine first as a basis for the practice on which he later expounds. In Romans, for example, after a long doctrinal discourse, Paul continues in 12:1 with the words, παρακαλῶ οὖν ὑμᾶς "I exhort you." This and similar formulations are found in his other letters (cf. 1 Cor 4:16; 2 Cor 10:1; Phil 4:2; 1 Thess 2:12; 3:2; 4:1, 10; 5:14; 2 Thess 3:12; 1 Tim 2:1; Phlm 9–10).[1]

This division of doctrine and duty is subtantiated statistically in the use of the imperative. The imperative is used sixty-two times in Romans: only thirteen times in chapters 1–11 and forty-nine times in chapters 12–16 (though fifteen times with reference to greetings in chap. 16). In Ephesians the imperative is used forty-one times: only once in chapters 1–3 (2:11) and forty times in the last three chapters. Granted, there may be implied exhortations without the use of the imperative. However, in reviewing the first three chapters of Ephesians there are only three instances of implied exhortations. Two of them are in Paul's two prayers: first, that believers might know God more intimately and thus realize that he has directed his great power toward them, implying that this power is to be appropriated for their

1. For a more detailed study of Paul's application, see Carl J. Bjerkelund, *Parakalô. Form, Funktion und Sinn der parakalô-Sätze in dem paulinischen Briefen*, Bibliotheca Theologica Norvegica, ed. Åge Holter et al., no. 1 (Oslo: Universitetsforlaget, 1967): 13–19, 179–87. Bjerkelund suggests that the παρακαλῶ-clause simply has an epistolary function but Schnackenburg (162) correctly points out that it functions as an apostolic admonition. Cf. also Ferdinand Hahn, "Die christologische Begründung urchristlicher Paränese," *ZNW* 72, nos. 1/2 (1981): 88–99, esp. 96–99; Mary Breeze, "Hortatory Discourse in Ephesians," *Journal of Translation and Textlinguistics* 5, no. 4 (1992): 313–47.

spiritual welfare (1:17–19); and second, that believers might be able comprehend the power of Christ's love in order to demonstrate Christ's love for one another (3:17–19). The only other place that indicates an implied exhortation is 2:10 where believers are to walk in the works God has prepared beforehand for them. Clearly, the first three chapters concentrate on doctrine and the last three on practice. In Ephesians the practical aspects of application are heightened by a repeated emphasis on the believer's "walk" (περιπατέω) found in 4:1, 17; 5:2, 8, 15. As discussed at 2:2, Paul uses this word thirty-two times and always metaphorically, referring to conduct or lifestyle both negatively (e.g., Eph 2:2; 4:17; 1 Cor 3:3; Col 3:7; 2 Thess 3:11) and positively (Eph 4:1; 5:2; Rom 6:4; Gal 5:16). The believers' conduct is implemented not by their own strength but by the utilization of God's power mentioned in Paul's prayers in chapters 1 and 3.

The conduct of believers that Paul addresses in these last three chapters is based on the knowledge given in the first three chapters. In other words, the revealed mystery of the union of Jews and Gentiles in Christ into one new person has practical ramifications for life here on earth. In these chapters the believer is charged to act out his or her position in a world governed by the devil (2:2; 6:12; cf. 2 Cor 4:4; 1 John 5:10).[1] This entire section has contemporary relevance. In fact, Ephesians contains more specific practical applications for daily life than any other NT book. Furthermore, the material presented not only applies to individual believers but also to the corporate body of believers in relationship to those outside the church. Spiritual growth and maturity of individual believers is measured in light of the body of believers. Individual spiritual growth that is not shared with the rest of the body is not true spiritual growth or maturity. Although today individualism highly prizes independence, the NT envisions individuals dependent on the Lord and fellow members of the body in a corporate setting.

The major divisions in these three chapters revolve around the "walk" (περιπατέω) in 4:1, 17; 5:2, 8, 15 combined with the inferential conjunction "therefore" (οὖν). The only exceptions to this are 6:10–20, where the believer's stand against evil is addressed,[2] and 6:21–24, which marks the conclusion and summation of the book.

1. For relevant literature on the ethical interests of Paul, see Nathan Larry Baker, "Living the Dream: Ethics in Ephesians," *SWJT* 22 (fall 1979): 39–44. On the other hand, Jeal (*Integrating Theology and Ethics in Ephesians*, 23–26, 202) does not see Ephesians 4–6 serving as the paraenetical portion of Ephesians derived from the theological material of chaps. 1–3. Although these two sections are distinguishable, each section shows continuity within itself as well as the fact that the first section has its own paraenetic material.

2. Cf. Weber, "'Setzen'-'Wandeln'-'Stehen' im Epheserbrief," 478–80.

A. Walk in Unity (4:1–16)

The revelation of the unification of Jewish and Gentile believers positionally as “one new person” (2:15), the body of Christ, and the prayer that this unity would result in a mutual experience of Christ’s love (3:16–19) leads Paul to demonstrate the manner of walk expected of this unified body. This can only be accomplished by God’s own power through the ministry of gifted believers who Christ gives to the church. The purpose is to bring all the members of the body to the unity of faith and to the full stature of Christ with the result that they will be a stable and growing body in living union with Christ the head.

1. The Basis of Unity (4:1–6)

First, Paul exhorts believers to have a proper attitude toward unity (vv. 1–3) and then illustrates how the three persons of the Trinity serve as the basis of this unity (vv. 4–6). This sentence, the sixth of eight lengthy ones in this epistle (cf. 1:3–14, 15–23; 2:1–7; 3:2–13, 14–19; 4:1–6, 11–16; 6:14–20), has seventy-one words.

a. Exhortation to Unity (4:1–3)

Because of the new position in Christ both individually and corporately, unity should exist among the believers in Christ. Paul, therefore, exhorts them to maintain this unity.

Text: 4:1. Παρακαλῶ οὖν ὑμᾶς ἐγὼ ὁ δέσμιος ἐν κυρίῳ ἀξίως περιπατῆσαι τῆς κλήσεως ἧς ἐκλήθητε, **4:2.** μετὰ πάσης ταπεινοφροσύνης καὶ πραΰτητος, μετὰ μακροθυμίας, ἀνεχόμενοι ἀλλήλων ἐν ἀγάπῃ, **4:3.** σπουδάζοντες τηρεῖν τὴν ἑνότητα τοῦ πνεύματος ἐν τῷ συνδέσμῳ τῆς εἰρήνης·

Translation: 4:1. “I, therefore, the prisoner in the Lord, exhort you to walk worthy of the calling with which you were called, **4:2.** with all humility and gentleness, with patience, forbearing one another in love, **4:3.** making every effort to keep the unity of the Spirit in the bond of peace."

Commentary: 4:1. Παρακαλῶ οὖν ὑμᾶς ἐγώ, "I, therefore, exhort you." The first three words are the same Greek words as in Rom 12:1 where, likewise, they follow a doxology that has concluded the preceding chapter. The conjunction οὖν draws an inference or a result from what precedes. In this passage, Meyer would limit its inference to the immediately preceding verse (3:21).[1] Ellicott, however, thinks it refers to the passages in the preceding chapter that relate to spiritual privileges as well as the calling of the Ephesians, both of which are mentioned in verses 6 and 12, or, more particularly, the prayer in verses 14–21, which discloses the great "calling."[2] Salmond relates it back to the great things done by God's grace in 3:6–21.[3] Alford thinks that possibly the οὖν is a resumption of τούτου χάριν in 3:1 and 14 and thus refers back to the contents of chapters 1 and 2.[4] It is not necessary to choose whether it refers to the prayer or the portion which precedes the prayer. It aptly refers to both since the prayer simply concludes Paul's previous statements. Furthermore, it is not uncommon for Paul to use this conjunction along with παρακαλέω (Rom 12:1; 1 Thess 4:1; 1 Tim 2:1; cf. also 1 Pet 5:1) after long doctrinal sections in order to draw inferences from the preceding discussion. Therefore, this conjunction is drawing an inference from all the preceding chapters of Ephesians.

We see the calling first in chapter 1 where we have been blessed with all spiritual blessings in that the Father selected us, the Son redeemed us, and the Spirit sealed us (1:3–14). Because of these blessings Paul prays that the believers might know God and thus know the hope of their calling, God's inheritance in the saints, and God's power toward or in the believers (1:15–23). This calling is further seen in the salvation of the unregenerate by God's grace and their placement in the heavenlies in Christ (2:1–10). This calling proceeds from the individual to the union of the Jews and Gentiles into one body, called the church (2:11–3:13). Because of this call of Jews and Gentiles into one body, Paul prays for Christ's strengthening love in order that the union would not only be true theologically but also experientially among the believers (3:14–21). Because of this calling to individual salvation and to a corporate body of believers, Paul draws the inference that we should walk worthy of that calling (4:1).

1. Meyer, 193.

2. Ellicott, 76; cf. Eadie, 266. Luz thinks that the paraenesis in Eph 4–6 has the prayers in 1:15–23 and 3:14–21 as its basis (Ulrich Luz, "Überlegungen zum Epheserbrief und seiner Paränese," in *Neues Testament und Ethik für Rudolf Schnackenburg*, ed. Helmut Merklein [Freiburg: Herder, 1989], 379–86).

3. Salmond, 319.

4. Alford, 3:112.

Having discussed the connecting conjunction οὖν, the first word of this section, παρακαλῶ can be considered. The three main senses of this verb are: (1) to comfort (Matt 2:18; 5:4; Luke 16:25; Acts 20:12; 2 Cor 1:4; 7:6–7, 13; Eph 6:22; Col 2:2; 4:8; 1 Thess 3:7; 2 Thess 2:17); (2) to appeal, entreat, request (Matt 8:5; 14:36; 18:32; Mark 1:40; 5:18, 23; 6:56; Luke 8:41; 2 Cor 9:5; 12:8, 18); and (3) to exhort (Luke 3:18; Acts 2:40; Rom 12:1; 2 Cor 10:1; Phil 4:2; 1 Thess 4:1; 1 Pet 2:11; 5:1).[1] The third use fits best here, since Paul's use of περιπατέω as an imperative in 5:2, 8 reinforces the idea "to exhort." This use not only gives it a sense of urgency but also a note of authority. This is borne out by Paul's use of the personal pronoun ἐγώ, "I," which gives it greater emphasis[2] and the reminder that he was "the prisoner in the Lord" for their sake. Most of the versions translate the word as "beseech" (AV, RV, ASV), "beg" (RSV, NRSV), "urge" (TEV, JB, NIV, NJB), or "entreat" (NASB). These translations seem to be a little too mild, implying that Paul is pleading for a favor. Thus, although the verb can have more than one English meaning, it seems the context demands the primary idea of exhortation.[3] This conclusion is viable even though Paul is addressing fellow believers because friendship does not exclude authoritative exhortation.[4] In fact, his close relationship to the readers makes the exhortation all the more effective.[5]

ὁ δέσμιος ἐν κυρίῳ, "the prisoner in the Lord," is a further extension of the personal pronoun ἐγώ.[6] This is similar to the beginning words of chapter 3 but with two differences: (1) here, instead of "Christ Jesus" he uses "Lord," and (2) in place of the possessive genitive construction "of Christ Jesus," he uses the dative with the preposi-

1. For further study of this word in biblical and extrabiblical contexts, see BAGD 617; BDAG 764–65; Otto Schmitz and Gustav Stählin, "παρακαλέω, παράκλησις," *TDNT* 5 (1967): 773–99, esp. 793–99.

2. MHT 3:37.

3. Cf. Barr, *The Semantics of Biblical Language*, 232–33.

4. Bjerkelund (*Parakalô*, 185–87) seems to stress the friendly aspects and thus tones down the exhortative emphasis; cf. also Schlier, 178–79; idem, *Die Zeit der Kirche*, 74–89; S. R. L[lewelyn], "Petitions, Social History and the Language of Requests," in *New Documents Illustrating Early Christianity*, vol. 6, *A Review of the Greek Inscriptions and Papyri Published in 1980–81*, ed. S. R. Llewelyn and R. A. Kearsley (Sydney: Macquarie University, 1992), 145–46.

5. Cf. Barth, 426. Barth (426 n. 3) may misrepresent Abbott by saying that he translated it "I beseech." Abbott (105), however, thinks that "exhort" is too weak and states: "More than exhortation is implied, especially as it is an absolute duty to which he calls them."

6. Strictly speaking, a repetition of the article (ὁ) should have preceded the prepositional phrase ἐν κυρίῳ. However, it is common for the NT writers not to repeat the article (cf. Robertson, *Grammar*, 783; MHT 1:84, 236; BDF §272). The construction in the present context makes it clear that ἐν κυρίῳ is to be joined with ὁ δέσμιος rather than ὑμᾶς. If ἐν κυρίῳ were to be joined to ὑμᾶς, it would have been placed after ὑμᾶς (Winer, *Grammar*, 169). The construction in the present context "gives the true emphasis to the exhortation which follows" (ibid.).

tion ἐν, "in," the Lord. As noted in 2:21 the phrase "in the Lord" refers not to God but to Christ as it is consistently used throughout the epistle (2:21; 4:17; 5:8; 6:1, 10, 21). It denotes the sphere or locale, indicating Paul's connection or union with Christ (cf. 1:2).[1] Hence, the reference to him as a prisoner in 3:1 focuses on both the possessive and causal ideas, for it was the cause of Christ that made him a prisoner, whereas in the present context, he stresses his union with Christ.[2] This union with Christ resulted in his obedience to the will of God. Consequently, he became a missionary among the Gentiles, including the Ephesians, and was imprisoned for their sake. He now exhorts them likewise to obey their Lord with whom they too have union.

ἀξίως περιπατῆσαι τῆς κλήσεως ἧς ἐκλήθητε, "to walk worthy of the calling with which you were called." The word περιπατέω, "to walk," was discussed at 2:2. In brief, it was found that in most instances it has a literal sense in classical literature, the LXX, the Gospels, and Acts. In the rest of the NT, forty-seven out of forty-nine times and all eight times in Ephesians (2:2, 10; 4:1, 17*bis*; 5:2, 8, 15), it is used metaphorically referring to conduct or lifestyle, whether negatively (e.g., Eph 2:2; 1 Cor 3:3; Col 3:7; 2 Thess 3:11) or positively (Eph 4:1; 5:2; Rom 6:4; Gal 5:16). Certainly, in this context, it refers to the lifestyle of the believer. The aorist tense is ingressive, indicating that the believer is to change his or her conduct from what it was previously.[3] The adverb ἀξίως, "worthy, worthily, suitably," literally means "'bringing up the other beam of the scales,' 'bringing into equilibrium,' and therefore 'equivalent'"[4] or "worthily, a manner worthy of, suitability."[5] This word appears six times in the NT, and outside of 3 John 6 it is used only by Paul. In Phil 1:27 its connotation is that the believer's life should be worthy of the gospel of Christ and in Col 1:10 its connotation is that the believer is to live a life worthy of the Lord (cf. Rom 16:2; 1 Thess 2:12). In the present context the emphasis is on conduct that is in balance with or equal to one's "call."

The noun κλῆσις, "call," appears three times in Ephesians (1:18; 4:1, 4). In the study of the word in 1:18, we concluded that it normally refers to a religious "call" or an "invitation, summons" by God (Rom 11:29; Eph 1:18; 4:4; 2 Thess 1:11; Heb 3:1). It is often linked with election (1 Cor 1:26; 2 Pet 1:10; 2 Tim 1:9) because in the verb form it is used of those whom God foreknew and predestined, thus called and justified (Rom 8:29–30). In the present context, the reference is not

1. Cf. Nigel Turner, "The preposition *en* in the New Testament," *BT* 10 (July 1959): 116–17.

2. In this context the preposition ἐν denotes the state rather than the idea of "for Christ's sake" (Winer, *Grammar*, 484–85 n. 3). Chrysostom (*Eph* 4:1 [*PG* 62:56–58]) and Theophylact (*Eph* 4:1 [*PG* 124:1080]) render it "for Christ's sake" (διὰ τὸν Κύριον).

3. Fanning, *Verbal Aspect*, 361.

4. Werner Foerster, "ἄξιος, ἀνάξιος," *TDNT* 1 (1964): 379.

5. BAGD 78; BDAG 94.

only to salvation by election and adoption by the Father (cf. 1:4–5),[1] but also to their union into one body, the church. Therefore, the call to walk worthy of the calling refers not only to the individual believers but also the corporate body of believers.

The noun is followed by the relative pronoun (ἧς), which is a genitive rather than a cognate accusative or possibly a dative. The genitive construction is probably attracted from the accusative because of the genitive noun preceding it.[2] The cognate verb ἐκλήθητε, "to call,"[3] is passive, indicating that it was God who called them to salvation and to their position in the body of Christ and their union with Christ. The aorist tense is ingressive, to "express the coming about of conduct which contrasts with prior conduct."[4]

In conclusion, in 3:13 Paul asks the Ephesian believers not to be concerned about his imprisonment; in 4:1 Paul exhorts them about their conduct during his imprisonment. It is interesting to note that the instructions Paul is about to give apply not only to the first century. His exhortation to holy living is equally relevant today. Next, in verses 2–3, Paul states the manner in which believers are to walk worthy of their calling.[5]

4:2. μετὰ πάσης ταπεινοφροσύνης καὶ πραΰτητος, "with all humility and gentleness." Rather than using imperatives, Paul employs two prepositional phrases followed by two participial clauses which function as imperatives. The quality of this walk or lifestyle is clearly delineated by these two prepositional phrases. The preposition μετά is virtually synonymous with σύν, although "*syn* is more suited to express intimate personal union (e.g., Col 3:4), and *meta* is more suited to denote close association or attendant circumstances (e.g., 1 Thess 3:13)."[6]

The word ταπεινοφροσύνη does not occur before NT times. It appears seven times in the NT (Acts 20:19; Eph 4:2; Phil 2:3; Col 2:18, 23; 3:12; 1 Pet 5:5). In Phil 2:3 it is in contrast to "self-seeking" (ἐριθεία) and "vainglorious boasting" (κενοδοξία) and in 1 Pet 5:5 it is in contrast to the proud (ὑπερήφανος). It conveys "lowliness of mind" or, better, "humility."[7] Since humility is not considered a virtue by human beings, it

1. Cf. Wiederkehr, *Die Theologie der Berufung in den Paulusbriefen*, 210–23.

2. Robertson, *Grammar*, 478, 716; MHT 1:93; 2:419; Winer, *Grammar*, 203.

3. For a study of καλέω and κλῆσις and their association with words like "grace," "peace," and "fellowship," see Oscar Andrés Rodríguez M., "La vida cristina como una vocación en las cartas de San Pablo. Ensayo de Moral Biblica Neotestamentaria basado en el Ef 4,1," *Estudios teológicos* 2 (Julio–Diciembre 1975): 9–25.

4. BDF §337 (1).

5. Dahl ("Ephesians and Qumran," 132–35) lists Qumran texts that parallel with ethical prescriptions mentioned in Eph 4–5. He is careful to note both the similarities and dissimilarities between Ephesians and the Qumran texts.

6. Harris, "Appendix: Prepositions and Theology in the Greek New Testament," 1206–7; cf. BAGD 509; BDAG 636–37.

7. Cf. Walter Grundmann, "ταπεινός κτλ.," *TDNT* 8 (1972): 21–22.

is understandable why this word did not exist before NT times.[1] In fact, Epictetus (A.D. 50–130) listed ταπεινοφροσύνη first among the qualities not to be commended.[2] On the other hand, Paul used this term when he mentioned to the Ephesian elders that he had served the Lord in Asia with all "humility" (Acts 20:19). He was their example. In other Scripture passages it should be noted that believers are warned to avoid false humility, but rather to be cognizant of who they are in God's program (cf. John 3:30; Rom 12:3). It is significant that this virtue is listed first. There are two possible reasons for this. First, Paul has emphasized unity—pride provokes disunity whereas humility engenders unity. Second, he was aware of their past pride and wished to encourage obedience to and dependence on God. Christ is the supreme example of humility (Phil 2:6–8).

The next word, πραΰτης is similar in meaning. It has the idea of "mildness" or "gentleness," the opposite of "roughness."[3] In the discussion of virtues, Aristotle makes the distinction between intellectual virtues and moral virtues, and he categorizes this word as a moral virtue along with temperateness.[4] In describing this word Aristotle states that it is the mean between "excessive anger against everyone and on all occasions" and "never being angry with anything." He states further: "Praise is not for him who is deficient in anger, nor for him who is therein excessive; but for one whose state is between the two. This man is gentle [πρᾶος]; and gentleness [πραότης] will be a mean state between these two affections."[5] In the LXX it occurs only nine times and in the canonical books it appears only three times where it combines ideas of humbleness and righteousness (Pss 45:4 [MT 45:5; LXX 44:5]; 90:10 [LXX 89:10]; 132:1 [LXX 131:1]; Sir 3:17; 4:8).

In the NT it appears eleven times and only in the epistles (1 Cor 4:21; 2 Cor 10:1; Gal 5:23; 6:1; Eph 4:2; Col 3:12; 2 Tim 2:25; Titus 3:2; Jas 1:21; 3:13; 1 Pet 3:16). It is mentioned as a fruit of the Spirit (Gal 5:23). Throughout the NT it has the idea of "gentleness." However, it must not be confused with the idea of weakness. Paul asked the Corinthians if they wanted him to come to them with a rod or in the spirit of gentleness (1 Cor 4:21). He later speaks of the gentleness of Christ (2 Cor 10:1). Jesus was gentle and humble in heart (πραΰς εἰμι καὶ ταπεινὸς τῇ καρδίᾳ, Matt 11:29) but not weak. This is illustrated by his display of anger toward Jews who had transformed the temple into a den of thieves (Matt 21:12–13). Likewise, Moses cannot be construed as weak, demonstrated by his wrath when he descended from

1. Cf. Carsten Peter Thiede, "Der Brief an die Epheser. 36. Teil: Kap. 4,1–6," *Fundamentum* 20, no. 1 (1999): 19.

2. As noted by Best, 362; Epictetus *Dissertationes* 3.24.56 (ταπεινῶς is used in 3.24.54).

3. Plato *Symposium* 197d.

4. Aristotle *Ethica Nicomochea* 1.13.20 §1103a.4–10.

5. Aristotle *Magna Moralia* 1.22.2–3 §1191b.31–41 [trans. G. Cyril Armstrong in Loeb].

the mountain and found Israel sinning against God by their creation of the golden calf (Exod 32). Yet he was more gentle (πραΰς σφόδρα) than anyone else on earth (Num 12:3). The word never connotes the idea of weakness. Rather, it implies the conscious exercise of self-control, exhibiting a conscious choice of gentleness as opposed to the use of power for the purpose of retaliation. Barclay states it well when he writes, "The man who is *praus* is the man who is always angry at the right time and never angry at the wrong time."[1] This term is used of the taming and training of animals. For instance, controlled by the master's will, a well trained dog is always angry at the master's foes and never angry at the master's friends. Only the person who is controlled by the Spirit of God can truly be gentle—angry at the right time and never angry at the wrong time. When such a person is wronged, he or she does not seek revenge, but when a wrong has been committed toward a brother or sister, or the body of believers, he or she has the power to address the situation. In Ephesus, where there was the probability of great differences between believing Jews and Gentiles, believers needed to have both humility and gentleness.

The adjective πάσης, "all," modifies both humility and gentleness. When this adjective is used with anarthrous singular nouns it can denote the highest degree, "full, greatest, all,"[2] for example, "with all perseverance in prayer" (Eph 6:18).[3] Hence, though it could be translated "every kind of humility and gentleness," in English it is better to render it "all humility and gentleness."

μετὰ μακροθυμίας, "with patience," is the third characteristic of the believer walking in conformity to his or her calling. Commentators have related this prepositional phrase to the rest of the sentences in three ways. First, some suggest that it has been connected with the following participial clause, ἀνεχόμενοι ἀλλήλων ἐν ἀγάπῃ, "forebearing one another in love."[4] But the repetition of the preposition μετά, "with," points backward making it parallel to μετὰ πάσης ταπεινοφροσύνης καὶ πραΰτητος. There is no need to connect with the following prepositional phrase because ἀνεχόμενοι has ἐν ἀγάπῃ to qualify it and does not need μετὰ μακροθυμίας.[5] Meyer remarks, "Besides, μετὰ μακροθ., if it belonged to ἀνεχόμ., would have an undue emphasis, since without long-suffering the ἀνεχόμενοι ἀλλήλων would not exist at all; Col. iii.12f."[6] Second, others would unite this prepositional phrase with

1. William Barclay, *Flesh and Spirit: An Examination of Galatians 5:19–23* (London: SCM, 1962), 120; cf. also Horsley, *New Documents Illustrating Early Christianity*, vol. 4, *A Review of the Greek Inscriptions and Papyri Published in 1979*, 169–70.

2. BAGD 631; BDAG 783.

3. Bo Reicke, "πᾶς, ἅπας," *TDNT* 5 (1967): 888.

4. Calvin, 171; Harless, 340; Olshausen, 208.

5. Eadie, 269.

6. Meyer, 195.

the former (μετὰ πάσης ταπεινοφροσύνης καὶ πραΰτητος) and attach it to the following participle ἀνεχόμενοι.[1] But this ignores the parallelism of the prepositions (μετά). Furthermore, besides creating one long sentence it "obscures the transition from idea to idea and makes the several clauses less distinctive."[2] The prepositions bring out the distinctives. Finally, this view obscures "the gradual transition from the general ἀξίως περιπατ. τ. κλ. to the special ἀνεχόμ. ἀλλήλ."[3] And third, some think that this prepositional phrase is parallel with the immediately previous prepositional phrase beginning with the same preposition μετά and that these prepositional phrases define the attendant circumstances of the believer's walk in accordance with his call.[4] This construction is the simplest. Although these prepositional phrases describe the attendant circumstances, the present context gives them an imperatival force. A walk worthy of their call demands humility, gentleness, and patience. In other words, these words do not describe an automatic response but one that demands conscious effort on the part of the believer who relies on the Spirit.

The noun μακροθυμία is late and rare in the classical writings. It is used for person's endurance of grief[5] or the indomitable patience of the inhabitants of a city under siege who plant turnips and hope to eat the ripened result before the city's ultimate defeat.[6] It appears only five times in the LXX depicting the patience of rulers and saints (Prov 25:15; Isa 57:15; Sir 5:11; 1 Macc 8:4) and the patience or forbearance of God (Jer 15:15). It translates the Hebrew אֶרֶךְ אַפַּיִם and אֶרֶךְ אַפַּיִם meaning to "delay the outbreak of his wrath."[7] As seen in 1 Macc 8:4, Rome epitomized this kind of patience: "μακροθυμία expresses there that Roman persistency which would never make peace under defeat."[8] In the NT it occurs fourteen times, ten times in Paul's writings (Rom 2:4; 9:22; 2 Cor 6:6; Gal 5:22; Eph 4:2; Col 1:11; 3:12; 1 Tim 1:16; 2 Tim 3:10; 4:2). In Rom 2:4 and 9:22 (cf. 2 Pet 3:15) it exhibits the staying of God's wrath, which indicates his long-suffering. The delay of his wrath is derived from the Semitic אֶרֶךְ אַפַּיִם.[9] This quality of long-suffering by God is, also, a fruit of the Spirit to be demonstrated by Christians (Gal 5:23). For the believer, patience is that cautious endurance that does not abandon hope. It pertains to waiting patiently

1. Theodoret *Eph* 4:2, 3 (*PG* 82:532–33); Oecumenius *Eph* 4:1–6 (*PG* 118:1213); Bengel, 4:88.

2. Salmond, 320.

3. Meyer, 195.

4. Alford, 3:113; Eadie, 269; Ellicott, 77; Meyer, 195; Abbott, 106; Salmond, 320; Schlier, 181; Gnilka, 197; Schnackenburg, 164.

5. Menander *Fragment* 549.2.

6. Strabo 5.4.10.

7. BDB 60, 73–74; Johannes Horst, "μακροθυμία, μακροθυμέω, μακρόθυμος, μακροθύμως" *TDNT* 4 (1967): 376.

8. Trench, *Synonyms of the New Testament*, 197.

9. Horst, *TDNT* 4 (1967): 382.

without immediate results, like the farmer who waits for his harvest and the OT prophets who waited for God's action (Jas 5:7–11). It includes patient endurance while awaiting the inheritance of the promises even as Abraham had (Heb 6:12–15). God is the greatest example of all. He stayed his wrath when he was wronged by human sin (Rom 2:4). Thus must the believer stay his or her impatience or vengeance when wronged by another believer, exhibiting patience one toward another, especially in the light of the union of believing Jews and Gentiles into one body. It is clear that patience is not only a virtue but a necessary ingredient for the life of Jewish and Gentile believers who comprise the body of Christ.

ἀνεχόμενοι ἀλλήλων ἐν ἀγάπῃ, "forbearing one another in love." Next Paul uses two participial clauses. The first participle ἀνεχόμενοι from ἀνέχω is used frequently in the classical literature. It means "to take up, to bear up, to endure."[1] In the LXX it occurs sixteen times and in the canonical books it appears eleven times. It is used of God's endurance of the Israelites' vain offerings (Isa 1:13) or Job's endurance through great trials (Job 6:11, 26; cf. also Isa 46:4). It also has the idea of restraint, as when God withheld the rain (Amos 4:7; Hag 1:10) or restrained himself from destroying people (Isa 42:14; 63:15; 64:12 [MT & LXX 64:11]). In the NT it is used fifteen times (always in the middle voice), ten times by Paul (1 Cor 4:12; 2 Cor 11:1*bis*, 4, 19, 20; Eph 4:2; Col 3:13; 2 Thess 1:4; 2 Tim 4:3). In addition, it is used when Jesus asks how long he should bear with the disciples (Matt 17:17 = Mark 9:19 = Luke 9:41) or when Gallio bore with the Jews' accusation against Paul (Acts 18:14). Outside of this text, Paul speaks of enduring in persecution (1 Cor 4:12; cf. 2 Thess 1:4), asks the Corinthians to bear with him in his boasts (2 Cor 11:1*bis*), and bemoans their tendency to endure false teaching (v. 4) and teachers (vv. 19, 20). Hence, this word has reference to bearing or enduring with respect to things or persons.[2] In the present context and in Col 3:13 Paul asks them to bear with those in the assembly. Thus, to translate this word "forbear" is appropriate. Robertson suggests that it is a direct middle meaning "holding yourselves back from one another."[3] In other words, differences between believers are to be tolerated.

The final prepositional phrase ἐν ἀγάπῃ, "in love," further qualifies how they are to forbear one another. Although Olshausen unites this with the following participle,[4] it is best to modify the immediately preceding participle because it is normal for the qualifiers to follow the verbs or participles (cf. 1:4),[5] and Olshausen's configuration "dis-

1. E.g., Homer *Ilias* 1.586; 5.285; *Odyssea* 11.375; Herodotus 4.28.

2. For further study, see Heinrich Schlier, "ἀνέχω, ἀνεκτός, ἀνοχή," *TDNT* 1 (1964): 359–60.

3. Robertson, *Grammar*, 807–8.

4. Olshausen, 208.

5. Cf. Bruce, 334.

turbs the symmetry of the two participial clauses."[1] This same phrase is used in 1:4 where we concluded that ἀγάπη is not a possessive love but a giving love. This kind of love seeks the highest good in the one loved, and more particularly for the believer, it has the idea of seeking the will of God in the one loved. It is an unconditional love that does not seek a response in kind. The prepositional phrase may be taken adverbially, namely, forbearing one another lovingly, or it may denote manner or instrument, namely, to forebear with or by love. The latter alternative appears to be the best. Hence, forbearance left unqualified could result in resentment or anger rather than love.

How this participle relates to the other elements of this passage is a matter of discussion. Some think that mutual forbearance expresses the action of μακροθυμία.[2] This may be true logically with respect to Col 3:12–13, but it does not work grammatically in the present context since the preceding nouns are genitives. It is more likely that this participle is parallel with the next one (σπουδάζοντες) since both are nominative plurals. These two nominative plural participles relate back to the infinitive in verse 1 (περιπατῆσαι) and the logical subject of the infinitive is ὑμεῖς.[3] Moule states that this construction may be due to Semitic influence.[4] They could be circumstantial participles of manner or means, meaning that Paul exhorts the Ephesians to walk worthy of their calling in the manner of or by means of forbearing one another in love.[5] However, it seems better to view them as carrying an imperatival force.[6] This conclusion is based on verse 1 where Paul exhorts them to walk worthy of their call by forbearing one another in love (v. 2) and making every effort to keep the unity of the Spirit (v. 3).

In conclusion, there was undoubtedly some tension between Jewish and Gentile believers even though they were now united into one body. Therefore, Paul has explained how their walk must be exemplified by humility, gentleness, and patience, forbearing one another in love, and thus excluding resentment. Such qualities could only be accomplished by the power of the Spirit in their lives, individually (3:16) and corporately (2:22).

4:3. σπουδάζοντες τηρεῖν τὴν ἑνότητα τοῦ πνεύματος, "making every effort to keep the unity of the Spirit." Lincoln observes, "This clause is parallel to the previous one in that it too begins with a participle and ends with a prepositional phrase with ἐν."[7] The second participle σπουδάζοντες is from σπουδάζω, which, in the intransitive use, as

1. Ellicott, 78.

2. Ibid.; Abbott, 106; Salmond, 321.

3. Meyer, 195; Abbott, 106.

4. Moule, *Idiom Book*, 31, 105.

5. Wallace, *Greek Grammar*, 652.

6. Robertson, *Grammar*, 946; MHT 1:181, 182; 4:89; BDF §468 (2); Winer, *Grammar*, 716; Fanning, *Verbal Aspect*, 386–87; Porter, *Verbal Aspect*, 374, 376–77.

7. Lincoln, 237.

it is here, means "to be busy, eager, to make haste."[1] It appears eleven times in the LXX and eight times in the canonical books: once it translates חוּשׁ, meaning "to be in haste, make haste, hasten" (Job 31:5), and the other times it translates the Niphal of בָּהַל, meaning "to be disturbed, dismayed, terrified" (Eccl 8:2 [MT 8:3]; Job 4:5; 21:6; 22:10; 23:15, 16; Isa 21:3).[2] It seems that the LXX translators have "not taken over the Gk. content of σπουδάζω,"[3] or they struggle to find a Greek verb for the Hebrew. Josephus' use of the word is "to be zealously engaged"[4] with less emphasis on haste.[5] In the NT it occurs eleven times denoting "haste" (e.g., 2 Tim 4:9, 21; Titus 3:12) but more prominently indicating "to be zealous, eager, make every effort" (Gal 2:10; Eph 4:3; 1 Thess 2:17; 2 Tim 2:15; Heb 4:11; 2 Pet 1:10, 15; 3:14). Actually, all the passages would be acceptable with the second nuance.[6] Certainly in the present context the second nuance is more fitting. The AV translation "endeavoring" could imply an attempt that might fail. Newer translations are varied but are more forceful by variously translating it "giving diligence" (RV, ASV), "being diligent" (NASB), "eager" (RSV), "spare no effort" (NEB), "take/make every effort" (JB, NIV, NJB, NRSV), "do your best" (TEV). All of these basically convey the same idea of a zealous effort, and the translation chosen for the commentary, "make every effort," is used in the NIV. It is parallel to the immediately preceding participle (ἀνεχόμενοι), thus meaning that it also has an imperatival force[7] as both participles relate back to the infinitive (περιπατῆσαι) in verse 1.

The infinitive τηρεῖν from τηρέω essentially means "to keep, preserve" what is already in existence. It is not the establishment of a new entity, but rather to keep and not lose[8] or destroy "something already in our possession."[9] The object of the infinitive is τὴν ἑνότητα τοῦ πνεύματος, "the unity of the Spirit." This term ἑνότητα from ἑνότης, "unity," is rare and in biblical literature it is used only here and verse 13 where it talks about the unity of faith to be obtained.

The following genitive (τοῦ πνεύματος) is a genitive of author,[10] a

1. Sophocles *Oedipus Coloneus* 1143; Euripides *Hecuba* 817; Xenophon *Oeconomicus* 9.1; *Memorabilia* 1.3.11.

2. BDB 96; Benedikt Otzen, "בהל *bhl*; בֶּהָלָה *behālāh*," *TDOT* 2 (1977): 3–5.

3. Günther Harder, "σπουδάζω, σπουδή, σπουδαῖος," *TDNT* 7 (1971): 563.

4. Josephus *B.J.* 1.22.1 §431.

5. Harder, *TDNT* 7 (1971): 563; cf. Josephus *B.J.* 2.20.2 §559.

6. BAGD 763; BDAG 939; Adai, *Der Heilige Geist als Gegenwart Gottes* 208. Harder (*TDNT* 7 [1971]: 565 n. 9) disagrees with this assessment for he thinks that there is a definite distinction between 1 Thess 2:17 and Eph 4:3. It seems that both passages could be rendered with the second sense without difficulty.

7. Robertson, *Grammar*, 946; MHT 1:181, 182; BDF §468 (2); Winer, *Grammar*, 716.

8. BAGD 815; BDAG 1002.

9. Salmond, 321; James D. G. Dunn, *The Theology of Paul the Apostle* (Grand Rapids: Eerdmans; Edinburgh: T & T Clark, 1998), 562.

10. BAGD 677; BDAG 835.

genitive of originating cause,[1] or a genitive of production/producer,[2] referring to the one who produces unity. The Spirit here is neither the human spirit[3] nor the spirit of the body of believers[4] but the Holy Spirit.[5] Nothing in the epistle suggests that unity is brought about by humans, only by the Holy Spirit (2:22; cf. 1 Cor 12:13). Furthermore, the immediately following context talks about the unity based in the three persons of the Godhead.

ἐν τῷ συνδέσμῳ τῆς εἰρήνης, "in the bond of peace." The noun σύνδεσμος primarily means "that which binds together," like the binding together of a defense structure[6] or the fastening of garments.[7] Metaphorically it is used of the bond that keeps a state together, namely, its good citizens,[8] or the bond between children and parents.[9] In the LXX it appears ten times (only in canonical books) and translates six different Hebrew words. There it is rendered, in the literal sense, the binding together of buildings (1 Kgs 6:10), and in the metaphorical sense, being bound to wickedness (Isa 58:6, 9). In the NT it is used only four times, each of these in the metaphorical sense (Acts 8:23; Eph 4:3; Col 2:19; 3:14). The concept of binding is vividly portrayed in Col 2:19 where it refers to the "ligaments" of a body.[10] Hence, Paul chained as a prisoner of the Lord (3:1; 4:1) speaks of the binding or chaining together of peace.[11]

The preposition ἐν is taken by some as instrumental, thus having the idea that the unity of the Spirit is preserved through the bond of peace.[12] However, the unity does not come by means of "the bond of peace" but by the Holy Spirit. It is better to consider ἐν as denoting the place or sphere[13] in which the unity of the Spirit is to be preserved and manifested, namely, in the bond of peace.

Peace appears eight times in this epistle (1:2; 2:14, 15, 17*bis*; 4:3; 6:15, 23) and was discussed at 1:2. Here it has reference to peace among believers. Some have taken τῆς εἰρήνης as an objective genitive

1. Ellicott, 78; Salmond, 321.

2. Wallace, *Greek Grammar*, 105.

3. As do Calvin, 172; Westcott, 57; Gaugler, 164–65. Some think it is a subjective genitive (see Schlier, 184; Adai, *Der Heilige Geist als Gegenwart Gottes*, 210).

4. As suggested by Theodore of Mopsuestia *Eph* 4:3 (*PG* 66:917).

5. Bengel, 4:88; Hodge, 201; Alford, 3:113; Eadie, 271; Ellicott, 78; Abbott, 107; Salmond, 321; Schlier, 184; Gnilka, 199; Caird, 72; Barth, 428; Schnackenburg, 164; Bruce, 334–35; Adai, *Der Heilige Geist als Gegenwart Gottes*, 209–20.

6. Thucydides 2.75.5.

7. Euripides *Bacchae* 697.

8. Plato *Respublica* 7.5 §520a.

9. Aristotle *Ethica Nicomachea* 9.12.7 §1162a.27.

10. McGrath, "'*Syn*' Words in Saint Paul," 223.

11. Robert Jewett, "The Bond of Peace and *Places in the Heart*: Reflections on 'The Dialogue on Theological Diversity'," *Quarterly Review* 18 (winter 1998): 358.

12. Aquinas, chap. 4, lec. 1, vv. 1–4 (153); Schlier, 184–85; Gaugler, 164.

13. Eadie, 271–72; Ellicott, 78; Abbott, 107; Salmond, 321; Winer, *Grammar*, 483.

and propose that unity is preserved by that which forms the bond of peace, namely, love, as the parallel passage in Col 3:14 states.[1] However, Col 3:14 expressly names love as the object of the "bond" and, thus, it is not entirely parallel to the present passage. The Ephesian readers would not regard "love" as the object especially when ἐν ἀγάπῃ has just been mentioned at verse 2.[2] The meaning of the Colossian passage should not be forced on the present passage. It seems preferable to view the genitive either as epexegetical, "the bond that consists in peace,"[3] or as appositional "the bond which is peace."[4]

In summary, believers are to make every effort to preserve the unity which has its origin in the Holy Spirit. This unity is portrayed by the bond between Jews and Gentiles who have become one new person in Christ. The bond consisting of peace is possible because Christ brought peace between these two former entities (2:14–16). Hence, there is no exhortation to establish peace because it has been done in Christ. Nor is there an exhortation to organize unity because this has been accomplished by the Holy Spirit. Instead, Paul's concern is to preserve, maintain, or protect that unity.

Verses 1–3 may be thus summarized. As a prisoner in the Lord, Paul exhorts the Ephesians to maintain a lifestyle worthy of their call to salvation and to the body of believers. Their lives should demonstrate humility, gentleness, and patience, which are accomplished by forbearing one another in love and making every effort to preserve the unity that comes from the Holy Spirit. Paul had explained in chapters 2 and 3 the work of the three persons of the Trinity in accomplishing this unity. His next topic will deal with the elements of unity that are centered on the Trinity.

b. Elements of Unity (4:4–6)

Paul now gives the basis by explaining in more detail how elements of the Christian faith revolve around the three persons of the Trinity. Unity is stressed by the sevenfold use of "one" (εἷς, μία, ἕν).

With an abrupt change of style, various suggestions have been made as to what form these verses represent.[5] It is thought by some that this is an early Christian confession or hymn.[6] However, one can-

1. Theophylact *Eph* 4:3 (*PG* 124:1080–81); Bengel, 4:88; Harless, 342–43.

2. Alford, 3:113.

3. BAGD 785; BDAG 966; Schlier, 185; Best, 365; Wiederkehr, *Die Theologie der Berufung in den Paulusbriefen*, 216. Adai (*Der Heilige Geist als Gegenwart Gottes*, 211) labels it a genitive of content.

4. Alford, 3:113; Eadie, 271; Ellicott, 78; Abbott, 107; Salmond, 321.

5. For a brief summary of the views, see Adai, *Der Heilige Geist als Gegenwart Gottes*, 195–96.

6. Gnilka, 200–201; Barth, 429; Bruce, 335; cf. Wengst, *Christologische Formeln und Lieder des Urchristentums*, 136–41; Martin Dibelius, "Die Christianisierung einer hellenistischen Formel," *Neue Jahrbücher für das klassische Altertum. Geschichte und deutsche*

not assert, as Hanson does, that if this is a hymn it was not created by the author of this epistle.[1] If, indeed, this is a hymn or confession it is most probable that Paul created it, as in 1 Cor 12:4–6. Nevertheless, one of the problems in viewing this as a confession is the use of the second person "you" in verse 4b.[2] It is more likely a summary which Paul utilized to stir the memory of the recipients. On the other hand, it may have been used as a confession after the Ephesians had received and read the letter. There is certainly nothing inherently wrong for Paul to have quoted a hymn or confession, but many NT scholars are much too eager to designate as hymns those portions that seem to have some sort of meter.

Text: 4:4. ἓν σῶμα καὶ ἓν πνεῦμα, καθὼς καὶ ἐκλήθητε ἐν μιᾷ ἐλπίδι τῆς κλήσεως ὑμῶν· **4:5.** εἷς κύριος, μία πίστις, ἓν βάπτισμα, **4:6.** εἷς θεὸς καὶ πατὴρ πάντων, ὁ ἐπὶ πάντων καὶ διὰ πάντων καὶ ἐν πᾶσιν ἡμῖν.

Translation: 4:4. "There is one body and one Spirit, just as also you were called in one hope of your calling; **4:5.** one Lord, one faith, one baptism, **4:6.** one God and Father of all, who is over all and through all and in all of us."

Commentary: 4:4. ἓν σῶμα καὶ ἓν πνεῦμα, "There is one body and one Spirit." An abrupt change is made without a conjunction. Normally, Paul introduces a new section with a conjunction to indicate how it relates to what has been said. One would think that a conjunction like γάρ, "for," would have been appropriate here because of the relationship of verses 4–6 to verses 1–3, that is, the basis or reason for the unity just mentioned. The abruptness is telling, for it appears to indicate the importance Paul places on the Trinity in conjunction with unity.

The sevenfold use of "one" (εἷς, μία, ἕν) emphasizes unity. First, there is one body (ἓν σῶμα), which refers to the universal church already discussed (1:23; 2:16; 3:5–6). Briefly, this consists of the body of believers, an entirely new concept in the NT, never envisioned in the OT. As previously stated, it is not that Gentiles become Jews, as in the OT, nor Jews become Gentiles, but that unbelieving Jews and Gentiles become one body of believers when they place their faith in the work of Christ at Calvary. They are no longer two entities but one. Second, there is the one Spirit (ἓν πνεῦμα) referring to the Holy Spirit mentioned in 2:18, 22. The passage 2:16–22 explains how this body, reconciled to Christ, now has access to God in one Spirit and how it is por-

Literatur und für Pädagogik 35 (1915), 224–36; reprinted in idem, "Die Christianisierung einer hellenistischen Formel," *Botschaft und Geschichte*, ed. Günther Bornkamm, vol. 2 (Tübingen: Mohr, 1956), 14–29; Best, "The Use of Credal and Liturgical Materials in Ephesians," 65–66.

1. Hanson, *The Unity of the Church in the New Testament*, 149.

2. Barth, 429.

trayed as a temple in which the Spirit dwells. There is unity in the universal church and in the Holy Spirit and there also should be unity in the local body of believers.

καθὼς καὶ[1] **ἐκλήθητε ἐν μιᾷ ἐλπίδι τῆς κλήσεως ὑμῶν,** "just as also you were called in one hope of your calling." Third, there is one hope. With this clause Paul breaks from the pattern of verses 4a and 5–6 and refers back to the call mentioned in verse l. He does this in order to give a conceptual framework on which the rest of the exhortation is based.[2] Some of the earlier translations translated the adverbial conjunction καθώς as "even as" (AV, RV, ASV) but the more recent ones appropriately render it "just as" (RSV, NASB, TEV, JB, NIV, NJB, NRSV). This adverbial conjunction makes a comparison (or possibly, denotes cause) by showing that the following clause illustrates the unity expressed by the terms "one body" and "one Spirit." The conjunction καί being used adjunctively, "also," supports the idea of it being an illustration or proof. The aorist passive verb ἐκλήθητε, "you were called," indicates the sovereign call of the believer. By some the preposition ἐν is viewed instrumentally, "by one hope,"[3] but it is best to regard it as sphere, "in one hope," speaking of "the element in which the calling takes place."[4] It is similar in sense to εἰς "into."[5] In the NT the use of ἐν in connection with καλέω consistently denotes sphere (Rom 9:17; 1 Cor 7:15, 18, 20, 22, 24; Gal 1:6; Col 3:15; 1 Thess 4:17; Heb 11:18). In this context, the sphere refers to "hope."

The noun ἐλπίς, "hope," was discussed at 1:18 and was defined as eager expectation of the outworking of God's plan. The hope presented in Ephesians is the reality that all things will be headed up in Christ (1:9) and though the believers are presently seated with Christ, in the future they will be displayed in heaven as trophies of his grace (2:7). Further, they have been brought near to God, united into one body in Christ and reconciled to God (2:11–3:13). Before this they were without hope and without God in the world (2:12). Hence, there is the element of objective hope which is laid up for the believers (cf. Col 1:5; Rom 8:24), and this serves as the basis of the subjective hope. Hope for believers is not the world's "hope so" but the absolute certainty that God will deliver what he has promised. In this context the emphasis is on objective hope in line with many of the other elements in these three verses. Since both believing Jews and Gentiles have "one" hope, it would further support the concept of unity portrayed in these verses.

1. The conjunction καί is omitted from B 323 326 *pc* lat syr^{p} cop$^{sa, bo^{pt}}$. This is not sufficient evidence to warrant its omission.

2. Lincoln, 238.

3. Meyer, 198.

4. Eadie, 274; cf. also Alford, 3:114; Ellicott, 79; Abbott, 108; Salmond, 322.

5. MHT 3:263; Winer, *Grammar*, 519.

The following term κλῆσις, "call," was also discussed at 1:18, connoting a summons or invitation by God and thus closely linked with election. God chose them and adopted them into his family, and this was made a reality in the believer's life when he or she responded to God's call. The form of the word is genitive (κλήσεως) and has been rendered as a possessive genitive, "hope belonging to your call,"[1] but more likely it is either a genitive of origin, "hope has its origin in your call,"[2] or a subjective genitive, "hope produced by your call." The last option is preferred and is consistent with its significance in 1:18. The genitive personal pronoun (ὑμῶν) is possessive and means that the call belongs personally to believers. The call has its origin in God and they were called by God. Accordingly this becomes their personal call. Although in 1:18 it is "his" call, it belongs to believers and, therefore, can rightly be called "your" call.

In conclusion, then, the elements of unity are portrayed in the one body, the one Spirit, and the one hope of their calling. The third person of the Trinity is the unifier in this verse.

4:5. εἷς κύριος, "one Lord." Fourth, there is one Lord. In the previous verse the third person of the Trinity was discussed, Paul now considers the second person, Christ. The word κύριος logically refers to Christ since Paul has just discussed the Holy Spirit in verse 4 and will discuss the Father in the next verse. Christ is the "one Lord" who provided redemption (1:7), hope (1:12), and headship over the church (1:22–23). Indeed, it was Christ who brought the Jews and Gentiles into one body, both now having access to God (2:13–18; 3:6, 12). He was called Lord from the time of the earliest disciples (cf. Matt 16:15 = Mark 8:2 = Luke 9:20; Acts 2:36; 10:36; 16:31; 19:17; 1 Cor 8:5–6; 12:3).[3] Later, when the Gentiles were admitted, they too were unified under the same Lord.

μία πίστις, "one faith." Fifth, there is one faith. The "one faith" does not have reference to an objective faith, the body of truth be-

1. Eadie, 274; Abbott, 109.

2. Ellicott, 80; Salmond, 322.

3. Cf. Joseph A. Fitzmyer, "The Semitic Background of the New Testament *Kyrios*-Title," in *A Wandering Aramean: Collected Aramaic Essays*, Society of Biblical Literature Monograph Series, ed. Leander E. Keck and James L. Crenshaw, no. 25 (Missoula, Mont.: Scholars Press, 1979), 115–42; cf. idem, "New Testament *Kyrios* and *Maranatha* and Their Aramaic Background" in *To Advance the Gospel* (New York: Crossroad, 1981), 218–35; D. R. de Lacey, "'One Lord' in Pauline Christology," in *Christ the Lord. Studies in Christology Presented to Donald Guthrie*, ed. H. H. Rowdon (Leicester; Inter-Varsity; Downers Grove, Ill.: InterVarsity, 1982), 191–203; Larry W. Hurtado, *One God, One Lord: Early Christian Devotion and Ancient Jewish Monotheism* (Philadelphia: Fortress, 1988), esp. 93–124; Nils Alstrup Dahl, "Sources of Christological Language," in *Jesus the Christ: The Historical Origins of Christological Doctrine*, ed. Donald H. Juel (Minneapolis: Fortress, 1991), 113–36; W. C. van Unnik, "Jesus: Anathema or Kyrios (1 Cor. 12:3)," in *Christ and Spirit in the New Testament. In Honour of Charles Francis Digby Moule*, ed. Barnabas Lindars and Stephen S. Smalley (Cambridge: Cambridge University Press, 1973), 113–26.

lieved by Christians (as in Acts 6:7; 1 Tim 3:9; 4:1, 6; Jude 3, 20) as some propose,[1] but rather to the subjective faith which is exercised by all Christians in Christ their Lord (cf. Col 2:7). The latter usage is the most common in the NT. For instance, Paul declares to the Romans, "God is one, who shall justify the circumcision by faith and the uncircumcision through faith" (Rom 3:30). In the first chapter of this book, Paul mentions that the Ephesians had expressed their faith when they heard the message (1:13) and that their faith in the Lord Jesus was widely known (1:15). Thus, it is the one faith in the one Lord.

ἓν βάπτισμα, "one baptism." Sixth, there is one baptism. This phrase has caused some debate. There are two major views and a third should be considered. First, most commentators think it has reference to water baptism.[2] Certainly, in the early church faith in Christ is closely tied to water baptism (Acts 2:38; 8:16, 35–39; 19:5; 1 Cor 1:13–15). Believers were to be baptized in the name of the Lord. However, there are two problems with this view: (1) the rite of baptism, with all its different modes, seems to be more divisive than unifying (certainly in the later centuries); and (2) there is no mention of the other ordinance, the rite of the Lord's Supper, as a unifying element as Paul did in 1 Cor 10:17. Nevertheless, it was the one rite that outwardly demonstrated the believers' faith in their Lord. Second, some consider it to be a reference to the Spirit's baptism.[3] This view is un-

1. As suggested by Hanson, *The Unity of the Church in the New Testament*, 154; Best, 368–69; O'Brien, 283.

2. E.g., Hodge, 208–9; Alford, 3:114; Eadie, 274; Ellicott, 80; Meyer, 199; Abbott, 109; Salmond, 322; Barth, 468–70; Schnackenburg, 166; Bruce, 336–37; Lincoln, 240; Best, 369; cf. also Warnach, "Taufwirklichkeit und Taufbewußtsein nach dem Epheserbrief," 36–51; Markus Barth, *Die Taufe—ein Sakrament?* (Zollikon-Zürich: Evangelischer Verlag, 1951), 472–73; Dunn, *Baptism in the Holy Spirit*, 161–62, 227; Beasley-Murray, *Baptism in the New Testament*, 199–200; Halter, *Taufe und Ethos*, 242–48; David F. Wright, "One Baptism or Two? Reflections on the History of Christian Baptism," *VE* 18 (1988): 8–10; Lars Hartman, *'Into the Name of the Lord Jesus': Baptism in the Early Church*, Studies of the New Testament and Its World, ed. John Barclay, Joel Marcus, and John Riches (Edinburgh: T & T Clark, 1997), 102–4; Thiede, "Der Brief an die Epheser. 36. Teil: Kap. 4,1–6," 21. Cross suggests that "one baptism" refers to "conversion-baptism" whereby baptism cannot be separated from conversion that is often practiced by both those who espouse infant baptism and those who embrace believer's baptism. See Anthony R. Cross, "'One Baptism' (Ephesians 4.5): A Challenge to the Church," in *Baptism, the New Testament and the Church: Historical and Contemporary Studies in Honour of R. E. O. White*, ed. Stanley E. Porter and Anthony R. Cross, JSNTSup, ed. Stanley E. Porter, vol. 171 (Sheffield: Sheffield Academic Press, 1999), 173–209, esp. 206–8; Nils Alstrup Dahl, "The Concept of Baptism in Ephesians," in *Studies in Ephesians: Introductory Questions, Text- & Edition-Critical Issues, Interpretation of Texts and Themes*, ed. David Hellholm, Vemund Blomkvist, and Tord Fornberg, WUNT, ed. Martin Hengel and Otfried Hofius, vol. 131 (Tübingen: Mohr, 2000), 417–20.

3. Chafer, 124–25; Roels, *God's Mission*, 182; John F. Walvoord, *The Holy Spirit. A Comprehensive Study of the Person and Work of the Holy Spirit*, 3d ed. (Findlay, Ohio: Dunham, 1958), 140; D. W. B. Robinson, "Towards a Definition of Baptism," *RTR* 34

likely because: (1) the phrase is in the triad of elements that pertain to Christ, the second person of the Trinity; and (2) there is nothing in the broader context (vv. 1–16) referring to the Spirit's baptism. A third option that needs to be considered is that it refers metaphorically to the believer's baptism into Christ's death,[1] speaking of the believer's union with Christ in his death and resurrection. Baptism signifies identification as seen in the baptism of Israel into Moses as they went through the Red Sea (1 Cor 10:2) and the baptism of the disciples with reference to Christ's death (Mark 10:38). Both of these examples make no reference to water or to the Holy Spirit. This same concept is seen in other NT passages (Rom 6:1–11; Gal 3:27; Col 2:12). Furthermore, it fits well with the context, for the believer's baptism into Christ signifies union with Christ (Rom 6:5) and it occurs at the time of conversion (Rom 6:2–4). This inward reality is all too often missed. It serves as the basis of the outward ritual. Hence, the "one baptism" most likely refers to the internal reality of having been baptized into (identified with) the "one Lord" by means of the "one faith" mentioned in this verse.

In conclusion, there is unity in the one Lord in whom believers place their one faith expressed in one baptism signifying their identification in his death and resurrection. This verse revolves around the second person of the Trinity.

4:6. εἷς θεὸς καὶ[2] πατὴρ πάντων, "one God and Father of all." This is the third triad and it speaks of God the Father. This marks the climax, for God is the one unifying factor in both testaments, in spite of the fact that many gods are honored in the world (cf. 1 Cor 8:5–6). This form of "God and Father" is seen in only fourteen other places (Rom 15:6; 1 Cor 15:24; 2 Cor 1:3; 11:31; Gal 1:4; Eph 1:3; 5:20; Phil

(January–April 1975): 3–4; E. R. Rogers, "Yet Once More—'One Baptism'?" *RTR* 50 (May–August 1991): 41–49. Barth (*Die Taufe—ein Sakrament?* 472–73; cf. 352–62), Dunn (*Baptism in the Holy Spirit*, 161–62), and Bruce (337 n. 17) see a very close relationship between water and Spirit baptism.

1. Cullmann and Robinson have elements of this view, see Oscar Cullmann, *Baptism in the New Testament*, trans. J. K. S. Reid, SBT, ed. T. W. Manson, H. H. Rowley, Floyd V. Filson, and G. Ernest Wright, vol. 1 (London: SCM; Chicago: Henry Regnery, 1950); J. A. T. Robinson, "The One Baptism as a Category of New Testament Soteriology," *SJT* 6 (September 1953): 257–74, reprinted in idem, "The One Baptism," in *Twelve New Testament Studies*, SBT, ed. C. F. D. Moule, J. Barr, Floyd V. Filson, and G. Ernest Wright, no. 34 (London: SCM, 1962), 158–75. However, both of these scholars make this a universal baptism stating that since Christ died for the whole world so all mankind received baptism long ago and so faith is not even necessary (Cullmann, *Baptism*, 23). Moore examines the sixteen passages discussed by Robinson and shows that there is the need of faith (see W. E. Moore, "One Baptism," *NTS* 10 [July 1964]: 504–16). Certainly in the present context the "one baptism" is preceded by the "one faith." See O'Brien, 284.

2. The conjunction καί is omitted from 51 *pc* vg^{mss} syr^{p} cop$^{sa, bo^{pt}}$ Irenaeus^{arm}. The manuscript evidence is not weighty enough to warrant its omission.

4:20; 1 Thess 1:3; 3:11, 13; Jas 1:27; 1 Pet 1:3; Rev 1:6), but God as "Father" is given around twenty times (e.g., Matt 6:8, 9, 14, 15; John 5:18; 6:27; 8:41, 42; Phil 2:11). God is further described as the God and Father "of all," which refers not to all humans but to all believers (John 1:12; Gal 3:26). This is substantiated in the present context because Paul is exhorting Christians, and not all humans, to preserve the unity. Some commentators want to make God the universal Father, and Barth asserts that this view is "clinched by 3:14–15" where it speaks of Paul praying to the Father who names every family.[1] However, that is a different context where Paul tries to show that the God to whom he prays is all powerful and still active in the world today. The present context is talking about the unity of all believers as modeled by the Father of all believers. Furthermore, the next words of the verse would argue against the idea of a universal Father of all human beings since he is not only over all but through all and in all. The NT never envisions that God is in every human being but that he resides only in believers (Rom 8:9).

ὁ ἐπὶ πάντων καὶ διὰ πάντων καὶ ἐν πᾶσιν ἡμῖν,[2] "who is over all and through all and in all of us." This is a further identification of the God and Father of all. Paul accomplishes this through three different prepositions. "The variation of the preposition is a skilful way of condensing thought, each preposition adding a new idea."[3] There is some debate as to whether the adjectives πάντων . . . πάντων . . . πᾶσιν are masculine referring to people or neuter denoting things, that is, the universe. Some view these adjectives as neuter[4] because: (1) at significant points in Ephesians "all" refers to the whole universe (1:10, 22, 23; 3:9; 4:10) and (2) elsewhere in Paul (1 Cor 8:6; Rom 11:36; Col 1:16) God's or Christ's relationship to "all" regularly means "everything" and not just persons or believers. But normally Paul speaks of God not as Father of creation but as Father of believers (Rom 8:15; Gal 4:6; Col 1:2; 2 Thess 2:16; Phlm 3) or Father of our Lord Jesus Christ (Rom 15:6; 2 Cor 1:3; 11:31; Eph 1:3; Col 1:3). Others view

1. Barth, 471.

2. The exclusion of ἡμῖν is in 𝔓^{46} ℵ A B C P 082 0150 6 33 81 104 424^{c} 436 459 1739* 1881 1912* 1962 2464 *l* 60$^{1/2}$ cop$^{sa, bo}$ eth geo^{1} Marcion$^{acc. to Epiphanius}$ Origen$^{gr, lat}$ Gregory-Thaumaturgus^{vid} Eusebius Athanasius Marcellus Ps-Ignatius Gregory-Nyssa Didymus^{dub} Chrysostom^{lem} Cyril Victorinus-Rome$^{1/2}$ Ambrose Jerome Augustine. Its inclusion is found in D F G Ψ 075 0278 256 263 365 424* 1175 1319 1573 (1739^{c}) 1852 1912^{c} 2127 2200 *Byz* [K L] *Lect* it$^{ar, b, d, f, g, mon, o}$ vg syr$^{p, h}$ arm geo^{2} slav Irenaeus$^{gr, lat}$ Adamantius (Chrysostom^{com}) Theodore^{lat} Victorinus-Rome$^{1/2}$ Ambrosiaster Maximinus Pelagius. The reading πᾶσιν. ἀμήν is found only in 1241 (vg^{ms}). The omission of ἡμῖν is almost exclusively Alexandrian, but its inclusion is well represented by the Western and Byzantine text-types, and it has some representation in the Alexandrian tradition with Ψ and the vg.

3. Robertson, *Grammar*, 567; cf. also Winer, *Grammar*, 521.

4. Robinson, 93–94, 179; Gnilka, 204; Barth, 471; Lincoln, 240; Best, 371; O'Brien, 285–86.

these adjectives as masculine[1] because: (1) they harmonize with the immediately previous masculine πάντων; (2) they are individualized by ἑνὶ δὲ ἑκάστῳ ἡμῶν in the next verse;[2] (3) "to speak of God as 'through all *things*' and 'in all *things*' is not really characteristic either of the Bible as a whole or Paul's letters in particular";[3] and (4) if one accepts the textual variant ἡμῖν it makes the most sense—"in all of us." The latter view is preferred.

Regarding the further identification of God, there are three parts. First, he is over (ἐπί) all, indicating his sovereign position over all believers. This has reference not only to his spiritual authority over us[4] but also in every aspect of the life of the believer. God is "supreme and transcendent."[5] If believers take God's sovereignty seriously, the result is unity and contentment and joy for believers, even in the midst of trials. The believer will trust God in his wisdom and care for all things that transpire in life.

Second, not only is God sovereign in all believers' lives, he also works through (διά) all of them. Here the emphasis is on God's immanence.[6] He accomplishes his purposes through the instruments of believers. This is in keeping with 2:10 where the believer is God's workmanship created for good works which God prepared beforehand in order that he or she should walk in them. However, since God provides the power for good works, he is to receive all the glory. Such a wonderful provision shows that he is alive and active in the world today.

Finally, God is in all believers (ἐν πᾶσιν ἡμῖν). This signifies the indwelling Spirit (John 14:16–17; Rom 8:9; 1 Cor 2:12; 6:19–20; Gal 3:2; 4:6; 1 John 2:27; 3:24; 4:13), his intimate presence. In 3:17 Paul prayed that Christ might be at home in their hearts. Although Christ was already in them, Paul wanted him to be the very center of their lives. Believers have the joy of knowing that God not only is over them and working through them, but he is also residing in them. Whereas Paul spoke about God dwelling in the person of the Holy Spirit in the corporate body of the church (2:22), he now is talking about the personal dwelling of God in believers.

In concluding this section two observations should be noted. First, the Trinity is an integral part of this treatise on unity. The one body of believers is vitalized by one *Spirit*, so all believers have one hope. That body is united to its one *Lord* (Christ) by each member's one act of faith, and his or her identity with him is in the one baptism. One *God*,

1. Alford, 3:114–15; Eadie, 276; Ellicott, 81; Meyer, 201; Abbott, 109; Salmond, 323; Dibelius-Greeven, 80; Masson, 187; Schlier, 188–89; Gaugler, 166; Hendriksen, 188 n. 103; Mitton, 143; Schnackenburg, 167; Bruce, 337.

2. Meyer, 201; Abbott, 109; cf. also Salmond, 323.

3. Mitton, 143.

4. Calvin, 173.

5. Mitton, 143.

6. Salmond, 323.

the Father, is supreme over all, operative through all, and resides in all. All seven components are united in the Trinity. Some scholars such as Kirby think that baptism is central[1] and some like Hanson think that faith is central,[2] but in reality the Triune God is the center and model for unity. This is in keeping with the rest of Ephesians which is known for its abundant references to the Trinity (cf. 1:4–14, 17; 2:18, 22; 3:4–5, 14–17; 4:4–6; 5:18–20).

Second, the order in the listing of the three persons of the Trinity is interesting. It is in reverse order of the Apostles' Creed,[3] for Paul begins with the Holy Spirit rather than with the Father. The reason for this is that the context is about the unity of the Spirit (v. 3) and the gifts of the Spirit (vv. 7–13), hence the Spirit is mentioned first.[4] The same order of the persons of the Trinity is given in 1 Cor 12:4–6 where Paul also discusses the gifts of the Spirit.[5] Also, theologically he works back to the ultimate source since all proceeds from the Father.

2. The Preservation of Unity (4:7–16)

Having discussed the need to preserve unity (vv. 1–3) and the elements of unity which serve as a model for Christian unity (vv. 4–6), Paul now analyzes the means of preserving that unity of the body, namely, by the use of various gifts given to the church (vv. 7–16). Paul stresses unity in verses 1–6, diversity in verses 7–10, and a return to unity in verses 11–16.

a. The Donation of the Gifts (4:7–10)

Within the body of believers, God has bestowed gifts. The exercise of these gifts plays a vital role in the maintenance of unity within this unique body. This section expounds on the concept of gift bestowal and is divided into three parts: (1) description (v. 7), (2) validation (v. 8), and (3) interpretation (vv. 9–10).

(1) Description of the Giving of Gifts (4:7)

Paul will demonstrate that each believer is sovereignly and graciously given a gift or gifts. Such gifts are not, as some think, limited only to church leaders.

1. Kirby, *Ephesians, Baptism and Pentecost*, 151.

2. Hanson, *The Unity of the Church in the New Testament*, 151.

3. Reumann, *Variety and Unity in New Testament Thought*, 121.

4. It has been suggested that the order is based on experience. See R. R. Williams, "Logic *versus* Experience in the Order of Credal Formulae," *NTS* 1 (October 1954): 42–44.

5. Cf. Francis Martin, "Pauline Trinitarian Formula and Church Unity," *CBQ* 30 (April 1968): 199–219.

Text: 4:7. Ἑνὶ δὲ ἑκάστῳ ἡμῶν ἐδόθη ἡ χάρις κατὰ τὸ μέτρον τῆς δωρεᾶς τοῦ Χριστοῦ.

Translation: 4:7. "But to each one of us grace was given according to the measure of the gift of Christ."

Commentary: 4:7. Ἑνὶ δὲ ἑκάστῳ ἡμῶν ἐδόθη ἡ[1] χάρις, "But to each one of us grace was given." Significantly, the conjunction δέ, "but," marks a contrast from the preceding context, going from the whole church to every individual within the church. In the oneness of the body there is also diversity (cf. Rom 12:4–5; 1 Cor 12:4–29). The contrast here is seen when Paul moves from the πᾶς, "all," to the particular ἑνὶ δὲ ἑκάστῳ ἡμῶν "to each one of us." "In the addition of ἑνί to ἑκάστῳ ἡμῶν, the idea of distribution is expressed more distinctly than by the simple term."[2] Every single believer (changed from "you" in vv. 1 and 4 to "us") is included, no one is excluded, it is not only for the leaders of the assembly.[3] Paul proceeds to show that unity does not mean uniformity but harmony.

The word χάρις, "grace," was discussed at 1:2. It means unmerited or undeserved favor and denotes enablement. It is an abstract noun and by its very nature is general. However, when an abstract noun has an article, a particular aspect of the noun is stressed. In this context, it is a particular enablement given to each believer to empower them for ministry. It is very closely connected with χάρισμα, "grace-gift," which is used in the parallel passage on gifts (1 Cor 12:4, 9, 28, 30, 31). Furthermore, Paul places the two terms side by side in two passages (1 Cor 1:4, 7; Rom 12:6). Thus, it can be deduced that χάρισμα is a particular manifestation of God's enabling χάρις for various types of ministry.[4] The verb ἐδόθη meaning "to give" is a divine passive gnomic aorist and emphasizes that the individual receives the gift of enablement from the Lord and is to use it to minister for his glory. Some would argue that the subject of the verb, the one who gives the grace, is God,[5] but more likely it is Christ[6] for in this context it is Christ who

1. This article is omitted by B D* F G L P* Ψ 082 6 326 1505 1739 1881 *al* cop but is included in 𝔓[46] ℵ A C D[2] 0278 33 𝔐. The external evidence is quite mixed. It seems that on balance the inclusion of the article has a slight advantage for it is included in the Alexandrian, Western, and Byzantine traditions.

2. Eadie, 279.

3. Christfried Böttrich, "Gemeinde und Gemeindeleitung nach Epheser 4," *Theologische Beiträge* 30 (Juni 1999): 138–40. For a discussion of the relationship between spiritual gifts and office, see Ronald Y. K. Fung, "Ministry in the New Testament," in *The Church in the Bible and the World. An International Study*, ed. D. A. Carson (Exeter: Paternoster Press; Grand Rapids: Baker, 1987), 154–212, esp. 163–77.

4. Ronald Y. K. Fung, "Ministry, Community and Spiritual Gifts," *EvQ* 56 (January 1984): 5.

5. S. Hoekstra, "Wie is het subject van de verba in de pericope Efes. 4:7 vgg., God of Christus?" *Theologisch Tijdschrift* 1 (Januari 1867): 73–78; Masson, 188 n. 6; Barth, 429–30.

6. Gnilka, 206; Bouttier, 180 n. 423; Pokorný, 168.

descends and ascends and has the right to give the gifts. With the resurrection, Christ has been given all authority and power in heaven and on earth (Matt 28:18; Rom 1:4) and this is demonstrated in the present context by his bestowal of the gracious gifts for ministry.

κατὰ τὸ μέτρον τῆς δωρεᾶς τοῦ Χριστοῦ, "according to the measure of the gift of Christ." The preposition κατά with the accusative denotes standard. The person is a recipient of the gracious gift according to the measure (τὸ μέτρον) of the gift of Christ. It conveys that Christ not only gives each believer a gift but he also determines the amount of the gift. The first genitive (τῆς δωρεᾶς) is probably subjective[1] conveying the amount, which harmonizes well with Rom 12:3, which says, "to each as God measured out the measure of faith" (ἑκάστῳ ὡς ὁ θεὸς ἐμέρισεν μέτρον πίστεως). The term δωρεά already discussed at 3:7 has the idea of a gift graciously given by God. The second genitive (τοῦ Χριστοῦ) is a genitive of source (or agent). Hence, each believer has received from Christ a measure of a gift to be used in a particular function in the body. This entire phrase is in agreement with Paul in Rom 12:6–8 where he states that the gifts differ according to the grace given and they are to be used accordingly. Since the gift is measured out by Christ, there should not be any jealousy within the body. The difference of the gift does not determine the value. The difference of value is determined only by the individual's use of it within the body.

(2) Validation for the Giving of Gifts (4:8)

Paul has established that each believer has been given a gift and now links this provision of God with a quotation from the OT. This verse has had much scholarly ink spilled over it with various interpretations endeavoring to explain the rationale of Paul's use of Ps 68.

Text: 4:8. διὸ λέγει, **ἀναβὰς εἰς ὕψος ᾐχμαλώτευσεν αἰχμαλωσίαν, ἔδωκεν δόματα τοῖς ἀνθρώποις.**

Translation: 4:8. "Therefore it says, 'When he ascended on high he captured the captives, he gave gifts to people.'"

Commentary: 4:8. διὸ λέγει, "Therefore it says." This is an introductory formula to alert the readers that he is going to quote an OT passage (so also at 5:14 but not at 4:25; 5:31; 6:2, 3). The inferential conjunction διό means "therefore, for this reason."[2] Paul had just made a statement about the giving of gifts to each believer and this can be inferred from the OT passage of Scripture which he quotes. The subject

1. Alford, 3:115; Eadie, 280; Meyer, 203; Salmond, 323. Ellicott (82) thinks it is a possessive genitive to indicate "the measure which the gift has, which belongs to and defines the gift." For a discussion of the different options, see C. E. B. Cranfield, "Μέτρον πίστεως in Romans xii.3," *NTS* 8 (July 1962): 345–51, esp. 350.

2. BAGD 198; BDAG 250; Molland, "Διο, Einige syntaktische Beobachtungen," in *Serta Rudbergiana*, 43–52; reprinted in idem, "Διο: Einige syntaktische Beobachtungen," in *Opuscula Patristica*, 9–16.

of the verb λέγει, "says," could be neuter "it" referring to the Scripture or it could be masculine "he" referring to God.[1] The neuter is preferred. Abbott gives a long discourse as to why one cannot supply the word "God" here, that is, because "God" is never "expressed or implied as the subject, except where in the original context God is the speaker, as in Rom. ix. 15."[2] God is also specifically mentioned in Acts 2:17 and 2 Cor 6:16 (cf. also 2 Cor 6:2). Some think that it refers to God in the present verse because the Scriptures are God's words.[3] Yet since Ps 68 is quoted it most likely refers to Scripture. The Ephesians would have had no difficulty in accepting that what the Scripture says, God says.

ἀναβὰς εἰς ὕψος ᾐχμαλώτευσεν αἰχμαλωσίαν, ἔδωκεν[4] δόματα τοῖς[5] ἀνθρώποις, "'When he ascended on high he captured the captives, he gave gifts to people.'" This quotation resembles Ps 68:18 [MT 68:19; LXX 67:19]. In order to see the differences, one needs to lay the texts parallel to each other.

NT: ἀναβὰς εἰς ὕψος ᾐχμαλώτευσεν αἰχμαλωσίαν, ἔδωκεν δόματα τοῖς ἀνθρώποις.
LXX: ἀνέβης εἰς ὕψος ᾐχμαλώτευσας αἰχμαλωσίαν, ἔλαβες δόματα ἐν ἀνθρώπῳ.
MT: עָלִיתָ לַמָּרוֹם שָׁבִיתָ שֶּׁבִי לָקַחְתָּ מַתָּנוֹת בָּאָדָם

Immediately it can be observed that the LXX translates the MT verbatim. Paul makes six changes from the LXX: (1) he changes the finite verb ἀνέβης to the participle ἀναβάς; (2) he changes the person of both verbs from second person singular (ᾐχμαλώτευσας, ἔλαβες) to third person sin-

1. For a brief discussion of the introductory formulas, see E. Earle Ellis, *Paul's Use of the Old Testament* (London: Oliver and Boyd, 1957), 22–25.

2. Abbott, 110.

3. Alford, 3:115; Ellicott, 83; Meyer, 203; Salmond, 324; Barth, 431; Robertson, *Grammar*, 392; Winer, *Grammar*, 656; Wallace, *Greek Grammar*, 533; Benjamin B. Warfield, "'It Says:' 'Scripture Says:' 'God Says,'" *Presbyterian and Reformed View* 10 (July 1899): 475–78; reprinted in Benjamin Breckinridge Warfield, *The Inspiration and Authority of the Bible* (Philadelphia: Presbyterian and Reformed, 1948) 302–7.

4. The καί before ἔδωκεν is omitted from $\mathfrak{P}^{46}$ א* A C^{2} D* F G 33 1241^{s} 1962 2464 *l* 593 it$^{ar, b, d, f, g, mon, o}$ vg cop$^{sa, bo}$ slav Justin Marcion$^{acc. to Tertullian}$ Irenaeus^{lat} Eusebius Theodore^{lat} Hesychius Ambrosiaster Hilary Ambrose Rufinus Jerome Pelagius Augustine$^{3/5}$ Quodvultdeus Varimadum. The conjunction καί is inserted before ἔδωκεν in א^{2} B C$^{*, 3}$ D^{2} Ψ 075 0150 6 81 104 256 263 365 424 436 459 1175 1319 1573 1852 1881 1912 2127 2200 *Byz* [K L P] *Lect* syr$^{p, h}$ arm geo Chrysostom Cyril Victorinus-Rome Augustine$^{2/5}$. The reading καὶ ἔδωκας is found only in *l* 598 *l* 751 *l* 884 eth. The weight of the evidence seems to be for its exclusion because there is good representation from the Alexandrian and Western texts. The other reading has good representation of the Byzantine text but not as good in the Alexandrian text-type.

5. The preposition ἐν is inserted before τοῖς ἀνθρώποις in only F G 614 630 2464 *pc* vg^{ms} Jerome^{pt}. All the other manuscripts exclude it.

gular (ᾐχμαλώτευσεν, ἔδωκεν); (3) he changes the action of the last verb from "receiving" (ἔλαβες) to "giving" (ἔδωκεν); (4) he changes the singular ἀνθρώπῳ to the plural ἀνθρώποις; (5) he leaves out the preposition ἐν; and (6) he adds the article τοῖς. What is the effect of these changes? Basically, there are two: (1) he has changed from the second person singular "you ascended" to the third person singular "he ascended"; and (2) he has changed the action from the receiving of gifts from among the people, the defeated foes, to the giving of gifts to the people, the believers.

There are enormous problems in attempting to solve the differences listed above. Many attempts have been made.[1] Beyond these problems, Ps 68 is reckoned "as textually and exegetically the most difficult and obscure of all the psalms,"[2] and various attempted interpretations have been proposed.[3]

1. S. R. Driver, "Notes on Three Passages in St. Paul's Epistles," *Exp* 3d ser., vol. 9 (January 1889): 20–23; Johannes Dalmer, "Bemerkungen zu I Kor. 10,3–4 und Eph. 4,8–10," *Theologische Studien und Kritiken* 63, no. 3 (1890): 579–92; Henry St. John Thackeray, *The Relation of St. Paul to Contemporary Jewish Thought: An Essay to Which Was Awarded the Kay Prize for 1899* (London: Macmillan, 1900), 182; Str-B, 3:596–98; Barnabas Lindars, *New Testament Apologetic: The Doctrinal Significance of the Old Testament Quotations* (London: SCM, 1961), 52–56; J. Cambier, "La Signification Christologique d'Eph. iv.7–10," *NTS* 9 (April 1963): 262–75; G. B. Caird, "The Descent of Christ in Ephesians 4,7–11," in *SE II. Papers Presented to the Second International Congress on New Testament Studies held at Christ Church Oxford, 1961*, ed. F. L. Cross, TU, ed. Friedrich Zucher et al., vol. 87 (Berlin: Akademie-Verlag, 1964), 535–45; J. Dupont, "Ascension du Christ et don de l'Esprit d'après Actes 2:33," in *Christ and Spirit in the New Testament. In Honour of Charles Francis Digby Moule*, ed. Barnabas Lindars and Stephen S. Smalley (Cambridge: Cambridge University Press, 1973), 219–28; Martin McNamara, *The New Testament and Palestinian Targum to the Pentateuch*, 2d printing, with supplement containing additions and corrections, AnBib, vol. 27A (Rome: Biblical Institute Press, 1978), 78–81; Barth, 472–77; Richard Rubinkiewicz, "PS LXVIII 19 (= Eph IV 8) Another Textual Tradition or Targum?" *NovT* 17 (July 1975): 219–24; Gary V. Smith, "Paul's Use of Psalm 68:18 in Ephesians 4:8," *JETS* 18 (summer 1975): 181–89; Lincoln, *Paradise Now and Not Yet*, 155–63; idem, "The Use of the OT in Ephesians," 18–25; Max Wilcox, "Text Form," in *It Is Written: Scripture Citing Scripture: Essays in Honour of Barnabas Lindars, SSF*, ed. D. A. Carson and H. G. M. Williamson (Cambridge: Cambridge University Press, 1988), 198–99; Richard A. Taylor, "The Use of Psalm 68:18 in Ephesians 4:8 in Light of the Ancient Versions," *BSac* 148 (July–September 1991): 319–36. For a brief discussion of what the eastern church fathers did with this passage, see Roger E. Reynolds, *The Ordinals of Christ from Their Origins to the Twelfth Century*, Beiträge Geschichte und Quellenkunde des Mittelalters, vol. 7 (Berlin: de Gruyter, 1978), 10–16.

2. Mitchell Dahood, *Psalms II: 51–100*, AB, ed. William Foxwell Albright and David Noel Freedman, vol. 17 (Garden City, N.Y.: Doubleday, 1968), 133; Artur Weiser, *The Psalms*, trans. Herbert Hartwell, Old Testament Library, ed. G. Ernest Wright, John Bright, James Barr, and Peter Ackroyd (London: SCM, 1962), 481–83.

3. See W. F. Albright, "A Catalogue of Early Hebrew Lyric Poems (Psalm lxviii)," *HUCA* 23 (1950–51): 1–39; Samuel Iwry, "Notes on Psalm 68," *JBL* 71 (September 1952): 161–65; J. Gray, "A Cantata of the Autumn Festival: Psalm lxviii," *Journal of Semitic Studies* 22 (spring 1977): 2–26.

However, in dealing with the present text, over the years there have been basically two approaches. First, it is thought that Paul altered the text to bring out its full meaning.[1] The problem with this view is that instead of giving it a full meaning, this renders it a different meaning.

Second, it is thought that Paul replaced "receive" with "give" by quoting from the OT textual tradition found in the Targum.[2] Regarding Ps 68:18 [MT 68:19; LXX 67:19], the Targumist renders it:

> "You, Moses the prophet, ascended to the firmament;
> you took captivity captive,
> you learned the words of the Torah,
> you gave them as gifts to the sons of men."[3]

Since the Targumist perceived the "gifts" to be the words of the law, it is proposed that when he read the difficult expression "you received gifts from among the people," he did not see it fitting for God's majesty. So by a simple transposition of the radicals from לקח ("to receive") to חלק ("to give") he changed it to "you gave them as gifts to the sons of men."[4] The Midrash has the same interpretation, the gift being the Torah and given to humans.[5] It must be recognized that the latter two writings are considerably later (no earlier than fourth or fifth century A.D.) but it is felt that they represent a pre-Christian interpretation. Possible evidence that this interpretation has early roots is the use of this concept in a second century B.C. apocryphal work, *T. Dan* 5.10–11.[6] This reading of "giving gifts" is also found in Ps 68:18 of the

1. Allan M. Harman, "Aspects of Paul's Use of the Psalms," *WTJ* 32 (November 1969): 6. Lindars (*New Testament Apologetic*, 55) states that it was altered by the exegetes in the Christian community.

2. Thackeray, *The Relation of St. Paul to Contemporary Jewish Thought*, 182.

3. For the Aramaic texts, see *Hagiographa Chaldaice*, ed. Paulus de Lagarde (Leipzig: B. G. Teubner, 1873), 38; *Targum de Salmos: Edición Príncipe del Ms. Villa-Amil n. 5*, ed. Luis Diez Merino, Biblia poliglota complutense. Tradición sefardí de la Biblia Aramea IV, 1. Bibliotheca Hispana Biblica, ed. Domingo Muñoz León, vol. 6 (Madrid: Consejo Superior de Investigaciones Científicas, Instituto "Franciso Suárez", 1982), 127; and for an ET, see Thackeray, *The Relation of St. Paul to Contemporary Jewish Thought*, 182; W. Hall Harris III, *The Descent of Christ: Ephesians 4:7–11 and Traditional Hebrew Imagery*, AGJU, ed. Martin Hengel et al., vol. 32 (Leiden: Brill, 1996), 65.

4. McNamara, *The New Testament and the Palestinian Targum to the Pentateuch*, 80.

5. Midr. Ps. 68.11 [68:19].

6. Rubinkiewicz, "PS LXVIII 19 (= Eph IV 8) Another Textual Tradition or Targum?" 221–22. De Jonge would date this work late second century A.D. See M. de Jonge, "The Testaments of the Twelve Patriarchs and the New Testament," in *SE. Papers Presented to the International Congress on "The Four Gospels in 1957" held at Christ Church, Oxford, 1957*, ed. Kurt Aland, F. L. Cross, Jean Danielou, Harald Riesenfeld, and W. C. van Unnik, TU, ed. Kurt Aland, Walther Eltester, and Erich Klostermann, vol. 73 (Berlin: Akademie-Verlag, 1959), 556. However, most maintain a second century B.C. date. See H. C. Kee, "Testaments of the Twelve Patriarchs (Second Century B.C.)," in *The Old*

Syriac Peshitta, but it is impossible to know if it depended on the Targum or Eph 4:8.[1] Hence, it could be deduced that Paul may have relied on the Targum reading of Ps 68:18 or that he picked up the rabbinic technique of midrash pesher and applied it to Christ.[2] The second alternative is more probable because it is unlikely that Paul would have regarded the Targum reading as Scripture.[3] Caird carries this further by declaring that Ps 68 was one of the appointed psalms for the Feast of Pentecost since the Targum of Ps 68:18 mentions Moses' ascent of Mount Sinai to receive the Torah and his descent to give it to men. It is surmised then that the author of Ephesians christianized the rabbinic exegesis of this pentecostal psalm to correspond with Christ's ascent and the Spirit's descent on the Day of Pentecost.[4] But the claim that this is a pentecostal psalm has little, if any, evidence. Bock states: "There is no mention of Moses or the law in Acts 2, a fatal omission for those who wish to connect the Moses-Pentecost association of Judaism to the allusion of Ps. 68 here."[5] Furthermore, when one reads commentaries on Ps 68,[6] even Jewish commentaries,[7] there is no claim that this is related to the Feast of Weeks.

A more recent attempt to solve this problem is made by Gary Smith.[8] By use of an analogy from Num 8:6–19 where the Levites were taken "captive" by God and given as a gift to Israel for tabernacle service, Smith sees the leaders in the church as taken by God and given to the church for ministry. However, this fails to solve the prob-

---

Testament Pseudepigrapha, ed. James H. Charlesworth, vol. 1 (Garden City, N.Y.: Doubleday; London: Darton, Longman & Todd, 1983), 777–78.

1. Cf. Eb. Nestle, "Zum Zitat in Eph 4,8," *ZNW* 4, no. 4 (1903): 344–45; Martin, "Quelques remarques sur le texte syriaque de l'Épître aux Éphésiens," 101–2.

2. Cf. Dibelius, *Die Geisterwelt im Glauben des Paulus*, 162; Ellis, *Paul's Use of the Old Testament*, 144; Lindars, *New Testament Apologetic*, 53; Richard N. Longenecker, *Biblical Exegesis in the Apostolic Period* (Grand Rapids: Eerdmans, 1975), 124–25. Barth (475) put it well when he stated: "Certainly there is a possibility that the author of Ephesians was not a lonely distorter of Scriptures but belonged in the company of *bona fide* co-interpreters."

3. Best, 379–80.

4. Caird, "The Descent of Christ in Ephesians 4,7–11," 539–44; Kirby, *Ephesians, Baptism and Pentecost*, 97–98; Lincoln, *Paradise Now and Not Yet*, 161; idem, "The Use of the OT in Ephesians," 19–20; Harris, *The Descent of Christ*, 143–59; Lincoln, 242–44.

5. Darrell L. Bock, *Proclamation from Prophecy and Pattern: Lucan Old Testament Christology*, JSNTSup, ed. David Hill, vol. 12 (Sheffield: JSOT Press, 1987), 183.

6. Dahood, *Psalms II: 51–100*, 17:133–52; A. A. Anderson, *The Book of Psalms*, New Century Bible, ed. Ronald E. Clements (OT) and Matthew Black (NT), vol. 1 (London: Marshall, Morgan & Scott, 1972), 481–99; Marvin E. Tate, *Psalms 51–100*, WBC, ed. David A. Hubbard and Glenn W. Barker; Old Testament ed. John D. W. Watts, vol. 20 (Dallas: Word, 1990), 170–75.

7. A. Cohen, *The Psalms*, Soncino Books of the Bible (London: Soncino, 1958), 209–15; Samson Raphael Hirsch, *The Psalms*, vol. 1 (New York: Philipp Feldheim, 1960), 454–71, esp. 463.

8. Smith, "Paul's Use of Psalm 68:18 in Ephesians 4:8," 181–89.

lem of how the text was changed from "you receive gifts" in Ps 68:18 to "he gave gifts" in Eph 4:8 and further, the use of the analogy from Num 8 is unacceptable, for in Ps 68 the captives were enemies whereas in Num 8 those taken were within the camp of Israel. Furthermore, nowhere are the Levites viewed as captives in Num 8. They are taken from among Israel to be used among their own people.

Finally, it is quite possible that instead of trying to quote Ps 68:18 specifically, Paul is summarizing Ps 68 with words that resemble verse 18. It is similar, perhaps, to the way a news reporter summarizes a thirty-minute speech in just two or three sentences. It is possible that one sentence by the reporter is very close to a sentence in the speech. Some could accuse the reporter of inaccuracy because it was not identical. However, the reporter's purpose is not direct citation on any one sentence but a summary of the whole speech.

A study of this psalm reveals many examples of God's gifts to people, hence, it is classified as a song of victory.[1] The first portion speaks of God's presence and activity (vv. 1–6) protecting the widows, giving the desolate homes, and leading prisoners to prosperity (vv. 5–6). In the second part, he speaks of God's past activity (vv. 7–18), marching with Israel in the wilderness, providing rain, providing for the needy (vv. 7–10), giving them victory over their enemies, and prospering them with the spoils (vv. 11–14). Again, in David's time, he gained victory in Zion (2 Sam 5:6–10) and received gifts from the enemy (Ps 68:15–18). The third section describes God's deliverance, care for his saints, and the scattering of his enemies (vv. 19–23). The fourth portion describes the procession of God into the sanctuary (vv. 24–27). The fifth part speaks of kings bringing gifts to God and the removal of those who do unrighteousness (vv. 28–31). The final segment is a call to praise God whose power is in the skies, a power and strength which he gives to his people (vv. 32–35).[2] These are among the numerous gifts God gives to people. Hence, it appears that Paul takes this prevailing theme of God's gifts to people and applies it to the church.

Regardless of the interpretation one prefers, it must be acknowledged that Ps 68:18 has been changed by Paul to make it applicable to the present Ephesian context. He declares that the gifts to which he refers are of a spiritual nature and are given to the believers in the Ephesian assembly and by application, to the believers down through the ages.[3] The text will now be examined in the light of these introductory remarks.

1. Claus Westermann, *Praise and Lament in the Psalms*, trans. Keith R. Crim and Richard N. Soulen, rev. ed. (Richmond, Va.: John Knox; Edinburgh: T & T Clark, 1981), 90–93. There is no agreement on the historical setting of this psalm.

2. For a chiastic outline of the psalm, see Moritz, *A Profound Mystery*, 66.

3. For a similar conclusion, see Taylor, "The Use of Psalm 68:18 in Ephesians 4:8," 336.

As previously stated, the first clause of this quotation (ἀναβὰς εἰς ὕψος ᾐχμαλώτευσεν αἰχμαλωσίαν) is taken from Ps 68 and refers to God who, having been present at Sinai, has now come to reside in Zion. In order for him to ascend to the high (Zion) he had to conquer the Canaanites. This resulted in the taking of many captives. The verb αἰχμαλωτεύω is not used in classical Greek but in the LXX it occurs thirty-nine times and in the canonical books it appears thirty-four times where it translates four Hebrew words, eighteen times for שָׁבָה (e.g., Gen 14:14; 34:29; Num 24:22; Ps 68:18 [MT 68:19; LXX 67:19]), always meaning "to take captive, to capture."[1] In the NT it is used only in Eph 4:8 and has the same meaning. The cognate accusative derived from αἰχμαλωσία is a late word rarely appearing before NT times.[2] In the LXX it occurs 134 times and in the canonical books it appears eighty-nine times for five Hebrew words, thirty-seven of which translate שְׁבִי (e.g., Num 21:1; Deut 21:13; 2 Chr 6:37; Ps 68:18 [MT 68:19; LXX 67:19]), denoting "captivity."[3] It is used only three times in the NT (Eph 4:8; Rev 13:10*bis*) and with the same sense. It is interesting to note that it is consistently used of military captives who are captured.[4] Certainly this is the case in Ps 68. God has had victory over the foe.

The second clause of Paul's quotation of Ps 68 (ἔδωκεν δόματα τοῖς ἀνθρώποις) presents real problems due to the change from second to third persons and the reversal of the action from receiving to giving. Psalm 68 conveys the idea of captives bringing gifts of the spoils and kings bringing tribute or possibly offerings of homage to God. Paul turns this around by stating that Christ gives gifts to those who are on the victorious side with him. Although the two renderings seem to be opposites, they are not incompatible. If God receives the spoils of war from the enemies in Ps 68, it is not beyond understanding that he would give gifts to those who are on his side as a provision from him as is portrayed in Eph 4:8. Furthermore, if this is considered only an indirect quotation summarizing the whole psalm, then there is no need to harmonize completely the specific verse but rather to show that it is consistent with the content of the whole psalm. Thus, the essence is that God is the one who gives gifts to his children.

Who, then, are the captives? From Ps 68 it is clear that they were the enemies of Israel who were defeated when Jerusalem was captured. In Ephesians some have interpreted the captives: (1) as the enemies of Christ, namely, Satan, sin, and death;[5] or (2) as the people who have been the captives of Satan, sin, and death, and who are now

1. BDB 985; B. Otzen, "שָׁבָה *šāḇāh*; שְׁבִי *šᵉḇî*, etc.," *TWAT* 7 (1990): 950–58.

2. Diodorus Siculus 20.61.8.

3. BDB 985; Otzen, *TWAT* 7 (1990): 952–53.

4. Gerhard Kittel, "αἰχμάλωτος," *TDNT* 1 (1964): 195–97.

5. Chrysostom *Eph* 4:9–10 (*PG* 62:82); Theophylact *Eph* 4:8 (*PG* 124:1084); Calvin, 175; Bengel, 4:89; Alford, 3:116; Eadie, 288; Ellicott, 84; Meyer, 210; Abbott, 113; Dibel-

taken captive by Christ in redemption.[1] The first interpretation seems to be more fitting. Christ had victory over Satan, sin, and death and gives gifts of the Spirit to those who have been identified with him.

The point that Paul is trying to make is the fact that Christ, who ascended as victor, has the right to give gifts. For if Christ had been defeated, he would yet be in his grave and spiritual gifts would be useless to those whom he could not redeem. On the other hand, Christ does not receive gifts from the defeated foes as in Ps 68, for such would be useless to God and his children. Satan, sin, and death have been defeated by Christ's redemption. Consequently, those who were held in their bondage have been freed and have obtained the gifts of the Spirit from their victorious Lord and Savior Jesus Christ.

(3) Interpretation of the Giving of Gifts (4:9–10)

After quoting Ps 68, Paul now interprets the Psalm for believers in this age. His interpretation revolves around two words from the Psalm citation: ἀναβάς, which he expounds in verses 9–10, and ἔδωκεν, which he discusses in verses 11–16. His discussion of the first word in verses 9–10 is somewhat parenthetical because the main thesis in the context is the giving of gifts. However, although parenthetical, these verses are important in order to establish the fact that Christ after his descent to the earth did ascend and thus, as the victor over the enemy, has the right to give gifts.

Text: 4:9. τὸ δὲ ἀνέβη τί ἐστιν, εἰ μὴ ὅτι καὶ κατέβη εἰς τὰ κατώτερα [μέρη] τῆς γῆς; **4:10.** ὁ καταβὰς αὐτός ἐστιν καὶ ὁ ἀναβὰς ὑπεράνω πάντων τῶν οὐρανῶν, ἵνα πληρώσῃ τὰ πάντα.

Translation: 4:9. "Now what is the meaning 'he ascended,' except that he also descended to the lower parts of the earth? **4:10.** He who descended is himself also he who ascended above all the heavens, in order that he might fill all things."

Commentary: 4:9. τὸ δὲ ἀνέβη τί ἐστιν, "Now what is the meaning 'he ascended.'" The conjunction δέ is "a transitional explanation or inference"[2] that is best translated as "now." The neuter article τό may be "before quoted words, sentences, and sentence fragments."[3] However, in this context Paul explores the meaning of the predicate ἀνέβη

---

ius, *Die Geisterwelt im Glauben des Paulus*, 163; Mussner, *Christus, das All und die Kirche*, 44.

1. Justin Martyr *Dialogus cum Tryphone Judaeo* 39.4–6 (*PG* 6:560–61); Theodore of Mopsuestia *Eph* 4:5–8 (*PG* 66:920); Theodoret *Eph* 4:8 (*PG* 82:533); Oecumenius *Eph* 4:7–13 (*PG* 118:1217); Aquinas, chap. 4, lec. 3, vv. 7–10 (159–60); Harless, 356–57; Olshausen, 214–15; Murray, 65; Hendriksen, 191; Richard Dormandy, "The Ascended Christ and His Gifts," *ExpTim* 109 (April 1998): 207; John F. Brug, "Psalm 68:19—He Received Gifts among Men," *WLQ* 96 (spring 1999): 126.

2. Eadie, 289; Ellicott, 84; Salmond, 326.

3. BDF §267 (1); MHT 3:182; Robertson, *Grammar*, 735, 766.

which was not quoted from Ps 68 but rather is derived from the participle ἀναβάς in that passage.[1] Paul did not quote the particular participle because he wanted to take the concept of the participle and change it into a finite verb in order to make a corresponding comparison with the following finite verb κατέβη "he descended." Hence, the whole clause τὸ δὲ ἀνέβη τί ἐστιν translated literally, would be "Now what is the 'he ascended?'" but is better translated "Now what is the meaning of 'he ascended?'" or "Now what does 'he ascended' mean?"[2]

εἰ μὴ ὅτι καὶ κατέβη,[3] "except that he also descended." The εἰ μή ὅτι καί construction literally reads "if [it does] not [mean] that also." In other words, the meaning of Christ's ascension presupposes his former descent. The conjunction καί is used adjunctively meaning "also." The traditional interpretation has been that the descent refers to Christ's descent from heaven to earth at the time of his incarnation and that the ascent refers to Christ's ascent from earth to heaven after the resurrection.

Another view first proposed by von Soden,[4] accepted by Abbott,[5] revived by Caird among others,[6] and significantly refined by Harris[7] suggests that the descent refers not to Christ's descent at the incarnation but to Christ's descent at Pentecost to give his spiritual gifts to the church. It is thought that this makes good sense of the parenthesis in verses 10–11 in that Christ ascended and then gave gifts. His descent,

1. Winer, *Grammar*, 136 n. 2.

2. Cf. Harris, *The Descent of Christ*, 179; *pace* Wallace, *Greek Grammar*, 238.

3. The texts that read κατέβη πρῶτον are $\aleph^{2}$ B C^{3} Ψ 075 0150 104 256 263 365 424* 436 459 1175 1319 1573 1852 1912 1962 2127 2200 2464 *Byz* [K L P] *Lect* (*l* 170 ἀνέβη [*sic*]) it$^{f, mc, o}$ vg syr$^{p, h}$ cop^{samss} arm geo slav Eusebius Didymus^{dub} Chrysostom Theodore^{lat} Theodoret. On the other hand, the texts that have κατέβη alone are 𝔓^{46} ℵ* A C* D F G I^{vid} 082 6 33 81 424^{c} 1241^{s} 1739 1881 *l* 1439 it$^{ar, b, d, g, mon}$ vg^{mss} cop$^{sams, bo}$ eth Irenaeus^{lat} Clement$^{from\ Theodotus}$ Origen$^{gr, lat}$ Cyril Tertullian Victorinus-Rome Ambrosiaster Hilary Lucifer Jerome Pelagius Augustine. The preferable reading is κατέβη without πρῶτον because it is represented in many early manuscripts and it has good geographical distribution as well as a good genealogical relationship within the text-types. It is the shorter reading and a more difficult reading because πρῶτον makes it clear that the order is first descension before ascension. For a scribe to insert it is understandable, but to omit it is incomprehensible. Cf. Martin, "Quelques remarques sur le texte syriaque de l'Épître aux Éphésiens," 102.

4. Von Soden, 135–36.

5. Abbott, 116.

6. Caird, "The Descent of Christ in Ephesians 4,7–11," 536–37; Caird, 74–75; cf. also Meuzelaar, *Der Leib des Messias* 136–37; Roels, *God's Mission*, 161–63; Calvin L. Porter, "Descent of Christ: An Exegetical Study of Ephesians 4:7–11," in *One Faith: Its Biblical, Historical, and Ecumenical Dimensions*, ed. Robert L. Simpson (Enid, Okla.: Philips University Press, 1966), 47–48, 51; Martin, "Ephesians," in *The Broadman Bible Commentary*, 156; Lincoln, *Paradise Now and Not Yet*, 160–62; idem, "The Use of the OT in Ephesians," 22–24; Lincoln, 246–47.

7. Harris, *The Descent of Christ*, 1–197, esp. 143–97; idem, "The Ascent and Descent of Christ in Ephesians 4:9–10," *BSac* 151 (April–June 1994): 204–14.

then, was in the person of the Spirit. Furthermore, they suggest that it is parallel to the rabbinic tradition which associated Ps 68 with Moses' heavenly ascent of Mount Sinai to "capture" the words of the Torah (in connection with the Feast of Pentecost) and his descent from Mount Sinai to distribute to the people the "gifts" of the Torah. In addition, it is suggested that in Ephesians Paul does not distinguish between Christ and the Holy Spirit (3:16–17). This view has much to commend itself, yet it has some problems.

First, it assumes the recipients of this letter would have had an acquaintance with the rabbinic traditions needed for this view. Although, there are elements of rabbinic material which may be dated in the first century, much of it is fifth century A.D. or later.[1] Furthermore, even if these elements existed in the first century, how much was there and how much would the Gentile audience in Ephesus be acquainted with them?

Second, as mentioned above, the association of the rabbinic tradition of Moses' ascent to receive the Torah (in connection with Ps 68) with the Feast of Pentecost is completely absent from Peter's explanation (Acts 2) to the people of Israel regarding the advent of the Holy Spirit on the day of Pentecost. If this rabbinic tradition was so well known in Israel why was there no mention of it when Peter addressed the Jews in Jerusalem?

Third, in Acts 2:33 Peter states that Jesus is exalted (ὑψωθείς) at the right hand of God and having received (λαβών) from the Father the promise of the Holy Spirit, poured out (ἐξέχεεν) what the people then saw and heard. Here there is no mention of the giving the gifts (δόματα) as mentioned in the present context and in Ps 68:18.

Fourth, in the present context it seems that the descent is before the ascent. The conjunction καί in verse 10 is best translated "also" denoting Christ who had descended also ascended. In fact, Lincoln, an advocate of Christ's descent on Pentecost, admits that the descent, prior to the ascent, "has the advantage of following the order in the original meaning of the psalm, for the descent inferred from the ascent of Jahweh to Mt Zion would be the fact that he first came down to deliver his people and triumph over his enemies before going up to his dwelling place."[2] Therefore, if one accepts Christ's descent on Pentecost as the correct exegesis of verse 9, it makes verse 10 useless.[3]

1. Harris (*The Descent of Christ*, 64–95, 194–96) is extremely careful and fair with the use and dating of rabbinic evidence. His suggestion of a fourth century date for the Targum Psalms (72–73, 194) is an earlier date than recognized by most scholars.

2. Lincoln, *Paradise Now and Not Yet*, 160; cf. also Moritz, *A Profound Mystery*, 80–82.

3. Schnackenburg, "Christus, Geist und Gemeinde (Eph. 4:1–16)," 287; cf. K. S. Hemphill, "The Pauline Concept of Charisma: A Situational and Developmental Approach" (Ph.D. thesis, University of Cambridge, 1976), 230–31. For a revised and more popular treatment of this, see idem, *Spiritual Gifts: Empowering the New Testament Church* (Nashville: Broadman, 1988), 174.

Fifth, although Lincoln suggests that there is virtual interchange between Christ and the Spirit elsewhere in Ephesians (1:13 and 4:30; 3:16–17; 1:23 and 5:18),[1] these functions are not identical if one examines these verses. In the present context the same person, namely, Christ, has descended and ascended. The personal pronoun αὐτός, "himself," isolates it to Christ.

Sixth, since there is no explicit reference to the Spirit, Hui rightly contends that it would not have been obvious to the readers that the one who descended subtly changed from Christ to Christ-in-the-Spirit.[2] This is especially true if one accepts the rabbinic background of Moses' ascent of Mount Sinai that no other than Moses descended from the Mount.

Seventh, the climax of Christ's activity is his ascension because at that time he fulfills all things (v. 10). Thus, it seems best to accept the traditional order that Christ's descent at the incarnation precedes his ascent to heaven shortly after his resurrection.

εἰς τὰ κατώτερα [μέρη][3] **τῆς γῆς,** "to the lower parts of the earth?" This phrase gives the locale to which he descended. The preposition εἰς gives the direction of his descent, namely, "into," or even better, "to." The comparative adjective κατώτερα is derived from the adverb of place κάτω, "below,"[4] meaning "lower."[5] The plural τὰ μέρη conveys the idea of "the parts" of a country such as regions or districts.[6]

The real problem is identifying the syntactical relationship of the genitival phrase τῆς γῆς. There are three views. (1) Traditionally it has been taken as a genitive of comparison or a partitive genitive, which would be interpreted as parts lower than the earth or under the earth, that is, Christ's descent into Hades.[7] In support of this view, Meyer states, "had Paul intended only the descent *to earth* . . . , it would not be

1. Lincoln, 247.

2. Hui, "The Concept of the Holy Spirit in Ephesians," 96–97.

3. The omission of μέρη is found in 𝔓^{46} D* F G *l* 921 it$^{ar, b, d, g, mon, o}$ cop^{sa} eth Irenaeus^{lat} Clement$^{from\ Theodotus}$ Origen^{lat} Eusebius Tertullian Victorinus-Rome Ambrosiaster Hilary Lucifer Jerome which, with the exception of 𝔓^{46} and cop^{sa}, are all Western readings. Its inclusion is found in ℵ A B C D^{2} I Ψ 075 0150 6 33 81 104 256 263 365 424 436 459 1175 1241 1319 1573 1739 1852 1881 1912 1962 2127 2200 2464 *Byz* [K L P] *Lect* it^{f} vg syr^{h} cop^{bo} arm slav Eustathius Chrysostom Theodore^{lat} Cyril Theodoret Pelagius Augustine, which has good Alexandrian and Byzantine readings. The inclusion of μέρη is the preferred reading because of good representative manuscripts in the Alexandrian and Byzantine texts, giving it a better geographical distribution.

4. MHT 2:166; Robertson, *Grammar*, 278, 299; 665.

5. BAGD 425; BDAG 535.

6. BAGD 506; BDAG 633.

7. Jerome *Eph* 4:9 (*PL* 26:498–99); Ambrosiaster *Eph* 4:10 (*PL* 17:387); Aquinas, chap. 4, lec. 3, vv. 7–10 (160–61); Bengel, 4:90; Olshausen, 218–20; Alford, 3:116; Ellicott, 85; Meyer, 213–14; Robinson, 96, 180; Ewald, 189–90; Scott, 208–9; Beare, 10:689; Wilhelm Bousset, "Zur Hadesfahrt Christi," *ZNW* 19, no. 2 (1919/20): 50–56; Bousset, *Kyrios Christos*, 60–68; Odeberg, *View of the Universe*, 18–19; Friedrich Büchsel, "κάτω,

easy to see why he should not have written merely κατέβη ["he descended"], or at any rate simply κατέβη εἰς τὴν γῆν ["he descended to the earth"] or κατέβη εἰς τὴν γῆν κάτω ["he descended to the earth below"] (Acts ii. 19)."[1] Instead he used a phrase that implies that which is more than the earth. Furthermore, in the very next verse Paul makes a similar contrast by referring to Christ's ascension above all the heavens. Thus, since he went to the highest part of heaven, he must have gone to the lowest part of the earth. Consequently, Christ's triumph included the farthest extents of the universe. Hades or the abyss is the lowest part of the earth (Rom 10:7), the place of the departed (Phil 2:10), and the place of the evil spirits (Luke 8:31). Furthermore, it is thought by some that 1 Pet 3:19 portrays that between Jesus' death and resurrection he preached to the departed spirits in this region. This interpretation is questioned on several accounts. First, Wallace states, "a comparative gen. is syntactically improbable, if not impossible: the comparative adjective is in *attributive* position to μέρη."[2] Second, Hui suggests that one "would expect the superlative (τὰ κατώτατα τῆς γῆς) and not the comparative (τὰ κατώτερα μέρη) in 4:9 (cf. LXX Ps 62:10 [MT 63:10; ET 62:9]; 138:15 [MT & ET 139:15])."[3] Third, never is there any indication that Jesus ascended from Hades. On the other hand, there are references indicating his ascension from the earth (John 8:21–23; 16:28). Fourth, no time is indicated as to when Jesus would have gone to Hades. Fifth, the place where Jesus had victory over evil powers and sin (so that he could give gifts) was not in Hades but at the cross (Col 2:14–15; Eph 2:16) where he stated, "it is finished" (John 19:30).[4] Sixth, in Ephesians the warfare with satanic hosts is not in Hades but in the heavenlies (1:20–21; 2:2; 6:12).[5] Seventh, it is true

κατωτέρω, κατώτερος," *TDNT* 3 (1965): 641–42; Johannes Schneider, "μέρος," *TDNT* 4 (1967): 597–98; BDF §167; Anthony Tyrell Hanson, *The New Testament Interpretation of Scripture* (London: SPCK, 1980), 136–41, 150; Arnold, *Ephesians: Power and Magic*, 57–58. Cf. "The Descent of Christ into Hades. A Correspondence between Professor Franz Delitzsch and Professor von Hofmann," *Exp* 4th ser., vol. 3 (April 1891): 241–63, 361–74. For a brief history of this view, see Harris, *The Descent of Christ*, 4–14. Kreitzer suggests that the lower parts of the earth corresponds to the myth regarding Demeter, Persephone, and Hades; and on the basis of numismatic evidence of the Neronian period (A.D. 54–59) people of Asia Minor would have associated the "lowermost parts of the earth" with the Plutonium of Hierapolis (city east of Ephesus) which was "a small subterranean cavern situated next to the temple of Apollo in the centre of the city and commonly regarded as a passageway to the underworld." See Larry J. Kreitzer, "The Plutonium of Hierapolis and the Descent of Christ into the 'Lowermost Parts of the Earth' (Ephesians 4,9)," *Bib* 78, no. 3 (1998): 381, and 382–93. The evidence Kreitzer marshalls is interesting but not convincing.

1. Meyer, 214.

2. Wallace, *Greek Grammar*, 112.

3. Hui, "The Concept of the Holy Spirit in Ephesians," 94.

4. Eadie, 292.

5. Cf. Ragnar Leivestad, *Christ the Conqueror. Ideas of Conflict and Victory in the New Testament* (London: SPCK, 1954), 157.

that Paul could have used simpler terms to express Christ's descent to the earth but, on the other hand, he also could have used specific terms referring to Hades (ᾅδης)[1] or the abyss (ἄβυσσος).[2] On the whole, it seems unlikely that Paul refers to Hades.

(2) Other commentators think τῆς γῆς is an epexegetical genitive or a genitive of apposition signifying "the lower parts, namely, the earth,"[3] as distinct from heaven. Accordingly, the descent to the earth refers to Christ's incarnation. The support for this view is first, that Jesus' descent from heaven is always viewed as being to earth and not to Hades (John 3:13; 6:62; 16:28). Second, there is no indication in the Gospel narratives that after the burial of Jesus he went to Hades. It would seem likely that Jesus would have referred to this experience during the fifty days between his resurrection and ascension. Third, the use of the genitive of apposition is common in this epistle (2:2, 14, 15, 20; 3:4, 7; 4:3; 6:14, 16, 17*bis*). A real problem with this view is that it seems a simpler way could have been used to express this.

(3) Some think that τῆς γῆς is a partitive or possessive genitive indicating that Christ descended into "the earth's lower part, the grave."[4] This viewpoint includes both Christ's incarnation and his death where he won the victory over Satan and sin. His burial substantiates his death. His ascension could not be before his death. The support for this view is first, that it makes good sense of the comparative adjective κατώτερα signifying the earth's lower part, namely, in the ground. Second, the preposition εἰς could be translated "into" stressing that Jesus went into the earth. Third, there is a parallel between this verse and 1:20 in that the death of Christ (1:20; 2:16; 5:2, 25) is connected with his resurrection (1:20–23; 2:5) and not with his incarnation or to a de-

1. The term ᾅδης is used ten times in the NT (Matt 11:23 [= Luke 10:15]; 16:18; Luke 16:23; Acts 2:27, 31; Rev 1:18; 6:8; 20:13, 14).

2. The word ἄβυσσος is used nine times in the NT (Luke 8:31; Rom 10:7; Rev 9:1, 2, 11; 11:7; 17:8; 20:1, 3).

3. Theodore of Mopsuestia *Eph* 4:5–8 (*PG* 66:920); Calvin, 176; Hodge, 220–21; Harless, 364; Eadie, 293–94; Abbott, 115; Salmond, 327; Schlier, 192–93; Gaugler, 172; Hendriksen, 192–93 n. 111; Gnilka, 209; Ernst, 351; Mitton, 147–48; Barth, 433–34; Schnackenburg, 178–79; Bruce, 343; Best, 386; O'Brien, 295–96; Winer, *Grammar*, 666; MHT 3:215; Robertson, *Grammar*, 499; Zerwick, *Biblical Greek* §45; Wallace, *Greek Grammar*, 86, 99–100; Franz Joseph Dölger, "Hadesfahrt Jesu in Epheserbrief 4,9?" *Antike und Christentum* 2, no. 4 (1930): 316–17; Percy, *Probleme*, 273–74 n. 26; Mussner, *Christus, das All und die Kirche*, 28, 41–44; Pokorný, "Epheserbrief und gnostische Mysterien," 185; Cambier, "La Signification Christologique d'Eph. iv.7–10," 267–71; Ernst, *Pleroma und Pleroma Christi*, 136; Lindemann, *Aufhebung*, 219–21; Harris, "The Ascent and Descent of Christ in Ephesians 4:9–10," 202–4; idem, *The Descent of Christ*, 50–54; Moritz, *A Profound Mystery*, 78–79; Carsten Peter Thiede, "Der Brief an die Epheser. 37. Teil: Kap. 4,7–10," *Fundamentum* 20, no. 2 (1999): 19–20.

4. Chrysostom *Eph* 4:9–10 (*PG* 62:81–82); Theodoret *Eph* 4:9 (*PG* 82:533); Oecumenius *Eph* 4:7–13 (*PG* 118:1217); Theophylact *Eph* 4:9–10 (*PG* 124:1084–85); McNamara, *The New Testament and the Palestinian Targum to the Pentateuch*, 81.

scent into Hades.[1] Fourth, using the same construction (εἰς τὰ κατώτερα μέρη τῆς γῆς), David refers to the depths of the earth with reference to the grave (Ps 63:9 [MT 63:10; LXX 62:10]). The one objection which could be raised against this view is that it could have been more easily understood by stating that "he descended into the heart of the earth" (κατέβη εἰς τὴν καρδίαν τῆς γῆς) much like Matt 12:40. However, the comparative adjective in the present context implies this.

In conclusion, these three views all have their supporters. To summarize, view (1) denoting Hades seems unlikely. The most probable are views (2) or (3). On balance it seems that the last view fits the context well and has the least problems. Christ's death accomplished victory over the evil powers and sin and redemption for those who believe. The gifts are given to those redeemed saints.

4:10. ὁ καταβὰς αὐτός ἐστιν καὶ ὁ ἀναβάς, "He who descended is himself also he who ascended." The use of the participle ὁ καταβάς, "he who descended," is emphatic by its position and it relates back to the finite verb κατέβη, "he descended," in the previous verse. The personal pronoun with the verb "to be" and the conjunction (αὐτός ἐστιν καί) that is used adjunctively further stresses the emphasis and can be translated "he precisely is also" or "is himself also." The pronoun (αὐτός) is not "the same" (which would be ὁ αὐτός) as translated in some versions (AV, RV, ASV, TEV, NRSV) but is simply the emphatic "he" because it is anarthrous, being the subject and not the predicate. Some translations bring out the emphasis by translating it "no(ne) other than" (NEB, JB, NJB) or "the very one" (NIV). With this emphasis, Paul stresses that the very person who descended is the one who ascended. The order is first descent and then ascent. Therefore, the theory mentioned above, namely, that it refers to Christ's bestowal of gifts at Pentecost, seems highly unlikely. Rather it asserts that Jesus, who descended to earth and the grave, is the one who ascended. The destination of his ascension is discussed next.

ὑπεράνω πάντων τῶν οὐρανῶν, "above all the heavens." The adverb ὑπεράνω is used as an improper preposition with the genitive. Because it is not ἄνω but ὑπεράνω it is considered intensive and is translated "far above" in most translations (AV, RV, ASV, RSV, NASB, NEB, NRSV). However, this is not borne out in the LXX where it refers to a Jerusalem wall "above" a tower (Neh 12:38, 39), the house of the Lord on the highest mountains which will be raised "above" the hills (Isa 2:2; Mic 4:1), or the gourd that made shade "over" Jonah's head (Jonah 4:6). In the last instance, if it were "high above," no shade would have been provided. The same sense of "above" is found in koine Greek.[2] It is used two other times in the NT. In Eph 1:21 it speaks about Christ's rank over all other authorities. Hebrews 9:5 refers to the cherubim

1. McNamara, *The New Testament and the Palestinian Targum to the Pentateuch*, 81.
2. Horsley, *New Documents Illustrating Early Christianity*, vol. 3, *A Review of the Greek Inscriptions and Papyri Published in 1978*, 87.

"over" the mercy seat and this particularly cannot be translated "far above," but rather, "above, over." In the present context it conveys the same sense. In later Greek it gradually replaced ὑπέρ, "over, above,"[1] and again is probably best translated "above" (TEV, JB, NIV, NJB) instead of "far above." It is true that Christ is far above all the heavens but this is not defined by ὑπεράνω but by the combination of this adverb with the adjective πάντων, "all." "All the heavens" may be an allusion to three heavens mentioned by Paul (2 Cor 12:2) or the Jewish idea of the seven heavens,[2] but Paul does not lay any importance on the number of heavens.[3] Certainly, the picture in the NT is that Jesus passed into the highest heavens (Heb 4:14; 7:26; Phil 2:9). It is the locale of Jesus' present ministry and rule. Because of the similar wording in 1:21 (ὑπεράνω πάσης ἀρχῆς καὶ ἐξουσίας καὶ δυνάμεως καὶ κυριότητος), Harris suggests that in this text Paul refers metaphorically to the "powers" who are in the heavens (cf. 6:12) who are subjugated to Christ.[4] This is a possibility. However, the main point of the present verse is to pinpoint the locale of Jesus' ascension.

ἵνα πληρώσῃ τὰ πάντα. "in order that he might fill all things." The purpose of Christ's ascension above all the heavens is expressed by the conjunction ἵνα, "in order that." A study of the verb πληρόω was made in 1:23. It is used twenty-three times by Paul, four times in Ephesians (1:23; 3:19; 4:10; 5:18). Here it is active and basically means "to fill." The object of the filling is "all things." The designation "all things" does not limit Christ's filling to the church, otherwise Paul would have made the church the object of the filling. Also, it does not refer to the Lutheran doctrine of the ubiquity or omnipresence of Christ's body.[5] Rather, the object of Christ's ascension was to allow him to enter into a sovereign relationship with the whole world, and in that position he has the right to bestow gifts as he wills. How is the universe filled with all things? It is the benefits of the work on the cross and consequently the ministry of the church to which Christ gave gifted persons who can function in his power. In 1:23 Christ is filled with God's fullness (cf. Col 1:19, 20) and Christ fills the church with that fullness. Since the verb (πληρώσῃ) in the present context is active, it means that Christ is the subject, filling all things with God's fullness. This also fits with 1:10 where Christ unites all things under his head. Notice in that context, as in the present setting, Christ is head over all the universe (Col 1:17) and embodies the fullness of the Godhead (Col 2:9), fills the universe, and is head over it (Eph 1:22; cf. Col 1:18). In the present con-

1. Robertson, *Grammar*, 297, 550, esp. 646–47; cf. Moule, *Idiom Book*, 86.

2. MHT 3:25; 4:91.

3. F. F. Bruce, "St. Paul in Rome. 4. The Epistle to the Ephesians," *BJRL* 49 (spring 1967): 319; cf. Lincoln, *Paradise Now and Not Yet*, 78–80.

4. Harris, "'The Heavenlies' Reconsidered," 84.

5. As does Lenski, 524–25.

text Christ fills the universe with the message of love by the messengers on whom he has bestowed the gifts as he willed (vv. 7–8, 11).

In conclusion, this verse serves as a critical link between the preceding and succeeding verses. Christ's descent enabled him to gain victory over Satan, sin, and death, followed by his ascent where as conqueror he had the right to bestow gifts to the church.[1]

b. The Distribution of the Gifts (4:11–16)

The central point of this portion is the distribution of gifts to the church which are given to unify the church. In brief, Paul discusses the giving of gifts to each believer in verse 7. In verse 8 he quotes from Ps 68 and in verses 9–16 he applies it to the believers of this age by concentrating on two words from the psalm: (1) ἀναβάς, which he expounds in verses 9–10 in a somewhat parenthetical fashion, demonstrating that after his descent Christ did ascend victoriously over Satan, sin, and death and thus had a right to give gifts; and (2) ἔδωκεν where, in verse 11, he returns to the theme of the context regarding the giving of gifts to the church. Verses 11–16 with 125 words, make up the seventh of the eight long sentences in Ephesians (cf. 1:3–14, 15–23; 2:1–7; 3:2–13, 14–19; 4:1–6, 11–16; 6:14–20).

(1) The Provision: Gifted Persons (4:11)

The present verse is a commentary on ἔδωκεν, namely, Christ's bestowal of gifts to the church (v. 8b). Paul states that God has appointed people with various gifts to the church (v. 7). In verse 10 Paul states that Christ "ascended above all the heavens, in order that he might fill all things," and the present verse gives the details of that filling, that is, gifted people to the church.

Before discussing the particular gifted people listed in this verse, six preliminary items need to be noted. First, the structure of τοὺς μὲν . . . , τοὺς δὲ . . . , τοὺς δὲ . . . , τοὺς δὲ . . . , is to mark out distinctly different gifted people without implying a contrast as it would have in earlier Greek.[2] Second, the article (τούς) is used as a demonstrative pronoun and can be translated "some."[3] Third, each gifted person listed (e.g., τοὺς μὲν ἀποστόλους) is a predicate accusative and could be translated either "some apostles" (AV), "some as apostles" (NASB), or "some to be apostles" (RV, ASV, RSV, NEB, TEV, JB, NIV, NJB, NRSV). The last translation is preferred because it brings out the distinction that each gifted person has a particular function among the assembly of believers. Each is to function in the measure of the gift given (v. 7). Fourth, the order in the list of gifts is similar to 1 Cor 12:28 where

1. Cf. Moritz, *A Profound Mystery*, 84–86.

2. Robertson, *Grammar*, 1152, 424; cf. Merklein, *Das kirchliche Amt nach dem Epheserbrief*, 73–75; Schnackenburg, 180.

3. Robertson, *Grammar*, 694, 1394; Winer, *Grammar*, 130.

Paul states, "And God has appointed in the church first apostles, second prophets, third teachers, then workers of miracles, then healers, helpers, administrators, various kinds of tongues." In Ephesians Paul has the same order except he lists the evangelists and the pastors (these are not mentioned in 1 Corinthians) between the prophets and the teachers.[1] It must be realized that the lists in the three passages on gifts (Eph 4; Rom 12; 1 Cor 12) vary and thus there are overlaps as well as omissions from each list. Fifth, surprisingly there is no mention of the Holy Spirit, but it can be assumed because this passage in many ways corresponds to the text on the gifts of the Spirit in 1 Cor 12:4–11, 28.[2] Sixth, Paul is listing gifts and not offices. Although the terms used for office (ἐπισκοπή/ἐπίσκοπος) can have reference to "visitation" (Luke 19:44; 1 Pet 2:12) or "guardian" (Acts 20:28; 1 Pet 2:25), it normally has the idea of an office (Acts 1:20; 1 Tim 3:1) or the specific office of an elder (Phil 1:1; 1 Tim 3:1, 2; Titus 1:7). In the instance of Acts 20:28 Paul addressed the Ephesian elders (v. 17) and asked them to be "guardians" or carry out the function of their office with regard to the church. Interestingly, the term "office" is never used in the NT in connection with the gifts. There seems to be five and possibly six distinctions between the gift and the office. (1) The office appears to be limited to apostles (Acts 1:21–25), elders/bishops (1 Tim 3:1–7; Titus 1:5–11), deacons (Acts 6:1–6; 1 Tim 3:8–13), and possibly deaconesses (depending how one interprets 1 Tim 3:11 and Rom 16:1). (2) Those who were selected to any of these offices were either appointed (Acts 14:23; Titus 1:5) or elected by people based on qualifications (Acts 1:26; 6:3; 1 Tim 3:1–13) whereas the gifts are sovereignly bestowed by God (Eph 4:7; Rom 12:6; 1 Cor 12:11, 18, 28). (3) Everyone has a gift (Eph 4:7; 1 Cor 12:7, 11; Rom 12:4) but not everyone holds an office. (4) Marital status is mentioned for the offices of elders and deacons (1 Tim 3:2, 4–5, 12; Titus 1:6) but no such qualification is mentioned for those gifted. The office of an elder or deacon appears to require a married person, never divorced (although there is room for debate on "the husband of one wife"), whereas there is no such restriction on those who are given gifts. Hence, a person who has a change in marital status does not lose his or her gift. (5) Those holding office cannot be novices (1 Tim 3:6, 10; Titus 1:8–9) whereas the gifts are given to each person regardless of age or maturity. (6) Certain offices must be held by men (e.g., 1 Tim 3:2, 12; Titus 1:6), whereas those who have gifts may be either gender (e.g., Acts 21:9–10; 1 Cor 11:5). Inexplicably, many commentators mix gift and office,[3] yet they

1. The relationship between the gifts mentioned in Eph 4:11 is discussed by Böttrich, "Gemeinde und Gemeindeleitung nach Epheser 4," 141–47.

2. Fee, *God's Empowering Presence*, 707.

3. E.g., Calvin, 178–80; Eadie, 298; Abbott, 117; Barth, 438; Schnackenburg, "Christus, Geist und Gemeinde (Eph. 4:1–16)," 292, 295. Schweizer states that "the ministries of bishop and pastor are one and the same" (Eduard Schweizer, *Church Order in the*

are not confused in the NT. Certainly, there is nothing in the present context about an office.[1] It is true that those who have offices will have gifts because all believers have gifts.[2] However, the opposite is not true, that is, a gifted person may not necessarily have an office since only a handful of people will occupy the offices of elder and/or deacon. Maintaining the distinction of the gifts and offices would help to avoid much confusion.

Text: 4:11. καὶ αὐτὸς ἔδωκεν τοὺς μὲν ἀποστόλους, τοὺς δὲ προφήτας, τοὺς δὲ εὐαγγελιστάς, τοὺς δὲ ποιμένας καὶ διδασκάλους,

Translation: 4:11. "Namely, he gave some to be apostles, and some to be prophets, and some to be evangelists, and some to be pastors and teachers,"

Commentary: 4:11. καὶ αὐτὸς ἔδωκεν[3] τοὺς μὲν ἀποστόλους, "Namely, he gave some to be apostles." The conjunction καί, "and," could make a connection in one of three ways. (1) It could serve as a transition from the parenthetical section (vv. 9–10) and would be translated "and." (2) It could be explicative "namely, that is," by explaining ἔδωκεν of Ps 68 in verse 8 and making no direct connection with verses 9–10 since they are parenthetical. (3) It could serve as an explicative, "namely, that is," linking this verse with verse 7.[4] The thought would be that in verse 7 Paul states that each believer is given a gift according to the measure of the gift of Christ and that verse 11 explains it: "namely, he gave some apostles," and so forth. The structure would be that the statement is made in verse 7, scriptural proof from Ps 68 is given in verse 8, a parenthesis is inserted in verses 9–10 explaining ἀναβάς of verse 8a, and finally, in verse 11, a transition is made to explain the giving of gifts first introduced in verse 7 (ἐδόθη) and again mentioned in verse 8b (ἔδωκεν). Any one of these are viable; either of the last two seem to be the most likely because they seem to give a better understanding of the structure of the passage.

New Testament, trans. Frank Clarke, SBT, ed. C F. D. Moule, J. Barr, Floyd V. Filson, and G. Ernest Wright, vol. 32 [London: SCM, 1961], 200); George W. Knight III, "Two Offices (Elders/Bishops and Deacons) and Two Orders of Elders (Preaching/Teaching Elders and Ruling Elders): A New Testament Study," *Presbyterion* 11 (spring 1985): 9–10; William R. "Rick" Yount, "The Pastor as Teacher," *SWJT* 38 (spring 1996): 15–23; C. Mack Roark, "Interpreting Ephesians 4–6: 'God's People in a Walk Worthy of His Calling,'" *SWJT* 39 (fall 1996): 34; Böttrich, "Gemeinde und Gemeindeleitung nach Epheser 4," 140–49. Although there may be an overlap of ministries between the person who has a gift and one who has an office, the two must still not be confused.

1. L. Michael White, "Social Authority in the House Church Setting and Ephesians 4:1–16," *ResQ* 29 (fourth quarter 1987): 221, 224, 227.

2. For a discussion of the relationship between gifts and offices, see Ronald Y. K. Fung, "Ministry in the New Testament," 163–77.

3. The perfect form (δέδωκεν) found only in 𝔓[46] and Clement[pt] is not acceptable.

4. So Klein, *Die Zwölf Apostel*, 67–68.

The personal pronoun αὐτός, "he," is emphatic, linking it with the αὐτός of the previous verse and showing that "he" who descended and ascended is also "he" who gave gifts. The verb ἔδωκεν, "to give," is a resumption of the same word used in verse 8 (ἔδωκεν), which ultimately goes back to same verb in verse 7 (ἐδόθη). Paul prepares to explain what he stated in verse 7 about the bestowal of gifts to the church and proceeds, in this regard, to give a commentary on the quotation from Ps 68. The reference "he gave gifts to people" in Ps 68 is specifically applied to the church.

Preceding the presentation of the gifts of the Spirit, the Holy Spirit was given on the day of Pentecost (Acts 2:33): "Therefore, being exalted at the right hand of God, and having received the promise of the Holy Spirit from the Father, he has poured out this which you see and hear." This passage refers to the indwelling of the Holy Spirit within every believer. The Ephesians context is discussing something different. Although each believer is indwelt, with no distinction, the present context is talking about the gifts that are given to each with distinction. Ephesians 4:7 indicates that each believer is given a gift according to the measure of Christ. Therefore, each believer is not given the same gift and same measure. Paul is making a slight change from what he stated in verse 7. In verse 7 he mentions that a gift is given to each, but in verse 11 he refers to the giving of a gifted person. There need be no contradiction here because the person who receives a gift is a gifted person. Paul does the same thing in 1 Cor 12 where he lists the gifts (vv. 4–11) and then later in the same context talks about the gifted people (vv. 27–31). This is again repeated in the other passage on the gifts (Rom 12:4–8). In all three of these contexts the verb δίδωμι, "to give," is used (Rom 12:3, 6; 1 Cor 12:7, 8) which indicates that it is a gracious gift of God to the church.

The specific gifted persons will now be considered. The first mentioned is "apostles" (τοὺς μὲν ἀποστόλους). Since the term "apostle" was discussed in greater detail at 1:1, only a brief discussion is in order here. It was suggested that an apostle is an official delegate of Jesus Christ, commissioned for the specific tasks of proclaiming authoritatively the message in oral and written form and of establishing and building up the churches. There are three kinds of apostles mentioned in the NT: those who had been with Jesus in his ministry and had witnessed his resurrection (Acts 1:21–22); Paul, who was born out of season (l Cor 15:8–9); and those who received the gift of apostleship. The first two categories are to be regarded as offices, whereas the last is a spiritual gift to the church. In the present context the apostle refers to the third kind, the gift of apostle. There were people in addition to the original twelve who had not been with Jesus in his ministry and did not witness his resurrection but who are listed as apostles. To mention some, we cite Barnabas (Acts 14:4, 14; 1 Cor 9:5–7), James, the Lord's brother (1 Cor 15:7; Gal 1:19), Apollos (1 Cor 4:6, 9), probably Silvanus (1 Thess 2:6 [GT 2:7]), Titus (2 Cor 8:23), Epaphroditus (Phil

2:25), and possibly Andronicus and Junia[s] (Rom 16:7). These had the gift of apostleship. It seems then that the main function of an apostle is to establish churches in areas that have not been reached by others (Rom 15:20). They are God's messengers to open up new territories for Christ.

τοὺς δὲ προφήτας, "and some to be prophets." The second gifted person, the prophet, is also listed among the gifts in 1 Cor 12:28 and Rom 12:6. In the study of this word in 2:20 and 3:5 we concluded that the prophet was one who was endowed by the Holy Spirit with the gift of prophecy for the purposes of edification, comfort, encouragement (1 Cor 14:3, 31), and further, to understand and communicate the mysteries and revelation of God to the church (12:10; 13:2; 14:23, 30–31). The prophetic gift may include a predictive element (1 Thess 3:4; 4:6, 14–18; Gal 5:21). However, the prophet is not one who is overcome by some uncontrolled ecstatic force, but rather one who has self-control when receiving the revelation (1 Cor 14:30–32; Rev 1:9–10). In light of an incomplete canon, initially the prophets may well have received revelation to complete what was needed so that every person could be presented perfect before God (Eph 4:12; Col 1:28). In the present context the prophet is a NT prophet because he is listed after the apostles, as in 2:20 and 3:5. The NT prophet most likely corresponds with the OT prophet when revelation and authority are concerned. In the present verse the prophet is listed among the foundational gifted persons who prepare saints for ministry and build up this new body, the church, revealed from the mystery. In many ways the prophet and apostle had similar functions for they were both involved in revelation. They had overlapping functions, much like many ministries today, but their emphases differed. The emphasis for the apostle was more on the divine commission to a specific task of proclaiming authoritatively the message in oral and written form and of establishing and the building up of churches, whereas for the prophet it was the communication of divine revelation. For more discussion on NT prophets and apostles, see the comments on 2:20.

τοὺς δὲ εὐαγγελιστάς, "and some to be evangelists." The third gifted person listed is the evangelist. The term occurs only two other times in the NT: first, as a designation of Philip (Acts 21:8); and second, a kind of ministry Paul exhorted Timothy to perform (2 Tim 4:5). Chrysostom proposes that the evangelists' duty was specifically to preach the gospel and that this did not necessarily compel them to travel widely for this purpose.[1] Theodoret probably more correctly states that they went everywhere preaching the gospel.[2] In all likelihood they worked both inside and outside of the church.[3] Whereas the prophets spoke as the occasion required revelation, the evangelists

1. Chrysostom *Eph* 4:11–12 (*PG* 62:82).
2. Theodoret *Eph* 4:11–12 (*PG* 82:536).
3. Best, "Ministry in Ephesians," 153–55.

continually spoke of the message of Christ's salvation.[1] They are placed between the prophets and teachers in the list causing Hadidian to suggest that they were the "evangelists" who wrote the Gospels, but such an idea has no real basis from the NT.[2] Rather, their function resembles modern missionaries who bring the message to new territories.[3] For example, Philip brought the message to the area between Jerusalem and Gaza where he met the Ethiopian eunuch and explained the message of Jesus to him. When the eunuch believed, he baptized him. After this, Philip continued to preach the message in various places from Azotus to Caesarea (Acts 8:26–40). In the early church it was thought that the evangelists were those who preached the gospel and were the successors to the apostles in that they laid the foundations of the faith in new areas, appointed shepherds, and then moved to other lands and people.[4] In conclusion, the evangelists would win converts to the faith, the apostles would establish churches, and the prophets would fill in needed revelation for the perfection of the saints. Some of these functions seem to have overlapped.

τοὺς δὲ ποιμένας καὶ διδασκάλους, "and some to be pastors and teachers." Because one article is used for both these gifted people, scholars have debated over the centuries as to whether they represent two different gifted persons[5] or one person with a combination of two gifts.[6] The latter interpretation may consider the conjunction καί as explicative, "that is," thus giving "and some to be pastors, that is, teachers." Others think that the reason for one article is to designate these two gifts as functioning primarily in a local setting as distinguished from those gifts listed earlier which functioned more in an itinerate ministry.[7] Although one article used for two plural nouns does not necessarily denote identity, as seen in 2:20 where there is one

1. Eadie, 303.

2. Dikran Y. Hadidian, "*Tous de evangelistas* in Eph. 4,11," *CBQ* 28 (*July* 1966): 317–21; cf. Oecumenius *Eph* 4:7–13 (*PG* 118:1220).

3. Barth, 438.

4. Eusebius *Historia Ecclesiastica* 3.37.1–4; 5.10.2–4.

5. Theophylact *Eph* 4:11 (*PG* 124:1085); Calvin, 179; Dibelius-Greeven, 81; Schlier, 196–97; Gnilka, 211; Schnackenburg, 181–82; Merklein, *Das kirchliche Amt nach dem Epheserbrief*, 362–65.

6. Chrysostom *Eph* 4:11–12 (*PG* 62:82); Jerome *Eph* 4:11–12 (*PL* 26:500); Oecumenius *Eph* 4:7–13 (*PG* 118:1220); Aquinas, chap. 4, lec. 4, vv. 11–13 (164); Bengel, 4:91; Harless, 370–71; Olshausen, 222–23; Hodge, 226–27; Alford, 3:117; Eadie, 304–6; Ellicott, 87; Meyer, 218; Salmond, 330; Masson, 192; Rienecker, 146; Gaugler, 176; Hendriksen, 197; Barth, 438–39; Bruce, 348; Karl Heinrich Rengstorf, "διδάσκαλος," *TDNT* 2 (1964): 157–58; Joachim Jeremias, "ποιμήν κτλ.," *TDNT* 6 (1968): 497; Carsten Peter Thiede, "Der Brief an die Epheser. 38. Teil: Kapitel 4,11–13," *Fundamentum* 20, no. 3 (1999): 26–27.

7. Theodoret *Eph* 4:11–12 (*PG* 82:536); Westcott, 62; Robinson, 181; Abbott, 118; Dibelius-Greeven, 81; Masson, 192. The *Didache* 13.2 speaks of the teachers being worthy of support in the local community.

article for apostles and prophets, it does indicate that "groups more or less distinct are treated as one for the purpose in hand."[1] Accordingly, in the present context some sort of distinction should be maintained. After a study of the grammatical structure of one article followed by two plural nouns separated by a καί (as here), Wallace suggests that the first is the subset of the second and thus "all pastors are to be teachers, though not all teachers are to be pastors."[2] Hence, while there is a distinction between the two, the distinction is not total.[3]

The term ποιμήν is used in classical literature for a "herdsman"[4] or "shepherd"[5] and metaphorically for one who was a "shepherd of people,"[6] also called "captain, leader, chief."[7] In the LXX it occurs eighty-one times and in the canonical books it appears seventy-eight times and sixty-seven times where it translates רָעָה, sometimes used as a substantive, meaning "shepherd"[8] (Gen 4:2; 46:32, 34; 1 Sam 25:7; Isa 40:11) and other times it is used metaphorically to refer to a "leader of people" (Isa 63:11; Jer 2:8; 3:15; Zech 10:3; 11:3, 5, 8, 15, 16) and sometimes to Messiah (Zech 13:7). In the NT this word is used eighteen times, but it is used only once by Paul (Eph 4:11). It is used as a "shepherd" of sheep (Matt 25:32; Luke 2:8, 15, 18, 20; John 10:2, 12) or metaphorically as a "leader" of people (Matt 9:36; 26:3 = Mark 6:34; 14:27). Jesus claims himself to be the good "shepherd" of his flock (John 10:11, 14, 16), and twice the NT writers portray Jesus as the "shepherd" of believers (Heb 13:20; 1 Pet 2:25). In the present context the term is best translated as "pastor," one who cares for his or her flock as a shepherd cares for his or her sheep. This would include ministering to troubled saints, exhorting and comforting all believers, and administering the activities in the local assembly. Again, a caution must be made that the term refers to the use of the gift. Therefore, it describes a function with no hint of reference to an office.[9]

1. Robertson, *Grammar*, 787; MHT 3:181.

2. Wallace, "Semantic Range of the Article-Noun-καί-Noun Plural Construction," 83; idem, *Greek Grammar*, 284. See also Harris who sees four conceptual categories although five types of persons (Murray J. Harris, *Jesus as God: The New Testament Use of Theos in Reference to Jesus* [Grand Rapids: Baker, 1992], 308–9); cf. Hemphill, "The Pauline Concept of Charisma," 242–43; idem, *Spiritual Gifts*, 183–84.

3. Calvin (179) discusses the possible difference. For a study on Calvin and the gifts of the Spirit, see Leonard Sweetman Jr., "Gifts of the Spirit: A Study of Calvin's Comments on 1 Corinthians 12:8–10, 28; Romans 12:6–8; Ephesians 4:11," in *Exploring the Heritage of John Calvin*, ed. David E. Holwerda (Grand Rapids: Baker, 1976), 273–303; Best, "Ministry in Ephesians," 157–58.

4. Homer *Odyssea* 10.82–85.

5. Euripides *Bacchae* 714; Plato *Theaetetus* 174d; *Respublica* 1.16 §343a.

6. Homer *Ilias* 2.243.

7. Ibid., 2.85; Aeschylus *Supplices* 767; Euripides *Phoenissae* 1140.

8. BDB 945; G. Wallis, "רָעָה *rāʿāh*; רֹעֶה *rōʿaeh*," *TWAT* 7 (1990): 567–69.

9. Jeremias (*TDNT* 6 [1968]: 497–98) states that by the time Ephesians was written, the term "pastor" was not an established title.

The second term διδάσκαλος had from the earliest of times meant teacher,[1] appearing only twice in the LXX (Esth 6:1; 2 Macc 1:10). It occurs in the NT fifty-nine times, seven times in Paul's letters (Rom 2:20; 1 Cor 12:28, 29; Eph 4:11; 1 Tim 2:7; 2 Tim 1:11; 4:3), always with the same meaning. Basically, it depicts instruction, not only in factual matters and skills but most likely also in moral evaluation.[2] Jesus was called a "teacher" by both friend and foe (Matt 8:19; 9:11; 12:38; 17:24; 19:16; 22:16; John 3:2; 11:28) and even called himself such (John 13:13). He followed the role model of the Jewish rabbis where he not only taught content but also gathered disciples around him.[3] However, one marked difference between the teaching of Jesus and the scribes is that he taught with authority (Matt 7:29; Mark 1:22; Luke 4:32). Likewise, teaching in the local assembly should have authority when based on the Scriptures. Teachers should not be like the scribes who propounded a variety of views but never came to any conclusion. Rather, they should teach the revelation of God authoritatively. Whereas the prophet spoke "under the *immediate* impulse and influence of the Holy Spirit"[4] (cf. 1 Cor 14:30), the teacher would give instruction on that which was already revealed by the prophet or from Scripture.[5] Also, the predictive function included in the prophet's role was not a part of the province of the teacher.[6]

In conclusion, it seems that these two gifts, pastoring and teaching, are distinct although it could be said that all pastors should be teachers but not all teachers are pastors. Certainly, Jesus recognized that he was both shepherd and teacher and as such was and is a model for all others with like gifts. Shepherding includes instruction but probably is mostly concerned with administration and various ministries to the flock. Teaching includes instruction in doctrine and its application to daily life but the teacher may not have all the administrative and shepherding responsibilities of the pastor.

The gifts which Paul described to the Ephesian assembly have application to the present-day church. One gift mentioned in this passage which has engendered much discussion is the gift of prophecy. Some think there is little, if any, distinction between prophecy and teaching.[7] Others maintain there is a distinction in that the prophet

1. Homer *Hymnus Mercurium* 556; Aeschylus *Prometheus Vinctus* 110.

2. Rengstorf, *TDNT* 2 (1964): 149.

3. Ibid., 153.

4. Ellicott, 87.

5. Cf. W. Harold Mare, "Prophet and Teacher in the New Testament Period," *Bulletin of the Evangelical Theological Society* 9 (summer 1966): 139–48; Forbes, *Prophecy and Inspired Speech*, 228.

6. Forbes, *Prophecy and Inspired Speech*, 229.

7. M. Eugene Boring, "'What Are We Looking For?' Toward a Definition of the Term 'Christian Prophet'," in *Society of Biblical Literature 1973 Seminar Papers*, ed. George MacRae, vol. 2 (Cambridge, Mass.: Society of Biblical Literature, 1973), 149; Thomas

imparts new revelation directly from the Lord (1 Cor 14:30–31) whereas the teacher illumines the hearer about past events and revelations.[1] The distinction between these two gifted individuals seems more in keeping with the NT. The prophet was prominent in the early church but by the end of the second century he became "an endangered species."[2] One can only speculate the reason for the demise of the prophet. It may be due to the increasing institutionalization of the church or the abuse of prophecy in Montanism, but, more likely with the canon completed and closed, there was no need for further revelation. Hence, the gift of prophecy does not seem to be operative today. On the other hand, in the present day there are many examples of gifted believing men and women as evangelists, pastors, and teachers. Some may question the validity of women pastors or pastor-teachers, but it must be remembered that these are gifts and not offices. Surely, women who pastor-shepherd among women should cause no problem at all (Titus 2:3–4). But in fact, Priscilla, along with Aquila, taught Apollos the way of God more accurately (Acts 18:25–26) which would indicate that a woman may not be limited to teaching only women.

Regarding the gift of apostle for today, it would seem that those who have that gift would function similarly to those in the early church by establishing churches in areas not reached by the gospel.[3]

W. Gillespie, "A Pattern of Prophetic Speech in First Corinthians," *JBL* 97 (March 1978): 74–95; M. Eugene Boring, *Sayings of the Risen Jesus: Christian Prophecy in the Synoptic Tradition*, SNTSMS, ed. R. McL. Wilson and M. E. Thrall, vol. 46 (Cambridge: Cambridge University Press, 1982), 78–80; Thomas W. Gillespie, *The First Theologians: A Study in Early Christian Prophecy* (Grand Rapids: Eerdmans, 1994), passim, esp. 23–32, 199–263.

1. Ernest Best, "Prophets and Preachers," *SJT* 12 (June 1959): 147–50; Friedrich, *TDNT* 6 (1968): 854; Cecil M. Robeck Jr., "The Gift of Prophecy in Acts and Paul, Part II," *Studia Biblica et Theologica* 5, no. 2 (1975): 42, 47–49; E. Earle Ellis, "The Role of the Christian Prophet in Acts," in *Apostolic History and the Gospel. Biblical and Historical Essays Presented to F. F. Bruce on His 60th Birthday*, ed. W. Ward Gasque and Ralph P. Martin (Exeter: Paternoster; Grand Rapids: Eerdmans, 1970), 62–65; reprinted in idem, *Prophecy and Hermeneutic in Early Christianity*, 138–42; idem, "Prophecy in the New Testament Church—and Today," in *Prophetic Vocation in the New Testament and Today*, ed. J. Panagopoulos, NovTSup, ed. W. C. van Unnik et al., vol. 45 (Leiden: Brill, 1977), 51; David Hill, "Christian Prophets as Teachers or Instructors in the Church," in *Prophetic Vocation in the New Testament and Today*, ed. J. Panagopoulos, NovTSup, ed. W. C. van Unnik et al., vol. 45 (Leiden: Brill, 1977), 122–28; idem, *New Testament Prophecy*, 110–59, 186–213, esp. 137–39; Grudem, *The Gift of Prophecy in 1 Corinthians*, 139–44; idem, *The Gift of Prophecy in New Testament and Today*, 135–43; Aune, *Prophecy in Early Christianity and the Ancient Mediterranean World*, 19, 204–5; Turner, "Spiritual Gifts Then and Now," 13–15, 46–48; Forbes, *Prophecy and Inspired Speech*, 225–37.

2. Aune, *Prophecy in Early Christianity and the Ancient Mediterranean World*, 204; cf. Hill, *New Testament Prophecy*, 186–92; Forbes, *Prophecy and Inspired Speech*, 247–50.

3. *Contra* Hywel Jones, "Are There Apostles Today?" *Evangelical Review of Theology* 9 (April 1985): 107–16, esp. 114–16.

Possibly, this would include missionaries who are involved in establishing churches. The danger is to equate this gift with the office (i.e., ones who had been with Jesus and seen his resurrection body) with an attempt to exert the same authority as those in the NT who qualified for the apostolic office. However, this presents no more of a problem than those who have the gift of pastor-teacher but confuse that with the office of elder or deacon and attempt to exert the authority of an elder or deacon. The NT does not mix gift and office.

Christ has sovereignly given gifted people to the church. These gifts were not to be used for self-promotion but for building up the saints. Paul will now develop this concept.

(2) The Immediate Purpose: Prepare for Ministry (4:12)

Having described the gifted people given to the church, Paul states their purpose is to prepare believers for the work of the ministry for edifying the body of Christ.

Text: 4:12. πρὸς τὸν καταρτισμὸν τῶν ἁγίων εἰς ἔργον διακονίας εἰς οἰκοδομὴν τοῦ σώματος τοῦ Χριστοῦ,

Translation: 4:12. "for the preparation of the saints for the work of the ministry for the building up of the body of Christ,"

Commentary: 4:12. πρὸς τὸν καταρτισμὸν τῶν ἁγίων, "for the preparation of the saints." The main problem in this verse is to determine its structure in view of the three prepositions: πρός . . . εἰς . . . εἰς. . . . There are four ways these prepositions might be related to each other. (1) Some see them as coordinates modifying the main verb in verse 12, ἔδωκεν, "he gave," and punctuated by a comma after each prepositional phrase (AV, RSV).[1] It would connote that he gave gifts for the purpose of preparing the saints, for the work of the ministry, and for the building up of the body of Christ. As such, it portrays the gifted people in verse 11 as the ones referred to in all the above three phrases with the rest of the people having little responsibility, thereby making a definite distinction between the clergy and laity.[2] The problem with this view is that the three prepositions are not all the same and there are no coordinating conjunctions to indicate the parallel.[3] Although Paul may use a variety of prepositions, he does not use them indifferently.[4] Furthermore, to make such a distinction between clergy

1. Chrysostom *Eph* 4:11–12 (*PG* 62:82–83); Theophylact *Eph* 4:12 (*PG* 124:1085); Oecumenius *Eph* 4:7–13 (*PG* 118:1220); Bengel, 4:91–92; Lincoln, 253.

2. As do T. David Gordon, "'Equipping' Ministry in Ephesians 4?" *JETS* 37 (March 1994): 69–78; John Jefferson Davis, "Ephesians 4:12 Once More: 'Equipping the Saints for the Work of Ministry?" *Evangelical Review of Theology* 24 (April 2000): 161–76; J. C. O'Neill, "'The Work of the Ministry' in Ephesians 4:12 and the New Testament," *ExpTim* 112 (July 2001): 338–40; cf. Lincoln, 253.

3. Westcott, 63.

4. Alford, 3:117.

and laity goes against the thrust of this passage that promotes unity in the body of Christ.

(2) Some consider that the first preposition (πρός) gives the ultimate purpose to the main verb ἔδωκεν and that the last two prepositions (εἰς) are parallel to each other, referring to the immediate purpose of the main verb; thus, the last two prepositions are identical and different from the first (RV, ASV).[1] It has the sense that he provided gifted people for the immediate purpose of the work of the ministry and for the building up of the body of Christ, while the ultimate and final purpose of the gifts is for the preparation of the saints. This still maintains the distinction between the clergy and laity, though to a lesser degree. Although this view makes a distinction between the prepositions, there is no coordinating conjunction between the last two prepositions which are considered parallel. Furthermore, it seems to be an awkward construction reducing the force of the third prepositional phrase which would normally be considered as the one denoting the ultimate purpose of the gifted people.[2]

(3) Others propose that the first preposition (πρός) gives purpose to the main verb ἔδωκεν, the second preposition (εἰς) depends on the first preposition, and the third preposition (εἰς) is parallel with the first preposition, depending on the main verb; hence, there is no comma after "saints" but one after "ministry" (NA^{27}, UBS^{4}, NEB, NASB, NRSV).[3] It would signify that he gave gifts for the purpose of preparing the saints for the work of the ministry and for the purpose of building up the body of Christ. It does make some distinction between clergy and laity in that the gifted persons of verse 11 are involved in preparing and building up of the body. The problem with this view is that it makes the first and third prepositions parallel though they are different prepositions, but it makes a distinction between the last two prepositions though they are identical.

(4) This view proposes that the first preposition (πρός) gives the purpose to the main verb ἔδωκεν (v. 11), the second preposition (εἰς) depends on the first preposition, and the third preposition (εἰς) depends on the second preposition (TEV, JB, NIV, NJB).[4] It is suggested

1. Harless, 372; Olshausen, 223; Hodge, 229–30; Alford, 3:117; Eadie, 308; Ellicott, 88; Meyer, 219; Lock, 49; Hanson, *The Unity of the Church in the New Testament*, 157. Cf. also Bruce, 349; Roels, *God's Mission*, 192–93.

2. Salmond, 331.

3. Abbott, 119; Scott, 210–11; Schlier, 198–99; Hendriksen, 412; Johnston, 19; Mitton, 152; Merklein, *Das kirchliche Amt nach dem Epheserbrief*, 77. Another proposal is somewhat similar to this in that the second preposition (εἰς) is subordinate to the first preposition (πρός) and the third preposition (εἰς) is dependent on the previous prepositional phrases together, see Ronald Y. K. Fung, "The Nature of the Ministry according to Paul," *EvQ* 54 (July–September 1982): 141. This would have the same criticism as outlined for the third view.

4. Salmond, 331; Moule, 110; Robinson, 99, 182; Murray, 68; Scott, 210–11; Lenski, 529–30; Dibelius-Greeven, 81–82; Caird, 76; Gaugler, 178; Schnackenburg, 183; Best, 397–98; O'Brien, 301–3.

that the commas between the prepositional phrases be omitted. Further, it is recommended that one must not overdraw the distinction between the two different prepositions in this context. The same two are used in Rom 3:25–26 and seem to be synonymous. In this case, however, it seems that the first preposition (πρός) expresses the immediate purpose[1] while the other two prepositions (εἰς) denote direction or goal.[2] The progression indicates, therefore, that he gave gifted people for the immediate purpose of preparing all the saints with the goal of preparing them for the work of the ministry, which in turn has the final goal of building up the body of Christ. This eliminates the distinction between clergy and laity, a distinction with little, if any, support in the NT.

In brief, the point is that the gifted persons listed in verse 11 serve as the foundational gifts that are used for the immediate purpose of preparing all the saints to minister. Thus, every believer must do the work of the ministry. This is certainly supported from the context, for in verse 16 edification requires the work of each individual member and not a select group. The final goal evolves from the last, namely, that the work of the ministry by every believer is to build up the body of Christ. Therefore, view (4) seems to be the simplest interpretation and more importantly, it recognizes the function of each of the prepositions.

Before NT times, the term καταρτισμός was rare though used by Apollonius Citiensis forty-seven times within a work on the medical practice of setting a limb or bone or the restoration of a shoulder.[3] In NT times, it is used of furnishing a room or preparation of a garment.[4] It is found only in this verse in the NT. However, the verb καταρτίζω is found frequently and means "to adjust, put in order, restore, mend," as the reconciling of political factions,[5] as well as "to furnish, equip"[6] or "to be instructed, trained."[7] In the LXX it occurs seventeen times (appears only in canonical books) where it translates nine different Hebrew words. It has various meanings such as "to establish" (Ps 74:16 [LXX 73:16]), "to equip, restore" (Ps 68:9 [MT 68:10; LXX 67:10]), and "to complete, finish" (Ezra 4:12, 13, 16; 5:3, 9, 11; 6:14). It appears thirteen times in the NT and can mean "to restore or mend"

1. BAGD 710; BDAG 874.

2. Even in Rom 3:25–26 the first preposition (εἰς) is more indicative of the remote goal in that God was just with regard to the past sins. The second preposition (πρός) indicates immediate purpose or goal showing that Christ's death made it possible for God's righteousness to be vindicated, making possible his justification of believing individuals in the present day.

3. E.g., Apollonius Citiensis 1.1, 2; 2.1, 4; 3.4; 4.2; cf. first or second century A.D. Soranus *Gynaeciorum* 4.16.3; 37.1.

4. MM 332.

5. Herodotus 5.28, 30, 106.

6. Diodorus Siculus 13.70.2.

7. Polybius 5.2.11.

fishing nets (Matt 4:21 = Mark 1:19), "to restore" a fallen brother (Gal 6:1; cf. 1 Pet 5:10), "to prepare" (Rom 9:22; Heb 10:5), "to put into proper order, complete, furnish" (1 Thess 3:10; 1 Cor 1:10; Heb 13:21), "to perfect" (Matt 21:16), or "to instruct" (Luke 6:40). Hence, the verb offers a wide range of meaning. Returning to the noun in the present context, it "refers to the preparation of the church for becoming perfect, not to this perfection itself, as can be seen from the use of *teleios* (complete, mature; . . .), *hēlikia* (stature; . . .), and *plērōma* (fullness) in v. 13."[1] This preparation includes instructing and equipping believers so that they may minister effectively in the church. There is no idea in the passage of restoration from a disordered state.[2] The genitive following this noun (τῶν ἁγίων) is an objective genitive. The term "saint" was discussed at 1:1 and means believers. Therefore, gifted persons were given to the church for the immediate purpose of training or preparing believers. It is important to be endowed with the gift(s) of the Spirit but it is also important to learn to use the gift(s) effectively in the church for its edification.

εἰς ἔργον διακονίας, "for the work of the ministry." Here the preposition εἰς introduces the goal of these gifted people, namely, to prepare other saints for the work of the ministry. The noun διακονία is related to the noun διάκονος, "servant," used in 3:7. The term διακονία has the idea of "service" in its classical usage[3] and it is used once in the LXX in 1 Macc 11:58 as table "service" (two times in certain manuscripts of Esth 6:3, 5 meaning "servant"). There are thirty-four instances of it in the NT basically denoting service at the table (Luke 10:40; Acts 6:1) and also the activities of an apostle (Acts 1:17, 25) or the distribution of alms (Rom 15:31; 2 Cor 8:4). It is listed as one of the spiritual gifts (Rom 12:7) and listed in connection with the spiritual gifts to show that as there are various gifts so are there various services (1 Cor 12:5). However, the present text is not speaking of a specific gift for it includes every saint and not all saints have the same gifts (1 Cor 12:28–30). The most frequent use of the word is in connection with the ministry, the service of the Lord (Acts 20:24; 21:19; Rom 11:13; 1 Cor 16:15; 2 Cor 4:1; 5:18; 6:3; 1 Tim 1:12; 2 Tim 4:5, 11). It is this concept which is used in the present context. It conveys the idea of serving the Lord by ministering to one another. This word promotes the idea of activity. Gifted individuals are given to the church for the purpose of preparing all the saints toward the goal of service or ministry. The genitive in this case is either a genitive of apposition, meaning the work which is ministry, or a descriptive genitive, meaning a work which is characterized by service. The believer is being

1. Reiner Schippers, "Right [ἄρτιος]," *NIDNTT* 3 (1978): 350; Horsley, *New Documents Illustrating Early Christianity*, vol. 3, *A Review of the Greek Inscriptions and Papyri Published in 1978*, 70.

2. Robinson, 182.

3. Thucydides 1.133.

readied to become involved in ministry to others. The final goal of this service is described in the next phrase.

εἰς οἰκοδομὴν τοῦ σώματος τοῦ Χριστοῦ, "for the building up of the body of Christ." This final εἰς marks the final goal for providing gifted persons to the church, namely, to build up the body of Christ. The noun was discussed at 2:21 where we concluded that it has reference to a building or the act of building. In 2:21, as here, it refers to the act of building and, in particular, a building that is in the process of construction. This is not an inanimate structure but a living and growing organism composed of living believers. Two genitives follow: the first one is an objective genitive (τοῦ σώματος) showing that the building in process is the body; the second one is a possessive genitive (τοῦ Χριστοῦ) showing whose body it is. Hence, the goal depicted in these prepositional phrases is the building up of the body of Christ to which every believer belongs.

In conclusion, then, Christ gave foundational gifts to the church for the immediate purpose of preparing all the saints for the goal of service and in turn this service is for the final goal of building up the entire body of Christ.[1] As each believer functions with the gift given to each, Christ's body, the church, will be built up. The gifts are never for self-edification but for the edification of the whole body of believers. The concept that the ministry belongs to clergy is foreign to this context because every saint is given a gift (v. 7) and every saint is involved in the ministry.[2] The gifted people listed are not to be considered as officers of the church but rather gifted individuals who are foundational. Apostles and evangelists need to proclaim the message and establish churches. Prophets and pastor-teachers need to inform and instruct believers. But the work of the ministry does not stop there—it continues as these gifted individuals prepare all the saints for the work of the ministry with the ultimate goal of building up the body of Christ.

(3) The Final Goal: Attain Maturity (4:13)

Having established that the gifted people were given to the church for the immediate purpose of preparing all the saints to minister for the building up of the body of Christ, Paul explains the need for the process to continue until attaining the goal that believers mature to the measure of the fullness of Christ.

1. Cf. Best, "Ministry in Ephesians," 162–63.

2. For a critique of the classical interpretation of this passage with regards to clergy training laity, see Henry P. Hamann, "The Translation of Ephesians 4:12—A Necessary Revision," *Concordia Journal* 14 (January 1988): 42–49. Caird (76) states: "The *ministry* is Christ's own programme of service to the world, which he entrusts to the whole membership of the people of God, not to a group of clergy within the church."

Text: 4:13. μέχρι καταντήσωμεν οἱ πάντες εἰς τὴν ἑνότητα τῆς πίστεως καὶ τῆς ἐπιγνώσεως τοῦ υἱοῦ τοῦ θεοῦ, εἰς ἄνδρα τέλειον, εἰς μέτρον ἡλικίας τοῦ πληρώματος τοῦ Χριστοῦ,

Translation: 4:13. "until we all attain to the unity of the faith and the knowledge of the Son of God, to a mature person, to the measure of Christ's full stature,"

Commentary: 4:13. μέχρι καταντήσωμεν οἱ πάντες, "until we all attain." Normally μέχρι appears in the NT as a temporal adverb or improper preposition with the genitive meaning "up to the point of." It occurs three times as a conjunction (Mark 13:30; Gal 4:19; Eph 4:13) and always with an aorist subjunctive without ἄν to indicate an indefinite future.[1] Used with an aorist subjunctive, it means *"until,* of a punctiliarly conceived future event preceded in time by the action of the main clause."[2] This conjunction could depend on the immediately preceding prepositional phrase "for the building up of the body of Christ," but it is more probable that it relates back to ἔδωκεν, "he gave," in verse 11, denoting that he gave gifted individuals to the church and that will continue until the action of the following aorist subjunctive καταντήσωμεν "until we all attain."

The verb καταντάω occurs thirteen times in the NT, four times in Paul's writings (1 Cor 10:11; 14:36; Eph 4:13; Phil 3:11). Outside of Paul it occurs only in Acts, all of which (except 26:7) speak of travelers arriving or reaching their destinations. In other places Paul uses it to refer to the arrival of the end of the age (1 Cor 10:11), to ask the Corinthians if they are the only ones that the Word of God has reached (1 Cor 14:36), and to express the desire that he, Paul, might reach or attain the resurrection of the dead (Phil 3:11). Hence, it means to reach, arrive, or attain a goal. "The goal is set, the end determined, and καταντᾶν simply denotes the meeting of this set goal and prescribed conclusion."[3] Thus it can be translated "reach" (JB, NIV, NJB) or "attain" (RV, ASV, RSV, NASB, NEB).[4]

One should note that all (οἱ πάντες), not just some, are to attain the goal set before us. This does not mean all human beings but rather refers back to the "saints" mentioned in the preceding verse. The "all" is mentioned because we are all being prepared for the work of the ministry with the goal of building up the body of Christ of which we are all a part. Immediately following are three prepositional phrases, each introduced by the preposition εἰς, "to." Although the three preposi-

1. Robertson, *Grammar*, 975; BDF §383 (2).

2. MHT 3:111; Wallace, *Greek Grammar*, 479–80.

3. Otto Michel, "καταντάω," *TDNT* 3 (1965): 623.

4. For a study of how this word is translated in Latin versions in order to avoid Pelagian ideas of good intentions and human activity, see Israel Peri, "Gelangen zur Vollkommenheit. Zur lateinischen Interpretation von καταντάω in Eph 4,13," *BZ* 23, no. 2 (1979): 269–78.

tional phrases in verse 12 denote the purpose and goals for the giving of the gifts, the three prepositional phrases in verse 13 signify not three separate goals but three aspects of the one goal of attaining maturity.[1] This could be a stair-step attainment of the goal, that is, each step built on the previous or it could be that the three prepositional phrases are parallel to each other, though there are no conjunctions between them. The first alternative is preferred.

εἰς τὴν ἑνότητα τῆς πίστεως καὶ τῆς ἐπιγνώσεως τοῦ υἱοῦ[2] τοῦ θεοῦ, "to the unity of the faith and the knowledge of the Son of God." This is the first aspect of the goal. The preposition εἰς, "to," indicates direction or goal.[3] Hence, this aspect of the goal is the unity of faith. The only other time the word ἑνότητα (from ἑνότης), "unity," is used in biblical literature is in verse 3 where Paul exhorts believers to make every effort to keep the unity of the Spirit. Here in verse 13 the goal refers to the effort made in order to preserve the unity. The following genitive (τῆς πίστεως) is not a subjective genitive (i.e., the exercise of faith) but an objective genitive (i.e., the content of faith) indicating that believers are to reach the unity of the faith. Gifted individuals prepare the saints toward this ultimate goal. Unity of the faith comes with the realization that we all have one faith[4] in the one person, Jesus Christ. It corresponds to the "one faith" mentioned in verse 5 which was given as the evidence of unity among believers.[5] Further explanation is given in the following prepositional phrases, showing that it is not organizational unity but practical unity of the faith in conjunction with the body of believers.

Encompassed in the first component of the goal is not only the achievement of unity of the faith but also the unity in "the knowledge of the Son of God." The term ἐπίγνωσις, "knowledge," discussed at 1:17, is derived from two words: γνῶσις, which is knowledge in the fullest sense and in the abstract, and the prepositional prefix ἐπι-, which rather than intensity, denotes direction, that is, "knowledge directed towards a particular object, perceiving, discerning, recognizing."[6] The following genitive (τοῦ υἱοῦ) is an objective genitive indicating that the particular object of knowledge is the Son of God. The last genitive (τοῦ θεοῦ) is a possessive genitive which signifies that Christ

1. Hodge, 230; Caird, 76, Lincoln, 255; Best, 403; Roels, *God's Mission*, 199–200, 205–7.

2. The words τοῦ υἱοῦ are omitted in only F G it^{b} Clement^{pt} Lucifer. Their omission may be in harmony with 1:17 where its object is αὐτοῦ, referring to God. The overwhelming evidence is to accept the inclusion of these words as genuine.

3. BAGD 229; BDAG 289.

4. Chrysostom *Eph* 4:13 (*PG* 62:83).

5. For a discussion of unity in Ephesians, see Benoit, "L'unité de l'Église selon l'épître aux Éphésiens," 1:57–77. This is reprinted in idem, *Exégèsis et Theologie*, 3:335–57.

6. Robinson, 254.

belongs to the Father. It is the only place in Ephesians where Christ is called the Son of God. In 1:17 the emphasis was on knowing God and here it is on knowing his Son, Jesus Christ. The emphasis has changed because of the subject of the context, that is, Christ's bestowal of gifts (v. 7) and gifted persons (v. 11) to the church so that it may be built up not only in the unity of the faith but also in the unity of the knowledge of him. It must be asserted that such knowledge applies not only to individuals but to the body of believers who together come to a unity of the knowledge of Christ. This knowledge is not an abstract but a concrete knowlege of Christ, which is the opposite of the deceitful doctrines promoted by people as mentioned in verse 14.[1]

In conclusion, the first aspect of the goal is two pronged, as exhibited by the one preposition followed by two articular genitives joined by a conjunction. The concepts belong together. Noyen suggests that though they are closely related, they are distinct in that faith is static and knowledge is dynamic.[2] However, in this case it seems that both are dynamic in that a dynamic faith brings a dynamic knowledge of Christ, which in turn produces more faith. This is similar to the way love always supercedes our knowledge. The more knowledge of his love, the more overwhelming it is (cf. 3:19).

εἰς ἄνδρα τέλειον, "to a mature person." The preposition εἰς, "to," is used the second time in this verse to denote the second aspect of the goal to be achieved. The first aspect is to attain to the unity of the faith and the knowledge of the Son of God. Building on this, the next aspect is to attain to a mature person. The adjective τέλειος literally means "having reached its end (τέλος)."[3] It is used of sacrifices that are "perfect, without spot/blemish,"[4] of animals that are "fully grown,"[5] and of a person who is "fully grown" or "matured" as opposed to a child.[6] In the LXX it occurs nineteen times (fifteen times in the canonical books) and refers to an "unblemished" animal (Exod 12:5) or blamelessness before humans (Gen 6:9) or before the Lord (Deut 18:13; 2 Sam 22:26; 1 Kgs 8:61). Also, it is used of David's "perfect" hatred toward God's enemies (Ps 139:22 [LXX 138:22]) or of one who calls his or her lover the "perfect one" (Cant 5:2; 6:9). In later Greek it is used of a fully grown or mature person.[7] In the NT it is used nineteen times, eight times by Paul (Rom 12:2; 1 Cor 2:6; 13:10; 14:20; Eph 4:13; Phil 3:15; Col 1:28;

1. Roels, *God's Mission*, 206.

2. Noyen, "Foi, charité, espérance et «connaissance» dans les Epîtres de la Captivité," 907–10.

3. MM 629.

4. Homer *Ilias* 1.66.

5. Herodotus 1.183.

6. Plato *Leges* 11 §929c; Xenophon *Cyropaedia* 1.2.4, 12, 14; Philo *Sobr.* 2 §9; Plutarch *Moralia: Quaestionum convivalium* 5.7.1 §680d.

7. MM 629. For a study of this word in connection with the Qumran, see B. Rigaux, "Révélation des Mystères et perfection a Qumran et dans le Nouveau Testament," *NTS* 4 (July 1958): 237–62, esp. 248–52.

4:12). It can mean absolutely perfect as used by Jesus when he told his audience that they must be perfect like their heavenly Father (Matt 5:48; cf. Rom 12:2; 1 Cor 13:10; Heb 9:11; Jas 1:17, 25; 3:2). Also, it can mean wholly dedicated (Matt 19:21; 1 John 4:18), or it can refer to maturity as opposed to immaturity before God (1 Cor 2:6; 14:20; Phil 3:15; Col 1:28; 4:12; Heb 5:14; Jas 1:4).[1] In the present context it cannot have the ethical sense of complete perfection, since this only comes at the parousia (2 Cor 4:13–5:10; Phil 3:20–21), but rather it has the ethical idea of fully grown or mature.[2] This is in contrast to immature and unstable children mentioned in the next verse.[3]

Who then is the mature person that is set forth here? Some think this designation refers to individual believers.[4] In fact, in the next verse it refers to individuals as "infants." However, the context as a whole talks about the body composed of individuals. Interestingly, Paul does not use the plural form: "we attain to mature persons" (εἰς ἄνδρας τέλειους) but instead he uses the singular form with reference to the unity of the collective body of believers: "we attain to a mature person" (εἰς ἄνδρα τέλειον).[5] This strongly indicates that the "mature person" refers to the church, the corporate body of believers.[6] This is analogous to 2:15 where Jews and Gentiles were created into one new person (εἰς ἕνα καινὸν ἄνθρωπον) and brought into one body (2:16). The use of the generic ἄνθρωπος in 2:16 is to show that a new humanity has come into existence, whereas in the present context Paul uses ἀνήρ, a term used to distinguish between the sexes or in this case between a boy and an adult man. Yet one cannot conclude that this is a reference to males only because the present context makes reference to "all saints" (vv. 12–13), each receiving a gift (v. 7), all in one body (v. 4) which is called the body of Christ (v. 12). The singular form "mature person" points to a body of believers, not to individual believers in the body since the context refers to all believers in the body of

1. For a study of the word, see Paul Johannes du Plessis, *Τελειος: The Idea of Perfection in the New Testament*, Theologische Academie Uitgaande van de Johannes Calvijn Stichting te Kampen (Kampen: Uitgave J. H. Kok N. V., [1959]), esp. 188–93; cf. also Joseph Agar Beet, "Christian Perfection. I. The Word 'perfect' in the New Testament," *Exp* 5th ser., vol. 5 (January 1897): 30–41.

2. Hanson, *The Unity of the Church in the New Testament*, 159.

3. Lona, *Die Eschatologie im Kolosser- und Epheserbrief*, 330.

4. Calvin, 182; Ewald, 195–96; Masson, 194; Mitton, 154; Percy, *Probleme*, 322 n. 78; Allan, "The 'In Christ' Formula in Ephesians," 61.

5. Merklein, *Das kirchliche Amt nach dem Epheserbrief*, 104.

6. Harless, 380; Alford, 3:118; Eadie, 313–14; Ellicott, 90; Meyer, 223–25; Abbott, 120; Salmond, 332; Robinson, 183; Schlier, 200–201; Gnilka, 215; Caird, 76; Barth, 493–94; Schnackenburg, 184; Bruce, 350; Best, *One Body in Christ*, 148–49; Merklein, *Das kirchliche Amt nach dem Epheserbrief*, 103–4; Roels, *God's Mission*, 204–5; David Peterson, *Engaging with God: A Biblical Theology of Worship* (Leicester: Apollos, 1992), 209; Lilly Nortjé, "The Meaning of ἄνδρα τέλειον in Ephesians 4:13: A Full-Grown Person, as Perfect and Mature as Christ," *Ekklesiastikos Pharos* 77, no. 1 (1995): 57–61.

Christ. Accordingly, all believers are to do the work of the ministry for the goal of building up that body of Christ. This is to continue until "we all" attain the goal of the unity of faith and of the knowledge of our Lord and until "we all" attain the goal of the mature person. As the body matures unity results. In fact, a sign of immaturity is the disunity of the body. Often we tend to think of spiritual maturity as only individual growth in the Lord, but in this passage the emphasis is on the importance of body growth, resulting in unity. Inversely, immaturity is individual growth not shared with the body with the result that the body lacks maturity. This may render some of its members powerless against the enticements of cunning people (v. 14). Again, as the individual in his or her spiritual growth contributes to the body, the body as a whole can grow.[1] On the other hand, this mature person has nothing to do with the Gnostic primordial Christ enthroned in heaven to whom believers come as Schlier suggests.[2] Rather, it is the body of believers on earth who are growing into maturity.

εἰς μέτρον ἡλικίας τοῦ πληρώματος τοῦ Χριστοῦ, "to the measure of Christ's full stature." This is the third time the preposition εἰς, "to," is used in this verse and indicates the third aspect of the goal. The first aspect is to attain to the unity of the faith and of the knowlege of the Son of God. The second aspect is to attain to a mature person. Building on these two aspects, the third component is to attain to the measure of Christ's full stature. In classical times the noun ἡλικία had the general idea of "age"[3] but normally it referred to old age where discretion more likely would be exercised.[4] Also, it could refer to physical bodily stature.[5] In the canonical LXX it appears only twice (Job 29:18; Ezek 13:18) but in twenty other occurrences in the LXX the word has the general meaning of age (2 Macc 4:40; 6:18; Wis 4:9). In the Hellenistic period it also has the predominant meaning of age.[6] In the NT it

1. Richard L. Strauss, "Like Christ: An Exposition of Ephesians 4:13," *BSac* 143 (July–September 1986): 263–64.

2. Schlier, 201 n. 1; cf. also idem, *Christus und die Kirche in Epheserbrief,* 27–37; Pokorný, "Σῶμα Χριστοῦ im Epheserbrief," 458–62; idem, *Der Epheserbrief und die Gnosis,* 78–81; Vielhauer, *Oikodome,* 135–36. For a refutation of this view, see Hanson, *The Unity of the Church in the New Testament,* 159–60; Mussner, *Christus, das All und die Kirche,* 61–64; Josef Ernst, "Das Wachstum des Leibes Christi zur eschatologischen Erfüllung im Pleroma," *TGl* 57, no. 3 (1967): 180–82; Ernst, *Pleroma und Pleroma Christ,* 146–49; Barth, 489–96; Evans, "The Meaning of πλήρωμα in Nag Hammadi," 259–65; Perkins, 100–101.

3. Pindar *Olympian Odes* 4.27; Herodotus 1.26; 3.134.

4. Homer *Ilias* 22.419; Pindar *Pythian Odes* 4.157; Plato *Laches* 180d.

5. Herodotus 3.16; Plato *Euthydemus* 271b; Diodorus Siculus 3.35.6.

6. MM (279) state, "Lk 19^{8} is the only NT passage where the word *must* mean 'stature'; apart from it (and the rather different Eph 4^{13}) the NT represents the general *usus loquendi* of our vernacular sources. We are indeed unable to quote any example from these . . . in which 'stature' is the natural meaning, and hardly any in which it is possible; while for 'age' we can present a long list. Thus the word is very common in connexion with being 'under age' or coming 'of age,' which in Egypt took place at the age of 14 years."

occurs eight times with reference to physical stature (Luke 19:3), age (Matt 6:27? = Luke 12:25?; John 9:21; Heb 11:11), and maturity (Luke 2:52; John 9:23). In the present context the word connotes maturity.[1] This concept fits well with τέλειος in the preceding verse and νήπιοι in the next verse. It is best viewed as a genitive of apposition, to "measure," which could be rendered "to the measure, namely, the maturity of the fullness of Christ."

This is the fourth time πλήρωμα occurs in Ephesians (1:10, 23; 3:19; 4:13). In every NT use it maintains the idea of the result of filling is fullness, completeness, entirety (see Excursus 5: A Study of πλήρωμα). It can be used actively, "that which fills," or passively, "that which is filled." In the present verse it is active, namely, Christ is the fullness of God and is actively filling the church. The genitival relationship is difficult to decipher. A series of genitives was a style used in both classical and NT Greek, especially by Paul (cf. Eph 1:6, 18, 19; 6:10; Col 1:13, 27; 2:12; 2 Cor 4:4; 1 Thess 1:3; Rom 8:21; 9:23). Each genitive is dependent on the one preceding it, and usually the last genitive is possessive, as is the case here.[2] It is probably best to take ἡλικίας as a genitive of apposition, τοῦ πληρώματος as an epexegetical genitive, and τοῦ Χριστοῦ as either a subjective genitive or, better, a possessive genitive. It would thus be translated "attain . . . to the measure which is Christ's full stature."[3] Similarly, Moule translates it: "the full height [in the metaphorical sense, of course, of *spiritual* maturity] represented by Christ's completeness."[4] As the church is filled by Christ, so is the stature of the church filled by him.[5] But does not this make it impossible for any indvidual saint to come to Christ's full stature? It must be carefully noted that the text states that "we" are to measure up to this extent. Hence, not the individual believer but the corporate body is the focus. Each member is to use the gift that has been given to him or her in measure (v. 7) and as each member fulfills this, then the body will measure (v. 13) to Christ's full stature. This does not imply that the church completes Christ.[6] Rather, as the gifts from Christ are used then the church will measure up to Christ's full stature.

1. Reiner Schippers, "Age, Stature, Maturity [ἡλικία]," *NIDNTT* 1 (1975): 92–93; Johannes Schneider, "ἡλικία," *TDNT* 2 (1964): 942–43.

2. MHT 3:218; HS §172; BDF §168 (2); Robertson, *Grammar*, 503.

3. Sellin ("Über einige ungewöhnliche Genitive im Epheserbrief," 100–101) thinks that ἡλικίας is a genitive of quality, τοῦ πληρώματος is a genitive of apposition, and τοῦ Χριστοῦ is a genitive of quality, "the measure consists of the fullness of Christ."

4. Moule, "'Fulness' and 'Fill' in the New Testament," 82.

5. Eadie, 314.

6. As Overfield, "Pleroma: A Study in Content and Context," 393; cf. Benoit, "The 'plèrôma' in the Epistles to the Colossians and the Ephesians," 157. It is doubtful that this is a reference to some Jewish motif of a form of divinity as suggested by Charles Mopsik, "La datation du *Chi'our Qomah* d'après un texte néo-testamentaire," *RSR* 68 (Avril 1994): 131–44.

There is one other problem to consider. Does this maturity occur presently or in the future? Some commentators think it refers to the present[1] and some think it has reference to the future,[2] but many think that the apostle did not have a specific time frame in mind. Instead he emphasized the goal which could be attained at any time.[3] The third alternative is the best because no time frame is implied in the text. On the other hand, the potential that it could occur in the present time is real, otherwise, there would be no need for gifts to be given to each believer for the building up of the church. Furthermore, Christ's death and the Holy Spirit's power are sufficient to accomplish this end. Finally, the contents of verse 14, "in order that we might no longer be children, being tossed back and forth by the waves and carried about by every wind of doctrine," can hardly have reference to the eschatological consummation.[4] Therefore, if the potential of the fully mature church is not real for the present time, Paul offers a false hope. Thus, it is possible for this age but may not be completed until the future, possibly when the church meets her Lord.

Thus, Christ gave foundational gifts in order to prepare all the saints in ministry to edify the body. Further, the corporate body is to reach or attain the unity of faith and the knowledge of God, to a mature person as a corporate entity, and to Christ's full stature. This can be accomplished because believers who function in the body have the foundational gifts to prepare them and also because each individual believer has been given a gift in measure (v. 7). Hence, if every individual believer allows the Spirit to use that gift to the measure given to him or her, then all the body of Christ will grow to the measure of Christ's full stature. Maturity involves sharing individual spiritual growth and using one's spiritual gifts within the body. This not only is evidence of spiritual maturity for the individual but it also brings unity to the body and the possibility of measuring up to Christ's full stature. "The glorified Christ provides the standard at which his people are to aim: the corporate Christ cannot be content to fall short of the perfection of the personal Christ."[5] In 1:23 Paul states that the

1. Chrysostom *Eph* 4:13 (*PG* 62:83); Theophylact *Eph* 4:13 (*PG* 124:1088); Oecumenius *Eph* 4:7–13 (*PG* 118:1220); Ambrosiaster *Eph* 4:13 (*PL* 17:389); Aquinas, chap. 4, lec. 4, vv. 11–13 (167); Mitton, 154–55; Franz-Josef Steinmetz, "Parusie-Erwartung im Epheserbrief? Ein Vergleich," *Bib* 50, no. 3 (1969): 328–36, esp. 335; Steinmetz, *Protologische Helis-Zuversicht*, 118–21.

2. Theodoret *Eph* 4:13 (*PG* 82:536); Calvin, 182; Bengel, 4:92; Hodge, 232–33; Hendriksen, 200; Barth, 489–96; Markus Barth, "Die Parusie im Epheserbrief, Eph 4,13," in *Neues Testament und Geschichte Historisches Geschehen und Deutung im Neuen Testament. Oscar Cullmann zum 70. Geburtstag*, ed. Heinrich Baltensweiler and Bo Reicke (Zürich: Theologischer Verlag; Tübingen: Mohr, 1972), 239–50.

3. Olshausen, 224; Eadie, 312; Ellicott, 91; Abbott, 121; Salmond, 333; Hemphill, "The Pauline Concept of Charisma," 248–49; idem, *Spiritual Gifts*, 188.

4. Du Plessis, *Τελειος: The Idea of Perfection in the New Testament*, 193.

5. Bruce, 350–51.

church is filled by Christ with the fullness of the moral excellence and power of God, in 3:19 he prays that Ephesian believers would be filled with the fullness of God, and in the present context he declares that Christ gave gifts in order that the body of believers might attain to the measure of the full stature of Christ. The moral excellence and power of God is proclaimed and appropriated by the body of believers. The purpose of all this is to protect the members of the body from the deceitfulness of cunning people leading to a scheme of error (v. 14) and to provide growth for the body of Christ by building itself up in love (vv. 15–16). Paul addresses this next.

(4) The Ultimate Purpose: Grow in Unity (4:14–16)

The topics of the previous verses were gifted people were given to the church (v. 11) for the purpose of preparing believers for the work of the ministry (v. 12) and for the goal of attaining maturity to the measure of Christ (v. 13). Paul next discusses the ultimate purpose of growing in unity (vv. 14–16).

(a) For the Individuals (4:14–15)

(i) Negatively: Avoiding Instability (4:14)

Paul first states the negative purpose (v. 14) and then the positive purpose (vv. 15–16). First, in verse 14 he states that believers should no longer be children because this brings instability which, in turn, leads to disastrous consequences.

Text: 4:14. ἵνα μηκέτι ὦμεν νήπιοι, κλυδωνιζόμενοι καὶ περιφερόμενοι παντὶ ἀνέμῳ τῆς διδασκαλίας ἐν τῇ κυβείᾳ τῶν ἀνθρώπων ἐν πανουργίᾳ πρὸς τὴν μεθοδείαν τῆς πλάνης,

Translation: 4:14. "in order that we might no longer be children, being tossed back and forth by the waves and carried about by every wind of doctrine by the cunningness of people by deceitfulness towards the scheme of error,"

Commentary: 4:14. ἵνα μηκέτι ὦμεν νήπιοι, "in order that we might no longer be children." The conjunction ἵνα both serves verse 14, giving us the negative ramifications, and also looks forward to verses 15–16 where the positive aspects are stated.

There are two issues that need to be discussed regarding the conjunction ἵνα. First, how is it to be taken? It could denote result or contemplated result as many versions render it (RSV, NASB, TEV, JB, NIV, NJB). However, it more likely connotes purpose (AV, RV, ASV). The purpose is in order that the believers will not be deceived by the trickery of people (v. 14) but that they might grow up in him (v. 15). Actually, the contemplated result is not too different from purpose. However, purpose seems to be more in line with the context whereby it is the reason that Christ gave gifted individuals to the church.

Second, to what does the conjunction ἵνα go back? There are three alternatives. (1) It could depend on either the verb (καταντήσωμεν) or the last prepositional phrase (εἰς μέτρον ἡλικίας τοῦ πληρώματος τοῦ Χριστοῦ) in verse 13, "we as a body all attain . . . to the full measure of Christ's stature" in order that individual believers might not be deceived people (v. 14) but that we might grow up in him (v. 15).[1] (2) It could depend on the last prepositional phrase of verse 12, "the building of the body of Christ" in order that believers will not be deceived (v. 14) but might grow up in him (v. 15).[2] (3) It could be coordinate with verse 13 and immediately dependent on the main verb (ἔδωκεν) of verse 11, meaning that Christ gave gifted people in order that believers would not be deceived (v. 14) but that they might grow up in him (v. 15).[3] Construction (1) has the advantage of being a near antecedent. However, this is a temporal clause depending on verse 11. Furthermore, "one does not become a mature man in order to grow."[4] Alternative (2) is viable if one considers the conjunction μέχρι (v. 13) as parallel to ἵνα (v. 14) with both going back to the last prepositional phrase of verse 12. However, μέχρι in verse 13 fits better when not dependent on verse 12 but on verse 11. Again, the believer does not need to become mature in order to grow. View (3) is preferred because it includes the other two alternatives. It views the conjunction ἵνα as parallel to the conjunction μέχρι in verse 13 although admittedly there is no coordinating conjunction to clearly indicate this. Thus, Christ gave gifted people to the church not only to function until the body attains to Christ's full stature, but also for the purpose of protecting believers from deception.

The term νήπιος refers to infants[5] or to children up to puberty.[6] It connotes not only physical age but childish understanding, that is, foolishness, inexperience, or lack of insight.[7] In the LXX it is used forty-seven times (thirty times in the canonical books) meaning a child, as opposed to adults (1 Sam 15:3; 2 Kgs 8:12; Ps 8:2; Prov 23:13; Joel 2:16), but it can also denote an adult with childish understanding or, one who is simple (Ps 116:6 [LXX 114:6]; 119:130 [LXX 118:130]; Prov 1:32). In the NT it is used fifteen times, eleven times by Paul. It can be used to denote a physical child (Matt 21:16; 1 Cor 13:11*quin*; Gal 4:1; 1 Thess 2:7) or a childish understanding (Matt 11:25; Luke 10:21; Rom 2:20; 1 Cor 3:1; Gal 4:3; Heb 5:13).[8] In the present context it has reference to a child's

1. Ellicott, 91; Salmond, 333; cf. Schnackenburg, 186.

2. Hodge, 236; Alford, 3:118; Moule, 112; von Soden, 138; Meyer, 227; Abbott, 121.

3. Aquinas, chap. 4, lec. 5, vv. 14–16 (169–70); Harless, 381; Westcott, 63; Schlier, 203; Gnilka, 216; Barth, 441; cf. Lincoln, 226.

4. Abbott, 121; cf. Hodge, 236.

5. Homer *Ilias* 9.440.

6. Hippocrates *Epidemiae* 6.1.4.

7. Homer *Odyssea* 13.237; cf. 9.44; Euripides *Iphigenia Aulidensis* 1243–44.

8. Walter Grundmann, "Die νήπιοι in der Urchristenlichen Paränese," *NTS* 5 (April 1959): 188–205.

gullibility, lack of understanding, or lack of perception. Paul proposes that gifts are necessary so that believers are not as children in their perception. He is going to describe further how a child reacts to those who try to persuade him to their way of thinking and how it is contrary to the way that edified believers should react. The adverb μηκέτι expresses their state as children. It could have reference to their preconversion days (cf. Gal 4:1) but more likely it refers to their spiritual infancy. The believers' goal of maturity (v. 13) is for the purpose that they not be immature children (v. 14). Best observes that "mature man" (v. 13) is singular and "children" (v. 14) is plural, possibly suggesting that individualism is a sign of childishness and unity a sign of maturity.[1]

κλυδωνιζόμενοι καὶ περιφερόμενοι παντὶ ἀνέμῳ τῆς διδασκαλίας, "being tossed back and forth by the waves and carried about by every wind of doctrine." These two participles further describe one who is childish and lacks stability. The first participle κλυδωνιζόμενοι conveys the idea of being thrown around by the waves of the sea[2] and being thrown into confusion (Isa 57:20—only occurrence in LXX).[3] Thus, the meaning in the present context. Children are easily confused in their thinking and are easily influenced by others. The second participle περιφερόμενοι appears only four times in the LXX and means "to carry about or around"[4] (Jos 24:33; 2 Macc 7:27) or can denote "turn around, make dizzy, turmoil" (Eccl 7:7; Prov 10:24).[5] It appears three times in the NT: twice in the literal sense "to carry about or around" (Mark 6:55; 2 Cor 4:10) and in the present verse it is also used as a metaphor for confusion. Both of these participles are passive (although the first one may be a deponent), indicating that an outside force is causing the confusion. These participles adjectively modify "children" by indicating the manner in which they are exhibiting their childish lack of perception. This outside force is expressed by the next noun ἀνέμῳ, a dative of instrument or means, and hence denotes by means of the wind. This noun is modified by the anarthrous adjective παντί and is translated "every,"[6] indicating that the wind comes from all different directions. Finally, "every wind" is followed by τῆς διδασκαλίας, which is most likely a genitive of content. This teaching is designed to counteract the pastor-teachers' teaching mentioned in verse 11. Pastor-teachers bring stability and unity whereas these teachings came from every direction and brought only confusion, turmoil, and disunity.[7] They swirled one around violently

1. Best, *One Body in Christ*, 148; cf. Best, 401–2, 404.

2. LSJ 962.

3. Josephus *A.J.* 9.11.3 §239.

4. Herodotus 1.84; 4.36, 64.

5. Josephus *A.J.* 17.5.2 §92.

6. BAGD 631; BDAG 783.

7. For the role of teachers for the development of unity within a sociological framework, see Peter W. Gosnell, "Networks and Exchanges: Ephesians 4:7–16 and the Community Function of Teachers," *Biblical Theology Bulletin* 30 (winter 2000): 135–43.

causing dizziness. Since the singular articular ἡ διδασκαλία, "the teaching," refers to Christian doctrine elsewhere in Paul's writings (cf. Rom 12:7; 15:4), some suggest that in the present context it also has reference to Christian doctrine that has been perverted by various currents of wind.[1] But again this overlooks the preceding qualifiers παντὶ ἀνέμῳ "every wind" which indicate a variety of false teaching both from within and from without that is opposed to the true teaching delivered by Paul and those who had the gift of a teacher (v. 11).[2] Next, Paul demonstrates that these teachings are done with deceit.

ἐν τῇ κυβείᾳ τῶν ἀνθρώπων, "by the cunningness of people." As in verse 12, here we have three prepositional phrases with one of the prepositions different from the other two (ἐν . . . ἐν . . . πρός). Most likely, each depends on the immediately preceding prepositional phrase, building up to a climax in thought. Therefore, it is better to leave out the comma after this first prepositional phrase.[3] The first preposition ἐν indicates instrument or means by which the teaching is accomplished. Consequently, it is done by means of trickery. The noun κυβεία literally means "dice-playing"[4] and the verb (κυβεύω) means cheating or playing at hazard.[5] It may have indicated dice that were loaded, hence meaning "cunningness, craftiness, trickery." It does not appear in the LXX and appears only here in the NT. The following genitive (τῶν ἀνθρώπων) is a possessive genitive showing that childish understanding is influenced from every direction by means of the deceit of people. Paul adds more.

ἐν πανουργίᾳ, "by deceitfulness." This is the second preposition in a series of three and this again is ἐν, denoting instrument or means, modifying the immediately preceding prepositional phrase. The word πανουργία is a synonym to the preceding noun and etymologically means "to be able to work all things." Although it can convey a good sense as "prudence" (Prov 1:4; 8:5), normally it has a negative connotation, "knavery, villainy, trickery, craftiness."[6] It is used only eight times in the LXX, four times in the canonical books (Num 24:22; Josh 9:4; Prov 1:4; 8:5), and three times it translates עָרְמָה, meaning "craftiness, prudence."[7] In the NT it occurs five times (Luke 20:23; 1 Cor 3:19; 2 Cor 4:2; 11:3; Eph 4:14) with the evil implication of "craftiness, cunninigness, deceitfulness." This serves to reinforce the preceding prepositional phrase to show that the trickery of people was done by deceitfulness.

1. Merklein, *Das kirchliche Amt nach dem Epheserbrief*, 107; Schnackenburg, 186.

2. Lincoln, 258; Best, 405.

3. There is no comma after the first prepositional phrase in UBS[3] but there is a comma in NA[27] and UBS[4].

4. Plato *Phaedrus* 274d; Xenophon *Memorabilia* 1.3.2.

5. Epictetus *Dissertationes* 2.19.28; 3.21.22.

6. Aeschylus *Septem contra Thebas* 603; Sophocles *Philoctetes* 927; Plato *Leges* 5 §747c.

7. BDB 791; H. Niehr, "עָרַם *ʿāram*; עָרוּם *ʿārûm*; עָרְמָה *ʿormâ*," *TDOT* 11 (2001): 361–66.

πρὸς τὴν μεθοδείαν τῆς πλάνης,[1] "towards the scheme of error." This is the third preposition that is dependent on the preceding prepositional phrase. Instead of ἐν as in the first two prepositional phrases, it is πρός, which indicates direction.[2] The word μεθοδεία is not used before NT times but comes from the older word μέθοδος, which means "procedure, process, method."[3] The latter word is used only twice in the LXX (Esth 16:13 [8:12n]—not in MT; 2 Macc 13:18) where it involved military cunningness. In the NT μεθοδεία appears only here and in 6:11 and can be translated "method" or, better, "strategy" or "scheme," all with an evil connotation. The final word in this phrase is πλάνη, which in classical times meant "wandering, roaming."[4] Metaphorically, it conveys the sense of "going astray" or "leading astray."[5] In the LXX it occurs six times, three times in the canonical books (Prov 14:8; Jer 23:17; Ezek 33:10) where it translates three different Hebrew words meaning "error, deceit." In the NT it appears ten times (Matt 27:64; Rom 1:27; Eph 4:14; 1 Thess 2:3; 2 Thess 2:11; Jas 5:20; 2 Pet 2:18; 3:17; 1 John 4:6; Jude 11) and means "deceit, delusion, error."[6] In most instances the concept of error fits well.[7] This is the best way to render it in the present context. The article before the noun gives it an abstract sense with the force of personification, that is, "error."[8]

Its genitival relationship with the previous word is difficult to decipher. It may be an objective genitive having the idea "towards the scheme which produces the error."[9] It could be a possessive genitive "towards an erroneous scheme." It may be a subjective genitive whereby the error uses or produces the scheme.[10] On the other hand, it could be a descriptive genitive or characteristic genitive, which would be rendered "towards a scheme characterized by error." Of the alternatives, it is unlikely that it is an objective genitive because the scheme does not produce error, but the error is conveyed by the scheme and it is also impersonal. The second alternative, subjective genitive, is somewhat vague and impersonal. The last alternative is preferred because it is a little broader. As a descriptive or characteristic genitive, it allows the error to produce the scheme while, at the same time, regarding the scheme as erroneous.

1. The addition of τοῦ διαβόλου found only in A cannot be considered genuine.

2. Cf. Moule, *Idiom Book*, 53–54.

3. Plato *Respublica* 7.13 §533c.

4. Herodotus 1.30; 2.103.

5. Plato *Phaedrus* 81a; *Respublica* 6.17 §505c.

6. L&N §§31.8, 10.

7. The usage is also attested in the papyri, see Horsley, *New Documents Illustrating Early Christianity*, vol. 2, *A Review of the Greek Inscriptions and Papyri Published in 1977*, 94–95.

8. Salmond, 334.

9. Ibid.

10. Alford, 3:119; Ellicott, 92; Abbott, 122.

In conclusion, the passage conveys the idea that childish understanding is easily confused by all sorts of doctrines which are devised by the trickery of people. These people use deceitfulness for their own ends (plan) which are characterized by error (cf. 5:6). It suggests that error is propagated with the intent of luring others to embrace the error (cf. Rom 1:32). This is obvious in the machinations of present-day cults. They have a scheme of error they want to propagate. By trickery and deceit, especially in the use of Scripture, they confuse the immature believer who lacks a proper understanding of God and his Word. For the most part the cults do not really bother those who are well acquainted with the Scripture and the God of Scripture. Consequently, it is of utmost importance for believers to follow God's plan for edification of the body through the gifted people provided for this purpose.

(ii) Positively: Development (4:15)

In verse 14 Paul discussed the purpose negatively, namely, that the lack of spiritual growth causes instability. In verse 15 Paul discusses the purpose positively, namely, that each believer might grow to the measure of Christ (cf. also v. 13).

Text: 4:15. ἀληθεύοντες δὲ ἐν ἀγάπῃ αὐξήσωμεν εἰς αὐτὸν τὰ πάντα, ὅς ἐστιν ἡ κεφαλή, ὁ Χριστός,

Translation: 4:15. "but rather being truthful with love, we might grow up to him with reference to all things, who is the head, the Christ,"

Commentary: 4:15. ἀληθεύοντες δὲ[1] ἐν ἀγάπῃ, "but rather being truthful with love." The stark contrast with verse 14 is marked in three ways: (1) by the adversative conjunction δέ, "but"; (2) by the participle ἀληθεύοντες, "being truthful," as opposed to the nouns referring to deceit and error; and (3) by the subjunctives with the ἵνα, ("in order that"—v. 14) from the static condition, μηκέτι ὦμεν νήπιοι, "we might no longer be children" (v. 14), to the dynamic, "we might grow" (v. 15). Noting these factors, the adversative δέ should be rendered "but rather" to emphasize that contrast.

The meaning of the participle ἀληθεύοντες, which is from the verb ἀληθεύω, has been debated. In classical times the verb could mean "to speak the truth,"[2] or "to be true, to prove true."[3] In the LXX it appears five times (Gen 20:16; 42:16; Prov 21:3; Isa 44:26; Sir 34:4) and trans-

1. Only F G *ex* latt? have ἀλήθειαν δὲ ποιοῦντες. Dubois states that this reading also appears in cop[bo], see Jean-Daniel Dubois, "Ephesians IV 15: ἀληθεύοντες δὲ or ἀλήθειαν δὲ ποιοῦντες. On the Use of Coptic Versions for New Testament Textual Criticism," *NovT* 16 (January 1974): 30–34. However, even with this support, the manuscript evidence is insufficient to be considered a genuine reading.

2. Xenophon *Memorabilia* 1.1.5; Plato *Respublica* 9 §589c.

3. Aeschylus *Septem contra Thebas* 562; Hippocrates *Prognosticum* 25.16.

lates four different Hebrew words. It is an ethical term used of proving or being true and never with the idea of speaking the truth. The noun ἀλήθεια has in both OT and Greek literature the sense of reality or the real state of affairs.[1] Although this has been greatly debated, it is essentially correct.[2] For further discussion of this noun, see 1:13. In the Qumran literature, truth had the meaning of "foundation."[3] In the NT the only other place the verb appears is in Gal 4:16 where it means "to speak the truth." However, in Ephesians the concept of "being truthful" is the best sense of the word.[4] In contrast to the preceding verse, where there are three prepositional phrases to denote falsehood and deceit, the present word speaks of being real or truthful in both conduct and speech. Their deceit was not only in their words but also in their conduct (cf. John 3:21). In other words, the believers' conduct should be transparent, revealing the real state of affairs, as opposed to hiding or suppressing the truth (Rom 1:18) through cunning and deceit.

The connection of the prepositional phrase ἐν ἀγάπῃ has been debated. Although some would connect it with the following subjunctive verb,[5] most think it should be joined with the preceding participle.[6] The last view is best because the participle would be isolated without it and normally, as seen in 1:4, Paul uses qualifiers following verbs and participles. Furthermore, this same construction is seen in verse 14 and thus makes a stark contrast with it. Paul adds ἐν ἀγάπῃ to temper truth. Truth may be demonstrated in a harsh way but Paul is asking that it be done with love. The preposition ἐν denotes instrument, "with love." The word "love" was discussed at 1:4 where it was defined as that which seeks the highest good in the one loved. Again, this is in contrast to the preceding verse, for deceit is used for selfish ends whereas truth with love considers the interest of others supremely important. Furthermore, with this in mind, believers are not to use truth in a retaliatory manner against the deceivers, but rather are to show and speak the truth with love. This manner of life is far more powerful than a life of deceit because it has no fear that hidden motives or facts will be revealed. It is a transparency that is wedded to love, love with truth that enables individual believers to grow harmoniously with other members of the body with the resulting growth of the whole body.

1. Bultmann, *TDNT* 1 (1964): 238.

2. Thiselton, *NIDNTT* 3 (1978): 881–82, 885; L&N §§70.4; 72.2.

3. For a study of this, see Murphy-O'Connor, "Truth: Paul and Qumran," 179–230.

4. BAGD 36; BDAG 43; Rudolf Bultmann, "ἀληθεύω," *TDNT* 1 (1964): 251; L&N §33.251.

5. Theodoret *Eph* 4:15 (*PG* 82:536); Harless, 385–87; Eadie, 318–19; Meyer, 230; Salmond, 335; Mußner, 131.

6. Theophylact *Eph* 4:15 (*PG* 124:1088); Oecumenius *Eph* 4:14–16 (*PG* 118:1221); Aquinas, chap. 4, lec. 5, vv. 14–16 (169–70); Calvin, 184–85; Hodge, 239; Alford, 3:119; Ellicott, 93; Abbott, 123 (modifies both); Robinson, 185; Westcott, 64; Masson, 195 n. 1; Schlier, 205; Gaugler, 182; Hendriksen, 202; Gnilka, 216; Caird, 77; Mitton, 156; Barth, 444; Schnackenburg, 187 n. 51; Bruce, 352.

This participial clause modifies the following verb. It shows either the means by which we should grow or the manner in which we should grow. Although there is little difference, the second alternative is preferred because the words portray manner. The believer's growth is Paul's next concern.

αὐξήσωμεν εἰς αὐτὸν τὰ πάντα, "we might grow up to him with reference to all things." Rather than remaining children, we are to grow into him with respect to all things. This is accomplished by means of the gifts given to each as well as the foundational gifts given to the church. The aorist subjunctive αὐξήσωμεν is united to the conjunction ἵνα in verse 14 giving the positive aspect of the purpose of the gifts. Thus, the subjunctive should be translated "might grow" rather than "will grow" because the latter gives it the certainty of an indicative. The aorist is ingressive, denoting a state or condition and signifying entrance into that state or condition. The verb is used also in 2:21 and there, as here, it is used intransitively followed by the preposition εἰς.

The phrase εἰς αὐτόν has been interpreted: (1) "in relation to" Christ as head we grow up;[1] (2) "into him" (AV, RV, ASV, RSV, NASB, NEB, JB, NIV, NJB, NRSV) referring to our incorporation in him;[2] and (3) "unto him" (TEV) or "towards him" denoting the end or aim of our growth, namely, to the standard of Christ's full stature.[3] View (1) does not seem apropos to the phrase or to the context. Rendering (2) has plausibility, but in this context he is the head and we are growing up into the body, not the head. In fact, we are already "in him." View (3) seems to be the most viable, for Christ, as the head, is the example for believers to follow. This also fits the portrayal given in verse 13 where believers are to attain to (εἰς) the unity of faith and knowledge, to (εἰς) a mature person, to (εἰς) Christ's full stature. As such, Christ is both the source (v. 7) and the goal (v. 15).

The τὰ πάντα is the accusative of general reference and is used in conjunction with intransitive verbs. Thus it can be rendered "with reference to all things" and conveys the idea that we are to grow in all areas of spiritual life. Schlier thinks that the verb is transitive and thus those who speak the truth in love cause all things of the world to grow into Christ. In other words, the church takes over the world (because it belongs to the church) and causes it to grow into Christ.[4] However, there is no indication in the NT that the church is going to take over the world. In fact, the church will eventually lose ground because of its predicted apostasy (2 Thess 2:3–12; 1 Tim 4:1–3; 2 Tim 4:3–4). Rather, the verb is intransitive and speaks of believers who are to grow to Christ.[5]

1. Meyer, 231; Winer, *Grammar*, 496.

2. Ellicott, 93.

3. Alford, 3:119; Eadie, 319; Abbott, 124; Salmond, 336; Gnilka, 217; Barth, 445.

4. Schlier, *Die Zeit der Kirche*, 289–92; Schlier, 205–6; idem, *TDNT* 3 (1965): 681.

5. Gaugler, 182; Gnilka, 218; Barth, 444–45; Schnackenburg, 188; cf. Käsemann, "Das Interpretationsproblem des Epheserbriefes," 5–8; reprinted in idem, "Das Inter-

To summarize, as it is preferable for a child to develop in all areas of life rather than just in one or two areas, so is the child of God to develop in all areas of spiritual life. For example, an increase in knowledge must be accompanied by an increase in love and development of proper attitudes, and at the same time God-given gifts must be continually exercised. Believers are to grow to Christ who is our standard. Christ is the embodiment of love (Eph 3:19; 5:2, 25; Rom 8:35; 2 Cor 5:14) and truth (Eph 4:21; John 14:6). Briefly, in verses 11–13 Christ gives gifts to all believers to prepare them to do the work of the ministry for the purpose of building the body of Christ in order to attain the unity of the faith, to a mature person, and to the full stature of Christ. In verse 15 the same idea is conveyed, as gifts enable growth to that standard, namely, Christ. This is not numerical but qualitative growth. The goal is to grow in Christ. It is not referring to an eschatological future but a present goal that can be achieved by the utilization of the gifts in his power.

ὅς ἐστιν ἡ[1] κεφαλή, ὁ Χριστός,[2] "who is the head, the Christ." The antecedent of the relative pronoun ὅς is αὐτόν. This one to whom we are growing up is identified as the head, a description already given in 1:22. As discussed in that passage, Christ's headship implies preeminence or prominence. Although the term κεφαλή does not necessarily inherently denote authority or source, the context may emphasize one of those aspects. Certainly, the context of 1:22 portrays Christ as the head in the sense of ruler or one who has authority, because that passage speaks specifically about everything being subjected under his feet. In the present context the idea of authority or ruler is not prominent but the ideas of source (v. 7) and goal (v. 15) are. The present verse stresses that the goal or end of our growth is the standard of Christ's stature. Christ, then, is identified as the head and thus he is a model for the believer. Also, the idea of source is emphasized in the prepositional phrase (ἐξ οὗ) in the next verse (v. 16). This is similar to Col 2:19 where the head is not seen as directive but rather as the source of sustenance for the body.[3] Hence, Christ as head is both the

pretationsproblem des Epheserbriefes," in *Exegetische Versuche und Besinnungen*, vol. 2 (Göttingen: Vandenhoeck & Ruprecht, 1964), 259–61.

1. The article is missing in D* F G 6 1737 1881 *pc* Clement. It appears in 𝔓[46] ℵ A B C D[2] Ψ 33 𝔐. Its inclusion is represented well from the Alexandrian and Byzantine texts. Since the omission is basically from only the Western text there is not sufficient grounds for deleting the article.

2. The reading ἡ κεφαλή, ὁ Χριστός is in ℵ[2] D F G Ψ 𝔐. The reading ἡ κεφαλή, Χριστός is found in ℵ* A B C 6 33 81 1175 1241[s] 1739 1881 2464 *pc* Chrysostom Theodoret Oecumenius Theophylact. The reading ἡ κεφαλή τοῦ Χριστοῦ is found in only 𝔓[46] and is not acceptable. The second reading is found in NA[27] and UBS[4] but it is almost exclusively an Alexandrian reading. The first reading is preferred because it has good geographical distribution with solid genealogical relationships in the Western and Byzantine texts.

3. O'Brien, *Colossians, Philemon*, 147; Roels, *God's Mission*, 107; Arnold, "Jesus Christ: 'Head' of the Church (Colossians and Ephesians)," 362–63; Dawes, *The Body in Question*, 144–47.

goal and source of our growth. Again, the word κεφαλή does not inherently denote "source,"[1] but the context supplies this concept.[2] A note of caution must be made for those who attempt to use this verse as a basis of seeing "head" as source. The preposition with the masculine relative pronoun ἐξ οὗ, "out of whom, from whom," (v. 16) indicating the source of the growth of the body relates back to the immediately preceding masculine noun Χριστός and not the feminine noun κεφαλή.[3]

As mentioned in the discussion in 1:23, there has been development in the concept concerning the body of Christ. In 1 Cor 12:27–28 the church is the body of Christ, whereas in Ephesians and Colossians (Eph 1:22–23; 4:15–16; 5:23; Col 1:18; 2:19) the body of believers is the church and Christ is the head of that body.[4] Although in the illustration of the body in 1 Cor 12:21, the "head" is used as one of the members of the body, it is not identified as being Christ, as it is in Ephesians and Colossians. In other words, in 1 Corinthians the church is the body and the body is Christ, whereas in Ephesians and Colossians the church is the body and Christ is the head, and furthermore, the body and the head is Christ. This metaphor is richer and more complex. In the end, the body of believers by utilization of gifts is to grow to Christ, who is the head, the source of their growth.

Scholars debate whether to include the article before Χριστός. The reading with the article is better than its exclusion. Although the significance is not all that great, it does denote the title meaning "the Messiah." The same Messiah who was to come, save, and rule Israel is now the head of the church. It is this anointed one who is the measure for all the church.

(b) For the Body (4:16)

Having developed the negative and the positive purposes of growth for individuals who make up the body, Paul continues to discuss growth but with reference to the whole body of believers.

Text: 4:16. ἐξ οὗ πᾶν τὸ σῶμα συναρμολογούμενον καὶ συμβιβαζόμενον διὰ πάσης ἁφῆς τῆς ἐπιχορηγίας κατʼ ἐνέργειαν ἐν μέτρῳ ἑνὸς ἑκάστου μέρους τὴν αὔξησιν τοῦ σώματος ποιεῖται εἰς οἰκοδομὴν ἑαυτοῦ ἐν ἀγάπῃ.

Translation: 4:16. "from whom the whole body, being fitted and held together through every supporting connection according to the work-

1. As do Berkeley and Alvera Mickelsen, Payne, and Kroeger, see discussion in 1:22.

2. Grudem ("The Meaning of Κεφαλή ['Head']," 18–19) admits that in the present context head is seen as the source of nourishment. Cf. also Fitzmyer, "Another Look at ΚΕΦΑΛΗ in 1 Corinthians 11.3," 53–54.

3. Perriman, *Speaking of Women*, 47.

4. Cf. Benoit, "Body, Head, and *Pleroma* in the Epistles of the Captivity," 2:59–69; Perriman, "'His body, which is the church. . . .' Coming to Terms with Metaphor," 135–37; Yorke, *The Church as the Body of Christ in the Pauline Corpus*, 99–118; Field, "The Discourses Behind the Metaphor 'the Church is The Body of Christ'," 103–4.

ing in measure from each individual part, causes the growth of the body to building itself up in love."

Commentary: 4:16. ἐξ οὗ πᾶν τὸ σῶμα συναρμολογούμενον καὶ συμβιβαζόμενον, "from whom the whole body, being fitted and held together." The preposition with the masculine relative pronoun ἐξ οὗ, "out of whom, from whom," denotes the source of the growth of the whole body.[1] It relates back to the immediately preceding noun, namely, Christ (not "the head"). Christ is the origin as well as the goal of the body's growth. The adjective πᾶν with an articular singular noun is to be translated as "all," "the entire," or "the whole."[2] The body refers to the church.

Immediately following are two participles. The first participle συναρμολογούμενον, from συναρμολογέω, is used only here and 2:21. There it was discussed as a word that Paul coined by joining the prepositional prefix συν- either to the rare noun ἁρμός, referring to stones torn away from their "joints" (or the "crevice" of a door); or to the rare verb ἁρμολογέω, meaning "to join" or "pile together," as stones for a tomb. Hence, it would have the resultant meaning "to join, fit together," especially with reference to a construction made of stones. Today with mortar it is easy to fit stones together but in that day, with no mortar, the stones were cut and smoothed by an elaborate process so that they fit exactly with each other.[3] As the ancient masons used an elaborate process of fitting stones together, it is certain that God's grace carefully fits together persons with one another in order to bring inner unity that can allow them to grow together. The emphasis is on the skillful fitting of each member to the other, as opposed to being thrown together haphazardly.

The second participle συμβιβαζόμενον, from συμβιβάζω, literally means "to bring or put together" and used metaphorically means "to bring to terms, reconcile."[4] It was used philosophically to make analytical comparisons and to draw conclusions[5] and is used to bring arguments together in order to demonstrate or prove something.[6] It appears ten times in the LXX (Exod 4:12, 15; 18:16; Lev 10:11; Deut 4:9; Judg 13:8 [B text]; Ps 32:8 [LXX 31:8]; Isa 40:13, 14; Theodotion Dan 9:22) translating four Hebrew words and always means "to teach, instruct." Teaching is a process of bringing together facts and arguments.[7] In the

1. Delebecque ("L'hellénisme de la «relative complexe»," 229–38, esp. 233) thinks that this "double relative" or "complex relative" (ἐξ οὗ) was borrowed from classical Greek, having the idea "from whom."

2. MHT 3:200; Moule, *Idiom Book*, 94; BAGD 631; BDAG 784.

3. For a detailed study of this word, see Robinson, 260–63.

4. Herodotus 1.74; Thucydides 2.29.6; Plato *Protagoras* 337e.

5. Plato *Hippias Minor* 369d; *Respublica* 6 §504a; Aristotle *Topica* 7.5 §155a.25; 8.11 §161b.37–38; *Sophistici Elenchi* 28 §181a.22.

6. Aristotle *Topica* 7.5 §150a.36; 8.3 §154b.27; 8.11 §157b.37.

7. One should deduce that the LXX's use of the term means "directing" or "guiding," which can then be applied to the present passage, as does G. H. Whitaker, "The Building and the Body (Eph. ii.21 f., iv.16; Col. ii.19)," *Theology* 13 (December 1926): 335–36.

NT this word occurs seven times with various meanings, including "to conclude, infer" (Acts 16:10); "to prove, demonstrate" (Acts 9:22); "to instruct" (Acts 19:33; 1 Cor 2:16 [quoting Isa 40:14]); and "to unite, bring or knit together" (Col 2:2, 19). This last sense fits the present context and is parallel with Col 2:19 and is best translated "held together" (NASB, TEV, NIV, NRSV) or "intimately joined together."[1] Individual believers are brought together much like a lawyer marshalls evidence together in a logical fashion so as to make a case clear or like a teacher who tightly argues in a logical sequence to demonstrate a theory. However, the union between believers is not only external in that they are redeemed and gifted by the same Lord but also internal in that they are indwelt by the Holy Spirit.

Having discussed the meaning of the two participles, we need to understand their function in the context. To begin with, they are circumstantial participles of manner modifying the main verb, which is near the end of this relative sentence. They show how the body[2] is causing the growth. They are very functional words since the various members of a body do fit precisely and are united integrally with one another. Both of the participles have the prepositional prefix συν-, which is common in Ephesians and only intensifies the concept of fitting and holding together. It speaks of the inner unity of believers who were, before their conversion, at enmity with one another. Both are in the present tense, indicating a continuing action; and in the passive voice, denoting that they are recipients of God's grace. They grow by being carefully fitted and held together, rather than growing individually apart from one another. Thus, it is not self-initiative that causes the growth but the gracious action of God who is responsible for the "fitting and holding" together of believers. The whole body functions together as the individual parts contribute. It should be noted that this fitting and bringing together occurs in two areas: (1) between believing Jews and Gentiles combined into one body, and (2) the utilization of various gifts among individual believers. The means by which this is done is further described in the rest of the verse.

διὰ πάσης ἁφῆς τῆς ἐπιχορηγίας, "through every supporting connection." As is often the case with Paul's writings, it can be difficult to determine what each succeeding phrase modifies or depends on. With this particular phrase, some join it to the main verb (ποιεῖται),[3] which would render it "the whole body being fitted and held together, *by means of every supporting connection* according to the working in measure from each individual part, causes the growth of the body." Hence, the "every supporting connection" is the cause of growth. However, most think it depends on the two previous participles (συν-

1. McGrath, "'*Syn*' Words in Saint Paul," 221.

2. Not the head as suggested by G. H. Whitaker, "συναρμολογούμενον καὶ συμβιβαζόμενον Ephesians iv 16," *JTS* 31 (October 1929): 48–49.

3. Bengel, 4:94; Alford, 3:120; Meyer, 234.

αρμολογούμενον καὶ συμβιβαζόμενον),[1] which would render it "the whole body being fitted and held together *through every supporting connection*, according to the working in measure from each individual part, causes the growth of the body." Hence, Christ unifies the body by means of "every supporting connection." This accentuates the need for all believers to utilize their gifts in order for Christ to achieve his purpose of unity for the church. The connection of this phrase with the participles is preferable because of their proximity to each other and because the construction in the parallel passage in Col 2:19 supports it. While the first preposition (ἐκ) in this verse denotes source, the present preposition (διά) signifies the means through which the whole body is being fitted and held together. Paul commonly uses human physiology to illustrate the body of Christ.

It is difficult to decipher the meaning of ἁφή.[2] In classical literature, it could mean: (1) the special sense of "lighting or kindling" a fire (by contact of fire), derived from ἅπτω;[3] (2) "touch,"[4] or "contact" of surfaces, derived from ἅπτομαι;[5] (3) "sense or sensation of touch";[6] or (4) "ligament."[7] In the LXX it occurs sixty-nine times (appears only in canonical books) and sixty-five times it translates נֶגַע, meaning "stroke, plague, mark."[8] Of all its occurrences, it is used sixy-one times in Lev 13–14 as a technical term for a leprous "mark" regarded as a "heavy touch" or "stroke" of the disease.[9] Twice it is used as a stroke or assault inflicted by human beings (Deut 17:8; 21:5). Other times it is used metaphorically for a "stroke" of chastisement or affliction (2 Sam 7:14; 1 Kgs 8:38; 2 Chr 6:29). The common idea of the noun is "touch" or "contact." Even in its technical use it depicts the spread of disease to garments (Lev 13:47) and to houses and their walls (14:34–48) by means of contact. This is further supported by the verb form (נָגַע), which basically means "to touch" with the extended meaning "to reach, strike." Hence, meaning (2) is the one that prevails in OT usage while the concepts of (1), (3), and (4) are not found there.

1. Hodge, 243; Eadie, 322; Ellicott, 94; von Soden, 139; Abbott, 125; Salmond, 337; Westcott, 64; Masson, 196; Schlier, 207; Gaugler, 184; Schnackenburg, 189; Bruce, 353; Lincoln, 262.

2. For a study of the word, see Lightfoot, *Colossians*, 198–99; Abbott, 125–26; Robinson, 186; Barth, 448–49.

3. Herodotus 7.215; Dionysius Halicarnassensis 11.33; Diodorus Siculus 19.31.1.

4. Aeschylus *Prometheus Vinctus* 850; Plutarch *Pericles* 15.4.

5. Aristotle *Physica* 4.5 §213a.9; 5.3 §227a.17; *Metaphysica* 5.4.1 §1014b.22; 11.12.14 §1068b.12; *Generatione et Corruptione* 1.8 §326b.12; 1.9 §327a.12.

6. Plato *Respublica* 7 §523e; Aristotle *Ethica Nicomachea* 3.10.9, 10 §1118a.31, 33.

7. Lightfoot (*Colossians*, 199) cites references from Hippocrates, but I was not able to find them. LSJ (288) lists "ligament" and cites only Eph 4:16 and Col 2:19 for this usage.

8. BDB 619; L. Schwienhorst, נָגַע *nāgaʿ*; נֶגַע *negaʿ*," *TDOT* 9 (1998): 203–9.

9. BDB 619; Schwienhorst, *TDOT* 9 (1998): 207–9.

The correct meaning for the present context may be deduced by the process of elimination. Certainly meaning (1), "kindling," is not applicable for the present passage. Meaning (4), "ligament," which is rarely found in translations (NIV, NRSV), is a special use employed by Hippocrates to describe both the tissue that connects to the bones and a mass of muscle. Lightfoot correctly argues that since Hippocrates uses it peculiarly, one should not apply that special sense here.[1] Furthermore, in the parallel passage (Col 2:19), in addition to ἁφή, Paul uses σύνδεσμος, which would be the more appropriate term for "ligament." Hence, it is improbable that ἁφή means ligament in the present context.[2] Definition (3), "sense or sensation of touch," is accepted by Chrysostom who makes the term equivalent to the senses (διὰ τῆς αἰσθήσεως, "by the sense").[3] More explicitly Theodoret thinks that "touch" is one of the five senses.[4] Meyer accepts this definition and concludes that it refers to "every feeling [sense or sensation] in which the supply is perceived, experienced."[5] However, as Lightfoot argues, this usurps the meaning of ἁφή, and one cannot substitute it for αἴθησις anymore than one can substitute "touch" for "sense" in English.[6]

Before discussing the last classical rendering of the word, it is interesting to note that it is rendered "joint" in most of the translations (AV, RV, ASV, RSV, NASB, NEB, TEV, JB) and by most commentators.[7] The consensus is that just as the joints in the human body are crucial to bodily function, so the various connecting parts in a building are critical to the function of the building. The problem with this view is that it tends to limit the "joints" to some, but not all, members of the church who are to hold the church together.[8] Some believe it refers to the church leaders mentioned in verse 11.[9] However, the passage clearly teaches that all receive gifts (v. 7) and all need to participate in the growth (vv. 13, 15). This is also seen in the parallel passages on the gifts (Rom 12; 1 Cor 12). Furthermore, Barth doubts that philologically this term could mean "joint" in Paul's day and points out that when the lexicons cite Eph 4:16 and Col 2:19,[10] they opt for "ligaments" rather than "joint."[11] Beyond this, there is no classical justifi-

1. Lightfoot, *Colossians*, 199.

2. Barth, 448.

3. Chrysostom *Eph* 4:15–16 (*PG* 62:84).

4. Theodoret *Eph* 4:16 (*PG* 82:537).

5. Meyer, 235.

6. Lightfoot, *Colossians*, 199.

7. Hodge, 242; Eadie, 322; Ellicott, 94; Salmond, 337; Schlier, 208; Gaugler, 184; Gnilka, 219; Hugedé, 174; Schnackenburg, 189; Bruce, 353.

8. Barth, 448.

9. Schlier, 208; Schnackenburg, 189–90; Gnilka, 211; Schnackenburg, "Christus, Geist und Gemeinde (Eph. 4:1–16)," 290; Merklein, *Das kirchliche Amt nach dem Epheserbrief*, 114–15.

10. Cf. LSJ 288; BAGD 125; BDAG 155.

11. Barth, 448.

cation for this definition. It seems, then, that "joint" is not the best possible rendering for this word.

Thus meaning (2), "contact," is the most acceptable usage.[1] This sense of the word is the normal one. Aristotle defines two kinds of union: one is cohesion (σύμφυσις) and the other is contact (ἁφή). The first is organic unity whereas the latter is mere contact.[2] He illustrates by pointing out that water and air, when separated, are merely in contact with each other, which is different from when they become one in actuality.[3] He goes on to say that although contact does not necessarily mean continuity, there certainly must be contact before cohesion can ever occur.[4] He expands further by suggesting that two objects become one by touching and that the resulting whole will have the same sort of union as that which holds it together, as with a rivet, glue, contact (ἁφῇ), or organic union.[5] Again, in another work Aristotle discusses this word and observes that in order for two things to undergo mixture, they must have contact with one another.[6] Ramifications of Aristotle's remarks are noteworthy. When applied to the body of believers it is clear that the union and growth of the body can only come when there is contact with other members of the body. Although the body is one, the members are distinct. However, the interaction or contact between members, as the gifts are exercised, promotes both individual and corporate growth. Every believer is necessary to this process, not just a select few.

In conclusion, it seems apparent that ἁφή is best rendered "contact" because this is the predominant meaning of the word in classical and LXX usage and makes the best sense in the present context. It can be translated "contact" or "connection." Actually, the latter is preferred here as it denotes a connection between two objects or, in this case, believers when they "touch" or "contact" one another.

The next term is ἐπιχορηγία, a word that makes no appearance before NT times. Without the ἐπι- prefix, the verb χορηγέω and the noun χορηγός originally conveyed the idea of leading a chorus[7] or defraying the cost of presenting a chorus at the public festivals.[8] Later, however, the general sense became one of defraying expenses or supplying in abundance. For example, it referred to an army amply supplied with provisions[9] or a person well supplied financially.[10] In later Greek the

1. Oecumenius *Eph* 4:7–16 (*PG* 118:1221); Westcott, 64; Masson, 196 n. 1; Barth, 448–49; Ch. Bruston, "Le sens de ἁφή dans la Bible," *Revue des études grecques* 24 (1911): 77–82.

2. Aristotle *Metaphysica* 5.4.2 §1014b.23–24.

3. Aristotle *Physica* 4.5 §213a.10.

4. Aristotle *Metaphysica* 11.12.14–15 §1069a.11–13.

5. Aristotle *Physica* 5.3 §227a.16–17.

6. Aristotle *De Generatione et Corruptione* 1.6 §§322b.21–323a.34.

7. Plato *Leges* 2 (654a); *Gorgias* 482b.

8. Demosthenes *Orationes* 18.257.

9. Polybius 3.68.8.

10. Aristotle *Ethica Nicomachea* 1.10.15 §1101a.15; 10.8.11 §1179a.11.

compound verb took on the same meaning, such as, making provisions for an army[1] or a wife providing for her husband (Sir 25:22). The verb form is found only five times in the NT where it is used to give or grant entrance into the eternal kingdom (2 Pet 1:11), to supply or furnish seed to the sower (2 Cor 9:10), to provide the Holy Spirit for the believer (Gal 3:5), to supplement one's faith with virtue (2 Pet 1:5), and to provide nutriment to the body of Christ (Col 2:19). The noun form is found only once outside the present context and there it conveys the sense of the support of the Holy Spirit (Phil 1:19). Therefore, the best definition in the present context is "supply" or, even better, "support."

Finally, it must be determined how the genitive τῆς ἐπιχορηγίας relates to ἁφῆς. Exegetes vary greatly in this depending on how they define ἁφή. Some who translate it "joint" make it a genitive of description or quality[2] meaning that the joint is characterized by or designed for supply. Meyer, who prefers "sensation," views the genitive as an objective genitive that means that every feeling or sensation is experienced[3] when the supply or support is given by Christ. Barth paraphrases the prepositional phrase as "every contact serves for supply" or "he provides sustenance to it [body] through every contact."[4] Thus, though he does not label the genitive, he appears to think it denotes purpose. Still, it seems better to view this as an attributive genitive rendered "through every supporting contact or connection." Accordingly, it describes the whole body as being fitted and held together by means of each contact that contributes to the growth of the whole. This supports the ongoing concept that each member of the body has been gifted and as each member utilizes the gifts as he or she makes contact or connection with other members of the body, the body will grow. It is analogous to the human body where each cell is an entity to itself but is not in isolation from the rest of the body but rather makes its contribution to development of the body. The amount of contribution is the next subject.

κατ' ἐνέργειαν[5] **ἐν μέτρῳ ἑνὸς ἑκάστου μέρους,**[6] "according to the working in measure from each individual part." How the first prepositional phrase relates to the rest of this relative clause has been de-

1. Dionysius Halicarnassensis 1.42.4.

2. Alford, 3:121; Ellicott, 95; Schlier, 208; cf. Sellin, "Über einige ungewöhnliche Genitive im Epheserbrief," 102.

3. Meyer, 235.

4. Barth, 449.

5. The words κατ' ἐνέργειαν are omitted from F G it Irenaeus[lat] Lucifer Ambrosiaster but this omission is limited only to the Western text. These words are replaced by καὶ ἐνεργείας in 𝔓[46], but again this is the only manuscript that has this reading. It may be that the scribe had mistaken the καί for the κατ' and either corrected the ending of ἐνέργειαν to fit the case or mistakenly picked up the ending of ἐπιχορηγίας.

6. The reading μέλους is found in A C Ψ 365 *pc* it[a] vg syr[p] cop[bo]. This reading is not acceptable because it is limited to very few manuscripts in the Alexandrian text only.

bated. Three views have been proposed. First, some think it depends on the main verb (ποιεῖται), showing that the body grows in accordance with the function of each member.[1] However, it is Paul's pattern to place the qualifying prepositional phrases after and not before the main verb (cf. 1:4). Second, some propose that it belongs to the two participles (συναρμολογούμενον καὶ συμβιβαζόμενον), which explains the work of each member, that is, the fitting and holding together of the body.[2] It would be parallel with the immediately preceding prepositional phrase: the first prepositional phrase shows the means and the second the manner of the fitting and holding together. The weakness in this argument is that there is a great distance between the participles and this prepositional phrase. Third, others think it depends on the immediately preceding prepositional phrase (διὰ πάσης ἁφῆς τῆς ἐπιχορηγίας) indicating the work of each member in the supporting connections.[3] In this case, the string of participial phrases becomes long and involved; however, this is not uncommon for Paul. It is difficult to make a choice between these three options. Nevertheless, it seems that the last option is the best because it is most consistent with the text in that it includes the function of the members and the connections between believers. Also, this view considers the broader context because it relates to the two participles and ultimately to the main verb.

The first preposition κατά with the accusative denotes standard. The term ἐνέργεια appears two other times in this book (1:19; 3:7) along with four instances of the verbal form (1:11, 20; 2:2; 3:20). In 1:19 we concluded that it had the idea of actual power in operation rather than potential power. It is the word from which we derive our English word "energy" and in this context most translations render it "working," which does reflect power that is active. Thus, Barth's translation "according to the needs"[4] is inappropriate. Rather it is better translated "according to the working."

The second prepositional phrase discusses the amount of active power produced by each member of the body. Expressed literally, it is according to the activity "in measure of each individual part." The preposition ἐν, "in," denotes proportion as "according to" or "amounting to"[5] the measure of each individual part. It is not the same as κατά, which denotes standard,[6] but has more the idea of proportion and can

Also, it is easy to understand how a scribe would change it to "member," but it would be very unlikely that he would change "member" to "part."

1. Alford, 3:120; Eadie, 323; Ellicott, 95; Meyer, 236; Salmond, 338.

2. Harless, 396; Abbott, 127.

3. De Wette, 149–50; Rudolf Stier, *Der Brief an die Epheser als Lehre von der Gemeinde für die Gemeinde* (Berlin: Wilhelm Hertz, 1859), 263–64.

4. Barth, 449.

5. Robertson, *Grammar*, 589; Winer, *Grammar*, 483; BAGD 261; BDAG 330.

6. Salmond, 337.

be rendered "commensurate with"[1] or "in keeping with"[2] the measure. The word μέτρον, "measure," is used three times in this context and is very important. As Christ has given to each believer a gift according to measure (v. 7), he expects each believer to use that gift to the measure given, no less and no more. As a result, all the body of Christ will grow to the measure of Christ's full stature (v. 13). The present verse teaches that the body of Christ is being fitted and held together through every supporting connection according to the function in (to the) measure of each individual member as the member uses that measure of the gift given to him or her.

The genitives that follow (ἑνὸς ἑκάστου μέρους) could depend on κατ' ἐνέργειαν and thus be parallel with ἐν μέτρῳ, or they could depend on ἐν μέτρῳ,[3] which in turn depends on κατ' ἐνέργειαν. The first view's rendering "according to the working in the measure of each individual part"[4] seems to indicate that the working is directed toward each individual part, making μέρους an objective genitive. However, there is no idea of distribution in the passage or in the preposition ἐν.[5] It seems best then to accept the second alternative, which could be rendered "according to the working in measure from each individual," making μέρους a genitive of source. The individual gives in measure because he or she has been given a gift in measure (v. 7). These genitives emphasize the individual's responsibility to do his or her part and not depend on others to do the work of ministry nor to think that he or she is to do all the work of the ministry. The physical body is a good illustration of this principle. If, for example, the liver cells are more active than for what they are designed, they will ultimately do harm to the body. Likewise, if the liver cells stop functioning, the body will suffer dire consequences since other body parts cannot replace their function. Even in the fifth century B.C. Hippocrates remarked on his fascination with the precise functions of the human body. He observed that good health proceeds when the various parts of the body function proportionately to one another (adverb μετρίως is used). Pain occurs when one of the parts is in defect or excess or when it is isolated from the body.[6] Importantly, 1 Cor 12:14–26 also illustrates that the body of Christ operates precisely on this principle. Briefly then, each member of the body of Christ is to function to the measure Christ has given to him or her (v. 7). When members fulfill their responsibilities, then the body of Christ can grow properly as Paul proceeds to devleop next.

τὴν αὔξησιν τοῦ σώματος ποιεῖται, "causes the growth of the body." The noun αὔξησιν is used only here and Col 2:19 and means "growth,

1. Ellicott, 95.
2. Meyer, 236.
3. See discussion by Abbott, 126–27.
4. Alford, 3:120; Ellicott, 95.
5. Abbott, 127.
6. Hippocrates *De natura hominis* 4.1–12.

increase."[1] The genitive τοῦ σώματος is used instead of the reciprocal pronoun (ἑαυτοῦ) because of the distance of the subject, thus preventing ambiguity "as the pronoun might have been taken to refer to μέρους,"[2] and because Paul uses a reciprocal pronoun (ἑαυτοῦ) in the immediate context. The main verb ποιεῖται is a present middle indicative showing the body's growth from within as a living organism. It has a causative idea[3] much like the parallel passage (Col 2:19) where Paul uses the verb "to grow" with the cognate accusative "growth" (αὔξει τὴν αὔξησιν). The subject "the body" mentioned at the beginning of the verse united with the verb could be rendered "the body . . . causes (brings about, procures) the growth of the body." Isolated from the context it would appear that the body of believers produces its own growth. However, the context makes it clear that it is not the believers' inherent ability that produces growth but their utilization of the gifts that Christ gives to each of them. Furthermore, immediately preceding the subject "the body" the prepositional phrase "from whom" (ἐξ οὗ) clearly indicates that the head, Christ, is the source from which the church draws its ability to produce or cause growth.[4]

Barth points out that according to ancient doctors the head or the brain was considered the acropolis of the body, but he concludes they did not view the head as the source of the body's growth as Paul does here.[5] However, Barth is inaccurate in his deduction. There is evidence that in Paul's day they would have considered the head as the source of growth for the body. For example, the Hippocratic school (fifth century B.C.) thought of the head as central to the nervous system and as the source of all the veins.[6] Hence, it is possible that Paul thought in these same terms. Regardless, as Howard observes, the physical head/body concept is not crucial to Paul's argument. Even though Christ is the head, the emphasis is on Christ and not on the head, otherwise he would have written ὅς ἐστιν Χριστός, ἡ κεφαλή, ἐξ ἧς πᾶν τὸ σῶμα rather than ὅς ἐστιν ἡ κεφαλή, Χριστός, ἐξ οὗ πᾶν τὸ σῶμα.[7] Christ, therefore, is the source of the gifts that enables the individual to build up the

1. BAGD 122; BDAG 151.

2. Salmond, 338.

3. Herbert Braun, "ποιέω, ποίημα, ποίησις, ποιητής," *TDNT* 6 (1968): 484; Wallace, *Greek Grammar*, 412.

4. David P. Kuske, "Ministry according to Ephesians 4:1–16," *WLQ* 91 (summer 1994): 213.

5. Barth, 450.

6. Cf. Sebastianus Tromp, "«Caput influit sensum et motum» Col. 2,19 et Eph. 4,16 in luce traditionis," *Greg* 39, no. 2 (1958): 353–66; esp. 358–60; Carolyn Osiek and David L. Balch, *Families in the New Testament World: Households and House Churches*, The Family, Religion, and Culture, ed. Don S. Browning and Ian S. Evison (Louisville, Ky.: Westminster John Knox, 1997), 183.

7. Howard, "The Head/Body Metaphors of Ephesians," 354. One must not push this too far because Col 2:19 has τὴν κεφαλήν, ἐξ οὗ πᾶν τὸ σῶμα. But even in that passage there is such a strong concentration on Christ that Paul uses the masculine relative pronoun.

body of Christ, and Christ is also the source of the body's unification through the interaction of believers which causes growth of the body.

εἰς οἰκοδομὴν ἑαυτοῦ[1] ἐν ἀγάπῃ. "to building itself up in love." The preposition εἰς, "to," expresses the final goal of the growth of the body. There is a shift in metaphors, possibly referring back to verse 12 where the goal is the building up of the body (εἰς οἰκοδομὴν τοῦ σώματος).[2] But as in verse 12, the building here is not inanimate but a living and growing organism made up of living believers. Furthermore, it is not unusual for Paul to switch metaphors, for in 2:16–22 he moves also from the body to a building. The reciprocal pronoun (ἑαυτοῦ) emphasizes the body's own activity of growth.

The final prepositional phrase ἐν ἀγάπῃ denotes the sphere in which this is to occur. It is in the sphere of love. Again even though there is a change of metaphors, one must keep in mind that the building is a living and growing organism. Members are to contribute the measure of the gift that each has been apportioned to other members in the body in an atmosphere of love. Thus, love among the members is another prerequisite for growth. Earlier in the verse Paul spoke of the interconnectedness between members of the body of Christ. He now makes clear that love must be an integral part of this dynamic in order for growth to occur. As a child grows better in an atmosphere of familial love, so the church grows better in an atmosphere of love between believers. Paul enjoins believers to be truthful ἐν ἀγάπῃ (v. 15) and to grow ἐν ἀγάπῃ (v. 16).[3]

In conclusion, verses 7–16 are the final section of the first half of chapter 4 entitled "Walking in Unity" (vv. 1–16). Verses 1–6 give the basis of the unity to which Paul calls them, and then it lists the seven elements of unity. In verses 7–16, Paul states that each believer is given a gift according to the measure of Christ (vv. 7–10). Further, he demonstrates that the ascended Christ has the right to give gifts. In the last portion of this section (vv. 11–16), Paul explains the distribution of the gifts. The foundational gifts were given (v. 11) to enable all believers to minister (v. 12) toward the goal of edifying the body of Christ (v. 13). The distribution of the gifts has a twofold purpose: negatively, that the individual believer might not fall prey to any wind of doctrine presented by deceitful people (v. 14); and positively, that the individual believer might be able to grow in Christ with respect to all things (v. 15). Paul concludes

1. The reading αὐτοῦ is in the place of ἑαυτοῦ in א D* F G 1505 *pc*. The reading ἑαυτοῦ appears in 𝔓[46] A B C D[2] Ψ 33 1739 1881 𝔐 Irenaeus[lat]. The first reading is unacceptable because it is represented by the Western text-type and only one manuscript in the Alexandrian text.

2. It is doubtful that Paul meant that οἰκοδομή is the heavenly building and the σῶμα is its earthly expression, as suggested by Schlier, "Zum Begriff der Kirche im Epheserbrief," 13 n. 2.

3. Hemphill, "The Pauline Concept of Charisma," 252–53; idem, *Spiritual Gifts*, 190.

that the church enables itself to grow in love as its individual members use the gifts that have been measured out to them (v. 16).

Throughout, Paul makes it clear that the ultimate source of growth is Christ, the head of this body, the church. It is also important to note that this passage makes it clear that the ministry of the church is not the obligation of a few but rather the responsibility of every believer. The distinction between the clergy and laity is a human creation. This is due primarily to a confusion between gift and office.[1]

In this section one observes that there can be unity in diversity. Although there is oneness of structure, there is variety in function. The unifying force is the oneness of purpose, that is, the use of gifts for body edification, not self-edification. The use of the gifts will provide growth for individual members and the corporate body to prepare both to meet their Lord.[2]

Finally, Paul ends this discussion by reminding believers that everything he has stated thus far must have one all-important ingredient. That ingredient is love. This is most significant in light of the fact that he was addressing both Jewish and Gentile Christians. Historically, animosity existed between these two groups, but now in Christ they have been redeemed and reconciled with each other (2:11–18).

As a new people, united into one body, a significant change in conduct is required. In the following sections Paul will describe the guidelines for this conduct.

1. As does Gordon, "'Equipping' Ministry in Ephesians 4?" 75–78.
2. Peterson, *Engaging with God*, 209–10.

B. Walk in Holiness (4:17–32)

This is the second of five sections (4:1, 17; 5:2; 8, 15) delineated by the use of περιπατέω "walk" in conjunction with the inferential conjunction οὖν, "therefore." Having completed his discourse on unity, Paul now instructs believers on how to walk in holiness. Holiness is not a necessary result of unity. A political party may have unity but it may not desire to have holiness of life. However, for the believer both unity and holiness are essential. This portion is divided into two parts: negatively, how a believer should not walk (vv. 17–19); and then positively, how a believer should walk (vv. 20–32).[1]

1. Presentation of the Old Person (4:17–19)

In presenting the old person, Paul explains his manner of life and the nature that is the basis for that lifestyle. He then contrasts those characteristics with the lifestyle of the new person in verses 20–32.

a. His Nature (4:17–18)

Paul exhorts the believers at Ephesus not to live as the Gentiles. He delineates the conduct of unbelievers by showing that they are by nature alienated from the life of God because of their hardness toward God.

Text: 4:17. Τοῦτο οὖν λέγω καὶ μαρτύρομαι ἐν κυρίῳ, μηκέτι ὑμᾶς περιπατεῖν, καθὼς καὶ τὰ ἔθνη περιπατεῖ ἐν ματαιότητι τοῦ νοὸς αὐτῶν, **4:18.** ἐσ-

1. For a discussion of the catalogues of virtue and vices with a paraenetic function, see Ehrhard Kamlah, *Die Form der katalogischen Paränese im Neuen Testament*, WUNT, ed. Joachim Jeremias and Otto Michel, vol. 7 (Tübingen: Mohr, 1964), passim, esp. 34–38.

κοτισμένοι τῇ διανοίᾳ ὄντες, ἀπηλλοτριωμένοι τῆς ζωῆς τοῦ θεοῦ διὰ τὴν ἄγνοιαν τὴν οὖσαν ἐν αὐτοῖς διὰ τὴν πώρωσιν τῆς καρδίας αὐτῶν,

Translation: 4:17. "This I say therefore, and testify in the Lord, that you no longer walk just as the Gentiles also walk in the futility of their minds, **4:18.** their reasoning process being darkened, being alienated from the life of God because of the ignorance that is in them due to the hardness of their hearts,"

Commentary: 4:17. Τοῦτο οὖν λέγω καὶ μαρτύρομαι ἐν κυρίῳ, "This I say therefore, and testify in the Lord." The οὖν, "therefore," does not serve as an inferential conjunction but has a resumptive force resuming the thought of verses 1–3 that had been interrupted at verse 4.[1] In verse 1 Paul had exhorted them to walk worthy of their calling and now in verse 17 he is telling them that they are no longer to walk as Gentiles walk because this is not worthy of their calling. The demonstrative pronoun τοῦτο, "this," refers to the exhortation that follows. In effect Paul is saying, "In resuming my exhortation I say this."

The verb μαρτύρομαι, "I testify," is not an oath with the Lord as a witness, as though ἐν κυρίῳ meant "by the Lord."[2] Instead, Paul is solemnly declaring his exhortation in the sphere of or in connection with the Lord (cf. Rom 9:1; 2 Cor 2:17; 1 Thess 4:1; 1 Tim 5:21; 2 Tim 2:14; 4:1).[3] He is in the Lord and speaks as one who is in the Lord. Consistently throughout this letter (2:21; 4:1; 5:8; 6:1, 10, 21) the prepositional phrase ἐν κυρίῳ, "in the Lord," refers not to God but to Christ.

μηκέτι ὑμᾶς περιπατεῖν, καθὼς καὶ τὰ[4] ἔθνη περιπατεῖ, "that you no longer walk just as the Gentiles also walk." The infinitive used as an imperative in the indirect command μηκέτι ὑμᾶς περιπατεῖν, "that you no longer walk" (cf. Acts 21:2, 21; 23:12), is in apposition to τοῦτο, "this."[5] The adverb μηκέτι, "no longer," implies that the Ephesians at one time did walk as the Gentiles. Certainly many, if not most, of the believers in Ephesus were Gentiles and had a lifestyle that is described in these verses (17–19). The present infinitive περιπατεῖν, "walk," with the adverb indicates that believers in Ephesus were not to conduct themselves as they had in the past. The present tense de-

1. Theodoret *Eph* 4:17 (*PG* 82:537).
2. As does Theodoret *Eph* 4:17 (*PG* 82:537).
3. Allan, "The 'In Christ' Formula in Ephesians," 56–57.
4. Following the article, the word λοιπά (*loipa* "rest") is found in $\aleph^{2}$ $D^{b, c}$ Ψ *Byz* [K L P] vg^{ms} syr arm *al*. The omission is found in $\mathfrak{P}^{46, 49vid}$ ℵ* A B D* F G 082 33 255, 256 263 296 365 424^{c} 467 1175 1319 1241^{s} 1739 1881 2464 *pc* $it^{d, g}$ $cop^{sa, bo}$ Clement (6.81: *h. t.*). The age of the manuscripts, the geographical distribution, and the genealogical relationship within the Alexandrian and Western text-types for the second reading gives it preference over the first. Internally, it is not only a shorter reading, but it is also more likely that a scribe would add the word rather than omit it. Theologically, the omission is better because if the reading were genuine, it would imply that the believers were still Gentiles. Paul is clear that they are not Gentiles, but rather Christians.
5. Robertson, *Grammar*, 700, 1046–47, 1078.

notes that they are to make a habit of avoiding the way Gentiles walk.[1] As noted in verse 1 "walk" denotes the lifestyle of the individual.

The conjunction καί after the comparative conjunction καθώς is adjunctive and thus these two words should be translated "just as also" indicating some people walk contrary to Paul's exhortation to the believers. These people are Gentiles. They are what many of the Ephesian believers were, namely, Gentiles in the flesh (2:11–12). Once they became believers they were no longer Gentiles but they, with the Jews, were Christians (2:15). As Christians their lifestyle must differ from that of both Jew and Gentile. A description of the Gentile lifestyle follows.

ἐν ματαιότητι τοῦ νοὸς αὐτῶν, "in the futility of their minds." The noun ματαιότης is a word that is rarely used. It has the meaning of "futility" or "emptiness" of humans.[2] It occurs in the LXX fifty-four times (appears only in canonical books): thirty-nine times in Ecclesiastes, fourteen times in the Psalms, and once in Proverbs. It translates four Hebrew words, forty-three times for הֶבֶל, having the idea of vanity, purposelessness, absurdity, and worthlessness.[3] In the NT it occurs only three times. In 2 Pet 2:18 it talks about false prophets who utter loud boasts of complete folly. In Rom 8:20 it conveys the idea that creation is subjected to futility or purposelessness in that its goal cannot be achieved. In other words, the earth was to produce fruit to preserve life but was thwarted due to the curse. In 1 Cor 15:17 Paul uses the adjective μάταιος to indicate that if Christ had not been raised, their faith "could not achieve its goal" for they would still be in their sins (v. 17). But what in Ephesians cannot achieve its goal? The noun is used in connection with the "mind."

The term νοῦς, meaning "mind," has different nuances.[4] The basic idea is one of perceiving, understanding, or thinking ability.[5] It also can have the idea of disposition or moral attitude.[6] Further, it is used for the result of thinking and thus has the nuance of opinion, purpose, plan, or resolve.[7] It appears thirty times in the LXX (twelve times in the canonical books), six times for לֵב or לֵבָב, referring to the heart or the inner person (Exod 7:23; Josh 14:7; Job 7:17; Isa 10:7, 12; 41:22).[8] It is also used of the mind or disposition (Isa 40:13; Wis 4:12; Jdt 8:14). In the NT it occurs twenty-four times, twenty-one times in Paul's letters, and twice in Ephesians (4:17, 23). Again, it conveys the basic idea of "understanding" (Luke 24:45; 1 Cor 14:14, 15, 19; Phil

1. Cf. Fanning, *Verbal Aspect*, 382–83, 332–33.
2. Philodemus Philosophus *Volumina Rhetorica* 6.32.6.
3. BDB 210–11; K. Seybold, "הֶבֶל *hebhel*; הָבַל *hābhal*," *TDOT* 3 (1978): 313–20.
4. J. Behm, "νοῦς," *TDNT* 4 (1967): 951–60.
5. Homer *Illias* 15.461; *Odyssea* 13.255.
6. Homer *Odyssea* 18.381; Herodotus 7.150; Philo *De Congressu Quaerendae Eruditionis Gratia* 21 §118.
7. Herodotus 1.10; 109; 9.46; Plato *Respublica* 1 §344d.
8. BDB 523; Fabry, *TDOT* 7 (1995): 412–34.

4:7; 2 Thess 2:2) or the result of thinking, "opinion, resolve, thought" (Rom 11:34; 14:5; 1 Cor 2:16*bis*). In addition, the idea of disposition or moral attitude is seen in the NT (Rom 1:28; 12:2; Col 2:18; 1 Tim 6:5; 2 Tim 3:8; Titus 1:15). In the present passage the concept of disposition or moral attitude fits best.[1] The original purpose of the mind was to be able to comprehend God's revelation, but due to the fall a person's mind is unable to accomplish this goal (μάταιος). Hence, the "futility of their minds" conveys the idea of not being able to perceive the revelation of God for which it was designed. Thus, its moral attitude or disposition prevents it from achieving its goal of proper moral decisions which are necessary for life (Rom 1:18–32). The believer is not to walk in this kind of moral purposelessness displayed by the Gentiles. Jervell has drawn up a list of words from Eph 4:17–25 describing the Gentiles that correspond to the words in Rom 1:21–29.[2] It demonstrates that the unregenerate Ephesian Gentiles were exactly the same as those described in Romans.

4:18. ἐσκοτισμένοι[3] τῇ διανοίᾳ ὄντες, "their reasoning process being darkened." The futility of the Gentile moral attitudes is further abetted by the darkening of their reasoning process. Although the alternate reading uses the classical ἐσκοτωμένοι, coming from σκοτόω, the preferred reading is ἐσκοτισμένοι, which comes from σκοτίζω. Regardless, in the NT both verbs are always in the passive and both can be rendered "to be darkened."[4] The verb σκοτίζω is used to convey the idea of a clouded or darkened mind[5] in contrast to an illumined mind.[6] In the LXX σκοτίζω occurs seven times and in the canonical books it appears six times (σκοτόω appears six and four times respectively) for חָשַׁךְ, meaning "be, grow dark"[7] both astronomically (Pss 105:28 [LXX 104:28]; 139:12 [LXX 138:12]; Eccl 12:2; Isa 13:10) and spiritually (Pss 69:23 [MT 69:24; LXX 68:24]; 74:20 [LXX 73:20]). It appears in the NT five other times (σκοτόω appears two other times,

1. Behm, *TDNT* 4 (1967): 958; BAGD 544; BDAG 680; L&N §30.5.

2. Jacob Jervell, *Imago Dei. Gen 1,26f. im Spätjudentum in der Gnosis und in den paulinischen Briefen* (Göttingen: Vandenhoeck & Ruprecht, 1960), 289–90.

3. The reading ἐσκοτισμένοι (from σκοτίζω) is found in D F G P 082 1739 1881 𝔐 Clement Chrysostom Theodoret Oecumenius Theophylact, while the more classical form ἐσκοτωμένοι (from σκοτόω) is found in 𝔓[46, 49] א A B I Ψ 33 1241[s] *pc*. The first reading is preferred because it has good geographical distribution and has good genealogical relationships within the Western and Byzantine texts. The second reading (accepted reading of NA[27] and UBS[4]) is only in the Alexandrian text. Internally, it is more likely that a scribe would opt for a classical form than the reverse. Ultimately, it really does not matter because both words mean the same thing and nothing has changed in that it is a masculine plural perfect passive participle.

4. Hans Conzelmann, "σκότος κτλ.," *TDNT* 7 (1971): 424.

5. Dionysius Halicarnassensis *de Thucydide* 33.

6. Plutarch *Moralia: Adversus Colotem* 24 §1120e.

7. BDB 365–66; cf. H. Lutzmann, L. T. Geraty, H. Ringgren, and L. A. Mitchel, "חָשַׁךְ *ḥāšak*, etc.," *TDOT* 5 (1986): 245–59.

Rev 9:2; 16:10) and again it has reference to astronomical (Matt 24:29 = Mark 13:24; Rev 8:12) or spiritual (Rom 1:21; 11:10) darkness. Certainly, in the present context it speaks about a spiritual or moral darkness similar to Rom 1:21, "their senseless heart was darkened." The next word, διάνοια, "process of thinking, reasoning process," was discussed at 2:3 where we concluded that its meaning was influenced more by the LXX than Greek philosophy. It is parallel to the OT idea of the heart or the thoughts of the heart and expresses calculations formed by a thinking mind; thus, it is best translated as "thoughts, reasoning processes."[1] The dative may be a dative of sphere or reference denoting the sphere in which this darkness occurs.[2]

There are three ways the participle ὄντες can be related to the two participles surrounding it. (1) It could be joined to the second perfect passive participle ἀπηλλοτριωμένοι, suggesting that the reason for the darkness of the reasoning processes is alienation from God.[3] The verb εἰμί as a participle followed immediately by another participle appears only in the parallel passage of Col 1:21 where ὄντας is connected with ἀπηλλοτριωμένους and in Acts 22:5. However, the main objection to this is the lack of symmetry in the sentence. (2) It could be related to both participles, signifying that because the Gentiles' reasoning ability had been darkened and they had been alienated from the life of God, they walked in the futility of their minds. Nonetheless, it is not normal for the participle to serve two other participles. Furthermore, it leaves dangling the last prepositional phrase in verse 18. (3) Most commentators think it is related only to the first participle whereby the futility of Gentile minds is further explained.[4] The reason that they walked in the futility of their minds was because their reasoning process had been darkened. This construction better balances the parallelism of the two clauses in the sentence, making it the most plausible solution.

Two other observations are worth noting in regard to the participles. First, note the change of gender from the neuter (τὰ ἔθνη) to the masculine (ἐσκοτισμένοι), which most likely indicates the transition from a class to persons.[5] Second, only in this passage and in the parallel passage (Col 1:21) is the perfect periphrastic formed by two participles. This usage was probably employed to emphasize the new state

1. Cf. Alves, *Il cristiano in Cristo*, 92–94.

2. Robertson, *Grammar*, 523.

3. Eadie, 329; Robinson, 189.

4. Theodoret *Eph* 4:18 (*PG* 82:537); Bengel, 4:95; Harless, 401; Alford, 3:121; Ellicott, 97; Meyer, 238; Abbott, 129; Salmond, 339; Westcott, 66; Gnilka, 224 n. 1; Barth, 500. This view is also expressed in NA[27] and UBS[4] by the use of a comma after the participle ὄντες.

5. Abbott, 129; Robertson, *Grammar*, 405, 407, 412*bis*; BDF §134 (2). Winer (*Grammar*, 660) suggests that "ἐσκοτισμένοι does not belong to the subordinate sentence καθὼς καὶ τὰ ἔθνη, but to ὑμᾶς." But his translator W. F. Moulton states (n. 1): "This is surely impossible: the words which follow must have been for the moment overlooked."

of things.[1] Specifically, those Ephesians who were once Gentiles and walked in darkness were now enlightened believers (Eph 1:18). Conversely, the passage deals with unbelieving Gentiles who continue in the darkness of their reasoning processes. The perfect tense of these two participles expresses a completed action with continuing results in that dreadful state.

ἀπηλλοτριωμένοι τῆς ζωῆς τοῦ θεοῦ, "being alienated from the life of God." Their condition defined, their position before God is the next concern. Briefly, their condition was that of futileness of the mind, darkness of the reasoning process, and now alienation from the life of God which is Paul's next topic. The participle from ἀπαλλοτριόω, found three times in the LXX (Ps 69:8 [MT 69:9; LXX 68:9]; Ezek 14:5; 3 Macc 1:3), is used only two other times in the NT (Eph 2:12; Col 1:21), always in a perfect participial form, meaning "excluded" or "alienated."[2]

Again the perfect tense stresses a completed action with continuing results in their present state of alienation from God. The word ζωή, "life," generally does not have the idea of the course of life, but rather the existence of life as opposed to death. In the OT (appearing 294 times in the LXX, 183 times in the canonical books) life is God's gift to human beings.[3] Hence, it is not referring to the "virtuous life," "godly life," or "the life that is approved by God"[4] but "living existence." The distinction between the existence of life and the conduct of life is clearly seen in Gal 5:25. This word is used 135 times in the NT, approximately half the time in Johannine literature, thirty-seven times by Paul and only here in Ephesians. The genitive τῆς ζωῆς is a partitive genitive[5] and the following genitive τοῦ θεοῦ is a genitive of origin.[6] In other words, the Gentiles are separated from the life that comes from God. This does not imply that they once enjoyed that life, it simply means that they have never had it and continue without it. Conversely, it implies that the believer has a life that comes from God. This brings to mind Paul's declaration that they were alienated from the citizenship of Israel (2:12) but now they are reconciled to God and have access to him (2:13–18) and are fellow citizens with the saints and members of God's household (2:19). Yet there is no specific reference in Ephesians of their having the life of God. Although Paul speaks often of eternal life in other letters (Rom 2:7; 5:21; 6:22, 23; Gal 6:8; 1 Tim 1:16; 6:12; Titus 1:2; 3:7), there are only a few references to life from God (Rom 5:17, 18; 8:6, 10; 2 Tim 1:10). In these passages this life is described as "the supernatural life belonging to

1. BDF §352; Burton, *Moods and Tenses* §155; Robertson, *Grammar*, 910, 1117; MHT 3:89; Fanning, *Verbal Aspect*, 417; cf. Porter, *Verbal Aspect*, 475.

2. BAGD 80; BDAG 96.

3. Hill, *Greek Words and Hebrew Meanings*, 163–85, esp. 163–71.

4. As suggested by Theodoret *Eph* 4:18 (*PG* 82:537).

5. Robertson, *Grammar*, 518; MHT 3:235.

6. Winer, *Grammar*, 233.

God and Christ, which the believers will receive in the future, but which they also enjoy here and now."[1] In this present context the believer is exhorted not to walk as the Gentiles who are alienated from God. By inference, then, the believer does have the life of God and must walk according to a different lifestyle.

διὰ τὴν ἄγνοιαν τὴν οὖσαν ἐν αὐτοῖς, "because of the ignorance that is in them." This gives the cause for their alienation. The noun ἄγνοια is used of "ignorance, lack of perception."[2] In the LXX it occurs twenty-eight times and in the canonical books it appears seventeen times translating five Hebrew words. It is used of sin that is committed unwittingly or unknowingly (Lev 5:18; 22:14; Eccl 5:5). In the NT it is used only four times. In Acts 3:17 Peter mentions that the Jews acted in ignorance when they crucified Jesus. In Acts 17:30 Paul relates that God overlooked times of ignorance in reference to sins committed before the time of the cross. Further, Peter tells believers that they are not to be conformed to the passions of their former ignorance (1 Pet 1:14), their preconversion days. The present context speaks of the ignorance concerning God's revelation and will. This, however, is not innocent ignorance. It is parallel to Rom 1:18–23 where Paul outlines the degradation of mankind. He makes it very clear that human beings have rejected the manifest knowledge of God through creation, and thus, refused to glorify or thank God. As a result their reasoning processes became purposeless and their senseless heart became darkened. Their wisdom was foolishness as they exchanged God's incorruptible glory for corruptible idolatry. Such is not innocence but deliberate refusal of God and his will. Twice Paul states that people are without excuse (Rom 1:23; 2:1). Likewise, the ignorance in the present context is not innocent but also a flagrant refusal of the knowledge of God and his will. This ignorance is "in them." It is not an external but an internal cause for their alienation from the life of God. Thus the blame of their ignorance falls on them and not on God or external factors.[3]

διὰ τὴν πώρωσιν τῆς καρδίας αὐτῶν, "due to the hardness of their hearts." This prepositional phrase depends on the immediately preceding prepositional phrase, and thus it is best to omit the comma before it. Alienation from the life of God was due to the ignorance in the Gentiles and this in turn was due to the hardness of their hearts. The word πώρωσις has been disputed. Robinson has argued that πώρωσις, "hardness," and πήρωσις, "blindness," often have been confused by copyists and many of the versions have translated the first word as "blindness."[4] Although "hardness" is the primary sense of the word, he

1. BAGD 340; cf. BDAG 430.

2. Aeschylus *Agamemnon* 1596.

3. Barth, 501; O'Brien, 321–22.

4. J. Armitage Robinson, "πωρωσις and πηρωσις," *JTS* 3 (October 1901): 81–93; reprinted in his commentary, 264–74.

preferred to translate it "blindness." The NEB translated this word in the present context as "their minds have grown hard as stone," a rendering that prompted a lively debate among scholars.[1] The word conveys the idea of callus that serves as mortar (thus petrification) to reunite the surfaces of fractured bones[2] or a pus which comes out of the bone and produces callus.[3] Only the verb form (πωρόω) is found in the LXX and it is found only once. In Job 17:7 it refers to the eyes growing dim. It appears also in the Alexandrian text of Prov 10:20 where it refers to the hardening of silver (rather than purified by fire). In the NT the noun occurs only three times. Mark 3:5 and Rom 11:25 refer to the hardness of the heart. Its use in the present context appears to demand the concept of "hardness." The verb form is used five times, three times in reference to the hardening of hearts (Mark 6:52; 8:17; John 12:40), once to the hardening of the mind (2 Cor 3:14), and once to the hardening of people (Rom 11:7). Of all these passages John 12:40 is the most noteworthy in relation to the present text. It speaks of God as the one who has blinded their eyes and hardened their heart (τετύφλωκεν αὐτῶν τοὺς ὀφθαλμοὺς καὶ ἐπώρωσεν αὐτῶν τὴν καρδίαν). Certainly, in that context one would not translate πωρόω as "blinded" because it would be redundant. Furthermore, it is interesting to note, as Dodd did, that in the NT this word is never "associated, even in metaphor, with the eyes."[4] Thus, in the present verse it is best to translate it "hardened." As mentioned in Eph 1:18 (see also 3:17) the heart is the center of a person, the seat of thought and understanding, will or volition, and, as here, of religious and moral conduct. The singular usage denotes that this heart belongs to each person in the group[5] and thus each person is responsible for this hardness. Thus, the revelation of God and his will is not able to penetrate the individual's heart or understanding. Hence, this is the cause of their being ignorant of the revelation of God and his will.

In reviewing these two verses a series of causes and effects becomes apparent. The scenario could be reconstructed by reversing the direction of the statements. The hardness of their hearts toward God caused their ignorance. Their ignorance concerning God and his will caused them to be alienated from the life of God. Their alienation caused their minds to be darkened, and their darkened minds

1. Fisher of Lambeth, "Blind or Hard of Heart?" *Theology* 69 (January 1966): 25–26; Barnabas Lindars, "Blind or Hard of Heart?" *Theology* 69 (March 1966): 121; Colville of Culross, "Blind or Hard of Heart?" *Theology* 69 (April 1966): 171; C. H. Dodd, "Blind or Hard of Heart?" *Theology* 69 (April 1966): 223–24. The first two of these contributors favored "blindness," the third thinks it could be translated either way, and the last defended "hardness."

2. Hippocrates *De fracturis* 23.14; *De articulus* 15.9.

3. Aristotle *Historia Animalium* 3.19 §521a.21.

4. Dodd, "Blind or Hard of Heart?" 224.

5. MHT 3:23.

caused them to walk in the futility of mind. It must be remembered that this series of causes and effects has a Gentile frame of reference. Its system is diametrically opposed to those who are believers. It is understandable why Paul exhorted the Ephesian believers not to walk as Gentiles do.

b. His Practice (4:19)

The character of unregenerate people has been disclosed and now Paul demonstrates how their lifestyle is a natural outgrowth of their character.

Text: 4:19. οἵτινες ἀπηλγηκότες ἑαυτοὺς παρέδωκαν τῇ ἀσελγείᾳ εἰς ἐργασίαν ἀκαθαρσίας πάσης ἐν πλεονεξίᾳ.

Translation: 4:19. "who, having become callous, have given themselves over to indecency for the practice of every kind of impurity with greediness."

Commentary: 4:19. οἵτινες ἀπηλγηκότες,[1] "who, having become callous." The indefinite relative pronoun οἵτινες has its usual qualitative force indicating certain persons who belong to a certain class: "such a one," "the kind who." Before Paul begins a description of Gentile lifestyle, he enlarges a little more on their characteristics. The word ἀπηλγηκότες is a perfect participle from ἀπαλγέω, which is a rare word that can mean "to be despondent, to despair"[2] or "to cease to feel pain," "become callous, insensitive."[3] It does not appear in the LXX and occurs only here in the NT. In the present context, Paul is not portraying Gentiles as despondent, for there is no indication that they regretted their wicked ways. Rather, it shows that hardness of heart toward God and his will and alienation from the life of God have caused them to become insensitive or calloused to God and his ways. It reflects their moral apathy. The perfect active participle expresses the continued effects of callousness. This participle could be antecedent or

1. The reading ἀπηλγηκότες is found in 𝔓[46] א A B Ψ 075 0150 6 33 81 104 256 263 365 424 436 459 1175 1319 1573 1739 1852 1881 1912 1962 2127 2200 2464 *Byz* [K L] *Lect* syr[h, hgr] Clement Origen Chrysostom Theodotus-Ancyra Greek mss[acc. to Jerome]. The second reading ἀπηλπικότες appears in D P 1241[s] *l* 617 it[ar, b, d, f, g, mon, o] vg syr[p] arm slav Irenaeus[lat] Victorinus-Rome Ambrosiaster Jerome Pelagius Speculum. In the text of 𝔓[49] the critical two letters are damaged and either of the two above readings could be read (Stephen Emmel, "Greek Biblical Papyri in the Beinecke Library," *Zeitschrift für Papyrologie und Epigraphik* 112 [1996]: 294 recto line 7). The third reading ἀφηλπικότες is found only in F G (cf. Martin, "Quelques remarques sur le texte syriaque de l'Épître aux Éphésiens," 102). The last two readings "to despair, to give up in despair, to lose hope" would be natural in thought after v. 18. However, they are primarily represented only in the Western text and thus lack the geographical spread to warrant them. The first reading is preferred externally and internally.

2. Polybius 9.40.4.

3. Thucydides 2.61.4.

coincidental with the following aorist indicative[1] but more likely it is causal, giving the reason for their immoral conduct as next described with three nouns, namely, indecency, impurity, and greediness.

ἑαυτοὺς παρέδωκαν τῇ ἀσελγείᾳ, "have given themselves over to indecency." The reflexive pronoun ἑαυτούς indicates that it was their own initiative which propelled them into immorality. The verb παρέδωκαν means "to hand over, give over." This is not a contradiction of Rom 1:24, 26, 28 where God gives humans over to their immoral conduct because of their refusal to accept his revelation from heaven. Chrysostom tries to reconcile the two passages by saying that God permitted humans to be given over to immorality.[2] However, in Romans the same verb is used as in the present context and it has no suggestion of permission. God is the subject of the verb; he handed them over. A better way to resolve the apparent contradiction is to consider that there are two stages: (1) people exercise their perversion of free will and give themselves over to sin, and (2) God's response is then to give them over to the sin which will continue to enslave them.

The first noun ἀσελγεία has the idea of "licentiousness, undue freedom, freedom with no boundaries,"[3] referring to sensual appetites.[4] It is used of Alcibiades who hit an influential man with his fist just for the fun causing a public outcry.[5] Josephus uses it to describe a Roman soldier who publicly exhibited his genitals in the temple during the Passover, a public insult to the Jews.[6] It is the performance of blatant acts with no consideration of personal standards or social sanctions. It is doing something openly with no shame.[7] This word is found only two times in the LXX where it has reference to political excesses (3 Macc 2:26) and moral debauchery (Wis 14:26). In the NT it appears ten times, four times in Paul, and only here in Ephesians. It is used in connection with sexual lust (Mark 7:22; 2 Cor 12:21; Gal 5:19) and is connected with drunkenness (Rom 13:13; 1 Pet 4:3). Most of the time, however, it is used of the desire to perform unrestrained desires (2 Pet 2:2, 7, 18; Jude 4). It is this last category that best fits the word in the present context. It is the practice of sin without concern as to what God or people think. It can be translated "indecent conduct, indecency."

εἰς ἐργασίαν ἀκαθαρσίας πάσης, "for the practice of every kind of impurity." The preposition εἰς denotes conscious direction or purpose, not accidental. The noun ἐργασία connotes "work, profession."[8] It fur-

1. Porter, *Verbal Aspect*, 399.

2. Chrysostom *Eph* 4:17–19 (*PG* 62:93); cf. also Kohlgraf, *Die Ekklesiologie des Epheserbriefes in der Auslegung durch Johannes Chrysostomus*, 131–32.

3. Plato *Respublica* 4 §424e.

4. Polybius 36.15.4.

5. Plutarch *Alcibiades* 8.1.

6. Josephus *A.J.* 20.5.3 §§108–12.

7. Cf. L&N §88.272; Barclay, *Flesh and Spirit*, 31–33.

8. Plato *Respublica* 2 §371b.

ther suggests the idea of "exercise, practice" of something.[1] In the LXX it occurs forty-five times and in the canonical books it appears thirty-four times for five Hebrew words, half the times it translates מְלָאכָה, meaning "occupation, work, business" (1 Chr 9:13; 26:29; Ps 107:23 [LXX 106:23]).[2] In the NT it appears six times and means "profit, gains" (Acts 16:16, 19), "business, occupation" (Acts 19:24, 25), and "effort" (Luke 12:58). In the present context the concept of "occupation" fits best but with the slightly different nuance of "practice, behavior."[3] It conveys the idea of occupation which becomes practice.

The second descriptive noun ἀκαθαρσία is used of uncleanness, impurity, or foulness of a wound,[4] or it can refer to moral impurity, as in the case when Demosthenes committed perjury to cause injury to another person.[5] In the LXX it occurs sixty-three times and in the canonical books it appears forty-nine times translating five Hebrew words, twenty-seven times for the feminine noun טֻמְאָה referring primarily to cultic impurity (Lev 15:25; 16:16; 22:5), but there is also reference to religious uncleanness (Ezra 6:21; 9:11; Ezek 36:25, 29), or just plain filth (Ezek 24:11; 2 Chr 29:16).[6] It can also refer to sexual uncleanness (Lev 15:25, 26; 18:19; Ezek 36:17). It appears ten times in the NT, nine times in Paul. In one instance it refers to ceremonial impurity (Matt 23:27) and the other occurrences refer to moral impurity.[7] It is used of sexual impurity (Rom 1:24; Gal 5:19) or unspecified impurity (Rom 6:19; 2 Cor 12:21; Eph 5:3; Col 3:5; 1 Thess 2:3; 4:7). In the present context it is used to refer to moral impurity. It "indicates a general defilement of the whole personality, tainting every sphere of life."[8] This is substantiated by the adjective πᾶς which, when used with an anarthous noun, means "every kind of, all sorts of" impurity.[9] There are other kinds of impurity besides sexual impurity.

ἐν πλεονεξίᾳ,[10] "with greediness." The third noun πλεονεξία etymologically comes from πλέον and ἔχω which literally means "I have

1. Plato *Gorgias* 450c.

2. BDB 521–22; J. Milgrom, D. P. Wright, and H.-J. Fabry, "מְלָאכָה *mᵉlāʾkâ*," *TDOT* 8 (1997): 325–31.

3. L&N §41.20.

4. Plato *Timaeus* 72c; Hippocrates *De fracturis* 31.4.

5. Demosthenes *Orationes* 21.119 (553).

6. Cf. BDB 379–80; G. André and H. Ringgren, "טָמֵא *ṭāmēʾ*; טֻמְאָה *ṭumʾâ*," *TDOT* 5 (1986): 330–40.

7. L&N §§79.54; 88.261.

8. Barclay, *Flesh and Spirit*, 31.

9. BAGD 631; BDAG 783.

10. Instead of ἐν πλεονεξίᾳ, the reading καὶ πλεονεξίας is found in D F G (1241^{s}) *pc* it vg^{mss} Clement Victorinus-Rome Ambrosiaster. This would read: "every kind of impurity and greediness." The support for this reading is only in the Western text and thus not sufficent evidence to be considered a valid reading.

more" and can also mean "I want more."[1] It conveys the idea of "covetousness, greediness,"[2] doing things for one's own advantage.[3] In classical times it meant "'an arrogant greediness', the spirit which tries to take advantage of its fellow men."[4] It occurs eight times in the LXX (six times in the canonical books) and translates בֶּצַע, meaning "gain made by violence" (Judg 5:19) or "unjust gain" (Ps 119:36 [LXX 118:36]; Jer 22:17; Ezek 22:27; Hab 2:9).[5] In the NT it appears ten times, six times in Paul's writings, and twice in Ephesians (4:19; 5:3). It is included as one of a number of sins that come from within a person (Mark 7:22; Rom 1:29) and is used of one who is covetous for material things (Luke 12:15; 2 Cor 9:5) or just wants more of everything (Eph 5:3; Col 3:5; 2 Pet 2:14) and of one who takes advantage because of position (1 Thess 2:5; 2 Pet 2:3). In the present context it best conveys the idea of wanting more of whatever one desires irrespective of need.[6] In all the literature it is a word that conveys unfavorable or undesirable characteristics, extreme selfishness, the opposite of moderation.[7] In Col 3:5 it is identified as idolatry. When one covets a particular thing, that becomes the center of his or her life and is worshiped in place of the creator (Rom 1:23, 25). Basically, covetousness is desiring what belongs to your neighbor. The reason Christians are not to be covetous is because they must believe that God supplies their needs and that they have no need for what God has given to someone else.

This prepositional phrase depends on the immediately preceding prepositional phrase (εἰς ἐργασίαν ἀκαθαρσίας πάσης, "for the practice of every kind of impurity"). It shows the manner by which the practice of all sorts of impurity is accomplished, namely, with greediness. The three words of ἀσελγεία (indecency), ἀκαθαρσία (impurity), and πλεονεξία (greediness) are a powerful combination[8] used to describe unregenerate people as those who are totally consumed with themselves. The selfishness in which they are immersed is in direct contrast to Christ who gave himself over for us as a fragrant offering and sacrifice to God (Eph 5:2). It is love of self in contrast to love of others

1. For a study of the word, see Gerhard Delling, "πλεονέκτης, πλεονεκτέω, πλεονεξία," *TDNT* 6 (1968): 266–74; Friedel Selter, "Avarice, Greed, Love of Money [πλεονεξία]," *NIDNTT* 1 (1975): 137–38.

2. Herodotus 7.149; Thucydides 3.82.8; Plato *Respublica* 2.3 §359c.

3. Thucydides 3.84.1; Xenophon *Memorabilia* 1.6.12.

4. Barclay, *New Testament Words*, 233.

5. BDB 130; cf. Diether Kellermann, "בצע *bṣʿ*; בֶּצַע *betsaʿ*," *TDOT* 2 (1977): 205–8.

6. L&N §25.22.

7. Chrysostom *Eph* 4:17–19 (*PG* 62:94); Calvin, 189.

8. To suggest, as Kuhn does, that these three capital sins come from the tradition of the Essene paraenesis is overstating the case (Kuhn, "The Epistle to the Ephesians in the Light of the Qumran Texts," 121). Paul does the same thing in greater detail in Rom 1:18–3:8. These sins are the same as those from the beginning of time, making it unnecessary to borrow from another source.

and of God. It is no wonder that Paul exhorts the Ephesian believers not to walk the way the Gentiles do.

2. Presentation of the New Person (4:20–32)

Deists argue that God created the earth and allowed it self-determination. The God of the Bible reveals that he not only created the earth but also continually sustains it. It is the same for those who have been redeemed. God not only redeems but also demands and enables a new lifestyle. Paul has presented both the nature and practice of the old person, and will now discuss the position and practice of the new person.

a. His Position (4:20–24)

Before Paul exhorts believers about their conduct, he instructs them concerning their new identity. This is divided into three parts: (1) the statement of the instruction, that is, their knowledge of Christ (v. 20–21a); (2) the nature of the instruction, namely, Christ is the truth in Jesus (v. 21b), and (3) the content of the instruction, specifically, putting off the old person and putting on of the new person (vv. 22–24).

(1) The Statement of the Instruction (4:20–21a)

Text: 4:20. ὑμεῖς δὲ οὐχ οὕτως ἐμάθετε τὸν Χριστόν, **4:21a.** εἴ γε αὐτὸν ἠκούσατε καὶ ἐν αὐτῷ ἐδιδάχθητε

Translation: 4:20. "But you have not so learned Christ, **4:21a.** inasmuch as you heard about him and were taught in him"

Commentary: 4:20. ὑμεῖς δὲ οὐχ οὕτως ἐμάθετε τὸν Χριστόν, "But you have not so learned Christ." The emphatic contrast with the previous verses is noted by: (1) the adversative δέ; (2) the change from τὰ ἔθνη to ὑμεῖς, which is emphatically placed; and (3) the adverbial conjunction οὕτως, which applies what had been stated before (cf. 5:24, 28, 33), namely, that the conduct of Gentiles is not what believers learned regarding Christ. The οὐχ οὕτως is a litotes, expressing an affirmative by the negative of the contrary. The use of ἐμάθετε with the accusative of a person is unique. On the other hand, the accusative of a person is used in the NT in regard to preaching Christ (1 Cor 1:23; 2 Cor 1:19; Gal 1:16; Phil 1:15), to knowing him (Phil 3:10), and to receiving Christ Jesus the Lord (Col 2:6).[1] In the context there is also reference to the believer having "heard him" (Eph 4:21). Nevertheless, here it denotes learning Christ. In the NT the verb μανθάνω is used to learn about things (Matt 9:13; Acts 23:27; 1 Cor 14:35; Phil 4:11; Rev 14:3), learn doctrine (Rom 16:17), learn a lesson (Matt

1. Salmond, 340–41.

24:32 = Mark 13:28; 1 Tim 2:11; Heb 5:8), learn by example (1 Cor 4:6), and learn from persons such as Christ (Matt 11:29), God (John 6:45), and people (Gal 3:2; Phil 4:9; Col 1:7), but nothing about "learning a person" (the same principle is also true in English). Yet in the present context it is stated that the believer is to learn Christ. The implication is that factual learning is insufficient, the goal is to know Christ personally. The inceptive aorist points to the time of conversion. Gentiles and Jews who had previously opposed God, heard Christ preached and received him. This then is the beginning point of their "learning Christ." Believers continually "learn" Christ who is alive and seated at the right hand of God in the heavenlies (1:20; 2:6). The new person's ordered life is not concerned with learning the law but rather hearing about and thus "learning" the living Christ and ordering his or her life to please him.[1] Paul expands on this theme in the next verses.

4:21a. εἴ γε αὐτὸν ἠκούσατε, "inasmuch as you heard about him." This is very much like the construction in 3:2. The word εἰ is a conditional conjunction that introduces the reader to the first part of the protasis of a first class condition that continues until the end of verse 24. The apodosis of this conditional sentence is verse 20. The following enclitic particle γέ is often added, as is the case here, to the conjunction (εἰ) either to give emphasis to it ("if indeed") or to add a concessive nuance ("inasmuch as").[2] In this case, although both connotations seem to be included, the emphasis is on the latter. On the one hand, it heightens the protasis on the conditional sentence, on the other hand, it concedes that they had heard about Jesus and were taught in him. In translations the intensity is shown by rendering it "if so be" (RV, ASV) or "if indeed" (NASB), and the concessive idea is expressed when rendering it "assuming" (RSV), "certainly" (TEV), or "surely" (NIV, NRSV). Thrall suggests that the sense is: "At any rate if you have heard . . . as I know you have."[3] This particle is important, for if it were excluded it would imply that the Ephesians had not heard of Paul's ministry even though he had been with them two or three years. It would imply that the writer was a stranger to the Ephesians which, in turn, would cause legitimate questions regarding the Pauline authorship of this letter.[4] However, the enclitic particle gives assurance that the Ephesians had heard about Christ and were taught in him; thus, Paul can exhort them not to live as Gentiles because they "learned" Christ as expressed in the apodosis (v. 20).

1. Karl Heinrich Rengstorf, "μανθάνω κτλ.," *TDNT* 4 (1967): 410; *contra* Wegenast, *Das Verständnis der Tradition bei Paulus und in den Deuteropaulinen*, 131–32.

2. BAGD 152; BDAG 190; Robertson, *Grammar*, 1148*bis*; cf. BDF §439 (2); MHT 3:331.

3. Thrall, *Greek Particles in the New Testament*, 88; cf. also Baumert, *Täglich Sterben und Auferstehen*, 381–82.

4. As do Abbott, 135; Mitton, 162–63.

Since he had not been present in Ephesus for five or six years, Paul is, by this particle, gently reminding them of what they had heard when he was there. He then proceeds to spell out explicitly their new position in Christ in order to crystalize in their minds what they had been taught by him. Besides here the combination of εἴ γε is used only in 3:2; 2 Cor 5:3; Gal 3:4; Col 1:23. In Eph 3:2 it presupposes that they did hear of the mystery and Paul's ministry; in 2 Cor 5:3 and in Gal 3:4 it assumes that their sufferings were not vain;[1] and in Col 1:23 it denotes confidence that they will continue in the faith.[2] Here it could be translated "if as I assume it to be the case,"[3] but it is smoother to translate it "inasmuch as."

Their "hearing about him" was through the preaching of the gospel by Paul and by other preachers and teachers. Normally ἀκούω "to hear" is found with a genitive to denote persons whom we hear or with an accusative, as here, to denote persons about whom (or things about which) we hear.[4] The Ephesians did not hear Christ in person but they heard about him in the gospel message. This hearing of Christ is how they "learned" Christ. Again, the aorist points to the time of conversion as it does in verse 20.

καὶ ἐν αὐτῷ ἐδιδάχθητε, "and were taught in him." Not only had they heard about Christ but they were also taught in him. This does not express means, "taught by him," as suggested in the AV because the Ephesians never saw Christ. Rather, it is the sphere or locale of the teaching, "in connection with him" or "in communion with him."[5] Hence, Christ is the object and the sphere of a believer's learning. Meyer notes the progression from their first reception of gospel (αὐτὸν ἠκούσατε) followed by the further instruction after they believed (ἐν αὐτῷ ἐδιδάχθητε). Both of these elements were contained in the previous ἐμάθετε τὸν Χριστόν.[6] To "learn" Christ occurs not only at conversion but through daily growth by increased knowledge of him (most likely a constative aorist) through gifted people ministering in their midst. This is in contrast to many religions whereby followers may continue to study about their chosen religion but never experience an intimate knowledge of their leader and/or founder of their religion. Believers in Christ not only "learn" Christ at the time they heard the gospel but they continue to "learn" him as they study God's Word and as they are ministered to by gifted people in the body.

1. Lightfoot, *Galatians*, 135–36; Betz, *Galatians*, 135 n. 69; Bruce, *The Epistle of Paul to the Galatians*, 150.

2. O'Brien, *Colossians, Philemon*, 69.

3. Salmond, 341; Barth, 504; cf. Eadie, 335; Meyer, 243.

4. Robertson, *Grammar*, 507; Winer, *Grammar*, 249 n. 1; BDF §173.

5. Robertson, *Grammar*, 588; Winer, *Grammar*, 488.

6. Meyer, 243.

(2) The Nature of the Instruction (4:21b)

Paul's statement of instruction is concluded (vv. 20–21a), and now the nature of that instruction will be explained (v. 21b).

Text: 4:21b. καθώς ἐστιν ἀλήθεια ἐν τῷ Ἰησοῦ,

Translation: 4:21b. "just as the truth is in Jesus,"

Commentary: 4:21b. καθώς ἐστιν ἀλήθεια[1] ἐν τῷ Ἰησοῦ, "just as the truth is in Jesus." The adverbial conjunction καθώς is comparative. To what it relates will be discussed below. The noun ἀλήθεια, "truth," was discussed at 1:13 and 4:15 where it was concluded that it contrasts falsehood with reality.

Two things need to be discussed: What is the meaning of "truth" and how does this clause relate syntactically? Some see it as the moral truth (holiness) which is in Jesus, thus compelling believers to lay aside the old person.[2] The problem with this is that it gives "truth" a different nuance and causes the clause to be connected with that which follows rather than the preceding context. Meyer sees the following infinitive (ἀποθέσθαι ὑμᾶς) as the subject of the sentence: "truth in Jesus is that you put off the old person."[3] Again, this conveys a special nuance to truth and, furthermore, it seems much more natural for the infinitive to depend on ἐδιδάχθητε. Similarly, Abbott suggests that ἀλήθεια in verse 24 and John 3:21 means "true teaching" and hence would construe it, "as it is true teaching in Jesus that you put off."[4] This again appeals to a special meaning of truth and it is more likely that the infinitive depends on ἐδιδάχθητε. The marginal reading in the WH text is the dative ἀληθείᾳ and it could be rendered "as he (Christ) is in truth in Jesus" or "he (Christ) truly is in Jesus." Thus the believers not only believe in Christ but also acknowledge him in Jesus.[5] However, this makes a dichotomy between Christ and Jesus and this was not a problem in Paul's day. It is unlikely that Paul is combating either the Gnostic tendency to divorce the saving Christ from the historical Jesus who was crucified[6] or the dichotomy of the Bultmannians between the Christ of faith and the Jesus of history.[7] Both of these debates occurred long after Paul's time.[8] The assump-

1. The dative form of this word (ἀληθείᾳ) is found in the margin of the WH text. This will be discussed in the text.

2. Harless, 413–14; Olshausen, 235–36.

3. Meyer, 244; cf. C. Anderson Scott, "Ephesians iv.21: 'As the Truth is in Jesus,'" *Exp* 8th ser., vol. 3 (February 1912): 178–85; Robinson, *The Body* 42, 43.

4. Abbott, 135.

5. See the correspondence between Westcott and Hort in Westcott, 70–71.

6. As suggested by Schlier, 217.

7. As suggested by James M. Robinson, *A New Quest of the Historical Jesus*, SBT, ed. H. H. Rowley, C F. D. Moule, Floyd V. Filson, and G. Ernest Wright, vol. 25 (London: SCM, 1959), 76–80; cf. also Abbott, 135–36; *contra* Carsten Peter Thiede, "Der Brief an die Epheser. 39. Teil: Kapitel 4,14–24," *Fundamentum* 20, no. 4 (1999): 29.

8. See discussion in Barth, 533–36.

tion that the Christ of faith and the Jesus of history are one and the same person is implicit in Paul's writings. On the other hand, the use of the name Jesus must not minimized as only a stylistic variation as Lincoln suggests,[1] for if that were the case, Best counters, "a pronoun would have sufficed."[2] Rather, Christ is truth embodied in Jesus.

Truth here is to be understood as reality in contrast to that which is false or deceptive as seen in the next verse (ἀπάτη), a description Paul used to characterize the unregenerate Gentiles in verses 17–18. Here "truth" is anarthrous, which is common among abstract nouns but this does not make it indefinite.[3] Some think that in this particular context "truth" is the predicate[4] and "Christ" is the subject. It cannot be rendered "as the truth is in Jesus" "because this unparalleled construction would imply that the truth that is in Jesus is only partial and incomplete, and would thus run counter to the whole of Pauline theology."[5] Rather, it is better rendered "but you have not so learned Christ, inasmuch as you heard about him and were taught in him as [he/there] is truth in Jesus."[6] Jesus is the embodiment of truth. It may well be that "truth" is the subject of the clause[7] and can be translated "as truth is in Jesus," "as truth exists in Jesus," or "as there is truth in Jesus." "Truth is found in the person of Jesus, who is the Christ: He is Himself the truth (John xiv 6): hence we can be said to 'learn Him'."[8] This truth is not intangible and abstract.[9] The message they heard was about Christ and they were taught in him. The mention of Jesus anchors the discussion in history.[10] Truth existing in Jesus is not due to the fact that he is the express image of the Father (Col 1:15) but because "his life was the one perfect life which fully demonstrated the indispensible practical aspects of total truth."[11] Beyond his life on earth, the ultimate reality in Jesus is his death and resurrection.[12] Christ, the Messiah promised in the OT, is the one who lived on earth and was called Jesus. He died to pay for sins which brought forgiveness (Eph 1:7; 2:13–18), and he rose to guarantee the truth of his pre-

1. Lincoln, 281.
2. Best, 429.
3. Wallace, *Greek Grammar*, 249–50; Lincoln, 281.
4. Robertson, *Grammar*, 545.
5. Murphy-O'Connor, "Who Wrote Ephesians?" 1205.
6. I. de la Potterie, "Jésus et la vérité d'après Eph 4,21," in *Studiorum Paulinorum Congressus Internationalis Catholicus 1961*, vol. 2, AnBib, vol. 18 (Rome: E Pontificio Instituto Biblico, 1963), 45–48; cf. Alford, 3:123; Salmond, 342; Westcott, 67.
7. Lincoln, 281; my colleague Daniel B. Wallace also thinks that "truth" may be a subject (personal interaction); cf. Moule, *Idiom Book*, 112.
8. Robinson, 190.
9. F. J. Briggs, "Ephesians iv.20, 21," *ExpTim* 39 (August 1928): 526.
10. Ernest Best, "Ephesians: Two Types of Existence," *Int* 47 (January 1993): 41.
11. Roels, *God's Mission*, 208–9; Pierre Berthoud, "Vérité et foi," *La revue réformée* 48 (Mars 1997): 50–51.
12. La Potterie, "Jésus et la vérité d'après Eph 4,21," 2:56–57.

dictions and the validity of redemption. It is this message built around the person of Christ Jesus which they learned when they heard about him and were taught in him.

In conclusion, this clause could depend on the two immediately preceding verbs (ἠκούσατε and ἐδιδάχθητε) but most likely depends on the last verb as a crescendo of verses 20–21. They "learned" Christ who was introduced to them when they heard about him and were taught in him, as he is truth embodied in Jesus. Although the adverbial conjunction καθώς could be causal as in 1:4 ("you were taught in him because the truth is in Jesus"), it is best viewed as a comparative expressing the nature of the instruction ("you were taught in him just as he is the truth embodied in Jesus").

(3) The Content of the Instruction (4:22–24)

Having discussed the statement (vv. 20–21a) and the nature (v. 21b) of the instruction, Paul now discloses the content of the instruction (vv. 22–24).

In order to understand this section, two things first need to be clarified regarding these verses: (1) their context, and (2) their structure. Regarding the context, Paul has been preparing believers to walk a holy life. Up to this point he has given the negative, namely, that they are not to walk as the Gentiles (vv. 17–19). He has shown how they had given themselves over to greed, living with all sorts of impurity and hardness of heart which caused their ignorance of God and his will. Consequently, they were alienated from the life of God and their minds through a darkened reasoning process were futile because they could not receive the revelation of God. This is a bleak picture of the human race. The context following these verses is one of exhortations to believers to live a lifestyle diametrically opposed to selfish purposes and to please the Spirit of God by whom they were sealed until the day of their own redemption from the presence of sin (vv. 25–32). Sandwiched in between these two larger contexts is the transition from a very selfish life with no place for God to an honest and honorable life, which is to please God. This transition is given in verses 20–24. In verses 20–21 Paul states that believers had "learned" Christ. But what does that mean? In verses 22–24 Paul gives the content or substance of the instruction they had received.[1]

1. Rey ("L'homme nouveau d'après S. Paul," 173–84) thinks Paul did not write these verses but a redactor composed them from Col 3:9–10. Although some expressions in these verses are difficult, that does not mean Paul was not the author. Paul expressed himself differently to the Ephesians than he did to the Colossians. Cf. Pierre Benoit, "Rapports littéraires entre les épîtres aux Colessiens et aux Éphésiens," in *Neutestamentliche Aufsätze. Festschrift für Prof. Josef Schmid zum 70. Geburtstag*, ed. J. Blinzler, O. Kuss, and F. Mußner (Regensburg: Friedrich Pustet, 1963), 19–22 (reprinted in Benoit, *Exégèsis et Theologie*, vol. 3, 331–34); Murphy-O'Connor, "Truth: Paul and Qumran," 207–8.

As to the structure of these verses, it revolves around three infinitives. The first (ἀποθέσθαι) and third (ἐνδύσασθαι) are aorist middle infinitives, whereas the second (ἀνανεοῦσθαι) is a present middle infinitive. The significance of the variation will be addressed below. First, however, it is necessary to understand the role of these three infinitives. Most agree that they relate back to ἐδιδάχθητε, "you were taught," and serve as the objects of the verb.[1] It is difficult to determine their function in this context. Some commentators suggest that these infinitives of indirect discourse function as imperatives in direct discourse[2] (the infinitive is not to be taken as an imperative, for there are only two undisputed examples of an infinitive functioning as an imperative in the NT [Rom 12:15; Phil 3:16] and both have only the infinitive and not the infinitive plus an accusative ὑμᾶς, as is the case here).[3] Hence, the translation would be, "you were taught that you (should) put off the old person." The reasons for this position are fourfold. First, it is not uncommon to have infinitives of indirect discourse refer back to an imperative of direct discourse (e.g., Rom 12:1; 1 Cor 5:9, 11; 2 Thess 3:5–6, 10, 14). Second, it makes good sense of the tenses of the infinitives: the first and third are aorists well-suited to the notion of urgent actions,[4] that is, put off the old person and put on the new person, whereas the second infinitive is in the present tense exhorting believers to continually renew their minds by the spirit.[5] However, it would seem that a better order is to have the actions of "putting off" and "putting on" first, followed by the continual renewal of the mind by the spirit as in Rom 12:2 (though there is no mention of the spirit in that

1. Murray thinks that they are infinitives of result and relate back to ἐμάθετε (v. 20) and translates them "but you have learned Christ so as to put off the old man and to put on the new man." See John Murray, *Principles of Conduct: Aspects of Biblical Ethics* (Grand Rapids: Eerdmans; London: Tyndale, 1957), 214–19. It would seem that if they were infinitives of result, Paul would have introduced them with ὥστε, "so that" (see Lincoln, 284; cf. also Moule, *Idiom Book*, 139).

2. Calvin, 189–90; Hodge, 259–60; Alford, 3:123; Scott, 218–19; Schlier, 218–20; Gaugler, 188–89; Hendriksen, 213–14; Gnilka, 229–33; Ernst, 364–65; Mitton, 164–66; Barth, 543–45; Schnackenburg, 199–200; Bruce, 357–58; Lindemann, 85–86; Lincoln, 283–84; Best, 430–31; MacDonald, 304; Muddiman, 217; Larsson, *Christus als Vorbild*, 226; Robert A. Wild, "'Be Imitators of God': Discipleship in the Letter to the Ephesians," in *Discipleship in the New Testament*, ed. with an Introduction by Fernando F. Segovia (Philadelphia: Fortress, 1985), 133–34; Bock, "'The New Man' as Community in Colossians and Ephesians," in *Integrity of Heart, Skillfulness of Hands: Biblical and Leadership Studies in Honor of Donald K. Campbell*, 161–64.

3. Burton, *Moods and Tenses* §§364–65; Moule, *Idiom Book*, 126; BDF §389; MHT 3:78; Wallace, *Greek Grammar*, 605; Moule, 225–26. This is recognized by Lincoln, 283. My colleague Daniel B. Wallace has been helpful not only by his published works but also personal interaction regarding this problem.

4. Fanning, *Verbal Aspect*, 334, 339–40.

5. Fanning states that these aorist commands should be expressed by the present tense but the aorist commands are used for two reasons: theological and lexical (ibid., 358–62).

context). Third, it fits the context well in that they are first taught in principle to "put off" and "put on" (vv. 22, 24) and then they are given specific applications of putting off and putting on (vv. 25–32).[1] Fourth, since this is the paraenetic section of the epistle, it would seem to be most natural to see these infinitives function as imperatives.

Other exegetes think these infinitives of indirect discourse function as indicatives in direct discourse or as complementary infinitives to ἐδιδάχθητε.[2] The translation would be, "you were taught that you have put off the old person. . . ." The reasons for this view are sevenfold. First, it is common in the NT to have infinitives of indirect discourse after verbs of communication or perception.[3] The problem with this view, according to Burton, is that no aorist infinitive of indirect discourse represents the aorist indicative of the direct form.[4] Recent research of 150 instances of aorist infinitives of indirect discourse confirms Burton's observation that they do not go back to an indicative, but rather to an imperative. However, Burton did not analyze the controlling verb and the research indicates that in every one of the 150 instances, the controlling verb *implies* an imperative or exhortation.[5] For example, "I exhort you to present yourselves" (Rom 12:1). It is necessary, therefore, to look at the controlling verb in the present context, namely, διδάσκω, "to teach." In addition to the present passage, Paul uses διδάσκω six times in the indicative. Although it can focus on exhortation as in 1 Cor 11:14, "Does not nature itself teach you that it

1. Fanning thinks that "the 'old man' and the 'new man' are metonymies for the *deeds* of the old life and new life" (ibid., 363).

2. Eadie, 338; Ellicott, 101; Moule, 118–19; Meyer, 246–48; Abbott, 136–38; Salmond, 342; Robinson, 190; Rienecker, 161–63; Caird, 80–81; John R. W. Stott, *The Message of Ephesians. God's New Society*, The Bible Speaks Today, ed. J. A. Motyer and John R. W. Stott (Downers Grove, Ill.: InterVarsity; Leicester: Inter-Varsity, 1979), 180; Bruce, 358 n. 127; Patzia, 226–27; O'Brien, 326–27; Robertson, *Grammar*, 1089; Moule, *Idiom Book*, 127, 139; Winer, *Grammar*, 404; Jervell, *Imago Dei*, 236–40; Roels, *God's Mission*, 210 n. 115; Feuillet, *Le Christ sagesse de Dieu*, 265; cf. Grant R. Osborne, "Mind Control or Spirit-Controlled Minds?" in *Renewing Your Mind in a Secular World*, ed. John Woodbridge (Chicago: Moody Press, 1985), 60–63; Michael Parsons, "The New Creation," *ExpTim* 99 (October 1987): 3–4; Wedderburn, *Baptism and Resurrection*, 338–39.

3. Wallace, *Greek Grammar*, 603–4.

4. Burton, *Moods and Tenses* §114.

5. Wallace, *Greek Grammar*, 605. In personal correspondence with me, Wallace writes, "Although Burton's comment is sometimes taken as a rule of Greek grammar, it should in any event be considered only descriptive, not prescriptive. That is, it is not a *necessary* postulate that aorist infinitives of indirect discourse refer back to an aorist imperative. Even if the force of the controlling verb is ambiguous, the context may well point to an indicative for the aorist infinitive." Wallace cites Gildersleeve's example from Plato *Theaetetus* 191a, οὐ φήσω ἡμᾶς ὀρθῶς ὁμολογῆσαι ἡνίκα ὡμολογήσαμεν, *I will not say that we were right to acknowledge (it) when we acknowledged it*. See Basil Lanneau Gildersleeve and Charles William Emil Miller, *Syntax of Classical Greek from Homer to Demosthenes*, pt. 1 (New York: American Book, 1900), 137 §327. Wallace continues, "The trailing aorist indicative in this context [in Plato] makes it perfectly clear that the

is dishonoring for a man to wear long hair" (cf. also Rom 2:21; 1 Cor 4:17), the other three times Paul refers to the impartation of tradition. Interestingly, all three uses are aorist indicative passives as is the case in the present context. The first passage is Gal 1:12 where Paul states that he did not receive nor was he taught the gospel. The second passage is where the Thessalonians were told to stand firm and hold fast to the traditions which they were taught by Paul either by word of mouth or by letter (2 Thess 2:15). The third passage is more difficult to decipher. In Col 2:7 Paul uses three participles where he speaks of being rooted and built up in Christ and established in the faith just as they were taught. The teaching could refer back to the three participles or it could refer to the "faith" (most likely objective faith though this is debated) immediately preceding. Regardless, what was "taught" refers to that which was imparted. This same concept is also seen in the OT (e.g., Deut 31:22; 32:44; Jer 32:33 [LXX 39:33]). Hence, διδάσκω is used to refer to the impartation of tradition. In the present passage, then, "you were taught that you have put off the old person."

Second, this view suits the context well. Paul had exhorted them not to walk as the Gentiles (vv. 17–19), for they were taught in him (vv. 20–21), and in the present context he proceeds to give the content of what they were taught (vv. 22–24). Immediately following this (v. 25) he uses the inferential conjunction διό to make application to the content just stated. Furthermore, in verse 25 Paul picks up the metaphor of ἀποθέμενοι, "putting off," from verse 22 and assumes it to be true because the old person has been put off. In other words, he assumes that the practice of falsehood has been put off because the believer has already put off the old person at conversion. He follows this with the present imperative, for each is to speak the truth with his or her neighbor. In fact, in this chapter there are no imperatives before verse 25 but there are eleven imperatives in verses 25–32.[1] If verses 22–24 are imperatival, then verses 25–32 would seem to be redundant. Moreover, every other time the inferential conjunction διό is used in Ephesians (2:11; 3:13; 4:8; 5:14), it is making a point based on what they were taught and not on an exhortation. Third, it seems unlikely that a believer would be characterized as one who is corrupted according to desires resulting from deceit (v. 22a), which is the characterization of

infinitive refers back to an indicative. This usage is not shut up to classical Greek either." Wallace suggests the following four passages. Ecclesiastes 5:1 [LXX 4:17], οὔκ εἰσιν εἰδότες τοῦ ποιῆσαι κακόν, "for they did not know *that they have done* evil"; Dan 2:45, ἑώρακας ἐξ ὄρους τμηθῆναι λίθον, "you saw *that* a stone *was cut* out of a mountain"; Neh 13:27, ὑμῶν μὴ ἀκουσόμεθα ποιῆσαι τὴν πᾶσαν πονηρίαν ταύτην, "Do not hear about you *that you have done* all this evil?"; and Ps 63:2 [LXX 62:3], οὕτως ἐν τῷ ἁγίῳ ὤφθην σοι τοῦ ἰδεῖν τὴν δύναμίν σου καὶ τὴν δόξαν σου, "So in the sanctuary *I looked to see* your power and your glory."

1. Roark, "Interpreting Ephesians 4–6: 'God's People in a Walk Worthy of His Calling,'" 36.

Gentiles in the earlier context (vv. 17–19), and is then commanded to put off such behavior (v. 22b).[1] Fourth, the parallel passage in Col 3:9–10 supports this view. There the aorist passive participles indicate that the putting off and the putting on has already been accomplished. These participles are used in conjunction with imperatives (Col 3:8, 12), namely, they are commanded to put off sins like anger and wrath because they have already put off the old person. In addition, since they have already put on the new person, they are commanded to put on godly characteristics like compassion and kindness. Fifth, this view agrees with other passages in Paul where he speaks of the same concept, though sometimes he uses other metaphors. In Gal 3:27 he uses the metaphor to refer to those who were baptized as those who have put on Christ. Romans 6 depicts the believers as those who died to sin, were buried with Christ, and were crucified with him (vv. 2, 4, 6). Believers are then asked to consider this true in their own lives (v. 11). In 2 Cor 5:17 the believer in Christ is depicted as a new creature, that is, old things have passed away and new things have come into existence. Sixth, the "old person" found in Rom 6:6 and Col 3:9 refers to the unregenerate person. In Col 3:9 it states, as mentioned above, that the old person has been laid aside. Although some may dispute this interpretation for Col 3:9, no one can dispute Rom 6:6 where it states that the old person was co-crucified with Christ. The death of the old person, characterized by Adam, came to an end at the time of conversion. In Rom 6:6 the use of the indicative rules out the imperative. On balance, the clear passage should instruct the more obscure one. It seems that the old person in the present context must refer to what we were before our conversion rather than what we presently are which needs to be laid aside. Seventh, although this is in the paraenetic section of the epistle, not all of it is injunctive in nature. Indeed, it is a pattern of Paul to start with the indicatives of faith and then press on to the exhortation. For example, 4:1–6 contains the exhortation to unity based on the unity in the Godhead. In 5:1–6 believers are to walk in love based on Christ's love for us. In 6:10–20 we are to use the armor that has been given to us. Hence, exhortations are based on the indicatives of faith. Indeed, if the indicatives of faith are not in 4:22–24, then this is a noteworthy exception, since it would be the longest text in Ephesians in which Paul does not base his injunctions on the indicatives of the faith.[2]

In conclusion, the second view is to be preferred because it makes better sense of the passage grammatically and contextually. The particulars of the passage are examined next.

1. Murray, *Principles of Conduct*, 216.
2. Wallace suggested this observation when discussing this passage with me.

(a) Put off the Old Person (4:22)

Text: 4:22. ἀποθέσθαι ὑμᾶς κατὰ τὴν προτέραν ἀναστροφὴν τὸν παλαιὸν ἄνθρωπον τὸν φθειρόμενον κατὰ τὰς ἐπιθυμίας τῆς ἀπάτης,

Translation: 4:22. "that you have laid aside the old person according to the former lifestyle who is being corrupted in accordance with the desires coming from deceit,"

Commentary: 4:22. ἀποθέσθαι[1] ὑμᾶς, "that you have laid aside." The verb ἀποτίθημι means "to put away, to store,"[2] or in the middle voice it can be rendered "to put away from, to lay aside"[3] or "to put off" a garment.[4] It appears sixteen times in the LXX (eleven times in the canonical books), eight times for the Hiphil of נוּחַ, meaning "to put or place" in custody (Lev 24:12; Num 15:34), "to lay or set down" stones (Josh 4:8) or garments after one takes them off (Lev 16:23).[5] It is also used of taking off clothes (2 Macc 8:35).[6] In the NT it appears nine times (always in the middle voice), four times in Paul (Rom 13:12; Eph 4:22, 25; Col 3:8). It is rendered "to put away" in prison (Matt 14:3), "to lay aside, to get rid of" things that are detrimental (Rom 13:12; Col 3:8; Heb 12:1; Jas 1:21; 1 Pet 2:1), and "to take off" clothes (Acts 7:58). In the present context it has the idea of putting off and laying aside clothes with the contrast in verse 24 of putting on the new person.[7] The aorist middle infinitive has the idea of an inceptive act that may have reference to conversion. Also, the lexical verbs of putting off and putting on of clothing emphasizes accomplished events rather than the process in activities.[8] The middle voice emphasizes that the subject receives the benefits of his or her action. It is not a reflexive idea, for the person could not do it by his or her own strength. Hence, believers were taught that they have put off or have laid aside the old person at conversion.

1. 𝔓[49] may read the aorist imperative middle (ἀπόθεσθε) rather than the aorist infinitive middle (ἀποθέσθαι) that is found in virtually all the manuscripts, see Emmel, "Greek Biblical Papyri in the Beinecke Library," 293 and 294 recto line 11; S. R. Pickering, "Readings in a Papyrus Text of Ephesians at Yale University," *New Testament Textual Research Update* 4 (1996): 113–14.

2. Homer *Ilias* 16.254.

3. Ibid., 3.89.

4. Herodotus 4.78.

5. BDB 628; H. D. Preuss, "נוּחַ *nûaḥ*; מְנוּחָה *mᵉnûḥâ*," *TDOT* 9 (1998): 282–83.

6. Josephus *A.J.* 8.11.1 §266.

7. For the origin of the ideas of putting on and putting off, see P. W. van der Horst, "Observations on a Pauline Expression," *NTS* 19 (January 1973): 181–87. Horst (186) states: "We may conclude at any rate that in the third century B.C. the expression τὸν ἄνθρωπον ἐκδῦναι was used in philosophical language to denote the transition from, let us say, the unenlightened state to the enlightened state."

8. Fanning, *Verbal Aspect*, 362.

The pronoun ὑμᾶς is given for the sake of clarity.[1] If it were not there the reader might think the infinitive depends on the immediately preceding comparative clause, which might be read "just as there is truth in Jesus, put off the old person." The pronoun then makes it clear that one must go back to the subject of verse 21a: "you were taught in him that you have laid aside the old person."

κατὰ τὴν προτέραν ἀναστροφὴν τὸν παλαιὸν ἄνθρωπον, "the old person according to the former lifestyle." It is necessary to discuss the prepositional phrase and then see how it relates to the infinitival clause. The noun ἀναστροφή has a wide range of meaning like the verb of the same origin which was discussed at 2:3. Like the verb, the earliest literal meaning was "to turn upside down, turn around, overthrow,"[2] but it also had the meaning of "dwelling in a place" or "abode"[3] and the idea of "behavior, conduct."[4] In the LXX it appears only twice (Tob 4:14; 2 Macc 6:23) and is defined as "behavior, conduct." In the NT it appears thirteen times, three times in Paul (Gal 1:13; Eph 4:22; 1 Tim 4:12) and always has this latter sense. So in the present context Paul is talking about the manner of life or one's conduct or behavior. By NT times the word προτέραν which literally means "the first of two," had surrendered this meaning to πρῶτος and meant only "earlier."[5] In the NT it is used eleven times (four times by Paul: 2 Cor 1:15; Gal 4:13; Eph 4:22; 1 Tim 1:13) and is always used as an adverb, except in the present context where it is used as an adjective meaning "earlier, former."[6] The preposition κατά with the accusative normally denotes standard and thus would be rendered "according to, in accordance with."

How then does this prepositional phrase fit with the rest of this infinitival clause? It immediately precedes the object of the infinitive τὸν παλαιὸν ἄνθρωπον, "the old person," which is further defined by the following participle and another prepositional phrase (τὸν φθειρόμενον κατὰ τὰς ἐπιθυμίας τῆς ἀπάτης). It is thought by some that the first prepositional phrase fits better grammatically with the infinitive than with the "old person."[7] However, this theory demands a unique translation of the preposition "with reference to." A better alternative is to view this prepositional phrase as further defining "old person." Paul had to put this prepositional phrase before the object "old person" because immediately following the object is the participle which is further defined by the second prepositional phrase beginning with κατά. Where else would he have put

1. Robertson, *Grammar*, 1038, 1089; Winer, *Grammar*, 405; BDF §406 (2); MHT 3:148.
2. Euripides *Andromoche* 1007.
3. Aeschylus *Eumenides* 23.
4. Polybius 4.82.1.
5. BDF §62.
6. Robertson, *Grammar*, 280*bis*, 283, 662; BDF §62; BAGD 721–22; BDAG 888.
7. Eadie, 339; Ellicott, 101; Meyer, 247; Salmond, 342.

it? If he had placed it immediately after "old person" followed by the participle and the second prepositional phrase (τὸν παλαιὸν ἄνθρωπον κατὰ τὴν προτέραν ἀναστροφὴν τὸν φθειρόμενον κατὰ τὰς ἐπιθυμίας τῆς ἀπάτης), the participle would be too far removed from "old person," the words it was describing. On the other hand, if he had placed it after the participle (τὸν παλαιὸν ἄνθρωπον τὸν φθειρόμενον κατὰ τὴν προτέραν ἀναστροφὴν κατὰ τὰς ἐπιθυμίας τῆς ἀπάτης), it would then further describe the participle and this does not fit grammatically and contexually. It would mean that two prepositional phrases further describe the participle. It is more likely that Paul is using the first prepositional phrase to further define "old person" and the second prepositional phrase to further describe the participle "being corrupted." Taking all this into consideration, therefore, the preposition κατά can be translated normally "according to, accordance with." Also, Zerwick thinks that the prepositional phrase could be like a simple genitive, translated "the old person of former ways."[1] Simply stated, Paul shows that the conduct of the old person is an integral part of the person. Conversely, the lifestyle and the position of the new person should be integrally bound together.

The object of the infinitive is τὸν παλαιὸν ἄνθρωπον, "the old person," who stands in contrast to the τὸν καινὸν ἄνθρωπον, "the new person" in verse 24. The old person, found in Rom 6:6 and Col 3:9, is the preconversion unregenerate person. Paul then is teaching that, having been taught in him, believers should know that the old person according to the former lifestyle was laid aside at the time of their faith in the one who taught them, namely, Christ.

τὸν φθειρόμενον κατὰ τὰς ἐπιθυμίας[2] τῆς ἀπάτης, "who is being corrupted in accordance with the desires coming from deceit." This participle with the prepositional phrase further describes the old person. The participle φθειρόμενον comes from φθείρω, meaning "to destroy, ruin"[3] and the passive "to be destroyed, perish."[4] In a moral sense it conveys the idea "to corrupt, ruin, decay."[5] In the LXX it occurs twenty times and in the canonical books it appears eighteen times where it translates five Hebrew words, eight times for שָׁחַת (mostly in the Hiphil) meaning "to destroy, ruin" (Lev 19:27; 1 Chr 20:1) or "to corrupt" morally (Gen 6:11; Hos 9:9).[6] In the NT it appears nine times and can be rendered "destroy" (1 Cor 3:17*bis*; 2 Pet

1. Zerwick, *Biblical Greek* §130.

2. Instead of τὰς ἐπιθυμίας, the reading τὴν ἐπιθυμίαν is found in D cop^{bopt} Lucifer of Calaris. However, this reading is not acceptable not only because it is found mainly in the Western text but also because there is only a sparse representation in that text-type.

3. Homer *Odyssea* 17.246; Herodotus 1.76.

4. Sophocles *Ajax* 25.

5. Aristotle *Ethica Nicomachea* 7.8.4 §1151a.15.

6. BDB 1007–8; J. Conrad, "שָׁחַת *šāḥat*," *TWAT* 7 (1990): 1234–43.

2:12; Jude 10) or "corrupt, ruin" (1 Cor 15:33; 2 Cor 7:2; 11:3; Rev 19:2). In the present context it is best translated "to corrupt."[1] The present tense denotes continuing action, which indicates that the corruption continues in the unregenerate person. Also, it is the passive voice signifying an action being received. This is further expressed in the following prepositional phrase.

The preposition κατά is repeated with the accusative denoting standard. The object of the preposition is ἐπιθυμία. This word was discussed at 2:3 where it was concluded that it meant a "desire" that can be either good or bad. In the present context, as in 2:3, it connotes bad desires because of the following genitive τῆς ἀπάτης. The word ἀπάτη means "deception, deceit, deceitful"[2] or an illusional kind of "pleasure."[3] In the LXX it is used five times and only in the noncanonical books and it can always be rendered "deceit, deception" (Jdt 9:3, 10, 13; 16:8; 4 Macc 18:8; cf. Eccl 9:6 [Codex א]). In the NT it occurs seven times, defined as deception in general (2 Thess 2:10) or seduction or deception which might come from wealth (Matt 13:22 = Mark 4:19), pleasure (2 Pet 2:13), sin (Heb 3:13), or philosophy (Col 2:8). In the present context it has the idea of deception or deceit. The genitive could be attributive indicating that the desires are deceitful,[4] but it is more likely a genitive of source indicating that the desires come from or are based on deceit. It can be rendered "in accordance with the deceptive desires" or better "in accordance with the desires coming from deceit." It is the antithesis of "truth" in verse 24. Therefore, the unregenerate person is constantly being corrupted by the desires that come from deception, the deception which promises fullness of life, a promise it cannot fulfill.

This completes the first part of Paul's explanation to believers regarding what they were taught in Christ. Briefly, he describes their former state as that of the "old person" corrupted by the desires that feed on deceit or illusion. This illusion that brings a person to ruin is the false idea that fulfillment of natural desires is all that is necessary for human life. However, Paul reminds believers that they have laid aside this old person. This is analogous to the believers' baptism into Christ Jesus' death or their crucifixion with Christ in Rom 6:3–6. This marks the end of the discussion of who the believers were before conversion.

(b) Be Renewed by the Spirit (4:23)

Text: 4:23. ἀνανεοῦσθαι δὲ τῷ πνεύματι τοῦ νοὸς ὑμῶν

Translation: 4:23. "but you are being renewed by the spirit in your mind"

1. Günther Harder, "φθείρω κτλ.," *TDNT* 9 (1974): 103; BAGD 857; BDAG 1054.

2. Homer *Ilias* 2.114; *Odyssea* 13.294; Polybius 4.20.5.

3. Polybius 2.56.12.

4. MHT 2:440, 485. Sellin ("Über einige ungewöhnliche Genitive im Epheserbrief," 103) thinks it is a genitive of quality.

Commentary: 4:23. ἀνανεοῦσθαι[1] δὲ τῷ πνεύματι[2] τοῦ νοὸς ὑμῶν, "but you are being renewed by the spirit in your mind." Having clarified the condition of the old person that was laid aside at the time of conversion, Paul now discusses the renewing of the mind. The conjunction δέ marks the contrast with the previous verse, there the negative, here the positive. This infinitive, like the previous one, is related back to ἐδιδάχθητε in verse 21.[3] The infinitive ἀνανεοῦσθαι is from ἀνανεόω, generally meaning "to renew."[4] In the LXX it appears ten times (Job 33:24; Esth 13:2 [3:13b]; 1 Macc 12:1, 3, 10, 16; 14:18, 22; 15:17; 4 Macc 18:4) and is rendered "to renew." In Hellenistic Greek it has the same sense.[5] It is found only here in the NT and the same definition is consistent with the context. The form of the infinitive could be either middle or passive voice. When the middle form is used, it has the accusative as its object.[6] But here there is no accusative. Although some attempt to give it the reflexive meaning "to renew oneself," such usage is not found in the literature.[7] In light of these factors, it is best to view it not as a middle but as a passive where the believer is the recipient of the renewing. The present tense suggests that the renewal of the mind is a repeated process throughout the believer's life,[8] which is in contrast to the inceptive act involved in putting off the old person (v. 22) and putting on the new person (v. 24). Schnackenburg thinks it involves the newness of the Christian spirit in contrast to the triviality of the Gentile mind. He supports this theory by making a distinction between the adjectives νέος, referring to something that is recent in time, and καινός, newness in quality.[9] However, as discussed at 2:15, that distinction is not viable.[10] Furthermore, in the parallel passage, Col 3:10, the process of renewal for the new person is described by the present participle from ἀνακαινόω rather than from ἀνανεόω. Also, in the next verse the adjective καινός is used to describe the new person whereas in the parallel passage in Col 3:10 the adjective νέος is used.

1. Instead of the infinitive ἀνανεοῦσθαι, the indicative or imperative ἀνανεοῦσθε is found in 𝔓[46] D[1] K 33 323 1241[s] *pc* latt Cyprian. The manuscript evidence is not sufficient enough to accept this reading as the original reading. Also, internally the infinitive is in keeping with the other infinitives in vv. 22 and 24. The scribes would tend to favor the imperative over the infinitive.

2. Instead of τῷ πνεύματι, the reading ἐν τῷ πνεύματι is found in 𝔓[49] B 33 1175 1739 1881 *pc*. This reading does not have good representation from any one text-type and should not be considered genuine.

3. Winer, *Grammar*, 405.

4. Thucydides 5.18.9; 43.2; 46.4; 7.33.4.

5. MM 36; Horsley, *New Documents Illustrating Early Christianity*, vol. 3, *A Review of the Greek Inscriptions and Papyri Published in 1978*, 62.

6. Thucydides 5.80.2.

7. J. Behm, "νέος, ἀνανεόω," *TDNT* 4 (1967): 900; Winer, *Grammar*, 330.

8. Fanning, *Verbal Aspect*, 360.

9. Schnackenburg, 200.

10. Cf. Harrisville, "The Concept of Newness in the New Testament," 69–79.

Hence, these two words are used interchangeably and mean "new." The renewing is both qualitative and recent.

The next word "spirit" could refer to the human spirit or the Holy Spirit. Some think that here it refers to the Holy Spirit since "spirit" in all other references in Ephesians (except 2:2) refers to the Spirit of God.[1] The problem is that the Holy Spirit is never alluded to as the "Spirit of your mind" but rather is referred to as the "Spirit of holiness" (Rom 1:4), "Spirit of God" (Rom 8:9), or "Spirit of adoption" (Rom 8:15). In this context the human spirit is the more likely referent.[2] There is a distinction between the Spirit of God and the human spirit (Rom 8:16). There is also a distinction between the mind and the human spirit as suggested in 1 Cor 14:14, namely, the spirit prays but the mind is unfruitful. In fact, there is little about the human spirit in the Bible. The origin of the human spirit is God who is the father of the spirits of all flesh (Num 16:22; Heb 12:9). God gives the spirit to a person (Job 27:3; 33:4; 34:14) and it is returned to God when the person dies (Eccl 12:7). It is possible to consider that one distinction between animals and humans is that humans have a spirit. However, this spirit is latent in a person until the Holy Spirit quickens it to convert the soul. At conversion one does not receive the spirit of the world but the Spirit of God (1 Cor 2:12). This human spirit is revived and bears witness to the Holy Spirit (Rom 8:16). The spirit of a person is being transformed from glory to glory by the Spirit of the Lord (2 Cor 3:18). The inner person is being renewed daily (2 Cor 4:16). Such is possible only by the Spirit of God. Hence, some think that the "spirit" refers to both the Holy Spirit and the human spirit.[3] The dative is most likely instrumental[4] and is translated "by the spirit." The following genitive is difficult to classify. It is probably best to view it as a genitive of place, a rare usage.[5] It means that the human spirit operates in the believer's mind.

Only the Spirit of God can ultimately change our lives. As the Spirit of God quickens the human spirit, then believers are being renewed

1. Oecumenius *Eph* 4:20–24 (*PG* 118:1228); Theophylact *Eph* 4:23 (*PG* 124:1093); Masson, 202; Houlden, 319; Gnilka, 230–31; Schnackenburg, 200; Sellin, "Über einige ungewöhnliche Genitive im Epheserbrief," 104–5.

2. So Bengel, 4:98; Calvin, 190; Hodge, 263–64; Alford, 3:124; Eadie, 341–43; Meyer, 248–50; Abbott, 137–38; Robinson, 191; Westcott, 68; Dibelius-Greeven, 87; Gaugler, 189; Hendriksen, 215; Mitton, 165; Barth, 508; Lincoln, 286–87; Bouttier, 210; Pokorný, 189; Best, 435–36; O'Brien, 330; Parsons, "The New Creation," 4.

3. Cf. Ellicott, 103; Salmond, 343; Schlier, 220; possibly Bruce, 358.

4. Alford, 3:124; Ellicott, 103; Meyer, 248–49.

5. Wallace suggested this in personal correspondence. See also Houlden, 319. Others suggest that it is a genitive of subordination, "spirit governs the mind" (Eadie, 342; Salmond, 343 [labeled it as subjective genitive]; Meyer, 249–50); possessive genitive, "the mind's spirit" (Ellicott, 102–3); or genitive of quality or a genitive that specifies (Sellin, "Über einige ungewöhnliche Genitive im Epheserbrief," 105), which is difficult to understand in this context.

by that spirit which is in the mind.[1] In conjunction with the other Pauline passages listed above, the spirit of a person is being constantly renewed. The present tense suggests that it is a repeated or continual process, constantly reminding us of what we are in Christ. It receives the truth and will of God and appropriates it in our lives. This renewing will transform our lives in very practical ways.[2]

(c) Put on the New Person (4:24)

Text: 4:24. καὶ ἐνδύσασθαι τὸν καινὸν ἄνθρωπον τὸν κατὰ θεὸν κτισθέντα ἐν δικαιοσύνῃ καὶ ὁσιότητι τῆς ἀληθείας.

Translation: 4:24. "and [that you] have put on the new person who has been created after God's likeness in righteousness and holiness that comes from truth."

Commentary: 4:24. καὶ ἐνδύσασθαι[3] τὸν καινὸν ἄνθρωπον, "and [that you] have put on the new person." The conjunction καί is a simple connective with the previous verses. Ultimately it refers back to verse 22. The infinitive ἐνδύσασθαι parallels with the infinitive ἀποθέσθαι in verse 22 because it is both aorist and middle. These two infinitives are in contrast to the present middle infinitive ἀνανεοῦσθαι in verse 23. In verses 22 and 24 the infinitives denote an inceptive action while the one in verse 23 denotes a repeated action. Further, those in verses 22 and 24 are middle voice signifying that the subject is receiving the benefit of his or her action, whereas in verse 23 it is passive where the subject is a recipient of the action.

The infinitive in the present verse is from ἐνδύω, which has always had the idea of putting on clothing whether in the active "to clothe, dress" someone[4] or in the middle "to put on, clothe oneself, wear."[5] In the LXX it occurs 117 times and in the canonical books it appears ninety-one times and in all but a few instances it translates לָבֵשׁ/לָבַשׁ with the same meaning, "to put on (a garment), wear, clothe"[6] (active in Gen 3:21; Exod 29:5; Num 20:26; middle in 2 Chr 6:41; Ps 65:13

1. Fee (*God's Empowering Presence*, 712) concludes that the first referent is the human spirit but one should "recognize the Holy Spirit as hovering nearby."

2. Parsons, "The New Creation," 4.

3. The reading of ἐνδύσασθαι is found in 𝔓[49] A D* F G Ψ 33 1739 𝔐 Clement[pt] Jerome[pt]. On the other hand, the imperative ἐνδύσασθε is found in 𝔓[46] א B D[1] K 104 323 1241[s] 1881 *pc* latt Clement[pt]. For the 𝔓[49] reading, see Emmel, "Greek Biblical Papyri in the Beinecke Library," 293 recto line 15; Pickering, "Readings in a Papyrus Text of Ephesians," 114. The second reading has better attestation in the Alexandrian text. The first reading is preferred because it has better representation from the Western and Byzantine text-types and hence better geographical distribution. Internally, it is easier to explain why a scribe would change it from an infinitive to an imperative than the other way around.

4. Homer *Ilias* 2.42; 10.21; Herodotus 2.81.

5. Homer *Ilias* 2.578; 11.16; Herodotus 7.218; Thucydides 1.130.1.

6. BDB 527; J. Gamberoni and H.-J Fabry, "לָבֵשׁ *lāḇēš*," *TDOT* 7 (1995): 457–68.

[MT 65:14; LXX 64:14]; Jonah 3:5). In the NT it is used twenty-seven times, thirteen times by Paul, three times in Ephesians (4:24; 6:11, 14). It refers to putting on clothes literally (active in Matt 27:31; Mark 15:20; Luke 15:22; middle in Matt 6:25 = Luke 12:22; Matt 22:11; Mark 1:6; 6:9; Luke 8:27; Acts 12:21; Rev 1:13; 15:6; 19:14) or metaphorically (only in middle voice in Luke 24:49; Rom 13:12, 14; 1 Cor 15:53*bis*, 54*bis*; Gal 3:27; Col 3:10, 12; 1 Thess 5:8).[1] In the present context the aorist middle suggests that believers were taught that they had put on the new person when they laid aside the old person at conversion. Worthy of note is that the old person does not remain with the new person. Dualism is not suggested or implied. One cannot be a Christian and a non-Christian at the same time.

Who is this new person? In 2:15 the new person refers to the church, the new race composed of believing Jews and Gentiles. Roels thinks that this same concept continues in chapter 4.[2] It is true that chapter 4 does make reference to the corporate body of believers (4:13, 16). On the other hand, it can be argued that the new person in verse 24 speaks of the individual who has become new in Christ.[3] This view is more consistent with the present context. Paul states in verse 7 that Christ gave gifts to "each of us" and in verse 11 Paul mentions that Christ gave "some" to be apostles, prophets, evangelists, and pastors and teachers, all this indicating individual believers. This reference to individuality continues in verses 12–16, the preparation of the "saints" for ministry and the function of "each individual part" which causes the growth of the body. Clearly, the emphasis is on individual believers. In the end, this is not an "either/or" but more likely a "both/and" situation.[4] The individual and the corporate body cannot be divorced one from the other. Corporate growth is dependent on individual growth. In conclusion then it seems that the "new person" in the present verse has its primary emphasis on the individual but the corporate connotation must not be excluded.

The καινὸν ἄνθρωπον, "new person," is in contrast to the παλαιὸν ἄνθρωπον, "old person" (v. 22). As mentioned above, the parallel passage in Col 3:10 uses the adjective νέος rather than καινός, which indicates that they are synonyms denoting both temporal and qualitative significance pertaining to something new. Replacement of the old with the new occurred at a point in time, namely, conversion. The result is a qualitative difference in lifestyle as depicted in this text.

τὸν κατὰ θεὸν κτισθέντα, "who has been created after God's likeness." The participle τὸν κτισθέντα is aorist passive from κτίζω. As discussed at 2:10, 15 κτίζω refers to what God created in both the physical

1. Cf. Horsley, *New Documents Illustrating Early Christianity*, vol. 4, *A Review of the Greek Inscriptions and Papyri Published in 1979*, 257.

2. Roels, *God's Mission*, 128–33.

3. Parsons, "The New Creation," 3–4; Best, "Ephesians: Two Types of Existence," 41.

4. So also Lincoln, 287; O'Brien, *Colossians, Philemon*, 190–91.

and spiritual realms. In this context it speaks exclusively of the spiritual realm. The use of the passive and the prepositional phrase indicates that God does the work and believers are the recipients. The aorist tense again denotes the inceptive action of God that is contemporaneous action with the aorist infinitive and should be translated "has been created" and not "is created" (as in AV, TEV). This new person has been created by God and was "put on" at the time of conversion.

The prepositional phrase κατὰ θεόν defines the standard of the creation. It is in accordance with God. This phrase presents some difficulty. It is similar to Rom 8:27 where the Spirit intercedes on behalf of the saints according to God. In that context one would translate it "according to God's will." Because the parallel passage (Col 3:10) states that the new person is being renewed in knowledge according to the image of the one who created him, some have translated the present prepositional phrase "after the likeness of God" or something similar (RSV, NASB, TEV, NIV, NRSV). Certainly, in the present context the creation of the new person is according to God's standard, which would be "after his likeness." The prepositional phrases in the next part of the verse would substantiate this idea.

When God created Adam, he made him after his likeness or image (Gen 1:27). What Adam lost in the fall, has been regained by Christ, a new creation in the likeness of God's image. It is interesting to notice that the word "creation" is not used in connection with the "old person." God originally created human beings without sin and when they fell they lost that original state. This new person has been newly created after God's image. The new creation is spelled out in 2 Cor 5:17 where Paul states that if anyone is in Christ he is a new creation, the old has passed away, the new has come. Hence, it can be translated "in God's image"[1] or "who has been created after God's likeness."

ἐν δικαιοσύνῃ καὶ ὁσιότητι τῆς ἀληθείας,[2] "in righteousness and holiness that comes from truth." These prepositional phrases depend on the immediately preceding participle and further describe God's creation of the new person. The word δικαιοσύνη speaks of "righteousness, justice."[3] In the LXX it occurs 345 times and in the canonical books it appears 263 times and translates eleven Hebrew words. About 225 times it translates צַדִּיק/צְדָקָה/צֶדֶק, meaning, respectively, "rightness or righteousness; righteousness; just or righteous."[4] References allude to God's attribute of righteousness (Deut 33:21; 1 Kgs 8:32; 2 Chr 6:23;

1. MHT 3:268; Moule, *Idiom Book*, 59.

2. Instead of τῆς ἀληθείας, the reading καὶ ἀληθείᾳ is found in D* F G it vg^{mss} Cyprian Lucifer. This suggests that the new person has been created in righteousness, piety, and truth. This reading is not acceptable for it is found almost exclusively in the Western text-type.

3. Herodotus 1.96; Plato *Respublica* 4.10 §433a.

4. BDB 841; B. Johnson, "צָדַק *ṣādaq*; צֶדֶק *ṣedeq*; צְדָקָה *ṣ^e^dāqāh*; צַדִּיק *ṣaddîq*," *TWAT* 6 (1989): 898–924.

Hos 2:19 [MT & LXX 2:21]; Zech 8:8), God's dealing in righteousness (Ps 9:4, 8 [MT & LXX 9:5, 9]; Isa 5:16; 33:5; 58:2), and also to a person's own righteousness (Deut 9:4–6; 1 Kgs 3:6) or acting righteously (Lev 19:15; 1 Sam 26:23; 2 Sam 8:15; Isa 56:1). In the NT δικαιοσύνη occurs ninety-two times, fifty-eight times in Paul, and three times in Ephesians (4:24; 5:9; 6:14). It can refer to God's attribute of righteousness (Rom 3:25–26) or to a person who has a right standing before God (Rom 3:21–22; 4:3, 5). It can refer to a person's own righteousness (Matt 5:20; Rom 10:3) or to his or her dealings that are to be righteous (Rom 6:13; Phil 1:11).[1] In the present context it refers to righteous actions of the new person, a quality of life (cf. Eph 5:9).

The second noun in this phrase is ὁσιότης, which has the idea of a disposition of piety towards the gods[2] or parents.[3] It appears nine times in the LXX, six times referring to personal piety before God (Deut 9:5; 1 Sam 14:41; 1 Kgs 9:4; Prov 14:32; Wis 2:22; 5:19), three times to God's holiness (Ode 9:75; Wis 9:3; 14:30), and once to the divine law (Wis 18:9 [Codex א]). It appears twice in the NT: in the present context and in Luke 1:75 with reference to Zechariah's prophecy where both this word and righteousness (the reverse order from Paul) are used to denote service to God with an attitude of personal piety and righteousness. Basically, it means to have personal piety, devotedness, or reverence before God. While Plato would define piety as a right conduct before the gods, "the NT regards it as a consequence of the new birth."[4]

The difference between δικαιοσύνη, "righteousness," and ὁσιότης, "holiness," is not great. In using both of these words in connection with Abraham, Philo suggested that a person must exhibit both qualities: justice to humans and holiness to God.[5] This expresses it well and may be the nuance Paul intended. Furthermore, the preposition ἐν is probably not an instrumental, which would indicate that the new person was made by means of righteousness and piety, but it more likely indicates sphere, that is, the new person has been created in the sphere or element of righteousness and piety which denotes the quality of the new person. This characteristic will have ethical ramifications which are spelled out in more detail in verses 25–32. As the lifestyle of the old person was integrally bound with the person, so also is the conduct of the new person tied with the person both individually and corporately.

Finally, the genitive τῆς ἀληθείας demands only a brief explanation. The word appears in 1:13; 4:21, 24, 25; 5:9; 6:14 and basically has the

1. For a more detailed study of this vast subject, see Gottfried Quell and Gottlob Schrenk, "δίκη κτλ.," *TDNT* 2 (1964): 174–225; Morris, *Apostolic Preaching*, 251–304.

2. Plato *Protagorus* 329c; *Euthyphro* 14c–e; Plutarch *Alcibiades* 34.4.

3. Diodorus Siculus 7.4.

4. Friedrich Hauck, "ὁσιότης," *TDNT* 5 (1967): 493.

5. Philo *De Abrahamo* 37 §208.

idea of reality as opposed to that which is false. It can be rendered "truth." It is the opposite of τῆς ἀπάτης, "deceit, deception," in verse 22 and is connected to both preceding nouns.[1] Like τῆς ἀπάτης it probably denotes source, indicating that the source[2] of righteousness and piety is truth and thus is translated "that comes or originates from truth." Therefore, the new person has been identified as one who is characterized by a righteousness that has its source in truth. The new person is directly opposite of the old person whose desires and lifestyle have their source in deception.

In conclusion, believers have put on the new person. This occurred when they laid off the old person at the time of their conversion. Some want to relate this to baptism.[3] However, one cannot know this with any certainty. Barth says it well:

> Indeed Eph 4:22–24 is a piece of instruction well suited to the preparation for, or the liturgy of, baptism. But its usefulness for a given service does not necessarily demonstrate the original *Sitz im Leben*. As yet there is no evidence that the exhortation to "strip off," to "be renewed," or to "put on" is in substance to be identified with the command and promise, "Be baptized and you shall be a new man!"[4]

Even if this were a part of a water baptism ritual, the ritual did not put off the old person and put on the new person. Water baptism is not the basis of the believer's experience. Rather, regeneration is the basis of the believer's experience and water baptism is only an outward symbol of an inward reality.

Although there is an emphasis on the individual as the new person, the corporate entity must not be ignored. Individual growth must contribute to body growth. This new creation, both individually and corporately, is characterized by righteousness and holiness based on

1. Alford, 3:124; Eadie, 345; Ellicott, 104; Meyer, 251; Abbott, 138; Salmon 3:344; Robinson, 191; Schlier, 222.

2. Cf. Murphy-O'Connor, "Who Wrote Ephesians?" 1206. Again as in vv. 22 and 23, Sellin ("Über einige ungewöhnliche Genitive im Epheserbrief," 103–4) thinks it is a genitive of quality.

3. Schlier, 218–22; Gaugler, 189; Gnilka, 229–33; Ernst, 365; Schnackenburg, 200; Jervell, *Imago Dei* 239–40, 244, 261–62; Larsson, *Christus als Vorbild*, 227–30; Pokorný, "Epheserbrief und gnostische Mysterien," 186–87; Feuillet, *Le Christ sagesse de Dieu*, 265; Kirby, *Ephesians, Baptism and Pentecost*, 159; Fung, "The Doctrine of Baptism in Ephesians," 11, 13–14; Wayne A. Meeks, "The Image of the Andgrogyne: Some Uses of a Symbol in Earliest Christianity," *History of Religions* 13 (February 1974): 183–89, 207; Halter, *Taufe und Ethos*, 248–56; Nils Alstrup Dahl, "Kleidungsmetaphern: der alte und der neue Mensch," in *Studies in Ephesians: Introductory Questions, Text- & Edition-Critical Issues, Interpretation of Texts and Themes*, ed. David Hellholm, Vemund Blomkvist, and Tord Fornberg, WUNT, ed. Martin Hengel and Otfried Hofius, vol. 131 (Tübingen: Mohr, 2000), 401–3.

4. Barth, 544.

truth. Such attributes will be manifested in various ways, as seen in the following verses.

b. His Practice (4:25–32)

To review, Paul has exhorted the Ephesians not to walk as the Gentiles do. He described the lifestyle of the Gentiles as walking in the futility of the mind resulting from darkened minds and alienation from the life of God. Consequently, they have lost all moral sensitivity and have given themselves over to impurity based on selfishness (vv. 17–19). He then explained that they were taught they had put off the old person and had put on the new person (vv. 20–24). Now he is going to give practical applications of how the new person in Christ lives day to day (vv. 25–32). The structure of 4:17–32 is as follows: (1) description of the lifestyle of the old person (4:17–19); (2) statement regarding having put off the old person and having put on the new person (4:20–24); and (3) exhortation on living a new lifestyle in accordance with being a new person (4:25–32). Some conclude these exhortations at 5:2[1] while others would conclude them at 4:32.[2] As mentioned above, 5:1 is the most logical place to begin a new section for this conforms to the pattern in which the major divisions in these three chapters revolve around the "walk" (περιπατέω) in 4:1, 17; 5:2, 8, 15 in conjunction with the inferential conjunction "therefore" (οὖν) in 5:1.

This new section has five exhortations with regard to the believers' conduct.[3] Each of these exhortations has three parts: (1) a negative command, (2) a positive command, and (3) the reason for the positive command. All the exhortations have the three parts in the same order except the second one which reverses the first two parts.

(1) Do Not Use Falsehood But Speak Truth (4:25)

Text: 4:25. Διὸ ἀποθέμενοι τὸ ψεῦδος **λαλεῖτε ἀλήθειαν ἕκαστος μετὰ τοῦ πλησίον αὐτοῦ,** ὅτι ἐσμὲν ἀλλήλων μέλη.

1. Calvin, 196; Ellicott, 111; Abbott, 146; Robinson, 110; Masson, 204–5; Schlier, 222–23; Hendriksen, 216, 221; Schnackenburg, 204; Lincoln, 293–94; Best, 443; O'Brien, 335.

2. Alford, 128; Eadie, 362; Salmond, 350; Westcott, 72, 74; Lenski, 590; Gnilka, 242–43; Mitton, 174; Barth, 555; Bruce, 367; Kreitzer, 148.

3. Sampley suggests that the form of this series of exhortations is patterned after Zech 8:16–17, the passage from which Paul quotes for his first injunction in v. 25 (J. Paul Sampley, "Scripture and Tradition in the Community as Seen in Ephesians 4:25ff," *ST* 26, no. 2 [1972]: 101–9). This is interesting but one is hard pressed to demonstrate his thesis. Montagnini thinks that these exhortations are connected with the Lord's Supper but again one finds it difficult to demonstrate this from the context. See Felice Montagnini, "Echi di parenesi cultuale in Ef 4,24–32," *RivB* 37 (Luglio–Settembre 1989): 257–82.

Translation: 4:25. "Therefore, having laid aside falsehood, 'each one of you speak the truth with his neighbor,' because we are members of one another."

Commentary: 4:25. Διὸ[1] ἀποθέμενοι τὸ ψεῦδος, "Therefore, having laid aside falsehood." Paul begins this section with the strong inferential conjunction διό (from δι' ὅ), translated "therefore" or "for this reason."[2] Having established the believer's position as a new person, the inferential conjunction διό points to the desired application of this position.[3] The lifestyle of the old person is integrally tied to the person and so the lifestyle and the position of the new should be integrally bound together. Once the new person had been put on at conversion, one's subsequent life should reflect what he or she is. This inference is seen not only in the conjunction but also in the aorist middle participle (ἀποθέμενοι), which is the same word, tense, and voice as the infinitive in verse 22 that describes the laying aside of the old person. This is an excellent demonstration of how conduct is closely connected with position. In this case, the particular practice which has been laid aside is τὸ ψεῦδος. This word basically has the sense of "falsehood, lie."[4] In the LXX it occurs thirty-one times and in the canonical books it appears twenty-five times. It translates four Hebrew words, nine times it comes from שֶׁקֶר, meaning "false" (Jer 3:10, 23; 37:14 [LXX 44:14]), "falsehood" (Isa 28:15; Jer 9:3 [MT & LXX 9:2]), "swear falsely" (Zech 5:4; Mal 3:5), or "lie" (Isa 44:20; Jer 43:2 [LXX 50:2]; Mic 2:11).[5] In the NT it appears ten times, four times in Paul (Rom 1:25; Eph 4:25; 2 Thess 2:9, 11). Using this word, the Scriptures have much to say about falsehood. John states that the devil from the beginning has had nothing to do with truth because there is no truth in him; according to his own nature he lies, for he is the father of lies (John 8:44). Further John states that no lie is of the truth; they are antithetical (1 John 2:21, 27). Revelation 14:5 states that the 144,000 will be pure and no lie will be found in them. In the same book John states that no one who practices abomination or falsehood will enter the coming age (Rev 21:27; 22:15). Paul agrees in Rom 1:25 where he depicts a sinful person as one who has exchanged the truth of God for a lie. In addition, he speaks of the future lawless one who will give false wonders which will be believed by the people in that day (2 Thess 2:9, 11). Hence, in all contexts this word is used as the antithesis of truth.

1. This conjunction διό is omitted from 𝔓[46] it[b, m*] Lucifer Didymus of Alexandria. The manuscript evidence for its omission is not enough to be considered seriously.

2. Cf. Molland, "Διο, Einige syntaktische Beobachtungen," in *Serta Rudbergiana*, 43–52; reprinted in idem, "Διο: Einige syntaktische Beobachtungen," in *Opuscula Patristica*, 9–16.

3. Wallace, *Greek Grammar*, 605.

4. Homer *Ilias* 2.349; 9.115; *Odyssea* 14.387; 19.203.

5. Cf. BDB 1055; cf. H. Seebass, S. Beyerle, and K. Grünwaldt, "שׁקר *šqr*; שֶׁקֶר *šaeqaer*," *TWAT* 8 (1995): 466–72.

Possibly Paul chose this first negative assertion because of his statements about truth in the immediately preceding words (v. 24; cf. v. 21). Falsehood connotes that which is not genuine or real. The lifestyle of the old person was one of deception (v. 22). This kind of lifestyle has been laid aside.

λαλεῖτε ἀλήθειαν ἕκαστος μετὰ τοῦ πλησίον αὐτοῦ, "'each one of you speak the truth with his neighbor.'" There is no introductory formula (so also at 5:31 and 6:2, 3 but not so at 4:8 and 5:14) to alert his reader that he is going to cite an OT passage. Paul introduces an exact quotation of LXX Zech 8:16, except for the substitution of μετὰ τοῦ for πρὸς τόν, which is a better rendering of the Hebrew text. In the Zechariah context God informs the remnant that he purposes to do good to Jerusalem and to Judah and the first command he utters to them is, "Everyone one of you speak the truth to his neighbor." Interestingly, Paul likewise has this as his first command for the new person.

Rather than falsehood we are to speak the truth with one another. This is the first occurrence of λαλέω, meaning "to speak, communicate," in Ephesians (cf. 5:19; 6:20). Although there is a fine distinction, the synonym λέγω generally refers to the content of what is said whereas λαλέω generally refers to the sound of communication.[1] For example, the sound of a trumpet (Rev 4:1) or of thunder (Rev 10:4) communicates to John. However, in the present context the content of what is spoken is primary, namely, to speak "truth" to one's neighbor. In contrast to the aorist middle participle (ἀποθέμενοι), this is a present active imperative indicating that, having laid aside falsehood, they are to make a habit of speaking the truth. The word ἀλήθεια, "truth," was used earlier (1:13; 4:21, 24) and it is that which is in contrast to a lie or that which is reality or actual to that which is false. Since the new person's conduct of righteousness and holiness is based on truth (v. 24), he or she is to speak truthfully to others. The second person plural along with the substantival adjective ἕκαστος,[2] "each one, everyone," reinforces the idea of individual responsibility in this matter. The use of the preposition μετά instead of πρός (LXX) not only renders a better translation of the Hebrew but it is also more appropriate for indicating mutual interaction among individuals.[3]

The word πλησίον is an adverbial accusative meaning "near, close by,"[4] and when used with an article it means "neighbor."[5] In the LXX it occurs 218 times and in the canonical books 162 times. It translates ten Hebrew words, around 125 times for רֵעַ and its derivatives. Its ba-

1. A. Debrunner, "λέγω κτλ.," *TDNT* 4 (1967): 76–77; BAGD 463, 469; BDAG 582–83, 589; Trench, *Synonyms of the New Testament*, 286–89; L&N §§33.69, 70.

2. Here, as in other places, ἕκαστος rather than ἀνήρ is a translation of אִישׁ demonstrating an "independence of Hebrew literalism" (Robertson, *Grammar*, 746).

3. BAGD 508–9; BDAG 636–37.

4. Homer *Ilias* 3.115; *Odyssea* 14.14; Herodotus 4.111.

5. Euripides *Hecuba* 996; Aristotle *Politica* 2.4.9 §1267a.25; Plato *Protagoras* 315d.

sic idea is "to have dealings with someone," whether it be a friend (Ps 35:14 [LXX 34:14]), lover (Cant 1:9, 15), or neighbor (Exod 11:2; Lev 19:16–18; 1 Sam 28:17; 2 Sam 12:11).[1] In the NT it appears seventeen times and with the exception of John 4:5 (used as an improper preposition with the genitive) it appears in the noun form. Of the seventeen times it is used in the NT, eleven times it quotes or alludes to the OT. Leviticus 19:18 "you shall love your neighbor as yourself," is quoted in the NT nine times (Matt 5:43; 19:19; 22:39; Mark 12:31, 33; Luke 10:27; Rom 13:9; Gal 5:14; Jas 2:8). The reference to "neighbor" in Acts 7:27 is an allusion to Exod 2:13. In the present verse, "each one of you speak the truth with his neighbor" is a quotation from Zech 8:16.[2] Although in the parable of the good Samaritan (Luke 10:29–37) Jesus demonstrates that one cannot define a neighbor but only be a neighbor,[3] in the present context the neighbor refers primarily to Christians and not to human beings in general. This is concluded because: (1) in the context of Zechariah the prophet was directing his words toward the community of the remnant; and (2) the next clause in the present context speaks of being members of one another. The reason for stating that it refers "primarily" rather than "exclusively" to Christians is because the new person is to speak the truth at all times, even in his or her contacts with the unbelievers.[4] Believers base their lifestyle on reality; there is no need to bring falsehood into any relationship whether with believers or unbelievers. This has already been addressed in 4:15 where believers are to be truthful in love, referring to both conduct and speech, so that the body can grow up to Christ. The reason believers are to speak truth with their neighbors is discussed next.

ὅτι ἐσμὲν ἀλλήλων μέλη, "because we are members of one another." Though ὅτι has been used before in the book (2:11, 12, 18; 3:3; 4:9), it is the first time it introduces a reason. The reason we are to speak the truth is "because we are members of one another." The noun μέλος can refer to a limb or member of a body, whether it be human or animal,[5] or it can be used of a musical entity, such as a phrase, song, or lyric strain.[6] In the LXX it occurs twenty-seven times (ten times in the canonical books), once for הֶגֶה, where it refers to a lamentation (Ezek 2:10)[7] but seven times for נֵתַח, referring to limbs of people (Judg 19:29 [B text]) and animals (Exod 29:17; Lev 1:6, 12; 8:20; 9:13;

1. BDB 945–46; D. Kellermann, "רֵעַ *reaʿ*, etc.," *TWAT* 7 (1990): 549–54; Heinrich Greeven and Johannes Fichtner, "πλησίον," *TDNT* 6 (1968): 313–15.

2. Cf. Moritz, *A Profound Mystery*, 88–89.

3. Greeven and Fichtner, *TDNT* 6 (1968): 317.

4. Carsten Peter Thiede, "Der Brief an die Epheser. 40. Teil: Kapitel 4,25–32," *Fundamentum* 21, no. 1 (2000): 18.

5. Homer *Ilias* 7.131; Herodotus 1.119; Plato *Leges* 7 §795e); Pindar *Nemean Odes* 1.47.

6. Plato *Respublica* 10.8 §607d); Herodotus 2.135; 5.95.

7. BDB 211–12; *HALOT* 1 (1994): 237–38.

Ezek 24:6).[1] It is used thirty-four times in the NT, twenty-nine times by Paul, two of these in Ephesians (4:25; 5:30). It signifies members of a human body (Matt 5:29–30; Rom 6:13, 19; 1 Cor 12:12–26; Jas 3:5–6; 4:1) and members of the body of Christ (Rom 12:4–5; 1 Cor 6:15; 12:27; Eph 5:30) but it is never used of animal limbs or of a musical entity. Certainly in this context it is talking about members in the body of Christ. He uses this figure to portray the close-knit relationship with other members of the body. It is interesting to observe that this word μέλος is never used of members of an organization but always of members of an organism. In other words, members of an organization may not necessarily have a relationship to other members, but members of an organism demand a close-knit relationship to the other members and they are accountable to one another. The concept of a close relationship is enhanced by the use of the reciprocal pronoun ἀλλήλων, "one another." In order for this body to function smoothly and efficiently, truth must be expressed among the members. Deception by one member not only harms that member but the whole body suffers as well and in the end self-destruction occurs. Chrysostom wisely asks if the eye sees a serpent does it lie to the foot? Or if the nose smells a deadly drug will it lie to the mouth? Or if the tongue tastes something bitter will it lie to the stomach?[2] In this same vein, Paul points out that although there are many individual members, these members comprise one body (cf. Rom 12:5). Thus, as new persons, believers are commanded to speak the truth with one another.

(2) Do Use Anger But Do Not Sin (4:26–27)

Text: 4:26. ὀργίζεσθε καὶ μὴ ἁμαρτάνετε· ὁ ἥλιος μὴ ἐπιδυέτω ἐπὶ [τῷ] παροργισμῷ ὑμῶν, **4:27.** μηδὲ δίδοτε τόπον τῷ διαβόλῳ.

Translation: 4:26. "'Be angry and do not sin'; let not the sun go down on your irritation, **4:27.** nor do you give opportunity to the devil."

Commentary: 4:26. ὀργίζεσθε καὶ μὴ ἁμαρτάνετε, "'Be angry and do not sin.'" Breaking with the consistent pattern of this section, statement of the negative and then the positive, here Paul states the positive and then the negative. Again, Paul introduces an exact quotation of the LXX from Ps 4:4 [MT & LXX 4:5]. There are two present imperatives, positive and negative. The first is ὀργίζω/ὀργίζομαι, meaning "to provoke anger, irritate,"[3] more often used in the passive and meaning "to be angry."[4] It used seventy-nine times in the LXX (sixty-one times in the canonical books) and all but two times (Job 12:6; Prov 16:3) it is in the passive form translating twelve Hebrew words meaning "to be angry." It refers

1. BDB 677; Johannes Horst, "μέλος," *TDNT* 4 (1967): 557–58.

2. Chrysostom *Eph* 4:25–27 (*PG* 62:100); cf. also Kohlgraf, *Die Ekklesiologie des Epheserbriefes in der Auslegung durch Johannes Chrysostomus*, 272–73.

3. Aristophanes *Vespae* 223, 404; Euripides *Helena* 1646; Plato *Phaedrus* 267c.

4. Aristophanes *Vespae* 431; Plato *Phaedrus* 267d; Thucydides 4.128.4.

to a person's anger twenty-two times (Gen 31:36; Exod 32:19; Ps 112:10 [LXX 111:10]; Dan 11:11) and God's thirty-nine times (Exod 22:24 [MT & LXX 22:23]; Judg 2:14; 2 Chr 29:8; Ps 2:12). Six times ὀργίζω is a translation of רָגַז, meaning in the Hitpael "to rage" (2 Kgs 19:28), in the Hiphil "to provoke, enrage" (Job 12:6 [Codex A]), and in the Qal "to quarrel" (Gen 45:24), "to tremble" (Exod 15:14; Ps 99:1 [LXX 98:1]; Prov 29:9),[1] and "to be angry" (Ps 4:4 [MT & LXX 4:5]), sometimes having the sense of trembling with anger.[2] In the NT this word occurs eight times, always in the passive and, with the exception of the dragon (Rev 12:17) and the nations (Rev 11:18), it always refers to a person's anger (Matt 5:22; 18:34; 22:7; Luke 14:21; 15:28; Eph 4:26). Since the word sometimes is used in reference to God's anger it cannot be said that anger is intrinsically evil. Hence, the next command is important. The imperative is from ἁμαρτάνω, meaning in classical Greek "to miss the mark" such as when throwing a spear[3] or "to miss" the way.[4] Generally it means "to fail to accomplish one's purpose, go wrong."[5] In the LXX it occurs 263 times and in the canonical books it appears 195 times where it translates eight Hebrew words but 170 times for חָטָא, which is used in Ps 4:5 [ET 4:4] with the meaning "to miss (a goal or way), go wrong, sin."[6] In the NT it is used forty-three times, always in the passive, seventeen times by Paul and only here in Ephesians. Although it is used to signify sin against humans (Matt 18:15, 21; Luke 17:3, 4; Acts 25:8) and God and humans (Luke 15:18, 21; 1 Cor 8:12), in most instances it refers to sin against God (e.g., Rom 2:12*bis*; 3:23; 5:12, 14, 16; 1 Cor 8:12*bis*; 1 John 1:10; 2:1*bis*). It has the same basic idea as ἁμαρτία studied earlier (Eph 1:7; 2:1) in that it denotes a conscious and deliberate false step as opposed to an inadvertent mistake.[7] In this context, however, the sin is against a person and/or God.

Over the years commentators have been puzzled by these commands.[8] Some have thought that the first imperative is a condition: "If you do get angry, be sure you do not sin."[9] But this view ignores the

1. BDB 919; G. Vanoni, "רָגַז *rāgaz*, etc.," *TWAT* 7 (1990): 327–30.

2. Peter C. Craigie, *Psalms 1–50*, WBC, ed. David A. Hubbard and Glenn W. Barker; Old Testament ed. John D. W. Watts, vol. 19 (Waco, Tex.: Word, 1983), 81.

3. Homer *Ilias* 5.287; 10.372.

4. Aristophanes *Plutus* 961.

5. Homer *Odyssea* 21.155; 11.511; Aeschylus *Agamemnon* 1194; Herodotus 1.207.

6. BDB 306–7; K. Koch, "חָטָא *chāṭāʾ*, etc.," *TDOT* 4 (1980): 309–19.

7. For a more thorough study of the word, see Gottfried Quell, Georg Bertram, Gustav Stählin, and Walter Grundmann, "ἁμαρτάνω, ἁμάρτημα, ἁμαρτία," *TDNT* 1 (1964): 267–316.

8. Wallace lists seven alternatives but then quickly narrows them down to either conditional or imperatival and discusses them in more detail (Daniel B. Wallace, "Ὀργίζεσθε in Ephesians 4:26: Command or Condition?" *Criswell Theological Review* 3 [spring 1989]: 353–72).

9. Chrysostom *Eph* 4:25–27 (*PG* 62:101); Theophylact *Eph* 4:26 (*PG* 124:1097); Oecumenius *Eph* 4:25–29 (*PG* 118:1229); Olshausen, 241; Schlier, 224 n. 3; Gaugler, 193;

coordinating conjunction which makes the two statements equal. Also, this view would require a conditional protasis (ἐὰν ὀργίζεσθε). Another theory suggests the first imperative is permissive and the second is jussive: "Be angry (because I cannot stop you or you cannot help it), but do not sin."[1] The problem with this view is that it is strange to have two present imperatives joined by a coordinating conjunction with two different senses (permissive and jussive). A further problem with the imperative "be angry" is that in verse 31 Paul instructs them to put away anger. Albeit, in verse 31 malicious anger is in question. This differs from the type of anger in the present verse, an anger without sin.

Therefore, it is best to accept both of these imperatives as commands, one as positive and the other as negative.[2] The negative particle (μή) puts emphasis on the second imperative.[3] This is understandable because it is more difficult not to sin than to have anger. One should not conclude, however, that the positive imperative means that Christians were required to be angry. The present tense of these imperatives probably does not indicate a continuous but an iterative or repeated action.[4]

Are these commands a contradiction of terms? First, it must be understood that Paul is quoting Ps 4:4 [MT & LXX 4:5]. This psalm is classified as an individual lament[5] in which the psalmist acknowledges God's past help and asks to be heard (v. 1). He then addresses his enemies, asking how long they will persecute him and reminding them that God hears his prayers (vv. 2–3). In the next verse, which is the one quoted in the present context, the psalmist instructs his enemies: "be angry but sin not." Because the Hebrew word has the connotation of trembling with anger, Craigie states, "The psalmist advises his adversaries to keep their rage within themselves, to maintain control of their actions and their evil words."[6] This may well have become a proverbial statement which Paul uses for the situation in Ephesus. They can be angry but not act out their anger sinfully. The reason they

---

Lincoln, 301; Best, 449; Robertson, *Grammar*, 949, 1023; Zyro, "Ephes. 4,26, ὀργίζεσθε καὶ μὴ ἁμαρτάνετε," *Theologische Studien und Kritiken* 14, no. 3 (1841): 685–90; Gustav Stählin, "ὀργή," *TDNT* 5 (1967): 421; James L. Boyer, "A Classification of Imperatives: A Statistical Study," *GTJ* 8 (spring 1987): 39–40; cf. also Schnackenburg, 207.

1. Theodoret *Eph* 4:26 (*PG* 82:540); Aquinas, chap. 4, lec. 8, vv. 25–27 (184–85); Hodge, 269–70; Alford, 3:125; Barth, 513; Winer, *Grammar*, 391–92; BDF §387 (1).

2. Eadie, 348–49; Ellicott, 105; Abbott, 139–40; Salmond, 345; Bruce, 361; O'Brien, 339; Wallace, "Ὀργίζεσθε in Ephesians 4:26," 358–72; Porter, *Verbal Aspect*, 352–53; Fanning, *Verbal Aspect*, 339; Wallace, *Greek Grammar*, 491–92.

3. Ellicott, 105.

4. MHT 1:125; cf. Wallace, *Greek Grammar*, 722.

5. Anderson, *The Book of Psalms*, 1:76; Craigie, *Psalms 1–50*, 79.

6. Craigie, *Psalms 1–50*, 81.

are not to sin is given in verses 26b–27—they are not to let it become a prolonged irritation and let the devil get hold of the believer.

Second, it is necessary to acknowledge that anger is not intrinsically sinful. As mentioned above, God expresses anger. What causes God to become angry? When wrong has been done against a person or against God himself. However, when God is angry, he is always in control of his anger. Unlike God, however, people have a tendency to allow anger to control them. Hence, the second command "do not sin" is necessary. This agrees with the concept of πραΰτης, "gentleness," discussed at 4:2 where a believer who is controlled by the Spirit is angry at the right time and never angry at the wrong time. For example, when someone in the body of believers has been wronged, it is correct for one to be angry but not to be consumed by that anger. It is noteworthy that in the Qumran community they were allowed to rebuke but never become angry (1QS 5:25–6:1).[1]

ὁ ἥλιος μὴ ἐπιδυέτω ἐπὶ [τῷ][2] **παροργισμῷ ὑμῶν,** "let not the sun go down on your irritation." This injunction sets a time frame in regards to anger. Apparently, this was a proverbial saying, for Plutarch mentions the Pythagorean custom that if led by anger into recrimination, the sun should never go down before the involved parties joined right hands, embraced one another, and were reconciled.[3] The noun παροργισμός is not found in classical literature and the verb form (παροργίζω) is rare, meaning "to provoke to anger, stir up anger."[4] The noun occurs only seven times in the LXX mostly in the active sense of provoking anger, as Manasseh did when he provoked the Lord (2 Kgs 23:26; cf. also 1 Kgs 15:30; 2 Kgs 19:3; Neh 9:18, 26; *Pss. Sol.* 8:9) and in the passive sense of an angry mood or God's anger (Jer 21:5).[5] The corresponding verb occurs fifty-seven times in the LXX (forty-six times in the canonical books) and twenty-eight times it translates the Hiphil of כָּעַס, meaning "to irritate, provoke to anger."[6] In the NT the noun appears only here and is used in the passive sense, that is, a mood of anger. The verbal form is found only twice (Rom 10:19; Eph 6:4) and means "to anger, irritate." It seems that the prepositional prefix (παρα-) intensifies

1. Cf. J. Gnilka, "Paränetische Traditionen im Epheserbrief," in *Mélanges Bibliques en Hommage au R. P. Béda Rigaux*, ed. Albert Descamps and R. P. André de Halleux (Gembloux: Duculot, 1970), 403.

2. This article τῷ is found in ℵ^{2} D F G Ψ 1739^{c} 1881 𝔐 Clement but is omitted from 𝔓^{49} ℵ* A B 1739* and NA^{25}. Its omission is found only in the Alexandrian text whereas its inclusion is found in the Western and Byzantine texts and partially in the Alexandrian text. The first reading is preferred because of the geographical spread and the good genealogical relationships within those texts.

3. Plutarch *Moralia: De fraterno amore* 17 §488c.

4. Aristotle *Athenaion politeia* 34.1; Theophrastus *Historica Plantarum* 9.16.6; possibly Strabo 7.2.1.

5. Cf. BAGD 629.

6. BDB 495; N. Lohfink, "כָּעַס *kāʿas*; כַּעַס *kaʿas*," *TDOT* 7 (1995): 283–88.

this word. Whereas ὀργή is the disposition of anger, παροργισμός is provocation, exasperation, violent anger[1] or a "state of being intensely provoked."[2] A good rendering is "festering anger, provocation, or irritation."

When anger festers for long periods of time it leads to angry outbursts which causes one to sin. The present prohibition (μὴ ἐπιδυέτω) suggests that one is not to make a practice of harboring anger overnight.[3] It is essential to keep short accounts of anger, to settle the problem before another day begins. "The day of anger should be the day of reconciliation."[4] What then, about a situation where two people want to take this injunction literally by settling their disagreement before going to bed but it is 4 A.M. before their differences are resolved? Actually though they did not fulfill the words literally because the sun had already set, they fulfilled the spirit of the injunction. Fuller concurs, stating that the apostle's proverbial meaning takes precedent to his words.[5]

4:27. μηδὲ δίδοτε τόπον τῷ διαβόλῳ, "nor do you give opportunity to the devil." Paul now declares the danger of prolonged anger. The negative disjunctive conjunction μηδέ continues the preceding negation μή, and has the meaning "and not, but not, nor."[6] In the present context "nor" fits best. The present imperative δίδοτε with the negative particle may indicate that the action is ongoing and must be stopped or may be used in an iterative sense.[7] The noun τόπος literally means "place" but can be rendered "possibility, opportunity, chance" (cf. Acts 25:16).[8] "Opportunity" gives the best sense in this text.

The term διάβολος is used infrequently in classical literature and as a substantive it means "slanderer."[9] Only in biblical literature is this word used with some frequency. In the LXX it occurs twenty-two times (twenty times in the canonical books): once it translates צַר (Esth 7:4) and once צֹרֵר (Esth 8:1) meaning "adversary, foe";[10] and eighteen times for שָׂטָן, rendered as "Satan, adversary,"[11] with the exception of Ps 109:6 [LXX 108:6]) where it means "accuser." Satan is the great enemy of the people of God. It is he who incited David to number the people (1 Chr 21:1), caused the sufferings of

1. Salmond, 346.
2. BDAG 780.
3. Fanning, *Verbal Aspect*, 337, 339.
4. Eadie, 349.
5. Thomas Fuller cited by Eadie, 349 n. 1.
6. BAGD 517; BDAG 647; cf. MHT 3:340; BDF §445; Robertson, *Grammar*, 1185.
7. Fanning, *Verbal Aspect*, 335–36.
8. BAGD 823; BDAG 1012.
9. Aristotle *Topica* 4.5 §126a.31–32; Aristophanes *Equites* 44–45; cf. Plutarch *Moralia: Quaestionum convivalium* 8.7.2 §727d.
10. BDB 865; Werner Foerster, "διάβολος," *TDNT* 2 (1964): 72.
11. BDB 966; K. Nielsen, "שָׂטָן *śāṭān*," *TWAT* 7 (1990): 745–51; Foerster, *TDNT* 2 (1964): 72.

Job (Job 1:6–12; 2:1–7), and accused Joshua the high priest (Zech 3:1–2). As an adversary he seduces people to turn against God. This term is used thirty-seven times in the NT, eight times by Paul, twice in Ephesians (4:27; 6:11). Only three times is it in the plural referring to people who are slanderers (1 Tim 3:11; 2 Tim 3:3; Titus 2:3). Otherwise, it is used once of a human being when Jesus used it with reference to Judas (John 6:70). The other thirty-three times it is rendered "the devil" (cf. 1 Tim 3:7; 2 Tim 2:26). Jesus stated that the devil has nothing to do with the truth because there is no truth in him; he lies because he is the father of lies (John 8:44). John identifies the devil as Satan who is the deceiver of the whole world (Rev 12:9; 20:2). Such a characteristic clearly defines why Paul gave this command.

This is why Paul does not want believers to give the devil an opportunity by their anger. The devil twists and distorts the truth. If there is no quick restoration between parties, further anger mounts and dissension and revenge often result. Paul states in Rom 12:19 that the believer is not to avenge himself or herself but rather allow the wrath of God to avenge wrong-doing. It is interesting to note that in Ephesians Paul literally says, "you do not give place to the devil" (μηδὲ δίδοτε τόπον τῷ διαβόλῳ), but in Rom 12:19 he literally says, "you give place to the wrath [God's]" (δότε τόπον τῃ ὀργῇ). Since God's wrath is just and always under his control, justice will be meted out in righteousness and truth. On the other hand, Jas 1:20 points out that a person's anger does not work the righteousness of God.

The designation διάβολος is used by Paul only in Ephesians and the Pastorals. Since the term σατανᾶς "Satan" is used in Paul's undisputed letters, some have questioned the authenticity of Ephesians. However, van Roon rightly shows how spurious that objection is by noting that the term "Satan" is used infrequently by Paul and it is used in both the undisputed letters (cf. Rom 16:20; 1 Cor 5:5; 7:5) and Pastorals (cf. 1 Tim 1:20; 5:15).[1] Furthermore, Paul would have been well acquainted with the frequent use of διάβολος in the LXX. This is especially true since he had just quoted in verse 25 from Zech 8:16 and διάβολος is found three times only a few chapters earlier (3:1–2). In addition, in the present context the term διάβολος is fitting because the devil is a slanderer who wants to see divisiveness in the body, which is caused by festering anger.

In conclusion, the imperatives in verses 26–27 are to be angry and to abstain from sin. This is accomplished by settling issues quickly so as to thwart the devil who will attempt to manipulate the situation for his purposes. In this passage the devil does not cause the anger but simply would like to use it as an opportunity to work evil.[2]

1. Van Roon, *The Authenticity of Ephesians*, 174.
2. Wink, *Unmasking the Powers*, 20–21.

(3) Do Not Steal But Work to Give to Needy (4:28)

Paul now gives the third specific application. He again follows the pattern introduced in verse 25: first, a negative injunction; second, a positive command; and third, the reason for the positive command.

Text: 4:28. ὁ κλέπτων μηκέτι κλεπτέτω, μᾶλλον δὲ κοπιάτω ἐργαζόμενος ταῖς [ἰδίαις] χερσὶν τὸ ἀγαθόν, ἵνα ἔχῃ μεταδιδόναι τῷ χρείαν ἔχοντι.

Translation: 4:28. "Let the stealer no longer steal, but rather let him labor working with his own hands that which is good, in order that he might share with the one who has need."

Commentary: 4:28. ὁ κλέπτων μηκέτι κλεπτέτω, "Let the stealer no longer steal." There is an abrupt change from the previous verse with no connecting conjunction between the plural and the singular. The translation of the present active participle ὁ κλέπτων is debated among grammarians. Some suggest an iterative action that had occurred in the past and would translate it "the one who used to steal" or "he who stole."[1] However, it is more likely that the present participle denotes action rather than time; thus, it "is not 'he who stole' or 'he who steals,' but simply 'the stealer,' differing from ὁ κλέπτης 'the thief' only in being more closely associated with the verb κλεπτέτω which is coming."[2] The present imperative with a prohibition seems to indicate that the action is going on and it needs to stop.[3] The adverb μηκέτι, "no longer," adds emphasis to this idea.

To whom is Paul referring? Were these professional thieves, slaves stealing from their masters, or Christians stealing from fellow believers? Best gives a good analysis of the problem. He discounts slaves as thieves because their situation would not be conducive to such activity. Furthermore, they have their own exhortation later (6:5–9). Nor was it likely that fellow believers were stealing from one another. Some might think this to be the case due to the reprimand given to them about lying and anger (vv. 25–27). More likely it was laborers who stole the things they handled or shopkeepers who cheated the customers. Best rightly maintains that it helps to understand the milieu of Paul's day. When a laborer was out of work there was no welfare system to help him or her nor would most have had enough wages to be able to save for times of unemployment. At such times many were forced to steal to maintain themselves and their families. Therefore, the injunction against theft struck at a real problem of that day.[4] The present tense of the imperative seems to focus on the activity that was ongoing even among Christians. However, Paul insisted

1. BDF §§275 (6); 339 (3); Zerwick, *Biblical Greek* §274; Moule, *Idiom Book*, 206.

2. MHT 1:127; 3:151, cf. 81; cf. Robertson, *Grammar*, 892, 1116; Winer, *Grammar*, 444; Porter, *Verbal Aspect*, 379; Fanning, *Verbal Aspect*, 411–12.

3. Wallace, *Greek Grammar*, 722.

4. E. A. Best, "Ephesians 4:28: Thieves in the Church," *IBS* 14 (January 1992): 2–9.

that the one who is characterized by stealing must steal no longer because the person has put off the old person and its conduct and put on the new person and with its lifestyle. He now proceeds to define this new conduct.

μᾶλλον δὲ κοπιάτω, "but rather let him labor." Having stated the negative injunction, Paul now declares the positive command. The stark contrast from the negative is marked by μᾶλλον δέ, which could be translated "but instead" or, as above, "but rather." The imperative κοπιάτω, from κοπιάω, is an ingressive-progressive present, having the force to begin and continue to labor in contrast to beginning and continuing not to steal.[1] In classical literature κοπιάω had the idea "to be tired, grow weary."[2] Later, the same sense "to tire"[3] referred specifically to warfare but could also allude to great efforts or "to wear out in work."[4] In the LXX it occurs fifty times and in the canonical books it appears thirty-six times where it translates fourteen Hebrew words with sixteen occurrences for יָגַע meaning "to grow or be weary" (Deut 25:18; Isa 40:28, 30, 31), "to toil, labor" (Josh 24:13; Isa 49:4; 65:23), or "to be/grow weary" from toil or exertion (2 Sam 23:10; Pss 6:6 [MT & LXX 6:7]; 69:3 [MT 69:4; LXX 68:4]; Isa 57:10).[5] In the NT there are twenty-three instances of this word, fourteen times in Paul, and only here in Ephesians. Again it is used of being tired from a journey (John 4:6) or of endurance without weariness (Rev 2:3). Further, it is used of hard work, toil, physical struggle (Matt 6:28; Luke 5:5; Rom 16:6, 12; 2 Tim 2:6) and spiritual exertion (John 4:38; Gal 4:11; Phil 2:16; Col 1:29; 1 Tim 4:10; 5:17). The point is that the labor exerted is exhausting. In this context the stealer used to obtain things with little effort, but with the acquisition of the new person all things are acquired with labor that requires much effort.

ἐργαζόμενος ταῖς [ἰδίαις] χερσὶν τὸ ἀγαθόν,[6] "working with his

1. Wallace, *Greek Grammar*, 722.

2. Aristophanes *Thesmophoriazusae* 795; *Aves* 735.

3. Josephus *B.J.* 6.2.6 (142).

4. Philo *De Cherubim* 12 §41; *Mut*. 44 §254.

5. BDB 388; G. F. Hasel, "יָגַע *yāg̱aʿ*, etc." *TDOT* 5 (1986): 385–93.

6. There are several variants with the following words ταῖς ἰδίαις χερσὶν τὸ ἀγαθόν. Some manuscripts have a different order of words. The first order of words has two versions: (1) τὸ ἀγαθὸν ταῖς ἰδίαις χερσίν, translated "working the good with his own hands," found in 436 1912 1962 *Byz*^{pt} [K] *l* 60 *l* 422 geo^{2} Theodore^{lat} is not acceptable because of such a lack of manuscripts; and (2) τὸ ἀγαθὸν ταῖς χερσίν, leaving out ἰδίαις, is found in Ψ 424* 1852 2200 *Byz*^{pt} [L] *Lect* Origen Basil$^{1/3}$ Chrysostom Theodoret^{lem}, translated "working the good with the hands," again is unacceptable because of so few manuscripts. The reason for the second order is that the object is closer to the participle as in Rom 2:10. The second order of words has four versions: (1) ταῖς ἰδίαις χερσὶν appears in *l* 597 (*l* 599 omits ταῖς) (cop^{samss} Tertullian *omit* ἰδίαις) (cop^{sams}) and is an unacceptable reading because of the paucity of manuscripts. (2) τὸ ἀγαθόν, "working the good," is found in P 6 33 424^{c} 1739 1881 Clement Gregory-Nyssa Didymus Pelagius^{ms} Speculum, but is unacceptable because of the lack of manuscript support; (3) ταῖς χερσὶν τὸ ἀγαθόν

own hands that which is good." The participle describes the means[1] or manner of labor. The term ἐργάζομαι is the basic word for laboring or working in contrast to idleness or useless busyness.[2] The following datives are instrumental, indicating that the work is to be done with one's own hands. In other places Paul uses this idea of working with one's own hands as the correct conduct for believers (1 Cor 4:12; 1 Thess 4:11) of which he was a good example (Acts 20:34).[3] This does not necessarily imply that only manual work is valid, but Paul is using this expression as the normal portrayal of hard work for gain as opposed to gaining by stealing. It parallels with the idea that the robber uses his hands to gain something that is not rightfully his and now is to use his hands to obtain honest gain.

The object of the work is τὸ ἀγαθόν, "the good." In Eph 2:10 ἀγαθός denotes that good which is moral as well as beneficial. Here refers to beneficial good.[4] The robber had used his hands to work injury to others but now he is to work that which is good. Earlier Paul stated that the believer is God's workmanship, having been created for good works (2:10). The present context is consistent with this teaching in that the new person in Christ is not to steal but work the good for which he has been designed. The reason for this is stated next.

ἵνα ἔχῃ μεταδιδόναι τῷ χρείαν ἔχοντι, "in order that he might share with the one who has need." The purpose (ἵνα) for work is not self-indulgence but to benefit those who are in need. The infinitive is from μεταδίδωμι and means "to give part of, to give a share," as Greek cities shared in the use of a temple or shared in the benefits of the constitution.[5] It can also mean "to communicate," which is the sharing of information.[6] This word is used seven times in the LXX (only twice in the canonical books) meaning "to impart" (Job 31:17; Prov 11:26; Wis 7:13; 2 Macc 1:35; Bar 6:27) or "to communicate" (Tob 7:10; 2 Macc 8:12). In the NT the word appears five times, four times

---

leaving out ἰδίαις, thus translated "working with the hands the good," is found in 𝔓$^{46, 49vid}$ ℵ^{2} B it$^{ar, o}$ vg$^{ww, st}$ Ambrosiaster Pelagius but again this has too few good manuscripts to support it, all basically from the Alexandrian text; and (4) ταῖς ἰδίαις χερσὶν τὸ ἀγαθόν, translated "working with his own hands the good," is found in ℵ* A D F G 075 0150 81 104 256 263 365 459 1175 1241 1319 1573 2127 2464 *l* 596 it$^{b, d, f, (g), mon}$ vg^{cl} (cop$^{sa^{ms}, bo}$) arm (eth) geo^{1} slav Basil$^{2/3}$ Victorinus-Rome Jerome Augustine. This is the most acceptable reading because of the date and character of the manuscripts as well as the geographical spread. This order of the reading is far better than the first order when all the manuscripts are gathered in their respective orders.

1. Wallace, *Greek Grammar*, 630.

2. Bertram, *TDNT* 2 (1964): 635.

3. Bruce, 362.

4. W. D. Morris, "Ephesians iv. 28," *ExpTim* 41 (February 1930): 237, thinks the abstract τὸ ἀγαθόν, "the good," was originally the concrete τὸ ἄρτον, "the bread," but this lacks sufficient textual evidence.

5. Herodotus 1.143; 4.145; cf. Aristotle *Politica* 5.5.9 §1306a.25.

6. Polybius 29.27.4; 38.8.1.

in Paul, only here in Ephesians. It can be used of sharing spiritual things, as when Paul shared a spiritual gift to strengthen the Romans (Rom 1:11) or of sharing the gospel (1 Thess 2:8). Also, it can be used of sharing material goods. For example, a person with two coats is to share with one who has no coat (Luke 3:11; cf. also Rom 12:8). In the present context Paul is talking about sharing materially the good that has been gained with hard labor. He uses this term instead of δίδωμι, "to give," in order to avoid the idea that all that is earned must be given to others, but rather some earned good must be shared with others. This is a mean between two extremes. One is neither to hoard nor recklessly give all away. Next, Paul is specific about with whom goods should be shared.

The noun χρεία has the sense of need, necessity, lack, want.[1] It occurs fifty-four times in the LXX but only nine times in the canonical books. For example, it refers to the need of timber from Lebanon for the temple (2 Chr 2:16 [MT & LXX 2:15]), to Artaxerxes who supplied Ezra with what was lacking for the temple (Ezra 7:20), to a fool who has no need of wisdom (Prov 18:2), to the Medes who lacked no gold (Isa 13:17), and to Jeconiah and Moab who were viewed as discarded broken vessels, which no one needed or wanted (Jer 22:28; 48:38 [LXX 31:38]). In the NT it occurs forty-nine times, fourteen times in Paul, including here and the next verse. It is used of the disciples who are enjoined to pray to the Father for their needs (Matt 6:8), of the sick who need a physican (Matt 9:12 = Mark 2:17 = Luke 5:31), of David's need when he was hungry (Mark 2:25), and of the distribution of goods for those who lacked or had needs (Acts 2:45; 4:35).[2] Hence, working with his own hands, the believer is to share beneficial material goods with ones who have needs.[3]

The believer, then, is to sense real need and then share the fruit of diligent labor. In this instance as in other NT passages (Acts 2:45; 4:35; Rom 15:25–28; 1 Cor 16:1–4), those who benefit by such sharing are fellow believers. This is in agreement with verse 25 where the neighbors are considered fellow believers because they are members of one another. It does not mean that Christians are never to help the needy who may not be believers but their primary responsibility is to those who are of the household of faith. This will demonstrate a love for one another and the world will know that they are his disciples (John 13:35).

In conclusion, then, the stealer can no longer steal because he has put on the new person. The stealing must cease and diligent work

1. Aeschylus *Septem contra Thebas* 287; *Prometheus Vinctus* 481; Sophocles *Oedipus Tyrannus* 1443.

2. For further study of this word, see William L. Lane, "Want [χρεία]," *NIDNTT* 3 (1978): 956–58.

3. Cf. Joüon, "Notes philologiques sur quelques versets de l'Épître aux Éphésiens," 460.

must ensue in order to share with those in the community of believers who have real needs. The robber had taken with his hands what was not earned or rightfully his to the detriment of the one from whom he stole to use for his self-indulgence. Conversely, a believer is to work diligently with his or her hands to gain what is good for the purpose of sharing with those who have need. Work then has many benefits: it provides for a person's material needs, it provides something useful to do (something that is beneficial to oneself and others), and enables one to materially help others who are in need. If the scenario of laborers out of work were forced to steal is correct, then those within the believing community would need to trust the Lord to provide through the community of believers who were to share their material goods.

(4) Do Not Use Corrupt Words But Edify with Words (4:29–30)

Having stated how interaction between the Ephesian believers should embrace sharing rather than stealing, Paul now exhorts how they should verbally interact with each other. In verse 25 Paul exhorted believers not to lie and now he exhorts them not use unwholesome words.

Text: 4:29. πᾶς λόγος σαπρὸς ἐκ τοῦ στόματος ὑμῶν μὴ ἐκπορευέσθω, ἀλλὰ εἴ τις ἀγαθὸς πρὸς οἰκοδομὴν τῆς χρείας, ἵνα δῷ χάριν τοῖς ἀκούουσιν. **4:30.** καὶ μὴ λυπεῖτε τὸ πνεῦμα τὸ ἅγιον τοῦ θεοῦ, ἐν ᾧ ἐσφραγίσθητε εἰς ἡμέραν ἀπολυτρώσεως.

Translation: 4:29. "Let no unwholesome word come out of your mouths, but whatever is beneficial for the building up of that which is lacking, in order that it might give grace to those who hear. **4:30.** And do not grieve the Holy Spirit of God, by whom you were sealed for the day of redemption."

Commentary: 4:29. πᾶς λόγος σαπρὸς ἐκ τοῦ στόματος ὑμῶν μὴ ἐκπορευέσθω, "Let no unwholesome word come out of your mouths." Instead of the normal Greek form οὐδείς, Paul uses the Semitic πᾶς . . . μή to negate the verb.[1] Since πᾶς is before an anarthrous substantive, it means "every, each"[2] word that comes from the mouth is to be wholesome. Paul may well have wanted to stress "every word" as opposed to "some" important words. The adjective σαπρός is used of rotten wood,[3] withered flowers,[4] and rancid fish.[5] It generally refers to things or people who are worn out or useless[6] or that which is of little

1. Robertson, *Grammar*, 753; MHT 2:434; 3:196; 4:84; Winer, *Grammar*, 216, 728; Zerwick, *Biblical Greek* §446.

2. BAGD 631; BDAG 783; BDF §275 (3).

3. Aristophanes *Equites* 918.

4. Demosthenes *Orationes* 22.70.

5. Aristophanes *Acharnenses* 1101.

6. Aristophanes *Plutus* 323; *Pax* 698; *Ecclesiazusae* 884.

worth.[1] There is no occurrence of this word in the LXX but it continued to have the same meaning in the Hellenistic period.[2] In the NT it occurs eight times, used only here by Paul, the rest in Matthew and Luke. For example, it refers to worthless or withered trees that produce evil or worthless fruit (Matt 7:17–18 = Luke 6:43; Matt 12:33*bis*) and of bad or worthless fish (Matt 13:48). In the present context the word could not be rendered "rotten" but it could be "foul, putrid." However, because of the immediate following words the implication appears to go beyond just foul language. Since all words are to build up fellow believers, it may well be that the adjective σαπρός has the idea of "unprofitable"[3] and could be translated "unwholesome" (NASB, NIV). Pfitzner thinks it can be traced back to Jesus when he said that what comes out of person's mouth defiles him or her (Matt 15:11).[4] Although Paul is exhorting all believers, he uses the singular for "mouth," which is a Semitic distributive singular relating to each person in a group.[5] The prohibition in the form of the present imperative has the force of cessation of activity in progress,[6] hence, believers are enjoined to stop unwholesome words from proceeding out of their mouths.

ἀλλὰ εἴ τις ἀγαθὸς πρὸς οἰκοδομὴν τῆς χρείας,[7] "but whatever is beneficial for the building up of that which is lacking." Again, Paul follows the negative command with a positive one. The construction is somewhat different but the meaning is clear. Literally it would be translated, "but if there be any good [word] for the building up of the need." The conditional conjunction with the indefinite pronoun (εἴ τις) is nearly equivalent to the indefinite relative pronoun (ὅστις) and can be translated "everything that" or "whatever."[8] Therefore, it can be rendered, "but whatever is beneficial for the building up of that which is lacking." In other words, beneficial words should be used for the

1. Otto Bauernfeind, "σαπρός, σήπω," *TDNT* 7 (1971): 96.

2. MM 569.

3. Bauernfeind, *TDNT* 7 (1971): 97.

4. Victor C. Pfitzner, "The School of Jesus: Jesus-Traditions in Pauline Parenesis," *Lutheran Theological Journal* 13 (May 1979): 31.

5. Cf. MHT 3:25; 4:84, 92.

6. Wallace, *Greek Grammar*, 724.

7. The reading χρείας appears in $\mathfrak{P}^{46}$ ℵ A B D^{2} I^{vid} Ψ 075 6 33 81 104 256 263 365 424 436 459 1175 1241 1319 1573 1739 1852 1881 1912 1962 2127 2200 2464 *Byz* [K L P] *Lect* vg$^{ww, st}$ syr$^{(p), h, pal}$ cop$^{sa, bo}$ arm eth geo slav Clement Origen Chrysostom Theodore^{lat} Theodoret Jerome. In place of χρείας, there is the reading πίστεως found in D* F G it$^{ar, b, d, mon, o}$ vg^{cl} Basil Gregory-Nyssa Tertullian Cyprian Victorinus-Rome Ambrosiaster Chromatius Latin mss$^{acc. to Jerome}$ Pelagius Speculum. This alternative reading is not acceptable because it is found in only the Western text-type. The manuscripts of the first reading are early in date and are good in character, genealogical relationships, and geographical distribution.

8. MHT 3:321; Robertson, *Grammar*, 956; BAGD 220; BDAG 279; cf. Salmond, 347; Robinson, 193.

purpose of building up a needy individual or a needy body of believers. The word ἀγαθός, "good," was discussed at verse 28 where we concluded that it meant moral and beneficial good, the opposite of κακός, "bad, evil, injurious" (cf. Luke 16:25; Acts 28:5; Rom 1:30; 2:9; 3:8; 7:19, 21; 12:17, 21; 13:10; 14:20; 1 Thess 5:15; Jas 3:8; 1 Pet 3:9; Rev 16:2). It is important to note that the word is singular. The emphasis throughout this verse is that every word is to be accounted for. Therefore, any word that comes out of a believer's mouth should be good and not evil which causes injury. The preposition πρός, "for," could express result but probably, in this case, expresses purpose.[1] The word οἰκοδομή was discussed at 2:21 where we concluded that it referred to a building or to the act of building and was used in conjunction with building up the animate body of Christ. Also, in 4:12 and 16 reference is made to the organism of the body of Christ. Again, in the present verse, it seems to refer to the building up of the body of believers because of the plural "those who hear" in the final clause. The following word χρεία is identified in the immediately preceding verse as denoting need, lack, or want. The genitive is difficult to classify.[2] Some think it is a genitive of reference meaning "for the edification with reference to the need."[3] Others consider it an objective genitive meaning "for the edification applied to the need" or "for the edification of the need"[4] Finally, some consider it a genitive of substance or quality meaning "for the building up of that which is lacking."[5] The last two categories are virtually the same. Thus, the purpose of our speech is to supply that which is lacking in other believers' lives by the utterance of beneficial words, thus contributing to the spiritual growth of the body.[6]

ἵνα δῷ χάριν τοῖς ἀκούουσιν, "in order that it might give grace to those who hear." Having stated both the negative and positive commands, Paul further explains that the purpose (ἵνα) of obedience to the positive commands is to give grace to those who hear. The word "grace" was discussed at 1:2 where we concluded it to be the bestowment of unmerited favor and/or enablement. In the present context it seems that the emphasis is on enablement. The body of believers has many lacks or needs, and beneficial words contribute to their individual growth and enable them to fill up that lack or need among them.[7] Pfitzner thinks that this may be reminiscent of Jesus' own speaking where the people marveled at his gracious words that proceeded from

1. MHT 3:275; cf. Robertson, *Grammar*, 626.
2. For a brief discussion of this, see Pfammatter, *Die Kirche als Bau*, 115.
3. Ellicott, 108.
4. Alford, 3:126; Eadie, 353; Meyer, 257; Abbott, 143; Salmond, 347.
5. Schlier, 226; Gaugler, 195; Barth, 518–19; Sellin, "Über einige ungewöhnliche Genitive im Epheserbrief," 102–3.
6. Cf. Vielhauer, *Oikodome*, 143–44.
7. Pfammatter, *Die Kirche als Bau*, 115–16.

his mouth (Luke 4:22).[1] At any rate, he is indeed our model in this matter.

In conclusion, Paul states that believers are accountable for what they say. In fact every word is accountable. Care must be taken that each word is not useless or unprofitable but is beneficial for the building up of the body. While the preceding verse dealt with the physical needs of believers, this verse speaks to their spiritual needs.

4:30. καὶ μὴ[2] λυπεῖτε τὸ πνεῦμα τὸ ἅγιον τοῦ θεοῦ, "And do not grieve the Holy Spirit of God." The coordinating conjunction καί is the first in this section, which would suggest that this is not a new and separate injunction but is to be added to the last exhortation. It could be linked ad sensum to the immediately preceding purpose clause so that it would be a second motivation for speaking that which is beneficial. However, it is better rendered as a coordinate to the negative imperative in the previous verse. Therefore, it would read, "let no unwholesome words come from your mouths . . . and do not grieve the Holy Spirit of God." Both imperatives are in the present tense which portrays the action as an ongoing process.[3]

The word λυπέω has the basic idea of grief or sorrow.[4] In the LXX it occurs sixty-three times (thirty-one times in the canonical books) where it translates twelve Hebrew words. The following examples illustrate its usage. Joseph told his brothers not to be distressed or grieved for what they had done to him (Gen 45:5). David grieved over his son Absalom (2 Sam 19:2 [MT & LXX 19:3]), Elisha was distressed with King Joash (2 Kgs 13:19), Haman grieved that he honored Mordecai (Esth 6:12), and songs are sung to a grieving heart (Prov 25:20). It is used twenty-six times in the NT, fifteen times by Paul, and only here in Ephesians. It is used when Herod Antipas grieved because of the promise he had made to Salome (Matt 14:9), when the disciples were distressed or grieved over Jesus' announcement of his death (Matt 17:23), when the rich young ruler went from Jesus grieving because he was not willing to sell all his goods (Matt 19:22), and when Paul caused the Corinthians grief or sorrow (2 Cor 2:2–5; 7:8–11). This basic idea of grief, pain, sorrow, and distress has not changed over the years.[5]

Here Paul enjoins believers not to grieve the Holy Spirit. The Holy Spirit has been mentioned before in this letter but this verse, for the first time, uses the full title, the Holy Spirit of God (τὸ πνεῦμα τὸ ἅγιον

1. Pfitzner, "The School of Jesus," 31.

2. The negative particle μή is omitted only by 𝔓[46] and should not be seriously considered as a genuine reading.

3. Wallace, *Greek Grammar*, 716–17.

4. Hesoid *Opera et Dies* 401; Sophocles *Ajax* 554, 589; Euripedes *Iphigenia Aulidensis* 31–32.

5. For a more detailed study, see Rudolf Bultmann, "λύπη κτλ." *TDNT* 4 (1967): 313–24; L&N §25.275.

τοῦ θεοῦ). The genitive could be possessive or attributive, and thus, "God's Holy Spirit." If the Holy Spirit can be grieved, it must follow that he is a person. An inanimate object cannot grieve. But what does it mean to grieve him? Schlier suggests that one should not grieve the spirit of joy that results from being a Christian (since we are his workmanship).[1] However, the reference is not to the disposition of the believer, but to the sensitivity of the Holy Spirit. Therefore, it is similar to the situation in Isa 63:10 where the people rebelled against God and grieved the Holy Spirit.[2] In the NT, Ananias and Sapphira were put to death because they tested the Spirit of God by lying to him (Acts 5:1–10). To a certain extent, this parallels the Qumran teaching that the holy spirit of man (not God's) is defiled by their blaspheming tongues (CD 5:11–12; 7:4). In the present context then, unwholesome words are forbidden for two reasons: first, they impede spiritual growth of fellow believers; second, they grieve the Holy Spirit.

ἐν ᾧ ἐσφραγίσθητε εἰς ἡμέραν ἀπολυτρώσεως, "by whom you were sealed for the day of redemption." The preposition with the relative pronoun (ἐν ᾧ) could speak of the sphere in which we were sealed[3] but more likely refers to the instrument with which we were sealed (cf. 1:13).[4] As in 1:13 the verb "to seal" is aorist passive showing that believers are the recipients of the sealing. We further concluded in 1:13 that it primarily denotes ownership. We belong to God. Kirby's suggestion that the sealing refers to baptism (along with 1:13)[5] is foreign to the context and to the whole NT.

The last prepositional phrase denotes the period of time for which believers are sealed. As in 1:14 the preposition εἰς may denote purpose, that is, "we were sealed for the day of redemption,"[6] but a reference to time is more likely, namely, "we were sealed until or with a view to the day of redemption."[7] These two concepts are closely related, for if believers were sealed for the purpose of the day of redemption which is still future, then they are sealed until that day. The following genitive ἀπολυτρώσεως, "redemption," could be a temporal

1. Schlier, 227–28.

2. Gordon D. Fee, "Some Exegetical and Theological Reflections on Ephesians 4.30 and Pauline Pneumatology," in *Spirit and Renewal: Essays in Honor of J. Rodman Williams*, ed. Mark W. Wilson, Journal of Pentecostal Theology Supplemental Series, ed. John Christopher Thomas, Rick D. Moore, and Steven J. Land, no. 5 (Sheffield: Sheffield Academic Press, 1994), 131–34, 144; This reprinted in idem, *To What End Exegesis? Essays Textual, Exegetical, and Theological* (Grand Rapids: Eerdmans; Vancouver, BC: Regent College Publishing, 2001), 264–66, 275; cf. idem, *God's Empowering Presence*, 713–15; Moritz, *A Profound Mystery*, 92–93.

3. Alford, 3:126; Ellicott, 109; Salmond, 345.

4. Barth, 521; Bruce, 363–64.

5. Kirby, *Ephesians, Baptism and Pentecost*, 153.

6. Ellicott, 109

7. Eadie, 356; Abbott, 144; Salmond, 348; Winer, *Grammar*, 494; Kennedy, "St. Paul's Conception of the Spirit as a Pledge," 279.

genitive, the time of redemption,[1] but more likely it is a descriptive or characteristic genitive or a genitive of quality; hence, the day is characterized by redemption.[2] The redemption mentioned here is the same as the one in 1:14. We suggested that there are two phases in redemption: the first is the one that sets believers free from sin and its obligation; and the second is the one that occurs in the eschatological future when Christ comes for the saints, setting believers free from the presence of sin.[3] The present context has reference to the final phase of redemption which in 1:14 is described as the redemption of the purchased possession.[4] Lincoln has observed that the phrase "day of redemption" is unique to Ephesians and agrees that it most likely refers to the final day of salvation and judgment. Paul expresses it elsewhere as "the day of the Lord" (1 Thess 5:2; 2 Thess 2:2; 1 Cor 1:8; 5:5; 2 Cor 1:14) or "the day of Christ" (Phil 1:6, 10; 2:16).[5] It is a day to which believers look forward.

In conclusion, verse 30 revolves around the person of the Holy Spirit. Believers are reminded that he has sealed them for the day of redemption. They are warned against the use of worthless words because they not only hurt the body of Christ but also grieve the Holy Spirit.

(5) Do Not Be Malicious But Edify in Action (4:31–32)

The last exhortation in this section lists vices for believers to put away followed by three positive injunctions, all of which encompass the conduct of the new person and include every area of life.

Text: 4:31. πᾶσα πικρία καὶ θυμὸς καὶ ὀργὴ καὶ κραυγὴ καὶ βλασφημία ἀρθήτω ἀφ' ὑμῶν σὺν πάσῃ κακίᾳ. **4:32.** γίνεσθε [δὲ] εἰς ἀλλήλους χρηστοί, εὔσπλαγχνοι, χαριζόμενοι ἑαυτοῖς, καθὼς καὶ ὁ θεὸς ἐν Χριστῷ ἐχαρίσατο ἡμῖν.

Translation: 4:31. "Let every kind of bitterness and anger and wrath and shouting and abusive speech together with every kind of malice be put away from you. **4:32.** But become kind to one another, compassionate, being gracious to one another, just as also God in Christ was gracious to us."

Commentary: 4:31. πᾶσα πικρία, "[Let] every kind of bitterness." This is the first in the list of negative attributes that a believer is to put away. Again, the adjective πᾶς with anarthrous singular nouns refers to everything belonging to the class indicated by the noun (here, the

1. Eadie, 356.

2. HS §166b; Wallace, *Greek Grammar*, 81.

3. Lona, *Die Eschatologie im Kolosser- und Epheserbrief*, 423–24; Fee, "Some Exegetical and Theological Reflections on Ephesians 4.30 and Pauline Pneumatology," 137, 139–40; idem, *To What End Exegesis?* 269, 271–72; idem, *God's Empowering Presence*, 716–17.

4. *Contra* Lindemann, *Aufhebung*, 231–32.

5. Lincoln, 307.

following five nouns) and is thus translated "all sorts of, every kind of, every form of."[1]

The first noun πικρία is derived from the adjective πικρός that is used of a "pointed" or "sharp" arrow[2] and, with reference to the senses, is rendered "sharp" or "bitter" taste,[3] "pungent" smell,[4] a "sharp" or "penetrating" pain,[5] or "piercing" sound.[6] The noun πικρία can refer to a bitter taste of plants[7] and, with reference to temper, may also mean "bitterness, resentment."[8] In the LXX it occurs twenty-seven times and in the canonical books it appears twenty times and translates seven Hebrew words, nine for מַר and its derivatives meaning "bitter" taste (Deut 32:32), a bitter spirit, "bitterness, resentment" (Job 7:11; 9:18; 10:1; 21:25; Ps 10:7 [LXX 9:28]),[9] or a place name reflecting bitterness (Exod 15:23; Num 33:8, 9). In the NT it occurs four times and is always used of a bitter or resentful attitude (Acts 8:23; Rom 3:14; Eph 4:31; Heb 12:15). In the present context where it is used in conjunction with other words of verbal expression it has the idea of "bitterness, resentment"[10] which must be put away.

καὶ θυμὸς καὶ ὀργή, "and anger and wrath." These two words are discussed together because they are synonyms. The second noun θυμός in classical times had the idea of the spirit or passion of a person. Aristotle classifies it as passion[11] and it could also refer to spirit or courage[12] and the passion to do right.[13] Further, it was known to be the seat of anger or anger itself.[14] Plato regarded it as the passion to do right but in the same passage refers to it as that which causes murder for which discipline is necessary.[15] In the LXX it occurs 326 times and in the canonical books it appears 246 times and translates thirty Hebrew words, but ninety times it translates אַף, meaning literally "nose" (Isa 2:22), which comes from the verb אָנַף, "to snort," hence, "to be angry"[16] and it is used of human anger (Gen 49:6, 7; Prov 21:14)

1. BAGD 631; BDAG 783; BDF §275 (3); MHT 3:199–200.
2. Homer *Ilias* 4.118.
3. Homer *Odyssea* 5.323; *Ilias* 11.846.
4. Homer *Odyssea* 4.406.
5. Homer *Ilias* 11.271
6. Sophocles *Oedipus Coloneus* 1610; *Philoctetes* 189.
7. Theophrastus *De Odoribus* 32.
8. Demosthenes *Orationes* 21.204; 25.84; Aristotle *De Virtutibus et Vitiis* 5.6.3 §1251a.4; Polybius 15.4.11.
9. BDB 600; H. Ringgren, "מרר *mrr*; מַר *mar*, etc.," *TDOT* 9 (1998): 15–19.
10. Wilhelm Michaelis, "πικρός, πικρία, κτλ.," *TDNT* 6 (1968): 125; cf. also L&N §88.201.
11. Aristotle *Ethica Nicomachea* 3.2.3 §1111b.11.
12. Ibid., 3.8.10 §1116b.23; Homer *Ilias* 20.174.
13. Plato *Leges* 5 §731b.
14. Homer *Ilias* 1.429; 9.496; Herodotus 7.160.
15. Plato *Leges* 5 §731c–d.
16. BDB 60; Johnson, *TDOT* 1 (1977): 351.

and more often of divine anger (Exod 32:12; Deut 9:19; 29:28 [MT & LXX 29:27]; Isa 5:25). Another seventy-six instances it translates חֵמָה and its derivatives, meaning the "burning anger, rage" of a person (Gen 27:44; 2 Sam 11:20; 2 Kgs 5:12; Esth 7:10) or of God (2 Kgs 22:17; Isa 63:5; Lam 2:4).[1] In the NT it is used eighteen times, five times by Paul, and only here in Ephesians. Although it can refer to passion (Rev 14:8; 18:3), it is also used of the anger of the devil (Rev 12:12), of God (Rom 2:8; Rev 14:10, 19; 15:1, 7; 16:1, 19; 19:15), and of humans (Luke 4:28; Acts 19:28; 2 Cor 12:20; Gal 5:20; Eph 4:31; Col 3:8; Heb 11:27). It is obvious that the primary Pauline usage refers to human anger. This is the case in the present context.

The third term ὀργή was already discussed at 2:3. It is used of both human and divine anger. In the NT it is used thirty-six times, twenty-one times by Paul, three times in Ephesians (2:3; 4:31; 5:6). Only five times does it refer to human anger or wrath (Eph 4:31; Col 3:8; 1 Tim 2:8; Jas 1:19, 20), the other times it refers to God's wrath.

As mentioned above these two words are synonyms. The only possible distinction in the original usage was that θυμός was more passionate and temporary, that is, anger that boils up, whereas ὀργή was more settled and abiding, a state of anger.[2] However, this distinction is probably nonexistent in the biblical narrative. In the LXX many of the same Hebrew words are translated by these two words. Also, these two words are used together synonymously in other contexts as well (Deut 9:19; Psa 78:49 [LXX 77:49]; 102:10 [MT 102:11; LXX 101:11]; Mic 5:15 [MT & LXX 5:14]; Rom 2:8; Col 3:8; Rev 14:10; 16:19; 19:15). As previously discussed, anger is not in itself sinful (see Eph 4:26). When the last word of this verse is discussed, it will become clear as to why Paul gives the exhortation to put away anger.

καὶ κραυγὴ καὶ βλασφημία, "and shouting and abusive speech." The fourth noun κραυγή[3] has the idea of "crying, screaming, shouting,"[4] which is a display of bad taste.[5] In the LXX it occurs sixty-six times (fifty-three times in the canonical books) and translates twelve Hebrew words. For example, it is used of the cry of complaint (Exod 3:7, 9), shouting (1 Sam 4:6*bis*; 2 Sam 6:15; Eccl 9:17; Amos 1:14), the cry of fear (1 Sam 5:12), and crying out to God (2 Sam 22:7; Pss 5:1 [MT

1. BDB 404; K.-D. Schunck, "חֵמָה *chēmāh*," *TDOT* 4 (1980): 462–65.

2. Trench, *Synonyms of the New Testament*, 131–32; Oskar Grether and Johannes Fichtner, "ὀργή, θυμός," *TDNT* 5 (1967): 409; Barclay, *Flesh and Spirit*, 52; L&N §§25.19; 88.173, 178.

3. Skard thinks that κραυγή is placed here because it rhymes with ὀργή not because it is their natural order. His view that reversal of the order of these two words would be more natural is questionable. See Eiliv Skard, "Kleine Beiträge zum Corpus Hellenisticum Novi Testament," Symbolae Osloenses, ed. S. Eitrem and E. Skard, Fasc. 30 (Oslo: A. W. Brøgger, 1953), 101–3.

4. Euripides *Orestes* 1510, 1529; Xenophon *Cyropaedia* 3.1.4.

5. Aristotle *Rhetorica* 3.2.10 §1405a.33 citing Dionysius.

& LXX 5:2]; 18:6 [MT 18:7; LXX 17:7]; 102:1 [MT 102:2; LXX 101:2]; Isa 30:19). In the NT the noun occurs six times, but only here in Paul. In the other NT passages it is used of a shout to announce the bridegroom (Matt 25:6), a shout of joy by Elizabeth when acknowledging Mary's baby (Luke 1:42), the shouting or clamoring of the Pharisees against the Sadducees in an assembly (Acts 23:9), the crying or shouting of Jesus in his prayers (Heb 5:7), and the removal of shouting or crying at the appearance of the new heaven and new earth (Rev 21:4). In classical literature, as well as in the NT, the word is used for shouts of joy.[1] However, in relation to the other negative words in the present context, it refers to shouting or clamor, probably between members of the body of believers.

The fifth noun βλασφημία is used of profane or abusive speech[2] not to be used when offering a sacrifice.[3] It appears only seven times in the LXX (once in the canonical books) where it refers to abusive words against God (Ezek 35:12), speaking against God (Theodotion Dan 3:29 [LXX 3:96]), and the abusive language of the Gentiles against God and his people (1 Macc 2:6; 2 Macc 8:4; 10:35; 15:24; Tob 1:18). In the NT it appears eighteen times and means slander, defamation, or abusive speech (Mark 7:22; 1 Tim 6:4) against God (Matt 12:31*bis* = Mark 3:28; Matt 15:19; Rev 13:1, 5, 6; 17:3), slander against people (Rev 2:9), and blasphemy such as was attributed to Jesus by religious leaders when he made himself equal with God (Matt 26:65 = Mark 14:64; Luke 5:21; John 10:33). Similarly, in the present context and the parallel in Col 3:8 it speaks of abusive language or cursing.[4] These last two words can be paired together because they both have to do with speech.

To summarize, first noun "bitterness" in verse 31 deals with attitude. The next two nouns "anger and wrath" deal with disposition, and the last two "shouting and abusive" refer to the manner of speech. Next Paul conveys to the believers what should be the fate of the qualities expressed by these words.

ἀρθήτω ἀφ᾽ ὑμῶν σὺν πάσῃ κακίᾳ, "together with every kind of malice be put away from you." In the list of injunctions in verses 25–30 Paul uses the present imperative, but here he uses the aorist imperative possibly in an ingressive sense to denote that a change of behavior is expected or possibly to heighten the sense of urgency.[5] The passive idea may be used because the believer cannot change his or her behavior but must depend on the power of the Holy Spirit with whom he or she was sealed (v. 30). The verb αἴρω, from which ἀρθήτω comes,

1. LSJ 992.

2. Demosthenes *Orationes* 25.26.

3. Plato *Leges* 7 §800c.

4. For further study, see Hermann Wolfgang Beyer, "βλασφημέω, βλασφημία, βλάσφημος," *TDNT* 1 (1964): 621–25.

5. Cf. Fanning, *Verbal Aspect*, 359–61, 378.

fundamentally means "to lift with a view to carrying" but also means "to take away, remove" without the idea of lifting up (Matt 24:39; John 19:15).[1] As a flood swept away the inhabitants of the earth (Matt 24:39) so should all these negative characteristics be swept away "from you" (ἀφ᾽ ὑμῶν).

The prepositional phrase σὺν πάσῃ κακίᾳ should be joined with all the previous vices listed. Again, the adjective πᾶς with anarthrous singular nouns refers to everything belonging to the class indicated by the noun and is thus translated "all sorts of, every kind of, every form of."[2] The noun κακία means "badness, vice, evil."[3] It is the opposite of ἀρετή, "moral excellence, virtue."[4] Philo sees it as "wickedness" or "badness, vice" of the soul.[5] In the LXX it occurs 142 times and in the canonical books it appears 109 times. It translates eleven Hebrew words, and ninety-three of the 109 are for רַע and its derivatives, meaning "badness, evil, wickedness, misery" (Gen 6:5; Jer 1:16; 3:2; Hos 7:1–3).[6] In the NT it is used eleven times, six times by Paul and only here in Ephesians. Once it is rendered "trouble" (Matt 6:34) but it normally means "wickedness, evil, malice" (Acts 8:22; Rom 1:29; 1 Cor 5:8; 14:20; Col 3:8; Titus 3:3; Jas 1:21; 1 Pet 2:1, 16). It can denote a single act of iniquity like the envious desire of Simon Magus (Acts 8:22), but generally it denotes the evil that men do among one another.[7] It is the all-inclusive word for badness or wickedness. It casts a pall on any action with which it is connected. Hence, it is best to translate it "ill-will, malice, maliciousness."

This word colors all the other words mentioned earlier in the verse. Certain words like anger and wrath need not have an evil connotation but with this last noun united to them, they denote a malicious anger and wrath. Therefore, Paul urgently exhorts believers to put away all of these qualities which are defined by malice.

4:32. γίνεσθε [δὲ][8] εἰς ἀλλήλους χρηστοί, εὔσπλαγχνοι, "But become kind to one another, compassionate." Following the intensely negative injunction, Paul again states the positive. This contrast is marked out by the adversative δέ. The present imperative implies the

1. BAGD 24; BDAG 28–29; Joachim Jeremias, "αἴρω, ἐπαίρω," *TDNT* 1 (1964): 185–86.

2. BAGD 631; BDAG 782; BDF §275 (3); MHT 3:199–200.

3. Sophocles *Oedipus Tyrannus* 512; Xenophon *Memorabilia* 1.2.28; Plato *Symposium* 181e; *Respublica* 1.20 §348c; Aristotle *Rhetorica* 2.6.11, 12 §1384a.8, 17.

4. Xenophon *Memorabilia* 2.1.21; Plato *Symposium* 181e; *Respublica* 1.20 §348c.

5. Philo *Leg. All.* 3.12 §38; *Virt*. 32 §172; *Sobr*. 10 §45.

6. BDB 947; C. Dohmen, "רעע *r‘‘*, etc.," *TWAT* 7 (1990): 585–88.

7. Walter Grundmann, "κακία," *TDNT* 3 (1965): 484.

8. Instead of δέ, the reading οὖν is found in D* F G 1175 it^{b}, but this is limited to only the Western text. This conjunction is omitted from 𝔓^{46} B 0278 6 104* 1739* 1881 it^{t} vg^{ms} Clement, but it has very few manuscripts and these are limited basically to the Alexandrian text. The conjunction δέ is found in 𝔓^{49} א D^{2} Ψ 33 1739^{mg} 𝔐 lat syr^{h} Tertullian, which is the best reading because there is good representation from the various text-types.

idea that they are to become what they are not at the present time. Believers are to begin and continue to become kind to one another. The adjective χρηστός is similar to the noun χρηστότητος already studied in 2:7.[1] In classical times the adjective had the idea of "useful, serviceable, good of its kind."[2] It was used as a substantive to denote kindness or benefits.[3] In connection with persons it connotes the idea of "good, honest, worthy,"[4] or somebody who is "good, kindly."[5] Accordingly, in the LXX it occurs forty times (twenty-seven times in the canonical books) and twenty-three times it translates טוֹבָה/טוּב/טוֹב, meaning something that is "pleasant, agreeable, good."[6] It refers to the goodness of God (Pss 25:8 [LXX 24:8]; 34:8 [MT 34:9 & LXX 33:9]; 52:9 [MT 52:11 & LXX 51:11]), the goodness and kindliness of humans (Prov 2:21), good figs as opposed to bad figs (Jer 24:2–3, 5), kindly or pleasant speech (Jer 52:32), good, genuine, or precious stones (Ezek 27:22; 28:13), and good or fine gold (Dan 2:32). In the NT it is used seven times, three times by Paul and only here in Ephesians. It is used of the pleasant yoke of Christ (Matt 11:30), of the good taste of old wine mellowed with age (Luke 5:39), of being good or kindly to enemies (Luke 6:35), of the goodness or kindness of God in allowing time for repentance (Rom 2:4), of good morals (1 Cor 15:33), and of tasting the goodness or kindness of God (1 Pet 2:3). It encompasses that which is fitting or appropriate to a situation, such as a glove that fits well on the hand. In the present context it is best translated "pleasant, good, kind." The preposition εἰς with the accusative ἀλλήλους is similar to a dative and sets forth the disposition or attitude of mind: "become kind to one another."[7]

As mentioned above, the noun χρηστότητος is used in 2:7 where God has raised up and seated believers in the heavenlies that he might demonstrate his kindness in giving salvation. Now, in the present verse, the adjective has the same connotation and refers to believers' kindness to each other. This attitude does not come naturally nor is it an ability which can be self-produced. According to Gal 5:22 it is the fruit of the Spirit. Therefore, it is only as one relies on the Spirit of God that it is possible to become kind to one another.

The second positive quality that the believer is to reflect is εὔσπλαγχνος. This is a rare word and is a compound based on the noun σπλάγχνον,[8] which originally was used mostly in the plural to re-

1. Cf. Konrad Weiss, "χρηστός," *TDNT* 9 (1974): 483–89.

2. Herodotus 3.78; Euripides *Hecuba* 594.

3. Herodotus 1.41, 42.

4. Sophocles *Oedipus Tyrannus* 610.

5. Demosthenes *Orationes* 59.2.

6. BDB 373; Höver-Johag, *TDOT* 5 (1986): 296–317.

7. Cf. Robertson, *Grammar*, 594.

8. For a study of this word, see Helmut Köster, "σπλάγχνον κτλ.," *TDNT* 7 (1971): 548–59; Esser, *NIDNTT* 2 (1976): 599–601.

fer to the inward parts (heart, lungs, liver, kidneys) that were reserved in the sacrifices to be eaten by the devotees.[1] Later it had the metaphorical reference to the seat of feelings, the emotions like anger[2] or love.[3] In the LXX σπλάγχνον occurs seventeen times (always plural), only three times in the canonical books (Prov 12:10; 26:22; Jer 51:13 [LXX 28:13]). It is used of the inward parts (Prov 26:22; 2 Macc 9:5; Sir 33:5), feelings (Sir 30:7; 4 Macc 14:13; 15:23, 29), and compassion (Prov 12:10; Wis 10:5). It is used in the NT eleven times (always plural), eight times by Paul. It refers to the inward parts of Judas which gushed forth (Acts 1:18); the heart, the center of compassion (2 Cor 6:12; 7:15; Phlm 7, 12, 20; 1 John 3:17); human compassion (Phil 1:8; 2:1; Col 3:12); and the tender mercy or compassion of God (Luke 1:78). The verb form (σπλαγχνίζομαι) is used to demonstrate Jesus' compassion for the crowd who were like sheep without a shepherd (Matt 9:36; cf. 14:14), for the leper who wanted to be healed (Mark 1:41), and for the widow at Nain (Luke 7:13). The adjective (εὔσπλαγχνος) is found only once in the LXX (Ode 12:7 [Pr Man 7]) with reference to God's compassion and in the NT it appears twice (Eph 4:32; 1 Pet 3:8) as meaning tender-hearted, compassionate.

χαριζόμενοι ἑαυτοῖς, "being gracious to one another." The participle is from χαρίζομαι, which when used with the dative of persons, as here, essentially has the idea of "saying or doing something agreeable, showing favor, kindness, pleasantness."[4] In the LXX it appears twelve times, once in the canonical books. It is used to refer to Ahasuerus' graciousness to Esther when she was given Haman's house (Esth 8:7). It also refers to one who gives alms (Sir 12:3), expensive gifts (2 Macc 4:32), the favor shown by a king (2 Macc 1:35; 4 Macc 11:12), the graciousness in granting life (2 Macc 3:31, 33; 7:22; 3 Macc 7:6), and God's gracious bestowal of blessings (3 Macc 5:11). In the NT it occurs twenty-three times, sixteen times in Paul's writings, and twice in Ephesians, both of which are in this verse. It is used to refer to Jesus who bestowed favor by curing diseases (Luke 7:21), to forgiveness bestowed on another (Luke 7:42–43; 2 Cor 2:7, 10*ter*; Col 2:13), to the granting or giving of something undeserved (Acts 3:14; 27:24; Rom 8:32; 1 Cor 2:12; 2 Cor 12:13; Gal 3:18; Phil 1:29; 2:9; Col 3:13*bis*), and, finally, to give or grant (Acts 25:11, 16; Phlm 22). The concept of the gracious bestowal of something unmerited is pervasive. Thus, it seems best to translate it "to be gracious."

It is interesting to notice that some English translations render this word "to forgive one another." Although this is a legitimate translation, it is not the normal rendering of the word. There are three rea-

1. Homer *Ilias* 1.464; Herodotus 2.40.
2. Aristophanes *Ranae* 844, 1006.
3. Dionysius Halicarnassensis 11.35.4.
4. Homer *Ilias* 5.71; 11.23; *Odyssea* 8.538; 13.265; Herodotus 6.130; Thucydides 3.40.4.

sons to render it "being gracious to one another." First, "to be gracious" is not only the normal meaning of the word, but it is the most suited to the context. Graciousness is the antithesis of bitterness, anger, wrath, shouting and abusive speech. In other words, bitterness is counteracted by a gracious attitude, anger and wrath are counteracted by a gracious disposition, the shouting and abusive speech are counteracted by gracious speaking. Second, the participle functions as a circumstantial participle of manner, describing how they are to be kind and compassionate to one another. Third, this concept is broader than forgiveness and, in fact, includes forgiveness. Hence, in this context "to be gracious to one another" is a better and more natural rendering of the verb.

The reflexive pronoun ἑαυτοῖς, literally "to yourselves," functions like the reciprocal pronoun ἀλλήλων (as in 5:19), "to one another."[1] Their gracious actions should be reciprocal. Such a manner of life can only lead to the building up of the body of Christ.

καθὼς καὶ ὁ θεὸς ἐν Χριστῷ ἐχαρίσατο ἡμῖν,[2] "just as also God in Christ was gracious to us." Having stated the negative and positive commands, Paul now gives the reason or motivation for the positive command. As discussed at 1:4 and 4:4, the adverbial conjunction καθώς could be causative, for example, "because, since, inasmuch as," but in this context it seems to denote manner (cf. 1:4; 5:3, 25, 29).[3] Paul is exhorting them to behave in the same gracious manner that God did in his Son. Some of the earlier translations rendered the adverbial conjunction καθώς as "even as" (AV, RV, ASV) but the more recent ones generally render it "as" (RSV, NEB, TEV, JB, NJB, NRSV) or "just as" (NASB, NIV). The conjunction καί taken adjunctively ("also") supports the idea of its being a comparative. Hence, the best translation is "just as also."

1. BAGD 212; BDAG 269.

2. The personal pronoun ἡμῖν is debated. It reads ἡμῖν in 𝔓^{49} B D Ψ 075 33 104 424 436 459 1175 1241 1739 1852 1881 1912 1962 (2200 ἡμᾶς) 2464 *Byz* [K L]*Lect* vg$^{\text{ww, st}}$ syr$^{\text{p, h, pal}}$ cop^{bomss} arm (geo) slav Origen Chrysostom^{com} Nilus Proclus Tertullian$^{1/2}$ Jerome Augustine$^{2/3}$ Cassiodorus Theophylact. It reads ὑμῖν in 𝔓^{46} ℵ A F G P 0150 6 81 256 263 365 1319 1573 2127 *l* 593 *l* 596 *l* 884 *l* 1159 *l* 1365 it$^{\text{ar, b, d, f, g, mon, o}}$ vg^{cl} cop$^{\text{sa, bo}}$ eth Clement Origen^{lat} Basil Chrysostom^{lem} Theodore^{lat} Tertullian$^{1/2}$ Victorinus-Rome Ambrosiaster Pelagius Augustine$^{1/3}$ (NA^{27}, UBS^{4}). It is quite evenly divided but the first reading is more acceptable. First, it has good representation from the Alexandrian, Western, and Byzantine text-types. The second reading has a better representation in the Alexandrian text with the uncials and the Coptic versions but not as good in the Western uncials although better in the early Latin versions. It has virtually nothing in the Byzantine tradition. Hence, the first reading has good representation of manuscripts from the three text-types, indicating a wider geographical distribution. Internally, it fits better with the two pronouns in 5:2 where the textual evidence favors the first person plural.

3. Wallace, *Greek Grammar*, 675.

The aorist indicative is in contrast to the preceding present participle. God's act of graciousness was accomplished nearly 2000 years ago. The aorist is not concerned with the internal characteristics of the action but sees the event in summary form, viewed from the outside as a whole.[1] The prepositional phrase ἐν Χριστῷ speaks of the sphere or locale in which God has been gracious. This gracious act was directed toward "us" (ἡμῖν) and was demonstrated by sending his Son to die on the cross for us. It is spoken of in 1:7–12 and 2:4–10. In fact, 2:4 states that it was God's rich mercy expressed in love toward us who had been dead in transgressions that made us alive. All this gracious love and redemption was done in Christ. Therefore, God's gracious act in Christ serves as an illustration and example for believers in their relationship with each other. This concept is expanded in the following verse, "become imitators of God."[2]

In conclusion, in verses 25–32 Paul gives specific exhortations regarding the lifestyle of the "new person." The exhortations have a tripartite structure: (1) a negative command; (2) a positive command; and (3) the reason for the positive command designed to give motivation to follow the command. Only the second exhortation (vv. 26–27) reverses (1) and (2). Throughout this portion it becomes progressively clear that the new lifestyle is to be diametrically opposed to the conduct of the unbelieving Gentiles mentioned in 4:14–19. Clear contrasts are made between falsehood and truth, sinful anger and anger without sin; stealing for self-indulgence and working to share with those in need, corrupt speech and edifying speech. Positively, Paul commands the believers to be kind and compassionate to one another, exhibiting the same graciousness that God in Christ had already demonstrated toward them.

1. Fanning, *Verbal Aspect*, 97.

2. Lorenz Nieder, *Die Motive der religiös-sittlichen Paränese in den paulinischen Gemeindebriefen*, Münchener theologische Studien, ed. Franz Xaver Seppelt, Joseph Pauscher, and Klaus Mörsdorf, vol. 42 (Munich: Karl Zink, 1956), 82.

C. Walk in Love (5:1–6)

In applying the doctrines in the first three chapters, Paul now for the third time uses the term for "walk" (περιπατέω, 4:1, 17; 5:2). Since the term does not appear until verse 2 some think the break should be between verses 1 and 2, others between verses 2 and 3. However, the key to this section of the book has not only been the verb but also its tie with the conjunction οὖν, which is in verse 1. Therefore, this marks the third section in his discussion on the conduct of the believers. God's children are to walk in unity (4:1–16), in holiness (4:17–32), and in love (5:1–6). This particular section is divided into two parts: (1) the positive, walk in love (vv. 1–2); and (2) the negative, abstain from evil (vv. 3–6).

1. Positive: Walk in Love (5:1–2)

Paul had just stated in the previous verse that God had acted graciously in Christ for all the believers. He does not leave that thought but continues it in this section by stating that they should imitate God and walk in love as Christ loved them.

a. Imitate God (5:1)

Text: 5:1. γίνεσθε οὖν μιμηταὶ τοῦ θεοῦ ὡς τέκνα ἀγαπητά

Translation: 5:1. "Therefore, become imitators of God as beloved children"

Commentary: 5:1. γίνεσθε οὖν μιμηταὶ τοῦ θεοῦ, "Therefore, become imitators of God." The conjunction οὖν is a resumptive inferential conjunction that goes back to 4:1 and 17 making another application from the first three chapters. It also builds on the previous section (4:17–32) where Paul told them not to walk as the Gentiles do because they have put off the old person and have put on the new person and practices which concluded with reference to God's gracious action in Christ as a motivation for them to be kind, compassionate, and gracious to one another. Paul again uses, as he did in 4:32, the present imperative "to become" rather than "to be." They are to develop continuously into imitators of God.

The word μιμητής is a word used in classical times that means an "imitator, copier,"[1] as an actor who "impersonates"[2] or, in the bad sense, an "imposter."[3] A word from the same root can mean a counterfeit. A good counterfeit is as close to the original as possible. The noun is not used in the LXX but the verb is found four times (Wis 4:2; 15:9; 4 Macc 9:23; 13:9) where people are called to imitate others but never called to imitate God. In the NT it occurs six times always in conjunction with γίνομαι, "to become," and all uses are in Paul's writings except one. Paul asks the believers to be imitators of him (1 Cor 4:16; 11:1; 1 Thess 1:6; 2 Thess 3:7, 9 [verb form]) as he is an imitator of Christ, and it is also used of believers imitating other believers (1 Thess 2:14; Heb 6:12).[4] Therefore, it suggests an imitation of a good role model. Only in this context Paul enjoins the believers to become imitators of God.[5] The genitive is an objective genitive. They are to become imitators of the God who in 4:32 dealt graciously in Christ by likewise acting graciously. Apparently, Lindars had not considered this verse when he asserted that the imitation of God is "neither biblical nor true to the ethical position of Jesus and the early Church, in so far as these can be recovered from the New Testament."[6] Barth states that though not in the OT, the concept of imitating God is found in Hellenistic Jewish writers, particularly Philo.[7] From Plato's *Theaetetus*

1. Xenophon *Memorabilia* 1.6.3; Plato *Respublica* 10.4 §602a.

2. Aristotle *Problemata* 19.15 §918b.28; *Poetica* 24.13 §1460a.8.

3. Plato *Respublica* 10.2 §598d.

4. Cf. D. M. Stanley, "'Become Imitators of Me': The Pauline Conception of Apostolic Tradition," *Bib* 40, no. 3 (1959): 859–77; Willis Peter De Boer, *The Imitation of Paul. An Exegetical Study* (Kampen: J. H. Kok N. V., 1962), 75–80; Andrew D. Clarke, "'Be Imitators of Me': Paul's Model of Leadership," *TynBul* 49.2 (November 1998): 329–60.

5. It is interesting to see how Judaism deals with being imitators of God. See Martin Buber, "Imitatio Dei," in *Mamre, Essays in Religion*, trans. Greta Hort (Melbourne: Melbourne University Press, 1946), 32–42; Esteban N. Veghazi, "La idea de la 'imitación de Dios' en el judaismo," *Revista Biblica* 41, nos. 1–2 (1979): 91–95; cf. Fischer, *Tendenz und Absicht des Epheserbriefes*, 140.

6. Barnabas Lindars, "Imitation of God and Imitation of Christ," *Theology* 76 (August 1973): 395.

7. Barth, 556 n. 10; 588–92; Wild, "'Be Imitators of God'," 127–43. Best (466) makes some interesting observations. He states: "Certain factors operated against the appearance among Jews of the idea of the imitation of God: the initial sin of Adam and Eve as the desire to be like God, the existence of human sin, the second commandment forbidding the making of any likeness to God, the Hellenistic usage of imitation in relation to sculpture. Indeed the thought of the imitation of the invisible God is paradoxical."

(25 §176a–b) Philo concludes that we ought to flee from earth to heaven and this flight means to become like God as far as possible (ὁμοίωσις θεῷ κατὰ τὸ δυνατόν) and to become like him is to become holy, just, and wise,[1] similar to the present context where Paul enjoins them to walk in holiness (4:17–32), walk in love (5:2), and abstain from evil (5:3–6). More specifically Philo illustrates from Moses that a person should imitate God as much as possible (μιμεῖσθαι θεὸν καθ᾽ ὅσον οἷόν τε).[2] He states that the strength that God gave should be used to imitate God by graciously giving in the same way (ἵνα μιμήσῃ θεὸν τῷ παραπλήσια χαρίζεσθαι).[3] He also states that a person resembles God by showing kindness (or being gracious). Thus what greater good can there be than to imitate God (ὅτι παραπλήσιον οὐδέν ἄνθρωποι θεῷ δρῶσιν ἢ χαριζόμενοι. τί δ᾽ ἂν εἴη κρεῖττον ἀγαθὸν ἢ μιμεῖσθαι θεὸν)?[4] These last two references are fitting for they speak of being gracious to one another as a reflection of God's grace, which parallels this context (4:32). Hence, the concept of imitating God was known in Hellenistic Judaism in the first century, the setting of Paul's own time and training. Paul now goes on to state how we are to imitate God.

ὡς τέκνα ἀγαπητά, "as beloved children." The comparative conjunction ὡς, "as," gives the manner[5] in which believers become imitators of God, namely, as beloved children. The adjective ἀγαπητός in classical times, with reference to children, meant "beloved" or "contented" but particularly referred to an only child to whom the parents had devoted all their love.[6] In other words, because the child had received so much love, the child had the security of being loved and thus was contented. In the LXX it occurs twenty-five times and in the canonical books it appears eighteen times where it translates five Hebrew words, six times for יָחִיד, meaning "only one, only son" (Gen 22:2, 12, 16; Jer 6:26; Amos 8:10; Zech 12:10)[7] and five times for יָדִיד, meaning "beloved" (Pss 60:5 [MT 60:7; LXX 59:7]; 108:6 [MT 108:7; LXX 107:7]; 127:2 [LXX 126:2]).[8] In the NT it is used sixty-one times, twenty-seven times by Paul, twice in Ephesians (5:1; 6:21). Many times it is used of the only son, specifically Jesus as the only Son of God (Matt 3:17 = Mark 1:11 = Luke 3:22; Matt 17:5 = Mark 9:7; Matt 12:18; Luke 20:13). It also refers to Christian brothers who are beloved (Acts 15:25; Rom 12:19; 16:5, 8, 9, 12; 1 Cor 10:14) and saints who are beloved of God (Rom 1:7). Paul calls Timothy beloved (1 Cor

1. Philo *Fug*. 12 §63.
2. Philo *Virt*. 31 §168.
3. Ibid., 32 §168.
4. Philo *Spec*. 4.13 §73.
5. Takamitsu Muraoka, "The use of ΩΣ in the Greek Bible," *NovT* 7 (March 1964): 59.
6. Homer *Odyssea* 2.365; 4.817; *Ilias* 6.401.
7. BDB 402; H.-J. Fabry, "יָחַד *yāḥad*; יַחַד *yaḥad*; יָחִיד *yāḥîd*; יַחְדָו *yaḥdāw*," *TDOT* 6 (1990): 43–46.
8. BDB 391; H.-J. Zobel, "יָדִיד *yādîd*," *TDOT* 5 (1986): 444–48.

4:17; 2 Tim 1:2) as well as certain other men (Col 1:7; 4:7, 9, 14; Phlm 1, 16) and he calls the believers to whom he writes beloved (1 Cor 4:14; 2 Cor 7:1; 12:19; 1 Thess 2:8). Thus, it means the one who is loved and is translated "beloved." Here Paul exhorts believers to become imitators of God, that is, as beloved children. As stated above, ἀγαπητός was often used in reference to an only child and such a picture might be applied to Christ as the only son of the Father. Here, in the present context it cannot be pressed quite to that extent, but believers must realize God's ability to extend his love to each of his children as if he or she were the only child. They should be content because of the knowledge and security of his love. He uses the term τέκνα which connotes a closer relationship to the parent than the word υἱός (cf. 2:3).[1] It denotes dependency on the parent. Therefore, believers are to be imitators of God as ones who are his beloved children because of his love which has been experienced in Christ. The result will be harmony and growth to the body of Christ.

b. Walk in Love (5:2)

(1) Command: Love (5:2a)

Text: 5:2a. καὶ περιπατεῖτε ἐν ἀγάπῃ,

Translation: 5:2a. "and walk in love"

Commentary: 5:2a. καὶ περιπατεῖτε ἐν ἀγάπῃ, "and walk in love." Since beloved of God as though his only child, a believer is to walk in love. The καί serves as a coordinating or an epexegetical conjunction giving further specification of the injunction in verse 1. These two statements parallel each other, for to be an imitator of God is to walk in love.[2] Here is the third instruction "to walk." First, believers must walk worthy of the call (4:1), then they must walk in holiness and not as the Gentiles (4:17), and now they are instructed to walk in love. The present imperative conveys a customary idea to "make this your habit" and does not indicate whether the action has been going on.[3]

The sphere of this walk is ἐν ἀγάπῃ, "in love." The word ἀγάπη was discussed at 1:4 where we concluded that it is a love given quite irrespective of merit and it seeks the highest good in the one loved. That highest good for anyone is the will of God. This command to walk in love is reminiscent of Christ's command to his disciples in his farewell discourse where he tells them to love one another as he has loved them (John 13:34; 15:12, 17). Paul shows next the kind of love we should have.

1. Cf. Massie, "Two New Testament Synonyms, Υἱός and Τέκνον," 140–50.
2. Spicq, *Agape in the New Testament*, 2:74.
3. MHT 3:75; Wallace, *Greek Grammar*, 722.

(2) Comparison: Christ's Love (5:2b)

Text: 5:2b. καθὼς καὶ ὁ Χριστὸς ἠγάπησεν ἡμᾶς καὶ παρέδωκεν ἑαυτὸν ὑπὲρ ἡμῶν προσφορὰν καὶ θυσίαν τῷ θεῷ εἰς ὀσμὴν εὐωδίας.

Translation: 5:2b. "just as Christ also loved us and gave himself for us as an offering and sacrifice to God for a fragrant aroma."

Commentary: 5:2b. καθὼς καὶ ὁ Χριστὸς ἠγάπησεν ἡμᾶς,[1] "just as Christ also loved us." As in 4:32, the adverbial conjunction καθώς is a comparison of manner setting Christ's love as the model to follow. The conjunction καί is used adjunctively, which supports the idea that it is an illustration and thus is translated "just as Christ also."

Christ's love for us is stated for the first time in this book. Earlier Paul stated that God the Father loved us (2:4). However, in Rom 8:35 and 37 Paul makes specific statements of Christ's love—"who shall separate us from the love of Christ . . . we are more than conquerors through him who loved us." In John's Gospel (13:1, 34; 15:12) the love of Christ is also seen as a model for the disciples. The object of that love is believers. But how did he show his love? Paul mentions this next.

καὶ παρέδωκεν ἑαυτὸν ὑπὲρ ἡμῶν,[2] "and gave himself for us." The supreme example of love is that Christ gave himself for us. The aorist tense for both of these verbs point back to the particular action of the cross.[3] The verb παρέδωκεν means "to hand over, give over" and the re-

1. The reading ἡμᾶς is found in $\mathfrak{P}^{46}$ $\aleph^{2}$ D F G Ψ 075 0150 6 33 104 256 263 365 424 436 459 1319 1573 1739 1852 1881 1962 2127 2200 2464 *Byz* [K L] *Lect* $it^{d, g, o}$ vg $syr^{p, h, pal}$ arm geo $Clement^{1/2}$ Basil Chrysostom $Theodore^{lat}$ Cyril John-Damascus Ambrose Jerome Pelagius $Augustine^{6/8}$ Varimadum. The reading ὑμᾶς is found in ℵ* A B P 0159 81 1175 1241 1912 *l* $60^{1/3}$ *l* 593 *l* $597^{1/2}$ $it^{ar, b, f, mon}$ vg^{ms} $cop^{sa, bo}$ eth slav $Clement^{1/2}$ Victorinus-Rome Ambrosiaster $Augustine^{2/8}$ Speculum and NA^{25}. The first reading is preferred because it has good representation from the Western and Byzantine text-types, whereas the second reading is almost strictly from the Alexandrian texts. Also, the first reading permits uniformity of the pronouns in this verse and 4:32.

2. Although there is a transposition of words in this verse near this pronoun, the main problem is the choice of pronouns. The pronoun ἡμῶν is found in $\mathfrak{P}^{46, 49}$ ℵ A D F G Ψ 075 0150 0159 6 33 81 104 256 263 365 424 436 459 1241 1319 1573 1739 1852 1881 1912 1962 2127 2200 2464 *Byz* [K L P] *Lect* $it^{ar, d, f, g, o}$ vg $syr^{p, h, pal}$ arm geo Clement Basil (Ps-Ignatius) (Gregory-Nyssa) Chrysostom $Theodore^{lat}$ Cyril Ambrose Jerome Pelagius $Augustine^{9/10}$ Varimadum. The reading ὑμῶν is found in B 0278^{c} 1175 *l* 1356 $it^{b, mon}$ $cop^{sa, bo}$ eth slav Victorinus-Rome Ambrosiaster $Augustine^{1/10}$ Speculum. Clearly, the first reading is genuine because it has good representation in all the text-types while the second reading has only partial support from the Alexandrian text.

3. Raymond Corriveau, *The Liturgy of Life. A Study of the Ethical Thought of St. Paul in His Letters to the Early Christians*, Studia: Travaux de recherche, vol. 25 (Bruxelles: Desclée de Brouwer; Montreal: Les Editions Bellarmin, 1970), 197. This is a good study of verses 1–2. In a recent study the aorist tense in Ephesians is "used when the author does not intend to signal immediacy or closeness to the experience of the audience, and is instead relating, for example, the acts of God or Christ on their behalf *without* a hortatory or paraenetic (exhortative) emphasis" (Gustavo Martín-Asensio, "Hallidayan

flexive pronoun ἑαυτόν indicates that he took his own initiative in handing himself over (cf. 4:19; 5:25).[1] This shows how much Christ loved us. Paul reiterates this in Gal 2:20 and it can also be seen in Rom 5:6–8 where Paul presents Christ's death for the ungodly as evidence of God's love (cf. also Gal 2:20). This echoes Jesus' own words where he states that he is the good shepherd and he will lay down his life for the sheep (John 10:11, 15, 17), commenting that there is no greater love than when one who lays down his life for his friends (John 15:13). Jesus was not forced to die at the hand of human beings but rather laid down his own life. In John 10:18 he specifically says that he lays down his life on his own accord and that he has power to lay it down and power to take it again. Jesus freely obeyed the Father's will.

The prepositional phrase ὑπὲρ ἡμῶν shows the object for which Christ laid down his life. The preposition with a genitive signifies that it was done "for our sake, in our behalf,"[2] showing interest in the object[3] and has "been characterized as the particle of love."[4] He did it "for us." He was willing to leave heaven's glory and die on the cross to become sin that sinners might become the righteousness of God.

προσφορὰν καὶ θυσίαν τῷ θεῷ, "as an offering and sacrifice to God." These accusatives are in apposition to ἑαυτόν and therefore serve as predicate accusatives and are translated "as an offering and sacrifice." These two terms for sacrifice must be examined. The first word προσφορά has various meanings in classical literature. It can mean "application, use,"[5] "presenting, offering,"[6] and "food."[7] However, none of these apply. It appears sixteen times in the LXX, three times in the canonical books. It is used to refer to the showbread in the temple (1 Kgs 7:48) or to an offering to the Lord (Ps 40:6 [MT 40:7; LXX 39:7]; Dan 4:37b; 1 Esdr 5:52 [LXX 5:51]; Sir 14:11; 34:18, 19; 35:1, 6 [LXX 35:1, 5]; 38:11; 46:16; 50:13, 14). In the NT it is used nine times,

---

Functional Grammar as Heir to New Testament Rhetorical Criticism," in *The Rhetorical Interpretation of Scripture: Essays from the 1996 Malibu Conference*, ed. Stanley E. Porter and Dennis L. Stamps, JSNTSup, ed. Stanley E. Porter, vol. 180 [Sheffield: Sheffield Academic Press, 1999], 104).

1. Other passages depict God handing Jesus over (e.g., Rom 4:25; 8:32) but here Christ is the subject and the verb is in the active voice. For a brief discussion of Jesus as the object and subject of being handed over, see Wengst, *Christologische Formeln und Lieder des Urchristentums*, 60–62; cf. Norman Perrin, "The Use of (παρα)διδόναι in Connection with the Passion of Jesus in the New Testament," in *Der Ruf Jesu und die Antwort der Gemeinde. Exegetische Untersuchungen Joachim Jeremias zum 70. Geburtstag gewidmet von seinen Schülern*, ed. Eduard Lohse, Christoph Buchard, and Berndt Schaller (Göttingen: Vandenhoeck & Ruprecht, 1970), 204–12.

2. BAGD 838; BDAG 1030–31.

3. HS §259m.

4. Corriveau, *The Liturgy of Life*, 200.

5. Plato *Leges* 1 §638c.

6. Ibid., 7 §791e.

7. Theophrastus *Historica Plantarum* 7.9.4; 8.4.4.

twice by Paul (Rom 15:16; Eph 5:2). In Rom 15:16 he uses it to refer to the presentation of the offering of Gentiles as a priestly service to God, but in other NT instances, it has reference either to the levitical offerings (Acts 21:26; 24:17; Heb 10:5, 8, 18) or to the sacrifice of Christ (Heb 10:10, 14). In the present context it refers to the sacrifice of Christ on the cross. Earlier some thought that this word referred to unbloody sacrifices and the next word to bloody sacrifices, but this will not stand for this particular word is used for bloody sacrifices in the Apocrypha (Sir 46:16) and in the NT references regarding the sacrifice of Christ mentioned above. In light of the sacrifices in the OT, it is best viewed here as a sacrificial offering to the Lord.

The second word θυσία was used in classical times of a burnt offering or sacrifice.[1] It is a very prominent word in the LXX, occurring 388 times (328 times in the canonical books), and translating eight Hebrew words. Approximately 140 times it translates זֶבַח, meaning "sacrifice"[2] and around 150 times מִנְחָה, meaning "offering, grain offering."[3] This latter Greek word is used for both blood and nonblood offerings. Both of these words are used with great frequency in Num 7:13–88. In the NT it is used twenty-eight times, five times by Paul and only here in Ephesians. Most of those times the word refers to the sacrifice of animals as prescribed in the OT, but it also used of Paul as a libation sacrifice (Phil 2:17), the gift sent to Paul as a sacrifice (Phil 4:18), believers as living sacrifices (Rom 12:2), praise as the believers' offering (Heb 13:15, 16; 1 Pet 2:5), and Christ as the sacrifice to end all sacrifices (Heb 9:23, 26; 10:12, 26). Christ as a sacrifice (Heb 7:27; 9:26) is that to which the present context refers. Christ's supreme sacrifice of himself is the ultimate demonstration of his love. In Heb 7:26–27 the writer states that Christ, a blameless high priest, needed no sacrifices like other high priests, so he offered up himself once for all.

Taken together the two words convey that Christ handed himself over as the offering and sacrifice that would fulfill all the offerings and sacrifices in the OT. When one looks at the calendar of feasts (Lev 23) and all of the offerings and sacrifices for which each Israelite was responsible, and all the offerings and sacrifices which the priests had to offer for all the people (both the daily offerings as well as the annual celebrations), it is astounding that the one supreme offering and sacrifice of Christ met all their requirements. The Book of Hebrews (9:26; 10:10–12) carries a parallel idea when it speaks of the "one" offering and sacrifice of Christ.

With regard to the dative τῷ θεῷ "to God," some connect it to the following prepositional phrase (RSV, NEB, JB, NIV, NJB, NRSV),[4] while

1. Herodotus 1.50; 6, 105; 8.99; Pindar *Pythian Odes* 5.86.

2. BDB 257–58; cf. J. Bergman, H. Ringgren, and B. Lang, "זָבַח *zābhach*; זֶבַח *zebhach*," *TDOT* 4 (1980): 8–29.

3. BDB 585; cf. H.-J. Fabry and M. Weinfeld, "מִנְחָה *minḥâ*," *TDOT* 8 (1997): 407–21.

4. Olshausen, 245; Hodge, 279; Harless, 450; Eadie, 365; Masson, 205 n. 5; Schlier, 232; Gaugler, 198, 245 n. 6; Mitton, 176; Barth, 559–60.

others attach it to the two preceding substantives (AV, RV, ASV, NASB).[1] The first option, that it is linked to the following prepositional phrase ("a fragrant aroma to God"), argues that the OT is replete with the concept of a sweet-smelling aroma to God (cf. Gen 8:21; Exod 29:18, 25; Lev 1:9, 13, 17; 2:9, 12; 3:5). Using it to describe a gift sent to him, Paul states that it was a fragrant offering, a sacrifice that is acceptable and pleasing to God (Phil 4:18). Paul also speaks of believers being a sweet aroma to God (2 Cor 2:14–16). Therefore, Christ handed himself over as an offering and sacrifice for the purpose of being a fragrant aroma to God. The objection to this view is that if Paul had intended this meaning he most likely would have put this dative after the prepositional phrase, otherwise, it is awkward. In fact, this exact prepositional phrase (εἰς ὀσμὴν εὐωδίας) occurs twenty-six times in the LXX (all within the canon except Jdt 16:16) and only twice is κυρίῳ, "to the Lord," before the prepositional phrase (Exod 29:18; Lev 17:4) as in the present verse. Eighteen times it follows the prepositional phrase (six times it does not have the dative). The second option, that the dative is connected to the two preceding nouns ("as an offering and sacrifice to God"), is the best. It provides the simplest explanation for it is in close proximity to the nouns. It means that Christ handed himself over as an offering and sacrifice to God. Since these nouns are predicate accusatives, the sense would be that he handed himself over to God as an offering and sacrifice for a fragrant aroma. The dative could be classified as a dative of advantage or better as a dative of indirect object. The offering and sacrifice of Christ was offered to God the Father. God's justice was met at the cross by Christ's supreme sacrifice. Next, Paul further explains the kind of sacrifice Christ was.

εἰς ὀσμὴν εὐωδίας, "for a fragrant aroma." The term ὀσμή refers to an "odor, smell," whether it be unpleasant[2] or pleasant.[3] The word εὐωδία means "sweet smell."[4] In the LXX ὀσμή occurs seventy-nine times (sixty-eight times in the canonical books) and εὐωδία occurs fifty-eight times (forty-eight times in the canonical books). Significantly, they occur forty-nine times together (forty-seven times in the canonical books) meaning "fragrant aroma" (e.g., Gen 8:21; Exod 29:18, 25, 41; Lev 1:9, 13, 17; Num 15:3, 5; Ezek 6:13, 19). The same construction with the same meaning occurs at least twenty-six times in the Qumran texts (e.g., 1QS 8:9; 4Q258 6:3; 4Q265 frag. 7 ii:9; 11Q19 13:12). In the NT ὀσμή occurs six times (John 12:3; 2 Cor 2:14, 16*bis*; Eph 5:2; Phil 4:18) and εὐωδία occurs three times (2 Cor 2:15; Eph 5:2; Phil

1. Bengel, 4:101; Alford, 3:128; Ellicott, 113; Abbott, 147; Salmond, 351; Caird, 83. Meyer (264) connects the dative to the verb ("gave himself over to God") but this is unacceptable because it is so far removed from the verb. Furthermore, Christ had given himself over to God all during his ministry and the point here is that in the supreme sacrifice, Christ gave himself over as an offering and sacrifice that was pleasing to God.

2. Homer *Ilias* 14.415; *Odyssea* 4.406.

3. Euripides *Cyclops* 153.

4. Herodotus 4.75.

4:18). The first word is used alone once (John 12:3) and the other times it is used either in close promixity to the other word (2 Cor 2:14–16) or together with the second word (Eph 5:2; Phil 4:8). Hence, these two words together[1] refer to sacrifice and derive their background from the OT. Out of the forty-nine times the expression "fragrant aroma" is found in the OT, twenty-six times (twenty-five times in the canonical books) it is this exact prepositional phrase as in the present verse. In other words, Paul is capturing the OT sense of a sacrifice that is acceptable to God. The genitive (εὐωδίας) is attributive, "fragrant aroma." The preposition εἰς indicates purpose, that is, the offering and sacrifice to God is for the purpose of a fragrant aroma.

In the past, even when properly prepared, God did not receive every sacrifice as a fragrant aroma because the offerer had a wrong attitude and a heart far from him. In contrast, Christ willingly gave himself to be offered and he did it to be a pleasant aroma to God. Likewise, we as believers should walk in sacrificial love so that we may be a pleasant aroma not only to God but also to fellow believers (2 Cor 2:14–16). Christ's love cost him his life. Should our love be without cost?

2. Negative: Abstain from Evil (5:3–6)

Paul now gives another negative command. Note the chiastic structure. In 4:31 Paul states the negative, in verse 32 the positive, in 5:1–2 the positive, and in verses 3–6 the negative.

a. Responsibility: Abstain from Evil Practices (5:3–4)

Paul states that believers should have no place in their lives for evil practices. He singles out first their conduct (v. 3) and then their speech (v. 4). To walk as unregenerate sinners runs counter to walking in love. Having given the specifics of love in the sacrificial death of Christ, Paul now gives the specifics of conduct antithetical to love.

(1) In Conduct (5:3)

Text: 5:3. Πορνεία δὲ καὶ ἀκαθαρσία πᾶσα ἢ πλεονεξία μηδὲ ὀνομαζέσθω ἐν ὑμῖν, καθὼς πρέπει ἁγίοις,

Translation: 5:3. "But do not let sexual immorality and impurity of any kind or greed even be mentioned among you, as is appropriate for the saints,"

Commentary: 5:3. πορνεία δὲ καὶ ἀκαθαρσία πᾶσα, "But do not let sexual immorality and impurity of any kind." The contrast is denoted

1. Winer (*Grammar*, 756) states that these two words might be regarded as semi-pleonasm: "The words however mean *odour of fragrance*: ὀσμή is the scent as inhaled, εὐωδία its property."

by the adversative conjunction δέ, "but." Paul is going from positive to negative exhortations. He lists lifestyles that are diametrically opposed to the Christian life, which is to imitate God and walk in love. The first word πορνεία is rare in the classical literature but is used to refer to prostitution[1] or to homosexuality.[2] In the LXX it appears fifty times, forty-three times in the canonical books, and translates זָנָה and its derivatives, meaning "fornication."[3] It can refer to harlotry (Gen 38:24; 2 Kgs 9:22; Jer 13:27; Hos 1:2*bis*; 2:2, 4 [MT & LXX 2:4, 6]; Mic 1:7*bis*; 3:4*bis*), wickedness (Isa 47:10), and spiritual harlotry or unfaithfulness (Num 14:33; Jer 2:20; 3:2, 9; Ezek 16:15–41; 23:7–35; 43:7, 9; Hos 4:11, 12; 5:4; 6:10). Essentially it means aberrant sexual conduct or, metaphysically, a deviation from the true worship of God. In the NT it is used twenty-five times, ten times by Paul, only here in Ephesians. Similarly, it is used of extramarital relationships (Matt 5:32; 15:19 = Mark 7:21; Matt 19:9; John 8:41; Acts 15:20, 29; 21:25; 1 Cor 5:1; 7:2; Rev 2:21; 9:21) and spiritual and/or political prostitution (Rev 14:8; 17:2, 4; 18:3; 19:2). In this context it refers to sexual conduct. When it used of sexual relationships it is normally thought of as extramarital relationships (e.g., Matt 5:32), including incest (1 Cor 5:1). Thus, it is a broad term best translated "sexual immorality"[4] and this should not be any part of the lifestyle of the believer.

The second word ἀκαθαρσία was discussed at 4:19 and means moral "impurity," which indicates the general defilement of the whole personality. This defilement of the whole personality is reinforced by the following adjective πᾶς and, when used with an anarthous noun, means "every kind of, all sorts of" impurity.[5] Hence, the translation "of any kind" captures this idea. Because the term "sexual immorality" immediately precedes it, some may hold that "impurity" has reference strictly to sexual impurity but it is preferable to consider it as all sorts of impurity as in 4:19.

ἢ πλεονεξία μηδὲ ὀνομαζέσθω ἐν ὑμῖν, "or greed even be mentioned among you." Paul continues his list of vices by using the disjunctive conjunction ἤ, "or," to distinguish between two classes of sins: the preceding, external sins of the flesh; the following, general internal sins of attitude. The term πλεονεξία, which was discussed at 4:19, means "covetousness, greediness." The opposite of moderation, it is selfishness to an extreme degree. The internal attitude is tied to the sexual immorality and impurity. Some think it has reference to sexual greed that expresses itself in self-gratification at the expense of

1. Hippocrates *Epidemiorum libri* 7.122.

2. Demosthenes *Orationes* 19.200.

3. BDB 275–76; S. Erlandsson, "זָנָה *zānāh*, etc.," *TDOT* 4 (1980): 99–104.

4. For a study of the term, see Bruce Malina, "Does *Porneia* Mean Fornication?" *NovT* 14 (January 1972): 10–17; Joseph Jensen, "Does *Porneia* Mean Fornication? A Critique of Bruce Malina," *NovT* 20 (July 1978): 161–84.

5. BAGD 631; BDAG 783; Robertson, *Grammar*, 772.

others. It is certainly not an action of love and concern for the other person. Accordingly, the injunction in the tenth commandment against coveting one's neighbor's wife (Exod 20:17; Deut 5:21) may be in mind here.[1] On the other hand, it may simply be greed for material possessions[2] to be consumed by oneself rather than sharing them with the community of believers and depending on the Lord to supply them as the need arises. The negative disjunctive conjunction μηδέ is most likely ascensive and is best translated "not even."[3]

The present imperative is from ὀνομάζω, meaning "to name," a word that is also used in 1:21 and 3:15. In the present context the prohibition in the present tense may suggest that there should not even be an occasion for these vices to be mentioned.[4] It is true that in 1 Cor 5:1 Paul does, in fact, mention a sin of sexual immorality that was actually being committed in Corinth. This verse is not a contradiction to Paul's own practice. Paul is not saying that one cannot identify the sin when it occurs. Rather, he is asserting that these sins should be so universally absent from the body of believers that there should be no occasion to associate them with the church. Herodotus makes a similar statement when he asserts, "one may not speak about what one may not do."[5] Bruce states it well: "such unholy things should not be acceptable subjects of conversation among people whom God has called to be holy."[6] Therefore, believers must refrain from acts and thoughts of immorality which could lead to impure talk and action.

καθὼς πρέπει ἁγίοις, "as is appropriate for the saints." The adverbial conjunction καθώς can be taken as manner (cf. 1:4; 4:32; 5:25, 29), but it can also denote cause (1:4) as seems best here. The reason that such sins should not be mentioned is because it is not fitting for the saints. The verb πρέπω when used with the dative of the person means "to be fitting, proper, appropriate."[7] It is used only ten times in the LXX, three times in the canonical books (Pss 33:1 [LXX 32:1]; 65:1 [MT 65:2; LXX 64:2]; 93:5 [LXX 92:5]), where it can be translated "to befit, be fitting, proper." In the NT it is used seven times, four times by

1. Lincoln, 322; cf. Robinson, 190, 197; Westcott, 76; Hendriksen, 228; Mitton, 178.

2. Calvin, 197; Eadie, 370; Ellicott, 113; Meyer, 266; Abbott, 133, 148; Salmond, 351–52; Schlier, 233; Gaugler, 199; Gnilka, 246; Barth, 503, 561; Schnackenburg, 218; Boutier, 220; Pokorný, 199; Best, 423, 476.

3. Robertson, *Grammar*, 1173; BAGD 518; BDAG 647; Wallace, *Greek Grammar*, 671.

4. The present imperative itself does not indicate whether or not the action is going on but the context may suggest this, though even this is debatable. Cf. Fanning, *Verbal Aspect*, 337; Wallace, *Greek Grammar*, 724. Martín-Asensio states, "The present tense forms in Ephesians are used consistently by the author to communicate the verbal ideas that are most central to his purpose, or those related to the immediate experience or the behaviour of his audience" ("Hallidayan Functional Grammar as Heir to New Testament Rhetorical Criticism," 104).

5. Herodotus 1.138.

6. Bruce, 370.

7. Aeschylus *Agamemnon* 941; Plato *Charmides* 158c.

Paul, and only here in Ephesians. It consistently means that which is fitting or appropriate. The term "saints" refers to all believers (see discussion in 1:1). The dative is possibly a dative of reference or more likely a dative of advantage.[1] Therefore, Paul is stating that it is inappropriate for the aforementioned sins to be mentioned among them.

In conclusion, Paul gives the negative exhortation against the sins of self-love that are so diametrically opposed to the love seen in Christ's sacrificial death. It is inappropriate for believers to even mention these vices. Paul will next discuss both improper and proper speech for the new person. Conduct and conversation are very closely tied to each other.

(2) In Conversation (5:4)

The lifestyle of believers includes their speech as well as their conduct. This verse is a continuation of verse 3 and is dependent on the verb in verse 3.

Text: 5:4. καὶ αἰσχρότης καὶ μωρολογία ἢ εὐτραπελία, ἃ οὐκ ἀνῆκεν, ἀλλὰ μᾶλλον εὐχαριστία.

Translation: 5:4. "and [let there be no] obscenity and foolish talk nor sarcastic ridicule, which are inappropriate, but rather thanksgiving."

Commentary: 5:4. καὶ[2] αἰσχρότης, "and [let there be no] obscenity." The next three vices listed, which occur only here in the NT, describe inappropriate speech among Christians. The first noun αἰσχρότης appears rarely in the classical period where it meant "ugliness, deformity."[3] It never appears in the LXX and is only here in the NT. The adjective αἰσχρός is found in classical literature and means something which "causes shame, dishonoring"[4] or which is "shameful, base."[5] It occurs eleven times in the LXX, six times in a canonical book (Gen 41:3, 4, 19*bis*, 20, 21) where it translates רַע/רֹעַ, meaning "evil, bad."[6] In the NT αἰσχρός is used four times, all by Paul. He uses it to say it is "disgraceful" or "shameful" for a woman to be shorn or shaven (1 Cor 11:6) or for her to speak in church (14:35), to speak of things the people of darkness do in secret (Eph 5:12), and he uses it to describe false

1. Robertson, *Grammar*, 541.

2. The coordinating conjunction καί is found in 𝔓[46, 49] א[1] B D[2] 33 𝔐 syr[p] cop[(bo)] Clement Jerome, while the disjunctive conjunction ἤ is found in A D* F G Ψ 81 104 1241[s] *pc* latt cop[sa] Irenaeus[lat]. Both of these readings are split. The second reading has good Western representation but split Alexandrian text. The first reading is preferred because of better representation in the Alexandrian text and solidly in the Byzantine text. For the 𝔓[49] reading, see Emmel, "Greek Biblical Papyri in the Beinecke Library," 293 verso line 9; Pickering, "Readings in a Papyrus Text of Ephesians," 116.

3. Plato *Gorgias* 525a.

4. Homer *Ilias* 23, 473.

5. Herodotus 3.155; Aeschylus *Septem contra Thebas* 685.

6. BDB 947–49; Dohmen, *TWAT* 7 (1990): 585–86.

teachers who teach for "base" gain (Titus 1:11). Hence, the basic concept of both the adjective and the noun is that which is shameful, disgraceful, base.

It should be noted that even though the preceding verse is concerned with conduct and the present verse deals primarily with speech, the meaning of this particular noun cannot be limited to speech.[1] A more specific word for shameful speech is αἰσχρολογία, which is used in Col 3:8. Rather, αἰσχρότης is a general word for shame that includes both conduct and speech and is best translated "obscenity" (TEV, NIV, NRSV), which may refer to conduct or speech. This serves as a good transition from the previous verse.

καὶ[2] **μωρολογία,** "and foolish talk." This rarer term refers to "silly, foolish, senseless talk."[3] This word is not found in the LXX and is used only here in the NT. In combining this with other words, Bertram thinks that this has reference not only to silly talk but also talk that may be empty and speculative, even dangerous to salvation.[4] At any rate, it is at least likely to refer to futile talk that detracts from the issues of faith and edifying discussion. Accordingly, it is best translated "foolish talk."

ἢ[5] **εὐτραπελία,** "nor sarcastic ridicule." In classical times it is used in a good sense, that is, "witty, wittiness,"[6] and Aristotle alludes to it as the fondness of laughter characterized by the youth.[7] Further, Aristotle states that it is the mean between buffoonery and boorishness,[8]

1. As do Theophylact *Eph* 5:4 (*PG* 124:1104); Oecumenius *Eph* 4:3–8 (*PG* 118:1236); Harless, 453; Olshausen, 247–48; Bruce, 370.

2. The coordinating conjunction καί is read in 𝔓$^{46, 49}$ ℵ^1 B D^2 33 𝔐 syr^p cop$^{(bo)}$ Clement Jerome, while the disjunctive conjunction ἤ is found in ℵ* A D* F G P 0278 81 104 326 365 1175 1241^s 1739 2464 *pc* latt syr^h cop$^{sa, bo^{mss}}$ Irenaeus^{lat}. For the 𝔓^{49} reading, see Emmel, "Greek Biblical Papyri in the Beinecke Library," 293 verso line 9; Pickering, "Readings in a Papyrus Text of Ephesians," 116. The two readings are quite evenly divided making it difficult to decide. The first reading has fairly good Alexandrian witness and solid Byzantine witness, whereas the second reading has fairly good representation of the Alexandrian text-type and is solidly represented by the Byzantine text. Internally, the first reading is preferred if one takes the preceding word as referring to speech, and the second reading is preferred if one takes this as referring to the whole of life and sees the succeeding words in another class. It is best to go with the first reading.

3. Aristotle *Historia Animalium* 1.11 §492b.2 states that animals with large projecting ears are a sign of senseless talk; Plutarch *Moralia: De garrulitate* 2 §504b.

4. Georg Bertram, "μωρός κτλ.," *TDNT* 4 (1967): 844–45.

5. The disjunctive conjunction ἤ is replaced by the coordinating conjunction καί in 𝔓^{46} 629 *pc* Cyprian but lacks sufficient evidence to be the preferred reading.

6. Plato *Respublica* 8.14 §563a; Diodorus Siculus 15.6.4.

7. Aristotle *Rhetorica* 2.12.16 §1389b.11.

8. Aristotle *Ethica Nicomachea* 2.7.13 §1108a.24–27. For a good and thorough discussion on this word and humor in the ancient world, see P. W. van der Horst, "Is Wittiness Unchristian? A Note on εὐτραπελία in Eph. v 4," in *Miscellanea Neotestamentica*, ed. T. Baarda, A. F. J. Klijn, and W. C. van Unnik, NovTSup, ed. W. C. van Unnik et al., vol. 48 (Leiden: Brill, 1978), 163–77.

but there is a tendency to move from that midpoint because people are so fond of jokes and ridicule that they will do anything to get a laugh.[1] Again it is not found in the LXX and is used only here in the NT. In the context it most likely indicates jesting that has gone too far, thus becoming sarcastic ridicule that cuts people down and embarrasses others who are present. It is humor in bad taste. Believers should build up and not destroy, even in humor. Or, since in the context the preceding words were concerned with sexual sins, εὐτραπελία could even have reference to dirty jokes or humor with suggestive overtones. This does not mean humor cannot not be used by Christians. However, it should not be employed at someone's expense thus running counter to Paul's injunction to edify each other (4:29). Consequently, Paul gives this warning. Like anger, humor is to be controlled.

ἃ οὐκ ἀνῆκεν, "which are inappropriate." The relative pronoun is neuter plural referring back to the list of feminine nouns.[2] It is not unusual in Greek to use a neuter relative pronoun "where strictly a masculine or feminine might have been expected—presumably with reference to the 'whole idea' of the preceding clause rather than of the single word which is the immediate antecedent of the relative."[3] The verb ἀνῆκεν is the imperfect of ἀνήκω but is to be read like a present.[4] It means "to reach up to, have come up to" as one pyramid which did not reach up to the height of another or a wall which did not come up to a man's waist.[5] It appears nine times in the LXX, twice in canonical books (Josh 23:14; 1 Sam 27:8). For example, Josh 23:14 speaks of God measuring up or fulfilling his promises. It is used by Demetrius when he writes to the Jews that he is granting them money from "appropriate" places (1 Macc 10:40, 42) and in another letter that relates that he releases the Jews from the taxes that was "due to them" or "properly theirs" (11:35*ter*). Hence, the meaning has shifted slightly to specify that which is appropriate, fitting, and proper. In the NT it appears three times. It is used of wives who are exhorted to be subject to their husbands as it is fitting or appropriate in the Lord (Col 3:18). Elsewhere, Paul commands Philemon to do what is fitting with regards to Onesimus (Phlm 8). Then, in the present text it is used in conjunction with the negative particle (οὐκ), signifying that it is not proper or fitting for believers to have the conduct and speech just described.

It is difficult to know the specific referent of the inappropriate speech and conduct mentioned here. Kreitzer suggests that the author of Ephesians may be referring to the obscene language and conduct

1. Aristotle *Ethica Nicomachea* 4.8.3–10 §1128a.10–36.

2. Cf. Robertson, *Grammar*, 714.

3. Moule, *Idiom Book*, 130; cf. Robertson, *Grammar*, 713.

4. Ibid., 887, 920; BDF §358 [2]; MHT 3:90; Burton, *Moods and Tenses* §32; HS §§198i, 209k; Winer, *Grammar*, 338.

5. Herodotus 2.127; 7.60.

associated with the mother-goddess Demeter/Cybele[1] which would have been known in Asia Minor. Kreitzer gives an array evidence to support his theory. However, some of this is derived from the second century A.D., well after the composition of this letter. Also, if Paul were referring specifically to the mother-goddess practices, it seems likely that he would have been more pointed in his remarks. Furthermore, when the early church fathers comment on this verse they never associate it with the mother-goddess cultic practices. It is more likely then that Paul is speaking in general terms, namely, that vulgar conduct and speech often displayed by humans is inappropriate for believers. As a precedent, OT saints were instructed to avoid behaving in a foolish manner (e.g., Deut 32:6; Job 2:10; Prov 8:5; 15:20; 17:25; 30:32; Eccl 7:7; Jer 5:21; 10:8) or indecently (e.g., Lev 20:17; Deut 22:14, 17; 23:14; 24:1; Jer 3:23–25). Similar injunctions were given to those who were a part of the Qumran community (as discussed in the next paragraph). Rather than addressing specific religious practices that were known in Asia Minor, it is more likely then that Paul is referring to inappropriate conduct and speech that was pervasive in all cultures outside the believing community. Even in the present day, much of the language and conduct of unbelievers is inappropriate for believers.

ἀλλὰ μᾶλλον εὐχαριστία, "but rather thanksgiving." As in 4:28, the stark contrast from the negative is marked by μᾶλλον δέ, which can be translated "but instead" or as here ἀλλὰ μᾶλλον, "but rather." Brachylogy is employed here and either ἔστω or γίνεσθω needs to be supplied.[2] The noun εὐχαριστία is analogous to the verb form, which is discussed at 1:16 and 5:20. It has the idea of "thankfulness, graditude."[3] In the LXX it is used only four times (Esth 16:4 [8:12d]; Wis 16:28; Sir 37:11; 2 Macc 2:27), all with the same meaning as in classical times. The word has not changed its meaning in the Hellenistic times.[4] It is used fifteen times in the NT, twelve times by Paul, and only here in Ephesians. Schubert thinks "thanksgiving" may be the exclusive meaning of εὐχαριστία.[5] In the NT it always refers to thanksgiving to God with the exception of Acts 24:3.

1. Larry J. Kreitzer, "'Crude Language' and 'Shameful Things Done in Secret' (Ephesians 5.4, 12): Allusions to the Cult of Demeter/Cybele in Hierapolis?" *JSNT* 71 (September 1998): 51–77.

2. Salmond, 353.

3. Demosthenes *Orationes* 18.91 (in a decree); Polybius 8.12.8; Diodorus Siculus 17.59.7

4. F. J. A. Hort and J. O. F. Murray, "Εὐχαριστία—Εὐχαριστεῖν," *JTS* 3 (July 1902), 594–98. For an interesting discussion of εὐχαριστία in the first century, see J. P. Audet, "Literary Forms and Contents of a Normal Εὐχαριστία in the First Century," in *SE. Papers Presented to the International Congress on "The Four Gospels in 1957" held at Christ Church, Oxford, 1957*, ed. Kurt Aland, F. L. Cross, Jean Danielou, Harald Riesenfeld, and W. C. van Unnik, TU, ed. Kurt Aland, Walther Eltester, and Erich Klostermann, vol. 73 (Berlin: Akademie-Verlag, 1959), 643–62.

5. Schubert, *Form and Function of the Pauline Thanksgivings*, 93.

There have been suggestions that in the present context the word denotes gracious speech in contrast with the flippant and sarcastic speech previously mentioned.[1] However, the evidence for such a meaning is lacking elsewhere. Rather, it has the idea that instead of flippant speech that dishonors God, one should voice thanksgiving to God for who he is and what he has done.[2] Elsewhere, Paul cites the ingratitude of humans (Rom 1:21) "as the analogous form of vicious behavior."[3] It is a play on words where instead of εὐτραπελία ("sarcastic ridicule") there should be εὐχαριστία ("thanksgiving"). This exhortation closely parallels the rules of conduct in the Qumran community that state that a member of the community will not keep Belial (Satan) in his heart and that there will be no foolishness (= μωρολογία) and malicious lies and deceit coming from his lips . . . abominations (= αἰσχρότης) will not be found on the tongue but rather he will sing songs of thanksgiving (= εὐχαριστία) from his mouth (1QS 10:21–23).[4] When taking into consideration other passages of Scripture, it is clear that "thanksgiving" includes praise to God for himself, for his gifts, and for each other. The latter is in contrast to using speech to destroy each other. Paul models this in his salutation where he gives thanks to God for other believers (1:15–16).

b. Reason: No Inheritance for Evildoers (5:5–6)

Paul exhorts the new person not to live like the old person, explaining that the old person has no inheritance in the kingdom of Christ and God and can expect only the coming wrath of God. In verses 3–5 Paul listed vices characteristic of unbelievers which, consequently, exclude them from the kingdom of God (cf. also 1 Cor 5:9–11; 6:9–10; Gal 5:19–21; Col 3:5–8). Dahl thinks that the lost letter that was misunderstood by the Corinthians (1 Cor 5:9–11) had a similar list and that the author of Ephesians borrowed not only from Col 3:5–8 but also from that lost letter.[5] This is sheer speculation since no one has seen the lost letter. It is better to suppose that Paul repeated many of the same vices often in various contexts, orally as well as in the written texts listed above. Even if Pauline authorship of this letter is not accepted, the passages listed above would suffice as sources for the present passage.

1. Cf. Chrysostom *Eph* 5:4 (*PG* 62:118); Calvin, 197.
2. O'Brien, "Thanksgiving within the Structure of Pauline Theology," 59.
3. Barth, 563.
4. Kuhn, "Ephesians in the Light of the Qumran Texts," 122.
5. Nils Alstrup Dahl, "Der Epheser Brief und der verlorene, erste Brief des Paulus an die Korinther," in *Abraham Unser Vater: Juden und Christen im Gespräch über die Bibel. Festschrift für Otto Michel zum 60. Geburtstag*, ed. Otto Betz, Martin Hengel, and Peter Schmidt, Arbeiten zur Geschichte des Spätjudentums und Urchristentums, vol. 5 (Leiden: Brill, 1963), 65–77, esp. 69–72; updated in idem, *Studies in Ephesians*, 335–48, esp. 340–42.

(1) Evildoers Have No Inheritance in the Kingdom of God (5:5)

Text: 5:5. τοῦτο γὰρ ἴστε γινώσκοντες, ὅτι πᾶς πόρνος ἢ ἀκάθαρτος ἢ πλεονέκτης, ὅ ἐστιν εἰδωλολάτρης, οὐκ ἔχει κληρονομίαν ἐν τῇ βασιλείᾳ τοῦ Χριστοῦ καὶ θεοῦ.

Translation: 5:5. "For you certainly know this, that no immoral or impure or greedy person, who is an idolater, has an inheritance in the kingdom of Christ and God."

Commentary: 5:5. τοῦτο γὰρ ἴστε γινώσκοντες, "For you certainly know this." The conjunction γάρ serves a double function: (1) confirmation of what they already know and (2) reason for the negative injunctions in verses 3–4. The reason they should not act like unbelievers is because unbelievers are not going to inherit the kingdom of Christ and God. The demonstrative pronoun τοῦτο refers to the content which follows.

The periphrastic construction ἴστε γινώσκοντες is an interesting one. Normally a periphrasis has the verb "to be" but here it has the perfect imperative (or indicative) of οἶδα.[1] This results in a present periphrastic emphasizing the continuous action of knowing.[2] Many think that this is a Hebraism of an infinitive absolute, although here the two words for "know" are not the same.[3] Due to this, others rule out a Hebraism and translate it "for you must be assured of this (the following), knowing yourselves."[4] However, others, who suggest that it may not be a Hebraism, think of it much like the infinitive absolute and therefore ἴστε is to regarded as an imperative rather than an indicative,[5] thus, translated "you well know this" or, as we have it, "you certainly know this."

ὅτι πᾶς πόρνος ἢ ἀκάθαρτος ἢ πλεονέκτης, "that no immoral or impure or greedy person." The conjunction ὅτι, which is in apposition to the demonstrative pronoun τοῦτο, can be translated "that" or "that, namely"[6] and is used to introduce the contents of what they well know. As in 4:29 Paul again uses the Semitic πᾶς . . . οὐκ construction[7]

1. Cf. BDF §353 (6); MHT 2:203, 222; 3:303.

2. cf. Robertson, *Grammar*, 330, 890.

3. MHT 1:245; 2:22, 23; 3:85, 157; 4:84; Zerwick, *Biblical Greek* §61. Normally the second word is the same as the first, but there is one exception to this in the LXX (1 Sam 20:3).

4. Cf. Salmond, 353; Abbott, 150.

5. MHT 1:245; 2:203, 222; Robertson, *Grammar*, 330, 890; BDF §§99 (2); 353 (6); cf. Porter, *Verbal Aspect*, 286, 362, 465. However, Porter thinks that it is an indicative and suggests that this periphrastic phrase should be understood as a component of a chiastic structure in vv. 3–5 (Stanley Porter, "ἴστε γινώσκοντες in Ephesians 5,5: Does Chiasm Solve a Problem?" *ZNW* 81, nos. 3/4 [1990]: 270–76). However, elements of his chiastic structure do not readily fall into place and seem to be forced.

6. Wallace, *Greek Grammar*, 459.

7. MHT 1:246; 2:22, 433–34; 3:196, 287; Winer, *Grammar*, 215; Robertson, *Grammar*, 753.

(or πᾶς . . . μή[1]) for negating the verb (rather than putting the negative first). Since πᾶς is before an anarthrous substantive, it may mean "every, each" individual member of a class,[2] or better "everyone,"[3] or in this case "no one."

There is a triad of nouns where πᾶς is associated with each (cf. vv. 3, 9). Here, the three nouns describe the persons who commit the acts mentioned in verse 3. Paul deliberately refers to verse 3 as seen by his use of the same word roots and employment of the same order. The disjunctive conjunction ἤ, "or, nor," distinguishes each particular class of people although some persons may be characterized by more than one quality. However, even if a person is characterized by only one of these qualities, he or she still has no inheritance. This is not to say that a believer might not fall into one of these sins, but rather this concerns the person who is characterized by one or more of these sins. Conversely, a criminal may do a good deed, but this is not what characterizes him.

ὅ[4] ἐστιν εἰδωλολάτρης, "who is an idolater." The neuter relative pronoun agrees with neither its antecedent πλεονέκτης nor its predicate substantive εἰδωλολάτρης. The neuter relative pronoun "gathers the general notion of 'thing'"[5] or the "whole idea" and yet needs to be translated as "who" in English. The relative pronoun refers the reader back to the greedy person and not to all three of the preceding persons; the singular points to this. This is substantiated in Col 3:5 where the relative pronoun (ἥτις) refers only to greed and not to the preceding vices. To covet is idolatry. That which is coveted becomes the center of one's life and is worshiped instead of the Creator (Rom 1:23). The greedy person is willing to exchange the glory of the incorruptible God for a corruptible idol (Rom 1:25). This is a flawed perspective. For example, Esau was so coveteous of the pottage that he sold his

1. Robertson, *Grammar*, 753; MHT 2:434; 3:196; 4:84; Winer, *Grammar*, 216, 728; Zerwick, *Biblical Greek* §446.

2. BAGD 631; BDAG 782.

3. BDF §275 (3). Blass-Debrunner feel that ἕκαστος means "each one" whereas πᾶς means "anyone."

4. The neuter relative pronoun ὅ is found in 𝔓[46] ℵ B F G Ψ 33 81 256 365 424[c] 915 1175 1319 1505 1739 1881 2005 2127 latt vg *al* and the masculine ὅς is found in A D 0278 *Byz* [K L P] Clement Chrysostom Theodoret. The text of 𝔓[49] is broken here but Emmel ("Greek Biblical Papyri in the Beinecke Library," 293 verso line 12) thinks there is insufficient room for the second reading. Externally, it is difficult to decide but it seems that the first reading is slightly favored for it has strong Alexandrian support and fairly strong Western support, represented by a fair amount of minuscules. The second reading does have a key manuscript from the Alexandrian text and from the Western text and it is solidly represented in the Byzantine text. Internally, the first reading is the harder reading for it is easy to see a reason to change this to the masculine but not the reverse. This, too, favors the first reading.

5. Robertson, *Grammar*, 713; Moule, *Idiom Book*, 130; cf. BDF §132 (2); MHT 4:86.

birthright—a ten-minute transaction in exchange for a life's inheritance!

οὐκ ἔχει κληρονομίαν, "has an inheritance." The negative particle οὐκ goes back to the πᾶς earlier in the sentence. The verb goes back to the three persons described. The singular verb emphasizes that every person who is characterized by the qualities mentioned has no inheritance in the kingdom. The present tense of the verb may indicate that those who practice those vices do not presently have an inheritance in the kingdom or it may be a "future-referring present," meaning they will not have an inheritance in the kingdom.[1] The term "inheritance," discussed at 1:14 (cf. also 1:18), refers to the eternal inheritance that does not belong to the sinner but to the saint. This inheritance is obtained as a result of redemption and is not a future reward contingent on faithfulness. The contrast in this passage is between those who inherit and those who receive the wrath of God, not between faithful and unfaithful disciples. It is a contrast between heaven and hell and not a comparison of degree.

ἐν τῇ βασιλείᾳ τοῦ Χριστοῦ καὶ θεοῦ,[2] "in the kingdom of Christ and God." In the NT the kingdom of God is mentioned in sixty-five verses (e.g., Matt 12:28; 19:24; 21:31; Acts 8:12; 14:22; 19:8; Rom 14:17; 1 Cor 4:20; 6:9–10; 15:50; Gal 5:21; Col 4:11; 2 Thess 1:5) and the kingdom associated with Christ occurs at least ten times (Matt 16:28; Luke 1:33; 22:29, 30; 23:42; John 18:36; Col 1:13; 2 Tim 4:1, 18; 2 Pet 1:11), but only in the present verse are the two persons of the Godhead mentioned together in relation to the kingdom. Furthermore, it is interesting to notice that Christ is mentioned before God. Paul may have chosen this order because Christ's sacrificial love on our behalf is the focus (5:2).

When the copulative καί connects two singular nouns (adjectives or participles) of the same case with an articular first noun and an anarthrous second noun, the person of the two nouns is the same person. The second noun further describes the first-named person. This is called Granville Sharp's rule and it can be used to defend the deity of Christ.[3] However, the force of this rule is somewhat blunted here because θεός is frequently without an article[4] and occurs without it in βασιλείαν θεοῦ (1 Cor 6:9, 10; 15:50; Gal 5:21).[5] Furthermore, possibly

1. Porter, *Verbal Aspect*, 230–32.

2. There are various constructions for τοῦ Χριστοῦ καὶ θεοῦ. The reading τοῦ θεοῦ is found in 𝔓[46] 1245 2147. The reading τοῦ θεοῦ καὶ Χριστοῦ is found in F[gr] G it[g] cop[bomss] Ambrosiaster. And Χριστοῦ τοῦ θεοῦ is found in 1739* vg[ms] eth Theodoret. None of these readings have sufficient evidence to alter the present text. Internal evidence verifies the external evidence for normally in the Gospels the kingdom is referred to as βασιλεία τοῦ θεοῦ and not "of Christ" as we have in the present context.

3. Zerwick, *Biblical Greek* §185; Wallace, *Greek Grammar*, 276.

4. Winer, *Grammar*, 162–63 n. 3; Robertson, *Grammar*, 786; Ellicott, 116.

5. Salmond, 354.

the reason for the article before Christ is to denote his title, that is, his proper name, "the Christ" or "the Messiah." The point is that this kingdom belongs to both Christ and God, which is verified by the possessive genitives. According to 1 Cor 15:24, Christ will hand his kingdom to God the Father and the kingdom of Christ and the kingdom of God will become the same kingdom.[1]

The people described in this verse have no inheritance. This corresponds with other thoughts by Paul on the same subject. He states in Gal 5:19–21 that those who do works of the flesh such as sexual immorality, impurity, and idolatry will not inherit the kingdom of God. Likewise in 1 Cor 6:9–10 the unrighteous—the immoral, idolaters, thieves, and the greedy—will not inherit the kingdom of God. The Corinthian believers were counted among them before they were washed, sanctified, and justified in the name of the Lord Jesus Christ and in the Spirit of God (v. 11). There are two aspects of the kingdom. First, there is the present dimension. Paul states in Col 1:13 that we have been delivered from the authority of darkness to the kingdom of his beloved Son, and later in 4:10–11 he speaks of his coworkers for the kingdom of God. Second, there is also the future dimension where in the end Christ will hand the kingdom to God the Father (1 Cor 15:24). This kingdom cannot be inherited by flesh and blood (1 Cor 15:50) but only by those who have believed the gospel of Christ's death and resurrection (15:1–4).

Hence, the kingdom of God is not for saints who have never sinned but for sinners who have been redeemed by Christ's supreme sacrifice (Eph 1:7, 14; 2:4–10; 4:32). Here in Ephesians Paul, addressing believers, rightly assumes that they have inherited the kingdom of God.[2] However, Paul warns that those whose lives are characterized by immorality, impurity, and greed, even though they may claim to be Christians, are not included in the kingdom of God.[3]

(2) Evildoers Receive the Wrath of God (5:6)

Text: 5:6. Μηδεὶς ὑμᾶς ἀπατάτω κενοῖς λόγοις· διὰ ταῦτα γὰρ ἔρχεται ἡ ὀργὴ τοῦ θεοῦ ἐπὶ τοὺς υἱοὺς τῆς ἀπειθείας.

1. For a discussion of the grammatical possibilities for this passage, see Harris, *Jesus as God*, 261–63. Thiede asserts that the one article indicates that the kingdom of Christ and the kingdom of God are identical (Carsten Peter Thiede, "Der Brief an die Epheser. 41. Teil: Kapitel 5,1–8," *Fundamentum* 21, no. 2 [2000]: 20).

2. Hammer thinks that in Ephesians inheritance is not a present reality but is oriented toward the future ("A Comparison of *klēronomia* in Paul and Ephesians," 268–69). But Paul speaks about those characterized in v. 5 as those who do not "have" the kingdom of God rather than those who "will" not have the kingdom of God. Cf. Denton, "Inheritance in Paul and Ephesians," 157–58.

3. O'Brien, 363.

Translation: 5:6. "Let no one deceive you with empty words; for because of these things the wrath of God comes on the sons of disobedience."

Commentary: 5:6. Μηδεὶς ὑμᾶς ἀπατάτω κενοῖς λόγοις, "Let no one deceive you with empty words." Without any introductory conjunction, Paul concludes this section with a solemn warning. The negative pronoun μηδείς emphasizes that "no one" or "not any person" is to deceive them. Who these people are is a matter of debate. It probably refers to both unbelievers and believers who falsely think that worldly living is of no consequence. Believers can be influenced by their culture so that what is acceptable in the world becomes acceptable in the church. The text has described those in the world as immoral, impure, and greedy. Because it appears that the unbelievers were not presently suffering the consequences of this lifestyle, believers might easily slide into a similar mode of life. Thus, Paul warns against being deceived by the world or by those so-called believers who have bought into the world system. In other words, let no one—whether inside or outside the church—deceive you. It seems that the prohibition in the form of the present imperative indicates a general precept making no comment about whether or not any sinful action is taking place.[1]

The verb ἀπατάω has the same sense as the noun ἀπάτη discussed at 4:22, meaning "to deceive, mislead."[2] It is used in the NT two other times: Paul states that Adam was not deceived in the garden (1 Tim 2:14) and James states that one who thinks he is religious but does not control his tongue deceives his heart (Jas 1:26). The object of the verb is an instrumental dative best translated "with empty words."[3]

The adjective κενός means "empty"[4] and it can refer to "empty words"[5] (cf. Exod 5:9; Deut 32:47), meaning that they are void of content or without truth (appears in the LXX seventy-six times, sixty-one times in the canonical books). In the NT it occurs eighteen times, twelve times in Paul, only here in Ephesians. Paul uses it in reference to the resurrection where he argues that if Christ is not raised from the dead then both his preaching and the Corinthians' faith is void of content (1 Cor 15:14*bis*). Similarly, in this context it has the idea of words that are without content or without basis, hence, "empty words." This makes good sense here for he had told the believers that unbelievers had minds that were without purpose, being darkened in their reasoning processes and that they were alienated from the life of God (Eph 4:17–18). There may have been those who would try to convince believers that everyone has an inheritance and that there is no

1. Wallace, *Greek Grammar*, 724.
2. BAGD 82; BDAG 98.
3. HS §173b.
4. Homer *Odyssea* 10.42; 22.249; Plato *Leges* 7 §796b; Herodotus 1.73.
5. Plato *Laches* 196b.

judgment on those who practice evil. Paul considers this empty speech a lie. He also tells the saints not to participate in useless or unwholesome talk, which is so characteristic of unbelievers (4:29). Rather, they are to know that the truth is in Jesus, that they have put off the old person and put on the new person, and that there is a new lifestyle that goes with the position (4:20–32). The truth, that is, words with content, should be believed rather than words devoid of content.

διὰ ταῦτα γὰρ ἔρχεται ἡ ὀργὴ τοῦ θεοῦ ἐπὶ τοὺς υἱοὺς τῆς ἀπειθείας, "for because of these things the wrath of God comes on the sons of disobedience." This is strongly worded. It is the reason one must not be deceived with empty words. Paul expresses this not only by the conjunction γάρ, "for," but also with the prepositional phrase διὰ ταῦτα, "on account of these things, because of these things." The demonstrative pronoun ταῦτα refers not to "empty words" but to all the sins mentioned in the preceding verse.

The concepts of the wrath of God and the sons of disobedience were discussed at 2:2–3. God's wrath or anger is not directed toward those who are sons of God but toward those who are the sons of disobedience—unbelievers. The word "sons" conveys distinction, and here the distinctive sons of disobedience. It was pointed out that outside Ephesians and Colossians, "disobedience" has the idea of "unbelief"[1] (Rom 11:30, 32; Heb 4:6, 11). This idea fits well in the present context because these people do not believe that God judges and consequently they try to persuade all people of this, including believers. That is why Paul warns believers not to believe their words, which are void of content. Rather they are to believe the truth which is in Jesus.

The present tense of the verb ἔρχεται signifies "a solemn present"[2] nature of the wrath of God. But is not the wrath of God in the future? It is both present and future.[3] In Romans Paul states that the present wrath of God is revealed from heaven (Rom 1:18) and that there is a future wrath for those who are hard-hearted and who continue to store up wrath for the day of God's judgment (2:5). This present and future notion applies also to the kingdom mentioned in the preceding verse. We are presently in the kingdom (Eph 5:5; Col 1:13) and counted as fellow heirs (Eph 2:11–22), sealed with the Holy Spirit (1:13), and yet we will fully possess the kingdom later when we are finally redeemed from the presence of sin (1:14).[4]

In conclusion, Paul exhorts his readers to be imitators of God and to walk in love. Believers' conduct and speech is not to be destructive

1. Actually 𝔓[49] has ἀπιστίας instead of ἀπειθείας. See William H. P. Hatch and C. Bradford Wells, "A Hitherto Unpublished Fragment of the Epistle to the Ephesians," *HTR* 51 (January 1958): 34; Pickering, "Readings in a Papyrus Text of Ephesians," 111–12.

2. Salmond, 354.

3. The timing as well as the nature of God's wrath is debated by Origen and Jerome, see Layton, "Recovering Origen's Pauline Exegesis," 399–403, 410–11.

4. For a different view, see Fischer, *Tendenz und Absicht des Epheserbriefes*, 150–52.

but constructive for the purpose of building one another up in the faith, unlike unbelievers whose conduct and speech are destructive and they will face the wrath of God. The latter are the sons of disobedience or unbelief, having accepted the lie of the evil one. On the other hand, believers are sons of obedience or faith, having accepted the truth in Jesus.

D. Walk in Light (5:7–14)

God's children are to walk in unity (4:1–16) by preserving the unity they already have in Christ as modeled by the Trinity. Furthermore, they are to walk in holiness (4:17–32) because they are new people in Christ and their lifestyle should reflect their new position. This lifestyle manifests itself by walking in love (5:1–6) as Christ demonstrated by his sacrificial love. This walk also includes abstaining from the evil practices of unbelievers. In the next section Paul exhorts believers to walk in the light, which pleases God, rather than to participate in the works of the evildoers (5:7–14). This section is divided into three parts: (1) do not become involved with evildoers (vv. 7–10); (2) do not become involved with their works (vv. 11–13); rather (3) have the approval of Christ's light (v. 14).

1. Do Not Become Involved with Evildoers (5:7–10)

Before a discussion of individual verses, there is a need to justify the break here instead of between verses 5 and 6 or between verses 7 and 8. As for verses 5 and 6, verse 6 appears to be a good conclusion to the previous section, that is, the warning to believers against being deceived with the empty words that discount a future judgment, asserting that all will inherit the kingdom, therefore, making it acceptable to live like the unbelieving world. Although reasons vary as to why the break should be between verses 7 and 8,[1] the basic argument is that the key term in this last half of the book is "to walk" (περιπατέω, 4:1, 17; 5:2) and that this does not appear until verse 8. However, as mentioned in 5:1, another key to this portion of the book is to unite

1. Dibelius-Greeven, 90; Masson, 207; Schlier, 236–37; Gaugler, 201 Gnilka, 251; Schnackenburg, 216; Lindemann, 93.

this verb περιπατέω with the conjunction οὖν that appears in verse 7, thus making the break between verses 6 and 7 the best choice.

In the following verses Paul reminds believers that they are children of light and their walk must demonstrate this fact. He exhorts them to refuse to participate with unbelievers in their acts of disobedience.

a. Command: Do Not Get Involved (5:7)

Text: 5:7. μὴ οὖν γίνεσθε συμμέτοχοι αὐτῶν·

Translation: 5:7. "Therefore do not become fellow participants with them;"

Commentary: 5:7. μὴ οὖν γίνεσθε συμμέτοχοι αὐτῶν, "Therefore do not become fellow participants with them." The conjunction οὖν, "therefore," starts a new section, making an inference from what has just been said. Because the wrath of God is coming on the sons of disobedience, believers are not to become partakers with them. Again, Paul uses the present imperative (γίνεσθε) which may denote (in this context) the ingressive-progressive force to begin and continue.[1] Westcott thinks the present tense here "indicates the imminence of the danger."[2] It should not be translated as ἐστέ, "be" (as AV, RV, ASV, NASB, NIV, NRSV), but "become," which indicates the possibility of entering into the condition[3] of becoming a fellow participant. Accordingly, in the light of the coming judgment (v. 6), believers should not be deceived into thinking that it is harmless to become participants with unbelievers.

The term συμμέτοχος occurs only here and in 3:6 where the believer is called a fellow participant of the promise. The word means one who is a partner or an accomplice in a plot. "It is a participation in another's rights by becoming somehow identified with that other."[4] The pronoun αὐτῶν is a genitive of association[5] referring not to sins[6] but to the persons (τοὺς υἱοὺς τῆς ἀπειθείας, "sons of disobedience")[7] mentioned in verses 3–6 who are objects of God's wrath. Because believers are in a new fellowship with the Lord and his saints, they are not to be fellow participants with sinners who are going in the opposite direc-

1. Wallace, *Greek Grammar*, 721.

2. Westcott, 77.

3. BAGD 159; BDAG 198.

4. McGrath, "'*Syn*' Words in Saint Paul," 221.

5. Wallace, *Greek Grammar*, 129.

6. As Ellicott, 117; Masson, 207 n. 4; Gaugler, 201; Hendriksen, 231; Gnilka, 250–51; Best, 486.

7. As Theodoret *Comm. Eph.* 5:7 (*PG* 82:544); Aquinas, chap.5, lect. 3, vv. 5–7 (202–3); Alford, 131; Eadie, 379; Meyer, 270; Abbott, 152; Salmond, 355; Robinson, 117; Westcott, 77; Dibelius-Greeven, 90; Lenski, 603; Schlier, 236; Mitton, 182; Schnackenburg, 222; Bruce, 372; Lincoln, 326; Bouttier, 224; O'Brien, 365.

tion. This does not imply that believers should have no association with unbelievers but rather are not to participate in their lifestyle. If there were no association with those in the world, there would be no opportunity to function as lights in the world. This recalls an analogous misunderstanding by the Corinthians believers (1 Cor 5:9–10).

b. Reason: Christians Are Changed Persons (5:8a)

After warning believers not to become fellow participants with unbelievers because of God's impending wrath mentioned in verse 6, Paul gives an additional reason; namely, they are no longer of the darkness but of the light in the Lord.

Text: 5:8a. ἦτε γάρ ποτε σκότος, νῦν δὲ φῶς ἐν κυρίῳ·

Translation: 5:8a. "for you were formerly darkness, but now you are light in the Lord;"

Commentary: 5:8a. ἦτε γάρ ποτε σκότος, "for you were formerly darkness." The conjunction γάρ is explanatory, giving the reason why believers should not be fellow participants with those who are of the world. The verb is emphatic both by its position and because the tense changes from the present to the imperfect. It emphasizes a past condition. This is further verified by the enclitic particle of time ποτέ (cf. 2:2, 3, 11, 13), which stands in contrast to the following adverb of time νῦν (cf. 2:2, 13; 3:5, 10), which indicates the present time.[1] The term σκότος means "darkness, gloom."[2] In classical usage darkness encompasses death[3] and is used of the netherworld.[4] Metaphorically, it has the sense of being in obscurity.[5] It occurs in the LXX 119 times, ninety-seven times in the canonical books and translates nine Hebrew words. Seventy-five times it translates חֹשֶׁךְ and its derivatives which mean "darkness, obscurity."[6] It can refer to physical darkness (Gen 1:2–5, 18) but more often it has theological connotations such as the place where the God of light is not. It connotes evil (Job 19:8; 22:11) and wickedness (Ps 82:5 [LXX 81:5]); the disobedient are in darkness (Ps 107:10 [106:10]). There is much made of darkness in the Qumran community. It is depicted as the way of sin and wickedness (cf. 1QS 2:7; 3:19, 21; 4:11; 1QM 15:9; 4Q177 3:8; 4Q286 frag. 7 ii:4). In the NT, the word is used thirty-one times, eleven times by Paul, and three times in Ephesians (5:8, 11; 6:12). Only occasionally is it used of physical darkness as when the sun became darkened at the crucifixion (Matt 27:45 = Mark 15:33 = Luke 23:44). It often refers to those who

1. Cf. Tachau, *„Einst" und „Jetzt" im Neuen Testament*, 125–26.
2. Homer *Odyssea* 19.389; *Ilias* 5.47.
3. Homer *Ilias* 4.461; 13.672; Euripides *Phoenissae* 1453.
4. Pindar *Fragmenta* 130 (95); Sophocles *Oedipus Coloneus* 1701; Euripides *Helena* 62.
5. Plato *Leges* 8 §837a; Sophocles *Antigone* 494.
6. BDB 365; Lutzmann, Geraty, Ringgren, and Mitchel, *TDOT* 5 (1986): 245–59.

live in the realm of sin (Matt 4:16; Luke 1:79; John 3:19; Acts 26:18; Rom 2:19; 13:12; 2 Cor 6:14; Eph 6:12; Col 1:13; 1 Thess 5:4, 5; 1 Pet 2:9; 1 John 1:6) or to the future abode of the wicked (Matt 8:12; 22:13; 25:30; 2 Pet 2:17; Jude 13).[1]

Therefore, darkness signifies sin, both its realm and power. Those who are in darkness must grope through life without the light of God's revelation (4:18). Their future will be a continuation of darkness but to an even greater degree. Interestingly, in this present verse Paul does not say that the believers were *in* darkness but that they *were* darkness itself, that is, the embodiment of darkness. As such, they were held in sway by the power of sin and approved of others who practiced sinful deeds (Rom 1:32).

νῦν δὲ φῶς ἐν κυρίῳ, "but now you are light in the Lord." A contrast is highlighted both by the adversative conjunction δέ "but" and by the adverb of time νῦν, "now." They were darkness but now they are light in the Lord.

The word φῶς (contraction of φάος) means "light."[2] In classical times it denoted the physical light of day[3] and it was sometimes used metaphorically for happiness, victory, and glory.[4] It could also speak of life itself[5] or of a manifestation of the divine.[6] In the LXX it occurs 175 times and in the canonical books it appears 130 times and translates five Hebrew words. About a hundred times it translates אוֹר, meaning "light."[7] As in classical usage, it can refer to the physical light of day (Gen 1:3–5), but primarily it refers to the character and revelation of God. God is clothed with light (Ps 104:2 [LXX 103:2]). Light comes from God (Ps 4:6 [MT & LXX 4:7]; 89:15 [MT 89:16; LXX 88:16]); Isa 60:19–20) and dwells with him (Hab 3:4). God can turn darkness into light (Ps 139:12 [LXX 138:12]). The antithesis of light is darkness and God uncovers the darkness with his light (Job 12:22).[8] Hearts that are open to the light of God's revelation experience God's salvation, which in turn lights life's path (Ps 119:105 [LXX 118:5]; Prov 6:23). In the Qumran community much is written about the contrast between light and darkness. The claim is made, for example, that those who are born of truth come from a fountain of light and all the children of light are ruled by the Prince of Light and walk in the ways

1. For a more detailed study of the word, see Hans Conzelmann, "σκότος κτλ.," *TDNT* 7 (1971): 423–45; Hans-Cristoph Hahn, "Darkness (σκότος)," *NIDNTT* 1 (1975): 421–25.

2. For a study of light, see Hans Conzelmann, "φῶς κτλ.," *TDNT* 9 (1974): 310–58; Hans-Christoph Hahn, "Light (φῶς)," *NIDNTT* 2 (1976): 490–96.

3. Plato *Respublica* 6.19 §508c; Homer *Odyssea* 21.429.

4. Homer *Ilias* 6.6; 17.615; Sophocles *Ajax* 709; *Antigone* 600.

5. Homer *Ilias* 18.61; *Odyssea* 4.540; Sophocles *Oedipus Tyrannus* 375.

6. Euripides *Bacchae* 1082–83.

7. BDB 21; Sverre Aalen, "אוֹר *ʾôr*," *TDOT* 1 (1977): 147–67.

8. Cf. Kerrigan, "Echoes of Themes from the Servant Songs in Pauline Theology," 2:225–26.

of light (1QS 3:19–20). In the NT φῶς is used seventy-three times, thirteen times by Paul, and five times in Ephesians (5:8*bis*, 9, 13, 14). It has few references to physical light (Luke 8:16; Acts 16:29; Rev 22:5). Mostly, it is used metaphorically. In the transfiguration Jesus' garments are said to have become white as light (Matt 17:2). John particularly liked to use the imagery of light. In John's Gospel Jesus claims that he is the light of the world (John 8:12; 9:5; 12:46) and God is described as light, in whom there is no darkness (1 John 1:5). Also, John states that the natural person loves darkness rather than light (John 3:19). Since Jesus identified himself as the light, John promises that those who believe in the light become sons of light (John 12:35–36) and cannot remain in darkness (12:46). Here, too, in Ephesians Paul states that believers were once darkness but now they are light.

Light and darkness oppose each other (e.g., Isa 5:20; 9:2; 50:10; Amos 5:18; Mic 7:8; Matt 6:23 = Luke 11:34; John 3:19; 8:12; 1QS 1:9–10; 3:19–20, 24–25; 1QM 1:1, 11–16; 3:6, 9; 13:16). Light and darkness cannot coexist. However, with darkness there is no qualifier as there is with light. People in darkness are on their own or are there by their own doing, but not so with light. The prepositional phrase ἐν κυρίῳ indicates that the believer is light in the Lord. The source of light is God and Christ. In this context, Christ is identified as the source (vv. 8, 14). "Lord" in this prepositional phrase refers to Christ as it does elsewhere in this epistle (2:21; 4:1, 17; 6:1, 10, 21).

c. Command: Walk as Children of Light (5:8b–10)

Having warned that the wrath of God is coming on the sons of disobedience (v. 6), Paul by inference (οὖν) urged believers not to become fellow participants with them (v. 7) because they were formerly darkness but now they are light in the Lord (v. 8a). With such privilege comes responsibility, as seen in the following verses.

(1) Command to Walk as Children of Light (5:8b)

Text: 5:8b. ὡς τέκνα φωτὸς περιπατεῖτε

Translation: 5:8b. "walk as children of light"

Commentary: 5:8b. ὡς τέκνα φωτὸς περιπατεῖτε, "walk as children of light." Paul again repeats the command "to walk" (4:1, 17; 5:2). The imperative is in the present tense to denote a habitual conduct for those who are children of light.[1] The comparative conjunction ὡς conveys a standard of how they are to walk.[2] They are to walk as the children of light. The word τέκνα, "children," has already been discussed at 2:3 (cf. 5:1) and connotes a close relationship to the parent. Since God is light (1 John 1:5) and believers are the children of God (5:1),

1. Cf. Fanning, *Verbal Aspect*, 358–60.
2. Cf. Muraoka, "The use of ΩΣ in the Greek Bible," 59.

they are to walk as children of God or light. As light reflects the glory of God, so should the believers reflect his glory because they are to be imitators of God. The genitive (φωτός) is probably not a genitive of source[1] because the emphasis is on believers as light, not that they came from light. It seems better to label this as a descriptive genitive or a genitive of characteristic quality,[2] that is, children characterized by light since they are the imitators of God who is light (cf. 1QS 1:9; 2:16; 3:13, 24, 25; 1QM 1:3, 11, 13; 13:16).

Before conversion believers were darkness and hated the light (v. 8a; 2:1–3; cf. John 3:20). But light exposed them and they became the children of light. Since they are light, they should walk as children of light and hate the darkness. But what are the qualities of the children of light? Paul addresses these next.

(2) Characteristics of the Fruit of Light (5:9)

Text: 5:9. —ὁ γὰρ καρπὸς τοῦ φωτὸς ἐν πάσῃ ἀγαθωσύνῃ καὶ δικαιοσύνῃ καὶ ἀληθείᾳ—

Translation: 5:9. "—for the fruit of light consists in all goodness and righteousness and truth—"

Commentary: 5:9. —ὁ γὰρ καρπὸς τοῦ φωτός,[3] "for the fruit of light." The conjunction γάρ, "for," is explanatory. Paul proceeds parenthetically to explain what it means to walk as a child of light. Classically, the word καρπός literally meant fruit of the field,[4] but also it can simply mean fruit, product, or result of an action, whether good or bad.[5] Likewise, in the LXX it refers to the fruit of the earth (Num 13:26–27;

1. As Eadie, 380.

2. Robertson, *Grammar*, 497 although later he labels it a genitive of apposition (651); MHT 2:440–41; cf. Moule, *Idiom Book*, 174; HS §159d.

3. The following manuscripts have φωτός: 𝔓^{49} ℵ A B D* F G P 6 33 81 256 424^{c} 629 1175^{c} 1319 1739* 1881 1962 2127 2464 it$^{ar, b, d, f, g, mon, o}$ vg syr$^{p, pal}$ cop$^{sa, bo}$ arm eth geo^{1} Origen Gregory-Thaumaturgus Ps-Cyprian Victorinus-Rome Ambrosiaster Lucifer Jerome Pelagius Augustine. The reading πνεύματος is found in 𝔓^{46} D^{2} Ψ 075 0150 88 104 263 365 424* 436 459 614 1241 1573 1739^{mg} 1852 1912 2200 *Byz* [K L] *Lect* syr^{h} geo^{2} slav Chrysostom Theodoret^{lat} Theodoret. The first reading is to be preferred because it has good representation from the Alexandrian and Western text-types, whereas the second reading has only a few manuscripts from the Alexandrian text but is solidly represented in the Byzantine text. The first has the best geographical distribution and has good genealogical relationships in the Alexandrian and Western texts. Internally, the first reading is preferred because it is the more difficult reading, whereas the second reading corresponds with Gal 5:22. The first reading agrees with the context, for light is mentioned three other times (vv. 8*bis*, 13). See Moir, "A Mini-Guide to New Testament Textual Criticism," *BT* 36 (January 1985): 128. In conclusion then, the first reading is the preferred one.

4. Homer *Ilias* 6.142; Herodotus 1.212.

5. Aeschylus *Septem contra Thebas* 600, 618; Plato *Phaedrus* 260d; Pindar *Pythian Odes* 2.74.

Deut 1:25), fruit of the womb or posterity (Gen 30:2; Deut 7:13), and the fruit or product of an action (Prov 1:31; Hos 10:13; Amos 6:12). In the NT it is used sixty-seven times, twelve times by Paul, and only here in Ephesians. Again, it refers to the fruit of the land (Matt 21:19; Jas 5:7, 18), fruit of the womb (Luke 1:42; Acts 2:30), and result of an action (Matt 7:16; 21:43; Rom 1:13; 6:22; Gal 5:22). Obviously, in the present context fruit refers to the product of an action.[1] The genitive (φωτός) is a genitive of production,[2] namely, it is the light that produces the fruit. Paul now lists the fruit so that believers can measure their lives to see if their actions or works are a result of the light.

ἐν πάσῃ ἀγαθωσύνῃ, "consists in all goodness." Since there is no verb, the verb "to be" is supplied conveying the idea of "characterized by" or "consists in." The preposition ἐν, "in," denotes the sphere[3] in which the fruit of light expresses itself. The adjective πᾶς used with an anarthrous noun means "every,"[4] and it literally means "every act of goodness and righteousness and truth" but because it is used in conjunction with these abstract nouns it is best to translate it "all." As seen earlier (vv. 3, 5) πᾶς is used in connection with a triad of nouns, here virtues instead of vices.

The word ἀγαθωσύνη does not appear in classical Greek but occurs fifteen times in the LXX (thirteen times in the canonical books) where it occurs ten times for טוֹבָה, three times for טוּב, and once for טוֹב all of which mean "a good thing(s), benefit, welfare, goodness."[5] It is used of leaders who have done "good things" for the nation (Judg 8:35; 2 Chr 24:16) or the nation which dealt with "goodness" toward Jerubbaal and his house (Judg 9:16 [B text]). It speaks of the Lord's "goodness" (Neh 9:25, 35; 13:31), of a person preferring evil over good (Ps 52:3 [MT 52:5; LXX 51:5]), and of a sinner who can destroy much "good" (Eccl 9:18). Finally, it is used of a person who deprives himself of or enjoys himself with the "good things" or "prosperity" for which he toiled (Eccl 4:8; 5:18 [MT & LXX 5:17]; 6:3, 6; 7:14). Thus, in general terms it has the idea of goodness or prosperity. With reference to the goodness of the Lord it conveys the sense of the Lord's generosity.[6] In addition to this verse it is used three other times in the NT, as follows: Paul is convinced that Roman believers are full of goodness (Rom 15:14), a quality of the fruit of the Spirit is goodness (Gal 5:22), and Paul prays for the Thessalonians that God would make them worthy of his call and might fulfill every "good" desire (2 Thess 1:11). Even after examination of these three uses of this word, it is still diffi-

1. L&N §42.13.

2. Wallace, *Greek Grammar*, 104–5. Best (489) labels it as a subjective genitive meaning "the light has produced fruit."

3. Cf. Winer, *Grammar*, 230.

4. BAGD 631; BDAG 783; Robertson, *Grammar*, 772.

5. BDB 375; Höver-Johag, *TDOT* 5 (1986): 296–317.

6. Barclay, *Flesh and Spirit*, 105.

cult to know exactly what it means here. As mentioned earlier ἀγαθός has reference to moral and beneficial good (2:10; 4:28, 29), which is the opposite of κακός, "bad, evil, injurious" (cf. Luke 16:25; Acts 28:5; Rom 1:30; 2:9; 3:8; 7:19, 21; 12:17, 21; 13:10; 14:20; 1 Thess 5:15; Jas 3:8; 1 Pet 3:9; Rev 16:2). The same can be said of ἀγαθωσύνη. But, in addition, it can signify generosity in connection with the beneficial good. Therefore, the best translation is "goodness," which embraces generosity towards others.

καὶ δικαιοσύνῃ καὶ ἀληθείᾳ—, "and righteousness and truth—." The next two words have been discussed earlier. The first word (discussed at 4:24), δικαιοσύνη, "righteousness," has in mind the right standing of the believer who has trusted God's work on the cross in the person of Jesus Christ. The righteousness of God has been imputed to the believer (Rom 3:21–22; 4:3, 5). Another connotation of the word is the attribute of righteousness. This, of course, characterizes God (Rom 3:25–26). There are also references to a person's own inadequate righteousness (Matt 5:20; Rom 10:3) as well as to the believer's call to righteous behavior (Rom 6:13). Paul prays for the Philippians to be filled with the fruit of righteousness (Phil 1:11). Both in Eph 4:24 and in the present context it refers to this quality of life[1] from which righteous actions spring.[2] Therefore, the fruit of light consists not only in goodness with generosity but also righteous actions or works.

The second word ἀληθεία was discussed at 1:13 (cf. 4:21, 24, 25) and we concluded that it is reality or what is actual as opposed to that which is false. More concretely for this context, it has the idea of right action or living as opposed to false living. It is a quality that comes from God and from which springs the actions of truthfulness.[3] These last two qualities are identified with the new person (4:24).

This verse is a parenthesis (AV, RV, ASV, RSV, NASB, NIV, NRSV). Paul had exhorted them to walk as children of light and this parenthetical thought explains the product of this light. The fruit or product of light consist in all three of these qualities: goodness, righteousness, and truthfulness. Although some of these qualities are mentioned in Qumran writings (e.g., 1QS 1:5; 4:2–3, 24; 5:4; 8:2; 1QH[a] 9:26–27 [1:26–27]; 18:16–17 [10:16–17]; 19:9 [11:9]), it is not justified to suppose, as Murphy-O'Connor does, that the Ephesian author drew from the Essene community.[4] There is no mention of "goodness" nor the concept

1. Hill, *Greek Words and Hebrew Meanings*, 154.

2. J. A. Ziesler, *The Meaning of Righteousness in Paul: A Linguistic and Theological Enquiry*, SNTSMS, ed. Matthew Black, vol. 20 (Cambridge: Cambridge University Press, 1972), 154; Peter Stuhlmacher, *Gerechtigkeit Gottes bei Paulus*, 2d ed., FRLANT, ed. Ernst Käsemann and Ernst Würthwein, vol. 87 (Göttingen: Vandenhoeck & Ruprecht, 1966), 216.

3. Cf. Theron, "Aletheia in the Pauline Corpus," 6, 17.

4. Murphy-O'Connor, "Truth: Paul and Qumran," 204–6.

of "fruit."[1] Instead of the Qumran literature, Paul's remarks may be based on 2 Chr 31:20, which in similar terms speaks of Hezekiah doing good and right and being truthful before the Lord (cf. Mic 6:8).

Light characteristically will expose that which is opposite of these characteristics. It will not tolerate evil or falsity. Sinners, those in darkness, are characterized by the opposite of the fruit of light: evil, wickedness, and falsehood. The fruit of light consists in nothing but that which is good.

(3) Confirmation of God's Pleasure (5:10)

Text: 5:10. δοκιμάζοντες τί ἐστιν εὐάρεστον τῷ κυρίῳ,

Translation: 5:10. "approving what is pleasing to the Lord,"

Commentary: 5:10. δοκιμάζοντες, "approving." Following the parenthesis (v. 9), this participle relates back to verse 8 and depends on the imperative περιπατεῖτε as it shows the manner of the walk of children of light. The word δοκιμάζω has in mind "to put to the test" as testing witnesses for a trial.[2] Along with this it means "to approve, sanction"[3] or "to approve after scrutiny as fit," for example, for the priesthood[4] or for an office.[5] In the LXX it appears thirty-six times, twenty-three times in the canonical books. It translates five Hebrew words and fourteen times for בָּחַן, meaning "to examine, scrutinize, try."[6] It is used of an ear testing words (Job 34:3), David asking God to try his heart for wickedness (Ps 17:3 [LXX 16:3]), God testing his saints (Pss 66:10 [LXX 65:10]; 81:7 [MT 81:8; LXX 80:8]; 139:1 [LXX 138:1]; Jer 9:7 [MT & LXX 9:6]; 11:20; 12:3; 17:10; 20:12), Jeremiah testing the saints (Jer 6:27), and of the saints testing God (Ps 95:9 [LXX 94:9]).

In the NT this verb is used twenty-two times, seventeen times by Paul, and only here in Ephesians. In its use in the Gospels Jesus reprimands the people for their ability to test or scrutinize the weather but their inability to test his significance in their midst (Luke 12:56*bis*); in another instance a man tells Jesus he is going to test his oxen (Luke 14:19). Paul uses this word to relate that sinful human beings do not test or approve God in knowledge (Rom 1:28), that the Jews are able to approve what is excellent in matters of the law (2:18), that believers are to prove or test what the will of God is (12:2), and that a person is to examine or test oneself before partaking of the Lord's supper (1 Cor 11:28). Peter speaks of the genuineness of faith being tried as perishable gold tested by fire (1 Pet 1:7). It obviously means to test or scrutinize something or someone in order to approve that entity rather than

1. Bruce, 374.
2. Thucydides 6.53.2; cf. Herodotus 2.38.
3. Thucydides 2.35.3; 3.38.5; Plato *Respublica* 3.15 §407c.
4. Plato *Leges* 6 §759d.
5. Aristotle *Athenaion politeia* 45.3; Plato *Leges* 6 §765b.
6. BDB 103; M. Tsevat, "בחן *bḥn*; בָּחוֹן *bāchôn*," *TDOT* 2 (1977): 69–72.

testing with failure in mind. The other major word for testing is πειράζω, which tends to be more negative, conveying the idea of tempting someone to do evil as Satan tempted Christ.[1] In the OT this latter term always translates נָסָה, which means "to test, try, tempt,"[2] while δοκιμάζω never translates this word. Hence, the word in this context carries the hope of a positive outcome, that is, approval. What are we to approve? That is Paul's next topic.

τί ἐστιν εὐάρεστον τῷ κυρίῳ,[3] "what is pleasing to the Lord." The word εὐάρεστος is not used in classical times and is found only twice in the LXX where it speaks of the righteous person who is "pleasing" to God (Wis 4:10) and of the request for wisdom from heaven to teach Solomon what is "pleasing" to God (Wis 9:10). In the NT it is used nine times, eight times by Paul, and only here in Ephesians. In Romans Paul exhorts believers to present their bodies as living sacrifices that are "acceptable" or "pleasing" to God (Rom 12:1) and he urges believers not to be conformed to this age but to be transformed by the renewal of their minds in order that they might prove or test what the will of God is, that is, what is "pleasing, acceptable" to him (v. 2). He tells the Corinthians that his aim is to "please" God (2 Cor 5:9), the Philippians that their gift was pleasing to God (4:18), the Colossians that children are to obey their parents for this is "pleasing" to God (Col 3:20), and he enjoins Titus to tell the slaves to be "pleasing" to their masters (Titus 2:9). In the benediction to his letter, the author of Hebrews prays that God will equip believers with everything good that they might do God's will which is working in them to do what is pleasing in his sight (Heb 13:21). With the exception of Titus 2:9, εὐάρεστος always has reference to pleasing God. One other time in the NT it is used in connection with the word δοκιμάζω, where the believer is instructed to prove that which is the acceptable will of God (Rom 12:2).

Normally, εὐάρεστος is followed by the dative. The dative here would be the dative of indirect object, τῷ κυρίῳ, "to the Lord." In the twenty-six occurrences of "Lord" in Ephesians, with the possible exception of 6:5 and 9 (referring to human masters), it refers to Christ. Christ is the Lord whom believers are to please.

In verses 8–10, Paul has stated that believers are to walk as children of light and approve what is pleasing to God. Light exposes what is not pleasing to the Lord. This goes beyond the moral will of God because his moral will is revealed in specific commands which do not need to be tested. It is to test the will of God for every aspect of life and to approve what would be pleasing to him. The Word of God is a

1. Cf. Trench, *Synonyms of the New Testament*, 278–81.

2. BDB 650; F. J. Helfmeyer, "נָסָה *nissâ*; מַסּוֹת *massôṯ*; מַסָּה *massâ*," *TDOT* 9 (1998): 443–55.

3. Instead of κυρίῳ the reading θεῷ is found in D* F G 81* *pc* lat Ambrosiaster, but it is not acceptable because there are only a few manuscripts and those are only in the Western text-type.

guide for this purpose. However, certain situations in life are not directly addressed in the Scriptures. In such cases, believers need to find principles from the Scriptures whereby they might be able to make choices that will please the Lord. Although not mentioned here, as the Scriptures are consulted the Holy Spirit enlightens and enables believers to discern what is pleasing to the Lord.

2. Do Not Become Involved with Evildoers' Works (5:11–13)

Believers are not to be fellow participants with the evildoers, nor are they to become involved with their works. Rather they are to expose those works. The reason believers are not to become involved with such activity is because those works are too shameful even to mention.

a. Command: Do Not Get Involved But Expose (5:11)

Text: 5:11. καὶ μὴ συγκοινωνεῖτε τοῖς ἔργοις τοῖς ἀκάρποις τοῦ σκότους, μᾶλλον δὲ καὶ ἐλέγχετε.

Translation: 5:11. "and do not participate in the unfruitful works of darkness, but instead even expose them."

Commentary: 5:11. καὶ μὴ συγκοινωνεῖτε τοῖς ἔργοις τοῖς ἀκάρποις τοῦ σκότους, "and do not participate in the unfruitful works of darkness." The conjunction καί links this prohibition to the one in v. 7. Hence, believers are not to be fellow participants with sinners (v. 7) and are not to participate in the unfruitful works of darkness (v. 11). The present imperative from συγκοινωνέω means "to have a joint share in, a connection with."[1] It occurs in the LXX without the prepositional prefix (συν-) thirteen times, four times in the canonical books where it translates three Hebrew words. It refers to the partnership of two kings (2 Chr 20:35), to Elihu accusing Job of fellowshiping with evildoers (Job 34:8), to participation in the shedding of blood (Prov 1:11), and to being united with the living rather than the dead (Eccl 9:4). It has to do with fellowship (Sir 13:1, 2*bis*, 17) as well as with sharing in marriage (2 Macc 14:25). In the NT συγκοινωνέω occurs three times. Other than here it is used in reference to the Philippians becoming partners with Paul in his hardships (Phil 4:14) and the angel who tells the saints to come out of fallen Babylon lest they share in her sins, resulting in judgment (Rev 18:4). In this verse the prohibition again is in the form of a present imperative to denote that they are to make it a practice not to participate in the unfruitful works of darkness.

1. Demosthenes *Orationes* 57.2; Hippocrates *De articulis* 85.

In verse 7 Paul instructed them not to be fellow participants with the evildoers, "the sons of disobedience," and in the present verse Paul tells them not to participate in their unfruitful works of darkness. The "unfruitful" works is in contrast to the fruit of the light in verse 9. The adjective ἄκαρπος, "unfruitful, useless," is used of unproductive or useless land (Jer 2:6) or seed (Matt 13:22 = Mark 4:19), fruitless trees (Jude 12), and unproductive or useless deeds (Titus 3:14). Hence, unfruitful works are useless and unproductive and their source in "darkness" (genitive of source) corresponds to the darkness in which they once lived (v. 8). If they have been formerly darkness but are now the light in the Lord, why should they participate in the sins that come from the place to which they had previously been in bondage?

μᾶλλον δὲ καὶ ἐλέγχετε, "but instead even expose them." The contrast is given by the adversative conjunction δέ, "but," and the comparative adverb μᾶλλον, "rather, instead" (4:28; 5:4) as well as the conjunction καί, which is best taken ascensively, "even." Instead of participating in sins they are even to expose them.

The present imperative is from ἐλέγχω, which in classical times meant "to disgrace, put to shame,"[1] but its more prominent use is "to cross-examine, question, investigate,"[2] "to convict,"[3] or "to expose."[4] It appears sixty-five times in the LXX, forty-nine times in the canonical books. It translates five Hebrew words, forty-one times for יָכַח, meaning "to decide, adjudge, prove."[5] It is used "to decide, judge" (Gen 31:37), "to convict" (Gen 31:42; Job 32:12; Ps 50:21 [LXX 49:21]), "to rebuke" (Ps 50:8 [LXX 49:8]), and "to expose, reprove" (Job 22:4; Ps 105:14 [LXX 104:14]; Hos 4:4; Hab 1:12). In the NT it is used seventeen times, eight times in Paul, and twice in Ephesians (5:11, 13). Barth thinks that it has four meanings in the NT: "(a) to reveal hidden things; (b) to convict or to convince; (c) to reprove, to correct; (d) to punish, to discipline."[6] Bauer offers four similar senses: (1) bring to light, expose, set forth; (2) convict, convince; (3) reprove, correct; (4) punish, discipline.[7] After an extensive study, Engberg-Pedersen criticizes Bauer's first definition because it lacks classical and LXX support for its root meaning, though it did eventually acquire this meaning. However, a few OT passages may have the element of exposure. Engberg-Pedersen argues that the root idea "is that of '*confronting somebody or something with the aim of showing him or it to be, in*

1. Homer *Odyssea* 21.424.

2. Plato *Apologia* 18d; *Leges* 12 §946c; Sophocles *Oedipus Tyrannus* 333, 783.

3. Herodotus 1.24, 117.

4. Ibid., 2.115; Homer *Ilias* 7 (805c); Sophocles *Antigone* 260; Plato *Theaetetus* 171d; Xenophon *Memorabilia* 1.7.2.

5. BDB 406–7; G. Mayer and H.-J Fabry, "יכח *ykḥ*; תּוֹכַחַת *tôḵaḥaṯ*; תּוֹכֵחָה *tôḵēḥâ*," *TDOT* 6 (1990): 64–71.

6. Barth, 570–71.

7. BAGD 249; BDAG 315.

some determinate respect, at fault'."[1] His definition seems to have some element of exposing. Observing the NT passages other than Ephesians, the word can be narrowed down to two basic senses: (1) "to expose, convict" (Matt 18:15; John 3:20; 8:46; 16:8; 1 Cor 14:24; 2 Tim 4:2; Jas 2:9; Jude 15) and (2) "to reprove, rebuke" (Luke 3:19; 1 Tim 5:20; Titus 1:9, 13; 2:15; Heb 12:5; Rev 3:19). When wrong is exposed, a conviction must follow that should result in reproof or rebuke. This in turn should lead to discipline. Hence, exposing includes both convicting and rebuking. In the present context it is best translated as "expose" because the object of the imperative is not persons but works. This coheres with the whole passage. In verse 9 Paul speaks of actions or works of goodness, righteousness, and truth (fruit of light) and in verse 10 believers are enjoined to discover actions or works that please the Lord. Both of these verses speak about good actions or works that are associated with light. Furthermore, in verse 13 Paul speaks of "everything" (τὰ πάντα) and not "everyone" is to be exposed by light. Now in verse 11 Paul discusses the opposite kinds of actions or works, unfruitful works of darkness which must be exposed. The present imperative may well be iterative to denote repeated action.

The question needs to be asked: "Whose deeds are to be exposed?" It is all too easy to conclude that it is the deeds of those in darkness.[2] Nevertheless, it is more likely that it refers to believers[3] who are participating in unfruitful works of darkness. First, the context is speaking about believers. Second, Paul exhorts believers (not the world) not to participate in the works of darkness but rather to do the works or fruit of light. Thus, it appears that some believers were participating in the works of darkness, making the enjoinder necessary. Third, in the NT there is no reprimand of those in the world. Rather, Paul exposes, rebukes, and disciplines those in the church (cf. also Matt 18:15–17). He explicitly states that believers are to judge those inside the church and not to judge those outside the church because God alone is going to judge the latter (1 Cor 5:12–13). Furthermore, instructions in Proverbs (9:7; 15:12) and even in Qumran literature (1QS 9:16) warn against rebuking unbelievers. Hence believers, rather than participating in evil works, are to help those who have fallen by exposing their unfruitful works and showing them that participation in those works is totally inconsistent with light. In this respect, the Corinthians failed to expose the sin of incest that was practiced by one of the believers in the church. It is interesting to note that the same commentators who think this exposure has reference to unbe-

1. Troels Engberg-Pedersen, "Ephesians 5,12–13: ἐλέγχειν and Conversion in the New Testament," *ZNW* 80, nos. 3/4 (1989): 97, cf. 93–101.

2. So Calvin, 200; Alford, 132; Eadie, 384; Ellicott, 119; Salmond, 357; Hendriksen, 233; Mitton, 184; Schnackenburg, 226; Lincoln, 330; Carsten Peter Thiede, "Der Brief an die Epheser. 42. Teil: Kapitel 5,9–16," *Fundamentum* 21, no. 3 (2000): 31–32.

3. So Gnilka, 255–56; Barth, 571; Bruce, 375; Best, 493–94.

lievers also suggest that Paul was not referring to verbal exposure but rather exposure by example, that is, by maintaining a contrastive lifestyle that consists of deeds of light.[1] However, as stated above, the word ἐλέγχω includes both exposure and reproof. Thus the verbal aspect must be included. This idea is exemplified in other NT passages. For example, Matt 18:15–17 states that a brother is to go to the sinning brother and point out his fault. This is also true in 1 Cor 5. It is difficult to imagine Paul telling the Corinthians to remain silent, just live a good lifestyle and evil will disappear. No, to expose evil deeds includes verbal rebuke. In light of this, it is clear that it is the deeds of believers which are in question. The present context supports this with μᾶλλον δέ plus καί, for not only are they not to participate in the works of darkness "but instead even" expose them.[2] The reason for exposing their evil deeds is given next.

b. Reason: Their Works Are Shameful (5:12)

Text: 5:12. τὰ γὰρ κρυφῇ γινόμενα ὑπ᾽ αὐτῶν αἰσχρόν ἐστιν καὶ λέγειν,

Translation: 5:12. "For the things done in secret by them are shameful even to mention,"

Commentary: 5:12. τὰ γὰρ κρυφῇ γινόμενα ὑπ᾽ αὐτῶν, "For the things done in secret by them." The conjunction γάρ, "for," introduces the reason for exposing the unfruitful works of darkness and could be translated "because." The adverb κρυφῇ, a rare word in classical literature, means "secret."[3] It occurs in the LXX twelve times, nine times in the canonical books and translates four Hebrew words. Six times it translates סָתַר, meaning "to hide, conceal," or סֵתֶר, signifying "covering, hiding-place, secrecy."[4] Three examples include a woman who will eat the afterbirth and her children secretly due to stress from war (Deut 28:57), David's statement that God made him in the secret place of the womb (Ps 139:15 [LXX 138:15]), and the declaration that the Lord did not speak to his people in secrecy (Isa 45:19; 48:16). There are two passages of particular interest to the present context. The first is an interjection of woe to those whose deeds are done in secret (Isa 29:15) for they cannot be hidden from God. The second is Job's reply to Zophar when he uses the two words in the immediate context by saying that God will surely expose (ἐλέγχω) those who in secret (κρυφῇ) show partiality (Job 13:10). In the NT this adverb is used only here. It could be translated adverbially as "secretly," but it is best to accept this as a dative as indicated in the text by the inclusion of the iota sub-

1. Schnackenburg, 226; Lincoln, 330.

2. Schlier, 238; Engberg-Pedersen, "Ephesians 5,12–13: ἐλέγχειν and Conversion in the New Testament," 101.

3. Sophocles *Antigone* 85; Xenophon *Symposium* 5.8; Pindar *Olympian Odes* 1.47.

4. BDB 711–12; Wagner, *TDOT* 10 (1999): 363–68.

script as is consistently found in the LXX. Furthermore, when there is a preposition with the word in the LXX, it has ἐν, "in" (Ps 139:15 [LXX 138:15]; Isa 29:15; 45:19; 48:16),[1] which translates the Hebrew word prefixed with the preposition בְּ, "in." Accordingly, it is best translated "in secret." The dative is not instrumental but manner,[2] showing how these works were done. Thus, the unfruitful works of darkness are done in secret. Certainly, the concept of darkness enhances this idea of secrecy. Darkness tries to conceal sins that should be exposed. Best rightly observes that "the reference to secrecy is much more easily understood of members of the community"[3] for unbelievers sinned openly without shame (Eph 4:19).

The preposition ὑπό, "by," denotes agency and the object of the preposition αὐτῶν, "them," refers to those who are doing the unfruitful works of darkness. This personal pronoun does not refer back to the works of verse 11 because this would make no sense. Rather, it refers back to the personal pronoun in verse 7 where it reads "do not become fellow participants with them (αὐτῶν)," that is, those on whom the wrath of God comes. At one time believers were like those who are in darkness (v. 8).[4] This is consistent with what is discussed above where Paul states that believers are not to be fellow participants with unbelievers (v. 7) nor participate in the unfruitful works of darkness (v. 11) done by them in secret which are shameful even to mention (v. 12).

αἰσχρόν ἐστιν καὶ λέγειν, "are shameful even to mention." The adjective αἰσχρός was discussed at 5:4 where we concluded that it meant something that is "disgraceful" or "shameful." The conjunction καί functions as an adverb and should be taken ascensively, "even."[5] The infinitive λέγειν normally is translated "to speak" but this rendering seems clumsy here. Rather, the translation "to mention" would heighten the ascensive idea of the conjunction. Kreitzer suggests that those things too shameful to mention may have to do with the ritual obscene language associated with the mother-goddess Demeter.[6] Although this could be the case, there is nothing in the text to suggest such a specific reference. It is more likely that Paul has in mind useless deeds in which believers are not to participate. But if these works

1. Rudolf Meyer, "κρύπτω κτλ.," *TDNT* 3 (1965): 960 n. 4.

2. Robertson, *Grammar*, 530.

3. Best, 495.

4. The grammarians go back to σκότος in v. 8 and say that it has some ad sensum agreement (cf. Winer, *Grammar*, 177, 182; BDF §282 [2]; MHT 3:40). Is it not much better to go back to the personal pronoun (αὐτῶν) in v. 7, only four words before σκότος, which makes a concrete relationship rather than an ad sensum agreement? It is from that previous pronoun that the reader moves forward four words and sees that believers were formerly identified as darkness.

5. BAGD 393; BDAG 495.

6. Kreitzer, "'Crude Language' and 'Shameful Things Done in Secret' (Ephesians 5.4, 12)," 63–64, 73–76.

are so bad that it is shameful to even mention them, why expose them? Exposing such things not only reveals unfruitful works but teaches believers two important lessons. First, it reveals the ugliness of the deeds done in secret. Second, it impresses on them the importance of producing the fruit of light, the works of goodness, righteousness, and truth (v. 9). Deeds of darkness cannot be allowed, therefore, to spread and encompass the community of believers.

c. Explanation: Light Shows True Character of Works (5:13)

Believers have now been commanded to refrain from participation in the unfruitful works of darkness, have been called on to expose those works, and have been given the reason for exposing them. Paul now explains what will happen when those works are exposed.

Text: 5:13. τὰ δὲ πάντα ἐλεγχόμενα ὑπὸ τοῦ φωτὸς φανεροῦται, πᾶν γὰρ τὸ φανερούμενον φῶς ἐστιν.

Translation: 5:13. "but everything exposed by the light becomes visible, for everything that becomes visible is light."

Commentary: 5:13. τὰ δὲ πάντα ἐλεγχόμενα ὑπὸ τοῦ φωτὸς φανεροῦται, "but everything exposed by the light becomes visible." The conjunction δέ is adversative making the contrast with τὰ . . . κρυφῇ γινόμενα, "the things done in secret," in verse 12. The τὰ . . . πάντα "all that, everything," refers not to all things generally[1] nor all people,[2] but all that which is done in secret.[3] The participle ἐλεγχόμενα repeats the imperative ἐλέγχετε in verse 11, which meant "to expose."

The verb φανερόω appears only once in classical literature (and this has some textual problems) meaning "being visible" used in reference to one who was the center of attraction, such as the winner of an Olympian prize.[4] However, the adjective φανερός is used more frequently meaning something that is "visible, manifest"[5] so that "all that is in it can be plainly seen."[6] In the LXX the verb occurs once and is translated from the Piel גָּלָה, meaning "to uncover, disclose,"[7] alluding to God's promise that in the future he will restore Judah and "manifest" abundance (Jer 33:6 [LXX 40:6]). The adjective is used eighteen times in the LXX, nine times in the canonical books, four of which translates three Hebrew words and five of which have no Hebrew word as a basis. It means "manifest" or that which is made "known."

1. As Aquinas, chap. 5, lec. 5, vv. 12–14 (208); Alford, 3:132.

2. As Calvin, 201; Salmond, 358.

3. Jerome *Eph* 5:13 (*PL* 26:524); Harless, 470; Eadie, 384; Ellicott, 120; Meyer, 275; Barth, 572, 592–98.

4. Herodotus 6.122.

5. Ibid., 3.24; Euripides *Bacchae* 501; Sophocles *Trachiniae* 608; Plato *Leges* 1 §630b.

6. LSJ 1915.

7. BDB 163; Zobel, *TDOT* 2 (1977): 480–81.

In NT times the verb's meaning paralleled secular literature where it meant "to make visible, manifest" that which was hidden or unknown.[1] It is used forty-nine times, twenty-two times by Paul, twice in Ephesians (5:13, 14). In all its occurrences its sense is "to manifest, appear, make visible." It is thought by some to be synonymous with ἀποκαλύπτω because in the parallel passages regarding the revelation of the mystery, ἀποκαλύπτω is used in Eph 3:5 (see study of the word) and φανερόω in Col 1:26.[2] But as Bockmuehl points out, φανερόω "*never expresses* the idea of *revelation*" but "*always* implies that its object is, at least in principle *demonstrably evident*, and not just subjectively so."[3] Hence, in Col 1:26 the mystery was made manifest or visible to the saints by the incarnation of Christ (v. 22), whereas Eph 3:5 has no reference to the incarnation; instead, it simply states that the mystery is revealed to the apostles and prophets by the Spirit.[4] Therefore, φανερόω connotes the action of making something clearly visible to the human eye. It is used to convey the idea that all hidden things will be made manifest (Mark 4:22). Likewise, those who do what is true come to the light in order that their deeds accomplished in God may be clearly seen (John 3:21). Again these passages illustrate the importance of hidden things being made clearly visible.

There are two problems to solve in this verse: (a) deciding whether the prepositional phrase (ὑπὸ τοῦ φωτός, "by the light") depends on the preceding participle (ἐλεγχόμενα) or on the following finite verb (φανεροῦται); and (b) determining whether the finite verb is middle or passive. Four interpretations are offered. View (1) joins the prepositional phrase to the participle and takes the finite verb as middle: "all things which are exposed by the light and whatever makes manifest is light."[5] View (2) joins the prepositional phrase to the finite verb and renders the finite verb as middle: "all things which are exposed are by the light made manifest" (AV, RV, ASV).[6] View (3) joins the prepositional phrase to the finite verb and depicts the finite verb as passive: "all the things which are exposed are made manifest (become visible?) by the light."[7] View (4) joins the prepositional phrase to the participle and takes the finite verb as passive: "all the things which are exposed

1. Dionysius Halicarnassensis 10.37; Josephus *A.J.* 20.4.1 §76; *Vita* 45 §231; Philo *Leg. All.* 3.15 §47.

2. Rudolf Bultmann and Dieter Lührmann, "φανερόω," *TDNT* 9 (1974): 4.

3. Markus N. A. Bockmuehl, "*Phanerosis*: A New Testament Historical Word Study on the Manifestation of the Invisible" (M.C.S. thesis, Regent College, 1983), 164; cf. also idem, "Das Verb φανερόω im Neuen Testament: Versuch einer Neuauswertung," *BZ* 32, no. 1 (1988): 98–99.

4. Bockmuehl, "*Phanerosis*," 143–45; idem, "Das Verb φανερόω im Neuen Testament," 97.

5. Abbott, 156.

6. Eadie, 385–87.

7. Hodge, 294–96; Alford, 132; Ellicott, 120–21; Meyer, 275–77; Salmond, 358–59; Schlier, 239; Barth, 572–73; Schnackenburg, 226–27; Bruce, 376; O'Brien, 372.

by the light are made manifest [translation in the commentary: 'but everything exposed by the light becomes visible']" (RSV, NASB, TEV, NEB, JB, NIV, NJB, NRSV).[1]

View (1) is cumbersome as well as redundant. Furthermore, in all forty-nine occurrences of φανερόω in the NT, it is never in the middle. Certainly this same verb in the next clause should be rendered passive and it seems highly unlikely for it to be middle in this clause and passive in the next clause. View (2) has the same criticism that the finite verb is never in the middle in the NT and it forms a statement making very little sense. View (3) loads everything on the finite verb and makes the participle unnecessary. View (4) seems to be the best because it provides a good progression. In verse 11 believers are told to expose the unfruitful works of darkness and when these works are exposed by the light, they become visible. Also, Paul then continues this concept in the next clause. Further supporting this translation is the fact that Paul normally puts the modifiers after verbs and participles rather than before them. Thus the prepositional phrase more naturally qualifies the preceding participle and not the following verb (cf. comment in 1:4). The adjective πάντα used with a plural participle with the article is normally translated "all"[2] (cf. 6:24). However, in this context, it makes better sense to translate it "everything" especially in light of the next clause where, referring to the same thing, it is used with a singular participle with the article that normally is translated "every."[3] Translating it "everything" heightens the idea that every single thing that is being exposed by the light becomes visible. Not one thing is missed.

In conclusion, then, everything done in secret by believers should be exposed by the light. The light refers to both believers (v. 8) and their fruit (v. 9). Paul further explains this next.

πᾶν γὰρ τὸ φανερούμενον φῶς ἐστιν, "for everything that becomes visible is light." Some newer translations (TEV, JB, NIV, NJB, NRSV) make this clause a part of verse 14. This follows the break of many Greek texts (NA^{27}, UBS^{4}, but not GNTMT).[4] The break is not critical but it seems to make better sense to include this clause with verse 13 because it completes Paul's thought. It is curious that though the Greek texts place this clause in verse 14, there is a period not before this clause (hence at the end of their v. 13) but after it indicating that the thought is not complete until then. By including this clause with verse 13, it allows the quotation in verse 14 to serve as a concluding remark.

The conjunction γάρ, "for," is explanatory, used to introduce the concept of what it means to become visible. The participle φανερούμενον

1. Olshausen, 252; Robinson, 201; Westcott, 79; Hendriksen, 234; Gnilka, 258 n. 1; Lincoln, 330–31; Best, 495.

2. BAGD 632; BDAG 782.

3. BAGD 632; BDAG 782.

4. So also Schnackenburg, 227; Lincoln, 330–31.

must be passive[1] because it needs to be consistent with the finite verb in the preceding clause. Paul is simply saying that everything that becomes visible is light and no longer darkness. But what does Paul mean by this? Eadie contends "that light does not always exercise this transforming influence, for the devil and all the wicked are reproved by the light, without becoming themselves light."[2] Alford replies that Eadie's view lacks the comprehension of φῶς ἐστιν and that the statement *"every thing shone upon* IS LIGHT" is a truism.[3] Eadie then responds that Alford's definition of light here is different from light in the previous clause.[4] Moule suggests that possibly it should be translated "becomes light."[5] This is possible but it is an unusual meaning for ἐστίν. John 3:20 states that everyone who does evil hates the light and does not come to the light, lest one's deeds should be exposed. As mentioned above (v. 11), Engberg-Pedersen has made a contribution regarding the definition of the word ἐλέγχω meaning "to expose" and "to reprove," but he has misapplied it to the conversion of unbelievers[6] when the context is really addressing believers.[7] If it is applied to unbelievers, then automatic conversion would result, since darkness, when confronted with the power of the light of Christian truth, would automatically become light. However, the present context is not talking about unbelievers but believers who have become copartners in the works of unbelievers. These unfruitful works of darkness are to be exposed in order that offending believers might produce the fruit of light, namely, goodness, righteousness, and truth (v. 9).

3. Conclusion: Enlightenment of Christ (5:14)

Text: 5:14. διὸ λέγει,
Ἔγειρε, ὁ καθεύδων,
καὶ ἀνάστα ἐκ τῶν νεκρῶν,
καὶ ἐπιφαύσει σοι ὁ Χριστός.

Translation: 5:14. "Therefore it says,
'Wake up, O Sleeper,
and rise from the dead,
and Christ will shine on you.'"

1. Winer, *Grammar*, 323; *contra* MHT 3:55.
2. Eadie, 386.
3. Alford, 3:132.
4. Eadie, 386.
5. Moule, *Idiom Book*, 25.
6. Engberg-Pedersen, "Ephesians 5,12–13: ἐλέγχειν and Conversion in the New Testament," 101–10; cf. also King, "Ephesians in the Light of Form Criticism," 275–76; O'Brien, 372–77.
7. So Best, 498–99; Best, *Ephesians*, 52.

Commentary: 5:14. διὸ λέγει, "Therefore it says." This is the same introductory statement as in 4:8 to alert his readers that he is going to cite an OT passage (not so at 4:25; 5:31; 6:2, 3). The inferential conjunction διό means "therefore, for this reason."[1] It makes an inference from verse 13. Paul uses this quotation as a concluding remark. There has been a great deal of debate on the source of the quotation.[2] It has been identified as a quotation from Isa 26:19 ("You who dwell in the dust, awake and shout for joy!"); 60:1 ("Arise, shine; for your light has come, and the glory of the Lord has risen upon you.");[3] Jonah 1:6 ("How can you sleep? Arise, call on your god!");[4] or from the Secrets of Enoch ("Be of good cheer, Enoch, be not afraid; rise up and stand before My face for ever.").[5] A careful look at the Greek in these texts reveals little resemblance to Eph 5:14. Most consider this quotation to be an early hymn, possibly a baptismal hymn.[6] In support of this is the parallelism which is "comparable to that of Hebrew poetry."[7] Noack thinks it is a hymn about Christ's second coming or a resurrection hymn that may have been adopted for baptism.[8] However, the context does not clearly support the idea of a baptismal liturgy.[9] Rather than specifying it for some particular liturgy or event, Barth

1. BAGD 198; BDAG 250; cf. Molland, "Διο, Einige syntaktische Beobachtungen," in *Serta Rudbergiana*, 43–52; reprinted in idem, "Διο: Einige syntaktische Beobachtungen," in *Opuscula Patristica*, 9–16.

2. Cf. Bent Noack, "Das Zitat in Ephes. 5,14," *ST* 5, no. 1 (1951): 52–64; Moritz, *A Profound Mystery*, 98–112; Best, "The Use of Credal and Liturgical Materials in Ephesians," 67.

3. Hendriksen, 234–35; Paula Qualls and John D. W. Watts, "Isaiah in Ephesians," *RevExp* 93 (spring 1996): 254–55.

4. M. W. Jacobus, "The Citation Ephesians 5:14 as Affecting the Paulinity of the Epistle," in *Theologische Studien. Herrn Wirkl. Oberkonsistorialrath Professor D. Bernard Weiss zum seinem 70. Geburtstage dargebracht* (Göttingen: Vandenhoeck & Ruprecht, 1897), 9–29.

5. Eb. Nestle, "Eph. v.14 and the Secrets of Enoch," *ExpTim* 9 (May 1898): 376–77.

6. Abbott, 158; Robinson, 119; Dibelius-Greeven, 90–91; Masson, 208–9 n. 7; Schlier, 240; Gaugler, 203; Gnilka, 260–63; Mitton, 185–87; Barth, 574–75; Caird, 86; Schnackenburg, 229; Bruce, 376; Lincoln, 319; 331–32; Best, 497–98; O'Brien, 374–76; King, "Ephesians in the Light of Form Criticism," 274; Kirby, *Ephesians, Baptism and Pentecost*, 160; Kuhn, "Ephesians in the Light of the Qumran Texts," 124–25, 129–30; Delling, *Die Taufe im Neuen Testament*, 77; Schnackenburg, "»Er hat uns mitauferweckt«. Zur Tauflehre des Epheserbriefes," 156–66; Ernst Käsemann, "A Primitive Christian Baptismal Liturgy," in *Essays on New Testament Themes*, trans. W. J. Montague, SBT, ed. C. F. D. Moule, J. Barr, Peter Ackroyd, Floyd V. Filson, and G. Ernest Wright, no. 41 (London: SCM, 1964), 162; Halter, *Taufe und Ethos*, 276–80; Fischer, *Tendenz und Absicht des Epheserbriefes*, 140–46.

7. Moule, *Idiom Book*, 199.

8. Noack, "Das Zitat in Ephes. 5,14," 64.

9. Wedderburn, *Baptism and Resurrection*, 52–54, 80–82; Martin Hengel, *Studies in Early Christology*, trans. Rollin Kearns (Edinburgh: T & T Clark, 1995), 282, 284; Moritz, *A Profound Mystery*, 106–9, 115.

suggests it may be a hymn composed at the congregational meetings, as mentioned in 1 Cor 14:26.[1] Along the same lines Moritz suggests that it was an early Christian hymn which was heavily influenced by Isa 26:19 and 60:1–2.[2] Since the main emphasis in the present context is on the restoration of Christians who were copartners with the unfruitful works of darkness, it may well be a hymn of repentance and encouragement sung regularly by earlier believers.

Ἔγειρε, ὁ καθεύδων, "'Wake up, O Sleeper.'" The imperative ἔγειρε is used to rouse people from their sleep (Matt 8:25; Mark 5:41 = Luke 8:54?; Acts 12:7). The verb καθεύδω is used twenty-two times in the NT, five times by Paul (Eph 5:14; 1 Thess 5:6, 7*bis*, 10). Though normally used of physical sleep, Paul also uses it of spiritual lethargy and indifference (1 Thess 5:6). It is so used in the present context where some believers have become coparticipants with the unfruitful works of darkness and need to be restored. It is much like the disciples sleeping when Jesus was praying in the Garden of Gethsemane. He asked them why they could not be awake at that critical hour and urged them to watch and pray that they might not enter into temptation (Matt 26:40–41 = Mark 14:37–43 = Luke 22:46). Paul is addressing believers who had fallen in with the unfruitful works of darkness and he uses this quotation to say, "Wake up from your spiritual laziness!" As "sleepers" they possibly did not even realize their spiritual indifference. This is an interesting metaphor since most sleep is done in darkness. They were sleeping in the unfruitful works of darkness. Some suggest that this is a reference to the Gnostic awakening of the soul from the sleep of darkness by a spark from the world of light and thus the soul returns to the heavenly world of light.[3] Kuhn rightly asserts that the awakening in the present text is "not a question of knowledge about the nature of the actual self, but more a question of a decision of the will, *a change in one's walking*, away from sinful action towards actions which is pleasing to God."[4]

καὶ ἀνάστα ἐκ τῶν νεκρῶν, "'and rise from the dead.'" The imperative ἀνάστα, a shortened form of ἀνάστηθι,[5] which is also used in Acts 12:7, is aorist possibly denoting an urgency to rise up from death.[6] Normally the resurrection from the dead refers to those who are phys-

1. Barth, 574–75 and n. 83.

2. Moritz, *A Profound Mystery*, 100–105, 115.

3. Cf. Bultmann, *Theology of the New Testament*, 1:174–75; Schlier, 241–42; Pokorný, "Epheserbrief und gnostische Mysterien," 187–88; Fischer, *Tendenz und Absicht des Epheserbriefes*, 142–44; Lindemann, *Aufhebung*, 234–35 n. 167; Lindemann, 96; Pokorný, 207–10.

4. Kuhn, "Ephesians in the Light of the Qumran Texts," 127; cf. Perkins, 120–21. Perkins suggests that the "Gnostic parallels should be treated as dependent upon Ephesians rather than as its source."

5. Cf. Robertson, *Grammar*, 310, 328; MHT 2:210.

6. Wallace (*Greek Grammar*, 491) labels this as a conditional imperative, hence, "if you rise from the dead, Christ will shine on you."

ically dead, but in the present context it has reference to a spiritual deadening demonstrated by their unfruitful works of darkness. Believers are told that those who continually practice such things will not inherit the kingdom of Christ and of God but will receive the wrath of God (vv. 5–6). This has reference not only to spiritual death but also the second death: the separation of people from God forever. Paul enjoins believers not to be partakers in their unfruitful works because their source is darkness, which is the sphere of the ungodly who do not know or care about God. In fact, these unbelievers use deceitful words to persuade believers to reject the mutual ideas of an inheritance for believers and a wrath for unbelievers. Hence, in their spiritual indifference Paul exhorts them to awake and with urgency arise from the path that leads to death.

καὶ ἐπιφαύσει σοι ὁ Χριστός,[1] "'and Christ will shine on you.'" The verb ἐπιφαύσκω is not found in classical literature. It is used only three times in the LXX where it refers to the moon not "shining" (Job 25:5), the shining of the sun (31:26), and the spray of the crocodile's sneezings glistening or shining in the sunlight (41:18 [MT & LXX 41:10]). It is used only here in the NT with the same import "to shine." In brief, then, this quotation is directed to the believer who is a copartner of the unfruitful works of darkness. He is commanded to awake from his spiritual sleep and rise from his spiritual deadness, so that Christ will shine on him, probably indicating approval. It is analogous to verse 10 where the believer is told to approve what is pleasing to the Lord. Again, this is not a reference to the unbeliever but to the spiritual laxity of the believer. True believers will respond because the Holy Spirit will lead them to live a life consisting in the fruit of light—goodness, righteousness, and truth (v. 9).

In conclusion, it is easy to see why it is necessary for believers who once were darkness to expose other believers' unfruitful works of darkness. Their deviant path does not please the Lord and the light is necessary to expose these works of darkness, which are contrary to the Lord's will. They are commanded to awake from their spiritual sleep and rise from the path of death. Their repentant response will please God and Christ will shine on them with approval.

1. The reading ἐπιφαύσει σοι ὁ Χριστός is found in 𝔓^{46} ℵ A B D^{2} F G Ψ 048 075 0150 6 33 81 104 256 263 365 424 436 459 1175 1241 1319 1573 1739 1852 1881 1912 1962 2127 2200 2464 *Byz* [K L P] *Lect* it$^{\text{ar, f, g, mon, o}}$ vg syr$^{\text{p, h, pal}}$ cop$^{\text{sa, bo}}$ arm eth geo slav Marcion$^{\text{acc. to Epiphanius}}$ Clement Naassenes$^{\text{acc. to Hippolytus}}$ Hippolytus Origen Origen^{dub} Josippus Athanasius Didymus Epiphanius Chrysostom Marcus-Eremita Theodore^{lat} Cyril Ambrose Jerome Pelagius Augustine$^{18/19}$ Quodvultdeus Varimadum. The second reading ἐπιψαύσεις τοῦ Χριστοῦ appears in D* it$^{\text{b, d}}$ Origen^{lat} mss$^{\text{acc. to Chrysostom and Theodore lat}}$ Victorinus-Rome Ambrosiaster Latin mss$^{\text{acc. to Jerome}}$ Paulinus-Nola Augustine$^{1/19}$. The first reading has manuscripts that are early and good in character, have good genealogical relationship within the text-types, and there is good geographical distribution of the witnesses. This is preferred over the second reading which has little evidence, most of which is in the Western texts.

E. Walk in Wisdom (5:15–6:9)

As mentioned previously, in chapters 4–6 the clue for major breaks is the imperative "walk" (περιπατέω) used five times in connection with the inferential conjunction "therefore" (οὖν). Up to this point Paul has used these two words four times: (1) in 4:1 where, based on the believers' heavenly position in Christ in chapters 1–3, believers are called to walk in unity; (2) in 4:17 where believers are commanded to walk in holiness and not as the Gentiles; (3) in 5:1–2 where believers are told to walk in love; and (4) in 5:7–8 where believers are told to walk in light by not becoming involved with the evildoers and their works. Now, for the last time, in 5:15 he uses περιπατέω and οὖν to introduce his next challenge to believers, that is, to walk in wisdom. This serves as the basis for the many exhortations found in 5:15–6:9. The author instructs them to be wise in their walk or conduct by being filled by the Holy Spirit. This section deals with relationships in families and employment where intimacy and constant contact can at times be trying. Consequently, believers have urgent need of the Holy Spirit's power to live in a manner pleasing to the Lord. However, before Paul makes specific applications, he enjoins them to walk by means of the Holy Spirit. This is walking wisely.

1. Admonition (5:15–21)

These verses form the basis for believers' conduct before their families and employers or employees. This section is structured around three contrasts expressed by μή and ἀλλά (vv. 15, 17, 18), indicating both negative and positive admonitions to walk wisely. These contrasts inform the structure of our outline.

a. Proper Action: Walk Wisely (5:15–16)

Text: 5:15. Βλέπετε οὖν πῶς ἀκριβῶς περιπατεῖτε, μὴ ὡς ἄσοφοι ἀλλ᾽ ὡς σοφοί, **5:16.** ἐξαγοραζόμενοι τὸν καιρόν, ὅτι αἱ ἡμέραι πονηραί εἰσιν.

Translation: 5:15. "Therefore, look how carefully you are walking, not as unwise but as wise, **5:16.** taking advantage of every opportunity, because the days are evil."

Commentary: 5:15. Βλέπετε οὖν πῶς ἀκριβῶς[1] περιπατεῖτε, "Therefore, look how carefully you are walking." Some think that the inferential conjunction οὖν serves as a conclusion to verses 8–14, that is, the converted sinner who has been awakened should now walk circumspectly, not as unwise, but as wise.[2] Although Paul may be concluding the thought from the previous paragraph, it seems more likely that the conjunction is resumptive, beginning a new section after the quotation, that is, "to return to our exhortation."[3] Verse 14 is introduced with the inferential conjunction διό which serves as a fitting conclusion to verses 8–13. Robinson states, "The metaphor of darkness and light is dropped, and the contrast is now between ἄσοφοι and

1. There is a textual problem regarding the order of the words. The NA[27] and UBS[4] texts have οὖν ἀκριβῶς πῶς as seen in 𝔓[46] ℵ* B 0150 0278 33 81 104 436 459 1175 1241[s] 1739 1962 cop[sa] geo slav Origen[lem] Chrysostom[lem]. The second reading has οὖν πῶς ἀκριβῶς D F G Ψ 075 6 256 263 365 424 1319 1573 1852 1881 1912 2127 2200 *Byz* [K L P] *Lect* it[b, (d), f, g, mon] vg[mss] syr[p, h, pal] (arm) (eth) (Ps-Hippolytus) Basil (Chrysostom[com]) Theodore[lat] Victorinus-Rome Ambrosiaster Lucifer Jerome (Augustine). The third reading, οὖν ἀδελφοὶ πῶς ἀκριβῶς, appears in ℵ[2] A 629 2464 it[ar, o] vg cop[bomss, (bo)] Pelagius. The third reading, which is the same as the second reading with only the addition of ἀδελφοί, is supported by the Alexandrian text in A (possibly ℵ[2] 256 1573 2127) cop[bomss, (bo)] and vg and by the Western text-type only in the Itala. The addition of ἀδελφοί is strange since it is never used in Ephesians in a general sense until the salutation in 6:23 (the personal sense is found in 6:21). It seems to be an addition by a scribe rather than in the original text. The first reading is strongly supported by the Alexandrian text-type. The second reading has some support from the Alexandrian text-type (Ψ), good support in the Western text-type (D F G, Itala), some support from the Caesarean (?) (syr, arm), and excellent support in the Byzantine text. Furthermore, the third reading has the same word order (though it adds ἀδελφοί) as the second reading and thus it would further support the second reading with the Alexandrian manuscripts A and possibly ℵ[2] 256 1573 2127 as well as versions cop[bomss, (bo)] and vg that were probably based on the Alexandrian text-type. Externally, the first and second readings are fairly equal because the first reading has early support but the second reading has better geographical distribution. Internally, the second reading is preferred because the imperative βλέπετε is never modified by an adverb in the NT. Therefore, the second reading is preferred only slightly above the first.

2. E.g., Calvin, 202; Alford, 3:133; Kuhn, "Ephesians in the Light of the Qumran Texts," 125, 126; Martin Haug, "Kinder des Lichts," in *Kurze Auslegung des Epheserbriefes* (Göttingen: Vandenhoeck & Ruprecht, 1965), 149–52; Schlier, 243; Gnilka, 267; Barth, 577; Schnackenburg, 234.

3. Abbott, 159; cf. also Eadie, 391; Ellicott, 122; Abbott, 159; Salmond, 360; Robinson, 202; Best, 502.

σοφοί."[1] More importantly, as indicated in the introductory paragraph to 5:15–6:9, the inferential conjunction οὖν in connection with περιπατέω marks a new section of Paul's thought as it does in 4:1, 17; 5:1–5, 7–8.

Before discussing individual words of the clause, their order must be understood. Most translations follow the order of the NA[27] and UBS[4] where the adverb ἀκριβῶς, "carefully," modifies βλέπω, translating them "look carefully then how you walk" (RV, ASV, RSV, NASB, NEB, TEV, JB, NJB, NRSV), but the better order textually is for the adverb ἀκριβῶς to modify περιπατέω, "to walk," which would read, "therefore, look how carefully you are walking" (AV). This is not only a better textual reading, but it also makes more sense contextually. If one accepts the first reading Salmond states, "In that case the injunction loses its distinctive note, and instead of the charge to take heed how they walked 'with strict carefulness,' we have the plain exhortation to 'take heed carefully' how they walked."[2] The point is not how carefully one is to observe but how carefully one is to walk.

The word βλέπω literally "to see," refers here to spiritual perception.[3] Bauer suggests that the interrogative particle πῶς can have the same meaning as ὅτι, "that" (AV; the tendency of later Greek), citing that this is clearly the meaning in Matt 12:4 = Mark 2:26 and Acts 11:13.[4] However, on examination it is clear that it should not be translated "that," but rather as it normally is, "how." It refers to the mode of careful walking as a Christian duty.[5] Hence, it is best translated "look how carefully you are walking" (AV). The adverb ἀκριβῶς, meaning "accurately, carefully, well,"[6] modifies περιπατέω and thus giving, "to walk carefully." Earlier we established that περιπατέω refers to the lifestyle of the individual (2:2; cf. also 4:1, 17; 5:2, 8). Here, the present indicative connotes a customary sense—the believer is to make a habit or practice of walking carefully.

μὴ ὡς ἄσοφοι ἀλλ' ὡς σοφοί, "not as unwise but as wise." This is the first contrast. Paul now explains "how" (πῶς) one is to walk carefully by using the comparative conjunction ὡς with both negative and positive statements.[7] Negatively, not as unwise but positively, as wise. Here the adjectives ἄσοφοι and σοφοί appear for the first time in Ephesians (ἄσοφος is used only here in the NT). The noun σοφία, "wisdom," was discussed at 1:8, 17; 3:10 where we concluded that it refers to true insight into known facts. The best wisdom is that which has been given by God for insight into the true nature of God's plan. The adjective in

1. Robinson, 202.
2. Salmond, 361; cf. also Gaugler, 203.
3. BAGD 143; BDAG 179.
4. BAGD 732; BDAG 901.
5. Winer, *Grammar*, 376.
6. BAGD 33; BDAG 39.
7. Cf. Winer, *Grammar*, 595.

the present context carries the same sense in that the wise one's "wisdom is divine in nature and origin."[1] The opposite is true for those who are ἄσοφοι, "unwise," for they walk as those who despise or have no insight into God's plan. Kuhn states, "The closest parallel to this meaning of *asophoi* and *sophoi* is 1QS 4:24: *ythlkw ḥkmh w'wlt* '(the two antithetical groups of people—the sons of light and of darkness) *walk in wisdom* (on the one hand) *and in foolishness* (on the other hand)'."[2] Since they are God's children, believers are to walk carefully, not as ones who walk without true insight into God's plan for their lives; not unwisely, as characterized by the Gentile world (Eph 4:17–19), but in a new lifestyle in conformity to God's wise plan.[3] Next, Paul explains in concrete terms what has as yet been expressed abstractly.

5:16. ἐξαγοραζόμενοι τὸν καιρόν, "taking advantage of every opportunity." After contrasting two kinds of walks (negatively: unwise; positively: wise), Paul now begins with a participle of manner indicating how to walk wisely. The word ἐξαγοράζω in classical times meant "to purchase" or "buy" an item[4] or a slave's freedom.[5] It is used only once in the OT where עִדָּנָא אַנְתּוּן זָבְנִין in Theodotion Dan 2:8 is translated καιρὸν ὑμεῖς ἐξαγοράζετε which has the idea of trying to buy up time. This could be a proverbial saying[6] since ἐξαγοράζω and καιρός are both in the Septuagint and in the present context. Although in Eph 1:10 and 2:12 the word καιρός has little if any distinction from χρόνος,[7] it may well mean in this context "the opportunities offered by time."[8] In the NT, ἐξαγοράζω is used only four times (Gal 3:13; 4:5; Eph 5:16; Col 4:5). In Galatians it is similarly used in the simple form ἀγοράζω where it speaks of "redeeming" from the curse of the law. In Eph 5:16 and Col 4:5 this composite form may be used to intensify its meaning, that is, "to 'buy up intensively'; i.e., to snap up every opportunity that comes."[9] For example, in Dan 2:8–9, Nebuchadnezzar told the

1. BAGD 760; BDAG 935.

2. Kuhn, "Ephesians in the Light of the Qumran Texts," 125–26.

3. How the unbelievers are viewed by Christians and pagans is discussed by Best, "Ephesians: Two Types of Existence," 42–50.

4. Polybius 3.42.2; 30.31.6; Plutarch *Crassus* 2.4.

5. Diodorus Siculus 36.2.2; 36.2a*bis*.

6. Friedrich Büchsel, "ἀγοράζω, ἐξαγοράζω," *TDNT* 1 (1964): 128.

7. Cf. Barr, *Biblical Words for Time*, 127–29; Burns, "Two Words for 'Time' in the New Testament," 22.

8. Büchsel, *TDNT* 1 (1964): 128; *contra* [James Gow], "Entre Nous: 'Redeeming the Time,'" *ExpTim* 37 (November 1925): 96. He thinks that rather than time or opportunities, it refers to habits or opinions. Cullmann thinks καιρός refers to a divine plan of salvation into which the believer is placed and that he redeems the time when he advances the redemptive history. See Oscar Cullmann, *Christ and Time. The Primitive Christian Conception of Time and History*, trans. Floyd V. Filson (London: SCM, 1951), 42–43, 225.

9. David H. Field, "Buy, Sell, Market [ἀγοράζω, ἐξαγοράζω, πωλέω]," *NIDNTT* 1 (1975): 268.

Chaldeans that if they did not tell him his dream and its interpretation, they would be destroyed. They bargained with him to give them the dream and then they could give him the interpretation. In his refusal he accused them of trying to gain or buy time before their doom. Paul used the term in a more positive manner in Eph 5:16 and Col 4:5 where he tells his audiences not to seek delay but to intensively buy up the time, that is, "to take full advantage of any opportunity—'to make good use of every opportunity, to take advantage of every chance.'"[1] The participle ἐξαγοραζόμενοι is the middle (indirect) voice where the subject acts for its benefit, hence, "taking advantage of every opportunity [for yourself]."[2] Why? Paul next gives the reason.

ὅτι αἱ ἡμέραι πονηραί εἰσιν, "because the days are evil." This is the second time in Ephesians (cf. 4:25) that ὅτι, "because," introduces the reason for the previous statement. People are to make the most of the opportunity at hand because the days are evil. The word πονηρός is a much used word in classical Greek. It can have the idea of "troubling" or "disastrous"[3] and "wretched," "poor," or "incompetent."[4] Socially, it can have also the idea of those who are poorly educated[5] and politically it is used of those in power who are base and use power for selfish gain.[6] Out of these, the moral sense is derived indicating one who is base or despicable[7] which is synonymous with κακός, meaning "bad, evil injurious" (cf. 4:31), ἄχρηστος, "unkind"[8] (see opposite 2:7 and 4:32), ἄδικος, "unrighteous," and ἀσεβής, "ungodly."[9] Xenophon defines the πονηροί men as ungrateful, careless, selfish, faithless, and incontinent.[10] In the LXX it occurs 373 times, in the canonical books 295 times, and translates seventeen Hebrew words, around 200 times for רַע and its derivative רֶעַע. It carries the same idea as all of the above, "bad, evil." It refers to that which is ethically bad, evil, or wicked with reference to persons (Gen 13:13; 1 Sam 30:22; Ps 10:15 [LXX 9:36]; Job 21:30), thoughts (Gen 6:5; 8:21; Jer 3:17; 16:12), and deeds or actions (Deut 17:2; 19:20; Neh 9:35; Jer 18:11; 23:2; Ezek 13:22).[11] Harder sums up the OT concept well when he states, "The wicked, then, are those who do not seek Yahweh or His commands, who will not be guided by Him, Ez. 11:2. Who is wicked is thus measured by God, by His commands, and by obedience to them. God de-

1. L&N §65.42; cf. R. Martin Pope, "Studies in Pauline Vocabulary. Of Redeeming the Time," *ExpTim* 22 (September 1911): 552–53.

2. Wallace, *Greek Grammar*, 419–21.

3. Aristophanes *Plutus* 352.

4. Ibid., 221; *Vespae* 977; Xenophon *Cyropaedia* 1.4.19; *Anabasis* 3.4.35.

5. Aristophanes *Equites* 336–37.

6. Isocrates 15.99, 316–17; Aristotle *Politica* 5.4 §1304b.26.

7. Euripides *Hecuba* 596–97; 1191; Plato *Symposium* 183d.

8. Plato *Leges* 12 §950b.

9. Isocrates 8.120; Aristotle *Ethica Nicomachea* 4.1.42 §1122a.6.

10. Xenophon *Memorabilia* 2.6.19–20.

11. For its various uses, see BDB 947–49; Dohmen, *TWAT* 7 (1990): 585–86.

termines what is evil, and in this sense evil is to be understood simply as that which is contrary to God."[1] In the Hellenistic period the word continues to have the same meaning "'morally reprehensible,' 'useless,' 'bad,' 'evil.'"[2] It is set in contrast to that which is good.[3] The word occurs seventy-eight times in the NT: fifty-two times in the Gospels and Acts, thirteen times in Paul's letters, three times in Ephesians (5:16; 6:13, 16), and thirteen times in the rest of the NT, again with the same idea of that which is evil or bad, that which is opposed to God.[4] The NT attributes such evil to people (Matt 7:11 = Luke 11:13; Matt 12:34–35; 1 Cor 5:13; 2 Thess 3:2; 2 Tim 3:13), thoughts (Matt 15:19; 1 Tim 6:4; Jas 2:4), deeds (Col 1:21; 2 Tim 4:18; Jas 4:16), and the devil (Matt 13:19; John 17:15; Eph 6:16; 2 Thess 3:3). Also, it refers to the abstract concepts of evil (Rom 12:9; 1 Thess 5:22) and that which is descriptive of this present age, using the terms bad, harmful, or useless (Gal 1:4; Eph 6:13). In the present context πονηρός speaks of the present age as evil. Moral, not physical, evil is in mind here but there are various interpretations of Paul's statement.[5] Lindemann thinks that the present time (καιρός) is evil and thus, on the one hand, the believers can fully utilize it, but on the other hand, since it is evil they are not to show it any respect.[6] But this seems contradictory and certainly the context argues against this view in that the text explicitly states that one is to take advantage of the opportunity (not disregard it) because the days are evil. Harder (also Scott[7]) suggests that the days are evil because they are a part of the last days with impending judgment. However, Harder also suggests that it may be the evil nature of the days that are morally corrupt, and the believers' resources are required to exploit every moment for that which is good.[8] His first suggestion has no support in the immediate context. The latter suggestion is more probable although it does not go far enough. The days are evil because they are controlled by the god of this age (2:2) who opposes God and his kingdom and who will try to prevent any opportunities for the declaration of God's program and purposes. Hence, in this present evil age believers are not to waste opportunities because this would be useless and harmful to God's kingdom and to those who are a part of it. Paul would have felt this very keenly. Although the evil plots against him caused his imprisonment for the sake of the gospel, nevertheless he used every opportunity to proclaim the gospel while imprisoned (Phil 1:12–14). Though believers are redeemed and are

1. Günther Harder, "πονηρός, πονηρία," *TDNT* 6 (1968): 550–51.
2. Ibid., 549.
3. Philo *Leg. All.* 1.18, 32 §§60, 101; *Virt.* 35, 36, 41 §§189, 194, 227; *Praem.* 12 §67.
4. Ernst Achilles, "Evil, Bad, Wickedness [κακός, πονηρός]," *NIDNTT* 1 (1975): 565.
5. As does Chrysostom *Eph* 5:16 (*PG* 62:128).
6. Lindemann, *Aufhebung*, 232–34.
7. Scott, 233.
8. Harder, *TDNT* 6 (1968): 554.

prepared for the days to come, they still live in the present evil days as has been true for believers throughout history (Ps 49:5). It is interesting to notice that he is not recommending that they fear the present evil age or avoid interaction with it. Rather his exhortation is to walk wisely in the evil days by seizing every opportunity. Unrelenting warfare exists between the God of heaven and the god of this age. In essence, believers are commanded not to let the god of this age intimidate them, but to take advantage of every opportunity in this immoral environment to live a life that pleases God (cf. Gal 2:10). How this is done is explained more fully in the following verses.

b. Proper State: Become Wise (5:17–21)

(1) In Thought (5:17)

Having laid the groundwork in verses 15–16 by exhorting believers to walk wisely by making most of every opportunity, Paul now enjoins them to have a proper perspective so that they can live a life that will be pleasing to the Lord. His pattern is to first state the negative and then to give the positive. Once he has finished this section (vv. 17–21), Paul will make specific applications to daily life (5:22–6:9).

(a) Negative: Do Not Become Foolish (5:17a)

Text: 5:17a. διὰ τοῦτο μὴ γίνεσθε ἄφρονες,

Translation: 5:17a. "On account of this do not become foolish,"

Commentary: 5:17a. διὰ τοῦτο μὴ γίνεσθε ἄφρονες, "On account of this do not become foolish." As in 1:15 διὰ τοῦτο, "on account of this," concludes the foregoing discussion. In this text Paul is drawing a conclusion not from the immediately preceding clause, "because the days are evil," but from his discussion beginning in verse 15. Paul has summoned the believers to walk wisely, taking advantage of every opportunity because the days are evil. For this reason he warns them not to become foolish. It is a restatement of verse 15b with slightly different words.

In classical literature the word ἄφρων has the idea of "senseless, lack of understanding,"[1] "folly,"[2] and it can also mean "out of one's mind, demented."[3] In the LXX it occurs 133 times and in the canonical books it appears 113 and translates thirteen Hebrew words. Nearly sixty times it translates כְּסִיל, which describes a person who is a "fool" (Ps 49:10 [MT 49:11; LXX 48:11]; Prov 10:18, 23), who displays folly (Prov 13:16; 15:2), is careless (Prov 14:16; 21:20), and despises wisdom (Prov 23:9; 26:7, 9).[4] Similarly, when translated from the other

1. Homer *Ilias* 3.220; *Odyssea* 21.102; Xenophon *Memorabilia* 1.2.55; 1.4.4.
2. Aeschylus *Eumenides* 377; Thucydides 5.105.3.
3. Homer *Ilias* 5.761, 875; Sophocles *Electra* 941.
4. BDB 492–93; J. Schüpphaus, "כסל *ksl*, etc.," *TDOT* 7 (1995): 264–69.

Hebrew words, it is a person who lacks understanding (Prov 17:18) or despises knowledge (Prov 1:22).[1] In the Hellenistic period it carried the same connotation.[2] Josephus uses it twice where it connotes something senseless or foolish.[3] In the NT it is used eleven times: twice in Luke (11:40; 12:20), once in 1 Pet 2:15, the remaining eight times in Paul, and only here in Ephesians. In all the cases in the NT it is translated "fool" or "foolish" by the RSV, NASB, NIV, and the NRSV (also the AV, except in Eph 5:17 where it is translated "unwise"). For example, Jesus denounces the Pharisees as fools because they were hypocritically clean on the outside but wicked on the inside (Luke 11:40). Further, God labels the rich farmer a fool who wanted to build larger barns but yet was not prepared for eternity (Luke 12:20). In the present context it can be translated "foolish" or "careless conduct," "contrasted with σύνεσις as prudent observance of the will of God."[4]

In Eph 1:8 two nouns, σοφία and φρόνησις, are used and are antonyms to the two adjectives used in the immediate context, namely, ἄφρων in the present verse and ἄσοφοι in verse 15. The term σοφία means the "true insight of known facts" or "insight into the true nature of things." In contrast, the ἄσοφος person does not have the insight into the true nature of things. The term φρόνησις conveys more the concept of discernment or discretion in a practical way. Whereas σοφία emphasizes insight, φρόνησις emphasizes understanding. The ἄφρων is foolish because he lacks discernment in practical living. In other words, the ἄσοφος lacks mental insight whereas the ἄφρων is unable to apply knowledge practically.

As in 5:7, the present imperative verb γίνεσθε should not be translated as ἐστέ, "be" (as AV, RV, ASV, RSV, NASB, NEB, TEV, JB, NJB, NRSV), but "become," which indicates the possibility of entering into the condition[5] of becoming foolish.[6] The present tense may indicate the action as an ongoing process, but here in conjunction with this particular verb it seems to indicate an ingressive-progressive action, namely, they are not to begin to become foolish and continue in that state.[7] Believers are to walk carefully as wise persons, making the most of every opportunity because the days are evil, and for this reason they are urged not to enter into the condition of foolishness. The uncareful believer can easily be enticed by the god of this age to become foolish in the practical application of knowledge. With this negative command explained, Paul next explains its positive side, that is, the reverse of foolishness.

1. Cf. BDB 493; Georg Bertram, "φρήν, ἄφρων, κτλ.," *TDNT* 9 (1974): 224–25.
2. MM 99.
3. Josephus *B.J.* 1.32.3 §630; 2.14.8 §303.
4. Bertram, *TDNT* 9 (1974): 231.
5. BAGD 159; BDAG 198.
6. Salmond, 362; Westcott, 77; *contra* Alford, 3:134.
7. Cf. Wallace, *Greek Grammar*, 721.

(b) Positive: Understand the Lord's Will (5:17b)

Text: 5:17b. ἀλλὰ συνίετε τί τὸ θέλημα τοῦ κυρίου.

Translation: 5:17b. "but understand what the will of the Lord is."

Commentary: 5:17b. ἀλλὰ συνίετε[1] τί τὸ θέλημα[2] τοῦ κυρίου,[3] "but understand what the will of the Lord is." The second contrast is now stated. The adversative conjunction ἀλλά, "but," indicates a strong contrast from the preceding negative statement. In classical literature συνίημι conveys the idea of bringing together, whether with hostility, as in "to battle,"[4] or with friendliness (middle voice), as in "to come to an agreement," for example, in marriage.[5] The noun form was discussed at 3:4 using the image of two rivers which come together. In the metaphorical sense, it means to bring together or accept something primarily by perceiving what is heard.[6] Hence, it is not only hearing what is said but understanding it,[7] whether the construction is the genitive of the person or the thing heard[8] or the accusative of content,[9] which is the case in Eph 5:17. It also more broadly means "to take notice of" or "to observe."[10] It can simply mean "to understand," whether it is constructed with the genitive, "to understand one another's language,"[11] or it is constructed with the accusative of con-

1. The reading συνίετε is found in 𝔓[46] ℵ A B P 0278 6 33 81 365 1241[s] 1739 *pc* Jerome Augustine. The reading συνίεντες is found in D[2] (D* F G) Ψ 1881 𝔐 latt syr[h] Chrysostom Theodoret. The first reading is almost exclusively Alexandrian. The second reading has only Ψ in the Alexandrian text-type, lat and the variations of D F G from the Western text-type, and is definitely represented by the Byzantine text. Although the second reading has a better geographical spread, it is mixed in regards to genealogical relationships. With reservation, the first reading is preferred because of the date and character of the manuscripts. The participial reading may have been influenced by v. 10 where there is a similar construction: δοκιμάζοντες τί ἐστιν εὐάρεστον τῷ κυρίῳ. However, in the immediate context the first reading also fits well, for Paul exhorted them negatively (διὰ τοῦτο μὴ γίνεσθε ἄφρονες) and now gives a positive counterpart which seems better than an assumption expressed in a participle.

2. The reading φρόνημα is found only in ℵ* and thus lacks date, geographical distribution, and genealogical relationships.

3. The reading θεοῦ is found in A 81 365 614 629 2464 *pc* it[a, d] vg[cl] syr[p] cop[bopt] Jerome Cassiodorus and the reading Χριστοῦ is found only in 𝔓[46]. The first variant is represented by the Alexandrian text-type but not by the most weighty manuscripts. The second variant has only 𝔓[46] and probably is a scribal insertion so that the reader would think that it refers not to God but to Christ. The reading in the text is superior because it has good representation from the various text-types and thus has good date and character, good geographical representation, and good genealogical relationships.

4. Homer *Ilias* 1.8; 7.210.

5. Ibid., 13.381.

6. Homer *Odyssea* 4.76.

7. Homer *Ilias* 15.442; *Odyssea* 1.271.

8. Homer *Ilias* 2.26; Herodotus 1.47.

9. Homer *Ilias* 2.182; *Odyssea* 6.289.

10. Homer *Odyssea* 18.34.

11. Herodotus 4.414; Thucydides 1.3.4.

tent, to "comprehend" or "understand" deceit,[1] someone's speech,[2] a lesson,[3] or the meaning of something.[4] In the LXX it occurs 107 times and in the canonical books it appears eighty-two times and translates seven Hebrew words: forty-six times for בִּין, meaning "to discern, perceive" in the Qal (Ps 139:2 [LXX 138:2]; Jer 9:12 [MT & LXX 9:11]; Isa 6:9–10 [quoted in Matt 13:14–15; Mark 4:12; Luke 8:10]), "to understand" in the Hiphil (Prov 8:9; Neh 8:12; Mic 4:12), and in the Hitpael (Job 31:1; Ps 119:100, 104 [LXX 118:100, 104]; Isa 1:3; 52:15 [quoted in Rom 15:21]);[5] and twenty-six times for שָׂכַל, all of which, except 1 Sam 18:30, are in the Hiphil stem and mean "to consider, ponder, understand, have insight" (Deut 32:29; Ps 14:2 [LXX 13:2] [quoted in Rom 3:11]; 64:9 [MT 64:10; LXX 63:10]; 106:7 [LXX 105:7]; Prov 21:12; Jer 9:23 [MT 9:24]).[6] Conzelmann points out that, different from Greek thought, OT thought considered insight as a gift from God rather than native to human beings.[7] The verb occurs twenty-six times in the NT: twenty-two times in the Gospels and Acts; and four times in Paul's letters (Rom 3:11; 15:21; 2 Cor 10:12; Eph 5:17). It means "to perceive, understand, comprehend." This perception or understanding is more than just the understanding of facts (as γινώσκω); it is an intelligent grasp of knowledge[8] that has resulting consequences. As in the OT, the NT also teaches that the lack of understanding is not just a simple lack of knowledge but results from human beings' rejection of God.[9] Again, the present imperative indicates that believers are to make it a practice to understand what the will of the Lord is.

The verb συνίημι, "understand," is followed by the accusative of content τί τὸ θέλημα τοῦ κυρίου. The word θέλημα was discussed at 1:1 where we concluded that it has the idea of a desire, wish, will, or resolve. This word is followed by the possessive genitive τοῦ κυρίου showing that it is the Lord's will which is to be understood or comprehended. The question is who is the Lord: is it referring to God or Christ? Possibly it refers to God because wherever θέλημα is used in Ephesians it always refers to God, except 2:3 where it refers to the will of the flesh. However, the word κύριος is used twenty-six times in Ephesians and always refers to Christ (e.g., 1:3, 15, 17; 2:21; 3:11), except where it refers to human masters (6:5, 9). In any case, in the mind

1. Aeschylus *Persae* 361.
2. Herodotus 3.46.
3. Pindar *Pythian Odes* 3.80.
4. Aristophanes *Plutus* 45.
5. BDB 106–7; Ringgren, *TDOT* 2 (1977): 105–7.
6. BDB 968; Koenen, *TWAT* 7 (1990): 783–89.
7. Hans Conzelmann, "συνίημι, σύνεσις, συνετός, ἀσύνετος," *TDNT* 7 (1971): 890.
8. Alford, 3:134; Eadie, 395; Salmond, 362; Schlier, 245 n 1; Barth, 579. One must be careful not to overdraw the distinction between συνίμι and γινώσκω.
9. Harder and Goetzmann, *NIDNTT* 3 (1978): 132.

of believers Christ is God and therefore believers are to understand the will of their Lord Christ. This fits well with the context, for in verse 10 the believer is to walk in the manner of "approving what is pleasing to the Lord," that is, Christ. Hence, when believers understand the will of the Lord, they will be wise, not unwise and foolish by following the will of the flesh (2:3) as they did in their unregenerate days. This is a reminder of what he mentioned earlier, namely, that believers are not to live as Gentiles do (4:17–19) but to live as those who have learned Christ and were taught in him in conformity with the truth that is in Jesus (4:20–21). Christ is to be preeminent in the lives of believers.

In conclusion, believers are to understand by careful consideration of individual circumstances what is the will of the Lord and then to carry out his will. However, since there is agreement in both the OT and NT that the ability for people to understand the things of God is a gift of God, how can God's will be comprehended? Paul answers this in the next verse.

(2) In Life (5:18–21)

Paul has exhorted the Ephesian believers to conduct themselves circumspectly, not as unwise or foolish by doing the will of the flesh (2:3). Rather, they are to comprehend or understand the will of the Lord. The unwise are governed by the flesh, whereas the wise are governed by the mind as it understands the will of the Lord. Once they comprehend the will of the Lord, then they are to walk according to it. The will of the Lord is discerned by the gift of God's insight and it is carried out by the power of God's Spirit.

(a) Negative: Be Not Drunk with Wine (5:18a)

Text: 5:18a. καὶ μὴ μεθύσκεσθε οἴνῳ, ἐν ᾧ ἐστιν ἀσωτία,

Translation: 5:18a. "And do not get drunk with wine, in which there is dissipation,"

Commentary: 5:18a. καὶ μὴ μεθύσκεσθε οἴνῳ, "And do not get drunk with wine." Going from the general to the specific, Paul explains how this wisdom works out in the believer's conduct. As in verses 15 and 17 Paul first states the negative and then follows it with the positive. The conjunction καί, "and," particularizes the foregoing statement, contrasting foolishness and understanding. It may be an explicative conjunction which points to a further explanation of the preceding statement, thus translated "and so," "that is" or "namely."[1]

The verb μεθύσκεσθε meaning "to drink" is a present imperative. The prohibition expressed with the present imperative could suggest that Paul was exhorting them to stop an action[2] or prohibiting them

1. BAGD 393; BDAG 495.

2. MHT 1:122, 126; 3:76; Wallace, *Greek Grammar*, 487; cf. Alford, 3:134; Eadie, 395; Ellicott, 124; Abbott, 160; Salmond, 362; Schnackenburg, 236.

from a course of action, that is, "make it your habit not to do" it.[1] There is no indication in this epistle that the Ephesian believers indulged in drunken behavior and that Paul found it necessary to enjoin them to cease, as was the case in 1 Cor 11:21–22.[2] Rather, he is charging them not to allow such behavior to become a habit in their lives because this would be considered unwise or foolish conduct. Intoxicated people are not in control of their faculties and thereby act foolishly. Therefore, they are unable to comprehend intelligently the will of the Lord. Paul further explains this in the next phrase. The οἶνος, "wine," is an instrumental dative indicating the means of intoxication.[3] Wine was a common drink in that day and Paul is not prohibiting the drinking of wine but rather becoming intoxicated with it.[4] This prohibition is similar to that found in the Wisdom Literature of the OT (Prov 23:31)[5] which would be fitting, for the present context is concerned with wise living.

ἐν ᾧ ἐστιν ἀσωτία, "in which there is dissipation." The relative prepositional phrase (ἐν ᾧ) picks up not only the noun οἴνῳ, "wine," but the entire previous clause (μὴ μεθύσκεσθε οἴνῳ). Thus, it refers to drunkenness with wine as an excess.[6] The word family of the noun ἀσωτία originally had the idea of an "incurable" sickness[7] and was used of "shamelessness, dissipation, profligacy, debauchery."[8] Aristotle discusses the term ἀσωτία stating that people with this vice are prodigals who waste their substance and are in the path of ruination of their own lives.[9] Most prodigals squander their money in debauchery and have no high moral standards as they readily yield to the temptation of pleasure.[10] Foerster summarizes ἀσωτία as a "wild and undisciplined life."[11] In the LXX, the adjective ἄσωτος is found only in Prov 7:11 and the noun ἀσωτία is found only in Prov 28:7 and 2 Macc

1. Robertson, *Grammar*, 854, 890; Moule, *Idiom Book*, 21 and n. 1; Fanning, *Verbal Aspect*, 336; Porter, *Verbal Aspect*, 357; Wallace, *Greek Grammar*, 525, 717.

2. *Contra* James D. G. Dunn, *Jesus and the Spirit. A Study of the Religious and Charismatic Experience of Jesus and the First Christians as Reflected in the New Testament*, New Testament Library (London: SCM, 1975), 238; Schlier, *Die Zeit der Kirche*, 254; Schlier, 246; Gnilka, 269; Staab, 155; Adai, *Der Heilige Geist als Gegenwart Gottes*, 223, 226–27.

3. Robertson, *Grammar*, 533. One would expect a genitive construction rather than an instrumental dative (cf. MHT 3:240).

4. Chrysostom states that wine is the cause of drunkenness by immoderate use of it (Chrysostom *Eph* 5:16 [*PG* 62:128]).

5. Cf. Moritz, *A Profound Mystery*, 94–95.

6. Alford, 3:134; Eadie, 396; Ellicott, 124; Abbott, 161; Salmond, 362.

7. Aristotle *Problemata* 33.9 §962b.6; Plutarch *Moralia: Quaestiones naturales* 26 §918d.

8. Plato *Respublica* 8.13 §560e; Aristotle *Ethica Nicomachea* 2.7.4 §1107b.10; Polybius 32.11.10.

9. Aristotle *Ethica Nicomachea* 4.1.2–5 §§1119b.22–1120a.5.

10. Ibid., 4.1.35 §1121b.5–11.

11. Werner Foerster, "ἄσωτος, ἀσωτία," *TDNT* 1 (1964): 507.

6:4 where it continues to have the idea of "debauchery" and "profligacy."[1] Josephus uses the noun ἄσωτος twice: (1) Arion, Hyrcanus' steward in Alexandria, questioned Hyrcanus' son as to why he lived a "dissolute" life in contrast to his father who had accumulated wealth by hard work and by restraining his desires;[2] and (2) drunken Vitellius, knowing his end was imminent, gorged himself with the most lavish and "luxurious"[3] banquet. The word "luxurious" is used in the sense of wasteful or without any restraint. In the NT the adverb ἀσώτως is used only in Luke 15:13 where it relates how the prodigal son squandered all his money in "dissolute" living. The noun ἀσωτία occurs three times: (1) in Titus 1:6 where believers are told to select elders whose children are believers not accused of "debauchery"; (2) 1 Pet 4:4 mentions that those in the world are surprised that believers do not join them in their excesses of "dissipation" or "ruination"; and (3) in the present verse. Hence, it has the idea of a disorderly life resulting from the lack of self-control. It refers to people who waste their resources to gratify their own sensual desires.[4] They lack discipline that leads to excesses that can lead to ruination. The word literally means "incorrigibility."[5] A drunk person lacks understanding and control. Thus, in this context Paul instructs believers not to be drunk with wine which causes unrestrained, dissolute living, leading only to ruin. It is difficult to select one precise word that describes this condition but probably "dissipation" is the closest. It is the opposite of being wise which takes full advantage of every opportunity (vv. 15–16).

As mentioned above, Paul's command does not indicate that they were to stop a present practice. Some suggest that Paul is possibly referring to their religious background in the cult of Dionysus, the god of wine, where they filled themselves with the "spirit" of Bacchus by imbibing wine which lead to an uncontrolled, frenzied conduct.[6] Although this is possible, it is unlikely because Paul does not mention directly that this was their religious practice as he does in other places (Eph 2:1–5; 4:17–21; 1 Cor 5:1; 6:9–11, 15–20; Gal 4:1–11). Drunkenness occurred both inside and outside of the religious practices of the day. Nor is it probable that Paul is referring to communal gatherings

1. Debauchery is closely linked with drunkenness in the Testaments of the Twelve Patriarchs (*T. Iss.* 7:2; *T. Jud.* 11:2; 12:3; 13:6; 16:1 with exact wording as in the present verse in *T. Jud.* 14:1); cf. Gnilka, 269; Lincoln, "The Use of the OT in Ephesians," 43; James Moffatt, "Exegetica," *Exp* 8th ser., vol. 7 (January 1914): 95.

2. Josephus *A.J.* 12.4.8 §203.

3. Josephus *B.J.* 4.9.4 §651.

4. Trench, *Synonyms of the New Testament*, 55.

5. BAGD 119; cf. BDAG 148.

6. Barth, 580; James Moffatt, "Three Notes on Ephesians," *Exp* 8th ser., vol. 15 (April 1918): 315–17; H. Preisker, "μέθη, μεθύω, μέθυσος, μεθύσκομαι," *TDNT* 4 (1967): 548; Cleon L. Rogers Jr., "The Dionysian Background of Ephesians 5:18," *BSac* 136 (July–September 1979): 249–57; Dennis Leggett, "Be Filled with the Spirit: Ephesians 5:18," *Paraclete* 23 (fall 1989): 10–11; Moritz, *A Profound Mystery*, 94–95.

at mealtimes that included discussion, drinking, and singing.[1] Though certainly such gatherings took place, nothing in the context indicates that Paul is referring to those occasions. Rather, Paul is simply saying that since they have been supernaturally redeemed, they are not to live the life of the natural person that is wasteful and ruinous.

(b) Positive: Be Filled by the Spirit (5:18b–21)

As is his practice, Paul not only instructs believers concerning the way in which they are not to live but also how they are to live. He had told them not to be unwise but wise, not to become foolish but to understand what the will of the Lord is, not to be drunk with wine in which there is dissipation. Now he gives the positive exhortation: be filled by the Spirit.

(i) The Command (5:18b)

Text: 5:18b. ἀλλὰ πληροῦσθε ἐν πνεύματι,

Translation: 5:18b. "but be filled by the Spirit,"

Commentary: 5:18b. ἀλλὰ πληροῦσθε ἐν πνεύματι, "but be filled by the Spirit." This marks the third contrast. As in verses 15 and 17 the negative here is contrasted with the positive by the adversative conjunction ἀλλά, "but." The contrast is not between the wine and the Spirit but between the two states expressed by the two verbs: being drunk with wine leads to dissipation but being filled by the Spirit leads to joy in fellowship and obedience to the commands of the Lord's will. Some commentators think that the "spirit" here refers not to the Holy Spirit but to the human spirit, and thus we are to be filled in spirit.[2] However, this is unlikely.[3] What would it mean to fill a human spirit? With what would it be filled? Would it result in what is expressed in the next verses? It is interesting to note that those commentators who hold to this view have difficulty in explaining the nature of the filling. They ultimately think that the human spirit has to be related to the Holy Spirit, for the human spirit left on its own inclines toward evil. Consequently, Westcott, who holds this view, states, "It is assumed that the Spirit of God can alone satisfy the spirit of man."[4] Although he takes the referent as the human spirit, in the end he comes to the same conclusion. In addition, the writer to Ephesians uses the term "spirit" thirteen other times (1:13, 17; 2:2, 18, 22; 3:5, 16; 4:3, 4, 23, 30; 6:17, 18) and each time it refers to a spirit outside of a person. Once it refers to the spirit of the devil or his emissar-

1. Peter W. Gosnell, "Ephesians 5:18–20 and Mealtime Propriety," *TynBul* 44.2 (November 1993): 363–71.

2. Alford, 3:134?; Abbott, 161–62; Westcott, 81; Lenski, 618–19; Joüon, "Notes philologiques sur quelques versets de l'Épître aux Éphésiens," 461; also marginal reading in RV and ASV.

3. Schnackenburg, 237 n. 16; Best, 508.

4. Westcott, 81.

ies (2:2) but the other twelve times it refers to the Spirit of God (1:17; 4:3, 23 are disputed but these have been discussed). Thus, it is natural to assume that the "spirit" here refers to the Holy Spirit. Futhermore, two other times in the NT (Luke 1:15; Acts 2:13–18) the use of wine is contrasted with πνεῦμα, "spirit," and in both instances the "spirit" refers to the Holy Spirit. Moreover, if it had reference to the human spirit, the noun would have been "modified by a possessive pronoun or at least an article."[1] Therefore, in the present verse it seems likely that the writer is making reference to the Holy Spirit.

The term πληρόω has already been discussed (1:23; 3:19; 4:10). It is used of something which is filled with content, for example, "to fill" containers or, in the passive, "the house was filled with the fragrance of the ointment" (John 12:3). Metaphorically, in the passive it can mean "to be filled with unrighteousness" (Rom 1:29). To "be filled" can connote the idea "that a man is completely controlled and stamped by the powers which fill him."[2] In other words, the one who is filled is characterized by that which fills him, whether it be fruits of unrighteousness or righteousness (Phil 1:11). Many suggest that the content of the filling is ἐν πνεύματι, translated "be filled with the Spirit."[3] However, normally verbs of filling take a genitive of content (e.g., πληρόω + genitive in Acts 2:28; 13:52; Rom 15:13, 14; πίμπλημι + genitive in Luke 1:41, 67; Acts 2:4; 4:8; 9:17; 13:9). Moreover, nowhere in the NT does πληρόω followed by ἐν plus the dative indicate content.[4] Some commentators translate ἐν as "with" in order to combine the thoughts of "in" and "by," thus indicating that the Holy Spirit is not only the instrument by which believers are filled but also the sphere in which they are filled.[5] This is an attempt to have it both ways, but it is

1. Wallace, *Greek Grammar*, 215.

2. Gerhard Delling, "πληρόω," *TDNT* 6 (1968): 291.

3. Chrysostom *Eph* 5:18 (*PG* 62:129); Aquinas, chap. 5, lec. 7, vv. 18–21 (213); Hodge, 302–3; Eadie, 398; Moule, 135–36; Robinson, 121, 203–4; Schlier, 245–46; Hendriksen, 239–40; Mitton, 190; Barth, 582; Bruce, 379–80; Lincoln, 344–45; Snodgrass, 289–90; Liefeld, 134–38; Easley, "The Pauline Usage of *Pneumati* as a Reference to the Spirit of God," 307; Andreas J. Köstenberger, "What Does It Mean to Be Filled with the Spirit? A Biblical Investigation," *JETS* 40 (June 1997): 231–35; Carsten Peter Thiede, "Der Brief an die Epheser. 43. Teil: Kapitel 5,17–20," *Fundamentum* 21, no. 4 (2000): 16–17.

4. Wallace, *Greek Grammar*, 374–75, cf. also 93 n. 62, 94, 170–71; Abbott, 161–62.

5. Alford, 3:134; Ellicott, 124; Schnackenburg, 237. The idea of sphere is seen in Rom 8:9 where Paul states that the believer is not "in" the flesh but "in" the Spirit, meaning that the believer's sphere of influence is the Spirit rather than the flesh (cf. Oepke, "ἐν," *TDNT* 2 [1964]: 540–41). Masson thinks "by the Spirit" is too precise and "in the Spirit" is too vague. He proposes "seek the fullness which the Spirit gives" (Masson, 209 n. 3). Cf. also Fee, *God's Empowering Presence*, 721–22 and n. 196. Leggett translates ἐν as "with" to indicate that "the Spirit is both the agent and substance of that filling" ("Be Filled with the Spirit: Ephesians 5:18," 11). This is unlikely as discussed above.

imprecise, and implies more than the text conveys. It seems best to translate ἐν πνεύματι with an instrumental sense, "by the Spirit" or "by means of the Spirit."[1] This is analogous to 4:30 where the preposition with the relative pronoun (ἐν ᾧ) is translated "the Spirit . . . by whom you were sealed." Furthermore, other passages where ἐν πνεύματι is used (e.g., 1 Cor 12:3, 13; Rom 15:16) can be translated "by." The content of the filling is not specifically mentioned in the present verse, but it may refer to the fullness of the moral excellence and power of God mentioned in Eph 1:23. Later Paul prays that believers would be "filled up to all the fullness of God," that is, filled with the content of God's moral excellence and power,[2] which is to know the love of Christ (3:19). Also, in the preceding verse we are "to understand the will of the Lord," the Lord here referring to Christ. Hence, the Holy Spirit is the means by which believers are filled with Christ and his will. This is fitting because the parallel passage of the present verse is Col 3:16 where Paul states, "let the word of Christ dwell in you richly, in all wisdom, teaching, and admonishing one another with the singing of psalms, hymns, spiritual songs with thankfulness in your hearts to God."

This lifestyle is in contrast to those who are "drunk with wine." As previously mentioned, persons controlled by alcohol no longer control their actions, as exhibited when asked to walk a straight line and are unable to do so. Likewise, those filled by the Spirit no longer control their actions but rather relinquish their will to the Lord. Ironically, this sometimes results in unusual actions also, as in the case of the believers at Pentecost (Acts 2:4, 13, 15).[3] It must be noted that the present imperative passive verb πληροῦσθε, "be filled,"[4] probably indicates an iterative force, a repeated action of filling by the Spirit.[5] The imperative mood places the responsibilty on the believers. The passive voice suggests that believers cannot fill themselves. Rather, believers are to be filled by the Spirit. Thus, believers are exhorted to be filled repeatedly by the Holy Spirit no matter where they are or what they are doing.[6]

1. Moule, *Idiom Book*, 76, 77; Wallace, *Greek Grammar*, 93 n. 62, 94, 171, 375; Meyer, 285; Abbott, 161–62; Salmond, 362.

2. Cf. Wallace, *Greek Grammar*, 375.

3. V. C. Pfitzner, "Good Songs in Bad Times. An Exegetical and Homiletical Study of Ephesians 5:15–21," *Lutheran Theological Journal* 12 (August 1978): 48.

4. Usami (*Somatic Comprehension of Unity*, 134) suggests a middle voice, i.e., "but [you] fill yourself with (in) spirit." However, it seems that the passive makes much better sense in this context. Also, Usami cites Col 1:9 as support but that is invalid since it is an aorist passive. We are the recipients of the Spirit's filling.

5. Wallace, *Greek Grammar*, 485–86, 722. Wallace suggest that here the present tense has a gnomic sense, i.e., "*a general, timeless fact*" (523, 525).

6. Not only in a church service, as Schlier would limit it, but in all places at all times) Schlier, *Die Zeit der Kirche*, 254). Cf. Köstenberger, "What Does It Mean to Be Filled with the Spirit?" 233.

In Pauline literature outside of Ephesians the term "spirit" occurs 132 times. Although there are a few references to a person's spirit (e.g., Rom 1:9; 8:16; 1 Cor 5:3–5; 14:14; 16:18; 2 Cor 7:1; Phil 4:23) or attitude (e.g., 1 Cor 4:21; 2 Cor 11:4; 12:18; Gal 5:20; 6:1; Phil 1:27; Col 2:5; 2 Tim 1:7), most refer to the Holy Spirit. Besides the filling by the Spirit, in 1:13 and 4:30 Paul speaks of the sealing of the Spirit, which serves as a mark of identification or ownership showing that the believer belongs to God. He also mentions this sealing ministry in 2 Cor 1:22. The NT also mentions the indwelling ministry of the Spirit in every believer (Rom 8:9–11; 1 Cor 2:12; 6:19; 2 Cor 5:5; Gal 4:6; cf. John 14:17; 1 John 3:24; 4:13) as a resource for God's presence and power. In 1 Cor 12:13 the believer is baptized by the Spirit into the body of Christ (cf. also Acts 1:5; 11:16) so that every believer is identified with the one body of believers in Christ. In addition, the believers are enjoined to walk by the Spirit (Gal 5:16–18, 25; Rom 8:4). In examining these various passages regarding the injunction to walk by the Spirit, they seem to parallel being filled by the Spirit. According to Gal 5:16–18 the one who walks by the Spirit does not gratify the desires of the flesh which are against the Spirit. In Rom 8:4–6 those who walk according to the flesh are not walking according to the Spirit. Later, in 8:13–16, Paul states that those who live by the Spirit will put to death the deeds of the body by the leading of God. The point is that walking by the Spirit and being filled by the Spirit mean that the Spirit of God directs and empowers a believer to live a life pleasing to God and his will. Those who live under the control of their flesh will not please God and God does not control their lives.

It is interesting to note that the indwelling, sealing, and baptizing ministries of the Spirit are bestowed on every believer at the time of salvation. There are no injunctions for the believer regarding them because they are an integral part of the gift of salvation. For example, if you are not indwelt by the Holy Spirit, then you are not a believer (Rom 8:9). On the other hand, "be filled by" and "walk by" the Spirit expressed in the present imperative indicates that this is not an automatic bestowment at the time of salvation but an injunction for every believer to follow continually. The filling by the Spirit is more than the Spirit's indwelling—it is his activities realized in and through us. Believers are commanded to be filled by the Spirit so that they will understand the will of the Lord and allow God's control of their lives, thus providing enablement to make the most of every opportunity rather than succumbing to the desires of the flesh. If believers were only filled with wisdom, the influence would be impersonal; however, the filling by the Spirit adds God's personal presence, influence, and enablement to walk wisely, all of which are beneficial to believers and pleasing to God. With the indwelling each Christian has all of the Spirit, but the command to be filled by the Spirit enables the Spirit to have all of the believer. The wise walk, therefore, is one that is characterized by the Holy Spirit's control.

(ii) The Consequences (5:19–21)

Both negative and positive commands have been given: do not get drunk with wine; be filled by the Spirit. The following verses mention four resultant characteristics of being filled by the Spirit.

(aa) Speaking (5:19a)

Text: 5:19a. λαλοῦντες ἑαυτοῖς [ἐν] ψαλμοῖς καὶ ὕμνοις καὶ ᾠδαῖς πνευματικαῖς,

Translation: 5:19a. "speaking to one another by means of psalms and hymns and spiritual songs,"

Commentary: 5:19a. λαλοῦντες ἑαυτοῖς, "speaking to one another." The five participles (λαλοῦντες . . . ᾄδοντες καὶ ψάλλοντες . . . εὐχαριστοῦντες . . . ὑποτασσόμενοι . . .) in verses 19–21 are dependent on the imperative πληροῦσθε, "be filled," and thus are considered by some to take on an imperatival force.[1] According to this view, believers are commanded not only to be filled by the Spirit, but also to speak, sing songs and psalms, give thanks, and submit. However, if this is what Paul intended, it seems odd that he did not continue with imperatives. Furthermore, if the force of these participles are imperatival then it is possible that one might speak, sing, thank, and submit by sheer will and not necessarily with the Spirit's power and control. It is more likely that Paul is stating what will happen when one is filled by the Spirit. As dissipation issues from drunkenness, so also speaking, singing songs and psalms, giving thanks, and submitting issue from the filling by the Spirit. Accordingly, these could be categorized as participles of manner or possibly as participles of attendant circumstance.[2] However, participles of attendant circumstance precede the main verb and are usually aorists.[3] These factors are not true in the present context. It is better to see them as participles of result.[4] The resultant characteristics suggest visible manifestation of one filled by the Spirit. Furthermore, participles of result are normally in the present tense and follow the main verb as here. The present tense of the participles most likely indicates repetition or progression of the characteristics described by these five participles. Once again, the point of the passage is that wine's control produces the resultant characteristics of dissipation, whereas the Spirit's control produces the resultant characteristics described by these five participles. The repetition or pro-

1. Robertson, *Grammar*, 440; Porter, *Verbal Aspect*, 377; Fanning, *Verbal Aspect*, 386; Salmond, 364; A. P. Salom, "The Imperatival Use of the Participle in the New Testament," *AusBR* 11 (December 1963): 46.

2. Meyer, 285; Best, 509.

3. Wallace, *Greek Grammar*, 641–44.

4. Alford, 3:134; Eadie, 399; Schnackenburg, 237; Lincoln, 345; Snodgrass, 287; Kreitzer, 159; O'Brien, 387–88; Wallace, *Greek Grammar*, 639, 644–45.

gression of these characteristics is evidence that the believer is being filled by the Spirit.

The first participle λαλοῦντες, from λαλέω means "to communicate" (cf. 4:25; 6:20). Although it is a fine distinction, the synonym λέγω usually refers to the substance of what is said, whereas λαλέω refers to the sound which communicates.[1] For example, the sound of a trumpet (Rev 4:1) or thunder (10:4) communicated to the apostle John. In this context Paul states that believers are to use their voices to communicate to one another. This communication is probably the same or similar to the "teaching and admonishing one another" in the parallel passage in Col 3:16. It is not empty talk, for Paul exhorts, "let the word of Christ dwell in you richly, as you teach and admonish one another in all wisdom, with psalms, hymns, spiritual songs, singing with gratitude in your hearts to God." As in Eph 4:32 the reflexive pronoun ἑαυτοῖς literally, "to yourselves" (AV), functions as the reciprocal pronoun ἀλλήλων, "to one another" (RV, ASV, RSV, NASB, NEB, TEV, NIV).[2] The dative indicates direction—speaking "to" one another.[3] This clearly indicates that the education of community members took place through clear speech rather than unknown speech or glossolalia.[4]

[ἐν][5] ψαλμοῖς καὶ ὕμνοις καὶ ᾠδαῖς πνευματικαῖς,[6] "by means of psalms and hymns and spiritual songs." The manner or means of com-

1. Debrunner, *TDNT* 4 (1967): 76–77; BAGD 463; BDAG 582; Trench, *Synonyms of the New Testament*, 286–89; L&N §§33.69, 70.

2. Robertson, *Grammar*, 690; MHT 3:43; Wallace, *Greek Grammar*, 351.

3. Winer, *Grammar*, 265–66.

4. Wayne A. Meeks, *The First Urban Christians. The Social World of the Apostle Paul* (New Haven: Yale University Press, 1983), 145; Pfitzner, "Good Songs in Bad Times," 49.

5. The inclusion of ἐν is found in 𝔓[46] B P 0278 6 33 1739 *pc* lat Chrysostom Ambrosiaster. It is omitted from ℵ A D F G Ψ 1881 𝔐 vg[ms] Theodoret and NA[25]. Its omission has far better support because of the age and character of manuscripts from three text-types, it has good geographical spread, and it has good genealogical relationships. Its inclusion is only in the Alexandrian text. Internally, it may have been included because it appears in the previous clause. The sense is not different with its omission. Thus, the omission is the preferred reading.

6. The reading ᾠδαῖς πνευματικαῖς is found in ℵ[1] (ℵ* *add senseless κα after* ᾠδαῖς) D F G Ψ 048[vid] 075 0150 0278 6 33 81 104 256 263 365 424 436 459 1175 1241 1319 1573 1739 1852 1881 1912 1962 2127 2200 2464 *Byz* [K L P] *Lect* it[ar, f, g, mon, o] vg syr[p, h, pal] cop[sa, bo] arm geo slav Origen Basil[vid] Cyril-Jerusalem Didymus Chrysostom Hesychius Theodore[lat] John-Damascus Victorinus-Rome Jerome Pelagius Augustine. A second reading is ᾠδαῖς πνευματικαῖς ἐν χάριτι found only in A and Niceta. The third reading has only ᾠδαῖς found in 𝔓[46] B it[b, d] Ambrosiaster. The fourth reading omits both words of the first reading and is found only in Augustine. The external evidence favors the first reading because of the date and character of the manuscripts, the geographical distribution of its witness, and the good genealogical relationship in the three text-types. The third reading has good attestation only in the Alexandrian text. Internal evidence favors the second reading because it gives good balance to the prepositional phrase and it follows what Paul wrote in the parallel passage, Col 3:16. However, both the external and internal evidence favor the first reading with the inclusion of ᾠδαῖς πνευματικαῖς.

munication is by psalms and hymns and spiritual songs. Much discussion has surrounded these words and it is difficult to make a sharp distinction. The dative is most likely instrumental expressing the means of the speaking, that is, "by means of psalms and hymns and spiritual songs." First, they are to communicate with one another by means of ψαλμοῖς, "psalms." Originally ψαλμός meant "plucking" the string of a bow[1] or the sound of a stringed instrument.[2] In the LXX it occurs ninety-two times and in the canonical books it appears eighty times and translates seven Hebrew words. Forty-two times it translates מִזְמוֹר, which is only in the psalm titles (e.g., Pss 3, 4, 48, 100); three times for נְגִינָה (Ps 4:title [MT & LXX 4:1]; Lam 3:14; 5:14); and three times for זִמְרָה (Pss 81:2 [MT 81:3; LXX 80:3]; 98:5 [LXX 97:5]; Amos 5:23), meaning stringed instrument.[3] From these uses of the word we may surmise that the singing of the psalms was accompanied by stringed instruments. Josephus also uses this word to designate a stringed instrument like a harp.[4] In the NT ψαλμός is used seven times (Luke 20:42; 24:44; Acts 1:20; 13:33; 1 Cor 14:26; Eph 5:19; Col 3:16) and all the references outside of Paul pertain to the OT psalms. In the two references in Paul's letters it refers to communication through psalms. Most likely they were OT psalms. Although one cannot be dogmatic, the NT church may have followed the OT and Judaistic practice, as it had in other instances, by singing the psalms with a stringed instrument.

The second word ὕμνοις, which is from ὕμνος and from which we derive the English word "hymn," has an uncertain origin. It is generally poetic material that is either recited or sung, many times in praise of divinity or in honor of one of the gods.[5] In the LXX it occurs thirty-three times and in the canonical books it appears sixteen times and translates five Hebrew words. Nine times it translates נְגִינָה in psalm titles (Pss 6:title [MT & LXX 6:1]; 55 [MT 55:1; LXX 54:1]; 61:title [MT 61:1; LXX 60:1]; 67:title [MT 67:1; LXX 66:1]; 76:title [MT 76:1; LXX 75:1]), indicating stringed instruments. It also occurs in other Psalms (65:1 [MT 65:2; LXX 64:2]; 100:4 [LXX 99:4]; 119:171 [LXX 118:171]; 148:14), indicating "praise." Seven times it translates the Piel form of הָלַל (2 Chr 7:6) and its cognate תְּהִלָּה (Neh 12:46; Pss 40:3 [MT 40:4; LXX 39:4]; 65:1 [MT 65:2; LXX 64:2]; 100:4 [LXX 99:4]; 119:171 [LXX 118:171]; 148:14), which also means "praise."[6] In the NT the verb form (ὑμνέω) occurs four times (Matt 26:30 = Mark 14:26; Acts 16:25; Heb 2:12). In

1. Euripides *Ion* 173.

2. Pindar *Fragmenta* 125 (91); Aristophanes *Aves* 218.

3. Cf. Gerhard Delling, "ὕμνος, ὑμνέω, ψάλλω, ψαλμός," *TDNT* 8 (1972): 491, 494; Karl-Heinz Bartels, "Song, Hymn, Psalm [ὕμνος, ψαλμός, ᾠδή]," *NIDNTT* 3 (1978): 671; cf. BAGD 891; BDAG 1096.

4. Josephus *A.J.* 6.11.3 §214; 7.4.2 §80; 9.3.1 §35.

5. Aeschylus *Choephori* 475; Plato *Leges* 7 §801d; *Respublica* 10.7 §607; Arrian *Anabasis* 4.11.2.

6. H. Cazelles, "הלל *hll*, etc.," *TDOT* 3 (1978): 411–13; cf. Delling, *TDNT* 8 (1972): 489–90; Bartels, *NIDNTT* 3 (1978): 669; BAGD 836; BDAG 1027.

the Gospel accounts it refers to the singing of the hallel psalms at the close of the Passover meal. In Acts 16:25, Paul and Silas sing hymns of praise in the Philippian prison. In Heb 2:12 the author quotes Ps 22:22 [MT 22:23; LXX 21:23] where the psalmist is praising (Hebrew is the Piel form of הָלַל) God in the midst of the congregation. The noun form occurs only in Eph 5:19 and in the parallel passage, Col 3:16. Nothing from either of these verses would suggest anything different from what the word historically meant, namely, a song of praise to God.

The third word ᾠδαῖς is from ᾠδή (a contraction of ἀοιδή), from which we derive the English word "ode." It is used of a dirge in Greek tragedy[1] but more often it refers to songs of joy or praise or just simply singing.[2] In the LXX it occurs eighty-seven times (seventy-one times in the canonical books) and translates six Hebrew words. Thirty-seven times it translates שִׁיר or שִׁירָה, meaning "song"[3] (e.g., Exod 15:1; Deut 31:19*bis*, 21, 22, 30; Judg 5:12; 2 Chr 5:13; 7:6); thirty times in the psalm titles (e.g., Pss 30:title [MT & LXX 30:1]; 68:title [MT & LXX 68:1]). Bartels states, "With the one exception of Deut. 31:30, where *ōdē* is spoken, singing is always indicated. Sometimes muscial accompaniment is mentioned (e.g., 1 Chr. 16:42), and on occasion both music and dancing. David and the Israelites sang and danced before the ark (2 Sam. 6:5)."[4] This word occurs seven times in the NT (Eph 5:19; Col 3:16; Rev 5:9; 14:3*bis*; 15:3*bis*). In Revelation it refers to a song of rejoicing and praise for the Lamb of God's victory over evil. Hence, it is fitting that Eph 5:19 and Col 3:16 include songs of rejoicing and praise to God. The adjective πνευματικαῖς, "spiritual," could modify all three nouns,[5] but is better viewed as grammatically related only to the last noun.[6] The first two nouns normally have specific reference to the praise of God, whereas the last noun is more general suggesting that Paul wanted to ensure that believers sang spiritual songs, that is, songs which issued from hearts filled by the Holy Spirit rather than produced by wine.[7]

In conclusion, the means by which believers are to communicate with one another is psalms, hymns, and spiritual songs.[8] As men-

1. Sophocles *Electra* 88; *Ajax* 631; Euripides *Troades* 514.

2. Euripides *Electra* 865; *Cyclops* 69; Aristophanes *Ranae* 244; *Aves* 1729; Plato *Leges* 4 §722d; *Respublica* 3.10 §§398c, 399c.

3. BDB 1010; cf. H.-J. Fabry, G. Brunert, Martin Kleer, Georg Steins, and Ulrich Dahmen, "שִׁיר *šîr*; שִׁירָה *šîrāh*," *TWAT* 7 (1990): 1259–95.

4. Bartels, *NIDNTT* 3 (1978): 673.

5. As Abbott, 163; Schnackenburg, 238; Lincoln, 346; Dunn, *Jesus and the Spirit*, 238.

6. As Eadie, 400–401; Alford, 3:135; Ellicott, 125; Robinson, 204; Schlier, 247; Gaugler, 204; Adai, *Der Heilige Geist als Gegenwart Gottes*, 228.

7. Bo Reicke, *Diakonie, Festfreude und Zelos in Verbindung mit der altchristlichen Agapenfeier*, Uppsala Universitets Årsskrift 1951:5 (Uppsala: A.-B. Lundequistska Bokhandeln; Wiesbaden: Otto Harrassowitz, 1951), 316.

8. Alfred Gill, "Ephesians v.19: Psalms and Hymns and Spiritual Songs," *ExpTim* 2 (April 1891): 165; Alexander B. Grosart, "Psalms and Hymns and Spiritual Songs," *ExpTim* 2 (May 1891): 180.

tioned above it is difficult to make much of a distinction between them.[1] Hengel notes that "they are the three most important terms used in the Septuagint to describe a religious song"[2] and all refer to believers' songs of praise to God. Although it is difficult to say that psalms were definitely accompanied with stringed instruments, this is the most natural interpretation. The psalms refer to the OT psalms that praise God for his goodness and for victories over the enemies. If they did not always recite the OT psalms, at least they had a pattern for creating new ones. The hymns and the spiritual songs also express the joy of the believer and praise to God. The content of these songs may well be expressed in the parallel passage in Col 3:16 where it states that there was teaching and admonishing one another by means of psalms, hymns, and spiritual songs. Through these, believers learn and rejoice in the character and purpose of God and the application to their lives.[3]

Were these psalms, hymns, and spiritual songs a reflection of the worship of the early church? There has been a great deal of discussion concerning this.[4] Certainly, at the end of the first century and the beginning of the second century, Pliny describes the antiphonal singing of hymns regarding Christ as God.[5] Some think that portions of the NT are early Christological hymns (e.g., Phil 2:5–11; Eph 2:14–18; 5:14).[6] However, much of this is speculation which has no concrete evidence from the NT.[7] Admittedly, early in the church's life there was singing, as seen in 1 Cor 14:26 where, when the church assembled, believers were to have, among other things, a psalm. Consequently, as

1. Martin thinks that psalms refer to the OT psalms; hymns were Christological in nature, which were devoted exclusively to a recitiation of the events of salvation; and spiritual songs were the immediate inspiration by the Spirit used for worship as seen in 1 Cor 14:26. (Ralph P. Martin, *The Worship of God. Some Theological, Pastoral, and Practical Reflections* [Grand Rapids: Eerdmans, 1982], 51–53).

2. Martin Hengel, "Hymn and Christology," in *Studia Biblica 1978. III. Papers on Paul and Other New Testament Authors. Sixth International Congress on Biblical Studies, Oxford, 3–7 April 1978*, ed. E. A. Livingston, JSNTSup, ed. Ernst Bammel et al., vol. 3 (Sheffield: JSOT Press, 1980), 175.

3. Hengel, *Studies in Early Christology*, 272–73, 275.

4. Cf. Deichgräber, *Gotteshymnus*; Sanders, *The New Testament Christological Hymns. Their Historical Religious Background*; Ralph P. Martin, "Some Reflections on New Testament Hymns," in *Christ the Lord. Studies in Christology Presented to Donald Guthrie*, ed. H. H. Rowdon (Leicester: Inter-Varsity; Downers Grove, Ill.: InterVarsity, 1982), 37–49; Hengel, "Hymn and Christology," 173–97; Martin, *The Worship of God*; Ferdinand Hahn, *The Worship of the Early Church*, trans. David E. Green (Philadelphia: Fortress, 1973); Dunn, *Jesus and the Spirit*, 238–39; F. S. Malan, "Church Singing according to Pauline Epistles," *Neot* 32, no. 2 (1998): 509–24, esp. 509–13, 517–20.

5. Pliny the Younger *Epistulae* 10.96.

6. For a more extensive bibliography, see 2:14.

7. For example, Orlett thinks 5:19 refers to the singing of the hymn given in 5:14 at a baptismal ceremony. However, he gives no real evidence on which to base this speculation (Raymond Orlett, "Awake, Sleeper!" *Worship* 35 [January 1961]: 102–5).

singing had been important for the worship of Israel, so, too, was it important in the early church and to the life of the church throughout history.

(bb) Singing (5:19b)

Text: 5:19b. ᾄδοντες καὶ ψάλλοντες ἐν ταῖς καρδίαις ὑμῶν τῷ κυρίῳ,

Translation: 5:19b. "singing songs and psalms with your hearts to the Lord,"

Commentary: 5:19b. ᾄδοντες καὶ ψάλλοντες, "singing songs and psalms," The first result of being filled by the Spirit is introduced by a present participle, "speaking to one another." Now the second is introduced by two present participles, "singing and psalming." The two participles should be considered one unit because they are joined by the conjunction καί, "and," and because they are followed by a qualifying phrase. This, then, matches the first participle:

> "speaking to one another . . . by psalms and hymns and spiritual songs"
> "singing songs and psalms . . . with your hearts to the Lord"

These two participles are the verbal forms of the nouns (ψαλμοῖς and ᾠδαῖς) discussed above. The participle ᾄδοντες comes from ᾄδω (contraction of ἀείδω), and its meaning is like that of the noun ᾠδή discussed above. It is used of singing with reference to humans, animals (e.g., the crowing of a cock), or inanimate objects (e.g., wind whistling through the trees)[1] and is set in contrast to speaking.[2] In the LXX the verb occurs seventy-four times and in the canonical books it appears seventy-one times where it translates six Hebrew words. It translates שִׁיר sixty times (e.g., Exod 15:1, 21; Ps 13:6 [LXX 12:6]; Jer 20:13). In the NT it occurs five times (Eph 5:19; Col 3:16; Rev 5:9; 14:3; 15:3), the same verses in which the cognate noun appears. Revelation 5:9 and 14:3 speak of singing a new song of praise to the Lamb of God for his redemption. Like the noun, the verb refers to song.

The participle ψάλλοντες is from ψάλλω, "to pluck," primarily a stringed instrument.[3] In the LXX it occurs fifty-eight times (fifty-five times in the canonical books) for either זָמַר (thirty times: only in the Psalms, except for Judg 5:3 and 2 Sam 22:50) or נָגַן (ten times: outside the Psalms, except for 33:3 [LXX 32:3]; 68:25 [MT 68:26; LXX 67:26]). It means "to play a stringed instrument" without singing (1 Sam 16:16, 17, 23; 19:9) or with singing (Pss 27:6 [LXX 26:6]; 33:2 [LXX 32:2]; 57:7, 9 [MT 57:8, 10; LXX 56:8, 10]; 71:22–23 [LXX 70:22–23]; 98:5 [LXX 97:5]; 101:2 [LXX 100:2]; 105:2 [LXX 104:2]; 108:1, 3 [MT

1. LSJ 26.
2. Philo *Somn.* 1.43 §256; Xenophon *Cyropaedia* 3.3.55.
3. Aristophanes *Equites* 522; Aristotle *Problemata* 19.23 §919b.2; 19.24 §919b.15.

108:2, 4; LXX 107:2, 4]).[1] In the NT it appears five times (Rom 15:9; 1 Cor 14:15*bis*; Eph 5:19; Jas 5:13). Some think the word intrinsically means a stringed instrument,[2] but this reads too much of the earlier meaning into it.[3] None of these passages demand it. In fact, in Rom 15:9 where the mention of praises sung to God is juxtaposed to confession among the Gentiles (from Ps 18:49; 2 Sam 22:50), the playing of the instrument alone does not even seem to fit. Again, in 1 Cor 14:15 songs are sung and not just played by an instrument, for believers are to sing in the spirit and be mindful of the words they are singing. In Jas 5:13 the author asserts that those who suffer should pray and those who are cheerful should sing praises. Again this likely refers to verbalized praise rather than instrumental playing. The same could be said for Eph 5:19 where the filling by the Spirit is expressed by singing and praising. Hence, none of these passages demand instrumental playing in conjunction with the singing of praise although it would not forbid it. The main point is the verbalizing of praise through singing. Literally, it would be translated "psalming," rendering it "singing and psalming," which does not work well in English. More properly, it should be translated "singing songs and psalms."

ἐν ταῖς καρδίαις[4] **ὑμῶν τῷ κυρίῳ,** "with your hearts to the Lord." It is best to accept the textual reading that includes the preposition ἐν, "in/

1. Delling, *TDNT* 8 (1972): 493–94.

2. E.g., LSJ 2018; John Foster, "The Harp at Ephesus," *ExpTim* 47 (February 1963): 156; Barth, 583–84.

3. Cf. BAGD 891; BDAG 1096.

4. The prepositional phrase ἐν ταῖς καρδίαις is found in א^2 A D F G P 365 *pc* latt syr$^{p, hmg}$ cop. A second reading ἐν τῇ καρδίᾳ appears in Ψ 0278 33 𝔐 Chrysostom Theodoret Theophylact (GNTMT). A third reading τῇ καρδίᾳ is found in 𝔓^{46} א* B 1739 1881 (NA^{27}, UBS^4). Regarding external evidence, the first reading has early manuscripts, wide geographical distribution, and has genealogical relationships (especially in the Western text). The second reading has the support of the Byzantine text-type and many church fathers. The third reading has early support but only in the Alexandrian text and hence lacks geographical distribution. The first reading has better external support. Regarding internal evidence, the third reading is the shortest and most difficult. One can see why a scribe would insert the preposition ἐν. However, it is very common to have the preposition ἐν either before the singular ἐν τῇ καρδίᾳ (cf. Rom 10:6, 8, 9; 1 Cor 7:37; 2 Cor 8:16; Phil 1:7) or before the plural ἐν ταῖς καρδίαις (Rom 2:15; 5:5; 2 Cor 1:22; 3:2; 4:6; 7:3; Eph 3:17; Col 3:15, 16). In Pauline literature there are only two times outside of the present context when this phrase is not introduced by the preposition ἐν and both times it is in the singular form (Rom 9:2; 2 Cor 9:7). Therefore, outside the present context, the phrase either in the singular or in the plural form is preceded by the preposition ἐν fifteen times whereas it is omitted only two times. Thus, the normal style is to include the preposition. Both the singular and plural prepositional phrases are used by Paul. However, out of the six times the preposition is used with the singular, only once is it used with a plural pronoun (i.e., present context if the third reading is accepted), and when it is used in the plural, it is always followed by the plural pronoun. Furthermore, in the parallel passage Col 3:16 (and also v. 15) Paul has ἐν ταῖς καρδίαις. Thus, both externally and internally the preposition followed by the plural dative is the best reading.

with," with the plural ταῖς καρδίαις followed by the personal pronoun ὑμῶν, thus giving "in/with your hearts." The preposition ἐν, "in," could indicate the sphere in which this singing of songs and psalms occurs (AV, NEB, TEV, JB, NIV, NJB, NRSV) or the instrumental idea of singing songs and psalms with the heart (RV, ASV, RSV, NASB). Delling thinks that the ἐν corresponds to the Hebrew בְּ (Pss 9:1 [MT & LXX 9:2]; 86:12 [LXX 85:12]; 111:1 [LXX 110:1]; 138:1 [LXX 137:1]) and translates it "from the heart."[1] But in this case it would have been more natural for Paul to write ἀπὸ τῶν καρδιῶν ὑμῶν, "from your hearts" (cf. Matt 18:35).[2] It is better to translate the Hebrew בְּ as "in" or "with." Hence, ἐν can indicate either sphere or instrument. This denotes the involvement of the heart in the singing of songs and psalms. Thus believers sing not only with their lips but also with or in their hearts where the Holy Spirit resides (Rom 8:9). As mentioned in 1:18 (cf. also 3:17; 4:18) the heart is the center of a person, the seat of religious and moral conduct, or, as here, of will or volition "which makes the whole man move steadfastly and with undivided attention and devotion in a specific direction."[3] The next dative phrase τῷ κυρίῳ indicates direction, that is, the singing is directed "to the Lord," or specifically to Christ their new Lord[4] who has delivered them from wrath and gives them power to live a life that is pleasing to God. The singing of praises is part of the believer's individual and corporate worship. Music is the means by which believers minister to each other and worship the Lord.

(cc) Thanking (5:20)

Text: 5:20. εὐχαριστοῦντες πάντοτε ὑπὲρ πάντων ἐν ὀνόματι τοῦ κυρίου ἡμῶν Ἰησοῦ Χριστοῦ τῷ θεῷ καὶ πατρί,

Translation: 5:20. "giving thanks always for all things in the name of our Lord Jesus Christ to God the Father,"

Commentary: 5:20. εὐχαριστοῦντες πάντοτε ὑπὲρ πάντων, "giving thanks always for all things." This is the third participial clause describing the outcome[5] or characterization of being filled by the Spirit: first there is "speaking to one another," then "singing songs and singing psalms," and now "giving thanks always for all things."[6]

1. Delling, *TDNT* 8 (1972): 498 and n. 66; Schnackenburg, 238.

2. For a similar suggestion, see Abbott, 163. Baljon refutes Venema's suggestion that it should read ἐκ τῆς καρδία ὑμῶν, "out of your heart" ("Opmerkingen op het gebied van de Conjecturaalkritiek," 154).

3. Barth, *The Broken Wall*, 182.

4. Although the parallel passage in Col 3:16 refers to God (τῷ θεῷ), it more likely refers to Christ here. See Schlier, 248; Schnackenburg, 238; Hengel, "Hymn and Christology," 176; Mussner, *Christus, das All und die Kirche*, 149; Adai, *Der Heilige Geist als Gegenwart Gottes*, 229, 449 n. 70; Hengel, *Studies in Early Christology*, 276.

5. O'Brien, "Thanksgiving within the Structure of Pauline Theology," 58–59.

6. This threefold structure is also observed by Robinson ("Die Hodajot-formel in Gebet und Hymnus des Früchristentums," 225). He does not carry it far enough

The present participle εὐχαριστοῦντες is from the verb εὐχαριστέω which historically is used in "giving thanks." In the NT it is used primarily for thanksgiving to God (only twice for thanks to men: Luke 17:16 and Rom 16:4; for a short study of this word, see 1:15). In this context Paul states that the third result of being filled by the Spirit is the offer of thanks to God.[1] Schlier's suggestion that this thanksgiving occurs in the setting of the eucharistic celebration[2] is highly speculative for nothing in the context directly points in that direction. Rather, the adverb of time πάντοτε expresses that this thanksgiving is continual ("at all times" or "always") and not just for the Lord's Supper. The prepositional phrase ὑπὲρ πάντων shows the extent of the thanksgiving—"for all things." Although ὑπὲρ πάντων could be masculine and translated "for all people" as does Theodoret,[3] it is better to view it as neuter because the context implies more than the giving thanks for or on behalf of all people. Certainly, the parallel passage in Col 3:17 indicates this, for it states: "whatever you do in word or deed, do everything in the name of the Lord Jesus, giving thanks to God the Father through him." Thus, thanksgiving to God should encompass all things that come into life's path, and when believers are filled by the Spirit this will be their response[4] in lieu of dissatisfaction and complaints. In difficult circumstances an attitude of thanksgiving is easier to achieve with the knowledge that God is always in control. In addition, since Paul mentions blessings so frequently in this letter, no doubt he has these in mind when he enjoins believers filled by the Spirit to give thanks to God.

ἐν ὀνόματι τοῦ κυρίου ἡμῶν Ἰησοῦ Χριστοῦ τῷ θεῷ καὶ πατρί[5],[6] "in

---

because there is another participle in the next verse which denotes the fourth element in the structure.

1. For a discussion of the form of Paul's thanksgiving, see Schubert, *Form and Function of the Pauline Thanksgiving*, 82–94.

2. Schlier, 248–49; *Die Zeit der Kirche*, 252–56. Similarly, Schnackenburg thinks the thanksgiving was a manifestation of the Spirit's filling in divine worship (Rudolf Schnackenburg, *The Church in the New Testament*, trans. W. J. O'Hara [London: Burns & Oates, 1974], 172).

3. Theodoret 5:20 (*PG* 82:545).

4. Chrysostom goes too far in giving thanks for even hell and its torments (Chrysostom *Eph* 5:20 [*PG* 62:130]). Paul is referring to the things of this life, negative or positive, that affect the believers and for which they should respond with thanksgiving.

5. The reading θεῷ καὶ πατρί is found in ℵ A B D^{1} Ψ 0278 33 1739 1881 𝔐 it^{f} vg syr$^{(p)}$ cop$^{bo^{pt}}$ Jerome. A second reading is a transposition, πατρί καὶ θεῷ, which occurs in 𝔓^{46} D$^{*.2}$ F G 1175 2464 *pc* it Victorinus-Rome Ambrosiaster. The best reading is the first because of the age and character, the geographical distribution, and the genealogical relationships of the manuscripts. Internally, the first reading occurs four other times in the NT (1 Cor 15:24; Phil 4:20; Jas 1:27; Rev 1:6) whereas the second reading never occurs in any other NT book. The first reading is more natural, indicating to whom one gives thanks, further described as Father. Thus, the first reading seems best because of external and internal evidence.

6. At this juncture some texts are punctuated with a comma or semicolon (TR WH UBS^{3}, AV, RV, ASV, NASB). Others are punctuated with a period (NA$^{26, 27}$, UBS^{4}, RSV, NEB,

the name of our Lord Jesus Christ to God the Father." The prepositional phrase ἐν ὀνόματι or ἐν τῷ ὀνόματι, "in the name," is used thirty-nine times in the NT (forty times if one counts Mark 16:17). With the exception of John 5:43b and 1 Pet 4:16, it always refers to a divine name. Eleven times it refers to the name of God the Father (Matt 21:9 = Mark 11:9 = Luke 19:38 = John 12:13; Matt 23:39 = Luke 13:35; John 5:43a; 10:25; 17:11, 12; Jas 5:10). The other twenty-six times it refers to the name of Jesus. The disciples of Jesus performed miracles in the name of Jesus. For example, they cast out demons (Luke 10:17; Acts 16:18) and healed a lame man (Acts 3:6; 4:10). They also preached in the name of Jesus (Acts 9:27–28). Six times Jesus instructs his disciples to pray to the Father in Jesus' name (John 14:13, 14; 15:16; 16:23, 24, 26). Here the same procedure is spelled out, namely, that the believer, filled by the Spirit, should give thanks to God the Father in the name of the Lord Jesus Christ. Thus, the name,[1] used as a channel of power in many instances, should also be used as a channel for prayer and thanksgiving, as portrayed in this text. Bietenhard asserts, "The whole life of the Christian stands under the name of Jesus."[2] The full title "Lord Jesus Christ" with the personal pronoun "our" depicts the believer's possession of the Lord of Glory through whom thanksgiving is made.

The direction of the thanksgiving is expressed with the personal dative object τῷ θεῷ καὶ πατρί, literally, "to God and Father." As in 1:3 the Granville Sharp rule applies, where a singular articular personal noun followed by καί and an anarthrous personal noun in the same case further describes the first noun.[3] Here God is further described as father. Although some translations have the literal "to God and Father" (AV, NEB), other translations make this point clear by reading "to God the Father" (RSV, TEV, NIV, NRSV), "to God who is our Father" (JB, NJB), or make the conjunction καί ascensive, "to God, even the Father" (RV, ASV, NASB). The translation "to God the Father" is accurate. The word "Father" demonstrates that God has a very personal relationship to believers; to them he is not just the God of the universe. Thus, believers, filled by the Spirit, give thanks always for all things to God the Father in the name of Jesus Christ the Lord. Once again this is in keeping with other parts of Ephesians which mention the three persons of the Trinity (cf. 1:4–14, 17; 2:18, 22; 3:4–5, 14–17; 4:4–6; 5:18–20).

TEV, JB, NIV, NJB, NRSV). The punctuation with the comma is preferred because this would make the following participle the last of a series of participles dependent on the finite verb πληροῦσθε in 5:18. Starting a new sentence with a participle with no finite verb and no conjunction would be odd.

1. For a more thorough study of the use of "name" in the NT, see Hans Bietenhard, "ὄνομα, ὀνομάζω, ἐπονομάζω, ψευδώνυμος," *TDNT* 5 (1968): 270–81; Hans Bietenhard, "Name [ὄνομα]," *NIDNTT* 2 (1976): 652–55. It is suggested that the "name" has a Christological sense because it is accompanied by the title *Lord Jesus Christ* (Kramer, *Christ, Lord, Son of God*, 81).

2. Bietenhard, *TDNT* 5 (1968): 274.

3. Winer, *Grammar*, 162–63 n. 3; Wallace, *Greek Grammar*, 274.

(dd) Submitting (5:21)

Text: 5:21. ὑποτασσόμενοι ἀλλήλοις ἐν φόβῳ Χριστοῦ.

Translation: 5:21. "submitting to one another in the fear of Christ."

Commentary: 5:21. ὑποτασσόμενοι ἀλλήλοις ἐν φόβῳ Χριστοῦ,[1] "submitting to one another in the fear of Christ." This verse is not the beginning of a new section but a fitting conclusion to the broader context of wisdom beginning in 5:17 and more particularly to the section which deals with the filling by the Spirit beginning with 5:18.[2] Hence, as mentioned above (p. 714 n. 6), there should not be a period but a comma between verses 20 and 21.[3] This is substantiated by the fourth of five participial clauses denoting the results of being filled by the Spirit: first, "speaking to one another" (v. 19a), second, "singing songs and singing psalms" (v. 19b), third, "giving thanks always for all things" (v. 20), and now the fourth, "submitting to one another in the fear of Christ" (v. 21). Although some grammarians consider this participle along with the preceding ones as imperatival,[4] it is best to conclude that this, as the four preceding participles, is a participle expressing result.[5]

The present middle or passive participle ὑποτασσόμενοι of ὑποτάσσω, which was discussed at 1:22, means "to be subject, subordinate." It is a part of the ταγ- word group signifying order or arrangement (see τάγμα in 1 Cor 15:23) and with the prepositional prefix ὑπο-, the word literally means "'to order oneself under' a leader."[6] Some translations render it more as a middle "submitting or subjecting yourselves" (AV, RV, ASV, TEV, NIV) while others render it as a passive to "be subject" (RSV, NASB, NEB, JB, NJB, NRSV). This verb in the passive is normally followed with

1. The words Ἰησοῦ Χριστοῦ are found in (ˢ D) F G, κυρίου is found in K cop^{boms}, and θεοῦ appears in 6 81 614 630 1881 pm Clement Ambrosiaster^{mss}. None of these readings have sufficient manuscript evidence to replace the reading Χριστοῦ.

2. Cf. Else Kähler, *Die Frau in den paulinischen Briefen unter besonderer Berücksichtigung des Begriffs der Unterordnung* (Zürich: Gotthelf-Verlag, 1960), 99–100, 251 n. 453; J. Paul Sampley, *'And the Two Shall Become One Flesh.' A Study of Traditions in Ephesians*, SNTSMS, ed. Matthew Black, vol. 16 (Cambridge: Cambridge University Press, 1971), 116; *contra* E. Margaret Howe, *Women and Church Leadership* (Grand Rapids: Zondervan, 1982), 54.

3. Kähler, *Die Frau in den paulinischen Briefen*, 251 n. 453. So also Chrysostom *Eph* 5:22–24 (*PG* 62:135); Alford, 135–36; Ellicott, 126; Meyer, 288; Salmond, 364–65; Westcott, 82; Lenski, 623; Hendriksen, 243 n. 149; Bouttier, 236; Snodgrass, 307, 313; Best, 515–16; O'Brien, 399. Others make a major break between vv. 20 and 21, see Calvin, 204; Eadie, 406; Abbott, 164; Masson, 210; Schlier, 250; Gaugler, 207; Gnilka, 273; Ernst, 381–82; Caird, 87–88; Mitton, 195; Barth, 608; Schnackenburg, 244; Bruce, 382; Lincoln, 352; Martin, *Ephesians, Colossians, and Philemon*, 67–68.

4. Cf. BDF §468 (2); Fanning, *Verbal Aspect*, 378, 386; Porter, *Verbal Aspect*, 378. However, on the previous page, Porter thinks it might have an indicative force.

5. Wallace, *Greek Grammar*, 651, 659 n. 6; cf. Winer, *Grammar*, 441.

6. Spicq, *Theological Lexicon of the New Testament*, 3:424 n. 2.

a dative "to persons worthy of respect."[1] Here it is followed by the reciprocal dative pronoun ἀλλήλοις, "one another." The difference between the middle and passive is not great. The passive could connote that the subject has no control of the action as a drunken person controlled by the wine. The middle expresses the idea of cooperation where the subject acts as a free agent. The latter is more in keeping with the context, for the previous four participles (λαλοῦντες, ᾄδοντες, ψάλλοντες, εὐχαριστοῦντες) are active indicating the subject is taking action under the guidance and control of the Holy Spirit.

In this text a result of believers filled by the Spirit is submission to one another in the body of believers. Unbelievers tend to take great pride in individualism and independence, which leads to selfishness. However, believers are to act differently. Jesus instructed the disciples that the world would know that they are his disciples if they love one another (John 13:34–35). Also, in other contexts Paul instructs believers to love one another with brotherly love and to prefer one another by showing honor (Rom 12:10) and in humility to count the other better than themselves (Phil 2:3).

Here in Eph 5:21 the result is mutual submission. This certainly implies humility. As previously stated, this can only be done consciously and continuously under the power and guidance of the Holy Spirit. But how does mutual submission work? If A submits to B, then B is not submitting but ruling. It could be that A submits with respect to some things or areas to B and, on the other hand, B submits to A in other things or areas. But how does one know when or in what areas you are to submit? Certainly, in the next section (5:22–6:9) there are those who submit (wives, children, slaves) and there are those who do not submit (husbands, fathers, masters). More will be discussed below. According to Clark the idea of mutual submission may mean to "'let there be subordination among you' (i.e., 'let each of you subordinate himself or herself to the one he or she should be subordinate to')."[2] The word "subordinate" may not be the best word to use since it can imply inferiority. "Submission" is a better term and its application in mutual submission to one another would imply that one is willing to submit to those who have authority, whether it be in the home, church, or in society.

Paul continues by showing that submission to one another is not to be taken lightly but rather done ἐν φόβῳ Χριστοῦ, "in the fear of Christ." The noun φόβος[3] or the verb φοβέω[4] in Homer's use had the idea of "flight" or "running away" as a result of being startled. Later the idea of "panic, fear," or "terrified" became the predominant mean-

1. BAGD 848; cf. BDAG 1042.

2. Stephen B. Clark, *Man and Woman in Christ. An Examination of the Roles of Men and Women in Light of Scripture and The Social Sciences* (Ann Arbor, Mich.: Servant Books; Edinburgh: T & T Clark, 1980), 76 n. 4.

3. Homer *Ilias* 11.71; 15.396; 17.597.

4. Ibid., 16.583; 17.505 (active); 5.498; 16.294 (passive).

ing for both the verb[1] and noun.[2] In classical times the verb followed by an accusative of persons (as in 5:33) meant "to stand in awe of, dread."[3] The noun followed by an objective genitive (as in the present verse) meant "fear of" or "dread of"[4] and later included a sense of awe before God.[5] In the LXX the verb φοβέω occurs 456 times and in the canonical books it appears 343 and translates sixteen Hebrew words. Around 290 times it translates the verb יָרֵא with the idea of fear (Gen 3:10; 19:30; Pss 3:6 [MT & LXX 3:7]; 23:4 [LXX 22:4]) with reference to God (Eccl 3:14; 8:12, 13) or gods (2 Kgs 17:7), parents (Lev 19:3), or leaders like Moses and Joshua (Josh 4:14*bis*).[6] In the LXX the noun φόβος occurs 197 times (127 times in the canonical books) and translates nine Hebrew words translating thirty-four times יִרְאָה (the cognate of the verb just mentioned) (Exod 20:20; 2 Sam 23:3) and thirty times from פַּחַד (Job 31:23; Ps 119:120 [LXX 118:120]), meaning "fear, dread, awe" of God.[7] Although פַּחַד has the general idea of fear or terror, the most common meaning of יָרֵא and its cognates with the accusative is reverential fear or awe of God or people, or respect for God or people.[8] In the NT the verb occurs ninety-five times, seventy-two times in the Gospels and Acts but only nine times in Pauline literature and only once in Ephesians (5:33), whereas the noun is used forty-seven times in the NT, nineteen times in the Gospels and Acts, fifteen times by Paul, and twice in Ephesians (5:21; 6:5). Both the noun (Rom 3:18; 13:3; 2 Cor 7:11; 1 Pet 3:14) and the verb (Rom 13:3; Gal 2:12; Matt 14:30) convey a sense of being afraid or fearful of something or someone. It also carries the idea of reverence or respect for God (noun: Acts 9:31; 1 Pet 1:17; verb: Luke 18:2, 4; 1 Pet 2:17) or men (noun: Rom 13:7*bis*; 1 Pet 2:18; 3:2; verb: Eph 5:33).[9]

Obviously there is a wide spectrum of meaning ranging from absolute terror to respect. It is the context that determines the meaning. Bauer suggests that the noun "fear" in the present verse should be translated "reverence, respect,"[10] whereas Mundle suggests "fear, awe, and reverence."[11] Although this second alternative is stronger, Barth thinks that even "awe

1. Herodotus 7.235; Aeschylus *Septum contra Thebas* 262 (active); Herodotus 9.70; Euripides *Troades* 1166.

2. Herodotus 7.10; 9.69; Aeschylus *Septum contra Thebas* 240; Euripides *Troades* 1165.

3. Aeschylus *Supplices* 893; Sophocles *Philotetes* 1250; Plato *Leges* 11 §927b.

4. Aeschylus *Persae* 116; Thucydides 3.54.5; Xenophon *Anabasis* 3.1.18.

5. LSJ 1947. For a more detailed study of the classical period, see Horst Balz, "φοβέω, φοβέομαι, φόβος, δέος," *TDNT* 9 (1974): 189–97.

6. BDB 431; cf. H. F. Fuhs, "יָרֵא *yārēʾ*; יָרֵא *yārēʾ*; יִרְאָה *yirʾâ*; מוֹרָא *môrāʾ*," *TDOT* 6 (1990): 290–315.

7. BDB 808; H.-P. Müller, "פָּחַד *pāḥad*; פַּחַד *paḥad*," *TDOT* 11 (2001): 517–26.

8. Günther Wanke, "φοβέω, φοβέομαι, φόβος, δέος," *TDNT* 9 (1974): 199–204.

9. For more references, see BAGD 862–64; BDAG 1060–62.

10. BAGD 863–64; BDAG 1062.

11. Wilhelm Mundle, "Fear, Awe [φόβος]," *NIDNTT* 1 (1975): 623.

and reverence" (RSV, NEB, TEV, JB, NIV, NJB, NRSV) are not strong enough. He suggests that only the English term "fear" (AV, RV, ASV, NASB) is suitable as long it is exercised in the context of love.[1] Which is the better meaning for the present verse? In the present context the noun is followed by the objective genitive Χριστοῦ, "Christ." There are only four other times in the NT when φόβος, "fear," is followed by one of the persons of the Godhead as an objective genitive. First, in Acts 9:31 the church throughout Judea, Galilee, and Samaria is described as increasing and walking in the fear of the Lord and the comfort of the Holy Spirit. Second, in Rom 3:18 Paul writes that the depraved sinfulness of human beings is caused by their lack of the fear of God. Third, in 2 Cor 5:11, in view of each believer's appearance before the judgment seat of Christ, Paul asserts that the fear of the Lord should motivate believers to participate in the ministry of reconciliation. Finally, in 2 Cor 7:1 Paul states that believers are not to be unequally yoked with unbelievers but rather cleanse themselves from defilement of body and of spirit, perfecting holiness in the fear of God. In all of these examples, the softer term "respect" is not adequate. The first passage is in the context of the church that was walking in the fear of the Lord, that is, fear in the sense of awe and reverence. The other three references are in the context of judgment where "fear, reverence, and awe" are well suited to the context. Käsemann states, "The fear of the Lord is no empty rhetorical phrase here."[2]

The discussion in the present context revolves around the believer who, filled by the Spirit, submits to others out of fear or reverence for Christ. Such fear conveys more than just respect. One could have respect for Christ but not be submissive. On the other hand, it is doubtful that it is a fear that comprises terror. Consequently, since the word is used in the context of Christ's love that is so amply demonstrated in this letter, it is best to view it as a reverential fear or reverential respect. This quality of "fear" motivates believers to submit to others within the body. The practice of mutual submission to one another in the fear of Christ must not be relegated merely to a church service,[3] but rather it is to be applied in daily life whenever and wherever they meet. It may be at a church service, at the workplace, at home, or at a social gathering of two or more believers.

Although this verse describes the concluding characterization of the believer filled by the Spirit that was begun in 5:18, it serves as a hinge verse to the entire following section.[4] The idea of submission

1. Barth, 608–9, 662–68.

2. Ernst Käsemann, "Ministry and Community in the New Testament," in *Essays on New Testament Themes*, trans. W. J. Montague, SBT, ed. C. F. D. Moule, J. Barr, Peter Ackroyd, Floyd V. Filson, and G. Ernest Wright, no. 41 (London: SCM, 1964), 78.

3. As Nieder, *Die Motive der religiös-sittlichen Paränese*, 98.

4. Angelico S. Di Marco, "Ef. 5,21–6,9: teologia della famiglia," *RivB* 31 (Aprile–Giugno 1983): 198; Richard D. Balge, "Exegetical Brief: Ephesians 5:21—A Transitional Verse," *WLQ* 95 (winter 1998): 41–43; Wallace, *Greek Grammar*, 651, 659.

will now be developed in the next section of 5:22–6:9. This is a critical verse, for the submission of any believer is really dependent on being filled by the Spirit.

2. Application (5:22–6:9)

Paul has admonished believers to walk wisely, making the most of every opportunity because the days are evil (vv. 15–16). This is accomplished by believers who comprehend the will of God and then carry it out by the enabling power of the Holy Spirit (vv. 17–18). The outcome of being filled by the Spirit is given by the four present participial clauses (with five participles—λαλοῦντες . . . ᾄδοντες καὶ ψάλλοντες . . . εὐχαριστοῦντες . . . ὑποτασσόμενοι) which describe the resultant characteristics of the believers filled by the Spirit (vv. 19–21). These characteristics are relatively easy to manifest in a church setting because fellow believers may only see each other a few hours each week. However, Paul's injunction to be filled by the Spirit extends beyond merely a church service or a casual gathering to the believer's life at home and at work where he or she will be observed twenty-four hours a day. Unfortunately, all too often this section of 5:22–6:9 is isolated from the previous context. Interestingly, no conjunction introduces this section,[1] which may indicate that this is not a new section but a continuation of the thought of walking in wisdom which began with 5:15.

While the first four participles relate primarily to a church setting, the last participle regarding submission relates both within or outside a church setting. Expressing the believers' submission to one another in the fear of Christ, it not only serves as a final characteristic of a life filled by the Spirit, but it also serves as an introduction to the next section. Here Paul discusses three sets of relationships: wife/husband, children/parents, and slaves/masters. In each instance the one who is to submit is discussed first, namely, the wife, the children, and the slaves. Paul then discusses the responsibility of those in the position of authority, namely, the husband, the parents, and the masters.

Excursus 7
Household Code

Before commenting on Paul's exhortations regarding family relationships, it is necessary to review the discussion on the *Haustafel* (Luther's designation) or household code, the rules for the household given in Eph 5:22–6:9; Col 3:18–4:1; 1 Pet 2:18–3:7; 1 Tim 2:8–15; 6:1–10; Titus 2:1–10. Much has been written on this subject[2] since it was introduced

1. Wallace notes that this is the first major section after 1:3 that does not begin with a conjunction, see Wallace, *Greek Grammar*, 659.

2. Crouch has surveyed the discussion up to time of his publication (James E. Crouch, *The Origin and Intention of the Colossian Haustafel*, FRLANT, ed. Ernst

early in the twentieth century by Dibelius in his commentary on Colossians. Much effort has been expended in attempting to identify the source of the NT household codes. Dibelius suggested that the household code in Colossians was a lightly Christianized version of a Stoic code.[1] NT phrases such as "it is proper" (Col 3:18) or "it is pleasing (to the Lord) (Col 3:20; Eph 5:10; Rom 14:18) were key phrases in Stoic literature. This idea was expanded by Dibelius' student, Karl Weidinger, who thought that the Stoic sense of duty was an adaptation of unwritten Greek laws regarding one's duties to the gods, country, parents, friends, and relatives. He claimed that the form of these codes was essentially the same in Stoic, Hellenistic Jewish, and Christian circles[2] and remained basically unchanged throughout the Hellenistic period.[3] On the other hand, early in this discussion, Lohmeyer suggested that the origin of the household code was not a Hellenistic but a pre-Christian Jewish code. He thinks "the Lord" (Col 3:18, 20, 22, 23, 24a; 4:1) is a reference to God (not Christ) of the original Jewish code.[4] This view was never widely accepted.

In reaction to Dibelius and Weidinger, two scholars in the 1950s argued that the household codes were uniquely Christian. Rengstorf proposed that the Christian household rules were sufficiently different and did not warrant the characterization of lightly Christianized Hellenistic codes. He suggested, for example, that the submission of the wife was uniquely Christian. He tried to bolster his argument for submission from the childhood stories of Jesus (Luke 2:51) and John the Baptist and also noted the role of Joseph and Zechariah as heads of their respective families.[5] However, the Christian household code is not easily

---

Käsemann and Ernst Würthwein, vol. 109 [Göttingen: Vandenhoeck & Ruprecht, 1972], 10–31). Balch has written an article which gives a survey as well as an annotated bibliography on this vast subject of household codes (David L. Balch, "Household Codes," in *Greco-Roman Literature and the New Testament: Selected Forms and Genres*, ed. David E. Aune, SBLSBS, ed. Bernard Brandon Scott, no. 21 [Atlanta: Scholars Press, 1988], 25–50). Cf. Marlis Gielen, *Tradition und Theologie neutestamentlicher Haustafelethik: Ein Beitrag zur Frage einer christlichen Auseinandersetzung mit gesellschaftlichen Normen*, Athenäum Monografien/Theologie: Bonner Biblische Beiträge, ed. Frank-Lothar Hosseld and Helmut Merklein, vol. 75 (Frankfurt am Main: Anton Hain, 1990), 24–67; Georg Strecker, "Die neutestamentlichen Haustafeln (Kol 3,18–4,1 und Eph 5,22–6,9)," in *Neues Testament und Ethik: für Rudolf Schnackenburg*, ed. Helmut Merklein (Freiburg: Herder, 1989), 349–75; Karl-Heinz Fleckenstein, *Ordnet euch einander unter in der Furcht Christi*, 111–41; Johannes Woyke, *Die neutestamentliche Haustafeln: Ein kritischer und konstruktiver Forschungsüberblick*, Stuttgarter Bibelstudien, ed. Erich Zenger, vol. 184 (Stuttgart: Verlag Katholisches Bibelwerk, 2000). Best discusses the place of the household code in the flow of Ephesians' argument (E. Best, "The Haustafel in Ephesians [Eph. 5.22–6.9]," *IBS* 16 [October 1994]: 146–60).

1. Martin Dibelius, *Die Briefe des Apostels Paulus: An die Kolosser, Epheser, an Philemon*, HNT, ed. Hans Lietzmann, vol. 3.2 (Tübingen: Mohr, 1912), 91–92.

2. Similar obligations are mentioned by several writers from different philosophical backgrounds. See Aristotle *Politica* 1.2.1–23 §§1253b–1255b; Seneca *Epistulae* 94.1–26; Plutarch *Moralia: De liberis educandis* 10 §7e; Epictetus *Dissertationes* 2.10; 3.7.

3. Karl Weidinger, *Die Haustafeln, ein Stück urchristlicher Paränese*, Untersuchungen zum Neuen Testament, ed. Hans Windisch, no. 14 (Leipzig: J. C. Hinrichs'sche Buchhandlung, 1928), 27–39, 40–42, 48–49.

4. Ernst Lohmeyer, *Die Briefe an die Philipper, an die Kolosser und an Philemon*, 8th ed., KEK, vol. 9 (Göttingen: Vandenhoeck & Ruprecht, 1930), 152–56, 158, 159–60 [identical to 9th ed., ed. Werner Schmauch, 1953].

5. Karl Heinrich Rengstorf, "Die neutestamentlichen Mahnungen an die Frau, sich dem Manne unterzuordnen," in *Verbum Dei Manet in Aeternum. Eine Festschrift für*

derived from the early chapters of Luke since Luke depicts Jewish households. Schroeder concurred that it was a uniquely Christian household code which neither in form nor content was Stoic. He argued that Paul created it to counter the problem of his own teaching regarding the equality of all persons (Gal 3:28). He felt that although the household code draws from the clear teaching of the OT law (e.g., honoring of parents, Deut 5:16) with the addition of Greek ("it is proper") and Christian elements (love), it ultimately goes back to the teaching and example of Jesus himself.[1] The problem remains, however, of identifying Jesus' teaching on the duties of the husband-wife, parent-child, and master-slave. As a result of a lack of this material, most scholars have not adopted the idea of a uniquely Christian household code.

The 1970s saw a resurgence of study on the household codes. The new studies also thought that Stoic influence was minimal because the Stoic codes addressed individuals rather than social classes (e.g., husbands, parents, masters, slaves) which were addressed in the NT. Rather, it was once again suggested that the origin of the NT household codes came from Hellenistic Judaism,[2] a syncretism of Jewish injunctions to obey God's will combined with Greek ethical codes employed by Hellenistic Judaism in their Gentile missionary outreach. The main sources of support for those who held this view were Philo (*Hypoth.* 7.1–8, 14 §§628–31; *Decal.* 165–67 §207), Josephus (*C. Ap.* 2.22–30 §§190–219), and an Alexandrian Jew (*Pseudo-Pholcylides* 175–227), all of whom lived between 100 B.C. and A.D. 100. These ancient writers linked Noachian laws (laws given to Noah after the flood that were applicable to the whole human race) with Hellenistic "unwritten laws" and attempted to show their relevance to Gentile and Jewish cultures.

More recently, scholars have argued that the source for the form of the NT codes is not Stoic, Jewish, or Hellenistic Judaism but rather the Hellenistic discussion regarding household management in the ancient world.[3] Adherents of this view propose that early in the

---

Prof. D. Otto Schmitz zu seinem siebzigsten Geburtstag am 16. Juni 1953, ed. Werner Foerster (Witten: Luther-Verlag, 1953), 131–45.

1. David Schroeder, "Die Haustafeln des Neuen Testaments. Ihre Herkunft und ihr theologischer Sinn" (D.Theol. diss., Hamburg Universität, 1959) 151–52, cited from Crouch, *The Origin and Intention of the Colossian Haustafel*, 27; David Schroeder, "Lists, Ethical," in *The Interpreter's Dictionary of the Bible*, ed. George Arthur Buttrick et al., Supplementary vol. (Nashville: Abingdon, 1962), 546–47.

2. Crouch, *The Origin and Intention of the Colossian Haustafel*, 84–101; Wolfgang Schrage, "Zur Ethik der neutestamentliche Haustafeln," *NTS* 21 (October 1974): 1–22; Eduard Schweizer, "Traditional Ethical Patterns in the Pauline and post-Pauline Letters and Their Development (Lists of Vices and House-tables)," in *Text and Interpretation: Studies in the New Testament Presented to Matthew Black*, ed. Ernest Best and R. McL. Wilson (Cambridge: Cambridge University Press, 1979), 201–2; Ralph P. Martin, "Virtue, Blameless [ἀνέκλητος, ἀρετή]," *NIDNTT* 3 (1978): 930–32; cf. also O'Brien, *Colossians, Philemon*, 217. For a different perspective, see Sampley, *'And the Two Shall Become One Flesh,'* 16–76, 103–8; William Lillie, "The Pauline House-tables," *ExpTim* 86 (March 1975): 179–83.

3. Dieter Lührmann, "Wo man nicht mehr Sklave oder Freier ist. Überlegungen zur Struktur frühchristlicher Gemeinden," *WD* 13 (1975): 53–83; Dieter Lührmann, "Neutestamentliche Haustafeln und antike Ökonomie," *NTS* 27 (October 1980): 83–97; Klaus Thraede, "Ärger mit der Freiheit. Die Bedeutung von Frauen in Theorie und Praxis der alten Kirche," in *Freunde "in Christus werden . . ." Die Beziehung von Mann und Frau als Frage an Theologie und Kirche*, ed. Gerta Scharffenorth and Klaus Thraede (Gelnhausen: Burckhardthaus; Stein/Mfr.: Laetare, 1977), 35–108; Klaus Thraede, "Zum his-

Hellenistic period the management of the state was compared to the family hierarchy where there were those who rule and those who were ruled.[1] For example, after comparing the family with the state, Aristotle states that three relationships must be examined: the master and slave, husband and wife, and the father and child.[2] Balch has shown how this Aristotelian framework continued into the first century A.D.[3] Interestingly, Peripatetics who followed Aristotle wrote treatises in his name with the same household management concerns. For example, one work from the third century B.C. attributed to Aristotle discusses the husband's treatment of his wife, the master's treatment of his slaves, while it only minimally mentions children.[4] In the latter half of the second century B.C. another who wrote in his name also treated the three relationships mentioned in the NT.[5] In the first century B.C. the Stoic Arius Didymus, Augustus Caesar's friend and philosophical teacher, continued to discuss household management in comparison with the various management forms of the political state: parents to children as monarchic, husbands to wives as aristocratic, and children to one another as democratic. He discusses how the man of the house relates to his wife, children, and slaves in a philosophical way rather than in ethical exhortations as exhibited in Col 3:18–4:1 and Eph 5:22–6:9.[6] Seneca of the first century A.D. attributes the concept of "household management" to Aristotle.[7] The Aristotelian household management concepts are seen in the Jewish writers Philo and Josephus. Philo compares managment of a household with Joseph's preparation to manage a city or nation.[8] He shows the proper conduct of the husband-wife, parents-children, and master-servants.[9] Building on the fifth command-

torischen Hintergrund der ›Haustafeln‹ des NT," in *Pietas. Festschrift für Bernhard Kötting*, ed. Ernst Dassmann and K. Suso Frank, Jahrbuch für Antike und Christentum, vol. 8 (Münster: Aschendorffsche Verlagsbuchhandlung, 1980), 359–68; David L. Balch, *Let Wives Be Submissive: The Domestic Code in 1 Peter*, Society of Biblical Literature Monograph Series, ed. James Crenshaw and Robert Tannehill, no. 26 (Chico, Calif.: Scholars Press, 1981); John H. Elliott, *A Home for the Homeless. A Sociological Exegesis of 1 Peter, Its Situation and Strategy* (Philadelphia: Fortress, 1981); David C. Verner, *The Household of God: The Social World of the Pastoral Epistles*, SBLDS, ed. William Baird, no. 71 (Chico, Calif.: Scholars Press, 1983); Franz Laub, *Die Begegnung des frühen Christentums mit der antiken Sklaverei*, Stuttgarter Bibelstudien, ed. Helmut Merklein and Erich Zenger, vol. 107 (Stuttgart: Verlag Katholisches Bibelwerk, 1982); Winsome Munro, *Authority in Paul and Peter. The Identification of a Pastoral Stratum in the Pauline Corpus and 1 Peter*, SNTSMS, ed. R. McL. Wilson and M. E. Thrall, vol. 45 (Cambridge: Cambridge University Press, 1983); Lincoln, 357–60; cf. also Reggie M. Kidd, *Wealth and Beneficence in the Pastoral Epistles: A "Bourgeois" from Early Christianity?* SBLDS, ed. David L. Petersen and Charles Talbert, no. 122 (Atlanta: Scholars Press, 1990).

1. Xenophon *Oeconomicus* 7.4–10.13; Plato *Leges* 3 §690a–c; 6 §§771e–7 §824c; Aristotle *Politica* 1.2.1–3 §1253b.1–22; 1.5.1–2 §§1259a.37–1259b.18; *Ethica Nicomachea* 8.10.1 §§1160a.31–11.8 §1161b.11.
2. Aristotle *Politica* 1.2.1 §1253b.1–10.
3. Balch, *Let Wives Be Submissive*, 33–49.
4. Aristotle *Oeconomica* 1.1 §1343a.1–5.6 §1344b.22.
5. Aristotle *Magna Moralia* 1.33.15–18 §1194b.5–28.
6. Arius Didymus 147.26–152.25; cf. translation of text in Balch, "Household Codes," in *Greco-Roman Literature and the New Testament: Selected Forms and Genres*, 41–44.
7. Seneca *Epistolae Morales* 89.10.
8. Philo *Jos*. 8 §§38–39.
9. Philo *Post. C.* 53 §181; *Hypoth*. 7.3, 6 §358.

ment of the Mosaic law, Philo shows the place of parents and children as well as slaves.[1] Josephus also writes about the relationships of husbands and wives, parents and children, and masters and slaves.[2] Others in the first century B.C. and A.D. such as eclectic Stoics like Ariston, Hecaton, Hierocles, Dionysius of Halicarnassus, and Neopythagoreans like Bryson and Callicratidas reflect the Aristotelian view of household management.[3]

The last view, the Hellenistic concept of household management, has much to commend itself because it deals with social classes similar to those mentioned in the NT. Although similarities may exist between the Hellenistic and NT household codes, there is little, if any, indication that the source of the NT household codes are the Hellenistic household codes. Elements in these codes are not evident in the NT. First, the NT does not compare the household with a political entity such as a city or nation, a common theme with Aristotle and the Peripatetics. For example, when Paul discusses the state in Rom 13, he makes no mention of the household. Also, when he discusses household regulations, he does not mention the state (Eph 5:22–6:9; Col 3:18–4:1; 1 Pet 2:18–3:7; 1 Tim 2:8–15; 6:1–10; Titus 2:1–10). Second, Greek literature addresses those in the position of authority (e.g., the husband, father, and master) but not those who are asked to submit to authority (e.g., the wife, children, and slave) whereas the NT addresses both the husbands and the wives, the fathers and the children, the masters and the slaves.[4] Third, the NT does not deprecate those who are to be submissive. For example, the woman in Greek literature is portrayed as being inferior in all things[5] and, in particular, her capacity to think deliberatively (τὸ βουλευτικόν).[6] In the NT the woman is exhorted to choose to be submissive. In Hellenistic writings, slaves are thought to have no deliberative faculty (τὸ βουλευτικόν) at all,[7] whereas in the NT slaves are enjoined to be obedient to the master and to render their service as to the Lord. Arius portrays slaves as stupid people who are unable to live by themselves thus benefiting from slavery.[8] In contrast, the Book of Philemon and 1 Cor 7:21 encourage slaves to win freedom and thus to take care of themselves as free people. The

1. Philo *Decal.* 31 §§165–67; *Spec.* 2.38–39 §§225–27.

2. Josephus *C. Ap.* 2.24 §199; 27 §206; 30 §§215–17.

3. For more details, see Balch, *Let Wives Be Submissive*, 51–59.

4. Yoder observed the same thing in Stoic literature (John H. Yoder, *The Politics of Jesus: Vicit Agnus Noster* [Grand Rapids: Eerdmans, 1972], 174–75).

5. Euripides *Hippolytus* 614–68; Plato *Leges* 6 §781b; Aristotle *Magna Moralia* 1.33.18 §1194b.25; Josephus *C. Ap.* 2.24 §201. χείρων used in these texts could mean inferior only in bodily strength, virtue, rank, or it could have reference to intelligence. Josephus states women are inferior in all things. Aristotle (*Politica* 1.2.12 §1254b.14) states that the male by nature is superior and is to rule, and the female is inferior and is to be ruled. Later when he discusses the man's relationship to his family, the husband is to rule over his wife in the mode of a republican form of government and over the children using a monarchical form. In government the king may be superior in rank to his subjects but qualitatively the same as his subjects. The male is by nature more fit to rule than the female (the reverse is contrary to nature) but in the husband-wife (not the male-female) relationship, there may be rank in rule without distinction regarding essence (*Politica* 1.5.2 §1259b.1–18). In 1 Pet 3:7 the wife is described as weaker (ἀσθενής) physically, but the husband is to honor her as she is a joint heir with him in the grace of life. Hence, there is no deprecation of her as a person for she is equal with man before God. Aristotle (*Oeconomica* 1.3.4 §§1343b.30–1344a.6) is much more even-handed for he uses ἀσθενής to describe physical weakness of women in comparison to men and describes men as inferior (χείρων) to the woman in some areas of domestic responsibility.

6. Arius Didymus 149.7; possibly Aristotle *Politica* 1.5.6 §1260a.13.

7. Aristotle *Politica* 1.5.6 §1260a.12; Arius Didymus 149.7.

8. Arius Didymus 149.2.

NT, therefore, does not deprecate the person who is to be submissive to another. Fourth, the Greek writings include instructions regarding the duties of the husband, father, and master, but no real example or motivation is offered to follow those instructions; however, the NT has the example of Christ's love and care for the church as well as the motivation to please the Lord.[1] Fifth, Greek and Hellenistic household codes discussed how the head of the house should manage the finances of the household but this is entirely absent in the NT household codes.[2] These are the primary differences between the Hellenistic and NT household codes.

Philo, who is thought to have adopted the Hellenistic household management, is more in line with what the NT presents. Along with the work attributed to Aristotle, Philo discourages the husband's mistreatment of his wife and children.[3] However, Philo differs from the Hellenistic view on slaves. He thinks that slaves are to render affectionate loyalty to their masters and, in turn, the masters are not to be arrogant or contemptuous towards them but to show gentleness and kindness to equalize the inequality.[4] Philo's view on slavery is influenced by the OT. The people of Israel, once slaves of the Egyptians (Lev 26:13; Deut 6:21; 15:15; 16:12; 24:18, 22), were instructed in how to treat their own slaves. They were to allow their slaves to be free after six years of service unless they chose to continue as slaves (Exod 21:2–6; Lev 25:39–46). The OT was an advocate for those who were weak, unfree, and who could not protect themselves. So Philo adopted the Hellenistic household management code only through the grid of the OT. The question is, however, did Paul adopt these Hellenistic codes?

Coming from the same background and period of time, Paul most likely would have been familiar with Hellenistic household management schema and most certainly was familiar with the teachings of the OT as well as the general principles regarding relationships taught by Jesus himself. Although the household code in Eph 5:22–6:9 contains similarities to those of the Hellenistic codes, Paul's instructions, as pointed out above, are quite different. The most important difference is the model or basis for the codes. Whereas in Hellenism the model was political, the Christian model is Christ himself, and he is also the motivating force. For example, while a Hellenistic writer would propose that if slaves were treated well they would be more productive,[5] Paul states that slaves should not be mistreated because the Lord is master of both parties and both are answerable to him (6:9).

Since there is so little agreement on the source of the NT household codes, Hartman, among others, rightly cautions against identifying them with any particular source.[6] It is natural that any given society would adhere to specific rules for the order of life, politically, domestically, socially, and religiously. It is also natural that since believers then and now are a part of society, they too need a code of conduct. The household code of Ephesians addresses this by advancing a distinctly Christian ethic.[7] As mentioned above, Rengstorf and Schroeder sug-

1. Similar circumstances in Stoic literature (see Yoder, *The Politics of Jesus*, 179–80).

2. Carolyn Osiek, "The Ephesian Household Code," *TBT* 36 (November 1998): 362.

3. Aristotle *Oeconomica* 1.3.4–4.1 §1344a.1–10; Philo *Hypoth.* 7.3 §358; *Post. C.* 53 §181.

4. Philo *Spec.* 3.25 §137; *Decal.* 31 §167.

5. Aristotle *Oeconomica* 1.5.2–6 §§1344a.29–1344b.22.

6. L. Hartman, "Some Unorthodox Thoughts on the 'Household-Code Form'," in *The Social World of Formative Christianity and Judaism: Essays in Tribute to Howard Clark Kee*, ed. Jacob Neusner, Peder Borgen, Ernest S. Frerichs, Richard Horsley (Philadelphia: Fortress, 1988), 228–30; cf. Philip H. Towner, "Households and Household Codes," in *DPL*, 418–19; idem, "Household Codes," in *DLNT*, 515; Lincoln, 360.

7. Cf. John M. G. Barclay, "The Family as the Bearer of Religion in Judaism and early Christianity," in *Constructing Early Christian Families: Family as Social Reality and Metaphor*, ed. Halvor Moxnes (London: Routledge, 1997), 66–80, esp. 76–78; Stephen C. Barton, "Living as Families in the Light of the New Testament," *Int* 52 (April 1998): 141.

gested that these household codes were distinctly Christian on the basis of OT law and the life and teachings of Jesus. However, the NT household codes seem to be a new Christian ethic in the life of the church rather than a teaching of Jesus handed down to the church. It is similar to Paul's instructions to the Corinthians, first, when he applies the teaching of Jesus by stating, "Not I but the Lord" (1 Cor 7:10) and second, when there was no specific teaching of Jesus he states, "Not the Lord, but I say to you" (1 Cor 7:12–24). There are no household codes as such in the teaching of Jesus, though Jesus may have touched on elements of them. Therefore, it seems best to view Paul under God's direction to present distinctly Christian household codes to instruct believers in their conduct with one another and within the secular society.

The purpose of the household codes has engendered a great amount of discussion. For many, the difficulty lies in different concepts of equality of persons and lines of authority (functional distinctions). As mentioned above, Schroeder feels that Paul created household codes to counter his own teaching regarding the equality of all persons mentioned in Gal 3:28. Caird suggests that though Gal 3:28 teaches about the liberation of women and slaves, Paul enjoins them to follow the old order of submission because many of their husbands and masters respectively may not have been a part of the believing community. To confront head on the social realities of the NT world regarding this new emancipation may have been "politically dangerous and religiously misleading" and could have spelled disaster for the church.[1] But there is no indication in the text that wives and slaves are to be submissive if only their husbands and masters are believers. They are to be submissive whether they are believers or unbelievers. Again, Caird does not make the distinction between women and wives. Walker suggests that the difference between egalitarianism in Gal 3:28 and the patriarchal structure of the household codes is because Galatians was written by Paul and the source for the household codes was a postapostolic Paulinist.[2] However, Gal 3:28 in no way contradicts the household codes. All persons are equal before God whether Jew or Gentile, bond or free, male or female. Though all are equal before God, this does not exclude lines of authority. On the other hand, where there are lines of authority in a hierarchical[3] pattern, equality is not negated. For example, all citizens of a country are equal but there are also many different ranks in the power structure of the country. It does not mean that those in authority are better citizens of the country than those whom they rule. There is no qualitative difference between rulers and citizens.[4] More importantly, another example of equality and yet subordination is the persons of the Godhead. All three persons of God are qualitatively equal (Matt 28:19; 2 Cor 13:14; Eph 4:4–6; 1 Pet 1:2; cf. also John 13:16; 17:21) yet the Son is subordinate to the Father (Matt 10:40; 26:39, 42; John 8:29, 42; 12:49), the Holy Spirit to the Father (John 14:26; 15:26; 16:13–15), and the Holy Spirit to the Son (John 16:7; cf. 14:26; 15:26). Thus, subordination does not imply a qualitative difference.[5]

Galatians 3:28 is a source of controversy on the point of equality versus authority.[6] In this

1. G. B. Caird, "Paul and Women's Liberty," *BJRL* 54 (spring 1972): 279–80.

2. William O. Walker Jr., "The 'Theology of Woman's Place' and the 'Paulinist' Tradition," *Semeia* 28 (1983): 101–12.

3. O'Brien (406–7) correctly suggests that it is better to label the model hierarchical rather than patriarchal. The hierarchical pattern is more fitting with the analogies used above regarding governmental authority and the roles of the three persons of the Godhead.

4. This same sentiment is expressed by Aristotle *Politica* 1.5.2 §1259b.1–18.

5. Bilezikian thinks there cannot be equality if there is subordination. See Gilbert Bilezikian, "Hermeneutical Bungee-Jumping: Subordination in the Godhead," *JETS* 40 (March 1997): 57–68.

6. Motyer attempts to reconcile this problem (Stephen Motyer, "The Relationship between Paul's Gospel of 'All One in Christ Jesus' [Galatians 3:28] and the 'Household Codes'," *VE* 19 [1989]: 33–48). For a more recent study on this, see Richard W. Hove, *Equality in Christ?: Galatians 3:28 and the Gender Dispute* (Wheaton, Ill.: Crossway, 1999), 93–142.

regard, a distinction must be made between male/female or free/slaves and husbands/wives or masters/slaves in the household codes (parents/children are not addressed in Gal 3:28 and Jew/Gentile are not addressed in the household codes). Though lines of authority are given to the husbands/wives or masters/slaves of the household codes, this is not true in Gal 3:28. For example, while wives are commanded to be submissive to their husbands, it does not mean that they are to be submissive to all men. Similarly, slaves are commanded to be submissive to their masters, but that does not mean that they are to be submissive to all masters.[1] Therefore, there is really no contradiction between Gal 3:28 and the household codes because they do not address the same thing. Accordingly, Paul is not correcting his earlier teaching nor are the household codes written by a postapostolic Paulinist. It is simply a matter of the qualitative (Gal 3:28) versus lines of authority (Eph 5:22–6:9).

What, then, is the intended function of the household codes? This has been greatly debated, as demonstrated briefly in the following arguments. Crouch, for instance, suggests that Paul is combating the social unrest of slaves due to his teaching of the manumission of slaves (1 Cor 7:21).[2] However, MacDonald sees no evidence for such a problem in the Colossian church[3] and the same can be said of the Ephesian church. Balch asserts that the function of the household code in 1 Pet 2:18–3:7 is apologetic in order to silence unbelievers' slanders against the Christians (1 Pet 2:11–15; 3:15–16) and also for the believing wife to win her unbelieving husband (1 Pet 3:1).[4] On the other hand, Elliott thinks that Balch has overemphasized the external concerns and minimized the function of the household code as a vehicle to promote the internal cohesion of the community.[5] In these and other arguments an apologetic function is proposed. However, this is clearly not the case with the Ephesian household code.[6] The theme in Ephesians is the unity of the church (Eph 2:11–3:13; 4:1–16) and the practical outworking of this unity in the present context is for believers to walk wisely by being filled by the Spirit (5:15–21). Therefore, the function of the Ephesian household code (5:22–6:9) is to enhance this unity. Furthermore, Dudrey rightly points out that the purpose of the household codes "is *not* to repress the socially downtrodden, but to transform spiritually all who are in Christ—husbands, fathers, and masters included."[7] It was to be a display to the Roman world how believers who are transformed and empowered by the Holy Spirit function within the family structure.

The form of the household code in Eph 5:22–6:9 is identical to the one in Col 3:18–4:1 and is similar to the one in 1 Pet 2:18–3:7.[8] First, this household code addresses six groups

1. So also George W. Knight III, "Husbands and Wives as Analogues of Christ and the Church: Ephesians 5:21–33 and Colossians 3:18–19," in *Recovering Biblical Manhood and Womanhood: A Response to Evangelical Feminism*, ed. John Piper and Wayne Grudem (Wheaton, Ill.: Crossway, 1991), 169.

2. Crouch, *The Origin and Intention of the Colossian Haustafel*, 126–27.

3. MacDonald, *The Pauline Churches*, 111–12.

4. Balch, *Let Wives Be Submissive*, 81–116.

5. Elliott, *A Home for the Homeless*, 217–19, 263 n. 237. For further discussion between Balch and Elliott, see John H. Elliott, "1 Peter, Its Situation and Strategy: A Discussion with David Balch," and David L. Balch, "Hellenization/Acculturation in 1 Peter," in *Perspectives on First Peter*, ed. Charles H. Talbert, NABPR Special Studies Series, no. 9 (Macon, Ga.: Mercer University Press, 1986), 61–78, 79–101.

6. MacDonald, *The Pauline Churches*, 109.

7. Russ Dudrey, "'Submit Yourselves to One Another': A Socio-historical Look at the Household Codes of Ephesians 5:15–6:9," *ResQ* 41 (first quarter 1999): 40; cf. Horrell, "From ἀδελφοί to οἶκος θεοῦ: Social Transformation in Pauline Christianity," 305–6.

8. Sampley, *'And the Two Shall Become One Flesh,'* 17–27. For a structural analysis of the *Haustafel*, see Gielen, *Tradition und Theologie neutestamentlicher Haustafelethik*, 208–38.

in three pairs: wives-husbands, children-fathers, and slaves-masters. Second, the subordinate partner is addressed first followed by the partner in authority. Third, the first of the pair is given longer instruction regarding their duties than the second of the pair. The notable exception to this in the Ephesian household code is the first pair where the husbands are given far more instruction regarding their duty than the wives. Fourth, each of those addressed are ultimately answerable to the Lord. Fifth, there is a symmetrical pattern "in which every class of individuals has its corresponding class immediately after it. Thus, admonitions to husbands follow those to wives, those to parents follow those to children, and masters are addressed after slaves."[1] Sixth, the elements of the form are: the party is addressed, the imperative is stated, amplification is given, and the motivation is presented.[2]

The elements of the Ephesian household code form

Verse	Address	Imperative	Amplification	Motivation
5:22–24	wives	submit to husbands	as to the Lord	husband is head of the wife as Christ is head of the church
5:25–33	husbands	love wives	as their own body	Christ gave himself for the church
6:1–3	children	obey parents	in the Lord	Command to honor parents and promise of a long life
6:4	fathers	provoke not children	but nurture	in discipline and admonition of the Lord
6:5–8	slaves	obey masters	as to Christ	Lord will reward
6:9	masters	do right by slaves	forebear threats	Lord will judge

The form of the Ephesian household code appears patriarchal or hierarchical in structure.[3] In early Greek and Roman households the patriarchal structure, the male head, had extensive authority over the wife, children, and slaves (*pater familias*). However, by NT times most marriages took place *sine manus* (without power transferred from the wife's father to the husband) so that women exercised a greater degree of independence from

1. Sampley, *'And the Two Shall Become One Flesh,'* 24.
2. Verner, *The Household of God,* 87–89.
3. Some who propound the feminist viewpoint think the household code contradicts the first three chapters of Ephesians where the author advocated equality of Jew and Gentile, whereas 5:22–6:9 is not about equality but about hierarchy. Even much of chaps. 4–6 is concerned about putting into practice what was taught in the first three chapters. Hence, 5:22–6:9 is out of character with the rest of the book, which may indicate a later addition. See Tanzer, 2:136–49, esp. 138–41, 145–49. However, it is not likely that an addition would be made in the midst of the last three chapters rather than at the end. Furthermore, a hierarchical structure does not deny equality, as mentioned above. Ådna suggests that 5:21–33 should not be seen as a patriarchal structure of marriage or as a design to limit women's ministries and functions in society and the church (Jostein Ådna, "Die eheliche Liebesbeziehung als Analogie zu Christi Beziehung zur Kirche. Eine traditionsgeschichtliche Studie zu Epheser 5,21–33," *ZTK* 92 [Dezember 1995]: 464–65; cf. also Groupe Orsay, "Une lecture feministe des «codes domestiques» par un groupe de femmes," *Foi et Vie* 88 [Septembre 1989]: 59–69). Mouton proposes that the patriarchal structure mentioned in Ephesians needs to be reoriented in terms

their husbands. To some degree even the Jewish household (especially in Hellenistic Judaism) followed suit.[1] Paul's injunctions reflect a hierarchical structure but still there is no suggestion of misogyny or the sweeping powers of the male head which were practiced in the early Greek household and even to a greater degree in the early Roman household. There is more space given to exhortations for the husband than the wife.

In conclusion, then, the Ephesian household code was for the purpose of fostering unity of believers in that community in Asia Minor. Specific groups of believers are addressed regarding their responsibilities to other groups who may or may not have been believers. The believers are to carry out their responsibilities as to the Lord in the power of the Holy Spirit.

Before embarking on the exegesis of the household code, it is important to emphasize its context again. Paul has enjoined believers to walk wisely by making the most of every opportunity. He has explained that this is done by understanding the will of the Lord by means of being filled by the Spirit. The resultant characteristics of this filling are described by the five participles, the last of which is submission to one another in the fear of Christ (5:21). This verse not only concludes the section that began in 5:15, but it also is a hinge verse to the present section (5:22–6:9). The present context is very much related to the previous context, for only believers filled by the Spirit are able to please the Lord by fulfilling their duties and are able to live blameless lives in close and continual contact with their family or employment relationships.

a. Wives and Husbands (5:22–33)

The first of the three pairs in the household code is concerned with wives and husbands. This is a disproportionately large section of twelve verses. The second pair, namely, children and parents, is discussed in four verses (6:1–4) and slaves and masters utilizes five verses (6:5–9). In Colossians (3:18–19) only one verse is devoted to wives and one verse to husbands.

(1) Responsibility of Wives' Submission (5:22–24)

According to the pattern, wives, who are to submit, are discussed first. It is the wife and then the husband, the children and parents, and slaves and masters. The discussion regarding wives in Ephesians has forty-one words, which is four times longer than that of Colossians but is less than half as long as 1 Pet 3:1–6, which uses ninety-

---

of today's culture (Elna Mouton, "The Transformative Potential of Ephesians in a Situation of Transition," *Semeia* 78 [1997]: 121–43). Rather than a reorientation of Ephesians in terms of today's culture, there needs to be a serious reexamination and proper application of the text where it will be discovered that the hierarchical structure should not demean women anymore than Christ demeans the church.

1. Verner, *The Household of God*, 27–81; *contra* Kroeger, "Appendix III: The Classical Concept of *Head* as 'Source'," 280–81.

seven words. A possible reason why Peter uses many more words is that some of the husbands may have been unbelievers and Peter is instructing wives how to win them over to the Lord. Here in Ephesians Paul instructs the wives to submit because the husband is the head of the wife as Christ is the head of church, and as the church submits to Christ so should the wife to her husband. The imagery of the church being a spouse of Christ is new.[1]

(a) Imperative: Submit to Husbands (5:22)

Text: 5:22. αἱ γυναῖκες [ὑποτάσσεσθε] τοῖς ἰδίοις ἀνδράσιν ὡς τῷ κυρίῳ,

Translation: 5:22. "Wives [submit] to your own husbands as to the Lord,"

Commentary: 5:22. αἱ γυναῖκες [ὑποτάσσεσθε][2] **τοῖς ἰδίοις ἀνδράσιν,** "Wives [submit] to your own husbands." The words αἱ γυναῖκες can refer to women in general, but the context demands that they have reference to wives. The wives' responsibilities are addressed first, followed by the husbands'.

The wives are [ὑποτάσσεσθε] τοῖς ἰδίοις ἀνδράσιν, "to submit to your own husbands." Although the verb is missing in some manuscripts, it is included in the majority of manuscripts from the earliest times, either as a second person plural present middle or passive imperative (ὑποτάσσεσθε) or as a third person plural present hortatory subjunctive (ὑποτασσέσθωσαν). If the original text omitted the verb, one can easily see why the scribes would have inserted ὑποτάσσεσθε for the

1. Benoit, "L'Église corps du Christ," 974 (reprinted in idem, *Exégèse et Théologie*, 4:210).

2. There are four variant readings for this verse. The first reading, γυναῖκες τοῖς ἰδίοις ἀνδράσιν ὡς, is supported by 𝔓[46] B Clement Theodore[latcom] Greek mss[acc. to Jerome] Jerome[com] (NA[27], UBS[4]). The second reading, γυναῖκες τοῖς ἰδίοις ἀνδράσιν ὑποτάσσεσθε ὡς, occurs in 075 0150 424* 1852 1912 2200 *Byz* [K L] *Lect* it[f] syr[h] geo slav Chrysostom. The third reading, γυναῖκες ὑποτάσσεσθε τοῖς ἰδίοις ἀνδράσιν ὡς, is found in D F G it[d, gtxt]. The fourth reading, γυναῖκες τοῖς ἰδίοις ἀνδράσιν ὑποτασσέσθωσαν ὡς, is found in ℵ A I P (Ψ ὑποτασσέσθωσαν *after* γυναῖκες) 6 33 81 104 256 263 365 424[c] 436 459 1175 1241 1319 1573 1739 1881 1962 2127 2464 *l* 596 *l* 895 *l* 1178 it[ar, b, gv,r, mon, o] vg syr[pal] (cop[sa, bo]) arm eth Origen[grlem, lat] Basil Theodore[latlem] Victorinus-Rome Ambrosiaster Ambrose Jerome[lem] Pelagius Theodoret Augustine. There are basically three readings: (1) omission of a main verb found in the first reading; (2) inclusion of the second person plural present passive imperative ὑποτάσσεσθε, "be subject," before or after τοῖς ἰδίοις ἀνδράσιν found in the second and third readings; and (3) inclusion of third person plural present hortatory subjunctive ὑποτασσέσθωσαν, "let them be subject," before or after τοῖς ἰδίοις ἀνδράσιν found in the fourth reading. Regarding the external evidence, the first reading has 𝔓[46] and B and no other manuscript support. The second and third readings have the support of the Western and Byzantine text-types with good genealogical relationships. The fourth reading has Alexandrian support with good genealogical relationships. Most would argue for the omission of the verb because it is the shorter reading and it is easy to explain the inclusion of the verb for the sake of clarity (cf. Metzger, *Textual Commentary*, 2d ed., 541). Regarding the internal evidence, the most natural would

sake of clarity since the preceding and the succeeding contexts use the second person plural present imperatives (see the textual critical discussion at p. 730 n. 2). It would be identical to the parallel passage of Col 3:18. Furthermore, if there were no main verb then the participle in the previous verse is appropriated with an imperatival force, though the participle would not agree with αἱ γυναῖκες in gender.

The verb in question is the present middle or passive of ὑποτάσσω discussed at 1:22 and 5:21 and basically means "to be subject, subordinate." It is rendered "submit yourselves or subject yourselves" (AV), "be in subjection or be subject" (RV, ASV, RSV, NASB, NEB, TEV, JB, NIV, NJB, NRSV), or "submit" (TEV, NIV). Some think this verb is passive and is normally followed with a dative "to persons worthy of respect."[1] Here it is followed by τοῖς ἰδίοις ἀνδράσιν, "to your own husbands." Others suggest that this verb is middle,[2] although most commentators never discuss the issue. There is a difference though it is not great. The passive could convey the idea that a person submits because he or she is forced to submit, for example, as one is submissive to a dictator; however, the middle definitely connotes that the subject volitionally exercises the action of submission, an act of a free agent. The middle seems in keeping with the context for three reasons. First, there is no indication that the church's submission to Christ is forced.

---

be the second or third readings (ὑποτάσσεσθε, "be subject") because in the immediately preceding context there are second person plural present passive imperatives in 5:18 negatively, μὴ μεθύσκεσθε οἴνῳ, "not to be drunk with wine," and positively, πληροῦσθε ἐν πνεύματι, "be filled by the Spirit," and in the succeeding context there are second person plural present active imperatives for the husbands to ἀγαπᾶτε, "love," the wives (5:25), children to ὑπακούετε, "obey," their parents (6:1), fathers μὴ παροργίζετε, "not to provoke," their children (6:4), slaves to ὑπακούετε, "obey," their masters (6:5), and masters ποιεῖτε, "do," the same to their slaves (6:9). Furthermore, the parallel passage in Col 3:18 includes the second person plural present passive imperative ὑποτάσσεσθε, "be subject." Because of these factors one could see how the scribes would have inserted it for the sake of clarity. The more difficult reading in the present context would be the fourth reading (ὑποτασσέσθωσαν, "let them be subject"), which is found in the early witnesses in the Alexandrian text-type. It is not unusual for the Alexandrian text to have a harder reading. In the end, whatever reading is adopted, the meaning remains the same. If there is an omission of the main verb, then one surmises that the participle in the previous verse is picked up in this verse with an imperatival force (MHT 1:181, 222–23; 4:85; Robertson, *Grammar*, 946). The second or third readings are preferred because of internal evidence, but the inclusion of ὑποτάσσεσθε, "be subject," is easily explained if the first reading were the original.

1. BAGD 848; cf. BDAG 1042; see Norbert Baumert, *Woman and Man in Paul: Overcoming a Misunderstanding*, trans. Patrick Madigan and Linda M. Maloney (Collegeville, Minn.: Liturgical Press, 1996), 221.

2. Robertson, *Grammar*, 807; MHT 1:163; Delling, *TDNT* 8 (1972): 42–45; Barth, 610–11, 708–10 and n 392; Stephen Francis Miletic, *"One Flesh": Eph. 5.22–24, 5.31: Marriage and the New Creation*, AnBib, vol. 115 (Rome: Pontificio Istituto Biblico, 1988), 29–30; John Wick Bowman, "The Gospel and the Christian Family. An Exposition of Ephesians 5:22 to 6:9," *Int* 1 (October 1947): 443–44.

Second, the duty of the husband is phrased in the active imperative in which the subject takes the action to love his wife. Third, in the previous context (5:18–21), four out of the five participles dependent on the imperative "to be filled by the Spirit" are active and the fifth participle is best seen as middle where the subject is responsible for the action. Therefore, the submission here is better taken not as a passive but as a middle, with the wife acting as free agent before God.

Originally the adjective ἴδιος had the idea of that which is one's own, that which is private or personal, in contrast to that which belongs to another or is public or common (κοινός).[1] However, by NT times it no longer had that significance and it differed little, if at all, from a reflexive or a possessive pronoun.[2] Its absence in Col 3:18 does not indicate any difference[3] nor does its absence in Eph 5:25 connote anything but for the husband to love his own wife. Paul means that the wife is to submit to her husband as opposed to men in general.[4] If Paul had meant that all females are to be submissive to all males, he would have used the adjectives θῆλυς, "female," and ἄρσην, "male," as he does in Gal 3:28 rather than the nouns γυνή, "woman, wife," and ἀνήρ, "man, husband" (cf. Matt 5:28, 31–32).[5]

How does this instruction correlate with 5:21 where Paul states that all believers are to be submissive to one another? Some suggest that 5:21 contains the controlling thought of mutual submission and, therefore, the rest of the passage (vv. 22–33) should be seen as mutual submission of husbands and wives rather than the submission of wives only.[6] However, though Paul states in 5:21 that all believers are to be submissive to one another, we see in the household code that specific roles of submission are related to certain lines of authority.

1. LSJ 818.

2. BAGD 369–70; BDAG 466–67; Deissmann, *Bible Studies*, 123–24; MHT 1:87–90; 3:191–92; Schnackenburg, 246 n. 14; Bruce, 384.

3. Abbott, 165.

4. Ben Witherington III, *Women in the Earliest Churches*, SNTSMS, ed. G. N. Stanton, vol. 59 (Cambridge: Cambridge University Press, 1988), 57; cf. also Ben Witherington III, *Women and the Genesis of Christianity*, ed. Ann Witherington (Cambridge: Cambridge University Press, 1990), 157.

5. Barth, 610 n. 9.

6. Else Kähler, "Zur »Unterordnung« der Frau im Neuen Testament. Der neutestamentliche Begriff der Unterordnung und seine Bedeutung für die Begegnung von Mann und Frau," *ZEE* 3 (Januar 1959): 8–10; Cindy Weber-Han, "Sexual Equality according to Paul: An Exegetical Study of 1 Corinthians 11:1–16 and Ephesians 5:21–33," *Brethren Life and Thought* 22 (summer 1977): 169–70; Kähler, *Die Frau in den paulinischen Briefen*, 99–103; Jules-Marie Cambier, "Doctrine paulinienne du mariage chrétien. Étude critique de 1 Co 7 et d'Ep 5,21–33 et essai de leur traduction actuelle," *Église et Théologie* 10, no. 1 (1979): 49–58; Howe, *Women and Church Leadership*, 54–55; Eric Fuchs, "De la soumission des femmes. Une lecture d'Éphésians 5,21–33," *Le Supplément* 161 (Juillet 1987): 73–81; Robert W. Wall, "Wifely Submission in the Context of Ephesians," *Christian Scholar's Review* 17 (March 1988): 276, 280–84; James R. Beck, "Is There a Head of

There is no indication in the household codes that the husbands are to be submissive to their wives,[1] Christ to the church, the parents to their children, or the masters to their slaves. Is this a contradiction of 5:21? It seems very unlikely that Paul would say one thing and then another in the same breath, so to speak.[2] Rather, Paul's statement concludes the section regarding the characteristics of believers filled by the Spirit (5:15–21). The last of the characteristics of believers filled by the Spirit is submission to one another, that is, in the midst of the body of believers. However, moving to the household code he restricts the command to wives alone (5:22–24). This is analogous to the command to all believers to walk in love (5:2), similar to Christ's command to love one another (John 13:34; 15:12, 17) but in the household

the House in the Home? Reflections on Ephesians 5," *Journal of Biblical Equality* 1 (1989): 61–66; Francois Wessels, "Ephesians 5:21–33 'Wives, Be Subject to Your Husbands, Love Your Wives . . .'," *Journal of Theology for Southern Africa* 67 (June 1989): 71, 75; Sharon Hodgin Gritz, *Paul, Women Teachers, and the Mother Goddess at Ephesus: A Study of 1 Timothy 2:9–15 in Light of The Religious and Cultural Milieu of The First Century* (Lanham, Md.: University Press of America, 1991), 90–91; Craig S. Keener, *Paul, Women & Wives: Marriage and Women's Ministry in the Letters of Paul* (Peabody, Mass.: Hendrickson, 1992), 157–83; Kroeger, "Head," 376–77; Matthew Vellanickal, "Family Relationship: A Pauline Perspective," *Bible Bhashyam* 20 (June 1994): 109–10; David M. Scholer, "The Evangelical Debate over Biblical 'Headship,'" in *Women, Abuse, and the Bible: How Scripture Can Be Used to Hurt or to Heal*, ed. Catherine Clark Kroeger and James R. Beck (Grand Rapids: Baker, 1996), 43–44, 51; Carol J. Schlueter, "Revitalizing Interpretations of Ephesians 5:22," *Pastoral Psychology* 45 (March 1997): 317–339; cf. also Heinrich Greeven, "Ehe nach dem Neuen Testament," *NTS* 15 (July 1969): 388. For a more tempered view of mutual submission, see Baumert, *Woman and Man in Paul*, 218–19, 224; Dudrey, "'Submit Yourselves to One Another'," 27–44.

1. *Contra* Stagg who thinks that the exhortation to the husbands to love their wives "in effect calls for a radical subordination (the word not used) of husband to wife" (Frank Stagg, "The Domestic Code and Final Appeal: Ephesians 5:21–6:24," *RevExp* 76 [fall 1979]: 546). However, he admits that the word "to submit" is not used for the husband. For a discussion of this problem, see Turid Karlsen Seim, "A Superior Minority? The Problem of Men's Headship in Ephesians 5," *ST* 49, no. 1 (1995): 167–81; reprinted as idem, "A Superior Minority? The Problem of Men's Headship in Ephesians 5," in *Mighty Minorities? Minorities in Early Christianity—Positions and Strategies: Essays in Honour of Jacob Jervell on His 70th Birthday 21 May 1995*, ed. David Hellholm, Halvor Moxnes, and Turid Karlsen Seim (Oslo: Scandinavian University Press, 1995), 167–81; cf. also Los Santos, *La novedad de la metáfora κεφαλή-σῶμα*, 290–93, 306–7.

2. Erdmann suggests that this is not unlike 1 Pet 5:5 where the younger believers are exhorted to be subject to the elders and immediately following there is the admonition that all are to be clothed with humility. The second imperative does not cancel the first. See Martin Erdmann, "Der Brief an die Epheser. 44. Teil: Kapitel 5,21–24," *Fundamentum* 22, no. 2 (2001): 27. Thériault's suggestion that Paul theologically endorsed equality but culturally adapted to the wife's submission to the husband is unlikely (Jean-Yves Thériault, "La femme chrétienne dans les textes pauliniens," *ScEs* 37 [Octobre-Décembre 1985]: 304–5).

code the command to love is addressed specifically to husbands (Eph 5:25, 28, 33).[1]

There has been a great deal of discussion regarding the wife's submission as presented in NT literature. As an example, Kroeger maintains that ὑποτάσσω has many meanings and can mean "to attach one thing to another or to identify one person or thing with another."[2] In this context she suggests that it is the wife who leaves her family and attaches herself to her husband, to be identified with him. To substantiate this rendering she cites Polybius (3.36.6–7; 38.4; 18.15.4), Rom 8:20, and Luke 2:51. Granted there may be some variations in meaning but, as Dawes points out, none of the references in Polybius support her interpretation.[3] Neither do the NT references. Thus, the normal rendering "to be subject, subordinate, to submit" is preferable. Others observe that Paul uses ὑποτάσσω, "be subject," for the wife and not ὑπακούω, "obey," as he does for children (6:1) and slaves (6:5), suggesting that this indicates that the wife is on a more equal basis with the husband.[4] Furthermore, commentators frequently note that outside of the NT the term ὑποτάσσω is used only two times[5] of the wife's submission to her husband[6] whereas commonly in Hellenistic Judaism the wife is to ὑπακούω, "obey,"[7] or δουλεύω, "serve,"[8] her husband. Thus, it is argued that there is a definite distinction between ὑποτάσσω and ὑπακούω. In fact, some think that ὑποτάσσω was a uniquely Christian term for the wife's relationship to her husband.[9] However, there are three problems with making a distinction between ὑποτάσσω and ὑπακούω. First, the term ὑποτάσσω historically has the idea of a subordinate role of one individual to that of another, whether it be politically, militarily, or socially.[10] Second, Paul and Peter also use the term ὑποτάσσω, "be subject," for the slaves in their household codes (Titus 2:9; 1 Pet 2:18). Furthermore, when Peter in the same household code

1. Dawes, *The Body in Question*, 222–25.

2. Kroeger, "Appendix III: The Classical Concept of *Head* as 'Source'," 281.

3. Dawes, *The Body in Question*, 210–12, esp. 210 n. 34.

4. Bengel, 4:106–7; Barth, 714; Bowman, "The Gospel and the Christian Family," 443–44; Kähler, *ZEE* 3 (Januar 1959): 7–9; Kähler, *Die Frau in den paulinischen Briefen*, 102, 254 n. 470; Baumert, *Woman and Man in Paul*, 219.

5. Plutarch *Moralia: Coniugalia praecepta* 33 §142e; Pseudo-Callisthenes *Historia Alexandri Magni* 1.22.4.

6. Rengstorf, "Die neutestamentlichen Mahnungen an die Frau," 132; Barth, 709; Lincoln, 367.

7. Josephus *C. Ap.* 2.24 §201.

8. Philo *Hypoth*. 7.3 §358.

9. Kähler, *ZEE* 3 (Januar 1959): 1–13; Kähler, *Die Frau in den paulinischen Briefen*, passim; Rengstorf, "Die neutestamentlichen Mahnungen an die Frau," 132.

10. LSJ 1897; Delling, *TDNT* 8 (1972): 39–46; Barth, 708–11; Ehrhard Kamlah, "Ὑποτάσσεσθαι in den neutestamentlichen »Haustafeln«," in *Verborum Veritas. Festschrift für Gustav Stählin zum 70. Geburtstag*, ed. Otto Böcher and Kaus Haacker (Wuppertal: Brockhaus, 1970), 238–40.

instructs wives to "be subject" (ὑποτάσσω) to their husbands, he illustrates this subordination by Sarah's "obeying" (ὑπακούω) her husband Abraham (3:5–6). Thus, the two terms seem to be used synonymously. Third, it is not suggested that the one who is subject to another is qualitatively inferior, as was discussed above.

True, in Roman times Hellenistic Judaism considered women inferior to men and because of this believed that women should be submissive to their husbands.[1] This view of women was a regression from that of the OT where a woman, though secondary in position, was nonetheless influential and appreciated as the helpmeet of the husband.[2] In fact, although Hellenistic Judaism viewed women as inferior, both Philo and Josephus stated that women should not be mistreated or humiliated.[3] Philo, who wanted to syncretize Greek and OT thinking, most likely would have known the Peripatetics' views of the wife's role in the family. These views are expressed in the third century B.C. by one who wrote in Aristotle's name. He proposed that the wife was actually superior to the husband in certain activities in the home and that both shared equally in the raising of children,[4] and he gave a long treatise of the proper conduct of both in the relationship.[5] Another writing in Aristotle's name in the second century B.C. mentions that, though the wife is inferior to her husband, she is more equal to her husband than are children to parents or slaves to masters. She is portrayed as a partner much like citizens are fellow partners of the state.[6] But what was Paul's view? Was he a man of his times? Paul clearly considered husbands and wives to be partners as is evidenced by his teaching on equal conjugal rights (1 Cor 7:2–4), a concept which was unheard of in that day (in fact, the wife is cautioned against this idea by one of the Peripatetics![7]). This is evidence that Paul viewed the wives as equal to husbands qualitatively even though

1. Crouch, *The Origin and Intention of the Colossian Haustafel*, 108–9; Craig S. Keener, "Marriage," in *DNTB*, 688–89. However, White gives evidence of the improved status of women in the Hellenistic period (John L. White, "The Improved Status of Greek Women in the Hellenistic Period," *BR* 39 [1994]: 62–79).

2. Albrecht Oepke, "γυνή," *TDNT* 1 (1964): 781–82. For studies and bibliographies on Jewish women and their roles, see Phyllis A. Bird, "Women in the Ancient Mediterranean World: Ancient Israel," *BR* 39 (1994): 31–45; Tal Ilan, *Jewish Women in Greco-Roman Palestine: An Inquiry into Image and Status*, trans. Jonathan Price, Texte und Studien zum Antiken Judentum, ed. Martin Hengel and Peter Schäfer, vol. 44 (Tübingen: Mohr; Peabody, Mass.: Hendrickson, 1995).

3. Philo *Hypoth*. 7.3 §358; Josephus *C. Ap*. 2.24 §201.

4. Aristotle *Oeconomica* 1.3.4 §§1343b.24–1344a.8.

5. Ibid., 3 §§140–47.

6. Aristotle *Magna Moralia* 1.33.18 §1194b.23–28.

7. Aristotle *Oeconomica* 1.4.2 §1343a.13–14. For a brief survey of recent studies of women in NT times, see Carolyn Osiek, "Women in the Ancient Mediterranean World: State of the Question—New Testament," *BR* 39 (1994): 57–61.

subordinate with regard to the lines of authority.[1] The motivation and rationale are given next.

ὡς τῷ κυρίῳ, "as to the Lord." Who is the Lord in this phrase? Normally, if this had reference to husbands, the author would have used a plural dative (τοῖς κυρίοις) corresponding to the plural τοῖς . . . ἀνδράσιν, "to the husbands." Nevertheless, because of 1 Pet 3:6 where Sarah called Abraham "lord," Aquinas, among others, argues that a wife is to be subject to her husband "as a lord."[2] Sampley also suggests that this may refer to the husband because the author has switched from the plural to the singular [Eph 5:23] and continues in the singular until verse 24b.[3] However, this interpretation is untenable for five reasons. First, as mentioned above, one would expect grammatically a plural dative to have been used to refer to husbands. The switch to the singular does not begin until verse 23. Second, the context supports this as a reference to Christ as seen in the next two verses which explain why the wife should submit as to Christ. God has ordained a hierarchy where the husband is head over the wife as Christ is head over the church. This gives a proper motivation for the wife to be submissive. Third, the adverbial phrase ὡς τῷ κυρίῳ is used in two other places in the NT. It is used in 6:7 where slaves are to serve with goodwill as to the Lord and not to people. There, the masters are called οἱ κύριοι, "the lords" (6:5, 9), but the singular use of "lord" in this adverbial phrase cannot refer to a servant's master but to Christ. Furthermore, in 6:9 the word "lord" occurs in both the singular and plural, stating that the "lords" (masters) are to treat the slaves properly because the "Lord" of the slaves is also the "Lord" of the masters and there is no partiality with him. The only other place this phrase occurs is in Col 3:23 where servants are to work in singleness of heart, fearing the Lord (3:22), to work wholeheartedly as to the Lord (ὡς τῷ κυρίῳ) and not to men (3:23), and because they will receive a reward from the Lord (3:24). Here also the masters are called "lords" (3:22; 4:1), and they are to treat the slaves fairly because they have a κύριον ἐν οὐρανῷ, "Lord (Master) in heaven." Again, there is both the singular and plural use of "lord" with the singular use of "lord" in the adverbial phrase having reference to Christ. Since the adverbial phrase ὡς τῷ κυρίῳ in the other two instances (Eph 6:7; Col 3:23) refers to Christ and not to humans, it is reasonable to think in

1. Erdmann, "Der Brief an die Epheser. 44. Teil: Kapitel 5,21–24," 25–27, 31.

2. Aquinas, chap. 5, lec. 8, vv. 22–28a (217); Gaugler, 20; Mussner, *Christus, das All und die Kirche*, 148; Mußner, 156; Schweizer thinks it is "the return of the traditional Hellenistic idea of an all-embracing cosmic order. Even the wonderful and deep interpretation of married life in the light of Christ's love towards the church in Eph. v.22–33 could lead to the concept of a universal hierarchy in which women are subject to men as these to Christ (cf. already I Cor. xi.3)." See Schweizer, "Traditional Ethical Patterns in the Pauline and post-Pauline Letters," 205.

3. Sampley, *'And the Two Shall Become One Flesh,'* 111–12, 122.

the present text it also refers to Christ and not to husbands. Fourth, this adverbial phrase is similar to that in Eph 6:5 where slaves are to be obedient to their "lords" with fear and trembling in singleness of heart ὡς τῷ Χριστῷ, "as to Christ."[1] Fifth, although the phrase is not identical (ὡς ἀνῆκεν ἐν κυρίῳ, "as is fitting in the Lord") in the parallel passage in Col 3:18, the similarity suggests that this has reference to Christ and not the husband.

The adverbial conjunction ὡς, "as," also requires examination. The various interpretations of it have been summarized well by Barth and Miletic[2] in the following four views. (1) It could have a causal force, namely, wives submit to your husbands because, as Col 3:18 states, "it is fitting in the Lord" or, as in Eph 5:21, because "you fear Christ." The problem with this view is its overdependence on Col 3:18 which does not use the same exact phrase. Furthermore, it would not likely be causal when immediately following this phrase there is a causal clause introduced by ὅτι, "because."[3] (2) It could have a comparative force, namely, wives submit to your husbands to the same degree as you do to the Lord. This is supported in Eph 5:24 where the wife is to submit to her husband "in everything." View (1) looked at motivation for submission while view (2) accentuates the act of subordination. The problem with view (2) is that the NT never calls for submission to another human being to the same degree as to the Lord. (3) It could be a combination of motivation and comparison,[4] rendered "as" or "just as." Barth states, "Subordination to Christ and subordination to the husband are then as related and inseparable as the love of God and the love of man or, perhaps, as the love of the neighbor and the love of self." He compares this with those who visit, feed, and cloth the poor and are told by Jesus, "As you did it to one of the least of these my brethren, you did it to me" (Matt 25:40).[5] As the wife submits to the husband she also submits to Christ. This combination of views (1) and (2) eliminates the exclusive problems of each view and yet keeps the elements of both views, creating a balance. It entails both motivation by fear of Christ and comparison with submission to Christ. (4) The wife's submission is seen as supremely or exclusively to Christ and her submission to her husband is the mere occasion of or training ground for her higher allegiance to Christ. Barth writes, "In 6:6–7 Paul appears to recommend even this attitude to slaves, and in

1. Schnackenburg, 245–46.

2. Barth, 612; Miletic, *"One Flesh": Eph. 5.22–24, 5.31*, 34–38.

3. Miletic, *"One Flesh": Eph. 5.22–24, 5.31*, 35.

4. Chrysostom *Eph* 5:22 (*PG* 62:136); Calvin, 205; Alford, 3:136; Eadie, 409; Ellicott, 127–28; Meyer, 290; Abbott, 166; Salmond, 366; Robinson, 123–24; Masson, 211 n. 1; Schlier, 253; Gaugler, 207–8; Gnilka, 275–76; Schnackenburg, 246; Bruce, 384; Lincoln, 368; Miletic, *"One Flesh": Eph. 5.22–24, 5.31*, 35–38; cf. also Muraoka, "The use of ΩΣ in the Greek Bible," 59.

5. Barth, 612.

Col 3:23 it is explicitly stated that slaves shall do their work 'as for the Lord, and not for men.'"[1] The problem with this view is that the text specifically states that wives are to submit to their husbands as well as to Christ, so it cannot refer exclusively to Christ. Submission to the husband becomes merely a by-product of her submission to the Lord. The main point of the text is submission to her husband and not the other way around. Furthermore, in regards to the slaves the command is built on the negative, that is, to carry out obedience not for people but as for Christ. Also in both Col 3:23 and Eph 6:6–7 Paul states how a slave carries out the orders of the master, not as people-pleasers but in singleness of heart, and this is to be done as to Christ or in the fear of the Lord. It seems that which is done in singleness of heart is not one and the same "as to Christ" or "fearing the Lord." In conclusion, view (3) seems most likely—as she submits to her husband she also submits to her Lord. Miletic uses the helpful mathematical analogy of a set, the wife's relationship to her Lord, and a subset, her relationship to her husband. She is subordinate in both sets. He writes, "Yet in her one act of subordination to her husband she acts as one who is subordinate to the Lord and therefore is related to the Lord in a manner correlative to her married status. Only when the injunction is viewed from the larger set can definition and perspective be given to it in the subset."[2]

(b) Reason: Husband Is Head (5:23)

Text: 5:23. ὅτι ἀνήρ ἐστιν κεφαλὴ τῆς γυναικὸς ὡς καὶ ὁ Χριστὸς κεφαλὴ τῆς ἐκκλησίας, αὐτὸς σωτὴρ τοῦ σώματος.

Translation: 5:23. "because the husband is the head of the wife as also Christ is the head of the church, he himself is the savior of the body."

Commentary: 5:23. ὅτι ἀνήρ ἐστιν κεφαλὴ[3] τῆς γυναικὸς ὡς καὶ ὁ Χριστὸς κεφαλὴ τῆς ἐκκλησίας, "because the husband is the head of the wife as also Christ is the head of the church." The causal conjunction ὅτι introduces the reason why the wife is to submit to her husband, that is, because he is the head of the wife. With the use of the comparative conjunction ὡς, "as,"[4] and the adjunctive conjunction καί, "also," Paul elaborates by saying that this headship of the husband over the wife is like Christ's headship over the church. In light of

1. Ibid.

2. Miletic, *"One Flesh": Eph. 5.22–24, 5.31*, 37. Cf. also Gielen, *Tradition und Theologie neutestamentlicher Haustafelethik*, 241–45.

3. The words ἐστιν κεφαλή are transposed in B 0278 104 365 1175 *pc* lat Tertullian, which is not sufficient enough evidence to stand.

4. The conjunction ὡς should not be understood causally (so Barth, 613) but comparatively as it consistently functions in the present context (Best, 535). Furthermore, the causal notion is already expressed by ὅτι at the beginning of the verse.

this, it is very important to understand the meaning of the headship of Christ in relationship to the church in order to more clearly understand the implications of the husband as head of the wife.

In recent times much ink has been spilled over the concept of head. As discussed at 1:22 and 4:15 some think "head" means "ruler" or "authority"[1] while others think it refers to "source."[2] However, it is better to view κεφαλή not as inherently denoting either authority or source, but rather "preeminence" or "prominence" with the context emphasizing either authority or source.[3] Certainly, the context of 1:22 portrays Christ as the head in the sense of "ruler" or "authority over" because it stipulates that everything is subjected under his feet, whereas the context of 4:15–16 emphasizes Christ as the "source" from which believers grow and from whom the whole body is being fitted and held together. In the present context Christ's headship is like that of 1:22 where he is the "ruler" or has "authority over" the church.[4] This is substantiated in 5:24 where the wife's subjection to her husband is

1. So Grudem, "Does κεφαλή ('head') Mean 'Source' or 'Authority Over' in Greek Literature?" 38–59; also printed in Knight, *The Role Relationship of Men and Women: New Testament Teaching*, 49–80; updated in Piper and Grudem, *Recovering Biblical Manhood and Womanhood*, 425–68, 534–41; Grudem, "The Meaning of Κεφαλή ('Head'): A Response to Recent Studies," 3–72; idem, "The Meaning of κεφαλή ('Head'): An Evaluation of New Evidence, Real and Alleged," 25–65; Fitzmyer, "Another Look at ΚΕΦΑΛΗ in 1 Corinthians 11.3," 503–11; cf. also Schlier, *TDNT* 3 (1965): 673–81; Brown and Munzer, *NIDNTT* 2 (1976); 156–63; BAGD 430; BDAG 542; David M. Park, "The Structure of Authority in Marriage: An Evaluation of *Hupotasso* and *Kephale* in Eph 5:21–33," *EvQ* 59 (April 1987): 120; Los Santos, *La novedad de la metáfora κεφαλή-σῶμα*, 300–302.

2. As does Bedale, "The Meaning of κεφαλή in the Pauline Epistles," 211–15; cf. also idem, "The Theology of the Church," 68–72. Others who have argued for source are Berkley and Alvera Mickelsen, "The 'Head' of the Epistles," 20–23 [264–67]; idem, "What Does *Kephalē* Mean in the New Testament?" 97–110; Payne, "Response: What Does *Kephalē* Mean in the New Testament?" 118–32; Kroeger, "Appendix III: The Classical Concept of *Head* as 'Source'," 267–83; Fee, *The First Epistle to the Corinthians*, 502–3 n. 42; Bilezikian, *Beyond Sex Roles*, 215–52; Kroeger, "Head," 375–76.

3. Cervin, "Does Κεφαλή Mean 'Source' or 'Authority over' in Greek Literature? A Rebuttal," 85–112; idem, "ΠΕΡΙ ΤΟΥ ΚΕΦΑΛΗ: A Rejoinder," 1–39; Perriman, "The Head of a Woman: The Meaning of κεφαλή in I Cor. 11:3," 602–22. Cf. Perriman, *Speaking of Women*, 49–60. Perriman suggests that the headship of man and the subordination of the woman is not a theological directive but since they are the social realities of the first century, Paul is showing how these realities "must somehow be reconciled with the inner reality of Christian fellowship and the headship of Christ over his church" (ibid., 59). This is not convincing in the light of the present context for Paul is giving theological directives when he enjoins the wives to submit to their husbands and the husbands to love their wives.

4. Seim, "A Superior Minority? The Problem of Men's Headship in Ephesians 5," 178–81; cf. Fitzmyer, "Another Look at ΚΕΦΑΛΗ in 1 Corinthians 11.3," 52–59. Best (535) rightly observes: "in the light of the contemporary patriarchal attitude to marriage, had AE [author of Ephesians] wished to suggest the husband was the source of the wife, he would have needed to made [*sic*] this clearer."

compared with church's subjection to Christ. Likewise, the husband is not the "source" of the wife, but the "head" over his wife. The context supports this supposition on two grounds. First, the preceding and succeeding verses state that the wife is to subject herself to her husband. Second, in the context of the household code the issue is not source but the lines of authority.

As mentioned in 1:23, some suggest that the "head" and "body" in Ephesians and Colossians are two distinct metaphors which, though related to each other, should not be combined as one metaphor. Otherwise in the present context one could postulate that the church without Christ lacks the head and likewise wives apart from their husbands are incomplete persons.[1] However, whenever "head" is mentioned in Ephesians (1:22; 4:15; 5:23) and Colossians (1:18; 2:10, 19), the "body" is mentioned in the same context, indicating that the two metaphors are combined.[2] It is the same in the present context with regards to marriage. Metaphorically, the husband and wife have become one flesh.[3]

Again it needs to be restated that the headship of the husband does not connote any sense of qualitative superiority to the wife. In social psychology the husband's rule over the wife is called "positional power," a power by virtue of one's position. In God's administration the role of the husband's headship is positional power.[4] His headship and the wife's submission are for the sake of harmony.

It is important to note that the concept of the wife's submission to her husband as well as the fact of the husband's authority over the wife would have had a direct impact on the structure of the Roman family in Paul's day. Then, the father had absolute control over all his family, called *patria potestas*.[5] He had the power of life and death

1. Ridderbos, *Paul*, 379–81; Yorke, *The Church as the Body of Christ in the Pauline Corpus*, 104–11; McVay, "Head, Christ as," 378.

2. Perriman, "'His body, which is the church. . . .' Coming to Terms with Metaphor," 136; Dawes, *The Body in Question*, 119–20; cf. Caird, 49, 78.

3. The complex metaphorical language used in Eph 5:21–33 is ably discussed by Annegret Meyer, "Biblische Metaphorik—gesellschaftlicher Diskurs: Rezeptionsästhetische Betrachtung über die Wirkung von Metaphern am Beispiel Eph 5,21–33," *TGl* 90, no. 4 (2000): 645–65.

4. A. Duane Litfin, "A Biblical View of the Marital Roles: Seeking a Balance," *BSac* 133 (October–December 1976): 335–36. Litfin lists the other four social powers that one human being has over another: information power, referent power (recipient desires to be like the one who leads), coercive-reward power, and expert power.

5. Crook, "Patria Potestas," 113–22; Saller, "*Patria potestas* and the Stereotype of the Roman Family," 7–22; cf. also Emiel Eyben, "Fathers and Sons," in *Marriage, Divorce, and Children in Ancient Rome*, ed. Beryl Rawson (Oxford: Clarendon, 1991), 114–16; Lacey, "*Patria Potestas*," 121–44; Gielen, *Tradition und Theologie neutestamentlicher Haustafelethik*, 146–58; Nicholas and Treggiari, "Patria Potestas," 1122–23; Lassen, "The Roman Family: Ideal and Metaphor," 104–6; Gardner, *Family and* Familia *in Roman Law and Life*, 1–4, 117–26, 270–72.

over his children. Although this authority was used primarily with regard to newborns, he could legally put to death any of his offspring for serious transgressions. This control over his children continued even after they married. However, the nature of the father's control of the daughter after she married differed according to the period in Roman history. Much has been written on marriage in the Roman family.[1] In brief, when a woman married in the early Roman Republic it involved *manus*, the husband's authority over his wife much like *patria postestas*. However, in the later Republic and in the early Roman Empire (Paul's day) there was a trend toward the bride entering *sine manus*, that is, the father, not the husband, had authority over her as long as he lived.[2] Therefore, she was independent from and not legally subject to her husband, she could seek divorce from him in conjunction with her father, and, in fact, the father could even initiate a divorce.[3] Thus, Paul's injunction of a wife's submission to the husband as the head of the family confronts the family structure of that day. Paul states that the husband, not the father, has the authority over the wife, and consequently, he is the head of the new family (cf. v. 31 which quotes Gen 2:24).

αὐτὸς[4] **σωτὴρ τοῦ σώματος,** "he himself is the savior of the body." Most commentators understand that this clause refers solely to

1. Percy Ellwood Corbett, *The Roman Law of Marriage* (Oxford: Clarendon, 1930); Jane F. Gardner, *Women in Roman Law & Society* (London: Croom Helm, 1986), 31–80; cf. also Beryl Rawson, "The Roman Family," in *The Family in Ancient Rome: New Perspectives*, ed. Beryl Rawson (Ithaca, N.Y.: Cornell University Press, 1986), 1–57; Susan Treggiari, *Roman Marriage: Iusti Coniuges from the Time of Cicero to the Time of Ulpian* (Oxford: Clarendon, 1991); Suzanne Dixon, *The Roman Family*, Ancient Society and History (Baltimore: Johns Hopkins University Press, 1992), 61–97; Richard P. Saller, "*Pater Familias, Mater Familias*, and the Gendered Semantics of the Roman Household," *Classical Philology* 94 (April 1999): 182–97.

2. John K. Evans, *War, Women and Children in Ancient Rome* (London: Routledge, 1991), 7–49; Rawson, "The Roman Family," 19–20; Susan Treggiari, "Divorce Roman Style: How Easy and How Frequent Was It?" in *Marriage, Divorce, and Children in Ancient Rome*, ed. Beryl Rawson (Oxford: Clarendon, 1991), 31–33; Treggiari, *Roman Marriage*, 28–36, 441–46, 459–61.

3. Gardner, *Women in Roman Law & Society*, 81–95; Richard Saller, "Slavery and the Roman Family," in *Classical Slavery*, ed. M. I. Finley (London: Frank Cass, 1987), 76–77; Mireille Corbier, "Divorce and Adoption as Roman Familial Strategies (Le Divorce et l'adoption 'en plus')," in *Marriage, Divorce, and Children in Ancient Rome*, ed. Beryl Rawson (Oxford: Clarendon, 1991), 58.

4. The present reading is found in $\mathfrak{P}^{46}$ ℵ* A B D* F G I^{vid} 048 33 1175 1739 1881 *pc* lat Clement. Another reading, καὶ αὐτός ἐστιν is found in $ℵ^2$ D^1 Ψ 0278 $\mathfrak{M}$ ($it^{a, b, m}$ vg^{mss}) vg^{ms} syr. The first reading has the support of much better external evidence, in date and character, geographical distribution of the Alexandrian and Western text-types, and genealogical relationship within the text-types. Internally, one can see why the scribes would have inserted the words of the second reading so as to make it clear to the reader that this clause refers to Christ and not to the husband. Hence, both externally and internally the first reading is superior.

Christ,[1] although there are some who think it has reference both to Christ and to the husband (ἀνήρ) in the first part of the verse,[2] making the husband the savior of his wife also. This is unlikely for the following reasons. First, the personal pronoun αὐτός in apposition to ὁ Χριστός is emphatic by its presence and its position.[3] It must refer only to that which immediately precedes (ὁ Χριστός) and cannot also refer to the husband (ἀνήρ) in the preceding clause.[4] This personal pronoun emphasizes Christ's exclusive work as the savior of the body, the church. The translations bring this out in various ways: "and he is the saviour of the body" (AV); "*being* himself the saviour of the body" (RV, ASV); "the body, and is himself its Savior" (RSV); "He Himself *being* the Savior of the body" (NASB); "Christ is, indeed, the Saviour of the body" (NEB); "and Christ is himself the Saviour of the church, his body" (TEV); "as Christ is the head of the Church and saves the whole body" (JB, NJB); "his body, of which he is the Savior" (NIV); and "the body of which he is the Savior" (NRSV). We translate it "he himself is the savior of the body" to emphasize that the pronoun refers to Christ. Second, nowhere in the context is the wife viewed as the husband's body in the same way as the church is Christ's body. True, the husband and the wife are one flesh (5:31) and husbands are to love their own wives as their own bodies (5:28). However, "as their own bodies" refers to husbands' bodies and not the wives, otherwise the exhortation would be nonsensical because it would be saying that the husbands are to love their own wives as their own wives (= bodies). Hence, since the wife is not the husband's body, this clause must refer to Christ alone. Third, as some suggest, the spouse's salvation mentioned in 1 Cor 7:16 is not parallel to the present context. In that context the believing spouse is to be an instrument in the unbelieving spouse's salvation, whereas in the present context both spouses are assumed to be believers.[5] Furthermore, in 1 Cor 7:16 the spouse is not the savior who gives salvation to the other spouse but is the instrument who leads the other spouse to the salvation which Christ offers. Fourth, the term "savior" is used twenty-three times in the NT outside the present con-

1. Alford, 3:136; Eadie, 410–11; Ellicott, 128; Meyer, 290–93; Abbott, 166; Salmond, 366; Westcott, 84; Dibelius-Greeven, 93; Masson, 211; Schlier, 254–55; Gaugler, 208; Gnilka, 277–78; Barth, 615–17; Schnackenburg, 247; Lincoln, 370; Muddiman, 262–63.

2. Oecumenius *Eph* 5:22–24 (*PG* 118:1241); Theophylact *Eph* 5:23 (*PG* 124:1113); Robinson, 124, 205; Scott, 238; Hendriksen, 248–49; Foulkes, 163; Bruce, 385; MacDonald, 327; Sampley, *'And the Two Shall Become One Flesh,'* 124–25; Werner Foerster, "σωτήρ," *TDNT* 7 (1971): 1016; Efren Rivera, "Wives, Be Subject to Your Husbands," *Philippiniana Sacra* 3 (May–August 1968): 239–40; Wall, "Wifely Submission in the Context of Ephesians," 281–82; implied by Chrysostom *Eph* 5:24 (*PG* 62:136); Martin, "Ephesians," in *The Broadman Bible Commentary*, 168; cf. Pierre Benoit, "L'horizon paulinien de l'Épître aux Ephésiens," *RB* 46 (Octobre 1937): 516.

3. Robertson, *Grammar*, 399, 416; Winer, *Grammar*, 665.

4. Abbott, 166.

5. Cf. Lincoln, 370.

text and always has reference to Jesus (Luke 2:11; John 4:42; Acts 5:31; 13:23; Phil 3:20; 2 Tim 1:10; Titus 1:4; 2:13; 3:6; 2 Pet 1:1, 11; 2:20; 3:2, 18; 1 John 4:14) or God (Luke 1:47; 1 Tim 1:1; 2:3; 4:10; Titus 1:3; 2:10; 3:4; Jude 25) and never to human beings. Fifth, if these words applied to the husband, it would be difficult to know what is intended. A husband's role is not to save or rescue from doom as does Christ. It could imply that he is the wife's protector, but this could not go as far as to imply protection from doom.[1] Sixth, some propose that the apocryphal story of Tobias' marriage to his cousin Sarah to save her (Tob 6:18) is a parallel to the husband as savior of his wife. This suggestion is not valid because it was not Tobias who saved her but incense and their prayer that saved both of them from the demon.[2] Therefore, in this context it seems best to assert that "savior" has reference only to Christ. Sampley summarizes it well when he says, "Christ, unlike the husband, is the savior of his own body."[3]

What, then, did this unique phrase mean for the believers in Ephesus? In fact, it is an ancillary comment[4] to reinforce Christ as the head, a reminder perhaps of his ultimate authority, the one who rescued the church from eternal separation from God (Eph 2:1–10, 12–19). Although nowhere else in the NT is Christ called the "savior of the body," it fits with this epistle, namely, Christ's redemption of individual sinners resulting in reconciliation to God and also to each other within the body of believers. Some suggest "savior of the body" reflects the concept of the Gnostic redeemer myth where the first man (Urmensch) fell, saved himself, and became both the redeemer/savior and head of the entire universe which is his body.[5] However, this is foreign to this context.[6] As already discussed at 1:23, the church, not the entire universe, is the body of Christ. Simply put, for Ephesian believers, the phrase "savior of the body" alludes to the body of Christ who was delivered by Christ from eternal doom. As to its application to the husband-wife relationship, the most that can be said is that the husband is the protector of the wife much in the same manner as described in verses 29–30. He should protect her in times of danger, both in a physical or in a spiritual sense. For example, under Mosaic law the husband could protect his wife from carrying out a rash vow (Num 30:6–14) and thus protect her reputation. Adam, as a husband,

1. Bruce, 385.

2. Cf. Sampley, *'And the Two Shall Become One Flesh,'* 59–60; Bruce, 385; Lincoln, 370.

3. Sampley, *'And the Two Shall Become One Flesh,'* 125; *contra* Otto Perels, "Kirche und Welt nach dem Epheser-und Kolosserbrief," *TLZ* 76 (Juli 1951): 395.

4. *Contra* Miletic (*"One Flesh": Eph. 5.22–24, 5.31*, 43, cf. 43–45) who thinks that 5:23c "is both the structural core and theological center of the address to the wives."

5. Schlier, 254–55, 264–76; Fischer, *Tendenz und Absicht des Epheserbriefes*, 181–200; more bibliography in comment on 1:23.

6. Lincoln, 371; Mußner, 157; MacDonald, 327.

failed in this regard in that he did not protect Eve from the serpent's lie. The husband, then, does not save the wife from eternal doom as Christ does the church but rather acts as her protector in a temporal sense.

Therefore, Christ, the savior of the body, is also the head of the church. The head in this context has the idea of "ruler" or "authority over," as seen in the present and the preceding verses. In light of this, the husband's position of authority over the wife must encompass a protective quality, which is exemplified in Christ who is "the savior of the body."

(c) Illustration: Church's Submission (5:24a)

Text: 5:24a. ἀλλὰ ὡς ἡ ἐκκλησία ὑποτάσσεται τῷ Χριστῷ,

Translation: 5:24a. "But as the church submits to Christ,"

Commentary: 5:24a. ἀλλὰ ὡς[1] ἡ ἐκκλησία ὑποτάσσεται τῷ Χριστῷ, "But as the church submits to Christ." This clause begins with the adversative conjunction ἀλλά. The variations in English translations of this conjunction indicate a problem. It is translated "therefore" (AV), "but" (RV, ASV, NASB, NEB), "and" (TEV, JB, NJB), "now" (NIV), and left untranslated (RSV, NRSV). The disparity is due to a difference of understanding in how the conjunction relates to the previous clause. Some see the conjunction as resumptive of the clause "as also Christ is the head of the church" (v. 23), with the possible translation of "consequently."[2] Yet the main thought has not been interrupted and it is more likely Paul would have used the conjunction οὖν if that were his intention. Eadie thinks that ἀλλά is an antithetic reference that expects an implied negative answer, that is, "do not disallow the marital headship, for it is a Divine institution—ἀλλά—but as the church is subject to Christ."[3] However, there is no negative answer expected here. Most think that it is a strong contrast to the immediately preceding clause where Christ is described distinctively as the savior of the body, and could be rendered, "but notwithstanding this difference (or "nevertheless") as the church submits to Christ. . . ."[4]

1. The reading ὡς is omitted by B Ψ *pc* it[b] Ambrosiaster. Its omission is based on insufficient evidence.

2. Robinson, 124, 205; Miletic, *"One Flesh": Eph. 5.22–24, 5.31*, 102–3 n. 6; Gaugler, 208; Gnilka, 278; Bruce, 385–86; Sampley, *'And the Two Shall Become One Flesh,'* 125–26; Rivera, "Wives, Be Subject to Your Husbands," 241–42; cf. BAGD 38–39; BDAG 45.

3. Eadie, 413.

4. Cf. Calvin, 205; Alford, 3:136; Ellicott, 128–29; Meyer, 291–93; Abbott, 166–67; Salmond, 366–67; Westcott, 84; Dibelius-Greeven, 93; Masson, 211; Schlier, 254; Barth, 619; Schnackenburg, 247; Lincoln, 372; Winer, *Grammar*, 565; Best, *One Body in Christ*, 173–74; Henri Maillet, "Alla . . . Plén . . . Métaphore et pédagogie de la soumission dans les rapports conjuaux, familiaux, sociaux et autres selon Éphésiens 5/21–6/9," *ETR* 55, no. 4 (1980): 566–67, 570.

The comparative conjunction ὡς, "as," begins the comparison of the submission of the church to Christ with the submission of the wife to the husband. The verb ὑποτάσσεται is the present middle or passive indicative of ὑποτάσσω, meaning "to be subject, subordinate." As previously discussed (5:21, 22) it is best seen as a middle where the subject acts as a free agent. The church subjects itself or is submissive to Christ, its head. This is explained in 1:22–23 where God gives Christ to the church as head, and it is he who fills the church with the fullness of God's power and attributes. The church benefits from the headship of Christ and so also should the wife's submission enhance her well-being.

(d) Application: Wives' Submission (5:24b)

Text: 5:24b. οὕτως καὶ αἱ γυναῖκες τοῖς ἀνδράσιν ἐν παντί.

Translation: 5:24b. "so also wives should submit to their husbands in everything."

Commentary: 5:24b. οὕτως καὶ αἱ γυναῖκες τοῖς ἀνδράσιν ἐν παντί, "so also wives should submit to their husbands in everything." This is the application to the first half of the verse. It is introduced by the adverbial conjunction οὕτως, "so," followed by an adjunctive conjunction καί, "also." The "wives" are the subject and the present middle/passive imperative ὑποτασσέσθωσαν needs to be supplied.[1]

The real problem comes with the last two words of the verse, namely, ἐν παντί, "in everything." A similar expression (κατὰ πάντα) is used for children's obedience to their parents (Col 3:20) and slaves to their masters (Col 3:22; ἐν πᾶσιν, Titus 3:9). It is difficult to know the precise meaning of this. It certainly would not mean that a wife should submit to her husband in anything that is contrary to the commands of God, for one needs to obey God more than humans (Acts 5:29).[2] In other words, the wife is not to submit to her husband in anything sinful,[3] including abuse.[4] Having said this, most likely it refers to the full submission of wives to their husbands[5] as the church is

1. Robertson, *Grammar*, 394.

2. Barth, 621.

3. Rivera, "Wives, Be Subject to Your Husbands," 242.

4. Feminists have rightly made a point about abuse, see Susan Brooks Thistlethwaite, "Every Two Minutes: Battered Women and Feminist Interpretation," in *Feminist Interpretation of the Bible*, ed. Letty M. Russell (Oxford: Basil Blackwell, 1985), 104–6; idem, "Epheser 5,21–33: Mißbrauch führt zu Mißhandlung [trans. Hilgegard Schneck]," in *Feministisch gelesen: 32 ausgewählte Bibeltexte für Gruppen, Gemeinden und Gottesdienste*, ed. Eva Renate Schmidt, Mieke Korenhof, and Reate Jost, vol. 1 (Stuttgart: Kreuz, 1988), 253–59.

5. Scholer thinks that wives' submission "in everything" must be seen in the first-century context where wives were perceived as inferior, uneducated, and very young and he argues that this would not apply today (David M. Scholer, "Feminist Hermeneutics and Evangelical Biblical Interpretation," *JETS* 30 [December 1987]: 416–17). But

to submit to Christ. The impact of these words must not be minimized, for that would detract from the first part of the verse. In essence, the church is to submit to Christ in everything. As the church benefits from submission to Christ so also ought wives benefit from their submission to their husbands. In conclusion, there are two words of caution. First, there is no indication that a wife's submission is to be based on the degree to which her husband demonstrates his love. In fact, it is very likely that some husbands did not respond to the gospel and see no need to be loving, yet the Christian wife is responsible before the Lord to submit to her husband whether or not he is a believer.[1] Second, her submission is to be of her own accord in obedience to the Lord (5:22),[2] not by the demand of her husband. As will be demonstrated next, the demands on husbands in the next verses are clearly as great, if not greater, than the injunction to wives.[3]

(2) Responsibility of Husbands' Love (5:25–32)

Having established the responsibility of wives to husbands, Paul turns to the responsibility of husbands to wives. To address the duty of husbands in Col 3:19 Paul uses only ten words; in 1 Pet 3:7 Peter uses twenty-five words; in the present context (Eph 5:25–31) Paul uses 116 words (125 words if the long reading of v. 30 is accepted) as compared with the forty-one words he uses in his enjoinder to wives. In the present text Paul continues to use the analogy of Christ and the church as he instructs husbands to love their wives as Christ sacrificially loved the church. The amount of space given to the subject and the analogy of Christ's love signifies the importance of husbands' responsibility to their wives. Whereas verses 22–24 state the measure of the wives' submission, verses 25–32 give the measure of the husbands' love. Fulfilling this responsiblity will not only enrich their wives but

---

how does Scholer know that the reason for the wives' submission "in everything" is due to first-century perception of women? There is nothing in the text to indicate this. This is selective application. Would Paul's injunction be applicable in parts of the world today where wives are considered inferior, uneducated, and very young? Also, can one infer that husbands were instructed to love their wives because in the first century wives were inferior, uneducated, and very young age and thus argue that the husbands' love is not required in today's world?

1. Los Santo seems to imply that although the wife is to be submissive to her husband as a duty before the Lord, she is to be submissive to a Christian husband who will love her as Christ loves the church (Los Santos, *La novedad de la metáfora κεφαλή-σῶμα*, 294–99). Although the letter is addressed to believers, the wife is to be submissive to her husband whether or not he is loving or whether or not he is a believer.

2. Kähler, *Die Frau in den paulinischen Briefen*, 101–3; Gielen, *Tradition und Theologie neutestamentlicher Haustafelethik*, 241–45.

3. Seim ("A Superior Minority? The Problem of Men's Headship in Ephesians 5," 166, 177–81) argues that the emphasis in the Ephesian household code is not on the submission of the wives but on the husband's ruling role in marriage.

will also bring harmony to the marriages and thus to the believing community.

(a) Imperative: Love Wives (5:25a)

Text: 5:25a. Οἱ ἄνδρες, ἀγαπᾶτε τὰς γυναῖκας [ἑαυτῶν],

Translation: 5:25a. "Husbands, love your wives,"

Commentary: 5:25a. Οἱ ἄνδρες, ἀγαπᾶτε τὰς γυναῖκας [ἑαυτῶν[1]], "Husbands, love your wives." Beginning a new group by use of the article to distinguish it from the other groups is not uncommon.[2] The imperative is clearly stated. Husbands are called to love their wives. The term ἀγαπάω, "to love," is a key word in this section being used six times (5:25*bis*, 28*ter*, 33). It refers to love irrespective of merit, even to the undeserving (see discussion of the word in 1:4). The present imperative reinforces the idea that a husband's love for his wife is to be an ongoing process. Thus in this context husbands are to love their wives even when they may seem undeserving and unloving, in other words, unconditionally. Its intent is to seek the highest good in the one loved. This is similar to the instruction for the wife. Her submission is not dependent on her husband's response; likewise, a husband's love is not dependent on his wife's response. Neither are governed by the vagaries of emotion, rather by an act of the will. This is not to say that love is an act of the will entirely devoid of any emotions, but rather if based entirely on emotions the husband's love would be based only on a good response. This concept is in agreement with the rest of Scripture as in the command to love one's neighbor (Lev 19:18; Matt 5:43; 19:19) where volitional love is expected regardless of response. The reflexive pronoun ἑαυτῶν functions as a possessive pronoun, indicating that husbands are to love their own wives

1. There are three readings. The first reading omits any pronoun after γυναῖκας as found in א A B 048 33 81 1241^{s} *pc* vgst Clement^{pt} (NA^{27}, UBS^{4}). The second reading adds the personal pronoun ὑμῶν found in F G it vg$^{cl.\ ww}$ syr Theodoret^{1}. The third reading adds the reflexive pronoun ἑαυτῶν found in D Ψ 0278 𝔐 (^{s} P 629 1739 1881 2464 *pc*) Clement^{pt} Chrysostom Theodoret^{2} Oecumenius Theophylact. The first reading has strong attestation in the Alexandrian text but in none of the other text-types. The second reading has only F and G of the Western text-type and some suspect that the personal pronoun in Greek was a result of Latin influence. The third reading is represented in one Western (D), some Alexandrian, and the whole Byzantine tradition. It also has strong evidence from the church fathers. Internally, the first reading is the shortest and most difficult reading because one would naturally want a pronoun to follow, but it would be difficult to understand why either ὑμῶν or ἑαυτῶν would be dropped. The third reading is the easiest to explain because it would be similar to ἰδίοις in v. 22 and would make it clear that husbands are head over their own wives and not all wives. In conclusion, the third reading is preferred by external evidence and the first reading is preferred by internal evidence. It is probably best to include the reflexive pronoun in brackets [ἑαυτῶν] to indicate uncertainty. The meaning is not altered, regardless of the reading.

2. Robertson, *Grammar*, 757; Wallace, *Greek Grammar*, 229.

and not other women, thus reinforcing monogamy. Even if the reflexive pronoun is not accepted as genuine, the article τάς before γυναῖκας functions as a possessive pronoun and is to be translated as above, namely, "your wives."[1]

This exhortation to husbands to love their wives is unique. It is not found in the OT, rabbinic literature, or in the household codes of the Greco-Roman era. Although the hierarchical model of the home is maintained, it is ameliorated by this revolutionary exhortation that husbands are to love their wives as Christ loved the church.[2]

Finally, the fact that Paul restates this exhortation two more times signifies its importance (vv. 28, 33; cf. also Col 3:19). Likewise, the length of the exhortation emphasizes its unavoidable importance.[3]

(b) Illustration: Christ's Love (5:25b–27)

Text: 5:25b. καθὼς καὶ ὁ Χριστὸς ἠγάπησεν τὴν ἐκκλησίαν καὶ ἑαυτὸν παρέδωκεν ὑπὲρ αὐτῆς, **5:26.** ἵνα αὐτὴν ἁγιάσῃ καθαρίσας τῷ λουτρῷ τοῦ ὕδατος ἐν ῥήματι, **5:27.** ἵνα παραστήσῃ αὐτὸς ἑαυτῷ ἔνδοξον τὴν ἐκκλησίαν, μὴ ἔχουσαν σπίλον ἢ ῥυτίδα ἤ τι τῶν τοιούτων, ἀλλ᾽ ἵνα ᾖ ἁγία καὶ ἄμωμος.

Translation: 5:25b. "just as Christ also loved the church and gave himself for her, **5:26.** in order that he might sanctify her having cleansed her with the washing of the water in connection with the word, **5:27.** in order that he might present the church to himself, glorious, not having a blemish or wrinkle or any such thing, but in order that she might be holy and blameless."

Commentary: 5:25b. καθὼς καὶ ὁ Χριστὸς ἠγάπησεν τὴν ἐκκλησίαν, "just as Christ also loved the church." The adverbial conjunction καθώς serves as a comparison which denotes manner,[4] illustrating Christ's love. The conjunction καί is used adjunctively, supporting the idea that this is an illustration and is translated "just as Christ also." Paul's exhortation to husbands "to love" is illustrated by "love" in the person of Christ. This is similar to 5:2 where he exhorts all believers

1. Wallace, *Greek Grammar*, 216.

2. Elisabeth Schüssler Fiorenza, "Marriage and Discipleship," *TBT* 102 (April 1979): 2031, reprinted in idem, *In Memory of Her. A Feminist Theological Reconstruction of Christian Origins* (New York: Crossroad; London: SCM, 1983), 269–70; cf. also Ron Highfield, "Man and Woman in Christ: Theological Ethics after the Egalitarian Revolution," *ResQ* 43 (third quarter 2001): 140–42, 145–46.

3. Cf. Wessels, "Ephesians 5:21–33 'Wives, Be Subject to Your Husbands, Love Your Wives . . .'," 73–75.

4. Some think καθώς has both a comparative and causal sense (Romaniuk, *L'Amour du Père et du Fils dans la Sotériologie de Saint Paul*, 47; Schlier, 255; O'Brien, 419; Haug, "Kinder des Lichts," in *Kurze Auslegung des Epheserbriefes*, 154; Corriveau, *The Liturgy of Life*, 220); Martin Erdmann, "Der Brief an die Epheser. 45. Teil: Kapitel 5,25–27," *Fundamentum* 22, no. 3 (2001): 32. It seems unlikely that the causal idea is in view otherwise the adverbial conjunction ὡς would have the same function in v. 24, namely, the wives' submission is because of the church's submission to Christ.

to become imitators of God and walk in love, just as Christ also loved us and gave himself for us as an offering and sacrifice to God for a fragrant aroma. It should be noted that the analogy between husbands and Christ is not concerned with headship but love, that is, not "be heads over your wives" but "love your wives."[1]

The verb "to love" (ἀγαπάω) is the same as used in the exhortation to the husbands in the previous verse. This verb form has already been described in previous contexts as a love that is not selfish. Instead it is concerned with the highest good in the one loved. For example, in 2:4 it is God's action of love to take sinners and make them alive with Christ, raise them, and seat them together in the heavenlies in Christ Jesus. In the present context the specific object of Christ's love is the church. Interestingly, this is the only time the NT specifically mentions Christ's love for the church.[2] What is the evidence of his love for her? This is given next.

καὶ ἑαυτὸν παρέδωκεν ὑπὲρ αὐτῆς, "and gave himself for her." The supreme test of Christ's love is that he gave himself for the church (redemption). The structure is similar to 4:19 and more particularly 5:2. The aorist tense of this verb along with the previous verb points back to the particular action of the cross. The verb παρέδωκεν, meaning "to hand over, give over," indicates that he took his own initiative in handing himself over.[3] This is in agreement with Jesus' statement that he is the good shepherd and he will lay down his life for the sheep (John 10:11, 15, 17); also, there is no greater love than when one lays

1. Knight, "Husbands and Wives as Analogues of Christ and the Church," 171.

2. Schlier, 255; Steinmetz, *Protologische Heils-Zuversicht*, 91. Steinmetz deduces that since this is the singular mention of Christ's love of the church, it shows that the author of the epistle was unfamiliar with the proper expression of Christ's love for us. This kind of reasoning is unacceptable because in most contexts Paul was dealing with individuals, but here he is speaking about the body of believers and thus he states Christ's love for the believers collectively. It does not in any way demonstrate that the author must have been unacquainted with the correct saying, for in the near context of 5:2 he mentions that "Christ loved us." The Syriac versions specifically state that Christ loved "his" church (cf. Martin, "Quelques remarques sur le texte syriaque de l'Épître aux Éphésiens," 102). Käsemann thinks that the concept of Christ's love for the church is not Pauline and the author of Ephesians is addressing issues from a perspective of the early Catholic era with Christology becoming a function of ecclesiology (Ernst Käsemann, "The Theological Problem Presented by the Motif of the Body of Christ," in *Perspectives on Paul*, trans. Margaret Kohl, The New Testament Library, ed. Alan Richardson, C. F. D. Moule, C. F. Evans, Floyd V. Filson [London: SCM, 1971], 120–21). However, although ecclesiology is emphasized in Ephesians, it is not at the expense of Christology, for the church did not come into existence by itself but on the basis of what God has done in Christ (Arnold, *Ephesians: Power and Magic*, 163–64; Lincoln and Wedderburn, *The Theology of the Later Pauline Letters*, 138; Barrett, *Paul: An Introduction to His Thoughts*, 155–56).

3. Romaniuk thinks that the formula "Christ died (or suffered) for us" appearing from his earliest to his latest epistles (Gal 1:4; 2:20; Eph 5:2, 25; 1 Tim 2:6; Titus 2:14) was a result of Paul's independent reflection (he added "Christ loved us [church]") on

down his life for his friends (John 15:13). The reflexive pronoun further enhances his supreme love by indicating that he was not forced to die at the hand of human beings but that he laid down his own life for the church. This is in concord with John 10:18 where he specifically states that he will lay down his life of his own accord and that he had power to take it again. He did the Father's will but was not forced to do it.

The prepositional phrase ὑπὲρ αὐτῆς indicates the object for which Christ laid down his life, namely, the church.[1] The preposition with a genitive signifies that it was done "for the sake of, in [on] behalf of,"[2] showing interest in the object[3] and has been characterized as the particle of love.[4] Whereas in 5:2 Christ's death was characterized as on behalf of individual believers, here it is represented as on behalf of the church, the body of believers. His supreme sacrifice is the evidence of his love.

With this kind of sacrificial love as the model for the husbands to follow, the submission of the wives "can never mean slavish subjection. For the Church never feels her relation to Christ to be such."[5] Westcott states, "Christ loved the Church not because it was perfectly lovable, but in order to make it such."[6] Next, Paul demonstrates how this is accomplished.

5:26. ἵνα αὐτὴν ἁγιάσῃ καθαρίσας, "in order that he might sanctify her having cleansed her." Paul presents the purpose or goal of Christ's love for the church by the three ἵνα clauses: that he might sanctify her (v. 26); that he might present to himself a glorious church (v. 27a); and that she might be holy and without blame (v. 27b).

The conjunction ἵνα at the beginning of this verse marks the initial purpose of Christ's love for the church, namely, her sanctification. As an individual believer is redeemed and sanctified, so also is the church purchased by Christ's death and sanctified. The personal pronoun αὐτήν, immediately after the ἵνα, suggests the importance Christ places on the church. The verb ἁγιάσῃ is an aorist active subjunctive

---

the Servant Song of Isa 52:13–53:12 (Kazimierz Romaniuk, "L'origine des formules pauliniennes 'Le Christ s'est livré pour nous', 'Le Christ nous a aimés et s'est livré pour nous'," *NovT* 5 [January 1962]: 55–76); cf. also Perrin, "The Use of (παρα)διδόναι in Connection with the Passion of Jesus in the New Testament," 204–12.

1. Schnackenburg ("Christus, Geist und Gemeinde [Eph. 4:1–16]," 284–85) thinks that the church already existed at the time of Christ's death. There is no reason to hold to this because Paul is not giving a chronology of events but the theological significance of his death.

2. BAGD 838; BDAG 1030–31.

3. HS §259m.

4. Corriveau, *The Liturgy of Life*, 200.

5. J. N. Sevenster, *Paul and Seneca*, NovTSup, ed. W. C. van Unnik et al., vol. 4 (Leiden: Brill, 1961), 199.

6. Westcott, 84.

of ἁγιάζω. The substantive and adjective (ἅγιος), discussed at 1:1, is used to describe God's character as unique or wholly other, but it also can refer to things, places, and persons who are not inherently holy but are set aside or consecrated to God or to God's service. The verb ἁγιάζω is rare in extrabiblical sources. In the LXX it occurs 194 times, in the canonical books it appears 168 times and translates eight Hebrew words, 131 of which translates the verb קָדַשׁ, meaning "to be set apart, consecrated" (Exod 19:23; 29:21; 1 Chr 23:13; Neh 3:1*bis*; Isa 13:3; Jer 1:5; Ezek 48:11).[1] In the NT it is used twenty-eight times, nine times in Paul and only here in Ephesians. It continues to express the idea of being set aside or consecrated to God or God's service. For example, things are set aside "to make them suitable for ritual purposes" (Matt 23:17, 19; 1 Tim 4:5);[2] Jesus prays for his disciples to be set aside to God's truth (John 17:17, 19); and people who are redeemed are considered sanctified or set apart to God (Acts 20:32; 26:18; 1 Cor 1:2; 6:11; 1 Thess 5:23; Heb 2:11; 10:10, 14; 13:12). Only the Lord's Prayer differs, where the Father's name is to be hallowed or considered holy (Matt 6:9; Luke 11:2).[3] It is proposed that in some rabbinic literature קָדַשׁ can mean "to separate to oneself as a wife." Thus, in the present context it would mean that Christ gave himself in order to betroth her, the church, for himself.[4] However, it is unlikely that Paul had this special meaning of the term in mind.[5] Rather, it is better to view ἁγιάσῃ in broader terms because the normal function of the aorist subjunctive is to view it as "a whole without regard for its internal details of its occurrence."[6] In this context the purpose of Christ's sacrifice was in order to set aside the church to God.

The next word καθαρίσας is an aorist active participle of καθαρίζω which is found in later Hellenistic writings. Josephus used it to speak of a religious cleansing of the land in reference to the reforms of Josiah.[7] In the LXX it occurs 124 times (101 times in the canonical books) and translates thirteen Hebrew words but sixty-six times it translates טָהֵר, meaning "to cleanse, purify."[8] It is used of the cleansing of food (Lev 13:6, 23), ceremonial cleansing (Lev 15:13, 28*bis*), and the moral cleansing of the people (Lev 16:30; Jer 13:27; Ezek 36:25). It occurs thirty-one times in the NT but is used only three times by Paul (2 Cor 7:1; Eph 5:26; Titus 2:14). Again it is used of the cleansing of

1. BDB 872–73; cf. Kornfeld and Ringgren, *TWAT* 6 (1989): 1185–1200.

2. BAGD 8; BDAG 9–10.

3. Otto Procksch, "ἁγιάζω," *TDNT* 1 (1964): 111.

4. Karl Georg Kuhn, "ἁγιάζω," *TDNT* 1 (1964): 97–98; Sampley, *'And the Two Shall Become One Flesh,'* 42–43.

5. Bruce, 387.

6. Fanning, *Verbal Aspect*, 393.

7. Josephus *A.J.* 10.4.5 §70.

8. BDB 372; H. Ringgren, "טָהֵר *ṭāhar*; טָהוֹר *ṭāhôr*; טֹהַר *ṭōhar*; טָהֳרָה *ṭohᵒrâ*," *TDOT* 5 (1986): 287–96.

food (Mark 7:19; Acts 10:15; 11:9), ceremonial cleansing (Matt 23:25–26), and the moral cleansing of the people (1 Cor 6:11; 2 Cor 7:1; Titus 2:14; Heb 9:14).[1] In the present passage it applies to the moral cleansing of the church for whom Christ gave his life. There is debate about the relationship of the aorist active participle καθαρίσας with the aorist subjunctive active main verb ἁγιάσῃ. Some view the action as antecedent to the main verb, thus "having cleansed it" (RV, ASV, RSV, NASB, TEV, NRSV);[2] others view it as contemporaneous with the main verb, "cleansing it" (AV, NEB, JB, NIV, NJB).[3] Abbott may have captured it best by noting that καθαρίσας is chronologically contemporaneous with ἁγιάσῃ but logically precedes it.[4] Thus the participle conveys the means, manner, or cause of the sanctification. Christ sanctifies (constative aorist) the church because (logically) he had cleansed (or by having cleansed) her by his sacrificial death. Temporally both actions occurred at the cross. However, since the subjunctive does not indicate the temporal aspect, it is best to indicate this in the participle though both the actions of the sanctification and cleansing occurred at the same time. Hence, it is best translated "in order that he might sanctify her having cleansed her." Again, this brings out more clearly not only the temporal aspect but also the manner, means, or the cause of the sanctification. Cleansing deals with the negative aspect, that of being cleansed from defilement of sin, whereas sanctification is the positive aspect, that of being set apart to God.[5] They are two sides of the same coin.

τῷ λουτρῷ τοῦ ὕδατος, "with the washing of the water." Paul continues the sanctification metaphor. The noun λουτρόν refers to "bath, bathing place"[6] or "water for bathing, washing, bathing."[7] In the LXX it occurs only three times (Cant 4:2; 6:6; Sir 34:25) and consistently has the meaning of washing. Josephus mentions that the prescribed Mosaic law regarding purification rites for the cured leper was to cleanse himself in a bath of water (ὑδάτων λουτροῖς).[8] In the NT it appears only twice (Eph 5:26; Titus 3:5). Needless to say, its meaning

1. BAGD 387; BDAG 488–89; Rudolf Meyer and Friedrich Hauck, "καθαρός, καθαρίζω, κτλ.," *TDNT* 3 (1965): 418–26.

2. Alford, 3:137; Eadie, 417; Ellicott, 130; Meyer, 294.

3. Eadie, 40; Ellicott, 12; Meyer, 28; Abbott, 168; Salmond, 368; Robinson, 205; Westcott, 84; Gaugler, 209; Gnilka, 280; Barth, 626; Schnackenburg, 249; Bruce, 387; Lincoln, 375; Best, 542; O'Brien, 421–22; a computer-based study of Pauline literature shows that when the aorist participle precedes the main verb, it tends to have antecedent action and when it follows the main verb, it tends to have contemporaneous action (Porter, *Verbal Aspect*, 383–84).

4. Abbott, 168.

5. Ibid.; Gnilka, 280; Hendriksen, 250.

6. Homer *Ilias* 22.444; Aeschylus *Choephori* 670; Sophocles *Trachiniae* 634.

7. Xenophon *Cyropaedia* 7.5.59; Sophocles *Antigone* 1201; *Oedipus Coloneus* 1599; Aristophanes *Lysistrata* 377, 469; Josephus *A.J.* 8.13.8 §356.

8. Josephus *C. Ap.* 1.31 §282.

here is controversial. Many think this refers to baptism.[1] Unfortunately, this is reading patristic and modern liturgy into the first century, and, moreover, there is nothing in the present context or in Titus 3:5 to indicate that this has reference to a baptismal rite. Furthermore, the rite of baptism does not cleanse one from sin. Even in the Qumran community the ritual washing was not considered as that which cleansed them (1QS 3.4–5, 8–10).[2] Rather, it was God who wiped out their transgressions and justified them (1QS 11.2–3, 5, 10, 12–14; 1QH[a] 19:10–12 [11.10–12]). Also, as Erdmann rightly observes, nowhere in the NT is the rite of baptism used in connection with the entire Christian community but only in connection with individual believers.[3] On the other hand, Barth and Dunn think it is a reference to the baptism of the Spirit.[4] Once again, nothing in the present context suggests the Spirit's baptism.

It is probably best to see it as a metaphorical expression of redemption with the imagery of the bridal bath practiced in the first century. Christ gave himself for the community of believers, the church. The purpose of this was to set apart the church because she had been cleansed with the washing of water. In 1 Cor 6:11 it also mentions washing. There, unlike those who will not inherit the kingdom of God, believers were washed, sanctified, and justified in the name of the Lord Jesus Christ and in the Spirit of God. Here, too, the washing has reference to the cleansing accomplished by Christ and not the ritual of baptism. In Titus 3:5 it refers to the washing of regeneration, indicating a cleansing that comes with salvation making us acceptable be-

1. Oecumenius *Eph* 5:25–33 (*PG* 118:1244); Theophylact *Eph* 5:26 (*PG* 124:1115); Aquinas, chap. 5, lec. 8, vv. 22–28a (219); Alford, 3:137; Eadie, 417; Ellicott, 130; Meyer, 295; Abbott, 168; Salmond, 368; Robinson, 206–7; Westcott, 84; Masson, 212; Schlier, 256–57; Gaugler, 209; Hendriksen, 251; Gnilka, 281–82; Schnackenburg, 249–50; Lincoln, 375; Hanson, *The Unity of the Church in the New Testament*, 138; David Michael Stanley, *Christ's Resurrection in Pauline Soteriology*, AnBib, vol. 13 (Rome: E Pontificio Instituto Biblico, 1961), 230; Beasley-Murray, *Baptism in the New Testament*, 201–4; Delling, *Die Taufe im Neuen Testament*, 100–101; Warnach, "Taufwirklichkeit und Taufbewußtsein nach dem Epheserbrief," 44; Schnackenburg, *Baptism in the Thought of St. Paul*, 74, 134–35; Anthony Tyrell Hanson, *Studies in the Pastoral Epistles* (London: SPCK, 1968) 85–89; Kirby, *Ephesians, Baptism and Pentecost*, 151–52; Corriveau, *The Liturgy of Life*, 215–16; Fung, "The Doctrine of Baptism in Ephesians," 11–14; Sampley, *'And the Two Shall Become One Flesh,'* 131; Halter, *Taufe und Ethos*, 283–84; Meeks, "The Image of the Andgrogyne," 205–6; Meeks, "In One Body," 216; Wedderburn, *Baptism and Resurrection*, 79; Fleckenstein, *Ordnet euch einander unter in der Furcht Christi*, 223–24; Maclean, "Ephesians and the Problem of Colossians," 42; Hartman, *'Into the Name of the Lord Jesus': Baptism in the Early Church*, 105–8; Dahl, "The Concept of Baptism in Ephesians," 420–24.

2. Cf. Joachim Gnilka, "Die essenischen Tauchbäder und die Johannestaufe," *Revue de Qumran* 3 (Mai 1961): 185–207.

3. Erdmann, "Der Brief an die Epheser. 45. Teil: Kapitel 5,25–27," 33.

4. Barth, 695–98; Dunn, *Baptism in the Holy Spirit*, 163–64.

fore a Holy God. Why is the term "water" used? The most likely explanation is that water is the most common element used for washing. Along with the above mentioned, Heb 10:22 refers to the new covenant that promises forgiveness of sins as fulfilled by Jesus' death allowing those who trust in that death to come to God because their hearts were sprinkled clean from an evil conscience and their bodies washed with pure water. Again, these are picturesque ways of expressing the cleansing effected by Christ's death. None of these passages have any suggestion of a sacramental setting. Nothing appears to be part of a formula associated with baptism such as "in the name of Jesus" or "in the name of the Father, Son, and the Holy Spirit." Furthermore, the idea of washing involves bathing rather than just a few drops of water or a quick dip into the water. In addition, baptism is always administered individually whereas this context speaks of the effect of Christ's death on the body of believers. As initially stated then, the washing of water is a metaphorical way to express cleansing.

As mentioned above, not only is this a metaphorical expression of redemption, but it also evokes the imagery of the bridal bath. This is significant since the present passage deals with the relationship of the husband to his wife. The prenuptial bath in Jewish marital customs[1] reflected the imagery of God's marriage to Israel related in Ezek 16. At the time of her birth, Israel was in a pitiable state, lying in blood, uncleansed by the washing of water, and was abhorred by all (16:4–6). When she grew up God entered into a covenant with her and bathed her with water (ἐν ὕδατι), washed off the blood, anointed her with oil, and clothed her with the finest materials, making her exceedingly beautiful, fit to be a queen (16:8–14). The custom of prenuptial bathing seemed to be practiced also among the Greeks.[2] Analogous to this bridal bath,[3] the present verse relates that Christ's death on behalf of the church was to cleanse her by the "washing of the water."

ἐν ῥήματι, "in connection with the word." This prepositional phrase causes two problems for the interpreter: to discern its meaning and to what it is connected. First, with regards to its meaning,

1. S. Safrai, "Home and Family," in *The Jewish People in the First Century. Historical Geography, Political History, Social, Cultural and Religious Life and Institutions*, ed. S. Safrai and M. Stern in co-operation with D. Flusser and W. C. van Unnik, Compendia Rerum Iudaicarum ad Novum Testamentum, ed. M. de Jonge and S. Safrai et al., sec. 1, vol. 2 (Philadelphia: Fortress; Assen: Van Gorcum, 1976), 758.

2. Corriveau, *The Liturgy of Life*, 215; J. Heckenbach, "Hochzeit," in *Paulys Real-Encylopädie der classischen Altertumswissenschaft*, ed. Wilhelm Kroll, vol. 8.2 (Stuttgart: J. B. Metzlersche Buchhandlung, 1913): 2129; Christiane Sourvinou-Inwood, "Marriage Ceremonies, Greek," *OCD*, 927.

3. Odo Casel, "Die Taufe als Brautbad der Kirche," *Jahrbuch für Liturgiewissenschaft* 5 (1925): 144–47; Meyer, 295; Abbott, 168–69; Bruce, 287; Dunn, *Baptism in the Holy Spirit*, 162–63; Halter, *Taufe und Ethos*, 282–83; Str-B, 1:506 n. c; 511 n. i; Sampley, *'And the Two Shall Become One Flesh,'* 42–43, 129–33; Pierre Benoit, "Christian Marriage according to Saint Paul," *Clergy Review* 65 (September 1980): 319.

the term ῥῆμα (ἐρῶ) from the earliest time denotes "that which is said/spoken, word, saying."[1] In the LXX it occurs 538 times (470 times in the canonical books) and translates eight Hebrew words. Around 350 times it translates דָּבָר (e.g., Gen 44:2; Deut 5:22; 1 Kgs 16:12; 1 Chr 21:4; Isa 16:13; 40:8), meaning "speech, word, message."[2] Many times it refers to the command or the word given by God. In the NT the term occurs sixty-eight times, fifty-two times in the Gospels and Acts, eight times it is used by Paul (Rom 10:8*bis*, 17, 18; 2 Cor 12:4; 13:1; Eph 5:26; 6:17), and eight times in the rest of the NT. Like λόγος, ῥῆμα can mean "thing, event," but the predominant idea is "word, saying, message, statement," focusing on communication.[3] With the exception of one time (2 Cor 13:1), Paul uses it to refer to words that come from God or Christ. How, then, is this word used in the present context? Is it the word spoken at baptism or in a gospel message? Most commentators think it refers to baptism. Yet, it must be noted that it is never used in the NT in connection with a ritual like baptism. Consequently, it is unlikely that it is used here either as a pronouncement of the persons of the Trinity by the one officiating the baptism[4] or a confession of faith by the recipient of baptism.[5] Rather, it is more probable that it is the message or word from God in which one places his or her trust (Rom 10:8*bis*, 17, 18; Eph 6:17; cf. also Matt 4:4; John 5:47; 6:68; 8:47; Acts 5:20; 10:37, 44; 11:14; Heb 6:5; 1 Pet 1:25; 2 Pet 3:2; Jude 17). In Hebrews it is used four times (1:3; 6:5; 11:3; 12:19) where it refers to words proceeding immediately or ultimately from God. As mentioned above, Paul uses it eight times and in all but one case (2 Cor 13:1) it refers to the word of God. It is the preached word or gospel[6] as re-

1. Herodotus 7.162; 8.83; Aristophanes *Pax* 521; Plato *Protagoras* 343b, *Respublica* 5.11 §464a.

2. Cf. BDB 182–84; J. Bergman, H. Lutzmann, and W. H. Schmidt, "דָּבַר *dābhar*; דָּבָר *dābhār*," *TDOT* 3 (1978): 84–125.

3. BAGD 735; BDAG 905; L&N §§13.115; 33.98.

4. Chrysostom *Eph* 5:26–27 (*PG* 62:137); Theodoret *Eph* (*PG* 82:548); Oecumenius *Eph* 5:25–33 (*PG* 118:1244); Theophylact *Eph* 5:26 (*PG* 124:1116); Aquinas, chap. 5, lec. 8, vv. 22–28a (219); Abbott, 169; Robinson, 125, 206–7; Dibelius-Greeven, 94–94; Masson, 212; Schlier, 257; Gaugler, 209; Zerwick, 155; Gnilka, 282; Schnackenburg, 250; Lincoln, 376; Best, 543–44; Colpe, "Zur Leib-Christi-Vorstellung im Epheserbrief," 185; J. Cambier, "Le grand mystère concernant le Christ et son Église. Éphésiens 5,22–33," *Bib* 47, no. 1 (1966): 71–75, 229; Sampley, *'And the Two Shall Become One Flesh,'* 132; Halter, *Taufe und Ethos*, 284; Fleckenstein, *Ordnet euch einander unter in der Furcht Christi*, 225–26; Hartman, *'Into the Name of the Lord Jesus': Baptism in the Early Church*, 106.

5. Westcott, 84–85; Martin, "Ephesians," in *The Broadman Bible Commentary*, 169; Mitton, 203; Bruce, 388; Kirby, *Ephesians, Baptism and Pentecost*, 152.

6. Alford, 3:137; Eadie, 420; Ellicott, 130; Salmond, 369; Murray, 95; Hendriksen, 252; Caird, 89; Barth, 689–91; Foulkes, 166; Lincoln, 376; O'Brien, 423; Barth, *Die Taufe-ein Sakrament?* 472; Dunn, *Baptism in the Holy Spirit*, 164–65; Richard A. Batey, *New Testament Nuptial Imagery* (Leiden: Brill, 1971), 28.

flected in τὸ ῥῆμα τῆς πίστεως, "the word of faith" (Rom 10:8); ἡ δὲ ἀκοὴ διὰ ῥήματος Χριστοῦ, "and the hearing of [faith] comes through the word (proclamation) of Christ" (Rom 10:17); and ῥῆμα θεοῦ, "word of God" (Eph 6:17). It often refers to the "preached word" which unbelievers hear (Eph 6:17; John 6:68; Acts 10:37; 11:14; Rom 10:8, 17; Heb 6:5; 1 Pet 1:25). The one problem that is raised against this view is that normally an article would be expected to precede ῥήματι. However, there are many instances where this word is anarthrous (Rom 10:17; Acts 11:14; cf. also Luke 3:2; 20:26; John 6:68; Acts 10:37; 2 Cor 12:4; Eph 6:17; Heb 6:5; 11:3). Furthermore, many words that are unique (no doubt about them being definite or indefinite) and almost equivalent to proper names (e.g., νόμος, χάρις, κόσμος, κύριος) are often anarthrous.[1] The ῥῆμα in the present context is the preached word of Christ's love for the church in that he gave his life for her for the purpose that he might sanctify her by having cleansed her with (instrumental dative) the washing of water. This is analogous to Jesus' words that one is clean through the word (λόγος) which he has spoken (John 15:3) and to his prayer to the Father on behalf of the disciples where he petitions, "sanctify them in the truth, your word is truth" (John 17:17). In Jewish customs at the time of betrothal the young man would present his bride-to-be with a gift and say to her, "Behold, you are consecrated unto me, you are betrothed to me; behold, you are a wife unto me."[2] With this spoken word they would be betrothed and then married about a year later. Just before the wedding she was bathed, symbolizing the cleansing that would set her apart to her husband. It was the spoken word that set her apart to the husband and not the bathing itself.

Second, to what is this prepositional phrase connected? Basically, there are three views. First, some suggest that it is linked to the verb ἁγιάσῃ, thus indicating that the church is sanctified by the word which would make "cleansing her by the washing of the water" parenthetical.[3] Although it makes good sense, the verb is far removed from the prepositional phrase. Second, many think it is coupled with τῷ λουτρῷ τοῦ ὕδατος, indicating that with baptism the word of the gospel or the word of confession of faith is spoken.[4] Although this construc-

1. Ellicott, 130; Meyer, 295; Salmond, 369; Winer, *Grammar*, 147–55, esp. 153.

2. *b. Qid.* 5a. How many of these Jewish customs were practiced in the first century is difficult to know with certainty. For an overview of Jewish marriage customs, see Richard Batey, "Paul's Bride Image: A Symbol of Realistic Eschatology," *Int* 17 (April 1963): 176–82.

3. Meyer, 295; Barth, 624, 626, 696; Cambier, "Le grand mystère concernant le Christ et son Église," 75; Winer, *Grammar*, 173.

4. Calvin, 207; Robinson, 125, 207; Westcott, 84–85; Masson, 212; Schlier, 257; Gaugler, 209; Hendriksen, 251–52; Gnilka, 281; Schnackenburg, 249–50; Bruce, 388; Lincoln, 376; Best, 544; Rudolf Schnackenburg, *Baptism in the Thought of St. Paul*, 6; Sampley, *'And the Two Shall Become One Flesh,'* 132–33.

tion flows naturally, one would expect the repeat of an article (τῷ or τοῦ) before ἐν ῥήματι.[1] Further, as noted above, the ritual of baptism is unlikely in this context. Third, others think it should be connected to the participle καθαρίσας meaning that the cleansing is accompanied with the word.[2] This would view the preposition ἐν as accompaniment[3] or in connection with the word. The third alternative seems best, rendering the cleansing instrumental by the washing of the water and accompanied with or in connection with the preached word or Gospel message of Christ's sacrifice for the church. This speaks of the body of believers' positional sanctification, which serves as the basis for their progressive sanctification. Hence, the reason that Christ gave himself for the church (redemption) was in order that he might sanctify her because he has cleansed her with the washing of the water, speaking metaphorically of his sacrificial death and this is in connection with the proclaimed word of Christ's death.

5:27. ἵνα παραστήσῃ αὐτὸς ἑαυτῷ ἔνδοξον τὴν ἐκκλησίαν, "in order that he might present the church to himself, glorious." This is a further purpose of Christ's death. The first concern here is to what the conjunction ἵνα refers. It could be parallel to the first ἵνα, that is, the first purpose for which Christ gave himself for the church was to sanctify her, now the second purpose is to present her to himself a glorious church. However, this is not likely because there is no coordinating conjunction to indicate this. Rather, it seems that this purpose is subordinate to or built on the first ἵνα, that is, the purpose for which Christ sanctified the church was in order that he might present to himself a glorious church. In other words, the immediate purpose for Christ's giving himself for the church was to set her apart (because he cleansed her) with the further ultimate purpose of being able to present to himself a glorious church.

The word παραστήσῃ is an aorist active[4] subjunctive of παρίστημι or παριστάνω. In classical times the term in the active voice basically meant "to cause to stand, place beside"[5] or "to set before, present"[6] with the idea "to render." In the LXX it occurs ninety-two times, in the canonical books it appears seventy-two times. It translates twelve Hebrew words, thirty-two times for עָמַד, meaning "to stand" or a more special

1. Alford, 3:137; Eadie, 418; Ellicott, 130; Meyer, 296; Abbott, 169; Salmond, 368; Barth, 689–90.

2. Alford, 3:137; Eadie, 419–20; Ellicott, 130–31; Abbott, 168; Salmond, 369; Westcott, 85; Masson, 212 n. 5; Lincoln, 376; O'Brien, 423.

3. Moule, *Idiom Book*, 78.

4. Schick notes that the RSV renders this passive, "that the church might be presented before him" (George G. Schick, "The RSV and the Small Catechism," *Concordia Theological Monthly* 27 [March 1956]: 177). However, the NRSV renders it active "so as to present the church to himself."

5. Polybius 3.72.9; 3.113.8; Demosthenes *Epistulae* 18.175.

6. Xenophon *Anabasis* 6.1.22; *Oeconomicus* 13.1; Demosthenes *Epistulae* 3.1; 18.1; 21.72; Polybius 3.94.7.

meaning "to serve."[1] In the NT it is used forty-one times, sixteen times by Paul and only here in Ephesians. It basically continues to have the meaning "to place beside, put at someone's disposal" (Rom 6:13*bis*, 19*bis*) or "to present, represent" (Luke 2:22; 2 Cor 11:2; Col 1:22; 2 Tim 2:15).[2] It is this last nuance, "to present" or "to render,"[3] that fits well with the present passage. It could have the technical idea of "giving away" a bride much as Paul describes when he likens himself to the "father of the bride" who presents the church of Corinth as a pure virgin to her husband, Christ (2 Cor 11:2).[4] The personal pronoun αὐτός, "he," following the verb places emphasis on the subject, Christ, who gave himself for the church. This is followed by a reflexive pronoun ἑαυτῷ, "to himself," to make it more emphatic that Christ not only sanctified the church in order that he might present her but that he might present her to himself.[5] In the present context Christ presents the universal church to himself. In a human wedding in the first century, the bride prepares herself for the bridegroom and he presents her to his father. Here Christ, the bridegroom, prepares the bride by sanctification and also presents her to himself.

The subject and the indirect object of the presentation is Christ. But what does Christ want to present to himself? That is spelled out in the next three words: ἔνδοξον τὴν ἐκκλησίαν. The term ἔνδοξος is used in classical times of honored or esteemed persons[6] and notable or glorious things[7] and also has the idea of something probable or generally admitted.[8] The last use is not found in biblical texts.[9] In the LXX it occurs sixty-nine times (forty-four times in the canonical books) and translates fifteen Hebrew words. Again it is used of honored or esteemed people (Gen 34:19; 1 Sam 9:6; 2 Sam 23:19, 23; Nah 3:10; Isa 5:14) and glorious things (Exod 34:10; Deut 10:21; Job 5:9; 9:10; Isa 12:4; 13:19; 64:3, 11 [MT & LXX 64:2, 10]). In the NT the word is used only four times: once it is used of people (1 Cor 4:10) and the other three times of things: splendid clothing (Luke 7:25), glorious things Jesus did (Luke 13:17), and the glorious church (Eph 5:27). It is placed before the article and the noun τὴν ἐκκλησίαν, making it emphatic in its description of what kind of church Christ was to present to himself. Commentators list it as a

1. BDB 763–65; H. Ringgren, "עָמַד *ʿāmad*, etc.," *TDOT* 11 (2001): 178–87; Georg Bertram, "παρίστημι, παριστάνω," *TDNT* 5 (1968): 838.

2. BAGD 627; BDAG 778; Bo Reicke, "παρίστημι, παριστάνω," *TDNT* 5 (1968): 839–40.

3. BAGD 627–28; BDAG 778; Baumert, *Täglich Sterben und Auferstehen*, 285–86.

4. Zerwick, 155. Best (545) points out differences between the present passage and 2 Cor 11:2.

5. Meyer, 298–99.

6. Xenophon *Memorabilia* 1.2.56.

7. Aeschines 3.231; Plutarch *Pericles* 28.3; *Moralia: De fortuna* 6 §99f.

8. LSJ 561.

9. Gerhard Kittel, "ἔνδοξος, ἐνδοξάζομαι," *TDNT* 2 (1964): 254.

tertiary predicate and thus it could be translated "in order that he might present or render the church to himself, glorious."[1] The tertiary predicate further emphasizes the qualitative character of the glory in which Christ is going to present the church. Normally in an ancient wedding the bride would prepare herself by washing in the bridal bath after which the bridegroom would go with his friends to her house to procure her and bring her to his house to present her to his father (Matt 25:1–13). In brief then, Christ prepares (redemption and sanctification) the bride, the church, with the purpose that he might present her to himself in the character of gloriousness. It is he himself who prepares her, he alone presents her, and he alone receives her all-glorious. Lincoln rightly sees the parallel in Ezek 16:10–14 where God clothes his bride Israel with luxurious clothing and adorns her with beautiful jewelry so that she would go forth among the nations perfected by God's splendor.[2] The nature of this glorious character is further explained next, first negatively and then positively.

μὴ ἔχουσαν σπίλον ἢ ῥυτίδα ἤ τι τῶν τοιούτων, "not having a blemish or wrinkle or any such thing." Paul's last statement was positive. The church is presented all glorious. Now negatively he states that the all glorious church will not be tainted in any way. For emphasis he begins with the negative particle μή, "not." The word σπίλος originally meant "rock, cliff"[3] but later meant "spot, stain, blemish" as blood stains[4] or a blemish on the body.[5] Metaphorically, it could refer to the stain of impurity in a person's character, such as criminals who were viewed as "dregs" of humanity.[6] It does not appear in the LXX and occurs in the NT only here and in 2 Pet 2:13. In the present context it refers to a metaphorical blemish on the body of the bride which a bridal bath could not erase.[7] In contrast, the cleansing from Christ's death can cleanse any blemish caused by sin. Following the disjunctive ἤ, "or," the second term ῥύτις occurs in classical literature but not in the LXX and appears only here in the NT. Normally, it appears in the plural to describe "wrinkles, puckers, folds" of skin.[8] Here it has the idea of wrinkles, connoting imperfections characteristic of age. Both σπίλον and ῥυτίδα are singular, possibly to emphasize that not one blem-

1. Eadie, 421; Ellicott, 131; Abbott, 170; Salmond, 370.

2. Lincoln, 377. Later in a second century A.D. document the city of Ephesus is described as being made more glorious (ἐμδοξοτέρα) "through the benefaction and divinity of the Ephesian Artemis" (see Oster, "Holy Days in Honour of Artemis," 78).

3. Aristotle *De Mundo* 3 §392b.30.

4. Josephus *A.J.* 13.11.3 §314.

5. Lucian *Amores* 15.

6. Dionysius Halicarnassensis *Antiquitates Romanae* 4.24.6; MM 584.

7. Schnackenburg, 251.

8. Aristophanes *Plutus* 1051; Plato *Symposium* 191a*bis*; Plutarch *Moralia: An seni respublica gerenda sit* 9 §789d.

ish or one wrinkle marks the church.[1] To be sure nothing is missed, Paul adds the catchall ἤ τι τῶν τοιούτων, "or any such thing." Hence, the church has no blemish nor any wrinkle nor anything else that would suggest imperfection in its gloriousness.

ἀλλ' ἵνα ᾖ ἁγία καὶ ἄμωμος, "but in order that she might be holy and blameless." Three things are to be noted. First, the adversative conjunction ἀλλά, "but," marks a contrast between the negative just stated and the positive to be stated. The second thing to be noted is the change in structure, a structure similar to that in verse 33. One would normally think that the conjunction would be followed by the participle οὖσαν, "being," without the negative particle μή, "not." However, after ἀλλά, he introduces the positive side by a purpose clause: "in order that she might be holy and without blame." This is the third ἵνα in this passage: the first states that Christ's love for the church demonstrated that the giving of himself was in order that he might sanctify it (v. 26) and the second states that Christ sanctified the church in order that he might present it to himself (v. 27a). What then, does the third ἵνα in verse 27b relate back to? The conjunction ἀλλά denotes the contrast with the previous negative statement ("blemish or wrinkle") and the ἵνα here introduces the purpose in a positive way ("holy and blameless") in contrast to the negative just stated. Hence, this ἵνα relates back to the expected οὖσαν (mentioned above) after the conjunction ἀλλά. The third item to notice is the difference in description. In the previous statement Paul described the bride as having no physical imperfection, whereas here Paul is speaking of moral purity. Physical perfection is a metaphorical way of describing moral perfection. Paul states that the church in her gloriousness does not have any imperfection whatsoever in order that she might be morally holy and blameless.

The above statement is identical in most respects to 1:4 where Paul states that God chose us in Christ before the foundations of the world that we might be holy and without blame before God (εἶναι ἡμᾶς ἁγίους καὶ ἀμώμους κατενώπιον αὐτοῦ). The differences are: (1) there the nouns are plural while here they are singular because in chapter 1 Paul is talking about individual believers whereas here he is discussing the corporate body of believers, the church; and (2) in chapter 1 believers are to be holy and blameless before God, whereas here the church is holy and blameless before Christ. Thus, the differences are not really significant. The meaning of these two adjectives ἁγία and ἄμωμος was discussed at 1:1 and 1:4 respectively where it stated that "holy" reflects God's character in its uniqueness, and "without blame"

1. For the interpretation of "no blemish nor wrinkle" from patristic times until the seventeenth century, see Charles Journet, "Note sur l'Eglise sans tache ni ride," *Revue thomiste* 49, nos. 1–2 (1949): 206–21; cf. also Denis Faul, "Ecclesia, Sponsa Christi. Orígenes y Agustín ante la exégesis de Eph. 5,27," *Augustinus* 15 (Julio–Septiembro 1970): 263–80.

denotes absence of defects. This agrees with 2 Cor 11:2 where Paul's stated desire was to present the church as a chaste virgin to Christ and Col 1:28 where he speaks of presenting everyone perfect in Christ.

The allusion to the church's holiness and blamelessness is important not only in the immediate context but it also serves as a climax to the argument and theology of the whole book. In Eph 1:4 God chose believers in order that they might be holy and blameless before him in love. All this is accomplished by the father's selection, Christ's redemption, and the sealing of the Holy Spirit (1:4–14). This is achieved by giving new life to sinners (2:1–10) and placing them into a new entity, the church, a body composed of believing Jews and Gentiles (2:11–3:13). This new body of believers is to live in unity (4:1–16), holiness (4:17–32), love (5:1–6), light (5:7–14), and wisdom (5:15–6:9). Finally, that which was planned in eternity past (1:4) will be accomplished when Christ presents to himself the church that is holy and without blame (5:27).

When will this presentation occur? Some think that it refers to a realized eschatology that speaks of Christ's relationship to the church presently.[1] However, is the church in the present day without any blemish or wrinkle? Is it holy and blameless? As the obvious demands a negative response, it has to be assumed that it refers to a future day at the coming of Christ when the church will be holy and without blame.[2] In fact, whenever the presentation of the bride (i.e., the marriage) is pictured, it always speaks of the future (e.g., Matt 22:1–10; 25:1–13; Rev 19:7–10; 21:9). Presently, the church is seen as the body of Christ but in the future she becomes the bride of Christ.[3] Nevertheless, even if accepted as a future occurrence, application to the present church is no less appropriate. Although in the future, sanctification will be complete, but the process is ongoing. Holiness of life for believers is enjoined (4:17–32).

In conclusion then, Paul had exhorted husbands to love their wives (5:25a). The model of their love is Christ's sacrificial love for the church, which had the immediate purpose of her sanctification,

1. Bengel, 4:108; Schlier, 258; Schnackenburg, 250–51; Lincoln, 377; Best, *One Body in Christ*, 175 n. 3; Steinmetz, *Protologische Heils-Zuversicht*, 92.

2. Jerome *Eph* 5:25–27 (*PL* 26:532–33); Calvin, 207; Alford, 3:138; Eadie, 422; Moule, 141; Meyer, 297, 299; Abbott, 169–79; Salmond, 370; Gaugler, 209; Hendriksen, 253–54; Barth, 628, 669, 678; Bruce, 389; I. A. Muirhead, "The Bride of Christ," *SJT* 5 (June 1952): 183–87; J. Jeremias, "νύμφη, νυμφίος," *TDNT* 4 (1967): 1104–5; Mussner, *Christus, das All und die Kirche*, 152 n. 358; Batey, *New Testament Nuptial Imagery*, 65–69; Renzo Infante, "Immagine nuziale e tensione escatologica nel Nuovo Testamento. Note a 2 Cor. 11,2 e Eph. 5,25–27," *RivB* 33 (Gennaoi–Marzo 1985): 57–58. For a development of Augustine's thought in this area, see Adolar Zumkeller, "Eph. 5,27 im Verständnis Augustins und seiner donatistischen und pelagianischen Gegner," *Augustinianum* 16 (December 1976): 457–74.

3. Roels, *God's Mission*, 142; Fung, "Some Pauline Pictures of the Church," 98; *contra* Bedale, "The Meaning of κεφαλή in the Pauline Epistles," 215.

which, in turn, served as the basis for the ultimate purpose of Christ to present the church to himself glorious, with full moral perfection (5:25b–27). From this illustration of Christ's all-encompassing love for the church, Paul applies the truths to these husbands who read this letter.

(c) Application: Husbands' Love (5:28–32)

It must be remembered that the purposes expressed in verses 26–27 are related to Christ's sacrificial love stated in verse 25. Verse 25 is not meant to be a doctrinal treatise on Christ's love but rather serves as an illustration of how the husbands are to love their wives. The doctrine of Christ's sacrificial love for sinners has already been explained (cf. 1:4–12; 2:2–10; 2:13–16; 3:6, 8; 4:20; 5:2) and is reinforced in verse 25 in order to illustrate the necessary depth of love husbands should demonstrate toward their wives. If Christ could love sacrificially those who hated him, should not husbands love their wives who do not have such animosity (we must be careful not to impose our modern western culture of mate selection into the first century for, in some cases, the marriages were arranged)? The purpose of Christ's love for the church was for her ultimate good, which should be the goal of a husband's love. Feuillet suggests that Gen 2:18–24 shows the dignity and role of the woman in her union with man by making her Adam's companion and not his servant. Paul portrays Christ in Eph 5:25–27 as the church's eternal fiancé and asserts that the husbands' relationship to their wives is one of a perpetual engagement.[1] Christ's love for the church is further applied to the husbands' love for their wives in the next verses.

(i) Responsibility: Love Wives as They Love Their Own Bodies (5:28)

Text: 5:28. οὕτως ὀφείλουσιν [καὶ] οἱ ἄνδρες ἀγαπᾶν τὰς ἑαυτῶν γυναῖκας ὡς τὰ ἑαυτῶν σώματα. ὁ ἀγαπῶν τὴν ἑαυτοῦ γυναῖκα ἑαυτὸν ἀγαπᾷ.

Translation: 5:28. "So ought also the husbands to love their own wives as their own bodies. He who loves his own wife loves himself."

Commentary: 5:28. οὕτως ὀφείλουσιν [καὶ] οἱ ἄνδρες[2] ἀγαπᾶν τὰς ἑαυτῶν γυναῖκας ὡς τὰ ἑαυτῶν σώματα, "So ought also the husbands to love their own wives as their own bodies." First, the referent of οὕτως must be identified. Some think that Paul is beginning a new thought by renewing his exhortation to the husbands, and so the ad-

1. A. Feuillet, "La dignité et rôle de la femme d'après quelques textes pauliniens: comparaison avec l'Ancien Testament," *NTS* 21 (January 1975): 173–74.

2. The first reading οὕτως ὀφείλουσιν [καὶ] οἱ ἄνδρες is found in 𝔓[46] B 33 1175 1505 *pc* syr[h]. The second reading οὕτως ὀφείλουσιν οἱ ἄνδρες appears in ℵ Ψ 0278 1739 1881 𝔐 syr[p]. The third reading οὕτως [καὶ] οἱ ἄνδρες ὀφείλουσιν occurs in A D F G P 048[vid] 0285[vid] 629 *pc* lat Clement. The first reading is found in only a few manuscripts of the Alexandrian tradition. The second reading has some Alexandrian support but its main

verbial conjunction οὕτως, "so," looks forward to the comparative conjunction ὡς later in the verse (like v. 33) and would read, "so also husbands ought to love their wives as their own bodies."[1] Others think that the οὕτως serves as a conclusion to what was begun with καθὼς καί in verse 25b and would be rendered: "just as also Christ loved the church . . . so also ought husbands to love their wives."[2] This view is preferable since the stylistic construction of the οὕτως καί in the present verse is similar to that of verse 24. In verse 24 Paul writes that as (ὡς) the church is subject to Christ, so also (οὕτως καί) are wives to be subject to husbands. Therefore, in verse 25 just as (καθὼς καί) Christ loved the church, so also (οὕτως καί, v. 28) ought husbands to love their wives. This structure is not uncommon in Paul's writings. For example, in Rom 5:12 Paul begins the comparison with ὥσπερ and concludes it in 5:18b with οὕτως καί. The same structure is also seen in Rom 5:19, 21, and 6:4. Part of the problem in the present context is a textual problem. If καί is accepted, then οὕτως must refer back to the καθὼς καί in verse 25b.[3] Barth states, "This *kai* makes unmistakably clear that the word *houtōs* ("so," "in the same manner") at the beginning of vs. 28 points back to the love of Christ described in vss. 25–27, not forward to an egotistic love. Only if *kai* were placed before 'bodies' (*somāta* [*sic*]), would this verse clearly affirm that husbands must love their wives, as (or because) they 'love also their bodies.'"[4] Furthermore, the slight change in wording in verse 28a in comparison to

---

support is from the Byzantine text. The third reading has some support from the Alexandrian text but its main support is the Western text. The first and third readings are identical except for word order. The second reading leaves out the conjunction καί, which does not change the meaning but only makes it slightly more emphatic. The third reading has a slight edge over the second reading with regards to geographical spread and genealogical relationships. It seems best to accept either the first or the third reading on the basis of external evidence. Internally, the third reading has a parallel in v. 24 where it states that just as the church is subject to Christ, so also (οὕτως καί) should the wives be subject to their own husbands. In conclusion, the first or third readings are preferred over the second. Although there is really no difference in interpretation between the two, the first is preferred because it is a harder reading. One would expect οὕτως καί, for this construction is frequent in Paul's letters (e.g., Rom 5:18b, 19, 21; 6:4; 1 Cor 2:11; 12:12; 14:9, 12; 15:22; cf. Matt 23:28; Mark 7:18; John 5:21, 26), but a word between these two words is rare (e.g., Rom 11:5; cf. Matt 24:39; Luke 11:30; 17:26; Rev 2:15).

1. Alford, 3:138; Schlier, 260; Hendriksen, 254; Schnackenburg, 252; Bruce, 391.

2. Eadie, 423; Ellicott, 132; Meyer, 299–300; Abbott, 170; Salmond, 370; Robinson, 208; Westcott, 85; Gnilka, 283; Barth, 629–30; Lincoln, 378; Best, *One Body in Christ*, 177; Sampley, *'And the Two Shall Become One Flesh,'* 141. Bouwman thinks that the οὕτως is apodosis to the καθώς of v. 25, G. Bouwman, "Eph. v 28—Versuch einer Übersetzung," in *Miscellanea Neotestamentica*, ed. T. Baarda, A. F. J. Klijn, and W. C. van Unnik, NovTSup, ed. W. C. van Unnik et al., vol. 48 (Leiden: Brill, 1978), 179–90.

3. Salmond, 370.

4. Barth, 630.

verse 24b suggests that the οὕτως καί serves as a concluding application to verses 25–27. In verse 24b the verb "to submit" is not repeated because it is obvious to the reader since it has just been stated in the first part of the verse. However, in 28a Paul repeats his main exhortation for husbands "to love" (ἀγαπᾶν) their wives probably because he had not mentioned this since verse 25b (ἀγαπᾶτε) and he wanted to prevent readers from getting lost in his elaboration on the purposes of Christ's love for the church in verses 26–27. In addition, Paul introduces the verb ὀφείλω, meaning "one must, one ought" when followed by an infinitive,[1] with the repeat of the verb "to love." In other words, Paul directs them back to the main point of verse 25 by exhorting husbands to love their wives and he reinforces this with a verb that stresses obligation. Therefore, it is best to accept οὕτως καί as a conclusion to the foregoing discussion of Christ's love for the church.

It should be observed that as with the exhortation to the wives, so also here the subject is a free agent. Husbands are commanded to love their wives unconditionally, not only if the wives are submissive. Rather, husbands are to love their wives in obedience to the Lord and because of the example of Christ's love. It is not the duty of the wife to tell him to love her. It is his duty to the Lord to love her.

In this verse Paul expands the example of Christ's love, namely, that of a person's love for his own body (ὡς τὰ ἑαυτῶν σώματα).[2] The word "body," which occurs nine times in Ephesians, is used metaphorically in all the instances except here where it refers to the literal physical body. This example is mundane but easily understood. Husbands are to love their wives in the same way that they are concerned about their own bodies. How is the adverbial conjunction ὡς to be taken? It could carry a comparative force: husbands are to have a love "similar" to their love for their own bodies.[3] In Jewish tradition it is written, "Our Rabbis taught: Concerning a man who loves his wife as himself, who honors her more than himself."[4] Others suggest that it is more than a simple comparison and think that it introduces the characteristic quality of a person (or thing or action) referred to in the context and so, in this case, would mean that husbands are to love their wives "as being" their own bodies.[5] There seems to be a combination of both ideas but with emphasis on the second because Paul states in the latter part of verse 28 that the one who loves his own wife loves himself

1. BAGD 598; BDAG 743.

2. The plural σώματα does not deny the individuality of each person (Gundry, Sōma *in Biblical Theology*, 220–21; MHT 3:24; *contra* Robinson, *The Body*, 29). This is also true of the plural reflexive pronoun ἑαυτῶν, see HS §139i.

3. BAGD 897; BDAG 1103.

4. *b. Yeb.* 62b.

5. BAGD 898; BDAG 1104; Eadie, 424; Salmond, 371; Masson, 213 n. 6; Best, *One Body in Christ*, 177; Muraoka, "The use of ΩΣ in the Greek Bible," 60; Dawes, *The Body in Question*, 97–99, 153.

and in verse 31 Paul quotes Gen 2:24, which states that the husband and wife are one flesh. Certainly, throughout the context the head corresponds to the body, and the head, Christ, loves the body, the church; so also husbands ought to love their wives who, as it were, are their own bodies.[1] On the other hand, the truism in verse 29, that no one ever hates his own flesh but nurtures it, cannot refer to the wife because husbands are capable of hating their wives and so the flesh must refer to one's own physical body. It should be noted that in verses 28–29, or in the entire context, there is no command to love oneself or the assertion that self-love is necessary before one can love another. It is a natural aspect of the human condition to love, nurture, and protect oneself.

Sampley thinks that in verses 28–29a Paul was influenced by Lev 19:18, which says, "Love your neighbor as yourself."[2] However, Lincoln rightly comments that this is entirely unnecessary "for understanding the flow of the argument at this point."[3] The present context is talking about a husband/wife relationship and not a relationship with one's neighbor even though the phrase "love as yourself" is used.

ὁ ἀγαπῶν τὴν ἑαυτοῦ γυναῖκα ἑαυτὸν ἀγαπᾷ, "He who loves his own wife loves himself." Abbott writes, "This is neither identical with the preceding nor an inference from it, but rather an explanation of ὡς τὰ ἑαυτῶν σώματα."[4] It is to make clear that the preceding phrase is not intended to focus on a person's love of his own physical body. Rather, the focus is directed on the extent of love a husband should have for his wife, that is, the same way that Christ loves the church. This love is not to be seen as a duty but as something that is consistent with his nature. As he does not think about loving himself because it is natural, so also, should the husband's love of his wife be something that is as natural as loving himself.

(ii) Illustration: One Cares for His Own Flesh (5:29a)

Text: 5:29a. Οὐδεὶς γάρ ποτε τὴν ἑαυτοῦ σάρκα ἐμίσησεν ἀλλὰ ἐκτρέφει καὶ θάλπει αὐτήν,

1. There is quite a debate between Jerome and Rufinus over the relationship of Christ with the church and the husband with the wife. Rufinus accuses Jerome of closely following Origen's restitution of all things where there could be another fall, which would mean men could be born as women and a virgin might become a prostitute. See Origen *In Epistolam ad Ephesios* 5:28–29 (*PG* 14:1297–98); Jerome *Eph* 5:28–29 (*PL* 26:533–34); Kazimierz Romaniuk, "Une controverse entre saint Jérôme et Rufin d'Aquilée à propos l'épître de saint Paul aux Ephésiens," *Aegyptus* 43 (Gennaio–Giugno 1963): 84–106; Clark, "The Place of Jerome's Commentary on Ephesians in the Origenist Controversy," 154–71.

2. Sampley, *'And the Two Shall Become One Flesh,'* 32–34, 139–42.

3. Lincoln, 379.

4. Abbott, 171.

Translation: 5:29a. "For no one ever hates his own flesh but he nurtures and takes tender care of it,"

Commentary: 5:29a. Οὐδεὶς γάρ ποτε τὴν ἑαυτοῦ σάρκα ἐμίσησεν, "For no one ever hates his own flesh." The conjunction γάρ, "for," is used to introduce an explanation of what has just been said. Best suggests that γάρ refers back to verse 28a ("So ought also the husbands to love their own wives as their own bodies . . . for no one ever hates his own flesh")[1] rather than 28b. Barth labels this as absurd for there is no textual evidence that verse 29 follows immediately after 28a, and it is more natural to relate γάρ in 29 to 28b than to 28a ("He who loves his own wife loves himself . . . for no one ever hates his own flesh"). Furthermore, this allows verses 29–30 to be a unit that explains that husbands' love of wives as their own bodies is the same way that Christ loves his body, the church.[2] Hence, it is best to assume that γάρ is introducing an explanation to what Paul said in verse 28b. Having stated that he who loves his wife loves himself, Paul becomes even more personal. He makes a categorical denial by saying "no one." This is followed by the enclitic particle ποτε, which should be translated "ever" in this context,[3] reinforcing the categorical denial. The term σάρξ, "flesh," used is instead of continuing with σῶμα, "body," as elsewhere (vv. 23, 28, 30). He uses these terms interchangeably.[4] It is possible that σάρξ is used in preparation for the quotation from Gen 2:24 in verse 31 which carries a nonethical sense. The reflexive pronoun ἑαυτοῦ emphasizes it is toward one's own flesh that there is no hatred. The verb ἐμίσησεν is an aorist indicative of μισέω, meaning "to hate." It is used forty times in the NT, four times by Paul, and only here in Ephesians. Here it is a gnomic aorist expressing "a general or proverbial truth, a maxim about occurrences which take place not only in the past but in the present and future as well,"[5] in this case, the general truth being that no one ever hates his own flesh, a fact which can be applied to people in general, not just to husbands.

ἀλλὰ ἐκτρέφει καὶ θάλπει αὐτήν, "but he nurtures and takes tender care of it." The adversative conjunction ἀλλά, "but," marks the contrast to "no one ever hates his own flesh." Paul uses two words "from the language of the nursery"[6] that are "charged with affection"[7] to describe the contrast. The first word ἐκτρέφω means "to bring up

1. Best, *One Body in Christ*, 177.

2. Barth, 633.

3. Robertson, *Grammar*, 1147; H. E. Dana and Julius R. Mantey, *A Manual Grammar of the Greek New Testament* (New York: Macmillan Company, 1927), 262.

4. Sand, *Der Begriff »Fleisch« in den paulinischen Hauptbriefen*, 136; Gundry, Sōma *in Biblical Theology*, 167.

5. Fanning, *Verbal Aspect*, 265; BDF §333 (1); cf. Porter, *Verbal Aspect*, 75, 78, 218–19, 222–23.

6. Martin, "Ephesians," in *The Broadman Bible Commentary*, 170.

7. Hugedé, 218.

from childhood, rear up."[1] In the LXX it occurs twenty-seven times and in the canonical books it appears nineteen times and translates six Hebrew words, eleven times from גָּדַל meaning "to grow up" (1 Kgs 12:8, 10; 2 Chr 10:10) or "to rear, bring up children" (2 Kgs 10:6; Isa 23:4; 49:21; Hos 9:12).[2] In some cases it was used "to nurse" a child.[3] In the NT, it is used only here and Eph 6:4. In 6:4 it refers to fathers who rear their children. Similarly, here it has the same connotation, that of a parent who nurtures a child. Many translations have "to nourish" (AV, RV, ASV, RSV, NASB, NRSV) and some have "to feed" (TEV, JB, NIV, NJB) or "to provide" (NEB). The translation "to feed"[4] limits it too much to the physical realm, whereas the word "nurture" possesses a broader scope encompassing the physical, psychological, and spiritual nature of a person. The words "to nurture" or "to care" are the best translation for this context. The second word θάλπω means literally "to heat"[5] and metaphorically with regards to passion "to inflame"[6] but also "to comfort, cherish, warm."[7] It occurs only four times in the LXX where it translates three Hebrew words and means "to warm" (Deut 22:6; 1 Kgs 1:2; Job 39:14) or "to nurse" (1 Kgs 1:4). It can also mean "to care" for a person or an entity.[8] In the NT it is used only here and in 1 Thess 2:7 where Paul states that he was gentle among them like a nurse or mother taking care of her own children. In the present context the English versions translate the word "cherish" (AV, RV, ASV, RSV, NASB) or "cares" (NEB, TEV, NIV, NRSV). Here, its import is "to care" or "to take tender care of" in the same way that a man cares for his own body, even with all its imperfections.[9] The present tense of both of these verbs gives it a repeated or customary force which fits well with the gnomic aorist in the preceding clause.

(iii) Illustration: Christ Cares for His Body (5:29b–30)

Text: 5:29b. καθὼς καὶ ὁ Χριστὸς τὴν ἐκκλησίαν, **5:30.** ὅτι μέλη ἐσμὲν τοῦ σώματος αὐτοῦ[, *ἐκ τῆς σαρκὸς αὐτοῦ καὶ ἐκ τῶν ὀστέων αὐτοῦ*].

Translation: 5:29b. "just as also Christ does the church, **5:30.** because we are members of his body[, out of his flesh and out of his bones]."

1. Herodotus 1.122; Aeschylus *Choephori* 750; Sophocles *Oedipus Tyrannus* 827; LSJ 523.
2. BDB 151; Jan Bergman, Helmer Ringgren, and R. Mosis, "גָּדַל *gādhal*, etc.," *TDOT* 2 (1977): 390–416.
3. MM 199.
4. As suggested by L&N §23.6.
5. Homer *Odyssea* 21.179; Sophocles *Antigone* 417.
6. Aeschylus *Prometheus Vinctus* 590.
7. Theocritus 14.38; LSJ 783.
8. MM 283.
9. L&N §35.36.

Commentary: 5:29b. καθὼς καὶ ὁ Χριστὸς[1] τὴν ἐκκλησίαν, "just as also Christ does the church." The adverbial conjunction καθώς introduces the comparison, and the conjunction καί is used adjunctively to add emphasis. As it is natural for man not to hate his own flesh but to nurture and take care of it, so it is also the natural thing for Christ to nurture and take care of his body, the church. He redeemed it (1:7–12; 2:1–10), sealed it (1:13–14), empowered it (1:19–23), brought it into one body (2:16), filled it with God's fullness (3:19), gifted it (4:7–16), and loved and sanctified it (5:25–26). Even with all its imperfections Christ nurtures and takes tender care of his body, the church. Christ did not give birth to the church and leave it stranded. He nurses her with the warmth of his love and power so that she will able to cope in the world. Christ, as head of the church, is not only a ruler or authority over the church but also the source of sustenance by which it is nurtured.

5:30. ὅτι μέλη ἐσμὲν τοῦ σώματος αὐτοῦ, "because we are members of his body." The conjunction ὅτι is causal[2] introducing the reason why Christ nurtures and takes tender care of the church, that is, because we are members of his body. Earlier in Ephesians, Paul mentioned that the church is Christ's body (1:22–23; 5:23), but now replacing impersonal statements with the first person plural he becomes more personal by claiming that he and the Christians in Ephesus are members of that body. In a different context Paul shows that though believers may have different gifts, all are members of the body of Christ by the baptism of the Spirit (1 Cor 12). The noun μέλος, "member," discussed at Eph 4:25 has reference to limbs or members of a body, whether human or animal. It is never used of a member of an organization but always used of a member of an organism. The use of this term demonstrates the close-knit relationship of the members with Christ. He nurtures and takes tender care of the church, the members of his body, as shown by his sacrificial death for the church (v. 25) and in his continuing care of his body of which all believers are

1. There are two readings. The first reading has Χριστός and is found in 𝔓[46] ℵ A B D* F G P Ψ 048 0278 0285 33 81 104 365 1175 1241[s] 1505 1739 1881 2464 *al* latt syr cop. The second reading has κύριος and occurs in D[2] 𝔐. The first reading has manuscripts that are early and are of good character with good genealogical relationships and wide geographical distribution. The second reading has limited geographical distribution, has no really early manuscripts, and has good genealogical relationships only within the Byzantine text-type. Internally, the second reading is more difficult because the use of κύριος in connection with σῶμα or ἐκκλησία is not found in the NT. On the other hand, the use of Χριστός in connection with σῶμα (e.g., 1 Cor 12:12, 27; Eph 4:12) or ἐκκλησία (Eph 5:24, 25, 32; Col 1:24) is often found. Hence, in the present context the first reading is easy to understand while the reason for a scribe to change it to κύριος would be difficult to understand. However, with such overwhelming external evidence and with consistency internally in the immediate context, the first reading is preferred.

2. Moritz (*A Profound Mystery*, 134) softens the causal force of ὅτι and renders it "after all" rather than "because."

members.[1] Although the "body" is used metaphorically of the church, it is not used as an analogy of the wives' role of submission as earlier in this context.[2]

[, ἐκ τῆς σαρκὸς αὐτοῦ καὶ ἐκ τῶν ὀστέων αὐτοῦ].[3] "[, out of his flesh and out of his bones]." The longer reading is accepted with great hestitation. It has good external evidence and it is the harder reading (see p. 769 n. 3 on the textual discussion). It may be said that the reading is too hard to justify its inclusion. Also, if this reading were the original, it is difficult to explain why it was omitted unless it was omitted by homoeoteleuton (αὐτοῦ . . . αὐτοῦ). On the other hand, Rodgers asserts that its inclusion allows for a better flow of the argument, which begins with believers as members of Christ's body and ends

1. Colpe ("Zur Leib-Christi-Vorstellung im Epheserbrief," 185–86) sees this in the sacramental setting of the Lord's Supper.

2. Gielen, *Tradition und Theologie neutestamentlicher Haustafelethik*, 566.

3. There are three readings. First, αὐτοῦ standing alone is found in 𝔓^{46} ℵ* A B 048 6 33 81 424^{c} 1739* 1881 2464 *l* 422 it^{s} vg^{ms} cop$^{sa, bo}$ eth Origen^{lat} Methodius Jerome Augustine^{vid} Ps-Jerome (NA^{27}, UBS^{4}). The second reading (Gen 2:23) αὐτοῦ καὶ ἐκ τῶν ὀστέων αὐτοῦ is found only in 0150. The third reading (Gen 2:23) αὐτοῦ ἐκ τῆς σαρκὸς αὐτοῦ καὶ ἐκ τῶν ὀστέων αὐτοῦ occurs in ℵ^{2} D G P Ψ 075 0278 0285^{vid} 104 256 263 365 424* 436 459 1175 1241 1319 1573 1739^{c} 1852 (1912 *omits first* αὐτοῦ) 1962 2127 2200 *Byz* [(K τοῦ σώματος *for* τῶν ὀστέων) L P] *Lect* (*l* 147 *adds* καί *after first* αὐτοῦ; *l* 1154 *omits* καί) it$^{ar, b, d, f, g, mon, o}$ vg syr$^{(p), h}$ arm geo slav Irenaeus$^{gr, lat}$ Chrysostom Theodore^{lat} Victorinus-Rome Ambrosiaster Ambrose Pelagius Theodoret. Regarding the external evidence, the first reading has manuscripts that are early and good in character but are limited to the Alexandrian text-type. The second reading has only one manuscript. The third reading has manuscripts that are early and good in character and have good geographical spread and good genealogical relationships. The third reading is the best from the viewpoint of the external evidence. Regarding the internal evidence, it is thought that the first reading is the best because it is the shortest reading and it avoids unnecessary confusion. Some think that the reason for the omission of the words in the second and third readings is due to homoeoteleuton (αὐτοῦ . . . αὐτοῦ). However, the inclusion of the words of the second and third readings is most likely due to scribal expansions derived from Gen 2:23 in anticipation of the quotation of Gen 2:24 in v. 31 (Metzger, *Textual Commentary*, 2d ed., 541). The third reading (ἐκ τῆς σαρκὸς αὐτοῦ καὶ ἐκ τῶν ὀστέων αὐτοῦ) is a paraphrase of Gen 2:23 (LXX: ὀστοῦν ἐκ τῶν ὀστέων μου καὶ σὰρξ ἐκ τῆς σαρκός μου) with two basic changes: (1) the word order is changed from flesh and bones to bones and flesh; and (2) the wording is changed from "bone of my bones and flesh of my flesh" to "out of his flesh and out of his bones." These changes are significant because Paul's quotation of Gen 2:24 in v. 31 has only minor changes. This may indicate that this was a scribal insertion based on memory rather than looking at the text of Gen 2:23. However, a scribe would tend to give a word-for-word account whereas Paul would more likely paraphrase (Moule, 142). If these words are not a scribal insertion, then Paul could be paraphrasing Gen 2:23 for his own purpose leading up to the quotation in v. 31 from Gen 2:24. Internally, the third reading is preferred because it is the more difficult reading because of the changes and because it causes inconsistency in Paul's argument, namely, how are we who are members of his body out of his flesh and out of his bones? Schlier thinks that its insertion was due to an anti-Gnostic polemic as Irenaeus (*Adversus Haereses* 5.2.3) and Tertullian (*De anima* 11) had so used it (Schlier,

with the quotation which depicts the concept of becoming one flesh.[1] If it is genuine, it is difficult to interpret. In fact, commentators who have accepted its inclusion have been anything but uniform as to its meaning. Some think it has reference to the believer's union to Christ in baptism[2] or the Lord's Supper.[3] But nothing in the immediate context is about baptism or the Lord's Supper. Moreover, "body and blood" are terms used for the Lord's Supper, never "flesh and bones," and a change in terminology would be unlikely since "blood" is so important in the Lord's Supper. Others think it refers to the shared humanity of believers and Christ.[4] The problem is that the shared humanity is with all human beings and not just believers. Furthermore, our humanity did not come from Christ but his humanity came from us (Rom 1:3; 9:5; John 1:14). Still others think that as Eve came into existence from Adam, we are members of his body by the rebirth achieved by Christ.[5] But there is nothing about the new birth in the present context. Although it is difficult to understand precisely why the physical terms "flesh and blood" are used, the most plausible explanation is that as Eve derived her physical life from Adam, we as believers derive our spiritual life from Christ.[6] This interpretation continues the concept of this context that Christ is the source of our spiritual union.

In conclusion, then, this verse teaches that Christ nurtures and takes tender care of the church because we are members of his body and are depicted as being from his flesh and from his bones.

(iv) Substantiation: Two Are One Flesh (5:31)

Text: 5:31. ἀντὶ τούτου καταλείψει ἄνθρωπος [τὸν] πατέρα καὶ [τὴν] μητέρα καὶ προσκολληθήσεται πρὸς τὴν γυναῖκα αὐτοῦ, καὶ ἔσονται οἱ δύο εἰς σάρκα μίαν.

---

261 n. 1). However, this will not stand because Gnostics used the expression "bone of my bones and flesh of my flesh" (see Peter R. Rodgers, "The Allusion to Genesis 2:23 at Ephesians 5:30," *JTS*, n.s., 41 [April 1990]: 92–94). In conclusion, the third reading is preferred with great hesitancy as indicated by its enclosure with brackets. It is accepted as the best reading because of its overwhelming external evidence and because it is the harder reading with regards to its internal evidence.

1. Rodgers, "The Allusion to Genesis 2:23 at Ephesians 5:30," 94.

2. Chrysostom *Eph* 5:30 (*PG* 62:139); cf. also Kohlgraf, *Die Ekklesiologie des Epheserbriefes in der Auslegung durch Johannes Chrysostomus*, 330–32.

3. Theodoret *Eph* 5:30 (*PG* 82:548); Calvin, 208–9.

4. Theophylact *Eph* 5:30 (*PG* 124:1117–18); Jerome *Eph* 5:30 (*PL* 26:534); Theodore of Mopsuestia *Eph* 5:30 (*PG* 66:919–20); Aquinas, chap. 5, lec. 9, vv. 28b–30 (223).

5. Chrysostom *Eph* 5:30 (*PG* 62:139); Ambrosiaster *Eph* 5:30 (*PL* 17:399); Oecumenius *Eph* 5:25–33 (*PG* 118:1244–45); Theophylact *Eph* 5:30 (*PG* 124:1117).

6. With various modifications, see Chrysostom *Eph* 5:30 (*PG* 62:139); Ambrosiaster *Eph* 5:30 (*PL* 17:399); Theodoret *Eph* 5:30 (*PG* 82:548); Oecumenius *Eph* 5:25–33 (*PG* 118:1244–45); Theophylact *Eph* 5:30 (*PG* 124:1117); Hodge, 344–47; Alford, 3:139; Eadie, 428–29; Ellicott, 134–35; Meyer, 302–3; Simpson, 133.

Translation: 5:31. "For this reason a man shall leave his father and mother and shall cleave to his wife, and the two shall be one flesh."

Commentary: 5:31. ἀντὶ τούτου καταλείψει ἄνθρωπος [τὸν][1] πατέρα καὶ [τὴν] μητέρα καὶ προσκολληθήσεται πρὸς τὴν γυναῖκα αὐτοῦ,[2] καὶ ἔσονται οἱ δύο εἰς σάρκα μίαν. "For this reason a man shall leave his father and mother and shall cleave to his wife, and the two shall be one flesh." Husbands have been commanded to love their wives as Christ loved the church and in the same way that they love their own bodies (v. 28). Now Paul goes one step further and claims that husbands and wives are in reality one flesh.

There is no introductory formula (so also at 4:25 and 6:2, 3 but not so at 4:8 and 5:14) to alert his reader that he is going to cite an OT passage. This verse is a quotation of Gen 2:24 and there are only two minor differences from the text in the LXX: Paul uses ἀντί τούτου whereas the LXX has ἕνεκεν τούτου and Paul leaves out the personal pronoun αὐτοῦ after πατέρα and after μητέρα. Genesis 2:24 is also quoted in Matt 19:5 and its parallel Mark 10:7–8 and the last part is quoted in 1 Cor 6:16. Mark's rendering is exactly like the LXX except it omits αὐτοῦ only after μητέρα, whereas Matthew's rendering omits the αὐτοῦ both

1. The textual problem is concerned with the article τόν before πατέρα and τήν before μητέρα. The first reading includes them and occurs in 𝔓[46] א A D[2] Ψ 048 0278 0285[vid] 1739 1881 𝔐 Origen. The second read omits them as seen in B D* F G. The first reading has an early date and good character of manuscripts with good geographical distribution of the Alexandrian and Byzantine text-types and good genealogical relationships in those two texts. The second reading has good representation from the Western text-type but only one major manuscript from the Alexandrian text. Although the meaning would remain the same regardless of the reading, the first reading is favored. Internal evidence would favor the inclusion of the articles because it would be the closest to the LXX. Their exclusion would make it a more difficult reading but not significantly so. Therefore, it seems that the inclusion of the articles should be accepted as the original reading.

2. There are four readings. The first reading καὶ προσκολληθήσεται πρὸς τὴν γυναῖκα αὐτοῦ is found in א[2] B D[2] Ψ 0278 1739[mg] 1881 𝔐 Origen. The second reading καὶ προσκολληθήσεται τῇ γυναικὶ αὐτοῦ appears in 𝔓[46] א[1] (א* *omits* αὐτοῦ) A P 0285 33 81 1241[s] *pc* latt. The third reading καὶ κολληθήσεται τῇ γυναικὶ αὐτοῦ occurs in D* F G. The fourth reading omits these words and is found in 6 1739* Cyprian Jerome. The fourth reading has too few weighty witnesses to be considered valid. The first reading has some support from the Alexandrian and Western texts and full support of the Byzantine tradition. The second reading has good support in the Alexandrian tradition and the third reading has support of the main manuscripts of the Western text. The second and third readings are the same except the third reading has κολληθήσεται instead of προσκολληθήσεται though both have the same meaning. The combination of the second and third readings strengthens the case for a preferred reading because the witnesses are early and of good character, good genealogical relationships, and good geographical distribution. In the end, however, the first reading is preferred because of good geographical distribution. Furthermore, this reading is an exact quotation from the LXX as is Mark 10:7 (though it is also disputed textually) whereas the third reading paraphrases the LXX similar to the way Matt 19:5 does. Whichever of the first three readings is preferred, the meaning is the same.

after πατέρα and μητέρα and has κολληθήσεται τῇ γυναικί instead of προσκολληθήσεται πρὸς τὴν γυναῖκα as found in Mark 10:7 and Eph 5:31. However, there is no change in meaning in any of these quotations from the LXX. The change in the present context is the use of ἀντί in the place of ἕνεκεν. Frequently עַל־כֵּן meaning "therefore, upon the ground of such conditions,"[1] is translated into ἕνεκεν τούτου (e.g., Gen 2:24; 16:14; 20:6; 32:32 [MT & LXX 32:33]; 42:21; 2 Sam 7:22; Ezek 7:20; 31:5; 44:12) or διὰ τούτου (1 Kgs 9:9; Jer 31:20 [LXX 38:20]) but never into ἀντί τούτου as it is in the present context. However, עַל is translated into ἀντί (Lev 26:24) or עַל אֲשֶׁר into ἀνθ' ὧν, both meaning "because" or "for (equivalence)" (2 Sam 3:30; 12:6; 1 Kgs 9:9; Jer 16:11; 22:9; Amos 1:3, 9, 13; 2:1, 6; Ezek 39:23). It is likely that Paul changed the improper preposition ἕνεκεν to the preposition ἀντί, which goes with the genitive to express "because of this, therefore, for this reason."[2] Having stated that Eve was one with Adam having come out of him, Gen 2:24 concludes that in the future man shall leave his father and mother and cling to his wife and they shall become one flesh. Likewise, as Paul has argued that husbands are to love their wives as their own bodies just as Christ loves the church because we are members of his body, he concludes by quoting Gen 2:24 to demonstrate that in marriage man and woman are one flesh. In other words, as Gen 2:24 was a fitting conclusion to 2:23, Paul utilized Gen 2:24 in Eph 5:31 as a fitting conclusion to 5:28–30. This reinforces the concept that the husband is compelled to love his wife because they are one flesh and no one hates his own flesh but rather nurtures and takes tender care of it in the same way that Christ loves his body, the church.[3]

The injunction for the man is to leave his father and mother and be united to his wife. The first verb καταλείψει is the future indicative of καταλείπω. In classical times it could mean "to leave behind,"[4] "forsake, abandon,"[5] or "to leave remaining."[6] In the LXX it occurs 282 times (220 times in the canonical books) and translates eighteen Hebrew words, forty-seven times of those for עָזַב "to leave, forsake, abandon" (e.g., Gen 2:24; 44:22*bis*; Ruth 1:16; Isa 54:6, 7; Jer 9:2 [MT 9:1]).[7] It is used twenty-four times in the NT, three times by Paul

1. BDB 487; cf. *HALOT* 2 (1995): 482–83.

2. BAGD 73; BDAG 88; Winer, *Grammar*, 456; Robertson, *Grammar*, 574; BDF §208 (1); Moule, *Idiom Book*, 71.

3. Raymond C. Ortlund Jr., *Whoredom: God's Unfaithful Wife in Biblical Theology*, New Studies in Biblical Theology, ed. D. A. Carson, no. 2 (Grand Rapids: Eerdmans, 1996), 154–55.

4. Homer *Ilias* 12.92; *Odyssea* 15.89; Herodotus 4.78.

5. Homer *Ilias* 12.226; 14.89; Sophocles *Philocetes* 809.

6. Xenophon *Anabasis* 4.2.11.

7. BDB 736–37; E. Gerstenberger, "עָזַב *ʿāzab*; עִזְבוֹנִים *ʿizzᵉbwônîm*," *TDOT* 10 (1999): 584–92.

(Rom 11:4; Eph 5:31; 1 Thess 3:1) of which the first two references are quotations from the OT. It is used of leaving a region (Matt 4:13; 16:4; 21:17; Heb 11:27), possessions (Mark 14:52; Luke 5:28; 15:4), or people (Mark 12:19, 21 = Luke 20:31; Luke 10:40; John 8:9; Acts 18:19; 24:27; 25:14; 1 Thess 3:1).[1] This idea of leaving, with reference to one's father and mother, is certainly the intent of Gen 2:24 and also where it is quoted in the NT (Matt 19:5; Mark 10:7–8; Eph 5:31). The second verb in this quotation, προσκολληθήσεται is also a future indicative passive of προσκολλάω. The verb κολλάω means "to glue, cement," as the welding of two metals together[2] "in contrast to nailing, to join together tightly."[3] The compound verb προσκολλάω in the passive has the same meaning, illustrated by the body and soul "being welded together,"[4] people "clinging" to each other,[5] or the sword "being stuck" to the hand with blood.[6] It is used eighteen times in the LXX (sixteen times in the canonical books) and translates three Hebrew words, twelve times for דָּבַק, meaning "to cling, cleave" to possessions (Num 36:7, 9; Deut 13:17 [MT & LXX 13:18]), to God (Deut 11:22; Josh 23:8), to people (Ruth 2:21, 23), or it simply refers to two things which are stuck together (2 Sam 23:10; Ezek 29:4; Theodotion Dan 2:43).[7] In the NT κολλάω occurs twelve times, always in the passive sense of "clinging" as dust to feet (Luke 10:11), to what is good (Rom 12:9), or "joined" as people, one to another (Luke 15:15; Acts 5:13; 9:26; 10:28; 17:34; 1 Cor 6:16) or to the Lord (1 Cor 6:17). The verb in this text, προσκολλάω, occurs only twice in the NT and both times it is in the passive and is quoted from Gen 2:24 (Mark 10:7; Eph 5:31). It has the same meaning as κολλάω and, in fact, Matt 19:5 uses it rather than προσκολλάω when quoting Gen 2:24. Hence, it has the idea of being joined to or cleaving to one's wife. It may even include the idea of sexual intercourse that represents the bond between husband and wife,[8] which is lacking with the man and his parents. It is actually used of sexual intercourse in 1 Cor 6:16 where it states that a person who has intercourse with a prostitute is one body with her. However, because of the broader context surrounding this verse, it encompasses more than physical union. In the present context this compound verb is followed by the preposition πρός, a seldom occurrence,[9] possibly to em-

1. Cf. Walther Günther and Hartmut Krienke, "Remnant, Leave [λεῖμμα, λείπω]," *NIDNTT* 3 (1978): 253.

2. LSJ 972.

3. Horst Seebass, "Join, Cleave to [κολλάομαι, προσκολλάομαι]," *NIDNTT* 2 (1976): 348.

4. Plato *Phaedo* §82e.

5. Plato *Leges* 5 §728b.

6. Josephus *A.J.* 7.12.4 §309.

7. BDB 179–80; G. Wallis, "דָּבַק *dābhaq*; דֶּבֶק *debheq*; דָּבֵק *dābhēq*," *TDOT* 3 (1978): 79–84.

8. Karl Ludwig Schmidt, "κολλάω, προσκολλάω," *TDNT* 3 (1965): 822–23.

9. Robertson, *Grammar*, 560; Moule, *Idiom Book*, 91.

phasize "to" whom the husband is joined,[1] that is, τὴν γυναῖκα αὐτοῦ, to his own wife.

Finally, the last part of the quotation further explains "cleave." When the husband leaves his parents and cleaves to his wife, καὶ ἔσονται οἱ δύο εἰς σάρκα μίαν, "the two shall be one flesh." Paul accepts the LXX reading οἱ δύο, "the two," over against the Hebrew text ("they shall be[come] one flesh") possibly to accentuate the concept of two becoming one.[2] There are those who allegorize this to mean that Christ left the Father in heaven to cleave to his wife, the church.[3] However, this is improbable for two reasons. First, this verse, both in the present context and in the context of Gen 2:24, is speaking of the union between husband and wife and not Christ and the church. Second, in this text the subject is the responsibility of the husbands. Christ and the church are used only for the pupose of illustration. On the other hand, because of the use of the future tense verbs, Meyer thinks that the union will occur at Christ's parousia.[4] This view also is not valid for two reasons. First, the use of the future tense cannot be pressed too far because Paul is quoting from Gen 2:24, which speaks of the future generations of the union of man and wife. Second, the future tense can be used to express commands,[5] but it is more likely that in this verse the three verbs have a gnomic sense expressing that which is expected under normal circumstances.[6] Hence, it is best as simply stating that a man leaves his parents and is joined to his wife and the two are one flesh.[7]

The prepositional phrase εἰς σάρκα μίαν is literally "to/into one flesh." One would normally expect a predicate nominative with ἔσονται, "shall be," but the use of the εἰς with the accusative is commonly

1. Cf. Robertson, *Grammar*, 623.

2. Barth, 720–21.

3. Chrysostom *Eph* 5:33 (*PG* 62:142); Jerome *Eph* 5:31–33 (*PL* 26:535–36); Theodoret *Eph* 5:31–33 (*PG* 82:547–50); Oecumenius *Eph* 5:25–33 (*PG* 118:1243–46); Theophylact *Eph* 5:31–32 (*PG* 124:1117–20); Aquinas, chap. 5, lec. 10, vv. 31–33 (225); Bengel, 4:109; Alford, 3:139; Lincoln, 380.

4. Meyer, 307–8.

5. BDF §362; Porter, *Verbal Aspect*, 419–20; cf. Fanning, *Verbal Aspect*, 122–23.

6. BDF §349 (1); MHT 3:86; HS §202i.

7. Merz attempts to show that the one flesh relationship of husband and wife (Gen 2:24) in a hierarchical structured marriage reflects the relationship of Christ and the church (Eph 5:22–33) and that by modifying genuine Pauline texts of 2 Cor 11:2 and 1 Cor 6:15–17, the pseudo-Pauline author attempts to defend marriage as a normative lifestyle (Annette Merz, "Why Did the Pure Bride of Christ [2 Cor. 11.2] Become a Wedded Wife [Eph. 5.22–33]? Theses about the Intertextual Transformation of an Ecclesiological Metaphor," *JSNT* 79 [September 2000]: 131–47). Although it is an interesting proposal, this theory rests on too many unproven assumptions. This "one flesh" concept relates not to the husband's headship over his wife as argued in Eph 5:22–24 but relates to the union between husband and wife as argued in 5:25–29 (S. Aaron Son, "Implications of Paul's 'One Flesh' Concept for His Understanding of the Nature of Man," *BBR* 11, no. 1 [2001]: 110–14).

due to a Semitic influence of the LXX's translation of the Hebrew לְ,[1] hence, "the two shall be one flesh." The man and the woman are two independent entities before they marry. When they marry the husband is to leave his father and mother (the implication is that this is true also for the wife) and they shall be glued or cemented to each other. It can be compared to two objects that have been glued together, each maintaining its distinctive features. It is not the same as an alloy, an admixture of metals, because in that case the distinctiveness of each person would be lost. Batey states it well: "Each personality is enlarged by the inclusion of the other, ideally effecting the perfect blending of two separate lives into one. Continuity with the old personality is not broken, but the radical transformation resulting from the intimate personal encounter creates a new self."[2] The result of this union is the nurture and tender care given to the wife by the husband.

(v) Conclusion: The Mystery Is Great (5:32)

Text: 5:32. τὸ μυστήριον τοῦτο μέγα ἐστίν· ἐγὼ δὲ λέγω εἰς Χριστὸν καὶ εἰς τὴν ἐκκλησίαν.

Translation: 5:32. "This mystery is great, but I speak with reference to Christ and the church."

Commentary: 5:32. τὸ μυστήριον τοῦτο μέγα ἐστίν, "This mystery is great." This declaration, made without the use of a conjunction, explains the previous verse. The adjective μέγα, "great," and the noun μυστήριον, "mystery," requires some discussion. As to the adjective μέγα some versions (AV, RSV, NEB, TEV, NIV, NRSV) use it as an attributive adjective modifying "mystery" and translate it, "this is a great mystery." Other versions (RV, ASV, NASB, JB, NJB) use μέγα as a predicate adjective and translate it as in this commentary, "this mystery is great." The second alternative is better grammatically because the demonstrative pronoun τοῦτο, "this," modifies "mystery" and because of the presence of the copula ἐστίν. The difference is not great. The first alternative stresses the difficulty in comprehending the mystery and the better alternative stresses the magnitude, importance, or profundity of the mystery.[3]

The term "mystery" was discussed at 1:9 and in Excursus 6: Mystery with the conclusion that it is something which was hidden in God and which humans could not unravel by their own ingenuity or study

1. MHT 2:463; cf. BDF §§145, 157; Robertson, *Grammar*, 458; Zerwick, *Biblical Greek* §32; Wallace, *Greek Grammar*, 47.

2. Richard Batey, "The μία σάρξ Union of Christ and the Church," *NTS* 13 (April 1967): 279; cf. also idem, *New Testament Nuptial Imagery*, 30–35; T. A. Burkill, "Two into One: The Notion of Carnal Union in Mark 10:8; 1 Kor. 6:16; Eph. 5:31," *ZNW* 62, nos. 1/2 (1971): 117–20.

3. BAGD 498; BDAG 624; Abbott, 174; Sampley, *'And the Two Shall Become One Flesh,'* 86–87.

but is revealed by God for all believers to understand. In Ephesians (3:3, 4, 9; 6:19) it refers to believing Jews and Gentiles as fellow heirs, in the same body, and as fellow partakers of the promise in Christ Jesus through the gospel. Although the present context does refer to believers as unified in one body with Christ as the head, it is not dealing with the mystery of Jews and Gentiles in one body as discussed in Eph 2:11–3:13.[1] Therefore, the meaning of "mystery" remains the same (i.e., a secret unveiled by God) though the content of the mystery has changed. In Scripture more than one mystery is revealed as seen, for example, in Rom 11:25 where the mystery refers to a partial hardening of Israel until the fullness of the Gentiles has come in.

So what is the mystery in this text? Many different suggestions have been made but it really narrows down to three views: (1) the human marriage explained in Gen 2:24; (2) the human marriage in Gen 2:24 as typological of the union between Christ and the church; and (3) specifically the union of Christ and the church. Each view will be examined respectively.

First to be considered is the view that the mystery is the human marriage mentioned in Gen 2:24. Many Roman Catholics, due to the Vulgate's translation of μυστήριον as "sacramentum,"[2] interpret the institution of marriage as a sacrament of the church that conveys grace.[3] This has its origins in pagan rituals where marriage is seen as equivalent to a *hieros gamos* ("holy wedding"), the union of the divine and the human, Elohim, father of all, and Eden, mother of all creation.[4] Thus, the Roman Catholic sacrament of marriage views the

1. Robinson, 239; Harvey, "The Use of Mystery Language in the Bible," 326.

2. Cf. J. J. Dougherty, "The Confraternity Version of Eph. 5:32," *CBQ* 8 (January 1946): 97.

3. Aquinas, chap. 5, lec. 10, vv. 31–33 (225); Schlier, 261 n. 1; Gnilka, 288–89; Schnackenburg, 256; cf. L. Johnston, "The Mystery of Marriage," *Scr* 11 (January 1959): 1–6; Engelbert Neuhäusler, "Das Geheimnis ist groß. Einführung in die Grundbegriffe der Eheperikope, Eph 5,22–29," *Bibel und Leben* 4 (1963): 155–67; Donal J. O'Connor, "The Concept of 'Mystery' in Aquinas's Exegesis," *Irish Theological Quarterly* 36 (October 1969): 276–77; Angelico Di Marco, "«Misterium hoc magnum est . . .» (Ef 5,32)," *Laurentianum* 14, no. 1 (1973): 56–80; Di Marco, "Ef. 5,21–6,9: teologia della famiglia," 189–94; Anne-Marie La Bonnardière, "L'interprétation augustinienne *du magnum sacramentum* de Éhes. 5,32," *Recherches Augustiniennes* 12 (1977): 3–45; Benoit, "Christian Marriage according to Saint Paul," 319–20. Barth has a good discussion on whether or not marriage should be considered a sacrament (Barth, 744–47). See also von Soden, "ΜΥΣΤΗΡΙΟΝ und *Sacramentum* in den ersten zwei Jahrhunderten der Kirche," 188–227. Mussner (*Christus, das All und die Kirche*, 151–52) thinks it refers to the sacrament of baptism and not marriage.

4. Schlier, 264–76; Gnilka, 290–94; Richard Batey, "Jewish Gnosticism and the 'Hieros Gamos' of Eph. V: 21–33," *NTS* 10 (October 1963): 121–27; Michael Theobald, "Heilige Hochzeit: Motive des Mythos im Horizont von Eph 5,21–33," in *Metaphorik und Mythos im Neuen Testament*, ed. Karl Kertelge, Quaestiones Disputatae, ed. Heinrich Fries and Rudolf Schnackenburg, vol. 126 (Freiburg: Herder, 1990), 220–54; Fleckenstein, *Ordnet euch einander unter in der Furcht Christi*, 142–55; Ådna, "Die eheliche Liebesbezie-

joining of a Christian man and woman as a reenactment of the marriage of Christ and the church.[1] However, this is unacceptable because Gen 2:24 gives no hint of a "Christian" marriage as opposed to a secular marriage. Regardless, secular or religious, marriage is the joining of two into one flesh. Furthermore, this view is based on second or third century Gnostic sources and there is no clear evidence that this understanding was evident in first-century Western Asia Minor.[2]

Second, some think that the mystery reflects a deeper meaning of the human marriage in Gen 2:24, namely, that it refers to the union of Christ and the church. Bockmuehl thinks it "an *exegetical* mystery: a deeper (in this case either allegorical or prophetic) meaning of a Scriptural text which has been elicited by means of some form of inspired exegesis. In other words, the deeper meaning of Gen 2:24 points typologically to Christ and the church."[3] The problem with this view is that, as Lincoln points out, "μυστήριον as a deeper meaning would not only be distinctive in Ephesians but also unparalleled in the NT."[4] Furthermore, the context (v. 30) is already talking about Christians being members of Christ's body, and Gen 2:24 only serves as a human illustration of that spiritual union.

Third, many see this mystery of the "two becoming one" as the union of Christ and the church.[5] This view is understandable because

---

hung als Analogie zu Christi Beziehung zur Kirche," 439–47; Barth, 748. Vonck suggests something entirely different when he proposes that the church *is* the body (1:23) and the Christian community *is* the flesh of Christ (5:29) and thus the one flesh is more than the human dimension (Pol Vonck, "This Mystery Is a Profound One [Ephes. 5:32]. A Biblical Reflection on Marriage," *African Ecclesiastical Review* 24 [October 1982]: 286–87).

1. Cf. Fleckenstein, *Ordnet euch einander unter in der Furcht Christi*, 233–41, 286–89.

2. Moritz, *A Profound Mystery*, 124–25.

3. Bockmuehl, *Revelation and Mystery*, 204; cf. also Brown, "The Semitic Background of the New Testament *Mystery*," 82–84, reprinted in idem, *The Semitic Background of the Term "Mystery" in the New Testament*, 64–66; Bornkamm, "μυστήριον, μυέω," *TDNT* 4 (1967): 823; Coppens, "'Mystery' in the Theology of Saint Paul and Its Parallels at Qumran," 146–47; Mussner, "Contributions Made by Qumran to the Understanding of the Epistle to the Ephesians," 162; B. Reicke, "Neuzeitliche und neutestamentliche Auffassung von Liebe und Ehe," *NovT* 1 (January 1956): 30–31; Heinrich Baltensweiler, *Die Ehe im Neuen Testament. Exegetische Untersuchungen über Ehe, Ehelosigkeit und Ehescheidung*, Abhandlungen zur Theologie des Alten und Neuen Testament, ed. W. Eichrodt and O. Cullmann, vol. 52 (Zürich: Zwingli, 1967), 230–31; Greeven, "Ehe nach dem Neuen Testament," 388; Kurt Niederwimmer, *Askese und Mysterium: Über Ehe, Ehescheidung und Eheverzicht in den Anfängen des christlichen Glaubens*, FRLANT, ed. Ernst Käsemann and Ernst Würthwein, vol. 113 (Göttingen: Vandenhoeck & Ruprecht, 1975), 152–53, 156; Penna, *Il «Mysterion» Paolino*, 75–79; Bruce, 394–95. Methodius of Olympus (d. A.D. 311) *Symposium* 3.2 cited by C. W. Macleod, "Bathos in 'Longinus' and Methodius," *JTS*, n.s., 27 (October 1976): 413–14; Moritz, *A Profound Mystery*, 117–52.

4. Lincoln, "The Use of the OT in Ephesians," 42; cf. Sampley, *'And the Two Shall Become One Flesh,'* 95–96.

5. O'Connor, "The Concept of 'Mystery' in Aquinas's Exegesis," 280–82; Cambier, "Le grand mystère concernant le Christ et son Église," 43–90, 223–42; Caragounis, *Ephesian*

the only other time Paul quotes Gen 2:24 is in 1 Cor 6:16 where he uses it in a similar fashion. In 1 Cor 6 he explains that believers are members of the body of Christ (v. 15) and therefore cannot partake in sexual immorality because when a man joins himself to a prostitute the two become one body (v. 16). As a proof of this Paul quotes Gen 2:24 and immediately follows with the declaration that the one who joins himself to the Lord is one Spirit with him (v. 17). In Ephesians, Paul moves from the spiritual (v. 30) to the quotation from Gen 2:24, which speaks of physical union (v. 31),[1] and then shifts back to the spiritual by proclaiming that this mystery is great, which refers to the spiritual union of Christ and the church (v. 32). In both passages Paul uses the same pattern of going from the spiritual realm to the physical realm (Gen 2:24) and returning to a spiritual application. Furthermore, the context portrays Christ as the model for the husband and the church as the model for the wife (Eph 5:24–27), and thus the union of the husband and wife into one flesh ("the two shall be one flesh") is a model for the union of Christ and the church (vv. 31–32). Therefore, this mystery is not the union of believing Jews and Gentiles nor of human marriage, but rather the union of Christ and the church.[2] This is made more clear in the next statement.

Mysterion, 30; Lincoln, "The Use of the OT in Ephesians," 30–36; Lincoln, 382–83; Best, 557; O'Brien, 432–35; Kostenberger, "The Mystery of Christ and the Church: Head and Body, 'One Flesh'," 79–94; Baumert, *Woman and Man in Paul*, 225–26; cf. Batey, "The μία σάρξ Union of Christ and the Church," 270–81; Piet Farla, "'The two shall become one flesh': Gen. 1.27 and 2.24 in the New Testament Marriage Texts [trans. Richard Rosser]," in *Intertextuality in Biblical Writings: Essays in Honour of Basil van Iersel*, ed. Sipke Draisma (Kampen: Uitgeversmaatschappij J. H. Kok, 1989), 74–75; Reynier, *Évangile et mystère*, 189–92; Ortlund, *Whoredom: God's Unfaithful Wife in Biblical Theology*, 157–58; Dawes, *The Body in Question*, 178–85, 190–91, 225–27. For a somewhat different interpretation of Paul's use of Gen 2:24, see Klara Butting, "Pauline Variations on Genesis 2.24: Speaking of the Body of Christ in the Context of the Discussion of Lifestyles," *JSNT* 79 (September 2000): 79–90, esp. 81–83, 88–90.

1. Miletic (*"One Flesh": Eph. 5.22–24, 5.31*, 21–22, 57–66, 89–98, 114–20) thinks this does not reflect the union of Adam and Eve but the union of the new Adam and Eve of the new creation (similarly Bedale, "The Meaning of κεφαλή in the Pauline Epistles," 215). But this is theological speculation for which there is no exegetical basis. Even Miletic (*"One Flesh": Eph. 5.22–24, 5.31*, 114) admits that there is no explicit identification of Christ as Adam and the church as Eve. Cf. also Roels, *God's Mission*, 140; Moritz, *A Profound Mystery*, 141–42.

2. Kostenberger asserts that the union of Christ and the church is the consistent use of "mystery" in Ephesians. On this point Kostenberger is confusing because earlier in his article when dealing with Eph 2:16; 3:3, 4, 9, he accepts Stott's definition of the mystery as a double union: union of believing Jews and Gentiles and the union of both entities with Christ, but later in his article when dealing with Eph 5:32, he defines the mystery as only the union of Christ and the church (Kostenberger, "The Mystery of Christ and the Church: Head and Body, 'One Flesh'" 83–84, 91–92). He cites the phrases τοὺς ἀμφοτέρους ἐν ἑνὶ σώματι (2:16) and οἱ ἀμφότεροι ἐν ἑνὶ πνεύματι (2:18) as being equivalent to οἱ δύο εἰς σάρκα μίαν (5:31 = Gen 2:24) (ibid., 83 n. 17). However, the phrases in 2:16 and 2:18 refer

ἐγὼ δὲ λέγω εἰς Χριστὸν καὶ εἰς[1] τὴν ἐκκλησίαν, "but I speak with reference to Christ and the church." A contrast is marked not only by the adversative δέ but also by the employment of the nominative pronoun ἐγώ.[2] This stark contrast ἐγὼ δὲ λέγω, "but I speak," indicates that he has not continued the discussion of the physical union of husband and wife. The only other place the expression ἐγὼ δὲ λέγω is used in the NT is in Matthew (5:22, 28, 32, 34, 39, 44) when six times Jesus gives his interpretation of the Mosaic law in contrast to what was generally accepted.[3] Why did Paul use this expression in the present text? Was it because there were other interpretations circulating among Ephesian believers which needed to be refuted? Some think he is refuting some Gnostic interpretations of Gen 2:24 which envision the copulation of heavenly beings when man and woman enact sexual intercourse.[4] However, this tradition is so late (second or third century A.D.) that it could not have been an issue in Paul's time.[5] There were other second-century interpretations of Gen 2:24 and marriage, including the Nag Hammadi literature,[6] but the Ephesians would not have heard of these either because they were also well after Paul's time.[7]

On the other hand, Sampley thinks some literature in Paul's day, such as extant in Philo, tannaitic literature, and intertestamental literature, indicate the reworking of the traditional interpretation of Gen 2:24. He attempts to make a case that some apocryphal literature

---

to the union of believing Jews and Gentiles and if one wants 5:31 to refer to the church, it would not be a union of believing Jews and Gentiles but a union of the church and Christ. Lincoln ("The Use of the OT in Ephesians," 32) and Roels (*God's Mission*, 144) think that the mystery in the present context is only a different aspect of the mystery mentioned in Eph 2:11–3:13. However, the union of Christ and church here is not the same as the union of believing Jews and the Gentiles in one body in 2:11–3:13.

1. This εἰς is omitted by B K *pc* Ptolemy[Ir] Tertullian Cyprian Epiphanius. There is not enough external evidence to verify its omission.

2. Robertson, *Grammar*, 677; BDF §277 (1); MHT 3:37.

3. Cf. Morton Smith, *Tannaitic Parallels to the Gospels*, Journal of Biblical Literature Monograph Series, ed. Ralph Marcus, vol. 6 (Philadelphia: Society of Biblical Literature, 1951), 28; David Daube, *The New Testament and Rabbinic Judaism*, Jordan Lectures in Comparative Religion, School of Oriental and African Studies, University of London, no. 2 (London: University of London, Athlone Press, 1956), 55–62.

4. Schlier, *Christus und die Kirche im Epheserbrief*, 60–75; Schlier, 262; Dibelius-Greeven, 95; Pagels, *The Gnostic Paul*, 127.

5. Percy, *Probleme*, 327–28.

6. Cf. Elaine H. Pagels, "Adam and Eve, Christ and the Church: A Survey of Second Century Controversies Concerning Marriage," in *The New Testament and Gnosis: Essays in Honour of Robert McL. Wilson*, ed. A. H. B. Logan and A. J. M. Wedderburn (Edinburgh: T & T Clark, 1983), 146–75; idem, "Exegesis and Exposition of the Genesis Creation Accounts in Selected Texts from Nag Hammadi," in *Nag Hammadi, Gnosticism, & Early Christianity*, ed. Charles W. Hedrick and Robert Hodgson Jr. (Peabody, Mass.: Hendrickson, 1986), 257–85.

7. For a brief discussion of some of these views, see Lincoln, 382–83.

along with Ezekiel and Song of Songs depict a special relationship between YHWH and Israel, similar to that of Christ and the church.[1] This is unconvincing for two reasons. First, the literature he examines gives the traditional interpretation of Gen 2:24, that is, man leaving father and mother and cleaving to his wife. Second, Sampley makes dubious associations of some apocryphal literature with OT canonical literature in order to demonstrate that there was a special relationship between YHWH and Israel similar to that of Christ and the church. He does this in a way that is not really germane to the quotation of Gen 2:24. In the end if Paul were acquainted with any of this literature, he would have considered it to be the traditional interpretation of Gen 2:24, that is, as the marital union of husband and wife and not as a special relationship between YHWH and Israel.

It is best, then, to accept that Paul had been interacting with the traditional interpretation of Gen 2:24. However, Eph 5:32 may be similar to Gal 4:24 where he informs the readers that he is going to allegorize an OT passage. The εἰς plus the accusatives Χριστόν and τὴν ἐκκλησίαν indicate the direction of the speaker's words:[2] "I speak with reference to Christ and the church." The Ephesian audience most naturally would have accepted that the Gen 2:24 passage refers to the union of the husband and wife as it was in the original context, an interpretation accepted also by other NT writers (Matt 19:5; Mark 10:7–8), Philo, Tannaim, and Apocrypha. But Paul applies Gen 2:24 to the mystery of the union of Christ and the church.[3] Moritz extends it further whereby Paul uses the words of Gen 2:24 to show the relevance of the union of Christ and the church for marriage.[4] Similarly, Dawes sees this as a double referent, that is, to the union of husband and wife and to the union of church and Christ.[5] This interlude or digression is not only marked off by ἐγὼ δὲ λέγω but also by the introductory adverb πλήν ("however, nevertheless, in any case"), which begins verse 33 and indicates his return to the subject of marriage.[6] This adverb "is used to conclude a discussion and emphasize what is essential,"[7] in other words, that which follows in verse 33.

Briefly then, in this verse Paul is referring to the mystery of the union of Christ and the church, which is already mentioned in verses 29–30. In the present verse Paul quotes "the two shall be one" in Gen

1. Sampley, *'And the Two Shall Become One Flesh,'* 51–61.

2. Ellicott, 136.

3. Bruce Kaye, "'One Flesh' and Marriage," *Colloquium* 22 (May 1990): 55–57; cf. Edward Schillebeeckx, *Marriage: Human Reality and Saving Mystery*, trans. N. D. Smith (London: Sheed and Ward, 1965), 112–15; Ådna, "Die eheliche Liebesbeziehung als Analogie zu Christi Beziehung zur Kirche," 459–63.

4. Moritz, *A Profound Mystery*, 144–48.

5. Dawes, *The Body in Question*, 182–85.

6. "New Testament Lexicography," *CQR* 29 (January 1890): 278.

7. BDF §449 (2); Robertson, *Grammar*, 1187; cf. BAGD 669; BDAG 826.

2:24 as support for that union. Although the readers would have naturally thought the Genesis passage refers to the physical union, Paul chose to explain clearly what he did mean, that in fact he was speaking about the union of Christ and the church. On the other hand, he also uses it to support the exhortation of the husband's tender care of his wife, his own body/flesh (vv. 28–30). Thus, Gen 2:24 is used in a two-pronged way. Hanson writes, "the Church is, on the one hand, an independent person, the object of Christ's love, and, on the other hand, so closely connected with Him, the Head, the Saviour, that together they constitute a unity."[1] This is the mystery.

(3) Responsibilities Reviewed (5:33)

Text: 5:33. πλὴν καὶ ὑμεῖς οἱ καθ' ἕνα, ἕκαστος τὴν ἑαυτοῦ γυναῖκα οὕτως ἀγαπάτω ὡς ἑαυτόν, ἡ δὲ γυνὴ ἵνα φοβῆται τὸν ἄνδρα.

Translation: 5:33. "Nevertheless also you, each one of you, should so love his own wife as himself, and the wife should fear her husband."

Commentary: 5:33. πλὴν καὶ ὑμεῖς οἱ καθ' ἕνα, ἕκαστος τὴν ἑαυτοῦ γυναῖκα οὕτως ἀγαπάτω ὡς ἑαυτόν, "Nevertheless also you, each one of you, should so love his own wife as himself." Before looking at this verse in more detail, two distinctions from his former exhortations need to be noted. First, he reverses the order, beginning with the husband and following with the wife.[2] Of course, this is not difficult to understand because he has just been dealing with the husbands' responsibility towards their wives and now he continues with the husbands. Second, he addresses each spouse in the singular rather than in the plural. The use of the singular for those addressed occurs only in this verse and nowhere else in the NT household codes. Perhaps the purpose of this was to emphasize individual responsibility. It also distinguishes the nature of this relationship from the following pairs in the household code (children/parents and slaves/masters).

The introductory adverb πλήν, used by Paul four times (1 Cor 11:11; Eph 5:33; Phil 4:11, 14), functions as a "balancing adversative,"[3] which "is used to conclude a discussion and emphasize what is essential"[4] and thus can be translated "only, nevertheless, in any case, however, but."[5] Having mentioned that the mystery is the union of Christ and the church (vv. 29–32), Paul uses this adverb to return to the main subject of his discussion, marriage.

The next words καὶ ὑμεῖς combine an adjunctive conjunction with a second person plural personal pronoun, "also you," and give further

1. Hanson, *The Unity of the Church in the New Testament*, 140.

2. Gnilka, 289.

3. Thrall, *Greek Particles in the New Testament*, 21.

4. BDF §449 (2); Robertson, *Grammar*, 1187; cf. BAGD 669; cf. BDAG 826; Maillett, "Alla . . . Plén . . . Métaphore et pédagogie," 566–67, 570.

5. BAGD 669; cf. BDAG 826.

indication that he is returning to the subject of marriage. The adjunctive conjunction is omitted from some translations (AV, RSV, NASB, NIV, NRSV), but it is important and needs to be retained because it stresses the application of both Gen 2:24 and the revealed mystery to the marriages of believers. The personal plural pronoun is emphatic by its use and position and, in addition, it indicates a return to the exhortations (vv. 22–25, 28) which were also in the plural. This is followed by the distributive phrase οἱ καθ᾿ ἕνα ἕκαστος, which individualizes[1] the ὑμεῖς by making "each one of you, each individual among you" responsible. No one is exempt. The verb ἀγαπάτω, "to love," is a third person singular present imperative relating back to the nearer ἕκαστος rather than to the more distant ὑμεῖς. The object of each husband's continuous love is his own wife (τὴν ἑαυτοῦ γυναῖκα). The intensity of the love is emphasized by the construction οὕτως . . . ὡς, "so . . . as," a construction already seen in verse 28. As in verse 28 the adverbial conjunction ὡς functions not only as a simple comparison where the husband's love for his own wife should be "like" his love for himself, but also introduces a characteristic quality of the husband, namely, that he should love his own wife "as being" himself. Therefore, he loves her because she is united with him, the "two becoming one." As stated earlier, it is not commanded that a person is to love himself or herself in order to love another. Love of self is a natural instinct. This verse, then, serves as a summary of what had been stated in verses 25–29, the only difference being that Paul gives a more personal touch by using the singular rather than the plural.[2] The husband is to love his wife as himself even with all her imperfections in the same way Christ loves the church. Christ demonstrated his love for the church by giving himself for her in order to present her to himself glorious. Meyer rightly observes that this passage gives a new quality to marriage. No longer is the relationship between husband and wife based exclusively on the creation model but also on Christ's personal love for his church.[3]

ἡ δὲ γυνὴ ἵνα φοβῆται τὸν ἄνδρα, "and the wife should fear her husband." The conjunction δέ makes a slightly adversative transition from the husband to the wife. "The wife" (ἡ γυνή) is most likely a nominative absolute[4] to give it more emphasis. Again, as is true for the husband, the wife is addressed in the singular, which, as stated earlier, may be in order to emphasize individual responsibility. It is interesting to note that while there was a repeat for the husband to love his wife, there is no repeat for the wife to submit to her husband but she should fear her husband. Rather than employing the imperative used

1. MHT 3:15; Moule, *Idiom Book*, 60; cf. Robertson, *Grammar*, 746.

2. Gundry, Sōma *in Biblical Theology*, 221.

3. Meyer, "Biblische Metaphorik—gesellschaftlicher Diskurs," 657; cf. also Niederwimmer, *Askese und Mysterium*, 129 n. 19, 155–56.

4. Alford, 3:140; Eadie, 435–36; Ellicott, 137; Meyer, 310; Abbott, 176; Salmond, 374.

for the husbands, Paul uses the conjunction ἵνα plus the subjunctive. Some think this expresses purpose or result, suggesting that each husband is to love his wife as himself in order that or so that the wife might fear her husband.[1] However, in that case the word order would have been ἵνα δὲ ἡ γυνὴ φοβῆται τὸν ἄνδρα rather than ἡ δὲ γυνὴ ἵνα φοβῆται τὸν ἄνδρα.[2] On the other hand, others think though not in classical Greek, the imperatival use of ἵνα with the subjunctive was used in Hellenistic times and at least in four recognized instances in the NT (Mark 5:23; 2 Cor 8:7; Gal 2:10; Eph 5:33).[3] The form of the subjunctive in these instances is either a middle or a passive present. Consistent with the usage within the context, it is best seen as a middle where the wife acts as a free agent before God (vv. 22, 24). The term φοβέω, "to fear," was discussed at 5:21 where all believers are called to submit to one another in the fear of Christ. There we concluded that φοβέω means "to fear, revere" and that the idea of "to respect" is too mild a concept. In the present context the object of fear is not Christ but the husband. Should it be taken as the same "fear" discussed at verse 21? Some commentators and versions translate it "to respect"[4] (RSV, NASB, NEB, TEV, JB, NIV, NJB, NRSV) but others translate it "to fear"[5] (AV, RV, ASV). Those who favor the first option suggest that "there is no fear in love but perfect love casts out fear, because fear has to do with punishment, and he who fears is not perfected in love" (1 John 4:18). However, the fear described here is one of terror.

In modern times people have a tendency to shy away from the stronger idea of fear. At times, they even have difficulty with the milder concept of respect. However, the philological evidence of this word never carries the idea of "respect" but always the idea of "fear."[6]

1. Margaret D. Gibson, "'Let the Woman Learn in Silence'," *ExpTim* 15 (May 1904): 380; Porter, *Verbal Aspect*, 331.

2. Alford, 3:140; W. H. Griffith Thomas, "'Let the Woman Learn in Silence'," *ExpTim* 15 (July 1904): 428.

3. Robertson, *Grammar*, 330, 933, 943, 994; BDF §387 (3); MHT 1:179; 3:95; Winer, *Grammar*, 396, 722; Moule, *Idiom Book*, 144–45; Zerwick, *Biblical Greek* §415; HS §210g; C. J. Cadoux, "The Imperatival use of ἵνα in the New Testament," *JTS* 42 (July–October 1941): 165–73; H. G. Meecham, "The Imperatival Use of ἵνα in the New Testament," *JTS* 43 (July–October 1942): 179–80; A. R. George, "The Imperatival Use of ἵνα in the New Testament," *JTS* 45 (January–April 1944): 56–60; A. P. Salom, "The Imperatival Use of ἵνα in the New Testament," *AusBR* 6 (January 1958): 123–41; cf. Porter, *Verbal Aspect*, 331.

4. Eadie, 435–36; Meyer, 310; Salmond, 375; Masson, 216; Hendriksen, 257–58; Gnilka, 289; Best, 559; Thraede, "Ärger mit der Freiheit," 118–19.

5. Chrysostom *Eph* 5:33 (*PG* 62:140–41); Oecumenius *Eph* 5:25–33 (*PG* 118:1245–46); Theophylact *Eph* 5:33 (*PG* 124:1119–20); Calvin, 211; Alford, 3:140; Ellicott, 137; Robinson, 127; Westcott, 87; Schlier, 263; Barth, 648–50, 662–68; Schnackenburg, 257; Lincoln, 385–86; O'Brien, 436–37.

6. Barth, 648–50, 662; cf. also Balz and Wanke, *TDNT* 9 (1974): 189–219; Mundle, "Fear, Awe [φόβος]," *NIDNTT* 1 (1975): 621–24.

Yet, there are different kinds of fear. There is the evildoers' fear of the wrath of the government officials. People are called to fear the Lord (Lev 19:14; 25:17; Deut 6:13; Josh 4:24; 24:14; Pss 67:7; 111:10; Acts 9:31; Rom 3:18; 2 Cor 5:11; 7:1; 1 Pet 2:17; Rev 14:7; 15:4; 19:5). These among other passages indicate that the word connotes more than respect.

Earlier, believers were called to fear or revere Christ (v. 21). As mentioned there the fear of Christ is more than respect, for a person could respect Christ and fail to be submissive to him. On the other hand, Louw and Nida observe that the fear of God is not "as though God were some kind of bogeyman," but rather it carries "the meaning of 'awe' (perhaps in a phrase such as 'to stand in awe of')."[1] Therefore, in the initial discussion of "fear" (cf. pp. 718–19) we concluded that it was best viewed as reverential fear or reverential respect. In regard to the wife, this fear could be defined as reverence for her husband's position as head of the home. Thus, as believers are to submit themselves to one another in the fear of Christ, so is the wife to submit to her husband with fear.[2] Oecumenius states it well when he attests that it is fitting for a wife to fear, but not as a slave.[3] This kind of fear could not be defined in terms of terror when it is directed toward the husband who is commanded to love her sacrificially. Again, the commands are given without conditions. Consequently, her submission is not dependent on her husband's response of Christlike love. This is similar to the instruction for the husband. His love is not dependent on her submission. Indeed, some wives may not have become believers and thus are not submissive, yet the Christian husband is responsible before the Lord to love his wife whether or not she is a believer.

In conclusion, this first part of the household code has been concerned with the responsibilities of wives and husbands. Wives are to submit to their husbands as the church does to Christ. Husbands are to love their wives as Christ loves the church. Although the responsibilities of the wives are outlined first, the most space is given to the responsibility of the husbands. Marriage is the union of two individuals into one flesh (Gen 2:24). Therefore, it should not be divisive but rather a loving and harmonious relationship. Believers' marital harmony is not to be dependent on their own ingenuity but rather motivated by obedience to God and by the enabling power of the Holy Spirit. The successful development of this relationship requires Spirit-filled partners who are truly concerned for each other and who have a real desire to see the work of God in their lives. The primary goal of

1. L&N §87.14.

2. Sevenster, *Paul and Seneca*, 199. Her submission is one of service in the fear of Christ, see Motyer, "The Relationship between Paul's Gospel of 'All One in Christ Jesus' (Galatians 3:28) and the 'Household Codes'," 43.

3. Oecumenius *Eph* 5:25–33 (*PG* 118:1245).

marriage is not to please oneself but to see the purposes of God work in and through each partner individually and corporately.

b. Children and Parents (6:1–4)

The second of the three pairs in the household code is concerned with children and parents. The broader context of these four verses includes the injunction to walk wisely by understanding the will of the Lord and by being filled by the Spirit (5:15–18) so that a proper harmony between children and parents can be achieved. There are similarities to other parts of the household code. First, the subordinate partner is addressed first, then the ruling partner. Second, each of those addressed are ultimately answerable to the Lord and not to the other partner of the pair. Third, the form is the same for each: the party is addressed, the imperative is stated, amplification is given, and the motivation is presented.

(1) Responsibility of Children's Obedience (6:1–3)

According to the pattern, attention is first given to those who have the submissive role, followed by the duties of those who have authority over them. When comparing this passage to the parallel one in Col 3:20–21, here in Ephesians thirty-five words are addressed to the children, thirteen in Colossians; sixteen words are addressed to the fathers in Ephesians and only ten in Colossians. In this portion there is nothing of the imagery of Christ's authority over the church or the church's submission to Christ as in the first portion of the household code.

(a) Imperative: Obey Parents (6:1a)

Text: 6:1a. Τὰ τέκνα, ὑπακούετε τοῖς γονεῦσιν ὑμῶν [ἐν κυρίῳ],

Translation: 6:1a. "Children, obey your parents in the Lord,"

Commentary: 6:1a. Τὰ τέκνα, ὑπακούετε τοῖς γονεῦσιν ὑμῶν [ἐν κυρίῳ[1]], "Children, obey your parents in the Lord." The article and the

1. ἐν κυρίῳ is found in 𝔓[46] ℵ A D[1] I[vid] Ψ 075 0150 0278 0285 6 33 81 104 256 263 365 424 436 459 1175 1241 1319 (1573 *omits* ἐν) 1739 1852 1881 1912 1962 2127 2200 2464 *Byz* [K L P] *Lect* it[a, ar, mon] vg syr[p, h] cop[sa, bo] arm (eth) geo slav Origen Basil Chrysostom Theodore[lat] Cyril Jerome Pelagius, but it is omitted in B D* F G it[b, d, f, g, o] Marcion[acc. to Tertullian] Cyril-Jerusalem[vid]; Cyprian Ambrosiaster. The first reading has early and good character manuscripts in the Alexandrian and Byzantine text-types with a few manuscripts in the Western text. It has good genealogical relationships and wide geographical distribution. The second reading has good but limited readings in the Alexandrian and quite strong in the Western text. It has good genealogical relationships only in the Western text-type and is quite limited with regards to geographical distribution. Therefore, the external evidence is strong for the inclusion of ἐν κυρίῳ. The internal evidence for its inclusion is that the copiest could have included it from Col 3:20 where it is used in connection with children or from Eph 5:22 where τῷ κυριῷ is used in connection with wives. However, if it were from Eph 5:22 it would seem that the copiest

noun τὰ τέκνα, "children," in plural form indicates that Paul is moving to a new group or class of people.[1] He makes a direct appeal to the children of the families in the Ephesian church. They must have been old enough to understand the concepts when the letter was read to the congregation.[2] This does not mean they had to be teenagers but certainly they would not have been infants. The five times the term τέκνον is used in Ephesians (2:3; 5:1, 8; 6:1, 4) it is always in the plural. The three previous references have to do with adults, referred to as the children of wrath (2:3), beloved children (5:1), and children of light (5:8). As suggested earlier, the term τέκνον denotes a closer relationship to the parent than the word ὑίος, "son." It implies a dependent relationship on the parent. In this context, Paul, no doubt, had in mind children old enough to understand and exercise their free will.

The children are instructed to obey both parents (τοῖς γονεῦσιν ὑμῶν) in spite of the fact that only the father is addressed in verse 4. The term ὑπακούω means "to obey, follow, be subject to" with the dative of the person.[3] Its import is "'to do what one is told' or 'to carry out someone's orders.'"[4] As discussed at 5:22 the terms ὑπακούω and ὑποτάσσω, "be subject," are basically synonymous, for in 1 Pet 3:5–6 wives are told to "be subject" (ὑποτάσσω) to their husbands, illustrated by Sarah "obeying" (ὑπακούω) her husband Abraham. In the same way children are to obey their parents. Although not stated in the text, the best model children can have is Christian parents who are obedient to the Lord (Rom 1:5; 6:17; 10:16; 15:18; 16:19, 26 2 Cor 10:5; Phil 2:12; 2 Thess 1:8; 3:14). The present imperative stresses that the obedience of children is an ongoing action.

The prepositional phrase ἐν κυρίῳ, "in the Lord," refers not to God but to Christ as it does consistently throughout the epistle (2:21; 4:1, 17; 5:8; 6:10, 21). In this context it would at first seem that the injunction to obey parents applies only to children whose parents are "in the Lord," that is, believers. However, the prepositional phrase "in the Lord" more likely qualifies the verb, thus emphasizing the children's ultimate obedience to the Lord. This is substantiated in the parallel passage in Col 3:20 where children are enjoined "to obey parents with respect to all things for this is pleasing in the Lord." Hence, the prepositional phrase does not define the limits of obedience, but rather it

---

would have had ὡς τῷ κυριῷ rather than ἐν κυριῷ or if he copied it from Col 3:20 he would have ἐν κυρίῳ following δίκαιον (see Metzger, *Textual Commentary*, 2d ed., 542). On the other hand, Munro ("Col. iii.18–iv.1 and Eph. v.21–vi.9: Evidences of a Late Literary Stratum?" 439–40; essentially reprinted in idem, *Authority in Paul and Peter*, 31) reverses this proposing that the prepositional phrase, along with with Eph 5:10, served as a basis of Col 3:20.

1. Robertson, *Grammar*, 757.
2. Moritz, *A Profound Mystery*, 168–71.
3. BAGD 837; BDAG 1029.
4. L&N §36.15.

shows the spirit in which the obedience is to be accomplished.[1] The verb "to obey" is active, demonstrating childrens' responsibility as free moral agents to carry out this instruction before God.

In the OT it frequently mentions the duty of children to obey their parents. In Exod 20:12 and Deut 15:16 children are commanded to honor their parents—these two passages are utilized in the next two verses in this context. In fact, the Mosaic law specifically states that a child who strikes or curses a parent should be put to death (Exod 21:15, 17). It is most likely that Paul is addressing those who are still home as dependent children, yet old enough to understand the instruction themselves.

(b) Reason: It Is Right (6:1b)

Text: 6:1b. τοῦτο γάρ ἐστιν δίκαιον.

Translation: 6:1b. "for this is right."

Commentary: 6:1b. τοῦτο γάρ ἐστιν δίκαιον, "for this is right." This is the motivation for children to obey their parents. It is the right thing to do before the Lord. Colossians 3:20 states it a little more explicitly: "for this is well-pleasing to the Lord" (τοῦτο γὰρ εὐάρεστόν ἐστιν ἐν κυρίῳ). Here, the conjunction γάρ, "for," introduces the reason or motivation for obedience. The neuter τοῦτο, "this," refers back to the command just given. The adjective δίκαιος is used both of the righteous character of God (Rom 3:26) and of Christ (2 Tim 4:8) as well as a person who is righteous, good, or just (Rom 5:7; 1 Tim 1:9; 1 John 3:7). It can refer to that which has been declared right or fitting: "masters treat your slaves with what is right and fair" (Col 4:1); "it is right for me to feel this way about all of you" (Phil 1:7); and "I will pay you whatever is right" (Matt 20:4). Although some think that "right" in the present context refers to the righteousness of God's commandment,[2] it seems to fit more naturally with the idea that it is right or fitting for children to obey their parents.[3] This concept is supported biblically in the next two verses, for ultimately one can only judge what is right or wrong in the light of God's own righteousness and righteous actions.

(c) Motivation: Old Testament Command and Promise (6:2–3)

Without an introductory formula (so at Eph 4:25 and 5:31 but not so at 4:8 and 5:14), Paul cites the OT to support his injunction that children

1. Abbott, 176.

2. Theodoret *Eph* 6:1 (*PG* 82:549); Calvin, 212; Meyer, 313–14; Salmond, 375; Robinson, 127; Masson, 217; Gottlob Schrenk, "δίκαιος," *TDNT* 2 (1964): 188; Haug, "Kinder des Lichts," 156.

3. Oecumenius *Eph* 6:1 (*PG* 118:124); Theophylact *Eph* 6:1 (*PG* 124:1120–21); Hodge, 357; Alford, 3:140; Eadie, 438; Ellicott, 138; Westcott, 87; Schlier, 281; Gaugler, 211; Hendriksen, 258; Gnilka, 295–96; Barth, 756; Schnackenburg, 261; Lincoln, 403; BAGD 196; BDAG 247; Stagg, "The Domestic Code and Final Appeal," 548.

should obey their parents. In 6:2–3 he quotes from the OT and in the middle of the quotation he adds a comment: "which is in fact the first commandment with promise." There is dispute regarding the passage from which he is quoting. Although the clause "that it may be well with you" does not appear in the MT of Exod 20:12, it does appear in both OT passages in the LXX. Most think that Paul is quoting from the LXX either from Exod 20:12 or Deut 5:16. It is more likely that he is quoting from the LXX of Exod 20:12 (τίμα τὸν πατέρα σου καὶ τὴν μητέρα, ἵνα εὖ σοι γένηται, καὶ ἵνα μακροχρόνιος γένῃ ἐπὶ τῆς γῆς) because his wording is closer to it. Paul makes only three minor changes: (1) he omits a second ἵνα before μακροχρόνιος; (2) he uses the verb ἔσῃ instead of γένῃ; and (3) he places the aforementioned verb before rather than after μακροχρόνιος. In addition, Deut 5:16 repeats the personal pronoun σου after "mother," which is followed by the clause "in the way/manner the Lord your God commanded you" (ὃν τρόπον ἐνετείλατό σοι κύριος ὁ θεός σου).

Text: 6:2. τίμα τὸν πατέρα σου καὶ τὴν μητέρα, ἥτις ἐστὶν ἐντολὴ πρώτη ἐν ἐπαγγελίᾳ, **6:3. ἵνα εὖ σοι γένηται καὶ ἔσῃ μακροχρόνιος ἐπὶ τῆς γῆς.**

Translation: 6:2. "Honor your father and mother, which is in fact the first commandment with promise, **6:3.** that it may be well with you and you may live long on the earth."

Commentary: 6:2. τίμα τὸν πατέρα σου καὶ τὴν μητέρα, "Honor your father and mother." As mentioned above this quotation is most likely from the LXX of Exod 20:12, although Deut 5:16 has only the one additional personal pronoun σου immediately following μητέρα. This is the fifth commandment in the Decalogue. The first four commandments deal with a person's relationship to God and the last six commandments deal with a person's relationship to other human beings. This commandment to honor one's father and mother encompasses a variety of related commandments. Anyone who strikes or curses his or her father or mother shall be put to death (Exod 21:15, 17); anyone who dishonors his or her father or mother shall be cursed (Deut 27:16); any stubborn, defiant, disobedient son shall be killed (Deut 21:18–21). Accordingly, it is commanded that "everyone shall revere/fear his mother and his father" (Lev 19:3). Hence, the OT writings maintain that to obey one's parents is to honor them; conversely, to disobey them is to dishonor them. It is interesting to note that honor/obedience and dishonor/disobedience include both father and mother and not just the father, the head of the hierarchical family. The mother was equal to the father and "had full claim on the obedience of the children (Ex. 20.12; Deut. 5.16)."[1] A child's honor and obedi-

1. J. J. Stamm and M. E. Andrew, *The Ten Commandments in Recent Research*, trans. with additions by M. E. Andrew, SBT, ed. C. F. D. Moule, James Barr, Peter Ackroyd, Floyd V. Filson, and G. Ernest Wright, vol. 2 (London: SCM, 1967), 96.

ence to the parents is the first important step in learning to honor and obey God. If a child dishonors and disobeys the parent, he or she will most likely have the same attitude toward God.[1] Of course, when children leave home and/or marry, they will be responsible for their own choices, and, if married, will leave their father and mother and cleave to their spouse (cf. Gen 2:24; Eph 5:32). Even then, though obedience may no longer be required, honor of one's parents must continue (Exod 20:12; Deut 5:16; Matt 15:4 = Mark 7:10; Matt 19:19 = Mark 10:19 = Luke 18:20). At any rate, young children are commanded to honor their parents by obedience to them. The present imperative reinforces the idea that children are to honor their parents continually.

ἥτις ἐστὶν[2] ἐντολὴ πρώτη ἐν ἐπαγγελίᾳ, "which is in fact the first commandment with promise." There is need to look at some of the particulars before discussing the interpretative problems of this relative clause. Some think that the indefinite relative pronoun ἥτις functions as a simple relative pronoun, "which is," having an explanatory force[3] but it is preferable to consider that it functions normally, giving a qualitative force "for such is, as it is"[4] and as translated here, "which is in fact." The next term ἐντολή signifies a "command" or "order."[5] According to Eph 2:15 "the law consists of commandments," meaning that the law has many specific commands.[6] Next, the adjective πρώτη, "first," is often in Greek without the article because an ordinal number is definite enough in itself.[7] Finally, with regard to the prepositional phrase ἐν ἐπαγγελίᾳ, "with promise," some think it is a dative of relation and translate it "in regard of a promise, in point of a promise," meaning that it is the first commandment which involves a promise.[8] Alford correctly states that this view of the dative "is too vague, and does not convey any definite meaning in English."[9] It seems better to accept it as a dative of accompaniment, "with a promise" meaning that it is the first commandment with a promise attached to it.[10]

1. Gerald Blidstein, *Honor Thy Father and Mother: Filial Responsibility in Jewish Law and Ethics*, The Library of Jewish Law and Ethics, ed. Norman Lamm (New York: KTAV, 1975), 1–59.

2. The verb ἐστίν is omitted only in B. The evidence for its omission is too slight to be seriously considered.

3. Salmond, 375; Robinson, 210.

4. Alford, 3:140; Eadie, 438; Ellicott, 138; Meyer, 314; Abbott, 176; Westcott, 88.

5. BAGD 269; BDAG 340; L&N §33.330.

6. Schrenk, *TDNT* 2 (1964): 551–52.

7. Robertson, *Grammar*, 793; Moule, *Idiom Book*, 113; Salmond, 375.

8. Chrysostom *Eph* 6:1 (*PG* 62:149); Jerome *Eph* 6:1 (*PL* 26:538); Oecumenius *Eph* 6:1–4 (*PG* 118:1245); Theophylact *Eph* 6:1–2 (*PG* 124:1121); Eadie, 439–40; Ellicott, 138; Meyer, 316; Salmond, 375; Gnilka, 297; Winer, *Grammar*, 488.

9. Alford, 3:141.

10. Ibid.; Abbott, 177; Robinson, 210; Westcott, 88; Gaugler, 211–12; Zerwick, 160; Schnackenburg, 261; Mitton, 211–12; Bruce, 398; Lincoln, 404–5. Wallace suggests the possibility of a dative of thing possessed (cf. *Greek Grammar*, 151, 372).

Regarding the relative clause, much discussion has been generated because it states that this is the first commandment with promise. How can this fifth commandment of the Decalogue be the first commandment with promise when the second commandment has promises attached to it, namely, punishment for those who hate God but steadfast love to those who love God (Exod 20:4–6; Deut 5:8–10)? There are five interpretations which attempt to solve this problem. (1) This fifth commandment is the first one of the second table of the law dealing with relationships to other people whereas the first four commandments deal with one's relationship to God.[1] The problem with this view is that there is more than one theory as to where the table of the law is divided.[2] For example, Philo, in one place, makes a division between the fourth and fifth commandments[3] and, in another place, he makes a division between the fifth and sixth commandments.[4] Hence, if there is no agreement on the division even by the same person, then there is no agreement that the fifth commandment is the first commandment of the second table. (2) The fifth commandment is the first commandment with a specific promise because the promises with the second commandment (Exod 20:5–6) are of a general nature applicable to all the commandments.[5] The promises are punishment for those who hate God but steadfast love to those who love God. Furthermore, it is suggested that these promises are not specifically related to the second commandment, "you shall not make a graven image," but refer to a "jealous God" who punishes and rewards. However, if this interpretation were correct, the fifth commandment of the Decalogue would not only be the first but the only commandment with a promise.[6] (3) Since it is addressed to children, it is the first commandment to be learned by children.[7] The problem is that it does not say it is the first commandment for children but the first commandment with a promise.[8] Furthermore, the first, not the fifth, of the Ten Commandments is the more important to learn first. (4) It is suggested that πρώτη has the intent of first in importance.[9] However, Jesus made it clear that the greatest and first (πρώτη) commandment is to love the Lord your God and the second is to love your

1. Ambrosiaster *Eph* 6:3 (*PL* 17:399–400); Schnackenburg, 261–62.

2. Eduard Nielsen, *The Ten Commandments in New Perspective: A Traditio-Historical Approach*, trans. David J. Bourke, SBT, ed. C. F. D. Moule, James Barr, Peter Ackroyd, Floyd V. Filson, and G. Ernest Wright, vol. 7 (London: SCM, 1968), 6–34.

3. Philo *Spec*. 2.47 §261.

4. Philo *Decal*. 24 §121.

5. Jerome *Eph* 6:1 (*PL* 26:538); Calvin, 213; Eadie, 439; Caird, 90; Bruce, 398; Lincoln, 404; O'Brien, 443.

6. Zerwick, 160.

7. Abbott, 177.

8. Hendriksen, 259.

9. Hodge, 358; Lenski, 648; Masson, 217; Hugedé, 224; Rienecker, 220; Gaugler, 211–12; Hendriksen, 260; Best, 567; Schrenk, *TDNT* 2 (1964): 352.

neighbor as yourself (Matt 22:36–40 = Mark 12:28–31). On the other hand, the proponents of this view would answer the objection by stating that, in the context, it is the most important commandment with a promise.[1] (5) Others suggest that πρώτη means first in the sense of being difficult to carry out.[2] Those who hold this view make reference to a rabbinic tradition that speaks of the easiest and the most difficult commands both of which promise to prolong life when carried out.[3] The "easiest commandment" refers to Deut 22:6–7, which states that when one comes across a bird's nest with both the mother and young in it, one is to let the mother go and keep the young. The "most difficult or weighty commandment" is the fifth commandment in Exod 20:12. Both the easiest and the most difficult commandments have the promise "that it may be well with you [not found in the Midrash] and that you may live long." Hence, the adjective "first" (πρώτη) is not to be understood numerically but in terms of difficulty. But this interpretation seems foreign to the present context.[4] In conclusion, views (2) and (4) appear to be the most plausible, and (2) is perhaps the best of these. Briefly, view (2) suggests that the promises given in the second commandment of the Decalogue are of a more general nature, applicable to all the commandments. In addition, the promises are not related to the second commandment regarding idolatry but related to a "jealous God" who punishes and rewards. On the other hand, the promise in the fifth commandment is more specific, addressed to a specific audience and directly related to the command to "honor your father and mother." The objection to this view is that it would not be just the first, but the only promise given. However, the commandments encompass more than the Decalogue. The whole law comprises many commandments with promises. Thus this would be the first promise included in the Ten Commandments which are an introductory summary of the whole law.[5]

6:3. ἵνα εὖ σοι γένηται καὶ ἔσῃ μακροχρόνιος ἐπὶ τῆς γῆς, "that it may be well with you and you may live long on the earth." In order to understand the broader implications of this verse, it is necessary to consider some of the particulars. The conjunction ἵνα introduces the purpose or result of both commands to obey and honor parents. The first verb, a second person singular aorist subjunctive of γίνομαι combined with the adverb of manner[6] εὖ can be rendered "that it may be well with you."[7] The second verb ἔσῃ, a second person singular future

1. Gnilka, 296–97.

2. Dibelius-Greeven, 95; Schlier, 281 n. 3; Zerwick, 160; Nieder, *Die Motive der religiös-sittlichen Paränese*, 85–86; cf. Str-B, 3:615.

3. *Deut. Rab.* 6.2 (Deut 22:6).

4. Gnilka, 297; Lincoln, 404.

5. Lincoln, "The Use of the OT in Ephesians," 33; Lincoln, 404.

6. Robertson, *Grammar*, 299; BDF §102 (3).

7. BAGD 159; BDAG 198.

indicative of εἰμί combined with the adjective and prepositional phrase μακροχρόνιος ἐπὶ τῆς γῆς is translated "and that you may live long on the earth." Normally, one would expect an aorist subjunctive to be used in connection with ἵνα. However, there are instances of the use of ἵνα with the future indicative, especially in the Book of Revelation (e.g., Luke 20:10; John 7:3; Acts 21:24; 1 Cor 9:18; Gal 2:4; 1 Pet 3:1; Rev 3:9; 6:4, 11; 14:13), and one other time where it is used with the verb "to be" (Rev 22:14) as in the present context.[1] Possibly Paul used the future indicative because there was no aorist construction of the verb to be[2] or possibly to heighten the expectancy missing in the subjunctive.[3]

The two promises given in this are difficult to define precisely since the Scriptures offer very little illumination. Generally under the old covenant, the promise of long life was given on the condition of keeping the law (cf. Deut 4:4; 5:33). The law, in this case, was to honor both father and mother, and as a result, God promised well-being and a long life in the land. The "land" in the OT had reference to the Promised Land of Israel. But what did the promise of well-being and long life mean for the OT saint and how is this to be interpreted in NT times?

In OT times the promise of well-being and longevity of life is not really defined. Due to this, commentators probably tend to skip over these promises, because there are no clear examples in the OT. Philo spiritualized the two elements by suggesting that "it may be well with you" means "virtue" and that "you may live long" refers to immortality.[4] However, this is not indicated in the OT. Perhaps the best clues in the OT context are given for those children who dishonored their parents. It states that a son who persistently disobeys his parents is to be stoned (Deut 21:18–21) and a son or daughter who strikes or curses his or her father or mother is to be put to death (Exod 21:15, 17 [LXX 21:15–16]). Conversely, then, when parents are honored, children are not punished by death and can expect physical well-being and longevity of life. The adverb εὖ, "well-being," is rather vague but probably, in the OT context, it refers to stability and discipline necessary to function well within the family and society. Therefore, as a general rule, obedience and honor foster self-discipline, which in turn bring stability, longevity, and well-being; disobedience and dishonor promote a lack of discipline, which in turn bring instability, a shortened life, and a lack of well-being. Generalities always must allow for exceptions, as is the case in the OT (e.g., Job 21:7; Pss 10:5 [LXX 9:26]; 73:3–9, 12 [LXX 72:3–9, 12]; Jer 12:1–3), but this should not prevent one from keeping this law.

1. Robertson, *Grammar*, 984; BDF §369 (3); MHT 3:100.

2. Abbott, 177.

3. Porter, *Verbal Aspect*, 415; cf. Robertson, *Grammar*, 875.

4. Philo *Spec.* 2.47 §262.

Does this principle still hold in the NT? Again, some spiritualize this passage in Ephesians by suggesting that "long life" refers to eternal life or a heavenly inheritance.[1] This view is foreign to this context for several reasons. First, if Paul had meant eternal life he more likely would have used the familiar combination of αἰώνιος and ζωή, "eternal life," which is used with great frequency in the NT (e.g., Matt 19:16, 29 = Mark 10:17, 30 = Luke 18:18, 30; John 3:15–16, 36; 5:24; Acts 13:48; Rom 2:7; 5:21; 6:22–23; Gal 6:8; 1 Tim 1:16; Titus 1:2; 3:7; 1 John 2:25, 5:11, 13; Jude 21). Second, the word μακροχρόνιος used only here in the NT, denotes a "long time,"[2] which "can never denote immortal duration."[3] Third, the prepositional phrase ἐπὶ τῆς γῆς, "in the land, on the earth," indicates that "long life" is to be located here on earth and not in heaven. Paul would have omitted this prepositional phrase if he had meant eternal life.[4] In short, Paul does not refer to a future eternal life but to a present temporal life.

In the end, the same general OT principle can be applied to the NT, namely, that obeying and honoring father and mother will bring well-being and a long life on earth. Again, there are going to be exceptions to the rule but the general principle holds. Children who have obeyed and honored their parents are more likely to lead disciplined lives, and the natural odds are for a balanced and long life. There is a basic difference in the promises to the Israelites in that these promises pertained to those who lived in the land which God had promised them. In the NT, the clause "which the Lord God gives you" is omitted because the church is not the continuation of Israel and has not received the promise of a specific land. Hence, rather than render ἐπὶ τῆς γῆς, "in the land," it is better to translate it "on the earth."[5] Thus, it refers to the place on earth where individual believers happen to live.

Because of the promise of long life on the earth, Lincoln contends that this could not have been penned by Paul who expected an imminent parousia. He suggests that it must have been written by a Jewish-Christian follower who had become more acclimatized to the reality of a longer period of time before the parousia.[6] This argument is not compelling, for Paul never predicted that the parousia would occur within his lifetime. Even the apostles did not presume to know the time of the parousia since Jesus had told them that even he did not know, only the Father knew (Matt 24:36 = Mark 13:32). No doubt, Paul, along with the other apostles and saints down through the centuries, hoped that the parousia would occur in his lifetime. On the other hand, he

1. Jerome *Eph* 6:1 (*PL* 26:538–39); Aquinas, chap. 6, lec. 1, vv. 1–4 (230); Schlier, 282; Zerwick, 160–61.

2. L&N §67.89; BAGD 488; BDAG 613.

3. Eadie, 441.

4. Schnackenburg, 262.

5. Alford, 3:141; Robinson, 210–11; Bruce, 398.

6. Lincoln, 406.

himself had long-range plans (e.g., to go to Spain), which would indicate Paul's uncertainity that the parousia would occur within his lifetime. In fact, there is a misconception surrounding the imminency of the parousia. The English term "imminent" can connote nearness of time but the NT idea of imminency, especially in connection with the parousia, is not so concerned with nearness of time, but rather the possibility of its occurrence at any time. Consequently, this encourages one to be prepared as if it could occur at any moment (Matt 24:36–44; 25:1–13). At any rate, the commands in these verses, as with all NT commands, must be obeyed regardless of when it is thought that the parousia will occur. In this verse, the child's obedience and honor promise longevity of life.

In conclusion, then, children are to obey and honor both fathers and mothers because it is right. This responsibility must be viewed in the larger context, that is, believers who are filled by the power of the Spirit. It is the child who is filled by the Spirit who will respond in obedience to this command.

(2) Responsibility of Fathers' Care (6:4)

As is his pattern, Paul has first addressed the ones under authority, namely, children. He now addresses the ones who have authority over the children, the fathers. Within the structure of the hierarchical family, Paul makes it very clear that the father must take responsibility for raising his children.

(a) Negative: Do Not Provoke to Wrath (6:4a)

Text: 6:4a. Καὶ οἱ πατέρες, μὴ παροργίζετε τὰ τέκνα ὑμῶν,

Translation: 6:4a. "And the fathers, do not make your children angry,"

Commentary: 6:4a. Καὶ οἱ πατέρες, μὴ παροργίζετε τὰ τέκνα ὑμῶν, "And the fathers, do not make your children angry." The coordinating conjunction καί, "and," closely ties the fathers' responsibility with the children's responsibility. The article οἱ is used to introduce a new group in order to distinguish it from another group.[1] In this case, fathers are distinguished from children. Interestingly, although children are commanded to obey both parents in verse 1 and honor father and mother in verse 2, only the fathers are addressed here. It could be that both the father and mother are in view,[2] but in light of the hierarchical structures, the father is responsible for his whole family. Although it was common for primitive societies to be matriarchal (lineage is traced through the mother), Israel followed the patriarchal structure with the father having absolute control over his children, even over his married sons and their wives if they lived with him.[3] He could

1. Robertson, *Grammar*, 757.

2. So BAGD 635; BDAG 786; Schnackenburg, 262.

3. Roland de Vaux, *Ancient Israel: Its Life and Institutions*, trans. John McHugh (London: Darton, Longman & Todd, 1961), 19–20.

stone his brother, son, daughter, or wife if they enticed him to serve other gods (Deut 13:6–11 [MT & LXX 13:7–11]). He was able to sell his daughter into slavery (Exod 21:7), and he and his wife could have their persistently rebellious son stoned (Deut 21:18–21). However, in a positive sense, the father also was responsibile for the education of his children (more particulary his sons) with respect to the Lord and his wonderful dealings with the nation Israel (Exod 10:2; 12:25–27; 13:8; Deut 4:9; 6:7, 20–21; 11:19; 32:7, 46).[1] Physical discipline was certainly a part of the educational process (Prov 13:24; 22:15; 29:15, 17; cf. Deut 8:5; 2 Sam 7:14). Likewise, in the Greek world the family was patriarchal in structure. The father had absolute authority over his children, much like a king over his subjects.[2] A son would learn from his father's example[3] and would receive formal education in the schools.[4] In Hellenistic Judaism, parents were considered as superior, similar to seniors, rulers, benefactors, and masters, while children occupied a lower position, that is, juniors, subjects, receivers of benefits, and slaves. Hence, parents were to children as God is to the world.[5] The fathers had a right to upbraid and severely admonish (νευθετεῖν) as well as beat, degrade, and lock up their children. If a child continued to rebel the father, with the consent of the mother, could execute the child in accordance with the Mosaic law (Deut 21:18–21).[6] Despite the severity of Greek parental control, the Romans thought that the Greeks were somewhat lax regarding the attitude of children toward their parents. In the Roman family, the father had absolute control over all his family called *patria potestas*.[7] The father's control over the son was for life. He could imprison his son, scourge, shame and punish him, sell him into slavery up to three times, or have him killed. The son's position in the community was of no consequence; for instance, though he might be a magistrate, he was still under his father's authority. The father had more power over his son than a master had over his slaves.[8] It would be unfair, however, to suggest that there was no tender loving care within families in the Roman

1. Ibid., 48–50.

2. Gottlob Schrenk, "πατήρ," *TDNT* 5 (1968): 949.

3. Plato *Leges* 5 §729b; *Protagoras* 324b–325a.

4. Frederick Arthur, George Beck, and Rosalind Thomas, "Education, Greek," *OCD*, 506–9.

5. Philo *Decal*. 31 §§165–67; *Spec*. 2.38 §§225–27.

6. Philo *Spec*. 2.41 §232; cf. Josephus *C. Ap*. 2.27 §206, 30 §217; *A.J.* 4.8.24 §264.

7. Crook, "Patria Potestas," 113–22; Saller, "*Patria potestas* and the Stereotype of the Roman Family," 7–22; cf. also Eyben, "Fathers and Sons," 114–16; Lacey, "*Patria Potestas*," 121–44; Nicholas and Treggiari, "Patria Potestas," 1122–23; Lassen, "The Roman Family: Ideal and Metaphor," 104–6; Gardner, *Family and* Familia *in Roman Law and Life*, 1–4, 117–26, 270–72.

8. Dionysius Halicarnassensis *Antiquitates Romanae* 2.26.3–27.5.

times.[1] Nevertheless, in this milieu Paul writes instructions to the believing fathers in Ephesus.

In giving the instructions, Paul brings to fathers a new perspective on the treatment of their children. He mentions nothing of their right to absolute power over them as in Roman law but, rather, prefaces a positive exhortation with a negative one, that is, to refrain from provoking their children.[2] The present prohibitory imperative παροργίζετε does not say "stop doing what has already started" but rather "make it a practice not to do it,"[3] that is, "do not provoke" your children. The verb παροργίζω occurs only here and in Rom 10:19, but the noun παροργισμός occurs in Eph 4:26. Along with the noun, the verb was discussed at Eph 4:26. Briefly, its use in classical literature, the LXX, and the NT was noted and said to mean "to irritate, provoke to anger." Applying it to the present context, fathers are not to make it a practice to cause their children "to become provoked or quite angry."[4] Although the prohibition in Col 3:21 uses a different word (ἐρεθίζω), its meaning is the same and there it is followed with "lest they become discouraged." Logically, the irritation caused by nagging and demeaning fathers in the context of everyday life may in turn cause children to become angry. This anger grows, no doubt, out of the frustration of never being able to please fathers who constantly nag or demean them. The personal pronoun ὑμῶν indicates that these children belong to the fathers and they are responsible for them.

(b) Positive: Care for Them (6:4b)

Text: 6:4b. ἀλλὰ ἐκτρέφετε αὐτὰ ἐν παιδείᾳ καὶ νουθεσίᾳ κυρίου.

Translation: 6:4b. "but bring them up in the training and admonition of the Lord."

Commentary: 6:4b. ἀλλὰ ἐκτρέφετε αὐτὰ ἐν παιδείᾳ καὶ νουθεσίᾳ κυρίου, "but bring them up in the training and admonition of the Lord." Having stated the negative, Paul does not continue as in Col 3:21 to state "lest they become discouraged" but moves on to a positive exhortation. The adversative conjunction ἀλλά, "but," denotes a strong contrast from the negative to the positive (μή—ἀλλά). The fathers are

1. For discussion on child raising, see Beryl Rawson, "Adult-Child Relationships in Roman Society," in *Marriage, Divorce, and Children in Ancient Rome*, ed. Beryl Rawson (Oxford: Clarendon, 1991), 7–30; Evans, *War, Women and Children in Ancient Rome*, 166–209; Eyben, "Fathers and Sons," 114–43; Richard Saller, "Corporal Punishment, Authority, and Obedience in the Roman Household," in *Marriage, Divorce, and Children in Ancient Rome*, ed. Beryl Rawson (Oxford: Clarendon, 1991), 161–64; cf. also Rawson, "The Roman Family," 1–57; idem, "Children in the Roman *Familia*," in *The Family in Ancient Rome: New Perspectives*, ed. Beryl Rawson (Ithaca, N.Y.: Cornell University Press; London: Croom Helm, 1986), 170–200.

2. Schrage, "Zur Ethik der neutestamentliche Haustafeln," 15.

3. Fanning, *Verbal Aspect*, 335–40; Wallace, *Greek Grammar*, 725.

4. L&N §88.177.

exhorted to "nurture" the children. The present imperative ἐκτρέφετε appears only here and in Eph 5:29 where we discussed it in more detail. It means "to bring up from childhood, bring up, rear up, nurture" or, as here translated, "but bring them up."[1] The sphere and influence[2] of this rearing is described in the prepositional phrase ἐν παιδείᾳ καὶ νουθεσίᾳ κυρίου, "in the discipline and admonition of the Lord." Next, two nouns need to be discussed. The first noun παιδεία is used of the "rearing of a child,"[3] "education, or training."[4] In the LXX it occurs 115 times and in the canonical books it appears fifty-seven times and translates ten Hebrew words, thirty-five times (mostly in Proverbs) for מוּסָר, which is used of "instruction" whether it be a body of knowledge (Prov 1:2, 7, 8; 4:1; 8:10; 15:32–33; 19:20) or specific content of knowledge (Job 20:3; Ps 50:17 [LXX 49:17]; Prov 24:32; Zeph 3:2, 7). It also refers to "discipline, punishment, correction" (Isa 26:16; 53:5; Jer 2:30; 5:3; 30:14 [LXX 37:14]).[5] In the NT it occurs five times outside the present context. It is used of "instruction" (2 Tim 3:16) and "discipline" (Heb 12:5 [quoting Prov 3:11], 7, 8, 11). In this context it reflects the idea of instruction in connection with correction or discipline of the Lord.[6] In the OT the fathers instructed their children about God's discipline as illustrated in his dealings with Israel throughout her history.

The second noun νουθεσία is used infrequently in classical literature. It is made up of νοῦς, "mind," and τίθημι, "to place," with the sense to exert influence on the mind,[7] and hence it is used of "counsel, admonition, correction."[8] In the LXX it is used only in Wis 16:6 referring to the plagues which served as a "warning" to the wilderness generation. It is used frequently by Philo as "admonition, warning, and correction."[9] In the NT it is used two other times outside the present context, "instruction" (1 Cor 10:11) and "admonition, warning" (Titus 3:10). In the Ephesian context "it denotes the word of admonition that is designed to correct while not provoking or embittering."[10] Dewitt points out that in Epicurus the word "signifies the gentlest sort of instruction in conduct, free from rebuke or reprimand and character-

1. Cf. MHT 3:311.

2. Winer, *Grammar*, 485.2; Alford, 3:141; Ellicott, 140; Meyer, 318; Salmond, 377.

3. Aeschylus *Septem contra Thebas* 18.

4. Thucydides 2.39.1; Aristophanes *Nubes* 961; Plato *Protagoras* 327d; *Gorgias* 470e; *Respublica* 2.17 §376e.

5. BDB 416; R. D. Branson and G. J. Botterweck, "יָסַר *yāsar*; מוּסָר *mûsār*," *TDOT* 6 (1990): 131–34.

6. Dieter Fürst, "Teach, Instruct, Tradition, Education, Discipline [παιδεύω κτλ.]," *NIDNTT* 3 (1978): 777.

7. Friedel Selter, "Exhort, Warn, Console, Rebuke [νουθετέω, νουθεσία]," *NIDNTT* 1 (1975): 568.

8. Aristophanes *Ranae* 1009; Diodorus Siculus 15.7.1; Plutarch *Moralia: De virtute morali* 12 §452c.

9. Philo *Mos*. 2.43 §241; *Leg. All.* 3.69 §193; *Spec*. 3.25 §141.

10. J. Behm, "νουθετέω, νουθεσία," *TDNT* 4 (1967): 1021.

ized by timely suggestions rather than sharp imperatives."[1] This analysis appears, however, to preclude any need for constructive rebuke. Although some translations render it "instruction" (RSV, NASB, TEV, NIV, NRSV), the term "admonition" (AV, RV, ASV) better brings out the nuance of correction or warning (NEB "correction"; JB, NJB "advice").[2]

The two nouns παιδεία, "training," and νουθεσία, "admonition," are more or less identical in meaning and thus seem to be redundant. Yet Philo has also used these two words when he compares God and humans in relation to "training and admonition."[3] The distinction between the two words is difficult to determine with any certainty. Several think that παιδεία is education emphasizing activity and discipline and νουθεσία is education, emphasizing the verbal aspect, whether it be encouragement or reproof.[4] This appears to be a reasonable explanation. Hence, παιδεία is the activity of education, best translated "training" and νουθεσία is the verbal aspect of education and best translated "correction" or "admonition," which is a part of instruction.[5]

The final word, κυρίου, "Lord," modifies both παιδεία and νουθεσία. The reference is to Christ who is their Lord.[6] In other words, the father's training and admonition is not to be anthropocentric as it was in Hellenism nor centered around the law as in the rabbinics but, rather, Christocentric.[7] Some consider κυρίου an objective genitive indicating that the training and admonition is concerning or about the Lord,[8] but in this context Paul is not speaking about the content of the training and admonition. Others consider it a genitive of quality and view the training and admonition in the light of the Lord.[9] However, this is unlikely because he is already denoting this by the phrase "in the training and admonition" (ἐν παιδείᾳ καὶ νουθεσίᾳ) and could have continued with the dative phrase ἐν κυρίῳ (as the construction in 1:3; 2:6; 1 Thess 2:14; cf. also 1 Tim 3:13; 2 Tim 1:13). The most likely view is that it is a subjective genitive (or possessive genitive), which indicates that the training and admonition come from the Lord or are

1. Norman Wentworth DeWitt, *St. Paul and Epicurus* (Minneapolis: University of Minnesota Press, 1954), 99.

2. Cf. Schick, "The RSV and the Small Catechism," 167.

3. Philo *Deus* 11 §54.

4. Trench, *Synonyms of the New Testament*, 113; Georg Bertram, "παιδεύω, παιδεία, κτλ.," *TDNT* 5 (1968): 624; Masson, 215 n. 5; Schlier, 283; Gaugler, 213; Gnilka, 298; Schnackenburg, 263; Lincoln, 407.

5. Barclay, "The Family as the Bearer of Religion," 76–77.

6. Gnilka, "Paränetische Traditionen im Epheserbrief," 410.

7. Werner Jentsch, *Urchristliches Erziehungsdenken. Die Paideia Kyriu im Rahmen der hellenistisch-jüdischen Umwelt*, Beiträge zur Förderung christlicher Theologie, ed. Paul Althaus and Joachim Jeremias, vol. 45; no. 3 (Gütersloh: Bertelsmann, 1951), 194–203, esp. 199–200; Barclay, "The Family as the Bearer of Religion," 76–78.

8. Theodoret *Eph* 6:4 (*PG* 82:549).

9. Jentsch, *Urchristliche Erziehungsgedanken*, 144; Schlier, 283; Gnilka, 298–99; Mitton, 213; Lincoln, 408; O'Brien, 446–47.

prescribed by the Lord[1] through fathers. The fathers are the Lord's agents and, therefore, raise their children according to his mandates. Such training and admonition would be sensitive to the children's responses and needs.

Again, in the larger context in which the life filled by the Spirit is supremely important (5:18), fathers must rely on the Holy Spirit to temper their conduct and attitude, thus enabling them to avoid provoking their children to anger. Also, the Holy Spirit gives them the wisdom and enablement they need to train and instruct. In the Roman world Seneca and Plutarch recommended that children should be led into honorable practices by encouragement and reason and not by brute force, which only discourages them.[2] While encouragement and reason are highly commendable, they are insufficient because a person's power of reason is not adequate to raise godly children. Paul exhorts believing fathers to train and admonish their children in ways prescribed by the Lord in the power of the Holy Spirit. The present tense of the imperative emphasizes the continued action of this responsibility.

In conclusion, this second part of the household code describes the responsibilities of children and parents in much the same way Paul described the duties of the husbands and wives. That is, he addresses each group directly. He takes great care not only to discuss the responsibility of children to obey their parents but also to explain that such conduct is for their well-being. This principle was first given in the OT but amplified to suit the context in which believers were now living. In the admonition to fathers his instruction to teach their children and to behave graciously towards them includes a caution, that is, not to provoke them to anger. The power of the Holy Spirit is to be the means by which all concerned will be able to fulfill these admonitions.

c. Servants and Masters (6:5–9)

The third of the three pairs in the household code is concerned with slaves and masters, again keeping in mind the broader context of these verses, that is, believers are to walk in wisdom by understanding the will of the Lord and to be filled by the Holy Spirit (5:15–18). With these principles in mind, a harmonious relationship between slaves and masters is fostered. As was the case for the previous two pairs in the household code, this pair has some similarities with the first-two pairs. First, the subordinate partner is addressed first; second, each of those addressed are ultimately answerable to the Lord; and third, the

1. Alford, 3:141–42; Eadie, 445; Ellicott, 140; Meyer, 318; Abbott, 178; Salmond, 377; Westcott, 88; Masson, 217 n. 6; Gaugler, 213; Barth, 755; Mußner, 163; Bouttier, 253; Best, 569–70; Winer, *Grammar*, 236–37; Bertram, *TDNT* 5 (1968): 624; Hans Schilling, *Grundlagen der Religionspädagogik. Zum Verhältness von Theologie und Erziehungswissenschaft* (Düsseldorf: Patmos, 1969), 410–15.

2. Seneca *De Ira* 2.21.1–3; Plutarch *Moralia: De liberis educandis* 12a §8.

form is the same: the party is addressed, the imperative is stated, amplification is given, and the motivation is presented.

Excursus 8
Slavery in Paul's Time

In the twentieth century, especially in the last forty years, much has been written on the subject of slavery in Greek and Roman times.[1] Slavery was defined by the mid-second

1. W. W. Buckland, *The Roman Law of Slavery: The Condition of the Slave in Private Law from Augustus to Justinian* (Cambridge: Cambridge University Press, 1908; reprint, 1970); R. H. Barrow, *Slavery in the Roman Empire* (London: Methuen, 1928); Isaac Mendelsohn, *Slavery in the Ancient Near East: A Comparative Study of Slavery in Babylonia, Assyria, Syria, and Palestine from the Middle of the Third Millennium to the End of the First Millennium* (New York: Oxford University Press, 1949); William L. Westermann, *The Slave Systems of Greek and Roman Antiquity*, Memoirs of the American Philosophical Society, vol. 40 (Philadelphia: American Philosophical Society, 1955); M. I. Finley, ed., *Slavery in Classical Antiquity: Views and Controversies* (Cambridge: W. Heffer & Sons, 1960); Solomon Zeitlin, "Slavery during the Second Commonwealth and the Tannaitic Period," *Jewish Quarterly Review* 53 (January 1963): 185–218; E. E. Urbach, "The Laws Regarding Slavery as a Source for Social History of the Period of the Second Temple, the Mishnah and Talmud," in *Papers of the Institute of Jewish Studies University College London*, trans. R. J. Loewe, ed. J. G. Weiss, vol. 1 (Jerusalem: Magnes Press, The Hebrew University, 1964), 1–94; Eduard Schweizer, "Zum Sklavenproblem im Neuen Testament," *EvT* 32 (September/Oktober 1972): 502–6; S. Scott Bartchy, *ΜΑΛΛΟΝ ΧΡΗΣΑΙ: First-Century Slavery and the Interpretation of 1 Corinthians 7:21*, SBLDS, no. 11 (Missoula, Mont.: Society of Biblical Literature, 1973); Joseph Vogt, *Ancient Slavery and the Ideal of Man*, trans. Thomas Wiedemann, Blackwell's Classical Studies, ed. Oswyn Murray (Oxford: Basil Blackwell, 1974); Roland Gayer, *Die Stellung des Sklaven in den paulinischen Gemeinden und bei Paulus. Zugleich ein sozialgeschichtlich vergleichender Beitrag zur Wertung des Sklaven in der Antike*, Europäische Hochschulschriften, vol. 23 (Bern: Herbert Lang; Frankfurt: Peter Lang, 1976); Keith Hopkins, *Conquerors and Slaves*, vol. 1, *Sociological Studies in Roman History* (Cambridge: Cambridge University Press, 1978); M. I. Finley, *Ancient Slavery and Modern Ideology* (London: Chatto & Windus, 1980); Franz Laub, *Die Begegnung des frühen Christentums mit der antiken Sklaverei*, Stuttgarter Bibelstudien, ed. Helmut Merklein and Erich Zenger, vol. 107 (Stuttgart: Verlag Katholisches Bibelwerk, 1982); K. R. Bradley, *Slaves and Masters in the Roman Empire. A Study in Social Control*, Collection Latomus, vol. 185 (Bruxelles: Latomus Revue D'Études Latines, 1984; reprint, New York: Oxford University Press, 1987); Saller, "Slavery and the Roman Family," 65–87; Alan Watson, *Roman Slave Law* (Baltimore: Johns Hopkins University Press, 1987); T. E. J. Wiedemann, *Slavery* (Oxford: Clarendon, 1987); Dale B. Martin, *Slavery as Salvation: The Metaphor of Slavery in Pauline Christianity* (New Haven: Yale University Press, 1990), 1–49; Saller, "Corporal Punishment, Authority, and Obedience in the Roman Household," in *Marriage, Divorce, and Children in Ancient Rome*, 144–65. For various texts on the different aspects of slavery, see Thomas Wiedemann, *Greek and Roman Slavery* (London: Croom Helm, 1981); Keith Bradley, *Slavery and Society at Rome*, Key Themes in Ancient History, ed. P. A. Cartledge and P. D. A. Garnsey (Cambridge: Cambridge University Press, 1994); idem, "Slavery, Roman," *OCD*, 1415–17; Richard A. Horsley, "The Slave System of Classical Antiquity and Their Reluctant Recognition by Modern Scholars," *Semeia* 83/84 (1998): 19–66. A series of monographs

century A.D. jurist Florentinus as "an institution of the *ius gentium* [common law of peoples] whereby someone, contrary to nature, is subject to the *dominium* [ownership] of another."[1] There is no doubt that much deprivation and degradation was experienced by most in servitude. But the institution of slavery existed long before Greek and Roman times, and, in fact, the Mosaic law included regulations for slaves and masters (Exod 21:1–11, 32; Lev 25:6, 39–55; Deut 15:12–18). In ancient Greece it was thought that a person who became a slave was, by fate, deprived of half his worth.[2] Many became slaves due to debt or capture in a war. Some viewed slaves as property, like chattel[3] or an inanimate tool rather than complete human beings[4] although according to Roman law they were considered persons.[5] In Hellenistic writings slaves were thought to have no deliberative faculty (τὸ βουλευτικόν)[6] and were considered stupid, unable to live by themselves; thus, the institution of slavery was really beneficial to them.[7] According to Greek law four differences distinguished a freedperson from a slave: (1) freedpersons were their own representative in legal matters whereas slaves had to be represented by their owner or by some other person legally empowered by their owner; (2) freedpersons were not subject to seizure as property whereas slaves were subject to seizure and arrest by anyone; (3) freedpersons could earn their own living as they desired whereas slaves had to do what their owner ordered; and (4) freedpersons could live where they wished whereas slaves had to live where their owner desired.[8]

However, as degrading as such slavery was, it must be realized that it was not the same as the slavery that existed in the United States.[9] First, the color of skin was not a factor. Slaves came from various nations and more than likely their appearance was no different from that of freedpersons.[10] Second, freedpersons could sell themselves into slavery knowing that they could later regain freedom.[11] Dio Chrysostom explicitly states that they sold themselves "under contract,"[12] which probably meant that there was a time limit on their slavery. There were various reasons for becoming a slave, such as "to find a life that was easier than they had as freedmen, to secure special jobs, and to climb socially."[13] For

beginning in 1967 focuses on the subject of ancient slavery: Forschungen zur Antiken Sklaverei, ed. Joseph Vogt, Hans Ulrich Instinsky, et al.

1. *Iustiniani Digesti* 1.5.4.1.

2. Homer *Odyssea* 17.322–23.

3. Aristotle *Ethica Nicomachea* 5.6.8 §1134b.11.

4. Aristotle *Politica* 1.2.4–6 §§1253b.23–1254a.8; *Ethica Nicomachea* 8.11.6 §§1161a.34–1161b.4; cf. Pseudo-Aristotle *Oeconomica* 1.5.1 §1344a.23–24 (third century B.C.).

5. Buckland, *The Roman Law of Slavery*, 3–4; cf. Seneca *Epistulae* 47.

6. Aristotle *Politica* 1.5.6 §1260a.12; Arius Didymus 149.7.

7. Arius Didymus 149.2.

8. W. L. Westermann, "Slavery and the Elements of Freedom in Ancient Greece," *Quarterly Bulletin of the Polish Institute of Arts and Sciences in America* 1 (January 1943): 10–11; reprinted in Finley, ed., *Slavery in Classical Antiquity*, 26–27.

9. For a discussion of Roman and American slavery, see Bradley, *Slavery and Society at Rome*.

10. Cf. Mary L. Gordon, "The Nationality of Slaves under the Early Roman Empire," *Journal of Roman Studies* 14, pts. 1 & 2 (1924): 93–111; reprinted in Finley, ed., *Slavery in Classical Antiquity*, 171–89.

11. *Iustiniani Digesti* 40.12.7; 13.1.

12. Dio Chrysostom *15th Discourse: on Slavery and Freedom II* 23.

13. Bartchy, *ΜΑΛΛΟΝ ΧΡΗΣΑΙ*, 46; cf. J. A. Crook, *Law and Life of Rome*, Aspects of Greek and Roman Life, ed. H. H. Scullard (London: Thames & Hudson, 1967), 59–63.

instance, Epictetus reports that when he was a slave he was provided with food, clothes, and shelter, and taken care of when sick. These benefits were not provided when he became a freedperson.[1] Furthermore, Crook states that in the *Digest* mention is made of "self-enslavement in order to secure the post of *servus actor*, the chief accountant of a big private household (and with normal luck to become later their freedman procurator in the same post and finish up a rich citizen with free-born children)."[2] In addition, Petronius of the Neronian era writes of a king's son who sold himself into slavery in order to become a Roman citizen so as not to have to pay taxes as a provincial.[3] Third, slaves could become highly trained and educated. In fact, some slaves became tutors (παιδαγωγός, Gal 3:24) and taught morals and manners to the sons of their owner's family. Some became professors of higher education (*litterator*, *grammaticus*, *rhetor*), and others, physicians.[4] Aulus Gellius, from the second century A.D., mentions slaves who became philosophers, most notable of whom was Epictetus.[5] Fourth, slaves could eventually become free and hence become Roman citizens. The jurist Gaius states that there were three requirements for this: (1) he must be over thirty years of age; (2) he must have been held by a Roman citizen; and (3) he must be freed by one of three recognized modes. The first was by *vindicta*—a fictitious claim made by a friend of the master (and the master puts up no defense) in which he asserts that the slave was a freedperson who was wrongfully held as a slave. The second was by enrollment (with the master's consent) on the census list of Roman citizens. The third was by the manumission testament of the master.[6] However, the manumission of a slave normally was for the benefit of the master.[7] For instance, the master may have promised manumission so that the slave would work harder and be more cooperative, or he may have freed the slave because he was sick or old and no longer effective. Even after he was freed, the Roman slave was still not completely free from his master. In a sense he was partially free (he may still have to work for his master a number of days a week or month), whereas under the Jewish law once a slave was free he was no longer responsible to his former master.[8] Hence, these are some of the differences between the slavery that existed in the first century and that which existed in the United States.

1. Epictetus *Dissertationes* 4.1.37, cf. also 33–36.

2. Crook, *Law and Life of Rome*, 60. Where in the *Digest* does it speak to this issue? Having discussed this with Crook, he felt that *Iustiniani Digesti* 28.3.6.5 (by Ulpian, d. A.D. 223) possibly could fit that requirement, but a better fit would be *Codex Theodosian* 4.8.6.1–2, which is a text two centuries later (A.D. 438).

3. Petronius *Satyricon* 57.

4. Vogt, *Ancient Slavery and the Ideal of Man*, 109–16. Harrill states, "In modern slavery, slave illiteracy was often required by law; in ancient slavery, an educated slave was prized (J. Albert Harrill, "Slavery," in *DNTB*, 1126).

5. Gellius *Noctes Atticae* 2.18.

6. Gaius *Institutes* 1.17; Buckland, *The Roman Law of Slavery*, 437–78; Barrow, *Slavery in the Roman Empire*, 173–207; Bradley, *Slaves and Masters in the Roman Empire*, 81–112; Watson, *Roman Slave Law*, 23–34; cf. J. Albert Harrill, *The Manumission of Slaves in Early Christianity*, Hermeneutische Untersuchungen zur Theologie, ed. Hans Dieter Betz, Pierre Bühler, Dietz Lange, and Walter Mostert, vol. 32 (Tübingen: Mohr, 1995), 53–56; Horsley, "The Slave System of Classical Antiquity and Their Reluctant Recognition by Modern Scholars," 48–53.

7. Thomas E. J. Wiedemann, "The Regularity of Manumission at Rome," *Classical Quarterly* 35, no. 1 (1985): 162–75; cf. also Bradley, *Slavery and Society at Rome*, 1–5, 12–21, 154–73.

8. F. Lyall, "Roman Law in the Writings of Paul—The Slave and the Freedman," *NTS* 17 (October 1970): 77–78.

In the first century slaves worked in many sectors of the economy. They were used in various types of agriculture and industry, as potters and miners of gold and silver.[1] Other occupations were public cooks, fullers, couch makers, and bakers; in the professions they were business agents and teachers, and in large households accountants and physicians.[2] Also, the Roman state owned slaves to carry out municipal services. Emperors used them throughout the empire in various capacities and some even managed and maintained the imperial properties. In the imperial palace slaves were used as physicians, chamberlains, overseers of furniture and palace lighting, selectors of jewelry for specific costumes, valets, tailors and clothing menders, butlers in charge of wine for the imperial table, official tasters, and stewards in charge of supplies.[3] It is clear that the use of slaves was pervasive in the first century of the Roman Empire. Ephesian slaves would have served in many of these capacities.

The treatment of slaves depended to a great degree on the owners. There are stories of very cruel treatment of domestic slaves.[4] The following are some examples. The emperor Augustus ordered that the legs of a slave named Thallus be broken because he had taken a bribe for betraying the contents of a letter.[5] Caligula had the hands of a slave cut off for stealing a piece of silver. He hung them around his neck and paraded him around the dining hall with a placard stating the reason for the punishment.[6] But such cruelty was not limited to the emperors. For example, Seneca portrays a master who gorged himself at dinner while surrounded by slaves whose lips could not move and the slightest noises—coughs, sneezes, or hiccups—were punished by a lash of the whip.[7] Juvenal reports about the master whose delight it was to have his slaves flogged, branded for stealing as few as two towels, and chained and imprisoned.[8]

However, there was a brighter side. Even early Greek literature included discussions regarding the better treatment of slaves. For instance, Pseudo-Aristotle (third century B.C.) declared that slaves should not be treated cruelly and proposed a proper balance between a slave's work, chastisement, and food. He pointed out that slaves who are severely punished and not fed would be sapped of their strength and unable to perform.[9] Columella, a large estate owner in central Italy in the first century A.D., gave a lengthy discourse on the fair treatment of slaves. He encouraged masters to have good relationships with their slaves, to be concerned about their well-being, their abilities, and their families. He practiced such himself.[10] Seneca, too, enjoined masters to treat their inferiors as they would like to be treated by their own superiors.[11] Nevertheless, even though there were advocates such as these, legislation restricting cruel treatment of slaves was sparse and the existing restrictions still were more for the benefit of masters rather than slaves.[12] Even when the empire became Christian, Constantine (324–361) issued decrees to protect the masters who had beaten their slaves to death.[13] Hence, a slave really had virtually no protection from the law.

1. Westermann, *The Slave System of Greek and Roman Antiquity*, 90–94; Hopkins, *Conquerors and Slaves*, 118–19; Bradley, *Slavery and Society at Rome*, 57–80; Craig S. Keener, "Family and Household," in *DNTB*, 362.

2. Westermann, *The Slave System of Greek and Roman Antiquity*, 73–74.

3. Ibid., 110.

4. Cf. Hopkins, *Conquerors and Slaves*, 118–23; Bradley, *Slaves and Masters in the Roman Empire*, 113–37; idem, *Slavery and Society at Rome*, 26–30.

5. Suetonius *Augustus* 67.2.

6. Suetonius *Caligula* 32.2.

7. Seneca *Epistulae Morales* 47.2–3.

8. Juvenal *Satura* 14.15–24.

9. Pseudo-Aristotle *Oeconomica* 1.5.2–5 §§1344a.29–1344b.22.

10. Columella *Rei Rusticae* 1.8–9.

11. Seneca *Epistulae Morales* 47.11.

12. Watson, *Roman Slave Law*, 115–33.

13. *Codex Theodosian* 2.12.1–2; Finley, *Ancient Slavery and Modern Ideology*, 122.

Slaves had no access to the courts and the death penalty awaited any slave who informed against the master.[1] In the end, therefore, masters made up their own rules.

The abolition of slavery is a modern phenomenon.[2] Certainly Paul and the early Christian church did not advocate the abolition of slavery as an institution.[3] Christianity's emphasis has always been on the transformation of individuals who will in turn influence society, not the transformation of society which will then transform individuals (1 Cor 1:18–2:16). Paul enjoins both slaves and masters to be servants of Christ as they carry out their duties. He depicts the slave as a free person in Christ and the free person as a slave of Christ (1 Cor 7:22). Furthermore, both slaves and masters are equal brothers in Christ (Gal 3:28; 1 Tim 6:2; Phlm 16) though they each may function in different roles. Nowhere does Paul suggest that slaves should give orders to their masters or masters to be submissive to the slaves. He was concerned, however, that both masters and slaves carry out their responsibilities as to Christ.

Why did not Paul advocate the abolition of slavery? First, he was more concerned with the big picture, eternity. He taught that suffering in this life was nothing in comparison with the joy of eternity (Rom 8:18–30). Second, in Rom 13 he advocated obedience to government. To propose the abolition of slavery would defy the government. Third, speaking speculatively, if he promoted the abolition of slavery, undoubtedly many slaves might have become Christians for the wrong reason. In the end, Christianity does not promise a release from the present circumstances but gives one power to endure those circumstances. Though Paul does not promote the abolition of the institution of slavery, he does instruct believers to avoid becoming slaves (1 Cor 7:23).[4] Furthermore, Paul enjoins those slaves who are able to gain freedom to avail themselves of the opportunity (1 Cor 7:21).[5]

(1) Responsibility of Servants' Obedience (6:5–8)

According to the pattern established with husbands and wives as well as with children and parents, those who are to submit are addressed first followed by those who had authority over them. Here fifty-nine words are used to address slaves as opposed to fifty-six in

1. Watson, *Roman Slave Law*, 128; Bradley, *Slaves and Masters in the Roman Empire*, 137.

2. For a discussion of the abolition of slavery and the history of ideas about slavery, see Vogt, *Ancient Slavery and the Ideal of Man*, 170–210; Finley, *Ancient Slavery and Modern Ideology*, 11–66; cf. also Wiedemann, *Slavery*, 1–10, 22–29.

3. For a discussion of Christianity and slavery, see Westermann, *The Slave System of Greek and Roman Antiquity*, 149–62; cf. C. R. Whittaker, "Circe's Pigs: From Slavery to Serfdom in the Later Roman World," in *Classical Slavery*, ed. M. I. Finley (London: Frank Cass, 1987), 105; John M. G. Barclay, "Paul, Philemon and the Dilemma of Christian Slave-Ownership," *NTS* 37 (April 1991): 185–86; Richard A. Horsley, "Paul and Slavery: A Critical Alternative to Recent Readings," *Semeia* 83/84 (1998): 153–200, esp. 167–94; I. A. H. Combes, *The Metaphor of Slavery in the Writings of the Early Church: From the New Testament to the Beginning of the Fifth Century*, JSNTSup, ed. Stanley E. Porter, vol. 156 (Sheffield: Sheffield Academic Press, 1998), 49–67. Bradley's view that Christianity made it worse for the slaves (*Slavery and Society at Rome*, 151–53) is unbalanced because he stresses only Paul's injunctions for the slaves and does not consider Paul's injunctions for the masters.

4. Bruce W. Winter, Slavery, "St. Paul as a Critic of Roman Slavery in 1 Corinthians 7:21–23," *ΠΑΥΛΕΙΑ* 3 (1997): 339–55.

5. Bartchy, *ΜΑΛΛΟΝ ΧΡΗΣΑΙ*, 37–120; J. Albert Harrill, "Paul and Slavery: The Problem of 1 Corinthians 7:21," *BR* 39 (1994): 5–28; Harrill, *The Manumission of Slaves in Early Christianity*, 68–128.

Col 3:22–25. Also, twenty-eight words are addressed here to the masters and eighteen words are used in Col 4:1. The differences between Ephesians and Colossians in regard to slaves are not as great as they are for the wives and husbands or children and fathers.

(a) Imperative: Obey Masters (6:5–7)

Text: 6:5. Οἱ δοῦλοι, ὑπακούετε τοῖς κατὰ σάρκα κυρίοις μετὰ φόβου καὶ τρόμου ἐν ἁπλότητι τῆς καρδίας ὑμῶν ὡς τῷ Χριστῷ, **6:6.** μὴ κατ᾿ ὀφθαλμοδουλίαν ὡς ἀνθρωπάρεσκοι ἀλλ᾿ ὡς δοῦλοι Χριστοῦ ποιοῦντες τὸ θέλημα τοῦ θεοῦ ἐκ ψυχῆς, **6:7.** μετ᾿ εὐνοίας δουλεύοντες ὡς τῷ κυρίῳ καὶ οὐκ ἀνθρώποις,

Translation: 6:5. "Slaves, obey your earthly masters with fear and trembling in singleness of your heart as to Christ, **6:6.** not according to eye service as people-pleasers but as slaves of Christ doing the will of God wholeheartedly, **6:7.** with goodwill rendering service as to the Lord and not to people,"

Commentary: 6:5. Οἱ δοῦλοι, ὑπακούετε τοῖς κατὰ σάρκα κυρίοις,[1] "Slaves, obey your earthly masters." The article and the noun οἱ δοῦλοι, "slaves," in the plural form indicates that Paul is moving to a new group or class of people.[2] Although the masculine is used, it undoubtedly included the female slaves.[3] Unlike the Stoics who usually addressed only their social peers, Paul directly addresses believing slaves[4] (cf. also Col 3:22–25) who were responsible to carry out his exhortations. Undoubtedly, they were a part of the church at Ephesus and heard the message directly. Otherwise, it is more likely that the Scriptures would have indicated that Paul had conveyed the message through their masters.

As in connection with Paul's exhortation to the children (6:1), so

1. The word order τοῖς κατά σάρκα κυρίοις is found in ℵ A B P 0278 33 81 104 365 1175 1245[s] 1505 1739 1881 2464 *al* Clement. The word order τοῖς κυρίοις κατά σάρκα appears in 𝔓[46] D F G Ψ 𝔐. The first reading has early and good character manuscripts and good genealogical relationships in only the Alexandrian text-type. The second reading has an early papyrus and one uncial in the Alexandrian text but has good character manuscripts and good genealogical relationships in the Western and Byzantine text-types. It also has good geographical distribution. External evidence tends to favor the second reading because of its geographical distribution. Internal evidence suggests that the scribes favored the first reading in order to be consistent with the parallel passage in Col 3:20. Also, the first reading would prevent confusion to the reader, for the second reading could suggest that slaves are to obey their masters in a fleshly manner or obey according the flesh with fear and trembling. The second reading is an easier reading because κυρίοις is not separated from the article. Internal evidence could go either way. It is difficult to decide which is the preferred reading. Either reading has basically the same sense.

2. Robertson, *Grammar*, 757; Wallace, *Greek Grammar*, 229.

3. Best, 575.

4. Bradley, *Slavery and Society at Rome*, 150.

here Paul uses the imperative ὑπακούετε with the dative of the person, meaning "'to do what one says' or 'to carry out someone's orders.'"[1] The object of the slaves' obedience, τοῖς κατὰ σάρκα κυρίοις, is literally translated "to the masters according to the flesh." As mentioned in the discussion on the textual critical problem (see p. 805 n. 1), this could be confused to mean that slaves are to obey their masters in a fleshly manner. However, the context demands that the prepositional phrase κατὰ σάρκα, "according to the flesh," refers not to the manner of obedience, because this is given in the next prepositional phrase, but to the kind of masters, that is, those who are composed of flesh, their human masters. Many versions translate these words in a cumbersome fashion such as "to those who are your masters according to the flesh" (AV, RV, ASV, NASB), "to those who are, according to human reckoning, your masters" (JB, NJB), or "to those who are your earthly masters" (RSV). Others translate it with much simpler wording as "your earthly masters" (NEB, NIV, NRSV) or "your human masters" (TEV) and these are preferable.

μετὰ φόβου καὶ τρόμου, "with fear and trembling." The preposition μετά denotes the attendant circumstances of mood or state of mind.[2] The noun φόβος was discussed at 5:21 in conjunction with the command that all believers are to submit to one another in the fear of Christ, which is accomplished in the power of the Holy Spirit (5:18). It was concluded that it was best viewed as reverential fear or respect. The same can be said for the verb form in 5:33 in connection with the wife's reverential respect for her husband's position as head of the home. Certainly, in connection with slaves the idea of "fear" or "dread" is appropriate. The use of fear was the way masters controlled slaves.[3] It was felt that fear produced greater loyalty.[4] Phaedrus (15 B.C.–A.D. 50), a slave of Thracian birth who may have been educated in Italy and was a freedman of Augustus, stated that slaves were punished for any offence.[5] Hence, fear was the order of the day. The second term τρόμος is used of "trembling" or "quivering" for fear.[6] It is used thirty times in the LXX (twenty times in the canonical books) and five times in the NT (Mark 16:8; 1 Cor 2:3; 2 Cor 7:15; Eph 6:5; Phil 2:12) and always has the idea of "shaking" or "trembling." The term specifically denotes the outward manifestation of fear, fear so great that it cannot be concealed. It is not uncommon for this word to

1. L&N §36.15.

2. BAGD 509; BDAG 637.

3. See the chapter entitled "Fear, Abuse, Violence" by Bradley in *Slaves and Masters in the Roman Empire*, 113–37.

4. Propertius 3.6.6.

5. Phaedrus *Fable* 3.prologue 33–37; Bradley, *Slaves and Masters in the Roman Empire*, 150–51.

6. BAGD 827; BDAG 1016; L&N §16.6.

be used in connection with φόβος, for the combination of these two words occurs thirteen times in the LXX and four times in the NT.

ἐν ἁπλότητι τῆς[1] καρδίας ὑμῶν, "in singleness of your heart." This prepositional phrase modifies the verb "to obey" and not the prepositional phrase μετὰ φόβου καὶ τρόμου, "with fear and trembling," which would have expected the construction τοῦ ἐν ἁπλότητι τῆς καρδίας ὑμῶν.[2] Gärtner observes that from Plato onwards, ἁπλότης is "compounded from *ha-*, together, and *pel-*, to fold" and means "singleness, single; the opposite being *diplous*, double. Beside this numerical meaning there grew up a positive ethical connotation for the word-groups. Hence, *haplotēs* [ἁπλότης] came to mean . . . straightness, openness, speaking without a hidden meaning."[3] In the LXX it occurs seven times (twice in the canonical books) meaning "simplicity" or "singleness of heart" (e.g., 2 Sam 15:11; 1 Chr 29:17; Wis 1:1; 1 Macc 2:37, 60). Although Josephus does use it with the idea of "generosity, liberality,"[4] he also uses it to mean "simplicity."[5] Philo uses this term in contrast to "cunningness, craftiness" (πανουργία)[6] or "wickedness, vice" (κακία).[7] The term is used eight times in the NT and only by Paul (Rom 12:8; 2 Cor 1:12; 8:2; 9:11, 13; 11:3; Eph 6:5; Col 3:22). Though it is used three times with the sense of "generosity" (2 Cor 8:2; 9:11, 13), the other five times it has the sense of "simplicity, singleness of heart, sincerity."[8] Some translate it "sincerity" (NASB, TEV, JB, NIV, NJB) while others translate it "singleness" (AV, RV, ASV, RSV, NEB, NRSV). It conveys the idea that slaves should obey wholeheartedly or completely.[9] The preposition ἐν denotes the manner in which obedience is carried out. As mentioned in 1:18 (cf. also 3:17; 4:18; 5:19) the word καρδία, "heart," is the center of a person, the seat of feelings and emotions, of will or volition, or as here, of religious and moral conduct. The Hebrew and Aramaic distributive singular "heart" (see a discussion of this word in 3:17), referring to the group, is commonly used by Paul.[10] Hence, slaves are to obey their masters in singleness of the heart, not duplicitous in their disposition and act. They

1. The article τῆς is omitted by ℵ 323 945 1739 1881 *al*. It should be retained because there is not enough good evidence for its omission.

2. Salmond, 378.

3. Buckhard Gärtner, "Simplicity, Sincerity, Uprightness [ἁπλότης]," *NIDNTT* 3 (1978): 572. Cf. Xenophon *Cyropaedia* 1.4.3; Polybius 1.78.8; Diodorus Siculus 5.66.4.

4. Josephus *A.J.* 7.13.4 §332.

5. Josephus *B.J.* 2.8.10 §151; 5.7.4 §319

6. Philo *Op. Mund.* 55 §156.

7. Ibid., 61 §170.

8. Otto Bauernfeind, "ἁπλοῦς, ἁπλότης," *TDNT* 1 (1964): 386–87. Bauerfeind thinks that Rom 12:8 refers to generosity, but even in that context it is best to see it as simplicity.

9. Heinrich Bacht, "Einfalt des Herzens—eine vergessene Tugend?" *GL* 29 (1956): 422–26.

10. MHT 3:23.

are not to pretend to labor while actually loitering. They should give undivided attention and effort to the task in hand.

ὡς τῷ Χριστῷ, "as to Christ." This adverbial phrase indicates who was the slaves' ultimate master (v. 6). In other words, slaves were to obey their earthly masters as they would obey their heavenly master, Christ.[1] This parallels 5:22 where wives are to be subject to their husbands "as to the Lord" (ὡς τῷ κυρίῳ). The slaves' obedience to their earthly master marked their obedience to their heavenly master. Paul makes no distinction between Christian and non-Christian masters in this regard. Briefly then, slaves' obedience must be more than outward appearance. It was to come from within with singleness of heart as they would do to Christ. No doubt, this injunction was not always easy to carry out. There may have been times when unbelieving masters would not let them fellowship with other Christians. Also, tension between a Christian master and a Christian slave was a possibility since the slave knew that in the eyes of God they were equal. Yet, as in the other two pairs, wife/husband and children/parents, certain lines of authority needed to be observed.

6:6. μὴ κατ' ὀφθαλμοδουλίαν ὡς ἀνθρωπάρεσκοι, "not according to eye service as people-pleasers." Paul has explained that slaves are to obey their earthly masters as they do their heavenly master and now he specifies the manner in which they are to obey. He first states the negative, then the positive. Negatively he states, μὴ κατ' ὀφθαλμοδουλίαν ὡς ἀνθρωπάρεσκοι, "not according to eye service as people-pleasers." The term ὀφθαλμοδουλία appears only here and in Col 3:22, the parallel passage. It is found nowhere else except in ecclesiastical writings. Literally, it means "eye service"[2] connoting "to serve with a view to impressing others."[3] It could convey the idea that the goal of performance is strictly to impress the master and to leave undone anything which would not be noticed by him. However, more likely it refers to the outward activity of work without the corrersponding inward dedication.[4] In other words, the service is outwardly correct "with no sense of inner obligation to the master for the sake of God and of Christ (the deceived ὀφθαλμοί of the master being contrasted with the deceitful ψυχή of the slave)."[5] The preposition preceding this word is κατά and when used with the accusative, as here, it denotes a standard. In other words, slaves were to obey their masters not "according to" the standard of mere outward performance. This prepositional phrase is followed by the comparative conjunction ὡς, "as," with ἀνθρωπάρεσκοι "people-pleasers," again a word that in the NT is used

1. Cf. Schweizer, "Traditional Ethical Patterns in the Pauline and post-Pauline Letters," 206.

2. BAGD 599; BDAG 743–44.

3. L&N §35.29.

4. C. F. D. Moule, "A Note on ὀφθαλμοδουλία," *ExpTim* 59 (June 1948): 250.

5. Karl Heinrich Rengstorf, "ὀφθαλμοδουλία," *TDNT* 2 (1964): 280.

only here and in the parallel passage in Col 3:22. The only other occurrences before the NT are in Ps 53:5 [MT 53:6; LXX 52:6] and *Pss. Sol.* 4:title, 7, 8, 19. In the latter work it is used of those who try to impress people, "with the implication of being in contrast to God or at the sacrifice of some principle," and can be rendered in the Ephesian context "as 'those who are just trying to make people like them.'"[1] They are ones "who have no real interest in their work, but only aim at making a favourable impression on their owners by fits of ostentatious zeal," doing the minimum of work.[2] The Christian slaves are enjoined not to obey their masters in that fashion.

ἀλλʼ ὡς δοῦλοι Χριστοῦ ποιοῦντες τὸ θέλημα τοῦ θεοῦ ἐκ ψυχῆς, "but as slaves of Christ doing the will of God wholeheartedly." With a strong adversative (ἀλλά) followed by another comparative conjunction (ὡς), Paul exhorts slaves to obey their masters as those who are slaves of Christ. The manner by which this is done is demonstrated by the participial clause ποιοῦντες τὸ θέλημα τοῦ θεοῦ ἐκ ψυχῆς "doing the will of God wholeheartedly." The present participle ποιοῦντες, "doing," expresses the manner in which the slaves of Christ are to obey (the verb "obey" needs to be supplied from v. 5). The word θέλημα was discussed at 1:1 where we concluded that it has the sense of a desire, wish, will, or resolve. This word is followed by the possessive genitive τοῦ θεοῦ showing that it is God's will that is to be done. The word θέλημα is always used in Ephesians with reference to God, except in 2:3 where it refers to the will of the flesh. The phrase ἐκ ψυχῆς,[3] literally, "from the soul," is translated "wholeheartedly" and actually means "from one's innermost being." In verse 5 "heart" is used synonymously. There are many references in the Bible to obey, serve, and love God with all the heart, soul, and/or strength (Deut 6:5; 10:12; 11:3, 13; 13:3; 30:2, 6, 10; Josh 22:5; Matt 22:37 = Mark 12:30, 33 = Luke 10:27). As obedient slaves of Christ, then, they were ultimately doing God's will, the emphasis being on wholeheartedly pleasing God rather than people. It should be noted that some commentators think that ἐκ ψυχῆς should be attached to the following clause (μετʼ εὐνοίας), denoting source of service accompanied with the feeling of goodwill in serving another.[4] Nonetheless, more agree that this is not the case because it would be redundant. Furthermore, its attachment to the preceding clause is a natural progression from serving with a disposition of goodwill towards one's master to doing the will of God whole-

1. L&N §25.98; cf. BAGD 67; BDAG 80; Werner Foerster, "ἀνθρωπάρεσκος," *TDNT* 1 (1964): 456.

2. Moffatt, "Four Notes on Ephesians," 96.

3. For a discussion of *ex animo* (ἐκ ψυχῆς) by the fourth-century Latin exegetes, see Jean Doignon, "«Servi . . . facientes voluntatem Dei ex animo» (Éph 6,6): un éclatement de la notion de servitude chez Ambroise, Jérôme, Augustin?" *Revue des sciences philosophiques et théologiques* 68 (Avril 1984): 201–11.

4. Bengel, 4:112; Alford, 3:142; Abbott, 179; Robinson, 211; Westcott, 89–90.

heartedly.[1] "It emphasizes an inner motivation that is unreserved and stands in direct contrast to the 'eye-service' of those who [are] 'men-pleasers' [v. 6]."[2]

6:7. μετ' εὐνοίας δουλεύοντες ὡς[3] τῷ κυρίῳ καὶ οὐκ ἀνθρώποις, "with goodwill rendering service as to the Lord and not to people." This gives a further amplification to the nature of the service. Parallel with the participle ποιοῦντες in verse 6, the present participle δουλεύοντες expresses also the manner in which slaves of Christ are to obey, namely, serving with goodwill. The noun εὔνοια appears only here in the NT. It occurs frequently in classical literature meaning "goodwill" or "affection."[4] It occurs eighteen times in the LXX (twice in the canonical books), primarily in Maccabees, and continues with the same sense (1 Macc 11:33; 2 Macc 9:21, 26; 11:19; 3 Macc 3:3; 6:26; 7:7; 4 Macc 2:10; 13:25). Specifically, it is used of the "goodwill" or "loyalty" of slaves toward their masters.[5] Some suggest that this word connotes "zeal, enthusiasm,"[6] but there can be a show of enthusiasm without goodwill. Thus, "goodwill" appears to be a more apt translation for this context.[7] Service with goodwill is to be done ὡς τῷ κυρίῳ καὶ οὐκ ἀνθρώποις, "as to the Lord and not to people." There is an ellipsis of a participle (δουλεύοντες) in connection with the comparative conjunction ὡς, which when included would be translated "serving with goodwill as if serving the Lord and not people."[8] Although ostensibly slaves are carrying out the orders of earthly masters, the attitude of goodwill that accompanies this service in the end seeks to please the perfect heavenly Lord and not the faulty earthly master. In the twenty-six times "Lord" is mentioned in Ephesians, it consistently has reference to Christ rather than to God, except twice when it refers to human masters (6:5, 9). Believers are to render service to their new Lord Christ. A story in Tacitus illustrates the opposite stance. He tells of the murder of a famous senator by a household slave, either because the master had refused to manumit the slave on a previously agreed price or because both the master and the slave had affection for the same slave boy.[9] In other words, the slave served with ill will. Likely, slaves have endless reasons to harbor resentment, especially when

1. Eadie, 451; Ellicott, 142; Meyer, 321; Salmond, 379; Masson, 218; Schlier, 285; Gaugler, 214; Gnilka, 301; Bruce, 401; Lincoln, 422; Best, 578.

2. O'Brien, 451.

3. The adverbial conjunction ὡς is omitted by D^2 K L Ψ 326 614 629 1241^{s*} 2495 *al* Ambrosiaster. The conjunction should be retained because there is not enough good evidence for its omission.

4. Herodotus 6.108; Thucydides 2.40.4; Plato *Protagoras* 337b.

5. Xenophon *Oeconomicus* 12.5–7; *P.Oxy.* 3:494.6; Lucian *Bis Accusatus sive Tribunalia* 16.

6. BAGD 323; BDAG 409; L&N §25.72.

7. J. Behm, "εὐνοέω, εὔνοια," *TDNT* 4 (1967): 972–73.

8. BDF §425 (4); MHT 3:158.

9. Tacitus *Annales* 14.42–45.

masters perpetrate great injustices against them. Thus, Paul, realizing that slaves could harbor many justified resentments, reminds them that ultimately their obligation is to the Lord and not to people. Accordingly, no matter what station in life Christians find themselves, they are always to render their conduct as to the Lord, as seen in the parallel comparative statements ὡς τῷ κυρίῳ found in 5:22 and 6:7 and ὡς τῷ Χριστῷ in 6:5.[1]

(b) Reason: God Rewards (6:8)

Why should slaves obey their masters with such honest diligence and positive attitude? Many masters would not necessarily reward such diligence and outlook. Yet there is a broader perspective than that of earthly gain. Hence, Paul continues by explaining the reason for proper Christian conduct.

Text: 6:8. εἰδότες ὅτι ἕκαστος ὃ ἐάν ποιήσῃ ἀγαθόν, τοῦτο κομίσεται παρὰ κυρίου, εἴτε δοῦλος εἴτε ἐλεύθερος.

Translation: 6:8. "knowing that whatever good each person does, this he will receive back from the Lord, whether slave or free."

Commentary: 6:8. εἰδότες ὅτι ἕκαστος ὃ ἐὰν ποιήσῃ[2] ἀγαθόν, "knowing that whatever good each person does." The participle εἰδότες, "knowing," most likely is causal relating back to the main verb ὑπακούετε, "obey," in verse 5. Slaves are motivated to obey because they know that their Master in heaven is going to reward them.[3] The conjunction ὅτι after verbs of mental perception serves to indicate the content.[4] This is followed by the distributive pronoun ἕκαστος, which refers to every individual (unlike the πᾶς before an anarthrous noun, which refers to every in the sense of any).[5] This is important because it means that no slave is excluded. No doubt, many slaves had done good deeds that went unnoticed by their masters who excluded them

1. Cf. Schrage, "Zur Ethik der neutestamentliche Haustafeln," 19.

2. The words ὅτι ἕκαστος ὃ ἐάν ποιήσῃ have different order in various manuscripts. The first order (ὅτι ἕκαστος ὃ ἐάν [or ἄν] ποιήσῃ) occurs in A D* F G P 0278 33 81 104 326 365 1175 1241[s] 2464 *pc*. The second order (ὅτι ἕκαστος ἐάν τι ποιήσῃ) is found in B it[d] and in WH, NA[27], and UBS[4]. The third order (ὅτι ὃ ἐάν τι ἕκαστος ποιήσῃ) appears in (ʃ D[2]) L[c] (Ψ) 𝔐. The fourth order (ὃ τι [or ὅτι] ἂν ποιήσῃ ἕκαστος) appears only in ℵ. The fifth order (ὃ ἕκαστος ποιήσῃ) is found in K vg[ms] Jerome. The sixth order (ἐάν τι ἕκαστος ποιήσῃ) occurs in L* 630 1739 1881 2495 *al*. The second, fourth, fifth, and sixth orders are found in very few manuscripts. The first order is represented in the Alexandrian and Western texts. The third order has many manuscripts but mainly in the Byzantine tradition. It would seem that the first order has preference. There is a slight difference in a literal translation but the meaning is the same. For the first order, see the translation above; the second order would be translated "knowing that each person, if he does anything good."

3. Nieder, *Die Motive der religiös-sittlichen Paränese*, 86.

4. BAGD 588; BDAG 731.

5. MHT 3:199.

from the credit they deserved. This is not the case with God, for he will notice the good deeds of every slave. Immediately following is the third class conditional clause (ὃ ἐὰν ποιήσῃ ἀγαθόν, "whatever good he does"), which indicates a probable future. It anticipates that the slaves will do good. As seen in 2:10 and 4:28, 29, the term ἀγαθός denotes that which is morally and beneficially good. In other words, the implication is that while the slave is doing good that is beneficial to the master, at the same time this good will be measured by God's standards as morally upright.

τοῦτο κομίσεται παρὰ κυρίου, "this he will receive back from the Lord." This is the apodosis of the protasis stated in the paragraph above. The demonstrative pronoun τοῦτο, "this," refers back to the ἀγαθόν and is emphatic by its position. In other words, "this" good and not something else will not go unnoticed. The verb κομίσεται is the future middle indicative of κομίζω. In the active voice it means "to bring" and the middle form used in classical Greek means "to receive, get (for oneself)."[1] The word occurs twenty-nine times in the LXX, eight times in the canonical books. This use of the middle continued in the LXX occurring eighteen times (e.g., Gen 38:20; Hos 2:11; 1 Macc 13:37; 2 Macc 8:33). In the NT it is used ten times, once in the active (Luke 7:37) and the other nine times in the middle, sometimes meaning "to get back, recover" (Matt 25:27; Heb 11:19) but more often meaning "to receive, obtain" (2 Cor 5:10; Col 3:25; Heb 10:36; 11:39; 1 Pet 1:9; 5:4).[2] The latter meaning makes good sense in this context. The preposition παρά followed by a genitive denotes "the point fr. which an action originates . . . after verbs of taking, accepting, receiving . . ." as is the case here.[3] Every slave who does good to his or her master shall definitely receive reward from the Lord, the supreme master. The future tense indicates that the slave will receive such recompense sometime in the future.[4] This future certainty rests not on the tense but God who makes the promise. This is important because masters sometimes promised freedom but never kept their promise.[5] Not so with the Lord (i.e., Christ). That future time most likely refers to the judgment seat of Christ when all believers will receive recompense for the deeds they have done (2 Cor 5:10).

εἴτε δοῦλος εἴτε ἐλεύθερος, "whether slave or free." The inclusiveness of this promise is now stated. Though the verb is omitted,[6] it is assumed that Paul is alluding to the future recompense for both slave and free believers. As the Lord treats both slaves and masters the same in the present time (cf. Gal 3:28; 1 Cor 12:13; Col 3:11), the

1. Thucydides 1.113.3; Aristophanes *Vespae* 690; Diodorus Siculus 17.69.1; 20.28.3.
2. BAGD 442–43; BDAG 557; L&N §§57.126, 136.
3. BAGD 609–10; BDAG 756.
4. Cf. Fanning, *Verbal Aspect*, 120–23.
5. Tacitus *Annales* 14.42.
6. MHT 3:333.

next verse reaffirms equal treatment as well in that future day. In the future, social status will not be important, only spiritual conditions. It will be a judgment based on righteous standards and not the whim of a master. Christian slaves were to give witness of their faith and the hope that one day they will be justly recompensed, even though they suffered for righteousness' sake in the present time (1 Pet 3:13–17).[1]

(2) Responsibility of Masters' Treatment (6:9)

Paul has completed his exhortation to slaves and now, following the pattern he began in 5:22, he turns his attention toward those in authority over them.

(a) Imperative: Forebear Threats (6:9a)

Text: 6:9a. Καὶ οἱ κύριοι, τὰ αὐτὰ ποιεῖτε πρὸς αὐτούς, ἀνιέντες τὴν ἀπειλήν,

Translation: 6:9a. "And masters, do the same things to them, stop threatening them,"

Commentary: 6:9a. Καὶ οἱ κύριοι, τὰ αὐτὰ ποιεῖτε πρὸς αὐτούς, ἀνιέντες τὴν ἀπειλήν, "And masters, do the same things to them, stop threatening them." The use of the article and noun οἱ κύριοι, "slaves," in plural form indicates that Paul is moving to a new group or class of people.[2] Although more space is devoted to the slaves and their duties toward their masters, the Christian masters also have specific responsibilities towards their slaves. The exhortation that they are to τὰ αὐτὰ ποιεῖτε πρὸς αὐτούς, "do the same things to them" is thought by Chrysostom to refer to δουλεύοντες in verse 7, indicating that masters are to serve slaves.[3] However, it probably refers to the more general idea of the spirit of integrity, dedication, and goodwill that the masters should exhibit toward their slaves as they do to the Lord. This is in keeping with Col 4:1 where Paul exhorts masters to treat their slaves justly and fairly (τὸ δίκαιον καὶ τὴν ἰσότητα). The phrase ἀνιέντες τὴν ἀπειλήν, "forbearing the threat," is a clear instruction to masters concerning their dealings with slaves. The word ἀνιέντες, present participle of ἀνίημι, can mean "to loosen, unfasten" or "to abandon, desert" or, as in the present context, "to give up, cease, stop."[4] The participle could function as imperatival but more likely functions as a participle of manner in relation to the main verb, namely, "masters, do the same things to them, stop using threats." The noun ἀπειλή, used mostly in the plural, can denote "boastful promises, boasts"[5] or, more com-

1. Barth, *The Broken Wall*, 225–26.
2. Robertson, *Grammar*, 757.
3. Chrysostom *Eph* 6:9 (*PG* 62:157).
4. BAGD 69; BDAG 82–83; L&N §68.43; Rudolf Bultmann, "ἀνίημι, ἄνεσις," *TDNT* 1 (1964): 367.
5. Homer *Ilias* 20.83.

monly, "threats."[1] It occurs in the LXX twenty-two times, only eight times in the canonical books, meaning "anger, wrath" (Prov 19:12; 20:2; Hab 3:12), "rebuke" (Prov 13:8; 17:10; Isa 50:2), and "threat(s)" (3 Macc 2:24; 5:18, 30, 33, 37; 4 Macc 4:24; 7:2; 8:19; 9:32; 13:6; 14:9). It appears in the NT only three times (Acts 4:29; 9:1; Eph 6:9; the verb appears twice: Acts 4:17; 1 Pet 2:23) and can be rendered "threaten."[2] It is "to declare that one will cause harm to someone, particularly if certain conditions are not met—'to threaten, threat.'"[3] In this text it can be translated, "stop threatening them." This prohibition is appropriate, for there was a proverbial statement that "all slaves are enemies" because masters were tyrants and abusive.[4] Abuse was displayed in various ways such as threats of beating,[5] sexual harassment of female slaves,[6] threats to sell the male slaves "away from the household so as to part him for ever from his loved ones,"[7] to name a few. Does Paul's exhortation prevent a master from threatening his slaves with punishment if they did wrong? If that were the case, slaves could refuse to work. It is more likely that Paul was enjoining Christian masters to treat their slaves with integrity and goodwill as he had asked the slaves to behave toward them.[8] No doubt, many times idle threats were made merely to engender fear in order to make slaves work harder. Paul urged them not to impose threats in the same way non-Christian masters might do.[9] Even Seneca had once remarked that it is more likely that slaves would perform good service when treated with integrity and goodwill.[10] According to Paul, both slaves and masters were to conduct themselves with integrity, compelled by their hearts and not by external forces.

(b) Reason: God Judges (6:9b)

Text: 6:9b. εἰδότες ὅτι καὶ αὐτῶν καὶ ὑμῶν ὁ κύριός ἐστιν ἐν οὐρανοῖς, καὶ προσωπολημψία οὐκ ἔστιν παρ᾽ αὐτῷ.

1. Ibid., 13.219; *Odyssea* 13.126; Sophocles *Antigone* 753; Herodutus 6.32; Thucydides 4.126.5.
2. BAGD 83; BDAG 100.
3. L&N §33.291.
4. Seneca *Epistulae Morales* 47.5.
5. Cf. Plautus *Amphitryon* 291–349.
6. Saller, "Slavery and the Roman Family," 68–76.
7. Wiedemann, *Slavery*, 27.
8. Cf. S. R. Llewelyn, *New Documents Illustrating Early Christianity*, vol. 8, *A Review of the Greek Inscriptions and Papyri Published 1984–85* (Sydney: Macquarie University; Grand Rapids: Eerdmans, 1998), 40.
9. Cf. Joüon, "Notes philologiques sur quelques versets de l'Épître aux Éphésiens," 462.
10. For Seneca's treatment on slaves, see *Epistulae Morales* 47; Robert J. Austgen, *Natural Motivation in the Pauline Epistles*, 2d ed. (Notre Dame: University of Notre Dame, 1969), 134.

Translation: 6:9b. "knowing that both their Master and yours is in heaven, and there is no partiality with him."

Commentary: 6:9b. εἰδότες ὅτι καὶ αὐτῶν καὶ ὑμῶν ὁ κύριός ἐστιν ἐν οὐρανοῖς, καὶ προσωπολημψία οὐκ ἔστιν παρ᾽ αὐτῷ, "knowing that both their Master and yours is in heaven, and there is no partiality with him." The participle εἰδότες, "knowing" (like that in v. 8), is most likely causal relating back to the main verb ποιεῖτε, "do," in verse 9a. The motivation for masters to deal with integrity toward their slaves is that they, too, have a Master and will be held accountable by that Master in heaven. In other words, they are servants of the same Lord as their slaves. This Master or Lord is the exalted Christ. The locale of their Lord is in heaven (ἐν οὐρανοῖς, lit. "in heavens"), the plural usage commonly used when referring to the place where God dwells.[1] This reference to the heavens serves to emphasize the contrast between the believers on earth and the sovereignty of the exalted Christ in heaven as the impartial judge.[2] In his next statement, Paul emphasizes the absence of partiality by the master in heaven. The word προσωπολημψία, "partiality," is developed from the two words πρόσωπον λαμβάνω "modelled closely on a Hebrew expression,"[3] literally translated "I receive a face," in reference to judgment on the basis of externals. For instance, an officer might not ticket a renowned person for a traffic violation because he recognizes his face. This, however, is not true of God, as is demonstrated in both the OT and NT (Deut 10:17; 2 Chr 19:7; Job 34:19; Ps 82:1–4; Acts 10:34; Rom 2:11; Gal 2:6; 1 Pet 1:17) as well as in other Jewish writings (Sir 35:12–13; *Jub.* 5:12–16; 21:3–5; *Pss. Sol.* 2:18; *1 Enoch* 63:8).[4] This same characteristic of impartiality is also attributed to Christ (Matt 22:16 = Mark 12:14 = Luke 20:21; Col 3:25; Eph 6:9). In the present context, Paul exhorts against the externals of conduct whether it be slaves who serve merely to impress (v. 6) or masters who use their power wrongly. Instead, both are to bear in mind that they will be judged by the same Master with no preferential treatment with regard to social status.[5] Whereas in Col 3:25 slaves are told that they will be judged

1. Horsley, *New Documents Illustrating Early Christianity*, vol. 3, *A Review of the Greek Inscriptions and Papyri Published in 1978*, 32.

2. Harris, "'The Heavenlies' Reconsidered," 85–86.

3. Eduard Lohse, "προσωπολημψία κτλ.," *TDNT* 6 (1968): 779–80.

4. Jouette M. Bassler, *Divine Impartiality. Paul and a Theological Axiom*, SBLDS, ed. William Baird, no. 59 (Chico, Calif.: Scholars Press, 1982). Since God's impartiality was such a popular concept in the OT and NT as well as in Jewish literature, it would be difficult to prove that the author borrowed from Rom 2:11 as suggested by Munro, "Col. iii.18–iv.1 and Eph. v.21–vi.9: Evidences of a Late Literary Stratum?"; essentially reprinted in idem, *Authority in Paul and Peter*, 28.

5. Bassler, *Divine Impartiality. Paul and a Theological Axiom*, 178. Schrage ("Zur Ethik der neutestamentliche Haustafeln," 9–10) does not think it refers to the future judgment, the "coming" Lord, but thinks it is a judgment of the Lord who is "presently"

impartially for wrongdoing, in this text the masters are told that they will be judged impartially for wrongdoing.[1]

The application of this passage to contemporary times must be done with caution. Paul was writing specifically for a society where slavery was a legal institution. However, there are certainly some principles from the passage that can be applied to employee/employer relationships in the present time. Primarily, Christian employees should serve their employers with fear, diligence, integrity, and goodwill and Christian employers should deal with their employees with integrity and goodwill, without threats. Both Christian employees and Christian employers need also to realize that they have a heavenly master to whom they are accountable for their attitudes and conduct. Furthermore, the behavior of both parties should be a testimony to the unbelievers with whom they work.

Paul's instruction to slaves and masters is the final part of the household code. As in the earlier portions of this code the instructions are directly given to each party, thus making each responsible to the Lord to obey them. The slaves are commanded to obey their masters, whether or not the masters are Christians or treat them properly. Their masters should not have to tell them to do so. Masters are enjoined to treat slaves properly and without partiality, whether or not the slaves are Christians or fulfill their obligations. How can these injunctions be implemented? It should be remembered that these instructions must be received in the light of the broader context of Eph 5:15–21 where the believer is admonished to walk wisely by being filled by the Holy Spirit.

In conclusion, the instructions given in the household code are God's formula for the wise walk of spouses, children, parents, slaves, and masters. Each of these must be filled by the Spirit in order to consistently carry out the exhortations given. This concept will be further demonstrated in the following verses where Paul addresses the present situation of all believers in an evil world where imminent attacks by the devil are a constant danger. He will introduce the spiritual armor necessary for believers to effectively engage in the battle against spiritual wickedness.

---

in heaven, which is typical of post-Pauline literature. However, one must see this in the light of the context, for in v. 8 it speaks of receiving the recompense in the future tense (which Schrage admits) and it would seem that the judgment of v. 9 is within the same time frame.

1. Schnackenburg, 266; Peter Richardson, *Paul's Ethic of Freedom* (Philadelphia: Westminster, 1979), 52.

F. Stand in Warfare (6:10–20)

In applying the doctrines presented in chapters 1–3, Paul uses the imperative "walk" (περιπατέω) five times in connection with the inferential conjunction "therefore" (οὖν). Believers are to: (1) walk in unity (4:1); (2) walk in holiness, not as the Gentiles (4:17); (3) walk in love (5:1–2); (4) walk in light, abstaining from involvement with evildoers and their works (5:7–8); and (5) walk in wisdom, controlled by the Holy Spirit (5:15). This last portion (5:15–21) is an extensive exhortation about the household code. Now Paul no longer uses the imperative "walk" in conjunction with the inferential conjunction "therefore." Rather, he begins this section with the articular adjective τὸ λοιπόν/τοῦ λοιποῦ, "finally," to indicate that these are his final thoughts before he ends the epistle. Looking at this section from the stance of rhetorical analysis, Lincoln suggests that this passage may well be a *peroratio* (normally a conclusion in recapitulating the facts and an emotional call to action based on those facts), an element of the *epilogos* outlined by Aristotle and Quintilian.[1] The *peroratio* was used by ancient rhetoricians and in speeches of generals before battle (1QM 15).[2] If this were the case in Ephesians, this conclusion would serve not only the paraenetic section of the book (4:1–6:9) but also as a stirring conclusion to the whole book. As such, the various pieces of armor would have links with the entire letter with Paul arousing them to action by the threefold use of the verb "to stand" (6:11, 13, 14).[3] While Lincoln's proposal has some merit, the author of Ephesians gives no obvious hints of links with the whole book nor is there any sort of recapitulation or an emotional call to action based on those facts, normally included in a *peroratio*.

1. Aristotle *Rhetorica* 3.19.1 §1419b; Quintilian *Institutio Oratoria* 6.1.1–55.

2. Generals would rouse their soldiers in order to empower them to stand firm in battle (Faust, *Pax Christi et Pax Caesaris*, 447).

3. Lincoln, xli–xliii, 432–33; Snodgrass, 335–36; Best, 585–86; Andrew T. Lincoln, "'Stand, therefore . . .': Ephesians 6:10–20 as *Peroratio*," *Biblical Interpretation* 3 (March 1995): 99–114; Kittredge, *Community and Authority*, 144–45.

Many of the Ephesian believers had been worshipers of Artemis prior to their conversion.[1] They depended on her for their protection. Arnold suggests that it was necessary for believers to understand that in reality Artemis represented spiritual wickedness empowered by wicked spiritual forces known as demons (cf. 1 Cor 10:19–21).[2] In the light of this he suggests that in 6:10–20 Paul is discussing the spiritual warfare of believers and their need to make use of God's resources for strength against such evil powers.[3] Certainly Ephesians mentions the operation of the wicked one (2:1–3) and the effect he has had on the unbelievers (4:17–19). This attack by the evil one is incessant and will continue until the day Christ comes back to judge the world, the devil, and his armies. In objecting to Arnold's view Strelan suggests that there is no evidence that the Ephesians depicted Artemis as evil and demonic.[4] Yoder Neufeld offers the suggestion that what is portrayed here is the imagery of the Divine Warrior in full armor that was developed from Isa 59, Wis 5, and 1 Thess 5. Particularly in Ephesians, then, the community of believers, the body of Christ, steps into the role of the Divine Warrior to conquer the cosmic hostile powers.[5] To the contrary, however, in Ephesians the body of believers does not appear to be portrayed in the imagery of the Divine Warrior but rather are enjoined to be soldiers strengthened in the Lord to stand defensively (not to conquer) against the onslaughts of the evil one. This ties in well with the beginning of the letter. Believers are enriched with all the spiritual benefits in the heavenly places (1:3) and are seated with Christ in the heavenlies (1:20; 2:6). Paul prayed that they would know God intimately and experience God's power that raised Christ to God's right hand in the heavenlies (1:19–23). Now in the present context Paul enjoins believers to be strengthened in the Lord to be able to stand against the spiritual wickedness in the heavenlies (6:10–12). The devil and his spiritual hosts desire to rob believers of their spiritual benefits. They must experience God's power that raised Christ to the heavenlies to stand defensively against the spiritual wickedness in the heavenlies. The exhortations expressed in this passage are primarily directed to individual believers but the corporate body is also in view.[6]

1. For a discussion of Ephesian worship, see the introduction (p. 84–86) and Arnold, *Ephesians: Power and Magic*, 14–29.

2. Arnold, *Ephesians: Power and Magic*, 66–68.

3. Cf. Ibid., 103–9.

4. Strelan, *Paul, Artemis, and the Jews in Ephesus*, 83.

5. Thomas R. Yoder Neufeld, *'Put on the Armour of God': The Divine Warrior from Isaiah to Ephesians*, JSNTSup, ed. Stanley E. Porter et al., vol. 144 (Sheffield: Sheffield Academic Press, 1997). For a discussion of the ancient mythologies and religions, especially Babylonian and Iranian, regarding wise people in battle as soldiers of the gods, see Kamlah, *Die Form der katalogischen Paränese im Neuen Testament*, 71–103, esp. 85–92.

6. Kitchen (119–26) understands this passage as a reference to the corporate and not individual believers. Best (586) thinks that Kitchen has gone too far because within Ephesians there are injunctions directed to individuals and not to the corporate body, e.g., the injunction against fornication (5:3) cannot be a reference to the church but to individu-

This section is divided into three parts: (1) putting on the armor (6:10–13); (2) standing with the armor (6:14–16); and (3) receiving the final pieces of armor (6:17–20).

1. Put on the Armor (6:10–13)

Verse 10 begins with the exhortation to "be strong in the Lord." With no conjunction this is followed by a second exhortation in verse 11 to put on the armor of God for the purpose (πρός) of being able to stand against the strategies of the devil. In verse 12 Paul gives the reason (ὅτι) for standing against the strategies of the devil. Verse 13 gives the conclusion (διὰ τοῦτο), that is, believers are to take up the whole armor of God that they may be able stand in the evil day. These verses are the basis for the following exhortations. Having put on the armor, they are exhorted not "to walk" but "to stand" (v. 14) against the onslaughts of the devil and "to receive" (v. 17) the final pieces of the armor.

a. What: Be Strong in the Lord (6:10)

Text: 6:10. Τὸ λοιπὸν ἐνδυναμοῦσθε ἐν κυρίῳ καὶ ἐν τῷ κράτει τῆς ἰσχύος αὐτοῦ.

Translation: 6:10. "Finally, be strengthened in the Lord, that is, in the might of his strength."

Commentary: 6:10. Τὸ λοιπὸν[1], [2] ἐνδυναμοῦσθε[3] ἐν κυρίῳ καὶ ἐν τῷ κράτει τῆς ἰσχύος αὐτοῦ, "Finally, be strengthened in the Lord, that

als. However, Best wants to make this passage exclusively refer to individual believers. It seems best to see this passage addressing primarily individual believers, but also the corporate body is not excluded from the spiritual warfare with the devil and his comrades.

1. The reading τὸ λοιπόν appears in א² D F G Ψ 𝔐 Chrysostom Theodoret Theophylact Oecumenius. The reading τοῦ λοιποῦ is found in 𝔓⁴⁶ א* A B I 0278 33 81 1175 1241ˢ 1739 1881 2464 *pc* (NA²⁷, UBS⁴). The second reading has good date and character of manuscripts but only in the Alexandrian text-type. The first reading has good date and character of manuscripts in the Western and Byzantine texts and it has good geographical spread with those two text-types and some Alexandrian texts. The first reading is preferred with regard to external evidence. Internal evidence could go either way. Both readings mean the same thing. Because of external evidence, the first reading is preferred.

2. After τὸ λοιπόν, the words ἀδελφοί μου occur in א² (ʃ A 0278) F G Ψ 𝔐 lat syr copᵇᵒ. A second reading ἀδελφοί is found in A (placed after ἐνδυναμοῦσθε) F G Ψ 0278 Theodoret. The omission of the first and second readings is in 𝔓⁴⁶ א* B D I 33 81 1175 1241ˢ 1739 1881 2464* *pc* itᵇ˒ ᵐ* copˢᵃ Lucifer Ambrosiaster Speculum. All three readings are represented with some good manuscripts. The omission has very good Alexandrian witness and a main Western reading. It is fairly good in geographical distribution. Internally, it would be difficult to explain its omission unless it was a slip of the memory or eye by the scribe. Other of Paul's epistles have either the first or the second reading in connection with τὸ λοιπόν (2 Cor 13:11; Phil 3:1; 4:8; 2 Thess 3:1). On the other hand, since these terms are not used in Ephesians, its inclusion seems to be a harder reading. Its omission is preferred.

3. The reading δυναμοῦσθε is found in 𝔓⁴⁶ B 33 but ἐνδυναμοῦσθε is found in the rest of the manuscript tradition and, hence, the preferred reading.

is, in the might of his strength." The words τὸ λοιπόν literally translate as "the rest, remaining," that is, "finally, in conclusion."[1] There is debate as to whether it introduces a logical conclusion like the inferential οὖν, "henceforth, therefore,"[2] or introduces the last member of a series, translated "finally."[3] The genitival form accepted in some readings (see p. 819 n. 1) has more the idea of "from now on, in the future" but may be translated "finally" in this context.[4] Having accepted the accusative reading, this word introduces the final portion of the letter, which contains some very practical exhortations similar to 2 Cor 13:11; 1 Thess 4:1; 2 Thess 3:1.[5] From Eph 4:1 to 6:9 Paul gives practical applications for the believers concerning how to live out their new position in Christ before both believers and unbelievers. Now, in his final section (6:10–20), he describes the continual warfare of wicked forces against believers and accordingly exhorts them to be strengthened in the Lord in order to be able to stand against the wicked schemes of the devil.[6] The struggle of believers ultimately is not a human conflict but is a battle against wicked spiritual forces.

The verb ἐνδυναμοῦσθε, "be strengthened," the present imperative passive of ἐνδυναμόω, occurs only here in Ephesians. Both the noun δύναμις, "power, ability" (1:19, 21; 3:7, 16, 20), and the verb δύναμαι, "to be able, capable" (3:4, 20; 6:11, 13, 16), appear five times each. ἐνδυναμόω in this context means "to endue with power, to become able, to become capable, to strengthen."[7] The same sense is found only once in the LXX (Judg 6:34 [B text]; although it is found two other times as a variant reading: 1 Chr 12:18 [MT & LXX 12:19]; Ps 52:7 [LXX 51:9]) and the six other occurrences in the NT (Acts 9:22; Rom 4:20; Phil 4:13; 1 Tim 1:12; 2 Tim 2:1; 4:17). Although in form it could be rendered as a middle,[8] it is best understood in the passive voice, "to be made strong" or "to be strengthened," as elsewhere in the NT (Acts 9:22; Rom 4:20; 2 Tim 2:1).[9] The power does not come from the believer but from an external source.[10] This usage is similar to that in Paul's prayer that the believers might be strengthened with power or

1. BAGD 480; BDAG 602; Moule, *Idiom Book*, 34; BDF §160; MHT 3:235, 336.

2. A. N. Jannaris, "Misreadings and Misrenderings in the New Testament," *Exp* 5th ser., vol. 8 (December 1898): 429–31.

3. Thrall, *Greek Particles in the New Testament*, 25–30.

4. BAGD 480; BDAG 602; Moule, *Idiom Book*, 39, 161.

5. J. B. Lightfoot, *Saint Paul's Epistle to the Philippians* [12th ed.] (London: Macmillan, 1898), 125.

6. Black, "Πᾶσαι ἐξουσίαι αὐτῷ ὑποταγήσονται," 77.

7. BAGD 263; BDAG 333; Walter Grundmann, "ἐνδυναμόω," *TDNT* 2 (1964): 286; Otto Betz, "Might [ἐνδυναμόω]," *NIDNTT* 2 (1976): 601, 604; L&N §74.7.

8. As Bruce, 403; Porter, *Verbal Aspect*, 359.

9. Ellicott, 145; Abbott, 180–81; Salmond, 381–82; Westcott, 92; Schlier, 289; Barth, 760 n. 7; Schnackenburg, 271; Lincoln, 441; Best, 590; O'Brien, 460.

10. Similar in Qumran literature, see Kuhn, "Ephesians in the Light of the Qumran Texts," 117–18.

might (δυνάμει κραταιωθῆναι) through his Spirit (Eph 3:16) and his final exhortation to the Corinthian believers to be strong (κραταιοῦσθε, 1 Cor 16:13).

The prepositional phrase ἐν κυρίῳ could be instrumental[1] but more likely denotes the sphere from which the strength comes, namely, in the Lord or in union with the Lord.[2] The sphere encompasses the source, again the Lord.[3] As noted in 2:21 the phrase "in the Lord" refers not to God but to Christ, which is consistent throughout the epistle (e.g., 2:21; 4:1, 17; 5:8; 6:1, 21). The immediately following καί is probably epexegetical ("that is"), explaining the preceding words "be strengthened in the Lord." Thus, the first part of the verse gives a general statement and the second part gives the particulars of being strengthened in the Lord.[4] The particulars are expressed in ἐν τῷ κράτει τῆς ἰσχύος αὐτοῦ, "in the might of his strength." This is similar to the genitival construction of the same words (τοῦ κράτους τῆς ἰσχύος αὐτοῦ, "the might of his power") in 1:19. The words κράτος and ἰσχύς were discussed at 1:19, the only other occurrences in Ephesians. To summarize that study, the word κράτος always has reference to supernatural power and has the sense of "strength, might, dominion, mastery." The word ἰσχύς generally denotes inherent strength or a power that one possesses.

To better understand this phrase, it is best to go from the last word to the first. Normally, the last of a series of genitives is possessive,[5] hence, αὐτοῦ, "his" strength refers to the Lord's inherent strength. The next words are the genitives τῆς ἰσχύος and these could be taken as an attributive genitive, "in his mighty power" (NEB, TEV, NIV), or as genitives of source, "in the might of his strength" (AV, RV, ASV, RSV, NASB, JB, NJB, NRSV). The latter fits better. It is supernatural power or might that has its source in the Lord's inherent strength. The last words to be considered are ἐν τῷ κράτει, "in the might," denoting not instrument[6] but sphere,[7] thus indicating the source of the strength.[8] Therefore, the believer is exhorted to be strengthened in the Lord, that is, in the might of the Lord's inherent strength.

In 1:19 Paul prayed that believers, by knowing God intimately, would understand his mighty power displayed through Christ's resur-

1. Allan, "The 'In Christ' Formula in Ephesians," 57; Yoder Neufeld, *'Put on the Armour of God,'* 114.

2. Ernest Best, "The Body of Christ," *Ecumenical Review* 9 (January 1957): 125; Eadie, 456; Salmond, 382; Robinson, 132; Westcott, 92; Lincoln, 441–42.

3. Schlier, 289; Arnold, *Ephesians: Power and Magic*, 108.

4. HS §294w.

5. MHT 3:218; HS §172; BDF §168 (2); Robertson, *Grammar*, 503.

6. As Meyer, 323; Barth, 760.

7. Eadie, 456; Ellicott, 145; Salmond, 382; Robinson, 132; Westcott, 92; Lincoln, 441–42.

8. Arnold, *Ephesians: Power and Magic*, 108.

rection and ascension. He further prayed that they would appropriate this power in their lives. Now Paul exhorts them to continue in that same might in the person of Christ. The passive imperative indicates that the believer receives the action of being strengthened and the present tense argues for a customary or habitual aspect[1] of that power or might in the believer. Verse 11a will explain how this is accomplished; verses 11b–12 will explain why this must be accomplished.

b. How: Put on God's Armor (6:11a)

Having identified the "what," namely, "be strengthened in the Lord" in verse 10, the "how" is explained in the first half of verse 11, namely, "put on the full armor of God."

Text: 6:11a. ἐνδύσασθε τὴν πανοπλίαν τοῦ θεοῦ

Translation: 6:11a. "Put on the full armor of God"

Commentary: 6:11a. ἐνδύσασθε τὴν πανοπλίαν τοῦ θεοῦ, "Put on the full armor of God." Without a conjunction, Paul introduces ἐνδύσασθε the aorist middle imperative of ἐνδύω. As discussed in 4:24, this word is used thirteen times by Paul, three times at Ephesians (4:24; 6:11, 14), and means "putting on clothes" either in a literal or metaphorical sense. The aorist imperative might well suggest a sense of urgency incumbent on the believers.[2] The middle voice indicates that they are responsible for putting on the full armor. They are to put on τὴν πανοπλίαν τοῦ θεοῦ, "the full armor of God." The term πανοπλία is used only three times in the NT (Luke 11:22; Eph 6:11, 13). In literature from classical to NT times it refers to the suit of armor of the foot soldier.[3] It appears eleven times in the LXX, though only twice in the canonical books; once having reference to clothing (2 Sam 2:21), and once a mistranslation of locusts (אַרְבֶּה) (Job 39:20). It continues to be used with reference to full armor (Jdt 14:3; Wis 5:17; Sir 46:6; 1 Macc 13:29*bis*; 2 Macc 3:25; 10:30; 11:8; 15:28). There is no Hebrew equivalent but there are descriptions of individual pieces of the armor of a foot soldier (1 Sam 17:38–39; 2 Chr 26:14; Jer 46:4 [LXX 26:4]). This full suit of armor "becomes heavier up to the Macedonian period, then lighter."[4] The defensive and offensive parts of the armor of the Roman foot soldier are mentioned in Polybius,[5] Josephus,[6] and the present passage (vv. 14–17). These will be discussed in more detail below. It is quite possible that Paul's vivid description of the armor may

1. Cf. Fanning, *Verbal Aspect*, 332–33.
2. Ibid., 378.
3. Herodotus 4.180; Thucydides 3.114.1; Aristophanes *Aves* 830; *Plutus* 951; Isocrates 16.29; Plato *Leges* 7 §796c; Diodorus Siculus 20.84.3.
4. Albrecht Oepke, "πανοπλία," *TDNT* 5 (1968): 295.
5. Polybius 6.23.
6. Josephus *B.J.* 3.5.5 §§93–95.

stem from the fact that, while writing this letter, he was in prison being guarded by Roman soldiers (cf. Acts 28:16, 20). The words τοῦ θεοῦ are genitives of origin,[1] indicating that God provides the armor. This is not a physical battle, but rather a spiritual one. Thus it requires supernaturally provided spiritual armor.

c. Why: Stand against the Devil's Strategy (6:11b–12)

Text: 6:11b. πρὸς τὸ δύνασθαι ὑμᾶς στῆναι πρὸς τὰς μεθοδείας τοῦ διαβόλου· **6:12.** ὅτι οὐκ ἔστιν ἡμῖν ἡ πάλη πρὸς αἷμα καὶ σάρκα, ἀλλὰ πρὸς τὰς ἀρχάς, πρὸς τὰς ἐξουσίας, πρὸς τοὺς κοσμοκράτορας τοῦ σκότους τούτου, πρὸς τὰ πνευματικὰ τῆς πονηρίας ἐν τοῖς ἐπουρανίοις.

Translation: 6:11b. "in order that you might be able to stand against the schemes of the devil; **6:12.** because our struggle is not against flesh and blood, but against the rulers, against authorities, against the cosmic potentates of this darkness, against the spiritual beings of wickedness in the heavenly realms."

Commentary: 6:11b. πρὸς τὸ δύνασθαι ὑμᾶς στῆναι πρὸς τὰς μεθοδείας τοῦ διαβόλου, "in order that you might be able to stand against the schemes of the devil." Having stated the "what" in verse 10, the "how" in verse 11a, Paul now explains the "why" in verses 11b–12. He indicates this with the preposition πρός followed by the articular infinitive τὸ δύνασθαι to express purpose.[2] The infinitive is the present middle/passive deponent of δύναμαι, a word already discussed at 3:4, 20, denoting "to be able, to be capable of." This is followed by the personal pronoun ὑμᾶς, "you," and στῆναι, the second aorist active (intransitive) infinitive of ἵστημι, meaning "to stand" or "to offer resistance to."[3] The term is used "to denote that which lasts and is stable, not subject to change or decay."[4] The one who stands is not pushed around but firmly holds his or her position. In terms of warfare, it does not connote an offensive, but rather a defensive stance, to hold one's ground. One needs to note that "you" put on God's armor in order that "you" might be able to stand. In this verse, specifically, the enemy is the devil. Thus, believers must hold fast πρὸς τὰς μεθοδείας τοῦ διαβόλου, "against the schemes of the devil." The preposition πρός with the accusative refers to a face-to-face relationship, either friendly or hostile, depending on the context. It is much like the English preposition "with" as used in such phrases as "walk with him" or "fight with him." The term μεθοδεία is not used before NT times and occurs

1. Eadie, 457; Ellicott, 145; Abbott, 181; Salmond, 382; Westcott, 92; Gnilka, 305 n. 6; O'Brien, 463; Winer, *Grammar*, 236.

2. Robertson, *Grammar*, 991, 1003, 1075; MHT 1:218, 220; 3:144; BDF §402 (5); Burton, *Moods and Tenses* §414; HS §226a; Wallace, *Greek Grammar*, 592.

3. BAGD 382; BDAG 482.

4. Walter Grundmann, "ἵστημι," *TDNT* 7 (1971): 651.

only in this verse and in 4:14 in the NT. As discussed at 4:14, it comes from μέθοδος, meaning "procedure, process, method," and can be translated "strategy" or "scheme." The plural may suggest many schemes as opposed to one grand scheme. In Ephesians the word διάβολος occurs only here and in 4:27. As a substantive it is used of a "slanderer," but more often it refers specifically to "the devil." Scripture states that he has sinned from the beginning (1 John 3:8). Jesus specifically stated that the devil has nothing to do with the truth because there is no truth in him, and he is a liar and the father of lies (John 8:44). In fact, John identifies the devil as Satan who is the deceiver of the whole world (Rev 12:9; 20:2). Due to this, one must always be cognizant that the strategies or schemes of the devil are based on lies and are designed to deceive believers. Consequently, Paul exhorts believers to put on the full armor of God for the purpose of being able to stand firmly against the lying strategies of the devil. In these strategies, the devil is crafty in that he "does not always attack through obvious head-on assaults but employs cunning and wily strategems designed to catch believers unawares."[1] They are told not to attack the devil or advance against him; they are only to "stand," hold the territory that Christ and his body, the church, have conquered. Without the armor of God it is certain that believers will be deceived and defeated by those "schemes" of the devil, which have been effective for thousands of years.

6:12. ὅτι οὐκ ἔστιν ἡμῖν[2] ἡ πάλη πρὸς αἷμα καὶ σάρκα, "because our struggle is not against flesh and blood."[3] Thus far Paul has instructed

1. Lincoln, 443.

2. The reading ἡμῖν is found in ℵ A D[2] I 075 0150 0278 6 33 104 256 263 365 424 436 459 1241 1319 1573 1739 1852 1881 1912 1962 2127 2200 2464 *Byz* [K L P] *Lect* (*l* 1154 ἡμᾶς) it[ar, g*] vg syr[h] cop[samss, bo] arm geo Marcion[acc. to Tertullian] Irenaeus[lat] Clement Origen[gr. lat20/23] Methodius Eusebius Asterius Ps-Athanasius Titus-Bostra Ps-Ignatius Gregory-Nyssa Didymus Ammon Macarius/Symeon Chrysostom Marcus-Eremita Theodore[lat] Cyril Hesychius[2/3] Theodoret Tertullian Cyprian Hilary Ambrose Jerome Pelagius. The reading ὑμῖν occurs in 𝔓[46] B D* F G Ψ 81 1175 *l* 422 *l* 592[2/3] *l* 593 *l* 597 *l* 1441 it[b, d, f, g2, mon, o] vg[ms] syr[p, pal] eth slav Origen[lat1/23] Nilus Ambrosiaster Lucifer Priscillian Gregory-Elivra Augustine Speculum. The pronoun is omitted from *l* 592[1/3] cop[samss] Origen[lat2/23] Hesychius[1/3]. The omission can be disregarded because its support is so sparse. Both the first and second readings have manuscripts that are early and with good character. The first reading has good geographical distribution in the Alexandrian and Byzantine text-types while the second reading has good geographical distribution in the Alexandrian and Western texts. Genealogical relationships are about equal in the first two readings. Externally, there is a slight preference for the first reading. Internally, the second reading is easier because the rest of paragraph is in the second person. Considering both the external and internal evidence, the first reading is preferred.

3. The Greek text order is αἷμα καὶ σάρκα ("blood and flesh") as in Heb 2:14. However, in Matt 16:17; 1 Cor 15:50; Gal 1:16 the Greek text has σὰρξ καὶ αἷμα ("flesh and blood"). Note also Wis 12:5; Sir 14:18; 17:31. The order does not seem to be important. Among the recent translations, only thus NRSV translates Eph 6:12 "blood and flesh," but not so in Heb 2:14.

believers to put on the full armor of God and has the explained the purpose for this, namely, to be able to stand against the schemes of the devil. Paul now explains the nature of the warfare for which the believers are to prepare. The conjunction ὅτι functions as a causal conjunction, introducing a further reason to put on the full armor of God. He points out that the struggle is not physical but supernatural. It is a spiritual battle against spiritual "Mafia." The next term πάλη normally refers to wrestling,[1] but it can also have the more general idea of "conflict, struggle."[2] It does not occur in the LXX and occurs only here in the NT. With regard to its usage in this text, if Paul meant "battle, conflict" in conjunction with armor, why did he not use the normal term μάχη rather than πάλη? Gudorf argues convincingly that the term πάλη was used to indicate that the fully armored soldier was an accomplished wrestler who on occasion would be involved in close-quarter struggle against a cunning opponent.[3] Due to the cunning schemes of the devil, believers need to be ready for both remote and close-at-hand assaults. The notion of a close encounter is enhanced by the following preposition πρός. As above, the preposition πρός with the accusative refers to a face-to-face encounter. The context determines whether it is friendly or hostile. In this context, it is a hostile conflict that is not directed toward or against αἷμα καὶ σάρκα, "blood and flesh." In other words, it is not a physical struggle or a wrestling match.[4] In fact, nowhere in this passage is there any indication of a human struggle. Although throughout the paragraph the second person plural is addressed, here the personal pronoun (ἡμῖν) is the first person plural, which indicates Paul's identification with the Ephesian believers in the spiritual conflict. It is a dative of reference ("the struggle with reference to us") though it is translated as a possessive ("our struggle").

ἀλλὰ πρὸς τὰς ἀρχάς, πρὸς τὰς ἐξουσίας,[5] "but against the rulers, against authorities." The conjunction ἀλλά, "but," is adversative and introduces the opposite of physical struggle, namely, the spiritual struggle. In Pauline literature, the present verse is the most explicit reference to the believers' struggle against evil spiritual powers. Carr

1. Homer *Ilias* 23.635; *Odyssea* 8.206; Thucydides 1.6.5; Plato *Leges* 7 §795b; Plutarch *Moralia: Quaestionum convivalium* 2.4 §638d; Philo *Leg. All.* 3.68 §190; *Mut.* 2 §14.

2. Aeschylus *Choephori* 866; Euripides *Heraclidae* 159; Heinrich Greeven, "πάλη," *TDNT* 5 (1968): 721.

3. Michael E. Gudorf, "The Use of πάλη in Ephesians 6:12," *JBL* 117 (summer 1998): 332–34.

4. Arnold mentions a parable from Pausanias about an Ephesian wrestler who was unbeatable because he wore a magical amulet around his ankle. In this light Paul could be saying that one should put on the armor of God rather than a magical amulet. Arnold is quick to say that this story is late and may not have been known to first century readers in Ephesus (*Ephesians: Power and Magic*, 117).

5. The words τὰς ἀρχάς, πρὸς τὰς ἐξουσίας are replaced with τὰς μεθοδείας in only $\mathfrak{P}^{46}$ which is insufficient evidence to be taken seriously.

suggests that it is uncharacteristic of the thought world of the first century A.D. and that this verse is a second century Gnostic interpolation not found in Ephesians originally.[1] However, there is no textual evidence for the omission of 6:12 and the concept of evil spiritual powers was characteristic of Jewish, pagan, and NT thought.[2]

Following the adversative conjunction, there is a series of prepositional phrases without conjunctions, a device which was most likely used to give greater prominence to those against whom the belivers are struggling.[3] The prepositional phrases are introduced with the preposition πρός with an accusative object and are best translated "against." The first two foes have already been discussed at 1:21 and 3:10. A study of the terms "ruler" and "authority" has been made at 1:21 where we concluded that ἀρχή signifies primacy in power, hence, "leader, ruler"; and that ἐξουσία comes from ἔξεστιν, which denotes the freedom to act. Accordingly, the noun implies the right to act and thus means "authority." Ten times these two powers are listed in the order of the present passage (Luke 12:11; 20:20; 1 Cor 15:24; Eph 1:20; 3:10; 6:12; Col 1:16; 2:10, 15; Titus 3:1) and can refer either to human or to angelic leaders. In the present context the plural indicates several leaders. Since it was already stated that the conflict is not human, it must refer to spiritual beings,[4] angelic leaders, or, as Black labels them, "cosmic or celestial potentates."[5] Furthermore, later in this verse he makes direct mention of the spiritual wickedness in the heavenlies.

πρὸς τοὺς κοσμοκράτορας τοῦ σκότους[6] τούτου, "against the cosmic potentates of this darkness." The third foe is called κοσμοκράτωρ. This

1. Carr, *Angels and Principalities*, 104–10.

2. For a devastating critique of Carr's view, see Clinton E. Arnold, "The 'Exorcism' of Ephesians 6:12 in Recent Research: A Critique of Wesley Carr's View of the Role of Evil Powers in First-Century AD Belief," *JSNT* 30 (June 1987): 71–87; cf. also O'Brien, "Principalities and Powers: Opponents of the Church," 127–28; Wink, *Naming the Powers*, 84–89; Robert A. Wild, "The Warrior and the Prisoner: Some Reflections on Ephesians 6:10–20," *CBQ* 46 (April 1984): 285; Michael Goulder, "Colossians and Barbelo," *NTS* 41 (October 1995): 618–19.

3. Winer, *Grammar*, 524; Robertson, *Grammar*, 566.

4. Gerhard Delling, "ἀρχή," *TDNT* 1 (1964): 483; cf. also Caird, 91; Lee, "Interpreting the Demonic Powers in Pauline Thought," 54–69; P. T. O'Brien, "Principalities and Powers and Their Relationship to Structures," *RTR* 40 (January–April 1981): 4–5; Reid, "Principalities and Powers," 746–52.

5. Black, "Πᾶσαι ἐξουσίαι αὐτῷ ὑποταγήσονται," 76.

6. There is the insertion of τοῦ αἰῶνος found in $\aleph^2$ D^2 Ψ 1739^{mg} 1881 𝔐 syr^{h**} Tertullian Chrysostom Theodoret Oecumenius Theophylact. The omission of these words are found in $𝔓^{46}$ ℵ* A B D* F G 0278 6 33 1175 1739* *pc* latt syr^p $cop^{sa, bo}$ Clement Origen Eusebius. The external evidence would support their omission because of the good date and character of the manuscripts, the good geographical distribution, and the good genealogical relationships. The internal evidence would support their omission because it would seem unlikely that a scribe would omit them, but it would be easy to understand why they would be inserted for it would be similar to 2 Cor 4:3–6 where the god of this age keeps unbelievers in darkness. Therefore, the omission of τοῦ αἰῶνος is preferred.

word has not been used before NT times and it occurs only here in the NT. It may well have been a term used in the first or second century A.D. of magical or astrological traditions.[1] In fourth-century magical papyri it is used as one of the magical titles of deities like Helios, Hermes, and Sarapis who were thought to aid the pagan petitioner. In astrology it is used of the sun (Helios) as master of all the planets in the universe, which determined the fate of the impersonal and personal universe. It appears in Jewish literature in the second century A.D. as "world rulers of the darkness" (*T. Sol.* 8:2; 18:2). The Hellenistic religions referred to gods who controlled parts of the universe, but in the Jewish religion they were seen as evil spirits.[2] Basically, the same terminology is used here by Paul when he describes them as "world/cosmic rulers of this darkness" in order to indicate "the terrifying power of their influence and comprehensiveness of their plans, and thus to emphasise the seriousness of the situation."[3] It may well be that the author of the *Testament of Solomon* derived his terminology from Paul. The use of the plural indicates that many of these rulers are under the leadership of the devil. These potentates are not earthly humans but supernatural beings,[4] and thus it is best to translate the word as "world rulers" or "cosmic potentates." Arnold suggests that Paul might even have been alluding to some of the pagan deities like Artemis of Ephesus who also represented demonic power as reflected in 1 Cor 10:19–21.[5] On the other hand, one needs to be cautious here since no texts identify Artemis in such terms[6] and even Arnold acknowledges that κοσμοκράτωρ is not used of Artemis in any text.[7]

The next noun σκότος, "darkness," was discussed at 5:8 and it refers to the realm and power of sin, the place where the God of light does not dwell (cf. 1 John 1:4). Hence, the cosmic rulers of darkness are in conflict with the God of light. This is not the only time that Paul uses the terms light and darkness to illustrate the contrasts between good and evil. For instance, in explaining his conversion to Herod Agrippa II, Paul states that when Christ spoke to him on the Damascus road, he appointed him to open the eyes of the Gentiles that they might turn from darkness to light and from the power of Satan to God (Acts 26:18). Again in his letter to the Corinthians, he states that the god of this world has blinded the minds of unbelievers to keep them in dark-

1. Arnold, *Ephesians: Power and Magic*, 65–68; cf. Macgregor, "Principalities and Powers: The Cosmic Background of Paul's Thought," 20–21.

2. D. C. Duling, trans., "Testament of Solomon," *The Old Testament Pseudepigrapha*, ed. James H. Charlesworth, vol. 1 (Garden City, N.Y.: Doubleday, 1983): 970 n. b.

3. Wilhelm Michaelis, "κοσμοκράτωρ," *TDNT* 3 (1965): 914.

4. Mussner, *Christus, das All und die Kirche*, 23.

5. Arnold, *Ephesians: Power and Magic*, 68. This is disputed by Strelan, *Paul, Artemis, and the Jews in Ephesus*, 83.

6. Strelan, *Paul, Artemis, and the Jews in Ephesus*, 156.

7. Arnold, *Ephesians: Power and Magic*, 193 n. 87.

ness in order to prevent them from the light of the knowledge of the glory of God that is revealed in the light of the gospel of Christ (2 Cor 4:3–6). He speaks of the Father who delivers believers from the dominion (ἐξουσία) of darkness and transfers them to the kingdom of his beloved Son (Col 1:13).

Therefore, Paul portrays the cosmic potentates of darkness as headed by the devil (v. 11) and in direct conflict with Christ and the believers. They have their abode in the heavens and from there "they extend their activity and authority to the regions below them."[1]

πρὸς τὰ πνευματικὰ τῆς πονηρίας ἐν τοῖς ἐπουρανίοις,[2] "against the spiritual beings of wickedness in the heavenly realms." This does not seem to depict a new foe but further describes the hostile rulers mentioned earlier and also identifies the locale of these foes.[3] The adjective πνευματικός occurs two other times in Ephesians and denotes spiritual benefits (1:3) and spiritual songs (5:19) that have their source in the Spirit of God. There are two theories regarding this adjective. First, some see it as an articular neuter plural (an abstract neuter)[4] with the quality of a substantive. It is considered as an alternative to τὸ πνεῦμα, "the things pertaining to the spirit," that is, "spiritual forces or elements"[5] (NASB, NEB, TEV, NIV, NRSV). Second, because it is an articular neuter plural followed by a genitive, others consider it a collective noun retaining the substantive quality. This interpretation serves "to indicate a categoric number of persons or things involved"[6] and they consider it an alternative to τὰ πνεύματα, "the spirits," that is, "spiritual armies or hosts"[7] (RV, ASV, RSV, JB, NJB). The second view has the support of Jewish literature that speaks of evil spirits (*Jub.* 10:5–13; 11:5; 15:31–32; *1 Enoch* 15:8–12; *T. Sim.* 4:9; 6:6; *T. Lev.* 18:12; CD 12:2; 1QM 13:2, 4). Furthermore, in this text, nouns such as ἀρχαί, ἐξουσίαι, and κοσμοκράτορες seem to indicate specific spiritual beings or armies rather than abstract spiritual forces.[8] In addition, this corresponds to the devil as a spirit in 2:2 and the unclean

1. Odeberg, *View of the Universe*, 16; Benoit, "Pauline Angelology and Demonology," 13.

2. The prepositional phrase ἐν τοῖς ἐπουρανίοις is omitted from 𝔓[46] and Didymus. This is not enough manuscript tradition to warrant its omission.

3. Cf. Dibelius, *Die Geisterwelt im Glauben des Paulus*, 164.

4. Robertson, *Grammar*, 763.

5. Salmond, 384; Abbott, 182–83; BAGD 679; BDAG 837; Hill, *Greek Words and Hebrew Meanings*, 283.

6. Van Roon, *The Authenticity of Ephesians*, 174; Wink, *Engaging the Powers*, 81, 349 n. 33; BDF §263 (4).

7. Eadie, 461; Ellicott, 147; Meyer, 327–28; Schlier, 291; Gnilka, 307; Barth, 803; Schnackenburg, 273–74; Winer, *Grammar*, 299; Baljon, "Opmerkingen op het gebied van de Conjecturaalkritiek," 155–56; Dunn, *NIDNTT* 3 (1978): 707.

8. Carr, *Angels and Principalities*, 107; Wink, *Engaging the Powers*, 8–9. These powers must not be demythologized bereft of spiritual essence by relegating them as institutional powers or oppressive political structures (idem, *Naming the Powers*, 60–67, 99–148). See comments on 1:21.

spirits called demons that Jesus exorcised (Mark 1:23, 26–27 = Luke 4:33, 35–36; Matt 8:16 = Mark 1:34). Thus, the translation "spiritual hosts" or "spiritual beings" is preferred. The term πνευματικός also depicts the character of the enemy as not human but supernatural.[1]

The following noun πονηρία, "wickedness," is descriptive of those spiritual beings. In classical times it was used of physical defect or sickness in people and animals[2] or of a moral sense of "depravity, wickedness."[3] In the LXX it occurs seventy times and in the canonical books it appears forty times and translates five Hebrew words. Twenty times it translates רָעָה, which can speak of "trouble, misfortune" (Neh 2:17) but most of the time it is used in the moral sense of "evil" (Exod 32:12; Neh 6:2; 13:7; Eccl 2:21; 6:1; 10:5) or "wickedness" (Ps 94:23 [LXX 93:23]; Isa 47:10; Jer 23:11; 33:5 [LXX 40:5]; 44:3 [LXX 51:3]).[4] In the NT the word occurs seven times (Matt 22:18; Mark 7:22; Luke 11:39; Acts 3:26; Rom 1:29; 1 Cor 5:8; Eph 6:12) and "only in a moral sense, especially in a very generalised way, as in the list of vices, e.g., R. 1:29."[5] Hence, it has the basic idea of "wickedness," "evil," or "iniquity." The genitive may be objective, that is, "spiritual beings concerned with evil,"[6] but it is more likely a genitive of quality, "spiritual beings whose essential character is wickedness."[7]

The final prepositional phrase ἐν τοῖς ἐπουρανίοις, "in the heavenlies" (occurs only in NT in Eph 1:3, 20; 2:6; 3:10; 6:12), states the locale of these spiritual hosts. However, for evil hosts to be located in the heavenly realms has been problematic to interpreters.[8] There are three major views. First, some think it suggests that the nature of the struggle is not concerned with earthly matters but heavenly ones.[9] In this case, one would expect the use of the preposition ὑπέρ, "on behalf of," διά, "on account of," or περί, "concerning," rather than ἐν, "in." Second, others think that the expression indicates that the church's conflict takes place in the heavenlies and the evil forces have invaded the church.[10] However, this view puts the emphasis on the conflict

1. Adai, *Der Heilige Geist als Gegenwart Gottes*, 267.

2. Plato *Hippias Minor* 374d; *Respublica* 10.9 §609c.

3. Xenophon *Memorabilia* 3.5.18; Aristotle *Ethica Nicomachea* 7.8.1.§1150b.35.

4. BDB 949; *HALOT* 3 (1996): 1269–70; Dohmen, *TWAT* 7 (1990): 585–87; David W. Baker, "רָעָה (*rāʿâ* I)," *NIDOTTE* 3:1154–58.

5. Harder, *TDNT* 6 (1968): 565.

6. BAGD 690; BDAG 851.

7. Eadie, 461; Meyer, 328; Salmond, 384; Harder, *TDNT* 6 (1968): 565.

8. For a discussion of some of the church fathers, see Christopher J. A. Lash, "Where Do Devils Live? A Problem in the Textual Criticism of Eph 6,12," *VC* 30 (September 1976): 161–74.

9. Chrysostom *Eph* 6:12 (*PG* 62:159; cf. also Kohlgraf, *Die Ekklesiologie des Epheserbriefes in der Auslegung durch Johannes Chrysostomus*, 293–94); Theodoret *Eph* 6:12 (*PG* 82:553); Oecumenius *Eph* 6:10–13 (*PG* 118:1249–52); Theophylact *Eph* 6:12 (*PG* 124:1128–29).

10. Eadie, 462–64; Robinson, 133; Westcott, 94.

whereas the word indicates the realm. Third, most think it refers to the seat or place of evil spirits or hosts.[1] This seems to be the plain sense of the verse.[2] This prepositional phrase is used four other times in Ephesians (1:3, 20; 2:6; 3:10) and each time it has reference to locale. In fact, earlier in the epistle (3:10) the church is told to demonstrate the manifold wisdom of God to both good and evil spiritual leaders in the heavenlies. Paul did not originate this idea. In the OT God and Satan converse with one another in heaven (Job 1:6–12). Also, good and evil angels struggle with each other in heaven and on earth (Dan 10:13, 20). As discussed earlier in this epistle, the heavenlies are also the abode of Christ and the church, for after Christ's death God raised and seated him at his right hand in the heavenlies (1:20–21) and also raised and seated believers with Christ in the heavenlies (2:6). Hence, both the devil and his followers and Christ and his followers are in the heavenlies.[3]

Although the prepositional phrase refers primarily to the realm of the spiritual hosts, not the place of the believers' struggle,[4] one cannot rule out that the locale of the conflict is in the heavenlies.[5] On the other hand, one cannot infer from this that the conflict is solely in the heavenlies. Although believers are blessed with all the spiritual benefits in the heavenly places (1:3) and are seated together with Christ in the heavenlies (2:6), they do live in the present evil age (5:16). Hence, believers are presently both on earth and in the heavenlies.[6] Furthermore, the devil and his followers are also presently both on earth and in the heavenlies. The devil is portrayed as the one who is "the ruler of the

1. Ambrosiaster *Eph* 6:11–12 (*PL* 17:401); Jerome *Eph* 6:11 (*PL* 26:547–48); Aquinas, chap. 6, lec. 3, vv. 10–12 (238); Calvin, 218–19; Hodge, 379–81; Bengel, 4:116; Alford, 3:145; Ellicott, 148; Meyer, 328–31; Abbott, 183; Salmond, 384; Schlier, 45–48, 291 (existentially); Gnilka, 307; Barth, 803; Schnackenburg, 273; Bruce, 406; Lincoln, 444–45; Percy, *Probleme*, 182 n. 7, 255–58; Lincoln, "A Re-Examination of 'the Heavenlies' in Ephesians," 474–76; Harris, "'The Heavenlies' Reconsidered," 86–87; cf. also Benoit, "L'horizon paulinien de l'Épître aux Ephésiens," 346–50; reprinted in idem, *Exégèsis et Theologie*, 2:57–62.

2. Bonnardière shows how Augustine attacks the Manichaean interpretation. Augustine reinterpretes this text by saying that evil does not refer to the "world/cosmic," namely, the "physical universe" but refers to "sinners." He further interprets that demons are not rulers of the universe but sinners who have submitted to them and that heaven which belongs to the evil spirits refers to a lower heaven (see A.-M. La Bonnardière, "Le combat chrétien. Exégèse augustinienne d'*Ephes*. 6,12," *Revue des études augustiniennes* 11, nos. 3–4 [1965]: 235–38).

3. Cf. Weber, "'Setzen'-'Wandeln'-'Stehen' im Epheserbrief," 479; Morrison, *The Powers That Be*, 45–46; Cargal, "Seated in the Heavenlies," 817–18.

4. Percy, *Probleme*, 182 n. 7; Lincoln, "A Re-Examination of 'the Heavenlies' in Ephesians," 475.

5. Cf. Charles, "The Seven Heavens: An Early Jewish and Christian Belief," 115; *contra* Clemens, "Note on the Phrase ἐν τοῖς ἐπουρανίοις," 140; Gibbs, *Creation and Redemption*, 130–32.

6. Harris, "'The Heavenlies' Reconsidered," 86.

realm of the air" (2:2), the one who controls this evil world (1 John 5:19) and is called "the god of this age" (2 Cor 4:4). The present battle, then, is played out in the heavenlies and on earth between those who align themselves with the devil and his angelic leaders and those who align themselves with Christ and his angels.[1] Although Christ has won the victory at the cross, the reality of conflict presently continues for the believers. The fact that Paul instructs believers to put on the armor of God argues for the present reality of the struggle. In conclusion, it must be realized that positionally believers have victory in Christ in the heavenlies, but in reality the victory will not be fully realized until the subjugation of evil yet in the future.[2] Therefore, this struggle is a present reality which will culminate with the defeat of the devil and his angels at the second coming of Christ (Eph 1:10, 21; cf. 1 Cor 15:24–28).[3]

d. Conclusion: Put on God's Armor in Order to Stand (6:13)

Up to this point Paul has urged the Ephesians believers: (a) to be strong in the Lord (v. 10), (b) to put on the armor of God (v. 11a), and (c) to stand against the schemes of the devil (vv. 11b–12). Now he concludes the believers need to put on the armor of God so that they can stand against the onslaughts of the devil (v. 13)

Text: 6:13. διὰ τοῦτο ἀναλάβετε τὴν πανοπλίαν τοῦ θεοῦ, ἵνα δυνηθῆτε ἀντιστῆναι ἐν τῇ ἡμέρᾳ τῇ πονηρᾷ καὶ ἅπαντα κατεργασάμενοι στῆναι.

Translation: 6:13. "On account of this, take up the full armor of God, in order that you may be able to resist in the evil day and having done everything, to stand."

Commentary: 6:13. διὰ τοῦτο ἀναλάβετε τὴν πανοπλίαν τοῦ θεοῦ, "On account of this, take up the full armor of God." This verse begins with διὰ τοῦτο, which introduces a causal conclusion. The previous verse outlines the formidable cosmic evil powers that are pitted against the believers and that possess superhuman power and strength. In this verse he essentially restates verse 11, namely, the exhortation to put on God's full armor. The verb ἀναλάβετε, an aorist active imperative of ἀναλαμβάνω, is used in a general way "to take up"[4] or

1. Whiteley attempts to apply the demonic powers to powerful destructive forces in the contemporary world (D. E. H. Whiteley, "Ephesians vi.12—Evil Powers," *ExpTim* 68 [January 1957]: 100–103). But the conflict outlined in Ephesians is between demonic hosts and the believers and not between the demonic hosts and the whole world.

2. Roy Yates, "The Powers of Evil in the New Testament," *EvQ* 52 (April–June 1980): 104.

3. Greeven, *TDNT* 5 (1968): 721; Caird, *Principalities and Powers*, ix; Lincoln, *Paradise Now and Not Yet*, 166; Wessels, "The Eschatology of Colossians and Ephesians," 190, 200; Harris, "'The Heavenlies' Reconsidered," 87. Lindemann (*Aufhebung*, 63–66) thinks that Ephesians blurs the distinction of a present and an eschatological culmination.

4. Herodotus 1.111.

in a military context "to take up" weapons,[1] allies,[2] or the wounded.[3] In the LXX it occurs ninety-seven times (sixty-eight times in the canonical books) and translates eleven Hebrew words. Of these, forty-one times it translates נָשָׂא, meaning "to lift, take up, carry" (Exod 10:13; 19:4; Num 14:1; Jer 7:29);[4] fifteen times it translates לָקַח, meaning "to take" (Gen 48:1; Exod 12:32) but also "to take up" or "lift" (Judg 19:28).[5] In a technical sense, it connotes the putting on or girding on of weapons (Deut 1:41; Jdt 6:12; 7:5; 14:2, 11). This idea is also found in Josephus.[6] In the NT it is used thirteen times: possibly once in the Gospels (questionable text), eight times in Acts, and four times in Paul's writings. Reference is made to Jesus taken up to heaven (Mark 16:19?; Acts 1:2, 11, 22; 1 Tim 3:16), the object in Peter's vision taken up to heaven (Acts 10:16), the tent of Moloch taken up (Acts 7:43), Paul taken on board ship (Acts 20:13, 14), and a travel companion taken along (Acts 23:31; 2 Tim 4:11).[7] It is used twice in Ephesians (6:13, 16) where it denotes the taking up or putting on of weapons, which is consistent with its usage in classical Greek, the LXX, and Josephus.[8] This is synonymous with ἐνδύσασθε in verse 11, namely, to take up the armor in order to carry it. The aorist imperative may suggest a sense of urgency incumbent on the believers. This makes sense in light of the preceding verse's description of the believers' conflict with the evil rulers in the heavenlies. The active voice indicates that believers are responsible for putting on the full armor. After the imperative, the next words are exactly the same as verse 11, namely, τὴν πανοπλίαν τοῦ θεοῦ, "the full armor of God." The armor has its origin (genitive of origin as in v. 12)[9] in God and is designed to protect the believer against the onslaughts of the devil and his hosts.

ἵνα δυνηθῆτε ἀντιστῆναι ἐν τῇ ἡμέρᾳ τῇ πονηρᾷ, "in order that you may be able to resist in the evil day." When Paul introduced the armor in verse 11, he stated that its purpose was to enable believers to withstand the formidable cosmic evil powers (vv. 11–12). Having now repeated his command to put on the armor, he again gives the purpose for believers to put on the armor. The clause is introduced with ἵνα plus δυνηθῆτε, the aorist passive/deponent subjunctive of δύναμαι. The verb δύναμαι, already discussed at 3:4, 20 and 6:11, means "to be able, to be capable of." This is followed by ἀντιστῆναι, a second aorist active

1. Ibid., 3.78; 9.46.

2. Thucydides 5.64.5.

3. Ibid., 8.27.4.

4. BDB 670–71; D. N. Freedman, B. E. Willoughby, H.-J. Fabry, and H. Ringgren, "נָשָׂא *nāśāʾ*, etc.," *TDOT* 10 (1999): 24–40.

5. BDB 543; H. Seebass, "לָקַח *lāqaḥ*; לֶקַח *leqaḥ*," *TDOT* 8 (1997): 16–21.

6. Josephus *A.J.* 20.5.3 §110; 6.1 §121.

7. BAGD 56–57; BDAG 66–67.

8. G. Delling, "ἀναλαμβάνω, ἀνάλημψις," *TDNT* 4 (1967): 7–8.

9. Winer, *Grammar*, 236.

infinitive from ἀνθίστημι. In classical literature it means "to set against, stand against, withstand," especially in battle.[1] In the LXX it occurs seventy-one times and in the canonical books it appears forty-six times where it translates fifteen different Hebrew words, ten times for עָמַד, "to make a stand, hold one's ground" in a military context[2] (Josh 23:9; Judg 2:14; Dan 10:13; 11:15–16); and six times for יָצַב, "to station oneself, take one's stand" in a military sense (Deut 7:24; 9:2; 11:25; Josh 1:5; 2 Chr 20:6).[3] In the NT the word occurs fourteen times: four times in the Gospels and Acts (Matt 5:39; Luke 21:15; Acts 6:10; 13:8), eight times in Paul's writings (Rom 9:19; 13:2*bis*; Gal 2:11; Eph 6:13; 2 Tim 3:8*bis*; 4:15), and two times in the General Epistles (Jas 4:7; 1 Pet 5:9). Essentially it means "to stand against, oppose, resist."[4] For example, it is used to withstand an idea or message (Luke 21:15; Acts 6:10; 2 Tim 4:15), to oppose a person through verbal confrontation (Acts 13:8; Gal 2:11; 2 Tim 3:8), to resist an evil person (Matt 5:39), to resist the devil (Jas 4:7; 1 Pet 5:9), or to resist God or his will (Rom 9:19; 13:2*bis*). Due to the military model in the present context, the idea "to resist, withstand, stand one's ground" is fitting. Thus, this term denotes a defensive rather than an offensive stance.[5]

The prepositional phrase ἐν τῇ ἡμέρᾳ τῇ πονηρᾷ, "in the evil day," has been explained five ways: (1) it is a final cataclysmic satanic outbreak just prior to the second advent of Christ;[6] (2) it refers to the entire span of the believers' life or the whole of the present age, which parallels with the "evil days" of 5:16;[7] (3) it refers to critical times in believers' lives when special diabolical hostility seems strongest;[8] (4) views (1) and (2) are combined, the present time being the evil day which will climax in the final outbreak of evil in a future day;[9] (5) views

1. Thucydides 4.115.2; Plato *Leges* 8 §834a; Homer *Ilias* 20.70, 72; Herodotus 6.117.

2. BDB 764; Ringgren, *TDOT* 11 (2001): 178–87.

3. BDB 426; *HALOT* 2 (1995): 427; Elmer A. Martens, "יצב (*yṣb*)," *NIDOTTE* 2: 500–501.

4. BAGD 67; BDAG 80; L&N §39.18.

5. *Contra* Wink, *Engaging the Powers*, 185.

6. Jerome *Eph* 6:13 (*PL* 26:550) (day of judgment); Meyer, 331; Dibelius-Greeven, 98; Schlier, 292–93; Gaugler, 224; Caird, 92.

7. Chrysostom *Eph* 6:13 (*PG* 62:159); Oecumenius *Eph* 6:13 (*PG* 118:1252); Theophylact *Eph* 6:13 (*PG* 124:1129); Aquinas, chap. 6, lec. 4, vv. 13–17 (239); Masson, 220. Lindemann (*Aufhebung*, 64, 235–36) thinks that the author uses apocalyptic terminology but with reference to the present age.

8. Theodoret *Eph* 6:13 (*PG* 82:553); Calvin, 219; Bengel, 4:116; Alford, 3:145–46; Eadie, 464–65; Ellicott, 148–49; Abbott, 184; Salmond, 384–85; Westcott, 95; Percy, *Probleme*, 259, 440; Hendriksen, 273; Mitton, 223; Mußner, 168; Harder, *TDNT* 6 (1968): 554.

9. Gnilka, 308; Barth, 804–5; Schnackenburg, 275–76; Lincoln, 446; Best, 596–97; S. Pietro Teodorico da Castel, "L'eschatologia nelle lettere della prigionia," *RivB* 9 (Ottobre–Dicembre 1961): 311; Pier Franco Beatrice, "Il combattimento spirituale secondo S. Paolo. Interpretazione di Ef 6,10–17," *Studia Patavina* 19, no. 2 (1972): 395–97.

(2) and (3) are combined, the present age referring to the present evil days (5:16) which are compounded with critical times of satanic hostilities against believers.[1] Which interpretation best fits the context? Paul does not appear to be referring to a future day (1) or he would likely have used the expression ἐν τῷ αἰῶνι τῷ ἐρχομένῳ, "in the coming age." In addition, the present context does not speak about preparation for a future battle but rather for the present conflict of diabolic hosts with the believers.[2] On the other hand, if he were speaking only of the present age (2), it seems that he would have used ἐν τῷ αἰῶνι τῷ πονηρῷ, "in this evil age"[3] or the expression similar to 5:16, namely, ἐν ταῖς ἡμέραις ταῖς πονηραῖς, "in the evil days." To refer to both present and future times (4), a more apt expression would be ἐν τῷ αἰῶνι τούτῳ καὶ ἐν τῷ μέλλοντι, "in this age and in the one to come," similar to Eph 1:21. It seems to speak more than to just certain critical days of diabolical attacks (3). On the other hand, Salmond states, "Regard must be had to the definiteness given to the ἡμέρα by the article, which marks it out as in some sense or other a single day, a critical day, a time of peculiar peril and trial."[4] Harder reinforces this idea by stating that it "is the 'evil,' 'dangerous,' 'critical' day, the day of distress, no matter whether it be regarded as a day in the present life, the day of death, the day of judgment, a day of conflict and peril, or the day when the devil has special power."[5] Therefore, view (5) is most appropriate because Paul appears to refer to the present evil times and at the same time to alert believers to the devil's extraordinary evil schemes leveled against them during these evil times. The believers should be aware that they must be prepared, not only for everyday evils but for the times of heightened and unexpected spiritual battles. For example, when the devil failed to tempt Jesus to sin, he left Jesus until an opportune time (Luke 4:13). In brief, then, Paul exhorts believers to take up the full armor of God in order to be able to stand in the evil day, always prepared for the vicious attacks that the devil will make at opportune times.

καὶ ἅπαντα κατεργασάμενοι στῆναι, "and having done everything, to stand." The final portion of this verse reinforces what Paul has just stated. The conjunction καί relates this infinitival clause as a parallel to the previous infinitival clause. Thus, the purpose of putting on the full armor of God is to enable believers to resist (ἀντιστῆναι) in the evil day and to stand (στῆναι), having done all. The anarthrous adjective

1. Bruce, 406; O'Brien, 471; Arnold, *Ephesians: Power and Magic*, 114; cf. Lona, *Die Eschatologie im Kolosser- und Epheserbrief*, 425–26.

2. This is a marked distinction from the Qumran community where they emphasized a great future battle against the powers of darkness (see Fischer, *Tendenz und Absicht des Epheserbriefes*, 167–71).

3. Cf. Salmond, 384.

4. Salmond, 384–85; cf. also Robertson, *Grammar*, 777.

5. Harder, *TDNT* 6 (1968): 554.

ἅπαντα (functions much like πᾶς, "all") without a noun can be translated "all, everybody, everything."[1] In form it could be either a masculine singular accusative or a neuter plural nominative or accusative. Here it can be construed as a neuter plural accusative since it does not speak of a specific enemy (which would have employed the accusative masculine plural) but rather everything pertaining to a conflict.[2] The participle κατεργασάμενοι is an aorist middle deponent participle from κατεργάζομαι. This verb historically meant either "to achieve, accomplish, do"[3] or (with an accusative of person) "to overpower, subdue, conquer."[4] It is used only thirteen times in the LXX (ten times in the canonical books) and translates eight Hebrew words. It conveys the idea "to prepare, equip" (Exod 15:17; 38:24 [LXX 39:1]; Num 6:3), "to make, do, accomplish" (Exod 35:33; Deut 28:39; 1 Kgs 6:36; Ps 68:28 [MT 68:29; LXX 67:29]; Ezek 36:9), "to overpower, subdue" (Judg 16:16?; Ezek 34:4; 1 Esdr 4:4). In the NT it occurs twenty-two times all in Paul's writings except twice (Jas 1:3; 1 Pet 4:3) and only here in Ephesians. Excluding the present context, the word has the sense "to do, achieve, accomplish" (Rom 1:27; 2:9; 7:15, 17, 18, 20; 15:18; 1 Cor 5:3; 2 Cor 12:12; 1 Pet 4:3), "to bring about, produce" (Rom 4:15; 5:3; 7:8, 13; 2 Cor 4:17; 2 Cor 7:10, 11; 9:11; Phil 2:12; Jas 1:3), or "to prepare" (2 Cor 5:5),[5] but never the idea "to overpower, subdue, conquer." But what is the sense in the present verse? There are two major views on its rendering in this text. (1) Some render it "having subdued or overcome all, stand" conveying the idea that victory has been accomplished, thus, believers can stand.[6] (2) Others contend that it should be rendered "having done all/everything, stand," suggesting that since all the necessary preparations are complete (i.e., all the armor is put on), believers are to stand or hold their ground against the attacks of the devil and his henchmen.[7] View (2) is preferred for the following rea-

1. BAGD 81; BDAG 98.

2. Eadie, 465–66; Ellicott, 149; Meyer, 332; Salmond, 385.

3. Sophocles *Electra* 1022; *Antigone* 57; Herodotus 5.24; Thucydides 4.65.3.

4. Herodotus 6.2; 8.100*bis*; Thucydides 4.85.2; Aristophanes *Equites* 842.

5. BAGD 421; BDAG 531; Georg Bertram, "κατεργάζομαι," *TDNT* 3 (1965): 635.

6. Chrysostom *Eph* 6:13 (*PG* 62:159–60); Oecumenius *Eph* 6:10–13 (*PG* 118:1252); Theophylact *Eph* 6:13 (*PG* 124:1129); Meyer, 331–32; Scott, 251; Schlier, 293; Mitton, 223; Baumert, *Täglich Sterben und Auferstehen* 349–50; Wink, *Naming the Powers*, 87–88; Yoder Neufeld, *'Put on the Armour of God,'* 128–31; BAGD 421; BDAG 531.

7. Alford, 3:146; Eadie, 465–66; Ellicott, 149; Meyer, 332; Abbott, 184; Salmond, 385; Robinson, 214; Westcott, 95; Dibelius-Greeven, 98; Masson, 220; Hendriksen, 272; Gnilka, 309; Barth, 765–66; Schnackenburg, 276; Bruce, 406–7; Lincoln, 446; Bouttier, 264; Best, 597; O'Brien, 472. Some think that Bengel's (4:116; cf. also Gaugler, 225) idea that it refers to all the necessary "preparations" is too limited (cf. Alford, 3:146; Eadie, 465; Meyer, 332; Salmond, 385) and if Paul meant that, he would have used the term for preparation (παρασκευασάμενοι) as he had in 1 Cor 14:8. However, the term κατεργάζομαι is used in 2 Cor 5:5 with the sense of preparation and thus could carry the same connotation in the present context. Furthermore, the context seems to indicate that

sons. First, the verb ἵστημι, "to stand," would have a consistent meaning throughout the context. If it connotes a victorious stand in verse 13, then it would differ from its meaning in verses 11 and 14. It is better to have it consistently mean a defensive stand.[1] The whole context speaks of a firm stand before the foe, not a victorious one.[2] Second, verses 14–17 are introduced by the inferential conjunction οὖν explaining that believers are to stand with the aid of the various pieces of armor. It would be unusual and certainly unnecessary to give details about armor subsequent to a victory. It is natural to describe such equipment for a defensive stand. Third, the imperative "stand" in verse 14 seems unnecessary and inappropriate if it has reference to a victorious stand but entirely appropriate if it refers to a defensive stand. Fourth, the grammatical relationship of the aorist participles in verses 14–16 (περιζωσάμενοι, ἐνδυσάμενοι, ὑποδησάμενοι, ἀναλαβόντες) with the aorist imperative στῆτε, "stand," in this verse would argue for holding ground rather than a victorious stand. The function of these participles also affects one's view. If seen as temporal participles, then they are most likely antecedent to the action of the imperative "stand." If the participles express means, then the believers are commanded to stand by means of putting on the various pieces of armor. This rendering would not point to a victorious stand. If they are causal, then believers are exhorted to stand because they are armed. This alternative is the most likely.

Finally, the function of the participle κατεργασάμενοι, "having done everything," in the present verse must also be ascertained. It is a consummative aorist stressing that everything has been done[3] to enable them to stand. Furthermore, in relationship to the infinitive (στῆναι) it is most likely causal (along with the succeeding participles), indicating once again that believers can stand defensively against the satanic hosts because they have made all the necessary preparations.

In conclusion, Paul exhorts believers to put on the full armor of God in order that they might be able to resist in the evil day and to stand defensively against satanic hosts. This is not about a victory or defeat. It is about holding fast to territory already won by Christ. The believer needs to realize that the devil and his angels are universal and strong, but not omnipotent. Accordingly, the strength of the Lord gained by utilizing the full armor of God is stronger than all the

---

"having done everything" means all the necessary preparations (viz., taking up the full armor of God) in order to be able to stand against the schemes of the superhuman power of the devil.

1. It is debatable as to whether there is any difference between ἵστημι and ἀνθίστημι for both have the idea of a defensive stand in this context (cf. Robertson, *Grammar*, 753*ter*; MHT 1:115).

2. Cf. Robert A. Guelich, "Spiritual Warfare: Jesus, Paul and Peretti," *Pneuma* 13 (spring 1991): 50–51, 60.

3. Fanning, *Verbal Aspect*, 415.

power of the wicked.[1] This is consistent with 4:27, which cautions against giving place or ground to the devil. Chafer summarized the believers' role well when he said, "In this connection, it is interesting to observe that as pilgrims we *walk*, as witnesses we *go*, as contenders we *run*, and as fighters we *stand*."[2]

2. Stand with the Armor (6:14–16)

Verses 10–13 discussed the armor of God in a general way. Now Paul gives details concerning the various pieces of the armor that will aid believers to stand against the assaults of wicked spiritual leaders. The next section with 113 words (vv. 14–20) is the last of the eight long sentences in this epistle (cf. 1:3–14, 15–23; 2:1–7; 3:2–13, 14–19; 4:1–6, 11–16; 6:14–20). It is divided into two parts indicated by the two aorist imperatives: (1) στῆτε, "stand," by putting on the various pieces of defensive armor (vv. 14–16); and (2) δέξασθε, "take," the final pieces of the armor together with prayer to be able to stand against the assaults of the spiritual forces of the devil (vv. 17–20).

a. The Mandate: Stand (6:14a)

Text: 6:14a. στῆτε οὖν

Translation: 6:14a. "Stand therefore"

Commentary: 6:14a. στῆτε οὖν, "Stand therefore." The inferential conjunction οὖν "therefore" indicates that Paul is introducing a result or an inference from that which he had just stated. Simply put, he had exhorted believers to put on the armor of God in order to stand firmly against spiritual wickedness. Now he exhorts them to do just that, to "stand." The aorist imperative probably "heightened the urgency of the instructions."[3] This urgency is further enhanced by the fact that this verb "to stand" (ἵστημι) is used for the third time in the immediate context (vv. 11, 13)[4] and also by a compound of this verb "to resist" (ἀνθίστημι) in verse 13. Therefore, the believers are told not to advance but to hold the ground and not to retreat in the face of wicked spiritual leaders led by the devil.

b. The Method: Arm (6:14b–16)

The command to stand is followed by a description of the believers' acquisition of the various pieces of the armor. Paul does this by a se-

1. O'Brien, "Principalities and Powers: Opponents of the Church," 140.
2. Chafer, 163.
3. Fanning, *Verbal Aspect*, 378.
4. Cf. Weber, "'Setzen'-'Wandeln'-'Stehen' im Epheserbrief," 478.

ries of aorist participles. These participles could denote the temporal aspect. If so, some studies indicate that the action of aorist participles are almost always antecedent to the main verb,[1] although newer studies suggest that this is more likely true when they precede the main verb but indicate simultaneous action when they follow the main verb.[2] However, if they do reflect a temporal aspect, it seems in this context they point to an antecedent action to the main verb. On the other hand, these participles may reflect a logical antecedent to the main verb expressing means or, more likely, cause. This appears to be the most consistent with the text. In other words, they are commanded to stand because they have put on the various pieces of armor.

Some of these pieces of armor are also listed by Polybius as will be pointed out below. They are also mentioned in Wis 5:18–22 but not always with the same spiritual designation (e.g., shield of holiness, helmet of justice), and thus it is unlikely that Paul borrowed from this source.[3] Interestingly, though the Qumran literature does speak of the weapons of warfare, the armor is not mentioned.[4] "In addition, unlike the Qumran community which expected to fight with actual physical weapons which were consecrated to God's cause, here the weapons are spiritual and supplied by God himself."[5]

(1) The Preparation: Girdle of Truth (6:14b)

Text: 6:14b. περιζωσάμενοι τὴν ὀσφὺν ὑμῶν ἐν ἀληθείᾳ,

Translation: 6:14b. "having girded your waists with truth,"

Commentary: 6:14b. περιζωσάμενοι τὴν ὀσφὺν ὑμῶν ἐν ἀληθείᾳ, "having girded your waists with truth." This is the first in the series of participles describing the articles of equipment the soldier needs for the conflict. The term περιζωσάμενοι is an aorist middle participle denoting a causal relationship to the imperative στῆτε, "stand,"[6] and is from περιζώννυμι or περιζωννύω. From the earliest of times it signified girding or binding something around the waist,[7] whether a girdle, belt, or apron. It occurs thirty-nine times in the LXX (thirty-four times in the canonical books) and translates four Hebrew words, twenty-two times for חָגַר, continuing with the idea "to gird" (e.g., Exod 12:11; Judg 3:16; 1 Sam 2:18; 2 Sam 3:31; Ps 109:19 [LXX 108:19]; Isa 15:3; Jer 4:8;

1. Moule, *Idiom Book*, 99; Fanning, *Verbal Aspect*, 407.
2. Porter, *Verbal Aspect*, 383–85.
3. *Contra* Casimir Romaniuk, "Le Livre de la Sagesse dans le Nouveau Testament," *NTS* 14 (July 1968): 498–514, esp. 505–11; Yoder Neufeld, *'Put on the Armour of God,'* 48–72, 119, 129–33.
4. Murphy-O'Connor, "Who Wrote Ephesians?" 1207.
5. Lincoln, *Paradise Now and Not Yet*, 165.
6. Cf. Wallace, *Greek Grammar*, 629 n. 41.
7. Aristophanes *Pas* 687; Josephus *A.J.* 11.5.8 §177; Plutarch *Romulus* 16.5; *Coriolanus* 9.2.

Ezek 7:18; Dan 10:5) and specifically the girding of weapons (Judg 18:11, 16, 17; Ps 45:3 [MT 45:4; LXX 44:4]).[1] In the NT the verb appears six times (Luke 12:35, 37; 17:8; Eph 6:14; Rev 1:13; 15:6) always with the same sense, "to gird."[2] Only in this text does the "girding" have a military application. The middle voice indicates that believers are responsible to gird themselves. The noun that follows is ὀσφύς, "waist, loins," the middle part of the body where a belt or girdle is worn.[3] It is used eight times in the NT, once to gird up the mind indicating alertness (1 Pet 1:13), three times of the hip or specifically the male genitals as a source of descendants (Acts 2:30; Heb 7:5, 10), and the other four times as the more common usage, a person's waist or loins (Matt 3:4; Mark 1:6; Luke 12:35; Eph 6:14). In Paul's day the girdle of the Roman soldier probably did not refer "to the protective girdle worn over the armour or to the sword belt" or to fastening his undergarments.[4] More likely, the girdle (*cingulum militare* or *balteus*) was a breech-like "apron which hung under the armour, which was made of loose or sewn thongs of leather" for protecting the thighs.[5] It was also used to fasten articles of clothing or tuck in the long skirts of a robe for greater freedom of movement. This word is followed by the instrumental dative ἐν ἀληθείᾳ, "with truth," indicating with what they are to be girded. The word "truth" has been discussed earlier (1:13; 4:21, 24, 25; 5:9) and has the basic idea of reality that is reliable and trustworthy as opposed to that which is false. Levine suggests that it is a spiritual wrestling belt of virtue that will replace the physical wrestling belt, the brute force of men.[6] This is unlikely in the light of the context. Nevertheless, the believer is to be girded with virtue, in this case truth. Is Paul referring to the objective truth of Christianity or the gospel[7] or is he referring to subjective truth, the believers' integrity and faithfulness?[8] It has been suggested that this refers back to Isa 11:5[9]

1. BDB 291–92; B. Johnson, "חָגַר *chāghar*, etc.," *TDOT* 4 (1980): 213–16.

2. BAGD 647; BDAG 801.

3. BAGD 587; BDAG 730; L&N §8.42. The singular ὀσφύς is used of a group (see Robertson, *Grammar*, 409; MHT 3:24).

4. Albrecht Oepke, "ζώννυμι κτλ.," *TDNT* 5 (1968): 307

5. Oepke, *TDNT* 5 (1968): 303; cf. also M. C. Bishop and J. C. N. Coulston, *Roman Military Equipment from the Punic Wars to the Fall of Rome* (London: B. T. Batsford, 1993), 96–99.

6. Étan Levine, "The Wrestling-Belt Legacy in the New Testament," *NTS* 28 (October 1982): 562.

7. As Oecumenius *Eph* 6:14–18 (*PG* 118:1252); Schlier, 295; Gaugler, 225; Best, 599; Oepke, *TDNT* 5 (1968): 307–8; Moritz, *A Profound Mystery*, 202.

8. As Chrysostom *Eph* 6:14 (*PG* 62:163–64); Calvin, 220; Alford, 3:146; Eadie, 467; Ellicott, 149–50; Meyer, 333; Abbott, 185; Salmond, 386; Westcott, 95; Masson, 221; Hendriksen, 276; Barth, 767–68, 796–97; Schnackenburg, 277; Bruce, 408; Lincoln, 448; Thiselton, "Truth [ἀλήθεια]," *NIDNTT* 3 (1978): 886.

9. Cf. Moritz, *A Profound Mystery*, 187–90; Kamlah, *Die Form der katalogischen Paränese im Neuen Testament*, 190 n. 5.

which states that the Messiah's righteousness and faithfulness will be the girdle of his waist, implying subjective truth inherent in the Messiah. Nonetheless, in this text it is possible that both objective and subjective truth are in view. Believers have girded their waists with God's objective truth, which in turn has become a part of them. This enables them to be reliable and faithful as God is reliable and faithful. This piece of armor is basic to all other pieces because truth and trustworthiness are basic to all the other qualities[1] that believers need in order to withstand diabolical attacks. As believers internalize God's truth they live and move in it.[2] Therefore, though objective truth may be partially in view, the subjective truth of God is the main emphasis.

(2) The Chest: Breastplate of Righteousness (6:14c)

Text: 6:14c. καὶ ἐνδυσάμενοι τὸν θώρακα τῆς δικαιοσύνης,

Translation: 6:14c. "and having put on the breastplate of righteousness,"

Commentary: 6:14c. καὶ ἐνδυσάμενοι τὸν θώρακα τῆς δικαιοσύνης, "and having put on the breastplate of righteousness." The second item of armor is introduced by the connective conjunction καί, "and," followed by another aorist middle participle ἐνδυσάμενοι denoting a causal relationship to the imperative στῆτε, "stand." It is from ἐνδύω, which means to put on clothes, either literally or metaphorically, as seen earlier (4:24; 6:11). The middle voice suggests that believers are responsible for putting on the breastplate. The term θώραξ can refer to the trunk or chest of the human anatomy[3] or it can refer to a coat of mail or scale plates that covers the trunk or chest.[4] In the OT the term is used for a coat of mail (1 Sam 17:5*bis*, 38), metal plates (1 Kgs 22:34 = 2 Chr 18:33), or metal armor (2 Chr 26:14; Neh 4:16 [MT & LXX 4:10]). The term is used in the NT only five times (Eph 6:14; 1 Thess 5:8; Rev 9:9*bis*, 17). In Paul's time it was probably a metal plate worn over a leather jerkin or a coat of mail[5] to protect the chest and back (metal plates in Rev 9:9, 17). Polybius wrote that the common soldier had a brass breastplate (*pectorale*) covering his chest to protect his heart, while wealthier soldiers had a coat of chain mail (*lorica jamata*).[6] Like the girdle around the waist, it is defensive armor. The word δικαιοσύνης, "righteousness," describes the breastplate

1. Cf. L. L. Barclay, "Ephesians vi.14," *ExpTim* 2 (February 1891): 118; cf. Yoder Neufeld, *'Put on the Armour of God,'* 133–35.

2. Similar in the Qumran literature (see Murphy-O'Connor, "Truth: Paul and Qumran," 205–6).

3. Aristotle *Historia Animalium* 1.7 §491a.29; 1.12 §493a.5; 1.13 §493a.17.

4. Homer *Ilias* 15.529–30; 23.560–62; Herodotus 9.22.

5. Bishop and Coulston, *Roman Military Equipment*, 85–91; Jonathan C. N. Coulston, "Arms and Armour, Roman," *OCD*, 174; cf. also BAGD 367; BDAG 463–64; L&N §8.38; Albrecht Oepke, "θώραξ," *TDNT* 5 (1968): 308–10.

6. Polybius 6.23.14–15.

and is probably a genitive of apposition,[1] that is, the breastplate which is righteousness. The word δικαιοσύνη appears in Eph 4:24 (where the word is discussed) and 5:9 and can refer to righteousness as an attribute, whether God's (Deut 33:21; 1 Kgs 8:32; Rom 3:25–26) or a person's (Deut 9:4–6; 1 Kgs 3:6; Matt 5:20; Rom 10:3). It can also refer to those who deal righteously, whether God (Ps 9:4, 8 [MT & LXX 9:5, 9]; Isa 5:16) or people (Lev 19:15; 1 Sam 26:23; Rom 6:13; Phil 1:11). Finally, it could refer to a person's right standing before God (Rom 3:21–22; 4:3, 5). In this text some regard it as justifying righteousness or a right standing before God,[2] but most regard it as sanctifying or subjective righteousness[3] (1 Cor 1:30), which, of course, has its basis in justifying righteousness. Isaiah 59:17 (cf. also Wis 5:18) refers to God putting on his attribute of righteousness as a breastplate. Likewise, in this context believers are, by appropriating God's righteousness, to act righteously in their daily dealings with God and humankind.[4] In other contexts, believers are exhorted to submit to God and resist the devil causing him to flee (Jas 4:7), and to endure by truthful speech and the power of God with the weapons of righteousness for the right hand and for the left hand (2 Cor 6:7). As a soldier's breastplate protected his chest from enemy attacks, so sanctifying righteous living (Rom 6:13; 14:17) guards believers' hearts against the assaults of the devil.

(3) The Feet: Gospel of Peace (6:15)

Text: 6:15. καὶ ὑποδησάμενοι τοὺς πόδας ἐν ἑτοιμασίᾳ τοῦ εὐαγγελίου τῆς εἰρήνης,

Translation: 6:15. "and having shod the feet with the preparation of the gospel of peace,"

1. Alford, 3:146; Ellicott, 150; Meyer, 334; Salmond, 386; Schlier, 295; Winer, *Grammar*, 666; HS §§165a, 295x; Wallace, *Greek Grammar*, 95; Jesús Precedo Lafuente, "El cristiano en la metáfora castrense de San Pablo," in *Studiorum Paulinorum Congressus Internationalis Catholicus 1961*, vol. 2, AnBib, vol. 18 (Rome: E Pontificio Instituto Biblico, 1963), 348.

2. As do Eadie, 468; Barth, 796–97; Oepke, "θώραξ," *TDNT* 5 (1968): 310; Moritz, "'Summing-up all Things'," 108.

3. As do Chrysostom *Eph* 6:14–17 (*PG* 62:164); Theodoret *Eph* 6:14 (*PG* 82:553); Oecumenius *Eph* 6:14–18 (*PG* 118:1253); Theophylact *Eph* 6:14 (*PG* 124:1132); Calvin, 220; Alford, 3:146; Ellicott, 150; Meyer, 333–34; Abbott, 185; Salmond, 386; Westcott, 96; Masson, 221; Schlier, 295; Gaugler, 226; Hendriksen, 276–77; Schnackenburg, 277; Bruce, 408; Lincoln, 448; Snodgrass, 342; O'Brien, 474–75; Theron, "Aletheia in the Pauline Corpus," 6, 17; Gottlob Schrenk, "δικαιοσύνη," *TDNT* 2 (1964): 210; Hill, *Greek Words and Hebrew Meanings*, 154; Stuhlmacher, *Gerechtigkeit Gottes bei Paulus*, 216; Ziesler, *The Meaning of Righteousness in Paul*, 153–54.

4. Cf. Moritz, *A Profound Mystery*, 190–92; Yoder Neufeld, *'Put on the Armour of God,'* 135–36; Kamlah, *Die Form der katalogischen Paränese im Neuen Testament*, 191.

Commentary: 6:15. καὶ ὑποδησάμενοι τοὺς πόδας, "and having shod the feet." The third item of armor is introduced by the connective conjunction καί, "and," followed by another aorist middle participle ὑποδησάμενοι denoting a causal relationship to the imperative στῆτε, "stand," and is from ὑποδέω/ὑποδέομαι. The verb always means to bind or fasten under, especially with reference to the feet because ancient sandals were bound on with straps. Thus it can be rendered "to shod" or "to put on shoes/sandals."[1] The middle voice indicates that believers are responsible for shodding their feet. It occurs only twice in the LXX (2 Chr 28:15; Ezek 16:10) and three times in the NT (Mark 6:9; Acts 12:8; Eph 6:15) and continues to have the same usage. The Roman legionaries wore heavy sandals (*caliga*, a low half-boot) with soles made of several layers of leather averaging 2 centimeters (3/4 inch) thick, studded with hollow-headed hobnails. They were tied by leather thongs half-way up the shin and were stuffed with wool or fur in the cold weather.[2] This verb ὑποδέω, "to shod," rather than the noun for sandal (ὑπόδημα as, e.g., in Matt 3:11 = Mark 1:7 = Luke 3:16) is used in this context. These were not running sandals but ones able to dig in with their hollow-headed hobnails and stand against the enemy.

ἐν ἑτοιμασίᾳ τοῦ εὐαγγελίου τῆς εἰρήνης, "with the preparation of the gospel of peace." Here the instrumental dative indicates with what believers are to be shod. The beginning prepositional phrase is ἐν ἑτοιμασίᾳ, "with the preparation." In classical times the noun ἑτοιμασία reflected the idea of "readiness"[3] or "preparation."[4] The verb form occurs more often, with the active meaning "to make ready, prepare"[5] and the passive "to be prepared."[6] In the LXX ἑτοιμασία occurs eleven times and in the canonical books it appears seven times and three times it translates the verb כּוּן, meaning "to establish, set up" (Ps 10:17 [LXX 9:38]) or "to make ready, prepare" (Ps 65:9 [MT 65:10; LXX 64:10]; Nah 2:3 [MT & LXX 2:4])[7] and three times from the nouns מָכוֹן, meaning "established place, foundation" (Ezra 2:68; Ps 89:14 [MT 89:15; LXX 88:15]) or מְכוּנָה, meaning "fixed resting place, base" (Zech 5:11).[8] The verb ἑτοιμάζω occurs 176 times and in the canonical books

1. LSJ 1879; Herodotus 1.155; Thucydides 3.22.2; Aristophanes *Ecclesiazusae* 36; Aristotle *Historia Animalium* 2.1 §499a.29; Josephus *B.J.* 6.1.8 §85; cf. BAGD 844; BDAG 1037; Albrecht Oepke, "ὑποδέω," *TDNT* 5 (1968): 310–11.

2. Bishop and Coulston, *Roman Military Equipment*, 100–101; Graham Webster, *The Roman Imperial Army of the First and Second Centuries A.D.*, 3d ed. (London: A & C Black, 1985), 121; Michael Grant, *The Army of the Caesars* (London: Weidenfeld and Nicolson, 1974), xx.

3. Hippocrates *De Decenti Habitu* 12.10.

4. Aeneas Tacticus 21.1.

5. Homer *Ilias* 1.118; Herodotus 6.95.

6. Thucydides 6.64.3; 7.62.1; Polybius 8.30.7.

7. BDB 465–66; K. Koch, "כּוּן *kûn*, etc.," *TDOT* 7 (1995): 89–90, 95–98.

8. BDB 467; Koch, *TDOT* 7 (1995): 90.

it appears 133 times and translates eighteen Hebrew words but translates the verb כּוּן nearly a hundred times with the same meaning. In the NT the verb occurs forty times with the same basic meaning "to make ready, prepare" (Matt 3:3 = Mark 1:3 = Luke 3:4; Matt 20:23 = Mark 10:40; Matt 22:4; John 14:2–3; Acts 23:23; 1 Cor 2:9; 2 Tim 2:21; Phlm 22). The noun ἑτοιμασία occurs only here in the NT. Some think that this should be translated "equipment" (cf. RSV), signifying "boots" to give them a "firm foundation" or "firm footing"[1] (NEB). Although consistent with this passage, the word is never so used elsewhere.[2] Therefore, the best translation is "preparation," "preparedness," or "readiness," which is consistent with its usage elsewhere. Accordingly, believers who have been shod with readiness will be able to stand. The following genitival phrase τοῦ εὐαγγελίου τῆς εἰρήνης, "of the gospel of peace," further describes this readiness. The first gentive is probably a genitive of origin or source and the second is most likely a genitive of content. Thus, readiness or preparedness has its source in the gospel, the contents of which is peace. The term "gospel" is used four times in Ephesians (1:13; 3:6; 6:15, 19) connoting "good news." In 1:13 it is the good news of salvation and in 3:6 it is the good news of the union of believing Jews and Gentiles into Christ. This latter reference is a parenthetical expansion of the mystery of Jewish and Gentile believers united in one body. The mystery, delineated in 2:11–22 (esp. vv. 14–18), alluding to Christ "our peace" is primarily horizontal in scope and secondarily vertical. In other words, the enmity between Jew and Gentile has been resolved (horizontal), the enmity between sinful mankind and God has been resolved (vertical). Paul states that he was privileged to preach this union and to enlighten all of humankind regarding the mystery (which was hidden from former generations) in order that through the church the manifold wisdom of God might be made known to the good and evil rulers and authorities in the heavenlies (3:8–10). Therefore, it is this gospel of peace with which the believers have shod their feet in readiness. What does this mean in the present context? Some would argue that in the midst of attacks from evil powers, believers have shod their feet in their readiness to preach the gospel of peace similar to Eph 3:8–10 or Isa 52:7 (cf. Rom 10:15) and Mic 2:1 (TEV, JB, NJB, NRSV).[3] However, this is un-

1. Hatch, *Essays in Biblical Greek*, 55; Amalric F. Buscarlet, "The 'Preparation of the Gospel of Peace'," *ExpTim* 9 (October 1897): 38–40; E. H. Blakeney, "A Note of the Word σιώπησις: Canticles iv.1, 3; vi.6," *ExpTim* 55 (February 1944): 138; John A. F. Gregg, "ἑτοιμασία in Ephesians vi.15," *ExpTim* 56 (November 1944): 54; Barth, 770, 797–98; cf. A. J. Th. Jonker, "Ἡ ἑτοιμασία τοῦ εὐαγγελίου τῆς εἰρήνης (Ef. 6:15)," *ThStud* 11, nos. 5–6 (1893): 443–51.

2. Cf. Alford, 3:146; Eadie, 469; Ellicott, 150; Meyer, 335; Lincoln, 449.

3. Theodoret *Eph* 6:15 (*PG* 82:553); Oecumenius *Eph* 6:14–18 (*PG* 118:1252–53); Theophylact *Eph* 6:15 (*PG* 124:1132); Aquinas, chap. 6, lec. 4, vv. 13–17 (241); Calvin, 220; Robinson, 215; Westcott, 96; Dibelius-Greeven, 98; Masson, 221; Schlier, 295–96;

likely for the following reasons. First, Paul specifically states, "having shod the feet with readiness of the gospel of peace," not "having shod the feet with the proclamation of the gospel of peace." Second, the context is about putting on defensive rather than offensive armor. Third, the main verb in the present context is "to stand" (v. 14) and not "to advance." Hence, Paul depicts believers as having put on another defensive piece of armor. Therefore, rather than preach the gospel of peace, believers are ready or prepared to stand against the onslaughts of the evil forces because they are firmly grounded in the gospel of peace.[1] It is the believers' "surefootedness" in the tranquility of the mind and security of the heart in the gospel of peace that gives them readiness to stand against the devil and his angelic hosts. It is somewhat paradoxical that the gospel of peace is the preparation for warfare against the hosts of evil.

(4) The Body: Shield of Faith (6:16)

Text: 6:16. ἐν πᾶσιν ἀναλαβόντες τὸν θυρεὸν τῆς πίστεως, ἐν ᾧ δυνήσεσθε πάντα τὰ βέλη τοῦ πονηροῦ [τὰ] πεπυρωμένα σβέσαι·

Translation: 6:16. "in addition to all these having taken up the shield of faith, with which you are able to extinguish all the flaming arrows of the evil one;"

Commentary: 6:16. ἐν[2] πᾶσιν ἀναλαβόντες τὸν θυρεὸν τῆς πίστεως, "in addition to all these having taken up the shield of faith." The

---

Gaugler, 226; Zerwick, 170; Gnilka, 311–12; Caird, 93; Schnackenburg, 278; Bruce, 408; O'Brien, 476–77; Walter Grundmann, "ἕτοιμος κτλ.," *TDNT* 2 (1964): 706; Oepke, "ὑποδέω," *TDNT* 5 (1968): 312; Schlier, *Principalities and Powers in the New Testament*, 59; Morris, *Apostolic Preaching*, 242; Romano Penna, "«L'évangile de la paix»," in *Paul de Tarse, apôtre de notre temps*, ed. Lorenzo De Lorenzi, Série monographique de «Benedictina» Section paulinienne, vol. 1 (Rome: Abbaye de S. Paul h.l.m., 1979), 175–76, 185; Arnold, *Ephesians: Power and Magic*, 111, 120; Arnold, *Powers of Darkness*, 157; O'Brien, *Gospel and Mission in the Writings of Paul*, 124; Moritz, *A Profound Mystery*, 192–95; Wendland, "Contextualizing the Potentates, Principalities and Powers in the Epistle to the Ephesians," 219.

1. Cf. Chrysostom *Eph* 6:14–17 (*PG* 62:168); Alford, 3:146–47; Eadie, 469; Meyer, 335; Abbott, 185; Salmond, 387; Hendriksen, 277; Lincoln, 449; Best, 599–600; Alfred Juncker, *Die Ethik des Apostels Paulus*, vol. 2, *Die Konkrete Ethik* (Halle: Max Niemeyer, 1904), 80; Roels, *God's Mission*, 217–19. Yoder Neufeld thinks it is an announcement of peace when the enemy has been vanquished (*'Put on the Armour of God,'* 138).

2. The preposition ἐν is found in 𝔓[46] א B P 0278 33 104 1175 1739 1881 2464 *pc* latt Methodius. The second reading ἐπί appears in A D F G Ψ 𝔐 Chrysostom Ambrosiaster Jerome Theodoret Theophylact. The first reading has the support of manuscripts with good date and character. However, it is limited to the Alexandrian text. It has good genealogical relationships within the Alexandrian text-type. The second reading has only manuscript A in the Alexandrian text-type but it has good date and character in the Western text-type. It is better than the first reading for geographical distribution and it has good genealogical relationships in the Western and the Byzantine text-types. The second reading has preference. Internally, the second reading is similarly used in Col 3:14 and

fourth item of the armor is introduced with two differences from the previous two clauses: (1) there is no connective conjunction καί, "and," but rather it is introduced by ἐν πᾶσιν, "above all"; and (2) the participle is not the aorist middle but the aorist active ἀναλαβόντες, also denoting a causal relationship to the imperative στῆτε, "stand," and is from ἀναλαμβάνω, which also occurs in verse 13. In a military context it means "to take up" or "to put on" weapons. The prepositional phrase at the beginning of this verse is either ἐν πᾶσιν or ἐπὶ πᾶσιν. Which reading is correct is difficult to decide. The AV accepted the ἐπὶ πᾶσιν reading and translates it "above all." Other translations accept ἐν πᾶσιν and variously translate it "withal" (RV, ASV), "above all" (RSV), "in addition to all" (NASB, NIV), "with all these" (NEB, NRSV), "at all times" (TEV), "and always" (JB, NJB). The preposition ἐν probably denotes accompanying circumstance,[1] thus giving the prepositional phrase the sense of "most especially," translated "above all," "at all costs" or "in all circumstances,"[2] or even better the sense of accession or addition, translated "with all these" or "in addition to all these."[3] This last rendering can also be attributed to ἐπὶ πᾶσιν.[4] Regardless of which reading one accepts, in this context it means "in addition to all" the weapons that have been previously listed.

The aforementioned pieces of armor had to be fastened to the body, as seen in the aorist participles (περιζωσάμενοι, ἐνδυσάμενοι, ὑποδησάμενοι),[5] but now believers are to take up τὸν θυρεὸν τῆς πίστεως, "the shield of faith." The term θυρεός, "shield," is used only here in the NT. In the LXX the term is used twenty-three times (all from canonical books) and translates three Hebrew words, nine times for צִנָּה, a shield covering the whole body and carried by an arm-bearer when not in conflict (1 Chr 12:9; 2 Chr 9:15*bis*; 11:12; Ezek 23:24).[6] Eleven times it translates מָגֵן, a smaller shield (buckler) used for hand to hand fighting (Judg 5:8 [B text]; 2 Sam 1:21*bis*; 2 Kgs 19:32; Neh 4:16 [MT & LXX 4:10]; Isa 21:5; Ezek 23:24).[7] In classical literature the term is used of

---

could be translated "over/above all" (AV) giving the sense of "most especially" or it could have the idea "in addition to all" (Salmond, 387). The first reading is similarly used in Luke 16:26 (which has the same textual variants) and could be translated "in/above all" with the sense of "most especially" (RSV) or "in addition to all" (NASB, NIV). Hence, the sense of either is about the same. In conclusion, it is difficult to indicate preference.

1. Robertson, *Grammar*, 589; Moule, *Idiom Book*, 78; cf. Joüon, "Notes philologiques sur quelques versets de l'Épître aux Éphésiens," 462–63.

2. Moule, *Idiom Book*, 78; Masson, 221 n. 6.

3. Robinson, 215; Westcott, 9; Dibelius-Greeven, 98; Schlier, 296; Gaugler, 227; Gnilka, 312; Barth, 771; Schnackenburg, 278; Bruce, 408; Lincoln, 449.

4. BDF §235 (3); Winer, *Grammar*, 490; Alford, 3:147; Eadie, 469; Ellicott, 151; Meyer, 336; Abbott, 186; Salmond, 387; Gnilka, 312 n. 2.

5. Eadie, 470.

6. BDB 857; D. N. Freedman, M. P. O'Connor, and H. Ringgren, "מָגֵן *māgēn*; גָּנַן *gānan*; צִנָּה *ṣinnâ*; שֶׁלֶט *šeleṭ*," *TDOT* 8 (1997): 84.

7. BDB 171; Freedman, O'Connor, and Ringgren, *TDOT* 8 (1997): 74–82, 85–87.

a *"stone put up against a door* to keep it shut"[1] and in the military it is used of an oblong shield (*scutum*) shaped like a door (θύρα is the word for door) that covers the whole man[2] as distinguished from the ἀσπίς (*clipeus*), a small round shield of approximately three-quarters of a meter (2 1/2 feet) in diameter. Polybius describes the θυρεός as having a convex surface measuring three-quarters by one and a quarter meters (2 1/2 by 4 feet) and a hand's breadth in thickness. It was made of two wood planks glued together with the outer surface covered first with canvas and then with calf skin. There was metal on the top and bottom edges to protect the wood when it hit the ground and on the center front there was an iron boss causing most stones and heavy arrows to glance off.[3] This shield not only covered the body but also the other parts of the armor described earlier; hence Paul uses the phrase "in addition to all these." He further describes this shield as a shield "of faith." The genitive is most likely a genitive of apposition, that is, the shield consists of faith.[4] Although some would consider this objective faith,[5] it is more likely the subjective faith of believers.[6] This is more consistent with the defensive parts of the armor previously mentioned. The possession of the shield of resolute faith helps believers stand firmly and resist the devil (cf. 1 Pet 5:8–9) and his schemes. In light of Isa 59, Yoder Neufeld suggests that the imagery is not primarily a defensive stand but "seeing the saints as Divine Warrior placing the powers under siege."[7] However, this is reading too much of Isa 59 into Eph 6. The entire present context speaks of a defensive rather than an offensive stance on the part of believers.

ἐν ᾧ δυνήσεσθε πάντα τὰ βέλη τοῦ πονηροῦ [τὰ][8] **πεπυρωμένα σβέσαι,** "with which you are able to extinguish all the flaming arrows of the evil one." The relative prepositional phrase (ἐν ᾧ) refers back to

1. LSJ 811; Homer *Odyssea* 9.240, 313; cf. MHT 2:347.

2. Polybius 2.30.8; 6.23.2; Plutarch *Pyrrhus* 26.5.

3. Polybius 6.23.2–6. Shields covered with animal skin are also mentioned in Homer *Ilias* 5.452; Herodotus 7.91; Thucydides 2.75.5; Pliny *Naturalis Historia* 8.39 §95; cf. also Bishop and Coulston, *Roman Military Equipment*, 82.

4. Winer, *Grammar*, 666; HS §§165a, 295x; Eadie, 469; Ellicott, 151; Meyer, 336; Abbott, 186; Salmond, 387; Best, 601; O'Brien, 479.

5. Lenski, 669; Masson, 222; Albrecht Oepke, "θυρεός," *TDNT* 5 (1968): 314.

6. Chrysostom *Eph* 6:14–17 (*PG* 62:169); Oecumenius *Eph* 6:14–18 (*PG* 118:1253); Theophylact *Eph* 6:1 (*PG* 124:1132); Aquinas, chap. 6, lec. 4, vv. 13–17 (241); Calvin, 220–21; Eadie, 470; Meyer, 337; Abbott, 186; Salmond, 387; Westcott, 96; Gaugler, 227; Hendriksen, 278 n. 175; Mitton, 226; Barth, 772–73; Schnackenburg, 278; Bruce, 408; Lincoln, 449; Best, 601; O'Brien, 479.

7. Yoder Neufeld, *'Put on the Armour of God,'* 139–40.

8. The article τά occurs in א A D^2 Ψ 0278 33 1739 1881 𝔐 but is omitted by $𝔓^{46}$ B D* F G. The first reading has some manuscripts with an early date and good character, good geographical distribution among the Alexandrian and Byzantine text-types, and good genealogical relationships in the Alexandrian and Byzantine texts. Its omission also has some early date and good character manuscripts and has good geographical

the shield and could denote the sphere "in which the flaming arrows are extinguished," but probably it is instrumental, "with which the flaming arrows are extinguished."[1] The verb δυνήσεσθε is a future indicative middle/deponent of δύναμαι. The verb δύναμαι is already discussed in 3:4, 20 and 6:11, 13, meaning "to be able, to be capable of." The future tense does not point to a great future conflict with satanic forces but rather looks at the whole duration of a contemplated conflict with evil forces or, as Best suggests, "refers to what follows after the picking up of the shield."[2] Thus, the shield will be able, at any time, to extinguish the fiery arrows. There are many references to arrows (βέλος) used in battle.[3] The term βέλος is a broad term used for any pointed missile-like weapon, especially an arrow or dart, but it can also refer to other weapons, such as a sword, a spear, or anything that is swift-darting.[4] It could refer to spears or javelins (ὑσσός, *pila*) that were 2 meters (7 feet) long, including an iron head 60 centimeters (2 feet) long, which had a killing range of about 30 meters (33 yards). When they were hurled, the tempered blade would sink into the shield and the soft shank would bend making the shield difficult to handle. Often the soldier would abandon the shield, leaving himself unprotected. Normally, the soldier had two spears and after throwing the second one, he would rush in and use his short thrust sword (to be discussed below). These spears could be wrapped with tow and smeared with pitch, then ignited, making them flaming javelins.[5] However, more likely this word refers to arrows (βέλη or ὀϊστοί, *malleoli*) that could be shot either from a bow or an engine.[6] They also

---

distribution among the Alexandrian and Western text-types and good genealogical relationships in the Alexandrian and Western texts. Internally, its inclusion is the easier reading. An adjective or a participle following a genitive takes an article unless it is to be understood predicatively (MHT 3:186). If the article were omitted then it would read "the arrows when/though they are flaming" (Winer, *Grammar,* 168). On the other hand, it could be that a scribe accidentally omitted it. Hence, internally its inclusion is preferred. Examining both the external and internal evidence, its inclusion is preferred, though with hesitation.

1. Moule, *Idiom Book*, 77; Eadie, 470; Ellicott, 151; Meyer, 337; Salmond, 387; Lincoln, 449.

2. Best, 601; O'Brien, 480.

3. E.g., Polybius 6.23.6; used forty-three times in the LXX mostly for חֵץ, "arrow," (BDB 346) e.g., in Deut 32:23, 42; 2 Sam 22:15; 2 Kgs 13:15*bis*, 17*bis*; Isa 5:28; 7:24.

4. LSJ 313; MM 108; Friedrich Hauck, "βέλος," *TDNT* 1 (1964): 608–9; Bishop and Coulston, *Roman Military Equipment*, 69, 79–81.

5. Polybius 6.23.8–11; Livy 21.8.10–12; 38.6.2; 42.64.2; G. R. Watson, *The Roman Soldier*, Aspects of Greek and Roman Life, ed. H. H. Scullard (London: Thames & Hudson, 1969), 58–59; Graham Webster, *The Roman Army: An Illustrated Study* (Chester, England: A Publication of the Grosvenor Museum, 1956), 25–26.

6. ὀϊστός in Herodotus 8.52; Thucydides 2.75.5; Apollodorus *Bibliotheca* 2.5.2; Arrian *Anabasis* 2.21.3; βέλος in Aeneus Tacticus 32.8–9; Polybius 11.11.3; Diodorus Siculus 20.88.2; 96.3, 4, 6; 97.2, 7; Apollodorus *Bibliotheca* 2.5.4; Arrian *Anabasis* 2.18.6; 23.3.

could be wrapped with tow and ignited, making them flaming arrows (πυρφόρα βέλη or πυρφόροι ὀϊστοί).[1] Flaming arrows are mentioned in the OT (Pss 7:13 [MT & LXX 7:14]; 77:17 [MT 77:18; LXX 76:18]) and in the Qumran literature (1QH[a] 10:26 [2:26]; 11:16, 27 [3:16, 27]; 1QM 6:16; 4Q177 1:8).[2] The genitive τοῦ πονηροῦ, "of the evil one," could be a possessive genitive, "the evil one's flaming arrows," but preferably it is a genitive of source, "the flaming arrows from the evil one." This is not referring to an abstract principle but a person (cf. also John 17:15; 1 John 5:19) who is called the "devil" in verse 11 and who heads the host of evil powers vividly described in verse 12. The σβέσαι is an aorist infinitive active of σβέννυμι, which occurs six times in the NT (Matt 12:20; 25:8; Mark 9:48; Eph 6:16; 1 Thess 5:19; Heb 11:34), and in all but one instance (1 Thess 5:19) it is in connection with fire and thus means "to quench, extinguish."[3] The skins and hides that covered the shields would extinguish the incendiary arrows, preventing the wood from catching fire.[4] Furthermore, before battle the shields were immersed in water, soaking the leather cover and canvas beneath the leather, which also aided in extinguishing the flaming missiles.[5] The adjective πάντα indicates that all the flaming arrows will be extinguished when they sink into the leather of the shield. No doubt some of the arrows were deflected to the ground, but those that did become implanted in the shield were extinguished.[6]

In conclusion, the metaphorical language depicts this shield of resolute faith that protects believers from spiritual harm aimed at them by the evil one. It not only stops the fiery weapons of attack but actually extinguishes them, thus rendering them useless. Believers must be wary of laying aside their shields of faith and attempting to fight the battle in their own strength.

3. Receive the Final Pieces of Armor (6:17–20)

The outline is divided here because Paul uses the imperative δέξασθε, "take," rather than another participle. This imperative is not parallel to the preceding participles in verses 14–16[7] but parallel to the

1. For details, see Ammianus Marcellinus 23.4.14–15.

2. Murphy-O'Connor, "Truth: Paul and Qumran," 205; Schnackenburg, 279 n. 34.

3. BAGD 745; BDAG 917; Friedrich Lang, "σβέννυμι," *TDNT* 7 (1971): 165–68.

4. Thucydides 2.75.5.

5. Colin Brown, "War, Soldier, Weapon [πόλεμος]," *NIDNTT* 3 (1978): 966.

6. Oepke thinks that the shield only deflected the arrows but did not absorb them and thereby did not extinguish them (Oepke, *TDNT* 5 [1968]: 314). However, there is enough evidence from military literature to indicate that the shield absorbs and extinguishes the flaming arrows.

7. As suggested by Meyer, 338; Abbott, 186–87; Salmond, 388; Masson, 222; Schnackenburg, 279; O'Brien, 480 n. 178; Arnold, *Ephesians: Power and Magic*, 105.

imperative στῆτε, "stand," in verse 14.[1] The connective conjunction καί, "and," indicates that this is not really a new sentence, as most translations suggest, but a continuation of the sentence beginning in verse 14 (as suggested by a semicolon for punctuation in NA[27], UBS[4], GNTMT). Verse 14 begins with an inferential conjunction οὖν, "therefore," indicating that Paul is introducing a result or an inference from what he had just stated in verse 13. In that verse, he has just reminded the believers that, having made all the necessary preparations, they can now stand against the evil one. From this the inferential conjunction makes the inference that believers are to stand because they have girded themselves with truth, have taken up the breastplate of righteousness, have shod themselves with the preparation of the gospel of peace, and have taken up the shield of faith (vv. 14–16). Now continuing with the connective conjunction καί, "and," Paul instructs believers to take the helmet of salvation and the sword of the Spirit, the last two pieces of the armor.

a. The Mandate: Take (6:17)

In physical warfare, the helmet and sword are the last two pieces a soldier takes up. The helmet, hot and uncomfortable, would be put on by a soldier only when he faced impending danger. He takes hold of his sword to defend himself against an approaching enemy. The sword is the only offensive piece mentioned in this context.

(1) The Head: Helmet of Salvation (6:17a)

Text: 6:17a. καὶ τὴν περικεφαλαίαν τοῦ σωτηρίου δέξασθε

Translation: 6:17a. "and take the helmet of salvation"

Commentary: 6:17a. καὶ τὴν περικεφαλαίαν τοῦ σωτηρίου δέξασθε,[2] "and take the helmet of salvation." The connective conjunction καί, "and," followed by the aorist imperative δέξασθε, "take," makes this parallel to the aorist imperative στῆτε, "stand," in verse 14. The word δέξασθε is an aorist imperative middle/deponent of δέχομαι meaning "to take, receive, take in hand, grasp."[3] It could actually mean "grab" since the context seems to indicate that the last thing a soldier does is grab his helmet and sword when he sees an approaching enemy. The aorist imperative may suggest a sense of urgency incumbent on the

1. Cf. Breeze, "Hortatory Discourse in Ephesians," 342–43; Best, 602.

2. The verb δέξασθε is omitted by D* F G it[b, m*] Cyprian Ambrosiaster Speculum. It is limited to the Western text and hence, not preferred as far as external evidence is concerned. Internally, its omission makes for an easier reading because it would be a continuation of the list, namely, "having taken up the shield of faith, . . . the helmet of salvation, and the sword of the Spirit." The inclusion of the verb breaks up the flow but it makes good sense. Therefore, both externally and internally, the inclusion of δέξασθε is preferred.

3. BAGD 177; BDAG 221.

believers.[1] The middle voice indicates that believers are responsible for grabbing the helmet and sword. The word περικεφαλαία means "head covering" but in a military context it refers to the "helmet."[2] The word occurs ten times in the LXX (nine times in the canonical books) and it is always used of a helmet (e.g., 1 Sam 17:5, 38; 2 Chr 26:14; Ezek 27:10; 38:4–5). In the NT it is used only twice (Eph 6:17; 1 Thess 5:8) and continues to have the military sense. Twice in the LXX the metal of the helmet is depicted as bronze (1 Sam 17:38; 1 Macc 6:35). In Roman times it had various shapes at different times and places, but it generally was made of bronze fitted over an iron skull cap lined with leather or cloth. During Claudius' reign (A.D. 37–41) the helmet was revised so that it covered the back of the neck, fitting slightly over the shoulder, a brow-ridge fitted above the face to protect the nose and eyes, and hinged cheek pieces were fastened by a chin-band to protect the face.[3] The next words τοῦ σωτηρίου, "salvation," describe the helmet and are probably genitives of apposition[4] (as in vv. 14, 16), that is, the helmet which is salvation. This helmet of salvation may well be an allusion to Isa 59:17 (as is the breastplate of righteousness in v. 14 above).[5] The use of the neuter adjective σωτήριον (common in the LXX) rather than the feminine noun σωτηρία confirms the allusion to Isa 59:17, for the neuter adjective is never used elsewhere by Paul and is used only three other times in the NT (Luke 2:30; 3:6; Acts 28:28), whereas the feminine noun is used forty-six times in the NT, eighteen times by Paul. The prophet in Isa 59:17 speaks of present salvation from wickedness, and in this context, Paul is referring primarily to a present-day experiential salvation from the attacks of the wicked one as opposed to salvation from a future judgment envisioned in 1 Thess 5:8 (περικεφαλαίαν ἐλπίδα σωτηρίας, "helmet, the hope of salvation"—note, in this instance, Paul substituted the neuter adjective for the normal feminine noun). It does not refer to salvation in the objective sense but a conscious possession of it in the midst of the onslaughts of the evil one. With his head protected, the soldier feels safe in the midst of battle. Likewise, believers' possession of salvation gives them confidence of safeness during the assaults of the devil.

1. Cf. Fanning, *Verbal Aspect*, 378.

2. Aeneus Tacticus 24.6; Polybius 3.71.4; 6.23.8; Diodorus Siculus 14.43.2.

3. Bishop and Coulston, *Roman Military Equipment*, 93–96; Webster, *The Roman Imperial Army of the First and Second Centuries A.D.*, 126; idem, *The Roman Army*, 26–27; Grant, *The Army of the Caesars*, xx; Erich Sander, "Die Kleidung des römischen Soldaten," *Historia* 12 (April 1963): 158; Albrect Oepke, "περικεφαλαία," *TDNT* 5 (1968): 314.

4. Alford, 3:147; Ellicott, 152; Meyer, 338; Salmond, 388; Winer, *Grammar*, 666; HS §§165a, 295x.

5. Cf. Moritz, *A Profound Mystery*, 190–92; Yoder Neufeld, *'Put on the Armour of God,'* 141; Kamlah, *Die Form der katalogischen Paränese im Neuen Testament*, 191.

(2) The Mouth: Sword of the Spirit (6:17b)

Text: 6:17b. καὶ τὴν μάχαιραν τοῦ πνεύματος, ὅ ἐστιν ῥῆμα θεοῦ,

Translation: 6:17b. "and the sword of the Spirit, which is the word of God,"

Commentary: 6:17b. καὶ τὴν μάχαιραν τοῦ πνεύματος, "and the sword of the Spirit." With the connective conjunction καί, "and," Paul mentions the second item to be grabbed just before the attacks of the devil and his armies. It is the μάχαιρα, "sword." It is a common term for a large knife that was used for many purposes,[1] including carving[2] and sacrifice.[3] As a weapon, it was a short sword or dagger,[4] later a sabre as opposed to the straight sword.[5] In the LXX it occurs 188 times (175 times in the canonical books) and translates four Hebrew words, but translates around 160 times for חֶרֶב, a common word for sword. In the LXX μάχαιρα denotes a flint knife used for circumcision (Josh 5:2–3), a barber's razor (Ezek 5:2, but 5:1 uses ῥομφαία for the barber's razor), but primarily a sword, a weapon of war (Exod 15:9; Judg 3:16; 2 Sam 20:8; Job 1:15; Jer 12:12; 47:6 [LXX 29:6]; Ezek 31:17–18).[6] In the NT the word is used twenty-nine times, only three times by Paul (Rom 8:35; 13:4; Eph 6:17). It is used as a military sword in all instances but two, once referring to believers who are persecuted or slain with a sword (Rom 8:35), and once referring to a surgeon's knife (Heb 4:12).[7] The other word for sword (ῥομφαία) is used only seven times in the NT (Luke 2:35; Rev 1:16; 2:12, 16; 6:8; 19:15, 21) and is the large and broad Thracian sword. Although in the LXX both terms translate primarily the same word (חֶרֶב), somewhat blurring the distinction, it is generally thought that ῥομφαία does refer to a large, broad sword[8] whereas μάχαιρα is used of a relatively short sword (or dagger).[9] This latter is in keeping with the Roman soldier's sword (*gladius*), known as the Spanish sword. Its double-edged blade was "two inches [5 centimeters] wide and two feet long [60 centimeters] and was admirably suit-

1. Homer *Ilias* 18.597; Aristotle *Politica* 1.1.5 §1252b.2.
2. Herodotus 2.61.
3. Homer *Ilias* 19.252.
4. Herodotus 6.75; 7.225; Pindar *Nemean Odes* 4.59.
5. Xenophon *Cyropaedia* 1.2.13; *Hellenica* 3.3.7.
6. BDB 352–53; O. Kaiser, "חֶרֶב *ḥereḇ*; חָרַב *ḥāraḇ*," *TDOT* 5 (1986): 155–65.
7. Michaelis thinks the references to sword in Matt 10:34; Luke 22:35, 38; Rev 6:14; Eph 6:17; Heb 4:12 are not speaking of military swords (see W. Michaelis, "μάχαιρα," *TDNT* 4 [1967]: 526). However, outside of Heb 4:12 it seems that all these have reference to military swords. Certainly Eph 6:17 is speaking of a military sword in light of the armor outlined in vv. 14–17, although it is talking about in the context of spiritual warfare.
8. BAGD 737; BDAG 907; Wilhelm Michaelis, "ῥομφαία," *TDNT* 6 (1968): 993–94; L&N §6.32.
9. BAGD 496; BDAG 622; Michaelis, *TDNT* 4 (1967): 524–25; L&N §6.33.

able as a cut-and-thrust weapon for close work."[1] It was placed in a sheath attached to the girdle high on the right side of the body so it would be clear of his shield-bearing left arm and not become entangled with his legs. It is the only offensive weapon of the armor mentioned in this context. This sword is further described as the sword τοῦ πνεύματος, "of the Spirit." The genitive is most likely not a genitive of apposition[2] because the following clause explains that the sword of the Spirit is not the Spirit itself but the word of God (ὅ ἐστιν ῥῆμα θεοῦ). Neither is it attributive, as the spiritual sword of the word,[3] nor a genitive of quality,[4] but, rather, a genitive of origin or source[5] ("sword given by the Spirit") similar to the "preparation of the gospel" in verse 15. Possibly, it could be a possessive genitive, "belonging to the Spirit."[6] More specifically, it could be the genitive of author since it mentions a personal name, the Holy Spirit. Thus, in accordance with the offensive nature of this weapon it has the idea of offensive empowerment by the Holy Spirit necessary in a spiritual battle (v. 12). The sword of the Spirit is held in the girdle or belt (*balteus*) of truth.[7]

ὅ ἐστιν ῥῆμα θεοῦ, "which is the word of God." This relative clause further describes the sword of the Spirit. The neuter relative pronoun does not refer to the neuter πνεύματος as its antecendent[8] but is attracted to the predicate neuter ῥῆμα (cf. 3:13).[9] Ultimately, it refers back to the whole phrase "the sword of the Spirit" as an explanatory clause giving a further description.[10] In verse 14 reference was made to Isa 11:5 in connection with the girdle of truth. It may be that Paul is again referring to the imagery of the LXX, for Isa 11:4 states that the Spirit of the Lord will rest on the Messiah who will smite the earth with the word (λόγος) of his mouth and with the breath (ῥῆμα) of his lips he shall destroy the wicked.[11] The Isaiah passage refers to the fu-

1. Webster, *The Roman Imperial Army of the First and Second Centuries* A.D., 12; Webster, *The Roman Army*, 25; Grant, *The Army of the Caesars*, xviii; cf. also Bishop and Coulston, *Roman Military Equipment*, 69–79.

2. As Olshausen, 279; Harless, 551.

3. Oecumenius *Eph* 6:14–18 (*PG* 118:1253); Theophylact *Eph* 6:17 (*PG* 124:1133).

4. As Chrysostom *Eph* 6:14–17 (*PG* 62:169); Masson, 222 n. 5; Schlier, 298.

5. Theodoret *Eph* 6:17 (*PG* 82:556); Alford, 3:148; Eadie, 473; Ellicott, 153; Meyer, 339; Abbott, 187; Salmond, 388; Westcott, 97; Mitton, 227; Barth, 776–77; Schnackenburg, 279–80; O'Brien, 481–82; Michaelis, *TDNT* 4 (1967): 526 n. 21; Lafuente, "El cristiano en la metáfora castrense de San Pablo," 2:349; Adai, *Der Heilige Geist als Gegenwart Gottes*, 138, 145.

6. Cf. Fee, *God's Empowering Presence*, 728.

7. F. R. Montgomery-Hitchcock, "Latin Expressions in the Prison Epistles," *Exp* 9th ser., vol. 2 (October 1924): 298.

8. As Mußner, 170.

9. Robertson, *Grammar*, 712; Wallace, *Greek Grammar*, 338.

10. Burton, *Moods and Tenses* §295; Robertson, *Grammar*, 411–12, 954; Wallace, *Greek Grammar*, 662.

11. Barth, 777; Caird, 93; Schnackenburg, 280; Bruce, 409; Lincoln, 451.

ture when the Messiah will smite the nations (cf. Rev 19:15). As previously mentioned, this text does not speak about a future battle, but instead the present battle with the wicked in the heavenlies. The term ῥῆμα was discussed at 5:26 where it was understood to mean the spoken or proclaimed word. Although a synonym of λόγος, ῥῆμα may "be seen more exclusively as a means of confrontation and judgement."[1] This is followed by θεοῦ, "God," which may be a subjective genitive or a genitive of origin, that is, the word which comes from God.[2] Briefly, then, the sword of the Spirit is the offensive weapon, the spoken word of God to be used against the spiritual wickedness of the devil. Christ demonstrated its use during his three encounters with the devil at the time of his temptation where he used the written word against the devil (Matt 4:1–11 = Luke 4:1–13). For instance, in reply to the devil's first temptation, Jesus quotes Deut 8:3, stating, "man shall not live by bread alone but by every word [ῥῆμα] that proceeds out of the mouth of God" (Matt 4:4). This is not preaching the gospel[3] but speaking God's word against his foes.[4] It should be noted that God's word is not to be recited as a magical formula. On the contrary, it is speaking the words of God in Christ's name empowered by God's Spirit. The spoken word of God is the "instrument" of the Spirit.[5] Again, it must be remembered that although this is the only offensive weapon listed among the pieces of the armor, in the present context it is not used to make advances but rather to enable the believer to stand firmly in the midst of satanic warfare. The devil and his forces must not be allowed to gain new territory in Christ's kingdom or to rob believers of their spiritual blessings in Christ. With this piece, the description of the armor comes to an end.

The entire armor is absolutely necessary in the spiritual warfare against the devil and his angels. As in other parts of this book, the exhortation is directed to both the individual and the corporate body. This is in keeping with the dominant theme of the book, unity of believing Jews and Gentiles in one body. Thus the church, the body of believers, is in this warfare together. As the Roman soldier did not fight alone, so must believers as a body, united under their

1. Yoder Neufeld, *'Put on the Armour of God,'* 145; cf. Kamlah, *Die Form der katalogischen Paränese im Neuen Testament*, 191 n. 5.

2. Adai thinks it could be a genitive of origin or a genitive of content (*Der Heilige Geist als Gegenwart Gottes*, 141).

3. As Alford, 3:148; Ellicott, 153; Salmond, 388; Mitton, 227; Barth, 777, 800; Schnackenburg, 280; Lincoln, 451; O'Brien, 482; Dunn, *Jesus and the Spirit*, 227; Arnold, *Ephesians: Power and Magic*, 120–21, 170; Arnold, *Powers of Darkness*, 157–58; O'Brien, *Gospel and Mission in the Writings of Paul*, 125.

4. Eadie, 473; Meyer, 339; Schlier, 298; Gaugler, 228; Caird, 93; Mitton, 227–28; Bruce, 409–10; Best, 603–4; Arnold, *Powers of Darkness*, 156.

5. Adai, *Der Heilige Geist als Gegenwart Gottes*, 139.

commander-in-chief, stand against spiritual wickedness in heavenly places.

b. The Method: Care (6:18–20)

These verses mark the concluding remarks regarding the believers' warfare. First, Paul exhorts them to be strengthened (ἐνδυναμοῦσθε) in the Lord and to put on (ἐνδύσασθε) the full armor so that they can stand against the devil's strategies (vv. 10–13). Second, he exhorts believers to stand (στῆτε) by appropriating the various pieces of the defensive armor (vv. 14–16). Finally, he commands them to grasp (δέξασθε) the last two pieces of armor, the helmet of salvation and the sword of the Spirit (v. 17), and continues by stating the need for prayer and alertness (vv. 18–20). Praying and maintaining alertness are depicted by the two participles προσευχόμενοι . . . ἀγρυπνοῦντες, "praying . . . keeping alert," in verse 18. The way in which these participles relate to the context is a matter of debate among interpreters. First, some think that "praying" is the seventh piece of armor.[1] However, Paul appears to have finished the armor metaphor for he does not mention any specific piece of armor representing prayer.[2] Second, most think that the participles relate back to στῆτε, "stand," in verse 14 rather than the nearer imperative δέξασθε, "take," in verse 17.[3] It is suggested that since the whole context is concerned with the believer's stand against wicked forces, this stand involves prayer and alertness. The main problem with this view is that the antecedent is quite remote from these participles. If such were the case, Paul most likely would have repeated the imperative στῆτε, "stand," so that it would have been closer to the participles. Furthermore, it should not be assumed that the imperative δέξασθε, "take," in verse 17 is subordinate to στῆτε in verse 14 because they are joined by the coordinating conjunction καί, "and." Third, others suggests that the antecedent is the imperative δέξασθε in verse 17 because it is in close proximity while στῆτε in verse 14 is quite remote.[4] This makes the most sense syntactically. In the wake of an imminent attack, believers are to take up the last two pieces of armor, the helmet of salvation and the sword of the Spirit. The manner in which this is done is to be in a constant state of prayer and alertness.[5] This is necessary because the battle is superhuman and needs to be fought with supernatural means and power.

1. Schlier, 298, 300; Gaugler, 228; Wink, *Naming the Powers*, 88.

2. Barth, 785–86.

3. Alford, 3:148; Eadie, 474; Ellicott, 153; Meyer, 341; Abbott, 187; Salmond, 389; Bruce, 411; Lincoln, 451; Best, 604; O'Brien, 483 n. 197.

4. Olshausen, 280; Schlatter, 7:248; Masson, 223; Schlier, 300; Gaugler, 228; Gnilka, 315; Snodgrass, 344; Wild, "The Warrior and the Prisoner," 288.

5. For a discussion on prayer in Ephesians, see James E. Rosscup, "The Importance of Prayer in Ephesians," *The Master's Seminary Journal* 6 (spring 1995): 57–78.

(1) Manner: Praying and Watching (6:18)

Text: 6:18. διὰ πάσης προσευχῆς καὶ δεήσεως προσευχόμενοι ἐν παντὶ καιρῷ ἐν πνεύματι, καὶ εἰς αὐτὸ ἀγρυπνοῦντες ἐν πάσῃ προσκαρτερήσει καὶ δεήσει περὶ πάντων τῶν ἁγίων

Translation: 6:18. "through every prayer and petition praying at every opportunity in the Spirit, and to this end keeping alert with all persistence and petition for all the saints"

Commentary: 6:18. διὰ πάσης προσευχῆς καὶ δεήσεως προσευχόμενοι ἐν παντὶ καιρῷ ἐν πνεύματι, "through every prayer and petition praying at every opportunity in the Spirit." Having commanded believers to take up their helmet of salvation and sword of the Spirit, Paul now describes the attitude that they should continually maintain. He does this by the use of two participles, προσευχόμενοι and ἀγρυπνοῦντες, "praying" and "keeping alert."[1] These participles could express the means, but more likely they show the manner in which believers are to take up their helmet of salvation and sword of the Spirit. In a certain sense they express exhortations,[2] not parallel to the imperative (δέξασθε) in verse 17 but subservient to it. Hence, the punctuation at the end of verse 17 should be a comma (as in WH, NA^{25}, UBS$^{1-3}$, and GNTMT) rather than a period (as in NA$^{26, 27}$ and UBS$^{3corr., 4}$). In other words, keep praying and watching when you take up the last two pieces of armor because the attack is imminent, the schemes are cunning, and God's power and insight are needed.

The prepositional phrase introducing these verses, διὰ πάσης προσευχῆς καὶ δεήσεως, "through every prayer and petition," expresses the means by which they pray.[3] In the context, the words used for prayer are προσευχή, προσεύχομαι, and δέησις. First, the noun προσευχή, discussed at 1:16, always has the idea of prayer or supplication to the eternal God or refers to the place of prayer. Second, the verb προσεύχομαι from the earliest times was used to suggest communication with deities, whether in the form of a vow or petition.[4] It occurs 108 times in the LXX and seventy-seven times in the canonical books translating four Hebrew words but sixty-eight times for פָּלַל and all but two times for the Hithpael stem meaning "to intercede, pray" (Gen 20:17; 1 Sam 1:10; 1 Kgs 8:28–30, 33, 35, 42, 44, 48, 54; Isa 16:12).[5] It occurs in the NT eighty-five times, forty-four times in the Synoptics, sixteen times in Acts, nineteen times in Paul and only here in Ephesians, and five

1. Evald Lövestam, *Spiritual Wakefulness in the New Testament*, LUÅ, n.s. Avid. 1, vol. 55, no. 3 (Lund: Gleerup, 1963), 70–75.

2. Cf. Barth, 777; Adai, *Der Heilige Geist als Gegenwart Gottes*, 233–34; O'Brien, *Introductory Thanksgivings in the Letters of Paul*, 251; cf. Wallace, *Greek Grammar*, 652.

3. Turner (MHT 3:267) and Moule (*Idiom Book*, 57) think it expresses attendant circumstances.

4. Plato *Symposium* 220d; Aeschylus *Agamemnon* 317.

5. BDB 813; Gerstenberger and Fabry, *TDOT* 11 (2001): 568–78.

times in the rest of the NT. It is the comprehensive word for prayer to the God of heaven[1] and is the vehicle of believers to address their heavenly Father in the name of Christ and in the power of the Holy Spirit. The third word is the noun δέησις, which in classical times connoted "need, lack, want."[2] Subsequently, it developed the meaning of "request, petition, entreaty."[3] In the LXX it appears eighty times (fifty-six times in the canonical books) translating nine Hebrew words and twenty-two times for תְּחִנָּה (1 Kgs 8:30, 38, 52*bis*, 54; 2 Chr 6:29, 39; Ps 6:19 [MT & LXX 6:10]) or תַּחֲנוּן (2 Chr 6:21; Ps 28:2, 6 [LXX 27:2]; Dan 9:17, 23), meaning "supplication for favor";[4] six times for שׁוּעַ or שַׁוְעָה (Job 36:19; Pss 5:2 [MT & LXX 5:3]; 34:15 [MT 34:16; LXX 33:16]; 39:12 [MT 39:13; LXX 38:13]; 40:1 [MT 40:2; LXX 39:2]; 145:19 [LXX 144:19]) "cry for help";[5] and seven times for תְּפִלָּה (1 Kgs 8:45; 2 Chr 6:35, 40; Pss 66:19 [LXX 65:19]; 102:17 [MT 102:18; LXX 101:18]; Isa 1:15) with the general idea of "prayer."[6] In the NT it appears eighteen times, twelve times in Paul's writings and only twice in Ephesians, both times in this verse. It is a derivative of δέομαι, "to plead, beg," and thus it is "that which is asked with urgency based on presumed need—'request, plea, prayer.'"[7] It can be used as a general term for prayer (Luke 2:37; 5:33; Phil 1:4, 19) but for the most part, in the NT it refers to specific petitions made to God. Often, however, the actual request is not stated, making the exact usage difficult to determine.[8] When it is used in conjunction with προσευχή (Phil 4:6; 1 Tim 2:1; 5:5; Jas 5:16–17), as it is here, δέησις probably is the more specific word for petition or supplication and the former the more general word for prayer. The singular anarthrous adjective πάσης signifies every incident of the believers' prayer and petition. Thus, the prepositional phrase can be translated "through every prayer and petition."

This prepositional phrase is followed by the participle προσευχόμενοι, which is further described by two prepositional phrases, ἐν παντὶ καιρῷ ἐν πνεύματι, "at every opportunity or occasion in the Spirit." The first phrase ἐν παντὶ καιρῷ occurs only here and in Luke 21:36. The preposition ἐν expresses the temporal idea "at" or "on."[9] The term καιρός occurs four times in this epistle (1:10; 2:12; 5:16; 6:18). As discussed in earlier passages the distinction between καιρός

1. BAGD 713–14; BDAG 879; Greeven, "προσεύχομαι, προσευχή," *TDNT* 2 (1964): 807–8; Hans Schönweiss, "Prayer [προσεύχομαι]," *NIDNTT* 2 (1976): 867–69.

2. Aristotle *Politica* 1.3.12 §1257a.23; *Rhetorica* 2.7.3 §1385a.

3. Plato *Epistulae* 7 §329d; Isocrates 8.138; Demosthenes *Orationes* 29.4; Josephus *B.J.* 7.5.2 §§103, 104, 107, 110.

4. BDB 337; H. Ringgren, "תַּחֲנוּנִים *taḥ*ᵃ*nûnîm*; תְּחִנָּה *t*ᵉ*ḥinnāh*," *TWAT* 8 (1995): 641–43.

5. BDB 1002–3; J. Hausmann, "שׁוע *šwʿ*, etc.," *TWAT* 7 (1990): 1187–91.

6. BDB 813; cf. Gerstenberger and Fabry, *TDOT* 11 (2001): 568–72.

7. L&N §33.171.

8. Heinrich Greeven, "δέομαι, δέησις, προσδέομαι," *TDNT* 2 (1964): 41; Hans Schönweiss, "Prayer [δέομαι]," *NIDNTT* 2 (1976): 861.

9. Moule, *Idiom Book*, 76, 78.

and χρόνος may be little, if any. As in 5:16 καιρός in the present context could have the idea of opportunities offered by time, hence, "opportunity, occasion." In the LXX its use suggests a "critical time."[1] Again, the singular anarthrous adjective παντί is used to signify every occasion or every opportunity that is available or "at every critical time." So when the enemy attacks, believers not only grab the helmet of salvation and the sword of the Spirit but also pray. It is unceasing prayer.[2]

The second prepositional phrase ἐν πνεύματι gives the sphere of their prayers, namely, "in the Spirit." This does not refer to the human spirit[3] but the Holy Spirit because it alludes to prayer in the midst of spiritual battle (cf. v. 17). There are other instances of instruction to pray in the Holy Spirit, for example, Jude 20. The Holy Spirit indwells the believer (Rom 8:15–16; Gal 4:6) and is a vital part of the believer's spiritual well-being. He gives strength in weakness and intercedes on behalf of the saints (Rom 8:26–27). Thus, prayer is directed to God in the power of the Holy Spirit.[4] This is in keeping with the rest of this epistle with regard to the Trinity in that through Christ both believing Jews and Gentiles have access to the Father in the one Spirit (2:18).[5] In the immediate context, praying in the Spirit may well be connected to the sword of the Spirit. The sword of the Spirit is, on the one hand, God's spoken word to put his enemies to flight and, on the other hand, the believers' utterance to God in prayer in the power of the Holy Spirit to aid in the struggle against the evil powers.[6] In the larger picture, however, this context relates prayer to the taking of the helmet of salvation and the sword of the Spirit, the last piece of defensive armor and the only piece of offensive armor respectively. It is the believers' cry to God on the occasion of assault. Trust in God's wisdom is necessary, for he provides the helmet of salvation and enables them to use their swords effectively in defense against the hosts of the wicked one.

καὶ εἰς αὐτὸ ἀγρυπνοῦντες ἐν πάσῃ προσκαρτερήσει καὶ δεήσει περὶ πάντων τῶν ἁγίων, "and to this end keeping alert with all persistence and petition for all the saints." The connective conjunction καί, "and," ties what had just been stated with the next clause in a coordi-

1. See Eynikel and Hauspie, "The Use of καιρός and χρόνος in the Septuagint," 385.

2. Lövestam, *Spiritual Wakefulness in the New Testament*, 72; Schlier, *Principalities and Powers in the New Testament*, 64–65; Moule, *Idiom Book*, 94. O'Brien thinks that rather than unceasing prayer it should refer to his regular times of prayer (*Introductory Thanksgivings in the Letters of Paul*, 21–22; idem, "Thanksgiving within the Structure of Pauline Theology," 56, 65 n. 37). However, in this context with the "at any moment" assault of the wicked one, it probably means to be ready to pray at any or all times.

3. As Ewald, 259; Westcott, 97; Lenski, 676; Johnston, 26–27.

4. For a discussion of prayer and the Spirit, see Peter R. Jones, "La prière par l'Esprit: Ephésiens 6:18," *La revue réformée* 27, no. 3 (1976): 128–39; Adai, *Der Heilige Geist als Gegenwart Gottes*, 237–43.

5. Jones, "La prière par l'Esprit: Ephésiens 6:18," 134.

6. Robinson, 135–36.

nate manner.[1] The εἰς αὐτό, "to this end" or "for this purpose," relates back to the preceding discussion of the necessity for prayer at the moments of attack from the evil one. It is for this reason that believers are to keep alert. Although some suggest that these two participles form a hendiadys—two coordinating words or expressions indicating a single concept,[2] the εἰς αὐτό would render this unlikely. The present participle ἀγρυπνοῦντες is from ἀγρυπνέω, which is used in classical times and means "to lay awake at night"[3] or "to watch" sheep.[4] It occurs only eleven times in the LXX (eight times in the canonical books) and primarily translates שָׁקַד, meaning "to lie awake" (Pss 102:7 [MT 102:8; LXX 101:8]; 127:1 [LXX 126:1]) or "to watch, guard" (Ezra 8:29; Job 21:32; Prov 8:34; Dan 9:14).[5] In the NT it appears only four times (Mark 13:33; Luke 21:36; Eph 6:18; Heb 13:17), meaning "to watch" and in particular in the present text "to watch" for a possible threat and thus "to be alert, vigilant."[6] Jesus had instructed his disciples to watch or to be alert for his second coming. In this text believers are urged to take the helmet of salvation and the sword of the Spirit by prayer and maintaining alertness. The following prepositional phrase ἐν πάσῃ προσκαρτερήσει καὶ δεήσει could express manner but, more likely, denotes accompaniment. The noun προσκαρτέρησις is rare, found only once in classical literature; however, the verb is used more frequently and means "to persist obstinately in."[7] Also, in the LXX the noun is not used but the verb form (προσκαρτερέω) appears three times (Num 13:20; Tob 5:8; Theodotion Dan 13:6 [Sus 6]) having the same idea of persistence. The noun is found only here in the NT although the verb form occurs ten times.[8] It is a compound word made up of καρτερέω (appears only in Heb 11:27 and means "to endure") and προς-. The compound "has the same basic meaning, but gives greater emphasis to the time element: to hold out, to persist, persevere with a person, persist in an opinion or activity."[9] In the NT the verb can mean "to be devoted or dedicated" to someone or some task (Acts 1:14; 2:42; 6:4; Rom 12:12; 13:6; Col 4:2). Hence, both the verb and the noun mean "to continue to do something with intense effort, . . . 'to devote oneself to,

1. Not in an epexegetical manner as suggested by Winer, *Grammar*, 546.

2. Cf. Abel, *Grammaire du Grec biblique*, 366; Winer, *Grammar*, 786 n. 3; Louis-Marie Dewailly, "Finns det många hendiadys i Nya Testamentet?" *Svensk exegetisk årsbok* 51–52 (1986–87): 56.

3. Xenophon *Cyropaedia* 8.3.42; *Hellenica* 7.2.19.

4. Plato *Leges* 3 §695a.

5. BDB 1052; E. Lipiński, "שָׁקַד *šāqaḏ*, etc.," *TWAT* 8 (1995): 445–49.

6. L&N §27.57; BAGD 14; BDAG 16; Albrecht Oepke, "γρηγορέω, (ἀγρυπνέω)," *TDNT* 2 (1964): 338–39; Colin Brown, "Guard, Keep, Watch [ἀγρυπνέω]," *NIDNTT* 2 (1976): 137.

7. Polybius 1.55.4; Diodorus Siculus 14.87.5; Josephus *B.J.* 6.1.3 §27.

8. Cf. Edward Lee Hicks, "Προσκαρτέρησις (Ephesians VI 18)," *JTS* 10 (April 1909): 571–72.

9. Wilhelm Mundle, "Patience, Steadfastness, Endurance [κρατερέω]," *NIDNTT* 2 (1976): 767.

to keep on, to persist in.'"[1] Thus, in this particular context it can be rendered "with all persistence and petition" (the latter word was discussed earlier in this verse). The point of this is that prayer is for the purpose of maintaining alertness. Prayer causes alertness and alertness keeps believers in prayer. If they are not alert, they do not see the dangers and thus see no need to pray. With the enemy making his assaults, the believers are to be enveloped with prayer and to this end they are continuing to be alert with all persistence and petition.

The final prepositional phrase περὶ πάντων τῶν ἁγίων, "for all the saints," indicates that all believers are involved in this struggle against evil powers. The preposition περί means "around, about, concerning" and when it is followed by a genitive after verbs or nouns regarding prayer, it "introduces the pers. or thing in whose interest the petition is made. Thus it takes the place of ὑπέρ ["concerning, on behalf of"]."[2] Here it is "concerning" all the saints. Reference to all the saints occurs twice previously in this epistle, namely, in 1:15 where Paul expresses thanksgiving for their love toward all the saints and in 3:18 where Paul prays that they may comprehend with all the saints the love of Christ. In 6:18 Paul demonstrates that individual saints involved in warfare compose an entire army that collectively battles against the enemy, this being true in human and spiritual warfare. Thus, in this spiritual battle there should be mutual concern for one another, demonstrated by prayer for each other.

It is important to note the repetition in this verse. Prayer and petition are mentioned four times. This is not tautology but done for the sake of emphasis. It suggests the thoroughness and intensity in regards to prayer. The adjective πᾶς ("every, all") is also mentioned four times. As believers take up the helmet of salvation and the sword of the Spirit, they should pray at *every* opportunity, through *every* prayer and petition, with *all* persistence and petition for *all* the saints. In the midst of spiritual warfare Paul emphasizes the vital importance of prayer. Paul certainly modeled this as seen twice in Ephesians (1:15–23; 3:14–21).[3]

Briefly, nuclear wars cannot be won with rifles. Likewise, satanic wars cannot be won by human energy. Thus, Paul has warned the saints to constantly pray and remain alert, ready to don the helmet of salvation and grasp the sword of the Spirit in order to do battle at a moment's notice. Neither of these pieces of armor, nor all other pieces, are available as the result of human endeavor.

(2) Petitions: For Utterance and Bold Speech (6:19–20)

Having instructed believers to pray for all saints, Paul now mentions, in verses 19–20, two specific requests for the Ephesian believers

1. L&N §68.68.
2. BAGD 644; BDAG 797; cf. also Wallace, *Greek Grammar*, 363.
3. Rosscup, "The Importance of Prayer in Ephesians," 66.

to pray on his behalf. These two verses are similar to Col 4:3–4. They can be outlined as follows:[1]

Ephesians 6:18–20	Colossians 4:3–4
προσευχόμενοι . . . ὑπὲρ ἐμοῦ	προσευχόμενοι . . . περὶ ἡμῶν,
ἵνα μοι δοθῇ λόγος ἐν ἀνοίξει τοῦ στόματός μου	ἵνα ὁ θεὸς ἀνοίξῃ ἡμῖν θύραν τοῦ λόγου
ἐν παρρησίᾳ γνωρίσαι τὸ μυστήριον τοῦ εὐαγγελίου,	λαλῆσαι τὸ μυστήριον τοῦ Χριστοῦ,
ὑπὲρ οὗ πρεσβεύω ἐν ἁλύσει,	δι᾽ ὃ καὶ δέδεμαι,
ἵνα ἐν αὐτῷ παρρησιάσωμαι ὡς δεῖ με λαλῆσαι.	ἵνα φανερώσω αὐτὸ ὡς δεῖ με λαλῆσαι.

The differences are minimal. In Colossians Paul and his companions are included in the request for prayer whereas in Ephesians it is for him alone. In Colossians Paul mentions "the mystery of Christ," which he earlier described as "Christ in you the hope of glory" (1:27). On the other hand, in Ephesians he mentions "the mystery of the gospel," which he earlier delineated as the unification of believing Jews and Gentiles into one body (2:11–3:13). Although minimal, these differences suggest that neither Colossians nor Ephesians depend on the other.[2]

Text: 6:19. καὶ ὑπὲρ ἐμοῦ, ἵνα μοι δοθῇ λόγος ἐν ἀνοίξει τοῦ στόματός μου, ἐν παρρησίᾳ γνωρίσαι τὸ μυστήριον τοῦ εὐαγγελίου, **6:20.** ὑπὲρ οὗ πρεσβεύω ἐν ἁλύσει, ἵνα ἐν αὐτῷ παρρησιάσωμαι ὡς δεῖ με λαλῆσαι.

Translation: 6:19. "especially for me, that utterance might be given to me in opening my mouth, to make known with boldness the mystery of the gospel **6:20.** for which I am an ambassador in chains, that I might speak boldly about it as I ought to speak."

Commentary: 6:19. καὶ ὑπὲρ ἐμοῦ, ἵνα μοι δοθῇ λόγος ἐν ἀνοίξει τοῦ στόματός μου, ἐν παρρησίᾳ γνωρίσαι τὸ μυστήριον τοῦ εὐαγγελίου,[3] "especially for me, that utterance might be given to me in open-

1. From Bockmuehl, *Revelation and Mystery*, 205.

2. Best, "Who Used Whom?" 79; Best, 604–5; O'Brien, 17.

3. The words τοῦ εὐαγγελίου are found in ℵ A D I Ψ 075 0150 0278 6 33 81 104 256 263 365 424 436 459 1175 1241 1319 1573 1739 1852 1881 1912 1962 2127 2200 2464 *Byz* [K L P] *Lect* it$^{\text{ar, d, f, o}}$ vg syr$^{\text{p, h, pal}}$ cop$^{\text{sa, bo, fay}^{\text{ms}}}$ arm eth geo slav Origen Basil Chrysostom Theodore^{lat} Jerome Pelagius. These words are omitted by B F G it$^{\text{b, g, mon}}$ cop$^{\text{fay}^{\text{ms}}}$ Marcion$^{\text{acc. to Tertullian}}$ Victorinus-Rome Ambrosiaster. Externally, the first reading has manuscripts that are early and with good character. This reading also has good geographical distribution, represented primarily by the Alexandrian and Byzantine texts among the uncials, as well as the Western texts among Itala. It has good genealogical relationships within the text-types. The omission is a strange combination of the Alexandrian B and the Western G in agreement. Otherwise, the manuscript tradition does not really support the omission. Internal evidence favors the first reading because there is no other read-

ing my mouth, to make known with boldness the mystery of the gospel." The structure of the argument in the broader context must combine verses 17 and 18 with the two ἵνα clauses in verses 19 and 20. In other words, believers are armed with the helmet of salvation and the sword of the Spirit (v. 17) and are now praying and keeping alert for the moment of imminent attack (v. 18). In verse 18 Paul instructs believers to pray for all saints. Now in verses 19 and 20 Paul asks them to pray for him specifically, the content of their prayers expressed by the use of the two ἵνα clauses.

Now, let us examine the particulars. Paul introduces verse 19 with the connective conjunction καί that has an adjunctive or ascensive force "also, even" or "particularly, especially."[1] The following prepositional phrase ὑπὲρ ἐμοῦ is rendered "in behalf of me," "in my behalf," or "for me." This is parallel with the immediately preceding prepositional phrase περὶ πάντων τῶν ἁγίων, "for all the saints." In the previous verse he had urged the saints to be prayerful and watchful for the sake of each other, but Paul now asks the saints to pray on his behalf. There is a change in prepositions, for in verse 18 he uses περί followed by a genitive, which means "concerning," "for," and in verse 19 he uses ὑπέρ followed by a genitive, which means "in behalf of, in the interest of, concerning, for."[2] In this instance, the prepositions mean the same thing[3] and hence the translation "for." On other occasions, Paul has requested prayer for himself and his fellow workers (2 Cor 1:11; Col 4:3–4; 1 Thess 5:25; 2 Thess 3:1–2) or for himself specifically with regards to particular needs (Rom 15:30–32; Phil 1:19). This presents a real problem for those who hold that the author of Ephesians was someone other than Paul. If Paul were dead, how could he ask for prayer or does the pseudonymous author ask prayer for Paul who is dead? Realizing this problem, Lincoln suggests that since the request is specifically for Paul's needs, a pseudonymous author adopted material from Col 4:3–4.[4] He argues that it is adopted because in Colossians Paul requests prayer for Paul and his fellow workers, whereas in Ephesians the author requests prayer for himself only. Best rightly asserts that if the author of Ephesians used Colossians, "his omission of a reference to others is surprising."[5] It is easier to assume that the au-

---

ing in its place like μυστηρίου τοῦ θεοῦ (Col 2:2) or μυστήριον τοῦ Χριστοῦ (Eph 3:4; Col 4:3), the last passage parallel to the present verse (see Metzger, *Textual Commentary*, 2d ed., 542). Therefore, both external and internal evidence favor the first reading.

1. Alford, 3:148; Eadie, 476; Ellicott, 154; Abbott, 188; Salmond, 390; Westcott, 98; Barth, 779; Bruce, 412; BAGD 393; BDAG 495; BDF §442 (12); Wallace, *Greek Grammar*, 670–71.

2. BAGD 838–39; BDAG 1030–31.

3. Robertson, *Grammar*, 618; MHT 3:270; Moule, *Idiom Book*, 63; Zerwick, *Biblical Greek* §96; Harris, "Appendix: Prepositions and Theology in the Greek New Testament," *NIDNTT* 3 (1978): 1174.

4. Lincoln, 453.

5. Best, 607.

thor is not copying Colossians but expressing a similar request with some differences. Possibly, when Paul wrote Ephesians the fellow workers were no longer with him, hence, he made requests for only himself. Also, often the same ideas are expressed in different ways by the same person. This is evident in present day commentaries when the author uses different words and phrases in covering the same content in the different sections of a commentary. Are there two different hands? No one would suspect that to be the case.

The specific content of Paul's first request is introduced by the ἵνα of content.[1] The subject, λόγος, has been used previously in the literal sense "word" (1:13; 4:29; 5:6) but here it has the idea of the use of words, that is, an utterance or a speech. The verb δοθῇ is an aorist passive subjunctive from δίδωμι, "to give," implying that this utterance or speech was to be graciously given to him by God. The following expression ἐν ἀνοίξει τοῦ στόματός μου may be a Semitic expression[2] indicating that God will give him utterance when he opens his mouth. The preposition ἐν seems to denote the time period[3] in which he is to speak this word or utterance, thus the translation "in/when opening my mouth." Robinson states, "It is not, as our Authorised Version renders it, 'that I may open my mouth'; but rather 'that God may open my mouth'."[4] Paul has precedence for the prophets of old were to speak as God opened their mouths (e.g., Isa 59:21; Ezek 3:27; 29:21; 33:22; Ps 39:9 [MT 39:10; LXX 38:10]; 78:2 [LXX 77:2]; Hos 9:7; cf. also Matt 10:19; Mark 13:11).

The final clause is introduced by the prepositional phrase ἐν παρρησίᾳ, which indicates the manner with which Paul was to make known the mystery. The noun παρρησία was discussed at 3:12 denoting freedom to speak with no restraints, hence, to speak freely, boldly, or openly.[5] Its position in the clause gives it emphasis. The aorist infinitive γνωρίσαι, indicating purpose or, more likely, a hypothetical result,[6] means "to make known, reveal." This was discussed at 1:9 with reference to the revelation of the mysteries that have been kept secret (Rom 16:26; Eph 1:9; 3:3, 5, 10; Col 1:27). Paul is to boldly make known τὸ μυστήριον τοῦ εὐαγγελίου, "the mystery of the gospel." The genitive is difficult to label though probably not subjective genitive ("the gospel proclaiming the mystery"),[7] but it could be objective geni-

1. MHT 3:129; Winer, *Grammar*, 363.

2. MHT 2:485; 4:84, 92.

3. Alford, 3:149; Eadie, 478; Ellicott, 155; Meyer, 345–46; Salmond, 391; Westcott, 98; Gnilka, 317; Lincoln, 454.

4. Robinson, 136; cf. Schlier, 302–3; Gnilka, 317; Schnackenburg, 283.

5. For a study of the word, see Marrow, "*Parrhēsia* and the New Testament," 431–46; Fredrickson, "Παρρησία in the Pauline Letters," 163–83.

6. Robertson, *Grammar*, 1090; Wallace, *Greek Grammar*, 594.

7. As Alford, 3:149; Ellicott, 155; cf. Brown, "The Semitic Background of the New Testament *Mystery*," *Bib* 40, no. 1 (1959): 82, reprinted in idem, *The Semitic Background of the Term "Mystery" in the New Testament*, 64.

tive ("the mystery about the gospel"),[1] genitive of content ("mystery is contained in the gospel"),[2] or, more likely, an epexegetical genitive ("the mystery, namely, the gospel").[3] In 3:10 Paul states that the mystery, that is, the union of believing Jews and Gentiles into one body, was to be made known to the angelic hosts by the church. In the present context Paul is speaking not about the gospel per se, but the mystery of the gospel, which is the union of believing Jews and Gentiles into one body. Paul asks believers to pray that he would be given utterance when he opens his mouth to make known with boldness the mystery of the gospel. This is not preaching the gospel in an evangelistic sense[4] for the context is about a defensive stand and not an offensive advance. Instead, it seems more likely that he needs this requested utterance for when he is attacked by the powerful hosts of the wicked one.[5] More specifically it may well refer to his trial before Caesar (Nero) in Rome (when and if the Jewish accusers would make charges against him). The Roman government looked on the Christians as a sect of the Jews and the Jews considered them a heretical group. In his trial before Caesar, Paul needed to make clear that Christians are neither a Jewish sect nor a heretical group but an entirely new entity, the church, the body of Christ, composed of Jewish and Gentile believers.

6:20. ὑπὲρ οὗ πρεσβεύω ἐν ἁλύσει, "for which I am an ambassador in chains." Paul continues by giving two further details about the phrase "mystery of the gospel." The first detail is introduced by a prepositional phrase with the relative pronoun οὗ, which relates back to τὸ μυστήριον, "the mystery" (not to τοῦ εὐαγγελίου, "the gospel"), "for this is the object of γνωρίσαι, and γνωρίσαι is in substance connected with πρεσβεύω."[6] Accordingly, in the parallel passage (Col 4:3) Paul uses δι᾽ ὃ καὶ δέδεμαι, "on account of which I am bound," and likewise, the neuter accusative relative pronoun refers back to its antecedent, τὸ μυστήριον. The preposition is again ὑπέρ followed by a genitive which generally means "on behalf of, in the interest of, concerning, for." Here it is translated "on behalf of which" or "for which." Thus, Paul was imprisoned not for the gospel but for the mystery of the gospel, that is, the union of believing Jews and Gentiles into one body. The verb πρεσβεύω means "to be the elder/eldest"[7] or "to occupy first

1. As Meyer, 346; Masson, 224 n. 2.

2. As Salmond, 390–91; Westcott, 98; Schlier, 303; Barth, 781; O'Brien, 488.

3. As Gnilka, 318 n. 1; Bruce, 412 n. 94; Lincoln, 453; Bouttier, 268; cf. Bockmuehl, *Revelation and Mystery*, 205; Dawes, *The Body in Question*, 189.

4. As van Unnik, "The Christian's Freedom of Speech in the New Testament," *BJRL* 44 (March 1962): 474–75; Marrow, "*Parrhēsia* and the New Testament," 446; Fee, *God's Empowering Presence*, 732.

5. Jones, "La prière par l'Esprit: Ephésiens 6:18," 138–39.

6. Abbott, 189.

7. Sophocles *Oedipus Coloneus* 1422; Herodotus 7.2; Plato *Leges* 12 §951e.

place"[1] but also "to be sent," "to be an ambassador," or "to serve as an ambassador"[2] and thus represent someone. Though the verb does not appear in the LXX, the noun πρέσβυς appears fourteen times (ten times in the canonical books) and means "messenger, envoy, ambassador" (e.g., Num 21:21; 22:5; Deut 2:26; Isa 57:9; 1 Macc 9:70; 10:51; 11:9; 13:14). In the NT the verb is used only here and in 2 Cor 5:20 meaning "to be a representative of, to be an ambassador of."[3] Accordingly, Paul is an ambassador for the mystery of the gospel. Also, he is ἐν ἁλύσει, "in chains," for this mystery. The word ἅλυσις is used eleven times in the NT, always to denote the binding with chains whether it refers to the Gerasene demoniac (Mark 5:3–4; Luke 8:29) or to imprisonment (Acts 12:6–7; 21:33; 28:20; 2 Tim 1:16; Rev 20:1). It is a collective singular, thus it does refer to a specific chain that bound him to a soldier (cf. Acts 28:16, 20). Paul, an ambassador in chains, is an incongruity[4] for normally the position of ambassador commands respect and as such is immune to incarceration by those to whom he was sent. Instead, commissioned by the mightiest of all sovereigns, Paul has been imprisoned.[5] In regards to this, the prepositional phrase "ἐν ἁλύσει is in distinct opposition to ἐν παρρνσίᾳ"[6] in the previous verse. In other words, since ambassadors had diplomatic immunity, they could speak boldly whatever they wished in behalf of the government they represented; however, prisoners had no such freedom. This is why Paul makes a further request in the next part of this verse. He does not ask for sympathy, for he had stated earlier that his imprisonment is the Ephesian believers' glory (3:13). Rather, he asks for boldness in the time of satanic attacks.

ἵνα ἐν αὐτῷ[7] παρρησιάσωμαι ὡς δεῖ με λαλῆσαι, "that I might speak boldly about it as I ought to speak." Here is the second detail about Paul's situation in relationship to the phrase "mystery of the gospel." The conjunction ἵνα is thought by some to relate back to the immediately preceding words πρεσβεύω ἐν ἁλύσει, suggesting that Paul, as an ambassador in chains, might be emboldened to speak about his situa-

1. Sophocles *Antigone* 720; Euripides *Heraclidae* 45.

2. Herodotus 5.93; Andocides 4.41; Xenophon *Cyropaedia* 5.1.3.

3. L&N §37.88; cf. BAGD 699; BDAG 861; Günther Bornkamm, "πρεσβεύω," *TDNT* 6 (1968): 681–83.

4. It is called a paradox (Bengel, 4:117–18; Gnilka, 319), an oxymoron (Westcott, 98; Lincoln, 454), or both (Barth, 782).

5. Wettstein, 2:261; Eadie, 480; Barth, 782; Lincoln, 454.

6. Abbott, 189.

7. The reading ἐν αὐτῷ is found in A D F G I Ψ 075 0150 6 33 81 256 263 365 424 436 1175 1241 1319 1573 (1852) 1912 1962 2127 2200 2464 *Byz* [K L P] *Lect* it$^{b, d, f, g, mon, o}$ vg syr$^{h, pal}$ arm (eth) geo slav Basil Chrysostom Theodore^{lat} Victorinus-Rome Ambrosiaster Jerome Pelagius. The second reading transposes ἐν αὐτῷ after παρρησιάσωμαι and is found in א 104 459 cop$^{sa, bo, fay}$. The third reading has αὐτό in place of ἐν αὐτῷ and is found in 𝔓^{46} B 1739 1881 syr^{p}. The dative pronoun αὐτῷ without the preposition is found only in *l* 921. The first reading has the overwhelming external evidence and is the preferred reading.

tion when necessary.[1] Although there is no connective conjunction, it seems best to consider this ἵνα as parallel with the preceding ἵνα (v. 19), denoting the content of his first personal prayer request.[2] Briefly, then, when the wicked hosts attack, believers are to take the helmet of salvation and the sword of the Spirit (v. 17) by praying and remaining alert on behalf of "all the saints" (v. 18). Paul next asks for prayer specifically for himself, and he expresses the content of their prayers by the two ἵνα clauses in verses 19 and 20. The first request was that he would be given the words to make known the mystery of the gospel (vv. 19–20a) and the second, that he would speak as boldly as he ought about the mystery (v. 20b). After this second ἵνα, the ἐν αὐτῷ refers back to the relative pronoun οὗ (which in turn refers back to τὸ μυστήριον, "the mystery," in v. 19) and can be translated "in it, therein, with regard to it," or perhaps better, "about it."[3] The verb παρρησιάσωμαι is an aorist subjunctive deponent of παρρησιάζομαι, which appears nine times in the NT (Acts 9:27, 28; 13:46; 14:3; 18:26; 19:8; 26:26; Eph 6:20; 1 Thess 2:2). It has the same basic meaning as the noun παρρησία (3:12; 6:19) denoting freedom to speak with no restraints, hence, to speak freely, boldly, fearlessly, or openly,[4] thus translated, "that I might speak boldly about it." Finally, he states ὡς δεῖ με λαλῆσαι, "as I ought to speak" (see 4:25 and 5:19 for use of λαλέω). This could have reference to his proclamation of the mystery of the gospel to prisoners as he had formerly done (Acts 28:30–32; Phil 1:12–13), but it more likely refers to the time when he would have to face his Jewish accusers before the Roman tribunal (Acts 25:11–12, 21; 26:32; 27:24; 28:17–19). Not only would Paul have to face his accusers, but he would have need to face the emperor Nero whose megalomania was a factor in the early 60s of the first century. He would have to defend the message of the mystery of the gospel against the assaults of the wicked one who would want to confuse the issue by having the Roman tribunal dismiss the trial on the grounds of mistakenly thinking that Paul's message simply led to the formation of another sect of the Jews.[5] Instead, the message of the mystery of the gospel described in this context is that believing Jews and Gentiles are one body, a new entity, and

1. Chrysostom *Eph* 6:18–20 (*PG* 62:169); Bengel, 4:118; von Soden, 153.

2. Alford, 3:149; Eadie, 480; Ellicott, 156; Meyer, 347; Abbott, 189; Salmond, 392; Westcott, 98; Schlier, 304; Gaugler, 230; Gnilka, 319; Best, 609.

3. The preposition ἐν is described as a "maid-of-all-work" in late Greek (MHT 1:103) and became more vague which contributed to its ultimate disappearance in modern Greek. Turner ("The Preposition *en* in the New Testament," 118) thinks that in conjunction with παρρησιάζομαι it should be rendered "in" or "in the sphere of."

4. BAGD 631; BDAG 782; L&N §§25.159; 33.90; cf. Joüon, "Notes philologiques sur quelques versets de l'Épître aux Éphésiens," 464.

5. Already in the first century the Christians were known as a sect or faction of the Jews (Acts 24:5) and were so considered in the second and third centuries. Cf. William Horbury, *Jews and Christians in Contact and Controversy* (Edinburgh: T & T Clark, 1998), 241.

not another sect of the Jews.[1] This is what Paul as ambassador wanted so urgently to make clear.

As has been previously mentioned, Paul's authorship of Ephesians has been questioned by some. However, if this epistle had been written in the last two decades of the first century, as some claim, then this call for prayer in behalf of the imprisoned Paul would be rather pointless. Wild attempts to overcome this dilemma by claiming that verses 19–20 depict "a typological model of the true Christian existence in the world," that is, all Christians are "in bonds."[2] But these verses specifically indicate that Paul is asking for prayer on behalf of himself (καὶ ὑπὲρ ἐμοῦ, v. 19) and not for all believers. Furthermore, nothing in the passage suggests that all Christians are in bonds. Lincoln, who asserts that a follower of Paul wrote this letter, is fully aware that this is problematic, for why would the author ask for prayer for Paul if he was already deceased? He responds by suggesting that the author of the epistle is presenting the triumph of the gospel in the midst of opposition and adversity and that the recipients of the letter understood that it was the Pauline representative asking "for prayer for his own bold proclamation of the Pauline gospel."[3] However, this is begging the question for this does not explain why the author identifies himself as Paul the prisoner who needs prayers in order to speak boldly about the mystery of the gospel. Is the pseudonymous author also in prison as his request implies? It is highly unlikely and Lincoln does not suggest this. If then the author falsely represents this part of the letter, is he to be trusted anywhere else in the epistle?[4] Furthermore, why would he ask for prayer for Paul when the readers would have known that Paul was already deceased and also would have known the outcome for which he requested prayer? It makes much more sense to see this as truly Paul asking his readers for prayer in a most difficult situation, in prison and facing a possible tribunal before Casear. In addition, in light of the political situation in Rome, Smillie demonstrates that the prayer concerns made in this letter must have been written by Paul in the early 60s and not by another writer sometime in the last three decades of the first century. Nero's paranoia in the early 60s fits well with Paul's need of utterance and bold speech in that time period that would not be true later.[5]

1. Nor was Paul trying to portray that Christians were a legitimate fulfillment of Judaism and should be entitled to Judaism's privileges as Smillie suggests (Gene R. Smillie, "Ephesians 6:19–20: A Mystery for the Sake of Which the Apostle is an Ambassador in Chains," *TJ* 18 [fall 1997]: 221).

2. Wild, "The Warrior and the Prisoner," 294.

3. Lincoln, 455.

4. In rejecting Pauline authorship of Ephesians, it is suggested that the writer was not speaking of a real imprisonment but one of appearance only (see Robert A. Wild, "'Put on the Armor of God'," *TBT* 36 [November 1998]: 369).

5. Smillie, "Ephesians 6:19–20: A Mystery for the Sake of Which the Apostle is an Ambassador in Chains," 218–20.

G. Conclusion (6:21–24)

Having discussed the calling of the church (chaps. 1–3) and the conduct of the church (chaps. 4–6), Paul now gives a short conclusion. Here he states that Tychicus is being sent to them and will provide further information about Paul's circumstances for the purpose of their encouragement.

1. Information (6:21–22)

Before commenting on these verses, it is interesting to note the verbal correspondence with Col 4:7–8, which is in the following chart.

Eph 6:21–22	Col 4:7–8
Ἵνα δὲ εἰδῆτε καὶ ὑμεῖς τὰ κατ᾽ ἐμέ, τί πράσσω, πάντα γνωρίσει ὑμῖν Τυχικὸς ὁ ἀγαπητὸς ἀδελφὸς καὶ πιστὸς διάκονος ἐν κυρίῳ, ὃν ἔπεμψα πρὸς ὑμᾶς εἰς αὐτὸ τοῦτο, ἵνα γνῶτε τὰ περὶ ἡμῶν καὶ παρακαλέσῃ τὰς καρδίας ὑμῶν.	Τὰ κατ᾽ ἐμὲ πάντα γνωρίσει ὑμῖν Τυχικὸς ὁ ἀγαπητὸς ἀδελφὸς καὶ πιστὸς διάκονος καὶ σύνδουλος ἐν κυρίῳ, ὃν ἔπεμψα πρὸς ὑμᾶς εἰς αὐτὸ τοῦτο, ἵνα γνῶτε τὰ περὶ ἡμῶν καὶ παρακαλέσῃ τὰς καρδίας ὑμῶν.

A total of thirty-two words are in verbatim agreement except the addition of τί πράσσω in Eph 6:21 and καὶ σύνδουλος in Col 4:7. It certainly suggests that the author of the second document copied from the first.[1] It is very possible that both epistles were written at the same

1. Best thinks the ἵνα clause in Eph 6:21 (Ἵνα δὲ εἰδῆτε καὶ ὑμεῖς) is clumsy and the author of Ephesians does not normally write clumsily which may suggest that author of Ephesians may have used Colossians. However, there are other factors in Eph 6:21–22 and Col 4:7–8 that would mitigate against that assumption. Best declares that it is difficult to determine who borrowed from whom and if both letters were by the same author then it is possible that the author repeated what he had already written. See Best, "Who Used Whom?" 77–79; Best, 613–14.

time or that the author still had the first letter while he was penning the other. It may well be that if Paul were the author of both epistles, as it is argued in this commentary, Tychicus took both letters with him when he went to Asia Minor.

Text: 6:21. Ἵνα δὲ εἰδῆτε καὶ ὑμεῖς τὰ κατ᾽ ἐμέ, τί πράσσω, πάντα γνωρίσει ὑμῖν Τυχικὸς ὁ ἀγαπητὸς ἀδελφὸς καὶ πιστὸς διάκονος ἐν κυρίῳ, **6:22.** ὃν ἔπεμψα πρὸς ὑμᾶς εἰς αὐτὸ τοῦτο ἵνα γνῶτε τὰ περὶ ἡμῶν καὶ παρακαλέσῃ τὰς καρδίας ὑμῶν.

Translation: 6:21. "Now in order that you may also know about my circumstances, how I am doing, Tychicus, the beloved brother and faithful servant in the Lord, will make everything known to you, **6:22.** whom I am sending to you for this very purpose, that you may know how we are and that he may comfort your hearts."

Commentary: 6:21. Ἵνα δὲ εἰδῆτε καὶ ὑμεῖς[1] τὰ κατ᾽ ἐμέ, τί πράσσω, πάντα γνωρίσει ὑμῖν[2] Τυχικὸς ὁ ἀγαπητὸς ἀδελφὸς καὶ πιστὸς διάκονος ἐν κυρίῳ, "Now in order that you may also know about my circumstances, how I am doing, Tychicus, the beloved brother and faithful servant in the Lord, will make everything known to you." The conjunction δέ makes a transition from the foregoing material and is translated "but" or "now." This is followed by ἵνα . . . εἰδῆτε καὶ ὑμεῖς τὰ κατ᾽ ἐμέ, "in order that you may also know about my circumstances." The main problem in this verse is the conjunction καί translated adjunctively "also." To what does it refer? There are five suggestions. First, it could

1. The words εἰδῆτε καὶ ὑμεῖς are found in B Ψ 0278 1739 1881 𝔐 vg^{ms} Chrysostom Ambrosiaster Jerome Oecumenius Theophylact. The second reading has the same words in a different order, καὶ ὑμεῖς εἰδῆτε, found in ℵ A D F G I P 81 326 630 1241^{s} 2464 2495 *al* lat Theodoret. The third reading has only εἰδῆτε appearing in 𝔓^{46} 33 f vg^{mss}. Externally, the third reading can be omitted because it lacks manuscript support. The first reading has some good representation in the Alexandrian text and it has the support of the Byzantine text. The second reading has good support in the Alexandrian and Western text-types. Both the first and second readings are about the same in geographical distribution and the second reading has a slight edge in genealogical relationships. Both the first and second readings are about equal with regard to external evidence. Internally, the third reading is favored because it is the shortest but it lacks in external evidence. The first reading is preferred over the second because it is unlikely that δέ would be followed by καί. Therefore, the first reading is preferred externally and internally.

2. The words are γνωρίσει ὑμῖν found in 𝔓^{46} ℵ B D F G P Ψ 0278 33 81 104 326 365 1175 1241^{s} 1739 1881 2464 *pc* (it$^{a, b, m}$ vg$^{st, ww}$) Ambrosiaster. The second reading is in reverse order, ὑμῖν γνωρίσει, found in A 𝔐 vg^{ct} Chrysostom Theodoret Oecumenius. The first reading is preferred from the standpoint of date and character of the witnesses, geographical distribution in the Alexandrian and Western text-types, and genealogical relationships. Internally, the first reading is also preferred because out of the eight other times these words are used together in the NT, seven times they are in this order (John 15:15; 1 Cor 12:3; 15:1; 2 Cor 8:1; Gal 1:11; Col 4:7; 2 Pet 1:16) and only once in the reverse order (Col 4:9). Thus, the more normal order is the first reading. In short, both external and internal evidence support the first reading.

refer to letters sent to other recipients (e.g., Colossians), which were also delivered by Tychicus "in order that you as well as the others may know about my circumstances."[1] Second, it could refer to the Ephesian saints whom Paul does not know personally, as he does those in other cities, that they "also" would know about Paul's situation.[2] Third, as Paul had heard about the believers in Ephesus (1:15; 4:20–21), now they "also" shall hear about him in his imprisonment.[3] Fourth, the believers had received doctrinal and practical instructions from Paul and now he "also" will apprise them of his personal condition.[4] Fifth, Paul had asked for prayer for his defense of the mystery of the gospel, and now he "also" will tell them about his circumstances.[5] The third view seems unlikely because it is so far removed from the earlier contexts to which it refers. The fourth and fifth views seem forced because he appeared to have finished his argument, and the transitional conjunction δέ "now," would indicate he is beginning a new section. The second argument makes an unproved assumption. With some reservation, the first view is probably the most viable. Since Tychicus was going to Asia Minor, Paul penned a letter to the Ephesians which contained information about his condition in prison. The words τὰ κατ᾽ ἐμέ are an idiom used to describe a person's situation and thus can be translated "in my circumstances,"[6] which likely refers to verse 20 where he stated that he was "in chains." The following words τί πράσσω are not referring to "what I am doing" for that has already been expressed in verse 20, but rather "how I am doing," which would be of interest to the readers.[7]

Here Paul relates that Tychicus will make everything known to them. Until this time papyri letters were sent by a relay of several messengers. However, in the first century, Augustus changed the Roman postal system from relays by messengers to a single messenger who would personally deliver the letter. Therefore, the delivery by Tychicus was in keeping with this newer method for the delivery of messages, enabling the recipients to receive first-hand information about the sender from the messenger, as indeed was the case here.[8]

1. Bengel, 4:118; Ellicott, 157; Meyer, 22, 348; Salmond, 392; Robinson, 217; Westcott, 99; Masson, 224; Schlier, 305–6; Hendriksen, 283; Bruce, 414; Bouttier, 271; Wallace, *Greek Grammar*, 563.

2. Abbott, 190; Barth, 809.

3. Alford, 3:149–50; Gaugler, 231.

4. Chrysostom *Eph* 6:21–22 (*PG* 62:170); Calvin, 223; Dibelius-Greeven, 99; Gnilka, 321; Percy, *Probleme*, 389–90.

5. Aquinas, chap. 6, lec. 5, vv. 18–24 (246–47); Schnackenburg, 285.

6. Herodotus 7.148; 2 Macc 3:40; Acts 24:22; 25:14; Phil 1:12; Col 4:7; cf. also Robertson, *Grammar*, 608; Dana and Mantey, *A Manual Grammar of the Greek New Testament*, 107.

7. Eadie, 481; Abbott, 190.

8. S. R. Llewelyn and R. A. Kearsley, *New Documents Illustrating Early Christianity*, vol. 7, *A Review of the Greek Inscriptions and Papyri Published in 1982–83* (Sydney: Macquarie University, 1989), 56.

Tychicus is described here and Col 4:7 as ὁ ἀγαπητὸς ἀδελφὸς καὶ πιστὸς διάκονος ἐν κυρίῳ,[1] "the beloved brother and faithful servant in the Lord." Here the Granville Sharp rule comes into play where the articular personal noun is followed by a καί and an anarthrous noun which further describes the person mentioned in the first noun.[2] Hence, Tychicus is a brother who is a (faithful) servant. In Colossians Tychicus is further described as a fellow servant (σύνδουλος). Outside of these two references, his name appears in three other places (Acts 20:4; 2 Tim 4:12; Titus 3:12). He and Tromphimus were the two Asians who accompanied Paul immediately after the Ephesian riot (Acts 20:4). Tychicus may well have come from the vicinity of Ephesus or Colossae. We are not told if he continued with Paul at the end of his third missionary journey, which included Jerusalem, Caesarea, and finally, Rome, or if he was with Paul a short time and then later went to Rome and ministered with Paul there. Later in his second Roman imprisonment, Paul sent Tychicus to Ephesus to relieve Timothy in order that Timothy could come to Paul (2 Tim 4:12) and Paul sent either Tychicus or Artemas to Crete to relieve Titus so that Titus could visit Paul in Nicopolis (Titus 3:12). Tychicus, then, bore five letters (Colossians, Philemon, Ephesians, 2 Timothy, Titus) and probably relieved two of Paul's apostolic legates. It is no wonder that he was called a "beloved brother and faithful servant in the Lord." As seen in 3:7 the word διάκονος, "servant," emphasizes the activity of the servant and in this case signifies faithfulness in his activities for the Lord. As noted in 2:21, the phrase ἐν κυρίῳ, "in the Lord," refers not to God but to Christ, as it consistently does throughout the epistle (e.g., 2:21; 4:1, 17; 5:8; 6:1, 10). It connects to both ἀδελφός, "brother," and διάκονος, "servant."[3] The words πάντα γνωρίσει ὑμῖν indicate that Tychicus will "make known or reveal (cf. word usage in 1:9) everything" about Paul to the Ephesian believers. These believers would have had great interest in Paul's welfare since it was his ministry to the Gentiles which caused his imprisonment. He had been arrested because of his message concerning the mystery of the gospel, which is the unification of believing Jews and Gentiles into one body (2:11–3:13). He had been preaching this message to the Gentiles, including those at Ephesus.

6:22. ὃν ἔπεμψα πρὸς ὑμᾶς εἰς αὐτὸ τοῦτο ἵνα γνῶτε τὰ περὶ ἡμῶν καὶ παρακαλέσῃ τὰς καρδίας ὑμῶν, "whom I am sending to you for this very purpose, that you may know how we are and that he may comfort your hearts." As mentioned above, this verse is verbatim in

1. It is normal not to have the repetition of the article after the first of many epithets (see Robertson, *Grammar*, 785).

2. Wallace, *Greek Grammar*, 274.

3. Allan thinks the phrase simply means "Christian" and thus "Tychicus is described as a beloved Christian brother and a faithful Christian minister." See Allan, "The 'In Christ' Formula in Ephesians," 57. However, it is more than just the appellation "Christian." It refers to his position in Christ as a brother and faithful servant.

wording and word order with Col 4:8. Paul is sending Tychicus with this letter. The verb ἔπεμψα is an epistolary aorist, that is, it views the action from the viewpoint of the recipients as they read the letter[1] and thus should not be translated "sent" (as AV, RV, ASV, RSV, NASB) but "am sending" (as NEB, TEV, JB, NIV, NJB, NRSV). If translated in the past tense it might be interpreted that Paul had sent Tychicus before he wrote this epistle. The wording εἰς αὐτὸ τοῦτο expresses the aim or purpose, "for the express purpose" or "for this very reason." This refers to what follows, namely, ἵνα, which occurs often in the NT (John 18:37; Acts 9:21; Rom 14:9; 2 Cor 2:9; 1 Pet 3:9; 4:6; 1 John 3:8).[2] Paul had two purposes for sending Tychicus. These purposes are introduced by a ἵνα and two aorist subjunctive clauses separated with the connective conjunction καί. The first purpose is ἵνα γνῶτε τὰ περὶ ἡμῶν, literally, "that you may know the things concerning us" but better translated "that you may know about us" (NASB, NEB, JB, NJB) or "that you may know how we are" (RSV, TEV, NIV, NRSV). Here the verb γινώσκω is used in the same way as οἶδα in verse 21, in this case, meaning "to find out" something about Paul the readers did not know previously.[3] This is followed by the second purpose for sending Tychicus, namely, καὶ παρακαλέσῃ τὰς καρδίας ὑμῶν, "and that he may comfort your hearts." The word παρακαλέσῃ is an aorist subjunctive of παρακαλῶ. As discussed at 4:1, it is used in three senses: (1) comfort; (2) appeal, entreat, request; and (3) exhort. In this text the first meaning fits best. Accordingly, Tychicus will tell them everything about the apostle and his ministry while in prison and this will encourage the hearts of the Ephesian believers. As mentioned in 1:18 (cf. also 3:17; 4:18; 5:19; 6:5) the word καρδία, "heart," is the center of a person, the seat of religious and moral conduct, of will or volition, or, as here, of feelings and emotions. Believers were to be comforted by the news of Paul's circumstances.

Verses 21 and 22 make no sense unless Paul is the author of this letter. What would be the point?[4] Certainly, if Tychicus was the author, as some suggest, it makes no sense at all. Why would the congregation want to know of Paul's situation when he was already dead? Were they to pray for the dead? It is incongruous for a pseudonymous author to ask the Ephesian believers to pray for Paul when he knew Paul was no longer living. It is even more preposterous to think that Tychicus would report about Paul's situation if the letter were not by Paul himself. It would mean that Tychicus would be part of the fraud. If

1. Robertson, *Grammar*, 845–46; MHT 1:135; 3:72–73; Burton, *Moods and Tenses* §44; Moule, *Idiom Book*, 12; Porter, *Verbal Aspect*, 228; Fanning, *Verbal Aspect*, 281–82.

2. Winer, *Grammar*, 200; John A. F. Gregg, "'Therefore . . . because' (διὰ τοῦτο . . . ὅτι) and Parallel Uses," *ExpTim* 39 (April 1928): 307.

3. Silva, "The Pauline Style as Lexical Choice: ΓΙΝΩΣΚΕΙΝ and Related Verbs," 190, 202, 207 n. 42; Porter, *Verbal Aspect*, 286.

4. Hunter, *Introducing the New Testament*, 121; cf. Muddiman, 296–98.

the author was pseudonymous, then the Ephesians would not have known who he was, and if they knew who he was, the letter is not pseudonymous!

Briefly, then, Paul sent his trusted brother and servant, Tychicus, to Ephesus. His mission was to deliver Paul's letter to the Ephesian believers and also to give them an oral report about Paul's situation. Paul's intention in all this was to comfort them. This was, in fact, a common practice in ancient times.[1]

2. Salutation (6:23)

Paul closes the epistle with a salutation and benediction (for a discussion of letter closing, see "Genre" in the Introduction).[2] The words "peace and grace" introduce verses 23 and 24. Both are found in the prologue of the epistle (1:2) but are repeated in the last two verses of this letter in reverse order.[3] In fact, seven other times Paul uses the exact same wording in his greetings as in 1:2 (χάρις ὑμῖν καὶ εἰρήνη ἀπὸ θεοῦ πατρὸς ἡμῶν καὶ κυρίου Ἰησοῦ Χριστοῦ, Rom 1:7; 1 Cor 1:3; 2 Cor 1:2; Gal 1:3; Phil 1:2; 2 Thess 1:2 [some manuscripts omit ἡμῶν]; Phlm 3).[4] It is unlikely that an imitator of Paul would have deviated from the normal Pauline order.

Text: 6:23. Εἰρήνη τοῖς ἀδελφοῖς καὶ ἀγάπη μετὰ πίστεως ἀπὸ θεοῦ πατρὸς καὶ κυρίου Ἰησοῦ Χριστοῦ.

Translation: 6:23. "Peace to the brothers and love with faith from God the Father and the Lord Jesus Christ."

Commentary: 6:23. Εἰρήνη τοῖς ἀδελφοῖς,[5] "Peace to the brothers." The blessing of peace is found frequently in the NT letters just prior to the final benediction (Rom 15:33; 2 Cor 13:11; Gal 6:16; 1 Thess 5:23; 2 Thess 3:16; Heb 13:20) and infrequently as a part of the benediction (1 Pet 5:14; 3 John 15).[6] The word εἰρήνη is used seven other times in

1. Ronald F. Hock, "The Greek Novel," in *Greco-Roman Literature and the New Testament: Selected Forms and Genres*, ed. David E. Aune, SBLSBS, ed. Bernard Brandon Scott, no. 21 (Atlanta: Scholars Press, 1988), 141.

2. See Weima, *Neglected Endings*: idem, "Pauline Letter Closings: Analysis and Hermeneutical Significance," *BBR* 5 (1995): 177–98.

3. Bruce, 414.

4. For a discussion of the form, see Mullins, "Benedictions as a NT Form," 59–64.

5. In place of ἀδελφοῖς, the word ἁγίοις is found only in 𝔓[46]. Externally, the first reading has overwhelming support. Internally, the normal way the believers are addressed in Ephesians is "saints" (1:1, 4, 15; 3:5, 18; 5:3; 6:18) and nowhere are they addressed "brothers." However, this may be an influence from Colossians where Paul twice addresses them as brothers (1:2; 4:15). The first reading is preferred because the second reading's manuscript evidence is so slight.

6. Cf. Weima, *Neglected Endings*, 87–100; idem, "Pauline Letter Closings," 183–87.

Ephesians (1:2; 2:14, 15, 17*bis*; 4:3; 6:15) and denotes "well-being," much like the OT שָׁלוֹם (cf. 1:2). Generally, in Ephesians it signifies a lack of hostility between God and the believer (1:2; 2:14, 17*bis*; 6:15) as well as between individual believers (2:15; 4:3). It not only expresses objective peace but also a subjective feeling of well-being. In the present context "peace" refers to the peace that comes from God, but indeed, peace of God within believers should produce peace between believers. Here the benediction of "peace" is addressed in the third person (τοῖς ἀδελφοῖς, "to the brothers") rather than the normal Pauline style where the readers are addressed directly in the second person (ὑμῖν, "to you").[1] It is unlikely that a pseudonymous author would have departed from the normal Pauline style.[2] Although Paul speaks in this letter of the household of God (2:19), this is the only time here that he uses the familial term "brothers."[3] It may well be that, if this is an encyclical letter, those referred to as brothers include people in various churches (cf. 1 Pet 5:9, "your brotherhood in all the world").[4] Briefly, then, Paul reminds believers of the peace of God, which is theirs and should flow through them to their fellow believers.

καὶ ἀγάπη[5] μετὰ πίστεως, "and love with faith." The next phrase, joined by a connective conjunction καί, "and," is ἀγάπη μετὰ πίστεως, "love with faith." Barth suggests that μετὰ πίστεως, "with faith," indicates the priority of faith,[6] but that is unlikely.[7] First, the preposition μετά with the genitive expresses association with, rather than superiority over, and in this context it shows a close connection with the two nouns, with the emphasis on the first noun.[8] Second, the usage of these two nouns in this epistle suggests that they are on equal par rather than faith being superior. Earlier Paul commended them for their faith in Christ and love toward the saints (1:15) and stated that Christ indwelt their lives through faith as they were rooted and grounded in love (3:17). Faith is joined with love and not with peace and is not to be considered a separate attribute along with peace and love. Thus it is not "peace, love, and faith"[9] but "peace and love." This

1. Lincoln, 465; Weima, *Neglected Endings*, 95; idem, "Pauline Letter Closings," 187.

2. Cf. Abbott, 190.

3. Lincoln, 465.

4. Schnackenburg, 289; Lincoln, 465.

5. In place of ἀγάπη, the word ἔλεος is found only in A. However, ἔλεος is never used in conjunction with πίστις in Paul but ἀγάπη is frequently used in conjunction with πίστις by Paul (1 Cor 13:13; Gal 5:6, 22; Eph 1:15; 3:17; Col 1:4; 1 Thess 1:3; 3:6; 5:8; 2 Thess 1:3; 1 Tim 1:5, 14; 2:15; 4:12; 6:11; 2 Tim 1:13; 2:22; 3:10; Titus 2:2; Phlm 5). Although the second reading would be a harder reading and thus preferred on the basis of internal evidence, the first is preferred because of the overwhelming manuscript evidence.

6. Barth, 811.

7. Lincoln, 466.

8. BAGD 509; BDAG 637.

9. As Dibelius-Greeven, 98; cf. Lincoln, 466; Kuhn, "Ephesians in the Light of the Qumran Texts," 120.

love not only presupposes faith but is enlightened from the knowledge faith gives in understanding God's love for the believer.[1] As stated in the Introduction, the theme of love has dominant place in Ephesians and hence, the purpose of the book is to promote love. Here love is combined with faith.

ἀπὸ θεοῦ πατρὸς καὶ κυρίου Ἰησοῦ Χριστοῦ, "from God the Father and the Lord Jesus Christ." As mentioned in the introduction to this section, Paul uses the prepositional phrase ἀπὸ θεοῦ πατρὸς ἡμῶν καὶ κυρίου Ἰησοῦ Χριστοῦ as a source of grace and peace eight times (including Eph 1:2) in his greetings. The only difference in the present verse is that it excludes ἡμῶν immediately after πατρός, "Father." God the Father is mentioned in 1:2, 3, 17 and 5:20. To the believer he is not only God but a personal father. In the present verse this prepositional phrase indicates that the attributes of peace and love with faith have their origin in God the Father and the Lord Jesus Christ.

3. Benediction (6:24)

Text: 6:24. ἡ χάρις μετὰ πάντων τῶν ἀγαπώντων τὸν κύριον ἡμῶν Ἰησοῦν Χριστὸν ἐν ἀφθαρσίᾳ.

Translation: 6:24. "Grace be with all of those who unceasingly love our Lord Jesus Christ."

Commentary: 6:24. ἡ χάρις μετὰ πάντων τῶν ἀγαπώντων τὸν κύριον ἡμῶν Ἰησοῦν Χριστὸν ἐν ἀφθαρσίᾳ, "Grace be with all[2] of those who unceasingly love our Lord Jesus Christ." Grace concludes the letter, just as it had introduced it in 1:2 where its meaning was discussed. Grace is the most common benediction in the NT books. Sometimes it is simply stated ἡ χάρις, "grace," with "with you/all of you" (Col 4:18 1 Tim 6:21; 2 Tim 4:22; Titus 3:15; Heb 13:25). Most of the time it contains all or most of the words ἡ χάρις τοῦ κυρίου ἡμῶν Ἰησοῦ Χριστοῦ, "the grace of our Lord Jesus Christ," with "with you/all of you" (Rom 16:20; 1 Cor 16:23; 2 Cor 13:14 [GT 13:13]; 1 Thess 5:28; 2 Thess 3:18; Rev 22:21) or "with your spirit" (Gal 6:18; Phil 4:23; Phlm 25). The benediction in this text is a mixture of both forms. It uses the simple noun "grace" though not with the prepositional phrase μετὰ πάντων ὑμῶν, "with all of you," but rather with the prepositional phrase μετὰ πάντων τῶν ἀγαπώντων τὸν κύριον ἡμῶν Ἰησοῦν Χριστόν, "with all of those who love our Lord Jesus Christ." Indeed, this is reminiscent of the expression "those who love God" often used in the OT (Exod 20:6; Deut 5:10; 7:9; Judg 5:31; Neh 1:5; Pss 5:11 [MT & LXX 5:12]; 69:36 [MT 69:37; LXX 68:37]; 122:6 [LXX 121:6]; 145:20 [LXX 144:20]) and NT (Rom 8:28; 1 Cor 2:9; 8:3;

1. Spicq, *Agape in the New Testament*, 2:83–84.
2. The adjective πᾶς used with a plural articular participle is translated "all" (see BAGD 632; BDAG 782).

Jas 1:12; 2:5; 1 John 4:20–21; 5:1).[1] In fact, Jesus indicated the importance of such love with his response to the lawyer's question as to which commandment is the greatest. He replied that it is to love the Lord your God with all your heart, mind, and soul (Matt 22:37 = Mark 12:30 = Luke 10:27). Here the object of this love is Christ. As mentioned in the Introduction, the key word for Ephesians is "love" and here it is used of the believers' love for Christ. Lincoln makes an apt observation: "Elsewhere the letter has referred to God's love for believers (cf. 2:4) and Christ's love for them (cf. 3:19; 5:2, 25), to believers' love for one another (cf. 1:15; 4:2), to believing husbands' love for their wives (cf. 5:25, 28, 33), and to believers' love in general (cf. 1:4; 3:17; 4:15, 16; 5:2; 6:23), but this is the only place where their love for Christ is made explicit."[2] This benediction of grace is for those who are committed to loving Christ and who need his grace in order to survive in a world that will hate them as it hated Christ (John 15:18–20). The counterpart to this benediction of grace is in 1 Cor 16:22 where Paul states, "if anyone loves not the Lord, let him be accursed" (1 Cor 16:22). The main verb most likely is the verb "to be," which could be rendered in three possible ways: (1) as an indicative (ἐστίν) declaring, "the grace *is* with all those who love our Lord Jesus Christ"; (2) as an imperative (ἔστω), "the grace *be* with all those who love our Lord Jesus Christ"; or (3) as an optative (εἴη) expressing a wish, "*may* grace be with all those who love our Lord Jesus Christ."[3] The last option seems to fit best in this context, especially in connection with the following words.

The prepositional phrase ἐν ἀφθαρσίᾳ, "unceasingly," is an unusual expression and in the present context it raises two questions. What does it mean and to what is it connected?[4] The term ἀφθαρσία, rare in classical literature, is used to signify "incorruption, immortality"[5] and is used "in contrast to the perishing of everything born of corruption."[6] It appears only five times in the LXX (Wis 2:23; 6:18, 19; 4 Macc 9:22; 17:12) where it continues with the same meaning. Outside the present context it occurs six times in the NT and only in Pauline literature (Rom 2:7; 1 Cor 15:42, 50, 53, 54; 2 Tim 1:10). For instance, in 1 Cor 15 where it is most frequently used, it is contrasted with the physical body which is perishable and cannot inherit eternal life. The new resurrected body is imperishable and will never decay or

1. Schlier, 310–11.

2. Lincoln, 466.

3. Cf. Weima, *Neglected Endings*, 83.

4. A Festschrift article on this expression could not be located, viz., Benedetto Prete, "Il senso dell' espressione ἐν ἀφθαρσίᾳ in Efes 6,24," *Studi sull 'Oriente e la Bibbia offerti al P. Giovanni Rinaldi nel 60° compleanno da alievi, colleghi, amici*, ed. G. Buccellati (Genova: Editrice Studio e Vita, 1967), 361–77.

5. Epicurus in Diogenes Laertius 10.123; Plutarch *Aristides* 6.2; *Moralia: De defectu oraculorum* 28 §425d.

6. MM 96.

die. Hence, ἀφθαρσία has the idea of "incorruptibility, immortality,"[1] a "state of not being subject to decay, leading to death—'immortal, immortality,'"[2] or "a continuous state or process, with the implication that the state or process in question is not interrupted by death—'unceasing, always, eternally, undying.'"[3]

Having suggested its meaning, the next problem is to determine to what part of the sentence it is connected. First, Barth translates it "in eternity." He proposes that it is not connected to only one part of the verse but to the whole verse and each of its parts.[4] However, if that were the case, it is not likely that Paul would have used a prepositional phrase that needs to be connected to something in the sentence. Second, some think it should be connected to the immediately preceding words "our Lord Jesus Christ," who is depicted as immortal.[5] They would support this with 1 Tim 1:17 which speaks of Christ as "the king of ages, immortal (ἀφθάρτῳ), invisible, the only God," and with Jas 2:1, which speaks of "our glorious Lord Jesus Christ." Further, they argue that in Ephesians Christ is portrayed as the resurrected Christ seated in the heavenlies. However, ἀφθαρσία denotes an attribute or a state and not a locale. Furthermore, if the author intended the prepositional phrase to refer to the immediately preceding words, he would have inserted an article before it—Ἰησοῦν Χριστὸν τὸν ἐν ἀφθαρσίᾳ. Third, some join it with the noun χάρις, "grace," thinking that the grace that is conferred by God on believers is immortal or indestructible. Thus it would be translated "grace and immortality" (NEB).[6] It is contended that the preposition ἐν is used to connect with other nouns (2:7; 3:12; 6:2).[7] There are three problems with this view. First, the prepositional phrase is far removed from that which it modifies—the last two words modifying the first two words of the verse. Second, though the preposition ἐν is used as a connective between two nouns earlier in the book, it never serves as a coordinating conjunction καί, "and,"[8] as this view

1. BAGD 125; BDAG 155; Harder, "φθείρω κτλ.," *TDNT* 9 (1974): 103–5; Robinson, 217–19.

2. L&N §23.127.

3. Ibid. §68.57. Moule (*Idiom Book*, 197) thinks it may have a double meaning, "to mean both *sincerely* (*in incorruption*) and *eternally* (*in incorruptibility*)."

4. Barth, 814.

5. Wettstein, 2:261; Dibelius-Greeven, 100 (possible); Staab, 166; Rendtorff, 85; Zerwick, 181 (possible); Martin, "Ephesians," in *The Broadman Bible Commentary*, 177.

6. Ambrosiaster *Eph* 6:24 (*PL* 17:404); Bengel, 4:118; Harless, 569–70; von Soden, 154; Lock, 69; Lenski, 687–88; Schlier, 311–12; Gaugler, 232; Gnilka, 325–26; Mitton, 232; Mußner, 174; Schnackenburg, 291; Lincoln, 467–68; O'Brien, 494–95.

7. Lincoln, 467.

8. Although sometimes in the Qumran materials ἐν is virtually a substitute for καί (see Kuhn, "Ephesians in the Light of the Qumran Texts," 119–20). Lincoln thinks this is a plausible interpretation for this verse (Lincoln, 467). For support he cites Eph 2:7; 3:12; 6:2, but interestingly he never translates ἐν as "and" in these verses except for the present verse.

proposes for this verse. Third, those who hold this view generally repeat "grace," that is, "Grace be with all who love our Lord Jesus Christ, grace and immortality." However, this is not implicit from the text. The fourth proposal found in most translations and commentaries prefers the idea that ἀφθαρσία is connected with the participle ἀγαπώντων, "love," describing an imperishable, immortal, or undying love (AV, RV, ASV, RSV, NASB, TEV, NIV, NRSV).[1] It is a love that is not corrupted by death, thus a love that is unceasing, undying, or endless. The unceasing or endless love of God and Christ is well demonstrated earlier in the letter (1:3–14; 2:1–10, 13; 3:17–19; 5:2, 25), which serves as a pattern for the believers to love Christ unceasingly. The preposition ἐν, "in," can denote the manner of this love, "in an unceasing way," or the phrase could be rendered adverbially, "undying, unceasing, endless love." Hence, the translation, "those who unceasingly love our Lord Jesus Christ." Unfortunately, some Ephesian believers later left or neglected their love and, accordingly, were reprimanded (Rev 2:4). However, in the present context he was able to give a benediction of grace to them because of their unceasing love for their Lord Jesus Christ. This is a very appropriate ending to the epistle.

Some manuscripts add an ἀμήν, "amen," after ἐν ἀφθαρσίᾳ.[2] Furthermore, there are various subscriptions in various manuscripts.[3] Any or all of these additions, if genuine, do not detract from the thought of the last verse of the epistle. None of these endings have suf-

1. Chrysostom *Eph* 6:24 (*PG* 62:174); Theodoret *Eph* 6:24 (*PG* 82:557); Theophylact *Eph* 6:24 (*PG* 124:1137); Calvin, 224; Hodge, 397–98; Alford, 3:150–51; Eadie, 484; Ellicott, 159; Moule, 164; Meyer, 351–52; Abbott, 191; Salmond, 394–95; Robinson, 138, 220; Westcott, 100; Scott, 257; Dibelius-Greeven, 100 (possible); Masson, 225; Hendriksen, 285; Johnston, 27; Thompson, 97; Zerwick, 180–81 (possible); Hugedé, 233; Bruce, 415–16; Best, 620; Spicq, *Agape in the New Testament*, 2:84–86.

2. An ἀμήν is added in א^{2} D Ψ 075 0150 104 256 263 365 424 436 459 1319 1573 1739^{c} 1852 1912 1962 2127 2200 2464 *Byz* [K L P] *Lect* it$^{ar, b, d, mon^{c}, r}$ vg$^{cl, ww}$ syr$^{p, h}$ cop$^{bo^{pt}}$ arm eth geo slav Chrysostom Victorinus-Rome. It is omitted by 𝔓^{46} א* A B F G 0278 6 33 81 1175 1241 1739* 1881 *l* 593 it$^{f, g, mon*, o}$ vgst syr^{pal} cop$^{sa, bo^{pt}, fay}$ Origen Theodore^{lat} Ambrosiaster Jerome Pelagius. Its inclusion is supported by the Byzantine texts and some Alexandrian manuscripts. Its omission is well supported by Alexandrian and Western texts. Therefore, it is omitted by manuscripts that are early in date and good in character, have good geographical distribution, and good genealogical relationships within the two text-types. Internally, it could go either way but normally there is no "amen" at the end of the letters. In conclusion, it seems better to argue for its omission. A third reading, namely, ἀφθαρσίᾳ εἰς αἰῶνας. ἀμήν is found in only one lectionary (*l* 921).

3. There are at least five different subscriptions. The first subscription πρὸς Ἐφεσίους is found in א A B* D Ψ 33 81 466 cop^{fay}. The second subscription ἐτελέσθη ἐπιστολὴ πρὸς Ἐφεσίους is found in F G. The third subscription πρὸς Ἐφεσίους ἐγράφη ἀπὸ Ῥώμης appears in B^{1} P. The fourth subscription πρὸς Ἐφεσίους ἐγράφη ἀπὸ Ῥώμης διὰ Τυχικοῦ occurs in K 0278 31 82 328 436 1739 1881 1908 TR. The fifth subscription ἐγράφη ἡ ἐπιστολὴ αὕτη ἡ πρὸς Ἐφεσίους ἀπὸ Ῥώμης διὰ Τυχικοῦ is found in L. The subscription is absent in 𝔓^{46} 365 629 630 1505 2464 *pc*. It is so varied it is difficult to judge. If one were to accept a subscription, probably the first one would be the best because it has good date and character in the

ficient manuscript support to consider them as a part of the original text. Regardless, the last verse of Ephesians has definite elements of Pauline style, except for ἐν ἀφθαρσίᾳ which is quite different from the rest of Paul's literature. It seems strange that a pseudonymous author would end with anything so different from the normal Pauline ending.

The conclusion of this letter (6:21–24) illustrates to believers the kind of love and oneness that Paul had been demonstrating throughout the book. Although imprisoned in Rome, his thoughts were for the welfare of the Ephesian believers. In light of this he sent Tychicus to them to report on his situation. His purpose was to comfort them. In addition, he sent a letter (now known as the Book of Ephesians) to instruct them in doctrine and their daily walk. His greetings to them were more impersonal than the greetings in some of his other letters. This may have been due to great changes in the congregation over the two years since he had seen them or it could have been because the letter was encyclical.

This epistle began with Paul's salutation of grace and peace (1:2) and ends with a benediction that also includes grace and peace. Indeed, the believer can have no peace without God's enabling grace.

Alexandrian tradition with some support from the Western text. It is also the shortest reading and it would be difficult to explain the omission of the other elements in the other subscriptions. It has better external support than its omission. The strength of the omission is that it is difficult to explain why scribes would have omitted any subscription.

Author Index

Scripture Index

John

Acts

Romans

1 Corinthians

2 Corinthians

Galatians

Philippians